PSYCHOLOGY & ADJUSTMENT
Values, Culture, and Change

RONALD JAY COHEN

St. John's University
Rockland Community College

ALLYN AND BACON

Boston ▪ London ▪ Toronto ▪ Sydney ▪ Tokyo ▪ Singapore

Vice President and Publisher: Susan Badger
Executive Editor: Laura Pearson
Acquisitions Editor: Kevin Stone
Editorial Assistant: Sarah L. Dunbar
Text Designer: Melinda Grosser
Photo Research: Ronald Jay Cohen, Mimi Moore
Cover Administrator: Linda Knowles
Cover Designer: Susan Paradise
Composition Buyer: Linda Cox
Manufacturing Buyer: Louise Richardson

Library of Congress Catalog Card Number 93-73777

ISBN 0-205-15456-5

Printed in the United States of America

10 9 8 7 6 5 4 3 2 1   98 97 96 95 94 93

The photo credits for this book are listed on pages 545–546, and are
considered an extension of the copyright page.

FOR HARRISON

BRIEF CONTENTS

CONTENTS

CHAPTER 4

C H A P T E R 5

A Developmental Perspective on Adjustment

Part 2 Problems, Coping, and Therapy

C H A P T E R   6

C H A P T E R   7

Coping   172

C H A P T E R   8

C H A P T E R 9

Part 3   The Person in Society

C H A P T E R   1 1

Friendship and Love

CHAPTER 12

CHAPTER 14

APPENDIX

Behavioral Science Research: What It Is, How It Is Done, and How It Is Used   436

PREFACE

TO THE STUDENT

An innovative science fiction television program called *The Outer Limits* aired from 1963 to 1965—before many of the readers of this book were born. For anyone who has watched the program, whether during one of its original broadcasts or during a wee hours rerun on cable, the most memorable thing about it was the way it began. The video image did strange things as a man with a deep, authoritative voice told us,

> There is nothing wrong with your TV set. We are controlling transmission. We can control the vertical. We can control the horizontal. For the next hour we will control all that you see and hear and think. You are watching a drama that reaches from the inner mind to . . . *The Outer Limits.*

Psychology textbook writers can identify with the deep-voiced man from *The Outer Limits*. After all, once you have been assigned our books for your courses, it is *we* who are at least partially responsible for the particular topics you are exposed to within that very broad field known as psychology. I take that responsibility most seriously, knowing full well that this will be the only course in psychology some students will ever take. For other students, this course may help them decide whether to pursue additional coursework in psychology—and possibly whether to become a psychologist!

Contemplate for a moment the wide range of psychology-related topics this author had to select from when deciding what topics to discuss, as well as how much discussion to give each topic. What topics would *you* like to see covered? What questions would *you* like to see answered? How much coverage should the topics and questions you've listed receive?

Am I "normal"?

How can I get along better with other people?

How can psychology be used to make the world a better place?

Perhaps these are the types of questions you are thinking about as you begin this course. Note that the first of these questions is at the level of the self, the second question is at a level that involves other people in a very immediate sense, and the third question is at a level that involves other people in a more global sense. In this book, issues of psychology and adjustment will be addressed at each of these levels and from many, varied perspectives. Let's state at the outset that psychologists having varied training, background, and experience may have vastly different responses to questions such as those posed above. In this book, we will explore those different perspectives, cite relevant research, and ask you to think about which of various positions work best for you.

A primary criterion in selecting topics was *your* interests. If you are like many students who take a course labeled as *Psychology of Adjustment, Personal Adjustment, Personal Development, Applied Psychology, General Psychology,* or *Toward Self-Understanding,* you are curious about psychology and "what's in it for you." Stated another way, you would like to gain an understanding, in fairly plain terms, of how and why people act as they do. You hope that you will take away from this course some knowledge of how psychology can be applied to everyday life, problems, and concerns. You are curious about ways that people—and, perhaps, in particular, you—can act more effectively and achieve more satisfaction from life.

In these pages, you will discover—if not absolute answers—new and more effective ways of thinking about some of your concerns. You will learn about what makes psychological research scientific, and how such research can be applied to, and made to work in the service of, everyday, real-life experience. From some classic studies to current research, the objective is to present a well-balanced and scholarly survey of the field of psychological adjustment. Throughout, an attempt has been made to keep the writing conversational—this the better for us to engage in a kind of dialogue. It is my hope that every time you pick up this book, your reading will be an active experience; an active exchange between me and you. As you read this book, if I pose a question—and I pose many—try to avoid the temptation to keep reading. Rather, pause for a moment to give some thought to the question. Mentally respond to it, then go on. Evaluate and reevaluate your own thinking on the matter in the context of the discussion presented. In many instances, there are no right or wrong answers to the questions raised. What is most important is that you think about the issues.

By now, I hope you are aware that this author, unlike the man with the deep, authoritative voice on *The Outer Limits,* has no burning desire to control all that you see, hear, or think while using this book. Quite the contrary, I hope you will use the printed words and illustrations in this book as stimuli to the active generation of your own private words and images—all to enhance your own personal understanding of psychology and adjustment.

Ronald Jay Cohen
Chestnut Ridge, New York

ACKNOWLEDGMENTS

A French proverb defines gratitude as the heart's memory. From the heart, thanks to my family, with special thanks to my wife, Susan, for their constant support before, during, and after the writing of this book. Thanks also to my former editor, now good friend, Phil Curson, who first encouraged me to write this text. I must also thank Agnes Gelli at the Rockland Community College library, who cheerfully and competently assisted me in obtaining many of the volumes and journal articles required for the writing of this book. Thanks, too, to Paula Blumenthal who generously provided access to her private library of adjustment-related publications.

Reviewers play a critical role in the final form a manuscript ultimately takes. I am grateful to Rajan Nataraajan for his thoughtful comments on the Appendix on Research in Behavioral Science. Sincere thanks also to each of the following reviewers for their valuable insights and comments, the fruit of which may be found throughout this book: Marsha Beauchamp, Jackie Gerstein, Victor Joe, Carol Kremer, Salvador Macias, John Nield, Robert A. Reeves, and Norris D. Vestre. Thanks to Bernardo Carducci for his most professional work in developing ancillaries to accompany this text, to Martin Heesacker for developing *Portraits of Adjustment,* a collection of Washington Post articles relating to *Psychology & Adjustment,* and to Kevin Stone at Allyn and Bacon for his editorial input and support.

Finally, a special thanks to my students at St. John's University and Rockland Community College for all their help in teaching me about how students can become excited about psychology and the place of values, culture, and change in that process.

Chapter 1

The Study of Psychology and Adjustment...And How to Study It

O U T L I N E

*Y*ou win the huge grand prize in a lottery and quickly learn that you possess the power to adjust to an entirely new lifestyle—one complete with mansion, chauffeured Rolls Royce, and house staff waiting to serve you "hand and foot."

Your Peace Corps application has been accepted and the next years of your life will be spent in a country where you don't know the language or customs. Electricity, running water, and fresh fruit and vegetables are considered luxuries in this country. You resolve that no matter what the conditions, you will adjust.

Between these two extremes, there are countless other situations such as adjusting to a new school or roommate that may spring to mind when you think of the word *adjustment*. In any situation, **adjustment** is *change or adaptation made in response to a new situation or a new perception of a situation*. In this book we will focus on the **psychology of adjustment**—*the changes in thoughts, feelings, and behavior that contribute to effective adaptation*.

THE WORLD OF PSYCHOLOGY

psychology
the study of mental processes and behavior.

Psychology is *the study of mental processes and behavior*. Like medicine and some other disciplines, psychology is both a profession and a science. If you are like many students, you are probably most familiar with the profession side of psychology. The word *psychology* probably conjures up images of a person conducting therapy with individuals or groups. However, in addition to the practice of therapy, the science and profession of psychology encompass a wide world of varied areas of specialization. This is understandable when you consider that any human or animal organism capable of behavior is fair game for study by psychologists. All psychological research, whether using animals or humans and whether at the level of cells in the brain or political movements in the former Soviet Union, has in common the objective of bettering the human condition.

To understand just how broad psychology is, consider some of the many different types of behavior psychologists might study: instinctual behavior, abnormal behavior, normal behavior, maternal behavior, paternal behavior, sexual behavior, prenatal behavior, infant behavior, child behavior, adolescent behavior, and adult behavior. Psychologists study how we sense, how we perceive, how we think, how we learn, how we remember, and how we forget. They study motivation, emotion, personality, psychodiagnosis, and psychotherapy.

Psychologists may study humans at home, at school, at work, or at play. They may study animals in their natural habitat, in a zoo, in a laboratory, at work (for example, a police dog sniffing out drugs), or at play. Psychologists may study people who are in trouble, in prison, in love, in space, or in love *and* in space. They may study people who are out of a job, out of money, or just out of the hospital. They may study people who are under pressure, under orders, or under water. They may study people who are up in the air (literally, like pilots), or just "up in the air" about what to do about a career. Suffice it to say that this list of possible study areas barely scratches the surface of the many different research options behavioral scientists may pursue.

adjustment
change or adaptation made in response to a new situation or a new perception of a situation.

psychology of adjustment
the changes in thoughts, feelings, and behavior that contribute to effective adaption.

THE PSYCHOLOGY OF ADJUSTMENT

In the 100-plus years that psychology has existed, an impressive body of research studies has been amassed. These studies have much to tell us on a great many different topics. Cull from this large number of studies just the research that has relevance to the way that humans adapt to changing situations, and there you have the psychology of adjustment research literature. It is primarily from this body of literature that this book draws.

BEHAVIORAL SCIENCE AND ADJUSTMENT

In a broad sense, **science** entails *the observation, description, identification, experimental investigation, and/or theoretical explanation of natural phenomena.* **Behavioral science**, as its name suggests, refers to *the observation, description, identification, experimental investigation, and/or theoretical explanation of behavior-related phenomena.* In this definition, *behavior-related phenomena* applies not only to observed behavior, but to an extraordinarily broad category of unobservable behavior including thinking and feeling. Through centuries of human existence, much speculation and many myths about human behavior have been advanced. One objective of behavioral science is to separate facts from unexamined beliefs and hunches about human behavior. It would take too much space here even to begin to adequately explain the rationale for and methods used in behavioral science. Students interested in learning more about what is "scientific" about behavioral science are referred to the Appendix of this book and to other whole volumes devoted to that subject (for example, Koch & Leary, 1992).

It seems fair to say that the philosophy and methods of behavioral science represent the best systematic approach to the study of human behavior, as well as the best hope for the advancement of general human welfare. Still, other approaches to the study of behavior have not only preceded behavioral science, but have also always shared the world stage with it. Psychologist George A. Kelly taught that all human beings are, in a sense, behavioral scientists. In his writings on the study of personality, Kelly (1955) provided rich descriptions of how nonscientists share with scientists certain ways of thinking. In everyday life, people make observations, formulate "research questions" (even if they are not labeled as such), learn the answers to these questions through experience, and then generalize from the findings. Of course, Kelly's "person-as-scientist" view is simile (comparison), not fact. Because people think and behave in a fashion that may in some ways be similar to scientists, it does not make all people scientists. Working scientists may be distinguished from their "scientist-like" counterparts by the objectivity they bring to their methods, the replicability of their findings, and the quality of the evidence they accept or offer in support of their conclusions.

ADJUSTMENT AND VALUES

You may have witnessed by way of television the dramatic event captured in Figure 1–1 (on page 4). The photo, taken from a live broadcast from Tiananmen Square in China, captures a tense encounter between a lone demonstrator and a Chinese Army tank. Students had organized the demonstration in support of democracy and the tanks represented the government's intolerant response. Many demonstrators were killed on the spot, or arrested, tried, and sentenced to death or prison terms.

The photo can be used as a stimulus to thought-provoking discussions on a number of different topics, such as civil disobedience as a response to unjust government. From our perspective, however, the photo is useful in illustrating how interwoven values and what may be referred to as *adjustment, effective behavior,* or a *healthy personality* are. To better appreciate why, consider the following questions:

Was this effective behavior on the part of the student? Why or why not?

What would constitute effective behavior on the part of the tank's crew?

What would constitute effective behavior on the part of the civilian bystanders and the demonstrator's fellow students?

It is not always a simple and clear-cut matter to identify what effective behavior is, and what the "well-adjusted person" would or should do under different circumstances. Is it effective to block a moving tank with your own body in the interest of bringing democracy to your country? Are there more effective ways a "better adjusted" individual might attempt to accomplish the same goal? Some may argue that such behavior on the part of the demonstrator in Tiananmen Square was indeed effective because it dramatically documented the fervent yearning of many people for democracy in China. Others may argue that such behavior was highly ineffective because it was against Chinese law, could not in

science
the observation, description, identification, experimental investigation, and/or theoretical explanation of natural phenomena.

behavioral science
the observation, description, identification, experimental investigation, and/or theoretical explanation of behavior-related phenomena.

FIGURE 1–1 WHAT IS "EFFECTIVE BEHAVIOR"? Exactly what constitutes "effective behavior" is sometimes more a matter of opinion than of science. Consider in this context the action of this student protester as he stood in Tiananmen Square during a seemingly futile attempt in 1989 to institute democracy in China.

values

that which one believes in and/or prizes.

value system

one's priorities with respect to values.

itself succeed in changing anything, and placed in immediate jeopardy the life of the person engaged in the behavior. The view you find more compelling will to some extent be based on your **values**, that is, *what you believe in and prize.* Knowing something about an individual's **value system**, or *priorities with respect to values,* can be very revealing. Value systems can be helpful in explaining various aspects of motivation, including occupational choices. Traditionally, for example, people who value job security and a pension over a higher salary accompanied by less security have sought positions in government rather than in private industry.

For one person, we'll call him Ray, money is valued above all else, including the rule of law. Ray is a career criminal. For another person, we'll call her Faye, respect for justice and the rule of law are values she has grown up with and adopted as her own. Faye has chosen a career in law enforcement. Ray shakes his head in pity and amazement at the thought of someone like Faye, working for the salary she does to further the cause of justice. Faye shakes her head in pity and amazement at the thought of someone like Ray, pursuing such a dead-end "career." In contemporary society, there are thousands of Fayes and thousands of Rays. Whom you identify with more depends on your own value system.

The search for answers to questions of identity such as "Who am I?" may in large part amount to a search for an understanding of one's value system. A constant feeling of psychological discomfort, or the feeling, as it is sometimes put, that one hasn't quite "gotten one's demons out," may in some cases signal a need to understand better, and adjust better to, one's own value system. If you are a "Faye type" who has gotten involved in criminal enterprises, you will not feel very comfortable or well-adjusted. The same would be true for a "Ray type" who has pursued a career in law enforcement.

Living at odds with one's value system places day-to-day stress on an individual. In order ultimately to resolve the psychological discomfort such an individual feels, a resolution of value conflicts will be necessary. On the other hand, it is also possible to feel that one's values and lifestyle are in perfect synchronization—and yet be living a lie. As an example, consider the situation of thousands of members of religious cults who earnestly believe that they know themselves, know their values, and have achieved a sense of psychological comfort by living in conformity with these values. Others may argue that the psychological comfort achieved by such cult members is not genuine, because it derives from self-deception, not self-knowledge. For example, cult members may paradoxically enjoy a sense of freedom despite the fact that their cult leader controls their very lives (see Figure 1–2), as well as their personal relations, sleep, diet, and other aspects of daily living.

FIGURE 1–2 A PREVENTABLE TRAGEDY? Sequestered from the "real world" in the Branch Davidian compound in Waco, Texas, nearly 100 followers of cult leader David Koresh, including 17 children, lost their lives in this fiery inferno (Verhovek, 1993). The 1993 mass suicide drew an eerie parallel to a 1978 mass suicide, also orderd by a cult leader, in which 500 people died. In both cases, cult followers belived that they would be "saved" if they rigidly adhered to the teachings of the cult leader. Might this tragedy have been prevented? How? What role might values and the ability to think critically play in keeping people from joining cults?

If you are like most people, you have probably never given much thought to your value system. Yet among other things, what you talk about, whom you associate with, what you dream about, what you desire, what you fear, and *what is important to you* are all reflections of your value system. You may find it enlightening to take a moment now to complete the Exploring Your Values questionnaire on page 6 (see *A Question of Values*). Your values are forces that are always with you, guiding many aspects of your behavior. Beginning with this questionnaire, you will find many tools in this book to help you better come to know the nature of these forces.

ADJUSTMENT AND CULTURE

Culture as we are using the word here may be defined as *the socially transmitted behavior patterns, beliefs, and products of work of a particular population, community, or group of people.* In this sense, culture may play a role in defining one's identity, influencing to a greater or lesser degree everything from choice of occupation to choice of foods to choice of wardrobe.

Culture dictates the words that are spoken and rituals performed at all milestones in life, from birth to marriage to death. In Irish culture, for example, when someone has died it is customary to hold what is called a *wake* (or watch over the deceased) before burial. The wake may be accompanied by excesses in food, alcohol, and festivities. By contrast, in Jewish culture the deceased is buried quickly, usually within one day of death, and the immediate family follows strict rules for mourning and self-denial for a week. Both processes represent cultural mechanisms for adjusting to the emotional trauma of the loss of a family member. It is neither strange nor crazy for people of Irish heritage to behave as they do at a wake; it is behavior that can best be understood in terms of its cultural context. It is neither strange nor crazy for people of Jewish heritage to behave as they do in response to a family loss; it is also behavior that can best be understood in terms of its cultural context.

Throughout this book, a great deal of psychological research will be cited. One question it may be useful to keep in mind is how generalizable the findings are to people of different cultures in or out of our country. For example, consider research conducted in American restaurants on tipping behavior. Studies have found that diners tend to tip servers more if they interact with them than if they do not. Thus, if servers introduce themselves to diners by name (Garrity & Degelman, 1990), or if the interaction involves the

culture
the socially transmitted behavior patterns, beliefs, and products of human work of a particular population, community, or group of people.

A QUESTION OF  Values

Exploring Your Own Values

The role of values in individual adjustment will echo through much of this book. Some familiarity with your own value system will better prepare you to think about how what is being said does or does not apply to you. So, with the objective of formally exploring a sampling of aspects of your own value system—perhaps for the first time—complete the brief self-assessment exercise that follows.

Use a pencil to rank the 10 values in the list below in terms of which is most important to you (#1), and which is least important to you (#10) *today*. After you have done that, use the same ranking system to complete the spaces on the right, this time filling in the spaces with reference to how you would like your value system to be—*ideally*—in the future.

Surveying these completed scales, what have you learned about yourself and your value system? Do discrepancies exist between your values today and how you would ideally like them to be in the future? Do you anticipate that these discrepancies will be resolved? How?

Value	My Rank Number Today	My Rank Number "Some Time in the Future"	Comment
1. Being secure	4	3	
2. Being at peace	2	2	
3. Being excited	6		
4. Being free	10		
5. Being accomplished	7		
6. Being sexy	9		
7. Being liked	8		
8. Being respected	1	1	
9. Being wise	5		
10. Being ambitious	3	4	

server touching the diner (Crusco & Wetzel, 1984; Stephen & Zweigenhaft, 1986), the tip the diner leaves for the server is likely to be larger than if there is no such interaction. Do you think such a finding would hold true in, say, Japanese culture? In fact, diners in Tokyo, for example, may be put off by servers who touch them. Perceiving such behavior as a sign of disrespect, Japanese diners could well leave *less* of a gratuity than if the server had maintained what would be considered a respectful distance. Studies conducted in American restaurants frequented by recent Japanese immigrants might also yield findings that are contrary to the general trend.

ADJUSTMENT AND CHANGE

Just when you think you have adjusted the color on your television set, there is a power outage and the color must be readjusted. Just when you have adjusted the apples in your cart, a gust of wind upsets that order. Just when you think you could not eat another bite, you are hungry again. Change—unexpected as well as expected—is very much a part of everyday life. Adjustment, because it is a response to change, may also most usefully be thought of as a constant process.

Interestingly, however, our everyday use of words like *adjusted* may convey that adjustment is not a process, but rather a state that some people are or are not in. From this perspective, adjustment can be described as the end-product of the process of adjusting. There is no harm in viewing some people as adjusted, and others as not adjusted or maladjusted (poorly adjusted) as long as we keep in mind the changeable nature of these terms. The person who is adjusted today is capable of being less adjusted, maladjusted, or even not adjusted tomorrow. The person who is not adjusted today may be more adjusted, or even adjusted tomorrow. In short, because adjustment is an ongoing process, there are no guarantees that the adjusted person will be adjusted for life. Likewise, the individual who is not adjusted today may well be adjusted tomorrow. How adjusted we are on a given day depends on the complex interplay of many different things ranging from our genetic inheritance to our life experiences to acts of nature. A hurricane can do miserable things to a person's adjustment! Stated another way, adjustment depends in part on the demands and challenges made on an individual.

A subtle distinction can be made between *demand* and *challenge* when using these terms in the context of adjustment. **Adjustive demands** may be defined as *factors originating primarily in the environment that prompt us to respond constructively to change.* The term **adjustive challenges** speaks more to the *internal factors, such as unsureness, reluctance, or fear, that can impede us from responding constructively to change.* Another subtle distinction between these two terms concerns the potential for personal growth that is implied. As a result of meeting an adjustive challenge, there is usually the implication that one has somehow grown as a person in the process. This implication is not as strong when speaking of adjustive demands: for an individual who meets demands to "stay afloat," any personal growth that occurs in the process seems by chance. It is possible, for example, for one to meet the adjustive demands of a harsh winter but experience little or no personal growth as a result.

Change may be viewed in several different ways. Below we focus on change in the context of the world stage, and the various roles we may play on that stage.

CHANGING TIMES

I open my morning newspaper and find that the world has changed overnight. The news of change comes at an international, national, and local level. News at any of these levels is capable of affecting me personally, and is therefore capable of influencing my thinking and behavior. For example, if I read that my country is committing troops to a conflict in the Middle East, I might worry about the fate of my son or daughter or nephew or niece who is in the military. I might also think about what would constitute effective personal action under such circumstances (such as writing a letter to my representatives in Congress). As I read of natural disasters such as earthquakes, hurricanes, tornadoes, flooding, and fires, I feel sympathy for the victims, yet also worry about the possibility of such catastrophes striking closer to home. What could I do to earthquakeproof, floodproof, or fireproof my home? Should I move to a safer area? If I read about a rash of local muggings, I become uneasy regarding the safety of myself and my family. What kind of security system should I install in my home? What precautions should be taken while out and about in an effort to ensure personal safety? These are some of the questions and behaviors I might be prompted to consider.

Beyond merely thinking or worrying about news events, it is of course possible to become part of them personally. Ask anyone who has had a child drafted and sent to a combat zone about how they felt. What did they do to adjust to the prospect of having a child sent in harm's way? Ask someone who has been a victim of a natural catastrophe or mugging about the adjustive demands and challenges they faced as a result of such events. From these people you may hear richly detailed, firsthand accounts of the many thoughts and feelings that accompany the real-life struggle of adjustment to events that most of us are fortunate enough only to read about in newspapers. Can you think of topics you might see or hear about in a newspaper or news broadcast that could ultimately impact your own adjustment?

adjustive demands
factors originating primarily in the environment that prompt us to respond constructively to change. Contrast with *adjustive challenges*.

adjustive challenges
factors originating within the self, such as the mobilization of ability, energy, and resources to respond constructively to change. Contrast with *adjustive demands*.

Surveying changing events in contemporary life, it may also be useful to take a step back and reflect on just how far humankind has come from its humble beginnings as cave-dwellers. At one time, people were fascinated not with Nintendo or music videos, but with things such as lightning and the mysteries of creation. With the march of technology, we soon harnessed energy and made it work for us in all sorts of modern conveniences. However, in recent years, the march of technology has accelerated to a dizzying pace. We are bombarded with new technology that places ever-increasing adjustive demands on all of us. We have, for example, wonderful, time-saving computer software to accomplish all kinds of marvelous things—if only we could take the time to read the encyclopedia-length manuals that come with it!

In many instances, the appearance of new technology creates a demand to trade in what is known, understandable, and trusted for something that is unknown, confusing, and relatively untested. For example, as word processing became "in" and typewriting became "out," an adjustive demand was placed on thousands of secretaries and others who use mechanical devices to print words on paper. For these and other people, the adjustive challenge involved relinquishing the trusted and somewhat understandable IBM Selectric typewriter and embracing the unknown, untested, and somewhat mysterious IBM "hardware" and "software"—in the context of computing, two relatively recent additions to our vocabulary. We are also witnessing technological revolutions in other areas. For example, electrically powered automobiles will soon become common, and with them will come a whole new vocabulary for auto enthusiasts, as well as a need for retooling by auto repair shop owners (see Figure 1–3). Of course, the whole idea behind advances in technology is that they are supposed to enhance our quality of life and ultimately result in *fewer* adjustive demands. But has that really been the case?

The promise of electrical appliances such as the refrigerator, washing machine, sewing machine, and dishwasher in the "ancient" days before these electrical appliances existed was that they would give their purchasers more leisure time. Yet somehow, as modern technology has advanced, we seem to have less and less, not more and more, leisure time. Today we live in an age of laptop computers, cellular telephones, and fax machines, yet people seem to be working harder (and longer) than ever before. For the most part, shopkeepers who open at 9 and close at 5 are part of a bygone era. In the local mall, hours from 9 to 9 are more the norm. And leisure time for many shopkeepers and other business people may be spent punching keys on a personal computer, doing business-related work (such as bookkeeping) that they once delegated to others. The availability of relatively safe, high-speed travel by air has paradoxically increased, not decreased, the amount of time many business people spend away from home. A whole new breed of business "road warriors" has emerged. These people may spend days, weeks, even months on the road conducting business. In part, adjustment to them means knowing where to park at what airport, what seat

FIGURE 1–3 CARS OF THE FUTURE Electrically powered cars, such as the Impact from General Motors, boasting acceleration that "pushes you back against the seat" (Hazleton, 1992, p. 34), are now a reality. Still, they may not take you through the tunnel linking New York and New Jersey one bit faster.

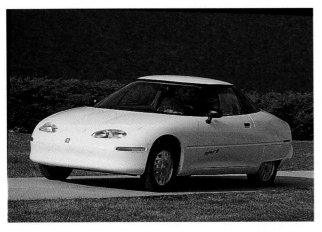

to request on the airline carrying the majority of their frequent-flyer miles, what room to request in their favorite hotel chain, and what to order on a restaurant's menu. Beyond these basics, the life of the frequent-business traveler carries a variety of other adjustive demands and challenges, not only for the business person living it, but for family members as well.

Perhaps the most impressive technological advances of all have been those related to diagnosis and treatment in medicine. Tools having names such as CAT scans, PET scans, and ultrasound technology have revolutionized diagnostic practices. Drugs have been developed that claim effectiveness against diseases as terrifying as AIDS. Yet a sad fact of life for too many Americans who desperately need such advanced diagnostic tools and medicines is that they cannot afford them. Even people who have paid for health insurance policies may find themselves abandoned by their insurer when the diseases they contract necessitate expensive drugs and treatment programs their insurers claim are experimental. Beyond potential abandonment by insurers, there is a disturbing new social trend of abandonment of the sick and the elderly by their own families (see *In the News* on page 10). In many respects, centuries of change have made life much easier. In some respects, however, modern life is more difficult—certainly a lot more complicated—than it was for our ancestors.

CHANGING ROLES

In the performing arts, the word *role* refers to a character or part. In the context of psychology, the word is used in a similar fashion. More specifically, **role** may be defined as *the characteristic and expected behavior in the context of a particular situation.* How would you characterize, for example, the behavior one generally expects of police officers as they write speeding tickets? Would "joking" be a good characterization? How about "empathic" or "sympathetic"? Probably "none of the above." Instead, words such as *serious, official,* and *professional* are probably better characterizations. It may well be that many police officers are joking, empathic, and sympathetic in their roles as husbands, wives, parents, or friends. However, in their role as law enforcement officers writing speeding tickets, few are anything but serious, official, and professional.

There are dozens of different roles any one person can play. To you, for example, Ronald Jay Cohen is the author of this textbook. But Ronald Jay Cohen is seen in different roles by different people, and he acts in different ways—I hope all role-appropriate—when interacting with these different people. To mention but a few of my different roles: I am somebody's son, somebody's husband, somebody's father, somebody's friend, somebody's neighbor, somebody's teacher, somebody's student, somebody's consultant, and somebody's therapist. Some of these roles may be further divided into different kinds of roles with different characteristics and expected behaviors depending upon the particular situation. For example, in my role as "author-interacting-with-students," much of my behavior may take the form of revealing further personal insights about the topics I write about. By contrast, in my role as "author-interacting-with-the-Department Chair," my insights might take a backseat to more administrative matters such as student attendance records.

What other kinds of roles do people play? A number of them are listed in Table 1–1 on page 11.

With time, our roles change. There comes a time when a child takes on the role of "nursery school class member," "kindergartner," or "first-grade student." There comes a time when, as they say, "you're not a kid anymore." There comes a time when a "law student" becomes a "lawyer," when a "benchwarmer" becomes a "team player," when a "politician" becomes "President of the United States." These types of role changes carry with them many benefits, as well as adjustive demands that must be dealt with. We have all heard, for example, of the many problems faced by previously unknown actors once they achieve stardom. Suddenly, they have precious little privacy. At every turn in public, there are paparazzi waiting to take their pictures, or autograph-seekers wishing signatures. At any time a story may appear in the tabloids that causes great anguish to them and their family members. Compounding this stress is the looming fear that their stars will fade and that their phones will stop ringing. Some actors who become stars are able to cope with the adjustive demands of fame. Others have used maladaptive means such as drugs in efforts to adjust—with tragic results.

As our roles change or become more complex, and as we take on additional roles, our obligations may compete. The term **role conflict** describes *being in a state in which the de-*

role
expected behavior in the context of a particular situation.

role conflict
a state in which two or more expected behaviors in a particular situation are at odds with each other.

"Granny Dumping" and the "Sandwich Generation"

On March 23, 1992, an elderly man in bedroom slippers and a sweatsuit with "Proud to be an American" imprinted on the shirt was left abandoned. He was found along with a bag of diapers outside the men's room at a dog racing track in Idaho. A note pinned to him identified him as John King, an 84-year-old suffering from Alzheimer's disease who had no income or savings, and in need of 24-hour care. All labels had been removed from his clothing and his wheelchair. The man was not able to identify himself or the people who had left him at the dog track. This inability to identify himself was consistent with the pattern of behavior observed in Alzheimer's disease, a brain disorder characterized by severe memory impairment and disorientation. Sufferers are usually, but not always, elderly.

The abandonment story made front-page headlines across the country. When the news reached Portland, Oregon, nursing home officials identified the abandoned man as John Kingery. An investigation showed that about 10 hours before Mr. Kingery had been abandoned at the dog track, he had been checked out of his nursing home by Sue Gifford, his daughter, who had been caring for him. In Idaho, as in other states, it is illegal to abandon a child or a dog, but there is no law that covers the abandonment of an adult who is dependent on others for care. Ms. Gifford was subsequently tried and convicted of kidnapping and theft of her father's pension checks ("Woman Convicted," 1992).

Perhaps the Kingery case attracted as much press as it did because of the site of the abandonment, a dog track—and the irony of the phrase "going to the dogs" (see for example, Baker, 1992). But the phenomenon called **granny dumping,** or the *abandonment of the elderly by relatives unable or unwilling to care for them,* is not new. Further, there is evidence to suggest that the problem will get worse in the future. Consider these facts:

- The American College of Emergency Physicians estimates that 70,000 elderly Americans were granny-dumped in hospital emergency rooms in 1991.

- Patients suffering from Alzheimer's disease may live 20 years or more in a condition in which they require round-the-clock supervision.

- It has been estimated that one in five families is currently caring for an aging parent.

- A 1989 survey conducted by the American Association of Retired Persons suggested that 14% of the people providing care to an elderly parent had left a full-time job to do so.

- There are about 30 million people now over the age of 65 and that number is expected to double to 60 million by the year 2030.

Family members who have been "squeezed between" caring for their own children and an elderly parent have been referred to in the press as the "sandwich generation." Legislation has been proposed that strives to ease the burden on the members of this generation in various ways. Until such legislation is passed, however, the only thing a member of the sandwich generation can do is try one's best to adjust and cope with the challenge. Apparently sympathetic to the plight of the convicted daughter of John Kingery, *The New York Times* editorialized that until Alzheimer's is cured, "the Sue Giffords of America will be as much the victim of an aging population as the John Kingerys" ("Granny Dumping," 1992, p. E16). Do you agree?

granny dumping
the abandonment of the elderly by relatives who are unable or unwilling to maintain their care.

mands and expected behaviors in the context of a particular situation are at odds with each other. The role of "volleyball team coach" may be in conflict with the role of "mother," for example, if the team's practice, travel, and game schedule seriously impairs the amount of quality time the coach can spend with her own children. The role of "friend" may be in conflict with the role of "parking enforcement agent" when the agent must decide whether to issue a summons to the illegally parked car of a friend. Catholic politicians and judges have in recent years been challenged by their church officials with respect to their views on abortion. The opinions such politicians and judges should have are well defined by their roles

TABLE I–I   ALL THE WORLD'S A STAGE . . .

From a social-psychological perspective, William Shakespeare was correct when he wrote, in *As You Like It*:

All the world's a stage,
And all the men and women merely players:
They have their exits and their entrances;
And one man in his time plays many parts . . .

On the "world's stage" today, it is possible to occupy many different roles. Survey the A-to-Z list of roles below. Could you see yourself in any of them? What other roles could you see yourself in?

Agent	Jungian	Salesperson
Bodyguard	Kindergarten teacher	Taxpayer
Cousin	Lab assistant	Underboss
Dog owner	Mentor	Veterinarian
Ex-convict	Nonsmoker	Warden
Forest ranger	Observer	X-ray technician
Grandmother/Grandfather	Purple Heart medal winner	Yankee
Harpist	Quitter	Zoologist
Idealist	Reader	

as "Catholics," but these views may be at odds with their views as elected representatives in the role of "politicians."

The role of someone such as you within the hallowed halls of the college or university you attend is that of "student." But have you ever thought about what it means to be a student, and how being a university or college student differs from being a high school student? What are the adjustive demands and challenges that operate with respect to the student role? Do you have any role conflicts with respect to your role as student? If you are attending school on an athletic scholarship, you may be faced with conflicting demands with respect to your roles as "student" and "athlete." If you have your own children at home, you may be faced with conflicting demands with respect to your roles as "student" and "parent." But whether or not you have any conflicts with respect to your role as student, and regardless of whether you are recently graduated from high school, an old hand at taking college-level courses, or returning to school after a long time away from it, there are a number of unique demands and challenges associated with this role. It will be helpful to you to take a few moments to consider those demands and challenges. As you do, think about the kinds of behaviors that will work best for you in successfully rising to meet those demands and challenges.

CHANGING PERSPECTIVES

An act of love, hate, crime, justice, adjustment, maladjustment, religious fervor, compassion, jealousy, rage, contemplation—any behavior—can be viewed from many different perspectives. A perspective is a *view,* and one's perspective of various phenomena often changes with different roles. For example, one's perspective on disability and disabled people may change dramatically if one becomes disabled. One's views on myriad subjects ranging from school systems to driving safety may change dramatically after one has had a child and assumes the role of parent.

Different perspectives yield different kinds of information regarding (1) the relationships between us and whatever we are looking at, (2) the relationships between the individual elements of whatever we are looking at, and (3) the relationships between the individual elements and the whole of whatever we are looking at. In filming a scene, for example, a director may vary camera shots in terms of distance from the subject. A close-up, a medium shot, a long shot, a bird's-eye view by means of an aerial shot, and a worm's-eye view from the ground upward are some of the many possibilities. The camera may be in focus, deliberately out of focus, or inadvertently out of focus. These are all possible metaphors for how people can view their own behavior as well as the behavior of others.

THE ROLE OF STUDENT

From the time you assumed the role of college student, how have some of your own views changed about things such as education, leisure, and time management? If you have not given much thought to such matters, now might be an excellent time to begin.

What does it mean to you to be a student? What values do you attach to being a student? What is important to you in your role as a student? What goals have you set for yourself? What time have you set aside in your schedule to meet these goals? What methods will you use to meet these goals? What strategies for meeting the demands and challenges of examinations have you developed?

Of all the things students do in their role as students, thinking is probably the activity that is most taken for granted. Because thinking about what one reads comes so naturally, it is very easy not to give much thought to it![1] But take a moment now to reflect on how you think while reading written materials such as this textbook, while listening to a lecture, watching a video, or doing any number of the education-related things that students do.

When you read something in a textbook, do you simply try to memorize it? Do you try to link what you have read to your own experience? If a general rule is discussed, do you find yourself thinking about exceptions to the rule? If a fact is expressed, do you ask yourself about the evidence that supports that fact? If a solution to a problem is being discussed, do you find yourself thinking about alternative solutions? In short, are you a passive thinker or an active thinker when you read a textbook? Does your learning energy tend to be used up in passive absorption? Or might the way you learn be better characterized by a term such as *active evaluation?* Aside from evaluating, do you ever try to view what is being said from a different perspective? Do you ever try to generate new thoughts on whatever it is that is being discussed?

Clearly, it seems meaningful to talk about different ways of thinking. Two ways of thinking that will be useful to you in your career as a student, and beyond, are *critical thinking* and *generative thinking.*

CRITICAL THINKING

As used in the term **critical thinking**, critical means *evaluative.* It means that your judgment capabilities are actively involved as you think. It means that you are weighing the merits and faults of the information with which you are confronted. It means that you are not passively receiving information and acting accordingly, but instead actively, carefully processing information and acting as a result of that information processing.

If you are like most people, critical thinking is something you do by habit, and you do quite a bit of it every day. In fact, almost any decision you make, major or minor, involves critical thinking. When you evaluate how sage your parents' advice is, you are engaging in critical thinking. When you watch an hour-long commercial (a so-called infomercial) on television that promises to make you rich if you order audiocassettes and a book, it is your capacity for critical thinking that prompts you to question whether the claim is true. If you are involved in a relationship in which intimacy may be a possibility, you may have already called upon your capacity for critical thinking and discussed the subject of AIDS and its prevention.

If all advertisers had their way, you would engage in very little critical thinking. The producers of that get-rich-quick infomercial, for example, would like nothing better than for you to act on impulse and order their product. In fact, by presenting a seemingly non-stop stream of wealth-related images and other verbal and nonverbal persuasive communications, they have done everything they know how to do to compel you to act uncritically. In a college or university classroom, however, it is quite the reverse. You will probably find that your instructors take extraordinary pains to compel you to think criti-

critical thinking
the active employment of judgement capabilities and evaluative skills in the thought process.

[1]This may sound like a contradiction, but is it?

cally. They may raise thought-provoking issues in class for discussion. They may not only entertain an individual student's question, but try to involve the entire class in arriving at an answer. Few instructors expect that you will uncritically write down what they say in class or that you will uncritically underline material in a textbook. Rather, instructors expect you to examine what is being said from the viewpoint of your own knowledge and experience and then to react to it. Weigh all the evidence, and be fair-minded about it. In some cases, you will find that you were right all along. In other cases, you will find that someone else was right. And in still other cases, you will discover that perhaps there never was any clearly right or wrong answer.

In the published literature in psychology, there are thousands of research studies purporting to have found one fact or another related to human adjustment. By what method would one critically evaluate which findings have merit, and which do not? The Appendix in this book provides some clues as to how behavioral scientists make such evaluations. After reading it, you may be better prepared to evaluate critically what exactly is "scientific" about scientific research.

GENERATIVE THINKING

In *On Becoming A Person* (1961), Carl Rogers, a renowned psychologist, recalled starting college in the agriculture program at the University of Wisconsin and the words of one professor there that forever stuck with him. In order to emphasize the futility of an encyclopedic knowledge gained for its own sake, Rogers's agronomy professor would tell his students, "Don't be a damned ammunition wagon; be a rifle!" Stated another way, "It isn't how many facts you know, it is how you use what you know!" As a target shooter who has extended the meaning of this bit of wisdom somewhat, I find the words useful also as a reminder of the value of knowing (1) what you are aiming at, (2) why you are aiming at it, and (3) what you need to do (in terms of concentration, for instance) in order to be right on the mark.

In my lectures, I raise questions from time to time, not to see if students recall facts, but to engage students, to hear their thoughts, and to learn from them myself. This practice of question raising for the purpose of provoking thought is also evident in my writing, including my other textbooks. A reviewer of my text on psychological assessment once praised my ability to "dialogue" with students in print. This prompted me to give more thought to my writing style, and what—in addition to teaching students about psychological assessment—I was trying to accomplish by such dialoguing. I concluded that what I was trying to do in print was in many ways similar to what I try to do in class lectures. I was trying to stimulate *generative thinking* in the minds of my readers.

As I will use the term, **generative thinking** refers to *the goal-oriented intellectual production of new or creative ideas*. Generative thinking is less random than everyday thinking; it is a goal-oriented activity. Generative thinking also seems close to how creative thinking might be defined except that generative thinking need not be creative in quality. By definition, creative thinking is creative. Generative thinking frequently entails creative thinking but it need not. Generative thinking may also be distinguished from *lateral thinking*, the term Edward de Bono (1970) used to differentiate this more creative form of thought from everyday kinds of thinking (what de Bono called *vertical thinking*). "You cannot dig a hole in a different place by digging the same hole deeper," explained de Bono (1970, p. 13). Yet in the pages of this book you will be called upon repeatedly to "dig deeper" in order to mine fresh insights. The behavior I am referring to as generative thinking may manifest itself in a number of ways such as:

generative thinking
the goal-oriented intellectual production of new or creative ideas.

- thinking of valued new uses for something familiar
- spontaneously creating humor that makes people laugh
- anticipating issues that will be discussed by your instructor during the class lecture
- seeing how something that seems to be wrong may actually be right
- seeing how something that seems irrelevant may actually be very relevant
- anticipating how something that is right for one cultural or ethnic group might be inappropriate for another
- perceiving something that no computer could perceive, only because you are human

- putting information to use in a way that no one has ever done before
- drawing on your own experiences to understand better an account of some phenomenon in a textbook
- using new ways of problem solving that work
- envisioning how things not yet created might function in the future
- finding ways to turn so-called negatives into positives
- discovering new and meaningful significance in writings, artworks, film, and other media

Generative thinking, whether described in these or similar terms, seems a desirable habit to get into. In my own classroom experience, students report more of a sense of mastery and comfort with material when they have been able to generate some original and meaningful thoughts about it. Generative thinking may occur informally or more formally through structured exercises (see Figure 1–4). Regardless of the route you take to thinking generatively, one objective seems worthy: "Be a rifle and not an ammunition wagon!"

GOAL SETTING

What are your personal goals with respect to each of the courses you are taking? Are your goals more related to learning something about the topics you study, or achieving a particular final grade in the course? For many students enrolled in degree-granting programs, the answers to such questions may vary depending upon the particular course. Certain required courses may be viewed as rites of passage—something just to get over with en route to some goal. Yet if you are going to take the time to try to learn something, a useful objective is to learn for the purpose of knowing, rather than knowing merely for the purposes of a course examination.

Beyond setting an overall goal that involves genuine learning in all of the course work you take, you may also find it useful to set "minigoals" for each day or week. For example, about how many pages per day of reading in which textbooks represents a realistic amount of material for you to cover? Your answer will depend in part on your own abilities, as well as the nature of external demands on your time. Your answer may also depend on how effectively the time you spend studying is actually spent.

STUDY BEHAVIOR

"I have to study." "Are you going to study?" "They went off to study."

We have all heard the infinitive *to study* used in sentences like these and we all believe that we know exactly what is meant by that word in each sentence. However, having dis-

FIGURE 1–4 THINKING GENERATIVELY These students are part of an annual "intellectual Olympics" for elementary and high-school students begun in 1978 and called the Odyssey of the Mind Program. Teams from schools throughout the world compete in events that tax their creative and generative thinking ability, including the preparation of original skits.

cussed the subject in depth with students, my own opinion is that studying is a very individual matter. What constitutes study for one person may not constitute study for another. Some students seek out the quiet and solitude of an empty apartment or a corner of the library off the beaten track. Other students prefer to study outdoors. Some students read every word in a textbook as it comes, while others skip around and may read, for example, all definitions of terms in the chapter first. Early birds prefer the crack of dawn, night owls the wee hours of the morning. Some students prefer dead silence while others report that they are incapable of studying without music or some other distraction in the background. Some students underline or highlight words in textbooks to the point that one might think the textbooks were impressionistic works of art. Others do not underline or highlight, partly out of fear of lessened returns on their investments when it comes to returning used books.[2] Some students keep notebooks of what they have learned from class and assigned reading while others take notes in the margins of their textbooks. Some students seem to manifest a strong sense of knowing what they are trying to accomplish during the time they study while others seem to be flying on a wing and a prayer.

How can you use the time you reserve for studying to optimum advantage?

When to Study: Time Management

From the era when the author was himself a university student, a popular folk-rock group called The Byrds had a hit song called *Turn! Turn! Turn!* With lyrics based on the Bible's *Book of Ecclesiastes,* the song opened,

To everything,
Turn! Turn! Turn!
There is a season,
Turn! Turn! Turn!
And a time for every purpose under Heaven . . .
A time to be born, a time to die
A time to plant, a time to reap
A time to kill, a time to heal
A time to laugh, a time to weep.

The song went on to mention other times in life, although there was never any mention of times such as "a time to go shopping," "a time to go out to eat," and "a time to go bowling." What was clear in the sage advice, however, was that there is indeed a time for *every* purpose—all of which brings us to the issue of planning time to study.

Have you ever felt that there just aren't enough hours in the day to accomplish all that you want to do? If so, you are not alone. At one university, 67% of the undergraduate students reported that their greatest personal need, of 40 needs listed on a survey questionnaire, was "to manage my time more effectively" (Weissberg et al., 1982). Indeed, how well you manage your time may have a far-reaching effect on how much you achieve in your college years and beyond.

If you think of your student role as a kind of occupation, then study is what you do. And just as people who go to work every day for a living tend to do so on a regular schedule, so it will be to your benefit to engage in "student-like" behavior, including study, on a regular schedule. Few people in the business world leave until the last minute all that they must do to succeed in their business or profession. Lawyers, for example, may spend months preparing to try a case in court. In a similar vein, trying to prepare for examinations by last–minute cramming not only leads to a highly stressful and painful way of life, it does not work as well as its more rational alternatives. A little study every day can be much more effective than a lot of study the night before an examination. Effective study behavior entails acknowledging that studying takes time. Given this reality, you need to set aside a realistic amount of time each day to study. When many different things compete on a daily basis for your time, it may be difficult to keep to that schedule. Still, it is in your best interest to make a schedule, and then to do your best to keep it. Research suggests that effective time management by students is positively related to final grade (Britton & Tesser, 1991).

Use the chart in this chapter's *Self-Assessment* exercise to create a daily study schedule for yourself. Your schedule should include an adequate and realistic amount of time allotted to activities such as socializing (including talking on the phone), sleeping, eating, recre-

[2]The present book excluded; you may find that this book contains too much useful information for you to exchange it for what the used-book vendor will give you for it.

SELF-ASSESSMENT

Time Management

HOUR				DAY			
	MONDAY	TUESDAY	WEDNESDAY	THURSDAY	FRIDAY	SATURDAY	SUNDAY
(A.M.)							
6:00							
6:30							
7:00							
7:30							
8:00							
8:30							
9:00							
9:30							
10:00							
10:30							
11:00							
11:30							
NOON							
(P.M.)							
12:30							
1:00							
1:30							
2:00							
2:30							
3:00							
3:30							
4:00							
4:30							

ation, and miscellaneous (including doing things like errands). Use a pencil, since you may find after a week or so of following this schedule that some changes are in order. Experiment with different schedules until you find one that you can live with and stick to. If it helps, imagine that you are under a "big bucks" contract to stick to this schedule and "produce."

Time management is life management. We all ultimately have only a certain number of days, hours, and minutes, and it is to our great advantage to make maximum use of our time.

WHERE TO STUDY

In my role as a clinical psychologist and psychotherapist, I conduct clinical evaluations and psychotherapy in a quiet office having few distractions. In my role as an instructor, I try to teach classes with as few competing influences as possible. If they are mowing the grounds outside my classroom, I sacrifice the ventilation an open window offers in order better to

SELF-ASSESSMENT

HOUR				DAY			
	MONDAY	TUESDAY	WEDNESDAY	THURSDAY	FRIDAY	SATURDAY	SUNDAY
5:00							
5:30							
6:00							
6:30							
7:00							
7:30							
8:00							
8:30							
9:00							
9:30							
10:00							
10:30							
11:00							
11:30							
MIDNIGHT							

Use this system of abbreviations to fill in each of the boxes (or create your own abbreviations):

ET= Eating (time spent daily eating meals and snacks)

EX= Exercise (time spent engaging in exercise whether simply taking a walk, or using equipment at the gym or health club)

M= Miscellaneous (time reserved for things that do not fit into any of the other categories)

R= Recreation (including a wide possible range of activities from listening to music to playing Monopoly)

SO= Socializing (this includes time talking on the phone and may overlap with "REC")

ST= Study (time reserved exclusively for study)

SL= Sleep (time reserved for sleep, including naps)

T= Travel (time commuting to school, getting to class, or other time spent in transit)

hear my students and to be heard by them. Because I encourage students (with points towards their final grade) to actively participate in class, few compete with me or a fellow student who has the floor by conducting conversations. When I decided to write this book, I made a commitment to spend many long hours sitting at my desk with little more than my computer and my library of professional journals to keep me company. Sacrifice in terms of spending less time than I would like to with my family, friends, and other people, and in terms of missing television programs that I enjoy all go with a writer's territory. I bring this up only to emphasize that your role, that of student, also requires some sacrifice and that you need to understand, expect, and to the extent that it is possible, be comfortable with that simple fact.

Unlike me, many people do have jobs and roles that allow them to divide their attention between what they are doing and other activities. For example, the butcher, the baker, and the shoemaker can all listen to music, interact with other people, even watch some television while they are, respectively, butchering, baking, or shoemaking. By contrast, the role of student demands more. Study, learning, and thinking are the things that students do, and although it is possible to do such things in a group, these activities are, for the most part, solitary endeavors. Psychologists and educators who have studied how people study are in general agreement that the same quiet place, one with as few distractions as possible, is the very best environment for study. Pick an appropriate place in your house or apartment where you will do little else but study. A good idea might be to have a "study chair" and a "study desk/table" that you will use only to study in. Sitting in that chair in front of that desk or table signals to you that you will be studying. Sitting in that chair in front of that desk or table becomes associated with learning. The chances are good that you will learn most effectively if you study without music or the television on in the background. If you feel you must have such distraction—and it is a distraction—you might try turning the volume as low as possible.

Using your bed as study headquarters is *not* a good idea. You have already built up associations with your bed as a place for sleeping and you shouldn't be surprised if you become somewhat sleepy when you get into it, even to begin a night's reading. Similarly, the use of the kitchen table for studying purposes also comes with baggage that is counterproductive to study. Because the table is so associated with food and eating, you may find yourself mysteriously getting hungry as you read. If you live in a very small apartment with few options for a dedicated study chair and desk, then an out-of-the-way nook in the campus library where you can study without distraction may represent the best available alternative.

Many students in urban areas have become quite adept at studying while on a subway or bus. Students in areas of the country where there are stretches of coastline have perfected the art of seaside study. Some students report success with in-home study in places other than a desk, such as a bubble bath. My own feelings about the more exotic places students can study is that they are probably fine for reviewing material that was orginally studied in a quiet place with few distractions.

HOW TO STUDY

An evaluation of the writing skills of approximately 2,000 American 4th-grade and 8th-grade students commissioned by the United States Department of Education suggested that most children are given little encouragement to write in school. When they do write, the quality of the writing is usually not very good (DeWitt, 1992). At the root of the problem is the fact that elementary school children receive only about 10 to 20 minutes per week of writing-related instruction. The question arises: Are there other skills we expect students to be proficient in that they receive *no* instruction in? What about studying skills? Thinking skills?

No analogous data on the classroom cultivation and evaluation of student-related skills such as studying and thinking exists, yet it would probably surprise no one if results were comparably poor. Although few students receive formal training in how to study or how to think, probably even fewer students would admit to needing remediation in these areas. Because we have the ability to think, we can mentally assure ourselves that we are thinking as effectively as possible. Because we have all had experiences "studying" (regardless of the unique methods and behaviors employed while engaged in that activity), we assume that we know how to study. Moreover, we may react defensively to the mere suggestion that we are not using study time as effectively as we might. Worst of all is the suggestion that we are not thinking as effectively as we might: That suggestion borders on insulting. Yet for most of us, it truly is possible to improve our study and thinking skills.

Perhaps the study system that itself has been studied most is the one called the SQ3R method. The first reference to this method was made by Francis P. Robinson over 50 years ago in a book that was also on the subject of psychology and adjustment. Robinson (1941) introduced a system that would greatly influence the study behavior of thousands of students for decades to come. Research on the system and its individual elements suggests that it really can work to improve students' reading comprehension, learning, memory, and grades (Adams et al., 1982; Anderson, 1985; Boker, 1974; Driskell & Kelly, 1980; Melton, 1978). Today, SQ3R is still helping students master material, although many professors (the author included) take some liberties in explaining the method to their students, giving it the spin they think will work best. Below, SQ3R is explained as Robinson introduced it, and then supplemented with (1) knowledge gained by my students' own experiences with it, and (2) my own views regarding the importance of thinking generatively while studying. If you have had prior acquaintance with the SQ3R system, consider the following section a review and amplification of what you already know. If you have never become acquainted with this useful system of study, you may find this section extremely helpful in terms of systematizing your study time, and making that time work more effectively for you.

SQ3R

SQ3R is a study system composed of five elements. The **S** stands for *survey.* The **Q** stands for *question.* The **3R** stands for *Read, Recite,* and *Review.* Each of these individual elements will be explained further. At the outset, however, understand that there is nothing magical about this system. If it works, it works because it fosters active mental involvement with the material that you read. Reading a textbook the same way that you might read some paperback novel is usually insufficient for the purposes of absorbing academic material. Reading a textbook may be pleasurable, but it is not like reading for pleasure. If you are reading to learn, you must actively work to be involved in what you read.

The first two steps in the SQ3R study system, that is, survey and question, are undertaken in preparation for reading, reciting, and reviewing.

To survey is *to examine* or *to determine the boundaries of.* The *S* in SQ3R means much the same thing; it refers to a survey of the material you are going to be reading. For the sake of example, let us say the material you are going to be reading is a chapter in this book. Your survey might begin with a reading of the outline that appears at the start of the chapter. You will almost immediately be able to tell from the outline what types of material will be covered in the chapter. Questions about various items in the outline will emerge naturally. If you do not find them emerging naturally, put on your "generative thinking cap" and generate some. The simplest way to do that would be to rearrange the wording of various statements in order to create questions. For example, if you see a heading such as *Adjustment and Values,* you might ask, "How does one's adjustment relate to one's values?" Write down all of the questions that occur as you read the outline. By engaging in such questioning, you will not only be prompting yourself to think generatively and critically about what you are reading, but you will be working to fulfill the Q or question element of the SQ3R system.

After surveying the chapter outline, the next step—still in the survey/question stage of the system—is to scan every page in the chapter, paying careful attention to headings and illustrative material before flipping the page. Again, as questions occur during your survey of the material, write them down for future reference. By the end of the chapter, you should have at least one question for each topic heading. In some chapters, that may amount to a lot of headings. However, the greater the number of headings, the greater the amount of learning that should be taking place.

I designed this textbook to contain a lot of interesting photo illustrations. In surveying and/or questioning, try looking at the photos in the chapter without reading the captions. Instead, write your own captions for the photo illustrations based solely on your knowledge of the chapter title and outline. When you go back and read the book, check your hunch about the caption against what is actually printed there. In using the survey/question elements of SQ3R, you now have the lay of the land for the chapter. You have some firsthand experience of what to expect in the chapter, and you will not be taken by surprise. It is now time to read and recite (the next 2 *Rs*). Later it will be time to review (the last *R*).

As you read the chapter, try to answer each of the questions you raised and wrote down. More specifically, after you have silently read the material that will help you answer any one question, close the book and recite aloud and in your own words the answer to the question. This may be one of the most difficult parts of the SQ3R system for many students, and perhaps the component that is most frequently ignored. Many students complain that they feel silly reciting material aloud. Others complain that it is too time-consuming to follow such steps. If you feel silly saying material aloud, keep in mind that you are not being asked to shout it from the roof top; low-grade muttering will pass!

SQ3R
a study method acronym for Survey, Question, Read, Recite, and Review. See also *supplemented SQ3R.*

The idea here is for you to understand the material well enough to rephrase it in your own words. Concerns about time must be dealt with by budgeting enough study time to study with optimum effectiveness. If you do not feel that you currently have enough time to do so, look at your time budget and see where you can obtain the study time you need.

You may find it useful to underline or highlight key points. Key points are underlined and highlighted not so much for purposes of mere memorization, but rather to stimulate your own thinking on the subject being discussed, as well as your own associations and related mental images. If you find yourself underlining virtually every sentence in the text-book, the author is either truly impressive, or you best be more selective about what does and does not constitute a key point. After all, it defeats the purpose of highlighting if everything is highlighted.

The final step in the SQ3R system is review. Go back to the beginning of the chapter and work back to the end. If you prefer, start at the end and work your way back to the beginning. Do you know the answer to all the questions you raised earlier on? If not, you can try the system once again. Additionally, you can try some of the techniques that follow. Because these techniques are designed to supplement, not replace, the basic SQ3R method I refer to this modified SQ3R study system as Supplemented SQ3R. As you will see, the *supplement* in Supplemented SQ3R amounts to 3 more *R*s.

supplemented SQ3R

the SQ3R study system supplemented with three additional *R*'s: Rewrite, Remember, and Record. See also *SQ3R*.

SUPPLEMENTED SQ3R

My own experience with students has demonstrated that while the SQ3R study system is very useful, there are add-ons that may enhance the study experience. Three such add-ons that I will briefly discuss here all begin with the letter *R*. They are *rewrite, remember,* and *record*.

Rewrite in your own words material from your lecture notes or textbook that you deem especially important. Think of personally meaningful examples to illustrate relevant points as you do this and incorporate these examples into your rewriting. These notes will summarize key points in a language that is maximally understandable to you. After all, you wrote them.

Remember refers to your private storehouse of memory techniques and tricks. Included are techniques that have worked for you in the past, as well as any new techniques you may pick up along the way—such as the ones in this chapter. If someone gave you a list of five grocery items to pick up, for example, what mechanism would you use to commit those items to memory? One method would be to keep repeating the names of the five items over and over again until you made it through the checkout counter. Referred to as *rehearsal,* this method would probably prove most laborious. Fortunately, psychologists who study how people remember and forget have delineated other fairly simple but effective ways of enhancing memory. As you read about them in this chapter's *Quality of Life,* you may find that some of them look familiar.

Record your rewritten notes and your "memory enhancers" on a handheld cassette recorder that can then be used to play back your reading of these notes through headphones. If you do not own one, buy one. They are usually relatively inexpensive. Given its great potential for use throughout your college career and beyond, it is a worthwhile investment. The immediate benefit is the one you will derive by reciting out loud your own rewritten notes. Many people who feel silly reciting material aloud do not feel silly at all if they are speaking into a tape recorder. The next benefit derives from hearing yourself talk about the material you are trying to learn. The SQ3R technique relies heavily on the sensory modality of vision as a learning technique. By supplementing SQ3R with a record-and-playback technique, you are bringing more emphasis to learning through another sensory modality—the auditory modality—thus increasing your chances for success in learning the material.

IN-CLASS BEHAVIOR

To this point, we have been discussing the role of student from an out-of-class perspective. That is, we have covered the kinds of things students do to study effectively to keep their objectives on-track. But the role of student also typically carries with it many in-class demands, including those related to listening, note taking, question asking, and test taking.

LISTENING

A special kind of listening takes place during class. You do not listen in class in the same way that you ordinarily listen to the radio when it just happens to be on in the car. Rather, listening in class is ideally more like having a very engrossing telephone conversation with your friend. You are hanging on every word your friend has to say, and perhaps even actively visualizing the things that your friend is describing. Stated another way, you are engaging in **active listening,** a type of listening that *entails your undivided attention to whatever it is you are attending to, and includes anticipation or visualization.* By anticipation, you actively give some thought not only to what the speaker says, but to what the speaker may say. If the speaker uses the phrase, "For example," try to think of your own example of what is under discussion. Active listening to a speaker may also entail **empathy,** *immersion in what is being said to such a degree that the listener actually shares some of the speaker's feelings or emotions as the speaker is speaking.*

To further illustrate the difference between mere listening and active listening, visualize a scene in which a group of people are listening to a particularly close Kentucky Derby as it is being broadcast on the radio. Some of the people are listening to the race out of sheer curiosity. Some people have placed some small wagers on the race and are a bit more attentive than those who have not wagered. And then there is that one person in the audience who, for whatever reason (he or she has placed a large wager, is close friends with one of the jockeys, etc.), is listening to the call of the race intently, virtually to the exclusion of all other voices, noises, and sounds. This person may also be keenly visualizing the changing field as the announcer provides additional information. Images of the emotions of the jockey, even of the horse, may be part of the mental picture. This type of active listening should serve as a model for the type of listening that will be most beneficial to you when attending class lectures.

Some students may argue that they cannot be active listeners in some classrooms because the instructors are too boring. Although it is true that some presentations are livelier than others, it is part of the student's role to listen actively to all educational presentations. Psychotherapists must listen attentively to material that some would rate as boring because it is their job to do so; to not listen would be irresponsible. Judges must listen attentively to arguments or testimony that some would find boring because it is their job to do so; to not listen would be irresponsible. Students will find over the course of their academic career that some presentations—lectures, films, videotape, or other media—vary in the degree to which they are engaging. But it is important to keep in mind that you are not attending classes to be entertained. If it happens that you are entertained during lectures, consider yourself very lucky. If you happen to be mentally stimulated by the material presented, better yet. But regardless of how you rate the quality of your class presentations, your job is to listen, learn, and actively process what you hear.

NOTE TAKING

What is the purpose of taking notes in class? Is it to provide a verbatim transcript of practically everything the instructor had to say? One might think so after reading some students' notes. In fact, note taking should ideally be reserved for things like important points, main ideas, and interesting examples or insights. You may also wish to incorporate into your class notes your own original thoughts or questions about what is being said. By doing that, you will be able to give more thought to the issues later or better develop questions you would like to raise.

Notes may take the form of words or pictures. If the notes are in the form of words, it is essential that they be legible. Have you ever experienced difficulty in deciphering your own notes? If so, prevention is the cure; write in a way that will make it easiest on you when it comes time to study from your notes. If need be, rewrite your notes after every class and use the rewriting time to review the major points. Your notes may also take the form of drawings, usually rendered quite quickly. Unlike doodlings, which are the work

active listening

a type of listening that entails one's undivided attention to whatever one is attending to; it includes anticipation or visualization.

empathy

in person-centered therapy, an active state of perceiving how another feels, almost as if one were the other.

QUALITY OF Life

Memory Enhancers

Many techniques can be used to improve memory. These memory-enhancing techniques are referred to as **mnemonic devices** (the *m* is silent and *mnemonic* sounds like *ni-mon-ik*). Some mnemonic devices are:

1. Rhyming
How many days "hath September"? In spelling, when does the letter *i* generally come before the letter *e*?

Did you find yourself answering the first of these questions with a rhyme that begins "30 days hath September"? Similarly, the second of these questions may be answered by the rhyme, "*i* before *e* except after *c,* or when sounded like *a* as in *neighbor* or *weigh*." Such examples provide convincing testimony that rhymes once learned are not readily forgotten.

To use rhyming as a study aid will require that you make up your own rhymes based on the material you need to learn. The rhymes may be relatively simple ("SQ3R will take me far"), or as complex as you would like. What follows is a little poem I devised to help prompt thoughts and images related to the student role and effective student behavior. Please pardon the last line and the obvious reference to Casey Kasem.

Being a student is very demanding;
it takes generative thinking to be outstanding.
Realistic goals are necessary too,
as is the time and the place that I do what I do.
I will give SQ3R a try,
If it doesn't work, I won't cry.
I'll simply supplement with 3 more *R*s,
and keep my feet on the ground while reaching for the stars.

If you're poetically inclined, take the time to create a rhyme. Who knows? As you become increasingly proficient at rhyming, you may discover your potential to become a poet, a textbook author—or even more lucratively, a rap artist!

2. The "First Letter" Technique
One way of memorizing a long list of things is to take the first letter or two of each word (or topic or whatever) and spell out a real word or nonsensical word or term that you can remember. You can remember a grocery list including items as diverse as milk, eggs, bread, nacho chips, diet soda, alfalfa, endive, and lollipops by taking the first letter of each item and linking it to letters in a real or nonsense word that you can remember. Does any come to mind as you look at this list? How about *mendable?*

Applying the method to the material in this chapter, suppose you were preparing for an essay test in which one of the possible questions was, "Discuss the specific types of behavior that, according to Cohen, make for effective studying." And let's further suppose that to be prepared to answer that question you wanted to include discussion of each of the following points: generative thinking, time management, where to study, SQ3R, Supplemented SQ3R, and study groups. One way to cue all of your memories regarding each of these topics might be to simply remember the following list of letters or nonsense phrase: SSS GT TM WT. In this phrase, SSS stands for the first letter in each of the following terms: SQ3R, Supplemented SQ3R, and Study Groups. GT stands for generative thinking. TM stands for time management. WT stands for "Where to?" as in where to study. Note that, in this mnemonic, the *S* words were placed before all the other expressions, each containing the letter *T,* even though the order of discussion in the text was reversed. Can you guess why? The answer is that the letter *S* comes just before the letter *T* in the alphabet and so it will be easier to remember *S* before *T* rather than the reverse.

3. The Method of Places
As a mnemonic device, the method of

---

mnemonic devices
memory-enhancing devices such as rhymes or acronyms.

product of the bored, the drawings that you create during class should be illustrations or diagrams that convey meaningful information about the material covered.

Another type of "drawing" that you may do during class has to do with drawing on what you already know. This type of drawing is done to enhance your understanding of the material by helping you to place it in the context of your own learning and experience. Because the subject of this particular course is adjustment, feel free to draw not only on academic knowledge, but also on relevant emotions, feelings, images, and memories.

places (sometimes called the method of *loci*; *loci* is Latin for places) involves pairing the material you want to learn with a series of places you already have firmly in mind. For example, you can probably visualize half a dozen houses in your neighborhood quite easily. If you wanted a convenient way of reminding yourself about the various aspects of adjustment that we discussed earlier in this chapter (science, values, culture, and change), you might visualize the "Science family" living in one of the houses, the "Values family" living in another, the "Culture family" living in another, and the "Change family" living in a two-family dwelling with the "Changing Times family" living in one half, and the "Changing Roles family" living in the other. The method of places may be applied in many different ways although the basic premise of pairing material you wish to learn with familiar places or locations is common to all applications.

4. Other Mnemonic Devices

A number of other mnemonic devices may be used to enhance memory. In what has variously been referred to as the "keyword" or "pegword" method, the material you are trying to remember is symbolically "hung on the pegs" of a list of things you have already remembered. For example, suppose you commit to memory a pegword or keyword list that goes, "One is a bun, two is a shoe, three is a tree," and so forth. Whatever list you are trying to remember is then paired with the imagery created by the previously memorized list of pegwords or keywords. For example, if you wanted to remember the names of three people you were introduced to at a party, Mr. Smith, Ms. Jones, and Dr. Cavanaugh, you might picture Mr. Smith eating a bun, Ms. Jones shopping for shoes, and Dr. Cavanaugh in a tree. Note that all three people are actively doing something in these mental pictures and that these images tend to the offbeat or bizarre. In trying to memorize material, you may find that active, offbeat, or even bizarre images may help in the memory process.

5. "Remindering"

Beyond the use of mnemonic devices, there are a number of things you can do to remind yourself of the things you need to learn to succeed in school. For example, you may try taping notes on the door to your room, on your bulletin board, or on your bathroom mirror to remind you of facts that you must remember for school. Of course, if you have roommates, you may need to obtain their consent before going great guns with this educational initiative.

Flash cards are not just for elementary school children. They can be used as reminders and tutors for adults as well. The only difference is that they cannot be store-purchased; you must make your own. On a set of index cards, write out one question to a card on one side of the cards, and print the answers on the reverse sides. Carry the cards with you as much as possible and review them every chance you get.

Many people write out "To Do" lists to remind themselves about what they have to do that day, and depending upon how you study, you may find the creation of a similar "To Study" list helpful. Tying a yellow ribbon to a tree has become a reminder to all who see it that we want someone or some group of people to come home. The wearing of a red ribbon is gaining increasing recognition as a sign of sensitivity and concern regarding AIDS. Pick your favorite hue of ribbon and wrap it around some object that you are going to see on a daily basis. Let it serve as a reminder to you regarding some school-related material or practice. For example, because one of the associations people have to green is freshness and growth, a piece of green ribbon might serve as a reminder to think generatively.

Ultimately, you will get the most out of your note taking if it represents not stenographic skill, but your personal classroom account based on active listening.

QUESTION ASKING

Neither teacher nor student has a monopoly on asking questions; *both* students and teachers raise questions to stimulate thought on the material being covered. For the student, the course-work-related questions that come to mind may be categorized as public, semi-public, and private. Public questions are those raised in class for everyone to hear. Semi-private questions are those that you may, for whatever reason, choose only to voice to people with whom you are in a special relationship (such as your instructor, a close friend, etc.). Perhaps most of the course-related questions that will come to mind will be private in nature. This is so because you may be actively questioning a great deal of what you read and you may not wish to verbalize all such questions in class (or elsewhere).

As an example of a private question, consider again the photo of the student protester in front of the tank that appeared on page 4. When you first saw the photo, a question that may have occurred to you immediately is, "Why is this man standing in front of the tank?" As you read on, another question that may have occurred is, "What must this man be feeling at such a time?" And as you began to think generatively about this scenario, your questions may have generalized to include not only the thoughts and feelings of the man in front of the tank, but the thoughts and feelings of the crew members inside the tank, the bystanders in the crowd, the government officials condoning the use of military force against unarmed civilians, and so forth.

Well thought-out questions raised in class can help stretch your own understanding of the matter under discussion as well as that of your fellow students. Further, questions provide needed feedback to instructors regarding how well the course material is being conveyed.

SEIZING THE OPPORTUNITY FOR PERSONAL GROWTH

personal growth
change in the self for the better.

Personal growth may be defined simply as *change in the self for the better.* Sometimes this beneficial variety of change will arise out of positive experiences, such as reading an inspiring book. Other times, it may arise from not-so-positive experiences, as when one learns something new and important about oneself under emergency or adverse conditions.

Among all the courses you are currently taking, you will probably find this one to be most special. This is because in addition to being about people in general, this course is about *you*. In addition to being about theories, it is about theories that apply to *you*. This course is not merely about values, it is about *your* values. While answering a question posed in one of the many *A Question of Values* sections presented in these pages, you may discover something particularly insightful about your own values as they pertain to "who you are." As you read about the relationship between physical health and mental health, you may think about the last time you were at a chinning bar. When reading about defense mechanisms, it may occur to you that one or another of them has been interfering with the achievement of some of your most cherished objectives. In short, expect from the outset that some of the material presented in this book and discussed in class may have great personal relevance to you.

Perhaps more than any other undergraduate course you will take, this course may start you thinking about yourself in a new way. You may find yourself experiencing various feelings as you read. What kinds of feelings? Feelings of apprehension—because you think some description of an abnormal behavior pattern matches your own behavior. Feelings of relief—because you are happy to read that some behavior on the part of your child is perfectly normal. Feelings of social urgency—because you find yourself developing strong sympathies towards one or another political movement, such as the environmental movement. Feelings of enlightenment—because you have been exposed to issues that you never gave much thought to before. Feelings of pride—because you've gotten in touch with "who you really are" and discovered that you like what you find. Feelings of uncertainty—because as you read about topics such as marriage, divorce, aging, death, work, and leisure, you wonder what life holds in store for you.

The key to dealing with such thoughts and feelings is to grow and become a better person as a result of them. If you feel comfortable enough to do so, you may wish to make a habit of sharing some of these thoughts and feelings with your classmates, either in or out of class. Like you, your classmates may be thinking about the same things—and personally growing as a result.

The following four chapters in this unit focus on various perspectives helpful in understanding human behavior and the psychology of adjustment. In the chapter that immediately follows, we focus on psychological frameworks. As you read, keep in mind that human behavior is extremely complex; no theory advanced to date has been entirely comprehensive or completely satisfactory. Also note that various frameworks for understanding human behavior are, like everything else, the product of a particular time period. Sigmund Freud's perspective on people, for example, is through the eyes of a clinician writing in Vienna nearly 100 years ago. Many of his ideas have required creative updating by contemporary Freudians. Freud's understanding of personality development in children, for example, was based on the premise of a two-parent family, not a one-parent, zero-parent, or modified-by-divorce family. In subsequent chapters in this unit, we will look at people from biological, cultural, and developmental perspectives.

SUMMARY

THE WORLD OF PSYCHOLOGY *Psychology* is the study of mental processes and behavior. This science and profession is very broad in scope, covering many varied aspects of human and animal behavior.

THE PSYCHOLOGY OF ADJUSTMENT The *psychology of adjustment* refers to that portion of behavioral science that deals with the way humans adapt to changing situations. Individual or cultural values often influence what is perceived as effective behavior or behavior that reflects a healthy psychological adjustment. Change—unexpected as well as expected—is very much a part of everyday life. Because adjustment occurs in response to change, adjustment can best be thought of as a constant process. The roles people play in life also change over time and sometimes role conflict occurs. Successful adjustment entails effectively dealing with such conflict.

THE ROLE OF STUDENT The role of student carries its own adjustive demands and challenges. Some of the behaviors expected of people in their role as students include thinking, studying, processing of information imparted in class, test taking, and personal time management. Two types of thought

processes emphasized in this book are *critical thinking* and *generative thinking*. Critical thinking is a thought process characterized by an active weighing of the merits and faults of information. Generative thinking is the intellectual production of new, novel, or creative ideas. Both types of thinking encourage students to process information they receive thoroughly and to look at it in new, perhaps original ways. Both types of thinking discourage students from being passive recipients of information.

One system for studying is the *SQ3R* method wherein *S* stands for survey, *Q* stands for question, and *3R* stands for read, recite, and review. In addition, effective in-class skills (such as active listening) and test-taking skills are most helpful for success in the student role.

Personal growth may be defined simply as change in the self for the better. Because this course deals with the psychology of adjustment, the student is encouraged to seize the opportunity to use this course not just to obtain credits on a transcript, but to achieve personal growth.

Psychological Perspectives

O U T L I N E

Describe the personality of someone who is an accomplished business person. What is your vision of the personality of someone who is a great psychotherapist? A great academic researcher? How about the personality of someone who is excellent in the art of making and keeping friends? How would you describe your own personality as compared to each of these types of people? How do you suppose personalities develop?

These questions pertain to the *psychological construct* of personality. In psychology, a **construct** may be defined as an *informed, scientific idea that is fabricated or "constructed" to describe or explain behavior.* In contrast to things that can be physically observed and directly measured in reality, constructs do not have a physical existence and can be measured only indirectly. For example, *anxiety* is a construct. It has no physical existence. It cannot be observed or measured directly although it may be inferred from certain visible signs (such as an apprehensive facial expression and clammy palms) as well as from verbal self-report (as in the statement, "I am nervous"). The construct *anxiety* can be used to help explain varied phenomena ranging from reluctance to engage in public speaking to difficulty in falling asleep at night.

Intelligence is another psychological construct. The construct *intelligence* can be used, among other ways, to help explain varied phenomena ranging from a person's grade on a vocabulary test to a person's knowing the answers to questions asked on *Jeopardy*. Can you think of any other psychological constructs? What about *motivation? Depression? Self-esteem?* Like other psychological constructs, these have no physical existence and must be inferred from behavior. Psychological constructs are thought to exist in different magnitudes in people and psychological tests and other assessment procedures (such as interviews and role-playing exercises) are the tools used to measure them. Psychological theories of personality advance notions about how or why people differ with respect to psychological constructs. Stated another way, theories of personality advance ideas about how people come to be psychologically unique. In this chapter, we will introduce many psychological constructs believed by different theorists to have great utility in explaining personality. Before exploring these personality-related constructs and theories, some discussion of the construct *personality* will be useful.

WHAT IS PERSONALITY?

construct

an informed, scientific idea that is fabricated or "constructed" to describe or explain behavior.

In every day conversation, people generally use the word *personality* as a kind of shorthand for describing the sum total of an individual's ability to relate to others. A "great personality" describes someone who generally elicits favorable reactions, while terms like "no personality" and "bad personality" describe people who tend to leave others feeling neutral at best.

Perhaps because psychologists having different types of education, training, and experience tend to view the construct of personality differently, various definitions of personality exist. For our purposes, we will define **personality** after Cohen et al. (1988, p. 401) as *an individual's unique constellation of psychological traits and states.* Having defined personality in terms of traits and states, we next consider the meaning of these, as well as related, terms.

personality

an individual's unique constellation of psychological traits and states.

PSYCHOLOGICAL TRAITS

trait

a characteristic.

psychological trait

any distinguishable, relatively enduring way in which one individual varies from another.

A **trait** may be defined simply as *a characteristic.* The term *physical trait* as applied to people refers to some characteristic of the body such as blue eyes or a cleft chin. The term **psychological trait** has been defined in many different ways. Here we will define it, after Guilford (1959, p. 6), as *any distinguishable, relatively enduring way in which one individual varies from another.* Guilford's use of the phrase "relatively enduring" must be emphasized because psychological traits do not necessarily exhibit themselves in consistent fashion. This point was emphasized by Cohen et al. (1992):

> The modifier "relatively" serves to emphasize that exactly how a particular trait manifests itself is, at least to some extent, situation-dependent. For example, a "violent" parolee may generally be prone to behave in a rather subdued way with her parole officer and much more violently in the presence of her family and friends. John may be viewed as "dull" and "cheap" by his wife, but as "charming" and "extravagant" by his secretary, business associates, and others he is keenly interested in impressing. (p. 402)

Personality-related trait terms are part of our everyday vocabulary and they have probably been around for as long as people have talked about individual differences. One psychologist, Gordon W. Allport (1897–1967), spent much of his professional life developing and writing about a complex theory of personality that relied heavily on the concept of personality traits. The two most comprehensive presentations of his theory can be found in *Personality: A Psychological Interpretation* (1937) and *Pattern and Growth in Personality* (1961). Although Allport's trait-related writings never attracted a great following, they served as a strong influence on others. Scholars have criticized Allport's theory of personality for its emphasis on the individual person, and its insufficient emphasis on social and environmental factors in behavior.

"PRIMARY" OR "SOURCE" TRAITS

Walk into a paint store and ask for white paint and you might be shown a dozen or two shades of white—a reality that was driven home to me when my wife and I decided to paint the interior of our house. After examining samples of white until they all seemed to blur, we decided on "linen white" for the house, except for the kitchen and bath where we chose "decorator white."

The array of available paint colors, either ready-blended or custom-mixed, was truly astounding. Yet that seemingly infinite array of colors can be reduced to three primary ones; red, yellow, and blue. Can the same be true for the seemingly infinite number of trait terms used to describe people? Can we specify a limited number of "primary" psychological traits?

A number of researchers have cited a need to devise a listing of personality traits that constitute the essential or "source traits" of personality (Eysenck & Eysenck, 1984; Kline & Barrett, 1983; Wiggins, 1979). Such a list, if it enjoyed widespread agreement, could provide psychologists with a uniform way to evaluate personality for clinical, research, or other purposes. However, devising such a listing of source traits, also referred to by some as "primary factors," has proven to be no easy matter. For example, one issue to be dealt with is comprehensiveness—how representative this listing of source traits actually is of that broad concept, "personality" (Goldberg, 1982; Peabody, 1984). Another issue concerns the extent to which the listing of source traits is grounded in a particular theory of personality (Hogan, 1983). Yet another issue concerns the extent to which any proposed listing of source traits can be found in existing psychological tests and assessment methods, including self-descriptions, and observer ratings (McCrae & Costa, 1987).

Raymond Cattell (1957) studied upwards of 18,000 trait-related terms in the English language (Allport & Odbert, 1936), and after using some sophisticated data reduction methods, concluded that 16 personality traits represent the primary or source traits of human personality (see Table 2–1). As you might expect, the methods used in such a data reduction process are controversial—much more so than determining which colors are primary—perhaps because so much more subjectivity and human judgment are involved (Cattell & Krug, 1986). It is not debatable, nor controversial, to say that red mixed with white makes pink. By contrast, it *is* debatable to say, for example, that the combination of the psychological traits *commitment, challenge,* and *control* yields a trait called *psychological hardiness,* a trait you will be introduced to in the following chapter.

Other personality theorists (Amelang & Borkenau, 1982; Digman & Takemoto-Chock, 1981; Goldberg, 1981; Norman, 1963; Tupes & Christal, 1961) have suggested that only five factors are needed for a model of personality. This view has most recently been popularized by Paul T. Costa, Jr., and Robert R. McCrae (1989; McCrae & Costa, 1987; Costa, 1991; McCrae, 1991) and it has received an enthusiastic reception (Digman, 1990; Piedmont & Weinstein, 1993). The five factors in the five-factor model of personality are:

- *Conscientiousness* including dimensions such as laziness versus hardworking, and punctual versus late;
- *Agreeableness* including dimensions such as lenient versus critical, and good-natured versus irritable;

TABLE 2–1 WHAT ARE THE "SOURCE" TRAITS OF PERSONALITY?

16 Source Traits of Personality According to Cattell (1957)

Trait Term	Range of Behaviors
1. Sociable	cool and reserved to warm and easygoing
2. Intelligent	dull, concrete thinking to bright, abstract thinking
3. Mature	easily upset to emotionally stable and calm
4. Dominant	obedient and submissive to assertive
5. Cheerful	sober and serious to enthusiastic
6. Persistent	undependable to conscientious
7. Adventurous	shy and timid to venturesome
8. Effeminate	tough-minded to sensitive
9. Suspicious	trusting to suspicious
10. Imaginative	practical to imaginative
11. Shrewd	naive to sophisticated
12. Insecure	self-assured to self-doubting
13. Radical	conservative and traditional to experimenting and nontraditional
14. Self-sufficient	group-dependent to self-sufficient
15. Controlled	undisciplined to self-disciplined
16. Tense	relaxed and laid back to tense and driven

- *Neuroticism* including dimensions such as worrying versus calm, and even-tempered versus temperamental;
- *Openness to Experience* including dimensions such as original versus conventional, and preference for routine versus preference for variety; and
- *Extroversion* including dimensions such as loner versus joiner, and sober versus fun-loving.

Note that as the number of primary factors or source traits decreases, the broadness of the meaning of the factor must increase. For example, *Openness to Experience* is one of the five factors in the five-factor model, and traits as diverse as *original, imaginative, creative, independent, liberal,* and *daring* are all subsumed under it. It would be possible to derive a four-, three-, two-, or even one-factor model by collapsing even more trait terms under one primary or source descriptor term. The problem, of course, is that the descriptor becomes so broad in meaning as to be rendered meaningless. Another potential problem with using very few factors is the higher probability that different dimensions of the factor will overlap. For example, while Costa (1991) cited the "passive-active" dimension to describe the *Extroversion* factor, these dimensions might arguably also describe the *Openness to Experience* factor.

THE USE OF TRAIT TERMS

Personality trait-related terms are very much part of the vocabulary of psychologists and laypeople. Many contemporary psychologists use interviews, tests, and other measures to gauge the degree to which certain personality traits exist in a person. The resulting data may be used in a psychological description of that person and/or evidence to prove or disprove predictions made by a particular theory of personality. For example, the results of a test used to measure the trait of *aggression* in a convicted armed robber might be used simply to describe the robber or to help understand the robber's behavior in the context of some theory of personality. The same trait terms have been used within the contexts of many different theories of personality and the meanings and connotations of the terms may differ depending on the context. For example, as you will appreciate as you read further in this chapter, the trait *dependent* in the context of Freud's personality theory implies "fixation at the oral stage of development." *Dependent* carries with it no such implication when it is used free of the context of Freud's theory.[1]

[1]Even within the basic theoretical framework of Freudian theory, the same trait term may have different meanings depending upon the user's interpretation. For example, *anxious* would have different meanings for Freud and for another famous Freudian psychoanalyst, Karen Horney. This point about trait terms will become clearer as we explore different theories of personality.

In using trait terms, it is very easy for both psychologists and laypeople to fall into what could be called "the tautology trap." A *tautology* may be defined as a needless repetition of something in different words. Suppose, for example, your friend John goes out to dinner with Mary, a newly arrived exchange student from Switzerland. According to John's recounting of the evening's events, "When the check came, Mary insisted on paying it. I noticed that she didn't leave a tip. The service was good and I thought it was cheap not to leave a tip."

"Why didn't Mary leave a tip?" you ask.

"Because she's cheap!" John responds.

Note that John used the trait term *cheap* in a tautological manner: it served both to *describe* and to *explain* Mary's behavior. John might have been more accurate in both his description of Mary's behavior and his explanation of its cause had he reserved judgment until he (1) knew Mary better and had observed her behavior across a wide range of situations, (2) defined in his own mind exactly what *cheap* means as a description and as an explanation of behavior, and (3) discussed with Mary her general thoughts about spending money and tipping restaurant staff. Had he discussed the matter with Mary, he may have learned the great value of a cultural as opposed to psychological perspective in this particular case. John would have learned, for example, that Mary was raised in Europe where many restaurants add a service charge directly to the bill so that tipping is not necessary. Often, cultural, biological, and other perspectives contribute greatly to our understanding of the psychological traits used to describe or explain human behavior.

PSYCHOLOGICAL STATES

The word *state* has also been used in different ways in the personality theory literature. In one usage, **state** is defined as *a transitory exhibition of a trait*. For example, when you first received notice of your acceptance to college you may have been in a state of elation. "Elated" would not be a trait that accurately describes you in your everyday life. It would, however, accurately describe the transitory state you were in.

state
a transitory exhibition of a trait.

PSYCHOLOGICAL TYPES

Another basic term in the vocabulary of personality theory is *personality type*. For our purposes, we may define a **personality type** as *any distinguishable, relatively enduring way in which one group of personality traits varies from another group of personality traits*. Many personality theories, such as those developed by Carl Jung (1923) and Alfred Adler (1927/1965), rely heavily on the notion that meaningful typologies of people can be developed. For example, Adler distinguished between what he called the *Good Man type* (people concerned with fellow human beings), and the *Ruling type* ("bossy," and, at worst, homicidal people). Certain psychological tests, such as the Myers-Briggs Type Indicator, have as their objective the use of different personality types to label the test-taker.

personality type
any distinguishable, relatively enduring way in which one group of personality traits varies from another group of personality traits.

With this brief background, let's proceed to consider some of the different personality theories and related perspectives on people that have dominated psychology.

A PSYCHOANALYTIC PERSPECTIVE

For psychology, the twentieth century began with a landmark event. In 1900, Sigmund Freud's book, *The Interpretation of Dreams,* was published. The book was important not only because it set forth Freud's thinking on the subject of dreams, but also because its final chapter detailed the first-ever theory of personality—a comprehensive one based on Freud's own clinical experience.

Freud called the method of psychotherapy he devised **psycho-analysis** (the hyphen has since been dropped), a term which refers quite literally to *the study of the mind*. As you will see, Freud believed that it was useful to study the mind in terms of three constructs he called the *id,* the *ego,* and the *superego*. The term **psychoanalytic theory** refers both to *the theory of personality that Freud developed, as well as the theory underlying Freud's system of*

psychoanalysis
a method of psychotherapy originated by Sigmund Freud.

psychoanalytic theory
refers both to the theory of personality that Freud developed and to the theory underlying Freud's system of therapy.

psychoanalytic perspective
a view or understanding of human behavior, thought, and motivation having reference to psychoanalytic theory.

therapy. The term **psychoanalytic perspective** refers to *a view or understanding of human behavior, thought, and motivation having reference to psychoanalytic theory.*

THE LIFE AND TIMES OF SIGMUND FREUD

Sigmund Freud (1856–1939) was one of eight children in a relatively poor family from what is now Czechoslovakia. Because he was born with a streak of some dark black hair on his head, cultural lore foretold his greatness. Looking back on that lore many years later, Freud shrugged it off, attributing it to the usual optimism experienced by "so many happy and expectant mothers" (cited in Jones, 1961, p. 6). Still, his mother is supposed to have reminded him of his "fate" while he grew up. In this context, it is noteworthy to draw parallels to Freud's theory which is indeed very fatalistic, in that childhood events are critically important to adult personality. To a large degree, one's behavioral fate becomes sealed in childhood according to psychoanalytic theory.

Freud studied biology at the University of Vienna. As a Jew, he was restricted to the professions of law and medicine by the anti-Semitism of the day. Freud was interested in scientific research, but not necessarily in becoming a physician. In fact, he would only begin seeing patients out of financial necessity. He earned his MD in 1881, became engaged to Martha Bernays in 1882, and married her four years later after what has been described as a stormy courtship. The couple would have six children and family life was never very easy due to continual financial problems. Even later in life, the burden of Freud's jaw cancer and the surgeries that cancer required exacted a heavy toll in terms of finances and stress.

While studying biology and medicine, Freud was exposed to the writings of many German philosophers and scientists who had speculated about the nature of the relationship between the brain and behavior. For example, in the early eighteenth century, Gottfried von Leibniz (1646–1716) had introduced the idea that perception could exist below the level of consciousness. Johann Herbart (1776–1841) elaborated on Leibniz's ideas by conceiving of the notion of a conflict between perceptions for representation in consciousness. Gustav Fechner (1801–1887) conceptualized the unconscious as a kind of iceberg—imagery that would later have a profound effect on Sigmund Freud (see Figure 2–1).

In addition to academic influences, one can also look to social influences on Freud's thinking. Freud grew up in a Victorian society in which sex was something to be thought about, not talked about freely. There were no *Cosmopolitan* surveys on sexual satisfaction, no *Sally Jessy Raphael* shows dealing with sexual frustration, no Masters, no Johnson, and no condoms dispensed in classrooms. It was a very different world. Rarely discussed in public, sex was a subject surrounded by mystery and brimming with confusion. In retrospect, it is little wonder that a mental health professional of the day might believe so passionately that many psychological "hang-ups" were in some way related to sex. In a culture that provided few outlets other than a physician's office to raise personal questions and discuss highly sensitive problems, Freud's "talking cure" provided a much needed form of therapy.

psychophysics
the study of how physical stimuli are perceived.

FIGURE 2–1 THE ICEBERG ANALOGY As part of his experimental work in the area of **psychophysics,** *the study of how physical stimuli are perceived,* Gustav Fechner likened the mind to an iceberg. According to this analogy, the majority of the mind is hidden below the surface of consciousness, where it is influenced by unobservable forces. Sigmund Freud would later describe and explain the significance of this submerged mass in terms of unconscious influences on behavior. Additionally, Freud would innovate techniques designed to explore this large and uncharted territory below the surface.

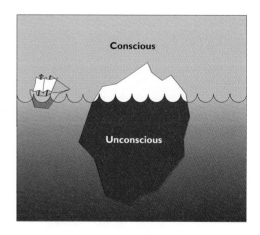

One of Freud's early mentors was Josef Breuer, a physician who was experimenting with hypnosis in the treatment of mental disorders. Freud became interested in this method of treatment, and in 1885 spent four months in France studying the technique with Jean Charcot, director of a renowned neurological clinic. One evening at a reception, Freud heard Charcot insist that in certain kinds of mental disorders, the root of the problem was always sexual in nature (Boring, 1950, p. 709). It is thought that this view made an impression on Freud as he too would soon express a similar position.

Freud practiced hypnosis for a while upon his return to Vienna but soon gave it up in favor of his own creation, **free association,** *a technique wherein patients recline on a couch and say everything that comes into their minds without censoring anything.* Free association was a technique designed to make the unconscious conscious. In the years that followed, Freud would devise a number of other techniques having the same objective. The analysis of dreams and the analysis of slips of the tongue (see *In the News*) are also techniques designed to illuminate the unconscious.

Recognition of Freud's work was slow in coming because many of his ideas were viewed as outlandish, if not offensive, by much of the established Viennese medical community. Still, he slowly gained increasing acceptance. In 1909, Freud was invited to speak at a celebration of the 20th anniversary of Clark University in Massachusetts (see Figure 2–2). On this occasion, Freud was awarded an honorary doctorate and met some of America's most prominent psychologists, including the president of Clark University, G. Stanley Hall, a man Freud perceived as a "kingmaker" (Rosenzweig, 1993). Freud viewed the invitation and the honorary degree he was awarded as a validation of his efforts—one of the few such validations and official honors bestowed on him during his life.[2]

Progress in psychoanalysis and science in general was impeded by World War I. However, by the 1920s, Freud was again heavily involved in his work, and it was during these years, on the basis of clinical experience rather than formal research, that Freud refined his theory of personality.

free association

a psychoanalytic technique, designed to make the unconscious conscious, in which patients say everything that comes to mind without censoring anything.

[2]Rosenzweig (1993) reconstructed this historic trip in great detail, including Freud's visit to New York upon arrival from Europe. On the day before his party would travel to Clark University, Freud wet his pants. Rosenzweig tells us that Freud asked his colleague Carl Jung to analyze that accident. Jung, who in later years would become Freud's rival, interpreted the behavior as indicative of Freud's need to call attention to himself no matter what the cost.

IN THE

Mario Cuomo's Freudian Slips

Moments in two speeches given by New York's governor Mario Cuomo in March 1992, after he had elected not to seek the Democratic Party's nomination for president, are of interest from a psychoanalytic perspective. While making reference to his life in politics, he began, "When I got elected Presid—." He then stopped himself and became flushed as the audience applauded enthusiastically. In another speech, he had to stop himself again when he began, "As I said in my State of the Union speech this year—" ("Cuomo's Freudian Slips," 1992).

In a book entitled *The Psychopathology of Everyday Life,* Freud described how slips of the tongue, forgetting, and accidents are reflective of the struggle of unconscious thoughts to gain mental expression. Interpreting what Cuomo said according to Freud (1904), might lead one to suspect that the presidency was very much on Cuomo's mind—somewhere, conscious or unconscious. How else might Cuomo's slips of the tongue be interpreted?

FIGURE 2–2 FREUD AT CLARK UNIVERSITY Freud's only trip to the United States was to make a presentation and to be honored himself at Clark University. Seated from left to right, Sigmund Freud (note trademark cigar in his left hand), G. Stanley Hall (the first president of the American Psychological Association), and Carl Jung (one of Freud's disciples). Standing, from left to right, are Abraham A. Brill (an American psychiatrist), Ernest Jones (a psychoanalyst and prolific writer who has left us with richly detailed accounts of Freud's life), and Sandor Ferenczi (a psychoanalyst in Freud's inner circle whose kissing and hugging of patients did not win approval from Freud once Freud got wind of the practice).

THE PSYCHOANALYTIC THEORY OF PERSONALITY

As a medical student, Freud was taught that the laws of physics and chemistry could be applied to the living organism as a system. This view of the body has been referred to as a "dynamic" perspective because the laws of physics and chemistry allow for energy exchanges. **Dynamic** in this sense means *of or pertaining to energy or force.*

Freud expanded the model of the human body as a dynamic system to include a model of the human mind as a dynamic system. This is why the psychoanalytic theory of personality, and its many variations, are sometimes referred to as **psychodynamic** (literally, *mind/energy*) in nature.

From a biological perspective, an organism derives energy from food and then depletes it in activities that are both voluntary (such as running), and involuntary (such as breathing). Freud created an analogous construct called *psychic energy.* As mechanical energy is involved in mechanical activity, and as chemical energy is involved in chemical activity, so psychic energy was thought to be involved in psychological activity. Some psychic energy was thought to be employed in conscious thinking, while much more of it was thought to be involved in unconscious processes. Freud also believed that exchanges and transformations between different forms of energy were constantly occurring, although he left for future researchers the problem of how these exchanges actually took place. Thoughts (psychic energy) about turning the page in this book, for example, could be translated into movement (muscular energy) at any time. The phone rings and the transformation of the sound (mechanical energy) into a perception that the phone is ringing (psychic energy) similarly involves an energy transformation. As illustrated in Figure 2–3, Freud's model of energy exchanges within the mind included three constructs that he referred to as the *id,* the *ego,* and the *superego.*

The **id** is *the seat of the instincts.* According to Freud, an **instinct** is *an inborn condition that drives psychological processes.* For example, hunger is an instinct that drives an organism to seek out and consume food. Organisms strive to quell the excitation of instinctual urges when they arise. Whether or not the instincts are quelled in a socially appropriate way will depend on a number of interactive factors such as the age of the person. According to Freud's theory, infants cannot be expected to behave socially appropriately due to the lack of development of their ego and superego. A lack of development, or faulty development of the ego and superego, are presumed to be the cause of socially inappropriate behavior in adults. Stealing an apple from a fruit stand is not a socially appropriate way of quelling hunger pangs. Paying the vendor for the apple is. The id is not equipped to comprehend socially appropriate ways of behaving but only to want what it wants when it wants it. In stealing as in other socially inappropriate forms of behavior, the id is presumed to be playing too dominant a role in the individual's behavior.

The **ego** is *the structure designed to control the id and the superego.* In the well-adjusted individual, the ego does just that. In the maladjusted individual, either the id or the super-

dynamic

of or pertaining to energy or force.

psychodynamic

of or pertaining to mental energy exchanges.

id

in psychoanalytic theory, the mental structure governing one's instincts.

instinct

an inborn, unlearned condition or motivating process, as in hunger.

ego

in psychoanalytic theory, the mental structure that controls the id and the superego.

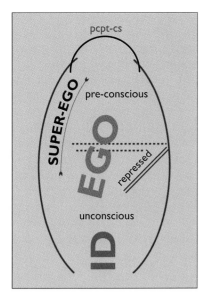

FIGURE 2–3 THE MIND ACCORDING TO FREUD In this redrawn sketch, Freud (1933, p. 111), illustrated his theory of personality. At the top of this sketch are the letters *pcpt-cs* which stand for "perceptual-conscious" or, stated simply, conscious. The flow of psychic energy in this model is bidirectional. Something you perceive may be pressed into—or, more accurately, repressed into—the unconscious, while repressed material in the unconscious may surface to consciousness. The ego has elements that are unconscious (containing repressed material) as well as elements that are preconscious. Exerting a "supervisory influence" of sorts over both the pre-conscious and unconscious material in the ego is the superego. At the base of this reservoir of psychic energy lies the id, with its sexual, aggressive, and other instinctual urges demanding satisfaction. In the well-adjusted individual, the instinctual urgings of the id are held in check by the ego and the superego.

ego may exert excessive control over the ego. Whereas the id is said to be governed by the **pleasure principle** (that is, it *seeks pleasure and avoids pain*), the ego is governed by the **reality principle**, *seeking gratification through appropriate means with appropriate objects*. Thus, while young children may place virtually anything in their mouths (illustrating the id and the pleasure principle at work), older children (having more developed egos) will only place food, lollipops, gum, and other suitable objects in their mouths. Freud used the term **displacement** to refer to *the process by which psychic energy is shunted from one object to another*. As they age, children typically displace the desire to suck their thumb to more appropriate objects. The degree of resemblance between the two objects will be one factor that will influence the exact form a displacement will take. A second influence on the form a displacement will take has to do with what is socially acceptable. It is socially acceptable, for example, to suck a lollipop. It is not socially acceptable to suck one's thumb.

Although the ego primarily serves reality, it is also capable of distorting it. In daydreaming and fantasizing, for example, reality is intentionally distorted in favor of the pleasure principle. The ego's distortion of reality may take less constructive forms, however, as when it acts to deny or falsify.

The **superego** is *the keeper of the mind's morals and values*. In essence, it is the superego that serves as a reminder that there are loftier considerations than the mere seeking of pleasure and dealing with day-to-day reality. The superego represents the internalization of the lessons one has learned from one's parents or society in general about what is good, proper, ethical, or moral. Rather than seeking pleasure or reality, the superego seeks perfection. But just as dominance of the id in the mind of an individual may lead to maladjustment, so might dominance of the superego. This potential for maladjustment is due in part to the fact that both the superego and the id have in common the ability to falsify reality. For example, a psychoanalytic interpretation of the eating disorder bulimia, which is characterized by, among other things, binge-eating and purging, excessive exercise, and perfectionism, would make reference to the dominance of the individual's superego, and its falsification of reality. The perfectionistic falsification might take the form of a young woman whose weight is in reality within normal limits perceiving herself as "too fat."

Another key concept in Freudian theory is **anxiety.** Defined in psychoanalytic terms, anxiety is *a conscious and painful experience of tension or dread produced by internal organs of the body in response to internal or external stimuli*. The source of anxiety may be an internal event, such as one's own thoughts, or some event external to the person, such as war. Freud distinguished three different types of anxiety. **Reality anxiety** may be defined as *fear arising from something that exists in the external world*. If you have ever borrowed money from a loan shark who has threatened to have your legs broken if you missed a payment, you

pleasure principle

in psychoanalytic theory, a striving to seek pleasure and avoid pain.

reality principle

in psychoanalytic theory, seeking gratification through appropriate means with appropriate objects.

displacement

process by which psychic energy is shunted from one object to another.

superego

in psychoanalytic theory, the keeper of the mind's morals and values.

reality anxiety

in psychoanalytic theory, fear arising from something that exists in the external world.

moral anxiety
in psychoanalytic theory, a fear of the superego, usually characterized by feelings of guilt or shame, as in the case of disturbing sexual or aggressive urges or fantasies.

neurotic anxiety
in psychoanalytic theory, a fear of one's own id and instinctual impulses.

phobia
irrational fear characterized by the generation of great anxiety and avoidance behavior.

psychosexual stages
in psychoanalytic theory, periods in maturation linked to the discharge of sexual energy in various ways.

have probably suffered reality anxiety. **Moral anxiety** is a *fear of the superego, usually characterized by feelings of guilt or shame.* Sexual or aggressive urges or fantasies—too shocking for you in spite of the fact that they are your own—are likely to result in moral anxiety. Society in Freud's day, as well as today, imparted mixed messages regarding the expression of sexuality and aggression. When one is not certain whether one's thoughts or actions are morally right, moral anxiety may result. **Neurotic anxiety** is a *fear of one's own id and instinctual impulses.* Included under the category of neurotic anxiety are all **phobias**, or *irrational fears.* Freud characterized phobias as manifestations of neurotic anxiety because he believed that the object of a phobia was only a symbol of some instinctual impulse pressing for expression. So, for example, the person who is agoraphobic (that is, fearful of venturing outdoors into the street), may in reality harbor a fear of unconscious sexual urges such as the urge to become a "streetwalker" or prostitute.

It is the ego's task to deal with danger and threats that may arouse anxiety. The ego may deal with danger and threats in any number of different ways. Some ways are more effective than others, and some ways are more reality-oriented than others. In Table 2–2, a number of different ego defense mechanisms are defined and discussed.

HUMAN DEVELOPMENT ACCORDING TO FREUD

Many theorists who have sought to understand human behavior from birth onward have devised developmental theories that outline stages of development. In Freud's theory, the person is said to go through **psychosexual stages**, *periods in maturation linked to the discharge of sexual energy in various ways.* Sexual energy, synonymous with the psychoanalytic concept of *libido,* has a very broad meaning, a fact Freud himself pointed out in one of his lectures at the University of Vienna:

> Whereas, for most people, the word "mental" means "conscious," we found ourselves obliged to widen the application of the term "mental" to include a part of the mind that is not conscious. In a precisely similar way, most people declare "sexual" identical with "pertaining to reproduction"—or, if you like it expressed more concisely, with "genital"; whereas we cannot avoid admitting things as "sexual" that are not "genital" and have nothing to do with reproduction. (Freud, 1952, p. 330)

Freud's use of the term *sexual* was equivalent to *pleasurable,* especially with reference to the subject of "infantile sexuality." In the first or oral stage of development, the object of sexual gratification is something to wrap one's mouth around and suck on. An infant sucking on a nipple (flesh or otherwise) is in this context having a "sexual" experience. As teeth erupt, the infant obtains pleasure not only from sucking and incorporating food into its body, but from biting as well. At this stage of development, psychic energy may be displaced into what are called "oral incorporative" personality traits. Such traits may be manifested in adults through incorporative activities as diverse as eating, incorporating knowledge, and sunning oneself. Alternatively, the psychic energy may be displaced into what are called "oral aggressive" personality traits. A film critic who spends much of his adult life gleefully preparing reviews with "biting sarcasm" is one who would be presumed to have obtained great pleasure from biting as an infant.

The second psychosexual stage is the anal stage (see Table 2–3). Toilet training typically begins at age 2, and it is at this time that the child first begins to experience the pleasure of releasing tension through evacuation or of maintaining tension in the intestines by fighting urges to evacuate. Freud believed that the nature of the toilet training experience was capable of leaving a lasting impression on an adult's personality (see Figure 2–4 on page 38).

During the third, or phallic stage of development, the focus of sexual gratification shifts to the genitals and, according to Freud, children experience sexual (this time, in the more traditional use of that word) feelings and urges, usually toward the opposite-sex parent. The condition as it applies to the development of both boys and girls was called the "Oedipus complex" by Freud. This name stems from the story of the Greek king Oedipus who unwittingly killed his father and married his mother. Some latter-day analysts have preferred to differentiate this condition in girls as the "Electra complex," another reference to Greek mythology. Both boys and girls are said to experience "castration anxiety." In boys,

TABLE 2–2   EGO DEFENSE MECHANISMS

As you read about these mechanisms, try to recall if you or someone you know may have ever used any of them. Is the use of a defense mechanism always good? Always bad? Can you think of situations in which the use of each of these defense mechanisms would be a sign of adjustment? A sign of maladjustment?

Defense Mechanism	Definition	Explanation
Repression	*The forcing of anxiety-provoking material out of consciousness, or maintaining out of consciousness material that was never conscious in the first place.*	Repression as an ego defense may be instituted by the ego or the superego. If something one witnesses is too emotionally painful, for example, the mechanism of repression may result in hysterical blindness (an inability to see even though there is nothing physically wrong).
Projection	*The process of causally attributing anxiety generating from the id or superego to the external world.*	In Freudian terms, projection involves an attempt by the ego to convert moral or neurotic anxiety into reality anxiety. For example, if it is too anxiety-provoking to think, "I am so angry at John I could kill him," one might instead project or attribute such aggressive thinking to John: "John is so angry at me he could kill me."
Rationalization	*The process of finding an excuse in the real world to justify something that might be frowned upon by the superego.*	Freud subsumed rationalization in projection, because rationalization so frequently accompanies projection. In the example offered above, the person thinking that "John is so angry at me he could kill me," might then rationalize aggressive thoughts towards John.
Reaction Formation	*Dealing with the anxiety aroused by one instinct by thinking or acting on its opposite.*	Freud viewed every instinct as having two opposite poles. For instance, he believed in a life instinct and a death instinct. Anxiety aroused by unacceptable impulses resulting from one instinct, such as a desire to hurt one's spouse, might be held in check through reaction formation. This would lead to totally opposite thinking and what could be described as "overly loving" behavior. When someone "protests too much," a reaction formation may be operating.
Fixation	*Cessation of emotional development in response to fear or anxiety.*	Fear of failure, fear of punishment, or other fears and sources of anxiety may prevent one from achieving emotional growth. For example, committing to love and marriage represents a momentous step in the lives of most people. Yet some people are unable to take this step due to debilitating fear. Freudians would say that such people are *fixated* in development. To protect their egos against what they perceive as the overwhelming anxiety that marriage will bring, they unconsciously remain at the same stage of emotional development.
Regression	*Moving backward in emotional development in response to fear or anxiety.*	Fear or anxiety can cause people to attempt to employ coping mechanisms that worked for them in the past, even when they may be inappropriate in some subsequent context. A dramatic example of regression can be seen in many school-age children on the first day of school. Rather than separate from parents and be left in the care of a teacher, children may throw tantrums. The child's fear of abandonment is overwhelming, and the result is regression to a more infantile stage of development. Such a regressive episode is usually temporary, although it may recur depending upon how it is resolved and other related factors.

TABLE 2-3 FREUD'S PSYCHOSEXUAL STAGES

Freud wrote of four psychosexual stages with a "latency period" between the third, or phallic stage, and the fourth, or genital, stage. The transition from one psychosexual stage to another tends to be smooth and gradual rather than abrupt. Therefore, the age given here for each of the stages must be considered approximate.

Psychosexual Stage	Age (According to Freud)
1. The Oral Stage	Birth to 1 year
2. The Anal Stage	1 year to 3 years
3. The Phallic Stage	3 years to 5 or 6 years
Latency Period	6 years to puberty (no occurrence at all is also possible)
4. The Genital Stage	From puberty onward

identification

a process of association with another to the point of emulation of the other's behavior and/or thinking.

latency period

in psychoanalytic theory, the period of development after the third or phallic stage and before the fourth or genital stage.

this condition arises out of fear of the father's wrath for having sexual feelings towards the mother. In girls, this anxiety was thought to arise as a result of the discovery of a cavity in place of a protruding sexual organ—a phenomenon Freud referred to as "penis envy." According to Freud, the sequence of events that occurs in resolving such anxiety, and the Oedipus complex in general, will have long-lasting implications. Some of the consequences may concern the individuals' **identification** (meaning *association* or *affiliation*) with their own genders, as well as the individuals' attitudes towards the opposite sex and people in authority.

After the phallic stage, and before the fourth or genital stage, there comes an in-between period that was not formerly labeled by Freud as a stage. Freud referred to this in-between time as the **latency period** to emphasize that the child is in *a transitional period during which the potential for adult sexual gratification is present, but for most children, inactive.* Freud (1952) put it this way:

> From about the sixth or eighth year onwards a standstill . . . is observed in the sexual development, which . . . deserves to be called a *latency period.* This latency period, however, may be absent; nor does it necessarily entail an interruption of sexual activities and sexual interests over the whole field. Most of the mental experiences and excitations occurring before the latency period then succumb to the infantile amnesia . . . (p. 335)

FIGURE 2-4 PERSONALITY AND THE POTTY Freud firmly believed that the child is parent to the adult: The nature of the child's experiences during the first five years of life will permanently shape the individual's personality. Toilet training that is a relatively pleasant experience, for example, will encourage traits such as productivity and creativity according to Freud. Harsh toilet training may cause the child to hold back from "creating" and to develop what Freud called an "anal retentive personality"—marked by the tendency stubbornly to hold back in many ways. Alternatively, very strict toilet training may cause the child to expel feces at the most inappropriate times, and the result may be an adult who is messy and expulsive in various ways (such as being prone to temper tantrums).

According to Freud, then, we do not remember details of our infantile and childhood sexuality before the latency period due to **infantile amnesia**, *the absence, in adulthood, of many childhood memories after the age of 2 and up to at least the age of 6* (Mosher, 1993). Following the oral, anal, and phallic stages and the latency period (if it occurs) comes the genital stage of development. In this stage, the primary source of pleasure generalizes from one's own body to that of another. Thus, through the life span, if the individual is well-adjusted, she or he progresses from an indiscriminate, pleasure-seeking infant to a discriminating, reality-oriented adult.

If you have never before read an account of Freud's theory of personality, you might find this summary a bit jarring. Just think how jarring it must have been to laypeople and professionals alike almost a century ago!

PSYCHOANALYSIS AFTER FREUD

As the founder of the first systematized method of psychotherapy, Freud attracted many followers who have in some sources been referred to as "disciples"—a word that conveys the religious-like fervor with which these followers learned, practiced, and sought to teach others this new perspective on human understanding. But Freud constantly found himself fending off criticism of his views, not only from disbelievers from without, but also from disciples within. Disputes among psychoanalysts about the meaning or importance of observed behavior were common because psychoanalytic theory allowed for the same behavior to be interpreted in several different ways. Before long, Freud was in the unenviable position of having disciples who thought they knew more about psychoanalysis than did their teacher. Such a frustrating state of affairs at one point moved Freud to assert, "Psychoanalysis is my creation. . . . For ten years I was the only one occupied with it. . . Nobody knows better than I what psychoanalysis is" (Miller, 1962, p. 238). In the end, many of Freud's most famous disciples, including his heir apparent, Carl Jung, would develop their own modifications of Freud's theory and their own schools of treatment. Perhaps one of the most influential "neo-Freudians" (referring to psychoanalysts who had modified Freud) was Karen Horney (pronounced "horn-eye"; see Figure 2–5). Horney focused more attention than any of her predecessors on the role of social factors in development. Poor social conditions and/or a poor parent-child relationship fostered what she referred to as "basic anxiety." How the child copes with this basic anxiety has critical implications for adult personality (Horney, 1945, 1980).

Freud did not use experimental methods to examine whether his theory of personality was correct or whether his methods of psychotherapeutic treatment worked. Rather, his entire body of work is based on the case study method, a method of proof that is viewed by most behavioral scientists as at best weak and at worst unacceptable. Having said that, any further criticisms to be leveled at psychoanalysis as a theory of personality and as a method of treatment are anticlimactic. One may criticize Freud, for example, for the way he wrote about women, the way he wrote about homosexuals, the way he seemed to assume that every child grows up with two parents in a home, and so forth. However, when all is said and done, it seems reasonable to say that *no one person living or dead has had a greater impact on psychology than Freud.* This is particularly amazing because Freud, living only miles away from Leipzig, Germany (where the first psychology laboratory in the world was set up), used entirely different methods to study, explain, and treat behavior from the "mainstream psychologists" of his day. Freud's training was medical/biological, a fact reflected in his theory of personality and method of treatment. Yet he was first to recognize the role and influence of childhood experiences in adult personality development. He was the first to exploit the significance of the unconscious and the idea of unconscious motivation. And he was the first to categorize various types of behavior and thinking patterns (such as behavior and thinking patterns used in defense mechanisms) within a comprehensive theory of personality. His ideas stimulated writers and experimental researchers whose works would fill libraries. His influence—whether his ideas are used as a source of support or as something to react against—is undeniable.

Psychoanalysis as taught by Freud and interpreted by dozens of his disciples is still taught in schools, some exclusively devoted to such study. Journals devoted to

infantile amnesia

in psychoanalytic theory, the absence, in adulthood, of many childhood memories after the age of 2 and up to at least the age of 6.

**FIGURE 2–5
KAREN HORNEY
(1885–1952)**

psychoanalysis are still published, and scholarly books about Freud, psychoanalysis, and other psychodynamic theories of personality and methods of treatment are still being written. In Chapter 9, we will further explore psychoanalysis, focusing on its utility as a method of psychotherapeutic treatment. For now, we shift our attention to what is called a behavioral perspective, and begin by focusing not on Europe or the United States, but on the area of the globe where the roots of this alternative approach to human understanding were planted: Russia.

A BEHAVIORAL PERSPECTIVE

A one-sentence summation of human (or animal) behavior as the behaviorist understands it might be, *All behavior is learned.* There are a few exceptions to this general rule, such as instinctual behavior (like geese following the first moving thing they see after birth), reflexive behavior (like an eye-blink), and involuntary behavior (like the expansion and contraction of the chest during breathing). But generally speaking, an understanding of people from a behavioral perspective entails an understanding of the process of learning. What then is learning? How do organisms learn? What relevance does learning have to adjustment?

learning

a process that brings about a relatively enduring change in behavior or knowledge as a result of experience.

Learning may be defined as *a process that brings about a relatively enduring change in behavior or knowledge as a result of experience.* From research using animals and humans, psychologists have constructed a number of models of how learning takes place. Here we will briefly describe three such models, and then discuss how such models provide a framework for understanding behavior. We begin with a look at a type of learning or conditioning that you have probably heard something about before. Does the name Pavlov ring a bell?

CLASSICAL CONDITIONING

conditioning

a type of learning that entails the acquisition of relatively specific patterns of response to the presence of well-defined stimuli.

Conditioning, a type of learning, may be defined as *the acquisition of relatively specific patterns of response in the presence of well-defined stimuli.* The kind of learning that caused Ivan Pavlov's dog to salivate at the sound of a bell is an example of one type of conditioning now referred to as Pavlovian or classical conditioning. It is somewhat ironic that Pavlov, one of the most frequently cited names in the psychology literature, "never considered himself in any sense a psychologist and, in fact, had little use for the psychologists of his time" (Lundin, 1972, p. 124). Pavlov was a physiologist and he rejected psychological explanations of the phenomena he studied. In fact, his assistants were subject to a fine if he caught them using psychological as opposed to physiological terminology (Schultz, 1969). For most of his life, Pavlov's opinion of the field of psychology was that it was "completely hopeless" (Watson, 1963). He considered it an uncontested fact that success in studying the nervous system could not be achieved unless "we utterly renounce the untenable pretensions of psychology" (Woodworth & Sheehan, 1964, p. 77). Towards the end, however, Pavlov's views of psychology became more charitable.

**FIGURE 2–6
IVAN PETROVICH PAVLOV
(1849–1936)**

As a physiologist studying the process of digestion in dogs, Pavlov's initial interest was in measuring salivary and gastric (stomach) secretions in response to various stimuli placed in the mouth. During the course of those studies, Pavlov observed salivation not only in response to food placed in the mouth, but also salivation in response to anticipation of food. Stimuli such as the sight or smell of food, even the sound of the attendants' approaching footsteps at feeding time, were all capable of eliciting salivation.

Pavlov shifted the focus of his research. Instead of studying salivary and gastric secretions in response to *physical* stimulation of the salivary and gastric glands, he began studying such secretions in response to what he called *psychical* stimulation. In numerous experiments, Pavlov demonstrated that salivation could be elicited by means other than food placed in the mouth. Various stimuli, such as a metronome, a tuning fork, a bell, a light, even the stimulus of stroking the dog, were all found capable of eliciting salivation when paired with the presentation of food. In Figure 2–7, we take a closer look at how a

FIGURE 2–7   CLASSICAL CONDITIONING

Prior to conditioning, some meat powder is placed in Lucky's mouth, and he reflexively salivates. In the language of Pavlovian conditioning, we have just elicited an *unconditioned response* (UR), salivation, by presenting the subject with an *unconditioned stimulus* (US), the meat powder. Essentially, all we have done is feed the dog meat powder, and a reflexive response (salivation) occurred. No conditioning has taken place to this point.

Prior to conditioning, the presentation of the unconditioned stimulus leads to the unconditioned response.

Still prior to conditioning, if we ring a bell, light a light, or pet Lucky, what response might we expect from him? We really have no reason to expect anything except maybe a "Why-on-earth-are-you-doing-that?"-type look. Certainly, we would have no reason to expect Lucky to salivate at the sound of a bell, the sight of a light, or the feel of being petted. At this point, such stimuli are referred to as *neutral stimuli* because they have little or no effect, one way or the other, on the subject's behavior. This can be illustrated as follows:

Prior to conditioning, the presentation of a neutral stimulus leads to no predictable response.

What happens if the presentation of the meat powder is paired with the sounding of a bell?

The answer is, conditioning begins. Lucky savors the US (the meat powder), and the UR occurs (saliva flows). Repeated pairings of the sounding of the bell with the presentation of the meat powder will prompt Lucky to salivate at the mere sound of the bell. Prior to conditioning, only the US (the meat powder) elicited the UR (salivation). As a result of conditioning, the bell, now referred to as the *conditioned stimulus* (CS) is eliciting salivation. To distinguish the salivation elicited by a US (such as meat powder) from the salivation elicited by a CS (such as a bell), the salivation elicited by a conditioned stimulus is referred to as a *conditioned response* (CR). The conditioning process can now be illustrated as follows:

During conditioning, a conditioned stimulus paired with an unconditioned stimulus leads to an unconditioned response.

Repetitions of this procedure will lead to Lucky salivating at the sound of the bell. Once Lucky does salivate at the sound of the bell, conditioning has taken place.

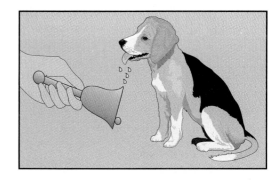

After conditioning, the presentation of the conditioned stimulus leads to the conditioned response.

dog—we'll call him Lucky—comes to salivate at the sound of a bell or some other stimulus such as the sight of a light or the feel of being petted. As you read, try to think beyond salivating dogs, meat powder and bells; how might Pavlovian conditioning be at work in contexts involving humans?

A formal definition of **classical** or **Pavlovian conditioning** is *a process in which relationships between events are learned, such that behavior comes to be elicited by a conditioned stimulus, due to a prior pairing of the conditioned stimulus with an unconditioned stimulus.*

Contemporary psychologists have characterized the writings of Pavlov, as well as the writings of many other learning theorists who have written on what we now call classical conditioning, as deriving from a rather narrow, "reflex" tradition or perspective. Within that tradition, the process of classical conditioning is thought of as a rather simple substitution process wherein a conditioned stimulus (such as a bell) comes to replace an unconditioned stimulus (such as food), in its ability to elicit a reflexive response (such as salivation). But decades of research since Pavlov first published his studies have suggested that the subject in a classical conditioning study is more of an active information processor than investigators first thought. Stated another way, salivation in response to a bell in the Pavlovian situation is probably not as reflexive and as automatic as researchers once believed. There is evidence to suggest that the end-product of classical conditioning—a conditioned response—is better conceived as being *not* like a simple reflex. Rather, the end-product of classical conditioning—a conditioned response—is a response that occurs as the result of an organism learning relations among events in its environment. Robert A. Rescorla, a psychologist who has championed this more cognitive perspective of classical conditioning, has argued that this form of conditioning is not one in which "the organism willy-nilly forms associations between any two stimuli that happen to co-occur. Rather, the organism is better seen as an information seeker using logical and perceptual relations among events, along with its own preconceptions, to form a sophisticated representation of its world" (Rescorla, 1988, p. 154.)

Pavlovian conditioning was once referred to as *respondent* conditioning, since the organism was thought to be a kind of *reflexive respondent* in Pavlovian conditioning situations. However, with the increasing realization that the organism is more of an active information processor than a reflexive respondent in such situations, the term *respondent conditioning* has gone out of vogue.

A behavioral perspective on understanding people entails understanding how classical conditioning takes place in people. Were you able to think beyond salivating dogs to generalize to situations that might involve classical conditioning in people? If not, an example that I find many students can readily identify with has to do with salivation upon entering a movie theater. Many of us have learned to pair the presentation of movies with the presentation of popcorn. In fact, one of the first sensations you are likely to experience upon walking into the movie theater is the smell of fresh popcorn. Repeated pairings of movies with popcorn has led many people to develop cravings for popcorn when watching movies. Well aware of the phenomenon, although perhaps not aware of its roots in classical conditioning, businesses that rent videos for home use also sell popcorn and other snacks.

Classical conditioning has many other everyday manifestations in human behavior. For example, there are some people who emit a classically conditioned anxiety response to the sight of needles in the doctor's or dentist's office. Repeated pairings of needles (originally, the UCS) with pain (originally, the UCR), has led to squeamishness (the CR) in response to needles (the CS).

An understanding of people from a behavioral perspective also entails understanding other processes of learning such as instrumental conditioning. As you read about this process, it will be instructive to think about ways instrumental conditioning can be used to explain human behavior.

INSTRUMENTAL CONDITIONING

Instrumental conditioning *entails the learning of relationships between an organism's own actions and the consequences of those actions in a particular context.* For example, in the context of some situations, the classroom among them, people learn to raise their hands in order to be given

---

classical conditioning

a process in which relationships between events are learned such that behavior comes to be elicited by a conditioned stimulus due to a prior pairing of the conditioned stimulus with an unconditioned stimulus.

Pavlovian conditioning

see *classical conditioning*.

instrumental conditioning

the learning of relationships between an organism's own actions and the consequences of those actions in a particular context.

the floor to speak. In other contexts, however, such as in placing an order in a fast-food restaurant, it would be inappropriate to raise one's hand in order to be given the floor to speak.

The roots of instrumental conditioning can be traced to the work of a psychology graduate student by the name of Thorndike and the development of what he called *the law of effect*. Another landmark event in the evolution of the behavioral perspective came with the publication in 1913 of a paper on how the behaviorist views psychology. The behavioral perspective on psychology was further sharpened through the experimentation and writings of American psychologist B. F. Skinner. We briefly overview the development of knowledge about instrumental conditioning using these three reference points.

THE LAW OF EFFECT

A Columbia University Ph.D. thesis by Edward Lee Thorndike (1898) entitled *Animal Intelligence: An Experimental Study of the Associative Processes in Animals* was to have a profound effect on researchers who studied the phenomenon we now refer to as instrumental conditioning. Among other things, Thorndike reported that hungry cats placed in a "puzzle box" attempted to escape to freedom, and food, waiting outside. The box was equipped with a mechanism, such as a loop or button, which, when properly clawed, would open the door's latch. Cats placed in such a box would typically spend about ten minutes or so trying to squeeze through any opening, clawing or biting at the box, and reaching through the bars of the box to grasp anything in range. And then, during desperate, sometimes random clawing and pawing, the cat would happen to hit the puzzle-solving loop or button in the box. Repeated placements in the box tended to lead to shorter response times in getting the box open. Thorndike (1898) said that "gradually all the other nonsuccessful impulses will be stamped out and the particular impulse leading to the successful act will be stamped in by the resulting pleasure, until, after many trials, the cat will, when put in the box, immediately claw the button or loop in a definite way" (p. 13).

Thorndike couched his findings in terms of **the law of effect**, which in essence says that *behavior is controlled by its effect or consequence*. In the case of the cats, the behavior of clawing a loop in the puzzle box led to the satisfying consequence of freedom. Clawing the loop was a response that tended to be "stamped in," while fruitless, unsatisfying responses such as attempting to squeeze through the bars tended to be "stamped out." Learning, according to Thorndike, was a matter of an association or connection between a stimulus and a response. Stimuli, such as a loop in a cat puzzle box, had come to be associated or connected with specific responses. For Thorndike (1931, p. 165), "learning is connecting" and if it were possible to analyze someone's brain for the learning that has taken place, Thorndike felt you would find "connections of varying strength." In fact, Thorndike believed that the key to understanding people lay in understanding these connections: "If all these [connections] could be completely inventoried, telling what the man would think and do and what would satisfy and annoy him, in every conceivable situation, it seems to me that nothing would be left out."

Law of effect

a behavioral principle which states that behavior is controlled by its effect or consequence.

Thorndike believed that connections between a stimulus and a response were strengthened when they were accompanied or followed by a satisfying state of affairs. He also felt that such connections were weakened when accompanied or followed by a nonsatisfying or annoying state of affairs. In later years, he modified his view with respect to how much a nonsatisfying state weakened the connection, concluding that punishment was less effective than reward.

General receptivity to what has become known as S-R (stimulus-response) or "connectionist" learning theory led to thousands of published studies further exploring the phenomenon. Psychologists as well as other behavioral scientists reported on the law of effect at work in myriad aspects of everyday existence. Behavioral researchers devised various devices to explore how the law of effect operated in different species and situations. Figure 2–8 presents a sampling of these devices.

WATSONIAN BEHAVIORISM

In 1913, a strident call to arms was made by American psychologist John B. Watson in an article entitled *Psychology as the Behaviorist Views It*. Watson called for the field of psychology to reject speculation about mental activity and instead to focus attention primarily on

FIGURE 2–8   DEVICES USED IN THE STUDY OF INSTRUMENTAL CONDITIONING

In his turn-of-the-century investigations, Thorndike employed puzzle boxes, like the one pictured below (A) to observe how confined cats clawed their way to success. While a graduate student studying with William James at Harvard, shortly before he accepted a fellowship to continue his graduate training in psychology at Columbia, Thorndike studied maze-running behavior in chicks using home-made mazes (B). Experimenters have devised a variety of other devices to explore the phenomenon of instrumental conditioning in other species. Pigeons have been taught to peck or not to peck at various stimuli in apparatuses (C).

Learning in rats has been studied, among other ways, by various types of mazes (D), the Lashley jumping stand (E), and perhaps the most popular device of all, a specially-equipped cage developed by B.F. Skinner— the "Skinner box" (F). The relatively simple learning processes noted in animals, such as laboratory rats, were widely believed to be applicable in the study of human learning. By using laboratory rats, readily available from commercial breeders and relatively easy to maintain in a laboratory, experimenters could have complete control over most of the relevant variables in an experiment.

A. A puzzle box of the type used by Thorndike. Thorndike also used dogs as subjects in his puzzle boxes, though his most oft-cited research was done with cats. The response measure of interest was time to solve the puzzle—similar, at least in that respect, to the game show *Wheel of Fortune*.

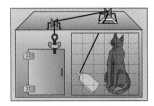

B. Thorndike initially used chicks as his experimental subjects, exploring instrumental conditioning by observing them running through mazes he created by standing books on end.

C. "To peck or not to peck?" That is the question. And the response of interest in studies of instrumental conditioning with pigeons might be number of pecks and/or number of errors depending upon the shape, size, and/or color of the pecking stimuli.

D. Rats may learn—or fail to learn—to negotiate mazes such as those pictured in order to obtain rewards (such as satisfaction of their appetite for food, water, or sex), as well as to avoid aversive stimuli such as electric shock. Responses measured in such studies include variables such as number of trials to some pre-determined criterion, and number of errors.

E. The Lashley jumping stand requires rats placed on it to visually discriminate between two (or more) cardboard doors. A jump to the correct door, and the cardboard will give way. A jump to the incorrect door leads to a fall to the net below.

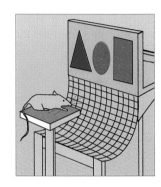

F. A Skinner box is a chamber that is typically equipped with a bar the rat can press (to obtain food or water or some other reward, or to avoid electric shock or some other aversive stimulus), or to produce whatever consequence the experimenter has set it up to produce. Depending on the objectives of the study, the box may also contain other bells and whistles—literally—as well as other things such as a light to act as a discriminative stimulus, or a grid floor which can be electrified. A typical response measure in studies using a Skinner box is number of bar presses; the number of times the animal will press a bar to obtain a reward or to avoid or terminate the administration of an aversive stimulus.

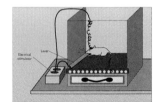

observable behavior. He wrote, "I believe we can write a psychology, and. . . never use the terms consciousness, mental states, mind. . . .It can be done in terms of stimulus and response, in terms of habit formation, habit integrations and the like."

Watson's passionate rejection of the way psychology was then conceptualized struck a responsive chord in the minds of many of his contemporaries. Among the many psychologists who would find Watson's arguments compelling was Burrhus Frederick Skinner. As one observer put it, "Watson's spirit is indestructible. Cleaned and purified, it breathes through the writings of B. F. Skinner" (MacLeod, 1959, p. 34).

BEHAVIORISM ACCORDING TO SKINNER

Skinner used animals such as rats and pigeons to study and devise principles of learning that he believed had applicability to all living organisms, including humans. His preference was to avoid reference to learning *theory* when he spoke of his work. Skinner believed that the task of researchers was to observe and describe behavior . . . period. To create a "theory of learning" and then test hypotheses from the theory was, for Skinner, putting the cart before the horse. In an article entitled, "Are Theories of Learning Necessary?", Skinner (1950) advocated building knowledge of learning based on behavioral experimentation and observation rather than the more traditional way of formulating a theory and then testing hypotheses derived from it by means of experimentaiton. Skinner also preferred the use of the term *operant conditioning* to instrumental conditioning. An **operant**, according to Skinner, *is an observable behavior that, once emitted, has an observable effect on the environment.*[3] **Operant conditioning** is *a learning process whereby the probability or frequency of emission of a particular response is altered as a result of a change in the consequences of emitting that response.* To better understand what is meant by these terms, consider a rat placed in a Skinner box that has been deprived of food for 24 hours. At some point in its exploration of this new environment, the rat will happen to press the bar—by chance or on purpose (it makes no difference at this point in the conditioning). In the case of the rat in the Skinner box, bar pressing is said to be the operant. The frequency of emission of this operant will vary according to its consequence. In general, if food arrives as a result of a bar press, bar-pressing behavior will increase. If electric shock is the result of a bar press, bar-pressing behavior will decrease. For Skinner, it would be inappropriate to speculate about how "hungry" the rat is or how much it "dislikes" electric shock. The emphasis in such research is strictly on observable behavior. "A food-deprived rat's frequency of bar-pressing increases when food is delivered as a consequence of bar-pressing" would be one way to summarize such research in the Skinnerian tradition.

Instrumental conditioning and operant conditioning would appear to be quite similar in meaning. Yet there is a difference. The difference relates to the implication of what is going on mentally in the organism between presentations of stimuli such as food or electric shock, and the probability or frequency with which the organism emits a particular response. The use of the term instrumental conditioning carries with it the implication that behavior is instrumental in achieving some consequence or effect, such as the satisfaction Thorndike (1905) referred to in his law of effect. Operant conditioning, Skinner's preferred description of the process of instrumental conditioning, carries with it no such implication. When certain stimuli are presented under certain conditions, they either strengthen or weaken the tendency of the organism to respond in a certain way. Skinnerians report what happens under specified conditions, without reference to unobservable, intervening variables such as mental state. Because behaviorists in the Skinnerian tradition so strongly focus on behavior and reject any reference to mentalistic notions, the Skinnerian brand of behaviorism has sometimes been referred to as radical behaviorism.

Operant behavior is so called because the organism, such as the rat pressing the bar, "operates" on the environment. What follows this operation will influence the frequency with which the operant behavior will be emitted. Conditions preceding the emission of an operant response are also important and this fact is acknowledged in the term *stimulus control of operant behavior,* which refers to the fact that stimuli in the environment can affect an organism's operant response. One such stimulus in the environment is light. For example, an animal in the wild may learn to forage for food only during daylight hours because it is only during those hours that its efforts have a great likelihood of being rewarded.

**FIGURE 2–9
BURRHUS
FREDERIC SKINNER
(1904–1990)**

operant
an observable behavior that, once emitted, has an observable effect on the environment.

operant conditioning
B. F. Skinner's nonmentalistic term for instrumental conditioning, a learning process whereby the probability or frequency of emission of a particular response is altered as a result of a change in the consequences of emitting that response.

[3]An aid to memorizing the meaning of operant is to think of *operating* on the environment. Operants are defined by the action they have on the environment. When a rat presses a bar to get food, for example, the operant is "bar pressing which activates the feeder mechanism and releases food."

In the laboratory, a rat in a Skinner box may be taught to press a bar only when a light above the bar is turned on. If the rat receives food for bar presses only when the light is on, it will learn to press the bar only when the light is on.

The concept of *reinforcement* (as well as various derivatives of this word including reinforce, reinforcing, and reinforcer) is central to an understanding of operant conditioning. Skinner's (1953, p. 21) modification of Thorndike's law of effect made reference to the concept of reinforcement in this way: "If the occurrence of an operant is followed by the presentation of a reinforcing stimulus, the strength is increased." So what is a reinforcer?

reinforcer
a general term for any stimulus—such as a food pellet or a jolt of electric shock—received by the organism after it emits an operant behavior such as pressing a bar in a Skinner box. See also *positive reinforcer* and *negative reinforcer.*

A **reinforcer** is *a stimulus*—such as a food pellet or an electric shock—*received by the organism after it emits an operant behavior,* such as pressing a bar in a Skinner box. Reinforcers may be positive or negative. Positive and negative reinforcers are similar in that they both tend to increase the probability or rate of the emission of the operant behavior that precedes them. But they are also different.

positive reinforcer
a reinforcer that increases the probability or rate of the operant behavior that precedes its administration.

A **positive reinforcer** is *a reinforcer that increases the probability or rate of the operant behavior that precedes its administration.* A food pellet delivered to a food-deprived rat contingent on the rat's pressing of a bar is a positive reinforcer. The delivery of this stimulus under conditions of food deprivation increases the possibility of the occurrence of the operant behavior. In general, organisms will work to receive positive reinforcers. Organisms will also work *not to receive* negative reinforcers. A **negative reinforcer** is *a stimulus that is avoided or terminated after an operant behavior is emitted, which tends to increase the frequency with which the operant behavior is emitted.* What would you expect to happen to the rate of bar pressing, for example, if a rat placed in a Skinner box is conditioned to bar press to terminate the administration of an electric shock or to avoid it altogether? It's a good bet that the rat's frequency of bar-pressing behavior will rise over what the bar-pressing rate would have been had no such contingency been in place. Electric shock, loud noises, and foul odors are all examples of possible negative reinforcers. Because the concept of a negative reinforcer is a bit difficult to grasp without devoting some thought to what it is and how it operates, it is readily confused with a different concept, punishment. However, negative reinforcement is *not* synonymous with punishment (see *A Question of Values*).

negative reinforcer
a stimulus that is avoided or terminated after an operant behavior is emitted and that tends to increase the frequency with which the operant behavior is emitted.

reinforcement
in general, describes the operation of contingently related stimulus events or consequences that tend to increase the probability or rate of emission of operant behaviors.

According to Skinner, the term **reinforcement** in general describes *the operation of contingently related stimulus events or consequences that tend to increase the probability or rate of emission of operant behaviors.* In this definition, "contingently related stimulus events or consequences" refers to events such as food pellets being delivered as a consequence of a bar press. Simply stated, reinforcement (such as food pellets for a food-deprived rat) given for an operant behavior (such as bar pressing in a Skinner box) will increase the probability or rate of the operant behavior. Practically speaking, the terms *reinforcer* and *reinforcement* are used interchangeably in many contexts. For example, an experimenter may say, "The rat was administered a reinforcer," or, "The rat was administered reinforcement."

experimental analysis of behavior
the study of how operants are conditioned and extinguished.

Skinner believed that principles of operant conditioning have profound applicability to society in general and he devoted his research to what he termed the **experimental analysis of behavior,** *the study of how operants are conditioned and extinguished.* Other researchers whose perspective could also be described as behavioral have differed with Skinner regarding how mentalistic behavioral research should be. A more mentalistic, or "cognitive behavioral," model of learning can be found in the social learning perspective on human behavior.

SOCIAL LEARNING

The general term used to describe *learning that occurs as a result of watching or observing the behavior of others* is **social learning.** Social learning occurs through "observation" by means of any of the senses.

social learning
a general term used to describe learning that occurs as a result of watching or observing the behavior of others.

In social learning terms, the object of imitation—a person, an animal, anything else—is called the *model.* The behavior to be imitated is said to be *modeled,* and the person imitating the modeled behavior is referred to as the *observer* or *learner.* For example, a foreign language teacher might model the pronunciation of a particular word, and the learner will then attempt to mimic that pronunciation.

Crime and Punishment

Punishment is *the condition of having an aversive stimulus administered or some favored stimulus being withdrawn as a consequence of the emission of a particular behavior.* Punishment is most typically administered to reduce the frequency or probability of a particular behavior. In experimental research, a punisher is an aversive or unpleasant stimulus, such as electric shock, or the withdrawal of something the organism finds positively reinforcing.

The terms *punishment* and *punishers* should not be confused with the terms *negative reinforcement* and *negative reinforcers.* In operant learning situations involving punishment, the consequence of the operant behavior is an aversive stimulus, and the probability or frequency of emission of the operant behavior tends to *decrease.* By contrast, in operant learning situations involving negative reinforcement, there tends to be an *increase* in the emission of the operant behavior.

If the consequence of lever pressing for a rat is the administration of shock, the animal is punished for lever-pressing behavior and the frequency of lever pressing will tend to decrease. But if the apparatus is set up so that the consequence of lever pressing was not the administration of shock but rather the avoidance of or escape from shock, the animal is negatively reinforced for lever-pressing behavior and the frequency of lever-pressing behavior would tend to increase.

Laboratory research, mostly with rats, suggests that:

(1) The effects of punishment on behavior are more immediate than other consequences of behavior such as the cessation of positive reinforcement.

(2) Timing and consistency in the application of punishment are important correlates of its effectiveness. The shorter the duration between the targeted operant behavior and the punishment, the more effective punishment is in deterring the operant behavior. The more consistently the targeted behavior is punished, the more effective punishment will be.

(3) In humans, punishment is most effective when combined with the teaching of positively valued behavior and an explanation for the punishment. As a practical example, it may not be enough to punish someone for failing to "just say no" to drugs. Any punishment contingent on such a failure would ideally be accompanied by sound counsel on the subject of what the person should "just say yes" to—including things like self-esteem, a goal-oriented work ethic, and other components of a healthy, drug-free lifestyle.

The use of punishment carries with it many potential pitfalls, including the possibility that the emotional and physical scars and effects left by the punishment will be irreversible. Another possibility is that the punishment will not be construed as punishing. The class clown scolded by the teacher for his antics may find it desirable and exciting to be spotlighted with this sort of attention. The effects of the punishment itself are often unpredictable because punishment merely discourages specific behavior, and does not necessarily encourage any more acceptable behavior.

Corporal punishment of students by means of paddling (hitting of the buttocks with a wooden paddle) and other forms is legal in most states. Should it be? Your answer to this question will depend, at least in part, on your value system. Do students have a right not to be struck while in the classroom? Should society take that right away from students who are disruptive? What purpose should corporal or other punishment serve?

The table below lists 10 states by the percentage of their pupils being paddled each year. The only other legally sanctioned corporal punishment by government-appointed officials used to take place in the military. That practice was outlawed in 1874.

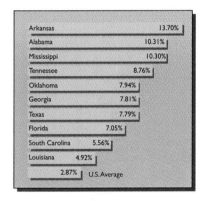

State	Percentage
Arkansas	13.70%
Alabama	10.31%
Mississippi	10.30%
Tennessee	8.76%
Oklahoma	7.94%
Georgia	7.81%
Texas	7.79%
Florida	7.05%
South Carolina	5.56%
Louisiana	4.92%
U.S. Average	2.87%

Legal forms of punishment inflicted on people are, of course, not restricted to school rooms. Courts may impose punishments on people ranging from fines to imprisonment to the ultimate punishment, capital punishment—a fact that should make consideration of values with respect to the use of punishment all the more compelling.

Children as young as 16 to 28 months are capable of imitating the actions of peers. At this age, such imitation may be communicating a message such as, "Let's do this together," or, "This is what we're doing" (Eckerman & Stein, 1982; Nadel, 1986; Uzgiris, 1984). Imitative acts may beget more imitative acts (Eckerman et al., 1989) and set in motion social-influence processes that lead to imitation games (Eckerman & Stein, 1990). By the time children reach nursery-school age, they are old hands at social learning processes. They have learned to imitate others, and they have seen the effect of their own actions on others when they serve as a model.

Albert Bandura first gained wide prominence as a social learning theorist with his now classic research on how aggressive behavior can be modeled and learned. In a series of studies that employed nursery school children as subjects and a film depicting an adult hitting a large, inflatable doll, Bandura and his colleagues demonstrated the power of exposure to a model's aggressive behavior. In one condition of an experiment, child subjects observed an adult female model who hit the doll and was then rewarded for such behavior. These subjects gave evidence of having learned this aggressive type of behavior by watching the model. When left alone to play with a similar doll they too evidenced aggression towards it. In another condition of the experiment, child subjects were exposed to a film that had a different ending—one wherein the adult model was scolded for what she did. These subjects were far less likely even to play with the doll, much less evidence aggressive behavior towards it. Bandura (1965) noted that although the children in this latter group did not behave aggressively, they gave evidence of having nonetheless learned by observation the same number of aggressive responses as other children in the study. What was critical, then, was the *consequence* of the aggressive behavior, that is, whether it was rewarded or punished.

In subsequent research, Bandura (1969, 1979) as well as other researchers have sensitized us to the great power of social learning and the critical influence the mass media can have in influencing prosocial and antisocial behavior. Given that children in the United States spend more time watching television than they do engaged in any other single activity except sleeping (Huston et al., 1990), issues in social learning have increasingly become social issues. Congress and other governmental and private interest groups have inquired into the relationship between violence as portrayed in film and television and real-life aggression. In general, psychologists have argued that mass media portrayals of violence contribute to real-life violence. The violence is not only presented in the context of weekly series or movies, but also in the form of news broadcasting. According to Bandura (1977), social learning will take place when a learner is paying attention to a modeled behavior and the learner has the capacity to store mentally a representation of that behavior either through words or images. When and if the learner is motivated to engage in the same behavior, the behavior will be said to have become part of the learner's behavioral repertoire.

AN EVALUATION OF BEHAVIORAL PERSPECTIVES

Social learning, as well as learning by classical or instrumental conditioning, has great appeal to researchers because so many things human beings experience or do can be explained with reference to learning principles. A basis for any act—good or bad—can be found in a person's learning history. Cognitive behaviorists would extend that explanatory power to thoughts and feelings as well.

Although a behavioral perspective offers a powerful basis for explaining and understanding behavior, many psychologists feel that there are many issues that are not convincingly addressed by such approaches. For example, consider the expression, "Every person has a price." From a strictly instrumental standpoint, one might say that this statement is true; pay somebody enough money, and they will do anything within their power. But in fact, this is not the case. There are people who would not under any circumstances do certain things, such as hurt another person or betray their country. In fact, there are people who would readily sacrifice their own lives for someone else or their country. Uniquely human concepts such as values and dignity must be introduced into the discussion to understand fully why people behave as they do. It is not impossible to define such terms behaviorally, but it is difficult to account for them in an entirely satisfactory way.

Understanding people from a behavioral perspective is limited in other ways. For example, topics such as creativity, faith, freedom, and pride tend to be handled only awkwardly within a strictly behavioral framework. In short, behavioral explanations have been most impressive when the behavior in question can be observed and experimented on. Situations in which most of the variables operating in the environment can be controlled, such as the situation that exists within the confines of a Skinner box, provide an ideal laboratory for the study of behavior from a behavioral perspective. The explanatory power of strictly behavioral explanations tends to lessen as one moves farther and farther from such confines and closer and closer to abstract principles that humans experience and live by. Although there are indeed many important similarities between conditions operative in all environments, and although behavioral researchers have made great contributions to our understanding of people, the natural environment for human beings has in many respects proven itself to be a most complex and challenging one for behaviorists. In the early days of behaviorism, John Watson bragged that he could raise newborn infants to grow up to be anything he wanted using behavioral principles. It appears that it is not that easy.

We will be looking at behavior from a behavioral perspective elsewhere throughout this book. Right now, however, consider another approach which, as its name implies, focuses on all that is uniquely human.

A HUMANISTIC PERSPECTIVE

I know that I speak to only a fraction of psychologists. The majority—their interests suggested by such terms as stimulus-response, learning theory, operant conditioning—are so committed to seeing the individual solely as an object, that what I have to say often baffles if it does not annoy them.

—Carl Rogers (1961, p. viii)

During the 1940s, Freud's view of personality was much in vogue among clinicians, while academic psychologists were actively studying behavior from a behavioral perspective. A diligent effort had even been launched to understand psychoanalysis in terms of stimulus-response theory (Dollard & Miller, 1950). Anyone attempting to advance an alternative to a psychoanalytic or behavioral conception of people would be swimming against a very strong tide and, indeed, be speaking to only a fraction of psychologists.

Yet the 1940s also witnessed the rise of a framework for understanding people that has come to be known as a third force in psychology, one that has had great appeal to many counselors, clergy, psychotherapists, and others who have occasion to conduct counseling and psychotherapy. In common with the psychoanalytic perspective and unlike the behavioral perspective, this third perspective arose primarily from clinical experience with people, not from the research laboratory. Also, in common with the psychoanalytic perspective and unlike the behavioral perspective, the province of this third perspective is human, not animal behavior. Unlike the Freudian view of people as being driven by instinctual impulses that struggle for expression, however, this third force focused on the boundless potential for good within each person. Carl R. Rogers and Abraham Maslow are the two theorists most identified with what has come to be known as **humanism**, *an approach to thought and behavior that tends to focus on ideals, potential, moral dilemmas, and other aspects of living that are uniquely human.*

humanism
a view of human behavior and cognition that tends to focus on ideals, potential, moral dilemmas, and other aspects of living that are uniquely human.

ROGERS'S PERSON-CENTERED MODEL

In a distinguished career that spanned more than a half-century, in places such as University of Chicago, the University of Wisconsin, Stanford University, Western Behavioral Sciences Institute, and the Center for the Study of the Person in La Jolla, California, Carl R. Rogers (see Figure 2–10) continually professed his unbridled belief in the good within each

**FIGURE 2–10
CARL RANSOM ROGERS
(1902–1987)**

actualization

in humanistic theory, the inborn tendency of personal growth that results in an adjusted person; when thwarted, maladjustment is presumed to result.

genuineness

openness and honesty.

unconditional positive regard

acceptance of the person no matter what.

empathy

in person-centered therapy, an active state of perceiving how another feels, almost as if one were the other.

self-concept

how one defines who one is.

ideal self

the person one would like to be.

person. He wrote for example, "*It has been my experience that persons have a basically positive direction. In my deepest contacts with individuals in therapy, even those whose troubles are most disturbing, whose behavior has been most antisocial, whose feelings seem most abnormal, I find this to be true. When I can sensitively understand the feelings which they are expressing, when I am able to accept them as separate persons in their own right, then I find that they tend to move in certain directions. And what are these directions in which they tend to move? The words which I believe are most truly descriptive are words such as positive, constructive, moving toward self-actualization, growing toward maturity, growing toward socialization*" (1961, pp. 26–27, emphasis in the original).

According to Rogers, biology and environmental opportunity (or the lack thereof) both play a role in human development. But there also exists an inborn tendency to **actualize**—that is, *to grow, to move forward, and to become a better person.* This actualizing tendency will result in an adjusted person but it must be allowed to thrive. Maladjustment is thought to result when this actualizing tendency is somehow thwarted. A person who grows up in a home without love, acceptance, and understanding will probably not have a good sense of who he or she is. A lack of a sense of identity makes the individual more vulnerable to various pressures, such as the pressure to take drugs. Stated another way, you will have more trouble deciding whether or not to take drugs if you must stop and decide whether taking drugs is "you" or not.

From a humanistic perspective, a primary function of counseling or psychotherapy is to put people back on track to positive growth by helping them to discover their senses of self—who they really are. The counselor or therapist creates an environment for growth by conveying to the person the very human qualities of **genuineness** (*openness and honesty*), **unconditional positive regard** (*acceptance of the person no matter what*), and **empathy** (*an accurate understanding of what the person is saying*). In early descriptions of his approach, Rogers contrasted it to psychoanalysis by noting that it was present- as opposed to past-oriented. He also noted a difference between it and psychoanalysis in terms of objectives:

This newer approach differs from the older one in that it has a genuinely different goal. It aims directly toward the greater independence and integration of the individual rather than hoping that such results will accrue if the counselor assists in solving the problem. The individual and not the problem is the focus. The aim is not to solve one particular problem, but to assist the individual to *grow,* so that he can cope with the present problem and with later problems in a better-integrated fashion. If he can gain enough integration to handle one problem in more independent, more responsible, less confused, better-organized ways, then he will also handle new problems in that manner. (1942, pp. 28–29)

For Rogers, the primary means of understanding people was to listen intently to them, not diagnose them, or otherwise label them as suffering from one or another complexes. Everything the person has to say is of interest to the counselor, especially references to oneself and to one's **self-concept** (*how the individual defines who she or he is*). In some situations, most typically in research, a formal test designed to measure the disparity between how people see themselves and how they would like to see themselves is administered. The extent of the difference between the self as one is, and the **ideal self** (*the self one would like to be*) is presumed to represent the extent of maladjustment. The larger the gap between these two perceptions, the more distance to be traveled on the road to adjustment, or as Rogers would put it, the road to becoming a fully functioning person. The notion of an index of maladjustment being obtained by examination of the self-ideal discrepancy has subsequently been applied by others in efforts to assess various groups such as families (Olson et al., 1985; see also *Self-Assessment*). In general, however, Rogers believed that formal assessment by means of tools such as psychological tests was not really necessary because "it is the *client* who knows what hurts, what directions to go, what problems are crucial, what experiences have been deeply buried" (1961, p. 12). As we will see in Chapter 9, the Rogerian therapist is relatively nondirective as the person finds his or her own way.

The Rogerian framework for understanding people was highly original. It grew out of a sincere effort to understand how counseling actually worked with children and adults.

SELF-ASSESSMENT

The Family Evaluation Test

Here is an example of the type of test from which a measure of difference might be obtained between one's "real family" and one's "ideal family." Keep in mind that this is not a real test and that no conclusions that are valid in the psychometric sense can be drawn from your test results. In Part 1 of this test, you will respond to each item by indicating whether the statement is generally true or false as things are right now. In Part 2, respond to each item by indicating whether the statement is generally true or false according to the way you would like things to be. After you have completed all of the items in both parts, compare your responses. For each area of discrepancy, think about what might be done to help close the gap between the reality of how things are and how you would like them to be.

Part 1: Respond to these items by indicating whether the statement is generally true or false as things are right now.

	T	F
1. I would describe the relationship between the members of my family as close.		
2. My family members are loving towards one another.		
3. My family members do not really communicate well with each other.		
4. As a family, we generally have good times together.		
5. Everyone is equal in my family.		
6. I am proud to be a member of my family.		
7. We have problems just as other families do, no more and no less.		
8. I seem to need more than I get from my family.		
9. My family is a family in name only.		
10. I feel like I can say just about anything to any member of my family.		

Part 2: Respond to these items by indicating whether the statement is generally true or false regarding the way you would like things to be.

	T	F
1. I would describe the relationship between the members of my family as close.		
2. My family members are loving towards one another.		
3. My family members do not really communicate well with each other.		
4. As a family, we generally have good times together.		
5. Everyone is equal in my family.		
6. I am proud to be a member of my family.		
7. We have problems just as other families do, no more and no less.		
8. I seem to need more than I get from my family.		
9. My family is a family in name only.		
10. I feel like I can say just about anything to any member of my family.		

Another influential figure in the development of this third force in psychology, Abraham Maslow, was drawn to the study of people and the humanistic perspective from a more academic setting.

MASLOW AND THE SELF-ACTUALIZING PERSON

Abraham Maslow grew up in Brooklyn and was educated at the City College of New York and the University of Wisconsin. At Wisconsin, he was the first graduate student of Harry Harlow, a psychologist who would achieve fame for innovative work on the effect of maternal deprivation in monkeys. Much of Maslow's early work was with monkeys as he explored motivation (Maslow & Harlow, 1932; Maslow, 1935a) and social relations in non-human primates, and then attempted to generalize this knowledge to motivation and social relations in humans (Maslow, 1935b, 1936, 1937, 1939, 1940). Although once enamored of the behavioral perspective as a framework for human understanding, Maslow would later quip that, "anyone who had a baby couldn't be a behaviorist" (Hall, 1968, p. 56). According to Maslow, babies exhibit "biological wisdom" and it is they—not the people who would attempt to influence their behavior—who know best when to eat, when

**FIGURE 2–11
ABRAHAM HAROLD
MASLOW
(1908–1970)**

to sleep, and so forth. As you might expect even having only this little bit of background, here is what Maslow (1971) thought of John Watson's boast regarding the power of behaviorism in shaping the destiny of children:

> Having a second baby, and learning how profoundly different people are even before birth, made it impossible for me to think in terms of the kind of learning psychology in which one can teach anybody anything. Or the John B. Watson theory of "Give me two babies and I will make one into this and one into the other." It is as if he never had children. We know only too well that a parent cannot make his children into anything. Children make themselves into something. The best we can do and frequently the most effect we can have is by serving as something to react against if the child presses too hard. (p. 169)

Maslow questioned whether the objective of psychology as a science should be the prediction and control of behavior. In *The Psychology of Science,* Maslow (1966) asked, "Do we ourselves want to be predicted and predictable? Controlled and controllable?" Another compelling question Maslow raised and looked at in a new way was, "Do people live by bread alone?" For Maslow, the answer to this question is not a simple yes or no, but one that may fluctuate depending on the general circumstances a person is living in, as well as on more specific daily fluctuations in those circumstances. For example, you may have food on your mind going in to the restaurant, but something else on your mind coming out. If you are living in the street, hungry, and wondering how you are going to survive from day to day, you may very well be preoccupied with obtaining food to the exclusion of all other interests—and in essence, live by bread alone. If you live in the lap of luxury, you may be more concerned with things such as entertaining yourself and your friends, writing your memoirs, or launching a campaign for political office.

In what was perhaps his most cited contribution, Maslow identified a hierarchy of human needs. Maslow's **hierarchy,** or *a graded series,* was of five needs that emerge in people. At the base of the hierarchy are physiological needs. At its top is **self-actualization,** *a relatively rare state in complete potential, and in particular complete emotional potential, has been obtained.* Self-actualization is achieved by self-actualizing people. According to Maslow, openness to experience, clarity of experience, growth-oriented choices, and movement towards fulfillment of one's potential are all characteristic of self-actualizing people (see Figure 2–12). From Maslow's writing, as well as from the writing of other humanists who have offered further interpretation of Maslow, we can offer some guidelines for getting on track to becoming self-actualized (see the *Quality of Life*).

hierarchy
a graded series.

self-actualization
a relatively rare state in which one's complete potential has been attained.

AN EVALUATION OF THE HUMANISTIC PERSPECTIVE

The humanistic perspective has great appeal, especially because, in contrast to the behavioral or psychoanalytic perspective, it views people very positively and focuses on their potential for good. Common to the writings of Rogers, Maslow, and other humanists is a very optimistic view of human beings. It is a view, one might say, that is empowering;

FIGURE 2–12 MASLOW'S HIERARCHY OF NEEDS This pyramid of human motives could be called a first-things-first approach to human understanding. First, a person strives to meet biological or physiological needs, such as the needs for food, water, and a normal body temperature. Having gratified these needs, the person looks to gratifying safety and security needs. Belongingness and love needs come next followed by esteem needs, including the need for self-respect and respect from others. At the top of the hierarchy is self-actualization, which is a process, not an end in itself. Self-actualizing persons are characterized by the ability to experience fully, vividly, selflessly, and with full concentration.

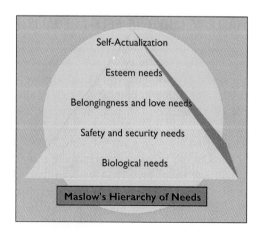

Climbing the Self-Actualization Pyramid

One of the key contributions Abraham Maslow made to our study of human motivation was his emphasis on the interdependent nature of motives. Stated another way, the strength of one motive, such as the need to belong, will depend on the strength of another motive, such as the need to eat or sleep. Although he did not explicitly outline a step-by-step program for climbing the self-actualization pyramid, he did leave a sufficient number of clues. Once you have your biological, security, belongingness, and esteem needs satisfied or relatively satisfied, it's time to think about the challenge of making it to the top. It will not be easy, but few things worthwhile in life are. Here are some tips for moving in that direction.

1. Be Open to Experience
The self-actualized person is willing to try new types of food, listen to new types of music, go to exotic places for exposure to different cultures. In short, the self-actualized person is open to experience. "Bungee jumping?" you ask . . . well, not necessarily quite that open to experience. You see, you have to keep those security needs met as well.

2. Appreciate Your Experiences for What They Are
Self-actualized people sees things clearly and tend not to habitually exaggerate or minimize what they see. An exception to this rule are self-actualized artists who may deliberately distort reality in the service of communicating through their art.

3. Believe in Yourself
Self-actualized people are people who have achieved a high degree of autonomy in their lives. This means that to the extent it is humanly possible, they are beholden to no one, free of restraint, and responsible for their own fate. Needless to say, strong beliefs in yourself must be tempered by the feedback you get from reality. For example, you may have a strong belief in your ability to pick winners at the racetrack. However, if the result of this belief is an unhealthy erosion of your finances, it is time to reevaluate your beliefs.

4. Make Growth-Oriented Life Choices
When faced with the many choices that must be made during the course of your life, you may ask yourself many different questions such as, "How will I make more money?" or "Which choice will look better to my neighbors?" For the self-actualized person, one guiding question is, "Which choice will best help me to grow as a person?" Of course, it is not always as simple as that. For example, spouses may have vastly different ideas about what decision will be best for *their* personal growth and your own decisions may have to be made in partnership with the person who is helping you to fulfill your belongingness and love needs.

5. Become All That You Are Capable of Being
Take a moment right now to consider what you are realistically capable of being or becoming in the following spheres of your life:
■ your occupation
■ your relationships with your family members
■ your relationships with your friends
■ your value system

Are you moving towards being all that you can be in each of these spheres? If not, what obstacles are in your way? How can these obstacles be overcome?

6. Cultivate a Sense of Humor if You Do Not Have One Already
Maslow saw self-actualized people as people who have senses of humor. If many people through the years have told you that you do not have a sense of humor or that you need to lighten up, they may be right. A sense of humor is an asset that will help you through what you may perceive to be some very dark moments in life. There are no rules for cultivating a sense of humor, but in their book *How to Be Funny*, Steve Allen and Jane Wollman (1987) advise that attitude is everything; even with all of its tragedy, the world can be a very funny place when and if you choose to see it that way.

people are empowered with a strong sense of good within them, and with the knowledge to know what is wrong in their lives, what needs to be changed, and how to change it.

In practice, however, many people approach the psychotherapeutic situation in great emotional need. It is precisely because they believe that they do not have the answers within them that they are seeking counseling. If the therapist in such an instance fails to take an active role in providing guidance, the danger exists that the person will become disillusioned with counseling, leave it, and gradually deteriorate. As a clinician who has had the unique experience of conducting psychotherapy in settings that were variously humanistic, behavioral, and psychoanalytic, I can verify from firsthand experience such danger. Many people are either too in need or too impatient to respond to even the most accepting but nonauthoritative therapist. In practice, the more severe the presenting problem, the less appropriate is the humanistic perspective as a treatment alternative. Additionally, there are people who because of ingrained cultural beliefs will respond more to a very directive as opposed to nondirective therapist.

Many concepts proposed by humanistic theorists do not readily lend themselves to research because of vague or multiple and different definitions. For example, it is very difficult to develop a tool that will measure what Rogers described as an actualizing tendency or the process of self-actualization as described by Maslow. Maslow (1970) described one study in which he used various psychological assessment devices to identify self-actualizing people. After screening 3,000 students at Brandeis University, he found only one person he thought might meet the criteria. The vast majority of the people Maslow uses in his descriptions of self-actualizing people are from history books, not from consulting rooms. One wonders whether even these historical figures would be deemed self-actualizing if Maslow had had the opportunity to assess them personally!

There is also the irksome issue of the very name of this perspective, and the argument that humanists have no monopoly on being or acting human or on treating people with human dignity. Most psychotherapists describe themselves as operating from a perspective of personality theory and psychotherapeutic treatment that is eclectic (or *composed of elements from different approaches depending upon the presenting problem*). Many of these therapists are quite humanistic in their outlook to the extent that they believe in the individual person's unique potential for growth.

In this chapter, we explored several theories regarding human behavior. In Chapters 7 and 9, we will take a look at how some of these perspectives have been pressed into the service of helping people with psychological problems. Along the way we will take a closer look at stress (Chapter 6) as well as severe thought and behavior problems (Chapter 8). More immediately, however, our attention will be focused in the following chapter on understanding behavior and adjustment from a biological and health-related perspective.

SUMMARY

WHAT IS PERSONALITY? The construct "personality" has been defined in many ways. Some definitions make reference to *psychological traits* (any distinguishable, relatively enduring way in which one individual varies from another), *states* (a transitory exhibition of a trait), and *types* (any distinguishable, relatively enduring way in which one group of personality traits varies from another group of personality traits). For our purposes, *personality* was defined as an individual's unique constellation of psychological traits and states. Different perspectives on personality include the *psychoanalytic* perspective, the *behavioral* perspective, and the *humanistic* perspective.

A PSYCHOANALYTIC PERSPECTIVE Freud introduced the first ever systematic theory of personality and psychotherapeutic treatment. *Psychoanalytic theory* and the corresponding

method of treatment called *psychoanalysis* have been described as dynamic systems because they suppose that different types of energy are transferred between the mind and the body. Essential to the theory is the existence of three functional divisions of the mind labeled by Freud as the *id* (which can be likened to the primitive self), the *ego* (which can be likened to the more mature self), and the *superego* (which can be likened to one's moral conscience). For Freud, most mental activity, including activity relating to motives for conscious action, takes place out of awareness and is unconscious.

A BEHAVIORAL PERSPECTIVE If behavior as the behaviorist understands it had to be summed-up in a single word, that word would be *learning*. According to this view, all behavior, with relatively few exceptions, is learned. In their exploration regarding the mechanisms by which organisms learn, behaviorists have identified various processes including those referred to as classical conditioning, instrumental conditioning, and social learning. Cognitive-behavioral theorists, including the social learning theorists, have applied learning principles to the learning of various types of thought patterns and the experience of emotion.

A HUMANISTIC PERSPECTIVE The two theorists best identified with what has become known as humanism, are Carl Rogers and Abraham Maslow. Both have written on the boundless potential for good within each person, and the inborn tendency within each person to grow, move forward, and become a better person. From a humanistic perspective, a primary function of counseling or psychotherapy is to put people back on track to positive growth by helping them to discover their sense of self—who they really are.

Chapter 3

Health:
A Biopsychosocial
Perspective

O U T L I N E

To what age do you think you will live?

For people born at the beginning of the twentieth century, making it to age 50 or beyond was an accomplishment. Microbes such as viruses and bacteria could cause acute illness and quick death. Knowledge about nutrition and diet was not used to prevent the onset of chronic diseases like cancer. Today, in the wake of some truly remarkable advances in medical technology and health research, the chances are excellent that many readers of this book will live into their 70s and beyond. Those chances can be improved all the more by certain decisions made regarding how one lives one's life.

From a strictly biological/medical perspective, maintenance of health is primarily a matter of identifying and treating, if possible, the genetic deficiencies, microorganisms (such as viruses or bacteria), and/or structural damage (such as a broken blood vessel or bone) that pose threats to health. According to this view, physicians and members of allied professions are the guardians of health; patients go to them when they are ill, and physicians use their knowledge and skill in an effort to restore patients' health.

A new perspective on health places greater emphasis on lifestyle in the maintenance of health. It takes into account not only biological factors but psychological, behavioral, social, and cultural factors as well. This newer way of looking at health and illness is the subject of this chapter.

A BIOPSYCHOSOCIAL PERSPECTIVE

biopsychosocial perspective
a view of how biological, psychological, and social factors may independently or in combination affect wellness and illness.

From a **biopsychosocial perspective**, *health is viewed from the standpoint of how biological, psychological, and social factors may independently or in combination with each other affect wellness and illness* (Engel, 1977; Schwartz, 1982). The biopsychosocial perspective grew out of a relatively simple but powerful realization: *one's behavior, thoughts, and feelings can play a critical role in health and its maintenance*. It grew out of eye-opening findings regarding the relationship between health and a wide variety of voluntary behavior, including eating behavior, smoking behavior, sexual behavior, drinking behavior, drug-taking behavior, behavior related to rest, sleep, and relaxation, behavior related to compliance with physician's orders, and other behavior. To the extent that how one thinks and behaves has an effect on physical health and well-being, psychological adjustment and physical health are intimately intertwined.

health psychology
growing specialty area in psychology seeking to understand how psychological variables can influence illness and disease.

The biopsychosocial perspective is at the heart of a young but rapidly growing specialty area in psychology called **health psychology**. Health psychologists seek to understand *how psychological variables can influence the onset, course, treatment, and/or cure of illness and disease*. Health psychologists may be involved in research, teaching, delivery of health-related services, administration of health-care programs, and other such activities having to do with the promotion of health and the prevention of illness, disease, and disability. In this chapter, we will survey some of the exciting research that has been done in the field of health psychology and explore the relationship between physical health and psychological adjustment. We begin with a description of some basic biological concepts and systems.

GENETICS

chromosome
a substance within the cells of plants and animals that is responsible for the determination and transmission of hereditary characteristics.

gene
a substance that typically occupies a fixed location on a chromosome and has responsibility for the determination and transmission of hereditary characteristics.

You may recall from your high school biology course that all living things are composed of cells, and that all cells contain "information" of a hereditary nature to be passed from one generation to the next. Chromosomes and genes are the carriers of such information. For our purposes, we may define a **chromosome** as *a substance within the cells of plants and animals that is responsible for the determination and transmission of hereditary characteristics*. A **gene** may be defined as *a substance that typically occupies a fixed location on a chromosome and has responsibility for the determination and transmission of hereditary characteristics*. The statement is qualified with "typically occupies" because it is possible for mutant genes (the product of random change) to violate expectancies regarding location or other characteristics. In certain genetic (that is, gene-related) abnormalities it is even possible that extra genes are observed or that genes that should be present are lacking. **Genetics** is defined as *the study of the biological mechanisms of variation and hereditary transmission in living organisms.* Through genetics, a great deal of knowledge has been amassed regarding the inheritance of physical and other characteristics.

Cells of different species typically contain different numbers of chromosomes. The cells of peas contain 7 pairs of chromosomes, mice have 20 pairs, humans have 23 pairs, and monkeys have 27 pairs. In humans, each of the billions of cells found in a normal adult contains 23 pairs of chromosomes, or a total of 46 chromosomes altogether (see Figure 3–1). The exception to this general rule are certain male and female cells involved in reproduction which undergo a special process of cell division to yield sperm and egg cells, which each contain 23 chromosomes. The sperm and egg cells combine to create a new person with his or her own 23 *pairs* of chromosomes.

A BIOLOGICAL PERSPECTIVE

It has been estimated that some 4,000 diseases and disorders have a genetic component (Bajardi, 1992). Locating which gene is responsible for which disorder is seen as a first step in identifying people at risk for such diseases and developing treatment procedures. Recent years have witnessed impressive breakthroughs as the genes responsible for diseases such as cystic fibrosis, muscular dystrophy, neurofibromatosis ("elephant man's disease"), and Huntington's disease have been identified. Within weeks after a gene identified as causal in Lou Gehrig's disease (also known as ALS, or amyotrophic lateral sclerosis) was identified in 1993, a patent was granted for a synthetic gene that might one day be used to replace the defective one. As envisioned by its developers, the synthetic gene might be self-administered in much the same way a diabetic self-administers insulin (Chartrand, 1993).

The federal government is sponsoring a large-scale program called the Human Genome Project which has as its objective the comprehensive mapping out of the some 100,000 genes found in human beings. The fruit of this project, and of the work of many independent laboratories, will be a detailed and comprehensive understanding of the

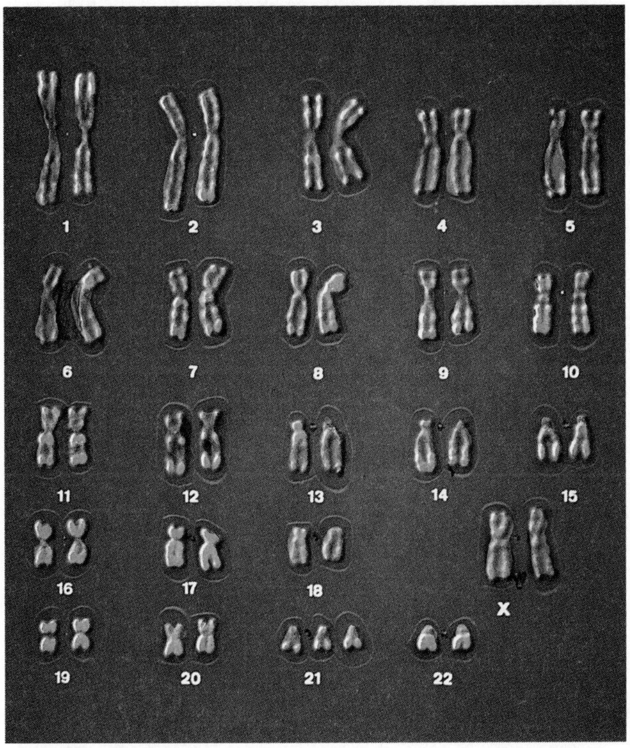

genetics
the study of the biological mechanisms of variation and hereditary transmission in living organisms.

FIGURE 3–1 CHROMOSOMES Pictured are pairs of human chromosomes as magnified through an electron microscope. The composition of the 23rd pair of chromosomes will determine the gender of the offspring. When what is called an X chromosome combines with an X chromosome, female offspring will result. When an X chromosome combines with what is called a Y chromosome, male offspring will result. Note that the 21st pair in the photograph is not a pair at all; there is an extra chromosome, three in all. The presence of an extra 21st chromosome is characteristic of children with **Down syndrome,** *a hereditary disorder marked by mental disability, heart defects, and other physical abnormalities.* Another disease, neurofibromatosis (a disfiguring condition that is also known as "elephant man's disease") arises from a rare abnormality of the 17th pair of chromosomes, wherein one large gene contains three little genes. Genes have also been found to play a role in the development of Alzheimer's disease (Goldgaber et al., 1987), although the role they play remains a subject of intensive research.

human genetic code. Progress on this ambitious project has been brisk (Angier, 1992a) and a number of genetic breakthroughs are expected in the near future (Leary, 1993). But such breakthroughs do not come value-free. Rather, new genetic knowledge and the technology it spawns may carry with it a multitude of ethical issues and questions. Consider in this context a hair-like piece of genetic material called a *telomere*. Some scientists suspect that telomeres act as a kind of timepiece for human life. The length of telomeres decreases with age. Death ensues when telomeres fall below a critical length (Angier, 1992b). If such findings are consistently replicated, and as accuracy and facility in the measurement of telomeres improve, one can envision the day when it will be possible to foretell the length of one's life, barring accidents and the like, based on the length of one's telomeres. If that day ever comes, the next logical question is, "Who should be privy to such information?" Today, life insurance companies and prospective employers are among those who are legally entitled to obtain medical records and perform their own medical examinations before issuing a life insurance policy or hiring or promoting an employee. If detailed genetic information was available, life insurance companies would almost certainly lobby for access to such information. Should they be given it? Prospective employers might argue that they have a right to such information before investing in the career of an employee. Should employers be given access to such information? What criteria should determine who should be given access to such genetic information?

For many people who have been diagnosed as having genetic disorders, advances in genetic mapping may be viewed with apprehension regarding possibilities for high-tech invasion of privacy (Bajardi, 1992). True, it has become easier to diagnose many different genetic disorders. Technology can also better predict the likelihood with which genetically transmitted diseases may in fact be transmitted. However, treatment of genetic disorders at the level of the gene is currently seen as a long way off for most people. The fear is that advances in identification of genetic disorders will work against people stricken with such disorders. They could be denied insurance, employment, or other benefits. Other controversies surrounding the use of genetic technology range from its use in identifying criminals through so-called "genetic fingerprints" (Kolata, 1992a) to its use in the creation of new, "genetically engineered" foods (Burros, 1992). Advances in genetic technology frequently prompt value-related debates (see *A Question of Values*).

A PSYCHOLOGICAL PERSPECTIVE

behavior genetics

the study of biological mechanisms of variation and hereditary transmission that affect behavior.

Behavior genetics, a sub-specialty of genetics, may be defined as *the study of the biological mechanisms of variation and hereditary transmission in living organisms that affect behavior.* Studies in behavior genetics are sometimes referred to as studies on the effect of nature versus nurture or heredity versus environment because they seek to determine the respective contributions of heredity and environment in targeted behaviors. Researchers in the field of behavior genetics explore the influence of heredity on behavior using many different methods. Subjects are typically **identical twins** (*two siblings who have exactly the same genetic inheritance because they developed from the same fertilized egg*) or **fraternal twins** (*two siblings who share the same father and mother and who were carried together in the mother's uterus but who developed from two separate fertilized eggs.* In one type of behavioral research design, reared-together identical twins are compared to reared-together fraternal twins on behavioral variables of interest. How much similarity on these variables exists between the identical twins as compared to the fraternal twins? If there is more similarity between the identical twins, heredity may be playing a greater role than environment with respect to the behavior in question. The strength of the conclusion would in part depend on the comparability of the environments to which the two sets of twins were exposed.

In general, although single genes have been found to be responsible for physical traits such as eye color, single genes have not been found to be responsible for any behavioral variables. Rather, to the extent that many behavioral variables have a basis in genes, that basis has been found to be **polygenic** in nature, that is, *deriving from more than one gene.* Also, to the extent that any behavior has a genetic basis, environmental and cultural variables typically play no small role in whether or not the behavior will be emitted. Lucy may inherit a set of genes that would predispose her to becoming a brilliant rocket scientist. However, if Lucy was born in the 19th century, the odds were heavily against such

identical twins

two siblings who have exactly the same genetic inheritance because they developed from the same fertilized egg.

fraternal twins

two siblings who share the same father and mother and who were carried to term together in the mother's uterus but who developed from separate fertilized eggs.

polygenic

deriving from more than one gene.

Biotechnology and Genetic Engineering

Advances in methods for examining and altering genes has led to a relatively new and growing industry that involves "genetic engineering." The term **biotechnology** refers to *the application of biological science for commercial or industrial objectives.* In practice, it refers to experimentation by genetic engineers that is designed, among other things, to create new forms of life, including new species of animals, new species of plants, and new species of microorganisms. Since a Supreme Court decision in 1980, these new forms of life have been deemed patentable inventions rather than products of nature.

The biotechnology industry has been virtually unregulated by the federal government since its inception. In February 1992, the president of the United States, citing possible economic benefits in the form of new jobs and the potential for the development of new sources of food, announced that even less regulation would be applied to the biotechnology industry ("Bush to Ease Rules on Products Made by Altering Genes," 1992). Government agencies are prevented from doing anything to interfere with such experimentation unless "unreasonable risk" is proved. However, as observed by Keppel (1992), "That would be fine if we were trying to decide whether rattlesnakes are poisonous. But the question with novel organisms is far more complicated. It lies in their interaction with thousands of other organisms." The government policy also leaves unclear the question of whose burden it is to prove that risk exists.

Critics of this "leave the genetic engineering industry alone" attitude on the part of the government fear that public health and welfare may be threatened as a result of genetic engineering. Consumers are already eating genetically engineered food, and many have wondered what, if any, will be the long-term effects of ingestion of the novel substances contained in them. Consumers having various food allergies may find themselves unwittingly eating foods containing substances to which they are allergic. Beyond the potential threat to individuals, there is the potential threat to the environment. Genetically engineered fish, for example, grow larger and faster than their "Nature-engineered" counterparts. Further, unlike their counterparts, they are capable of surviving in cold, northern waters (Bruggeman, 1992). What effect will the introduction of these fish into northern waters have on the environment and other aquatic organisms?

Genetic breakthroughs in medicine and other fields promise to increase our quality of life. Still, nagging values-related questions linger regarding the mixing and matching of genes by genetic engineers. History records countless actions done with the noblest of intentions that have backfired into natural disasters. For example, a few gypsy moth eggs innocently imported from Europe in the late 1860s by an entrepreneur seeking to create a silk industry in Boston turned out to be an environmental catastrophe. Although the importer's silk business was never launched, the moths sur-

vived. The catastrophic legacy of those moths is millions of acres of defoliated trees.

Perhaps some of the most far-reaching consequences of genetic technology may be in the area of human reproduction and the very radical changes it will bring in "the family" and the concept of "kinship" as we presently know them (Edwards, 1991). As we will see when we discuss family planning in Chapter 13, advances in genetic engineering are bringing new meaning to "tailor-made" and "build to suit" when it comes to the creation of human beings.

What is in these foods? If current trends continue, only a genetic engineer will be

a genetic gift bearing fruit. Not only would the requisite technology for rocket science be nonexistent but also a strong cultural bias against women in science would have militated against a successful career in science for Lucy. In general, studies in behavior genetics have supported the notion that heredity sets an upper limit on our behavioral capabilities. En-

biotechnology

the application of biological science for commercial or industrial objectives.

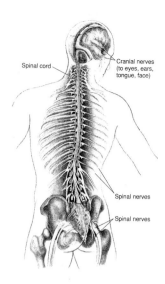

Spinal cord
Cranial nerves
(to eyes, ears,
tongue, face)

Spinal nerves

Spinal nerves

**FIGURE 3–2   THE NER-
VOUS SYSTEM** The nervous
system may in some ways be
likened to a central command
post with extensions and
branches throughout the body.
The **central nervous system**
consists of *the brain and the spinal
cord.* The other major part of the
nervous system is the **peripheral nervous system,** which
consists of *the tissue that connects
the central nervous system to the
rest of the body.* It is through sensory input to the brain that we
perceive light, touch, sounds, temperature, taste, and other sensory
input. It is through commands issued from the brain that we walk,
talk, lift weights, and engage in
other voluntary movements. It is
also through commands of the
central nervous system—at the
level of the brain or in some cases
the level of the spinal cord—that
certain involuntary movements
occur. For example, pulling a hand
away from a hot stove, having the
pupils of the eye constrict in response to bright light, or experiencing a quickening of heartbeat
in response to an alarm are all
dictated by the central nervous
system.

branching
growth and interconnections in a
nervous system.

gland
an organ that extracts from the
blood specific substances in order
to manufacture other substances.

vironmental and cultural factors play a role in determining how close to that upper limit
we can come.

THE NERVOUS SYSTEM

The brain, the spinal cord, and the entire network of nerves "wired" to it, including the
electrical and chemical activity that goes on within it, can be referred to collectively as the
nervous system (see Figure 3–2). A number of intriguing questions exist about the nature
of the relationship between the brain and psychological adjustment. Some of these questions are:

- Do adjusted people have brains that are in some way physically different from those
  of severely maladjusted people?
- Do the brains of severely maladjusted people function in a way that is somehow different from those of adjusted people?
- How does damage to the brain, the spinal cord, or any other part of the nervous
  system affect adjustment or other aspects of behavior?
- How does the nervous system physically change over the course of time and what
  are the behavioral manifestations of these changes?
- What effect, if any, does environment have on the brain?

Some preliminary answers to such questions have begun to be developed. For example, there is evidence from animal studies to suggest that exposure to more enriched environments leads to observable changes in the brain. Psychologists have observed that animal
subjects housed in more enriched and varied environments tend to develop more **branching** (*growth and interconnections*) in their nervous systems as compared to animals housed
in restricted environments (Camel et al., 1986; Greenough et al., 1988; Renner & Rosenzweig, 1987; Rosenzweig, 1984; Rosenzweig et al., 1972). For laboratory animals, a *restricted environment* refers to a barren cage while an *enriched environment* refers to a cage
filled with visually stimulating objects, toys, wheels to spin on, and so forth.

Branching patterns have also been found to change in humans as they age. Although
loss of nerve cells is common in aging, the pattern of nerve branching will differ as a function of a number of factors including one's health. Branching may increase, perhaps to compensate for the nerve cells lost, in people who remain healthy, relatively active, and alert
(Buell & Coleman, 1981). Branching may decrease or cease altogether in people who become senile. Exactly why branching patterns increase, decrease, or totally cease with age
remains an important research question currently under investigation.

Do the brains of very violent people differ from the brains of average, everyday people? In some rare cases, the answer to this question is yes. For example, on a summer night
in 1966, Charles Whitman murdered his mother and his wife. The next morning, Whitman perched himself at the top of a tower at the University of Texas at Austin and began
firing his hunting rifle at anyone who came into range. Before police ended this random
homicide spree by shooting and killing Whitman, 14 innocent people had been killed and
another 24 wounded.

In accordance with Texas law, an autopsy was performed on the perpetrator's body.
The autopsy revealed that Whitman had a large tumor in an area of the brain that is associated with the emission of aggressive and rage-like behavior. Presumably, this tumor had
a causal role in Whitman's murderous behavior, although the exact extent of its role can
never be known. Other people have developed tumors in the same area of the brain and
have not felt compelled to kill, let alone commit multiple murders. Still, the case is an oft-
cited example of the extent to which disease in the nervous system can radically affect one's
behavior and adjustment.

THE ENDOCRINE SYSTEM

Normally working in well-coordinated fashion with the nervous system is the system of
glands that make up the endocrine system (see Figure 3–3). A **gland** is *an organ that extracts from the blood specific substances in order to manufacture other substances.* Some glands,

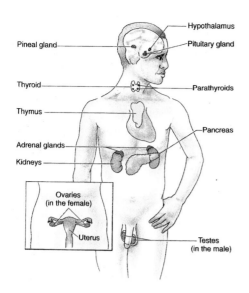

FIGURE 3–3 SOME OF THE GLANDS IN THE ENDOCRINE SYSTEM Organs in the endocrine system include the hypothalamus, the pituitary, the thyroid, the parathyroids, the adrenal glands, the pancreas, the ovary (female), and the testis (male). *Renal,* from the Latin *renes,* refers to the kidneys. The term *ad renal* literally means "near or adjacent the kidneys." Note that the adrenal glands are actually perched on top of the kidneys. It is the adrenal glands that produce adrenaline.

such as tear glands, secrete their products (tears in the case of tear glands) into *tubular passageways in the body* called **ducts**. The hallmark of glands in the endocrine system is that they are all ductless; the material they produce is secreted directly into the bloodstream. Specific products of various endocrine glands, referred to as **hormones** (*chemical messengers produced by one tissue that travels through the blood to affect another tissue*), play a role in growth, metabolism, sex and reproduction, mood, stress regulation, and exertion. Hormones may be released in automatic fashion in response to substances circulating in the blood, or they may be released as a by-product of mental activity, including thoughts, emotions, and imagery (Clark & Gelman, 1987). Some endocrine glands play an important role in situations of perceived danger in which "fight or flight" is required. For example, the adrenal glands release adrenaline into the bloodstream which in turn causes a number of physical changes, such as a faster heart rate, that are all designed to help the body cope with stress.

ducts

tubular passageways in the body.

hormone

a chemical messenger produced by one tissue that travels through the blood to affect another tissue.

THE IMMUNE SYSTEM

The human body's immune system is an elaborate system of external and internal defenses against **pathogens**, *harmful or potentially harmful agents including microorganisms and toxins.* Pathogens may enter the body in several ways, including through physical contact with the skin, inhalation (breathing), and ingestion (eating). Once a pathogen has broken through an external line of defense such as the skin, the body's network of internal defenses goes to work. This internal defense system may be likened to the armed forces because it includes squadrons of various types of cells each designed to perform some specific defensive function. Some cells act as "lookouts" combing the body for the presence of pathogens. Other cells act to sound the body's alarm or the all-clear signal when the danger has passed. Some cells will actually battle the pathogens while others will clean up after the battle is over.

In recent years, the attention of many researchers has increasingly been focused on the structure, function, and behavior of the helper T-cells. Helper T-cells engulf and attempt to destroy pathogens that enter the body. Unfortunately, when they attempt to engulf and destroy some kinds of pathogens, they are overpowered and, in a manner of speaking, taken over. In the disease AIDS (an acronym for *acquired immunodeficiency syndrome*), a virus referred to as HIV (*human immunodeficiency virus*) overpowers the helper T-cells that engulf it. Worse yet, HIV commandeers the reproductive mechanism of the helper T-cells and uses it to reproduce even more HIV. During the course of the disease, the number of helper T-cells will decline and the AIDs victim will come down with what are called **op-**

pathogens

harmful or potentially harmful agents including microorganisms and toxins.

opportunistic disease

a condition arising from a weakened immune system as a result of a disease such as AIDS.

immunization

a process that stimulates the formation of protective antibodies to infectious organisms.

antibody

the general term used to describe protein molecules in the blood that defend the body against invading pathogens.

vaccine

minute amounts of inactive or live organisms or toxins introduced into the body for the purpose of bringing about immunization to a disease.

portunistic diseases which the body's helper T-cells could have fought off. The actual cause of death for many AIDS patients is an opportunistic disease such as pneumonia.

The body's natural immunity to many different types of diseases can be enhanced through **immunization**, *a process that stimulates the formation of protective antibodies to infectious organisms.* An **antibody** is the general term used to describe *protein molecules in the blood that defend the body against invading pathogens.*[1] In immunization, an immunizing substance, usually referred to as **vaccine** (*minute amounts of inactive or live organisms or toxins*), is introduced into the body in order to stimulate the body to produce antibodies to those organisms or toxins. Immunization dates back to 1796 and the use of cowpox virus to produce human immunity to the disease smallpox. The technical term for cowpox virus is *vaccinia* (from the Latin root *vacca,* meaning *cow*) and it is in that term that words such as *vaccine* and *vaccination* (synonymous with immunization) have their origins. Through the years, vaccines for many different diseases, including polio, whooping cough, and rabies, have been developed. Vaccines vary in the length of time they actively produce immunity to disease. For example, a vaccination against yellow fever confers immunity for 10 years while one against plague may only work for 6 months. In recent years, a national debate has been going on regarding the need for universal vaccination of all American children (see *In the News*).

ADJUSTMENT AND HEALTH

Have you ever wondered about how your physical state of health could affect your mental state? Have you thought about how your mental state might affect your physical state of health? If your answer to one or both of these questions was "Yes", you may be pleased to learn that your curiosity in such matters is shared by many research scientists. In matters of illness and wellness, evidence increasingly points to a reciprocal relationship between the mind and the body; one influences the other.

STATE OF HEALTH AFFECTS STATE OF MIND

Physical illness, disease, aches, pains, or discomfort can dramatically affect moods, thoughts, competency in performing cognitive and behavioral tasks, and assorted aspects of personal and interpersonal behavior (Friedman & DiMatteo, 1989). Consider in this context an adult who is suddenly experiencing severe and irreversible hearing loss. In an era in which the volume of music is often cranked up and played through multiple speakers in one's car, at rock concerts, and in other places, irreversible hearing loss has become an increasingly common phenomenon (New York League for the Hard of Hearing, 1993).

A hearing disability robs the individual of more than hearing. It takes away the pleasures of theater, films, television, and other media in which sound plays a key role. Such an impairment might also seriously impact one's ability to drive a car safely, ride a bicycle safely, even walk on the street safely. In social situations, friends, family, co-workers, and others might frequently be asked to repeat things. Fast one-liner-type jokes that people whiz by would do just that—whiz by without being heard. How do you think the people around an adult suddenly stricken with hearing impairment might begin behaving towards such a person? How do you think the hearing-impaired person would begin responding to those people? What other social consequences might you envision in terms of relations at school, on the job, and at home? What consequences might you envision in terms of the hearing-impaired person's self-concept and self-esteem?

If you envisioned worsening psychological adjustment due to factors such as increasing social isolation, then you accurately anticipated what typically happens to many people as a hearing impairment worsens. Because this type of physical disability so often has immediate and negative personal, psychological, and social consequences, people having such a disability are typically urged by professionals to undergo counseling, in addition to training in skills such as lipreading and communication by signing.

[1]In *auto-immune diseases* such as lupus, for example, the body misidentifies some of its own cells as pathogens and proceeds to produce antibodies to destroy them.

Universal Vaccination for Children

Diphtheria is a highly infectious, sometimes fatal disease that is sweeping across Russia in epidemic proportions (Bohlen, 1993). The disease has virtually been eliminated in the United States due to early childhood immunization against it and the administration of regular booster immunizations until the age of 12. Could diphtheria and other diseases virtually eradicated by vaccination programs return to our country? Yes, according to health experts who remind us not to let our collective guard down by thinking of many infectious diseases as things of the past.

Recent years have witnessed the comeback in this country of various diseases, such as tuberculosis and measles, thought by many to have been medically conquered years ago. We live in a very mobile society, one in which an infected person from one area of the world is capable of introducing an infectious disease in another area at the other side of the planet in a matter of hours. Even an infected mosquito or other organism that somehow gets onboard an airliner may be capable of starting a deadly outbreak of infection. Americans have little reason to feel complacent about outbreaks of infectious disease in Africa, Asia, South America, or anywhere on the globe; it can be brought to their doorsteps with a vengeance in a matter of hours or days.

Vaccinations that will prevent many diseases are currently available. New types of vaccines that employ recently developed genetic technology have already been successfully employed with laboratory animals and are on the near horizon for use with humans (Henig, 1993a). In recent years, some have urged the universal vaccination of children in the United States at government expense (Graham, 1993; Henig, 1993b). Others cite the staggering costs of such a program (Rosenthal, 1993a) and raise questions regarding the rights and responsibilities of all involved parties (DeParle, 1993). Henig (1993b) proposed that an adult's failure to have a child immunized be treated by law much as child abuse is.

Currently, only about half of all 2-year-olds in the United States, and less than that ratio in some communities, have had all of the recommended childhood vaccinations (Henig, 1993b). In the past decade, some 168,000 people in the United States, mostly children, have become sick with diseases for which effective vaccinations exist (Graham, 1993). Conditions seem ripe for a comeback of several infectious diseases if widespread immunization programs are not implemented.

Even relatively minor, everyday kinds of fluctuations in health can carry negative personal and social effects. For example, think of the last time you had a bout with the flu, a bad cold, or a sore throat. Simply resting out a virus at home may well contribute to negative emotional states such as anxiety, anger, or depression. In turn, anxiety, anger, and depression may affect the way one deals with other people, which in turn will affect the way other people think about and behave towards anxious, angry, or depressed people. You probably have a full schedule of things to do and not a whole lot of time to get done what you have to do; such is the nature of contemporary living. A doctor's order to take days of bedrest might therefore, somewhat paradoxically, prove quite stressful.

STATE OF MIND AFFECTS STATE OF HEALTH

Emotions, beliefs, expectancies, and other thoughts and images in the mind can have physical effects on the body that have short- or long-term consequences (Engel, 1977; Schwartz, 1982; Taylor, 1986).

EFFECTS OF SHORT-TERM STRESS

Both men's voices trembled slightly as [the prosecutor's] cross-examination began. . . . (Mydans, 1993a, p. A14)

So went one journalist's account of an emotion-charged cross-examination in the federal trial of four Los Angeles police officers charged with violating the civil rights of a motorist. Trembling voices, trembling hands, quickened heartbeats, raised blood pressure, visible perspiration, and fainting (see Figure 3–4) are some possible short-term effects of stress. Another usual accompaniment of stress is the release of a chemical into the blood that makes the blood stickier and therefore able to clot faster. If one were to be cut, the ability of the blood to clot faster would be a great benefit. However, blood that clots faster is typically not a benefit to anyone predisposed to suffering a heart attack. A blockage of blood flow in the heart is the cause of the heart attack, and stickier, faster-clotting blood can therefore be a causal factor. Thus, because of the physiological changes that accompany stress, it is possible for one having heart trouble to die as a result of stress. It does not matter whether the stress is of a cognitive or emotional nature (as in being told bad news), or of a physical nature (as in exerting oneself by shoveling snow).

In people having heart problems, even the momentary stress suffered in response to a bad dream may be fatal. All of us dream every night. Dreaming occurs in progressively longer periods of sleep called **rapid eye movement (REM) sleep**, so-called because of the *quick, side-to-side movement of the eyes that is highly correlated with dreaming* (Carskadon & Dement, 1989; Dement, 1974). The longest REM period occurs just prior to waking. It is then, according to Virend K. Somers, a sleep researcher at the University of Iowa, that the physical arousal caused by dreams can be so powerful as to cause a heart attack in a person predisposed to cardiovascular problems. If this is true, one would expect many heart attacks to occur in the wee hours of the morning just before waking. In fact, this has been shown to be the case ("Now, a Report That Sleeping," 1993). The findings of Somers and his colleagues (1993) suggest that sleep and bedrest can actually be fatal to a person predisposed to both cardiovascular problems and stressful dreams.

Another consequence of momentary emotional stress includes loss of temper and a loss of judgment that can quickly end in harm to oneself or others. Driving, operating machinery, or engaging in any activity that demands concentration and/or good, clear judgment is certainly not recommended while one is in an emotional rage. You may also want to stay away from Greek tragedies (see Figure 3–5).

EFFECTS OF LONG-TERM STRESS

In contrast to sources of stress that affect health in a sudden and dramatic fashion, there are myriad other sources of stress that tend to do their destructive work to the body in

rapid eye movement (REM) sleep

sleep characterized by quick, side-to-side movement of the eyes that is highly correlated with dreaming.

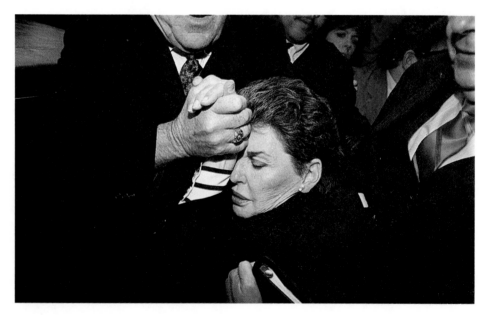

FIGURE 3–4 OVERCOME BY EMOTION Hotel owner Leona M. Helmsley collapsed outside the federal courthouse in Manhattan in March 1992 after a judge ordered that she begin serving a prison sentence for tax fraud. Cynics might say Mrs. Helmsley feigned weakness in the hope of gaining sympathy. However, what goes on in the mind is capable of exerting a powerful effect on the body. Can you think of some incident from your own experience in which your mental response to something may have influenced your physical response?

FIGURE 3–5 OEDIPUS, KING OF THEBES
The ancient Greeks, in their literature, mythology, and drama, evidenced a keen sensitivity to chains of events that began with emotional upset and ended with some catastrophic result. In many Greek tragedies, for example, various kinds of stress and emotional conflicts lead to maladjustment and/or abnormal behavior which in turn lead to suicide, homicide, or both. In the play *Oedipus, King of Thebes,* for example, the title character (played here by Laurence Olivier) blinds himself after learning that he has inadvertently killed his father and married his mother. For her part, the Queen of Thebes, Oedipus's mother and wife, commits suicide once she learns she has been living in an incestuous relationship with her son. As we saw in the preceding chapter, the tragedy of Oedipus was so compelling from a psychological standpoint to Sigmund Freud, that he used the term "Oedipal" to describe a special type of emotional conflict involving incestuous desires.

nondramatic ways, usually over the course of many years. The ongoing stress of an unhappy marriage or work situation is the type of stress referred to here. For years or even decades, the chemical aftermath of the body's reaction to chronic or prolonged stress may produce wear and tear that eventually manifests itself in terms of many varied physical problems (Cohen & Williamson, 1991; Kurstak et al., 1987; Light, et al., 1992). Hans Selye (1976) referred to such problems as *diseases of adaptation* based on his belief that the diseases developed as the body physically adapted to stress. **Psychosomatic disease** (sometimes referred to as *psychophysiological* or *psychogenic* disease, disorder, or illness) is another term used to describe *physical conditions that result from infection or weakness and are thought to be caused, maintained, or affected in intensity by psychological factors.*

In the term *psychosomatic, psycho* refers to the mind, and *somatic* refers to the body. The term *psychosomatic* as a descriptor of disease serves to emphasize the fact that some diseases can be caused, maintained, or intensified by psychological factors such as stress. *Psychosomatic, psychophysiological,* and *psychogenic* do *not* mean that a disease is "all in the mind." Suggestive evidence linking psychological factors to many physical conditions have been found (Herbert & Cohen, 1993), including illnesses and conditions as diverse as the common cold (Cohen et al., 1992; Cohen et al., 1993; Totman et al., 1980), backaches (Holmes, 1979), high blood pressure (Egan et al., 1983), gum disease (Green et al., 1986), and the recurrence of genital herpes (Kemeny et al., 1989; Longo & Clum, 1989).

The precise mechanisms by which stress acts on the body to produce these various conditions are not known. It may be that stress contributes to a predisposition to become ill by weakening the immune system in general (Holmes & Masuda, 1974). According to this notion, the organ or system representing the weakest link in the body would be the one affected by stress. In a person having a weak heart, for example, stress might provoke heart problems. In other people, stress might provoke headaches, stomach problems, a skin rash, back problems, even cognitive, emotional, or behavioral problems. A weakness in a particular organ or organ system may be the result of genetic inheritance or some other factor.

psychosomatic disease or disorder

terms used to describe physical conditions that result from infection or weakness and are thought to be caused, maintained, or affected in intensity by psychological factors.

THE MIND-BODY CONNECTION

Thousands of people inexplicably survive fatal diseases they are "supposed to" die from (Levoy, 1989). They may survive as a result of undergoing what most legitimate medical practitioners would describe as placebo or fraudulent treatment. For example, such patients may survive by taking sugar pills that they believe to be powerful medicine or by undergoing some ritual (such as one designed to remove a curse) that they fervently believe will cure them. It is also true that thousands of people die from conditions they should by all rights survive. Bernie Siegel, a retired surgeon, cited the case of a woman who died shortly after she overheard her doctor refer to her as "a classical case of TS." Although the patient had interpreted these initials as standing for "terminal situation," the doctor was actually referring to the cause of the patient's heart murmur (tricuspid stenosis). Siegel (1991) attributes such unnecessary deaths, as well as all of the beat-the-medical-odds survival stories to the fact that feelings, beliefs, hopes, positive expectations, and peace of mind all have physiological underpinnings. Stated another way, Siegel believes that the mental experience of certain thoughts, emotions, and imagery can actually affect one's health.

Not everyone agrees with the view of the mind as healer or slayer. Skeptics in the medical community have argued that even diseases widely thought to be affected by psychological factors have not been satisfactorily proven to have any psychological basis (Levenson & Bemis, 1991; Pickering & Gerin, 1990). Marcia Angell, a deputy editor at the prestigious *New England Journal of Medicine,* once wrote a stinging editorial that dismissed the role of psychological factors in disease. Angell (1988) likened the use of psychology to combat disease to "a rain dance." In a similar fashion, researchers who publish findings suggesting that mental factors play a role in improving or worsening physical health have been attacked as generating an "epidemic of false hope" (Cassileth, 1988). Yet as we will see, evidence is mounting that psychological factors may indeed play a role in the onset and course of an ever-widening list of diseases and conditions.

IN SEARCH OF THE LINK

In 1964, a study by George Solomon and Rudolf Moos at Stanford University suggested a link between emotional and physical health. Among women who were genetically disposed to develop rheumatoid arthritis, emotionally conflicted subjects tended to develop the disease, while emotionally healthy subjects did not. Recalling that study, Solomon (1989) reflected, "We felt that emotional health protected them from rheumatoid arthritis." Some 30 years ago, such a finding generated widespread skepticism among fellow professionals. Today, however, such findings have a much more receptive audience. Solomon and his colleagues are still at work in this area, trying to better define the nature of the mind-body link (Solomon et al., 1985).

Analyzing data from 3 decades of research begun in 1937 on a group of Harvard University students, George Vaillant concluded that subjects who did not cope in mature fashion with their difficulties were 4 times more likely to become ill than their better-adjusted peers. Mature coping strategies were reality-oriented methods, while immature coping strategies were methods that employed a distortion of reality. In addition to psychological variables seeming to exert an effect on physical variables, Vaillant (1967) also reported that the psychological variable of coping style affected many other spheres of life. Realistic in contrast to unrealistic coping styles were associated with higher rate of self-report of happiness, higher income, more friends, more harmonious marriage, and less mental illness.

Janice Kiecolt-Glaser and her husband Ronald Glaser, both of Ohio State University, have explored the effects of stress on the immune system in a number of studies (Kiecolt-Glaser & Glaser, 1985; Kiecolt-Glaser et al., 1991). In one oft-cited experiment that employed first-year medical students as subjects, measures of immune system functioning were taken at periods presumed to be either high or low in stress. A high stress period was exam week, a low stress period was return from summer vacation. Kiecolt-Glaser et al. (1984) found that during periods of high stress, immune system functioning decreased in terms of both the number of cells available to battle pathogens and the performance quality of the available cells. Normal vigor returned to the immune system after summer vacation. The study suggested to Kiecolt-Glaser (1989) that "even commonplace events that we associate with emotional arousal or discomfort can be associated with [decreases] in immune functions."

If you have ever thought that being stressed out made you more vulnerable to catching a cold, there is now experimental evidence to support your claim. Cohen et al. (1991) used three different measures of stress to derive an index of stress for each of the more than 400 volunteer subjects in their study. They also administered numerous other lifestyle-related measures after which the experiment began. Subjects were isolated for 2 days before and 1 week after the treatment they received. For subjects in the experimental condition, the treatment was exposure to one of five cold viruses administered by nasal drops. Subjects in the placebo group were given nasal drops of a harmless and inactive salt solution.

All subjects were in good health at the beginning of the study, and their health was monitored over the course of it. Measurements taken ranged from number of facial tissues used daily to sophisticated analysis of various cellular components of the immune system. The results indicated that stress was significantly related both to respiratory infection and to the appearance of cold symptoms (see Figure 3–6). The researchers speculated that stress somehow weakens the body's defense against viral infection. For example, it may be that stress somehow affects the amount and consistency of nasal mucous or other natural antiviral agents.

In light of studies such as these, the conclusion that stress weakens immune system functioning seems reasonable (Ader & Cohen, 1984; Antoni et al., 1990; Antoni et al., 1991; Jemmot & Locke, 1984). Weakened immune system functioning may be a causal factor in many diseases, disorders, and conditions thought to be psychosomatic in nature. Cancer, cardiovascular disorders, skin problems, gastrointestinal disorders, eating disorders, and headaches are some conditions currently thought to be affected by a stress-related weakening of the immune system (Kaplan, 1985).

PSYCHONEUROIMMUNOLOGY

Psychoneuroimmunology refers to *the study of how the nervous system interacts with the endocrine and immune systems.* This relatively new field of inquiry is based on the premise that the body's various systems communicate with each other and affect each other's functioning. Today, some of the most exciting research in this field is aimed at uncovering the actual mechanism by which mental experience, such as positive or negative thoughts or images, can weaken or strengthen the immune system. Psychoneuroimmunologists have developed some intriguing leads regarding the possible structure of the mind-body communication system. For example, previously uncharted links between the nervous system and immune system have been documented. Karen Bulloch of the University of California at San Diego has traced nerve threads that run from the central nervous system to the thymus, a ductless gland located just behind the top of the sternum (breastbone). The thymus releases thymic hormone, which is thought to play a role in immunological response, especially in childhood. David Felten of the University of Rochester Medical School has traced similar threads from the nervous system to the spleen. The spleen is located in the upper left abdominal cavity in contact with the left kidney and the pancreas. The spleen removes worn-out red blood cells and some pathogens from the blood stream. It also has a role in red blood cell and antibody production.

Complementing leads on the possible structure of the "mind-body connection" are intriguing observations regarding the actual mechanisms by which the intercellular "dialoguing" might take place. According to one line of research that employs highly sophisticated biochemical techniques, messages between the nervous system and the immune system may be transmitted and received through tiny molecules in various biochemical products such as neurotransmitters and hormones (Hall, 1989). The consequences of the chemical dialogues that take place between the nervous system and the immune system are presumed to affect one's emotional state as well as one's health. For example, because the stomach area is believed to be heavily "wired" for such chemical dialoguing (Pert, 1989), molecules released from that area in response to a meal tend to be soothing and can readily contribute to a feeling of well-being. However, it is also true that we can feel pain in the stomach and have a very negative "gut reaction" in response to thoughts, emotions, or imagery to which are attached negative cognitive labels, such as "frightening" or "stressful."

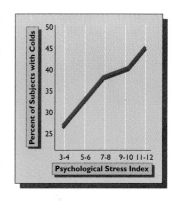

FIGURE 3–6 STRESS AND THE COMMON COLD With greater stress, the percentage of subjects who evidenced clinical illness rose.

psychoneuroimmunology the study of how the nervous system interacts with the endocrine and immune systems.

Cutting-edge research on the mind-body connection has exposed as a myth the notion that the immune system acts with complete independence inside the body. Contemporary findings, both in animal and human studies, suggest that the immune system not only defends the body against foreign invaders but also actively communicates with the brain; the immune system receives messages from the brain, and sends messages to it (Ader & Cohen, 1984). As Barber (1988) put it, psychoneuroimmunologists "have discovered that anxiety, joy, love and hate leave distinctive footprints in the exquisitely complex dance of molecules and cells that wards off disease in the human body."

Different people seem to exhibit different degrees of tolerance to stress. No one knows for sure exactly why this is so but there has been no scarcity of proposed explanations. From a biological perspective, differences in stress tolerance are typically presumed to be a function of the strength of one's genetic constitution. From a psychological perspective, a variety of factors have been suggested as relevant.

PSYCHOLOGICAL FACTORS IN STRESS TOLERANCE

Factors such as psychological hardiness, positive thinking and optimism, personality, and social support have all been proposed as possible explanations for observed differences between people in stress tolerance.

HARDINESS

Do some personality characteristics decrease or buffer the illness-related effects of stressful life events? Suzanne Kobasa (1979a, 1979b) identified a number of telephone company executives in high stress positions. According to these executives, some had remained physically healthy despite the stress of their work while others had developed what were presumed to be stress-related illnesses. All the executives were examined with psychological tests of personality. From her analysis of the differences on tests between the executives with the healthy versus the not-healthy histories, Kobasa developed a profile of what she termed a hardy personality. According to Kobasa (1982a, 1982b; 1984; Kobasa et al., 1982), the three personality traits essential for the "hardy personality" are *commitment, challenge,* and *control.* Hardy people are more committed to their goals and have a strong sense of purpose. They are more drawn to challenging tasks and accept change not as a burden but as just another part of life. They are also apt to see themselves as more in control of their own destiny as contrasted with their less hardy counterparts. Kobasa as well as others (Ganellen & Blaney, 1984) suggest that hardy people suffer fewer illnesses because of their healthy approach to life.

Critics of Kobasa fault her with respect to the methodology of her analysis and her possible confusion of hardiness with maladjustment. People who feel alienated, powerless, and out of control may be viewed as less hardy by Kobasa's methods (Funk & Houston, 1987). Others have suggested that such intertwinement of variables may be inevitable (Epstein & Katz, 1992). Hull et al. (1987) argued against the view of "hardiness" as a unitary construct. They found *commitment* and *control* to be related to health, although they questioned the value of *challenge* in this context. Kobasa herself noted another possible area of concern with her findings; the fact that self-report measures were used. It is possible that hardy individuals are people who are less willing to acknowledge illness "because it conflicts with their self-image as persons who are vigorous and in control of their lives" (Kobasa, 1982b, p. 24).

Is hardiness a causal factor in resistance to stress? Might it merely be an accompaniment of resistance to stress? Could it even be a consequence of resistance to stress? How does hardiness interact with other psychological variables? These are questions still to be explored. In one study, it was found that people identified as having a hardy personality responded to stress with more positive thoughts than members of a control group (Allred & Smith, 1989). Such findings compel one to wonder about the role of positive thinking and optimistic outlook in stress tolerance.

POSITIVE THINKING AND OPTIMISM

Although the term *positive thinking* enjoys widespread popular usage, references to it in the professional psychology literature have been relatively sparse.[2] **Positive thinking** may be defined as *a process of interpreting information in its best possible light, anticipating and mentally working towards the best possible outcome, and/or focusing on whatever is best or most hopeful.* **Optimism** may be defined as *a general tendency to envision the future as favorable.* **Pessimism** may be defined as *a general tendency to envision the future as unfavorable.*

Some intriguing research suggests that optimists tend to enjoy good health and that optimism may be positively related to stress tolerance (Humphries, 1986; Peterson et al., 1988; Reker & Wong, 1985; Scheier & Carver, 1985). For the person who expects to achieve success, stress may be viewed as an obstacle to be overcome rather than as an obstacle that cannot be hurdled. Optimistic college students tend to be more problem-focused in coping with stress than are their pessimistic counterparts (Scheier et al., 1986).

TYPE A AND TYPE B PERSONALITIES

William Harvey, personal physician to King James I, discovered circulation as well as the heart's role in that process. Harvey (1628) was among the first to speculate that the mind might play some role in circulatory disorders. Sir William Osler (1892), a Canadian cardiologist, made reference to the causal role of stress in heart attacks. Two American cardiologists, Meyer Friedman and Ray Rosenman (1959, 1974), identified specific behavior patterns that they believed placed people at high risk for heart attacks. One pattern was characterized by impatience, competitiveness, and feelings of time pressure. This Type A behavior pattern, as they called it, placed an individual at higher risk for a heart attack than the more mellow and laid-back behavioral pattern of what they called Type B behavior[3]. A number of psychological tests to determine if an individual was more a Type A or Type B personality were soon developed, the most popular being the Jenkins Activity Survey (JAS) (Jenkins et al., 1979). The JAS has been employed in a number of studies that have examined the relationship between personality and health, particularly in coronary heart disease.

Friedman and Rosenman (1974) and their colleagues (Rosenman et al., 1975) presented an impressive argument for the relationship between Type A behavior and coronary heart disease. They, along with other researchers, amassed a great deal more data to support this hypothesis (Haynes, et al., 1980; Jenkins et al., 1976). One line of research suggested that people classified as Type A are more physiologically reactive to stress than people classified as Type B (Krantz & Manuck, 1984; Williams, et al., 1982). In response to stress, sympathetic changes in hormonal secretions, blood pressure, and pulse rate of the Type A's tend to be higher than of the Type B's.

The relationship between the A/B typology and coronary heart disease may not be as straightforward as the initial reports suggested. Certain elements of the Type A personality seem to be more critical than other elements in disposing one towards coronary heart disease. "Which ones?" you may ask. The list of suspects include potential for hostility (Engebretson & Matthews, 1992; McCann & Matthews, 1988) and negative emotions that well up inside with no outward expression (Diamond, 1982; Endicott, 1989; Lai & Linden, 1992). These and other individual elements of the Type A behavior pattern have been discussed in the literature although research is ongoing and there is currently little consensus among researchers (Hearn et al., 1989; Ragland & Brand, 1988; Shekelle et al., 1985). An obstacle to demonstrating a clear and consistent relationship between Type A behavior and coronary heart disease may lie in the broadness of the Type A/Type B construct, and/or in differences related to the measures used to define this construct (Dimsdale, 1988; Fischman, 1987; Krantz & Glass, 1984; Matthews, 1982).

No listing of the individual elements of the Type A behavior pattern that is linked to cardiovascular disease have presently been agreed upon. Still, treatment and prevention programs to help Type A's slow down, become more patient, and do only one thing at a time have been attempted (Powell et al., 1984)—but with questionable success: the Type A behavior pattern is particularly resistant to change (Rosenman & Chesney, 1982). It may

positive thinking

a process of interpreting information in its best possible light, anticipating and mentally working towards the best possible outcome, and/or focusing on whatever is best or most hopeful.

optimism

a general tendency to envision the future as favorable.

pessimism

a general tendency to envision the future as unfavorable. Opposite of *optimism.*

[2]Even definitions of this term in the pop psychology literature may be hard to come by. For example, in *The Power of Positive Thinking*, a popular self-help book by the Reverend Norman Vincent Peale (1952), the term *positive thinking* is never even mentioned after the title page. Instead, the reader will find a curious mixture of counsel—some quite questionable—and New Testament-based teachings and exhortations (such as to repeat "I can do all things through Christ which strengtheneth me," from *Phillippians* 4:13).

[3]As an aid to remembering the differences between the Type A and Type B lifestyles, it might help to think of the *A* as standing for *Active* or *Achievement-oriented,* and the *B* as standing for the *B* in *Laid-Back.*

take a rather extensive overhaul of one's life view and everyday lifestyle to make the move from A to B. Further, teaching people to relax may paradoxically increase their stress (see *Quality of Life*).

SOCIAL SUPPORT

social support

understanding, acceptance, empathy, advice, guidance, and/or expressions of care, concern, agreement, trust, and love from friends, family, community caregivers, or others in one's social environment.

Social support may be defined as *understanding, acceptance, empathy, advice, guidance, and/or expressions of care, concern, agreement, trust, and love from friends, family, community caregivers, or others in one's social environment.* The source of social support varies. Social support may come from your mother, father, brother, sister, uncle, aunt, friend, classmate, priest, rabbi, police officer on the beat, the person sitting next to you on the bus, the person at the other end of a pay-per-call telephone service, or any other person you can communicate with in person, by telephone, by fax, or by any other means.

Research has suggested that social support may be related to activity of the heart during stress and/or immune functioning (Gerin et al., 1992; House et al., 1988; Kamarck et al., 1990). Lonely medical student subjects have been found to have poorer immune functioning than less lonely counterparts (Glaser et al., 1985; Kiecolt-Glaser et al., 1984). Immune functioning may also be affected by family care giving (Kiecolt-Glaser et al., 1991) and by marital disruption, whether by divorce or some other cause (Irwin et al., 1987; Kiecolt-Glaser & Glaser, 1985; Schleifer et al., 1983).

THE SICK ROLE

Much like many other good things, even the most well-meaning social support can yield paradoxically negative effects. One such negative effect is a reinforcement of the "sick role" (Parsons, 1978, 1979). We all appreciate the concern of family, friends, and co-workers when we are ill, but some people can thrive on it a bit too much. A lesson about illness, responsibility, and concern from others is learned early by most of us. Fever may lead to staying home from school, which in turn leads to watching cartoons all day while Mom or some other caretaker is at our beck-and-call. The lesson learned from such an incident is that illness need not be all that bad; it absolves one from responsibility and earns one extra individualized attention. For most of us, however, there are more rewards and more sources of fulfillment in remaining healthy. And today perhaps more than ever before in the history of the world, it is possible to *choose* health.

CHOOSING HEALTH

You may have seen a television commercial that begins with actress Sally Struthers raising and answering this question: "Do you want to make more money? Sure, we all do." Struthers then goes on to list various courses offered by a correspondence school (gun repair, veterinary assistant, etc.) and to make the suggestion that enrollment might help viewers make more money. In essence, the message is that viewers can *choose* to make more money or not.

Now let's think about another television commercial—a hypothetical one created by you designed to convince people that they can *choose* wellness. What words would you write to persuade viewers of the value of a biopsychosocial approach to health? The script might begin: "Do you want to be healthier? Sure, we all do. Well, here are some of the things you need to do . . ." What comes next? How would you fill the remaining seconds in a 60-second television commercial? Consider that question as you read, and actually write the script after you have completed this chapter.

LIFESTYLE AND HEALTH

The importance of lifestyle to health and health maintenance has been increasingly recognized (Amler & Doll, 1987; Hamburg et al., 1982; McKinlay et al., 1989). The life expectancy of women is about 78 years of age while the life expectancy of men is about 71. Although no one knows for certain what accounts for this 7-year gap, lifestyle is strongly suspected as causal. Statistically, women and men die at different rates from different

Relaxation as an Antidote to—and a Paradoxical Cause of—Stress

It is generally the case that the experience of relaxation and the experience of stress are two incompatible, mutually exclusive experiences. Operating on this assumption, many therapists teach their clients relaxation skills as a way of countering stress and making them more receptive to the acquisition of other coping skills.

One of the more popular methods used in teaching relaxation was first described by Edmund Jacobson (1938). This technique entails tensing and relaxing each muscle group within the body until every muscle group has been tensed and relaxed. To get a sense of how this "progressive relaxation" progresses, try following these directions:

> Clench your right hand in a fist. Squeeze it tight and concentrate on the feeling of tension in the muscles. Now relax it. Feel the relaxation flow into your hand. Note the difference in the feelings between the tensed state and the relaxed state. Now repeat the exercise.

After concentrating on the difference between the tensed state and the relaxed state with respect to the muscles in your right hand, you would then move on to do the same exercise with your left hand—followed by your forearm, shoulders, and so forth until every muscle group in your body had been tensed and then relaxed. This exercise of tensing and relaxing can be time-consuming if done properly. However, the time spent may be well worth it in terms of the gains in being able to recognize tension and stress in the body immediately. Once you have focused and concentrated on the differences between the tensed state and

the relaxed state in the back of your neck, for example, you can more easily recognize when you are physically becoming tense or stressed, even if you have not as yet labeled yourself as "stressed." Further, the end product of the exercise is one very relaxed person. In such a relaxed state, the individual might be more receptive than otherwise to the acquisition of other kinds of coping skills. Alternatively, progressive muscular relaxation may be useful in promoting sleep for those people kept awake by anxiety.

A number of other relaxation-related skills and techniques, such as meditation and biofeedback, are taught in efforts to help people to learn to relax. One method which might be called the "Your Favorite Place" technique simply involves vividly visualizing the most appealing place you can possibly imagine. You think of this place in all its detail as you breathe deeply and try to become more and more relaxed with every breath. Other relaxation techniques may be those that clients report having had success with in their own past experience. Taking a warm bath, quietly reading, watching television, playing with a child or a pet, playing a musical instrument, knitting, tinkering in a workshop—these are but a sample of the things people do to relieve stress and achieve a sense of relaxation.

A problem arises, however, when in the course of teaching a client relaxation skills, the tension level of the client *increases* instead of decreases. Although contrary to what might be expected, some clients, especially those having generalized anxiety to begin with, may find relaxation training stressful (Borkovec & Grayson, 1980; Lazarus, 1965). In one study involving

progressive relaxation treatment for general tension, many of the clients reported paradoxical increases in tension over the 4-week course in learning to relax (Borkovec & Hennings, 1978). Heide (1981) reported that more than half the subjects in his study reported increases in tension during relaxation sessions, and Heide and Borkovec (1983; 1984) introduced the term *relaxation-induced anxiety* to alert fellow professionals to the nonobvious side effects of relaxation training. The use of relaxation training has been found to be ill-advised with patients who have specific types of respiratory (Kinsman, et al., 1980; Lehrer, et al., 1986) or gastrointestinal problems (Luthe & Schultz, 1969). Lazarus and Mayne (1990) listed a number of possible unpleasant side-effects of relaxation training, including unpleasant sensations of warmth, dizziness, and fear of losing control.

Generally, following doctor's orders is good for us. In fact, it is all too often the case that noncompliance with a health professional's prescription leads to health problems (Becker, 1985; Di-Matteo & DiNocola, 1982; Haynes et al., 1979). In some cases, however, even the prescription to relax can bring with it adverse consequences. Any such adverse consequences and any other questions one might have about a behavioral prescription or a medication that has been prescribed, should be discussed with the health professional who prescribed it.

causes—causes which in turn are linked to behaviors such as smoking and drinking. As the proportion of female smokers has gradually grown since the 1950s, so the gender gap in mortality rates as a result of diseases such as lung cancer has narrowed considerably (Wingard & Cohn, 1990).

Simply stated, **lifestyle** refers to *an individual or group's relatively consistent day-to-day patterns of living.* Patterns of living in this context refers to a wide range of variables related to what daily life is like; how one dresses, shops, vacations, and otherwise spends or invests money; the kinds of people one associates with, the kinds of restaurants one eats at, and the kind of car one drives; the number of calories one typically consumes and expends daily, the number of cigarettes smoked, the amount of alcohol consumed; the number of hours per day spent in work, play, and sleep—all of these variables and more reflect one's lifestyle.

Perhaps because the concept of lifestyle is so broad, a lifestyle-related reference can convey quite a bit of information and conjure up many different visual images. For example, information and images related to one's values (as in *a decadent lifestyle*), motivation (as in *a drug-free lifestyle*), physical activity (as in *an athletic lifestyle*), and willingness or ability to commit to a lifelong relationship (as in *a single lifestyle*) may all be conjured by the use of such terms. If you were going to describe your own lifestyle in one word or term, what would it be? Why? What specific aspects of your own lifestyle are you pleased with? What aspects of it would you improve? Specifically focusing on aspects of your lifestyle that have to do with your own health, what area do you think you would like to work on?

Some research has suggested that health-related concerns in areas such as nutrition, dieting, exercise, and sleep are quite common (Harris & Guten, 1979). Some general guidelines in each of these areas follow below. If you happen to have special dietary, exercise, or sleep needs, whether due to a physical condition, an eating disorder, pregnancy, or some other cause, these general guidelines are *not* necessarily good for you; when in doubt, consult your physician.

NUTRITION

In 1894, Willard O. Atwater of the United States Department of Agriculture recommended a diet that consisted of 52% of calories from carbohydrates, 33% from fat, and 15% from proteins. Since that time, the government has issued several different modifications of dietary recommendations, but its most recent one (see Figure 3–7) comes quite close to those recommended by Atwater ("Uncle Sam's Groceries," 1992). The federal guidelines are developed from many authoritative sources regarding the food intake needs of the average adult. Related information is also available from many private organizations regarding the

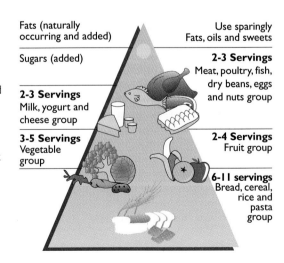

FIGURE 3–7   THE FOOD PYRA-MID Since the 1950s, the United States Department of Agriculture (USDA) has been teaching that food from four food groups should be consumed. In April of 1992, however, that teaching was updated with the food pyramid in which "fruits and vegetables" was split into two separate food groups. The USDA believes that Americans as a group consume too much fat and it now recommends that fat be used only sparingly.

Fats (naturally occurring and added)

Sugars (added)

2-3 Servings Milk, yogurt and cheese group

3-5 Servings Vegetable group

Use sparingly Fats, oils and sweets

2-3 Servings Meat, poultry, fish, dry beans, eggs and nuts group

2-4 Servings Fruit group

6-11 servings Bread, cereal, rice and pasta group

role of diet in preventing certain diseases. For example, material on lowering cancer risk through diet is available through your local branch of the American Cancer Society (ACS). In general, a diet that is low in animal fat and high in fresh fruit, vegetables, fish, and calcium is presumed to lessen cancer risk (Kromhaut et al., 1985; Willet et al., 1990).

To conform to the food pyramid guidelines, the challenge for most Americans will be to drastically reduce the proportion of fat in their diets. Yet reducing fat in one's diet is much easier said than done, particularly because of deceptive advertising and food labeling practices. According to registered dietitian Densie Webb (1993):

- Minifoods like minicookies may yield more fat per ounce than their "maxi" counterparts.
- Foods labeled "fat-free" are not necessarily entirely free of fat.
- "Light" brands of certain foods may contain the same amount of fat as the regular brand. For example, peanut butter and "light" peanut butter contain about the same amount of fat.
- Margarine in stick form contains the same amount of fat as a comparable serving of butter. Margarine in a tub contains slightly less only because it is whipped and there is more air in it.
- Ground turkey and ground beef can contain about the same amount of fat. The reason for this is that dark-meat turkey is more fat-dense than white-meat turkey and ground turkey may contain both types of meat. Turkey breast is the leanest cut of turkey.
- Milk labeled "2% fat" contains 45% of its calories as fat which is very close in ratio to whole milk, which contains 50% of its calories as fat. By the way, according to the labeling system used, whole milk might be labeled "3% milk." Skim milk is the only type of milk that provides none of its calories as fat.
- Carob candy bars contain about the same amount of fat as chocolate bars.
- Cholesterol-free mayonnaise contains the same amount of fat as regular mayonnaise: about 11 grams per tablespoon.
- Light cooking oils contain the same amount of fat as regular cooking oils: about 14 grams per tablespoon.

If you have questions about a particular food, many companies now have toll-free information lines you can call for answers. Additionally, many local public health centers, as well as many federal and corporate agencies, sponsor free information lines during regular business hours. For example, a call to 800-535-4555 will put you in touch with a government home economist or dietitian working for the United States Department of Agriculture meat and poultry division. One caller to the American Seafood Institute's hotline (800-328-3474) wondered if it was safe to cook fish in her dishwasher. The operator responded, "Well I guess you could. But wrap the fish well in foil, use a short cycle to avoid overcooking and don't use soap" ("Food Facts," 1992).

It is one thing to know what to eat and quite another thing to eat right. **Obesity** is said to exist *when body fat exceeds 20% of total weight in men, and 30% of total weight in women* (Williams, 1986). The number of obese individuals varies with respect to age group but on average, about one in four Americans is obese (National Center for Health Statistics, 1985). Obesity is widely believed to place an individual at high risk for heart disease as well as a variety of other diseases ranging from diabetes to cancer (Bray, 1986; Cohen, 1987; Hamilton et al., 1990; Jeffrey & Lemnitzer, 1981; Van Italie, 1979; Whelan & Stare, 1990). In one study of 2,000 women, it was found that nonsmokers who had high amounts of saturated fat in their diet were about four times as likely to develop lung cancer as usual (Alavanja, 1993). John Laszlo (1993), research director of the American Cancer Society wondered if obesity may have been a causal factor as well because high fat consumption is also linked to obesity.

For health reasons, but perhaps more for aesthetic reasons, many Americans, at any given time, consider themselves to be on a diet.

obesity

a condition said to exist when body fat exceeds 20% of total weight in men or 30% of total weight in women.

DIETING

In the hope of obtaining some assistance in losing weight, Americans spend about 32 billion dollars annually on diet programs, diet books, and other diet aids, according to Thomas Wadden, an obesity researcher at Syracuse University. Wadden et al. (1992) reported that in the long term, dieters in one study who used a low-calorie liquid diet fared no better in their weight-loss efforts than dieters who ate regular food and received behavioral counseling. Like many of the dieters in Wadden's study, most people who begin diets and diet programs—any diet, and any diet program—do not follow them through to completion and maintenance of a goal weight. About one in five adult Americans are on a diet right now, and most of them are destined to gain back every pound they will lose (Toufexis et al., 1986). With so many Americans hoping to shed some unwanted pounds, and with methods ranging from diet pills to aerosol spray desserts, a frequently raised question is, "What is the best way to diet?"

My own clinical experience has taught me the great value of a biopsychosocial perspective when it comes to the subject of weight loss. Yet, it seems that almost *any* dieting technique will work as long as (1) the dieter remains committed to the weight loss program, and (2) the biological "hand" one has been "dealt" is not too heavily stacked against the dieter. As evidence that virtually any diet can help the person determined to lose weight, consider a bestseller entitled *I Eat Therefore I Get Thin* (*Je Mange Donc Je Maigris*), by Michel Montignac. The book has been so successful in France that it has spawned a cottage industry of food boutiques, spas, and restaurants (Cohen, 1993). Montignac contends that calories are not important while indulging oneself with foods like chocolate and *foie gras* (prepared goose liver) is important. Experts in Europe and this country have dismissed Montignac as a quack, and the book is winked at as "a delightful, joyful swindle" (Cohen, 1993). Marian Apfelbaum (1993), a professor of nutrition at the Bichat medical school in Paris, speculated that the Montignac diet "worked essentially because its prescriptions as to which foods may not be eaten together obliged people to concentrate on what they were eating, consume less and thus get thin." Thus, the success of the Montignac diet may be due more to the determination of the dieter than to the diet itself. Such a phenomenon is not new to the United States; from time to time, a fad diet, usually with little scientific grounding, becomes all the rage. Personal testimonials as to the success of the diet multiply daily and are usually publicized over the protests of medical, psychological, and nutrition experts.

Being overweight has origins and/or consequences that are biological, psychological, and social in nature. Its treatment will ideally address each of these areas (see Table 3–1). If you wish to begin a diet program, it is a good idea to consult a physician to be assured that it is medically safe for you to do so. You may also use the consultation to explore the possibility of (1) any biological obstacles, cautions, or restrictions in this undertaking, and (2) any obstacles, cautions, or restrictions related to the companion exercise program which you will also want to initiate. Ask the physician to recommend a diet and an exercise program that will be safe for you. You may also seek a referral to a dietitian or nutritionist who can tailor-design a diet program for you. Note also that a recorded announcement regarding nutrition, and a free question-answer service with a registered dietitian is available from The American Dietetic Association (800-366-1655).

With diet and exercise program in hand, it will be up to you to keep yourself motivated enough to follow through on both. Right from the beginning, I would strongly encourage dieters to write down certain thoughts or draw certain images designed to keep them motivated when, some time in the future, their motivation may falter. Various books and articles that focus on psychological aspects of dieting (for example, Brownell, 1991; Cohen, 1979; Mahoney & Mahoney, 1976; Stuart, 1978) and other psychologically oriented tips can help to keep dieters on track. Underlying every successful diet program is a healthy, ongoing dose of self-esteem and self-love.

On a practical note, it is a good idea to eat slowly, at regular times, and at regular intervals with the caloric intake of all snacks planned. You may wish to put up a picture of yourself at your goal weight if you have one, just to encourage you to get there. Do not begin a weight loss program in a rush to lose weight; unrealistic goals will be your down-

TABLE 3–1   UNDERSTANDING WEIGHT AND WEIGHT LOSS FROM A BIOPSYCHOSOCIAL PERSPECTIVE

	Biological	Psychological	Social
Excess Weight			
Origins	genetic metabolic bone structure	self-esteem high emotion fatigue	loneliness competition cultural ideals
Consequences	fat accumulation	negative self-image depression	teasing ostracism
Treatment	medication surgical correction	psychotherapy counseling introspection	social support group memberships exercise with friend

The origins and consequences of excess weight may lie in biological, psychological, and/or social factors, and so must the treatment. Only a few sample factors in each category are cited. For example, low self-esteem can be a causal factor with respect to weight gain. Low self-esteem, as well as negative self-image, may also be a *consequence* of excessive weight gain. In the social sphere, the cultural ideal of being ultra-thin may actually compel some people to be countercultural and gain weight. However, for most people, the social consequences of being overweight are not pleasant. Social support from family, friends, a therapy group, even fellow members of a commercial weight control program can be extremely helpful in the process of weight loss and weight maintenance. We might also add to this chart educational factors; thinking in terms of what *nutrients to consume* rather than *foods to eat* will facilitate sound nutrition and weight loss.

fall. Keep in mind that exercise is likely to be an extremely important part of your weight loss program.

EXERCISE

Although exercise may not be for everyone, regular exercise for most people is something that in all probability will extend the number of years they live (Hamilton et al., 1990). One long-term study of over 10,000 men found that those who exercised regularly in some moderately vigorous sport lived on average 10 months longer than those who remained sedentary (Paffenbarger et al., 1993). Moderately vigorous activity included sports such as tennis, jogging, brisk walking, and biking. The findings also suggested that exercising subjects lived not only longer but also better in terms of being victims of disease. Perhaps some of the most dramatic findings concerned subjects who both gave up smoking and began an exercise program; Paffenbarger et al. (1993) believed the two actions taken together extended life by about 3 years.

The key to a successful program of exercise is to start slowly and work up to the point where exercise becomes a regular and enjoyable part of your day. If possible, design your program with an exercise expert such as a personal trainer. The consultation with such a professional will be worth it if the person can devise a program tailor-made to your own objectives. It is also recommended that you consult a physician before beginning any exercise program, especially if you have any chronic health problems such as heart disease.

Make time for your exercise program and then stick to your schedule. You may even want to combine an exercise such as walking with studying—using your "Walkman" as "Learnman" to listen to recorded notes. Don't forget to warm-up before beginning and to cool down at the end of exercise. A good general warm up is gentle stretching, as in reaching for your toes without bending your knees and then stretching your arms in the air. Alternatively, you may wish to gently sway the trunk of your body from side to side, letting your arms remain loose. More specific warm-up exercises will vary as a function of the specific exercise you wish to engage in. For example, if you are going to be playing tennis, warm-up may entail hitting some forehands and backhands. Cooling down means not stopping abruptly, but continuing to exercise at an increasingly lower level even though you have for all intents and purposes finished your exercise. One way to keep track of time when warming up or cooling down is to cue them to a song or two of some targeted duration. For example, when 10 minutes of music stops, you know that your warm-up or cool-down time is up.

The popular expression "no pain, no gain" is incorrect with respect to physical exercise. If you are feeling pain—muscle pain, burning, whatever—you are either overdoing it or doing something wrong. "No pain, no gain" is sometimes used to refer to "pain" in the sense of discipline and/or motivation—as in doing one more "painful" push-up to top your old record. Here the "pain" refers not to an injury, but to not letting yourself give up when the easiest, least "painful" thing to do would be to give up. For the purposes of competition, coaches typically demand such "pain" from their athletes. Whether you demand such "pain" from yourself is your decision.

It is important that exercise be pleasant. The activities you choose to engage in must be activities that you can stick to for more than a few days, weeks, or until swimsuit season is over. If you do not feel good while you are actually engaging in the exercise, or if you feel extremely "charley-horsed" afterwards, you probably will not stick to your program. Another way to make exercise pleasant is by combining it with something you like, such as music, conversation with an exercise buddy, or a television program or video you can watch while exercising in place.

One injury can bring your exercise program to an untimely end. Injuries can be avoided during exercise by concentrating on what you are doing at all times, and by taking precautions in terms of wearing the proper clothing and using the right type of equipment for the exercise you are engaging in. Injuries can also be avoided by monitoring how hard you work at exercise. In general, the harder you work out, the greater your chance of injury. The more moderate your workout is, the less your chance of injury. As in dieting, results from exercise occur over time, and unrealistic expectations can do you in.

In general, working out a little bit for 5 days a week is probably better for you than working out a whole lot just 1 or 2 days per week. For example, let's say you have set a goal for yourself to walk 5 miles per week. Would you be better off walking that distance very vigorously all in 1 day? Or would you be better off walking only 1 mile a day for 5 days? All other things being equal, the physical benefits and the number of calories burned would be the same whether you walked the 5 miles in 1 day or over the course of 5. Perhaps the major difference concerns the risk of injury, which is much higher if you walked the 5 miles all in 1 day.

If weight loss is one of the goals of your exercise program, then you need to think about the number of calories you are taking in and the number of calories you are expending as you exercise. The only way you will lose weight on a regular basis is if you burn more calories than you take in. So, if you limited your caloric intake, for example, to 1,600 calories per day, and you burned a total of 2,100 calories per day, the balance sheet would show a daily loss of 500 calories. Over the course of a 7-day week, that would result in about 3,500 calories lost. Since it takes 3,500 calories to create or drop 1 pound of weight, you would have lost 1 pound in that week. Should you continue on such a program for a full year, you could lose as much as 52 pounds—assuming it is medically safe for you to do so. Exactly how and where this weight loss will show on you is very much an individual matter. However, you should know that the idea that you can "spot reduce" (that is reduce the amount of fat in one specific part of your body) is a myth. For a listing of calories contained in different foods, consult a calorie-counting handbook. A sample of calories burned in different activities is presented in Table 3–2.

SLEEP

Although some of us would like to deny our need for it, sufficient sleep is as important to good health as things such as sound nutrition and sufficient exercise. Sleep serves a restorative function although exactly how and why it does this remains unclear (Crick & Mitchi-

TABLE 3–2   CALORIES BURNED IN DIFFERENT ACTIVITIES

The number of calories a person will actually burn while engaged in any activity will depend on a number of factors such as the person's weight and how strenuously and continuously he or she engages in the activity. In the table below, some activities are listed along with the number of calories that would be burned off when a person of approximately 175 pounds engaged in the activity nonstop for 10 minutes. In general, the number of calories expended will be more for heavier people and less for lighter people.

Activity	Calories expended
Sleeping	14
Sitting and writing	21
Walking at 2 mph	40
Light gardening	42
Table tennis (ping pong)	45
Golfing	48
Swimming	56
Volleyball	65
Tennis	80
Shoveling snow	89
Racquetball	104
Running at 5 mph	122
Cycling at 13 mph	178

son, 1983; Smith & Lapp, 1991; Webb, 1982). Experiments have found that sleep deprivation in the short term can lead to symptoms such as irritability, distractibility, and concentration problems. Long-term sleep deprivation greatly increases the severity of such symptoms and produces others such as hallucinations. Worry, anxiety, physical pain, external noise, stimulant drugs or medication, and light are some of the obstacles to getting a good night's sleep. Exactly how much sleep a person needs can be a very individual matter, one based on factors as diverse as genes (Webb & Campbell, 1983) and activities engaged in (Smith & Lapp, 1991). Insufficient sleep may be due to varied medical problems (Kryger et al., 1989) or simply to poor sleep habits.

If you are experiencing sleep difficulties as a function of poor sleep habits, one strategy for sleep will entail *prevention* and *diversion*. Prevention involves (1) following a regular schedule, including regular exercise and a realistic bedtime; (2) avoidance of caffeine and any other stimulants that might keep one up during the night; and (3) maintenance of an environment conducive to sleep—comfortable mattress and pillows, darkness, quiet.

Diversion may be defined as distraction—something that entertains or relaxes. Part of one's daily schedule should include some relaxing towards the end of the day—watching television, taking a hot bath, getting out the stereo headphones, or some other such nonstrenuous activity. The end of the day is *not* the time for contemplation of personal, financial, academic, or other woes. For poor sleepers, such sleep-robbing worry can only compound difficulties. To the extent that it is possible, poor sleepers should be careful to use the bedroom for sleeping and resting, not for studying, watching television, arguing, worrying, or any other such activities. The danger in using the bedroom for worrisome or anxiety-provoking activities is that it might become mentally associated with—that is, classically conditioned to—such activities. It is also a good idea to avoid getting into bed and wondering whether you will be able to get to sleep. Rather, divert your attention to other, less worrisome thoughts and images. Try creating and visually sustaining the most relaxing, soothing fantasy imaginable as you drift off to sleep.

If all else fails and you feel you absolutely must get out of bed and do something, try to pick some fairly routine, nonexciting activity such as rearranging your desk drawers or pairing socks. If sleeping problems persist or become particularly troublesome, a visit to someone specializing in the treatment of sleep disorders is in order. If possible, avoid the use of drugs for the purpose of falling to sleep. Unwanted effects of sleeping pills include their potential for *tolerance* and *addiction*, two terms to be defined later.

DRUG USE AND ABUSE

Drugs can play an important role in maintaining good health. If the body's immune system is viewed as a standing army ready to fight off harmful invaders, then medication prescribed by a competent physician can be viewed as "reinforcements" that help get the job done. Of course, not all drugs that people take are prescribed by physicians. As with so many other tools, drugs may be used or abused. A listing of some commonly abused drugs is presented in Table 3–3.

All drugs are capable in different strengths and concentrations of affecting human health and behavior. Interestingly, even two different brands of the same prescription medicine, thought by doctors to be interchangeable can yield dramatically different effects ("Opposite Mental Effects," 1993). Such was the case in a study of two brands of blood pressure medicine, one made by Bristol-Myers Squibb, and the other made by Merck Sharp & Dohme (Testa et al., 1993). The risk of unintended negative consequences rises dramatically with respect to drugs illicitly sold on the street due to the possibility of non-sterile manufacture or handling and other potential dangers.

Life-threatening and fatal accidents represent another class of unintended and indirect effect of many drugs, particularly so-called recreational drugs that cloud consciousness (National Academy of Sciences, 1982). Alcohol and other drugs are factors in most automobile accidents with fatalities and there is an automobile accident in which someone dies every 10 minutes in the United States.

Other unintended consequences of drug use may be addiction, withdrawal, or tolerance. **Addiction** refers to *a physiological or psychological dependence on the drug*. **Withdrawal** refers to *the unpleasant feelings or thoughts one experiences when one refrains from using a drug for which a physiological or psychological dependence has been established*. For example, habitual cigarette smokers who refrain from smoking (whether by choice because they are trying to quit, or by chance, because they have run out), may develop withdrawal symptoms such as headaches or general irritability. As illustrated in Figure 3–8, the power of withdrawal symptoms created by smokers' nicotine deprivation goes well beyond mild cravings; some people would rather "fight than switch." **Tolerance** refers to a *situation wherein the body begins to tolerate a particular dosage of the drug and increasingly higher dosages are needed to achieve the same effects*. Long-term users of amphetamines, for example, may find that they must progressively raise the dosage of the drugs they take in order to achieve the same effect. As dosages are raised, the more severe the withdrawal reaction can be when the user finally decides to quit.

addiction

physiological or psychological dependence on the drug.

withdrawal

the unpleasant feelings or thoughts one experiences when one refrains from using a drug for which a physiological or psychological dependence has been established.

tolerance

a situation wherein the body begins to tolerate a particular dosage of the drug and increasingly higher dosages are needed to achieve the same effects.

FIGURE 3–8 NICOTINE-INDUCED CIVIL UNREST Shortages of cigarettes led to demonstrations and rioting in some Russian cities (Ramirez, 1990). In one demonstration in August 1990, angry smokers blocked traffic in downtown Moscow. Here, the smoking Muscovites argue with a driver who was attempting to pass through their human blockade.

TABLE 3–3 SOME COMMONLY ABUSED DRUGS

Drug Category	Effect	Examples	Comment
Stimulants	In general, stimulants increase heart rate, respiration rate, and blood pressure and tend to make people feel more alert and "up" than they would feel without them. Users may also experience a mild euphoria with some stimulants.	Caffeine (found in coffee, tea, chocolate, and many soft drinks), nicotine (found in tobacco), amphetamines (including benzedrine, methedrine, methamphetamine, and dexedrine), and cocaine (including the cocaine derivative that goes under the street name "crack").	Nicotine and caffeine are relatively low in potency as stimulants go yet even they may have dramatically adverse effects on newborn infants if used by pregnant or nursing mothers (American College of Obstetricians and Gynecologists, 1990). Stimulants are legally prescribed and used for medical conditions such as narcolepsy. They may be abused by dieters seeking to speed metabolism to lose weight, students wishing to study continuously without sleeping, truckers wishing to prolong their endurance on the road, and others seeking to defy the need for sleep. Addiction and tolerance are possible consequences of sustained use. Sudden death due to cardiac failure, associated especially with highly potent stimulants such as cocaine, are always a possibility. Other possible unintended consequences of cocaine use include panic attack, paranoia, delusions, hallucinations, depression, impotence, insomnia, violent behavior, and disruption in vocational or family life.
Depressants	Depressants depress central nervous system activity, making the user feel drowsy and less jittery. In some cases, depending upon the particular depressant used and the context of its use, depressants may also induce a feeling of euphoria.	Depressants can be found in many forms ranging from alcoholic beverages to narcotics such as heroin, morphine, and opium. Sedatives are legally prescribed depressants used to sedate or calm. Referred to as "downers" in the street, sedatives may chemically be either barbiturates (marketed under names such as *Seconal, Tuinal,* and *Nembutal),* or nonbarbiturates (marketed under names such as *Quaalude, Sopor,* and *Parest).* Tranquilizers, including "minor tranquilizers" (such as *Librium)* and "major tranquilizers" (such as *Thorazine* and *Stelazine)* are depressants that may be prescribed in the treatment of severe psychiatric disorders.	Alcohol, like other biologically active agents that depress central nervous system functioning, impairs motor coordination, perception, and judgment. Driving under the influence of alcohol (or any other central nervous system depressant) is against the law and is an abuse of alcohol that may be fatal to the driver, passengers in the driver's vehicle, pedestrians, and occupants of other vehicles. Regular use of alcohol and other depressants, with the exception of tranquilizers, carries with it a risk of addiction and tolerance. Interestingly, while narcotics may be addictive in street addicts, they may be taken for years under medical supervision for relief of pain with no addiction and no tolerance effects (Rosenberg, 1993b).
Hallucinogens	A hallucination is *the perception— seeing, hearing, smelling, tasting, and/or feeling—of something that is not really there.* Many drugs from different categories, including alcohol and other depressants, are capable of inducing hallucinations. Drugs classified as hallucinogens are especially potent in inducing hallucinations, even when taken in relatively minute amounts.	LSD (lysergic acid diethylamide), psylocybin, mescaline, PCP, marijuana, and hashish. LSD has been synthesized in a number of forms including tablets, capsules, and sugar cubes. It has also been liquefied and placed on the back of paper, where it is licked like a postage stamp. Mescaline occurs naturally in the peyote cactus and psylocybin occurs naturally in a variety of mushroom. PCP (phencyclidine hydrochloride), also known by its street name, "angel dust," is a synthetically manufactured drug that has hallucinogenic properties. Its inclusion in this category is somewhat arbitrary because it may also have stimulant and depressant effects, as well as numerous other unpredictable effects. The inclusion of marijuana and hashish in this category is also somewhat arbitrary because these drugs may also have depressant as well as stimulant properties under certain conditions. The potential for hallucinogenic effects with marijuana or hashish intoxication rises as a function of the potency of the THC exposure.	Some naturally occurring hallucinogenics such as mescaline and psylocybin have a long history of ritual use among South American Indians and native Americans attempting to achieve spiritual enlightenment. Similarly, some more contemporary users of hallucinogenics, particularly of LSD, have sought out such drugs for their alleged consciousness-expanding properties. Yet far from romanticized notions about "learning the true nature of the universe," for example, lies the reality of a class of drugs that grossly distorts sensation and perception; it is analogous in some ways to a person with perfect vision looking through inch-thick bifocals. Some drugs in this category are much more potentially dangerous than others. Ingestion of PCP, for example, may result in severe mental disorientation (linked to accidents, suicide, and violent behavior), memory and speech difficulties, convulsions, and even death due to respiratory failure.

The Health Self-Management Experiment

Most everyone believes there is at least one area in which they could be doing more to preserve, maintain, or enhance their own personal health. What concerns do you have about your health? Here is your opportunity to target one of those concerns and to make a meaningful change—for life!

In this experiment, you are the experimenter, and there is only one subject (also you). No special equipment is required, although one piece of graph paper and the discipline of a serious behavioral scientist is mandatory. In general, this simple experiment calls upon you to (1) *identify a problem and target a specific behavior for change*, (2) *baseline your current behavior and then change it in some way designed to address the problem*, and (3) *keep records to evaluate your progress*. The experiment can be done and later repeated with different treatment methods and behavioral objectives. Some problem areas you may wish to focus on include nutrition, dieting, sleeping, smoking, or exercise.

1. Identify the problem or behavior targeted for change and set a behavioral objective.

"The problem" is a behavior targeted for change that has been identified in terms of *the number of* something, usually within some frame of reference such as time (*per second, per minute, per hour, per day, per week*, and so forth), and/or in terms of place (*at home, at work, at school*, and so forth). If, for example, the behavior targeted for change was smoking, the problem might variously be identified as *the number of cigarettes smoked per week* or *the number of cigarettes smoked per day at home*, depending upon the objectives of the study. If the goal was complete elimination of smoking behavior, the objective would be to reduce the number of cigarettes smoked to 0 and to keep it there. As another example, if you are overweight and have targeted for change your overall daily intake of food, the problem would be identified as *the number of calories consumed per day*. Behavior change would be designed to ensure a safe and gradual weight loss over time through the reduction of some targeted number of calories consumed on a daily basis. In every statement of the problem, as well as the objective, all of the terms used must be operationally defined. For the purposes of this experiment, set daily goals for yourself.

2. Change behavior in a way designed to address the problem.

This is the stage of the experiment in which some treatment method is introduced. Many different possible types of treatment are possible. For example, some treatments reward targeted behavior, others punish targeted behavior, other methods selectively reward and/or punish targeted behaviors. In some experiments, the experimental treatment is simply information provided to the subject; variables of interest may be related to how the subject processes and acts on the information. In a self-managed stop-smoking study, the experimental treatment might entail a mental contract in which a financial penalty of $1 is assessed for every cigarette smoked during time periods designated as smoke free. Dollars accumulated due to a failure to abstain from smoking might be donated to a charity that would not be among the subject's first choices.

For our purposes, let's say that the "treatment" will entail a contract with yourself stating that if you conform to your behavioral objective, you will purchase an item that you would really like (a desired article of clothing, a compact disc, a book, or whatever) that costs about $21 including tax. Ideally, the desired item should be something very special—something you might not buy under ordinary circumstances, perhaps because you consider it a bit of an extravagance. Each day during the week that you behave in a manner consistent with your daily objectives, you will reward yourself by putting away $3 towards your special purchase. At the end of the 7-day period, assuming you

Explanations of why some people abuse drugs have been offered from a variety of different perspectives. Each of these perspectives may contribute something to our understanding of the problem or raise important issues and questions. For example, from a biological perspective, knowledge about what drugs do at the level of the neuron may help us to better understand addiction, tolerance, and physical withdrawal symptoms. In drug addiction, for example, it may turn out that the addict is actually trying to self-medicate some chemical deficiency in the brain. From a genetic perspective, greater knowledge about the relationship between genes and drugs will help scientists determine if and how a predisposition to drug or alcohol abuse can be inherited. From a sociocultural perspective, we can learn about patterns of drug abuse that may be culturally reinforced, as well as possible ways to reverse such maladaptive trends. From a behavioral perspective, drug

have complied with the terms of your mental contract, you go straight to the store and make your purchase. If, due to deviations from your stated objectives, you were not able to put away $3 per day, you have some options. You can, for example, spend the amount you were able to put away on a lesser-priced item, or put the money back into savings and repeat the experiment at a later date. The option you choose should be based on your assessment of what would best promote self-management of health in the future.

3. Keep records and evaluate your progress.
Use a graph similar to the one below to gauge your progress. Note that both the horizontal and vertical axes of the graph begin at zero. On the horizontal axis is the time frame in which your study was run, and on the vertical axis is the total number of servings you consumed each day from the targeted food group. Graph your baseline week in one color (say, blue) and the week that you instituted "treatment" in a second color (say, red). Looking at the graph below, how would you say this person responded to treatment?

In addition to graphing your daily progress, it may also prove helpful to you to keep a personal diary of the thoughts, images, and emotions that occur to you as you attempt to manage your behavior. With respect to the treatment method, for example, what works? What doesn't work? What thought or image best seems to motivate you towards your goal? How can you incorporate such thoughts and images into your daily routine to keep you on track?

This sample health self-management experiment should be thought of as only one of many ways that people can motivate themselves to make positive change in their lives. For truly meaningful change to occur in one's life, external, store-bought rewards must ultimately be exchanged for the inner ones that money can't buy.

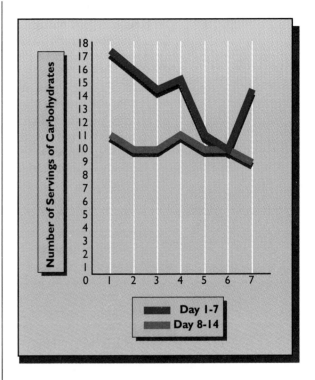

This graph traces the progress of one student to conform to government recommendations regarding the number of daily servings of food in the bread/cereal/rice/pasta group. How is this student doing?

as possible ways to reverse such maladaptive trends. From a behavioral perspective, drug abuse can be explained with reference to learning principles.

hallucinations
sensory experiences of things that are not really there.

Values, Choice, and the Biopsychosocial Perspective

A biopsychosocial perspective on health has a number of important implications for thinking about wellness maintenance and the treatment and prevention of disease. It places emphasis on the need for people themselves to prevent problems by engaging in wellness-promoting behaviors. It places emphasis on the need of health professionals to understand disease, disorder, deficits, and other problems not solely within a biological/medical context but within a psychological context as well. As a biopsychosocial perspective becomes more integrated into "mainstream" medicine, we can expect physicians to ask questions about people's behavior—ranging from what they had for breakfast to how they are feeling about themselves to what precautions they took during sex—in addition to questions about medical symptoms.

I once shared an office suite with a psychologist who made a determined effort to keep himself in good physical shape. He ate right, rested sufficiently, and exercised regularly on a stationary bicycle. On one occasion, I asked him if he found riding a stationary bicycle boring. He said that he had been doing it for years and that he found it horribly boring. Yet, he added, "My grandfather died when he was 40 of a heart attack. My father also died at 40 of a heart attack. I'm 36. It depends how important it is to you."

How important is it to you? Do you value your physical health? What one thing can you do right now to start taking better care of yourself? The *Self-Assessment* exercise that follows asks you not only to identify a health-enhancing behavior but also to act on it.

In this chapter we explored some of the mysteries of the mind-body connection and the complex relationship between biological, psychological, and social factors. From a biopsychosocial perspective, we saw that health is not merely the absence of disease, it is more a way of living one's life.

How much one values one's life and health may depend on a number of interactive factors such as self-esteem, financial circumstances, cultural background, even one's gender. Recalling the years he practiced as a surgeon, Bernie Siegel observed differences as a function of gender in response to the diagnosis of terminal cancer. Siegel (1991) believes that men tended to lose their will to live more quickly than did women. Siegel recalled that, in response to being informed of a diagnosis of cancer, a typical male might say, "What's the purpose of living if I can't work?" By contrast, a woman might typically respond with something like, "Keep me alive until my son's wedding." After the woman survived to see her son married, she would return to the office and remind Dr. Siegel: "And don't forget I have another son." Not coincidentally, the role of gender in adjustment is explored in the chapter that follows.

SUMMARY

A BIOPSYCHOSOCIAL PERSPECTIVE A *biopsychosocial perspective* on health is a view that takes into account how biological, psychological, and social factors may independently or in combination with each other affect wellness and illness. This perspective is at the heart of *health psychology,* a discipline in which biological, psychological, and social variables are studied regarding their influence on the onset, course, treatment, and/or cure of illness and disease. *Genetics* is defined as the study of the biological mechanisms of variation and hereditary transmission in living organisms. In the study of behavior genetics, research suggests that heredity sets an upper limit on capabilities and that environmental and cultural factors play a role in determining how close to that upper limit we can come.

The *nervous system* consists of the brain, the spinal cord, and the entire network of nerves "wired" to it, including the electrical and chemical activity that goes on within it. The human body's immune system is an elaborate system of external and internal defenses against *pathogens,* harmful or potentially harmful agents including microorganisms and toxins. The body's natural immunity to many different types of diseases can be enhanced through *immunization,* a process that stimulates the formation of protective *antibodies* to infectious organisms.

ADJUSTMENT AND HEALTH Research strongly suggests that the relationship between mind and body is reciprocal; one affects the other. The specific site and mechanism of the mind-body link is not known but some intriguing speculation points to communication between the nervous system and the immune system. The emerging field of *psychoneuroimmunology* is the study of how the nervous system interacts with the endocrine and immune systems.

CHOOSING HEALTH Knowledge regarding what is healthy combined with contemporary medical technology makes it likely that if a young person today dies young, there is a good chance that the death will be related to poor nutrition, obesity, lack of exercise, lack of sleep, use of drugs, an accident, or some other aspect of the person's lifestyle. To the extent that one's lifestyle does contribute to one's health, one can choose health.

Chapter 4

Gender and Culture

O   U   T   L   I   N   E

In the previous chapters, we have focused on some of the many ways that an individual person is unique. From a biological perspective, each of us has a unique genetic inheritance and physical constitution. From a psychological perspective, each of us has unique learning experiences, as well as unique mental and behavioral potentials. In this chapter, our focus shifts to a cultural perspective and a consideration of some of the things that make groups of people similar to each other, yet different from other groups of people. We begin with a consideration of females and males in biological and societal contexts.

GENDER, THE INDIVIDUAL, AND SOCIETY

Do you think that your life would be very different had you been born the opposite sex? Other than transsexuals, few can answer such a question with certainty, but it is a fact that males and females differ biologically in many nonobvious ways (Hoyenga & Hoyenga, 1993a, 1993b). Further, in cultures throughout the world, females and males are seldom viewed or treated equally (Brislin, 1993). Let's briefly explore some of the biological differences between males and females as well as the different ways that females and males are perceived and treated in a cultural context. The term **gender** technically refers to *cultural, social, and psychological aspects of being male or female in contrast to purely biological ones* (Unger, 1979). As a reference to biological males and females, however, the terms *gender* and *sex* have been virtually interchangeable in common usage.

gender

1. biological sex 2. cultural, social, and psychological aspects, in contrast to purely biological ones, of being male or female.

BIOLOGY AND GENDER

People differ biologically as a function of sex. Of particular interest to many physiologically oriented psychologists is the wide-ranging, powerful, and differential influences that hormones exert on the behavior of men and women.

HORMONES AND BEHAVIOR

The relationship between hormones and behavior is reciprocal. Hormones, among other variables, influence behavior, and behavior, among other variables, influences hormonal output. Hormones play a role in sexual, aggressive, maternal, and paternal behavior, and they affect our experience of anxiety, fear, and stress (Baum et al., 1985; Brown, 1985; Crews, 1984; Rodriguez-Sierra et al., 1984). Research suggests that hormones play a role in immunity to disease (Galaburda et al., 1987; Geschwind & Galaburda, 1985a, b, & c; Schachter et al., 1987; Sherman et al., 1985). Sex hormones may provide females with greater immunity than men to bacterial and viral diseases, but less immunity to autoimmune disease (Hoyenga & Hoyenga, 1993a, 1993b). Hormones may affect emotions experienced by people differentially as a function of gender. They can affect a cell's biochemistry (Angelbeck & DuBrul, 1983; Garcia-Segura et al., 1987), growth (Juraska et al., 1989), and electrical activity (McEwen, 1991; Schiess et al., 1988). Hormones can "turn on" or "turn off" a gene within the cell (Edwards et al., 1991; Maiter et al., 1991; Spranger et al., 1991).

Levels of the male sex hormone (testosterone) and the female sex hormone (estrogen) are characteristically different throughout life in males and females. Measured blood levels of these hormones can vary from day to day, even from minute to minute, within the same person. Hormone levels vary as a result of internal events, such as pregnancy, and external events, such as the amount of stress an individual is under. In laboratory animals, level of sex hormones has been found to vary as a function of the position of the fetus in the uterus. Hoyenga and Hoyenga (1993a) reported that a fetus's position in the uterus between two males or two females will differentially affect the fetus's exposure to male or female sex hormones, and perhaps also later gender-related behavior.

The fetus's exposure to hormones influences postbirth gender-related behavior, including emotional expression (Jacklin et al., 1983). High **prenatal** (*before birth*) levels of testosterone in fetal boys have been associated with masculine play activities at age 4 (see Lytton & Romney, 1991).[1] Analyses of hormone levels of the human infant at birth (as sampled from the umbilical cord) have been found to be related to the development of various gender-related behaviors (Jacklin et al., 1988; Marcus et al., 1985). Hormone levels associated with positive mood have been found to differ as a function of a child's sex (Marcus et al., 1985). In males, some evidence suggests that a relationship exists between testosterone level and the likelihood of violent (Dabbs et al., 1991) or antisocial (Dabbs & Morris, 1990) behavior. In the process of aging, estrogen levels decrease in women and increase in men (Bartsch & Voight, 1984).

The human brain is so exquisitely sensitive to male and female hormones that it is even meaningful to speak of "male brains" and "female brains" in terms of structural and related differences (Allen & Gorski, 1990; Allen et al., 1989; Hofman & Swaab, 1991; Ojemann, 1991). Other organs of the body in mammals are also sensitive to female and male hormones and in this sense it is also meaningful to speak of "male" and "female" livers, kidneys, and adrenal glands (Aguilar et al., 1987; Bardin & Catterall, 1981; Mooradian et al., 1987; Pak et al., 1985, Tsim et al., 1985).

Another biological difference between women and men for much of their reproductively mature lives is the monthly female menstrual period. Throughout history and around the world, attitudes towards this biological reality have fostered a number of myths. For example, in the 1920s, the official view of administrators in education in Great Britain was that "the periodic disturbances, to which girls and women are constitutionally subject, condemn many of them to a recurring . . . diminution of general mental efficiency" (Richardson, 1991, p. 318). As a result of premenstrual changes, relatively slight changes in mood (including increased levels of tension, anger, and depression) may occur in women (Hampson, 1990). However, for most women, these changes are viewed as no more severe than the changes many people experience in going from weekends to weekdays (Mansfield et al., 1989; McFarlane et al., 1988).

The female menstrual cycle may affect sexual activity, and sexual activity may affect the menstrual cycle (Cutler et al., 1979; Cutler et al., 1985). While a number of other factors, including psychological ones, strongly influence and handily overrule purely hormonal dispositions, some of the research on hormones and sexual and other behavior is nonetheless fascinating. For example, in the human female, from a purely hormonal standpoint, shortly after midday appears to be the optimal time for female orgasm to take place (Palmer et al., 1982). In the human male, hormonal shifts may make positive moods more likely in the afternoon as compared to the morning (Taub & Berger, 1974), while cognitive tasks might better be performed in the morning (Klaiber et al., 1982).

OTHER SEX DIFFERENCES

A number of other differences have been observed between people as a function of sex, including differences in observed electrical activity of the muscles (Greenwald et al., 1989) and the brain (Smith et al., 1987; Smith et al., 1989) in response to emotion-evoking stimuli. For some reason, men seem better able than women to identify internal states (Pennebaker & Roberts, 1991). Perhaps the "ultimate" biological difference between women and men is that women get pregnant and nurse babies while men do not.[2] Many analyses of the differential treatment of women and men across various societies are strongly tied to this biological fact of life (D'Andrade, 1966; Murdock & Provost, 1973; Sidanius et al., 1991).

SOCIETY AND GENDER

Ever since people first began living in groups, divisions of responsibility and labor have been made, and different social roles for women and men have evolved. Women bore children, nursed them, and did not travel very far with or from their newborn infants. Child rearing was a full-time job that could not be interrupted by activities such as food-hunting or warring. By contrast, whatever males of the culture did locally might be interrupted

prenatal
before birth.

[1]These levels were taken through an analysis of amniotic fluid obtained by a procedure called *amniocentesis*. The amniotic sac (or bag of waters as it is sometimes called) envelops the fetus and contains fetal cells. Using ultrasound imaging equipment to guide the placement of a needle, the physician inserts the needle through the abdomen and into the amniotic sac. In a medical, nonresearch context, amniocentesis may be ordered by a physician about 9 to 12 weeks into a pregnancy if the parents' histories indicate that the fetus is at risk for chromosomal abnormalities. As a result of the procedure, the gender of the child becomes known, and the mother is usually given the option of being told or not.

[2]In the history of the world, the option of purchasing formula is a relatively recent innovation.

by an extended, long-distance hunt, by a battle, or by other nondomestic tasks. Men have historically been more competitive than women, competing for, among other things, food, other resources, and mates. Remnants of this most primitive notion that women are commodities to be possessed or bartered survive in contemporary Western society, perhaps most blatantly in pimp-prostitute relationships. Yet this idea finds expression elsewhere as well. For example, a report by the Pentagon's inspector general on misconduct by Navy aviators at their Tailhook Convention in 1991 contained a photograph of one participant wearing a T-shirt that read "Women Are Property" (Gordon, 1993). The woman-as-commodity notion also finds expression in the popular media, such as in the film comedy *Honeymoon in Vegas,* wherein Sarah Jessica Parker is bartered for her fiancé's gambling debts. Other recent films, such as *Mad Dog and Glory* and *Indecent Proposal* have had similar premises.

Over a century ago, Charles Darwin wrote of differences between men and women in their tendency to express emotion. From an evolutionary perspective, he believed, males tended to be more aggressive, more competitive, and less communicative than females. Females tended to be more social than males, and factors such as communication skills, including conveying and understanding emotional expression, tended to be more critical to their social role. The belief that females are more adept than men at expressing emotions (Berenbaum et al., 1987) and are more attuned to the emotions of others (Custrini & Feldman, 1989) survives to the present day, and can be supported by research (Heesacker & Prichard, 1992). Later in this chapter, the issue of how best to deal with such differences in emotion-related communication is addressed.

Another artifact of our long history of male/female role differentiation has to do with the value assigned to labor that is stereotypically female or male in nature. Rosaldo (1974) conceptualized the traditional difference between the work of women and men as being private (domestic) or public in nature. It was part of the traditional male role to venture out into the world for purposes such as hunting or warring. It was part of the traditional female role to stay close to home to tend to the children. Rosaldo believes a longstanding tendency has existed to value public over domestic roles. Even in modern times, the primary responsibility for domestic tasks such as child rearing is largely perceived as a woman's (Katz & Konner, 1981; Whiting & Edwards, 1988). In the opinion of some, the generally lower status of women across cultures is due to such devaluation of the domestic role (Williams & Best, 1982, 1990), although not everyone agrees that women hold lower status across cultures (Mukhopadhyay & Higgens, 1988; Silverblatt, 1988).

PSYCHOLOGY AND GENDER

In an age when more parents than ever before in history know the sex of their children before they are born, many new babies have a room decorated in shades of pink or blue waiting for them upon arrival. In addition to the decor of the room, the parents' selection of clothing for the infant, blankets, and other furnishings will also typically depend on the sex of the child being brought home from the hospital. As is illustrated in the *Cultural Close-Up,* many more parental behaviors throughout the life of the child are likely to vary as a function of the child's sex.

A DEVELOPMENTAL PERSPECTIVE

As you might expect after reading Chapter 2, different theories exist to account for how and why male and female infants come to exhibit behavior that tends to be viewed as masculine or feminine. Social learning theory places great emphasis on parental reinforcement of behavior judged to be gender-appropriate; children observe traditionally masculine and feminine behaviors, imitate them, and are subsequently rewarded only for emission of the behavior deemed to be gender-appropriate. For example, boys may receive rewards and encouragement from parents or others for imitating the behaviors of combat troops they watch on television, while girls may not receive such rewards and encouragement. Girls may receive rewards and encouragement for imitating ballerinas, while boys may not. According to this view, children need not even be old enough to have knowledge about the concept of gender in order to begin acquiring what is culturally viewed as gender-appropriate behavior (Mischel, 1966).

Culture, Gender, and Child-Rearing Practices

A number of researchers have examined child-rearing practices in different cultures. Low (1989) reanalyzed some of the data from such research and some of her findings are graphically illustrated below. It can be seen that relative to boys, there tends to be greater emphasis on sexual restraint in the training of girls across different cultures. Also on a cross-cultural basis, boys tend to receive more training than girls in areas such as self-reliance, competition, aggression, and fortitude.

Low argued that there is probably an evolutionary basis for this emphasis on traits such as achievement, self-reliance, competition, aggression, and fortitude. Especially in societies in which men are permitted to have more than one wife, a man's resources or status (or both) might be a determining factor in how many wives and children he will have. Low's analysis of

the data suggested that a relationship does in fact exist in many societies between resources (such as material goods) controlled by a man, the status a man has in his culture (such as that attained by being a great warrior), and the number of children the man has.

Similar studies in a number of different cultures have also found a relationship between a man's achievement and the number of his children (Betzig, 1986; Chagnon, 1979, 1988; Daly & Wilson, 1983; Irons, 1979; Turke & Betzig, 1985).

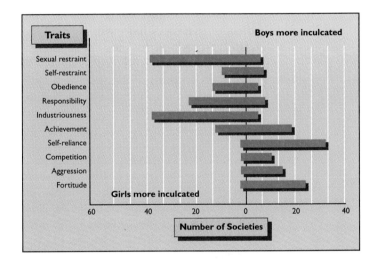

An alternative to social learning theory as an explanation for gender role development is cognitive developmental theory (Kohlberg, 1966; Kohlberg & Ullian, 1974). As its name implies, cognitive developmental theory is indeed a theory of development—development that occurs in stages which Kohlberg refers to as *gender identity, gender stability,* and *gender constancy.* Here, gender identity refers to the knowledge of one's sex. Most children reach this stage by age 3 or so (Marcus & Corsini, 1978; McConaghy, 1979). Within the next year or so, children develop gender stability, or the recognition that gender assignment is permanent. This recognition probably influences the way that children think about and mentally organize gender-related observations. The notion of gender stability solidifies further as it transforms to gender constancy, a stage most children reach by age 8 or so. By that time, children better understand the constancy of gender, and can appreciate that a woman who dresses like a man is still a woman and a man who dresses like a woman is still a man. Also by age 8 or so, children are presumed actively to seek out information related to gender-appropriate behavior, the better to behave in a gender-appropriate fashion (Perry & Bussey, 1979).

Some of the assumptions and conclusions of cognitive-developmental theory have been questioned on various grounds, including the extent to which the processes described are applicable to girls as well as boys (Gilligan, 1982). Additionally, children seem to develop gender-related knowledge much earlier than cognitive-developmental theory presumes (Levy & Carter, 1989; Serbin & Sprafkin, 1986). Gender-related behaviors and preferences have been observed in children as young as 2 (Jacklin, 1989).

Sandra Bem (1981) advanced an explanation for gender role development that she referred to as *gender schema theory*. Gender schema theory blends elements of cognitive developmental theory with social learning theory. According to this view, as soon as children can identify themselves as male or female, they begin actively to process gender-related information and then act accordingly. Children as young as 2 are rewarded for attending to gender-related information and actively organizing information they receive in a way that is deemed gender-appropriate (Bem, 1985; Fagot et al., 1992; Martin & Little, 1990).

OTHER GENDER-RELATED DIFFERENCES

"What constitutes a romantic act?"

When Raymond Tucker and his colleagues asked university students that question, an analysis of the responses as a function of gender yielded some interesting findings. Most frequently cited by both women and men was taking walks. Next in frequency for women were sending or receiving flowers and kissing. For men, kissing and candlelight dinners were next most frequently cited. Men also cited making love as an act of romance. Women did not. Women cited hearing or saying "I love you" as romantic. Men did not. Tucker et al. (1991) speculated that their findings might be explained by the fact that men in America are expected to be less emotional than women. How would *you* explain the findings?

The Tucker et al. (1991) research is but one of thousands of published studies that have examined differences between people as a function of gender with respect to some cognitive, behavioral, emotional, or other psychological variable. Such studies have taught us that women and men are to some extent different psychologically—yet to what extent and for what reasons has remained a matter of debate. For example, however *aggressive* is defined, and it has been defined in many different ways, boys are repeatedly found to be more aggressive than girls. Yet the extent to which differences in aggressiveness are due to genetic, psychological, cultural, or other factors is very much a matter of debate. The male hormone testosterone has been linked to aggressiveness in both humans (Erhardt & Baker, 1974; Olweus et al., 1980; Parke & Slaby, 1983) and animals (Edwards, 1969; Joslyn, 1971; Young et al., 1964). Yet beyond hormonal differences, we know that boys and girls are treated differently. Other factors, such as individual differences in personality, may also account in part for observed differences in aggressiveness. The net result has been ongoing controversy about the relative contribution of biological, psychological, and social factors in aggressiveness.

The finding that boys are more aggressive than girls has been stable over time. Other findings concerning gender-related differences have not been so stable, and the reason for their instability may also be a matter of debate. For example, a number of studies in the 1970s and 1980s suggested that significant differences as a function of gender existed in cognitive abilities such as verbal and mathematical skills. Girls were purported to be more verbal than boys, and boys were purported to be more mathematical than girls. By the late 1980s, such differences were believed to be relatively small and insignificant (Hyde & Linn, 1988; Linn & Hyde, 1989). If indeed a change in these measured abilities took place over time, what accounts for that change? While acknowledging that differences in thinking and behavior do exist, some researchers have questioned the magnitude of these differences as well as their importance (Basow, 1992; Hyde, 1990). *Perceived* gender roles may overshadow actual gender as an influence on thought and behavior (Basow, 1992).

gender identity
the sense that one is female or male.

[3]A very small percentage of the population never develops this sense of gender identity based on their own biological sex, and instead develops the gender identity of the opposite sex. Such children may be diagnosed as a *gender identity disorder*. As adults, some people with gender identity disorder will undergo a surgical procedure that physically transforms them into a person of the opposite sex.

GENDER IDENTITY, ROLES, AND STEREOTYPES

Differential treatment of boys and girls by parents, peers, and others serves to establish the child's **gender identity** or *the sense that one is female or male*. Typically, a sense of gender identity is established some time between the 2nd and 3rd year of life.[3]

Along with acquiring a sense of gender identity, the developing person learns from family, friends, television, films, storybooks, toys, and other sources about **gender roles**; that is, *culturally defined expectations of behavior formed on the basis of sex*. These expectations may involve everything ranging from occupational choice to household chores. Widely held notions about gender roles may lead to the development of *gender stereotypes*.

STEREOTYPES AND GENDER STEREOTYPES

In the printing trade, a stereotype is a metal printing plate; the raised type of the stereotype will print the same thing over and over. In psychology, **stereotype** also refers to something fixed and repetitive—usually *a belief about a person or a group of people that is derived primarily from perceptions regarding the group to which the individual belongs*. Can you think of any person whom you have stereotyped on the basis of a particular group to which that person belongs? What about stereotypes related to these three people: A woman having blonde hair? A citizen who is a registered Democrat? A person who is a psychologist?

Years ago, one manufacturer of hair dye sought to persuade brunette and red-headed women to dye their hair blonde by the widespread promotion of the stereotype that "blondes have more fun." In advertising during political campaigns in recent years, the Republican political party has promoted the stereotype of the Democratic party as "the party of higher taxation for higher government spending." A widely held belief about psychologists, psychiatrists, and other professionals in the field of mental health is that "you have to be crazy yourself to go into that field." Are any of these stereotypes true?

As you might expect, stereotypes may lead to inaccurate perceptions of people and unfair conclusions about individuals within the group being stereotyped. For example, in the face of the widespread belief that "blondes have more fun," a woman who happens to have blonde hair may have undue difficulty being taken seriously in employment interviews and in employment or other settings. A Democrat who has an innovative plan for raising revenue without increasing taxes may be summarily ignored or viewed with distrust if voters tend to view Democrats as being intent on "taxing and spending." Individuals working in the mental health field may unfairly be subjected to doubts about their own mental health when, in reality, they are human beings like everyone else with many of the same everyday kinds of problems.

Stereotypes can be positive in nature, too. However, even if the stereotype itself is positive, it does not necessarily follow that the effects of the stereotype are positive. For example, consider the stereotype that "all Asians are excellent students." Because this statement is not true, belief in it will set unrealistic expectations on the part of all parties who believe it—including Asian students themselves, parents of Asian students, non-Asian fellow students, and instructors. When and if the (unrealistically) high expectations are not met, negative feeling states, such as disillusionment, depression, and anger, may result.

In many instances, stereotypes can be understood as learned phenomena that result from inappropriate generalization. For example, some Democratic administrations did substantially raise taxes in order to fund public works programs, yet this does not necessarily mean that all Democrats favor such policies. Some psychologists, like other mortals, do experience emotional problems. Yet because psychologists hold themselves out to be experts in human behavior, many people unfairly tend to hold them to a higher standard of conduct than others (Cohen, 1993). If and when a psychologist does not behave appropriately, the incident may be blown out of proportion and contemptuously regarded as indicative of the behavior of all psychologists—hence the stereotype of mental health professionals who are "themselves crazy." The image of the glamorous blonde who "had more fun" was certainly reinforced in various films of the 1950s and 1960s featuring movie stars such as Marilyn Monroe, Jayne Mansfield, and Brigitte Bardot. Still, it is at best debatable whether these women indeed had more fun in their personal lives (see Figure 4–1 on page 94).

Part of the appeal of stereotypes, even the more absurd and groundless ones, is the seeming ease with which individual people can be categorized and pigeonholed by other people. In a nonrational sense, then, stereotypes take the guesswork out of speculation about someone's personality, needs, values, and motives; stereotypes cut to the quick and seemingly reveal all that seems important to know about a person. Of course, life would

gender roles
culturally defined expectations of behavior formed on the basis of sex.

stereotype
a belief about a person or a group of people that is based primarily on the basis of perceptions regarding the group to which the individual belongs.

FIGURE 4–1   DID THEY REALLY HAVE MORE FUN? Movie stars such as Marilyn Monroe inspired an advertising campaign that claimed "blondes have more fun." In reality, this stereotype had little truth to it, least of all with respect to the Hollywood blondes to which it was readily applied. Monroe suffered persistent bouts of depression and eventually committed suicide. Jayne Mansfield, another glamorous blonde film star, also suffered emotional difficulties. She died in a car accident along with the leader of a Satan-worshipping cult. The French film star Brigitte Bardot suffered from depression and attempted to take her own life on more than one occasion.

indeed be simple if we knew for a fact, for example, that "blondes have more fun"—especially if we wanted to know which of several job candidates was the more serious-minded. Unfortunately, stereotypes may obscure more information than they convey. People who stereotype other people may be especially watchful for information that confirms the stereotype and not attend to information that counters it.

Stereotyping can alter one's memory of events. In one study, college student subjects were provided with a description of various aspects of the life of "Betty." One week later, all subjects were given a bit of additional information about Betty just prior to being asked to recall what they had already been told about her. Half the subjects were informed that Betty was living with her husband and the other half were told that Betty was a lesbian. The researchers concluded that subjects' recall of information about Betty's life was colored by their expectations and mental categorizations made on the basis of this new bit of information. For example, the subjects informed that Betty was a lesbian tended to forget that she had gone out on many dates in college but remembered that she had never married (Snyder & Uranowitz, 1978, cited in Snyder, 1984). The study is representative of a great deal of research that suggests that everything from expectations about what a person is capable of doing to beliefs about what a person has done may be influenced by one's mental stereotypes (Cordua et al., 1979; Deaux & Major, 1987; Furnham & Duignan, 1989; Jones, 1986; Jussim, 1986; Leone & Ensley, 1985; Rodin, 1987; Ruble & Stangor, 1986).

From the perspective of the person being stereotyped, the process of stereotyping can either work for them and be a blessing or work against them and be a curse—or worse. If, for example, a prospective employer harbors a stereotype that more intelligent people wear glasses and, due to genetic defect (or whatever reason), you happen to wear glasses, the employer's unfounded stereotype might work in your favor. But what if you don't wear glasses? Worse yet, what if you don't wear glasses and happen to be far and away the most qualified person to apply for the job? Throughout history, many people have been denied not only jobs but also housing, human rights, liberty, and even their right to survive on the basis of unfair, inaccurate, and, in some cases, cruel stereotypes. In Nazi Germany, for example, the German people were taught to hate Jews, blacks, homosexuals, and other minorities. Although many Jews were among the struggling poor, Hitler stereotyped them as rich and the people who, as a group, were responsible for Germany's great economic problems. In turn, such stereotyping led to governmental denial of Jewish people's basic human rights and to the grisly, unjust, and inhumane execution of millions of people in Nazi death camps.

Currently, we live in times of great political awareness and there appears to be an encouraging trend towards recognizing and remedying stereotyping errors. Special interest groups have successfully brought economic pressure to bear on private industry. Products or services that perpetuate detrimental stereotypes have been boycotted. For example, in October 1992, the American Association of University Women (AAUW) worked to eliminate a *gender stereotype* that it believed existed in one well-known product. A **gender stereotype** is based on *a belief about a person or group of people based solely on the sex of that person or group of people.* The AAUW fought to obtain, and eventually did obtain, a promise from the manufacturer of the talking Barbie doll to remove the phrase "Math class is tough" from the doll's microchip. The AAUW had complained that this phrase "could undermine confidence among girls in their mathematical abilities" ("No More Math Phobia," 1992).

gender stereotype
a belief about a person or group of people based solely on the sex of that person or group of people.

What gender stereotypes come to mind when you think of men? What gender stereotypes come to mind when you think of women? Explore some of your own thoughts about what makes a man a man and a woman a woman in the *Self-Assessment* exercise below.

Words such as *tough, protective, breadwinner,* and *gentlemanly* tend to be associated with the stereotypic male, while words such as *gentle, dependent, caring,* and *homemaker* tend to be associated with the stereotypic female (Atkinson & Huston, 1984; Cartwright et al., 1983; Deaux & Lewis, 1984; Eagly & Steffen, 1984; Hoffman & Hurst, 1990; Myers & Gonda, 1982). Such gender-related stereotypes find expression in a variety of ways ranging from casual conversations with peers to the pictures displayed on the boxes of children's toys and games. As a result of gender stereotypes, there was once a day in the United States when few men were nurses or homemakers and few women were doctors, lawyers, politicians, or corporate leaders. Awareness of the potentially negative effect of these and other gender stereotypes has led to constructive change in the form of laws designed to promote greater equality of opportunity between the sexes. Constructive change is also evident in, and can be helped along by, depictions of women and men in songs, stories parents tell to children, books, and the entertainment media in general. In a thoughtful review of how the media can erode harmful gender role stereotypes and influence the formation of more healthy ones in the minds of children—a process referred to as *counterstereotyping*—Durkin (1985) concluded that building on a child's social knowledge was a more effective method of change than directly contradicting what the child believes to be true. In this context, it might be interesting to speculate about the relative effectiveness of different depictions of females in changing gender-related stereotypes (see Figure 4–2 on page 96).

SELF-ASSESSMENT

Real Men, Real Women

Satire abounds about what "real women" or "real men" do or do not do (such as the humorous notion that "real men don't bond"). Beyond all the humor regarding what constitutes a real man or a real woman lie our own most personal thoughts regarding differential behavioral expectations as a function of gender. *Jot down a description of the ideal female and the ideal male in terms of various psychological and behavioral variables.* Some issues you may wish to address concern their different thought processes and the different ways they communicate or express

emotion. In what ways are your ideal woman and ideal man similar? In what ways are they different?

After you have committed some of your thoughts to paper, evaluate them. Regardless of your own gender, how are you similar to your ideal female? How are you similar to your ideal male? What gender-related psychological variable or behavior would you most like to change about yourself? What obstacles exist to making such a change?

FIGURE 4–2   GENDER STEREOTYPES AND THE MEDIA Which of these female leads would you presume to be most and least useful in changing stereotypical images about women? Why? Pictured are: Angela Lansbury as the detective/author in *Murder She Wrote*, Sigourney Weaver as a spaceship crew member and leader in *Aliens*, and Bridget Fonda as an ex-federal agent in *Point of No Return*.

PREJUDICE AND SEXISM

prejudice
preconceived judgments and opinions.

sexism
a gender-related form of prejudice that derives from a basic view that one sex is superior to the other.

discrimination
preferential, exclusionary, or differential behavior towards a person or group of people on the basis of race, religion, ethnic origin, gender, or other factors related to the person's or group of people's group membership.

A danger of gender stereotypes, as well as of other stereotypes, is that they can lead to prejudice. **Prejudice**, from the Latin *praejudicium*, which means "before judgment," refers to *preconceived judgments and opinions*. Perhaps most frequently, the term is used to refer to prejudgments that are negative, although the term may also be used to refer to prejudgments that are positive. Later in this chapter we discuss one specific type of prejudice called *racism*. For now, let's look at **sexism**, *a gender-related form of prejudice which derives from a basic view that one sex is superior in some way to the other*. The notion that a physically attractive woman is probably not well-suited to a position that requires keen mental ability or management skill is an example of a sexist view of businesswomen (Heilman et al., 1988, 1989).[4] Sexism and other forms of prejudice may carry with them unfortunate consequences such as discriminatory behavior.

Discrimination may be defined as *preferential, exclusionary, or differential behavior towards a person or group of people on the basis of race, religion, ethnic origin, gender, or other factors related to group membership*. For centuries, discriminatory behavior and practices in various social settings ranging from the classroom to the boardroom have worked against females. Events such as Take Our Daughters to Work Day (see Figure 4–3) represent one attempt to begin to address such past inequities.

SEXISM IN THE WORKPLACE

According to the Bureau of Labor Statistics, approximately 54 million women representing several generations are currently in the American work force. Generally, women still earn about 30% less than their male counterparts. In the wake of legislation that makes such practices illegal, job discrimination on the basis of gender remains but has become more subtle (Morrison & Von Glinow, 1990). Only about 3% of this country's top corporate executives are women, and this figure has not changed appreciably in the last decade (Saltzman, 1991). Discrimination against women may take the form of obstacles to joining prestigious country clubs, where many corporate deals are sealed (MacLean, 1991). There are also many jobs, typically very low-paying ones, that have remained "women's work" (the position of chambermaid, for example). In the military, the question of whether women should be allowed to fight in infantry combat missions is as much an equal-opportunity issue (in this case, the opportunity to earn more pay and advance in rank) as any other type of issue. Sexual harassment in the workplace remains a problem for both men and women, but women are more apt to be targets of harassment (Fain & Anderson,

[4]Interestingly, it has been demonstrated that physical attractiveness is an asset that pays. Once a physically attractive woman or man is hired or promoted, the odds are good that she or he will earn more than her or his unattractive counterparts (Frieze et al., 1991).

FIGURE 4–3 DAUGHTERS IN THE WORKPLACE April 28, 1993 was the first annual "Take Our Daughters to Work Day," an event designed to introduce girls to various opportunities that await them in the workaday world. Nationwide, an estimated 200,000 to 1,000,000 girls participated (Kleinfield, 1993), including 10-year-old Kate Martuscello shown here trading a bond under the supervision of Chase Manhattan employee, Craig Sanger. Begun as a local event in New York City by the Ms. Foundation for Women, the idea attracted a national audience after it was mentioned in a *Parade* magazine interview with feminist Gloria Steinem. As Kleinfeld (1993) observed, it was also "National Leave Our Sons at School Day" by default. Some schools set up in-class programs for boys, including discussion groups that addressed topics such as sexual harassment and why boys were left in class (McLarin, 1993).

and women, but women are more apt to be targets of harassment (Fain & Anderson, 1987).

Analyses by Harvard economist Claudia Goldin, Baruch College economist June O'Neill, and University of Illinois economists Francine Blau and Marianne Ferber indicate that genuine progress is being made by women in the workplace (Nasar, 1992). Unlike the temporary advances made by women as a result of World War II—gains that were lost when the fighting men came home and returned to their jobs—the workplace gains made by women in recent years are not transient (see Figure 4–4 on page 98). To deny such solid gains would not be constructive, according to Karlyn Keene of the American Enterprise Institute: "If you continue to see yourself as a society that's not doing well by women, the implication is that it could become a self-fulfilling prophecy" (Keene, 1992, p. F10). Indeed, at an individual level, it has been suggested that less self-confidence on the part of women on the job may be a factor impeding advancement (McCarty, 1986).

In the 1970s and 1980s, the low numbers of women in management positions meant there were few role models for aspiring businesswomen (Fitzgerald & Crites, 1980). Yet as the twenty-first century dawns, perhaps a question of greater interest concerns the kinds of role models women want. It is at best questionable whether women want to fashion their careers after the current female leaders of American industry. Consider in this context the views of 18 of the most powerful women in corporate America. The group met at Queens College in New York City in September 1992 to discuss various issues related to women in management. Participants included the president and chief operating officer of Mattel, the president of Liz Claiborne, the publisher of *People Magazine*, and the vice president and general manager of a division of Eastman Kodak. The mood in the conference room was subsequently described by one of the participants (a president of a life insurance company division) as "bittersweet" and lacking in optimism (Lyne, 1992). There was a general feel-

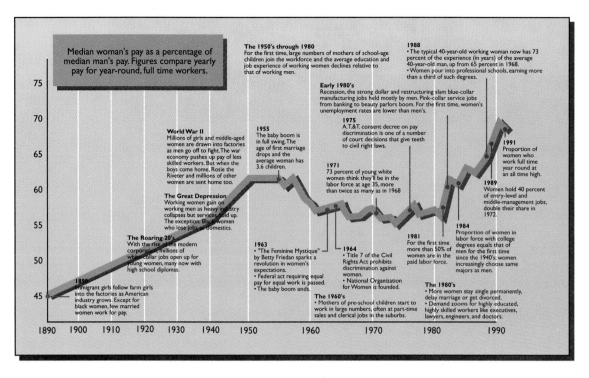

FIGURE 4-4   PROGRESS OF WOMEN IN THE WORKPLACE Source: Nasar (1992).

ing on the part of the participants that the contemporary woman wants a more balanced lifestyle earlier on (Wagonheim, 1992). Ann S. Moore (1992), publisher of *People Magazine,* put it this way: "I've begun hearing young women saying, 'Holy smokes, I would never do what she does.' Now, I had a great time doing it. I have a child, I'm married to the same man, I have a great job and it didn't seem like hard work to me when I was doing it. But it's a sobering thought that no one wants to do what I'm doing."

Indeed, when a working woman is not subjected to interpersonal conflicts, she may subject herself to what might be termed "intrapersonal conflicts"—or self-made conflicts regarding one's varying roles. Especially for the woman who has children and is working out of economic necessity, an almost constant source of conflict may concern the investment of time in work versus in nurturing activities. One mother who returned to her demanding career only 10 days after her child was born expressed these reservations: "I knew I would never stay home full time with a child. There are times I have regretted it. I've missed a lot. Sometimes I think, 'Wouldn't this be great to spend more time and be here?' But you can't have both" (Richardson, 1992). On the other hand, stay-at-home women who opt for a family instead of a career may not be free of work-related conflicts either. They may feel intimidated by women who have been able not only to work but to raise their children as well. One stay-at-home mother who sought psychotherapy for her feelings of inadequacy confided that she felt most awkward meeting women who had both high-powered careers and children. She described her feelings of intimidation around working women: "It's like show-and-tell time and I don't have anything to show and tell" (Richardson, 1992). She also believed that rude or bratty behavior emitted by children of working moms was excusable while such behavior from children of stay-at-home mothers was inexcusable.

Any guilt suffered by a working family woman in the 1970s was only intensified by a theory of "infant bonding" that became popular in that decade. The theory held that it was critical for mother and infant to spend a great deal of quality time together shortly after birth. Although useful in the sense that it stimulated the opening of obstetrics wards to fathers as well as mothers, the theory unnecessarily aroused guilt in many working parents, as well as in mothers who were slow to recover from childbirth. Subsequent research did not support the theory, nor its claim that children's emotional or physical health was jeopardized by mothers working (Easterbrooks & Goldberg, 1985; Eyer, 1993). Some research even supports the notion that having a working mother yields positive effects on children, in terms of enhanced self-reliance and academic competence (Hoffman, 1987). A more urgent concern for most working mothers today is not whether or not they have "psychologically bonded" but whether or not they have competent and reliable child care.

SEXISM IN HEALTH CARE

AIDS in women may manifest itself quite differently from AIDS in men. This fact is probably responsible for countless misdiagnoses of AIDS in women and the subsequent loss of vital, potentially life-saving time in the treatment of infected women (Corea, 1992). For Gina Corea (1992), widespread misdiagnoses of AIDS is only the tip of the iceberg of many problems related to health care for women. The more entrenched and fundamental problem is that women have served as "the other" in medical research, diagnosis, and treatment—"other" referring here to the individual other than the "standard male."

The problem of the "standard male" as a subject in medical research has its roots in many decades of using a conveniently available pool of people—college students and medical students—as the subjects in medical research. Decades ago, when many large-scale medical research projects were first initiated, most college students and medical students were male. Males were used as subjects not only in original research on, say, cancer or heart disease, but for purposes of consistency and comparability in follow-up studies as well. The result has been volumes of medical research on males and relatively little clinical research on women. In many instances, the findings of long-term studies that employed men as subjects are simply generalized to women ("Cholesterol at 20," 1993)—a variety of guesswork with which many women have become impatient (McGuire, 1993). In 1993, the National Institutes of Health formally acknowledged the use of men as the normative standard in medical research, and launched a 15-year, $625 million study to explore the causes of cancer, heart disease, and osteoporosis, as well as other medical issues, in women ("U.S. Health Study," 1993).

SEXISM IN EDUCATION

In 1993, a newly elected president took office and sought to deliver on a promise to appoint the first female attorney general of the United States. The president had unexpected difficulty in filling that cabinet post with a female. Part of the problem stemmed from the relatively small pool of qualified applicants from which to choose. As Labaton (1993) noted, past inequities in females' access to law school was one of the reasons cited for the dearth of qualified applicants. Law schools only began admitting women in significant numbers in the 1970s, and few leading law firms have women in their top ranks. Finding a highly qualified woman who was a Democrat and had a "clean" record was unexpectedly difficult (see Figure 4–5).

FIGURE 4–5   THE FIRST FEMALE ATTORNEY GENERAL Janet Reno, a prosecutor from Dade County, Florida, was confirmed by the Senate as the nation's first female attorney general—but not before the rejection of two other Clinton administration candidates. Zoe Baird, the woman the president first nominated, had never generated any excitement from members of the American Bar Association. According to insiders of that association, Baird's most memorable address concerned hourly billing (Margolick, 1993). Baird's nomination was not confirmed by the Senate because she had employed illegal immigrants as household help. Judge Kimba M. Wood's name was withdrawn from consideration for the position on similar grounds. The rejections of Baird and Wood sparked discussion of "the pitfalls of seeking public office in an age of poorly defined and ever-changing morality . . . " (Margolick, 1993).

Problems concerning sexism in education tend to be far more subtle than the ones brought to light in the search for a female attorney general. Such problems may relate to images in children's picture books, the pictures on the boxes of games and toys, or the content of books that reinforce gender stereotypes. Sexism may manifest itself in differential encouragement by teachers or parents to express oneself, to succeed academically, or to experience a sense of control. A large research literature has pointed to these types of differences and, in general, to a more advantaged educational environment for boys (Dweck et al., 1980; Eccles, 1985; Etaugh & Harlow, 1975; Fox et al., 1985; Good et al., 1973; Matlin, 1987; Meece et al., 1982; Schnellman & Gibbons, 1984; Women on Words and Images, 1972).

SEXISM IN OTHER SETTINGS

Gender stereotyping, prejudice, and discrimination have placed women at a disadvantage in terms of many varied opportunities. Physical abuse and violence against women is all too prevalent in the home (Wolfe, 1991), and homicide is the leading cause of death of women in the workplace. As Bell (1990) observed, "If a woman's going to die from an injury at work, she's probably going to be murdered." Knowledge of legally sanctioned prejudice, discrimination, and violation against women in countries other than our own might well make many Westerners cringe (Quindlen, 1993). Recently, one woman from Saudi Arabia sought political asylum in Canada because she was unable to travel alone or without a veil in her native country and was not free to pursue the education she wanted (Farnsworth, 1993). In a landmark decision, the woman was allowed to remain in Canada after it was established that she might be in danger for her "feminist" beliefs were she to return to Saudi Arabia.

TOWARDS GENDER EQUITY

What can be done about gender inequity in the workplace, health care system, educational settings, and other areas? Beyond equal opportunity legislation and laws designed to ensure equal treatment of people by sex, much thought has been given to how best to modify gender-related prejudice.

MINIMIZING GENDER DIFFERENCES: ONE APPROACH TO EQUITY

In a musical called *My Fair Lady,* first produced on the Broadway stage long before the time of many of the readers of this book, the male lead sings a song entitled "Why Can't a Woman Be More Like a Man?" More in step with current trends, a chorus of voices in the social science community has raised the flip-side question: *Why can't a man be more like a woman?* This view is reflected in the writings of many males and females who support what has been referred to as the "antisexist men's movement" (Pleck, 1984, p. 79).

THE ANTISEXIST MEN'S MOVEMENT PERSPECTIVE

According to the antisexist men's movement perspective, male thinking and behavior patterns, and in particular those patterns related to emotional behavior, are the product of biological instincts that have not kept pace with cultural evolution. According to this radical view, it would be desirable for men to shed their "toxic levels of masculinity" (Pittman, 1990, p. 42) and, in essence, become more like feminist women (Good et al., 1990; Hearn & Morgan, 1990; Kimmel, 1987; Scher, 1990). One implication drawn from a reading of the antisexist male literature is that there is one right and one wrong role model for males—and nothing in between. Yet, as a puzzled Wagenheim (1990, p. 42) queried, "Why do today's men have to choose between Rambo and Richard Simmons?"

After a scholarly review of the antisexist men's perspective, Martin Heesacker and Shawn Prichard of the University of Florida ultimately rejected it as the product of a "one size fits all" mentality. Heesacker and Prichard (1992) faulted the perspective for its failure to appreciate biological and other influences on the male expression of emotion and for its implication that "people can socialize themselves out of biology" (p. 279). They argued that a middle ground exists between views of biology as either all-powerful or totally sub-servient to socialization. They also argued that therapists and counselors need to rethink their treatment of male clients so that the treatment allows for male "ways of being" (p. 282), not just feminine ones. As they put it, "Like those dangerous few feet near the left rear fender of one's car on the freeway, counseling has a blind spot when it comes to men and their emotions" (p. 284).

THE ANDROGYNY ALTERNATIVE

A less radical perspective on minimizing gender differences was advanced by Sandra Bem. The term **androgyny** refers to *the coexistence of culturally stereotyped masculine and femi-nine thoughts, emotions, physical appearance, and other aspects of behavior and personality in one person.* Bem (1974, 1975a, 1975b, 1983, 1985) and others (for example, Basow, 1992; Bem et al., 1976; Eagly & Steffen, 1984; Lott, 1985) see a societal movement towards an-drogyny as a psychologically healthy phenomenon. According to this view, such a meld-ing would place a wider range of personality traits, behaviors, and adjustment strategies at the disposal of both males and females. Not everyone agrees. For example, it has been argued that a gender-neutral society would impact negatively on family life as well as on other societal institutions (Gilder, 1986). Whiteley (1983) suggests that psychological benefits to be derived from any such movement towards androgyny would stem from greater acceptance of traditionally masculine behavior on the part of women, not more traditionally feminine behavior on the part of men. From a feminist perspective, Lott (1981) argued that society's challenge was to do away entirely with gender-related label-ing of learned behaviors, not simply to make such behaviors more accessible to people of each gender.

androgyny
the coexistence in one person of both masculine and feminine thoughts, behavior, emotions, and physical appearance as culturally stereotyped.

SENSITIVITY TO GENDER DIFFERENCES: A BETTER APPROACH?

Writing in the *Harvard Business Review,* and referring to various studies in different indus-tries, Felice N. Schwartz (1989) advanced some rather jarring realities regarding women in management:

- In general, women in management cost a company more than men in management.
- The rate of turnover of top-performing corporate women is 2.5 times greater than that for men.
- About one-half of the women in a large, packaged goods company return late or not at all from maternity leave.
- In general, women have a greater tendency than men to interrupt their career growth in ways that will limit their promotability.

If such assertions are generalizable to many areas within the corporate world, it would not be surprising to find companies hesitant about recruiting, training, and developing fe-male managerial talent. Sensitive to charges of sexism, as well as to the possibility of liti-gation or government prosecution, many companies only begrudgingly comply with equal employment opportunity guidelines and requirements.

One solution to this very real, dollars-and-cents dilemma would appear to lie in greater sensitivity and responsivity to the needs of people based on gender, as well as to all other aspects of their life circumstances. In the workplace, there are single and married women who have no intention of ever having children and are every bit as career-focused as their male counterparts. Schwartz refers to such women as *career-primary* and she ar-gues that equal opportunity for these women, as for career-primary men, is clearly in the best interest of both the woman and the employer. To foster equal opportunity for the ca-reer-primary woman, men in business will have to be more sensitive and responsive to is-sues regarding female socialization, including all the possible additional sources of stress that may impact on females in a traditionally male corporate culture.

Schwartz also argues for more sensitivity to the needs of the person she refers to as *the career-and-family woman.* This woman wishes to pursue seriously a career while actively partaking in family matters. The flexibility to balance a career and a family is what the ca-reer-and-family woman wants, and she is usually willing to make some sacrifices in order

job-sharing

two or more people sharing a particular job with prorated salaries and benefits.

to have that flexibility. The flexibility might take the form of work-at-home tasks, part-time employment, even **job-sharing** (*two or more people sharing a particular job with prorated salaries, and benefits,*). There are costs and benefits to such flexibility, and it will take some corporate experimentation to make such programs work in the best interests of all. However, one of the immediate benefits of such a program might be the removal of corporate awkwardness regarding equal employment regulations. Ideally, such awkwardness would be replaced by a new candor between employer and employee, and more enthusiastic utilization of the entire pool of available talent by employers—including mothers and fathers who might wish to take a more active role in family life.

The need for more appreciation of and sensitivity to gender-related differences extends far beyond the workplace. As Heesacker and Prichard (1992) explained, women and men have different emotional voices that need to be heard and understood. Men may profit from exposure to women's "ways of being," as women might profit from exposure to men's "ways of being." In a much more general sense, it is also true that people can profit from more sensitivity and tolerance to the "ways of being" of people from different cultures.

CULTURE AND ADJUSTMENT

Gender identity, roles, and stereotypes all emerge within a cultural context and each can exert great influence on one's personal adjustment. In the remainder of this chapter, we look at culture from several different perspectives, beginning with a brief consideration of its many varied functions.

THE FUNCTIONS OF CULTURE

norms

in sociology, guidelines for most aspects of everyday living.

customs

behavior arising from cultural tradition.

sanction

a culturally mandated social consequence for adherence or non-adherence to a culture's guidelines; positive sanctions express social approval and negative sanctions express social disapproval.

We can imagine that culture first evolved as a force that brought order and stability to an environment where interpersonal chaos reigned. People need to communicate with one another and an important aspect of culture is the verbal and nonverbal language it provides people for doing just that. But more than means for communicating, culture provides what sociologists refer to as **norms**, or *guidelines for most aspects of everyday living.*[5] These cultural guidelines vary widely in importance. At one extreme, there are those cultural prescriptions that have momentous, even life-or-death consequences. For example, culture prescribes what is right, what is just, and what is worth dying for. At the other extreme are cultural prescriptions which by comparison are fairly trivial. For example, culture prescribes how one should eat pasta and prepare chicken soup. Some cultural guidelines take the form of **customs**, or *relatively specific behaviors usually engaged in by people as a result of cultural tradition.* On New Year's Eve, for example, it is customary to stay up at least until midnight and to make a toast with someone for good luck in the new year. There is no law that says you have to do it, but many people do.

Culture not only provides guidelines for personal and interpersonal conduct, it also provides what sociologists refer to as **sanctions** (or *social consequences*) for adherence or nonadherence to such guidelines. *Positive sanctions* express social approval and may take varied forms ranging from a warm smile to a Congressional Medal of Honor. *Negative sanctions* express social disapproval and may take the form of anything from a dirty look to capital punishment. To some extent, cultural sanctions may become internalized. For example, one will not be arrested or socially condemned for violating the custom of calling one's mother or sending her a card on Mother's Day, although guilt may well result.

In what other areas of life does culture provide us with norms or customs? Quite a few, once you stop to think about it. Culture prescribes a society's answers to questions as diverse as, "How close does one stand to a stranger?" and, "What shall I wear to the wedding?" Culture tells us about socially appropriate and inappropriate ways of earning a living, finding a spouse, serving food, and maintaining personal hygiene. It provides guidelines for interacting with parents, children, grandparents, friends, enemies, women, men, elders, physicians, criminals, the physically ill, the mentally ill, the elderly, and other people who assume various social roles. It conveys information and expectations about people, such as who is considered an adult, who is in love, and who is worthy of respect, esteem, or reverence. It tells us whether we should look forward to growing old or to use

[5]Should you go on to take a course that deals with the subject of psychological testing and assessment, you will learn about a different meaning of this term in that context. There, the term *norms* refers to a standard used to compare test scores. (Cohen et al., 1992)

any means possible to retard aging. It tells us what to save and hand down to future generations, and what to throw away. It provides guidelines for judging qualities ranging from intelligence, to social worth to physical attractiveness (see Figure 4–6).

Culture provides us with cues about the types of activities deemed appropriate for people of different genders. For example, in the United States, there is no rational reason why fathers can't take their babies out for a walk in a stroller or baby carriage. Still, one is much more likely to see mothers than fathers out walking their babies in this fashion. No rational reason exists to explain why women tend to be socially prohibited from smoking cigars or pipes. Yet it still strikes people in the United States as odd to see a woman engaging in such activity. By the way, in cigar factories in Cuba, many male and female workers sit at their workbenches hand-rolling their goods while puffing on the profits. No eyebrows are raised, and no one thinks any less or more of a woman who enjoys a fine cigar.

Culture provides us with cues that may lead us to make inferences about a wide range of people, places, and things (Crocker & Major, 1989; Kashima & Triandis, 1986; Marcus & Kitayama, 1991). For example, from repeated media presentations of therapists sporting beards, smoking pipes, and speaking with thick Viennese accents, one might well attribute great psychological prowess to someone who fits such a description.[6] Our culture has instilled in us certain images and expectations regarding leadership—not necessarily consistent with the images and expectations of people from other cultures. In the broadest sense, culture provides a way of thinking about oneself, others, and the world in general (Adelman, 1988; Berry, 1990; Bond, 1988; Furnham & Bochner, 1986; Grove & Torbiorn, 1986; Hannigan, 1990; Harwood & Miller, 1991; Lambert & Taylor, 1990; Miller & Bersoff, 1992; Moghaddam & Solliday, 1991; Paige, 1990; Taylor, 1991; Whiting & Edwards, 1988; Yu & Wu, 1988).

VALUES AND CULTURE

Acculturation refers to *an ongoing process by which an individual's thoughts, behaviors, and values develop in relation to the general thinking, behavior, and values of a particular cultural group.* The process begins in infancy with the primary agent of acculturation being the newborn's family or caretakers. Later, other agents of acculturation may include peers, teachers, clergy, co-workers, other acquaintances, newspapers, television programs, films, theater, music, and other media.

Few, if any, culture-related messages are value-free. Varying in degree from blatant to subtle, a values-related point of view tends to be inherent in cultural teachings. Culture teaches that people are basically good, basically bad, or something in between. Culture teaches people to live for the past, present, or future. Culture teaches people to respect and value all living things or to look out for "Number 1." Culture provides guidelines regarding what is worth fighting for and what is not. Culture teaches us that certain ways of being are prized, while others are tolerated and yet others are despised. Culture imparts lessons relevant to perceiving and dealing with people of other cultures.

The term *cultural universal* refers to a concept taught by all cultures. Because few, if any, veritable cultural universals have been identified, the term is more a hypothetical construct than a reality. Many general types of events, such as ceremonies associated with birth, marriage, and death appear to be universal, although specific aspects of such events differ as a function of culture (Murdock, 1945). Researchers have also been hard put to identify universal *taboos* (cultural prohibitions). It was once thought, for example, that incest and cannibalism were universal taboos, yet cultures that condone such practices under certain conditions have been identified (Albert, 1963; Beals & Hoijer, 1965; La Barre, 1954). In the past, it has been presumed that one important function of culture was to preserve a people's biological continuity through reproduction (Kabagarama, 1993). Certainly this has been the case in China, for example, where married couples have been taught for centuries to believe that they will dishonor their ancestors if they do not have a male child to continue the blood line. However, China now has about 22% percent of the world's population living on only 7% percent of the world's arable land. Through strict government regulations, China is now attempting to reverse this cultural teaching. In essence, it is at-

FIGURE 4–6 DON'T HATE HER BECAUSE SHE THINKS SHE'S BEAUTI- FUL In a television commercial for a shampoo, Kelly LeBrock implored: "Don't hate me because I'm beautiful." For many viewers, and certainly for those from cultures that have different standards of beauty from hers, Ms. LeBrock has nothing to worry about.

acculturation

an ongoing process by which an individual's thoughts, behaviors, and values develop in relation to the general thinking, behavior, and values of a particular cultural group.

[6]This despite the fact that, in reality, many therapists are physically incapable of growing a beard and others, myself included, find them too itchy to bother.

tempting to preserve its culture and its biological continuity through a drastic program designed to *limit* reproduction. The value that the government places on this policy is evident in its strict laws designed to lower the birth rate and in the harsh penalties imposed for the transgression of those laws. Violators are subject to monetary fines, forced sterilization, physical beatings, or worse (Kristof, 1993).[7]

Although culture plays a very important part in daily living, it is an aspect of life that is easily taken for granted. For example, after working up a sweat, many Americans will say "Uh-huh!" to Pepsi or believe that "Coke is it." Under similar circumstances, few Americans would say "Uh-huh!" to warm, fresh camel blood—yet that is a brew of great appeal to the Sinai Desert Arab (Henslin, 1993). You may have reflexively responded with "Uccchhh!" as you read the last sentence. Yet understanding customs from cultures different than our own sometimes entails suspending judgment, if only long enough to learn about the history, folklore, and values attached to the custom.

VALUES, SUBCULTURE, AND COUNTERCULTURE

Similar to descriptions of people, descriptions of cultures tend to employ trait terms that convey a notion of broad uniformity and consistency—uniformity and consistency that seldom exist in reality. For example, the culture of the United States has been described in terms such as *individualistic, achievement/success-oriented, progress-oriented, democratic,* and *humanitarian* (Williams, 1970). How applicable such terms are to the American citizenry as a whole is arguable. Individual citizens of the United States certainly vary greatly in the degree to which they conform to such descriptions. This is so because we live in what is variously described as a culturally diverse or **pluralistic society**, *a social group comprised of people from many different cultures.* Within the context of the larger culture, there exist many **subcultures** or *groups that can be distinguished from the dominant culture by their unique sets of values, norms, and sanctions.* Most subcultures, including those as diverse as high school football teams, labor unions, and nursing home occupants, exist in harmony with the dominant culture. Other subcultures are **counterculture** (literally, *against culture*) in social orientation; that is, they subscribe to values, norms, and sanctions that are inconsistent with the dominant culture.

Organized crime families, street gangs, religious cults, and terrorist organizations are some examples of counterculture groups. One of the oldest, continually active counterculture groups in this country is the Ku Klux Klan (KKK). The organization's name is derived from the combination of a phonetic spelling of the Greek word *kuklos,* meaning *circle* (Randel, 1965), and a phonetic spelling or misspelling of the word *clan.* Founded in 1866 in Pulaski, Tennessee, by six former officers of the Confederacy, the KKK's initial mission was to maintain and reassert white supremacy over blacks in the post-Civil War period (Shelton, 1968). Initially a prankish group that used disguises in an attempt to scare and intimidate people, mostly blacks, it quickly degenerated into a secret terrorist organization that targeted not only blacks but also Jews, Catholics, foreigners and anyone else it viewed as obstacles to its social agenda. Intent on enforcing its white supremacist view of the world through various means, legal as well as illegal, it employed tactics such as lynching, bombing, flogging, tar-and-feathering, and mutilation (Salmony & Smoke, 1985). The Klan's symbol, a burning cross, was designed to convey its "fiery zeal" (Shelton, 1968). The KKK grew so violent that its leader, the "Grand Wizard," disbanded the organization in 1869. Still, local KKK organizations remained active on their own for years thereafter. In 1915 the roots of the modern day KKK were planted with the incorporation of the Invisible Empire, Knights of the Ku Klux Klan by a former preacher in Georgia. Economic uncertainty and social unrest after World War I are thought to have helped the reincarnated KKK to thrive. Membership was further boosted by the passage of the Civil Rights Act of 1964. Traditionally clad in white sheets, Klan members held meetings at night in isolated spots, burned crosses, listened to inflammatory rhetoric, and then dispersed to engage in actions that they believed would advance their objectives. Recently, law enforcement officials who infiltrated the Klan, as well as legislators who have passed and upheld laws against its interests, have effectively extinguished much of the Klan's "fiery zeal" (see Figure 4–7). As a result, the KKK has been increasingly forced to employ legal means to achieve its ends, such as running candidates for political office (Mannes & Carter, 1992).

pluralistic society

a social group comprised of people from many different cultures.

subculture

a group that can be distinguished from the dominant culture by its unique sets of values, norms, and sanctions.

counterculture

a group that subscribes to values, norms, and sanctions that are inconsistent with the dominant culture (literally, "against culture" in social orientation).

[7]For example, Kristof (1993) described the tragic case of one woman who did not conform to the government-mandated timetable for birth. Government officials forcibly took her to an unsanitary first-aid station when she was only 7 months pregnant and proceeded to induce labor. The baby died 9 hours later and the mother was left emotionally and physically crippled.

FIGURE 4–7   UNDER THE HOOD In February 1990, a Klansman challenged a 1952 Georgia law prohibiting him from wearing his hood in public by arguing that the law violated his constitutional right to free speech. However, the Georgia court and other courts have upheld such laws, denying Klansmen the right to hide their faces under disguises. As we will see in Chapter 10 when we discuss a famous experiment by Stanley Milgram, it tends to be easier for people to act aggressively under the cloak of anonymity as opposed to face-to-face contact. Thus we might expect police officers who wear name tags, such as Officers Long and Gentry in the photo to be much more judicious in their public displays of aggression than people who wear masks and do what they will anonymously.

Today, when sincere people of all racial, ethnic, and religious persuasions are actively seeking ways of living in peace together, hate groups advocating divisiveness seem hopelessly out of step with the times. Yet an unfortunate reality in the United States is that no group of people, minority or majority, has any monopoly on espousing hatred and violence. As a contrast to one of America's oldest counterculture groups, consider the values expressed by one of this country's newest, the so-called gangster rappers (see *A Question of Values*).

LIVING IN A MULTICULTURAL SOCIETY

In describing a multicultural society, sociologists may speak of a **culture-defining group** (CDG), usually *the majority,* and its relation to **non-culture defining groups** (NCDG), usually *minority groups.* Whether persons are viewed as members of the CDG or NCDG is a relative matter. For example, a Haitian family from Port-au-Prince that has immigrated to Missoula, Montana, is the NCDG, just as an American family that has immigrated from Missoula to Port-au-Prince is the NCDG. For members of the NCDG, many of their adjustive demands, challenges, and conflicts involve balancing adaptation to the CDG culture with retention of one's own culture. Neighborhood Chinatowns, as well as other neighborhoods-within-neighborhoods in which many people from NCDGs reside, represent one response to this adjustive challenge. These neighborhoods emerge in response to the need for social support from members of a cultural group with whom one identifies (Tyler, 1992).

The adjustive demands, challenges, and conflicts of CDG members will concern the extent to which they tolerate, encourage, or prohibit expressions of cultural diversity by various NCDGs. Philosophical, verbal, and sometimes even physical clashes arise between CDG and NCDG members, and between groups of people from different NCDGs. These clashes stem in part from strong beliefs instilled by cultural teachings and from the impassioned behavior such beliefs sometimes arouse. As Hymowitz (1993) has observed, "culture is an essentially conservative force. It binds people to a past laden with powerful traditions and beliefs and often obligates them to strict, customary discipline."

A SOCIOECONOMIC PERSPECTIVE

The term **socioeconomic** is *a contraction of the words "social" and "economic" typically used to refer to one's status or class in society* (such as "lower class" or "upper class") *which, in turn, is typically tied to family income and number of people in the family.* Although no guarantees

culture-defining group
in sociology, a reference to the majority group in a culture, in contrast to a minority group.

non-culture defining group
in sociology, a reference to the minority group.

socioeconomic
a contraction of the words *social* and *economic,* typically used to refer to one's status or class in society (such as "lower class" or "upper class"), which, in turn, is typically tied to family income and number of people in the family.

Gangster Rap

Insights into the thinking, feeling, values and aspirations of a particular culture or subculture can be found in the oral, written, and artistic traditions and expressions of the culture, as well as in its institutions. The rhymes of the gangster rappers provide a frightening but revealing glimpse into the concerns, desires, and value systems of many gang members. Perhaps even more disturbing is the widespread support such messages receive in the form of fan clubs, product purchases, and sold-out concert tours. In your view, what accounts for the appeal of the gangster rapper's message?

Gangster rap had its origins with a rap group called NWA (an abbreviation for Niggas With Attitude) from Compton, California. In its 1988 debut album *Straight Outta Compton,* the group rapped about hatred for the police, about gunplay, and drug dealing. NWA's second album, entitled *Niggaz-4Life,* which advocates, among other things, gang rape and forced oral sex, reached number 1 on the pop album charts in June 1991 (Rule, 1992). Other rap artists, such as a group called Public Enemy, would soon be recording raps having similar messages and selling them to receptive audiences. Within 2 weeks after the Los Angeles riots of 1992, rap singer Sister Souljah was quoted by the *Washington Post* as saying, "I mean, if black people kill black people every day, why not have a week and kill white people?" In June 1992, more controversy erupted over a rap entitled "Cop Killer" contained on the album *Body Count.* In "Cop Killer," rap artist Ice-T chants, "I'm 'bout to dust some cops off . . . Die, pig, die!" Like Sister Souljah, Ice-T argued that the meaning of his controversial words was misinterpreted. Ice-T described the rap as the first-person

story of a character "who is fed up with police brutality" ("Vice President Calls," 1992). In July 1992, amidst protests from police associations and threats of possible lawsuits if police officers were killed, the manufacturer and distributor of *Body Count* began to withdraw it from shelves. The album sold about 300,000 copies, 100,000 of which were sold after the protests over the "Cop Killer" song began (Pareles, 1992).

One of the original members of NWA, O'Shea Jackson (now better known as Ice Cube), struck out on his own in 1989 with a million-selling album entitled *AmeriKKKa's Most Wanted.* An album entitled *Death Certificate* released in 1991 contained raps that variously (1) glorified guns ("Man's Best Friend"), (2) belittled white women ("Horny Lil' Devil"), (3) chided upwardly mobile African-Americans for wanting to be white or Jewish ("True to the Game"), and (4) encouraged African-Americans nationwide to boycott or burn Korean groceries ("Black Korea"). "I Wanna Kill Sam" characterized Uncle Sam as a white supremacist and "My Summer Vacation" told of a drug-dealing gang from Los Angeles that sets up shop in St. Louis and engages in drive-by shootings. The St. Louis police are depicted as racist. Homosexuals are demeaned throughout.

The messages contained in gangster rapper's rhymes, including their widespread use of pejorative and offensive terms such as *nigger,* has been a great source of controversy to people from varied racial groups. Black proponents of the language used by the gangster rappers argue that their use of words such as *nigger* will serve to deracialize the impact of such words. They "liken it to the way some homosexuals have

started referring to themselves as 'queers' in a defiant slap at an old slur" (Marriott, 1993). Yet others fear that the continued use of such negative epithets serve the interest of no one. Rather than a step forward, the use of such language in the popular media may represent a step backward in the direction of self-hate (Cathcart, 1993). They argue that rather than neutralizing the emotional impact of such slurs, the use of such language may have the reverse effect, acting to make bigotry more socially acceptable.

How can we best understand the gangster rap phenomenon? Jon Pareles (1991, p. 28), in his review of Ice Cube's *Death Certificate* album, put it this way: "Ice Cube speaks for parts of a suffering community, but suffering doesn't necessarily build nobility. Sometimes it just leaves scars, and those scars are revealed on Death Certificate." Listening to the rhymes of gangster rappers may indeed prompt many to wonder how the suffering and scars Pareles speaks of can more effectively be addressed by mental health professionals, politicians, and society at large.

O'Shea Jackson, better known as the tough-talking rap artist, "Ice Cube."

of psychological adjustment come with high socioeconomic status, it is true that lower socioeconomic status seems to be associated with higher rates of emotional and behavioral problems (Eron & Peterson, 1982). A number of reasons may account for this correlation, including poor nutrition, inadequate housing, unemployment or low job satisfaction, and unstable family situations. In addition, people who are higher up the socioeconomic ladder are more apt to seek and obtain professional mental health services for their problems. People who are lower down on the socioeconomic ladder, and in particular minority group members, are more apt to be victims of prejudice and discrimination with respect to employment opportunities, housing availability, and other necessities of life.

By race, two out of every three poor people in this country are white (Henslin, 1993). However, in proportion to their representation in the total population, only 10% of whites are poor as compared to about 31% of blacks and about 26% of Hispanics. For many Americans, being poor amounts to a life sentence in the inner city and a consequential barrage of destructive forces that erode one's chances for healthy adjustment. Death by gunfire, drugs, and AIDS is an everyday occurrence, and the death of one adult may make orphans of one or more children. When one or both parents are not absent as a result of death or abandonment, they may be absent as a result of imprisonment. Upwards of 10% of all children live in what have been called "zero-parent" homes. Many of these children live with nonrelatives, in group homes, or are homeless (Gross, 1992a).

Homelessness among children and adults has been on the rise in the United States. It has been estimated that on any given night, approximately 700,000 people in the United States are homeless (Congressional Budget Office, 1990). The total number of homeless people and the proportion of women and children within that total are believed to be growing, although conducting research on this population is difficult. Moreover, definitions of homelessness have varied from study to study (Trotter, 1983; Fischer & Breakey, 1991), with some studies defining homeless as living in sheltered institutions (including jails and homeless shelters) and others defining it as living in public settings (such as streets, parks, and beaches).

Consistent in studies on homeless people—however homelessness is defined—is the finding of alcohol and other drug abuse (McCarty, Argeriou, Huebner, & Lubran, 1991). Abuse of alcohol is perhaps the single most prevalent health problem in the homeless (Fischer, 1989; Institute of Medicine, 1988). It has been estimated that the rate of alcohol abuse among the homeless is about 6 to 7 times greater than that in the general population. The destructive effects of chronic alcoholism in many cases worsen already poor health conditions and family relations and heighten an already high risk of accident and trauma. Because alcohol abuse impairs judgment, it may also contribute to high-risk sexual behavior and possible exposure to the virus that causes AIDS. One study in Atlanta determined that as many as 70% of homeless people's deaths were alcohol-related (Hanzlick, 1984).

Studies of drug abuse other than alcohol abuse among homeless people suggest that between 25 and 50% of the members of this population are drug abusers (Fischer, 1989). Preferences for particular drugs may change with the times (depending on factors such as cost and availability of a drug in its various forms), but abuse of marijuana, hashish, cocaine, opiates, barbiturates, and amphetamines is common. Drug habits bring with them the risk of arrest as well as the risk of contraction of AIDS through the use of HIV-infected needles. To support drug habits, many homeless people must engage in illegal acts, including mugging, burglary, prostitution, and drug-dealing.

The development of policies to address poverty, homelessness, and related problems of powerlessness has been hampered in part by an overabundance of varying views on how best to deal with the problem. Still, the degree of maladjustment and suffering that exists among poverty-stricken people, and especially among homeless women (Milburn & D'Ercole, 1991; Robertson, 1991) and children (Rafferty & Shinn, 1991; Rotheram-Borus et al., 1991) demands study and the development of effective interventions. Toward the objective of treatment and rehabilitation, many experts have designed ways to meet the mental and physical health needs of the homeless through innovative outreach and detoxification programs. After completing such programs, the individual is ideally provided medical and social support, as well as alcohol- and drug-free housing. In general, an objective of such programs is to empower those with little power, thus restoring dignity.

RACE, ETHNICITY, RELIGION, AND PREJUDICE

The term **race** may be defined as *any group of people classified together on the basis of genetic characteristics that are more or less distinct.* **Racism** refers to *notions of the superiority of one race over another.* In recent years, the recognition that extensive intermarriage has occurred through the centuries has compelled some to label the entire concept of race as a myth (Montagu, 1965). In contrast to calls to abolish the concept of race altogether are calls for much greater specificity in references to racial and ethnic backgrounds (Hevia, 1993). The 1990 United States Census listed white, black, American Indian/Alaskan Native, and Asian/Pacific Islander as options for the racial background item, yet 10 million Americans categorized themselves as "Other." According to the acting director of the Census Bureau, Harry Scarr, about 8% of the nearly 2 million people who identified themselves as American Indian listed their tribe membership using terms as diverse as African-American, Arab, Haitian, Hispanic, and Polish. Scarr (1993) observed that, "Some advocates argue that Census procedures—in fact all governmental and administrative systems—do not allow persons of mixed parentage to report their 'true' racial identity" (p. E3).

Ethnicity, from which the term *ethnic* is derived, refers to *the quality of belonging to a group having a common religious, linguistic, or ancestral heritage.* People of different races may be, for example, Catholic, Hungarian, or Hispanic in ethnic origin. According to U.S. Census data, African Americans make up the largest single minority group in the United States (over 30 million people), followed by Hispanics (over 20 million people), Asian Americans (about 4 million people), and Native Americans (about 1.5 million people). By the way, controversy also surrounds the merits of the use of the term *Hispanic* (a term that refers to Spain and to a European heritage) as compared to the use of *Latino* (a term that refers to a Latin-American heritage). Consistent with the practice of the U.S. Census, the term *Hispanic* is used in this text.

Religion may be defined generally as *a system of expressing belief in a higher power that created the universe and oversees it.* Just as stereotyping on the basis of gender can and does occur, so may stereotyping on the basis of race, ethnic background, religion, and related variables. Harmful upshots of such stereotyping include racism, prejudice, and discrimination. One group of people, the Jews, has the unenviable distinction of having the longest unbroken chain of prejudice and discrimination in the history of the world (Wistrich, 1992). **Anti-Semitism**, or *political, social, and economic discrimination and aggression against Jews*, dates back to antiquity and still exists today (see Figure 4–8).

race
any group of people classified together on the basis of genetic characteristics that are more or less distinct.

racism
notions of the superiority of one race over another.

ethnicity
the quality of belonging to a group with a common religious, linguistic, or ancestral heritage.

religion
a system of expressing belief in a higher power that is believed to have created the universe and continues to oversee it.

anti-Semitism
political, social, and economic prejudice, discrimination, and aggression against Jews.

FIGURE 4–8 ANTI-SEMITISM IN THE ANCIENT WORLD In the ancient Roman empire, few Jews were allowed the privileges of Roman citizenship. An uprising in the year 66 met with harsh reprisals as depicted in an engraving by Flavius Josephus entitled *Ten Thousand Jews Massacred in One Day by the Inhabitants of Damascus.* Throughout history, Jews have been targets of massacres, as well as crippling economic and other restrictions. This rendering depicts the Middle Ages era practice of condemning Jews to death for practicing their religion.

In Russia, beginning in the 1880s, legislation was passed to limit the ability of Jews to own land or attend institutions of higher learning. Government-sanctioned massacres of Jews along with looting of their property occurred in some 600 cities in Russia following an unsuccessful revolution in that country in 1905. Anti-Semitism was official government policy in Nazi Germany, where legislation passed in 1933 excluded Jewish people from protections of German law and the property of Jews was summarily seized by the government. Local and sporadic killing of Jews by Nazi gangs spiraled into more systematic, government-sanctioned efforts when concentration camps began to be constructed in 1938. Jews in Germany (and later in countries allied with or conquered by Germany including Italy, France, and Poland), if not simply executed, were used as slave labor, subjected to heinous medical experimentation, or otherwise employed in unspeakably inhumane ways. By the mid-1940s, nearly two-thirds of the Jewish population had been killed by massacre, starvation, or other means, and a new word came into the world's vocabulary—**genocide**, referring to *the systematic annihilation of a group of people based on their religious or political beliefs, racial or ethnic origin, or other such factors.*

In the post-World War II era, anti-Semitism has been unrelenting in various parts of the world. For example, in 1971, soon after Muammar al-Qadaffi seized power in the country of Libya, a series of laws were announced that permitted the state to confiscate all the assets of Jews. Violent expressions of state-sponsored anti-Semitic terror has taken many forms. Two relatively recent examples include Iraq's launching of missiles into the Jewish state of Israel in 1991 during the Persian Gulf War (despite the fact that the two countries were not at war), and the 1992 bombing of the Israeli Embassy in Buenos Aires, Argentina. The latter bombing killed 28 people and, according to the U.S. State Department, is believed to have been sponsored by the government of Iran. Anti-Semitism is widespread throughout the world (Cowell, 1992; Riding, 1992a, 1992b; Whitney, 1992a). In Tokyo, *The Secret of Jewish Power to Control the World*, by Aisaburo Saito, a Japanese legislator, was a bestseller (Hier, 1993). Another Japanese bestseller called *The Jewish Conspiracy* identifies a convenient scapegoat for Japan's economic woes (Hier, 1993). Jews have also been scapegoated as the group of people responsible for everything from the economic decline of the former Soviet Union to the downing of Korean Airlines Flight 007 (Hier, 1993). In the newly reunified Germany, there has been a rise in neo-Nazism (Kinzer, 1991, 1992).

Closer to home, a large-scale survey found that 1 in 5 Americans harbor strong prejudice against the Jews ("Twenty Percent in U.S.," 1992). Other evidence of anti-Semitism is not difficult to find (Berger, 1990; "Campus Journal," 1993; "Canadian Convicted in Anti-Semitism Case," 1992; Fischer, 1992; Levin, 1992; McFadden, 1992). A Federal Bureau of Investigation report on hate crimes covering 32 states for the year 1991 indicated that Jews were second only to blacks as victims of such crimes. Even the bomb blast in the garage at the World Trade Center in February 1993 may have been motivated by anti-Semitism, among other possible motives. A note received by *The New York Times* four days after the bombing explained that the bombing was motivated in part as a "response for the American political, economical, and military support to Israel" (Mitchell, 1993). The letter threatened future terrorist activity within the United States if it continued such support, and it demanded that the United States cease "all diplomatic relations" with Israel.[8]

As you read about such longstanding, widespread, and, in some instances, government-sanctioned prejudice and discrimination, what thoughts come to mind? Were you to be the victim of such widespread prejudice or discrimination, how do you think it might affect the way that you view the world or other people? How would you cope? What thoughts might offer personal comfort or solace from such hatred? What kind of behavior would you engage in to effectively respond to it? For millions of Americans who have been targets of prejudice or discrimination for nothing more than their religion, skin color, or ethnic background, such questions hold more than academic interest.

THE ROOTS OF RACISM, PREJUDICE, AND DISCRIMINATION

Racism, prejudice, and discrimination can be traced back to the founding of the United States. The Declaration of Independence provided for the freedom of property-owning

genocide

the systematic annihilation of a group of people based on their religious or political beliefs, racial or ethnic origin, or other such factors.

[8]Blumenthal et al. (1993) summed up the results of months of intensive investigation in a most detailed account of the bombing according to federal investigators. According to Blumenthal et al. (1993), the text of the letter sent to *The New York Times* matched that found on computer disks seized at the home of one of the suspects, Nidal Ayyad, a naturalized American citizen having Palestinian parents. Investigators traced calls from where they believe the bomb was made to Ayyad, and they asserted that Ayyad accompanied another suspect, Mohammed Salameh, to rent the van believed to have carried the bomb. The guilt or innocence of the parties charged remain a matter for a jury to decide upon hearing all the evidence. The motivation for the bombing remains something of a mystery despite the letter from one of the suspects. As Blumenthal et al. (1993) observed, it was "still not clear what blend of Palestinian grievance, Islamic militance or anti-Americanism may have finally motivated the attack on the 110-story twin towers, which dominate lower Manhattan and shine as a symbol of Western wealth and power" (p. B4).

white men, not property-owning (or non-property owning) women, African Americans, Native Americans, or slaves. It would take the Civil War to bring about the abolition of slavery, and not until a century after that historic conflict would federal legislation guaranteeing the rights of African Americans and others be passed into law. In the meanwhile, racism, prejudice, and discrimination prevailed at different times, in different places, and against various groups of immigrants to the United States, including the Irish, the Japanese, the Jews, the Italians, Mormons, Puerto Ricans, Catholics, Mexicans, and the Chinese (see Figure 4–9).

What factors foster prejudice against an individual on the basis of religious, racial, or ethnic background? One answer to this question makes reference to the operation of a group stereotype in a particular culture. If Tom believes that all people from *X* group are *Y*, and Henrietta belongs to group *X*, then Henrietta is *Y*, at least in Tom's eyes. Another useful perspective in understanding prejudice has to do with the values, needs, education, and motives operating within the prejudiced person. Over a half-century ago, researchers discovered a correlation between the number of lynchings and the price of cotton in the South (Hovland & Sears, 1940). One explanation of this correlational finding is that the tighter things became financially for the majority, the greater the need for minority scapegoats to blame. A similar finding, also interpreted in terms of scapegoating as a motivation, had to do with self-satisfaction and prejudice against Jews; the less one was satisfied with one's economic status, the more likely one was to be prejudiced against Jews (Campbell, 1947). Although scapegoating theory has been influential, its chief drawback concerns the complexity—read "impossibility"—of predicting just which group will be scapegoated by whom and to what degree. Scapegoating theory may sometimes seem stretched, for example, as an explanation for the prejudices of the rich and privileged against the poor. Another problem for scapegoating theory is the fact that many different but related variables may contribute in various degrees to the observed prejudice (Schuman et al., 1985). So, for example, consider the case of a prejudiced person having little formal education and low socioeconomic status. Whether the prejudice can be accounted for by the socioeconomic status variable, the level of education variable, some combination of these variables, or some other variable(s) entirely, is unknown.

FIGURE 4–9 DISCRIMINATION AGAINST THE CHINESE IN THE 1870S
This cartoon editorialized against thinly veiled racist notions that prevailed in the form of patriotism and "hire American" policies.

THE ARGUMENT OF NATIONALITY.

Excited Mob—" *We don't want any cheap-labor foreigners intruding upon us native-born citizens.*"

Another phenomenon of relevance to an understanding of prejudice has been called the **in-group/out-group phenomenon**, or *the tendency for one to view as outsiders all people who are not members of the same group.* Even when you were a child choosing sides for some informal team play, you may have experienced an immediate "bonding" with your team-mates and the feeling that you and your other team members were somehow better than the other team. In this context, you were in the in-group, and everyone else was in the out-group. The in-group/out-group phenomenon is a force that is also very much at work among adolescents (your high school was probably better than the neighboring one, right?), and adults (the team that you root for is going to win the championship next year, right?) (Tajfel, 1970). Unfortunately, the in-group/out-group phenomenon may also divide people along racial, ethnic, and religious lines, sometimes with tragic consequences.

in-group/out-group phenomenon

the tendency for one to view as outsiders all people who are not members of the same group.

The contemporary consequences of past and present racism, prejudice, and discrimination can in part be seen in the high rates of crime and drug abuse that plague the inner city. As Cornel West (1993), the director of Afro-American studies at Princeton University has observed, it is inappropriate to highlight immoral behavior among urban city dwellers while ignoring the immoral circumstances that contributed to their plight. According to psychologist Gordon Allport, prejudice must be considered as a contributing factor in the plight of minorities in urban America. Allport (1954) wrote that treating any group of people in a prejudiced and discriminatory way will evoke either self-hate or rebellious anger in the group so treated. Either of these reactions may have the effect of becoming a self-fulfilling prophecy, thus perpetuating the prejudice. For example, consider the effect on a minority group of people of being consistently labeled as *lazy* by the dominant group. Such labeling might well affect the self-esteem and/or work motivation of the group members. The result of either effect could conceivably be a work slowdown—with consequential validation of the *lazy* stereotype. Allport's (1954) classic work in the area of prejudice, and in particular his ideas about the scapegoated group rebelling, make for compelling reading in the light of recent events (see *In the News*).

THRIVING IN A MULTICULTURAL SOCIETY

We live in a culturally pluralistic society in which daily contact with people from a variety of different backgrounds has become more the rule than the exception to it. The great degree of cultural diversity in America is evident from sources as diverse as current census data (Yetman, 1991), immigration trends ("Coming to America," 1992), even changing American tastes in food. In 1992, for example, salsa soundly displaced ketchup as the best-selling condiment in the United States (O'Neill, 1992).

For all the benefits and opportunities for personal growth that living in a culturally diverse society brings, there are also many potential problems. Conflicts between people of different racial, religious, or ethnic backgrounds have taken many forms ranging from children scapegoating one another to an armed group of people attempting to annihilate some other group of people. At a global level, such conflicts must be addressed by political leaders, religious leaders, schools, and the media.

At a personal level, the acronym CUT seems appropriate because calls for *communication, understanding,* and *tolerance* have been common to many proposals designed to cut down intergroup conflict. In stark contrast to the physical confrontations people seem all too ready to partake of, leaders such as the American clergyman Martin Luther King, Jr., combated violence with nonviolence, understanding, tolerance, and steady movement towards the goal of eliminating racial oppression. He fought the Klan, neo-Nazi groups, and other enemies not with weapons that physically kill but with words of reason and nonviolence. Personally living by a doctrine of nonviolent persuasion based on *Satyagraha,* the doctrine of nonviolence taught by Gandhi in India, King fought and won battles not in the street but in the halls of the Supreme Court of the United States. Although King was assassinated, his words, deeds, and contributions to humankind have been immortalized.

At Harvard University's 1992 commencement exercises, that institution's president, Neil L. Rudenstine, addressed the issue of problems that people from different backgrounds encounter when they must live and work together. For Rudenstine (1992), the essential problem is that the human race "has tended throughout history to be quite tribal

Civil Unrest in Los Angeles

On April 29, 1992, a verdict of "Not Guilty" on charges of excessive use of force was returned for three Los Angeles police officers, and a fourth officer was cleared of most charges against him. The four officers had been charged as a result of the videotaped beating of motorist Rodney King as they subdued him after a high speed chase on the night of March 3, 1991. Within hours after the verdict was announced, there was widespread rioting, looting, and arson in Los Angeles. Thousands of fires burned out of control as firemen dodged debris and bullets from onlookers. Before it was over, more than 50 people were dead, 9,000 arrests had been made, and economic losses were estimated at upwards of one billion dollars.

Critics viewed the jury verdict as a reaffirmation of the impossibility for blacks in white America to obtain justice. Outrage focused on the setting in which the trial took place, a community that had a history of positive interactions with the police. The racial composition of the jury—6 men and 6 women, 10 of whom were white, one of whom was Asian, and one of whom was Hispanic—was also criticized and deemed to be a contributory factor in the verdict.

Individual jurors who have commented on such charges have repeatedly stated that they were swayed by the weight of the evidence, not by racism or undue sympathy for the police (Mydans, 1993b). By law, the only criteria applied in selecting the site of the trial were factors such as the convenience of the location for the parties and witnesses, and the expense of the trial. Both the defense and prosecuting attorneys agreed that the trial would have to be tried where it was tried. The scarcity of black jurors was due in part to the fact that a representative from a black advocacy organization contacted black potential jurors about the case on the second day of jury selection, thus causing them to be excused from sitting on that jury.

For Colman (1992), the causes of the riots can be found in institutionalized racism in American society. Colman wrote that "Anyone who looks at the videotape of Mr. King's beating and says this was not a case of assault with a deadly weapon is missing a vital body nerve center. . . . The white suburban jury is simply a reflection of the polarization of black and white communities over the last 20 years" (p. E16). The perspective of the rioters was brought in to sharper focus in October of 1992 with the findings of a bipartisan, 17-member committee of legislators

and sectarian." He urged students and faculty alike to invest more time in getting to know one another.

Everyday experience tells us that people do not remain prejudiced for want of exposure to strong antiprejudice messages. In fact, most people are exposed to multiple antiprejudice messages in sources as diverse as textbooks and MTV. The editor of *Teaching Tolerance,* a magazine published by the Southern Poverty Law Center, notes that, "[W]e choose whom we will learn from and appreciate, whom we will ignore, whom we will fight to reconcile with and whom we will allow to alienate us forever . . ." (Bullard, 1993, p. 50). In this context, then, perhaps we need to think a little *less* critically when investing time in getting to know people from other cultures. Perhaps we need to give culturally different ideas and behavior a thorough, honest, and fair mulling-over before rejecting them as inconsistent with our own ways.

Some may believe communication, understanding, and tolerance do not go far enough in lessening the gaps that exist between various social groups. They say, in essence, "Let us

headed by Assemblyman Curtis Tucker. The Tucker committee concluded that the causes of the Los Angeles riots were similar to the causes of rioting in Los Angeles in the 1960's including poverty, lack of employment opportunity, unequal consumer services, and widespread perceptions of police abuse ("New Riots, Old Story," 1992). One rioter was quoted in *The Los Angeles Times* as saying, "If you've been oppressed and suppressed for so long, crying out for change and not being heard, you take the matter into your own hands." Another person at the scene was quoted as saying, "We're wrong, they're wrong, everybody's wrong."

Rioting in response to racial injustice in this country is certainly not unprecedented. In August 1965 in Los Angeles, the arrest of a black motorist in Watts section of the city on the charge of drunken driving sparked a riot in which 34 people were killed. In July of 1967, rioting in Newark, New Jersey, and Detroit, Michigan claimed a total of 69 lives. Yet some have won-

dered aloud about the motivation for the 1992 Los Angeles riots. One view was that "failed expectations created by the mass media" (Nogee, 1992) were actually at fault. According to this view, repeated presentation of the prosecution's videotape—edited for maximum audience impact—was what convicted the defendants in the eyes of the public. Although the jury was privy to defense arguments, those arguments received scant, if any coverage in the popular press. As Nogee (1992), p. E16) put it, "The mass media left no room for doubt, reasonable or otherwise. . . [and the result was] the terrible loss of life and destruction of property we experienced." Another perspective on the rioting focuses on the role of opportunistic looting. One resident of South Central Los Angeles was quoted as saying, "A lot of people probably never even heard of Rodney King. They're doing it because it's like Christmas in the springtime" (Terry, 1992, p. A24). Chicago's mayor, Richard M. Daley (1992) echoed such sentiments in response to rioting occa-

sioned by his hometown team winning a national basketball championship: "When people have an excuse to loot, they loot . . . " (Daley, 1992, p. A16).

Yet another perspective focuses on the fact that Korean-owned business were disproportionately targeted. The former director of the Korean American Grocers Association saw 20 years of his own work go up in flames, and he reported that about 600 Korean-owned businesses had been looted, destroyed by fire, or damaged (Park, 1992).

In organized demonstrations or other lawful means, many thousands of people in cities throughout the United States demonstrated their concerns about justice for all. Federal officials retried the case against the four officers on the grounds that Rodney King's civil rights had been violated. Convictions were won against two of the LAPD officers in the federal case (Mydans, 1993c). From what you know about the videotape, the evidence against the officers, the officers' defense, and the rioting, what are your thoughts?

celebrate, not merely *tolerate* differences." At first glance, the idea of celebrating diversity may have great appeal. Yet a harsh reality of cultural diversity is that some subcultures (for example, the KKK) have been built on prejudiced, racist, sexist, or otherwise unacceptable ideologies. For many people, the demand to "celebrate" such diversity would amount to asking too much. In situations when a person or group is espousing divisive, hate-related messages, it stretches the goodwill of decent, law-abiding people to *tolerate* free—if hate-mongering—speech, much less *celebrate* it. Values have a very definite place in the discussion of multiculturalism and tolerance; neither tolerance nor multiculturalism can be allowed to justify moral blindness.

Many different kinds of tools might be brought to bear to help promote the kinds of communication and learning to which Rudenstine made reference. Some of these tools, as well as others, are illustrated in the *Quality of Life* feature. As you read about them, think about which ones might be particularly effective or ineffective. Can *you* think of any teaching tools or devices to add to this list?

QUALITY OF  *Life*

Education for Multicultural Living

The English novelist/moralist Graham Greene once wrote, "Hate is a failure of imagination." In this context, there is clearly a need for more imagination in teaching related to multicultural living. On the bright side, more imaginative approaches are increasingly in evidence, and some of them are illustrated here. Education for multicultural living must also include a strong message regarding society's intolerance of individuals and groups intent on violating the rights of others. It is important that perpetrators of hate crimes be apprehended and tried in a court of law so that would-be perpetrators are not led to believe that they can act above the law.

A long tradition of research by social psychologists suggests that group cooperation to achieve some shared goal can reduce "us-versus-them" prejudices (Aronson, 1990; Cook, 1985; Finchilescu, 1988; Gaertner et al., 1990; Wright et al., 1990). Here, people come together to rebuild Los Angeles after the 1992 riots.

Down the road from the site of the Los Angeles riots of 1992, the Simon Wiesenthal Center's *Museum of Tolerance* opened in February of 1993. Like other exhibits at the museum, this one helps children understand prejudice from various perspectives. Here, a child is encouraged to generate thoughts about how his life would be different as a function of factors such as gender, role, or race.

A conference at a historical society in New Mexico is where a Jewish poet from Jerusalem (at left), and a Hispanic businesswoman from Pasadena, California (at right) learned that their ancestors may have come from the same city. Such conferences can be a fun way to explore one's own heritage, as well as all that one has in common with others.

Ethnic events, commercial as some may seem, can still provide an opportunity to acquaint oneself with interesting aspects of other cultures. *Powwows,* for example, provide an opportunity to partake of Native-American storytelling, crafts, music, and art.

SUMMARY

GENDER, THE INDIVIDUAL, AND SOCIETY Males and females differ biologically in many nonobvious ways and are seldom viewed or treated equally in cultures throughout the world. Biological differences range from the action of male and female sex hormones to the electrical activity of muscles in response to emotion-provoking stimuli. Perhaps the ultimate biological difference between women and men is that women get pregnant and nurse babies, men do not. Many analyses of the differential treatment of women and men across various societies are strongly tied to this biological fact of life. From a developmental perspective, baby girls and boys are treated differently by parents and others, and these environmental differences will typically lead to a sense of gender identity, gender stability, and gender constancy.

GENDER IDENTITY, ROLES, AND STEREOTYPES *Gender identity* refers to a knowledge of one's sex, gender stability refers to the recognition that gender assignment is permanent, and gender constancy refers to the recognition that gender assignment is constant despite physical appearances. Along with acquiring a sense of gender identity, the developing person learns from family, friends, television, films, storybooks, toys, and other sources about *gender roles;* that is, culturally defined expectations on the basis of sex. A *stereotype* refers to a belief about a person or a group of people that is derived primarily on the basis of perceptions regarding the group to which the individual belongs. Stereotypes may lead to inaccurate perceptions of people and unfair conclusions about individuals within the group being stereotyped. Potentially harmful upshots of stereotyping include prejudice, racism, and discrimination.

TOWARDS GENDER EQUITY Beyond equal opportunity legislation and laws designed to ensure equal treatment of people by sex, one approach to minimizing differences between the sexes to widely broaden what is considered to be gender-appropriate behavior. Another approach is to learn about and develop sensitivity to gender differences.

CULTURE AND ADJUSTMENT An individual is unique in terms of genetic inheritance, biological constitution, and experience, but a person shares a common culture with other people. Culture places similar demands on individuals within it to speak a common language, dress a common way, perhaps even to think in a way consistent with ways that the group as a whole values. Learning such social facts of life is the process of *acculturation,* and one's family, friends, instructors, and the media are some of the teachers. From a cultural perspective, the study of adjustment may also focus on differences between people as a function of social status differences, differences in material resources, and differences as a function of racial or ethnic variables. Communication, understanding, and tolerance are needed if people are to thrive in a multicultural society.

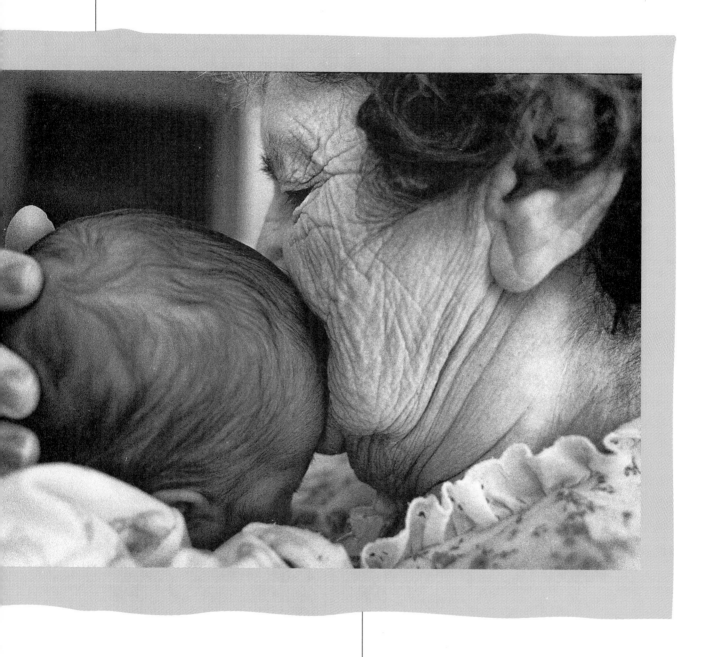

A Developmental Perspective on Adjustment

O U T L I N E

The process of adjustment begins before birth. The fetus adjusts as best it can to the environmental conditions within the mother's womb. These conditions are in part a consequence of the mother's behavior—what she eats, what she drinks, what she breathes, and what otherwise enters her bloodstream and passes into the developing baby's bloodstream. If the mother has taken steps to create as safe an environment as possible for her child, her chances of having a healthy baby will be that much increased. If the mother has not taken such steps, the chances of having a healthy baby decrease. Infection, radiation, alcohol, drugs, tobacco smoke, improper nutrition, physical overexertion, and excessive emotional distress are among many factors known to affect the developing baby adversely.

In this chapter we survey human adjustment from infancy through adulthood.[1] The demands and challenges of adulthood will be given somewhat less emphasis because many of these adjustment-related issues, such as finding a mate and deciding upon a career, are covered in detail in subsequent chapters. As you read, think about the applicability of the various personality theories you read about in Chapter 2. Which theoretical approach to personality seems to make the most sense to you? Why?

infancy

the period between birth and 2 years of age.

INFANCY

Infancy is typically defined as *the period between birth and 2 years of age.* In general, physical challenges during this period relate primarily to the development of motor skills such as sitting, standing, and walking. Cognitive challenges include those related to perceiving the self, the external world, and the boundaries between the two. Many emotional challenges are related to the development of an attachment to caregivers. Social challenges include learning to trust people. But we are getting ahead of ourselves . . .

PRENATAL ADJUSTIVE CHALLENGES

[1]As you might anticipate, the nature of the adjustive challenges we face from birth onward can be quite diverse. Here we can only discuss relatively few of them, and then primarily with respect to the average or "normal" person. More detailed coverage of various aspects of human development from birth onward can be found in textbooks devoted to developmental psychology.

Numerous prenatal influences on the human fetus can influence the child's future health and adjustment (see Figure 5–1). For example, a very high or low anxiety level in the mother can lead to physical and/or mental problems in the infant (Joffe et al., 1985; Oakley, 1985; Ramsey et al., 1986; Reeb et al., 1987; Stott, 1971; Van den Bergh et al., 1989). Maternal use of drugs, including nicotine, alcohol, cocaine, and other substances capable of being transmitted to the fetus through the uterus can have extremely harmful effects including miscarriage, premature birth, birth defects, lifelong mental or physical difficulties, and death shortly after birth (American College of Obstetricians and Gynecologists, 1990;

FIGURE 5–1 CHALLENGES IN LIFE As life begins, so does the challenge of survival. In many instances, newborn infants will require more than simple tender loving care to meet this challenge. This baby is receiving treatment with bright light for a condition known as jaundice, a yellowing of the skin. Jaundice occurs in about two thirds of all full-term babies and may range from mild to severe. It has a number of possible causes, the most common being a failure of the baby's liver to remove a yellow substance from the blood called bilirubin (pronounced "Billy Reuben"). As the baby's liver and other organs become fully functional, the jaundice will go away, usually within a week or so after birth. Treatment with natural or artificial light, also known as phototherapy, has been found to help speed the liver's removal of bilirubin. When the laboratory analysis of the bilirubin level in the blood indicates that it is safe to do so, phototherapy will be discontinued.

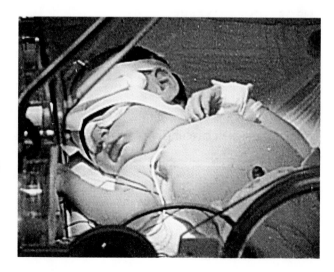

and death shortly after birth (American College of Obstetricians and Gynecologists, 1990; Streissguth et al., 1989; Treaster, 1993; Weiss & Mirin, 1987).

THE FIRST 2 YEARS OF LIFE

Soon after bringing the newborn home from the hospital, parents are faced with numerous choices regarding their treatment of the baby. For example, parents must make decisions about sleeping and feeding schedules. Wolfson et al. (1992) described a program to help ease such decision making by helping infants establish stable sleeping patterns. Another sleep-related decision has to do with whether to lay the infant in its crib on its back, side, or stomach to sleep. Increasing general awareness about sudden infant death syndrome (SIDS), in which a baby thought to be healthy dies in its sleep, has added new significance to questions regarding infants' sleeping position. SIDS strikes about 1.5 per 1,000 babies born alive, typically within the first 6 months of life. It has been observed that the risk of SIDS in children whose mothers are smokers is double that for children whose mothers are not smokers (American College of Obstetricians and Gynecologists, 1990). Still, the cause of SIDS has remained a medical mystery and there is no known prevention or cure (see Figure 5–2).

At a most general level, we can say that the human infant progresses from a state of total helplessness, incompetence, and dependency to one that is far more self-reliant, competent, and independent. At some point well into the aging process, or as a result of disease, disability, or environmental factors, the trend may reverse and move once again in the direction of helplessness, incompetence, and dependency. Throughout the process of development, a great deal of love and acceptance on the part of the child's caregivers is essential (Sears et al., 1957). But love is not enough. For optimal development, caregivers must provide proper nutrition and protection from the elements, disease, injuries, abuse, and neglect (see *In the News*). Caregivers must also institute effective measures of discipline, impart socially acceptable values, build the child's self-esteem and self-confidence, and provide the guidance the child needs to meet life's daily challenges. Once physical, cognitive, and emotional needs have been provided for, and if the environment is such that it stimulates curiosity, exploration, and the satisfaction of learning and discovery, the human being is capable of a most remarkable evolution. From a state of total self-absorption at birth, the infant may transform into someone capable of acts that will benefit the human condition worldwide. Yet even a journey of a million miles, must begin with a single step . . . literally.

MOTOR DEVELOPMENT

Motor skills in the present context refer to *proficiency related to placing the body in motion.* Newborn infants cannot so much as turn over on their own; place them down on their

motor skills
proficiency related to placing the body in motion. See also *gross motor skills* and *fine motor skills*.

FIGURE 5–2 UP, DOWN, OR SIDEWAYS? Noting a slightly higher risk of sudden infant death syndrome (SIDS) for babies who are placed on their stomach to sleep, a panel of the American Academy of Pediatrics now recommends that healthy, normal, full-term babies sleep on their sides or backs. The recommendation does not apply to babies who vomit excessively or those who have certain breathing or gastrointestinal problems. No upper-age limit was placed on the recommendation, but by the time babies are 4 or 5 months old, as one member of the panel put it, "they're going to decide what position they sleep in, not you" (Brooks, 1992). For babies placed on their stomachs to sleep, a number of factors have been found to raise the risk of SIDS: (1) a cold or other recent illness, (2) constraint of movement such as the constraint that occurs through swaddling in sheets or blankets, (3) a mattress so soft that recesses under the body are formed, and (4) a heated room (Ponsonby et al., 1993). Parents are advised to discuss with their pediatrician which sleeping position is best for their infant.

Child Abuse and Neglect

In August 1990, husband-and-wife baby-sitters Mary and Eugene Wong were sentenced to 8 to 25 years in prison on the charge of manslaughter for killing a 2-month-old baby in their care. The baby was found to have died from *shaken baby syndrome,* a form of child abuse involving the shaking of a baby by the arms or shoulders thereby causing a tear in its fragile blood vessels. In May 1991, a 16-year-old New York woman drowned her baby in the Harlem River. In September 1991, the Bronx mother of an 8-year-old was arrested and charged with child abuse. The girl had reportedly been handcuffed by her ankle to the bathtub, scalded with hot water, whipped with a cord, and scoured with a scouring pad. In April 1992, a North Carolina man was convicted of abusing children at the day-care center he owned. The abuse was considered so heinous that the man received a sentence of 12 consecutive life terms. In June 1992, a Roman Catholic priest charged with rape and indecent assault against several children plead guilty in a Massachusetts court. This list of atrocities against children can unfortunately be expanded to fill volumes. It is a sad fact of life that if you open a daily newspaper there is a very good chance that there will be some child abuse or child neglect-related story in it.

Over 2 million children are abused or neglected annually in this country (House of Representatives, 1990). In New York State alone, there are an average of 1,500 reports of child abuse each day (Dugger, 1992). Many abusers were abused children themselves, a fact that has led some professionals to conceive of lack of parental love as a kind of "communicable disease."

Whatever the cause of child abuse, health professionals, teaching professionals, and other licensed professionals in all 50 states now have a legal obligation to report child abuse when they encounter it. Cohen et al. (1992, pp. 562–564) reviewed in detail many of the physical and emotional signs of abuse and neglect. For example, physical signs of abuse include injuries on both sides of a child's face; in most veritable accidents, only one side of the face is injured. Unusual marks or impressions on the child's skin may form identifiable and familiar patterns such as those that could be made by human teeth, the tines of a fork, or a rope. A glove-like redness on the hands or feet may betray the aftermath of exposure to scalding water. Patches of hair that are missing may betray abusive hair pulling. Physical signs of neglect include clothing that is inappropriate for the season, poor hygiene, and lagging physical development.

Emotional signs of abuse and neglect can be a great deal more subtle than the physical signs. And like many of the physical signs, the emotional signs *may* reflect abuse or neglect, but do *not necessarily* reflect abuse or neglect. Some emotional indicators include fear of going home, fear of adults in general, and reluctance to remove outer garments. Unusual or extreme emotional reactions to hearing other children cry may also be another sign of abuse or neglect. If a child having younger siblings has taken the role of caregiver at home, some signs of abuse or neglect may include fatigue and frequent tardiness or absence at school.

Child abuse is an injustice that, like many other kinds of crimes, inflicts an incalculable but heavy toll on its vic-

tims in terms of trauma and emotional scars. But as we remain vigilant to signs of child abuse and child neglect when they occur, equal vigilance must be exerted not to make a case for child abuse where no child abuse has occurred (Ackerman, 1987; Besharov, 1985; Coleman, 1989; A. Green, 1986; Jones & McGraw, 1987; Raskin & Yuille, 1987; Wong, 1987). The charge of child abuse can in some instances represent no more than a legal strategy in a child-custody dispute (Corwin et al., 1987). Child witnesses in child-abuse cases, especially younger ones from the ages of 2 to 7, do not have as highly developed memory capabilities as older children. They may confuse events referred to only in conversations subsequent to the alleged abuse with events that actually occurred (Ceci et al., 1987; Goodman & Reed, 1986).

Anatomically correct dolls are widely used by therapists, police, attorneys, social workers, and others when interviewing children suspected of being sexually abused. Yet their value in this context is debatable because the dolls themselves may be suggestive, prompting sexually related ideation where such ideation may or may not have existed before (Gardner, 1989; Moss, 1988; Raskin & Yuille, 1989; Terr, 1988). One recent review of experimental work in this area led to the conclusion that, "the techniques for using anatomical dolls have not been developed to the level that they allow for a clear differentiation between abused and non-abused children" (Ceci & Bruck, in press).

stomachs, backs, or sides, and there is an excellent chance that they will be in that same position until you move them again. The infant's very first exhibition of motor ability may be an attempt to raise the head or grab at some moving object. It will not be until about 6 months that the baby will be able to grab successfully at something. Any success at grabbing a dangling object before that time may be the result of simple grasping reflexes rather than a deliberate effort to visually aim at the object and snatch it. At about 6 months of age, the infant will also acquire the motor skills needed to roll over. A few months later, the child may be creeping around on all fours.

By age 1, many children have acquired the skill to stand on their own without any assistance. It is at about this age that children may begin to be referred to as toddlers. The noun *toddle* refers to *a slow, uncertain walk,* and the verb *to toddle* refers to *walking in a slow, uncertain manner.* Because many infants take their first tentative steps on their own between the ages of 1 and 2, the term **toddler** has become widely used to refer to a child of this age. By age 2, most children are typically walking, running, and, in general, engaging in a great deal of exploration. A potential problem, however, is that the toddler's newfound motor skills and exploration needs can easily invite physical injury if the child is not properly supervised. For many years it was believed that infants should be maintained in cribs until they learned the ability to perceive depth. Yet a now classic series of experiments conducted by Gibson and Walk (Gibson, Tighe, & Walk, 1957; Gibson & Walk, 1960; Walk, 1966; Walk, 1969; Walk & Gibson, 1961) suggested that depth perception was inborn in many animal species and may be inborn in humans as well. Psychologist Eleanor Gibson had debated with her husband, the experimental psychologist James J. Gibson, whether their young children were capable of detecting the hazardous drop from the edge of the cliffs at vacation spots they stopped at. Psychologist Richard Walk's interest in the study of depth perception grew out of experimental work with Army paratroopers at Fort Benning, Georgia. Together, Gibson and Walk conceived of an apparatus called a visual cliff to explore depth perception in human infants and species who live in different types of habitats (see Figure 5–3).

In one study, 27 infants ranging in age from 6 to 14 months were tested on the visual cliff. The procedure entailed placing each on the center board and having the child's mother call it from the deep side. Only three of the infants ventured onto the deep side of the cliff to respond to the mother, suggesting to Gibson and Walk (1960) that "most human

toddler

a child between the ages of 1 and 2, the age at which toddling, a precursor to walking, typically begins.

FIGURE 5–3 DEPTH PERCEPTION IN INFANTS
A visual cliff apparatus contains a shallow side with a distinctively patterned floor, a "deep" side with the same distinctively patterned floor, and a divider in-between (which may or may not contain the same pattern). Although perceived as deep, the deep side has no appreciable drop to it; both the shallow and deep sides are glass-covered surfaces. In different experimental procedures, human or animal subjects were placed either on the shallow side, the deep side, or on the cliff itself. Another variable in such research is the height of the perceived drop from the cliff.

FIGURE 5–4
JEAN PIAGET
(1896–1980)

infants can discriminate depth as soon as they can crawl." This finding alone does not prove that depth perception is innate. Still, Gibson and Walk argued that there was strong evidence for such an interpretation based on comparable research with animals such as newborn goats, chicks, turtles, rats, lambs, pigs, kittens, and dogs. A newborn chick, for example, always hops off the board of the cliff on the shallow side.

Subsequent research using the visual cliff and a heart-monitoring procedure yielded fascinating results (Campos et al., 1970). When a child was initially placed at the deep side of the cliff, the heart rate of subjects over 8 months of age sped up significantly, while younger subjects showed no significant difference in heart rate as a function of the side that they were placed on. Interestingly, very young subjects, including those as young as 2 months of age, appeared to react to being placed at the deep side of the cliff with a *decrease* in heart rate, suggesting to the experimenters that these subjects did indeed perceive the depth but were not afraid of it. Campos et al. concluded that it is not until about 8 months of age that a child will become fearful of falling over an edge, although the ability to perceive depth may be present earlier. An alternative interpretation for the decrease in heart rate is that the very young infants perceived the depth but felt more helpless than the older infants to do anything about it; they were, in essence, resigned to their fate.[2]

COGNITIVE DEVELOPMENT

In 1892, psychologist William James described the world of the infant as one of "blooming, buzzing confusion." It is easy to see how much of the newborn's behavior—including seemingly random crying and cooing—can easily be interpreted as confused. A newborn infant does not have the ability to focus visually, and most behavior, such as sucking, is merely reflexive in nature. However, research on babies as young as 3 or 4 months of age has indicated that these subjects are capable of learning to make simple discriminations between auditory and visual stimuli (Colombo et al., 1990; Kaplan et al., 1992; Yonas, 1988). Infants seem particularly interested in faces (Walker-Andrews, 1988), exposure to which may change infants' internal feeling states (Kaplan et al., 1991).

During the 1920s, the Swiss developmental psychologist Jean Piaget (see Figure 5–4) used his observations of his own children to derive a theory of how children develop their thinking and reasoning skills. Piaget referred to the first 2 years of life as the period of *sensorimotor development*. This contraction of *sensory* and *motor* is most apt in light of the fact that infants spend so much of their time sensing or perceiving things and then attempting to deal with those things primarily through some sort of motor response, such as sucking and grabbing. Piaget characterized infants as active explorers who become increasingly creative and knowledgeable in their means of exploration. By the end of the first 2 years of life, a differentiation of the self from the external world begins to occur.

EMOTIONAL DEVELOPMENT

Newborn infants exhibit many differences from each other that are presumed to be innate (Birns, 1964; Eisenberg et al., 1961; Freedman, 1965; Horowitz, 1969; Lipton et al., 1961; Westman, 1973). **Temperament** refers to *emotional and behavioral dispositions presumed to be inborn*. Infants differ at birth in temperament, as evidenced by observable behavior such as crying. What is the significance of such differences? Is temperament at birth related to future emotional development?

Answers have been difficult to find due to the complexities and practicalities inherent in research directed by such questions. Some research suggests that "difficult" temperament in infants may be linked to future poor performance in school (Keogh, 1982), increased susceptibility to childhood accidents (Carey, 1985), and increased frequency of behavior problems (Earls, 1981; Graham et al., 1973; McInery & Chamberlin, 1975; Prior et al., 1987). But given that the relationship between temperament and these variables has not been strongly established, perhaps the most reasonable conclusion is that temperament alone is not predictive of future emotional development or adjustment problems (Earls & Jung, 1987). In combination with other factors, however, temperament may be an important factor in predicting later maladjustment, especially in children from families who are at high risk of maladjustment (Oberklaid et al., 1991; Sanson et al., 1991).

temperament
emotional and behavioral dispositions presumed to be inborn.

[2]Some research to be reviewed in the following chapter suggests that laboratory animals placed in a hopeless and helpless situation may die due to a slowed heartbeat resulting from a comparable kind of resignation (Richter, 1957).

It is also during infancy that a child is thought to develop a basic sense of security as well as trust in other people. According to Erikson (1963), the child who can expect consistently to receive love, care, and attention during the first year of life is more apt to develop basic feelings of trust and security than a neglected or abused child. In turn, a basic feeling of trust and security frees the child to grow intellectually (as well as in other ways) without worrying about whether physical and emotional needs will be met. According to Erikson, the abused or neglected child may be much more suspicious of people. In essence, if you cannot trust your own parents to be loving and attentive to your needs, who can you trust?

SOCIAL DEVELOPMENT

Closely related to the concept of trust in infancy is the concept of **attachment**, or *the emotional ties that develop between the infant and others.* As the child gets older, signs of attachment tend to become more evident (Ainsworth, 1973). Such signs may be evidenced in expressions of fear or protest when a caregiver leaves the room or expressions of delight when a caregiver returns. At 18 months or so, pleasure prompted by the presence of a caregiver may still be expressed, although the agitation in response to the caregiver's departure may begin to diminish. By this age, it is presumed that the infant is beginning to achieve an understanding of the fact that departure is not permanent; the child has begun to trust that the caregiver will return. Studies of babies reared in institutions such as orphanages as compared to babies reared at home indicate that institutionally reared babies tend to develop more slowly in most ways and in general tend to be less healthy. Exactly why this is true is not known although quality of care (Bowlby, 1969; Spitz, 1965) and lack of sufficient stimulation (Dennis, 1973) are both thought to be involved (Rutter, 1974). Laboratory experimentation with monkeys has confirmed that early social deprivation can leave animals with profound social and emotional deficits (Harlow, 1958, 1959; Harlow & Harlow, 1962).

attachment
in developmental psychology, the emotional ties that develop between the infant and others.

THE PRESCHOOL YEARS

During the preschool years (age 2 to age 6 or so), children continue to develop physically. Round faces and bodies tend to thin as children grow more in an upward than an outward direction. **Gross motor skills,** *abilities involving large muscle movements,* such as running, jumping, hopping, skipping, throwing, climbing, kicking, pushing, and pulling, continue to develop rapidly, while **fine motor skills,** *abilities involving relatively small muscle movements,* such as tying one's shoe or pouring milk, are not quite developed at this age. Preschoolers as young as 3 years of age may proudly ask (or demand) that adults watch them engage in various motor behavior such as riding a tricycle. Complementing burgeoning motor skills are burgeoning cognitive abilities. Preschoolers experience a boundless curiosity about the world around them. They are curious about people they meet, the food they eat, and almost everything that crosses their path. Their efforts to satisfy this curiosity lead to a great deal of exploration along with excitement, satisfaction, surprise, and pride when they somehow manage to influence outcomes. At mealtime, the need to explore may outweigh the need for food—leading to mushed peas or comparably messy consequences.

gross motor skills
abilities involving large muscle movements, such as running, jumping, hopping, skipping, throwing, climbing, kicking, pushing, and pulling.

fine motor skills
abilities involving relatively small muscle movements, such as tying one's shoe or pouring milk.

PLAY AND THE PRESCHOOLER

It has been said that the "work" of the preschooler is play. Interestingly, the work of many other species at a comparable stage of life is also play. For example, kittens play with a moving ball of yarn in much the same manner that an adult cat might crouch and pounce on a food source such as a mouse. In this sense, the kittens' play helps develop skills that would be necessary if they had to fend for themselves in the wild. Young monkeys playing together not only develop many of the motor skills useful for survival in adulthood, but also skills of cooperation and communication that are equally necessary if the individual, as well as the species, is to thrive and survive. Similarly, the almost nonstop play of the preschooler is thought to have adaptive value (Garvey, 1977; Vandenberg, 1978). There is joy in discovering the world through touch, sight, sound, smell, and other experiences.

For adults, play may amount to being a couch potato on a Sunday afternoon. Similarly, infants may be fascinated by the visual stimulation of a mobile as they lie flat on their backs in cribs. Such a low level of activity would hardly constitute play for a preschooler. Preschoolers seem to be able to find feasts for their senses in almost any environment— playground, sandboxes, bathtubs, whatever. They may whirl by themselves just to experience dizziness, play with others in rough-and-tumble fashion, or dress up by applying mom's make-up or putting on dad's hat. Mobiles are for manipulating or taking apart, not merely watching in fascination, if you are a preschooler.

One categorization of preschoolers' play lists five different types, each thought to be more advanced than the next in terms of the level of social skills required for participation: *solitary play* (in which a child, even among a group of children, plays alone); *onlooker play* (in which a child watches another child or group of children play); *parallel play* (in which children may appear to be playing with each other but are actually playing by themselves and not interacting); *associative play* (in which children interact but are not really playing the same game); and *cooperative play* (in which children interact and really play the same game) (Parten, 1932). Onlooker play may be observed in children as young as 2 years or less, while associative and cooperative play typically do not emerge until age 5 or so. Transitions from one type of play to another have been found to proceed at different paces depending upon the level of social stimulation in the child's environment (Rubin et al., 1976).

CHILD INJURY PREVENTION

With increasing recognition of the role of behavioral factors in health, the field of injury control has become fertile ground for psychologists (McGinnis, 1991; Spielberg & Frank, 1992). Injury is the leading cause of death for persons between the ages of 1 and 45, and injury kills more children than the next 6 causes of death combined (Dershewitz & Williamson, 1977). Approximately 16 million children are treated annually in hospital emergency rooms as a result of injury, about 600,000 are hospitalized, and about 30,000 are permanently disabled (Rodriguez, 1990). Injuries to children in this country occur at a higher rate than in many other industrialized nations (Fingerhut & Kleinman, 1989). It has been argued that despite lip service about the priority people in the United States place on our children, the political reality is quite shocking; little priority is placed on children relative to other special interest groups (Margolis & Runyan, 1983). For example, a strong lobby exists against government intervention on the part of child safety in consumer products. Government intervention in the toy and child-products industry is seen as a threat to corporate profits and freedom (Berger, 1981; Garbarino, 1988). Another possible reason child-injury prevention is not a high priority has to do with widespread misperceptions regarding the cause of such injuries. Most people prefer to believe that child injuries are either the result of willful child abuse by an adult or of an unavoidable accident (Peterson & Roberts, 1992). Although child injuries most certainly may result from abuse or accidents, there are nonetheless many things parents, children, and manufacturers of products can do to help prevent them. As Peterson and Roberts (1992) persuasively argue, it is time to start researching the causes of injuries as well as to implement effective strategies of injury prevention.

Governmental efforts to lessen injuries may be undertaken at many different levels. Laws and regulations are variously aimed at influencing the behavior of manufacturers (as in setting certain standards), caregivers (as in requiring that children use child safety seats in cars), and the children themselves (as in prohibiting children under a certain age from driving a motor vehicle). The most effective forms of prevention appear to be those that do not rely on education for the caregiver or the child, but rather on the manufacture of products (Peterson & Roberts, 1992). For example, laws regulating the manufacture of cribs and the packaging of medicines have saved untold numbers of children from strangulation and poisoning.

Regardless of their own exercise habits, many parents would like to see their children become active in play, exercise, and sports. Often one of the first sites of a child's involvement in exercise and sports are playgrounds—sites at which approximately 150,000 injuries to children, and 20 or so deaths occur annually. Falls are responsible for about three-fourths of the injuries and about a third of the deaths in playgrounds (Sloane, 1992). Additionally, children are hit by moving swings when they walk near them, or strangled by equipment that has an opening small enough for a child's head to fit through. Thus, while preschoolers should be heartily encouraged to exercise, they must be properly supervised. The need for adult, responsible supervision is particularly necessary in urban areas where too often the street becomes the preschooler's playground.

COGNITIVE DEVELOPMENT

In Piaget's theory of cognitive development, the period of time between ages 2 and 7 is referred to as one of **preoperational thought**. "Operational" in this sense refers to logical operations and/or connections with thoughts. Thus, the stage of preoperational thought is *the stage during which the child has not yet acquired the ability to perform logical operations on thoughts.* For example, on the basis of logic, a cup of liquid, whether placed in a long, tall glass, or a short, wide container, is still equal to a cup of liquid. But try telling that to a child who, in Piagetian terms, is preoperational. The child will inevitably conclude that the taller container contains more water—this even if the child has watched an adult pour exactly one cup of water into each container (see Figure 5–5). Preoperational thinking is also evident in the preschooler's inability to understand cause and effect, the concept of change over time, and other abstract concepts that require logical operations or connections between thoughts.

The world of the preschooler has often been termed "egocentric" because a child in this stage of development believes the world, and everything in it, exists much as he or she sees it. Unlike egocentrism as that term is used with reference to adults, egocentrism as applied to preoperational children refers to a typical stage of cognitive limitation, not a personality trait. The "me-only" view of the world of the preschooler is the only world they are cognitively capable of appreciating. And the egocentrism is indeed wide-ranging in scope. Preschoolers may attribute life to everything from a teddy bear to a doorknob. Their reasoning here is that since they are alive, everything else must be alive too. Because a particular food is viewed as mush, it could only be the case that everyone else in the entire world must also view this food as mush. Because they know what they are talking about when they speak in not-always-coherent sentences, they assume that everyone else knows what they are talking about. Two preschoolers may even carry out what from outward appearances seems like a conversation—until one listens carefully to what is being said. In actuality, the two children are engaging in what has been termed a *collective monologue*; each is talking without really listening or reacting to what the other child is saying. With growing maturity, the preschooler's me-only view will broaden to allow for the appreciation of another person's perspective.

preoperational thought
in Piaget's theory of cognitive development, the period of time between age 2 and age 7 in which the child has not yet acquired the ability to perform logical operations on thoughts.

FIGURE 5–5   AN EXPERIMENTAL DEMONSTRATION OF PREOPERATIONAL THINKING A classic demonstration of preoperational thinking begins with two glasses of liquid, in the exact same type of glass, and filled to the exact same amount. Pour the liquid from one of the glasses into a tall container, and pour the liquid from the other glass into a short container. Now ask the child which container contains more liquid. Up to the age of about 6 or 7 or so, most children will say that the taller one contains more liquid, simply because it now appears larger. The logical operation required to answer correctly is based on the ability to retain mentally or conserve the amount of something, despite its change in shape. For example, we know that two equal amounts of clay remain equal in quantity even after one is rolled into a ball, and the other is pounded flat. In Piagetian terms, we are able to retain mentally or conserve images of the amount of matter, despite subsequent images that may otherwise be viewed as contradictory. Numerous experiments with children in the Piagetian stage of preoperational thought have demonstrated Piaget's principle of conservation not only with respect to liquid, but also with respect to matter (as when clay in different shapes is used), number, volume, and area.

With the development of the cognitive ability to represent things mentally at about the age of 2 or so comes the ability to fantasize and pretend. Stated another way, imaging ability precedes the ability to imagine. In the beginning of the preschool years, for example, children may pretend that there is liquid in an empty cup which they can drink. As the child gets older, the cup of liquid may be complemented by an entire "meal" such as a cardboard steak or a plastic dessert. Towards the end of the preschool years, the saucer under the cup may be imaginally transformed into a flying saucer, a shield, a weapon, or something else. Preschool children may also create imaginary playmates with whom they talk, play, or otherwise interact. Especially when the ability to engage in symbolic thought is relatively new, children evidence great difficulty in distinguishing reality from fantasy. Dreams and nightmares can be as real as reality to the preschooler

FORMAL EDUCATION AND THE PRESCHOOLER

"Schooling for the preschooler" may sound like a contradiction in terms. Still, school-like preschool experiences, in the form of government-sponsored Head Start programs or privately sponsored Montessori school experiences, are very available. In a study that compared the effectiveness of different approaches to preschool education, Miller and Dyer (1976) concluded that programs that emphasize self-motivation and curiosity were preferable to programs that focused mainly on the acquisition of academic skills. Gains made by children in programs that focused on academic skills tended to be temporary, and nonexistent by second grade or so. By contrast, gains made by children in programs that sought to enhance the child's curiosity and motivation to learn seemed to last longer. The matter is by no means closed, however, and the topic of philosophy of education has remained a subject of lively debate.

EFFECTIVE PARENTING

"Effective parenting" sums up a collective group of skills that any parent or prospective parent would do well to acquire before the birth of his or her first child. The need for this skill does not end when the child becomes an adolescent, a young adult, or even a "grown" adult. Effective parenting must ideally be a lifelong skill for anyone who has a child. Here we focus briefly on early childhood, particularly the preschool years.

Ideas about what constitute effective parenting may change with time and place (LeVine & White, 1987), and ironclad rules of parenting are surprisingly few. The warm/cold dimension also appears to be of great importance in childrearing; as you might expect, an approach to parenting that is warmly affectionate has been found to be preferable to one that is generally cold, rejecting, or hostile (Greenberger & Goldberg, 1989). Parents who routinely demonstrate to their children how much they love, value, and prize them help to build their children's self-esteem.

Parents will find different focuses of parenting interest as their children go through different developmental stages. During the preschool years, and for some time subsequent to them, one focus of parents is discipline and limit-setting. For the school-aged child, focus might shift to promoting academic success in school and satisfying social relationships.

Anyone who has ever had the unenviable task of trying to explain to a preschooler why only one or two toys may be taken home from a toy store can readily understand the concept of limit-setting, or placing restraints on behavior. Preschoolers sometimes seem as if they are creatures of impulse, and it is difficult to say "no" to an impulsive person (of any age). In their efforts to teach children restraint and other values, parents inevitably find themselves in the position of having to set limits, administer some kind of discipline, or otherwise attempt to modify a child's behavior and thinking. The methods that a parent uses to accomplish these goals range from verbal persuasion to denial of privileges to corporal (physical) punishment. The consequences of the use of various methods in setting limits with the preschooler must be very carefully weighed. The preschool years are thought to be critically important in the child's formation of a self-concept, and traumatic blows to self-esteem may have harmful consequences. Preschool children perceive their parents as all-powerful and all-knowing. Consequently, criticism, contempt, and a lack of love from these all-powerful, all-knowing people may result in a self-concept complicated by feelings that one is blameworthy, contemptible, and/or unlovable.

On the basis of her observations of children and their parents in a nursery school setting, Diana Baumrind (1967) identified different general styles of parenting. Baumrind used *authoritarian, authoritative,* and *permissive* to categorize parenting as it was *generally* exhibited over time and across situations. The authoritarian parent is the one whose word is unquestionable law. If the child breaks the law, certain punishment results. Somewhat less dictatorial and more democratic in style is the authoritative parent. This type of parent also sets rules, but is not as absolute in enforcing them. Stated another way, the authoritative parent maintains a receptive ear to what the child has to say and stands willing to modify rules accordingly. Related differences between the authoritarian and the authoritative parent have to do with the warmth with which discipline is administered, and a willingness to explain why the rules are what they are. The permissive parent is the parent who always seems to be oblivious of what the child is doing. Rules and limits are kept to absolute basics, if that, and children are left in large part to do whatever they please. The categories need not be absolute; it is possible for the same parent to be authoritarian in one type of situation, authoritative in another, and permissive in yet another.

Baumrind (1967, 1971) and others have speculated about what children raised under these various types of parenting conditions would be like as they got older, although such speculation must be viewed with caution (Martin, 1975). In general, an authoritative style combined with love seems preferable to either the authoritarian or permissive approach. Although physical punishment or the threat of using it may be effective in the short run, explanation to the child of why an alternative way of behaving is preferable tends to be more effective in the long run. In asserting their rightful authority and power, parents ultimately walk a thin line between not doing enough to effect change and doing too much to the point of trauma and long-lasting emotional scars. This point will be revisited in the *Question of Values* feature in Chapter 7 (Coping) with a discussion of parental coping, assertiveness, and values.

The preschool years are also the time in which toilet training takes place—a significant life event according to Freud as well as other personality theorists. Some parents believe that when it comes to toilet training, the earlier the better. They may also harbor the belief that the speed with which the child becomes toilet trained is just another manifestation of the child's ability. Yet the ability of a child to become toilet trained depends in no small way on the maturity of the muscles used in toileting. From this biological perspective, to attempt to toilet-train a child before the child is physically ready may prove to be an exercise in futility for both parent and child. In infants, the muscles controlling bladder and bowel functions relax reflexively, allowing the body's waste products to escape. By about the age of 2 1/2 in girls, and slightly later in boys (usually 3 years of age or so), a child becomes physically ready to begin toilet training. Signs that an individual child is ready include behavioral indications that the child has an awareness of a "full" or "ready to go" sensation. For some children, this may mean a frenzied grasping of their genitals as they anticipate what will happen momentarily. Many different systems of toilet training have been proposed. In general, the use of praise and encouragement is preferable to criticism and blame. The use of models, including those found in specialized books and videos, may also prove helpful in the process of toilet training.

SOCIAL DEVELOPMENT

At a social level, preschoolers move from the self-centeredness of infancy to greater acknowledgment of, and interaction with, other people. Satisfaction, as well as dissatisfaction, can be derived not only from mother or father, but also from siblings and playmates. The development of language skills during the preschool period is intimately related to a growing sense of independence. Children now understand that they need not physically cling to a parent in order to know that the parent is "there for them." In addition, because the preschooler has developed the ability to represent parents (as well as other things) in thought, mental symbols survive partings. Departures therefore become less traumatic. The ability to be separated from parents or other caregivers for an extended period of time will be an important element in making the transition from the preschool-stage to the school-age stage of life.

THE MIDDLE CHILDHOOD YEARS

Different theorists have used different names to classify various developmental periods in childhood and adolescence. For our purposes, we will designate the developmental period between the ages of 7 and 12 as the *middle childhood* years. It is during these years that children's physical development continues to progress, and motor skills mature to adult-like capabilities. In fact, many children in this age group are already performing adult-like work in many cultures throughout the world. Social skills also progress at a brisk pace and it is not uncommon for children in middle childhood to be charged with the responsibility of baby-sitting younger siblings. Cognitively, there are many challenges to be met and conquered during this period of life, such as those related to reading, writing, and arithmetic. Unlike the preschool child, who seems consumed with self-experimentation and a passion for play, children in the middle childhood years evidence a greater ability to appreciate the perspective of others and can be more serious-minded about learning. The child's preoccupation with solitary play gives way to more social pursuits and a burgeoning interest in school-related tasks.

COGNITIVE DEVELOPMENT

Some time between the ages of 5 and 7, children acquire enhanced ability to concentrate, memorize, learn, and reason (White, 1965; Wright & Vlietstra, 1975). This time span is a transitional period between the stages of mental development that Piaget referred to as pre-operational thinking and *concrete operational thinking,* which begins at age 7 or so. In Piaget's theory, concrete operations refer to mental activities and logic that are applied with reference to specific, or "concrete" situations. Children capable of concrete operational thought may seem quite knowledgeable in many areas, but this knowledge usually is limited to things with which they have had direct experience, either personally or by observation. At the age of 12 or so, the child will begin to exhibit what Piaget calls *formal psychological thought.* The hallmark of this cognitive stage of development is the ability to generalize freely from specific experiences or things known to have a "concrete existence" (see Table 5–1). The first grade curriculum in most schools presumes that a child has reached the stage of concrete operations. Comprehension of concepts such as number, time, and space will be necessary for success in school.

Most of the types of Piagetian conservation tasks will be mastered during the middle childhood years. For example, by the age of 6 or 7, the child will be able to discern when

TABLE 5–1   WHY DEATH OCCURS, FROM THREE PIAGETIAN PERSPECTIVES

Psychologist Gerald Koocher (1973) asked children at three different Piagetian levels of development, "What makes things die?" As expected, the answers Koocher received became increasingly abstract (that is, less concrete) with children's increasing age. Answers from preoperational children tended to be least abstract, and in some cases, illogical. Children in the concrete operations group were able to generate specific causes of death, usually of a violent nature (such as those dramatized in the media). Most abstract were the responses of children in the stage of formal operations. These children were able to envision causes of death that did not have the concrete existence of, say, a gun.

Piagetian stage	Age span	Typical response
Sensorimotor	Birth–2 years of age	Not studied by Koocher
Preoperational stage	2–6 years of age	"Going swimming alone"
Concrete operations stage	7–12 years of age	"Guns"
Formal operations stage	12 years of age and older	"Worn out body"

two sets of beads having the same number of beads are arranged differently, the number of beads remains equivalent. Most significantly in the middle childhood years, children acquire the ability to think about their own thinking. This ability will affect their lives dramatically. In school, for example, they will be able to monitor their own learning, plan their own study strategies, and make corrections in their approaches—all provided they are motivated to do so, and have had appropriate guidance. Socially, they can plan how they are going to interact with different people—such as in telling a joke or asking a riddle—and anticipate the effect of their actions on others. Oral language skills of children in the middle childhood years may be impressive, but there are many linguistic subtleties that children have yet to learn (see Figure 5–6).

SOCIAL DEVELOPMENT

Being able to relate to other people effectively entails the ability to take another's perspective. Insights with respect to egocentrism and perspective-taking ability have been obtained through the study of how children play strategy games that involve anticipating an opponent's behavior. In a "hide the penny" game, for example, DeVries (1970) observed a developmental progression in the ability to develop strategies both in the role of "concealer" of the penny and in the role of "guesser." DeVries found that it was not until the age of 4 or 5 that children realized that the game was competitive. Even then, younger children in the role of concealer would hide the penny in predictable fashion, first in one hand and then the other. Children at this age are apparently unaware that the guesser could easily guess this pattern. Similarly, in their role as guesser, children in the 4 to 5 age range would also guess one hand and then the other, apparently assuming that the concealer would act just as they would. By the age of 5 or 6, children may begin to use a random concealment policy in a deliberate attempt to outwit the guesser. Interestingly, the child of this age in the role of guesser still tends to guess in predictable, alternating fashion. Such behavior is thought to be due to an apparent incapability of understanding that the concealer too is capable of using a random concealment strategy. It is not until the age of 6 or 7 that the child will begin to use an unpredictable strategy for both concealing and guessing. At that age, the child is presumed to have not only the ability to think about how someone else is thinking, but to understand that others may be thinking about how they are thinking as well.

As the child develops, the ability to take the perspective of another person will play a greater role in social relationships. Before the age of 10 or so, the choice of friends—perhaps more accurately labeled as playmates—is based more on convenience-related factors such as where the playmate lives or what time the playmate was picked up from an after-school center. Early on, parents have almost total influence over the choice of a child's playmates. Increasingly, parents have less and less influence over who their children socialize

FIGURE 5–6 COMMAND OF LANGUAGE IN MIDDLE CHILDHOOD Illustrating how arrangements of words, or syntax, can affect young children's understanding, Chomsky (1969) described an experiment wherein the experimenter asked children whether a blindfolded doll was "easy to see or hard to see." Seven-year-olds often interpreted this question as if they were being asked whether it was easy or hard for the doll to see. Just a year or so later, however, children tended to have a better knowledge of syntax and were able to understand the question in terms of the questioner's vantage point.

with. After the age of 10 or so, friendships may be based, at least in part, on the friends' perception of similar values. Friendships may also be based on the appeal of learning about the interesting lifestyle of a peer, even if that lifestyle is not consistent with one's own value system. Two children may become friends because one offers the other the opportunity to enjoy vicariously what is perceived to be a more exciting or rewarding lifestyle. A wild skateboarder, a child actor, a school athletic team member, a sexually precocious girl or boy, even a child involved in criminal activity may each be capable of providing a child with vicarious rewards. If parents disapprove of their child's association with one particular friend or "the wrong kind of crowd" in general, it will be important for them to keep lines of communication open about such matters. Discussion of what it is specifically that the child finds appealing about the association, and what it is specifically that the parent objects to may prove helpful (Steinberg, 1991).

Healthy middle childhood children may participate in various kinds of sports and play before, during, and after school. With their developing motor abilities and strength, children can handle baseball bats, footballs, skateboards, rollerblades, and other kinds of sports equipment that was simply too cumbersome for them in their preschool years. With their developing fine motor abilities, they have no problem with computer and video games that require great precision in finger movements, as well as sophisticated eye-hand coordination. Their developing cognitive and academic abilities make it possible for board games such as *Monopoly* and *Scrabble* to provide hours of fun.

MORAL DEVELOPMENT

moral development

the process by which people acquire and practice principles of right, good, proper, and/or ethical conduct.

Moral development refers to *the process by which people acquire and practice principles of right, good, proper, and/or ethical conduct.* References to instilling "family values" in children are typically references to moral development and the teaching of principles of right and wrong.

Research by Piaget (1965) and others (Damon, 1980; Kohlberg, 1976) has focused on the process by which children develop increasingly sophisticated moral judgment. A typical research study might entail presenting a subject with two different stories about two different children and then asking the subject to explain why one or the other child is nicer or naughtier. Careful interviewing of the subjects regarding their answers has led to a number of insights with respect to the development of moral reasoning. For example, in one set of stories, a child is said to have broken 16 cups by accident. Another child is said to have broken only 1 cup while doing something that he was not supposed to be doing. Six-year-olds judge the child who broke more cups to be naughtier. Similarly, 6-year-olds tend to judge a lie that greatly deviates from reality (such as "a goldfish the size of a dog") as worse than other lies older children might recognize as more damaging ("sugar is good for you"). Six-year-olds also judge stealing behavior by the criterion of amount stolen rather than the reason for the stealing. Thus, for example, if food is seen as more valuable than ribbon, a child who steals food to feed the homeless may be seen as worse in the eyes of 6-year-olds than one who steals a piece of ribbon for her hair. By contrast, 9-year-olds may see the ribbon stealing as worse because the child took the ribbon for herself, but the other child stole the food to feed the hungry (Piaget, 1965).

In general, Piaget observed a shift in the direction of more sophisticated moral reasoning and judgment between the ages of 5 and 10. By 10 years of age, children have shifted from making moral judgments primarily on the basis of physical factors such as damage or amount and come to use reasoning that takes into account people's intentions as well as other factors. Kohlberg (1969) devised an elaborate system of moral levels and stages that people presumably move through in sequential steps. Although useful in stimulating a great deal of thinking and theorizing, Kohlberg's system has been criticized on various grounds (Gilligan, 1977, 1982; Hoffman, 1984; Hogan, 1975; Rest, 1983; Sullivan, 1977; Trainer, 1977; Turiel, 1974; Wallach & Wallach, 1983). Ultimately, the morality of one's behavior is probably dependent upon a number of factors other than a knowledge or belief in what is right and wrong. Almost every day we hear news reports regarding corruption within the ranks of the criminal justice system and other people who cognitively know what they are doing is not right (see Figure 5–7). Knowing right from wrong—even when it seems possible *to* know right from wrong—is not enough. There are

FIGURE 5–7 MORAL DE-VELOPMENT IN ELECTED OFFICIALS After years of condemning corruption in Congress and calling for ethics and accountability in government, Representative Newt Gingrich of Georgia (shown here addressing government students in front of a mural in the school) overdrew his account at the House of Representatives bank 22 times. One overdraft included a check for $9,463 to the Internal Revenue Service. Before the overdraft was revealed, the House ethics panel had admonished Gingrich for his failure to report a 1986 real estate transaction involving the wife of a contributor to his campaign (Applebome, 1992). Over 300 former or present members of Congress overdrew their accounts at the House bank. What might Piaget or Kohlberg have to say about such behavior?

motivating forces, such as greed, that seem to work against moral development in children and adults.

TELEVISION AND THE CHILD

Most American homes are equipped with two or more televisions and one or more video-recorders. Most households subscribe to cable. Because television is so much a part of everyday life, it is easy to overlook what a potentially potent influence this electronic medium can be in the molding of thoughts and behavior.

It has been estimated that American children between the ages of 2 and 11 watch about 25 hours of television per week. On average, preschoolers watch slightly more than this amount—about 28 hours—while school-age children watch slightly less—about 23 hours (Nielsen, 1990). In general, children in homes where the mother's educational level is low tend to spend the greatest amount of time watching television (Bernard-Bonnin, 1992; Comstock et al., 1978). Cartoons tend to be most popular across all age groups while series, movies, and various kinds of children's shows, based on their specific content will capture different audiences by age. American children are exposed to an estimated 22,000 television commercials a year, many for high-fat, relatively non-nutritive products (Choate, 1975). Interesting in this context is the finding of a significant relationship between obesity and time spent watching television (Dietz & Gortmaker, 1985).

How children comprehend what they watch on television has been a topic of interest to researchers. As you might expect, very young children believe much of what they watch on television to be an accurate potrayal of reality. This fact can be painfully evident when a preschooler discovers that some food advertised on television tastes awful, or when some toy is not at all what it seemed to be in the commercials. For the young child, there may be little if any distinction made between the television program itself and the commercials. It is not until the age of 7 or so that children begin to understand the motivation of the characters they watch on television—and can begin to grasp the motivation of advertisers as well. It will not be until 5 or 6 years later that children will begin to understand more sophisticated aspects of television viewing such as the concept of plot.

The content of much of what is shown on television has been an ongoing source of concern for many parents. Acts of violence, the modeling of racist or sexist behavior, and the imparting of messages that one can change how one feels for the better simply by taking a drink or a drug are the kinds of communications many parents would prefer not to expose their children to. Yet programming that some parents may find offensive seems to be everywhere, even in the once more-innocent world of cartoons. Gone are the days when cartoon characters were by and large sweet and lovable. Popular cartoon characters today, such as the Simpsons, earn widespread appeal for *not* being sweet and lovable. Nickelodeon's *Ren and Stimpy Show* features Ren, a greedy chihuahua, and Stimpy, a pudgy cat who loves his cat litter. As one reviewer observed, "The show's humor stoops to seldom-seen cartoon levels. Ren sits in the bathtub and grins sheepishly when bubbles rise to the surface; walking through the house he steps on something squishy, which turns out to be one of Stimpy's hairballs" (Schoemer, 1992, p. C24).

Experts such as Jerome Singer of the Yale University Family Television Center advise concerned parents to view programs with their children and provide input about what is right, wrong, or questionable about what is depicted. Singer (1990; Singer et al., 1988) argues that family discussion and explanation of what is seen on television can help even preschoolers to better discriminate fantasy from reality. Such discussion may also be helpful in eliminating children's fear of victimization which may arise from watching televised violence. At its best, television entertains and/or teaches. It is a medium that has boundless potential for illustrating ways of thinking and behaving that will impact positively on society. Viewing with their parents can help make the experience of watching videos or televised programming maximally fulfilling for children (Collins et al., 1981; Grinberg-Levin, 1987; Salomon, 1977).

CHALLENGES TO HEALTH AND SAFETY

In the middle years, challenges to health may come in the form of poor nutrition (Johnson et al. 1992; Webb, 1992), allergic reactions to certain foods (Sampson et al., 1992), and the leading cause of death for this age group, accidents. Fatal or serious bicycle accidents (Friede et al., 1985) and skateboard accidents (Greensher & Mofenson, 1985) are usually preventable with proper training, caution, and the use of protective gear such as helmets. Many types of serious eye injuries, such as those sustained as the result of careless BB gun usage, could be prevented by means of proper training, caution, and the use of protective gear such as safety goggles (Grin et al., 1987). Pedestrian accidents, usually involving a child darting into the path of an oncoming car, claim the lives of about 2,000 children between the ages of 5 and 9 annually. To prevent such tragedies, parents are urged to begin teaching their children pedestrian safety early in the middle childhood years. However, even with such knowledge, it is questionable whether children even as old as 9 years will remember to look in all directions before attempting to cross a street (Rivara et al., 1989). It has therefore been recommended that adults not allow children to negotiate traffic unsupervised until the children reach about 9 or 10 years of age (Schickedanz et al., 1990).

Especially for members of minority communities in inner cities, the hazards to life and limb are not limited to activities like crossing the street, food allergies, or skateboard accidents. There is a risk of fatal abuse by caretakers (Christoffel, 1990), and a growing risk of violent death at the hands of a "friend" or acquaintance as the child moves into adolescence (Rodriguez, 1990). It has been estimated, for example, that the rate of death by homicide for African-American males between the ages of 10 and 14 is 4 times higher than that for white counterparts (National Center for Health Statistics, 1992). In an effort to address this growing problem, psychologists have been urged to focus research attention on African-American youngsters between the ages of 10 and 14 who live in urban areas, come from low-income homes, and have histories of aggression, victimization, or the witnessing of assaultive violence (Hammond & Yung, 1993; see *Cultural Close-Up* on page 133).

To be sure, middle childhood has its hazards. However, the greatest threats to the developing person's health and safety are yet to come in the period of adolescence. It has been estimated that as many as 25% of all adolescents in this country regularly engage in be-

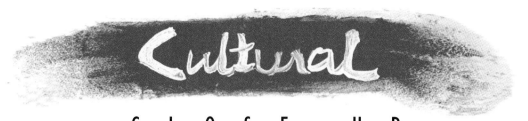

Assaultive Violence Among Young African-American and Hispanic-American Men

Writing in a recent issue of *American Psychologist*, Hammond and Yung (1993) made an impassioned plea for more psychologists to join in the search for a solution to an urgent public health problem: assaultive violence among young people, particularly young people from minority communities. In all ethnic groups between the ages of 12 and 19, males are almost twice as likely as females to be victims of violent crime (Christoffel, 1990). Nationwide, a leading cause of death among young African-American men, and to a somewhat lesser extent young Hispanic-American men, is assaultive violence committed by a "friend" or acquaintance (Christoffel, 1990; Fingerhut et al., 1992; Harlow, 1989, 1991; Smith et al., 1986; Sumner et al., 1986; Tardiff & Gross, 1986). Statistically, the young African-American victim of fatal violence is most likely to be killed at home by a gun, while young Hispanic-Americans are most likely to be killed in the street by a knife (CDC, 1991; Loya et al., 1986; Mercy et al., 1986; U.S. Department of Justice, 1991).

The most common cause of such assaults is retaliation or revenge for prior verbal or physical abuse, although jealousy conflicts and mere showing-off may also be factors (Wilson & Daly, 1985). Challenges to one's manhood (Roberts, 1990), economic frustration feeding aggressive impulses (Agnew, 1990; Parker, 1989), "free floating anger" (Ramey, 1980), and dysfunctional responding to racial discrimination (Oliver, 1989a, 1989b) are some of the explanations that have been offered as underlying mechanisms. A failing of many such explanations is that they do not satisfactorily account for why many minority community members who are

poor and presumably equally frustrated, angry, and disenfranchised do not engage in homicidal behavior (Bell, 1987; Hampton, 1986; Hawkins, 1990; Sampson, 1987).

Hammond and Yung's review of this public health problem suggests that it must be addressed in a number of different ways. Education regarding the problem and the relevant issues is extremely important. Many young African Americans seem to believe that most African Americans who die by gunshot are killed by the police (Price et al., 1991). They further believe that guns provide a sense of security and that a ban on them would be unfair to poor people. Subjects were generally unaware that African-American men are more likely than any other group of people to be killed by guns, most typically by other African-American men (FBI, 1987, 1989). Education regarding the role of alcohol and other drug abuse in predisposing people to violence, as well as to becoming murder victims (Lester, 1986; Mercy et al., 1986), is also necessary.

More psychological research will be needed to understand the role of cultural values in the commission of such aggression, as well as the role of ethnicity, socioeconomic status, and related factors. Hammond and Yung (1993) call for better tracking of nonfatal injuries from assault and more thorough reporting of accounts of such incidents from hospital emergency rooms. Research can also shed light on the utility of various types of public policy interventions being contemplated or already placed into effect, including metal detectors in schools and legislation enacting curfews and strong gun control measures. How can violence and aggression best

be curbed? What types of programs work best for members of various minority communities? Sound research addressed to such questions is a prerequisite to the development of effective interventions.

Currently, many different types of intervention programs are in operation. Programs involving mentors who promote positive racial identity and self-esteem have shown promise (Kunjufu, 1986; Wilson-Brewer & Jacklin, 1990; Wilson-Brewer et al., 1991), as have school-based programs involving training in social skills (Hammond, 1991; Hammond & Yung, 1991). Appropriate training for health professionals to conduct these types of programs as well as the research necessary to gauge their effectiveness will also be necessary (Hammond & Yung, 1993).

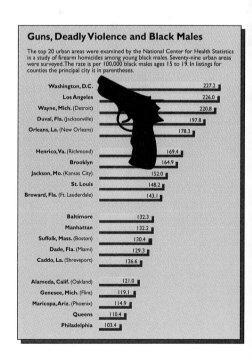

Guns, Deadly Violence and Black Males

The top 20 urban areas were examined by the National Center for Health Statistics in a study of firearm homicides among young black males. Seventy-nine urban areas were surveyed. The rate is per 100,000 black males ages 15 to 19. In listings for counties the principal city is in parentheses.

Washington, D.C.	227.2
Los Angeles	226.0
Wayne, Mich. (Detroit)	220.8
Duval, Fla. (Jacksonville)	197.8
Orleans, La. (New Orleans)	178.3
Henrico, Va. (Richmond)	169.4
Brooklyn	164.9
Jackson, Mo. (Kansas City)	152.0
St. Louis	148.2
Broward, Fla. (Ft. Lauderdale)	143.1
Baltimore	132.3
Manhattan	132.2
Suffolk, Mass. (Boston)	130.4
Dade, Fla. (Miami)	129.3
Caddo, La. (Shreveport)	126.6
Alameda, Calif. (Oakland)	121.0
Genesee, Mich. (Flint)	119.1
Maricopa, Ariz. (Phoenix)	114.9
Queens	110.4
Philadelphia	103.4

havior that is harmful to themselves or others. Another 25% engage in behavior that places them at more moderate level of risk (Camper, 1992). With adolescence comes feelings of invulnerability and immunity to danger—even in the face of many real and potentially fatal sources of danger including violence, drug abuse, and sexually transmitted diseases (Dryfoos, 1990; Hechinger, 1992; Quadrel et al., 1993). The period of the middle childhood years is an excellent time for parents to open—and keep open—lines of communication with their children on topics such as values, sex education, and the use of drugs. These lines of communication may prove invaluable to all parties concerned during the potentially turbulent times of adolescence.

ADOLESCENCE

Infancy may be characterized as a period of transition from the isolation of the womb to the physical, social, and other demands of the external world. The preschool period of development may be characterized as a time of play and exploration of one's own capabilities. The middle childhood period is a time for acquiring academic knowledge as well as worldliness in social and other spheres of life. And then comes adolescence—a period that we will somewhat arbitrarily define as beginning at **puberty** (a *time when hormonal and physiological changes are acting to transform a child into a person capable of reproduction*) and ending at the age of 18 or so. Adolescence may be thought of as a kind of crossroads between childhood and adulthood. It is a time when many individuals begin to grapple with a deceptively simple identity-related question: "Who am I?"

PHYSICAL DEVELOPMENT

At the onset of puberty, a biological alarm clock of sorts goes off and releases hormones that will produce a great deal of physical growth and other changes in a relatively short period of time. In females, more fat tissue will appear, with one bodily effect being the assumption of the more rounded look that is associated with women as distinguished from young girls. In males, more muscle tissue will appear. This fact, combined with increased heart and lung capacity as well as more social encouragement for physical strength training, makes most males physically stronger than females during adolescence. The term **primary sex characteristics** makes reference to the *somatic qualities necessary for reproduction*, such as ovulation and menstruation in females and sperm production and ejaculation in males. **Secondary sex characteristics** are *somatic qualities associated with sexual maturation but not necessary for reproduction,* such as pubic and underarm hair. Some secondary sex characteristics, such as facial hair and a deepening of the voice in males, and breast and hip development in females, typically occur in one and not the other sex. On average, primary sex characteristics appear in females at about age 12 or so and at about age 14 or so in males. Exactly when primary or secondary characteristics will actually appear is a highly individual matter, one based on many factors such as genes, general health, metabolism, and nutrition.

There is great potential for some aspects of the physical maturation process to be unsettling to the adolescent. The action of developing sweat glands may produce acne as well as a substance that creates body odor. Physical growth may not proceed at the exact same pace on both sides of the body, with the temporary result being a disproportionate appearance as well as muscular clumsiness. Imagine such changes occurring in your own body and you may better appreciate (or recall from your own experience) the plight of an individual trying to remain "cool" in the face of such physical and emotional upheaval. The good news is that at the same time as such dramatic changes, adolescents are able to develop their bodies to peak physical condition (see Figure 5–8).

COGNITIVE DEVELOPMENT

To think beyond what is and to dream about what could be—these are two of the mental processes that characterize adolescence. Compared to younger children, adolescents

puberty
a period of life marked by a number of hormonal and physiological changes beginning with the appearance of secondary sex characteristics and ending with the transformation of a child into an adult capable of reproduction.

primary sex characteristics
qualities necessary for reproduction, such as ovulation and menstruation in females and sperm production and ejaculation in males.

secondary sex characteristics
somatic qualities associated with sexual maturation but not necessary for reproduction, such as pubic and underarm hair.

 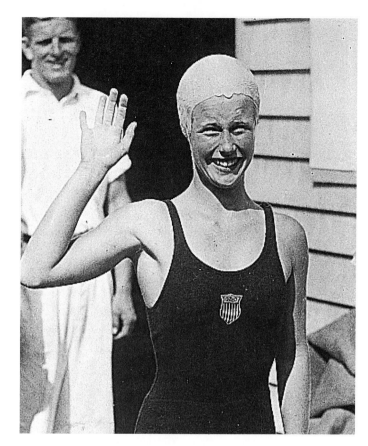

FIGURE 5–8 TWO GOLD MEDALISTS At the 1992 Summer Olympic games in Barcelona, Spain, Chinese competitor Fu Mingxia (left) won a gold medal for her performance in the women's 10-meter platform diving event. What makes this fact noteworthy is that she was just 13 years old and the second-youngest Olympic competitor ever to win a gold medal. The youngest was an American 13-year-old named Marjorie Gestring (right), younger by weeks than Fu, who won the women's diving competition at the 1936 games in Berlin. That many Olympic competitors are in their teens or 20s rather than their 30s or older, is rather telling evidence of the great physical capability and potential that exists during adolescence and early adulthood. After she won her gold medal in 1992, Fu Mingxia (13 years, 11 months) said through an interpreter that she likes Madonna, ice cream, and reading (Eskenazi, 1992).

are more capable of, and more prone to, speculation, hypothesizing, and fantasizing about possibilities. In Piagetian terms, it is during adolescence that the stage of formal operational thought is attained. Adolescents understand logic better than they have ever before in their lives and are even capable of recognizing illogical behavior in themselves (Flavell, 1977).

Adolescents move from the security of the elementary school and to a junior high school or middle school and a world of many varied courses such as Conversational Spanish, Introduction to the Computer, Business Law, and Journalism, to name but a few. About 12.5% of all adolescents nationwide will drop out before finishing high school (Youth Indicators, 1988). Teenage pregnancy is a major reason behind dropping out, even though school systems today no longer encourage dropping out as a consequence of pregnancy. Some of the correlates of dropping out of school include the educational level attained by parents, socioeconomic status, family income level, level of stress within the family, and students' in-school experiences (Entwisle & Alexander, 1990; Nelson, 1988). In general, the higher the parents' educational level and the higher the family socioeconomic status and income level, the better the chance that the adolescent will not drop out of school. Children of educated parents not only tend to have role models to emulate, but helpful and concerned tutors. They have parents who read to them when they were younger and evidenced a willingness to devote whatever time was necessary to help them with their homework and other school-related duties. Adolescents from higher socioeconomic status homes are not forced to leave school out of economic necessity. They are not pressured to make a choice between forestalling income by staying in school and getting a job and bringing home a full-time salary (however meager). The size of a school and/or the social climate within a school may also play some role in whether students tend to drop out or not. Some research suggests that the more participation in school activities, the less likelihood of dropping out (Pittman & Haughwout, 1987). Programs designed to deal with the dropout problem will optimally address both the academic and personal needs of adolescents who are contemplating dropping out or who have already dropped out. Work-study programs may also lessen dropout rates (Bloch, 1989).

SOCIAL DEVELOPMENT

A key source of input for adolescents in their struggle to establish an identity for themselves is how their peers relate to them. "Am I a nerd? An athlete? Am I desirable sexually? Am I intelligent?" These are the kinds of questions on which adolescents can get some subtle and not-so-subtle feedback from their peers. Such feedback may come in school, school-related activities, at after-school job sites, or at after-school meeting spots such as the local shopping mall (see Figure 5–9). The influence of the culture and the social environment that the adolescent is exposed to has increasingly been viewed as a focus of research interest for mental health professionals (see for example, Eccles et al., 1993; Jessor, 1992, 1993).

While striving for their own sense of identity, adolescents find support from peers who are going through the same process. This support is invaluable and may come in the form of long hours of "hanging out" with friends, as well as of numerous and lengthy telephone calls. A feeling of belonging and acceptance from peers is extremely important. Adolescents typically have unwritten dress, appearance, and even language codes that must be conformed to if one is to be accepted into a group. In some circles, for example, extremes such as spiked, completely shaven, or wildly multi-colored hair may be part of the code.

Conformity in behavior is another factor that has a bonding effect on groups of adolescents (as well as on adults). One type of group behavior, referred to as **prosocial** in nature, is *approved of by society and deemed to be beneficial in nature*. Participation in organized sports or a charity car wash are examples of prosocial behavior. By contrast, **antisocial** behavior is *disapproved of by society and/or not sanctioned by law*, usually because it is harmful to oneself, others, or animals. Some examples of antisocial behavior by adolescents include truancy, drug abuse, crimes, sexually irresponsible behavior, and cruelty to animals. Gangs are groups of individuals who socialize together and usually engage in antisocial behavior

prosocial

approved by society and deemed to be beneficial in nature.

antisocial

disapproved of by society and/or not sanctioned by law.

FIGURE 5–9 MEETING AT THE MALL In bygone eras, it was a malt shop, a diner, a disco. Today, the place where many adolescents congregate for "something to do when there is nothing else to do" (Tako, 1992) is a regional shopping mall. As Glaberson (1992) observed: "The food court has seen its loves and heartbreaks. It has become the venue for timeless experiments: drugs and liquor can be had for a price. Cars in the mall parking garage are as popular for intimate moments as they have always been. And shoplifting can be a badge of honor for those in search of a rebellious image" (p. A31).

in groups. In recent decades, the nature of adolescent gangs in the United States has changed rather dramatically for the worse. In a bygone era, gang members were groups of neighborhood youths who banded together to protect their "turf." In those days, few gang members owned or carried firearms, "rumbles" were with rival gang members, and deadly force against members of the public, the police, and innocent bystanders was rare. Today, youth gangs tend to be heavily armed and oriented towards making money through criminal activity. They may have "chapters" in different cities and exhibit wanton disregard for the lives of rival gang members, innocent bystanders, and the police.

FAMILY TIES

Depending upon the nature of the child-parent relationship that has been built up over the years, an adolescent may either turn towards or away from parents (or other caregivers) for guidance and support. Children who have been raised in a relatively democratic family environment have been found to be most likely to react positively to the advice of their parents (Kelly & Goodwin, 1983). Children from families where there has been little or dysfunctional communication and little or no emotional expressiveness and support are especially at risk for a troubled adolescence (Leflore, 1988). Abused or neglected adolescents are at risk for becoming some of the approximately 1.5 million people under the age of 18 who run away from home annually in this country (Farber, 1987; Morrow & Sorell, 1989). The average age of adolescent runaways is 15. About 25% of all runaways have a history of at least one suicide attempt. Runaway adolescents tend to be depressed, insecure, and impulsive, and most exhibit emotional and/or behavioral problems (Feitel et al., 1992). Most run away with less than a dollar in their pockets, and wind up staying with a friend, a relative, or at a shelter before going back home. Almost all will run away more than once. Because so many runaways have been found to be abused at home (Farber et al., 1984; Feitel et al., 1992), it has been suggested that society focus greater attention on running away as a symptom of a problem, rather than as the problem itself.

A TIME OF RISK

Surviving adolescence has become a challenge unto itself because the risk of death or serious injury from violence, accidents, and other causes is high. Let's take a closer look at some of the risks that contemporary adolescents face.

DRUG ABUSE

The temptations that exist for children and adolescents to experiment with drugs can be strong. Pressure to be part of the group by indulging in drug use, the promise of uniquely pleasing physical and/or mental sensations, the desire to prove to oneself or others that one is grown-up and can act like grown-ups who abuse drugs, and the desire to rebel against parents or other authority figures are a few of the factors that may induce a child or adolescent to experiment with drugs. The wide availability of drugs, including the fact that drugs may be bought and sold in or near most schools (see *A Question of Values*), ensures that precious few (if any) adolescents will make it through high school without having been urged by some peer to try some illegal drug.

Alcohol as well as other drugs may be used with the objective of lessening self-consciousness, reducing stress, or making socializing easier. It has been estimated that more than half of all high school seniors become drunk once a month (Leary, 1990). The leading cause of death in teenagers is alcohol-related accidents. Another type of drug used by adolescents, disproportionately by male adolescents, are synthetic male hormones otherwise known as anabolic steroids. Steroids are used to help "pump up" the body with massive muscles (*anabolic* means *building up*) and help to make boys look more like the idealized male images they see in muscle magazines and other media. Steroid use can help them to achieve their objectives, but not without exacting a heavy toll. Steroids' numerous dangerous side effects include the development of tumors of the liver, hardening of the arteries, the wasting away of the testes, and the development of male secondary sexual characteristics such as body and facial hair in females (Committee on Sports Medicine, 1989).

A QUESTION OF  Values

Cameras in the Schools

An English teacher in New Hampshire's Mascenic Regional High School entered the boys' rest room and found it enveloped in marijuana smoke. The police chief had heard that drugs were being stored behind and dealt from the paneling in that rest room and he asked permission of the school principal to place a hidden video camera there to catch the perpetrators in the act of dealing drugs. The principal consented, and for a little less than two weeks, the camera secretly recorded all that went on.

When a father was informed about the recorded actions of his son, his response was to complain to a local television station about the secret videotaping. The American Civil Liberties Union argued that the school had no legal right to videotape in the rest room with a hidden camera, and that

such videotaping amounted to a violation of the students' rights under the Fourth Amendment, which protects citizens from unreasonable search and seizure. The school responded that it had the right to use such means for the greater welfare of all the students. Further, as the chief of the Criminal Justice Bureau for the New Hampshire Attorney General's office pointed out, it was unclear whether a warrant would be necessary to place the camera because students had no "reasonable expectation of privacy" when entering the rest room anyway; other students in the rest room could see whatever the camera saw.

In general, there was overwhelming support among the students and the community for the action of the principal and the police. Although only one juvenile was charged with vandalism

and no pushers were arrested, the incidence of vandalism and drug use dramatically dropped as a result of the action.

How you see this situation—whether you are more sympathetic to the American Civil Liberties Union's position or to that of the police and the school—amounts to a question of values. Do you value your right to privacy and your right not to have government representatives secretly observing your behavior, or your right to have a drug-free rest room? If individual rights to privacy are to be infringed upon, who should make that decision? What constitutes sufficient ground for such an infringement to be made? What are your thoughts on these issues?

Drug abuse carries with it a strong potential for negatively impacting on the adolescent's life in physical as well as psychological ways. Physically, there is the risk of death or severe impairment. This risk need not result from the drug itself, but from consequences of the drug. For example, drinking beer and smoking marijuana do not ordinarily cause death. However, beer drinking and marijuana smoking have been linked to motor vehicle and other accidents. Thousands of teenagers are killed or seriously incapacitated in drug-related incidents annually (Blum, 1987). Many more suffer other negative consequences associated with drug abuse including physical or psychological dependency on the drug(s), memory loss, impaired judgment, loss of friendships, failed dating relationships or marriage, and job instability (Kandel et al., 1986; Newcomb & Bentler, 1988, 1989). Unfortunately, most adolescents enjoy a false sense of invincibility and maintain a "but-that-can't-happen-to-me" attitude when it comes to the prospect of drug-related tragedy. Issues related to the identification, treatment, and prevention of drug abuse and related problems may be viewed from several different perspectives (Takanishi, 1993).

VIOLENCE

A clipping from a New York newspaper describes how, in the case of adolescents, "looks can kill":

Mean looks exchanged on a sidewalk in the Bronx late Friday night escalated into gunshots only minutes later in a subway station, leaving one teenager dead and another wounded, the transit police said. (Rabinovitz, 1992)

Unfortunately, such violence among adolescents resulting in death by gunshot is not atypical. It has been estimated that every school day, about 135,000 students bring guns to school—a fact that has compelled many schools to install metal detectors at their entrances (Leary, 1992a). Gunshot wounds were second only to automobile accidents as the leading cause of death in all of this country's 15- to 19-year-olds (Hilts, 1992b). Homicide is the leading cause of death for blacks between the ages of 15 and 19 (Leary, 1992a). In the light of such shocking statistics, George Lundberg (1992), editor of the *Journal of the American Medical Association,* perceived a public health emergency, and "a grotesque picture of a society steeped in violence, especially by firearms, with such ubiquity and prevalence as to be seemingly accepted as inevitable."

In addition to death by firearms, adolescents may face the risk of death or injury from abuse at home or in social relationships. It has been estimated that before they graduate from high school, about one in every eight students will be involved in an incident of violence that arises from dating (Gardner, 1991). According to Leonardo Marano (1992), coordinator of a program to treat adolescent batterers, males who batter have been socially indoctrinated to believe that the man's role in a relationship is to be tough, macho, and in control. Therapy for batterers may entail exposing them to, and helping them to accept, a more realistic male role in a relationship. One way of helping to prevent teenage date violence is to teach teenagers about it in the high school curriculum (Braham, 1992).

SUICIDE

Suicide is the third leading cause of death for the 15 to 19 year-old age group (Garland & Zigler, 1993). The suicide rate among adolescents is approximately double what it was in 1968 and roughly 10% of adolescent males and 20% of adolescent females have attempted suicide (Leary, 1990). The actual incidence of suicide may be higher than official reports indicate because moral and other stigmas associated with suicide often cause suicides to go unreported (Jobes et al., 1987).

How can a potentially suicidal adolescent be identified? In fact, this is no easy task; even pediatricians have a poor record in this area (Fine et al., 1986; Goldberg et al., 1982; Hodgman & Roberts, 1982; Slap et al., 1992). Part of the problem is that complaints that suicidal adolescents typically voice are vague and nonspecific. In one study of adolescents who attempted suicide in Finland, it was concluded that adolescents who "were able to point out some definite difficulties that create a dead-end life situation seemed to have a smaller risk of completed suicide or violent death than those whose reasons for a suicide attempt remained unclear" (Kotila, 1992, p. 416). In that same study, it was found that adolescents who ingested alcohol and then exhibited suicidal thoughts and actions were at increased risk of a violent death by means other than suicide. Merely ingesting alcohol as part of a suicide attempt was not found to influence the outcome (Kotila, 1992).

In addition to what may seem like vague complaints about life in general, a suicidal child or adolescent may show signs of depression, including changes in eating, sleeping, or recreational habits, a decrease in time devoted to school work, an increase in difficulty concentrating, and signs of irritability, withdrawal, or fatigue. The suicidal adolescent may be living in a home where there is great marital discord, physical or emotional abuse, or where a parent or sibling has recently died. Other circumstances that can trigger children to contemplate suicide seriously include frustration with boyfriends or girlfriends, the loss of a close friend, or being placed in what the adolescent perceives to be a horribly humiliating situation.

Like the adult contemplating suicide, adolescents actively planning their own suicide may show signs of "getting the house in order." Quite literally, such individuals may clean their rooms, and, in this process, find prized possessions which, to the surprise of friends, are bestowed on them as unexpected gifts. Cherished pets may be given away during this housekeeping stage. The foreboding significance of such housecleaning may elude parents since many adolescents who engage in such behavior do it with confidence and reassurance to those around them: They are at peace with themselves having made this final solution.

Children, adolescents, or adults who display such subtle signs of or who openly express suicidal thoughts or plans must be seen by a mental health professional competent to deal with such problems. The need for treatment is especially urgent for people who have had a prior history of suicide attempts because it is likely they will act once more on their threats or musings. It is a myth that "people who talk about committing suicide never do it." In fact, the reverse is true. It must be conveyed to anyone who talks or muses about suicide that their words are being taken seriously. In those instances in which medical professionals deem individuals to be a danger to themselves, the suicidal individual may have to be forcibly confined in a mental hospital for treatment.

SEXUALLY TRANSMITTED DISEASES

Due perhaps to factors such as better nutrition and general health, puberty occurs at an earlier age on average than it did in years past. People tend to marry at an older age than they used to. The influence and control once exercised by the nuclear family has for the most part eroded, leaving children and adolescents with more autonomy than they have ever had, but not necessarily any better judgment. Children, adolescents, and adults are socially permitted—even encouraged—to behave in some ways that are very similar. For example, people from 8 months to 80 years of age can wear designer jeans, gym shoes, and jogging outfits without eliciting a second look. Beyond clothing styles, society's greater permissiveness seems also to have been extended to certain behavior patterns such as dating. Dating tends to begin at a younger age than it did in the past, and to go on longer than it customarily did as well. Peer pressure, sometimes even encouragement from parents, can push children as young as 9 or 10 into dating, although many parents refuse to go along with such proposals (Lawson, 1990). Compound these factors with strong, burgeoning biological urges and a bombardment of sex-related entertainment and advertising in the media, and it will probably come as no surprise that today's adolescents tend to be more sexually active than their predecessors (Sonestein, 1991). This fact and the widespread existence of various kinds of sexually transmitted disease (STD), including fatal diseases such as acquired immunodeficiency syndrome (AIDS), make for an unhappy reality for contemporary adolescents (CDC, 1992).

Approximately 1 million teenagers become pregnant in this country annually—a rate that approaches 1 pregnancy for every 10 female adolescents. About 2.5 million teenagers annually contract a sexually transmitted disease such as syphilis, gonorrhea, chlamydia, or AIDS. Sexually transmitted diseases will be discussed in greater detail in Chapter 12. According to the Centers for Disease Control, one in five high school students is at risk for contracting the AIDS virus. The results of a 1990 nationwide survey conducted with more than 11,000 students suggest that "a substantial proportion of students engage in behaviors that place them at risk" ("Teen-Agers and AIDS," 1992). As compared to 21% of the white males, 60% of the black males polled reported having had 4 or more sex partners—a finding that places black adolescent males at very high risk for contracting AIDS as well as other sexually transmitted diseases. Fewer than half of the sexually active participants in the study reported that they had protected themselves against AIDS and other sexually transmitted diseases. Other research, such as a study conducted with healthy, inner-city heterosexual adolescents, has suggested that even adolescents knowledgeable about AIDS engaged in high-risk sexual behavior (Keller et al., 1991). These researchers also found that occasional alcohol and marijuana use were strong predictors of high risk behavior; the occasional users were more apt than the nonusers to engage in high-risk sexual behavior.

Herbert Friedman, chief of the Adolescent Health division of the World Health Organization's Family Health Division, reminds us that "Sexuality is a fundamental quality of human life, important for health, happiness, individual development, and indeed for the preservation of the human race" (1992, p. 345). Yet Friedman is also keenly concerned about, and actively seeking solutions to, the adolescent health crisis that now exists. He believes that the key to the crisis is to involve adolescents in the process of modifying behavior (World Health Organization, 1986) and he describes young people as "the greatest resource for their own health. They are capable of planning, research, training, information provision, and establishing referral networks and evaluation, given appropriate technical help" (1992, p. 349).

ADULTHOOD

From birth, human beings go through a series of transitions that have been referred to variously as "stages" (Piaget & Inhelder, 1969), "passages" (Sheehy, 1976), and "seasons" (Levenson et al., 1978). These and other such terms typically define a specific time period (such as adolescence) with physical, mental, behavioral, or other characteristics that are presumed to characterize that period. Knowledge of the stages that people typically progress through can also be extremely helpful in identifying individuals who are exceptional, that is, advanced or backward with respect to average development. Yet a strong word of caution is also in order regarding the notion of stages in psychological development: Stages in human development are seldom absolute. There are many exceptions to the progression outlined in a typical stage-based developmental description; some people inevitably fall between the cracks. When, for example, does a child become an adult?

BECOMING AN ADULT

Tribal rites in primitive countries as well as religious traditions still followed in America today (such as Jewish *bar* or *bat mitzvahs* at the age of 13) once served as dividing lines between boyhood and manhood and girlhood and womanhood. In contemporary society, however, few would agree that a child becomes an adult at the age of 13 or any other arbitrary number of years.

One way of thinking about a distinction between adolescence and adulthood has to do with Erik Erikson's (1968) concept of **identity**—in this sense, *a consistency in one's self-image, a recognized role in society, and a commitment to various ideals* (Westen, 1985). According to this view, adolescence can be seen as a time of trying on different kinds of identities and seeing how they fit. The bridge from adolescence to adulthood is crossed when an individual becomes comfortable with a particular adult identity and in behavior, thought, and feeling commits to that identity. Of course, not everyone crosses the bridge at the same time, and, by Erikson's estimation, some people never do. Some people place an indefinite moratorium, or pause, on developing an identity for themselves. That is, they keep trying on different identities long past the time that they are chronologically in their adolescent years (Marcia, 1966). For other people, the failure to assume an adult identity is hardly as purposeful. These people simply drift aimlessly through life, exhibiting what Erikson referred to as *identity diffusion,* or no particular commitment to life goals or values and little motivation to develop any such commitment. At some point these individuals may develop adult identities, although they may well be maladaptive ones (such as criminal identities). Erikson also identified a maladaptive behavior pattern at the other end of the spectrum: a willingness to assume an identity, on the basis of others' opinions rather than of one's own well thought-out actions. Of course, whether or not an individual ever actually assumes an adult identity, the mere passage of time and the physical symptoms of aging will change adolescents to adults—at least in physical terms.

identity
according to Erik Erikson, a consistency in one's self-image, a recognized role in society, and a commitmen t to various ideals.

THE AGING PROCESS

After accepting an Oscar for best supporting actor during the *Academy Awards Show* in 1992, Jack Palance, then 72 years old, surprised the audience by performing numerous one-handed push-ups. The impromptu calisthenics was Palance's way of convincing anyone watching that getting older did not necessarily entail any slowing down or loss of strength (see Figure 5–10). Some aspects of aging (graying, thinning, or balding hair, wrin-

FIGURE 5–10   NO SLOWING DOWN HERE After the 72-year-old Jack Palance delighted millions of viewers with his one-handed push-ups, Billy Crystal, in a running gag, updated Palance's purported activities throughout the *Academy Awards* telecast, announcing that "Jack Palance is on the stairmaster," and "Jack Palance is bungee jumping."

kles, and so forth) are matters of genetics; nothing can be done about them. There are, however, many things adults can do to stave off some of the other typical accompaniments of age.

On average, Americans gain about half a pound in body weight each year beginning at age 30. Many people mistakenly attribute this weight gain to a slowed metabolism. Metabolism does slow by 2 to 3% on average for every 10 years after the age of 20. However, experts believe that the weight gain that occurs with advancing age is more attributable to a voluntary decrease in activity rather than to an involuntary decrease in metabolism. Progressive increases in weight can effectively be countered with increased exercise alone. Walking as little as half a mile a day will be of great value to some people. Other people may profit even more from an exercise program combined with relatively small reductions in average daily caloric intake.

People do slow down as they get older. Contributing factors to this slow-down include a decrease in the heart's pumping efficiency, a decrease in the lung's breathing capacity, and decreases in bone and muscle mass. In fact, the heart's pumping efficiency may drop by as much as one third during the period between age 30 and age 70. Similarly, the lungs may lose between one third and one half of their air capacity between these ages. Bone mass loss begins to occur at about age 40 or so. As much as 30 to 40% of muscle mass may be lost between the ages of 30 and 70. The good news is that all these losses are not inevitable; they can be slowed to various degrees by a program of regular and balanced exercise. Exercise, particularly weight training, can help strengthen bones and muscles, thus delaying loss in their mass. A regular program of physical exercise also helps to retard the loss of heart and lung efficiency over time. Also, if not used, connective tissue may shorten, thus producing feelings of stiffness and inflexibility. Regular use of connective tissue through exercise strengthens it, thus promoting flexibility.

Perhaps one key but seldom discussed reason people slow down is because they believe it is age-appropriate or role-appropriate to do so. They believe that because they are older, certain of their body parts may be worn out and not as good as they used to be. In fact, on many older Americans those body parts may simply be "rusted out" for lack of sufficient use—and just waiting for a little "elbow grease."

According to many stage theories, the final stage in human life is one that is typically referred to in terms such as "death and dying." In that stage, the adjustive challenge lies in confronting one's mortality. Yet it is very optimistic to believe that only people of advanced years must deal with the prospect of their own deaths. Annually, millions of young people die or become severely disabled as a result of disease, drugs, accidents, starvation, acts of war, terrorism, crime, or other aggression. Thus, although we consider the topic of death and dying below, we do so with the reminder that death and dying are unfortunately not activities reserved only for the old.

CONFRONTING MORTALITY

The French actor and showman Maurice Chevalier once said that he preferred old age to the alternative—the alternative being not living to reach old age. Equally relevant to the topics of aging and death is George Burns's observation that the best thing about being 90 years old is the lack of peer pressure. His quip was a not-so-subtle reference to the fact that as you get on in years, you are likely to live through the death of many of your peers and loved ones.

Despite a large (Cohen, 1976a, 1976b) and ever-growing (Feifel, 1990) literature on death and dying in the context of mental health, most of us find death and dying a subject very difficult to deal with. Moreover, the definitive guide on how mentally and socially to deal with one's own mortality, a dying loved one, or the death of a loved one, will probably never be written. Such matters defy simple or ready explanation. The research of Elizabeth Kübler-Ross (1969) involving dying patients, for example, had a most beneficial influence on helping to sensitize caregivers, family members, and others to the dying person's mental processes and anguish.[3] What is lacking from such works, however, are the magically consoling words you can say to a dying person, or to that person's family, or to yourself about death. Depending on one's depth of religious belief, one might find those words either in the Bible or in the words of a cleric. For most Americans, however, the harsh reality is that there are no magically consoling words. Perhaps the best that one can do is to convey one's love, caring, and feelings of loss as honestly as they have ever been communicated. Such communications may seem woefully inadequate under the circumstances, but if they are genuine and the very best you have to give, no one could ask more from you. You cannot demand more of yourself.

Ultimately, death must be viewed as a part of life; everything that has ever lived, or will live, will one day die. Thinking about this unpleasant reality of life does not necessarily make the prospect of death any more pleasant or acceptable. Still, the reality that death is a natural part of life may be useful in some way, however small, if it helps keep us on track and productive during the relatively brief time we have on Earth. In this context, consider the thoughts of Erik Erikson. Erikson (1963) viewed the period of late adulthood, a period that covers from age 60 onward, as a time of reflection on how meaningful and how full life has been. Life for most of us will contain assorted triumphs and failures. For Erikson, what is key to adjustment in this later period of life is how people view their lives on balance: Was it full? Empty? Meaningful? Meaningless?

For some people, an event or series of events that happened in the past, perhaps in childhood, has in essence acted as a kind of spoiler when it comes to future happiness. Many popular self-help books have touched on a related theme in their discussions of a construct they refer to as the "inner child." In this context, you may wish to try the *Self-Assessment* exercise that follows. You may find that, in a sense, "The child is the parent of the parent."

Just as it may be beneficial to give at least a passing thought to retirement at an early stage in one's work life, so it may be wise to anticipate the day when you will be looking back on your life—this despite the fact that you probably have your whole life in front of you at this moment. In your later years, what would you like to be able to say about your life? How consistent with this statement about your life in retrospect are your plans for the future? What can you do now to help insure that whatever it is you wish subsequently to say about your life becomes a reality?

[3]According to Kübler-Ross (1969) most dying people pass through stages of denial, anger, bargaining (characterized by thoughts and prayers such as, "If I am allowed to live, I will be more religious"), depression, and acceptance. Some researchers have disagreed about the order and occurrence of these stages, and others have proposed other stages.

SELF-ASSESSMENT

The Elusive "Inner Child"

With titles such as *Your Inner Child of the Past* (Missildine, 1983), *The Radiant Child* (Armstrong, 1985), *Self-Parenting* (Pollard, 1987), *Growing Up Again* (Clarke & Dawson, 1989), *Healing Your Aloneness: Finding Love and Wholeness Through Your Inner Child* (Chopich & Paul, 1990), and *Home Coming: Reclaiming and Championing Your Inner Child* (Bradshaw, 1990), a number of self-help books have promoted the notion that every adult has an "inner child" that can affect adult thinking, behavior, and emotion. A quick survey of such books suggests that they vary widely in scholarship and the extent to which they are grounded in psychology. Each of the books has its own definition of what "inner child" means, no two of the books define this construct in the same way, and the same author may use the term in wildly variant ways in the same book. The inner child is loosely linked by some authors to the Freudian concept of id, the Freudian concept of ego, Erik Erikson's theory of developmental stages, Carl Rogers's concept of self, and Albert Ellis's description of irrational beliefs. Additionally, the inner child is variously equated with inner power, inner vulnerability, inner control, inner lack of control, naiveté about the world, wisdom about the world, rigidity, creativity, being a leader, being a follower, a cure for aloneness, and a cure for social relationships. The adult may or may not be connected to the inner child depending upon which self-help book you read. The inner child may itself be "connected" to other constructs such as those labeled "toxic guilt" and "toxic shame" by Bradshaw (1990). While Namka (1989) seems content to focus on "inner wisdom," Borysenko (1990) variously refers to constructs such as the "healing inner child," the "internal Self" and the "inner self-helper" (with the definitional boundaries between such terms being slim) to help explain her views.

Of what value is the help offered in the self-help books that deal with the inner child? If one finds observations like, "It is when we love ourselves that our hearts fill up and the love overflows to others" (Chopich & Paul, 1990) helpful, then such books can be of great value. My own suspicion is that readers largely ignore popular book writers' fluctuating definitions of inner child and simply use that very vague construct to address some aspect of their personal histories about which they have doubts, insecurities, or other negative feelings. Most everyone has such feelings about one or another aspect of his or her past. And much as a child grows and moves on, most of us would like to grow and move on from that lingering doubt or insecurity.

Take a moment now to think about some significant incident from your own childhood. How did it affect you as a child? How might it still be affecting you as an adult? What types of thoughts, feelings, or behavior will help you grow and move on from any negative residue of this childhood occurrence?

SUMMARY

INFANCY The process of adjustment begins at conception; what the mother consumes, even her state of mind, may affect the child. Infancy is typically defined as the period between birth and 2 years of age. During this period, the child's motor, cognitive, emotional, and social skills will begin to develop.

THE PRESCHOOL YEARS During the years from age 2 to age 6, the child's *gross motor skills* (abilities involving large muscle movements) develop rapidly, while *fine motor skills* (abilities involving small muscle movements) will require some more time to develop. Burgeoning cognitive abilities and a growing capacity for symbolic thought blossom into curiosity, active exploration, and the joy of discovery.

THE MIDDLE CHILDHOOD YEARS By the age of 7, children in many different cultures are already performing adult-type functions such as baby-sitting or crop-gathering. It is also during these years that one's cognitive potential is typically developed through formal training in skills such as reading, writing, and arithmetic. The child in the middle years evidences a greater ability to take the perspective of another person, and this ability plays a greater role in social relations as well. Complementing such developing social skills is *moral development* or the process by which children acquire and practice principles of right, good, proper, and/or ethical conduct. Children acquire such principles, sometimes collectively referred to in the phrase "family values," from many sources, including parents, teachers, peers, and books and other media.

ADOLESCENCE Concern about a child's health and safety acquires new meaning for caregivers as the child moves into the teenage years. Adolescent feelings of invulnerability combined with various kinds of high-risk behavior, including high-risk sexual behavior, may jeopardize the health and well-being of people in this age group. Physically, adolescents must cope with rapid changes in their bodies and external appearance. Socially, they tend to look to peers rather than parents or others for support. Cognitively, they are more capable than ever before to think beyond what is and to contemplate what might be.

ADULTHOOD At one time, tribal rites and religious traditions provided unambiguous guidelines for who was a child and who was an adult in a particular society. Such clear guidelines are lacking in contemporary culture. Erik Erikson's notion of *identity* (a consistency in one's self-image, a recognized role in society, and a commitment to various ideals) is one construct of value in identifying when the bridge from adolescence to adulthood has been crossed. "Death and dying" is the final stage of life in many stage theories, although the aged have no monopoly on dying.

Stress

O U T L I N E

No one is immune from it. No one can avoid it. And most folks believe that they have more than their share of it. It's *stress*. Just mention the word to people and a knowing smile will come to their lips . . . *everyone* knows what stress is! Some of the following explanations may sound familiar:

It's something that you get as a result of something bad happening.

It's something that you get as a result of something good happening.

It's something that you get as a result of anticipating that something bad is going to happen.

It's something that you get as a result of anticipating that something good is going to happen.

It can come from just about anything, such as physical illness or watching reruns on television all day.

It can cause all sorts of things, such as physical illness or watching reruns on television all day.

It's powerful! I once saw somebody faint from it. You can even collapse and die from it.

A formal definition of stress is elusive. In everyday conversation, stress refers to diverse forces in the environment: Noise, crime, pollution, and the hazards of commuting to school or work might all be considered examples of stress. But stress also refers to diverse forces presumed to be within the body itself, such as tension, disturbing thoughts, and even involuntary behavior (trembling hands or a high-pitched voice).

So what is stress? Where does it come from? What happens as a result of it? These questions are explored below from a physiological and a psychological perspective.

WHAT IS STRESS?

stress

mental and/or physical strain resulting from anxiety, work, or adjustive demands or challenges.

Stress may be defined as *mental and/or physical strain resulting from adjustive demands or challenges.* This simple definition belies the fact that there is little that is simple about stress. A landmark book on the subject, *The Stress of Life* by physiologist Hans Selye (1956), first introduced many people to the great physiological and psychological complexities of stress. The book remains a respected resource long after Selye's death. But Selye had no way of predicting such a legacy for himself when starting out as a young research scientist. He had aspired to discover a new sex hormone. When he injected a substance into laboratory animals, the substance's physiological effects seemed to mimic that of a hormone. Elated, Selye believed he had discovered what he sought. Elation quickly turned to depression, however, when Selye found that various other substances injected into his subjects caused exactly the same response. Even totally different kinds of treatments, such as jolts of electric shock or immobilization by means of physical restraints, caused the same physical response. While brooding in his laboratory and not getting much work done, Selye decided to look at his findings in a totally different way. He began to think generatively about what he had found. This new perspective did not reveal anything about the body's reaction to a specific hormone, but rather something about the body's reaction to a nonspecific source of stress.

THE PHYSICAL EXPERIENCE OF STRESS

stressor

something capable of causing stress.

Selye's data provided evidence that the body goes through a predictable response to any kind of stress. This response is composed of three stages that proceed in the same order: the *alarm reaction,* the *stage of resistance,* and the *stage of exhaustion.* These three stages are collectively referred to as the *general adaptation syndrome* (GAS). Because virtually any **stressor** (*something capable of causing stress*) could cause the GAS, Selye defined stress as "a nonspecific response of the body to any demand." The response referred to in this definition is the GAS, and he described it as nonspecific because it was not specific to any particular source of stress. As examples of just how varied stressors can be, Selye (1974) presented images of harried business people, pressured air-traffic controllers, competitive athletes, and a person watching a loved one die of a terminal disease; although the source of stress varied in each case, the body's reaction was exactly the same.

Selye's claims regarding the nature of the body's response to stressors have not gone unchallenged and remain controversial (Mason, 1975). Still, it is true that the body under stress does respond in a number of stereotypical physiological ways.

THE GENERAL ADAPTATION SYNDROME

Understanding Selye's general adaptation syndrome requires some knowledge of how the nervous system (see page 62 in Chapter 3) responds to stress. The peripheral nervous system is subdivided into two branches: the *sympathetic* branch and the *parasympathetic* branch. The sympathetic nervous system may be described as being "sympathetic"; that is, on your side and doing absolutely everything to help you in times of stress and excitement. Dilating the pupils to admit more light in order to see better, dilating structures in the lungs to allow more oxygen in, and stopping digestion so that blood bound for the stomach can be diverted for use by the muscles are functions of the sympathetic nervous system.

During the first, or alarm stage, a number of hormones, collectively referred to as stress hormones, stream into the blood. These hormones create many mental and bodily changes that prepare us for "fight or flight." *Fight* refers to the type of response characterized by physically confronting the source of stress. Flight refers to the response to stress characterized by trying to get out of harm's way—running away from a wild beast, for instance. On some occasions in contemporary life, it remains important for the body to be able to respond in such ways to stress. Yet many physical, chemical, and emotional changes that take place in response to stress are outdated; they are more suited to the wild than to classrooms, business board rooms, social gatherings and city roads and highways. An appropriate reaction to stress in response to an announced examination, for example, is studying, not "fight or flight."

The sympathetic nervous system is in charge of "emergency measures" during the alarm stage. After the alarm stage is over, it is time to regroup, readjust, and repair any damage that may have occurred. Here the parasympathetic nervous system takes over, and the second, or resistance stage (also known as the *adaptive stage*) begins. During the resistance stage, heart and breathing rates return to normal, the secretion of saliva and mucus returns to normal, food digestion restarts, and the body attempts to return to the state it was in before it mobilized for a fight-or-flight response.

What if the stress continues for a long time? Selye explored this question employing laboratory rats as subjects and cold temperature as the stressor. He found that the rats could adapt to the cold but only for a limited time period. After several months, the rats' adaptive resources were depleted and they entered what Selye called the *exhaustion* stage. During this stage, the high levels of energy required to keep the body in a heightened state of alertness finally ran out. As the ability of the body to cope with stress faltered, sensory perception and muscular ability failed. Eventually, the animals died. Figure 6–1 on page 150 illustrates how the body's resistance to stress changes over the three stages of the general adaptation syndrome.

The general adaptation syndrome may help to explain some mysterious phenomena such as so-called voodoo death. Basedow (1925) offered a chilling description of an Australian aborigine being "boned," that is, having a bone aggressively pointed at him by a witch doctor. The body of the boned man reacts with violent, uncontrollable trembling. As Basedow observed, the man "finally composes himself, goes to his hut and frets to death."

Walter Cannon (1942) studied voodoo death and wondered whether the actual cause of death was a self-induced overstimulation of the sympathetic nervous system. Curt Richter, a psychologist at the Johns Hopkins Medical School, conducted a series of experiments using wild and domesticated rats as subjects, which he believed advanced our understanding of voodoo death. Subjects were stressed by being forced to "swim" in a tank under a constant stream of water until they sank. After autopsy, Richter (1957) found that many of his rats died not from overstimulation of the sympathetic nervous system, but from overstimulation of the parasympathetic nervous system. He interpreted the data as indi-

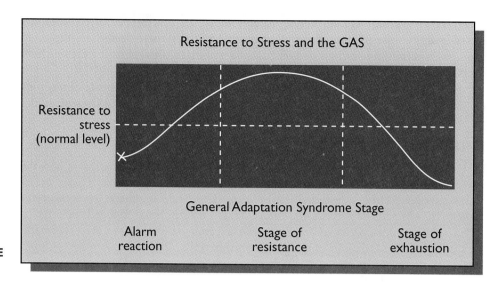

**FIGURE 6–1
RESISTANCE TO STRESS
AND THE GENERAL
ADAPTATION SYNDROME
STAGE**

cating that the rats had died of "hopelessness." Richter had previously observed that wild rats also seemed to simply "give up" (p. 196) after being held and restrained from moving. Richter speculated that, like the wild rat, the boned victim is resigned to his fate. Fight or flight are not alternatives in either situation because both situations seem hopeless.

Martin Seligman (1975) described a somewhat similar phenomenon that he called "learned helplessness." Seligman strapped dogs into a harness and subjected them to repeated electric shock which they had no way of avoiding. When subsequently placed in a situation in which they could escape the shock by jumping over a hurdle, Seligman's subjects simply endured the shock. The research literature is replete with generalizations about the phenomenon of learned helplessness in humans made from Seligman's research. Still, some of the most compelling studies on learned helplessness are probably those that have employed human subjects (Rodin, 1986).

Research by Richter (1957) and Seligman (1975) raise important questions from different perspectives. We might wish to explore further why Richter's rats died a "parasympathetic death," not a "sympathetic death." Also, one might ask if Richter's research is relevant to voodoo death or any other uniquely human phenomenon. How appropriate is it to attribute higher order cognitive processes and human-like motivation such as hopelessness or helplessness to laboratory animals? What are the ethical issues involved in research such as that conducted by Curt Richter? See *A Question of Values.*

FOUR TYPES OF STRESS

Selye (1974, 1976, 1980) expanded his ideas about stress and eventually distinguished four types. One type, **eustress**, is *pleasurable stress*, exemplified by the feelings one experiences while racewalking. Although physical and mental demands are placed on the body, these demands are voluntary and purposeful and the result seems to be beneficial. Exactly why this type of stress is beneficial is not known. This puzzling phenomenon may have something to do with the interplay between activities, physical sensations, and the mental labels attached to these physical sensations. Accordingly, racewalking may be accompanied by positive thoughts such as, "I am exercising and doing something good for my body." By contrast, engaging in the same behavior but thinking, "I must walk quickly to leave this aversive situation," may somehow evoke less healthful bodily responses.

Some people seem to prefer or need more eustress than others. According to psychologist Marvin Zuckerman (1971, 1978, 1979, 1984), people who thrive on eustress, as well as people who tend to seek out novel—positive or negative—stimuli, are "sensation seekers." Zuckerman (1979, p. 10) defined the trait of **sensation seeking** as *"the need for varied, novel, and complex sensations and experiences and the willingness to take physical and social risks for the sake of such experiences."* Zuckerman developed a 22-item Sensation Seeking Scale (SSS) (1972) to help identify people who are high and low in the trait of sensa-

eustress

as defined by stress researcher Hans Selye, a pleasurable type of stress, such as that experienced when racewalking.

sensation seeking

the need for varied, novel, and complex sensations and experiences and the willingness to take physical and social risks for the sake of such experiences.

tion seeking. High sensation seekers seem to thrive on the novel, exhilarating, and challenging types of experiences that low sensation seekers would shy away from as being too risky or stressful. Each SSS item, like the sample below, contains two choices. Examinees are instructed to select the one more applicable to them.

A. I would like to try parachute jumping.
B. I would never want to try jumping out of a plane with or without a parachute.

The SSS is based on the test-taker's self-report and is useful when the test-takers have great insight into themselves and are willing to be candid in their responses. However, test data based exclusively on self-report is of dubious value when test-takers do not have the requisite insight, and/or their responses are less than honest. Can you think of a more behavioral measure of sensation seeking? How about the "test" described in Figure 6–2?

The type of stress that most frequently comes to mind when we think of the word stress is the type that Selye referred to as **distress** (*a condition characterized by emotional upset and/or physical strain*). Distress frequently carries with it unpleasurable, if not harmful, consequences. According to Selye's stress classification system, then, what is commonly referred to as *stress* might more precisely be termed *distress*.

Two other types of stress distinguished by Selye were **hypostress** (*a condition involving too little stress, as in boredom*) and **hyperstress** (*a condition involving an excessive demand on our coping ability*). Selye's distinctions between these four types of stress have not found their way into everyday conversation. Still, the distinction between these terms reminds us that the physiological arousal we may experience in response to two vastly different events, one positive—the other negative—may be quite similar, if not exactly the same.

Later in this chapter we note that it is the cognitive label applied to physiological and psychological feelings that determines whether people consider themselves to be stressed. This same cognitive label tells what type of stress—good or bad—we are experiencing. For example, some people who are seasoned bungee jumpers secure the bungee cord to themselves with excited anticipation, telling themselves in essence, "This kind of stress is the good or positive kind." However, first-time jumpers may engage in exactly the same behavior but tremble under the weight of self-talk that says, "This kind of stress is the bad or negative kind." Both the experienced and the novice jumpers may be engaging in the exact same behavior, and both groups may even be experiencing the same physiological symptoms (quickened heartbeat and breathing, as well as other signs of sympathetic arousal). Still, the cognitive labeling of the feelings experienced by members of the different groups may be totally different.

distress
as conceived of by stress researcher Hans Selye, the variety of stress that carries with it unpleasurable and harmful consequences.

hypostress
as defined by stress researcher Hans Selye, a condition involving too little stress, as in boredom.

hyperstress
as defined by stress researcher Hans Selye, a condition involving an excessive demand on one's coping ability.

FIGURE 6–2 A BEHAVIORAL MEASURE OF SENSATION SEEKING?
Bungee jumping involves securing one or more rubber-like cords (*bungee cords*) to the body and jumping into the air from a position typically 150 to 250 feet off the ground. How would you predict people on line in an amusement park waiting to bungee jump would score on a valid measure of sensation seeking? How would you predict such a group would score as compared to age-matched golfers waiting to tee-off at fairways in the same general area, or as compared to a random sample of people at a shopping mall? Adolescents who score high on a paper-and-pencil measure of sensation seeking have been found to be more prone to use alcohol and tobacco than counterparts who score low (Newcomb & McGee, 1991). Would you expect differences in alcohol and tobacco use among bungee-jumping adolescents as compared to non-jumpers? Why?

A QUESTION OF  Values

The Study of Stress in People and Animals

Ethical constraints considerably narrow the types of stressors that can be employed in experimental research using humans. For this reason, dogs, cats, and other animals, mostly laboratory rats, are widely employed in such research. Many of the findings cited in textbooks are generalizations made from experimentation with animals. For example, generalizing from his work with rats, Richter (1957) sought to explain the phenomenon of voodoo death with reference to the construct of *hopelessness*. Increasingly, however, laypeople and professionals alike are raising questions regarding the ethics of such animal research. In particular, many have raised questions regarding the morality of inflicting pain or extreme emotional distress in animal subjects, especially for research that may be of dubious value.

James Rachels, a philosopher at the University of Alabama at Birmingham, acknowledges that great differences exist between people and animals, but argues that society's differential treatment of the two should be based on what the differences between the species actually are. For example, we needn't worry about a college scholarship program for chimpanzees because chimpanzees lack the cognitive capacity for such endeavors. However, according to Rachels (1990), if chimpanzees are going to be subjected to experimentation that entails hurt, pain, and surgical alteration, a relevant moral question concerns not whether

such animals are able to read, speak, or endure the rigors of college course work but rather whether they are able to suffer.

How generalizable are many of the findings resulting from animal research? As an exercise, you may wish to read Curt Richter's (1957) study in its entirety (it is probably available in your school library). Ask yourself what meaningful generalizations can be made about human behavior from it. Some might say that given the extreme complexity of phenomena such as voodoo death and hopelessness—involving as they do uniquely human cognitive, emotional, social, physical, and cultural factors—*no* meaningful generalizations about such phenomena can be made from the study of wild and laboratory rats. Still, there are those, including Richter (1957) himself, who suggest that rats are creatures of sufficient cognitive complexity to experience such motivations as hopelessness. If Richter is right, ethical questions would seem to arise regarding the appropriateness of conducting such research. On moral grounds, would it not be unacceptable to subject such marvelously mindful creatures to a procedure in which they are to swim until they drown in uncomfortably hot or cold water under a constant jet stream? Some of Richter's subjects "swam" for upwards of 80 hours until relief in the form of drowning finally came. Rachels (1990) makes the case that, in the interest of moral consis-

tency, society must either upgrade the value we place on animal suffering— the preferable choice—or downgrade the value we place on human suffering and consequently be prepared to employ human subjects in comparable experimentation.

Today, more than 20 million animals are used every year as subjects in research conducted at universities, research institutes, private laboratories, military installations, and hospitals (HSUS, 1992). Psychologists employ animals as subjects in behavioral research; manufacturers of various products (including pharmaceuticals, cosmetics, household cleaners, and pesticides) employ animals in commercial research. Some of the research inflicts no pain and suffering on the animals beyond that of life in a cage (which can be extremely stressful to dogs, cats, chimpanzees, and other nonhuman primates). Other research inflicts unspeakable pain and suffering on animals in experiments that can only be described as gruesome and inhumane. Animal rights groups have sought to engender public ire at research and other routine procedures that cause such pain and suffering including, for example, the use of the steel leg trap by fur trappers and the daily practice of scraping the genitals of civet cats to manufacture perfume.

In the United States, the Department of Defense (DOD) routinely employs animals to test the lethality of various kinds of weapons and the

PSYCHOLOGICAL EXPLANATIONS OF STRESS

Selye's orientation was physiological, not psychological. His thinking about stress was shaped largely by experimentation using laboratory animals, not people. Many psychologists have attempted to integrate Selye's ideas into what is known about stress from a psychological perspective. An immediate obstacle, however, is Selye's overly broad and clearly physiological definition of stress. Although the body's response to stress is remarkably sim-

safety of various kinds of protective gear. The experimentation may involve shooting, blasting, smashing, gassing, or other such treatment. A great deal of other stress-related research, by comparison more innocuous, including the Richter study, has also been funded in whole or in part by the military. In 1990, the DOD used more than 300,000 animals in research. According to the Humane Society of the United States (HSUS) (1992, p. 4), "military experiments are several times more likely to involve unrelieved pain than are other experiments. But the DOD's experimental programs are subject to almost no outside scrutiny; the public and the scientific community are kept in the dark."

The American Psychological Association (APA) strongly supports animal research and has promulgated a code of ethics and guidelines for humane conduct in such experimentation. In an editorial requesting member support for animal research, the APA's chief executive officer wrote,

> Research using animals has immeasurably benefited the advancement of knowledge in psychology, and the lives of innumerable members of society have been enhanced and enriched by the applications of psychology. . . . The pioneering work of Harry F. Harlow, Ph.D., with rhesus monkeys made significant contributions to theories of child development and psychi-

atry. Although his work involving maternal deprivation is sometimes criticized today, his research had an important impact on the treatment and care of institutionalized human infants. (Fowler, 1992, p. 2)

Extremist organizations violently opposed to all animal research have attempted to wreak havoc in animal laboratories throughout the country by illegally breaking and entering into private premises and attempting to rescue animals, disrupt research, and intimidate researchers. At the other extreme are those who would condemn all animal rights activists as misguided zealots who are antiscience and antihuman. In the middle ground, there are organizations such as the APA and the HSUS that both advocate humane treatment for animals. As an animal advocacy organization, HSUS goes a bit farther than the APA, calling for a reduction in the total number of animals used in research, for rigorous accountability in research, and for the development of research alternatives that do not employ animals. For example, instead of dropping an irritant into a rabbit's eye to test its toxicity, a membrane found in chicken eggs may be used as an alternative.

How do you feel about research using animals? For more information about the APA's position on animal research, you may write to the following address: American Psychological Association, Inc., 750 First Street, NE,

Washington, DC 20002. For more information on animal research from the perspective of HSUS, or a directory of cosmetics and personal care manufacturers that do not test on animals, send a stamped, self-addressed envelope to The Humane Society of the United States, 2100 L Street NW, Washington, DC 20037. To learn more about, or comment on the use of animals in research by the Department of Defense, you may write the Secretary of the Department of Defense, Room 3E880, The Pentagon, Washington, DC 20301, or write your representatives in Congress.

An anesthetized chimpanzee in a research study is carried past rows of cages. The chimp is one of more than 20 million animal subjects used in experimentation in this country every year.

ilar no matter what the stress is, the mental response to stress on the part of different people is remarkable for its dissimilarity. Psychologist Richard Lazarus and his colleagues (Holroyd & Lazarus, 1982; Lazarus & Folkman, 1984, 1987) have proposed what they call a *transactional model* of stress. According to this model, it is the unique aspects of the interaction—or transaction—between the person and the environment that will or will not produce stress. Later in this chapter, our own model of stressor perception is presented. This highly simplified model incorporates some of the findings of Lazarus and Folkman (1984), Schachter and Singer (1962), and others who have helped to illuminate the role that cognitive, social, and physiological determinants, as well as the cognitive labeling of emotional states, can have on one's perception of stress. Before that, however, some background regarding *arousal* and related concepts will be helpful.

THE CONCEPT OF AROUSAL

arousal

the state of nervous system activation.

In everyday conversation, the verb *to arouse* is synonymous with to stimulate, to excite, or to stir up. Psychologists also use *arousal* with reference to how stimulated, excited, or stirred-up one's nervous system is. More formally, **arousal** may be defined as *the state of nervous system activation.* A person's level of arousal may vary quite a bit during the course of an average day. After a good night's sleep, your level of arousal on the way to work or school might best be described as moderate. Encountering any stimuli that are anxiety-provoking, fear-provoking, anger-provoking, or otherwise emotion- or excitement-provoking, may cause your level of arousal to rise. Lying in bed and dropping off to sleep, your level of arousal lowers. A high state of arousal is characterized by a rapid heartbeat, shallow and quick breathing, and other physical symptoms.

On a purely physiological basis, it is difficult to discern what emotion is being experienced when an individual is in a high state of arousal; fear, anger, and sexual arousal are some of the possibilities. How do we identify or label our feelings when we are physiologically aroused? Different answers to this question exist. From a cognitive perspective, one may have to look beyond the internal world to cues in the external world.

COGNITION, AROUSAL, AND EMOTIONAL STATE

adrenaline

a hormone that arouses the sympathetic nervous system.

Is the state of physiological arousal alone sufficient to produce an identifiable emotion? To explore this question, Marañon (1924) injected 210 patients with **adrenaline**, *a hormone that arouses the sympathetic nervous system.* When asked what they were feeling, few subjects seemed to experience any strong emotion. If asked to talk about a specific topic, such as the death of a parent, the subjects became quite emotional, even when they had talked calmly about such matters prior to adrenaline administration. Marañon's findings were replicated by American researchers in the 1930s (Cantril & Hunt, 1932; Landis & Hunt, 1932). Trying to understand such findings, Stanley Schachter (1959) speculated that individuals in such an aroused state would have "evaluative needs," that is, a need to understand and label their own bodily feelings. Now the stage was set for a study that would explore cognitive, social, and physiological factors in emotional states.

Stanley Schachter (1964) and Jerome E. Singer (Schachter & Singer, 1962) argued that aroused states are cognitively identified with labels such as *joy, fear, anger,* and *love* on the basis of social, environmental, and other cues (see Figure 6–3). In one study (1962), they informed their subjects that they were interested in testing the effects of a vitamin supplement on vision. However, because the focus of the research was actually on environmental cues and arousal, the subjects did not receive a vitamin supplement; the injection subjects received contained either adrenaline or a placebo (*inactive substance*). Subjects randomly assigned to the experimental condition received the adrenaline, while subjects randomly assigned to the control condition received the placebo. After receiving the injection, subjects were then led to a waiting room where another person was already waiting to have his vision tested. This other subject, however, was actually a confederate, or collaborator, of the experimenter.

placebo

inactive substance or treatment, typically used in research as a control for an active ingredient or experimental treatment procedure.

In one experimental condition (the "euphoric condition"), the confederate in the waiting room followed a prescribed procedure that included sailing paper planes, shooting wads of paper, even playing with one of two hula hoops that had been left behind a portable chalkboard. In another experimental condition (the "anger condition"), the confederate acted sullen and bitterly complained about having to fill out forms.

The experimenters also manipulated the information subjects received about the physiological effects they could expect as a result of the injection. Subjects in the "informed condition" were initially given an accurate description of the physical effects they could expect to experience as a result of being injected with the vitamin supplement: "What will

The visual stimulus is perceived as a snake.

Snake comes into view and is seen.

Cognition that a snake is in sight engenders response of sympathetic nervous system, including rapid heartbeat, shallow breathing, and related physiological reactions.

Thoughts such as "I fear snakes" lead to a cognitive labeling of the physiological arousal as *fear*.

FIGURE 6–3 AROUSAL AND COGNITION ACCORDING TO SCHACHTER According to Schachter, a person experiences arousal and then cognitively labels that arousal. Above, the man has had a reflexive reaction of his sympathetic nervous system when seeing a snake. Feeling the arousal and seeing the snake, the man concludes, "I am afraid."

probably happen is that your hand will start to shake, your heart will start to pound, and your face may get warm and flushed." Subjects in the "misinformed condition" were told, "What will probably happen is that your feet will numb, you will have an itching sensation over parts of your body, and you may get a slight headache." Subjects in a third condition were given no information relevant to the side effects of the vitamin, nor any information about what to expect physiologically. The subjects' interaction with the confederate in the waiting room was observed by the experimenter through a one-way mirror. Following the waiting room experience, all subjects were interviewed as to their emotional feelings.

Schachter and Singer hypothesized that subjects given adrenaline but not informed of the hormone's true physical effects, that is, subjects in the adrenaline/misinformed and adrenaline/no explanation groups, would experience arousal and then cognitively try to explain their aroused feelings by looking towards the environment. If Schachter and Singer were correct, these subjects would be more likely than the others to behave euphorically if exposed to a euphoric confederate or to behave angrily if exposed to an angry confederate. They found this to be the case: Subjects not informed or misinformed about the effects of the adrenaline did look to the social environment to help explain what they were feeling. These subjects tended to behave in a euphoric or angry manner and subsequently rated themselves as being euphoric or angry, based on the behavior of the confederate they were paired with in the waiting room.

Twenty years later, a number of studies have echoed Schachter's beliefs about the cognitive mechanism by which arousal is labeled (Reisenzein, 1983). Still, the nature of the relationship between cognition and arousal is not as straightforward as Schachter's findings suggest. Questions have been raised regarding the replicability of the Schachter and Singer study (Leventhal & Tomarken, 1986; Marshall, 1976; Marshall & Zimbardo, 1979; Maslach, 1979; Rogers & Deckner, 1975), as well as regarding the notion that virtually any emotional label can be applied to a heightened state of arousal (Ekman et al., 1983). Others have faulted Schachter's theory for not giving adequate weight to the role of cues such as one's own facial expression in the experience of emotion (Izard, 1971; Ekman & Friesen,

1975). According to Robert Zajonc, people experience emotions much more quickly than Schachter's cognitive theory of emotions would suggest. For Zajonc (1980, 1984), it is possible for people to experience an emotion instantaneously and not even be consciously aware of why they are feeling happy, sad, or otherwise.

As Zajonc suggests, it is possible to experience an emotion without very much thought. But such lack of thought will usually be confined to relatively simple experiences, such as sampling a new food that instantly tastes good or bad. As situations become more complex, however, cognition probably plays more of a role. Consider in this context love— an emotion we will have much more to say about in Chapter 11.

A special person in one's life is capable of making one's heart beat faster and of producing other sympathetic nervous system responses. Exactly why this person has such an effect can be explained, in part, with reference to constructs such as interpersonal attraction. However, people may perceive themselves as angry at, even repulsed by, other people with whom they were once in love. Why? The answer has to do with cognitive labeling of physical arousal. How arousal is labeled—love or hate or something else—may in some instances fluctuate with the nature of the things being heard, seen, or otherwise perceived. Such insights from the behavioral laboratory lend credence to folk wisdom about the "thin line between love and hate."

WHAT ARE STRESSORS?

Heather makes plans to sleep over at her friend's house. Her friend lives in a neighborhood that is right near a major airport. Jets take off and land all day and all night. Is the sound of the jets a source of stress? Yes and no . . .

Heather lies in bed, only to toss and turn all night. At least the experience has been educational: she can now distinguish take-off and landing sounds. She has long gotten past her initial fear that every plane landing was dive-bombing for the bedpost. Still, it has all been intolerably stressful! Over breakfast, she learns that her friend has long ago gotten used to the jet-engine noise and can now sleep right through it without any problem.

The story illustrates that stress is not necessarily something out there in the environment, or something that automatically wells up as a result of exposure to annoying or threatening stimuli. The noise of the planes was stressful to Heather, but not to someone who has become accustomed to such noise.

Earlier, stress was defined in terms of the mental and/or physical strain resulting from adjustive demands or challenges. Adjustive demands or challenges may arise as a result of a number of different types of stressors, including real or perceived annoying, threatening, frightening, challenging, anxiety-provoking, or fatiguing stimuli. Let's look briefly at some physical, psychological, and cultural types of stressors.

PHYSICAL STRESSORS

A nationally representative survey involving 1,200 full-time undergraduate students from 100 campuses during the 1991–1992 school year indicated that the five leading issues facing America today are (1) AIDS, (2) drugs, (3) the environment, (4) the budget deficit, and (5) the quality of education. When the focus was shifted to the student's own campus, alcohol abuse, crime, and intergroup relations were also mentioned as primary concerns (Himmelfarb, 1992). More generally, disease, physical trauma, physical disorders, malnutrition, dehydration, lack of sleep, physical pain, foul air in a stuffy room, foul air in a polluted environment, physical discomfort from crowding, threats to life and limb posed by fire, water, drugs, or guns, are a few examples of the types of physical stressors to which people may be exposed.

PSYCHOLOGICAL STRESSORS

There are many potential sources of psychological stress. Psychological stress may be categorized broadly in terms of *change, conflict, frustration,* and *pressure.* These categories and the individual variables within them overlap to varying degrees with physical and cultural sources of stress. Thus, for example, although cultural stressors are grouped below as a separate category for emphasis, cultural factors could also have been discussed under the headings of change, conflict, frustration, or pressure.

CHANGE

Change and stress are intimately intertwined. Change can cause stress. Change may also result in the relief of stress. Over the course of a lifetime, people weather myriad physical, mental, emotional, social, and environmental changes, some of which are clearly more stressful than others. And according to statistical probabilities, some groups of events to which adjustment is required are more likely than others to play a part in the onset of illness (Rahe et al., 1964).

To understand better the relativity of stress, rate the events below on a scale of 0 (not stressful) to 100 (most stressful). *Stressful* is defined here in terms of both the average intensity of effort it would take to readjust, and the length of time it would take to readjust. As a point of reference marriage has a stress rating of 50 on this scale. To respond to the items, ask questions such as, "On average, would this adjustment take more or less effort than adjustment to marriage? Would this adjustment take less or more time than adjustment to marriage?"

Life Event	Stress Rating on Scale of 0 to 100
Marriage	50
Mortgage over $10,000	_____
Pregnancy	_____
Death of a close family member	_____
Death of spouse	_____

In the 1960s and 1970s, there was great interest in exploring and quantifying the relative degree of stress caused by various life changes. Thomas Holmes (1979) and his associates (Holmes & Masuda, 1974; Holmes & Holmes, 1970; Masuda & Holmes, 1967; Rahe & Holmes, 1965; Rahe et al., 1964) pioneered research in this area. Holmes and Rahe (1967) asked 394 people from different demographic groups (groups varied by gender, age, marital status, ethnic group membership and other variables) to assess the stressfulness of various changes. As in the brief exercise above, respondents were instructed to use the stress of marriage (arbitrarily set by the experimenters at 50) as a point of reference, and then to estimate the value of other life events accordingly. How does your rating of the mortgage, pregnancy, and death items compare to the findings of the researchers?

The findings of Holmes and Rahe (1967) generated a great deal of interest in stress and life change (Barrett et al., 1979; Elliott & Eisdorfer, 1982), including cautions to minimize life change if one's score on such a scale was high (F. Cohen, 1979). However, criticism of such scales, as well as criticism of putting too much faith in the scores derived from them, soon began to mount (Cleary, 1980; Depue & Monroe, 1986; Derogatis, 1982; Monroe, 1982; Perkins, 1982; Rabkin & Streuning, 1976; Schroeder & Costa, 1984; Zeiss, 1980; Zimmerman, 1983). There was also no shortage of suggestions for improvement (Dohrenwend et al., 1979; Paykel, 1974; Rahe & Arthur, 1978; Sarason et al., 1978). Concerns expressed by various researchers with respect to tests purporting to measure life stress and/or change included the following:

- The scales tended to concern themselves with specific life events rather than chronic problems or clusters of events.
- The scales did not appear to be methodologically sound because there was a great deal of subjectivity in the test taker's interpretation and scoring of the items. For example, "close family member" could be interpreted in vastly different ways by different people.
- The scales are insensitive to the relevance of individual items to people from various racial, ethnic, or other groups in society, and responses may vary systematically as a

consequence of group membership. For example, the pregnancy question on the Holmes and Rahe scale might be responded to in predictable and systematically different ways by groups of married versus single people.

- Some of the items on some of the older scales (such as the $10,000 mortgage question on the Holmes and Rahe scale) became dated.
- Many potential sources of life stress and life change are not tapped by the items on such tests. This raises questions concerning the adequacy of the tests in terms of their sampling of the variable (life stress or change) they purport to measure.
- There may be a confounding or confusion of the variable of change with other variables that may more accurately be pinpointed as a cause of stress. For example, it may be that change causes conflict or frustration or pressure, and it is these latter variables that are the veritable sources of stress, *not* change.

Few researchers would deny that change typically entails stress and adjustment. Consider in this context a proposed change at Mills College and student reaction to it (see *In the News*).

CONFLICT

The word *conflict* may conjure up images of nations at war or people brawling. In a psychological context, **conflict** more often refers to *opposing or incompatible thoughts, feelings, or behaviors that are competing for expression.* Three categories of conflict, *approach-approach*

conflict

1. an intrapsychic state in which two or more mutually exclusive wishes, impulses, or tendencies simultaneously exist. 2. an interpersonal state in which two or more people (or entities such as nations, organizations, or corporations) disagree, are opposed to one another, or are engaged in mutually aggressive behavior.

IN THE News

The Stress of Change

In the Spring of 1990, the trustees at Mills College in Oakland, California, one of this country's oldest colleges for women, voted to admit male students. Since the 1930s men had been admitted only as graduate students. The photograph to the right was snapped moments after the president of the trustees announced that financial considerations had dictated the change in the school's 138-year tradition. The students were told that the school could not survive unless this policy change was made. The announcement was greeted with screams, sobs, and vows of defiance. Before long, many students were boycotting classes and blocking entrances to buildings, while others were trying to coordinate the development of a legal defense fund. Some students were so profoundly af-

fected by the announced change in policy that they shaved their heads and placed the shaven hair on a makeshift "altar" to their "ancestors" on the steps of the student union.

Why were the students upset? According to Bishop (1990):

The students cited studies showing that women educated in women's colleges go on to achieve higher positions in private and public employment. They have also expressed fear that men would take over leadership roles on the campus and change the dynamics in the classroom, to the detriment of the women.

The story is useful in illustrating how not only change, but also the mere

threat of change can affect people so profoundly.

By the way, the trustees reversed themselves and Mills remains an undergraduate institution for women only.

conflict, approach-avoidance conflict, and *avoidance-avoidance conflict,* were first proposed in the 1930s and are still in use today. According to this way of thinking about conflicts, thoughts, feelings, and behaviors are categorized in terms of whether the intent behind them is to move towards or away from something.

In an approach-approach situation, conflict arises due to the desirability of approaching two or more positive alternatives. Deciding between television shows to watch, schools to attend, firms to work for, movies to go to, restaurants to eat at, clothes to wear—these are all examples of approach-approach conflicts. In an avoidance-avoidance situation, conflict arises due to the undesirability of two or more negative alternatives. The convicted murderer who is given a choice of capital punishment administered by means of lethal injection or hanging faces an avoidance-avoidance situation. In an approach-avoidance situation, conflict arises as a result of the mixed feelings that keep a person from feeling good about approaching or avoiding something. A person wanting to be environment-conscious and to support companies that sell recycled products but who finds that the recycled products are much costlier than the nonrecycled products is involved in an approach-avoidance conflict.

Approach-avoidance conflicts can be resolved by giving serious thought to the comparative costs and benefits of the various options and then making an informed decision. Many times, unfortunately, that is easier said than done. For example, shopping for food in many countries is often much more stressful than a trip to the local market in America. Due to great shortages of commodities, people must wait on long lines to get into stores. Once inside, the shopper is likely to be greeted by a poor selection of inferior offerings, all very highly priced. Still, one must eat to survive. This variety of approach-avoidance conflict is thus part of everyday life for millions of people. On a lighter note, some kinds of approach-avoidance conflicts can be avoided (see Figure 6–4).

Can you think of an avoidance-avoidance conflict that you have had to deal with? How did you deal with it? By what criteria did you decide that one option was more favorable than the other?

FRUSTRATION

Have you ever felt you were powerless to do something you very much wanted to do? If so, you have experienced firsthand **frustration**, *a source of stress resulting from the preven-*

frustration
a source of stress resulting from the prevention, blocking, or thwarting of efforts or wishes to achieve a desired objective.

FIGURE 6–4 AN APPROACH-AVOIDANCE CONFLICT Consumers stricken by Big Mac attacks on a Sunday afternoon in Moscow may have to wait hours to consume the object of their desire. The line on this day stretched for many blocks.

tion, blocking, or thwarting of efforts or wishes to achieve a desired objective. Training hard to complete a marathon run but finding that your body simply does not allow you to finish the race—that's frustration. Offering assistance that could be genuinely helpful to someone you love and learning that they refuse to accept it—that's frustration. If you would like to ask someone out on a date but somehow can never bring yourself to do so, even when the timing seems so right—that's frustration. If you ask someone out on a date but they refuse—that's frustration.

The best way to deal with frustration is to prevent it in the first place. Prevention means acquiring the competencies necessary to succeed. Another way entails monitoring and effectively altering demands on the self. How realistic are these demands? Too high? Too low? What constitutes a minimum level of performance that could reasonably be expected?

In some instances, it is physically impossible to acquire the competencies necessary to prevent frustration such as that suffered by disabled people, who must exert extraordinary effort to accomplish what most people take for granted (see Figure 6–5). Nachman (1992) described an incident in which he was asked by a Broadway theater manager to leave a performance of *Peter Pan* because his wheelchair, parked in the aisle, was considered a fire hazard. After Nachman quietly insisted on staying, the manager called the police to the theater. The police did not compel Nachman to leave and he was able to enjoy the show. Other firsthand accounts attest to other frustrations associated with even relatively minor physical disability (Samuels, 1992) and the rage such frustration can evoke (Hockenberry, 1992).

FIGURE 6–5 FRUSTRATION AS A SOURCE OF STRESS For years, disabled Americans suffered the stress of frustration in public places such as restaurants and theaters. The Americans with Disabilities Act of 1990 now requires businesses open to the public to be accessible to people with disabilities. It outlaws some of the discriminatory practices and requirements that some theater owners have in the past imposed upon patrons in wheelchairs, such as requiring the purchase of two seats, or the attendance of a chaperone who would carry the person up and down stairs. People who have reasonable grounds to believe that they have been discriminated against as a result of their disability may bring a civil action against the discriminatory business establishment. Further, the Department of Justice may investigate alleged violations of the law and prosecute offenders.

The stress of frustration is very much a part of every person's maturation process. From birth onward, frustration awaits and must be dealt with. Infants may feel frustrated at their inability to communicate, their inability to feed themselves, their inability to free themselves from the confines of a playpen, crib, or high chair. As a child gets older, the frustrations of learning to walk, talk, use the toilet, socialize, ride a two-wheeler, be liked by other children, and to conquer other such challenges await. Soon, more adult-like frustrations may become part of daily life, such as the frustration of waiting in the cold for a school bus, waiting on a long line for lunch in the cafeteria, and trying to master some difficult concept necessary for success on an upcoming test. As adults, it is quite easy to think back on childhood as a stress-free time of life. In reality, children have to deal with stress too.

PRESSURE

Pressure to get good grades. Pressure to earn a living. Pressure to finish work within a specified time limit. Pressure to get married. Pressure to excel. Pressure to conform. Pressure to perform. Pressure to "do the right thing." Pressure to "do the wrong thing." Internal pressure. External pressure. Parental pressure. Peer pressure. These are a few of the ways we think about **pressure**, or *internal or external demands, usually burdensome in nature, regarding ways of thinking, feeling, or behaving.* Inherent in the notion of pressure is the image of a weight pressing down. From a psychological perspective, it is worrisome cognitions that "weigh" on the mind.

pressure
burdensome internal or external demands regarding thoughts, feelings, or behavior.

Pressure may come from the environment. In an area of the world where there is a constant threat of terrorist activity, or the uncertainty of a sudden natural disaster (such as along the San Andreas fault in California), a certain amount of stress from such pressure can be expected to be part of daily life. Another external source of pressure may derive from the expectations and/or demands of parents, friends, or family. In Japan, for example, roughly 20% of all elementary school students, and 50% of students in grades 7 through 9, are enrolled in 50,000 to 60,000 *jukus* (cram schools that tutor students to pass entrance examinations). An 11-year-old student will typically rise at dawn, work a full day, spend 3 hours at the juku, and spend a couple more hours doing homework before going to bed at midnight. Children who attend jukus do not have time to take up after-school activities such as sports, hobbies, or music (Weisman, 1992a).

Another source of pressure is the self. Some people seem much more driven than others. They hope for high levels of success in relatively short periods of time. Sometimes the internal source of such behavior is an irrational belief such as, "I must earn enough money to retire before I am 30 or I am worthless." Such a thought would certainly be extreme. But it is just these types of extreme expectations and standards that many people judge and evaluate themselves by.

Albert Ellis (1958, 1962), Arnold Lazarus (Lazarus & Fay, 1975), Donald Meichenbaum (1977), and others (for example, Rohsenow & Smith, 1982) have helped focus attention on irrational thinking as a culprit in personal distress and related problems. Based in part on the seminal writing of Ellis, as well as on the writing of other therapists, this chapter's *Quality of Life* presents my own noncomprehensive sampling of irrational things that people can demand of themselves.

Pressure from the self may be a good thing. This fact was recognized nearly a century ago in a series of experiments that analyzed the relationship between self-imposed pressure to succeed at a task and the complexity of the task (Yerkes & Dodson, 1908). As a result of those experiments, the Yerkes-Dodson principle was formulated. In simplified form, that principle is: *There is an optimal degree of pressure for every task. In general, the more difficult or complex the task, the more a high degree of pressure will interfere or disrupt the successful completion of the task. Therefore, the higher the degree of task difficulty or complexity, the lower will be the optimal degree of pressure.*

For several decades, the Yerkes-Dodson principle enjoyed widespread acceptance and was even referred to as a law of human behavior. However, as with many such "laws," ex-

QUALITY OF  Life

The 10 Irrational Commandments

Do any of these irrational beliefs sound familiar? What rational thoughts would you personally use to counter such thinking? A more rational alternative to the often perfectionistic or otherwise illogical thinking inherent in the "commandment" is presented under each statement.

1. *I must be loved, accepted, and respected by everyone who knows me.*
It would be nice if everyone who knows me loves, accepts, and respects me, but in the real world that probably is not going to happen. People differ. I do not love, or even like, everyone I know, and it is unreasonable to expect that everyone is going to love me.

2. *I expect there to be justice in the world, and I cannot bear to live in a world without it.*
It is a sad fact of life that there is not as much justice as we would like. In the real world, bad things happen to good people, seemingly with no rhyme or reason. We can all hope for justice and do our best to work towards achieving justice, but it is unrealistic and inevitably upsetting to believe that justice will always prevail.

3. *I have no control over my happiness; whether I am happy or unhappy depends entirely on external events.*
To the contrary, you have a great deal of control over your happiness and your mood; it is your choice to see the glass as half-empty or half-full.

4. *I am a prisoner of my past and I can never escape it.*
You *are* a prisoner of your past as long as you continue to believe that you are. An alternative way of thinking about your past has to do with how you have profited from your experience and grown as a person.

5. *There must be some solution to every human problem.*
Although solutions to problems often exist, there is no guarantee that the solutions will always be desirable. In effect, some problems in life simply do not have desirable solutions and it becomes counterproductive and maladaptive to spend one's life searching for them.

6. *The way to happiness is by just trying to enjoy yourself at all times.*
The odds are against such a strategy working since it is immature to believe that it is possible to pursue such a course. Not all of life is going to be enjoyment. Further, as simple logic would dictate, if you are constantly working to enjoy yourself, enjoying yourself has become work. Balance in life's pursuits is preferable.

7. *Other people seem to be happier and better adjusted than I am, and I need to work towards being as happy and as adjusted as they are.*
The focus in working towards your own adjustment, happiness, and self-fulfillment is best kept on yourself, not on other people. Neither riches, nor fame, nor the things money can buy could save them from chronic unhappiness and a tragic end.

8. *I must express and ventilate my anger whenever I experience it.*
There is a difference between expressing anger and being assertive. For example, there is a difference between yelling at a cashier who short-changed you, "Thief!" and calmly but assertively informing the cashier of the error. Many things will happen in life that may generate feelings of anger. However, in the vast majority of instances in which interpersonal relations are concerned, an assertive response is preferable to an angry or aggressive one.

9. *The more isolated from other people I can be, the better I like it.*
Here we can turn to some sage words from Barbra Streisand in the classic song *People*: "People who need people are the luckiest people in the world." Moving towards isolationism in an attempt to shut out life's stresses has a terrible cost: many of life's greatest joys are shut out as well.

10. *No matter how outlandish a thought or belief seems to be, stick to it, because you are probably right, and everyone else is wrong.*
Follow your dream but cultivate relationships with people against whom you can bounce-off your innermost thoughts. In matters of health, consult a qualified mental health professional without hesitation. Your school may have a counselor available for consultation on a no fee or low fee basis. Some guidelines for selecting a therapist will be presented in Chapter 9.

ceptions began to mount (Fantino et al., 1970; Hochhauser & Fowler, 1975). Generalizations about pressure are difficult to make because it can improve as well as impair performance under different conditions.

CULTURAL STRESSORS

Change may be a source of stress, regardless of whether the change occurs as a result of major events, such as a new job, a new residence, a new spouse, or minor events, such as a new hairstyle. One type of change, however, seems to be unusually potent in producing negative thoughts and feelings, including feelings of alienation, uprootedness, and depression. It may bring with it sharp rises in drug and alcohol abuse, even suicide rates. This type of change can be called *cultural confusion* (see *Cultural Close-Up* on page 165).

OTHER TYPES OF STRESSORS

Other ways in which stressors may be categorized include their *source, magnitude, consequences, imminence, predictability, intensity, duration,* and *number.* Stressors may come from a very wide variety of sources and range in magnitude from relatively inconsequential to potent enough to cause one to faint, become sick, even die. Resigning from the school volleyball team, for example, is probably not as stressful as resigning from school. Arguing with a merchant whom you may never have to see again is probably a lot less stressful than arguing with a parent or other blood relative. The emotional and physical consequences of a diagnosis of an incurable disease are far more dire than a diagnosis of indigestion.

Stressors differ in the extent to which they are imminent. When committing crimes, for example, some criminals may see the stressor of prison (or other punishment) as in the vague and distant future. Other perpetrators of crime mentally deny that they will ever be punished for their acts; they believe they will never be caught. Once apprehended, criminals may try to cope in various ways, such as finding religion, getting tougher, trying to rehabilitate themselves, trying to escape, or trying to commit suicide. Karla Faye Tucker, the first woman scheduled for execution in the state of Texas since 1863, confided to friends shortly after her murder of two people that she had received sexual pleasure from each swing of the pick ax she used as a murder weapon ("Texas Set to Execute," 1992). While on death row, however, she found religion and attributed her earlier remarks to her friends to bragging. People may differ regarding the issue of Tucker's conversion to religion; would she have made such a dramatic conversion in her life were it not for her death sentence?

Stressors differ in predictability and, to some extent, in the degree to which they can be controlled. Some stressors, such as the stress that comes from giving a planned speech, can be anticipated. Other stressors, such as the stress of being in a fender-bender, cannot be anticipated. Intensity, duration, and number are also relevant factors. A physical stress such as a high-voltage electric shock may have a relatively minor effect if applied for a duration lasting only a small fraction of a second. On the other hand, such a shock may be life-threatening or even fatal if applied for an extended period of time. Like physical sources of stress, psychological sources of stress are also presumed to have effects that become more damaging if sustained over time and/or are present in large quantities (see Figure 6–6 on page 164). The sheer number of stressors an individual must cope with at any one time may present a serious problem (see the *Self-Assessment* exercise on page 166).

THE PERCEPTION OF STRESS

The sheep and the bear were walking in the woods when all of a sudden they were surrounded by a pack of hostile, hungry bears.

"Looks like we're done for, Winnie!" cried the sheep, her voice crackling with stress.

"What do you mean **we**, Lambchop?" replied her calm companion.

This parable is useful in emphasizing the relativity of stressors. Due to individual differences, including differences in genetic, cultural, and psychological factors, what is stressful to one person is not necessarily stressful to another.

THE PROCESS OF PERCEPTION

perception
the process whereby sensory stimuli are organized and interpreted into meaningful cognitions.

psychopathology
disease of the mind.

Perception may be defined as *the process whereby sensory stimuli are organized and interpreted into meaningful cognitions.* Seeing a sight, hearing a sound, or otherwise mentally organizing light energy, sound energy, or any other sensory input is said to be *perceiving.*

It is important to note that there is not necessarily any one-to-one relationship between what is out there in reality and one's perception of reality. For example, some people hear voices that are not really there or grossly distort the meaning of voices that are really there. **Psychopathology** (literally, *diseases of the mind*) is thus one kind of screen through which sensory input may be filtered. There are other kinds of screens or filters, each of which affect perception. Imagine two people looking at a specimen through a microscope. One person, a shipping clerk, looks through the lens and reports seeing "something out of a Madonna video." The second individual, a medical researcher, looks through the same lens, sees the same thing, and perceives a cure for Alzheimer's disease. In addition to psychopathology, factors such as education and experience may also play a part in perception. In general, we can group the key factors involved in human perception in terms of physiological factors, situational factors, and psychological factors.

PHYSIOLOGICAL FACTORS

Sensory input can be thought of as being screened through various kinds of physiological and psychological filters. From a physiological perspective, perception of sensory input will depend on factors including *the level of functioning* of sensory organs and the areas of the nervous system that process such input. In this sense, for example, color-blindness may be thought of as one filter through which visual input is processed. An individual who is red-green color-blind, for example, will experience red and green in a manner different from the individual having normal color vision. A person who has an exceptional sense of smell (olfactory sense) screens olfactory stimuli differently from people having average olfactory abilities. Perfume manufacturers typically seek out and employ people with higher-than-average olfactory ability for work in quality control and the development of new

FIGURE 6–6 OF DEATH AND LIFELONG STRESS On May 4, 1970, the Ohio National Guard was called to duty to quell anti-Vietnam-war demonstrations at Kent State University. After one of the guardsmen lobbed a tear gas grenade to disperse the crowd, student Jeffrey Miller picked up the grenade and lobbed it back in the direction of the Guardsmen. Miller was then shot dead. This photo of a woman kneeling in anguish alongside Miller's lifeless body came to symbolize the horror that took place that day. The event would haunt not only Miller's family and the families of other students who were killed, but Mary Ann Vecchio, the woman immortalized in this photo. At the time, she was a 14-year-old runaway from Florida. Five years after the shooting, she was quoted as saying, "I've been miserable since Kent State." In the intervening period, she had been arrested for crimes such as loitering and marijuana possession, and had been sent to a juvenile home. In May of 1990, Ms. Vecchio was approached by a reporter for comment on the twentieth anniversary of the Kent State tragedy. Then 34 years old and supervisor of cashiers at a Las Vegas casino, Ms. Vecchio declined to be interviewed saying, "It really destroyed my life, and I don't want to talk about it" ("Kneeling with Death," 1990).

CLOSE-UP

Cultural Confusion as a Source of Stress

In a classic work originally published in 1897, Durkheim (1951) advanced the idea that weakened links between individuals and their cultural community caused such great distress that widespread suicide could be expected to result. An unusually high number of suicides were recorded between 1979 and 1984 in Alaska. Were these record high data consistent with Durkheim's theory?

The annual suicide rate for Alaska natives for the period 1979 through 1984 was about twice that of sex- and age-matched groups in the entire United States population. Because some proportion of deaths certified as accidents in Alaska are also thought to be suicides, the actual suicide rate is in all probability much higher than the official data would lead one to believe.

Two investigators reviewed and analyzed official death certificates for native Alaskan suicide victims for the period 1979 to 1984 (Kettl & Bixler, 1991). These researchers concluded that, "Cultural confusion is probably the biggest culprit in the increase in native suicide rates . . ." (p. 61) They pointed out that Alaska had remained relatively isolated even after it became a state in 1959. In the mid-1960s however, oil was discovered, and Alaska and native Alaskans would never be the same:

> New money and technology brought television into every village, and Alaska natives found themselves culturally assaulted not only by newcomers but also by the propagation of American culture by movies and television. Alaskan natives would hunt whales in walrus-skin boats and return home to watch Johnny Carson on television. An ancient way of life began to dis-

sipate, and cultural confusion was left in its wake. Youngsters growing up would wonder whether they should follow traditional Eskimo ways, learn the newer American culture, or find some common ground between the two. (Kettl & Bixler, 1991, pp. 55–56)

Kettl and Bixler observed that their analysis of the suicide data was consistent with Durkheim's theory. Alaskan natives who were members of the two groups that benefited most from the discovery of oil, the Athabaskan Indians and the Inupiat Eskimos, had the highest suicide rates. The peak in the suicide rate for all people native to Alaska was 1976, a year that paralleled peak economic growth in that state. That year, suicides among native Alaskans were four times the national average.

Kettl and Bixler also observed that an analysis of the distribution of suicides for older native Alaskans, women, and young men also confirmed what would be expected from Durkheim's theory. Since elder native Alaskans were respected as depositories of cultural knowledge, their rate of suicide would

be expected to be low. In fact, there were no suicides among Alaskans who were aged 55 or over—a marked contrast to the relatively high rate of suicide in an age-matched group in the United States. According to Durkheim's theory, native women might also be shielded from the stress of the cultural transition in Alaska, due to their preoccupation with traditional roles such childcare and homemaking. In fact, as Durkheim's theory would have predicted, the great majority of suicide victims were young, single males. Kettl and Bixler explain:

> The young Alaska native was faced with a paradox. He had literally all of the careers in the world to pursue and yet did not have the choice of pursuing the lifestyles of his ancestors. The lifestyle of the past was gone, but no clear substitute took its place. Instead, a morass of American pop culture, alcohol, and money from the oil-rich north slope quickly moved in and truly overwhelmed young Alaskans. They became more familiar with TV reruns than subsistence hunting and fishing, and consequently less connected with their past, their identity, and themselves. (p. 60)

Interestingly, a similar process of cultural change is currently in progress in the independent states of the former Soviet Union and cultural confusion is rampant (Bohlen, 1992). A 16-year-old boy wrote a disturbing letter to a newspaper stating that he was a "citizen of a nonexistent state" and that he did not know where he lived (Bohlen, 1992). Bohlen commented that "Such confusion is not just a question of borders or competing claims of sovereignty. It is psychological and for some even traumatic."

SELF-ASSESSMENT

Hassles in the Lives of Students

There is research to suggest that daily hassles, or everyday kinds of stressors, may be highly predictive of adverse physical and mental conditions (Burks & Martin, 1983; DeLongis et al., 1982; Monroe, 1983; Eckenrode, 1984; Weinberger et al., 1987). *The Hassles Scale* (Kanner et al., 1981), perhaps the most commonly used measure of hassles, has been criticized by some as being not a pure measure of everyday stressors (Dohrenwend et al., 1984; Dohrenwend & Shrout, 1985; B. Green, 1986; Marziali & Pilkonis, 1986). Overreaction to everyday stressors may prompt some test-takers to overrate the hassles on the scale, thus inflating scores. Kohn, Lafreniere, & Gurevich (1990) attempted to remedy some of the deficiencies of the Hassle Scale by creating their own hassle scale—which they purposely did not call a hassle scale. Rather, they gave it the more "innocuous title" (p. 621) of the Inventory of College Students' Recent Life Experiences (ICSRLE).

Here then is the ICSRLE, a measure of college student hassles. If you wish, follow the directions and take this test as you would most of the other self-assessment instruments—*just for fun*. Do not sum scores to reach a composite score because the composite score would probably not be meaningful anyway. The ICSRLE is in a very early stage of development and was developed on the basis of data from relatively few students, all at a Canadian university, and in a ratio of about 3 females to every male. For this reason, no meaningful interpretations of total test scores could or should be made by American students. After you have completed the test, you may wish to derive your own insights simply by scanning the patterns of your responses.

INVENTORY OF COLLEGE STUDENTS' RECENT LIFE EXPERIENCES (ICSRLE)

Following is a list of experiences which many students have some time or other. Please indicate for each experience how much it has been a part of your life *over the past month*. Put a "1" in the space provided next to an experience if it was *not at all* part of your life over the past month (e.g., "trouble with mother in law—*1*"); "2" for an experience which was *only slightly* part of our life over that time; "3" for an experience which was *distinctly* part of your life; and "4" for an experience which was *very much* part of your life over the past month.

1. Conflicts with boyfriend's/girlfriend's/spouse's family _____
2. Being let down or disappointed by friend _____
3. Conflict with professor(s) _____
4. Social rejection _____
5. Too many things to do at once _____
6. Being taken for granted _____
7. Financial conflicts with family members _____
8. Having your trust betrayed by a friend _____
9. Separation from people you care about _____
10. Having your contributions overlooked _____
11. Struggling to meet your own academic standards _____
12. Being taken advantage of _____
13. Not enough leisure time _____
14. Struggling to meet the academic standards of others _____
15. A lot of responsibilities _____
16. Dissatisfaction with school _____
17. Decisions about intimate relationship(s) _____

18. Not enough time to meet your obligations _____
19. Dissatisfaction with your mathematical ability _____
20. Important decision about your future career _____
21. Financial burdens _____
22. Dissatisfaction with your reading ability _____
23. Important decisions about your education _____
24. Loneliness _____
25. Lower grades than you hoped for _____
26. Conflict with teaching assistant(s) _____
27. Not enough time for sleep _____
28. Conflicts with your family _____
29. Heavy demands from extracurricular activities _____
30. Finding courses too demanding _____
31. Conflicts with friends _____
32. Hard effort to get ahead _____
33. Poor health of a friend _____
34. Disliking your studies _____

35. Getting "ripped off" or cheated in the purchase of services _____
36. Social conflicts over smoking _____
37. Difficulties with transportation _____
38. Disliking fellow student(s) _____
39. Conflicts with boyfriend/girlfriend/spouse _____
40. Dissatisfaction with your ability at written expression _____
41. Interruptions of your school work _____
42. Social isolation _____
43. Long waits to get service (e.g., at banks, stores, etc.) _____
44. Being ignored _____
45. Dissatisfaction with your physical appearance _____
46. Finding course(s) uninteresting _____
47. Gossip concerning someone you care about _____
48. Failing to get expected job_____
49. Dissatisfaction with your athletic skills _____

fragrances. Such individuals in the French perfume industry—referred to as "noses"—are rare, extremely esteemed, and highly paid.

The *physical intactness* of any organ that may act as a receptor of sensory input (eyes, ears, skin, and nose) plays an important part in the sensory filter system. A break in the skin, for example, may alter the way you experience touch at that particular point. *Preexisting stimuli* may have a profound effect on perception. For example, try drinking orange juice immediately after brushing your teeth with toothpaste. The orange juice may now taste much different as a result of the toothpaste's residue in the mouth.

Our sensory apparatus has a limited range of sensitivity. For a stimulus event to be perceptible, it must fall within the physical limits of reception range. For example, a silent dog whistle will arouse the attention of a dog having normal hearing, although the frequency of the sound is beyond the range of most people's hearing.

SITUATIONAL FACTORS

Situational factors also play a part in perception. For example, consider the *background* against which something is perceived. A black speck will be readily spotted in a glass of milk but remain virtually invisible on a blacktopped driveway. Imagine going to a comedy club and finding that you are the only person in the audience. Under such circumstances, the comedians may not seem as funny as they would in a packed room in which roaring laughter greeted every line. For this reason, the producers of many television sitcoms add recorded laughter to the soundtrack in the hope that the laughter will be contagious.

Perspective also makes a difference in how things are perceived. The pyramids in Egypt, for example, might vary greatly depending upon whether seen from a ground-level perspective or from the vantage point of a helicopter. *Activity within the environment* is another factor that may influence perception. When you are sitting stationary in a train looking out the window, you may perceive movement of the train even though it is actually the movement of the train on the track next to yours that results in the perception.

A factor that can make a great difference in terms of what one visually perceives is *available light*. During the day, we remark at the many different colors we see gracing the houses and cars on the street. With only moonlight as illumination, however, it is nearly impossible to distinguish such colors, even from a relatively short distance.

Generally speaking, the kind of lifestyle one leads is also a great influence on perception. As we saw in Chapter 3, lifestyle refers to a relatively consistent day-to-day pattern of living. If you are living the lifestyle of the homeless, an apartment most people would find modest may seem like a palace. On the other hand, if you happen to be a privileged, pampered, but nonetheless unhappy member of royalty, even a palace may seem like a prison.

PSYCHOLOGICAL FACTORS

Numerous psychological factors, including level of psychopathology and education can affect perception. The fact that needs can strongly influence perception is captured in the imagery of the person dying of thirst in the desert who sees a water source, only to find a sandy mirage. Sensing something that isn't really there can sometimes represent the body's desperate way of attempting to meet its physical needs. The fact that motivation and past experience may affect perception is reflected in such homespun wisdom as, "You see what you want to see and you hear what you want to hear." The sheer number of stimuli coming in to the brain at any time may be thought of as a psychological factor in perception. For example, an air-traffic controller must typically monitor simultaneously more activity than a toll collector, who conducts only one transaction at a time. For this reason, the air-traffic controller's "filtering system" can be thought of as much sharper, well-defined, or finer than that of the toll collector—at least when they are on duty.

Psychological filters sort out new from old information, and integrate the new into the existing framework. However, under exceptional circumstances when the information being input is intolerably stressful, psychological filters are capable of shutting down. Alternatively, hypothetical filters may be capable of screening out things or parts of things that may be too painful to perceive. In those cases, the filters may block the assimilation (or incorporation into our fund of information and experience) of information that would prove extremely stressful (Shontz, 1975). For example, an abiding belief that we live in a humane and just world might block the assimilation of news of the death of an infant in cross fire. Other kinds of thoughts—rational or irrational—may act to block the assimilation of other kinds of stressful cognitions (Horowitz, 1976, 1979). These filters may also be thought of as being "tuned" differently in different people. Some people are more disposed than others to laugh at or construe in a humorous way input that others might find extremely stressful. Some people are more disposed to interpret stimuli some might find stressful in the best possible light. The person so disposed may thus be less likely to be negatively affected by the would-be stressor (Martin & Lefcourt, 1983; McCrae, 1984; Nezu et al., 1984).

Humans as well as other organisms strive to maintain what is called an *optimal level of arousal*. An optimal level is not one so high as to cause too much excitement and one not so low as to cause boredom. Rather, it is something between these two extremes. An optimal level of arousal may differ quite a bit for different people. For example, we might expect that a person who scores very high on Zuckerman's sensation-seeking scale has an optimal level of arousal that is much higher than that of an individual who scores very low. Similarly, individual differences in the perception of stress could be explained with reference to the psychological concept of an optimal level of arousal.

model

a representation of some person, place, object, or process, devised to facilitate general understanding and specific information about operation, utility, and structure.

A MODEL OF STRESSOR PERCEPTION

To understand stress perception and human perception in general, the stressor perception model in Figure 6–7 may be helpful. In this context, a **model** can be defined as *a representation of some person, place, object, or process, devised to facilitate general understanding and*

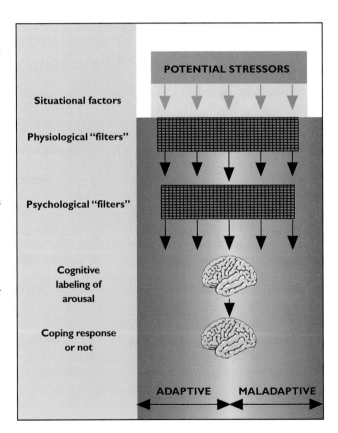

FIGURE 6–7 A MODEL OF STRESSOR PERCEPTION Within the context of the unique aspects of a particular situation, sensory input is screened by physiological as well as psychological filters. This screening or filtering process may be adaptive or maladaptive based on factors such as the presence, absence, and/or magnitude of psychopathology. Individuals make cognitive determinations about their perceived level of arousal, in essence answering questions such as, "Am I under stress?" and, "Is a coping response required?" The process of labeling one's state of arousal and the appraisal of the presence of stress as well as decisions regarding coping responses may all be adaptive or maladaptive.

specific information about operation, utility, and structure. Physiological filters and psychological filters are constructs that illustrate the process by which an individual ultimately labels a potential stressor as stressful or not; these "filters" have no physical existence in the brain.

It can be seen in Figure 6–7 that how someone perceives or experiences a sensory stimulus depends on the action and interaction of a number of factors including the nature of the potential stressor itself, situational factors, the individual's physiological and psychological filtering system, the degree and nature of the arousal precipitated, and the cognitive labeling of the arousal state experienced.

POTENTIAL STRESSORS

The term *potential stressor* is used in the model to emphasize the relative nature of forces that cause stress. What causes stress may depend on a number of factors that are unique to a particular situation (referred to in the model as *situational factors*), as well as on other factors that are unique to the individual (referred to in the model as *physiological filters* and *psychological filters*.)

SITUATIONAL FACTORS

The magnitude and intensity of noise that many construction workers are exposed to—such as constant hammering, jackhammering, and sawing—can be quite high. For the seasoned construction worker, however, such noise is all in a day's work, and much of it is probably not even perceived. For people whose work day is typically spent in a quiet office, library, or similar environment, the noise of a construction site might prove quite stressful. But after a day's work, and in the context of trying to relax by going to the movies, the construction worker would probably be as annoyed as the next person if noise like that at the construction site became audible in the theater. Such unanticipated and distracting noise would most likely be disturbing to everyone in the audience. Like many other potential stressors, noise must therefore be considered in its situational context before an informed appraisal can be made about how much stress it is causing.

THE FILTERING SYSTEM

Sensory stimuli are screened through a system composed of a complex network of physiological and psychological filters. Incoming sensory information, including one's own thoughts, may be thought of as being processed with respect to experience, to past and existing beliefs, opinions, and feelings, and to other information. As illustrated in Figure 6–7, this process may—as with the arousal and coping responses that follow—proceed in an adaptive or maladaptive fashion. Here, **adaptive** generally describes *a rational process that yields constructive thoughts or behaviors* and **maladaptive** generally describes *a typically irrational process that does not yield constructive thoughts or behavior. Maladaptive may also be thought of as being hurtful to oneself and/or others.*

The line separating adaptive from maladaptive is not always clear and may require a judgment call. There are also times when it seems obvious to all concerned, even laypersons, which responses are adaptive and which are maladaptive. Consider the thoughts of different high-school students receiving a letter grade of B in physics. Which types of perceptions seem adaptive to you and which seem maladaptive?

> "Wow! I got a B in physics! I'm going to go out and celebrate!"

> I think I deserved a higher grade than a B. I'm going to have to discuss this with the teacher.

> This grade is a crushing assault on me! I'm going to kill myself with a butcher knife! But first I'm going to kill the teacher who gave me this grade!

The first two responses are adaptive, while the third response is clearly maladaptive. In 1990, a high school physics teacher in a Florida public high school was stabbed with a butcher knife by a student to whom he had given a *B*—the student's first *B*. The teacher survived and testified at the trial that the student had lunged at him from behind. The teacher struggled to wrest the knife away from the student before more severe injury

adaptive

an adjective describing a rational process that yields constructive thoughts or behaviors.

maladaptive

an adjective describing a typically irrational process that does not yield constructive thoughts or behavior and may result to being hurtful to oneself or others.

could be inflicted. The student's defense attorney contended that his client was temporarily insane at the time of the incident, was obsessed with academic excellence, and was actually trying to kill himself, not the teacher. The student's course load included four honors classes and three advanced college-placement courses. The student believed that the physics grade jeopardized his dream of attending Harvard Medical School. The court found the student not guilty on the basis of temporary insanity and ordered that both he and his parents undergo psychotherapy for 12 months. Expelled from the public high school, the student graduated from a private high school in 1992 and gave the valedictory address. In the address, he said, "There's nothing wrong with reaching for the stars, but it takes slow and careful preparation" ("Student Who Stabbed Teacher," 1992). Presumably, the nature of this student's filtering system has been altered by his psychotherapeutic experience. Should he receive a grade in the future that for any reason displeases him, he will, we must hope, be prepared to deal with it more adaptively than he did in the past.

COGNITIVE LABELING OF AROUSAL

The state of arousal experienced in response to a stimulus is given a cognitive label by the person aroused. Two types of mental labels to describe the effect of potential stressors are *stressful* and *not stressful*. The label chosen may be the product of an adaptive or maladaptive labeling process. If maladaptive, sensory input that is in reality stressful (for example, life threatening) might be labeled *not stressful*. Maladaptive cognitive labeling may also result in input that is in reality not stressful (such as a noninsult that is perceived as an insult) being labeled *stressful*. Our labeling of a stressor as stressful or not stressful will in turn have consequences on the coping decision.

THE COPING DECISION

Like the process of perception, the process of deciding how to cope with stress may be adaptive or maladaptive. Adaptive decision making involving rational thoughts are likely to lead to constructive solutions. Maladaptive decision making involving irrational thoughts are not likely to lead to constructive solutions. Making no response at all to stress when adjustment is warranted is viewed as maladaptive behavior according to this model. However, where the stress is perceived as what Selye called eustress, a response of "no response" may be adaptive because such "good stress" need not require coping responses.

The coping decision, whether adaptive or maladaptive, will depend upon a wide range of overlapping factors such as the decision-maker's personality, physiological state, mental state, and learning history. In the following chapter, our stressor perception model will be extended to help explain some of the ways that people cope with stress.

THE POSITIVE SIDE OF STRESS

It bears repeating that stress is very much a part of life, and we all must learn to live with it. A little bit of stress is not only not a bad thing, it is quite normal. We sometimes even seek out moderate amounts of stress, such as the type of stress involved in riding a roller coaster or seeing an anxiety-provoking film, in order to keep from being bored—or as some psychologists might say, "to maintain an optimal level of arousal." Then there are those other kinds of stressful experiences that we do not seek out, experiences like academic examinations, public speeches, or emotional arguments with loved ones. One can expect the stress level to rise in response to such events. But perhaps more importantly, one can learn from these experiences. To cope adaptively with certain kinds of stress is often personally fulfilling. It is precisely the kind of experience that can make you feel and believe that you are truly growing as a person.

SUMMARY

WHAT IS STRESS? *Stress* may be defined as mental and/or physical strain resulting from adjustive demands or challenges. It may be viewed from physiological and psychological perspectives, among others. From a physiological perspective, the focus is on the changes that take place in the body as a result of the perception of stress, including all of the changes initiated by the sympathetic nervous system. From a psychological perspective, focus is placed on the cognitive aspects of arousal, and the cognitive factors that enter into the labeling of emotional states.

WHAT ARE STRESSORS? *Stressors* are forces capable of causing stress and they may be categorized in various overlapping ways. Stressors may be physical in nature, as in the case of a polluted or noisy environment. Stressors may be psychological in nature and take the form of mental conflict, frustration, or pressure. Stressors may also be viewed as being cultural, as in the case of sweeping societal changes that cause upheaval in individual identities and cultural traditions.

THE PERCEPTION OF STRESS *Perception* was defined as the process whereby sensory stimuli are organized and interpreted into meaningful cognitions. There is not necessarily any one-to-one relationship between what is out there in reality and one's perception of reality. Rather, perception is the product of physiological, situational, and psychological factors, all overlapping. A model of how stress is perceived took note of the role such factors may play in filtering stress-related information and in coping with it.

THE POSITIVE SIDE OF STRESS Certain types of stress can help stave off boredom, help us to maintain an optimal level of arousal, and serve as a stimulus for personal growth.

Coping

O U T L I N E

Stress is very much a part of everyday life, and in everyday life people **cope** or *contend* with stress. Coping may take place in response to a stressful or traumatic event. Coping may also take place in response to some anticipated stressful or traumatic event. **Adaptive coping** takes place when *the source of the stress is maturely and effectively addressed, thereby lessening the stress or making it more tolerable.* **Maladaptive coping** takes place when *the source of the stress is ineffectively or inadequately addressed and the stress either remains or is compounded.* Consider how one might cope adaptively and maladaptively with the stress of being rejected by one's first choice of graduate schools. An adaptive coping response would be to wait to hear from other schools one had applied to, or to send out applications to more schools. A maladaptive way of coping with that same rejection would be to begin plotting retaliatory acts against the rejecting school. Can you think of other ways that coping behavior might be categorized?

VARIETIES OF COPING BEHAVIOR

cope

contend, adapt, or adjust.

adaptive coping

contending with stress in a manner such that the source of the stress is maturely and effectively addressed as a result, and the stress is thereby lessened, eliminated, or made more tolerable.

maladaptive coping

contending with stress in a manner such that the source of the stress is ineffectively or inadequately addressed, and the stress either remains or is compounded as a result.

Coping can be a very private affair. Some people struggle daily with troubling thoughts, convinced that no one but they can effectively address their personal problems. But coping can also be public in nature, as in cases when people reach out to others, professionals or nonprofessionals, for counsel and guidance. Coping may be limited to thinking and feeling or take the form of observable behavior. That behavior may be targeted to deal directly with the source of the stress. Let's call this type of behavioral coping strategy *direct action*. Alternatively, behavior may be targeted to deal indirectly with the source of stress—a strategy of coping that we will refer to as *indirect action*. Direct or indirect action may also be adaptive or maladaptive in nature. For example, consider an employee who is scolded by the boss. The employee may cope adaptively with the stress directly, such as by talking to the boss with the objective of satisfactorily resolving the complaint, or indirectly, such as by taking an exercise class to blow off steam. The employee may deal maladaptively with the stress directly, such as by physically threatening or striking the boss, or indirectly, such as by getting drunk after work. These various coping strategies are illustrated in Table 7–1.

The alternative to coping, that is, not coping, is a rather extreme alternative. Most people attempt to cope with stress—some cope adaptively, some cope maladaptively, and the rest attempt to cope in a manner that could be described as somewhere between these two ends of the coping spectrum. To refuse or to be unable to attempt to cope is to be overwhelmed to the point of immobilization.

In this chapter, we will survey some of the ways—public and private, as well as adaptive and maladaptive—that people cope with stress. As you read about these methods of coping, think about the sources of stress in your own life and evaluate how you have coped with these sources of stress in the past. Later in the chapter, a model of coping behavior will be presented.

TABLE 7–1   DIRECT/INDIRECT COPING BEHAVIOR AND ADAPTIVENESS

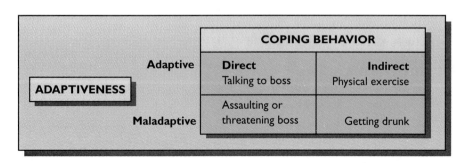

		COPING BEHAVIOR	
		Direct	**Indirect**
ADAPTIVENESS	Adaptive	Talking to boss	Physical exercise
	Maladaptive	Assaulting or threatening boss	Getting drunk

PERSONAL COPING

In the course of conversation with a friend of mine who is an adult professional male in his late 30s, I was quite surprised to learn how he characteristically coped with stress. His method was to get into his car, make certain that the windows were all rolled up tight, and then yell as loud as he could until he began to feel better. Driving the car was optional.

I am aware of no survey data that would provide information about how common this "secluded yell" technique is, nor any scientific reports of it having any value. Still, this report by a single person intrigued me sufficiently to prompt a review of the literature on coping behavior. By conducting that review, as well as by informally and unscientifically questioning students and others I know, I derived the list of coping strategies presented in Table 7–2. Each of these methods of coping—some of them adaptive, others of them maladaptive—could be elaborated on with interesting details and intriguing stories. For example, if you currently own a pet, you can probably generate a number of your own stories about how interacting with it can help reduce or buffer stress (see *Quality of Life*).

In what follows, we examine everyday kinds of thoughts, feelings, and behaviors people use to cope with stress. Although some of the coping techniques may sound like—indeed have the same name as—the defense mechanisms first described by Freud (see pages 36 to 37), the terms (such as *denial*) here have their everyday, familiar meanings.[1]

[1]Freud believed that ego defense mechanisms were largely unconscious and the result of exchanges of what he called psychic energy. The use of such terms in this discussion carries with it no such assumptions.

TABLE 7–2   SOME EVERYDAY WAYS ADULTS COPE WITH STRESS

Here is a nonexhaustive list of the ways people have devised to cope—or to attempt to cope—with stress. Which of the following techniques do you think are adaptive? Maladaptive? Is your preferred coping method listed? If not, please drop me a note in care of the publisher and let me know of this oversight.

Bubble bath indulgence	Music (playing an instrument)
Cleaning	Needlepoint
Crying ("having a good cry")	Playing with a child
Daydreaming	Playing with a pet
Drinking or other drug use	Prayer
Eating	Punching, kicking, or otherwise striking a pillow or something else
Entertainment as distraction (watching television, reading, etc.)	Rearranging drawers
Exercise (walking, running, sit-ups, weight training, etc.)	Self-indulgence
	Self-punishment
Gambling	Sewing
Gardening	Sex
Jacuzzi sitting	Shopping
Knitting	Sleep
Masturbation	Smoking
Meditation	Talking it out to yourself
Movies or video rental	Talking it out with others
Mowing the lawn	Throwing something
Music (hard rock with volume cranked up)	Working
	Yelling (publicly)
Music (classical with volume at a soothing level)	Yelling (secluded)

QUALITY OF *Life*

Pets Against Stress

Exhibiting her trademark contagious smile is the author's pride and joy, Sheena Cohen. I'll preface further description of Sheena by telling you that, as a psychologist, I was trained *not to* describe animal behavior in **anthropomorphic** (that is, *person-like*) terms, but rather to think of such behavior strictly in terms of instinct, stimulus, and response. I must confess, however, that I could no more think of this member of my family in strict stimulus-response terms than I could of any other member of my family.

Sheena has been my constant companion through many years of writing. During breaks away from the keyboard we play catch, hide 'n' sneak, or towel tug of war; or just spend some quality time cuddling. Like many dogs, she is quite transparent in communicating how she feels through verbal and nonverbal gestures. Tail wagging equals happy, while tail-between-legs equals anxious. A conspicuous lick of the chops says, "I'd like to sample what you're eating," while other types of licks administered to the hand or face convey affection or other messages, such as, "I'm hungry." Sometimes what she is trying to communicate by her behavior or wide range of vocalizations is not clear. Perhaps it is better that way. If dogs could talk, many dogs and their masters would probably not be talking. Disputes over food, feeding times, frisbee catching, and where and when to scratch would do in many a relationship.

I picked out Sheena about 7 years ago at my first and only trip to the ASPCA dog pound in Manhattan. Some fool had the poor judgment to abandon this beautiful creature in traffic (Sheena is a homebody, and I believe she did not run away, but must

instead have been abandoned by someone very determined to leave her). Her boundless love and eternally surprising displays of intellect have nourished in me a heightened respect and regard for animals. She has greatly and significantly enriched my life. Are my feelings about my pet unique?

Probably not. Adjamine (1992) described how what was once a battered, matted, injured, middle-aged, Shepherd-Labrador mix that no one wanted was cleaned up, brought to her home, accepted by her cats, and instantly became a well-behaved and affectionate member of her household. More than that, the dog helped to teach her an important lesson about hope: She wrote, "I have watched this symbol of neglect and despair become a loving animal, seemingly waking up to life and kindness for the first time. I have learned that there is life and hope even after the worst of inequities, pain and pessimism."

Owners may perceive their pets as social assets (Luborsky et al., 1973), supportive in times of stress (Smith, 1983), and a kind of peacemaker who

COPING BY THINKING AND FEELING

negative affect

an unpleasant state of tension that may take the form of anxiety or feelings of dread.

cognitive coping

a process of using thoughts as a means of diminishing, eliminating, or helping oneself to feel better about the negative affect associated with stress. Contrast with *behavioral coping*.

Negative affect, or *anxiety, feelings of dread, or an unpleasant state of tension,* is a frequent accompaniment or consequence of stress, if not a defining element. One way people cope with stress and the negative affect associated with it is cognitive (or *mental*) in nature. The term **cognitive coping** therefore refers to *a process of using thoughts as a means of diminishing, eliminating, or helping oneself to feel better about the negative affect associated with stress.* Cognitive coping may be distinguished from **behavioral coping**, which refers to *a process of using action in addition to thoughts as a means of diminishing, eliminating, or helping oneself to feel better about the negative affect associated with stress.*

Technically, there is not always a clear line between coping that is cognitive or behavioral in nature. Cognitions can influence behavior and behavior can influence cognitions. For example, you may *feel* confident (a cognition), and therefore *act* confidently (a behav-

can reduce tension between family members (Meer, 1984). Pets can help make people feel safer (Katcher & Friedman, 1980), and make humans more humane (Bustad, 1979). Just watching an aquarium prior to dental work can reduce dental anxiety (Katcher et al., 1984). Pets provide a focus of pleasurable daily activities for owners and a ready source of nurturance and contact comfort. For a retired person or one having no daily scheduled activities, a pet may serve as a kind of clock. Echoing the sentiments of Fox (1975), Friedmann et al. (1980) extol the benefits of pet ownership by noting that pets are always available to give or receive attention.

Petting a pet can lower the pet's blood pressure (Anderson & Gantt, 1966; Lynch et al., 1974; Lynch & McCarthy, 1969; Newton & Ehrlich, 1966) and positively affect the owner's cardiovascular functioning (Friedmann et al., 1983; Lynch, 1985). In a study of 1-year survival of patients after discharge from a coronary care unit, researchers concluded that pet ownership added significantly to chances of survival

(Friedmann et al., 1980). Exactly why this should be the case was left open to question. The answer may lie in the nature of the interaction between the owners and the pets or in other factors, such as the preexisting personality differences between the group of pet-owners and the group of nonowners.

Some studies on naturally occurring pet ownership (as opposed to cases in which subjects are given pets for the purpose of research) have concluded that there are no physical (Robb & Stegman, 1983) or psychological (Lawton et al., 1984; Ory & Goldberg, 1983; Robb & Stegman, 1983) benefits to owning a pet. However, there is growing research literature that suggests that pet ownership may serve as a buffer to stress and perhaps even to illness (Allen, 1985; Allen et al., 1991; Anderson et al., 1984; Gage & Anderson, 1985; Katcher & Beck, 1983). The use of "pet therapy," particularly when the pet is a dog, may provide a buffer against stress in the elderly (Siegel, 1990). Pets may also play a very humane role in the treat-

ment of the terminally ill because, unlike people, they do not avoid such patients. Muschel (1984, p. 457) further observed that the "animal's quiet, accepting, and nurturing presence strengthens and frees the patient to resolve his or her experience successfully."

Many high-power corporate executives own pets and bring them to work daily. One psychologist believes that such behavior may reflect either an effort "to be more human," or an effort to show "that you're in a position of power or favor and you can do anything you want" (Soder, 1992). However, an author and dog trainer for many corporate leaders (cited in Becker, 1992) believes on the basis of his experience that keeping a dog at the worksite not only reduces stress, but also increases productivity.

Almost half of the households in America have a pet of some sort. If you do not currently own one, you may wish to consider the possibilities.

ior), or you may act confidently (behavior) and therefore feel confident (a cognition). Further, what is viewed as cognitive as distinguished from behavioral is in some contexts more a matter of perspective than of meaningful difference. For example, is sleep a cognitive or a behavioral activity? In fact, it is both. With this caution in mind about the sometimes artificial nature of the dichotomy between cognition and behavior, let's take a closer look at some cognitive and behavioral coping techniques. We begin with a brief and noncomprehensive survey of some cognitive factors in coping.

COGNITIVE FACTORS IN COPING

For most of us, coping by thinking thoughts to counter the discomfort of stress is virtually automatic or reflexive. Some of the cognitive coping strategies we might use are listed in Table 7–3. Some of the ways we might categorize cognitive aspects of coping behavior

anthropomorphic

human-like or person-like.

behavioral coping

a process of using action in addition to thoughts as a means of diminishing, eliminating, or helping oneself to feel better about the negative affect associated with stress. Contrast with *cognitive coping*.

TABLE 7–3   A SAMPLE OF COGNITIVE COPING METHODS

Technique	Definition
Rational Thinking	Thinking reasonably about whatever the source of the anxiety is and not blowing it out of proportion or "catastrophizing."
Imagining or Fantasizing	Visualizing how things might have been done differently, how you would have liked things to occur, or how in fact they might occur in the future.
Denial	Consciously attempting to block out the source of the anxiety as if it had never happened.
Problem Solving	Mentally searching for alternative solutions; this is also referred to as "brainstorming" when this activity is engaged in by two or more people having a common objective.
Rationalization	Justifying the stress in some way.
Humor	Coping with stress by confronting it directly, yet allowing for positive affect or emotion.
Prayer	Appealing to a higher, spiritual authority for some wish to be granted.
Religious Faith	Coping by comforting oneself with the thought that whatever happened did so as a result of divine will.

include by whether they (1) are adaptive or maladaptive, (2) employ defense mechanisms such as denial or rationalization, (3) employ humor to minimize the impact of the stress, (4) use prayer or religious meditation as a coping tool, or (5) employ other techniques such as problem solving or brainstorming.

As an exercise in thinking about adaptive versus maladaptive cognitions in response to stress, imagine all that would take place if you returned from school to find that your residence had been burglarized. What would your initial reaction be? What would you think? How would you feel? What would you do? What things would you tell yourself in order to feel better?

Your initial reaction may be one of panic and your initial thoughts might race towards an assessment of the damage: "What was stolen? What was broken? How much worse off am I now than I was before the break-in?"

Within moments, however, you might progress from the stage of panic and damage assessment to active coping. You might, for example, begin to tell yourself things like this in order to feel better:

"Calm down; anything they took can be replaced."

"Thankfully, I wasn't personally harmed."

"I'll report this to the police; perhaps they will be able to recover my things."

"I am going to take more adequate precautions in the future, such as storing valuables in a more secure place and installing a security system."

Each of the responses above are adaptive because they address the source of stress in a mature and effective way that is designed to make the stress more tolerable. What about self-talk more like these sentences?

"My home was violated and my life has been destroyed!"

"They've taken everything of value that I had, and I now have nothing to live for!"

"I'm going to buy a gun and blow away who ever did this!"

These types of thoughts are maladaptive because they are out of proportion and do not address the stress effectively. In fact, thoughts such as these will most likely have the effect of *compounding* the stress.

Self-talk may also take the form of *denial* ("I am going to forget about this"). Denial as a coping strategy has the potential of being either adaptive or maladaptive, depending upon how it is used. To discover that one's residence has been burglarized and to respond immediately with denial—as if nothing has happened—would clearly be maladaptive. There are important papers that may have to be replaced or other tasks that must be tackled, and such a denial of reality would almost certainly have serious repercussions. True, denial under these, as well as other, circumstances does have what may seem to be some short-term advantages, such as the immediate reduction of stress. But, you may know from your own experience that if you put off—or deny, in a sense—some project due for class until the last week of the semester, the stress of doing it has a way of compounding itself over time.

Denial can be adaptive under certain circumstances. For example, after time has passed since the occurrence of a traumatic episode, it might well be very adaptive to use denial as a conscious coping strategy and to say, in essence, "I am going to place this negativity behind me and move on with my life." Here, denial does not represent self-deception but rather a conscious choice. In this way, denial can be adaptive (Strain, 1978). Like denial, the cognitive coping strategy of *rationalization* may be used adaptively or maladaptively. It is maladaptive when it is used for self-deception, but it may well be adaptive if the individual using it genuinely accepts the rationalization.

Humor occupies a very special place in the coping process (see Figure 7–1). Through its judicious use, problems of varying magnitude may be addressed with a smile or a laugh instead of, or at least along with, tears and sadness. For example, even after being burglarized, it may be possible to find something to smile about. You might remark about the broken-down bicycle that was stolen, "It is going to cost them more than the bicycle is worth to fix those gears and brakes!" In 1979, there were some very tense days as a catastrophic nuclear meltdown at the Three Mile Island facility threatened Harrisburg and hundreds of nearby Pennsylvania communities. A professor at a campus some 20 miles away from the nuclear facility observed that jokes about the imminent disaster began to circulate quickly, apparently in an effort to defuse the anxiety. An example: "Do you know the 5-day forecast for Harrisburg?" "Two days" (Kassovic, 1979). A more recent example of the crisis-defusing role of humor can be found in Jay Leno's inaugural monologue as the host of the *Tonight* show on May 25, 1992. The worst rioting this nation had seen had subsided in Los Angeles about a month prior to this appearance, but the images of federal troops on the streets were still fresh in everyone's mind. Leno quipped: "Have you seen the new recruitment posters? Join the Army and see Hollywood Boulevard . . . It was great for Bob Hope. It was the first time in his career he was able to entertain the troops while standing on his back porch!"

FIGURE 7–1 HUMOR AS A COPING DEVICE This comedy troupe called "Surrealist Hit Parade" has been a big hit in the war-torn European regions of Bosnia and Herzegovina. In a mock radio newscast, listeners might be treated, for example, to a comedic account of a SWAT team out seeking blood donors. The group's radio satires have become so popular that people in the region even tape the broadcasts and some bar owners replay them for patrons (Sudetic, 1993). As one member of Surrealist Hit Parade put it, "You have to find humor to be able to function during months of depression like those we've suffered here. Without this we'd all end up in an asylum" (Petrovic, 1993, p. A4).

In therapy, I have defused situations I have found stressful by using humor, in addition to other techniques. For example, shortly after I began in private practice, a severely disturbed woman who had been referred to me by a colleague at Bellevue Hospital said to me at the end of her first session, "Dr. Cohen, when I come in next week, I'm bringing a gun. I am going to shoot you and then I am going to shoot myself." My reflexive, anxiety-reducing reaction (not verbalized to the patient) was a self-question that I could smile about: "I need this?" My response to the patient, by the way, was to ask her about the type of gun she owned, with the objective of being able to assess the reality of her threat. Had she said, for example, "a Smith & Wesson .357 magnum revolver," I might have given her threat more credence than the response she did give me (which was simply to repeat "a gun"). At any rate, there I was the following week, unarmed and vulnerable when she came through the door. Fortunately for me, my assessment of the reality of her threat was accurate, although, admittedly, it could not have been (with one of the consequences being that you would be reading someone else's adjustment textbook). On another occasion, when a depressed female patient tearfully confided to me that she had been tempted to throw herself in front of the subway train on the way to my office, I responded by telling her it was time to clear up her outstanding bill. She laughed. And it was the first time she had laughed in weeks.

For millennia before psychotherapy existed, *prayer* and religious faith have helped countless millions of people to adjust and make it through even the most trying times. Research has shown that after the death of a spouse or a divorce, regular church- or temple-goers seem to adjust better than people who do not attend religous services regularly (Siegel & Kuykendall, 1990). The possibility exists, however, that the regular church- or temple-goers were better adjusted to begin with, and/or had more of a network of close friends for support all through their lives. It is also possible, that religious faith may interfere with coping. For some people, and for reasons that are not understood, exposure to certain religious ideologies may have an adverse or "blocking" effect on coping ability (Cohen & Smith, 1976).[2]

There are certain sources of stress that can be reduced or eliminated by *creative problem solving*. Trying to live within your means when you are on a limited budget is an example of one source of stress that can be addressed by problem solving—in this case, by making decisions about expenses that are or are not truly necessary and about how to manage from day to day with available funds. Finding suitable employment in a tight job market is another source of stress that can be addressed by problem solving. Strategies other than merely sending out résumés to companies, including creative ways of networking, may be what is necessary to get the job you want. If the source of stress is one that entails finding some sort of solution or compromise, then problem solving is the obvious strategy of choice. **Brainstorming** refers to problem-solving and the seeking of creative solutions, usually by two or more people who have a shared objective.

Another concept that is key to the subject of cognitive coping strategies has to do with effectiveness in accomplishing objectives, or *self-efficacy*.

THE CONCEPT OF SELF-EFFICACY

How long or hard will people work to combat stress or other factors they perceive to be working against them? Psychologist and learning theorist Albert Bandura (1982, 1986) believes that one answer to this question can be discussed in terms of **self-efficacy**, defined as *individual judgments and perceptions regarding how effective one's actions are likely to be with respect to particular situations*. According to Bandura, our perceptions regarding our self-efficacy can greatly affect the things we tell ourselves, as well as the things we do to cope, when under various types of stress. For example, if you believe it is absolutely impossible for you to deliver a speech in public, you may persist in mentally finding evidence to support this belief, with the result that you are indeed physically unable to deliver a speech in public. As we will see when we discuss coping with the assistance of others, one way self-efficacy can be boosted is through social support.

brainstorming

problem-solving and the seeking of creative solutions, usually by two or more people who have a shared objective.

self-efficacy

one's judgments and perceptions regarding how effective one's actions are likely to be with respect to particular situations.

[2]Interested students are encouraged to refer to Cohen (1977, 1978), Coyne (1976), Ellis (1978), Halleck (1976), London (1976), McLemore and Court (1977), and Stokes (1977).

COPING BY ACTING

Coping with stress frequently involves *doing* in addition to *thinking*. You probably know from your own experience, however, that things people do in response to stress are not always adaptive or direct in terms of eradicating the source of stress. Perhaps one of the most common maladaptive and indirect responses to stress is eating. Eating is an ineffective method of coping (except in situations where the solution to the problem requires weight gain), and one that frequently compounds stress and worry rather than minimizes or eradicates it. The experience of hunger is one of our most primitive negative feeling states. We are biologically programmed to experience hunger when our bodies require nourishment. The experience of hunger may thus be likened to a blinking light in the brain that is flashing, "Something is upsetting my **homeostasis** (or *bodily equilibrium*); feed me now!" In people having problem-eating habits, there is evidence to suggest that this same flashing light goes off not only when they are hungry, but also when they are stressed, depressed, extremely joyful—in short, anytime the bodily equilibrium is upset. This explanation for overeating is somewhat simplistic, does not apply to everyone, and is only one of several factors that may be causally responsible. Further, one literature review of the phenomenon known as *emotional eating* has concluded that many of the research studies on this topic have been seriously flawed (Allison & Heshka, 1993). Still, as many clinicians have heard from their clients, and as you may well know from firsthand experience, the refrigerator is often turned to in times of stress (see Figure 7–2).

homeostasis
bodily equilibrium.

DIRECT ACTION TO RELIEVE STRESS

The sources of most stress can be readily identified and some sort of direct action—adaptive or maladaptive—can be taken to relieve them. Suppose, for example, you are sitting in a movie theater enjoying the film, when suddenly a very young child seated behind you begins to rhythmically kick your chair. There are a number of forms of direct action you may take to relieve this stress. Perhaps the most socially appropriate form of direct action would be to turn and politely ask the child to stop or ask the child's parent to have the

FIGURE 7–2 CONSUMING PASSION According to one way of thinking about emotional eating, binge eating represents an attempt to escape from self-awareness by shifting attention from the self to food (Baumeister, 1989, 1990; Heatherton & Baumeister, 1991; Heatherton et al., 1991, 1992). A more adaptive response to the stress would be to focus one's attention on the stress itself, and to deal effectively with its cause (Cohen, 1979b).

child stop. If your reasonable appeals fail, you have a number of other direct action alternatives available to you, such as asking the management to intervene or simply changing your seat if another is available.

Direct action, if it is mature, appropriate, and adaptive, is one of the best ways human beings have at their disposal to deal with stress. Direct action that is immature, inappropriate, or maladaptive is one of the worst ways to deal with stress. In the movie theater example, the wrong move would be to stand up, turn around, and scream through gritted teeth, "I'm going to beat the living daylights out of you if you don't stop kicking my chair!" Such a confrontational response might provoke an even more aggressive response from the child's father, who may happen to be employed as the sparring partner to the world heavyweight kick-boxing champion. You do not have to be a psychologist to know that attempts to relieve stress should not, to the extent that it is humanly possible, put you in imminent peril of more stress, hospitalization, lifelong disability, or worse.

Another direct action approach to coping with stress involves acquiring the competencies needed to make potentially stressful situations as minimally stressful as possible. For example, if you find the week of final examinations to be extremely stressful, it may be less stressful if you over prepare for the examinations. Such over-preparation might take the form of spending more time studying than you might ordinarily over the course of the entire semester (or quarter). By being as prepared as you can possibly be to meet the demands of a particular situation, you can reduce the amount of stress associated with that situation.

Self-help books and self-help videos are widely used ways to acquire or enhance one's competencies in various areas. The advice in such media runs the gamut from very bad to very good, depending on the individual source. How is the layperson to know what advice is good and what advice is bad? Help in making such decisions comes from the work of two researchers who explored taxonomies (or *classification systems*) of advice. According to Gottlieb and Mayer (1988), advice "provides information about problems that can be used in the process of self-regulation and change" (p. 2) and varies on a continuum between "direct and honest" to "empathic and supportive." "Direct" in this sense may be interpreted in much the same way that we have described it above with reference to behavioral strategies. Gottlieb and Mayer add that advice may also be evaluated on a continuum from "bad" to "good." An example of advice that is direct and honest (as opposed to empathic or supportive) would be this advice to an escaped felon: "Turn yourself in to the authorities." Beyond being direct and honest, we would also describe this advice as "good," at least from the perspective of society at large. An example of advice to the same individual that is empathic and supportive (as opposed to direct and honest) but "bad" might be: "Don't turn yourself in to the authorities; you deserve to be free."

One might also envision the elements of the Gottlieb and Mayer taxonomy not on a continuum that ranges from direct to supportive, but as a matter of degree of directness of the advice. Accordingly, some varieties of advice could be at once direct and honest *and* empathic and supportive. For example, "good" advice that is at once direct and supportive might be: "Turn yourself in because you may receive a lighter sentence."

When reading a self-help book or watching a self-help video, it may be helpful to pause to evaluate how good or bad the advice seems to be and whether or not it falls more at the "direct and honest" or "empathic and supportive" end of the continuum. It is also a good idea to consult a number of such sources before rigorously adhering to the suggestions contained in any one of them.

Assuming that the self-help book or video you select contains good, direct, honest, valid, prudent, and safe suggestions for remedying a particular problem—and this is a very big assumption—the book will still only be of value to the extent that its prescriptions are followed. For example, if being overweight is a source of stress, there are many fine books available on the subject that contain good, honest, valid, prudent, and safe suggestions for slimming. However, the recommendations in books featuring a reasoned and sound approach to weight loss may seem dull, if not difficult and cumbersome to implement. Rather than learning about the need for regimented food intake from various food groups, exercise, and general lifestyle changes, most people would opt for a seemingly quick solution that holds out promises of rapid weight loss and simplicity of effort. It is for this reason that the faddish, "magical," and sometimes even dangerous dieting suggestions found in the splashy dieting books often have far greater popular appeal than do far more sensible approaches.

INDIRECT ACTION TO RELIEVE STRESS

In many more situations than we would like, direct action to relieve stress is simply not an option. If, for example, you are in freeway traffic that has come to a dead stop because the President is in town, there is little in the way of direct action to be taken to relieve the stress. You can think pleasant thoughts, you can think not-so-pleasant (even nasty) thoughts that will nonetheless distract you from the stress of sitting in traffic, you can listen to music, or take other forms of indirect action to relieve stress. However, you cannot take direct action to relieve the stress because you cannot make the cars that are in your way move.

Among the most popular indirect methods of coping with stress today is exercise. The human body was designed to be active—and designed to atrophy or become weak if it is not active. As we saw in Chapter 3, people who live a *sedentary lifestyle* (that is, a lifestyle that entails a great deal of sitting and little or no exercise) are exposing themselves to greater risk for disease and early death than people who are active. That fact alone, plus the benefits of looking and feeling good as a result of exercise, should be enough to motivate most people to engage in a regular exercise program. There is an added bonus, however: During exercise, substances called *endorphins* are released in the brain. These substances are thought to contribute to the "high" many athletes report experiencing when indulging in their sport. Exactly how these natural substances work is not known, although their chemical structure is similar to morphine and their action at sites in the brain seems similar as well.

From an evolutionary perspective, consider that stress produces autonomic arousal which, as you will recall, prepares the body for fight or flight. True, engaging in physical activity such as the use of a stair-climbing machine isn't quite the same as fighting or fleeing, but such activity does have the effect of putting muscles to work, making the heart beat faster, making respiration rate increase, and so forth—all bodily effects that were once elicited by autonomic arousal. Exercise thus represents one contemporary "natural" alternative way to deal with the physiological consequences of stress.

COPING WITH THE ASSISTANCE OF OTHERS

There is a middle ground between coping on one's own and seeking professional assistance. That middle ground consists of seeking help or advice from nonprofessionals—the people we know, or people who serve the community we live in, such as members of specialized support groups.[3] This kind of support and advice can sometimes be of critical value in maintaining coping efforts, as well as in keeping such efforts headed in the right direction.

SOCIAL SUPPORT

Social support may also be differentiated by whether it is problem-specific or nonspecific. An example of an organization that offers problem-specific social support is the nonprofit group Alcoholics Anonymous (AA). It is designed to provide social support for alcoholics combating alcoholism. Other groups, such as the commercial enterprise once known as Erhard Seminars Training (EST) and now known as The Forum, provide nonspecific sources of social support. The Forum, for example, is open to virtually anyone who pays the membership fees and attends the seminars. Perhaps one of the most important variables with respect to social support concerns the receiver's perception of its quality and value (Wetherington & Kessler, 1986). Some expressions of social support are superior to others because they are perceived as being more genuine, sincere, or valuable (see Figure 7–3).

[3]"Nonprofessionals" refers here to people who do not earn their livelihood in counseling, psychotherapy with, or medicating of people having mental and/or emotional problems or disorders.

FIGURE 7–3 QUANTITY AND QUALITY OF SOCIAL SUPPORT

Much like its physical counterpart, the less tangible variety of social support psychologists speak of varies both quantitatively and qualitatively. It can be measured in terms of the number of people available to supply support as well as the amount and quality of the support supplied (Wetherington & Kessler, 1986). Most of us rely on our family, friends, and "significant others" for emotional support. Yet as you probably know from your own experience, different people can express support in different ways. Some people may express support via a batch of home-baked chocolate chip cookies while others opt for more verbal means. In your own experience, who have you found to be most supportive? For you, what distinguishes social support that is genuinely supportive from less helpful attempts? How have you coped with a lack of social support or with social support that you did not find particularly meaningful?

SOCIAL SUPPORT AND ADJUSTMENT

A large and growing literature has linked perceived social support with adaptive adjustment as well as with enhanced general well-being (Cobb, 1976; Cohen & Wills, 1985; Cutrona et al., 1986; Gore, 1978; House, 1981; Jemmott & Magloire, 1988; Leavy, 1983; Seeman et al., 1987). The absence of perceived social support has been linked to maladjustment (Fiore et al., 1983; Rook, 1984; Sandler & Barrera, 1984; Shinn et al., 1984).

Of current interest to researchers in this area is the development of a model of how social support operates to foster adaptive adjustment (Heller et al., 1986; Major et al., 1990; Wallston, et al., 1983). One model has it that perceived social support acts as a kind of buffer to soften the blow of stressful events in one's life (Cohen & Syme, 1985; Shumaker & Brownell, 1984; Major, 1990; Thoits, 1986). However, interpretation of available evidence does not straightforwardly fit a simple buffer model of social support. Other variables, such as self-efficacy, are presumed to be operative.

The mechanism by which social support works has also been explored in a study with 821 female twins that explored various aspects of social support by means of a questionnaire (Kessler et al., 1992). On the basis of their analysis of the data, the researchers questioned the validity of many existing notions about how social support works. They rejected, for example, the notion put forth by Thoits (1988) that social support helps us to resist stress by providing assistance in evaluating coping alternatives. Rather, Kessler et al. suggested that other factors, such as genes and the environment, play a much greater role in buffering the effects of stress than had previously been suggested in the social support literature. Future research also employing pairs of twins will be necessary to isolate conclusively the critical factors involved in the process of social support.

How willing we are to seek support from family, friends, and others will depend on a number of variables. Such variables include the self-esteem of the person requiring the support, past experience with the party or parties from whom support is desired, and the present nature of the relationship between the parties involved. In certain situations, such as those in which the support may be viewed as threatening or demeaning, people may be reluctant to request aid. People may reject and/or devalue offers of social support from siblings for just these reasons (Fisher et al., 1982; Nadler et al., 1974; Nadler et al., 1983;

Searcy & Eisenberg, 1992). Cultural factors, too, must be considered when evaluating how willing an individual will be to accept social support in the form of professional help, or even from family or friends.

A CULTURAL PERSPECTIVE ON HELP SEEKING

Researchers have identified some general differences between groups raised in cultures or subcultures other than the culture-defining, or majority culture in terms of attitude toward, or social acceptability of, various types of help seeking (see *Cultural Close-Up*). According to Garcia-Preto (1992), people from Hispanic cultures tend to rely on their own families as great resources for advice and counseling. To go outside the family for counsel may be construed as a sign that the person has no one to turn to within the family. Given that background, it is not surprising that many Hispanics who undergo professional treatment do so as a result of referral by a court, a prison, or some other social service agency rather than by voluntary choice. Regardless of how they arrived at a professional treatment setting, the presenting problem that caused the referral has typically mushroomed to crisis proportions by the time treatment is initiated. Yet before therapists can effectively deal with the problem, they must develop a working relationship with the client. Garcia-Preto believes that, here again, the usual rules of the game will not play well for people of Hispanic back-

C L O S E - U P

An Asian Perspective on Coping

According to Chan (1992), Asian culture teaches a mystical linkage between body, mind, and spirit. Illness (physical or mental) may be thought of as one's punishment for wrongs in this or a past life. And because all illness is thought to have a physical cause, Asian-acculturated people may be very skeptical of the benefits of any approach to therapy that entails little more than talking. The cultural bias is towards more physical treatment techniques, such as therapy employing acupuncture, herbs, or medicine. There is also more cultural tolerance for the "sick" individual who seeks a physical, as opposed to a mental, cure.

Compounding a general discounting of the rationale for psychotherapy and

skepticism about its possible benefits, there are a number of other factors that militate against psychotherapeutic success for Asian-culture patients. For example, the expression of emotion is generally discouraged among Asians. Therapists not attuned to the culture may treat such inhibition as "resistance" or some other reaction, rather than recognize it as something that is culturally instilled. The Asian client may expect a rather rapid cure—comparable to that which is sometimes effected by physical means. If a rapid cure is not forthcoming, the client, as well as the client's family, may lose faith in the treatment method and believe it is not working. In general, the traditional Asian family cannot be expected to be a great source of support

for the patient. This attitude hails back hundreds of years to when it was perceived as a great shame on the individual and the family for any one outside the family to become aware that an individual has a problem.

Chan recommends that any attempts at giving advice to people raised in an Asian culture be couched as "educational" in nature because there is a high cultural value placed on education. Additionally, involvement of the entire family, not just the patient, is recommended. The family must be educated as to the benefits that can be obtained through therapy, the projected timetable of change, and what they can do to make meaningful differences in the patient's progress.

ground. Most therapists are trained to focus attention on the patient and not to be very revealing about what is going on in their own lives. Garcia-Preto believes that therapists would do well to bend the rules and be a bit more revealing about themselves when dealing with Hispanic patients. By being more revealing about themselves, the therapist not only creates more of a family-like atmosphere, but also models that it is safe to let one's guard down in therapy.

In a presentation that compared the help-seeking patterns of people from Irish versus Italian backgrounds, McGoldrick (1992) observed that for Italians, the family is the problem-solving resource of choice, and the resource to bring problems to before going "outside." By contrast, people of Irish background would sooner go to a therapist for help than to their own families. As McGoldrick quipped with reference to Irish culture, "If your family finds out that you have a problem, you now have two problems." Accordingly, organizations like Alcoholics Anonymous provide a better cultural fit for the Irish than for Italians: The Irish cultural tradition includes people meeting and socializing in pubs, talking in fairly intimate fashion to near-strangers. AA also represents a good cultural fit for the Irish because its spiritual overtones are very consistent with the Irish Catholic culture. By contrast, Italians do not have a long cultural tradition of speaking intimately to strangers. McGoldrick put it this way: "They do nothing with people whose names they don't know." The spiritual aspect of AA is also not as appealing to Italians as it is to the Irish.

Greene (1985, 1992) observed that because most psychotherapists are white, many African-Americans are reluctant to enter into psychotherapeutic treatment. Once the client has entered treatment, the initiation of a working relationship between the two parties may be delayed until initial anxiety—perhaps even distrust—can be worked through (Greenson, 1964). Initial therapy sessions may be marked by testing of the therapist through the use of techniques such as displaying open resentment, playing dumb, or ingratiation (Gardner, 1971).

Most Native Americans live under conditions ripe for fostering emotional difficulties. They tend to live in poverty (Levitan, 1990), with a home life that may be dysfunctional due to alcohol (Three Feathers Associates, 1989) or other problems (Horejsi et al., 1992), and with a world outside the tribal community that holds racism and prejudice (Three Feathers Associates, 1987). Yet even in the face of such adversity, Native Americans may evidence reluctance to seek professional help. There is lingering suspicion regarding government programs, including social welfare agencies (Goodtracks, 1973). Further, life in a Native-American tribe is very much like life in a very small American town. Many people are related or have done business with each other, and will therefore know each other, as well as each other's affairs (Horejsi et al., 1992). Such an atmosphere can be fertile territory for rumors and gossip and is not conducive to seeking professional help.

It should be emphasized that the observations cited above about attitudes towards help seeking on the part of people from different cultures are obviously not true of all people from the African-American, Asian, Hispanic, Irish, Italian, or Native-American culture. Rather, these observations should serve only to sensitize us to the fact that very real differences may exist between people as a function of culture or other factors with respect to their attitudes towards seeking help from others. The role of ethnic and cultural background in help-seeking behavior is increasingly becoming a topic of research interest (Atkinson et al., 1978; Attneave, 1984; Comas-Diaz & Griffith, 1988; Green, 1982; Ivey et al., 1993; Jackson, 1973, 1983; Kay, 1977; Kleinman, 1980; Maultsby, 1982; McGoldrick et al., 1982; Sue, 1981; Sue & Zane, 1987; Tseng & Hsu, 1970).

COGNITIVE-BEHAVIORAL CONSIDERATIONS IN COPING

"The only thing certain in life is death and taxes." To this oft-quoted bit of wisdom we might add another certainty: stress. Coping with stress is an ongoing necessity. Figure 7–4 is a simplified representation of how people cope with stress. The model is an extension

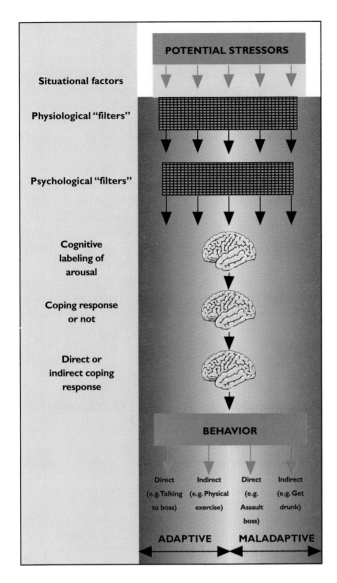

Situational factors

POTENTIAL STRESSORS

Physiological "filters"

Psychological "filters"

Cognitive
labeling of
arousal

Coping response
or not

Direct or
indirect coping
response

BEHAVIOR

Direct	Indirect	Direct	Indirect
(e.g. Talking	(e.g. Physical	(e.g.	(e.g. Get
to boss)	exercise)	Assault	drunk)
		boss)	

ADAPTIVE | **MALADAPTIVE**

FIGURE 7–4   A DECISION MODEL OF HUMAN COPING BEHAVIOR As illustrated by the model, an individual may decide to emit no coping response or may be incapable of emitting one. A coping response itself may be categorized according to this model as being either direct or indirect and adaptive or maladaptive.

of the stressor perception model presented in the previous chapter. Once stress is perceived, a coping decision is made. The coping decision may be adaptive or maladaptive and may take the form of direct action, indirect action, or no action.

In what follows, some very general considerations regarding whether a direct or indirect response is indicated are provided. Additional considerations regarding one's personal coping strategies can come from many sources. One such source is a system devised by Lazarus (1973) for organizing and effectively addressing problems of behavior and thought. It is introduced below and discussed in greater detail in Chapter 9.

DIRECT VERSUS INDIRECT COPING RESPONSES

As illustrated in the model, direct action, indirect action, or no action may represent an adaptive or maladaptive mode of coping. In previous research on stress researchers have made reference to concepts that are in many ways similar to *direct* and *indirect* responses as these two terms are used here. For example, Shontz (1975) discussed how the stress of a serious illness might be dealt with in terms of *encountering* and/or *retreating* from it (see also McGlashan et al., 1975).

In their extensive review of the professional literature on coping behavior, Roth and Cohen (1986) dichotomized the way that people deal with stress in terms of *approach* and *avoidance* strategies. The terms *direct* and *indirect* as applied to possible coping responses seem preferable for the present purposes than *approach* and *avoidance.* The word *direct,* in contrast to *approach,* better conveys the objective of the behavior or action; that is, to directly confront the stress for the purpose of minimizing or eliminating it. Avoidance may be action taken for the purpose of avoiding a specific source of stress, in which case the action is not taken to deal with the stress directly but instead indirectly. Avoidance may be action taken for the purpose of avoiding stress in general (that is, a nonspecific source of stress), in which case it may still be conceived of as action that is not dealing with stress directly but instead indirectly.[4]

Roth and Cohen proposed that the use of different coping strategies carry with them potential benefits and costs. For example, some of the potential costs cited for avoiding stress include interference with appropriate action, disruptive avoidance behavior, emotional numbness, intrusion of threatening material, and lack of awareness of relationship of symptoms to trauma (Roth & Cohen, 1986, p. 817). Table 7–4 builds on this notion of differential coping strategies with a listing of indications and cautions regarding the use of direct and indirect coping strategies.[5]

Will a perceived source of stress simply "roll off your back," "eat you up alive," or be handled in some way that represents a middle point between these two extremes? Setting aside for the moment the role of genetic and environmental factors (see Kessler et al.,

[4]So often, attempts to avoid stress result at best in minimizing it (rather than in no experience of stress at all). In this sense, the term *avoiding stress* may convey an outcome that is more of an ideal than a behavioral reality in most cases. Approach-avoidance should be used with this understanding.

[5]The development of Table 7–4 also benefited from the published work of R. S. Lazarus (1983) and S. Miller (1980).

TABLE 7–4   SOME CRITERIA FOR EMPLOYING DIRECT AND INDIRECT COPING STRATEGIES

Reaction to Stress	Indications for Use	Cautions
Direct Strategy	Useful for confronting the source of stress and venting negative feelings associated with the stress (including feelings such as anger, frustration).	Confrontation may escalate the nature of the stress and increase negative affect such as feelings of anger or frustration.
	Useful when the source of stress is a problem that can be solved.	It is futile to attempt a direct response if no solution to the problem can be found.
	Useful when the nature of the stress may change over time and an avoidance response would not allow the monitoring of the changing conditions.	Caution is called for when the nature of stress is capable of changing and a premature direct response eliminates the possibility of monitoring the situation.
	Useful when direct confrontation with the source of stress may minimize or eliminate present and future stress from the same source.	Caution is called for if attempts to minimize or eliminate stress may cause the same stress to repeat in the future or may simply postpone the stress.
Indirect Strategy	Useful when source of stress is a problem that seems incapable of being solved.	It is important to be certain that there is no direct solution. Otherwise, the same stress may have to be dealt with indirectly repeatedly, instead of directly once.
	Useful in minimizing the experience of negative feelings associated with stress because the deliberate objective is to minimize these feelings. On the other hand, positive feelings should be accentuated.	Because negative feelings regarding the stress are not vented, negative affect associated with the stress may linger, as may other negative thoughts and feelings associated with the stress.
	Useful when the nature of the stress is not anticipated to change over time.	Caution is called for when the nature of stress is capable of changing. An indirect response may eliminate the possibility of monitoring the situation.
	Useful when the source of stress is not anticipated to be long-term in nature.	It is important to be certain that the stress is not anticipated to be long-term in nature. If there is a strong possibility that the stress will be long-term in nature, a direct response may be preferable.

1992), according to the decision model of coping, the answer to this question is in your hands (actually, your mind).

A MULTIMODAL PERSPECTIVE

Psychologist Arnold A. Lazarus (see Figure 7–5) devised a system of therapy called *multimodal behavior therapy*, elements of which would seem to have great relevance to personal coping. Multimodal behavior therapy, as well as other therapist-administered systems of behavior change, will be discussed in greater detail in Chapter 9. Here, let's note that different systems of therapy often carry with them implications for personal coping efforts as well. For example, knowledge of Albert Ellis's rational-emotive approach to treatment (see pages 161–162 in Chapter 6, page 239 in Chapter 9), could lead one to pose to oneself questions such as, "What would constitute a rational response under these circumstances?" In like manner, knowledge of Lazarus's multimodal behavior therapy could prompt one to pose to oneself different types of questions. Let's see what those questions are, and how such questions may be relevant to categorizing personal problems and planning coping efforts.

FIGURE 7–5
ARNOLD A. LAZARUS

At the core of the multimodal approach are seven interdependent factors, each of which can be employed as one mode of effecting adaptive change in thinking and behavior. In multimodal behavior therapy, these seven interactive *modalities* serve as "a constant compass to orient therapists towards the client's entire network of interactive modalities" (Lazarus, 1976b, p. 6). The first letter of each of the modalities (Behavior, Affect, Sensation, Imagery, Cognition, Interpersonal Relations, and Drugs) spell out the acronym *BASIC ID* (see Table 7–5 on page 190).

In addition to serving as "a constant compass" for therapists, the BASIC ID may also serve as a guide for laypeople both in evaluating adjustive demands and in identifying areas where effort in personal coping can best be invested. For example, in contemplating how to meet a particular adjustive demand or challenge, one might use the BASIC ID as a checklist for posing questions relevant to the particular demand or challenge faced. The exact form of the questions will vary with the situation, but some general questions covering each of the seven elements of the BASIC ID would be:

1. What *behavior* needs to be changed?
2. Does my *affect* in this situation require adjustment? If so, how?
3. How does *sensation*—all that I see, hear, smell, touch, and so forth—play a part in the problem I must confront?
4. What *imagery* or mental pictures do I associate with this adjustive challenge, and how do those images need to be modified?
5. What *cognitions* or thoughts, fears, attitudes, beliefs, or values are relevant to the adjustive challenge? How do they need to be modified to be more adaptive?
6. Looking at this challenge from an *interpersonal* perspective, what effect does it have on the people touched by it? How might other people be enlisted to help address it effectively?
7. What additional light can be shed by looking at this challenge from a *biological* perspective (this being a reference to the *Drugs* modality)?

In some cases, the person facing the adjustive demand or challenge will lack the ability or motivation to effectively evaluate such considerations or considerations related to direct or indirect coping. For many readers of this text, however, Lazarus's BASIC ID can provide a handy checklist of points worthy of consideration when an adjustive demand, challenge, or crisis looms.

COPING IN EVERYDAY LIFE

The decision to deal directly or indirectly with a source of stress may depend upon your past experience with the same or similar sources of stress as well as upon other factors related to your preparedness to cope. Let's briefly survey some of these factors.

TABLE 7–5 MODALITIES IN MULTIMODAL BEHAVIOR THERAPY

Behavior

Of particular interest here are questions concerning the client's behavioral assets, excesses, and deficits, as well as the antecedents and consequences of behavior. If possible, quantification of behavior, in terms of counting, charting, and graphing of variables such as frequency, intensity, or duration of behavior is strongly encouraged. In addition to inquiring about situations when a client emitted a particular behavior, it is also important to probe regarding situations when the client did not emit a particular behavior.

Affect

This is the "feelings" modality and it encompasses everything from the rage expressed by some extremely violent patients to the apathy and apparent absence of affect expressed by other patients. Lazarus includes here not only feelings a client may be in touch with, but also those the client may be out of touch with, including anger. Feelings that require modification in therapy may be expressed in distorted fashion by the client and it is up to the therapist to discover the hidden meaning of such expressions. Pleasant affective states, including love, joy, and pride, are as important to explore as negative states.

Sensation

How does the client experience and utilize sensory input? For Lazarus, learning to fully utilize senses is an important part of personal fulfillment and development. Some clients may be oblivious to nuances of sensation, while others may be preoccupied with the same phenomena. Sensory exercises are used in the treatment of certain disorders such as those involving sexual dysfunction.

Imagery

The mental pictures people carry with them are capable of exerting an influence on behavior. Lazarus uses special exercises to probe the client's imagery, such as having clients picture their childhood home and what each of the people in the home are doing. Another assessment technique that employs the imagery modality entails having the client mentally picture a real or imagined "special safe place" and then having the client describe it to the therapist. Lazarus has found that dwelling on particular images while having clients report their associated feelings is a useful technique in getting past the rationalizations clients may otherwise provide for their behavior (Ahsen & Lazarus, 1972).

Cognition

Albert Ellis (1958) and Lazarus and Fay (1975) have discussed in detail illogical philosophies that many people share. All such irrational beliefs, thoughts, attitudes, and fears come under the realm of the Cognition modality, and it is here that they are identified and treated. Citing the psychoanalyst Karen Horney (1950), Lazarus (1976b) writes that "the tyranny of the should" must be explored in each patient—the things patients say to themselves that betray what they believe they "should" or "should not" be, and/or "should" or "should not" do. Lazarus prefers to infer "shoulds" from a person's behavior rather than to ask a patient directly about them. For example, in the case of a workaholic patient, a "should self-statement" that might be inferred is, "I need to work as much as possible to be personally fulfilled." More assistance in understanding the Cognition modality from a cognitive-behavioral standpoint can be obtained from Ellis (1962), Mahoney (1974), and Meichenbaum (1973).[6]

Interpersonal Relations

The multimodal therapist not only listens to what clients say about their interactions with other people but also observes their interactions, including therapist-client interactions and client-client interactions in group therapy. The therapist may interview not only the client, but also friends, family, and others in the client's life who can be helpful in providing a revealing picture of how the client behaves in the company of others.

Drugs

Physical health, physical complaints, medical history, physical fitness, physical habits, and chemical substances the client may be or was taking are some of the components of this extremely wide-ranging modality. It may be argued that this modality could have more appropriately been named something like "Physical Factors" or "Physiological Factors." However, to do so would have sacrificed the *D* in the BASIC ID acronym; BASIC ID is clearly catchier than BASIC IP. When the indications are such that the use of psychotropic drugs would be helpful, a multimodal therapist who is not a physician will refer the patient for medication to a psychiatrist. The use of medication within the context of multimodal therapy has been discussed in detail by psychiatrist Allen Fay (1976).

LEARNING FROM PAST EXPERIENCE

"Have I ever had to deal with the type of stress I am currently trying to cope with?" "What general coping strategies were or were not successful for me in the past and why?" "How might I change my approach for better results?" These types of questions may prove most important when deciding upon a general coping strategy. Your comfort level with a coping strategy that you employed in the past may be due to factors related to your own per-

[6]Some assistance in reaching such a perspective can be obtained from Ellis (1988) and Lazarus and Fay (1975).

sonality (Averill & Rosen, 1972; Miller & Mangan, 1983) or to the "goodness of the fit" between the coping style you employed and the demands of the situation (Cohen & Roth, 1984). As Roth and Cohen (1986, p. 819) noted, different people have different characteristic ways of coping and "it is not an easy matter to make 'approachers' avoid or 'avoiders' approach . . . ." A rule of thumb is that flexibility is adaptive and rigidity is not. Flexibility in this sense means being capable of altering the way you cope as a function of the unique demands of each new situation. As explained further below, it is also desirable not only to learn from your past coping experiences but also to use that learning in future situations that require coping. In this way, one profits from past experience of physical and psychological stress.

"From a *physical* perspective, how have I experienced this stress in the past, and what worked to relieve these physical symptoms?" As we saw in Chapter 6, stress is experienced differently by different people. A twinge in the stomach, a tightening of muscles in the back of the neck—any number of physical or mental events may signal the onset of stress. What are your own early warning signs? By being able to identify these signs and verify that you are indeed under stress, you will be able to respond that much more quickly. Should you decide to use relaxation exercises to counter the stress, you will be better able to focus in on the physical sites that seem most negatively affected by the stress. Alternatively, you may decide to counter the stress, anger, or other negative feelings you may be experiencing with other kinds of strategies. For example, you may attempt to assume the stressor's point of view (Feshbach & Weiner, 1982), or simply consider how important the stressful event really is in the grand scheme of things. On occasions when you have successfully used these or other coping strategies, you may find it useful to reward yourself cognitively with a compliment like, "I handled that pretty well this time" (Novaco, 1975).

"From a *psychological* perspective, how have I experienced this stress in the past?" This is a very broad question that may have many possible answers. Here we will focus on one that we have not yet previously discussed: *meaning*. In the context of meaning, the question might be rephrased as follows: "What is the meaning of the stress I have endured in the past or am currently enduring now?" This is the type of question that might be posed for your consideration by a therapist whose orientation to therapy is *existential* in nature. Loosely based on the philosophy of existentialism, the existential approach to psychotherapy is primarily concerned with general issues concerning aspects of human existence. Inherent in this approach is the premise that modern life, with its many sources of human misery and conflict (on a personal as well as a global level), is dehumanizing. War, crime, and other world events can make individual lives seem very meaningless. A typical goal in the existential approach to therapy is to restore meaning to people's lives and to help them to make life choices on their own. When people have experienced severe stress, even horror, helping them to find meaning in their experience is one of the objectives of the existential approach.

For centuries, religious counselors helped people find meaning in their lives, usually within the context of religion. In a sense, the existential approach to treatment does much the same thing but within a more secular context. Thinking about the meaning of stress may be helpful not only in assimilating and getting over negative experiences of the past, but also in developing useful insights for the present and the future. For some assistance in achieving such insights, you may want to complete The Stressful Event Analysis form in the *Self-Assessment* exercise on page 192.

There is one additional lesson that the professional literature in psychology teaches us about the power of past experience in coping with present or future stress. That lesson may be stated as: "Let the past be your guide, but not your warden." Stated another way, "Refuse to be a prisoner of your past." Times change and so do circumstances. Something you may have tried many years ago as a way to relieve stress may not have worked then, but may well work now or at some time in the future. Seligman (1975) illustrated that laboratory animals could be taught to feel as if they were helpless with respect to their fates. Humans too can learn to be helpless. In the face of adversity they give up, failing to realize that new solutions and opportunities—perhaps accessible by means of strategies that did not work in the past—are out there.

SELF-ASSESSMENT

The Stressful Event Analysis Form*

Recall an incident in the recent past (no more than a week or so back in time) that caused you a great deal of stress.

1. Describe the incident.
2. Describe what happened just before the incident, including your own thoughts, feelings, and behaviors.
3. To the best of your recollection, describe your thoughts, feelings, and behaviors at the time that the incident was actually happening.
4. Describe what happened just after the incident, including your own thoughts, feelings, and behaviors.
5. In retrospect, describe your actions during the stressful incident, including your thoughts, feelings, and behaviors, on each of the following dimensions. Place a checkmark at the point on each of the continua that you believe best describes your actions with respect to this particular incident.

(a) ADAPTIVE __ __ __ __ MALADAPTIVE
Why?
(b) UNREALISTIC __ __ __ __ REALISTIC
Why?
(c) RATIONAL __ __ __ __ IRRATIONAL
Why?
(d) UNINTENTIONAL __ __ __ __ INTENTIONAL
Why?
(e) PROPORTIONATE __ __ __ __ DISPROPORTIONATE
Why?

6. If a similar event happened tomorrow, how might you act differently? Explain why and be specific, including reference to your thoughts, behaviors, and feelings.
7. What has this exposure to stress taught you about yourself?
8. How have you grown as a person as a consequence of this exposure to stress?

PREPARING FOR THE FUTURE

Think of an upcoming situation in your own life that you are likely to find stressful and then ask yourself, "What makes this situation stressful?" An analysis of your answer may help point the way to what you need to do to prepare.

PREPARING FOR ANTICIPATED STRESS

It is not always possible to anticipate stressful situations or to prepare oneself to deal with stress. However, in those situations in which stress can be anticipated, it is a good idea to prepare yourself as much as possible for it. Preparation may involve imagining yourself performing at your peak in the stressful situation or actually engaging in behaviors that will help ensure that you perform at your peak when the time comes.

One route to preparation for a stressful situation entails *acquiring the relevant competencies*. For example, if the anticipated stress entails passing the hairdresser's licensing examination, acquiring the relevant competencies would mean knowing what you need to know to pass that examination. If the anticipated stress involves negotiating a big deal with a client of your corporation, acquiring the relevant competencies would mean learning everything you can about negotiation skills and giving some advance thought to the terms you can give up, the terms you can compromise on, and the terms that represent your own bottom line. If the anticipated stress entails caring for your sister's newborn infant while she is out of town for the weekend, acquiring the relevant competencies would entail learning everything you can about the care and feeding of newborn infants—and having your sister's telephone number, just in case!

Another way to prepare for an anticipated source of stress is to learn what you can about the stress and how it might affect you. Then, mentally and behaviorally rehearse adaptive ways of responding. At the appointed time, place into action the thoughts and behaviors that you have by now rehearsed well. Essentially, it is these three steps that underlie one approach to coping called *stress inoculation* (Meichenbaum, 1974, 1977). Meichenbaum emphasizes the importance of understanding the things you say in your own mind when anticipating stress and the things you can rehearse as alternatives. For example, a dental patient might be instructed to rehearse the phrase, "I am going to be a healthier person after I have this tooth extracted," as a replacement for the thought, "I am going to be toothless and in pain" (Ludwick-Rosenthal & Neufeld, 1988).

PREPARING FOR UNANTICIPATED STRESS

Stress will inevitably rear its head from time to time despite your best efforts to deal with it, ignore it, or prevent it. If you find that certain sources of stress more often than not stem from particular beliefs or values that you cherish, you may want to take a step back for perspective and reevaluate them.

Another approach to minimizing the effects of everyday stress entails cultivating relaxation skills and practicing them on a regular basis. In *The Wellness Book*, physician and stress expert Herbert Benson (1992) argued that over 50% of all office visits to physicians have stress-related causes and that the experience of stress can be minimized with regular relaxation exercises. Benson believes that it is critically important to shut down our everyday train of thought periodically and substitute sheer relaxation. He recommends a very simple technique for accomplishing this task. A word of caution, however, in attempting *any* relaxation technique: Some people suffer adverse effects when they attempt to relax (see Figure 7–6). If you are one of those people, stop the procedure immediately. It will be a good idea to discuss your experience with a trained health professional. Benson's technique can be described in five steps:

1. *Select a word, sound, or phrase that you wish to focus on.*
   The word (which Benson refers to as a "focus word") may be something like *relax, peace,* or *tranquillity.* If you prefer, you may choose a sound, such as *Ommm*—used by many people who practice meditation. An example of a phrase that you might use is, "I owe my body respect and protection."
2. *Close your eyes and relax all of the muscle groups in your body.*
   Feel relaxation permeate your entire body including the back of your neck, your arms, your chest, your thighs, and your feet.
3. *Concentrate on your breathing.*
   Deep, rhythmic breaths may help to deepen the relaxation you are experiencing.

FIGURE 7–6   A BONZAI GROWS IN BROOKLYN It may look like a suburb of Tokyo, but this photo of a man meditating was snapped at a Japanese Garden at the Brooklyn Botanic Garden. Although meditation may work for this man as a method of stress reduction, it is not a technique for everyone. There is evidence that some people may experience adverse effects in response to attempts to meditate, include *increased* tension (French et al., 1975; Kennedy, 1976; Lazarus, 1976a).

4. *Repeat the word, sound, or phrase that you have selected every time you breathe out.* Try to clear your mind of other thoughts except the focus word, sound, or phrase. If other thoughts intrude, just say to yourself something like, "Stop!" or "Oh well," and return to the focus word, sound, or phrase.

5. *Do this exercise for about 10 to 20 minutes several times a week.*
   Keep in mind that there is nothing magical about this exercise. Engaging in other types of diversion such as quiet reading, petting a pet, or even taking a catnap might have comparable antistress effects.

If in the past you have habitually regretted certain types of behavior—such as failing to stand up for your rights, being too aggressive, or not expressing love and affection as freely as you would like—some assertiveness training as a stress prevention technique may be in order. However, before signing up for a seminar or purchasing any self-help materials, it would be a good idea to clarify your personal objectives and values regarding self-assertion. Most discussions of assertiveness training offer relatively uncritical acceptance of such teaching while ignoring the critical role personal values can play in the process. In fact, values play a key role in determining the situations one will choose to be assertive in and the methods one will use to assert oneself. Learning assertiveness is not like learning the Heimlich maneuver; there is no one standard course with one expected, standard result. Values, sometimes a function of one's cultural background or gender, may also play a key role with respect to the way that the assertive behavior of others is interpreted. In *A Question of Values*, we explore further some of these oft-ignored considerations regarding the widely practiced art of assertiveness training.

COPING BEHAVIOR AND GENERATIVE THINKING

There are times when generative thinking, either individually or in a group, may be what is necessary to discover a nonobvious solution to a stress-causing problem. A group brainstorming session with friends or family may prove a helpful way of overcoming some stressful situation. In brainstorming, each member of the group contributes ideas, most typically with little forethought or mental "censorship," with one idea acting to generate others. The end product of a brainstorming session may be an innovative solution that no one member of the group would have thought of without the contribution of the others. Group brainstorming should be distinguished from another collective decision-making process called "groupthink." **Groupthink** is *a small-group phenomenon involving a drive for consensus at any cost in which consideration of highly innovative alternatives tend to be suppressed* (Janis, 1972). One way of avoiding groupthink is by brainstorming with more than one group. So, for example, it might be beneficial to brainstorm with groups of friends and family members separately.

groupthink
a small-group phenomenon involving a drive for consensus that is so strong that innovative alternatives tend to be suppressed.

If you use brainstorming or any other technique to derive a solution for a problem, evaluate how satisfactorily the solution addresses the problem. For example, one innovative and nonobvious solution to the problem of loneliness is to reconceptualize loneliness as an opportunity to get to know oneself better (Moustakas, 1961). How satisfactory is that solution? My own view is that almost *any* problem can benefit from enhanced self-insight. However, most people who describe themselves as lonely might better spend their time in efforts aimed at getting to know *other* people better. Merely relabeling a very real problem as a nonproblem is seldom a satisfactory coping strategy. Today, some types of therapeutic approaches for the problem of loneliness contain very specific behavioral prescriptions for building interpersonal relationships. Thinking generatively, what specific suggestions might you offer to a lonely college student? How could this hypothetical student work towards meeting people and building enduring relationships? What obstacles might you foresee to your suggestions? How could those obstacles be overcome?

Speaking of overcoming obstacles, consider the obstacles that had to be overcome by the astronauts whose mission it was to capture a whirling 9,000-pound satellite some 230 miles above the Earth (see *In the News*).

WHEN TO SEEK PROFESSIONAL ASSISTANCE

An individual is in need of a consultation with a trained mental health professional if a radical change in everyday behavior transforms that otherwise well-functioning individual into a clear danger to herself or himself or to other people. Beyond that, few hard and fast rules exist for seeking such a consultation. There are a number of situations in which it would certainly seem like a good idea to seek professional assistance, and some of those situations are summarized in Table 7–6. This list of situations could be greatly extended. Yet although there are those people who lack sufficient insight to know that they need professional help, most people reading this book will probably be their own best judge of when thoughts or behaviors are sufficiently troubling to require some sort of professional intervention.

OBTAINING PROFESSIONAL ASSISTANCE

Once it is determined that professional help is needed, the next question concerns which professional to choose. Again, there are few rules, but generally speaking, if the problem is so severe as to be immediately life-threatening to the patient or others, my own recommendation would be to proceed at once to a hospital emergency room. If the situation is not immediately life-threatening but capable of becoming life-threatening, you may wish to seek out the services of a board certified psychiatrist or licensed clinical psychologist who has hospital-admitting privileges, as well as training and experience in crisis management. Although some psychologists in some states have hospital-admitting privileges, most psychologists currently do not. Additionally, the training of most psychologists, relative to that of many psychiatrists, does not typically include as much supervised experience in the handling of life-threatening emergencies.

Beyond life-threatening emergencies, the choice of the profession of a therapist may be somewhat arbitrary. Some of the variables that may enter into your consideration of a potential therapist might include the therapist's expertise with your particular problem, the therapist's overall level of training (such as whether a psychologist is a diplomate of the American Board of Professional Psychology), the gender, race, and/or ethnic background

---

TABLE 7–6   WHEN ONE MIGHT SEEK PROFESSIONAL ASSISTANCE

You are overwhelmed by an onslaught of emotionally draining and burdening stresses in your life.

A medical doctor recommends psychotherapy as a possible means of improving a medical condition such as high blood pressure.

You can identify specific attitudes and/or behaviors that you would like professional help in ridding yourself of.

You have nonspecific daily anxiety, tension, depression, or fear that you would like professional help in ridding yourself of.

There are a number of issues in present life or in your past that you would like professional help in working through.

You feel "down" too much of the time and would like to feel better about yourself and life in general.

You feel like the thoughts and/or emotions you experience are out of synch with the reality of what is going on around you.

Negative feelings or thoughts have begun to interfere with your eating, sleeping, toileting, or other daily habits.

You feel plagued by thoughts or behaviors that seem out of your control.

Your relationships with other people, including or excluding family members, never seem to be as satisfactory as you would like them to be and you would like to work on self-improvement in this area.

A QUESTION OF  Values

Coping and Assertiveness

In a highly influential book entitled *Your Perfect Right*, Robert Alberti and Michael Emmons (1970) introduced the concept of assertiveness by asking readers questions such as, "Has anyone ever cut in front of you in a line?" and "Do you have difficulty saying 'no' to persuasive salesmen?" Readers who had such problems were advised that they needed to be able to stand up for their own interests without feeling anxiety about doing so; in short they needed some training in the art of being assertive. Other examples of assertiveness included feeling comfortable while engaging in activities ranging from talking to strangers at a party to expressing intimate thoughts to a loved one. Assertive behavior entails actively asserting one's rights and feeling good about it, as opposed to passively witnessing another violate one's rights. As distinguished from aggressive behavior, assertive behavior is not hostile; it entails only exercising one's "own rights without denying the rights of others" (Alberti & Emmons, 1974, p. 2).

It seems almost an understatement to say that people were very receptive to the concept of self-assertion. Within a few short years of its first edition in 1970, *Your Perfect Right* had spawned dozens of similar books, hundreds of journal articles, numerous tests purporting to measure the trait of assertiveness, and countless workshops, seminars, audiotapes, and videos offering "assertiveness training." Even today, when you open almost any psychology textbook containing a discussion of assertiveness, you will find an uncritical discussion of its merits. Is it true that assertiveness is universally good and nonassertiveness is universally bad?

A restaurant patron orders a dish well-done. The server delivers it from the kitchen and it is not well-done. The assertive response on the part of the patron would be to send the food back. A nonassertive response would be not to make waves and to eat the food, perhaps enjoying it not as much as if it been cooked to order. An aggressive response would be to insult or curse the server, the chef, or other restaurant staff within earshot.

In this hypothetical situation, few people would argue with the appropriateness of the assertive response, sending the food back. Yet daily living can serve up far more ambiguity regarding what the correct, assertive response should be, who is correct in standing up for their rights, how standing up for one's rights can best be accomplished, and where one person's rights end and the other person's rights begin. As an example, set aside the rather straightforward and oft-cited restaurant example and consider the dilemma of the parents of 18-year-old Jimmy.

Jimmy enjoys staying home, sleeping late, and piping the soundtrack from MTV through his six-foot blaster speakers. He spends most of his nights hanging out with friends who on occasion drink and do drugs. He has a part-time job as a bag boy at a local supermarket, but he is on the verge of being fired from that job due to excessive absences and tardiness. Jimmy needs no assertiveness training. When asked by his parents to "clean up his act," he assertively reminds them of his right to live his own life the way he sees fit. What should Jimmy's parents do?

Some people might reflexively answer that Jimmy's parents are the people in this story who need to be more assertive. If you agree—and since it is our hypothetical story—let's imagine that Jimmy's parents do take a course in assertiveness training, one designed especially for parents who have children like Jimmy living at home. Jimmy's parents learn very specific techniques for resisting Jimmy's influence and for asserting their rights as parents. They are taught, for example, that Jimmy must be presented with strict and unconditional rules for acceptable behavior. Jimmy must be told that if he does not follow rules set by his parents while he is living in their house, privileges will be withdrawn. If Jimmy fails to cooperate, even the privilege of living in his parents' home will be withdrawn.

The assertiveness training Jimmy's parents received may sound extreme.

---

of the therapist (and whether you feel you would work better with one type of person as opposed to another), as well as the financial sacrifices you are capable of or willing to make in order to undergo psychotherapy. Another extremely important variable to be considered is the therapist's approach to therapy (see Chapter 9).

Hypnosis (*an altered state of consciousness in which there is heightened suggestibility*) has the potential of being an extremely powerful therapeutic tool when employed by a knowledgeable and competent mental health professional. Psychologists, psychiatrists, and so-

hypnosis

an altered state of consciousness in which there is heightened suggestibility.

It is. Nonetheless, it is the same type of assertiveness training that many parents are receiving in programs aimed at managing live-at-home teenagers who are discipline problems. According to Pieper and Pieper (1992), this approach, referred to as "tough love," is based on the premise that parents must not allow themselves to be manipulated by their children. A teenager such as Jimmy must recognize that the security and comfort of his parent's home is a privilege, not a right, and it is a privilege that his parents can withdraw. Having attempted and failed to assert their rights in many less extreme ways, Jimmy's parents, like thousands of other parents in a similar position, might well be very receptive to the concept of tough love. Yet unlike the situation in the restaurant, in which a patron's assertiveness does not impact on anyone else's rights, questions arise regarding where Jimmy's rights end and his parents' rights begin. This is especially true when you consider, as the Piepers have pointed out, that parents who follow the policy of tough love "must be prepared to sacrifice their child to save the child from himself. This willingness to sacrifice the child in the service of reclaiming him is seen as the highest and most selfless type of parental love" (p. 371).

The uncritical acceptance of assertiveness in many psychology textbooks ignores the difficult values-related issues that are sometimes inherent in behaving assertively. Assertiveness is not, as many have been led to believe, an uncomplicated, straightforward, and universally "good" way of being in the world. Complex decisions about self-assertion, including method of self-assertion, magnitude of self-assertion, and consequences of self-assertion must frequently be made. In many instances, such as the case cited above, the parties must grapple with many complex, values-related questions as they mutually strive to "stand up for their rights," resist the influence of others, and exert their own influence. In the case of Jimmy, some of the questions the parents must grapple with include, "Shall I be skeptical or trusting? Shall I be rejecting or accepting? Do I better express my love towards my child by wrapping my arms around him, or by letting him go?"

As the concept of assertiveness is increasingly evaluated from a multicultural perspective, new values-related questions and issues are being raised. For example, Parham (1990; White & Parham, 1990) speaks of futility in teaching individual assertiveness skills unless the values of society at large change. Cheatham (1990) teaches that assertiveness training must always be taught within a multicultural context. What people from one culture might find assertive, people from another culture find aggressive. Kantrowitz and Ballou (1992) approached the content of many assertiveness training programs from the perspective of feminists. They wondered aloud whether such programs are gender-neutral and cautioned that assertiveness training can sometimes provide a forum for teaching women a man's "style of being."

A number of factors enter into—or should enter into—the decision to be assertive—even in those relatively noncontroversial situations often offered in support of assertiveness. For example, if someone cuts in front of you in line, it may make a difference to some people whether that someone is just anyone or if that someone is an angry member of the local Hell's Angels who happens to be in a hurry. It is true that people should not have difficulty saying "no" to a persuasive salesperson. But then again, a reflexive "no" may not be the best response if indeed the salesperson is making some compelling and persuasive points about the prospective purchase.

Perhaps most importantly, it is useful to keep in mind that life is seldom as simple as the relatively superficial examples consistently offered in support of assertiveness and assertiveness training programs. Beyond those tired examples lies a world where the boundaries between assertion of one person's rights and infringement of another person's rights are not always so clear.

cial workers, among other mental health professionals, may have received professional training in hypnosis, and may refer to themselves not only as therapists, but also as hypnotists. However, if you think you would like to try hypnosis for a particular problem (such as overeating or smoking), or if you think you would like to undergo an extended program of **hypnotherapy** or **hypnoanalysis** (*psychotherapy in which hypnosis is primary among the therapeutic tools employed*), you are strongly advised to exercise great caution in selecting a therapist. Terms like hypnotist, hypnotherapist, hypnoanalyst, clinical hypnotherapist, and

hypnotherapy
psychotherapy in which hypnosis is primary among the therapeutic tools employed.

hypnoanalysis
see *hypnotherapy.*

Improvisation in Space

On May 13, 1992, three NASA astronauts ventured from the space shuttle, *Endeavor,* to capture a telecommunications satellite that had fallen out of its orbit. The maneuver, suggested by the astronauts themselves and approved by NASA Mission Control, was historic in that it entailed an eight-and-one-half hour, 3-man space walk. More than historic, the accomplishment was inspirational. After the well-practiced exercises to capture the satellite by mechanical means had failed, it was only as a result of NASA personnel's innovation and "can do" attitude that the mission was accomplished.

numerous other variations having *hypno* in them have no legal meaning in most states. In such states, *anyone* can represent him or herself in newspaper or other advertising using the title of hypnotist, or any other, yet more creative, hypnosis-related title. Moreover, there exists a number of bogus associations and organizations having very official and scholarly sounding names that purport to train and accredit hypnotists. What can the consumer do?

Critically question the credentials of any hypnotist before entering into a relationship with one. Rule out immediately any hypnotists who maintain a side business doing stage hypnosis or performing at private parties. If you have any questions regarding a hypnotist's credentials, contact a local or national accrediting agency. As a psychologist who has received professional training in hypnosis, I can tell you that it takes only about 5 minutes or so to teach the average person how to hypnotize someone. Yet it may take years of training and supervised experience to know what to do therapeutically with a client placed in a hypnotic state. Hypnosis in the hands of a nonprofessional can be just as dangerous as psychotherapy in the hands of a nonprofessional. The danger is that it is relatively easy to get motivated clients to open up and start making relatively intimate revelations about themselves, but not so easy to handle such revelations properly and to properly achieve a sense of closure on them (Echterling & Emmerling, 1987; Finkelstein, 1989; Kleinhauz & Beran, 1981; Kleinhauz & Eli, 1987; MacHovec, 1988; Mott, 1987). A similar danger exists with therapy-like groups that are not run by mental health professionals. It may be relatively easy to open up in such groups, although the "closing" may be left for a psychiatric emergency room (Glass et al., 1977; Kirsch & Glass, 1977).

In the search for mental health services, *consumer beware* is perhaps the most appropriate advice that can be given. There are a number of unscrupulous, self-proclaimed therapists using legally protected titles and mail-order doctorates, framed and hung on their walls. It is important to carefully screen out not only potentially unqualified therapists but also legitimately licensed or otherwise credentialed therapists who may be qualified on paper only—they may lack the background, training, experience, or expertise to deal with the presenting problem. More advice for the prospective consumer of mental health services is presented in Chapter 9, Therapy.

SUMMARY

VARIETIES OF COPING BEHAVIOR People *cope* or contend with stress in different ways. Some ways are adaptive, some are maladaptive. Some ways are direct, some are indirect. Some people fail to cope at all.

PERSONAL COPING METHODS Personal coping can amount solely to a matter of cognitive activity, as in prayer or meditation. Personal coping may also entail behavior, as it does when exercise is used to work off stress.

COPING WITH THE ASSISTANCE OF OTHERS Friends, family, and others who care can help us to cope with stress by providing social support. Social support can be problem-specific (such as the social support offered in groups such as Weight Watchers), or nonproblem specific (as in many general support and self-help groups). Research has suggested that social support operates to foster healthy adjustment, perhaps by buffering the effect of life events that might otherwise be viewed as aversive.

COGNITIVE AND BEHAVIORAL CONSIDERATIONS IN COPING Once stress is perceived, a decision regarding coping must be made. A decision model of coping behavior was presented wherein action taken, if action is taken, can be direct, indirect, adaptive, or maladaptive. Different coping strategies carry with them different costs and benefits. Knowledge of a multimodal perspective on coping arms the individual with a checklist of important cognitive and behavioral considerations regarding the coping decision.

COPING IN EVERYDAY LIFE The nature of the coping decision one ultimately makes depends on numerous factors including how one has coped with the same or similar problems in the past, how prepared one is to cope in the future, and the creative capability of the problem-solver. Depending on the particular situation, coping with stress may entail acquiring certain competencies, using stress inoculation techniques, using self-relaxation exercises, or engaging in group problem-solving exercises.

WHEN TO SEEK PROFESSIONAL ASSISTANCE Few hard and fast rules exist regarding when a person should seek professional assistance. Most mental health professionals would probably agree, however, that an individual is in need of a consultation with a professional if a radical change in everyday behavior transforms that otherwise well-functioning individual into a clear danger to herself or himself, or to other people.

Abnormal Behavior

Suppose you observed a woman on her knees who said she was talking to the Creator. Would you consider her behavior abnormal? One answer to this question would be, "It depends on a number of factors, such as the context of the observation." If the woman was engaged in such behavior in a house of worship, the behavior might well be widely viewed as normal. On the other hand, if the woman was on line at the post office, most people would probably consider the behavior abnormal.

All of us seem to think we know abnormal behavior when we see it. But do we? And exactly what is it about behavior we label as abnormal that makes it not normal? In this chapter we address these and related questions.

WHAT IS ABNORMAL BEHAVIOR?

By definition, the adjective *abnormal*, from the Latin *abnormis,* means "departing from normal" or "away from the rule." But while a definition of this adjective is relatively clear, a definition of the term "abnormal behavior" is not. As applied to observable human behavior (action) and unobservable human behavior (cognition or thinking behavior), what constitutes abnormal behavior has in many cases been a matter of heated debate. Judgments about what behaviorally departs from normal or goes away from the rule are necessarily based on knowledge about what "normal" or "the rule" is. But which thoughts and behaviors shall we consider to be the rule? Studying abnormal behavior from different perspectives can provide some insights. Below we develop a definition of abnormal behavior that integrates statistical, cultural, and psychological perspectives.

A STATISTICAL PERSPECTIVE

If you were born with five fingers on each hand, you would be considered normal with respect to fingers on your hand. If you were born with four fingers on each hand, you would be considered abnormal with respect to fingers on your hands. Such judgments regarding what is normal or abnormal are not controversial and are based on a statistical interpretation of normality; what is in the majority is normal and what is in the minority is abnormal. According to a purely statistical frame of reference, behavior that most people engage in is normal, while behavior that only a minority of people engage in is abnormal. In your view, how satisfactory would that definition be?

Few mental health professionals would agree that a purely statistical approach to defining normality is satisfactory. One problem with it concerns the need to in some way quantify all behavior. For example, "the number of hours per week spent watching television" can easily be quantified. People who spend significantly more or fewer hours per week watching television than the average could be categorized on a purely statistical basis as abnormal. Realistically, however, other variables related to television watching are perhaps even more critical to judging normality. For example, the content of what is watched on television is important—how "weird" the programs selected are. Quantifying "weirdness" is not as straightforward as counting the number of hours; reasonable people will differ about which television programs are weird and how weird they are.

Another major problem with a statistical view of abnormality is that it makes no distinction between behavior that is socially valued and behavior that is socially abhorred. Consider in this context an act of heroism by an ordinary citizen who, at risk to life and limb, saves the life of a stranger. From a purely statistical perspective, this courageous act is abnormal. Still, few heroes are referred for therapy or sent away to mental institutions. To the contrary, people reward uncommon bravery with medals, plaques, cash, and other symbols of admiration and appreciation.

A SOCIOCULTURAL PERSPECTIVE

In a sociocultural perspective, the purely statistical perspective is modified to account for what is socially valued or not valued. According to this view, behavior that is culturally valued is not considered abnormal even if it is statistically infrequent. Thus, if acts of heroism are culturally valued, heroic behavior is not abnormal.

The sociocultural perspective represents an advance over a purely statistical approach. One problem with it, however, is that extreme differences may exist, even within the same culture, about the kinds of behavior that are socially valued. Consider for example, a group of physicians who stand up to a mob's threats to destroy their abortion clinic. Whether the physicians are viewed as courageous heroes or murderous scoundrels has to do with where an individual observer stands on the abortion issue.

Social values may change over time. In the era when the Communist party was all-powerful in the former Soviet Union, many people who held anticommunist beliefs were committed to mental institutions. The policy of committing dissidents to mental hospitals was enforced for the dual purpose of punishment and "reeducation" (or brainwashing to achieve conformity with the party line). The revolution in August 1991 abolished the Communist party and the practice of committing anti-Communists to mental hospitals abruptly ceased. Political dissidents who had been declared insane were suddenly deemed to be sane—even to be heroes.

From an international and multicultural frame of reference, a view of abnormality from one and only one sociocultural perspective may be misleading. Allowance must be made for the fact that people from other cultures may have been taught ways of thinking, behaving, and "being in the world" that are quite different from our own. These ways of being are not necessarily abnormal simply because they appear different, foreign, or strange from our own perspective (see Figure 8–1).

According to the 1990 census, approximately 20 million foreign-born people from a wide range of backgrounds reside in the United States (Barringer, 1992). These people, as well as generations of Americans born to foreigners, contribute to making this country very culturally and ethnically diverse. Living in such a country brings with it many benefits, such as the opportunity for exposure to a wide sample of ethnically and culturally diverse experiences including food, entertainment, language, art, history, music, and so forth.

FIGURE 8–1 A SCENE FROM THE SUDAN In southern Sudan, the Dinka tribe lives with cattle, which they regard as sacred. Is this abnormal? Why?

However, it also brings a need for understanding with respect to a wide variety of culturally prescribed ways of thinking and behaving.

The boundaries between normal and abnormal are not always clear, even with reference to the cultural majority exclusively. Most Americans include a great deal of red meat in their diet. They love hamburgers and prize a tender steak. Should vegetarianism be considered abnormal? Most Americans value clear, unblemished, and unmarked skin. Is having one tattoo abnormal? How about two tattoos? How many tattoos are needed before being tattooed is considered abnormal? What extremes of behavior exceed the boundaries of normality for a "hot" rock group (see Figure 8–2)?

A PSYCHOSOCIAL PERSPECTIVE

Does the behavior contribute to the well-being of the individual and others? This is a key question from a psychosocial perspective. Inherent in this perspective is a broad definition of well-being as well as two assumptions. One is that *it is normal for human beings to strive for the well-being of themselves and others.* Although such an assumption may sound reasonable enough, it is not without controversy. As we saw in Chapter 2, some psychological theorists, such as Carl Rogers, would readily embrace the notion that people are born with a basic predisposition to strive for the well-being of themselves and others. But other theorists, such as Sigmund Freud, held a far less optimistic view of human nature. For Freud, normality is a state in which one's basic instincts are firmly under the ego's control. According to this view, abnormality results from a failure to control basic human instincts. Freudians and others might not readily agree that it is natural for people to strive for their own and others' well-being.

The second assumption is that *people know and agree on the kinds of behavior that does and does not contribute to the well-being of the individual and of the group.* However, the issues being discussed in newspapers today reveal great public controversies about what does and does not contribute to public well-being. For example, should logging be allowed to continue in an area where such activity threatens the extinction of a particular species? Some would argue that the greater social good is advanced by the jobs that the lumber industry provides. Others would argue that the greater social good is advanced by maintaining our planet's diversity of animal and plant life. Especially in situations in which two or more socially advantageous goals are pitted against one another, what constitutes the best route to

FIGURE 8–2 HOW "HOT" IS TOO HOT? A group called the Red Hot Chili Peppers reportedly walked on stage for a concert wearing little more than their socks. Is that normal behavior? Why?

personal and social well-being is not straightforward. Rather, opinions, usually based on personal values, will vary greatly.

AN INTEGRATIVE PERSPECTIVE

What we will refer to as an *integrative perspective* integrates features of the statistical, sociocultural, and psychosocial perspectives. Accordingly, **abnormal behavior** may be defined as *overt action or thinking that is statistically rare in the population, counter to the prevailing cultural and/or subcultural norms, and usually harmful to the well-being of oneself or others.* The inclusion of the term *subcultural norms* alerts us to the need for viewing behavior not only in its broad cultural context but also in a subcultural context. The definition leaves open the question of what type of behavior is harmful to the well-being of oneself or others. History teaches, however, that such questions are more apt to be resolved by the courts than by mental health professionals.

abnormal behavior
overt action or covert thinking that is statistically rare in the population, counter to the prevailing cultural and/or subcultural norms, and usually harmful to the well-being of oneself or others.

WHAT CAUSES ABNORMAL BEHAVIOR?

Is abnormal behavior caused by biological factors? Psychological factors? Cultural factors? Other factors? Some combination? Think about these questions as you think back to that woman in the post office, on her knees, engaged in conversation with the Creator (or so she claims). Do you have any thoughts regarding what might be causing such strange behavior? Do you say to yourself something like, "That woman is sick!"? Implied in the latter statement is the belief that abnormal behavior results from mental illness, disease, or defect. **Disease** may be defined as *an abnormal biological condition that impairs normal functioning and arises from factors such as infection, inherent weakness, or environmental agents.* We consider the disease or biological model of abnormality, and the medical model subsumed under it, first.

disease
an abnormal biological condition that impairs normal functioning and arises from factors such as infection, inherent weakness, or environmental agents.

A BIOLOGICAL MODEL

Beginning in the late eighteenth century, biologists, physiologists, medical researchers, and other scientists began to develop a keen interest in the link between brain abnormalities and disordered behavior. Decade after decade, scientists researched the possible mechanisms and processes by which many different kinds of biology-related variables could play a role in producing abnormal behavior. One way of becoming mentally disordered was through infection by the sexually transmitted disease syphilis. Left untreated, syphilis in its advanced stages may attack the brain and cause **general paresis**. Named for the Greek term for *letting go,* this condition is characterized by *the loss of certain voluntary and reflexive motor capabilities, as well as by other mental and behavioral deficits.* By 1913, analysis of brain tissue from people who had died of advanced syphilis confirmed that syphilitic infection had caused the general paresis.

general paresis
the loss of certain voluntary and reflexive motor capabilities as well as the development of other mental and behavioral deficits, as seen in later stages of syphilis.

Potentially overlapping with infection in effect, other biological factors are capable of directly or indirectly causing abnormal behavior. For example, **stroke** (*a cutting off of blood to a site in the brain, usually due to a clot in an artery*) may have dramatic and differential effects on behavior depending upon the specific area of the brain affected. Genetic defects may cause Down's syndrome or related conditions known to impact mental functioning and behavior. Physical trauma, such as a blow to the head, can cause damage to the brain which in turn may cause abnormal behavior. Deprivation of biological necessities, such as oxygen, proper nutrition, or sleep, can also cause abnormal behavior. Exposure to **toxins** (*poisonous materials*) such as lead or ingesting a drug that affects brain functioning will also give rise to abnormal behavior. The process of aging may cause atrophy or death of brain cells which in turn may cause **senility**, *a condition characterized by diminished cognitive abilities, including memory loss, usually caused by advanced age.* Figure 8–3 on page 206 illustrates a biological model for understanding the causes of abnormal behavior.

stroke
a cutting off of blood to a site in the brain, usually due to a clot in an artery.

senility
a condition characterized by diminished cognitive abilities, including memory loss, usually due to advanced age but sometimes due to disease.

Perhaps because some types of abnormal behavior have been shown to be of biological origin, and perhaps because people engaging in abnormal behavior sometimes appear

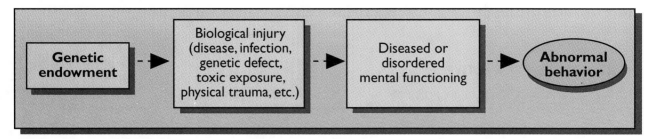

FIGURE 8–3 THE BIOLOGICAL MODEL OF ABNORMALITY According to a biological model of abnormality, abnormal behavior is a symptom of diseased or disordered mental functioning which in turn has resulted from compromised biological intactness. Biological intactness may be compromised by variables such as genetic deficit at birth, disease, infection, toxic exposure, physical trauma, and/or other such injuries. As the term is generally used in this context, *disordered functioning* is synonymous with *diseased functioning* except that no biological cause can be identified.

pathology

disease process.

psychopathology

disease of the mind.

diagnosis

a classification derived as a result of an attempt to identify or distinguish a disease, disorder, or deficit on the basis of signs and symptoms.

symptom

an observed manifestation of one or more known diseases or disorders. See also *sign* and *syndrome*.

syndrome

a pattern of symptoms that characterize a particular disease or disorder.

prognosis

a statement regarding the probable course of a disease.

relapse

a regression back into illness after whole or partial recovery.

remission

a condition in which the symptoms of a disease have abated.

cure

recovery from disease or a restoration of health.

as if there is something physically wrong with them, there exists a temptation to believe that all abnormal behavior may have a biological basis. Indeed, as early as the mid-nineteenth century, one of modern psychiatry's first textbooks (Griesinger, 1845) foretold the day when a biological basis would be found for all mental disorders. That day has yet to arrive and probably never will. Still, with sentiments echoing those expressed by Griesinger nearly 150 years before, one contemporary psychiatrist has argued that, "current modes of describing and defining psychiatric illness are seen as temporary expedients until biological markers . . . preceding the appearance of symptomatic behaviors, can be linked to . . . disorders" (Fabrega, 1992, p. 6). Stated another way, if a biological factor has not yet been linked to a particular mental disorder, hope springs eternal that such a link will eventually be made. That belief and hope are also inherent in the medical model.

THE MEDICAL MODEL

A fever may be viewed as a symptom of some underlying **pathology** (*disease process*). In like fashion, according to what has become known as the *medical model,* abnormal behavior is viewed as symptomatic of some underlying pathology. The symptom (such as a fever) can be treated with one kind of treatment (such as an aspirin), but it may take an entirely different type of treatment (anything ranging from antibiotics to laser surgery) in order to treat the underlying disease. As applied to abnormal behavior, the medical model holds that some underlying disease may be responsible for the observed psychopathology. Tranquilizers will relieve anxiety only temporarily; permanent relief of anxiety entails treating the physical cause of the anxiety.

The medical model has great logical appeal. Biological malfunctions do negatively impact on mental functioning and, ultimately, on behavior. The appeal of the medical model is so widespread and its influence so pervasive that the vocabulary of the mental health profession—including the term *mental health* itself—clearly reflects a medical model of behavior disorder. Terms such as mental illness, mental hospital, mental health professionals, psychotherapy, psychotherapist, **psychopathology** (literally, *disease of the mind*), **diagnosis** (*an opinion derived from an attempt to identify or distinguish a disease*), **symptoms** (*indicators of disease*), **syndromes** (*groups of signs or symptoms that define or characterize a disease*), **prognosis** (*a statement regarding the probable course of a disease*), **relapse** (*a regression back into illness after whole or partial recovery*), **remission** (*a condition in which the symptoms of a disease have abated*), and **cure** (*recovery from disease or a restoration of health*) all reflect the medical model.

In spite of the logical appeal of the medical model, many mental health professionals, particularly psychologists and other nonphysicians, only reluctantly employ such terminology. The terminology of the medical model is appealing in that it affords the convenience of a common language. What is objectionable, however, is the implication that all forms of behavior disorder have medical/biological causes and should thus be treated via medical/biological means. As you will see, the medical model is simply not comprehensive enough to account for all observed phenomena. Before reading on, what problems could you foresee with a strictly biological or medical model perspective on abnormal behavior?

A PSYCHOSOCIAL MODEL

Especially when the onset of a psychological disorder can be readily linked to an event that is external to a person, a medical model seems stretched as an explanation for observed behavioral abnormalities (see *In the News*). According to the psychosocial model, abnormal behavior is presumed to result from the complex interplay of one's learning or experiential history and environmental conditions. In this context, *learning or experiential history* is a broad term that encompasses diverse psychological and social experiences. Subsumed under the relatively broad heading of psychosocial model of abnormal behavior are all of the models of abnormal behavior in which psychological (including cognitive, behavioral, and emotional factors) and social factors are deemed to play a causal role. Not subsumed under the psychosocial model heading are models of abnormal behavior in which biological factors (such as infection or chemical imbalance) are key to etiology (cause). Four influential psychosocial models are the psychoanalytic model, the behavioral model, the cognitive model, and the humanistic model.

post-traumatic stress disorder

a variety of anxiety disorder caused by a reaction to a severe life stressor such as a natural disaster, a rape or other violent crime, or military combat.

IN THE News

Hurricane Andrew and Post-Traumatic Stress Disorder

In August 1992, Hurricane Andrew hit southern Florida and part of Louisiana and earned infamy as the single most costly natural disaster ever to occur in the United States. But the toll was not only financial; it was also emotional. As Wilkerson (1992 p.A1) observed, "Hurricane Andrew, a cruel aggressor in the view of rational adults, was the bogeyman come to life for the thousands of children who survived it but lost their life's treasures: their hamsters, Nintendo games, security blankets and other childhood possessions." The great emotional upset of the hurricane was the direct cause of various types of abnormal behavior in children such as crying spells (in some cases triggered by the onset of rain) and nightmares. Many children whose houses were left standing felt apprehension at going into them.

The hurricane left in its wake a variety of anxiety dis-order called **post-**traumatic stress disor-der** (PTSD). PTSD is *a reaction to severe life stressors including natural disasters, rape or other violent crime, military combat, and forced relocation* (as a result of political upheaval, the threat of toxic pollution, or other such events). It is characterized by symptoms such as mental reexperiencing of the event, avoidance of stimuli associated with the event, chronic tension, impaired memory or concentration, and lingering depression. A recently developed technique for treating PTSD is presented in Chapter 9 (pages 242–244). Here, however, consider the relevance of a disease model of abnormal behavior to understanding PTSD. Does it have any relevance?

Natural disasters can leave in their wake long-lasting psychological effects in children and adults. The trauma of Hurricane Andrew was reportedly causal in prompting the 10-year-old pictured above to return to drinking from a bottle (Wilkerson, 1992).

THE PSYCHOANALYTIC MODEL

neurosis

literally, "nerve related disease," a now antiquated term used to refer to nonpsychotic mental disorder.

Historically, Sigmund Freud's psychoanalytic model of personality contained within it the first comprehensive psychosocial model of abnormal behavior. Because Freud came from a medical background, one would think that he would have developed a medical model of disorder. In fact, a literal interpretation of Freud's early theorizing in this area would lead one to conclude that Freud's model was indeed better categorized as medical/biological than psychosocial. Freud interpreted much of the abnormal behavior his patients reported to him as symptomatic of an underlying disorder he called a **neurosis**, which literally means, *nerve-related disease*. As decades passed, however, the term *neurosis* evolved to mean something more like *as if the nerves were diseased*. Psychoanalytic theory, as well as the many different psychodynamic perspectives that flowed from it, have largely been viewed as psychosocial in nature.

Consistent with the psychosocial perspective, Freud viewed abnormal behavior as symptomatic of underlying intrapsychic conflicts. For example, a person who came to Freud complaining of a problem with alcohol might be treated for this problem, but only indirectly. Freud would have viewed the alcoholism to be symptomatic of an underlying neurosis, such as one related to frustrated oral dependency needs as a child. The treatment would be focused not on the symptom (the problem drinking or alcoholism), but on the "real problem" as presumed by psychoanalytic theory: frustrated childhood oral dependency needs. As we will see in Chapter 9, the emergence of competing theories and methods of therapy has made psychoanalysis far less attractive as a treatment method than it once was.

THE BEHAVIORAL MODEL

According to a behavioral model, abnormal behavior is the result of the same kinds of learning processes that give rise to normal and adaptive behavior. Abnormal behavior is understood in terms of principles of classical conditioning, operant conditioning, observational learning, and other principles of learning. As we will see in Chapter 9, therapy from a behavioral perspective is a matter of unlearning abnormal and maladaptive behavior, and relearning normal and adaptive behavior.

THE COGNITIVE MODEL

Cognitive perspectives on the etiology of abnormal behavior focus on the thoughts and images that serve to cause and maintain observed behavior, as well as more "covert" (or private) behavior such as thinking, feeling, and imaging. Perhaps the earliest application of a cognitive orientation to the study of abnormal behavior came with the efforts of John Dollard and Neal Miller. At a time when psychoanalytic therapy was all the rage and behavior therapy was in its infancy, these two psychologists sought to understand psychoanalytic theory in terms of learning theory. In their now classic work *Personality and Psychotherapy* Dollard and Miller (1950) wrote in a readable and inviting way about how cognitive representations of thoughts and feelings could be modified in systematic fashion with the objective being more adaptive thinking and behavior. They wrote, for example, that, "In the same way and by the same principles that bad tennis habits can be corrected by a good coach, so bad mental and emotional habits can be corrected by a psychotherapist" (Dollard & Miller, 1950, p. 8).

The cognitive perspective on behavior, personality, and mental disorders was also advanced by George A. Kelly. In his book *The Psychology of Personal Constructs*, Kelly (1955) sensitized readers to the relativity of perception, and the role of background and experience in the perceptual process. Kelly believed that people perceive the world through their own different kinds of lenses, so to speak. Accordingly, understanding an individual's behavior (normal or abnormal) was largely a matter of understanding the cognitive impressions and representations those lenses make. For example, suppose while you were working as a volunteer in a psychiatric hospital one of the patients said to you, "The sky is very patriotic today." Kelly might have advised you not to look to the sky for an explanation of this statement. Rather, look to the patient. More specifically, it would be useful to know more about what the constructs "sky" and "patriotic" mean to this individual.

On the matter of internal cognitive processes such as thinking, the behaviorist B. F. Skinner (1953, p. 35) taught that: "The objection to inner states is not that they do not exist, but that they are not relevant . . . We cannot account for the behavior of any system while staying wholly inside it; eventually we must turn to forces operating upon the organism from without." However, an increasing number of behaviorally oriented therapists and researchers would part company with Skinner regarding his views on the importance of "inner states" or "self-described covert events" such as thinking and feeling. These cognitive and cognitive-behavioral therapists and researchers would begin to focus their attention on the irrational and maladaptive thoughts, images, and feelings that underlie abnormal behavior and problems of adjustment. A person might suffer from depression, for example, not as the result of any intrapsychic conflict or environmental contingency but rather because he or she may be laboring under irrational beliefs about the possibility of being perfect, being liked by everyone, or living in a world that is totally just to everyone. The work of cognitive and cognitive-behavioral therapist/researchers such as Albert Ellis and Aaron Beck will be discussed in Chapter 9.

THE HUMANISTIC MODEL

A humanistic model of abnormal behavior tends to focus on the uniquely human processes of cognition and behavior such as values, self-fulfillment, meaning in life, and personal growth. Like the cognitive approach, there is clearly a focus on the disabling assumptions people may harbor about themselves or others. However, as distinguished from the cognitive approach, there is greater emphasis on topics such as inner experience, the concept of self, and the uniquely human potential for self-direction and personal growth. There is not the emphasis on stimulus-and-response that characterizes the behavioral perspective on abnormality. Neither is there the emphasis on intrapsychic conflicts that characterize psychoanalytic and other psychodynamic perspectives. From a humanistic perspective, abnormalities in behavior and cognition are viewed in terms of damage to the human spirit.

The overall contribution of the humanistic approach to conceptualizing abnormal behavior has been fairly limited. Its application to severe forms of mental illness is questionable. Humanistically oriented treatment approaches have appeared to have relevance in the understanding of a relatively narrow range of behavior disorders, particularly adjustment-related problems. One objective of humanistic treatment, as we will see in Chapter 9, often entails mobilizing an individual's inherent capacity for positive change.

A COMPARISON WITH THE MEDICAL MODEL

Figure 8–4 contains a general representation of the psychosocial model of abnormal behavior. In it, the term *learning history and experience* makes reference to an extremely broad array of cognitive, behavioral, and emotional experiences—so broad that psychodynamic, learning, cognitive, and humanistic perspectives of abnormal behavior can all be subsumed under it. *Environmental conditions* is an equally broad term referring to diverse events ranging from acts of people (parents, friends, teachers, strangers, and so forth), to acts of animals (such as your cat running away from home), to acts of Nature (such as beautiful days

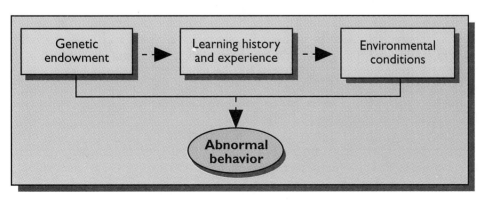

FIGURE 8–4   A PSYCHO-SOCIAL MODEL OF AB-NORMALITY According to this model, we begin life with our genetic endowment and then have various learning experiences while being exposed to various environmental conditions, all of which is capable of producing abnormal behavior. Unlike the biological model or the medical model, abnormal behavior in the psychosocial model is not viewed as a symptom of damaged mental functioning.

and merciless storms), to seemingly random events (such as a chance meeting with an old friend or winning the jackpot at Bingo!).

In contrast to the medical model, in which treatment almost always focuses exclusively on the identified patient, treatment from a psychosocial perspective may entail focus on the environment and the conditions in the environment acting to maintain the abnormal behavior. This is especially true in behavioral approaches but it is also true, for example, in humanistic approaches. From a humanistic perspective, an environment that stifles opportunities for self-expression, for example, might well be a target for therapeutic efforts. Treatment according to the medical model tends to be past-oriented. Because something in the patient's history (whether biological or emotional in nature) is believed to have caused the disease, treatment typically involves detailed scrutiny of the past in order to achieve insight as to the cure. By contrast, treatment from a psychosocial perspective may be past-oriented (as it generally is in psychoanalysis or even behavior therapy when it is necessary to better understand prior learning), but it may also be exclusively focused on the here-and-now.

One long-time advocate of a psychosocial model of abnormal behavior, psychiatrist Thomas Szasz, has written about many possible pitfalls of viewing abnormal behavior as symptomatic of "mental illness." For example, Szasz (1960) argued that because disease is presumed to be out of the person's control, people deemed to be mentally ill may freely engage in abnormal behavior without the personal, social, legal, and ethical restraints to which the rest of us must conform. If that is the case, it behooves society to be very certain about who is and is not mentally ill. In fact, as revealed in glimpses of highly publicized legal proceedings involving pleas of insanity, there are often great differences of opinion about who should be considered mentally ill as a matter of law.

Another long-time proponent of a psychosocial model of abnormal behavior, psychologist George W. Albee, has argued that society's reliance on the medical model to explain deviant behavior has spawned a mental health care system that is incapable of dealing with society's needs. Albee (1968) insisted that due to the advanced education and training necessary to become a mental professional, too few mental health professionals enter the work force annually. Albee envisioned replacing existing medical institutions (like hospitals staffed by doctors and nurses) with community centers and community programs staffed by trained community workers who need not have advanced degrees. For Albee, because contemporary society can be dehumanizing, it is the human touch—not necessarily the highly educated mental health professional's touch—that is critically needed.

The medical model has also been criticized for the resulting stigma attached to a psychiatric diagnosis, and for the personal and social consequences of this stigma. At best, a psychiatric label only describes some aspects of the way a person characteristically behaves and thinks. Yet it is very easy to lose sight of that fact. A tendency exists to view the diagnosed person primarily in terms of the diagnosis. On the basis of the psychiatric diagnosis, we may have certain expectations about how an individual will behave, even if those expectations have no basis in fact.

A BIOPSYCHOSOCIAL MODEL

Considered alone, neither the biological model, the medical model, nor the psychosocial model seems entirely satisfactory. This is so because a compelling case can be made that while certain mental disorders are indeed biologically based and may productively be thought of as diseases, other mental disorders seem only to be "disease-like" and are more productively conceptualized in purely psychosocial terms. Our solution to this problem is to view the roots of abnormal behavior not from a purely biological, medical, or psychosocial perspective, but rather from a perspective that combines features of each—a biopsychosocial perspective (see Figure 8–5).

From a biopsychosocial perspective, then, we may use the language of the medical model and the widely shared meaning of terms such as mental illness while remaining aware of the limitations of these terms. For example, when speaking of "mental illness," we may in some instances be speaking of a veritable illness, and in some instances be speaking of a condition that only resembles an illness. How do we know which conditions

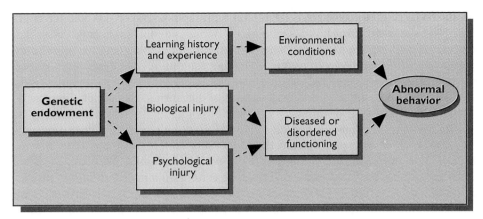

FIGURE 8–5 A BIOPSY-CHOSOCIAL MODEL OF ABNORMALITY A biopsychosocial model of abnormality allows that some types of abnormal behavior may arise from disordered or diseased mental functioning while other types of abnormal behavior may arise from the interplay of one's learning history with environmental conditions.

are veritable illnesses? It is sometimes difficult to tell, but the published research literature can be quite helpful as a guide. **Organic conditions**, or *conditions that have a documented biological, genetic, or physiological basis,* are usually acknowledged, even by psychologists with a strong psychosocial orientation, to be illnesses or diseases in the usual sense of those words. The disease status of *conditions that have no known biological, genetic, or physiological basis* (**functional conditions**) is far more controversial.

In the days when the medical model was first gaining widespread public and professional acceptance, it represented a most significant scientific and humanistic advance over preexisting notions of deviant behavior. Spirit possession and related notions were not only demystified but secularized. As a result, abnormal behavior could be classified, explained, humanely treated, and subjected to systematic study. Another positive consequence of the medical model has been the systematic accumulation of valuable information about the nature of abnormal behavior. Critics of the medical model argue that it has high costs attached to it, such as the stigma attached to being found mentally ill. Indeed, there is stigma attached to mental illness. However, there is no evidence to suggest that a purely psychosocial, behavioral, or other classification system for abnormal behavior would carry with it any less stigma.

Must there be a classification system at all? The best answer to this question is probably yes. Some sort of labeling or classification system seems necessary if people are to speak a common language about normal and abnormal behavior. A classification system is useful in research, the development of effective interventions, and record-keeping, to name but a few areas. "But," you may wonder, "how are diagnostic judgments regarding abnormal behavior made?"

organic conditions

presenting symptoms that have a biological, genetic, or physiological basis. Contrast with *functional conditions.*

functional conditions

presenting symptoms that have no known biological, genetic, or physiological basis. Contrast with *organic conditions.*

IDENTIFYING AND CLASSIFYING ABNORMAL BEHAVIOR

Identification and classification are two activities common to all areas of science. In behavioral science, the hope is that research on specific patterns of abnormal behavior will yield effective methods of treatment and prevention.

SYSTEMS OF CLASSIFICATION

Different systems of classification exist. One comprehensive classification system used to identify disease is the World Health Organization's *Manual of the International Statistical Classification of Diseases, Injuries, and Causes of Death* (ICD). Through its several editions, American psychiatrists have not found it useful due to certain omissions in diagnostic categories (Widiger et al., 1991). In this country, the reference work of choice for the classification of psychiatric disorders is the American Psychiatric Association's *Diagnostic and*

epidemiology

the medical science that explores the origins and distribution of disease within a population as well as the conditions that influence the spread or severity of the disease.

epidemic

the rapid or extensive spread of a disease, especially a contagious disease.

prevalence

the current rate of illness (or accidents or other events) in a specified population, including new, presently existing, or treated (or deceased) cases.

incidence

the current rate of new cases of illness (or accidents or other events) in a specified population over a specified period of time.

interview

a technique for gathering information by means of discussion.

mental status examination

a face-to-face interview in which the interviewer evaluates the interviewee on numerous variables, such as judgment and memory, in order to derive a diagnosis and/or behavioral assessment.

behavioral observation

watching an individual or group of people for psychodiagnostic, psychotherapeutic, or research purposes, typically while maintaining some kind of record of what is observed.

[1]Published glimpses of the decision-making process have revealed that a bit of politics sometimes enters into this process. See, for example, Millon (1981) regarding the criteria for defining *antisocial personality disorder* in DSM-III, and others (Gunderson, 1983; Kernberg, 1984; Michels, 1984) discussing the inclusion of a diagnostic category called *avoidant personality disorder*. Ideally, the selection for inclusion or exclusion of a diagnostic category or set of diagnostic criteria should not hinge on the political influence of any one committee member.

Statistical Manual of Mental Disorders (DSM). Currently in its fourth edition and referred to as DSM-IV, the manual contains descriptions of various patterns of abnormal behavior, a system of identifying the pattern of behavior by name and number, and notes on distinguishing one abnormal behavior pattern from other patterns. A DSM diagnosis is used by psychologists, psychiatrists, and other mental health professionals on insurance forms, state, hospital, and court records, and other official documents that call for a psychiatric diagnosis to be recorded.

Traditionally, decisions were made to include or exclude particular diagnostic categories on the basis of expert opinion (Kendell, 1988; Robins & Helzer, 1986; Spitzer, 1985). Committees of experts discussed various psychiatric disorders and came to some agreement about what should and should not be considered a mental disorder.[1] By contrast, in the creation of DSM-IV, the underlying objective was to create a diagnostic system that had a firm grounding in the published psychiatric literature (Frances et al., 1989; Widiger et al., 1990). Ultimately, however, as Pincus et al. (1992, p. 115) concluded, "There are no infallible rules to apply."

EPIDEMIOLOGICAL INFORMATION

In addition to information on diagnostic categorizations, the DSM includes information on the *epidemiology* of psychiatric disorders. **Epidemiology** is *the medical science that explores the origins and distribution of disease within a population, as well as the conditions that influence the spread or severity of the disease.* One term from the field of epidemiology that may already be familiar to you is **epidemic**; it refers to *the rapid or extensive spreading of a disease, especially a contagious disease.* Two epidemiological terms used by mental health professionals in their study of mental disorders are *prevalence* and *incidence*. **Prevalence** (derived from the Latin *praevalere* meaning *to be strong*) is defined as *the current rate of illness (or accidents or other events) in a specified population, including new, presently existing, or treated (or deceased) cases.* One variety of prevalence, referred to by epidemiologists as *period prevalence*, refers to prevalence for a narrowly specified period of time. **Incidence** refers only to *the current rate of new cases of illness (or accidents or other events) in a specified population over a specified period of time.* In these definitions, *rate* may be stated in terms such as "cases per hundred," "cases per thousand," "cases per million," and so forth. The *specified population* will vary widely as a function of the epidemiological focus of study. "People who attended the American Legion convention in Philadelphia in 1976" is one example of a specified population.

Epidemiologists are, in a sense, medical detectives. Using a variety of methods, these researchers attack mysteries related to the nature and course of disease. Comparable detective work is also going on in the behavioral sciences. Like medical epidemiologists, behavioral epidemiologists attempt to sort out and isolate the factors believed to cause and maintain varieties of abnormal behavior—even, on occasion, epidemics of abnormal behavior (see *Cultural Close-Up*).

THE TOOLS OF PSYCHOLOGICAL ASSESSMENT

Mental health professionals use tools of psychological assessment such as the interview, behavioral observation, case study material, and psychological tests to make psychodiagnostic judgments regarding research subjects, clients, people involved in legal proceedings, and others (Cohen et al., 1992).

THE INTERVIEW

An **interview** may be defined simply as *a technique for gathering information by means of discussion.* A special type of interview in the mental health field is called the **mental status examination**, *a face-to-face interview in which the interviewer evaluates the interviewee on numerous variables (such as judgment, behavior, and memory) in order to arrive at a diagnosis.*

BEHAVIORAL OBSERVATION

As its name implies, **behavioral observation** entails *watching an individual or group of people for psychodiagnostic or psychotherapeutic purposes, usually while maintaining some kind of*

Cultural CLOSE-UP

Koro Epidemics in Asia

Most Americans have never heard of a psychiatric disorder known as *koro,* although many thousands of cases of it have been reported through the years. The Malay word *koro* (in Chinese, *su yang*) describes a psychiatric disorder characterized by the unfounded belief that one's genitals are shrinking. In males, *koro* may manifest itself as a belief that the penis is melding into the abdomen. The man who believes that he has contracted *koro* also believes that once his penis has totally disappeared into his abdomen, he will die. To forestall such shrinkage—and death—until medical help can be obtained, *koro* victims may attempt a number of home remedies. The sufferer may clamp the penis to something that will keep it from shrinking, tie a red string around it (red being a color that is thought to ward off evil), or have his wife perform fellatio (Yap, 1951). In women, *koro* manifests itself as a belief that the breasts or female genitalia are

shrinking. In females too, death is thought to result once the shrinkage occurs, and comparable home remedies may be attempted until medical help can be obtained.

Although *koro* attacks are most typically sporadic (Hughes, 1985), there have been accounts of *koro* epidemics in China (Mo et al., 1987), India (Charkaborty et al., 1983), Singapore (Ngui, 1969), and Thailand (Sunwanlert & Coates, 1979). Such epidemics have involved hundreds or even thousands of reported cases within a relatively brief time span. Wen-Shing Tseng, a psychiatrist at the University of Hawaii School of Medicine, and colleagues (Tseng et al. 1988; Tseng et al., 1992) analyzed a *koro* epidemic in China from an epidemiological perspective. Among other things, they found *koro* victims to be younger, less educated, and more superstitious than nonvictims from the same geographic area. Interestingly, Tseng et al. (1992) observed

a correlation between periods of *koro* epidemics in China and periods of social change and turmoil. An epidemic in 1952 occurred at about the time land reform was in progress. Ten years later, another epidemic occurred, this one coinciding with a governmental program to hasten economic and industrial growth. A *koro* epidemic in 1966 came at the high point of the Cultural Revolution in China. An epidemic of *koro* in 1974 coincided with an epidemic of encephalitis (brain inflammation): the disease caused a great deal of social turmoil. Tseng et al. (1992) concluded that social tension might be a triggering factor for a *koro* epidemic in China. As a preventive strategy, Tseng et al. (1992) urged community mental health education in communities deemed to be at high risk for a future outbreak of *koro.*

record of the activity. In a family therapy setting, behavioral observation may be focused on the number of times a couple gets into an argument, as well as on the nature of the arguments. In a classroom setting, behavioral observation may be focused on the number of times children diagnosed as hyperactive leave their seats or otherwise engage in inappropriate behavior. In a psychiatric hospital inpatient setting, behavioral observation of an individual patient may be focused on the number of activities the patient engages in that are required for daily, independent living (such as making one's bed or washing out a mug). Data from behavioral observation are seldom used to make psychiatric diagnoses. Rather, such data can be used to support or refute a diagnosis. Behavioral observation is also useful as a research tool.

THE CASE STUDY

A **case study**, also referred to as a *case history,* consists of *a compilation of biographical data from as many different relevant sources as the person compiling the case study can find.* Sources

koro
an Asian psychiatric disorder characterized by the delusion that one's genitals are shrinking and by related symptoms.

case study
a compilation of biographical data on one person drawn from diverse sources including, among others, official government records, school records, police reports, medical and psychological records, employment records, family albums, family videotapes, and interview data.

may be as diverse as official government records (birth and hospital records, school records, police reports, etc.), medical and psychological records from private practitioners (including records of prior psychiatric evaluation or psychological assessment), employment records, and interview data obtained from the subject's friends, family, co-workers, and other associates. School yearbooks, photos in family albums, films and videotapes in one's home library, as well as other possessions and mementos may also be employed in the development of a case history.

Case study data alone are usually insufficient for the purpose of making a diagnosis. There are some special circumstances, however, in which case study data alone must suffice for diagnostic purposes. For example, in the aftermath of a suicide, researchers might use case study material to conduct a "psychological autopsy" of the suicide victim and arrive at a psychiatric diagnosis. Another instance in which case study material alone would suffice for diagnostic purposes is when the individual being diagnosed is some historical or famous personage, who is either deceased or alive but uncooperative.

PSYCHOLOGICAL TESTS

test

a guage, device, or procedure used to measure

psychological test

a gauge, device, or procedure used to measure psychological variables.

The noun **test** refers to *a gauge, device or procedure used to measure*. In classrooms, for example, students are typically administered academic tests to gauge or measure their knowledge in certain academic areas. A **psychological test** may be thought of as *a gauge, device or procedure used to measure psychological variables*. Psychological tests have been devised to measure categories and subcategories of psychological variables as diverse as intelligence, personality, social functioning, interests, fears, sources of satisfaction, level of adjustment in marriage, level of adjustment in occupation, magnitude of behavior disorder, thought disorder, or brain and nervous system functioning—the list goes on. It has been estimated that upwards of 20,000 new psychological tests are developed annually (American Psychological Association, 1993a). Psychological tests and related assessment procedures may take a variety of forms and may be administered orally, by means of paper and pencil or computer, or by other means. Moreover, existing instruments, procedures, even nontests can be pressed into service for use in measuring psychological variables (Cohen et al., 1992). For example, when commercially available video games were first gaining widespread popularity as a means of entertainment, psychologists were devising ways to use such technology as a means of evaluating abilities such as eye-hand coordination (Kennedy et al., 1982).

VARIETIES OF ABNORMAL BEHAVIOR

Humans are capable of an extraordinarily wide range of behavior. In the remainder of this chapter, we focus attention on behavior patterns within that broad spectrum that the DSM lists as abnormal. Keep in mind that the DSM does not represent the "last word" on the subject, just research findings and opinion. The very idea of a last word on a psychiatric disorder represents a kind of contradiction in terms; the hallmark of most psychiatric disorders is some degree of uncertainty about etiology, prevention, and/or treatment. The precise mechanisms through which many medications act to control specific symptoms of psychiatric disorders are simply not known. The ability to predict the later onset of most psychiatric symptoms on the basis of psychological or physical tests is quite limited. Indeed, if literally *everything* were to become known about a psychiatric disorder, and if it could be managed in a purely medical way, patients suffering from the disorder would more likely be treated by general practitioners and internists than by psychiatrists or other mental health professionals. The model for such a transition in care is general paresis, once regarded as a psychiatric condition and now viewed primarily as a medical one.

ADJUSTMENT DISORDERS

adjustment disorder

a condition diagnosed when a maladaptive or excessive response to a stressor occurs within three months of the stressful event or when everyday functioning has been profoundly impaired by the stressful event.

After reading Chapter 6, you may well appreciate that stressors—the loss of a loved one, victimization by criminal behavior, an act of Nature, whatever—may leave lasting imprints on one's thought and behavior patterns. An **adjustment disorder** is *present when a mal-*

adaptive response to a stressor occurs within 3 months of the stressful incident. In this context, *maladaptive* means that the response to the stress is excessive in intensity. It may also mean that the individual has been so affected by the stressor that everyday functioning has been profoundly impaired. If after 6 months or so an individual is still debilitated by the stressor, the diagnosis will be changed. For example, after the loss of a loved one, a bereaved person may be extremely depressed and be diagnosed as suffering from an adjustment disorder. If this individual is still severely depressed by the loss six months later, the diagnosis may be changed from adjustment disorder to major depression.

MOOD DISORDERS

Once widely referred to as *disorders of affect* or *affective disorders*, **mood disorders** are *emotion-related problems of behavior and thinking of such magnitude that everyday functioning is impaired.* **Mood** refers to *an average of affect over a period of time* (with "period of time" ranging from "over the course of an interview" to "over the course of a year" or more). **Affect** refers to one's *expression of emotion.* Normal affect is reflected in behavior that is appropriate to the situation. For example, it is normal, usual, and expected for people to be sad at funerals. Under ordinary circumstances, anyone who is particularly jubilant during a funeral would be said to be exhibiting *inappropriate affect.* Similarly, there is a very good chance that anyone who cries through a comedy presentation would also be exhibiting inappropriate affect. Another clinical characterization of affect concerns its "sharpness." The term *blunted affect* characterizes a condition wherein capacity to respond emotionally appears limited. *Flat affect* refers to a condition wherein there is little or no emotional responsivity.

References to mood are usually made in terms of two extremes or poles. Think of these extremes or poles as ranging from "very low" (as would be seen in depressed states) to "very high" (as would be seen in what are called manic states). A mood disorder that involves only one of these extremes, for instance, at the low end (depression) or the high end (mania), is said to be **unipolar** in nature (meaning, *involving one pole*). Some people exhibit disorders of mood having "highs" as well as "lows" and these types of disorders are referred to as **bipolar** (meaning *involving two poles*). **Mania** is *a condition characterized by highly emotional behavior—elation, anger, or sadness—combined with high energy, and rapid, usually faulty, thinking.* Whereas slowed speech and thinking characterize depression, rapid speech and **flight of ideas** (*a rapid stream of different thoughts and images*) are typical in mania. Poor judgment may also be evident in people during manic episodes. They may do things that they think other people will view as amusing only to find that their pranks are not considered funny at all. In extreme cases, people in manic states may develop a **delusion** (*false belief*), such as the delusion that they are someone else. Such manic symptoms are distinguished from a more severe form of psychopathology to be discussed subsequently (paranoid schizophrenia), in which the delusions are more entrenched, longer lasting, and more systematized.

It is not uncommon to feel down or depressed from time to time. However, the individual who is clinically depressed exhibits many changes from usual physical functioning. Changes in eating or sleeping patterns and general slowing of movement or speech are typically present. Additionally, the individual suffering from depression may cry frequently and suffer from irritability or frequent loss of temper. Lessened motivation to achieve, to relate socially, and to derive joy from life are frequent accompaniments. Negative thought patterns, including feelings of worthlessness, guilt, or apathy, and even contemplation of suicide may also be present. Depressive episodes are common among people who have been diagnosed as manic (Goodwin & Jamison, 1987). For this reason, where mania has been diagnosed, the disorder is considered to be bipolar in nature, that is, it is considered to have both manic and depressive elements.

MOOD AND HEALTH

The study of mood disorders, particularly depression, is of interest regarding the links between it and other mental and physical diseases. A growing body of research suggests that depression in medical patients may compound the negative effects of physical illness. In one study of 330 men who were infected with the AIDS-causing HIV virus, subjects who

mood disorder
an emotion-related problem of behavior and thinking of such magnitude that everyday functioning is impaired.

mood
an average of affect over a period of time.

affect
expression of emotion.

unipolar disorder
a mood disorder that involves only one affectual extreme, such as depression at the low end of the spectrum or mania at the high end. Contrast with *bipolar disorder.*

bipolar disorder
a mood disorder that involves the expression of affectual extremes, including "highs" as well as "lows." Contrast with *unipolar disorder.*

mania
a mood disorder characterized by highly emotional behaviorùelation, anger, or sadnessùcombined with high energy, and rapid, usually faulty, thinking.

flight of ideas
a condition symptomatic of the mood disorder, mania, in which there is a rapid stream of different thoughts and images.

delusion
false belief.

were depressed were found to die at a rate twice that of men who were not clinically depressed within the first three years after diagnosis (Burack, 1992). A study of kidney dialysis patients showed death was significantly more likely in extremely depressed than in nondepressed patients (Burton et al., 1986). In this study, it was speculated that the depression may have been responsible for making patients more careless about compliance with dietary and other medical prescriptions. In an extensive study of elderly women suffering hip fractures it was found that depressed women had hospital stays that were on average 8 days longer than women in the nondepressed group (Strain et al., 1991). In a study of 242 people having rheumatoid arthritis the patients who were most apt to report the greatest pain and the greatest difficulty sleeping were those who were severely depressed (Nicassio & Wallston, 1992). For those suffering from chronic diseases, treatment for depression may well lead to improvement (Von Korff et al., 1992).

The causes of many mood disorders of long-standing duration may lie in a combination of biological and psychological factors. Medication is typically prescribed for the more severe disorders, and such treatment, often in combination with psychotherapy, can give patients a new lease on life. Psychotherapy without prescription medication may be all that is needed to treat the less severe and more transient varieties of mood disorder.

ANXIETY DISORDERS

Sitting for an examination. Giving a speech. Being called on in class. Asking someone out for a date. Being pulled over by the police. These are all situations capable of inducing that familiar, uneasy feeling known as anxiety. Formally defined, **anxiety** is *a state of fear, dread, uncertainty, nervousness, or concern.* A certain amount of anxiety seems too often an accompaniment of many aspects of everyday existence—from walking down a dark street at night to sending in an employment application. Anxiety can be helpful and constructive. It may spur athletes on to their trophy-winning best or serve to inspire great writing, sculpting, painting, or other works of art. However, an anxiety level that has begun to impede one's quality of life and/or anxiety that has no rational or realistic cause signals the existence of what mental health professionals call an anxiety disorder. There are several varieties of anxiety disorder, including many that were once subsumed under the now defunct diagnostic category of neurotic disorders. Here we briefly describe some of them.

PHOBIC DISORDER

Phobias are *irrational fears characterized by the generation of great anxiety and avoidance behavior.* **Phobic disorder** refers to *the condition of being phobic.* Three general subcategories of phobic disorder are *agoraphobia, social phobia,* and *simple phobia.* **Agoraphobia,** *a fear of going outside or outdoors,* can be quite detrimental to one's quality of life, especially for people who might otherwise enjoy going shopping, frequenting restaurants, traveling abroad, or doing just about anything that involves leaving the house. **Social phobia,** as its name implies, refers to *fear of interacting with people.* Although we all may have experienced occasional shyness, public speaking anxiety, or stage fright, the magnitude of anxiety produced by such situations in persons diagnosed as being socially phobic is much higher (Turner et al., 1986) and much more injurious to one's overall quality of life (Liebowitz et al., 1985; Turner & Beidel, 1989).

The category **simple phobia** (*irrational fears of specific objects and/or situations*) includes fears of the widest possible array of **phobic objects** (*stimuli that are irrationally feared and capable of producing avoidance behavior*). Phobic objects may include situations (public speaking, standing in a high place, entering enclosed surroundings such as elevators or airplanes), things that are alive (such as animals or insects), things that were alive (human corpses, dead animals), inanimate matter (such as dirt or dust), acts of Nature (such as thunderstorms), even abstract ideas (such as humiliation). In common practice, and with some exceptions (such as agoraphobia for fear of open spaces and **claustrophobia** for *fear of closed spaces*), clinicians typically refer to most simple phobias with the use of the term *fear of* followed by whatever it is that is feared rather than use ancient linguistic roots for phobic objects and then appending these roots to *phobia*. For example, clinicians usually use *fear of snakes*, not *ophidiophobia*; *fear of storms*, not *brontophobia*; and *fear of crowds*, not *ochlophobia*.[2]

A great deal of research evidence supports the view that learning principles are involved in the development of most phobic disorders. A parent may have modeled a particular phobia for a child. Such is the case, for example, when a parent becomes anxious at the sight of cat and the child learns, from the parent's verbal and nonverbal behavior, to be fearful of cats. Alternatively, the pairing of a traumatic event with a particular object may account for why certain objects become phobic objects. Principles of learning may also be put to work to treat phobias. Treatment may involve graduated exposure to the phobic object, giving the phobic client the opportunity to see that nothing catastrophic happens as a result of the exposure.

PANIC DISORDER

A **panic attack** may be defined as *a condition of relatively brief duration (usually no more than a few minutes), not precipitated by the victim being the focus of others' attention, in which the victim experiences behavioral, cognitive, and physical terror with symptoms such as shortness of breath or related breathing difficulties, dizziness, shaking, trembling, sweating, nausea, and/or fear of dying or losing control.* Some evidence suggests that the origins of panic attack can be found in exposure to severe stress (Foa et al., 1984; Lelliott et al., 1989; Pollard et al., 1989). The actual occurrence of a panic attack may be triggered by internal sensations that are associated with threat and responded to with anxiety (Clark, 1986; Clark et al., 1988; Ehlers et al., 1988; Sanderson et al., 1989). When a panic attack occurs, the symptoms are so intense that some researchers have questioned whether the experience is simply intense anxiety or instead something qualitatively different (Barlow et al., 1985; Rapee, 1987). A sufferer's report of panic attacks and/or the fear that panic attacks will recur may prompt a diagnosis of **panic disorder.** The best available treatment for panic disorder is probably a combination of antidepressant medication and psychotherapy, although the side effects of antidepressant medication (such as drowsiness) can be debilitating (Mavissakalian & Perel, 1989).

OBSESSIVE-COMPULSIVE DISORDER

An **obsession** may be defined as *a mental preoccupation, usually with the same or similar thoughts being thought again and again.* For example, someone might have an obsession with cleanliness and think thoughts like, "I must keep myself clean and my hands free of germs." A **compulsion,** derived from *compel*, is *an urge or impulse, usually perceived as irresistible, to engage in some type of behavior.* An individual with a cleanliness obsession might develop a hand-washing compulsion or a compulsion to shower an inordinate number of times per day. This is so because compulsive behavior sometimes represents an effort—usually an unsuccessful effort—to relieve anxiety caused by obsessive thoughts (Steketee & Foa, 1985). The diagnosis of **obsessive-compulsive disorder (OCD)** reflects the fact that obsessions and compulsions are typically concurrent. However, either obsessive thoughts or compulsive behavior or both may be present in order for the diagnosis of OCD to be made.

Almost any type of thought pattern can become the basis for an obsession, although thoughts involving fear for one's safety and guilt over one's behavior or thoughts are common. It is also true that almost any type of behavior can be performed compulsively. In OCD, however, checking behavior (checking that the gas is off, checking that the door is locked, etc.) and cleansing behavior (cleaning oneself, cleaning one's home, etc.) are common (Rachman & Hodgson, 1980). Treatment for OCD may involve drug therapy, psychotherapy, or both. A behavioral treatment technique called *response prevention,* wherein the patient is prohibited from engaging in the compulsive behavior, has been shown to be particularly effective (Steketee & Foa, 1985). There is some evidence to suggest that behavior therapy for OCD produces not only behavioral improvement but also chemical changes in the brain (Baxter et al., 1992). These chemical changes are in some ways similar, though not identical, to changes that occur as a result of drug therapy for OCD (Blakeslee, 1992a; Swedo et al., 1992).

panic attack

a condition of relatively brief duration, not precipitated by the victim being the focus of others' attention, in which the victim experiences behavioral, cognitive, and physical terror with symptoms such as shortness of breath or related breathing difficulties, dizziness, shaking, trembling, sweating, nausea, and/or fear of dying or losing control.

panic disorder

an anxiety disorder characterized by recurrent panic attacks or fear that panic attacks will recur.

obsession

a mental preoccupation, usually with the same or similar thoughts being thought repeatedly.

compulsion

an urge or impulse, usually perceived as irresistible, to engage in some type of behavior.

obsessive-compulsive disorder (OCD)

an anxiety disorder characterized by obsessive thoughts and/or compulsive behavior.

[2]A fun exercise is to identify ancient Greek or Latin roots for modern words and then to come up with clinical-sounding names for different types of fears. For example, what clinical-sounding names ending with *phobia* might you devise for *fear of computers, fear of coupons,* or *fear of voice mail?*

GENERALIZED ANXIETY DISORDER

We all seem to carry a certain amount of anxiety with us during many of our waking hours—sometimes it is even carried with us into sleep in the form of nightmares. For some people, however, anxiety seems constant, unending, and not linked to any one specific life event. Such mental experience may be accompanied by physical symptoms and sensations, a partial listing of which would include trembling, aching muscles, restlessness, irritability, rapid pulse, frequent urination, gastrointestinal problems such as diarrhea, and difficulties in breathing, swallowing, sleeping, or concentrating. The diagnosis of **generalized anxiety disorder** will be made when the condition has lasted for a minimum of 6 months and cannot be linked to a single event or circumstance in one's life. In addition, the experience of anxiety must be accompanied by at least half a dozen physical symptoms or sensations of the variety listed above. Treatment for generalized anxiety disorder may entail drug therapy, psychotherapy, or most typically, a combination of both.

PSYCHOACTIVE SUBSTANCE USE DISORDERS

Beer is a psychoactive substance; so are other forms of alcohol and other drugs having the potential to alter one's state of consciousness, including nicotine, marijuana, amphetamines, sedatives, and hallucinogens. A **psychoactive substance use disorder** is diagnosed when, for a minimum of 1 month, (1) an individual continues to use some drug (a psychoactive substance) while aware that such usage may cause or aggravate psychological, social, or physical problems, or (2) an individual continues to use the psychoactive substance in situations in which its use is clearly dangerous to oneself and/or others (such as getting high before operating heavy machinery).

PERSONALITY DISORDERS

In Chapter 2, we defined *personality* after Cohen et al. (1988, p. 401) as an individual's unique constellation of psychological traits and states. From that definition, we might reasonably expect that a personality *disorder* involves some abnormality or dysfunction with respect to one's psychological traits or states. This is in fact the case. We may define a **personality disorder** as *a condition characterized by maladaptive psychological traits that causes significant impairment in the person's functioning in social, occupational, or other contexts.* The diagnosis is made only if the symptoms of this disorder have been present for at least one year prior to the diagnosis. Often, the symptoms of an adult personality disorder have been present since early adulthood or adolescence. The diagnosis is not made if the symptoms are sporadic or limited only to certain periods of one's life.

Common threads running through many different subtypes of personality disorder include disturbed interpersonal relationships, persistent patterns of trouble throughout life (as opposed to isolated incidents or episodes), and resistance to change. Many people diagnosed with personality disorders have no desire to conform to the demands of others or society at large. One subtype of personality disorder we read of frequently in the popular press is *antisocial personality disorder.*

ANTISOCIAL PERSONALITY DISORDER

From your own knowledge and experience, what traits would you expect to be dominant in an individual diagnosed as suffering from antisocial personality disorder?

If you are like most people, the term *antisocial* conjures up images of someone who shuns contact with people and prefers to be alone. This interpretation of the term is logical because *anti* means *against or opposed to* and *social* usually refers to *people* or *interpersonal relationships.* However, as is the case with many psychology-related terms, use of the term *antisocial* by members of the public differs somewhat from the more technical use of that term by members of the mental health profession. In the context of the diagnosis of antisocial personality disorder, *antisocial* may be defined as something more akin to *against adaptive, honest, or straightforward relationships with people* or *against the interests of society in general.* This is because the antisocial personality may actively seek out social relation-

---

generalized anxiety disorder

a chronic anxiety disorder that is seemingly not linked to any particular life event and which may be accompanied by physical symptoms or sensations.

psychoactive substance use disorder

a condition characterized by the use of drugs for one month or more when such drug use may be harmful to oneself or others.

personality disorder

a condition characterized by inflexible and maladaptive psychological traits that causes significant impairment in the person's functioning in social, occupational, or other contexts.

antisocial personality disorder

a condition characterized by disrespect for others and the authority of the law.

ships—but all too often for the wrong reasons. Far from being a recluse, the antisocial personality may appear to be a charming, engaging person, capable of earning people's trust, only to callously abuse this trust by manipulating, cheating, or otherwise exploiting people for his or her own ends.

Before age 15, a diagnosis of antisocial personality is made on the basis of history that includes behavior such as mugging, fire setting, rape, truancy, and wanton destruction of property. After age 15, the diagnosis is made on the basis of factors such as disrespect for the authority of law, failure to honor agreements or obligations, extended periods of unemployment despite the availability of gainful employment, and recklessness or willful disregard for the health, safety, or welfare of others. The ranks of people so diagnosed include criminals, prostitutes, and drug pushers as well as corrupt government officials, unscrupulous business people, and self-serving evangelists.

SEXUAL DISORDERS

Under the DSM category **sexual disorders,** there are two major subcategories: *sexual dysfunction* and *paraphilias.* **Sexual dysfunction** refers to *inability or impairment of ability to achieve sexual satisfaction.* The inability or impairment referred to may stem from varied sources including disorders of sexual desire or sexual arousal, orgasm disorders, and pain experienced as a result of intercourse. **Paraphilia** refers to *a disorder characterized by the choice of an inappropriate love object.* From its Greek roots, paraphilia is loosely translated as meaning *near or resembling love.* Implied in the prefix *para* (meaning *near, resembling, or beside*) is a judgment that the "love" (*philia*) is wrong, harmful, or unfavorable.[3] A diagnosis of paraphilia is made when an individual has urges and acts on, or reports sexual arousal from fantasies related to (1) inanimate objects (such as high-heeled shoes, leather, or underwear), (2) the infliction of pain, suffering, or humiliation (as in the practices of sadism and masochism), or (3) nonconsensual sexual partners. In voyeurism, the nonconsensual "partner" is someone being observed. In pedophilia, the nonconsensual sexual partner is a child.

PEDOPHILIA

Pedophilia entails *sexual abuse of children by adults* and does not include sexual activity between children (Gordon & Snyder, 1989). A child or **minor** (the *legal term for a person who has not reached adulthood as prescribed by law*) is defined by different ages in different states. In all states, however, a minor is not legally competent to give consent to sexual activity and an adult who engages in sexual activity with a child is subject to criminal penalties. An ominous exception to this policy recently occurred in Florida. Two 15-year-old girls argued that they had consented to sex with their boyfriends, ages 19 and 20, and that they did not want the men prosecuted as a result. Ordinarily, the men would have been convicted on the charge of statutory rape because the girls were below the age of consent as provided by statute. The judge ruled that Florida's statutory rape law violated minors' right to privacy. The decision, which only affects that local jurisdiction, left unresolved whether a child of any age was fair sexual prey for an adult. Citing constitutional guarantees that allow minors to obtain abortions, the judge found that, "If this constitutional right to privacy extends to the decision of a minor to have an abortion, it must extend to the decision to engage in sexual intercourse" ("Judge in Florida," 1992).

Pedophiles, also referred to in everyday parlance as child molesters, may attempt a wide range of sex-related acts with children (Knudsen, 1991). The age of the child molested varies, although girls are most likely to be molested first in the 6-to-12-years age range and boys in the 7-to-10-years age range (Knudsen, 1991). Molesters may attempt to exhibit their genitals to children or have children exhibit their genitals to them. They may attempt touching that ranges from kissing and fondling to oral sex, vaginal sex, or anal sex. It is difficult to estimate the true incidence of pedophilia because it is probably underreported. Parents who learn that their child has been molested may be reluctant to report it, especially if a relative was the perpetrator. According to one telephone survey of 2,600 adults in the United States, almost 10% of the men and almost 15% of the women reported being a victim of some sort of sexual abuse as a child (Finkelhor et al., 1990). Perhaps in

sexual disorders
a general diagnostic term referring to an inability or impairment in one's sexual functioning, or an inappropriate choice of sexual object.

sexual dysfunction
an inability or impairment in achieving sexual satisfaction.

paraphilia
a mental disorder characterized by the choice of an inappropriate sexual object, as in pedophilia.

pedophilia
sexual abuse of children by adults.

minor
the legal term for a person who has not reached adulthood as defined by law.

[3]It is interesting in this context to note that *para* in *paralysis* denotes a condition unfavorable to movement. *Paramilitary* refers to a military-like group, sometimes one operating without legitimate authority.

as many as 80% of molestations, the child was previously acquainted with the molester (Waterman & Lusk, 1986). The molester may be a family member, a relative, a teacher, a clergyman, or a neighbor, for example, and is statistically likely to be a male (Cooper et al., 1990; Finkelhor & Russell, 1984). Banning (1989) wondered whether the statistics on pedophilia underestimate the number of adult women who commit this crime since society grants women greater license than men to handle young children affectionately.

Strategies of pedophiles to gain the cooperation of their victims range from luring children with presents or money to more coercive techniques like threats or physical force. Personalities of pedophiles vary, particularly as a function of whether they molest their own children or someone else's (Ames & Houston, 1990). Pedophiles who abuse their own children may be extremely dominant or extremely passive individuals, while pedophiles who abuse strangers or others' children tend to be the more passive types, frequently unable to engage in mature sexual relationships with other adults (Wilson & Cox, 1983).

Pedophilia is not only a type of abnormal behavior, it is also a crime in every state. Perpetrators may be sentenced to treatment for committing pedophilia, but usually such treatment is administered within the context of a secure facility such as a prison. Treatment for male pedophiles may be gauged by means of a penile plethysmograph, a ring-like monitor placed around the penis that measures level of arousal. Child molesters are shown photos of children while such measures of arousal are taken (Haywood et al., 1990). Unfortunately, studies of psychotherapeutic treatment for pedophilia have not been encouraging (Rice et al., 1991), perhaps because many molesters deny that they are in need of treatment (Simkins et al., 1990). Until more effective treatment approaches can be developed, incarceration of known child molesters is in the best interest of society at large.

SCHIZOPHRENIC DISORDERS

The word *schism* refers to a *separation* or *division*. In the word *schizophrenia*, the Latin root *schiz* refers to *separation, division* or *splitting,* and *phrenia* refers to *mind.* *Schizophrenia* may therefore be interpreted literally to mean *split mind.* But what exactly is split in the "split mind"? Is "split mind" synonymous with "split personality"? From Hollywood representations of schizophrenia, one might think that a schizophrenic is a person of "two minds," each harboring a distinctly different personality. And much like the title character in Robert Louis Stevenson's (1896) story *The Strange Case of Dr. Jekyll and Mr. Hyde,* one personality is envisioned as pleasant enough (Dr. Jekyll in Stevenson's novel), while the other is the opposite, even evil (Mr. Hyde). Unfortunately, popular portrayals of schizophrenia in television and films have tended to be off the mark owing to widespread misinterpretation of what mental health professionals mean when they use the term schizophrenia. Schizophrenia does *not* refer to two personalities. The condition wherein an individual manifests two (or more) distinct personalities is called *multiple personality disorder* (discussed subsequently).

To appreciate the meaning of *split* in schizophrenia and the so-called *split mind,* consider how the normal, "whole" mind usually operates. Generally, a good working relationship exists between thoughts, emotions, sensory perceptions, behaviors, and the real world. For example, with respect to sensory perceptions, most normal people do not regularly hear voices speaking to them that in reality are not there. Also, most people do not organize their lives around beliefs that are so outlandishly untrue as to be impossible. People whom we consider normal tend to react with appropriate affect to stimuli, exhibiting tears on tragic occasions and smiles or laughs on joyous ones. People whom we consider normal are able to bring to daily life a certain degree of logic, and to communicate with others in ways that make sense to other people (whether or not other people agree with their opinions). In people whom we consider normal, logic may also be attributed to their movements. For example, students who wish to speak in class raise their hands as a signal to the instructor. A hand raised and then locked in that position, or a hand raised at random intervals by a student who had no wish to speak in class would be highly unusual and atypical behavior.

Contrast the general description of "normals" above with the way people diagnosed as suffering from schizophrenic disorder may think and behave, depending upon the specific subtype of schizophrenia they are diagnosed as having. In some forms of schizophrenia, sufferers experience hallucinations, or *sensory experiences of things that are not really there.* For example, they may see things that aren't really there, hear things that aren't really there, smell things that aren't really there, and so forth. Patients with some varieties of schizophrenia may also suffer delusions, firmly believing things that are patently untrue, even impossible. For example, a schizophrenic may believe that a neighbor across the street is inserting thoughts into his head against his will by means of a "thought machine" aimed at his window. Another schizophrenic might believe that her employer is somehow capable of hearing her thoughts. In addition to hallucinations and delusions, other problems with cognition may be evident, such as impaired ability to reason. The schizophrenic may reason, for example, "Jesus was concerned with the plight of the homeless; I am concerned with the plight of the homeless; therefore, I must be Jesus."

Beyond disorders of cognition, disorders of affect may be present in schizophrenia. Whereas a normal person may receive bad news and evidence depressed affect as a result, patients suffering from some types of schizophrenia may receive the same type of bad news and laugh, have no reaction at all, or otherwise react in an inappropriate manner. Mood may fluctuate wildly in short intervals of time, with little or no relation to external events. In normals, cognition seems linked to affect; cognition influences affect and affect influences cognition. In schizophrenics, there sometimes appears to be a break in that link; cognition and affect appear to operate independently. It is to this break or schism or division between cognition and affect to which the term *schizophrenia* refers. For our purposes, then, we may define **schizophrenia** as *a general category of behavior and thought disorder characterized by severe disturbances of thought, behavior, emotion, and/or perception.*

People having some types of schizophrenia are very poor communicators. Rather than making themselves understood, they seem more interested in verbally venting some of the chaos that is going on mentally. Their speech may be garbled and incoherent, and the logic of what they are talking about may be impossible to follow. In other forms of schizophrenia, speech may be very coherent but the ideas expressed are outlandish. Schizophrenics may make up new words and terms as they go along, rhyme words, or echo or repeat sentences, questions, or words. Alternatively, they may be totally nonresponsive and silent, or cleverly deceptive. Motor behavior in schizophrenia may be unpredictable, **negativistic** (*doing exactly the opposite of what one is directed to do*), or bizarre. In one subcategory of schizophrenia called **catatonic schizophrenia**, the patient may assume odd poses without moving for long periods of time (see Figure 8–6 on page 222).

Different constellations of symptoms characterize each of the subtypes of schizophrenia. For example, in **paranoid schizophrenia**, the patient has highly systematized delusions, sometimes accompanied by hallucinations. The delusions typically have themes of persecution (such as, "The FBI is plotting against me") or grandeur ("I am someone who is extremely important to national security"). In **disorganized schizophrenia**, the patient may experience hallucinations and delusions that are not very well organized at all. Formerly referred to as *hebephrenic schizophrenia*, disorganized schizophrenia is characterized by incessant giggling, laughing, or silliness. Disorganized schizophrenics typically evidence little concern about their personal appearance and hygiene, and may lose bladder or bowel control.

There has been no shortage of explanations for the profoundly dysfunctional behavior observed in the various types of schizophrenia. For example, psychodynamic theorists view such behavior as a regression to an id-level of functioning while behaviorists may conceptualize it in terms of the absence of effective social reinforcement and the consequential closing out of the external world. Behaviorally oriented therapy for schizophrenics, in which rewards are given for appropriate behavior, has shown to be of value in treating a wide range of specific behaviors. However, it is perhaps the researchers who have approached schizophrenia from the biological perspective who have made the most spectacular gains in recent years. Research focusing on elements within the brain that are functionally involved with the transmission of nerve impulses—material called *neurotransmitters*—suggests that they may play a causal role in some forms of schizophrenia. Medication that works at the site of neurotransmitters, affecting their action, has in some cases led to dramatically beneficial changes in thought and behavior. Such medication does not work for everyone, however, and it may take a high toll in terms of side effects.

schizophrenia
literally, split mind, a psychotic condition characterized by severe disturbances in thought, behavior, and/or emotion.

negativistic
doing exactly the opposite of what one is directed to do.

catatonic schizophrenia
a subtype of schizophrenia characterized by slowed or bizarre motoric responses, frequently accompanied by depressed, blunted, or flat affect.

paranoid schizophrenia
a subtype of schizophrenia characterized by highly systematized delusions, usually of persecution and/or grandeur.

disorganized schizophrenia
formally referred to as hebephrenic schizophrenia, this subtype of schizophrenia is characterized by inappropriate affect, prolonged periods of laughing, and/or little concern about personal appearance.

FIGURE 8–6 CATATONIC SCHIZOPHRENIA In their behavior, patients diagnosed as suffering from a variety of schizophrenia called catatonic schizophrenia seem to want to "stop the world." Their motor movements may be very slow and they may, at times, freeze in some peculiar position for hours on end. Upon such freezing, limbs may be made extremely rigid. More characteristic of catatonic schizophrenics, however, is the phenomenon known as *waxy flexibility*. Like a warm, melted candle, the catatonic schizophrenic's limbs may be bent into some position and the limb will remain in that position for as long as the patient continues to remain in the frozen posture.

amnesia

loss of memory related to one's identity.

dissociative disorder

a general term used to describe a condition characterized by a loss of association between identity, consciousness, and memory, as in amnesia and multiple personality disorder.

multiple personality disorder

a condition characterized by the development of one or more identities in addition to one's true identity.

DISSOCIATIVE DISORDERS

There is a strong association between identity, consciousness, and memory in most people. But what happens when strong *dissociation* exists between identity, consciousness, and memory? Answer: A condition known as a *dissociative disorder*. Examples of dissociative disorders include psychologically induced *loss of memory related to one's identity*, or **amnesia** (in contrast to physically induced amnesia, which is not considered a dissociative disorder), and *multiple personality disorder*.

MULTIPLE PERSONALITY DISORDER

In general, a **dissociative disorder** is characterized by a *breakdown in the links between identity, memory, and consciousness*. **Multiple personality disorder** (MPD), is *a condition characterized by the development of one or more identities, in addition to one's true identity*. The different personalities may prompt different styles of dress, speech, behavior, and thought on the part of the MPD sufferer, including different ways of perceiving and thinking about oneself. There is some evidence to suggest that the differences between the personalities of an MPD sufferer are so profound as to affect physical functioning as well. Differences in the same MPD person with reference to variables such as color blindness and allergic sensitivity have been observed as a function of the personality being manifest when testing occurred (Braun, 1988). Sometimes, however, what appears to be MPD may actually be a function of culture. Landrine (1992) notes, for example, that the Western notion of a clear distinction between the self and the non-self does not necessarily exist in certain Asian, African, and Mediterranean cultures. In such cultures, the notion of self is more closely linked to one's family. Western mental health professionals may confuse such a culturally different patient's empathy and identification with the experience of a family member with the symptoms of MPD.

As with many other mental disorders, there is much speculation, and no overabundance of hard evidence to suggest how multiple personality disorders evolve. Presently, a great deal of research attention is being focused on the life history of MPD sufferers, with particular focus on reactions to great emotional trauma. From a psychodynamic perspective, MPD may be viewed as a defense against or escape from severe psychological trauma; the individual escapes into the shelter of another personality. Such mental escape or defense maneuvers have been thought to occur both in children (Spanos et al., 1985; Wilbur, 1986) and adults (Bliss, 1984; Schafer, 1986). This view finds support from a behavioral perspective; behavioral clinicians might focus their attention on the reinforcement value of escaping into the world of alternative personalities. From a behavioral perspective one might also expect an increase in the incidence of the disorder given all of the publicity and attention it receives in the popular media. An increasing array of models are available from which to acquire detailed information about MPD and other dissociative disorders. Fictional accounts of identity-related difficulties are frequently the subject of films (ranging from *Psycho* to *The Hand that Rocks the Cradle*), and real patients may be found being interviewed on tabloid-type talk shows such as *Donahue* and *Oprah*.

CURRENT ISSUES IN DIAGNOSING ABNORMAL BEHAVIOR

The sample of diagnostic categories presented above makes up only a fraction of the many varieties of disorder presented in the DSM. But as you may have concluded on your own, no matter how large and purportedly comprehensive any list of mental disorders is, it is likely to be open to question on a number of grounds. What was left out? What was included in it that perhaps should have been left out? What is the scientific basis for including a particular disorder and the criteria listed for diagnosing it? These are some of the many questions critics have raised about various editions of the DSM (Achenbach, 1980; Bayer & Spitzer, 1982; Caplan, 1987; Dell, 1988; Fenton et al., 1988; Kaplan, 1983; Quay, 1986; Rey, 1988; Rutter & Shaffer, 1980; Schacht, 1985; Tryer, 1988; Zimmerman, 1988). Perhaps some of the more compelling questions being raised now with greater frequency are those related to the cultural relevance of various diagnoses.

THE NEED FOR CULTURAL SENSITIVITY

Traditionally excluded from the DSM are some culture-specific disorders that are very rare in this country such as *koro* (see page 213) and *piblokto* (see Figure 8–7). The danger in

FIGURE 8–7   A CASE OF *PIBLOKTO* This Eskimo woman, afflicted with a condition called *piblokto*, that was once common in the Arctic, has thrown herself in the snow. She may make sounds imitating the cry of birds or other animals, and/or tear off her clothes and run about wildly.

not developing greater cultural sensitivity in psychological evaluations is the possible injustice that flows from misdiagnoses based on cultural misunderstanding.

Cultural sensitivity in the diagnosis of mental disorders means, in part, looking to the prevailing norms of behavior for ethnic and cultural minorities in attempting to understand the individual. To overlook such influences is to risk labeling someone mentally ill for behaving or thinking in a way that the person has been taught from birth. Eisenbruch (1992, p. 8) made this point with respect to the psychiatric diagnosis of post-traumatic stress disorder, a diagnosis which "is often based on an ethnocentric view of health that prescribes how refugees should express their distress, how their disorders should be classified, and how the distress should be eliminated." Littlewood (1991) echoed this view, arguing that diagnostic classifications made strictly on the basis of a manual such as the DSM may make inadequate allowance for cultural background as a factor in understanding individual stress and distress. It has been estimated that approximately one third of the United States population will be composed of ethnic minorities by the year 2000 (Mezzich et al., 1992). One third of the population of the United States will therefore remain at risk for psychiatric misdiagnosis unless effective action is taken to systematically consider cultural and ethnic factors in abnormal behavior.

In this chapter we saw that various forms of abnormal behavior can be conceptualized in different ways. In the following chapter on the subject of therapy, we will see that how problem behavior is treated depends on how it is conceptualized.

SUMMARY

WHAT IS ABNORMAL BEHAVIOR? Human beings have an extraordinarily broad range of behaviors in their repertoire. What constitutes abnormal behavior may be viewed from different perspectives. From a *statistical perspective,* what is normal and abnormal is largely a matter of frequency; if most people do it, it's normal, and if most people don't, it's abnormal. A *sociocultural perspective* adds the element of social value. According to that view, behavior that is culturally valued (such as heroism) is not considered abnormal even if it is statistically infrequent. Of course, what is socially valued may change with time and place. From a *psychosocial perspective,* the critical issue is whether the behavior in question contributes to the well-being of the individual or others. From an *integrative perspective*—the one that we will subscribe to in this book—*abnormal behavior* may be defined as overt action or thinking that is statistically rare in the population, counter to the prevailing cultural and/or subcultural norms, and usually harmful to the well-being of oneself or others.

WHAT CAUSES ABNORMAL BEHAVIOR? Abnormal behavior may arise from a number of different biological and psychological factors. From a biological perspective, abnormal behavior is caused by *disease,* which is defined as an abnormal biological condition that impairs normal functioning and arises from causes such as infection, inherent weakness, or environmental agents. Subsumed under the biological model of normality is its more applied counterpart, the medical model. As applied to the study of behavior pathology, the medical model holds that abnormal behavior is a symptom of an underlying disease that requires treatment. An alternative to the medical model is a *psychosocial model,* which traces the roots of abnormal behavior not to disease, but—depending on the particular variety of psychosocial model—to factors such as learning, faulty thinking, and conditions not conducive to healthy development of the self. A *biopsychosocial model* combines the best features of the biological and psychosocial perspectives.

IDENTIFYING AND CLASSIFYING ABNORMAL BEHAVIOR The classification system most popular in the United States is the American Psychiatric Association's *Diagnostic and Statistical Manual of Mental Disorders* (DSM). The DSM contains descriptions of various patterns of abnormal behavior, epidemiological information, a system for identification, and notes on distinguishing the identified behavior pattern from other similar patterns. Tools used in the assessment of abnormal behavior include the interview, behavioral observation, the case study, and psychological tests.

VARIETIES OF ABNORMAL BEHAVIOR Varieties of abnormal hehavior include *adjustment disorders* (maladaptive responses to stress), *mood disorders* (emotion-related problems of behavior and thinking), *anxiety disorders* (recurring patterns of fear, dread, uncertainty, nervousness, or concern), *psychoactive substance use disorders* (use of drugs that affect mental state), *personality disorders* (conditions characterized by maladaptive psychological traits), *sexual disorders* (including disorders of sexual dysfunction, sexual desire, and sexual attraction), *schizophrenic* disorders (severe disorders of thought, emotion, and behavior), and *dissociative* (or identity-related) *disorders,* including *multiple personality disorder.*

CURRENT ISSUES IN DIAGNOSING ABNORMAL BEHAVIOR Perhaps some of the most compelling questions being raised are those related to the cultural relevance of various diagnoses. Greater cultural sensitivity in psychological evaluation is necessary to prevent misdiagnoses based on cultural misunderstanding.

Therapy

O U T L I N E

In his classic work *Counseling and Psychotherapy*, Carl Rogers (1942, pp. 19–20) observed that, "Throughout the centuries individuals have, in a variety of ways, used face-to-face situations in an endeavor to alter the behavior and change the attitudes of a maladjusted person toward a more constructive outcome." Included among older "methods in disrepute," as Rogers referred to them, were ordering and forbidding, reassurance and encouragement, and exhortation (that is, asking people to promise that they will not engage in some behavior, and sometimes to sign a pledge to that effect). Interestingly, some of the methods Rogers listed as in disrepute have in recent years been dusted off, dressed up, and given new life. For example, in a newer behavioral technique called *contingency contracting*, to be discussed subsequently, the client may in fact be asked to sign a pledge or contract. There are dozens—by some counts hundreds—of different approaches to psychotherapy. All of which compels us to raise at the outset one very basic question. . .

WHAT IS PSYCHOTHERAPY?

counseling
guidance or advice giving.

psychotherapy
psychological treatment of mental and behavioral disorders.

Counseling may be defined as *guidance or advice giving.* **Psychotherapy** (literally, "therapy of the mind or soul") may be defined as *the psychological treatment of mental and behavioral disorders.* Although psychotherapy is sometimes thought of as more intense, long-term, and systematic in application as compared to counseling, the two terms may in many contexts be used interchangeably—which is how we will use them here.

Precious few generalizations can be made about what psychotherapy is, although the following seem reasonable:

■ Psychotherapy is a process in which a client seeking assistance for psychological discomfort or a problem of some sort ("the presenting problem") enters into a therapeutic relationship with a therapist.

■ Psychotherapists approach the therapeutic situation with their own framework or perspective for understanding human behavior. Accordingly, a client's presenting problem is understood by the therapist within this framework or perspective.

■ Therapists treat clients using talk, behavioral homework assignments, and/or other means in accordance with their own framework for understanding and modifying human behavior. This treatment occurs during appointed hours, usually at a regular time and place.

rapport
in interviewing, assessment, counseling or psychotherapy, the working relationship or alliance.

■ Psychotherapy typically involves the establishment of a **rapport** or *working relationship or alliance* between the client and the therapist. Inherent in the relationship is the client's trust in and respect for the therapist. It is only for as long as this working relationship exists that the therapist can work to free the client of the problem behavior or thoughts.

expectancy of therapeutic gain
in counseling or psychotherapy, a belief that a positive outcome will result from a course of counseling or psychotherapy.

This last factor is a most important one: It is essential in order for the client to develop what is called an **expectancy of therapeutic gain** or *the belief that the therapist will be able to help.* Primitive therapists and shamans used masks and paraphernalia to build up expectancies of therapeutic gain on the part of their "patients." Contemporary therapists may employ other techniques, such as displaying diplomas and other certificates prominently.

Exactly what the experience of psychotherapy is for any individual person will vary as a function of a number of factors. The most obvious of these factors are those related to *the person seeking therapy*, *the person providing the therapy*, and *the therapeutic situation or context*. Below we look at these and related factors before proceeding to discuss different frameworks for psychological treatment.

THE PERSON SEEKING THERAPY

Individuals bring to therapy situations an enormously diverse array of presenting problems, personal abilities, assets, resources, skills, motivation, and liabilities. Some individuals, for example, are extremely articulate, insightful, mentally quick, and seemingly one step ahead of the therapist. At the other extreme are individuals who are barely verbal or totally nonverbal, and truly lacking in the cognitive ability to develop adaptive insights or behavior change strategies. Clearly, the experience of psychotherapy will be very different for these different types of people.

In a multicultural society such as ours, it is also important to recognize that clients are likely to come from a wide array of cultural backgrounds. Along with varying cultural backgrounds, clients bring with them varying values, beliefs, expectations, and styles of interaction. Formally recognizing such facts, the American Psychological Association established a task force in 1988 to study issues related to the delivery of psychological services to various cultural groups. In 1991, the APA published guidelines that were "intended to enlighten all areas of service delivery, not simply clinical or counseling endeavors" (APA, 1993b, pp. 45–46). One of the guidelines, for example, used this illustration to urge sensitivity to cultural beliefs and values:

> There is a disorder among the traditional Navajo called "Moth Madness." Symptoms include seizure-like behaviors. This disorder is believed by the Navajo to be the supernatural result of incestuous thoughts or behaviors. Both differential diagnosis and intervention should take into consideration the traditional values of Moth Madness. (APA, 1993, p. 46)

The individual seeking therapy is variously referred to as a *patient*, a *client*, or, simply, a *person*. In medically oriented institutional settings such as inpatient or outpatient psychiatric facilities, as well as in prisons and other institutional settings, *patient* is typically the term of choice. In psychotherapy and counseling in private practice settings, as well as in school, business, and industrial/organizational settings, the term *client* or simply *person* is favored. For our purposes, we may use the words *patient, client,* and *person* interchangeably to refer to a person in therapy.

THE PERSON PROVIDING THERAPY

Ideally, the psychotherapist has the background, training, knowledge, and experience necessary to use techniques known to be effective, at least with respect to the prevailing state of knowledge in the field of behavioral science. Unfortunately, people having a wide array of background, training, knowledge, credentials, experience, and competence hold themselves out to the public as psychotherapists. It is no easy matter for the prospective consumer of psychotherapy services to determine who is and is not qualified to undertake psychotherapeutic treatment. Some assistance is provided in this chapter's *Quality of Life*.

A partial listing of the different types of professionals who conduct psychotherapy and counseling would include psychologists, psychiatrists, clinical social workers, occupational therapists, and psychiatric nurses. Recent years have witnessed a dramatic rise in the number of clinical social workers practicing nationwide (see Figure 9–1 on page 232). There are also many different types of counselors and "human development professionals" who practice in a wide variety of settings. These professionals may have had relatively narrow training in areas such as addictions counseling, college counseling, multicultural counseling, and rehabilitation counseling. The actual credentials necessary to practice this profession may be as varied as the settings that offer such counseling.

In addition to mental health *professionals* who provide mental health-related services, are *paraprofessionals,* who may also provide such services. Considered as a group, paraprofessionals come from a wide array of backgrounds. Many do not have any formal degrees, although all have had some specialized training in the delivery of mental health-related services. A drug counselor at a local youth center, for example, may hold no formal degree, but due to superior "street smarts" and interpersonal skills, combined with some limited professional training, may be a great community asset. Others in the community, such as members of the police force, may be given some psychology-related training in order to be better prepared to provide community service (see Figure 9–2 on page 232).

QUALITY OF *Life*

A Consumer's Guide to Psychotherapists

The background, training, education, experience, and competence of people who hold themselves out to the public as psychotherapists is extraordinarily diverse. An untold number of psychotherapists are self-proclaimed psychotherapists whose legal authority to practice stems more from loopholes in the law than from compliance with it. Among those psychotherapists and counselors who are legal, bona fide practitioners, education and other professional requirements may range widely from state to state for various positions and titles. A person having no degree, a bachelor's degree, a master's degree, or a doctoral degree may be legally entitled to use the title *psychotherapist, therapist,* or something akin to one of those terms. States differ in terms of the mental health professions they recognize. For example, in California there is a profession called Marriage, Family, and Child Counseling (MFCC). Counselors in this profession have earned at least a master's-level degree from an accredited MFCC program and passed an oral and written examination. The MFCC profession does not exist, however, in most other states.

In general, a clinical or psychiatric **social worker** is *one who holds either a bachelor's degree, a master's of social work (MSW) degree, or a doctoral degree (either a Ph.D. degree or a doctor of social work—DSW—degree).* State licensing requirements typically include a requirement of clinical training in a mental health facility.

The description of the terms *psychologist* and *psychiatrist* that follows should be thought of as most general. If you are interested in learning more about the exact qualifications necessary for the use of these or other titles, contact the appropriate licensing or certification body in your state, the

American Psychological Association, or the American Psychiatric Association. The term **psychologist** generally refers to *an individual having doctoral-level training in psychology.* The most common doctoral degrees are the doctor of philosophy (Ph.D.), the doctor of psychology (Psy.D.) and the doctor of education (Ed.D.) degrees, although psychologists may hold other degrees as well. It is also possible in many states to use the title psychologist legally in settings such as schools, hospitals, and rehabilitation centers while having only a master's degree. However, the use of that title by persons having a master's degree may be legally limited to services that are provided only within those settings; use of the title *psychologist* outside those settings, as in independent practice, may constitute a violation of law.

Clinical psychologists typically *have a doctoral degree in clinical psychology, and background, training, and experience that prepares them for psychotherapeutic work and/or research with a very wide-range of clientele, including severely mentally disordered individuals.* **Counseling psychologists** typically *have a doctoral degree in counseling psychology, and background, training, and experience that focuses more on everyday problems in living, including school-related problems, occupational and career choices, and marital and family-related difficulties.* Both clinical and counseling psychologists may be found in a variety of settings including independent practice and academia (as instructors and/or counselors), and as consultants to business, industry, and other private and public organizations. In general, clinical or counseling psychologists are referred to as such by virtue of the type of program they pursued in graduate school. Simply be-

cause someone is represented as a clinical or counseling psychologist is no automatic guarantee that the person is licensed for independent practice.

Psychiatry may be defined as *a specialty area within medicine that deals with the research, diagnosis, treatment, and prevention of mental disorders.* As medical doctors, psychiatrists are legally permitted to prescribe medication and to use other **invasive procedures** (*procedures such as injections, electroshock treatment, and so forth directly affecting bodily tissues*). In no state are psychologists legally permitted to prescribe medicine or to conduct invasive procedures.

Like *psychologist,* the term *psychiatrist* is not as straightforward in definition as many people believe. In their training to become medical doctors, medical students may receive exposure to training in a number of different medical specialty areas including dermatology, surgery, neurology, and psychiatry. Upon graduation from medical school and the completion of a one-year internship and other state-mandated requirements, a medical doctor (M.D.) may legally begin a career in the practice of medicine. M.D.'s may decide to limit their practice to any specialty area within medical practice. It is possible then, for physicians to hold themselves out to the public as specializing in psychiatry (and legally to use the title psychiatrist) when in reality they may have had precious little education, training, background, or experience in psychiatry. As I have noted elsewhere, "Although it is commonly believed that a psychiatrist holds a specific license to practice psychiatry, the term 'psychiatrist' is generally not protected by statute. Rather, psychiatrists are regulated internally by professional medical associations" (Cohen & Mariano, 1982, p. 67).

Physicians may elect to take specialized training in psychiatry in order to become certified in this specialty area of medicine by the American Specialty Boards. Typically, such specialization requires a 3-year training *residency* or training program in psychiatry, including a specified number of hours in supervised patient contacts, as well as other requirements. Upon the successful completion of the residency, the physician is said to be a *board-certified psychiatrist*. How many physicians holding themselves out to the public as psychiatrists are actually board-certified psychiatrists? Little research has been done to address this question. However, consider the results of one study conducted in the state of Ohio, where over 800 physicians were listed in an American Medical Association directory of physicians who limited their practice to psychiatry. Only 229 of these physicians were found to be board certified in psychiatry. In this study then, almost three-quarters of the "psychiatrists" were found *not* to be board-certified psychiatrists (O'Keefe & McCullough, 1979).

If you or someone you know is considering a consultation with a psychotherapist, here are some questions you may wish to consider in advance:

Does it matter if one sees a psychiatrist, psychologist, social worker, or someone else?

If you think you may have to be prescribed medication and to be medically monitored, a psychiatrist is probably the best choice. It is true that you could see a nonphysician for psychotherapy and a physican for medication, but that will drive up the cost of therapy substantially. If you believe that you will not require medication, then the decision will best be made not on the basis of the therapist's professional degree, but on other factors including

(1) the therapist's background, training, and experience with the problem for which you are seeking help; (2) the therapist's track record in treating the problem; and (3) other practical considerations such as the geographical location of the therapist and the fees.

Should one see a male or a female therapist? What about the personality of the therapist?

Competence in a particular area of treatment is more important than the gender of the therapist. That said, it is also important that you feel comfortable with the therapist and be able to develop a rapport or working relationship with her or him. Therefore, whether to choose a male or female therapist is simply a matter of personal preference. It will also be useful to keep in mind that therapists having any title—counselors, psychologists, psychiatrists, social workers, ministers, rabbis, educators, trainers—are human beings, just like you. They have different personalities, just like people in general do. Therapists are subject to the same human foibles, stresses, mood variations, motivational assets, and motivational deficits as everyone else. For these and other reasons, one patient's experience of psychotherapy with one therapist may be extremely different from another patient's experience of psychotherapy with the same or different therapist. A trial of two to four sessions with a therapist may be a good investment in helping you to find someone with whom you feel you can work.

Does it matter if the therapist has a license?

There is no guarantee that an unlicensed therapist is ethical and competent to treat your particular problem. Sad to say, it is also true that there is no guarantee that a licensed therapist is ethical and competent to treat your particular problem. All other things

being equal— and they seldom are— the odds are in favor of going with the licensed professional. Licensed professionals are subject to ethical and other regulations of regulatory agencies and professional associations. Your communications with the licensed person will be legally privileged and confidential, much the same way that lawyer-client and priest-penitent relationships are legally protected. The confidentiality of communications with unlicensed therapists is not guaranteed by law.

How does one find a therapist?

Not very good places to start are places like newspaper ads, flyers on your windshield, ads in the yellow pages, and the like. I personally advise students to be especially wary of therapists who emphasize in their advertising that they are "warm" or "empathic," or that they have unusually high "success rates." Most therapists are "warm" and "empathic" to varying degrees. Few if any therapists are habitually "cold" and "nonempathic." Among professionally trained therapists, precious few have significantly higher success rates than others. Those professionals who do have significantly higher success rates than others are probably not advertising for patients. If they do happen to be advertising, they are probably not describing themselves in such fashion.

If you are in search of a therapist, you might begin by making some inquiries of people or agencies you trust and believe might be knowledgeable about such matters. The instructor teaching this course, the counselor at the campus counseling center, local community or municipal mental health centers or agencies, or national mental health organizations are all reasonable places where you can begin to seek out mental health professionals.

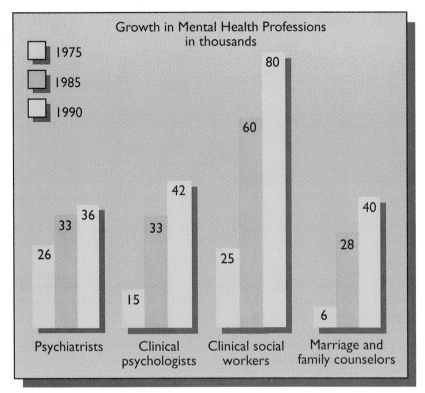

Growth in Mental Health Professions
in thousands

☐ 1975
☐ 1985
☐ 1990

Psychiatrists: 26, 33, 36
Clinical psychologists: 15, 33, 42
Clinical social workers: 25, 60, 80
Marriage and family counselors: 6, 28, 40

FIGURE 9–1   NUMBER OF MENTAL HEALTH PROFESSIONALS IN A SAMPLING OF PROFESSIONS Cutting across the membership of the professions represented above, as well as representing people who are not members of any of the professions above, is an organization of counselors called the American Association for Counseling and Development (AACD). AACD has a membership of more than 58,000 counselors, which includes members in the United States and 50 foreign countries.

Paraprofessionals and community workers who need not have formal degrees in the mental health field should not be confused with other people who may be self-proclaimed counselors or therapists and who may be fraudulently representing themselves to the public as mental health professionals. Although a psychologist, a psychiatrist, a social worker, or any other trained mental health professional can also be a psychotherapist, a psychoanalyst, a counselor, a hypnotist, or a marriage counselor, it is important to understand that titles such as psychotherapist, psychoanalyst, therapist, counselor, hypnotist, hypnotherapist, and marriage counselor carry with them *no legal standing* in most states. *Anyone*, including yourself, the local bartender, or your paper delivery boy could hang a shingle out and refer to themselves by any of these legally unprotected titles in most states.

THE CONTEXT OF THERAPY

The various kinds of situations in which therapy is conducted may also affect the character of the experience of psychotherapy. For example, the nature and conduct of court-or-

FIGURE 9–2   COMMUNITY MENTAL HEALTH WORK Mental health-related work can be carried out by virtually any "natural" member of a community including merchants, business people, and yes, even the police. At a talent contest in the Bronx sponsored by The Police Athletic League-Tactical Narcotics Team Playstreets Drug Education program, New York City Police Officer Colleen Curran was persuaded by some younger community residents to relearn "double dutch."

dered psychotherapy with a reluctant prisoner in the confines of a prison may have a very different character than psychotherapy conducted with a self-referred student in a school guidance counselor's office. The character of voluntary counseling with a motivated prisoner may have a very different character than counseling conducted with a reluctant spouse in a marriage counseling situation (see Figure 9–3).

APPROACHES TO THERAPY

There are many different approaches to counseling and psychotherapy. Each approach, having its own methods and objectives, is built upon a certain set of ideas about the nature of people and the nature of behavior change. Before reading on, consider in this context the half dozen positions regarding adjusted and maladjusted human behavior presented in Table 9–1 on page 234. Think about how the objective of therapy, as well as the methods used, might change as a function of each of these six different frameworks for understanding people.

The first of these frameworks for understanding normal and abnormal behavior has probably been the most popular in human history. It has existed for the longest period and has been practiced in the largest number of places around the world. In North America, Native Americans of the Plains long subscribed to such beliefs and dealt with abnormal behavior accordingly (see *Cultural Close-Up* on page 235). Having read the previous chapters, you may find the remaining frameworks for understanding people familiar by now. They respectively represent psychoanalytic, behavioral, humanistic, biological, and eclectic perspectives. In this chapter we revisit these related approaches for the purpose of better acquainting you with the rationale for, methods used in, and treatment objectives of different approaches to psychotherapy.

RESEARCH ON THERAPY

We often hear statements like, "Psychotherapy works" or, "Psychotherapy doesn't work," without pausing long enough to ask some important questions. "What is meant by *psychotherapy*? What was actually done, to whom, and for how long? What is meant by *work*?"

Psychotherapy outcome studies, or *research on the effectiveness of psychotherapy*, must take into account variables related to the client, the therapist, the presenting problem, and the context of treatment if the results are to be open to meaningful interpreta-

psychotherapy outcome study

research on the effectiveness of various approaches to psychotherapy.

FIGURE 9–3   THE RABBI OF SING SING Counseling and psychotherapy may take many forms as it is undertaken on a daily basis within the walls of diverse institutions. For over 40 years, Rabbi Irving Koslow has been counseling inmates once a week at Sing Sing, a maximum security institution referred to as "the Big House" in Ossining, New York. In those years, the Rabbi has counseled people convicted on a wide range of crimes from murder to embezzling. He was a source of emotional support to 17 inmates who he personally walked to the electric chair, including two convicted of treason in a controversial case, Ethel and Julius Rosenberg. Sometimes bringing traditional Jewish foods with him for distribution, the objective of Rabbi Koslowe's visits is to strengthen prisoners' faith and introduce positive mental and behavioral change. The Rabbi put it this way: "People ask me what I'm doing bringing matzoh ball soup to a bunch of killers, but maybe we can make some change. Maybe we can bring some good in their life... If I can have an inmate come into the chapel, put on a yarmulke and worship, I think that shows there's a positive change in behavior, a real step forward" (cited in "The Rabbi at Sing Sing," 1992). The Rabbi considers the Jewish prisoners at Sing Sing his personal congregation but freely admits that he "does not mind losing members" when they are deemed worthy to return to society.

TABLE 9–1 UNDERSTANDING OF HUMAN BEHAVIOR AND METHOD OF PSYCHOTHERAPY

Position Regarding Human Behavior	Objective of Therapy (Your thoughts?)	Methods Used (Your thoughts?)
1. The essential factors responsible for adjusted and maladjusted human behavior are best understood in terms of the actions of spirits in the spirit world.		
2. The essential factors responsible for adjusted and maladjusted human behavior are best understood in terms of unconscious processes.		
3. The essential factors responsible for adjusted and maladjusted human behavior are best understood in terms of classical conditioning, operant conditioning, and other known processes of learning.		
4. The essential factors responsible for adjusted and maladjusted human behavior are best understood in terms of the concept of self, and any discrepancy between one's ideal self and the reality of everyday experience.		
5. The essential factors responsible for adjusted and maladjusted human behavior are best understood in terms of physical, chemical, and electrical activity within the body.		
6. The essential factors responsible for adjusted and maladjusted human behavior are best understood in terms of unconscious motivation, principles of learning, uniquely human endowments, and biological factors.		

tion. The research must also be understood in terms of the particular treatment approach or approaches that were employed. Was the therapy psychoanalytic, behavioral, humanistic, or something else? How scientific was the research? Was a control group such as a wait list/no therapy group employed? These are some of the important questions to be raised.

Complementing psychotherapy outcome studies has been a flurry of exploration regarding cultural- and gender-related issues in therapy. Researchers have examined, for example, the relationship between cultural background of clients and use of mental health services (Cheung & Snowden, 1990; Sue & Sue, 1990), the therapist's treatment strategy (Comas-Diaz & Griffith, 1988), and outcome in treatment (Juarez, 1985). Many gender-

Cultural

C L O S E - U P

Therapist of the Plains

People today demand more than "a song and dance" from their therapists and physicians. However, in different times and places, song and dance were routinely employed to foster healing. Chanting, dancing, and other rituals, some including drugs, magical potions, and hypnosis, were all used by witch doctors, shamans, and medicine men in an effort to treat deviant behavior and restore afflicted people to society. Sometimes the healer himself had to ingest a drug—this to enable him to go into the spirit world and attempt to reclaim the soul of the afflicted person. This 1832 painting by George Catlin is of a Plains Native-American medicine man named Old Bear. He is holding his traditional medicine wands and fans, has medicinal herbs at his waist, and is sporting a bear cub apron.

related issues in therapy, including those related to cognitive and moral development (Gilligan, 1982), traditional male and female roles (McGoldrick et al., 1982), and one's view of the self (Okun, 1992) have begun to be discussed. Some researchers have begun exploring the specific skills therapists require for working with specific populations (Malgady et al., 1987; Root, 1985; Zuniga, 1988). One such skill is the ability of the therapist to view the individual as a member of one or more groups. In this context, Ivey et al. (1993) described the "culturally intentional counselor and therapist" who views individual clients as family and cultural group members. Such a therapist may convey this understanding to a client who engages in abusive behavior:

> We'll need to look at your issues from three levels. First we want to stop the abusive behavior, and we'll work on that by using some cognitive-behavioral techniques. Second, people tend to become more assaultive under oppressive conditions. For example, those who suffer economic oppression and the loss of a job are more likely to lose control. Third, we need to work together to focus on issues of injustice in our community and take direct action for a more humane system. (Ivey et al., 1993, p. 5)

Our survey of different approaches to therapy begins with a brief look at the first formal system of psychotherapy ever to be developed.

PSYCHOANALYTIC APPROACHES

Freud believed that most behavior was unconsciously motivated. Many of the techniques used in the psychoanalytic approach to counseling and psychotherapy have as their goal making the unconscious conscious. But how does one make conscious what is by its very definition *unconscious*?

PSYCHOANALYTIC TECHNIQUES

Freud did not have one answer to that question—he had several. Among the techniques he used to expose unconscious material were free association, dream analysis, analysis of resistance, analysis of transference, and analysis of events in everyday life.

FREE ASSOCIATION

Freud believed that people in a relaxed, stationary position, free just to let the mind wander, could get in touch with unconscious material. Patients lay down on the couch in Freud's office (see Figure 9–4) and were instructed to **free associate**, or *to disclose anything at all that came to mind, regardless of whether it seemed to make sense or not, and regardless of whether it was socially acceptable or not*. Freud sat behind the patient and took notes. By sitting behind the patient, the analyst did not distract the **analysand** (*the person being analyzed by the psychoanalyst*). Additionally, Freud personally had a distaste for the prospect of being stared at directly by free-associating patients for all of his working day. Sometimes the unconscious material would reveal itself in this manner but in disguised form, in which case it was the analyst's task to make sense of the patient's free associations.

The technique of free association is sometimes confused with *word association*. Both are techniques that may be used in psychotherapy, although word association is perhaps better associated with psychological evaluation. In **word association**, *the therapist or assessor provides a stimulus word and patients respond with the first word or words that come to mind*. Contrast with *free association*. For example, if you heard the word *chair,* what would be the first word you would think of? If you said, *sit,* the response would be considered a very common one and not uniquely useful in terms of providing insights into your unconscious mind. However, had you responded to the stimulus word of *chair* with a response that is not very common, say *fall,* that response might well provide grist for the analyst's mill. An analyst might wonder, for example, if you harbored concerns about your ability to support yourself.

DREAM ANALYSIS

The unconscious also reveals itself in dreams, according to Freud. The people and objects in the dream may appear in disguised or symbolic form. Freud believed that if the unconscious revealed itself in undisguised or nonsymbolic form, the stress might be too much for the dreamer. Objects such as guns, sticks, or horns were referred to as **phallic symbols** or *objects presumed to represent penises*. Objects such as closets, drawers, and boxes were presumed to be disguised vaginal representations. For Freud, dreams provided insights into one's innermost desires and fears. If you dreamed, for example, that someone you know had died, it could be interpreted, depending on other information, as meaning that you either feared or unconsciously desired that person to die.

ANALYSIS OF TRANSFERENCE

Transference may be defined as *a process by which feelings one has for one person are shifted to another.* Freud observed that as analysis proceeds, patients may begin to respond to the analyst in many of the same ways that they have responded to other important people in their lives. For example, analysands might respond to a male analyst as to their fathers and to a female analyst as to their mothers. Analyzing the transference is a very important part of psychoanalytic treatment. By the way, sometimes *analysts shift their own feelings, and begin treating analysands in ways that are characteristic of how they have dealt with other people—a*

free association

the process of verbalizing any and all things that come to mind as they come to mind. Contrast with *word association.*

analysand

in psychoanaltyic psychotherapy, the person being analyzed by the psychoanalyst.

word association

a psychotherapeutic and assessment technique whereby the therapist or assessor provides a stimulus word and clients respond with the first word or words that come to mind. Contrast with *free association.*

phallic symbol

in psychoanalytic theory, an object in fantasy or a dream presumed to represent or symbolize genitalia.

transference

in psychoanalytic psychotherapy, a process by which feelings the client has for one person are presumed to be projected to the therapist.

FIGURE 9–4   THE TOOL OF THE PSYCHOANALYTIC TRADE This is a photo of Freud's office couch on which so many of his patients reclined and free associated. It is a lush divan draped with an Oriental rug. Fred Brafman and Ira Bilus are co-owners of a company that has been selling analyst couches since the 1940s. They report that the company sells several hundred a year and ships them as far away as Alaska and Hawaii. Brafman observes that certain frills such as buttons or fringe trim are no longer incorporated on analysts' couches. Edgy analysands pick at buttons or unravel fringe trim, thus leading to maintenance problems for the analyst. Contemporary analysts have different taste than Freud, but they all take their purchase decision regarding a couch very seriously, and they all agree that a couch should not look like a bed. Many new analysts buy the same kind of couch their training analyst had which, according to Sulkowicz (1992, p. C6), "has to do with identifying with your analyst." Here are some thoughts on analytic couches as collected by Gordon (1992), along with a brief description of the couch and its owner:

"This is not just furniture . . . this couch is central to your professional life and to your identity as an analyst."—Male analyst having a low-key couch of light gray wool

"You wouldn't want a fire-engine red couch . . . You don't want anything dramatically distracting for the patient."—Male analyst having a Victorian oxblood-red couch

"I'm turned off by the hard look of many analytic couches, I wouldn't want to get on them."—Female analyst having an earthy brown suede sofa

process Freud called **counter-transference**. An analyst may consult with another analyst for assistance in dealing with counter-transferential feelings.

ANALYSIS OF EVENTS IN EVERYDAY LIFE

"Are you analyzing me?"

The answer to that question is almost always "no" when it comes to analysts at social gatherings—even analysts give their analytic abilities a rest when they are not working. Yet analysts since Freud have prided themselves on the ability to be personality detectives, gaining insights into people from what they say or do. Freud believed that he could tell a great deal about a person by the seemingly chance actions they engaged in upon entering his office. For example, consider this description of one patient's behavior:

> The first . . . chance actions of the patient . . . will betray one of the governing complexes of the neurosis . . . A young girl . . . hurriedly pulls the hem of her skirt over her exposed ankle; she has betrayed the kernel of what analysis will discover later, her narcissistic pride in her bodily beauty and her tendencies to exhibitionism. (Freud, 1913/1959, p. 359)

counter-transference
in psychoanalytic psychotherapy, a process by which the feelings the therapist has for one person are presumed to be projected to the client.

Missing an appointment, having an accident, saying something that you did not really mean to say (that is, making "a Freudian slip"), telling a joke—for psychoanalysts, these and many other behaviors may be very meaningful in terms of what they reveal about the unconscious.

In my own training at Bellevue, I was exposed to psychotherapy supervisors having different approaches to treatment. One of my supervisors was a highly trained and gifted psychoanalyst. In one supervisory session, I described to him how, in my last therapy session with a patient, the patient had told me that he had forgotten to take his medication. Then, in the middle of his therapy hour, the patient produced his pills, took one out, swallowed it, and then proceeded on. During my supervisory session, I related the incident to my supervisor who, as was his custom, asked me what I thought. I interpreted the behavior as the sending of a message to me that I was not helping him enough. The more experienced and knowledgeable supervisor thought differently. He informed me that his "antennae" would be alerted for suicidal ideation; taking the pill in the middle of the session was the patient's unconscious cry for help. The very next session, the patient came in and discussed how he had almost committed suicide by overdosing in the interim period.

PSYCHOANALYTIC APPROACHES IN PERSPECTIVE

Psychoanalysis, as a system of understanding people and as a therapeutic system, has been rightly criticized with regard to many of the points listed on pages 34–40 in Chapter 2. Yet its contributions must also be acknowledged as must its staying power and appeal.

Whether one wishes to make reference to the concept of an unconscious or not, it does seem to be true that many people seem baffled by their own motivations for thinking or behaving in ways that cause them personal difficulty. Sometimes simply pointing out how someone may have learned to behave in a particular way or how that person has the human potential to change is insufficient or unsatisfactory to the person in need. Setting aside the validity of the concept of an unconscious (which indeed has been challenged), the concept of unconscious motivation has great appeal to some patients. Similarly, a form of therapy that allows for dream interpretation and the like may be more engaging than other forms of treatment to some kinds of patients. Certain types of patients may not want an approach that is extremely problem-focused and problem-specific. Certain types of patients may not want an approach in which the burden to make progress in treatment appears to be placed on *their* shoulders instead of on the therapist's.

Fewer than 1,000 therapists are currently enrolled in analytic institutes accredited by the American Psychoanalytic Association—a number that is down substantially from the glory days of years past. Still, this form of treatment continues to have appeal to verbal patients who are not severely disordered and who believe that learning about their unconscious motivation will help them. From the perspective of the psychoanalytic therapist, this method of treatment has appeal for the intellectual challenge it provides in terms of uncovering, interpreting, and therapeutically dealing with unconscious material. A key part of the success of *any* therapeutic enterprise is the goodness of fit between the patient and the therapist. As long as analysts and analysands continue to find each other, psychoanalysis will continue to provide a vehicle by which people can discover intriguing self-insights and work towards self-improvement.

COGNITIVE, BEHAVIORAL, AND COGNITIVE-BEHAVIORAL APPROACHES

In the 1960s, when behavior therapy was first coming into its own, many behavior therapists were quite radical in that they insisted on focusing attention only on observable behavior; what clients said was very much secondary to what clients did. However, the door was soon opened to a consideration of clients' cognitions—including thoughts, beliefs, emotions, opinions, perceptions, self-statements—by a student of B. F. Skinner who conceived of cognitions as "operants of the mind" (Homme, 1965). For many years, the growth of this more cognitive perspective of behavior therapy—soon referred to as *cognitive-be-*

havior therapy—seemed to develop along lines parallel to, and separate from, its more radical predecessor. Today, although radical behaviorists still exist, as do those who urge a disentangling of cognition from behavior therapy (see for example, Hawkins, 1989; Sweet & Loizeaux, 1991), most practitioners do not deny a place to cognition in conceptualizing and behaviorally treating disorders. Nagging questions remain, however, about the precise nature of the relationship between cognition and behavior (Beck & Weishaar, 1989). For example, does cognition cause behavior, or is cognition merely part of behavior?

COGNITIVE APPROACHES

The three approaches to therapy discussed first below are sometimes described as cognitive in orientation because of their central emphasis on changing a client's maladaptive thought processes. However, because cognitive change is so intimately intertwined with behavior change, it would also be appropriate to refer to these approaches as cognitive-behavioral.

BECK'S COGNITIVE THERAPY

In his approach to treatment, Aaron Beck (1976; Beck et al., 1990) focuses on the thoughts and images that he believes are causing and maintaining maladaptive behavior. In therapy, Beck will stop and "freeze-frame" a maladaptive thought (such as, "I must be perfect," or, "I will kill myself if my spouse leaves me."), the better to expose it as maladaptive, illogical, or ineffective. Beck may direct patients to keep a home diary of such maladaptive thoughts and of troubling images as a reference source in treatment. Departing from strictly cognitive procedures, Beck may also employ techniques that rely heavily on behavior. For example, Beck finds it useful for clients to reenact through role-playing painful or highly emotional events in their lives, the better to work successfully through the lingering negative effects of those events. Most of Beck's writing has been on the subject of depression, and it is for this presenting problem that his techniques have the greatest applicability.

ELLIS'S RATIONAL-EMOTIVE THERAPY

As was illustrated in Chapter 6, people do not always think logically or rationally. A key objective in Albert Ellis's rational-emotive therapy (RET) is to identify irrational thoughts and beliefs, challenge them with more logical and rational alternatives, and ultimately replace them with effective thoughts and beliefs (Ellis, 1962, 1967). For example, consider an irrational belief such as, "All people to whom I am attracted and would like to date must also be attracted to me and want to date me." In therapy, this belief would be challenged in a number of ways, including one in which the irrational nature of the belief is turned around, perhaps with a question to the client such as: "Are *you* attracted to everyone who is attracted to you? If not, why would you expect this to be the case of anyone else?" Within the context of RET, dealing with such an irrational belief might also entail very behaviorally oriented homework assignments such as attendance at a singles group and careful observation of interpersonal interactions. RET has potential application for a wide spectrum of problems (Bernard, 1991; Ellis, 1991).

GLASSER'S REALITY THERAPY

Have you ever heard someone advise someone else to, "Get real!" or, "Start living in the real world"? In a sense, such advice sums up a key objective of reality therapy as developed by William Glasser. Glasser (1965, 1981, 1984) places great emphasis on self-management and personal responsibility for one's own actions. The approach is most likely to be used with emotionally troubled teenagers, people in drug abuse programs, prisoners, parolees, and probationers. In reality therapy, both formal and informal therapist-client meetings are used. Therapy may take place in a consulting room, over lunch, or while shooting hoops on the basketball court. Reality therapists freely use humor, sarcasm, "street stories," and examples from their own lives to help their clients to accept the realities of the real world and to encourage them to accept responsibility for their own actions. Drinking, drug taking, and other such behaviors are seen as attempts to obscure the real world. By identifying the needs the client has, as well as effective ways for the client to meet those needs, the reality therapist helps the client to achieve self-reliance.

BEHAVIORAL APPROACHES

As outlined by Bandura (1969) and others, behavioral approaches emphasize the role of learning processes in the development and treatment of abnormal behavior. Therapy is largely a matter of unlearning (or in behavioral terms, *extinguishing*) maladaptive behavior and learning more adaptive ways of behaving in its stead.

Behavior therapy begins with an assessment of the **contingencies** (or *events incidental to other events*) that are believed to have caused the presenting problem and that may be operating to maintain it. Sometimes contingencies maintaining behavior occur by chance and in this sense could be described as "coincidental." For example, a loud and unsettling crash of thunder coincidental to the presentation of a Raggedy Ann doll to a child might serve to instill in that child a fear of Raggedy Ann dolls. In the past, the (radical) behavior therapist might define contingencies only in terms of observable events and behavior; no reference would be made to supposed internal events (such as private thoughts) or unobservable constructs (such as *fear*). Fear of snakes, for example, might have been conceptualized as "the behavioral response of trembling contingent upon the presentation of the stimulus of a snake."

Contingencies may be divided into **antecedents** of the problem behavior (*what comes before the behavior*), and **consequences** (*what happens as a result of engaging in a particular behavior*). Behavior therapy designed to modify a particular behavior may intervene at the level of the antecedents and/or consequences of the problem behavior. Reeducation with regard to the behavior itself may also be part of the treatment. As an example, a behavioral approach to pedophilia might explore the pedophile's thoughts, mental images, and behaviors just prior to child molesting, during child molesting, and after child molesting. Therapy would seek to modify those thoughts, mental images, and behaviors. Reeducation might entail exposure to educational materials that describe in graphic detail the lifelong burden molested children carry with them.

Knowledge about the antecedents and consequences of a client's behavior may be obtained by an interview with the client and/or people who know the client well (such as family members, co-workers, roommates, cellmates, etc.). The assessment may also be aided by direct behavioral observation of the client by the therapist in an out-of-the-consulting room, "natural" setting (such as the client's home, a public place—anywhere the problem behavior is likely to occur). Formal psychological tests of personality, such as the Rorschach inkblot test, are typically of little interest to a behavior therapist because the focus of interest is squarely on behavior, not on personality trait constructs. Checklists such as the one that appears in the *Self-Assessment* exercise may provide a great deal of useful information about the client's behavioral patterns.

Clearly, behavioral assessment for treatment is very different than psychoanalytic assessment for treatment. Regarding the fear of snakes example, psychoanalytically oriented therapists do not focus their attention on the trembling behavior or its consequences. They are interested in its antecedents, but only to the extent that some trauma in the individual's personal history may have generated anxiety that now manifests itself in disguised form as a fear of snakes. According to this view, the snake may represent something other than a snake, perhaps a phallus. In psychoanalytically oriented therapy, then, working through the phallus-related problem will presumably lead to the patient's relief from the irrational fear of snakes. By contrast, behavior therapists focus their attention on the antecedents, consequences, and behaviors involved regarding a client's fear of snakes, and focus treatment on that fear.

Many different criteria may enter into a decision concerning choice of therapeutic technique. For example, some people are able to visualize things better than are others. For people who have difficulty with visualization, a behavior therapy technique that relies

---

contingency

an event incidental to another event.

antecedents

what comes before the behavior.

consequences

what happens as a result of engaging in a particular behavior.

SELF-ASSESSMENT

The Reinforcement Survey Schedule

Joseph R. Cautela and Robert Kastenbaum (1967) created a general checklist of various things and activities that people may find reinforcing. In the first three sections, respondents are asked to rate items on a 5-point scale in terms of the degree of joy or pleasurable derived from the stimuli. The fourth section taps behavior engaged in frequently. Information from such an instrument might be used by a therapist to structure a program whereby certain reinforcing behavior (for example, shopping) might be made contingent on other less appealing behavior (such as studying). Cautela and Kastenbaum (1967) also foresaw a use for their scale in research and in the training of new clinicians.

Some sample items from each section of the instrument follow below. You can use your responses to them to learn more about your personal likes, dislikes, and favored activities. Consult Cautela and Kastenbaum (1967) for a reprinting of the entire instrument.

Instructions

The items in this questionnaire refer to things and experiences that may give joy or other pleasurable feelings. Check each item in the column that describes how much pleasure it gives you nowadays.

	Not at all	A little	A fair amount	Much	Very much
SECTION 1					
1. Eating					
a. Ice Cream	___	___	___	___	___
b. Candy	___	___	___	___	___
c. Fruit	___	___	___	___	___
d. Pastry	___	___	___	___	___
e. Nuts	___	___	___	___	___
f. Cookies	___	___	___	___	___
2. Solving Problems					
a. Crossword puzzles	___	___	___	___	___
b. Mathematical problems	___	___	___	___	___
c. Figuring out how something works	___	___	___	___	___
SECTION 2					
3. Shopping					
a. Clothes	___	___	___	___	___
b. Furniture	___	___	___	___	___
c. Auto parts & supply	___	___	___	___	___
d. Appliances	___	___	___	___	___
e. Food	___	___	___	___	___
f. New car	___	___	___	___	___
g. New place to live	___	___	___	___	___
h. Sports equipment	___	___	___	___	___
4. Being Praised					
a. About your appearance	___	___	___	___	___
b. About your work	___	___	___	___	___
c. About your hobbies	___	___	___	___	___
d. About your physical strength	___	___	___	___	___
e. About your athletic ability	___	___	___	___	___
f. About your mind	___	___	___	___	___
g. About your personality	___	___	___	___	___
h. About your moral strength	___	___	___	___	___
i. About your understanding of others	___	___	___	___	___

SECTION 3: SITUATIONS I WOULD LIKE TO BE IN

How much would you enjoy being in each of the following situations?

1. You have just completed a difficult job. Your superior comes by and praises you highly for "a job well done." He also makes it clear that such good work is going to be rewarded very soon.

not at all ( ) a little ( ) a fair amount ( ) much ( ) very much ( )

2. You are at a lively party. Somebody walks across the room to you, smiles in a friendly way, and says, "I'm glad to meet you. I've heard so many good things about you. Do you have a moment to talk?"

not at all ( ) a little ( ) a fair amount ( ) much ( ) very much ( )

SECTION 4

List things you do or think about more than:

5	10	15	20 times a day?
___	___	___	___
___	___	___	___
___	___	___	___
___	___	___	___
___	___	___	___
___	___	___	___

guided imagery

in cognitive therapy, a technique that involves the client imagining different scenarios at the direction of the therapist.

indications

in psychotherapy, reasons for using a particular technique. Opposite of *contraindications*.

contraindications

in psychotherapy, reasons for not using a particular technique. Opposite of *indications*.

on exposure to real things would be preferable to a technique called **guided imagery**. Arnold Lazarus (1971) outlined a number of **indications** (*reasons for using a particular technique*), as well as **contraindications** (*reasons for not using a particular technique*) regarding various behavioral treatments. He, as well as others, have cautioned that even seemingly harmless techniques, such as teaching clients how to relax, are not without possible adverse effects (Borkovec & Grayson, 1980; Carrington, 1977; Edinger & Jacobsen, 1982; Lazarus & Mayne, 1990).

Some behavior therapists attribute great importance to their clients' perceptions and thoughts. Other behavior therapists give less credence to such self-reported mental activity and focus primarily instead on what their clients do. Most behavior therapists can perhaps best be described as being cognitive-behavioral in orientation. From that perspective, thoughts, self-statements, and other cognitions are seen as mediating factors that influence how environment-related variables are internally processed. Thus, for example, it would be important to know whether the thought in a client's mind after receipt of a mild electric shock is, "Ouch! That hurts! Stop it!" or something more like, "Hmmm! That tickles! More!" Operating on the assumption that cognitions are factors that work like intermediaries between the outside world and one's private experience, behavior therapists may work to alter cognitions by means of *cognitive restructuring* techniques. The cognitive therapists discussed above, as well as behavior therapists such as Meichenbaum (see page 192) and Lazarus (discussed below), all describe the use of various cognitive restructuring techniques to reshape their clients' thoughts, attitudes, and beliefs. A technique called *systematic desensitization* entails pairing muscle relaxation with an anxiety-provoking stimulus. One objective of a systematic desensitization program is to free one to be able to envision or actually face a formerly feared stimulus with markedly decreased anxiety. Systematic desensitization may be supplemented with other techniques involving such social learning (see Figure 9–5). A relatively new variant of systematic desensitization, one found to be particularly useful with clients suffering from post-traumatic stress disorder (PTSD), is called *eye movement desensitization*.

EYE MOVEMENT DESENSITIZATION

Eye movement desensitization (EMD) represents a modification of the classic muscle relaxation method of conducting systematic desensitization (Shapiro 1989a, 1989b, 1990, 1991). Based on Shapiro (1989a), here is a simplified, three-step description of the technique as it is used in the treatment of PTSD:

1. PTSD clients are asked to visualize an image that is representative of the distressing scene from which they wish relief. Clients are next asked to derive a "belief statement" that "best goes with the picture" such as, "I am helpless." Concentrating on both the traumatic image and the accompanying belief statement, clients assign a value of how disturbing the two are on a scale from 0 to 10 (in

**FIGURE 9–5
SOCIAL LEARNING
TO REDUCE FEAR**
Sometimes just observing a live or videotaped model encounter a feared object or situation will help reduce an observer's anxiety.

which 10 is most disturbing and 0 is not disturbing at all). They are also asked (1) to pinpoint where the anxiety is physically located, (2) how they would prefer to feel, and (3) what belief statement they would prefer to substitute for the one they currently have. For example, the client may wish to substitute "I am in control" for "I am helpless."

2. Clients are instructed that the therapist will be asking for feedback as to how they are feeling while the procedure progresses. Clients are then instructed to visualize the traumatic scene, think of the negative belief statement, and concentrate on the anxiety that the scene provokes.

3. While concentrating on the image, the belief statement, and the anxiety, clients visually track the therapist's index finger (see Figure 9–6).

Shapiro believes that if there is no reduction in the anxiety the client is experiencing after two sets of eye movements, there may be some kind of a mismatch between the image, the emotion, and the cognition. If the image fades but the bodily sensation remains, the bodily sensation remains the focus as the eye movements are made. Shapiro (1989a, p. 215) believes that "the predominant emotion will be desensitized during the first session . . ."

Initial reports by a number of clinicians who have used this technique with PTSD clients have been quite encouraging (Marquis, 1991; Puk, 1991; Wolpe & Abrams, 1991). Exactly why the EMD procedure may be effective will require further research. Shapiro (1989a) noted that the types of eye movements involved in the procedure are similar to

FIGURE 9–6 EYE MOVEMENT DESENSITIZATION According to Shapiro (1989a), eye movement desensitization (EMD) may be an effective method of treating post-traumatic stress disorder. In this technique, the client mentally conjures a disturbing mental image along with accompanying thoughts and emotions and then "holds it." The therapist places a finger about 12 inches in front of the client's face and then moves the finger rhythmically from the extreme left to the extreme right while the client visually tracks the finger. These repetitions continue at least a dozen or so times, at the relatively rapid rate of two back-and-forth movements per second. After the dozen repetitions, the client is instructed to "blank out" the picture, take a deep breath, and give some rating on a 1 to 10 scale as to how disturbing the image is. The procedure is repeated until the images and associated thoughts and feelings are diminished to an acceptable level. The procedure also calls for systematically exploring how the picture and its associated anxiety change during the course of the procedure. In some cases, new memories will have to be desensitized before the therapist returns to the original image, thoughts, and feelings.

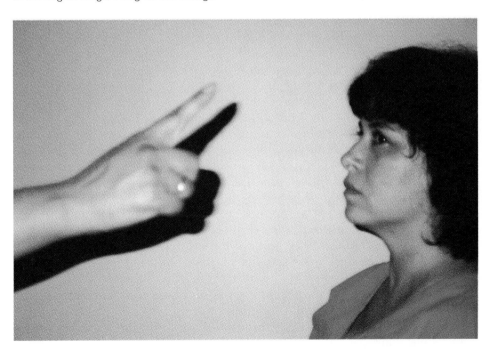

the rapid eye movement (REM) observed during the times during sleep that dreaming occurs. She speculated that such eye movements during sleep may serve some kind of naturally desensitizing function. Suggestive in this context are the findings from one study in which subjects suffering from PTSD were found to spend less time in REM sleep than a control group (Lavie et al., 1979).

OTHER BEHAVIORAL TECHNIQUES

More familiar types of learning tasks may be part of a behavior therapy program. For example, the therapist may employ in the treatment program homework assignments including **bibliotherapy** (literally, *reading therapy*). In Jane's case, the bibliotherapy might be the assignment of a book to read on the difference between poisonous and nonpoisonous snakes in her area. With increasing home ownership of videorecorders and the widespread availability of a large variety of videotaped material, behavior therapists may also employ **videotherapy** (*learning by watching videotapes*) as an *adjunct* (or aid) to treatment. Feature films may have value in terms of what they can teach directly. They may also have value as stimulus for further discussion in therapy sessions (Covino, 1992). The use of videotherapy (and related techniques such as bibliotherapy) by the way, is by no means limited to behavioral approaches to treatment, and is now commonly employed by many therapists from various schools of treatment.

Some behavioral procedures are designed to reduce the appeal certain potentially harmful things (such as drugs) have for some people. One such procedure is **aversion therapy**, *a process in which an unpleasant stimulus is applied, or a positive reinforcer is removed in an effort to lessen the positive appeal of an undesirable behavior.* Experimentation with aversion therapy dates back to the late 1920s and studies that explored the value of electric shock paired with the presentation of the sight, smell, and taste of various alcoholic beverages (Kantorovich, 1928; Razran, 1934).

In general, researchers have found aversion therapy to be of some value in the treatment of alcoholism and sexual perversions (such as child molesting). It is not a cure, however. As Bandura (1969) noted, its primary value seems to be that of providing a "time-out" window of opportunity: "The major value of aversive procedures is that they provide a rapid means of achieving control over injurious behavior for a period during which alternative, and more rewarding, modes of behavior can be established" (p. 554). In a political climate in which the use of aversive techniques such as electric shock by psychologists or others—even for the therapeutic gain of the patient—is widely frowned upon, aversion therapy is used most judiciously, and usually only as a last resort.

Other behavioral techniques include implosion and flooding. **Implosion** involves *exaggerated imaginal exposure to the feared or anxiety producing stimuli.* If the client was snake phobic, the imagery might involve dozens of snakes doing all kinds of horrendous things to the patient. According to the developers of this treatment method (Stampfl & Levis, 1967), at some point during such imaging the individual will spontaneously "implode," at which point snakes will cease to produce an emotional arousal. **Flooding** is *an in vivo form of implosive therapy,* although the anxiety-provoking stimuli need not be exaggerated in any way. In treating snake phobia by flooding, clients might be asked to spend an increasingly greater amount of time in a room with harmless snakes. Each time they emerge from the snake room with no ill effects they have presumably moved closer to a cure.

All forms of therapy, physical as well as psychological, even when conducted by highly trained professionals, may carry with them unanticipated ill effects. A danger in implosive therapy is that the therapist, in striving to create a scene as fear-arousing as possible, will describe imagery that even the client has never thought of—thus compounding the problem. *In vivo* exposure to the feared source of anxiety may be too much for some clients to bear. In one instance, for example, a client who had a fear of going outdoors "hid in a cellar out of fear of being sent into the street for 90 minutes by the therapist" (Emmelkamp & Wessels, 1975, p. 14).

Behavior therapy may involve the restructuring of contingencies based on assessment using information such as that found in the Reinforcement Survey Schedule (see p. 241). Especially with child clients, new behaviors not previously in the client's repertoire may be learned using things the client listed as positively reinforcing as rewards. For example,

(see p. 241)

---

bibliotherapy

the use of books in a psychotherapeutic context, as in learning some moral from a story.

videotherapy

using videos psychotherapeutically, as in the case of learning some moral from a story told in a film.

aversion therapy

in behavior therapy, a process in which an unpleasant stimulus is applied or a positive reinforcer is removed in an effort to lessen the positive appeal of an undesirable behavior.

implosion

a behavior therapy technique that entails the exaggerated imaginal exposure to the feared or anxiety-producing stimuli. Contrast with *flooding*.

flooding

an *in vivo* form of implosive therapy that entails increasing exposure to anxiety-provoking stimuli. Contrast with *implosion*.

learning how to load dishes into a dishwasher and start the wash cycle may be rewarded by 30 minutes of "quality time" with a parent. With adults, a technique known as **contingency contracting** involves *writing out an actual contract and specifying exactly what will happen under various conditions.* For example, a contract in the context of a behaviorally oriented stop-smoking program might specify that if the client does not reduce the total number of cigarettes smoked per day by 5 within 30 days of the agreement, the client will have to donate $50 to his least favorite political organization.

Behavioral techniques such as contingency contracting have application in group treatment as well as in individual treatment programs. A **token economy**, for example, is *a group application of contingency contracting in which tokens, gold stars, or other such "currencies" are awarded for socially valued behavior.* Patients in hospitals or other institutions may earn a certain number of tokens for making their own bed or drying the dishes. The tokens are subsequently cashed in for rights and privileges. Prison systems in many states use a similar system whereby prisoners may earn time off their sentences in exchange for good behavior.

At high schools where students have the option of driving to school or taking the school bus, the privilege of parking at school can and has been used as a reinforcer. This is so because for many suburban high school students, driving to school has high status attached to it, while taking the bus is seen as an embarrassment. The principal at New Milford High School, Joanne Mendillo, was hired with a mandate to reduce the number of dropouts. She found that many of the students were failing to do their homework or to get sufficient sleep because they were working at after-school jobs in order to pay for their cars. And whereas the school bus would ensure that students arrived on time and stayed there for the entire school day, students who drove themselves were more likely to come in late, leave early, and leave to go to local fast food places during lunch or study hall hours. From conversations with students, Mendillo believed that students had "too much freedom and want more structure in their lives." Mendillo gave them more structure by making a space in the school parking lot a privilege contingent upon the emission of appropriate behavior (Judson, 1992).

Beyond parking permits loom broader questions regarding value judgments that must be made when designing programs with the objective of behavioral control. For example, an important question to raise when attempting to control behavior is, "Is behavioral control being implemented for the benefit of the controller or the controllee?" In an often-cited debate between Carl Rogers and B. F. Skinner (1956), such value-related questions were raised and explored in depth.

COGNITIVE-BEHAVIORAL APPROACHES

Cognitive-behavioral approaches to treatment strike a balance between the most cognitive of the cognitive approaches and the most behavioral of the behavioral approaches. From the cognitive-behavioral perspective, thoughts, feelings, and behaviors are not separated by any theoretical boundaries and all are fair game for modification. Arnold Lazarus's multimodal behavior therapy exemplifies the cognitive-behavioral approach to treatment. In Chapter 7, the BASIC ID modalities were introduced (see pages 189-190). Here we look at how multimodal behavior therapy works in practice.

MULTIMODAL BEHAVIOR THERAPY

In the 1960s, Arnold Lazarus was involved in cutting-edge research and clinical work in the field of behavior therapy. By the next decade, however, Lazarus began to look beyond the framework of a strictly behavioral approach to clinical treatment. In his book *Behavior Therapy and Beyond*, Lazarus (1971) confessed that he had toyed with calling the book *Beyond Behavior Therapy,* but decided against it because the latter title "would imply a decisive break with behavior therapy" (1971, p.xi). Lazarus referred to the type of behavior therapy he practiced as *broad spectrum behavior therapy* and he soon broadened it yet further with what he called a *multimodal* approach.

Multimodal behavior therapy, as compared to the broad spectrum approach, "provides a more comprehensive and systematic assessment-therapeutic modus operandi" (Lazarus,

contingency contracting

in behavior and cognitive-behavior therapy, the technique of devising an agreement regarding the client's behavior and the consequences of that behavior, including rewards and punishments, for therapeutic purposes. See also *token economy*.

token economy

an institutional application of contingency contracting that entails the use of rewards such as tokens, gold stars, or other such "currency," exchangable for material goods, services, or privileges.

1976b, p.6). In practice, this means that the therapist has more systematic guidelines when undertaking psychological assessment and therapy and a wide array of diagnostic and treatment techniques to choose from. The seven interactive and interdependent modalities of the BASIC ID serve as "a constant compass" to orient treatment. As its name implies, the roots of multimodal behavior therapy are in behavior therapy. Yet although the approach is largely driven by learning principles, it is also extremely eclectic in terms of diagnostic and therapy techniques.[1] Multimodal therapy "presupposes a readiness to deploy any technique of promise, regardless of theoretical origins (if any), as long as there is demonstrable empirical support for its use" (Franks, 1976, p. ix). Although different techniques may be used, they must be used systematically; an eclectic treatment approach unsystematically applied is of questionable value (Lazarus, 1976b).

Lazarus has published numerous case illustrations of how the multimodal approach works in everyday applications (see for example, Lazarus, 1976b, 1987, 1989a, 1989b, 1992a, 1992b). The first published case history was of Mary Ann, an overweight and withdrawn 24-year-old woman who had been diagnosed as "chronic undifferentiated schizophrenia." Although she was heavily medicated, Lazarus could detect glimmers of warmth, wit, and insight. From the patient's responses to a life history questionnaire, Lazarus (1973) determined that well-meaning parents had "created a breeding ground for guilty attitudes, especially in matters pertaining to sex." The patient's vulnerability to peer pressure had made her vulnerable to drug abuse. Soon after her graduation from high school at age 18, Mary Ann began to hear voices and was hospitalized. She was subsequently hospitalized at age 21 following a suicidal gesture, and at age 24 after her sister died suddenly.

One of the first steps in multimodal therapy after history taking is to develop a modality profile, a listing of the seven modalities along with the specific areas of concern within each modality. Adjacent to the listing of concerns is a listing of the specific techniques to be used in addressing each of the modalities. The modality profile for Mary Ann is presented in Table 9–2. Many, but not all of the proposed treatment techniques, are techniques that have been written about in the behavior therapy and cognitive-behavior therapy literature. One exception, for example, is the "empty chair technique," a gestalt therapy procedure described by Fritz Perls (1969). Under the treatment method listed as "sexual education," Lazarus prescribed reading *Sex Without Guilt* (Ellis, 1965). Over the course of the 13-month treatment period, Mary Ann became engaged to be married, and was taken off medication. She was seen for premarital counseling, as well as for family counseling with her parents. She was also seen in group treatment for 30 weeks. A 1-year post-treatment follow-up found her "coping admirably without medication" (Lazarus, 1973).

Lazarus (1973) anticipated a major criticism of multimodal therapy in his article introducing the procedures. He wrote of Mary Ann's Modality Profile, "The Modality Profile may strike the reader as a fragmented or mechanistic barrage of techniques that would call for a disjointed array of therapeutic maneuvers. In actual practice, the procedures follow logically and blend smoothly into meaningful interventions." Although such skillful blending is thoroughly believable when as knowledgeable and as experienced a therapist as Lazarus is applying them, such a blending would seem to be much more of a challenge to the less experienced therapist. The same is true of instituting some of the treatments in the "proposed treatment" column of the Modality Profile. For example, under the problem of "excessive eating," the proposed treatment is "low calorie regimen." Yet motivating a client to stay on a low calorie regimen may in itself be a Herculean task. Presumably, the low calorie regimen, when combined with all of the other interventions listed would work, perhaps because of factors such as a general lessening of stress, a heightening of self-esteem, and so forth. For the novice therapist, however, this would be a great presumption, and the task of making the different proposed treatments "blend smoothly into meaningful interventions" might be more an exercise in optimism than an achievable reality.

A PERSPECTIVE

As behavior therapy began to earn widespread attention in the 1960s and 1970s, most objections to it centered around its supposed mechanistic, stimulus-response view of people. A hot topic of discussion concerned values in behavioral treatment and the ethics of be-

[1]Whether or not *eclectic* is the proper term to describe such an approach to psychotherapeutic treatment has been something of a controversy in the professional literature (see, for example, Lazarus et al., 1992; Norcross, 1989, 1990; Patterson, 1989, 1990; Thorne, 1973).

TABLE 9–2   MARY ANN'S MODALITY PROFILE

Modality	Problem	Proposed Treatment
Behavior	Inappropriate withdrawal responses	Assertive training
	Frequent crying	Nonreinforcement
	Unkempt appearance	Grooming instructions
	Excessive eating	Low calorie regimen
	Negative self-statements	Positive self-talk assignments
	Poor eye contact	Rehearsal techniques
	Mumbling of words with poor voice projection	Verbal projection exercises
	Avoidance of heterosexual situations	Re-education and desensitization
Affect	Unable to express overt anger	Role-playing
	Frequent anxiety	Relaxation training and reassurance
	Absence of enthusiasm and spontaneous joy	Positive imagery procedures
	Panic attacks (Usually precipitated by criticism from authority figures)	Desensitization and assertive training
	Suicidal feelings	Time projection techniques
	Emptiness and aloneness	General relationship building
Sensation	Stomach spasms	Abdominal breathing and relaxing
	Out of touch with most sensual pleasures	Sensate focus method
	Tension in jaw and neck	Differential relaxation
	Frequent lower back pains	Orthopedic exercises
	Inner tremors	Gendlin's focusing method (Lazarus, 1971a, p. 232)
Imagery	Distressing scenes of sister's funeral	Desensitization
	Mother's angry face shouting "You fool!"	Empty chair technique
	Performing fellatio on God	Blow up technique (implosion)
	Recurring dreams about airplane bombings	Eidetic imagery invoking feelings of being safe
Cognition	Irrational self-talk:	Deliberate rational disputation and corrective self-talk
	"I am evil."	
	"I must suffer."	
	"Sex is dirty."	
	"I am inferior."	
	Syllogistic reasoning, overgeneralization	Parsing of irrational sentences
	Sexual misinformation	Sexual education
Interpersonal relationships	Characterized by childlike dependence	Specific self-sufficiency assignments
	Easily Exploited/submissive	Assertive training
	Overly suspicious	Exaggerated role taking
	Secondary gains from parental concern	Explain reinforcement principles to parents and try to enlist their help
	Manipulative tendencies	Training in direct and confrontative behaviors

havior control. Values and ethics in behavior therapy and psychotherapy will always remain important considerations, but behavior therapists have been quite eloquent in their response to those who would argue that their techniques are less benevolent or more insidious than any other approach to therapy. As Bandura (1969, p. 85) put it, "All behavior is inevitably controlled, and the operation of psychological laws cannot be suspended by romantic conceptions of human behavior, any more than indignant rejection of the law of gravity as antihumanistic can stop people from falling." Others phrased it this way: "Either one manages the contingencies or they get managed by accident. Either way there will be contingencies, and they will have their effect" (Homme & Tosti, 1965, p. 16). Behavior therapists have also argued convincingly that all therapists exert varying degrees of control in their efforts to treat clients, but behavior therapists are most open about doing this. The relevant question thus shifts from *if* control should be exerted, to *how* control can best be exerted in the interest of the client.

As a framework for understanding behavior and a method of treating it, the behavioral approach has made great strides in a relatively brief period of time. Today, the etiology of many of the disorders found in psychiatric diagnostic manuals are widely understood not only in biological terms (as is the bias in medical manuals) but in learning terms as well. Many behavior therapists, cognitive-behavior therapists, and cognitive therapists conduct therapy with all of the rigor of an experiment, making systematic changes in techniques until the most effective ones are employed. Case studies in this literature are typically reported with exemplary detail and precision.

Research on the therapeutic value of behavioral approaches tends to be quite impressive, especially with respect to very circumscribed kinds of presenting problems, such as fears. For more vaguely defined kinds of problems, greater reliance on the cognitive aspect of cognitive-behavioral approaches seems to be what is needed to ensure therapeutic success. Again, it is worth emphasizing that approaches to therapy which were once thought to be exclusively behavioral, cognitive, or cognitive-behavioral have begun to meld in many respects. This trend can be expected to continue. Although some spectacular successes can be claimed as a result of this melding process, especially in the area of depression (Robinson et al., 1990), it is also true that there are some who would prefer to keep the cognitive and behavioral approaches more independent of each other (Sweet & Loizeaux, 1991).

A distinction has sometimes been made between "insight-oriented" approaches to therapy and "action-oriented" approaches. In psychoanalytically oriented therapy, for example, the ultimate objective of behavior change is typically achieved by helping patients to achieve insight with respect to the nature of their problems. The therapeutic philosophy in psychoanalysis is thus paraphrased as, "Once the patient has insight into the problem, behavior change will follow." By contrast, behavior therapy typically entails more "action-oriented" techniques including therapist-prescribed visualization exercises, behavioral exercises, and homework assignments. But more and more, the once so clear boundary line between action-oriented and insight-oriented approaches to therapy is becoming blurred (Jacobson, 1991). In a sense, insight is an objective in virtually any form of therapy, including humanistic approaches such as that practiced by Carl Rogers. Insight, at least with respect to how learning plays a role in behavior, has increasingly become a staple in behavioral approaches. It is also true that behavior change (or action) is, after all, a goal of the so-called insight-oriented approaches. For these reasons, the distinction between so-called insight-oriented approaches to therapy and other approaches to therapy is not as clear-cut as it has been in the past.

HUMANISTIC APPROACHES

Approaches to psychotherapy that are typically categorized as humanistic may take many different forms. For example, a humanistic approach to treatment called *gestalt therapy* (Perls, 1969) has as its objective an increase in one's self-awareness and self-acceptance through an unblocking of various sensory and cognitive obstacles. The most widely practiced and most representative therapy of the humanistic approach, however, is the client-centered approach developed by Carl Rogers. In Chapter 2, you were introduced to aspects of the framework that Rogers developed to understand human behavior. Here we extend that discussion and briefly survey the impressive body of Rogers's research and writing.

COUNSELING AND PSYCHOTHERAPY ACCORDING TO CARL ROGERS

In Rogers's approach, the client seeking treatment is viewed as being in emotional distress as a result of a denial or distortion of significant areas of experience. This denial or distortion is the result of a state of incongruence between the self and the ideal self. People strive to maintain a certain image of themselves in spite of what life experiences teach. To varying degrees, we may all deny or distort reality so that it better fits our own conception of self. However, as a consequence of such denial or distortion, certain feelings or thoughts are pressed out of awareness. According to Rogers, when experiencing certain feelings or thoughts would threaten the concept of self, such feelings and thoughts are kept from awareness.

Over the years however, the discrepancy between one's real and ideal self may widen. Rogers cites other factors, external to the person, that may contribute to what he calls an incongruency between one's real and ideal self. For example, being brought up in a home without love, support, and understanding contributes to a lack of congruence. Psychotherapy, then, entails a restoration of congruence between the self and the ideal self. The therapist's role in this restorative process is more that of a facilitator than of an architect. In the conduct of therapy, the therapist strives to create a climate conducive to congruence by becoming a party to a relationship in which there is genuine communication, caring, and understanding. The cultivation of this unique sort of working relationship may be the single most important "technique" in the client-centered approach to treatment. In such an environment, clients are thought to be freed to become "who they really are."

The humanistic notion of people "finding themselves" had great intuitive appeal. During the 1960s and 1970s, many Americans went in search of themselves in **encounter groups** which involved *seeking personal growth from different types of confrontation as directed by the group leader or other group members.* Closely related were **sensitivity training** sessions which involved *seeking personal growth by becoming more physically, mentally, or socially aware.* Many varied types of group experiences were available to focus on cognitive, sensory, or experiential aspects of being. The actual value of such groups, especially when run by novices and nonprofessionals, was open to question (see Figure 9–7).

Client-centered therapists diligently work to convey to their clients that they are hearing and understanding whatever it is that the client conveys. Perhaps for this reason, ever since its founding in the 1940s, the client-centered approach has had particular appeal for clients who are members of minority groups, including clients of color and gay and/or unmarried and pregnant clients (Gendlin, 1988). In the client-centered setting, people receive sincere, stated or unstated assurance from a professional therapist that they are being listened to with empathy, that the therapist is not being judgmental, and that the therapist is striving to understand them on their own terms.

The uncompromising trust of the humanist in the capacity of every person to grow is in some ways reminiscent of the Taoist teachings of Lao-tse. Attributed to this Chinese philosopher who lived in the sixth century B.C., the quote that follows might well have been from the lips of Rogers on the subject of psychotherapy: "To interfere with the life of

encounter group
a humanistic, group approach to personal growth and awareness typically derived from different types of confrontation.

sensitivity training
1. a group approach to personal growth by becoming more physically, mentally, or socially aware.
2. a general name for a specific type of counseling sometimes court-ordered for remedial purposes, as in the case of sensitivity training for a person who has engaged in sexual harassment.

FIGURE 9–7 FINDING YOURSELF—BUT WHERE?
Evaluated from a professional standpoint, it is unlikely that many encounter groups, especially those run by nonprofessionals—produced meaningful and sustained changes in their participants. As Lefebre (1963) noted, these groups tended to encourage momentary outbursts as opposed to sustained feelings and it is reasonable to assume that any gain associated with these outbursts were similarly fragmented. Back (1972) concluded that such activities offered comfort at best, not cures.

things means to harm both them and one's self. He who imposes himself has the small, manifest might; he who does not impose himself has the great secret might ... The perfected man does not interfere in the life of beings, he does not impose himself on them, but he helps all beings to their freedom" (Buber, 1957, pp. 54–55).

NONDIRECTIVE COUNSELING

In his book *Counseling and Psychotherapy,* Rogers (1942) expressed the belief that a warm and responsive therapist who creates a permissive and nonjudgmental environment would help the client to gain self-understanding. This newly acquired self-understanding would, in turn, enable the client "to take positive steps in the light of his new orientation" (p. 18). Rogers envisioned the therapist as one who was free from the burden of coming up with the correct diagnosis of the client.[2] Therapists were not yet free, however, to "be themselves." That requirement would be taken up by Rogers much later, as his conceptions about therapy constantly changed as a function of experience and research.

At the time that Rogers was working on *Counseling and Psychotherapy,* psychoanalysis and a treatment approach described by Rogers (1942, p. 115) as "directive" were dominant forces among therapists and counselors. Simply stated, the directive approach was based on the premise that the therapist knows best: The therapist knows how to categorize the client's problem, knows what is wrong with the client, and knows what the client needs to right whatever it is that is wrong. Yet even if every one of these conditions was true, there was never any guarantee of therapeutic progress. As Rogers would later recall of directive approaches, "Disillusionment with these techniques inevitably occurred as counselors discovered that even though they 'knew' what was wrong with a client and what he *should* do to help himself, neither this knowledge nor its communication was effective in changing his behavior" (Meador & Rogers, 1973, p. 122).

Rogers (1942) distinguished his nondirective approach from more directive approaches by allowing that goals in counseling should be set by the person being counseled, and that the focus of the process should be on the person, not the problem:

> . . . we find that the directive group tends to focus its efforts upon the problem which the client presents. If the problem is solved in a manner which can be approved by the counselor, if the symptoms are removed, the counseling is considered successful. The nondirective group places its emphasis upon the client himself, not upon the problem. If the client achieves through the counseling experience sufficient insight to understand his relation to the reality situation, he can choose the method of adapting to reality which has the highest value for him. He will also be much more capable of coping with future problems that arise, because of his increased insight and his increased experience in independent solution of his problems. (pp. 127–128)

Even before the publication of *Counseling and Psychotherapy,* the name of this new approach to counseling was drawing fire from many therapists who believed that Rogers had no monopoly on being nondirective. In a 1940 symposium on psychotherapy that featured representatives of different treatment approaches, including Rogers, *all* of the participants claimed that the values of therapists do not influence those of the patient. In a sense, they claimed that they too were nondirective. As an illustration, consider the view of one psychoanalyst:

> The basic idea of Freud's psychoanalysis . . . is impartiality toward the patient's inner conflicts . . . Without taking any part in these never-ceasing struggles, psychoanalysis aims exclusively at letting light and air into the battlefield by making conscious the unconscious elements of the conflicts. The idea is that if the mature ego of an adult has full access to all the forces involved, it should be capable of finding an adequate and tolerable, at least nonpathological, solution to these conflicts, and capable of finding a workable proportion between satisfying desires and keeping them under effective control. (Waelder, 1940, p. 705)

Is it true that all therapists are relatively value-free and nondirective as they conduct psychotherapy? A most interesting upshot of decades of dialogue on values and nondirectiveness in therapy has been a rather surprising turn-around of views on this issue. Many mental health professionals began to come to the realization that *no therapist, regardless of*

[2]Obviously no one had ever mentioned the term *insurance forms* to Rogers at this point in his career.

therapeutic approach, can be value-free or nondirective in the process of therapy. Therapists are human. Being human, they have value systems which they cannot help but bring to the therapeutic situation. A simple nod of the head may reflect a therapist's values in terms of whether the therapist agrees or disagrees with a value-laden statement a client is making. Even the decision to treat or not to treat a particular patient in the first place may reflect the therapist's values.

Rather than perpetuating a myth of therapeutic neutrality, many therapists have increasingly made their values known to clients, the better to let the clients know where they stand. It is true that psychotherapeutic methods, just like hammers, wrenches, and other tools, can themselves be value-free. However, *it is the way that tools are used that reflect the user's values.* This point was made by Albert Bandura (1969) with respect to behavior therapy, and in response to those who would mistakenly assume that:

> traditional psychotherapies fervently embrace humanism whereas behavioral approaches . . . are supposedly uninterested in the moral implications of their practices or are antagonistic toward humanistic values. In fact, behavioral therapy is a system of principles and procedures and not a system of ethics. Its methods, and any other effective procedures for that matter, can be employed to threaten human freedom and dignity or to enhance them. (p. 87)

CLIENT-CENTERED THERAPY

By the 1950s, the somewhat controversial *nondirective* name for the Rogerian approach to treatment had been dropped. The new name for this therapeutic approach was announced in the title of Rogers's new book: *Client-Centered Therapy* (1951). This new name shifted the focus of attention from therapists (and whether or not they were directive or nondirective) to the person in therapy. The use of the word *therapy* was also noteworthy. Rogers had previously preferred the term *counseling* when used with *nondirective* because *therapy* in the 1940s was better identified with the professional activity of psychiatrists. Another reason for the name change was that, "It indicated a shift in emphasis from the negative, narrower statement, 'nondirective,' to the positive focus on the growth-producing factors in the individual client himself" (Meador & Rogers, 1973, p. 123). This focus on the individual client led to intensive research and personality theorizing regarding the concept of self (Rogers & Dymond, 1954). In their efforts to learn as much as possible about their clients' self-concepts, Rogers and his colleagues studied not only the spoken words of their clients, but messages that might be "hidden" within those words. According to Rogers, a great effort was under way to respond to "the client's implicit as well as explicit affect. This required the therapists to get behind the words of the client and into his feeling world and precipitated a new look at accurate empathic understanding" (Meador & Rogers, 1973, p. 123).

Accurate empathic understanding is one of three factors that Rogers concluded are necessary and sufficient for therapeutic personality change to occur. In this context, **empathy** refers to *an active state of perceiving how another feels, almost as if one were the other.* The other two factors are *genuineness* and *unconditional positive regard.* **Genuineness** may be defined as *the absence of a "false front" on the part of the therapist and honest experiencing of the moment.* **Unconditional positive regard** may be defined as *a prizing, valuing, or unqualified acceptance of the self experiences of another.* Rogers attempted to specify behaviorally what is meant by each of these terms and to test his ideas in psychotherapy research. In practice, however, devising rigorous behavioral definitions of each of these terms and measuring therapeutic interactions in terms of them has proven to be fraught with methodological problems.

Beyond fostering human growth in people identified as "clients," Rogers sought to explore how the types of principles he had outlined for use in therapy might be applied to ordinary people as well. In books having titles such as *On Becoming a Person* (1961), *Freedom to Learn* (1969), *Carl Rogers on Encounter Groups* (1970), *On Becoming Partners: Marriage and Its Alternatives* (1972), and *A Way of Being* (1980), Rogers explored mechanisms by which normal people change, learn, and adjust. In 1969, Rogers founded the Center for the Study of the Person in La Jolla, California. In the ensuing period until his death in 1987, Rogers remained active in various client-centered (now renamed *person-centered*) ac-

empathy

in person-centered therapy, an active state of perceiving how another feels, almost as if one were the other.

genuineness

in person-centered therapy, an honest experiencing of the moment and the absence of a false front.

unconditional positive regard

in person-centered therapy, an interpersonal environment wherein there is unqualified acceptance, valuing, and prizing of the inherent worth of an individual.

tivities ranging from the teaching of workshops in foreign countries to applying his methods to the training of political leaders and policy makers.

HUMANISTIC APPROACHES IN PERSPECTIVE

Carl Rogers revolutionized the psychotherapeutic approaches of his day and developed a new approach to psychotherapeutic treatment. The person-centered approach has continually evolved and been actively refined over the course of 5 decades. Rogers was also a pioneer in the development of techniques used to evaluate the success of psychotherapy. In the interest of studying the process of therapy, he was the first to record actual therapy sessions—this at a time when recording technology was so primitive, that recordings were made on clumsy glass disks. Although Rogers was criticized at the time for violating the sanctity of the therapeutic relationship by such recording (Gendlin, 1988), audiorecording and videorecording of therapy sessions with the consent of the client for research purposes has become common practice today.

As you might expect, the elements Rogers listed as "necessary and sufficient" for psychotherapy to take place have not been universally embraced by practitioners of different schools of therapy. Albert Ellis (1959), for example, believes that although the conditions outlined by Rogers may be desirable, they are not necessary and sufficient. Additionally, Rogers's claims regarding the utility of his approach for virtually any type of client, including people identified as schizophrenic, have not been widely accepted by mental health professionals. More effective treatment programs, including biochemical approaches, are preferable in such cases. As with other approaches to therapy, the client-centered approach must provide an optimal fit of presenting problem, type of client, and therapist if it is to be effective. In addition to not being the treatment of choice for problems such as schizophrenia, client-centered therapy would probably not be the treatment of choice for many other types of conditions, including those related to very narrowly defined problems such as phobias. Client-centered therapy might well be the treatment of choice, however, for someone seeking occupational guidance, someone in the throes of a mid-life crisis, or someone wrestling with other problems and crises related to self-identity.

Rogers's works have been translated into many languages and his influence will be felt worldwide for many years to come. Client-centered practitioners can be found most everywhere, most notably in this country, Europe, and Japan. As his ideas have influenced business people and educators, the influence of Carl Rogers extends beyond consulting rooms into boardrooms and classrooms.

OTHER APPROACHES

A number of other approaches to psychotherapeutic treatment exist, some representing adaptations of treatment approaches we have already discussed. For example, psychoanalytic therapy, behavior therapy, and client-centered therapy may all be employed with couples, families, or with groups of unrelated people.

GROUP THERAPY

It is not easy to generalize about the benefits of group therapy because so many different activities can take place in the name of "group therapy." Still, any listing of the comparative benefits of group treatment would probably include the following:

- Group members receive support not only from the therapist, but from others in the group as well.
- People who are in need themselves help themselves by helping others.
- Group therapy permits one to see firsthand that many people are surviving and working towards positive behavior change even though their problems may seem much worse than one's own.
- Group therapy permits one to see firsthand improvement in some group members, who may then become models or sources of inspiration to other group members.

BIOLOGICALLY BASED APPROACHES

Based on the premise that the external exhibition of abnormal behavior is symptomatic of something wrong internally, biologically based treatment approaches are among the oldest in recorded history. Although the nature of the relationship between the brain and abnormal behavior in all of its varied forms remains a mystery, a number of impressive inroads have been made.

PSYCHOTROPIC MEDICATION

In the area of **psychotropic medication** (*drugs that have the psyche or mind as their target for the site of action*), advances in the development of antipsychotic, antidepressant, and anti-anxiety agents have literally worked wonders for many patients. New drug delivery methods, such as the wearing of a patch may prove helpful (see Figure 9–8). Although not a substitute for insight or self-managed behavior change, psychotropic medication can be extremely important in terms of helping patients reach a point where they will be more receptive to, and might benefit from, psychotherapy. [3]

BIOFEEDBACK

Biofeedback, an abbreviation for *biological feedback*, may be defined as *the external output of internal monitoring of bodily processes*. In this procedure, bodily signs of relaxation, such as heart rate or skin temperature, are magnified and "fed back" via auditory or visual signals, thus facilitating relaxation. Biofeedback has been used as an aid to treatment for a variety of conditions ranging from hypertension (Blanchard et al., 1986) to headaches (Satinsky & Frerotti, 1981) to hyperactivity (Omizo & Williams, 1981). Yet whether the use of biofeedback instrumentation is superior to simple relaxation training remains an open question (Blanchard et al., 1987).

ELECTROSHOCK TREATMENT

Electroshock treatment entails *the passing of an electrical current through the brain for therapeutic purposes*. Because this type of treatment causes a convulsion (or momentary seizure) to occur in the patient as a result of the passing electricity, it is also referred to as *electroconvulsive treatment* (ECT). The original rationale for inducing convulsions in people as a treatment method was amazingly simple and indeed quite "shocking." A Hungarian physician named Meduna (1936) speculated that convulsive disorders seemed not to be present in schizophrenics and other psychotics. He wondered whether schizophrenia and seizure activity were somehow incompatible physiologically. He further speculated that inducing convulsions could cure psychosis. Few medical practitioners of the day dared to attempt

psychotropic medication
drugs that have as their targeted site of action the psyche or mind.

biofeedback
an abbreviation for biological feedback which refers to the internal monitoring of bodily processes amplified through some type of external output such as light or sound.

electroshock treatment or therapy
the passing of an electrical current through the brain which causes a convulsion for therapeutic purposes.

[3]Recent years have also witnessed great controversies regarding extreme side effects of certain psychotropic medications. For example, drugs having trade names such as *Prozac* (an antidepressant) and *Halcyon* (the world's most prescribed sleeping pill), have been alleged to be causal in suicidal or homicidal behavior. After investigating such claims, the federal Food and Drug Administration has maintained that both of these drugs are safe when used as prescribed.

FIGURE 9–8   THE NICOTINE PATCH Marketed under names such as *Habitrol, Nicoderm,* and *Prostep,* a round adhesive patch that delivers a measured, reduced-over-time dose of nicotine is one of the newer biochemical weapons in the battle to stop smoking. Available only by prescription, the patch stops nicotine cravings while eliminating the need to purchase, handle, or otherwise behaviorally deal with cigarettes. Patients who employ this means of quitting should ask their doctor about the risks associated with it, including the risk of heart attack when smoking while wearing the patch. One hospital reported such a phenomenon after cardiac patients misused the patch in this way. Another possible side effect is sleep disturbances. In an effort to minimize that side effect, one company introduced a patch that is worn only while the user is awake (Fisher, 1992). Perhaps anticipating that such a biologically based treatment approach might work best if accompanied by some sort of psychological intervention, the makers of the *Habitrol* brand product enclose with their patch a "Declaration of a Smoke-Free Future" which users are encouraged to sign and display.

such a treatment because they feared causing irreversible brain damage or death. But Ugo Cerletti, an Italian psychiatrist, was undeterred. He experimented with electroconvulsive treatment using pigs at a Rome slaughterhouse. He then went on to be the first to use this treatment method on a human subject (see *A Question of Values*).

As practiced today, electroshock may be employed with severely depressed, sometimes suicidal patients, especially those who have not responded to antidepressant or other psychotropic medication (Weiner & Coffey, 1988). An electroshock treatment involves the passing of as little current as will induce a seizure in a patient for about 1/25th of a second. In previous years, the current was passed for as long as a full second. Muscle relaxants and anesthetics are administered prior to passing the shock, and oxygen may be administered during the procedure itself. Brain wave and heart activity may be monitored during the procedure. The treatments are typically given once, twice, or three times a week, usually totaling fewer than 10 treatments. Short-term memory loss is a side effect of the procedure, although this has been minimized by a procedure in which shock is only administered to one side (usually the right side) of the head. Although the total

A QUESTION OF

The First Electroshock Treatment

Today, with relatively few exceptions, society demands that people administered new or experimental medical treatments give their **informed consent** to treatment. This means that *they agree to undergo treatment after being given a full description of it, including a complete disclosure of all of its possible risks and benefits.* By contemporary legal/ethical standards, if the person for whom the treatment is intended is unable to provide informed consent to treatment, a family member or other legally authorized person has to give or refuse consent to treatment.

The story of the first electroshock administration in 1938 as described by Impastato (1960) is noteworthy on many counts, and useful as a stimulus for discussion on topics such as informed consent and decision making with respect to new and experimental treatments. The man who was to make history as the first human to be administered electroshock treatment had been admitted to a hospital speaking gibberish and was diagnosed as schizophrenic (catatonic type). He would not or could not identify him-

self, nor could anyone else identify him. In describing the procedure, Impastato (1960) noted that "adequate preparations" were made for this treatment, although it is not specified whether any anesthesia or muscle relaxants were administered. The first shock of 70 volts was delivered for 1/10th of a second. After a spasm which lasted a fraction of a second, the patient broke out into song. Cerletti believed that another treatment should be administered, this time with a higher voltage and a longer duration. Present in the room was Cerletti's staff (Accornero, Bini, Fleischer, Kalinowsky, and Longhi). Fearing that another shock administered right after the first might kill the patient, they argued that treatment should be postponed until the next day. Over their objections, Cerletti made the decision to continue. At that point, according to Impastato (1960), "the patient suddenly sat up and pontifically proclaimed, no longer in a jargon, but in clear Italian: `Non una seconda! Mortifera!'" ["Not again! It will kill me!"]

Although the patient's objection was cause for Cerletti to "think and swallow," Cerletti ordered that the treatment proceed with a higher voltage and a longer duration—an action which raises important ethical questions. For example, at what point should actual experimentation begin on a notion regarding treatment if the treatment is capable of causing death or irreversible brain damage? With reference to the case described, what rationale did Cerletti have for administering a second treatment at a higher voltage and longer duration? The patient had responded to the first treatment by beginning to speak "pontifically" and in clear, understandable language. Impastato (1960) implies that Cerletti was a courageous pioneer for conducting this research. Do you agree?

Impastato's account left unstated the fate of the patient. However, we learn from Brandon (1981) that the patient went on to receive over a dozen shock treatments over the course of two months and "was discharged completely recovered."

number of patients who receive electroshock treatment annually is not known, upwards of 100,000 Medicare claims are made for reimbursement for this procedure annually.

Meduna's idea regarding the physiological incompatibility of schizophrenia and seizure disorders was proven to be in error many years ago (Hoch, 1943; Kalinowsky & Hippius, 1969). Even Meduna himself eventually "recognized with admirable candor that the coma therapies were crudely empirical and compared them to kicking a Swiss watch" (Redlich & Freedman, 1966, p. 336). Recent reviews of the effectiveness of electroshock therapy in treating depression or other problems have yielded mixed findings (see, for example, Scott, 1989). Still, in 1990, the American Psychiatric Association officially recommended electroshock therapy for the treatment of severe depression. Additionally, some organized groups of mental patients have gone on record as being in support of electroconvulsive therapy. For example, the executive director of the 35,000-member National Depressive and Manic Depressive Association describes electroconvulsive therapy as "lifesaving" (Dime-Meenan, 1992). Given such broad-based support, use of this treatment method can be expected to increase in years to come.

BRIGHT LIGHT TREATMENT

Bright light treatment, also sometimes referred to as "phototherapy," is *therapy that entails systematic and regular exposure to intensely illuminated areas*. Sometimes recommended for patients with seasonal affective disorder or other affective disorders (such as depression), the patient sits at a comfortable distance from the source of light for an hour or two and engages in usual activities such as reading, watching television, or studying. Light is measured by an international unit of illumination called a *lux*. Normal room light at night is typically equivalent to about 500 lux. In phototherapy, the room is lit to 2,500 or more lux. Research suggests that this technique is effective as a treatment for seasonal affective disorder (James et al., 1985; Lewy et al., 1983; Wirz-Justice et al., 1986), although controversies exist with respect to exactly how the treatment should be implemented (Avery et al., 1991; Helleckson et al., 1986; Jacobsen et al., 1987) and the role of the patient's expectancy of therapeutic gain (Wehr et al., 1987). If you think that your moods may be affected by the level of light, try raising the level of illumination in the room that you stay in most. *Good lux!*

bright light treatment
the systematic and regular exposure to intense illumination for therapeutic purposes. Also referred to as *phototherapy*.

A PERSPECTIVE

In general, biologically based treatment approaches, and medication in particular, appear to have a future as bright as the lighting used to treat seasonal affective disorder. Mental problems have always carried with them more stigma than physical problems. For this reason, most people with any kind of mental or behavioral disorder would prefer to conceptualize their problem in biomedical as opposed to behavioral terms. Similarly, a pill or other physical treatment is generally preferred over a long and uncertain course of psychotherapy. An unfortunate by-product of the general public's receptivity to psychiatric medication has been a tendency to look to pills and other drugs as a means of coping with problems in living.

Another factor that continues to bode well for the future of biologically based treatment approaches is economic in nature. Ongoing psychotherapy, especially with a highly trained psychiatrist or psychologist, can be extremely costly as compared to the cost of management by means of medication. Most health insurance policies encourage policy holders having mental or behavioral problems to seek medically oriented treatment. A depressed, elderly policy holder may find that a course of treatment with electroshock therapy is fully reimbursable, while this may not be true for as little as one consultation with a nonmedical counselor. From the standpoint of the insurer, the nature and course of routine biologically oriented treatment is in many instances better known and more predictable than the nature and course of psychotherapeutic treatment.

A trend in the area of psychotherapy is increased sharing among the various schools of treatment methods shown to be of proven value in the treatment of particular disorders. There is even a movement afoot to afford psychologists the education and training that will legally entitle them to prescribe medication (Brentar & McNamara, 1991). Opponents to such a role for psychologists argue that the very nature of the profession of psychology would be radically changed for the worse were psychologists to begin to involve themselves in such biomedical enterprises (DeNelsky, 1991). Psychologists in favor of prescription privileges will not only have to battle forces from within their professional community but also formidable forces from without, including the American Medical Association which is lobbying against such efforts on economic as well as other grounds.

One therapeutic approach that we may see applied more frequently in the future is the use of highly educated mental health professionals to train community caregivers to dispense various kinds of mental-health-related services. State or privately funded community counseling programs may prove key in bettering the quality of life for us all. Consider in this context the words of Jerome Miller, president of a private organization called the National Center on Institutions and Alternatives. Referring to many of the child and adolescent looters who took part in the Los Angeles riots of 1992, and taking into account the high rate of single-parent and zero-parent homes in the inner city, Miller (1992) reflected that, "None of these kids has had someone who sat with them and talked to them for hours about their lives." This deceptively simple point about the therapeutic value of having someone with whom to talk about one's life—preferably a loving family member or a trained professional who genuinely cares—is well-taken. Having people in the community available for people to talk to is a critically important need that will not go away in the future. It is a need that, once fulfilled, will benefit us all.

On that note, we have already begun to look at adjustment from a more global and interpersonal perspective. We continue along those lines in each of the chapters of the unit to follow.

SUMMARY

WHAT IS PSYCHOTHERAPY? *Psychotherapy* (literally, "therapy of the mind or soul") may be defined as the psychological treatment of mental and behavioral disorders. *Counseling* may be defined as guidance or advice-giving. Individuals variously referred to as patients or clients bring to therapy situations an enormously diverse array of presenting problems, personal abilities, assets, resources, skills, motivation, and liabilities. Psychotherapists approach the therapeutic situation with their own framework or perspective for understanding and treating human behavior. Contexts of therapy vary from private practice consulting rooms to prison cells. Drawing conclusions about one method of psychotherapy as compared to another is most difficult given this welter of variables that must be accounted for in any comparative research.

PSYCHOANALYTIC APPROACHES Freud believed that most behavior was unconsciously motivated and many of the techniques used in psychoanalysis have as their goal making the unconscious conscious. Included among these techniques are free association, dream analysis, analysis of resistance, analysis of transference, and analysis of events in everyday life.

COGNITIVE, BEHAVIORAL, AND COGNITIVE-BEHAVIORAL APPROACHES Central emphasis in cognitive approaches to therapy is placed on modifying a client's maladaptive thought processes. However, because cognition change is so intimately intertwined with behavior change, it would also be appropriate to refer to these approaches as cognitive-behavioral. Behavioral approaches to therapy rely heavily on processes of learning to extinguish or unlearn maladaptive behavior patterns and relearn more adaptive ones. In a strictly behavioral approach, emphasis is placed on observable behavior and unobservables such as thought or emotion are deemphasized. Cognitive-behavioral approaches to treatment strike a balance between the most cognitive of the cognitive approaches and the most behavioral of the behavioral approaches.

HUMANISTIC APPROACHES Approaches to psychotherapy that are typically categorized as humanistic may take many different forms, including the client-centered approach of Carl Rogers. In that approach, a focus of interest is the denial or distortion people maintain about their senses of self. Client-centered therapy helps clients to find their "true" selves. The therapist does this by helping to foster a climate in which thera-peutic exploration can occur. The therapist demonstrates accu-rate empathic understanding, genuineness, and unconditional positive regard.

OTHER APPROACHES A number of other approaches to psychotherapeutic treatment exist. Biologically based treatment approaches include medication, biofeedback, electroshock treat-ment, and bright light treatment. For a variety of reasons, bio-logically based treatment approaches appear to be becoming increasingly popular.

Interpersonal Relations

O U T L I N E

Perhaps the most common regret people express as they near the end of life concerns insufficient time spent with loved ones—this despite the fact that interpersonal relations present some most stress-provoking demands (Holmes & Rahe, 1967). In this final unit, we will be looking at one-to-one relationships between people, as well as at selected aspects of relationships between groups of people. We will explore some general principles relevant to how we view other people and how we view ourselves. We will look at various kinds of relationships between people including those involving friendship, sexual relations, marriage, and divorce. We will look at adjustment in the workplace and in the environment in the broadest possible context. Let's begin with background about how people tend to perceive other people.

SOCIAL PERCEPTION

social perception

the process, act, or faculty of becoming aware of other people in relation to oneself.

Social perception may be defined broadly as *the process, act, or faculty of becoming aware of other people in relation to oneself*. A large and growing literature in psychology has focused on how observers look at themselves and others (Jones & Nisbett, 1971; Kihlstrom et al., 1988; Watson, 1982). Comparing oneself to someone else, anticipating another's behavior or motives, and wondering how one's own behavior might impact on someone else are some examples of social perception at work. Consider in this context what goes on in the minds of many as they watch an old Western movie. Audiences for such movies seldom had to invest much effort in figuring out who the good guys and who the bad guys were. The answer to this question was clear not from the justness of the cowboy's cause, but from the color of his hat. With few exceptions, the cowboys wearing the white hats were unswervingly allied with good and virtue. Cowboys partial to black hats tended to be partial to criminal activity. Audience members quickly learned to attribute good and benevolent motives to the actions of cowboys wearing white hats. By contrast, attributions regarding the motives of the cowboys in black hats were not very favorable at all.

Understanding how and why attributions are made is a topic that can take us far afield of old Western movies. Moreover, attribution is a social perception process of vital, real-world concern. Each day, for example, people are hurt, killed, sentenced to prison, released from custody, married or divorced on the basis, in whole or part, of other people's attributions about them. Each day, millions of dollars shift hands in stock markets and other business settings, largely on the basis of business-related attributions. After reading the section on the attribution process that follows, perhaps you can generate some additional examples of the great, everyday power attributions can have.

THE PROCESS OF ATTRIBUTION

attribution

derived from the verb to *attribute* (mentally assign), a social psychological term that refers to an inferred characteristic and/or causation.

The verb *to attribute* means *to regard* or *to mentally assign*. Such assignments frequently refer to characteristics ("John was fearful") and/or causation ("Jane acted out of anger"). The noun **attribution** refers to *an inferred characteristic and/or causation* (Jones & Nisbett, 1971). Every day, attributions are made, some of which have momentous consequences. For example, juries hear evidence as to a defendant's guilt or innocence and then impose their own attribution on this matter in the form of a verdict. A business person makes attributions about the motives of consumers before investing in a new product. The process by which people make attributions about the behvior of others as well as themselves can be understood in terms of some general, often interacting variables such as past experience, social comparison, and the apparent need people have for consistency.

PAST EXPERIENCE

Experience is a teacher. Burn your hand once on a hot oven and you'll be more careful the next time around. Stated another way, after you have burned your hand once on an oven from which smoke is wafting, you will be more likely to attribute heat to the oven door and you will therefore not touch it. In much the same way, people learn or are taught to make various kinds of attributions about things, themselves, and other people (see Figure 10–1).

SOCIAL COMPARISON

In addition to making attributions on the basis of past experience, people make attributions about themselves and others on the basis of comparisons with other people (Festinger, 1954). For example, we may think of ourselves as tall, rich, poor, cute, outgoing, and so forth. The popular media caters to people's fascination with and curiosity about other people by presenting, for example, surveys of public opinion, surveys of sexual practices, listings of people on best- and worst-dressed lists, listings of people and corporations by accumulated wealth, and rank-orderings of people based on variables such as sexiness or popularity.

Have you ever compared yourself in any way to the other students in your class? Chances are good that you probably have, just as other students may have compared themselves to you. Such social comparison was probably quite fleeting and informal. However, in the interest of learning something both about yourself and social comparison in the attribution process, try the *Self-Assessment* exercise on page 262.

THE NEED FOR CONSISTENCY

Are you a happy person? Is your best friend helpful? You may have answered each of these questions with a reflexive "yes." In doing so, you attribute consistency to the behavior of yourself and others. In reality, is such consistency there 100% of the time? Probably not. You may be a *generally* happy person, but if you are like most people, there are also times when you are not so happy. Similarly, there are occasions when even your best friend may not behave in a helpful fashion. In our perception of ourselves and others, we tend to gloss over exceptions to the rule and consequently think of ourselves and others as behaving more consistently than is the case in reality. We seem to have a need for such consistency, as it is frequently easier to think of the rule than of exceptions to it. But what happens when one is confronted with a rule *and* an exception to it? Such a situation may provoke a mental phenomenon known in psychology as *cognitive dissonance*.

FIGURE 10–1 AN "ARRESTING" ATTRIBUTION The police officer may transport this person either to jail or to a hospital depending upon the officer's attributions regarding the person's behavior. If the officer perceives the cause of the offensive behavior to be mental illness, then the man will be taken to a hospital for treatment, not jail for incarceration.

SELF-ASSESSMENT

The Social Comparison Test

Instructions: Respond "True" or "False" to each of the items as it applies to you. Next, take the test again, this time answering the questions as you believe "the average male student", and "the average female student" at your school would answer the same questions. Compare your three sets of answers. How is your perception of yourself different from your perception of the average female and male at your school? What do you think accounts for these differences?

Note: Keep in mind that this test is not a "real" psychological test in the sense that it has been satisfactorily proven to measure social comparisons. Rather, it is presented here only as a tool of self-study.

1. I think of myself as a success.
2. I have a lot of doubts about my abilities.
3. I pat myself on the back for a job well done.
4. I'm unhappy about what I see in the mirror.
5. I have a great sense of humor.
6. My life has not been very good so far.
7. I tend to be self-conscious in groups.
8. I like my speaking voice.
9. I am good at what I do.
10. I belong in a position of leadership.

COGNITIVE DISSONANCE

On occasion, each of us may think different thoughts that have competing implications for behavior. When such a situation arises, there is a natural tendency, in the interest of consistency in the way that one sees oneself, to change one of the competing or incongruent thoughts so that self-image will remain consistent. For example, consider the following two thoughts:

Thought 1. I believe in recycling recyclable materials.
Thought 2. It's too much trouble to participate in recycling programs.

These two thoughts clearly have contradictory implications for behavior. Thought 1 implies that the person will participate in recycling programs, while Thought 2 implies that the person will not participate in such programs. Thought 1 and Thought 2 can be thought of in psychological terms as being *dissonant* or inconsistent with one another and contradictory in terms of their implications for behavior. The dissonance might be resolved by a third cognition which weakens or nullifies one of the previous two. For example, the thought about one's belief in recycling might be replaced with something like, "Most people, even those who believe in recycling, do not do it, therefore I need not either."

cognitive dissonance

an unpleasant mental state owing to the simultaneous existence of two or more thoughts that have contradictory implications for behavior.

Cognitive dissonance may be defined as *a phenomenon in which two or more thoughts that have contradictory implications for behavior exist at the same time.* Cognitive dissonance arises when one or more thoughts suggest to you, "Do this," while, at the same time, one or more other thoughts suggest to you, "No, do that instead." According to Leon Festinger (1957), cognitive dissonance is an unpleasant state. The person experiencing such dissonance will act to relieve it by acquiring additional information, by eliminating one or more of the cognitions currently held, or by changing behavior.

As an example of cognitive dissonance in everyday life, Festinger (1957) considered why many smokers in the late 1950s continued to smoke even though strong advisories warned them to quit. Because the notion that smoking was hazardous to one's health was still relatively controversial in 1957, heavy smokers tended to resolve dissonant cognitions (such as "I smoke" and "Smoking kills") by refusing to believe the studies that found smoking to be harmful. Today, with much more accumulated evidence indicating that smoking is harmful, how do you think smokers resolve the same kinds of dissonant cognitions? Might self-deception still play some role?

In some contexts, such as a military situation, a critical part of basic training entails techniques to prevent or reduce dissonance. Most people are raised to believe that it is wrong to kill other people. New recruits understand that they may be compelled to kill and therefore must somehow resolve two dissonant cognitions: "It is wrong to kill" and, "I must kill." One dissonance-reduction technique employed by the military is to dehumanize the enemy; troops are trained to view foes as something other than human. For example, American aviators refer to enemy aircraft and aviators as *bogies*. Another dissonance reduction technique in the theater of war is to make killing as impersonal as possible. Consider in this context the emotional toll on a soldier of killing one person in hand-to-hand combat with a bayonet versus killing thousands of people by pressing a button in an office setting. Which do you think would exact a higher emotional toll? Why?

ERRORS IN SOCIAL PERCEPTION

Magicians and other illusionists remind us that errors in physical perception can be made quite easily. Whatever it is we think we saw or believe occurred need not necessarily mirror reality. And just as we can't always be 100% certain about the reality of what we physically perceive, so we can't always be entirely certain about our social perceptions. The attributions we make about others are subject to many sources of error. One such error has been found to be so common that it has come to be referred to as fundamental.

THE FUNDAMENTAL ATTRIBUTION ERROR

Which is more important in determining how a person will act in a given situation: factors presumed to be internal to the person (such as personality or intelligence), or factors external to the person (such as the particular circumstances of a specific situation)?

As you might guess, there is no simple answer to this question. From the vantage point of behaviorists such as B. F. Skinner, factors external to the person play a critical role. According to this view, behavior is a product of genes, past learning experiences, and current environment; there is no need to invoke unobservable constructs such as "personality" to explain behavior. However, laypeople, as well as many non-behaviorally-oriented psychologists, do not hold such an extreme view of the causes of behavior. In fact, according to attribution researchers, the causes of behavior are in many instances perceived to be either internal or external depending on various factors such as whether the people doing the perceiving are observing their own or someone else's behavior.

Jones and Nisbett (1971) found that people tended to explain their own behavior in terms of *external* or environmental rather than internal causes. By contrast, people observing other people's behavior tend to develop a different causal explanation; some *internal* attribute of the other people is presumed to have caused them to act the way that they did. This *tendency to attribute behavioral causation to internal factors for others and external factors for ourselves* has been called the **fundamental attribution error** (Ross, 1977; Harvey et al., 1981).

Success of outcome may be an important variable with regard to causal attributions (Forsyth & McMillan, 1981; Whitley & Frieze, 1985). Attributions of success or failure may differ as a function of the nature of the relationship between the observer and the person about whom the attribution is being made. For example, if one has a hostile relationship with the person about whom an attribution is being made, positive outcomes for that person may be attributed by the observer to external circumstances (as in, "That positive outcome was the result of sheer luck"). Negative outcomes may more likely be viewed by the hostile observer as being the result of internal circumstances ("The person brought this negative outcome on himself or herself").

In some instances, the consequences of the fundamental attribution error are particularly unfortunate. For example, too often in cases in which a victim is assaulted, raped, or hurt in some way, public opinion may take the form of sentiments like, "It was the person's own fault! One doesn't do such things!" In some instances, it may in fact be the case that an innocent victim's action or inaction heightened the risk of an unfortunate outcome.

fundamental attribution error

an error of social perception regarding the tendency of people to explain their own behavior in terms of external or environmental causes while explaining the behavior of others in terms of internal or personal causes.

Still, blaming veritable victims for unjust assaults adds insult to injury and diverts societal focus away from effectively addressing the external cause of the problem.

Attributions are but inferences or judgments that people make and they are not hard facts on which to base important decisions. Still, many people do act on attributions, and the result of their actions may actually influence the course of their lives in many ways. For example, you may attribute ill motives to a friend or family member and abruptly cease further communication with that person. Given that we all go through life only once and that it is probably better to go through it with as many friends, family members, and other possible sources of social support that we can possibly have, it is unfortunate that one misattribution can have such dramatic effects. Perhaps the most effective tool human beings can use to prevent misattributions and misunderstandings is effective communication (discussed in detail in the following chapter).

THE ACCURACY ERROR

Experience is a teacher but it is not a perfect teacher. Smoke wafting from an oven may well signal that an oven is hot, but it may not; shortly after turning an oven on that has not been cleaned, it is possible for some grease to ignite and cause a smoky fire within that will not make the oven exterior hot. Also, in the case of microwave ovens, wafting smoke may signal a fire within but relatively little exterior heat may be present. Of many attributions reflexively made on the basis of experience, then, some may be true and some may not be true. Even in the old Westerns, the good guys did not *always* wear white hats.[1]

Experience can also teach the wrong lessons in the first place. Some people grew up being told—wrongly—that they were not very bright, not very physically attractive, or not very something else that was desirable. The emotional scars left by such experiences still influence how such people think of themselves as adults. Some people are taught by parents or others to attribute consistent kinds of traits—usually negative traits—to all members of a particular racial or ethnic group. Through a personal negative experience with one member of a racial, ethnic, or other group, some people come to attribute negative traits to all members of that group. You will recall from Chapter 4 the powerful, sometimes highly destructive, effects that racial, ethnic, gender, and other stereotypes can have.

THE RELATIVITY ERROR

reference group
people with respect to whom some social comparison is made.

Attributions may be made on the basis of social comparisons. But whom do we tend to compare ourselves to? Most typically, one compares oneself to a **reference group**, *a group of people who are in one or more ways quite similar to oneself* (Rosenberg, 1979). It is easy to lose sight of the fact that comparisons made within one reference group may bear little or no resemblance to comparisons made within others. For example, an individual judged to possess the best body at the Mr. Flushing, New York, competition may have little in common with an individual judged to possess the best body at the Mr. Universe competition.

OTHER ATTRIBUTION ERRORS

"One sees what one expects to see in other people," serves as a summary statement for another possible type of attribution error, *the error of expectancy*. In a classic report entitled "The Warm-Cold Dimension in First Impressions of Persons," Harold Kelley demonstrated that one's expectancies regarding another person may influence impressions and evaluations of that person. In Kelley's (1950) study, college student subjects were given different descriptions of a teacher that differed only with respect to how "warm" or "cold" the person was reputed to be. After a 20-minute lecture and interaction with the teacher, the students then rated him. Although all that really differed was the description of the man prior to his lecture, students who heard the "warm" description were more apt to evaluate the man more positively than students who heard the "cold" description.

The *illusory correlation error* refers to another variety of social perception error, one based on an observer's belief that a relationship exists between two aspects of another person's behavior, appearance, or other variables (Hamilton & Gifford, 1976). The relation-

[1]A cowboy hero who comes readily to mind—at least to my mind, as it is probably before your time—is Hopalong Cassidy; "Hoppy" as his friends called him, always wore black.

ship is illusory because it is one that has not been proven to be true. Rather, it may be true only in the observer's own mind, and may be based on limited, if any, experience. Some statements reflecting the illusory correlation error would include, "People who smoke a pipe while they drive drive too slowly"; "Women who wear leather miniskirts and men who wear earrings are promiscuous"; and "Instructors who give take-home finals give more A's." From your own experience, what additional types of illusory correlations exist?

Walking in the downtown area of any large city around midday, we are likely to come across many different types of people. Different types of attributions may be made in the observer's own mind regarding various aspects of these people's backgrounds and lifestyles. As you look at each individual in Figure 10–2, what attributions come to mind?

SELF-PERCEPTION

Many principles of social perception are relevant to self-perception. Past experience, for example, clearly plays a role in how we perceive ourselves. Having experienced a certain amount of success or failure in various academic, athletic, and other ventures, we begin to develop a perception of ourselves in terms of who we are with respect to such abilities and traits. Social comparison and the need for consistency also play roles in the way that people perceive themselves.

SELF-CONCEPT

Self-concept may be defined as *the summary statement of all of one's accumulated information about oneself including one's interpretation of that information.* One view of the self-concept is that of a cognitive entity that processes incoming self-relevant information according to complex rules involving memory and other factors (Kihlstrom & Cantor, 1983; Markus, 1980). One's self-concept may make reference to an extraordinarily wide range of mental, physical, and social traits; what you do, who you are, and what you think you are "made of" are all components of your self-concept. You know yourself better than you know other people because you have access to your own internal feelings and thoughts. You may also, as Daryl Bem has argued, learn about yourself through your own behavior. According to Bem's (1972) **self-perception theory**, *inferences about one's own in-*

self concept
the summary statement of all one's accumulated information about oneself including one's interpretation of that information.

self-perception theory
a theory that holds that inferences about one's own internal states may be drawn from one's own outward behavior.

FIGURE 10–2 WHO ARE THESE PEOPLE? People routinely make inferences about the thoughts, feeling, and behavior of other people. One may cognitively try to match a newly encountered person with some category of person or set of characteristics previously encountered (Cantor & Mischel, 1977, 1979; Fiske & Taylor, 1984; Higgins & Bargh, 1987; Rosch, 1978; Schneider, 1973; Schneider & Blankmeyer, 1983; Taylor, 1981). What attributions come to mind about each of the people in this photo? Can you identify where your attributions may have originated? What sources of error may be affecting your attributions?

ternal states may be drawn from one's own outward behavior. Part of your self-concept, for example, may be an image of one who loves to listen to rock music and seldom if ever listens to classical music. Traditionally, such a behavior pattern would be thought to arise from thoughts:

THOUGHT		BEHAVIOR
"I enjoy rock music"	♦	Listens to rock music.
"I do not enjoy classical music"	♦	Does not listen to classical.

According to Bem's theory, it is possible for the arrow to go in the other direction, especially under circumstances in which we are unsure about our beliefs (Chaiken & Baldwin, 1981). Stated another way, Bem believes that people can learn about themselves and how they think from their own behavior:

THOUGHT		BEHAVIOR
"I enjoy rock music"	ℜ	Listens to rock music.
"I do not enjoy classical music"	ℜ	Does not listen to classical.

Although it may indeed be possible to learn about oneself through one's own behavior, a number of studies suggest that one's own private thoughts and feelings probably play a more critical role in the development of the self-concept (Andersen & Ross, 1984; Johnson, 1987; McGuire & McGuire, 1986).

ERRORS IN SELF-PERCEPTION AND SELF-CONCEPT

Just as the processes by which one perceives others are subject to error and distortion, so the way one perceives oneself is subject to error and distortion as well. One's self-perceptions and self-concept can be distorted or inaccurate as a result of being based on a social comparison with an inappropriate reference group. Distortions and inaccuracies in self-concept may also stem from past experience that teaches the wrong lesson. Being told by one's parents or significant others that one is ugly or worthless, for example, may lead to self-perception and self-concept problems. A stubborn need for consistency in the face of contrary information may also contribute to self-perception-related difficulties. For example, a belief that one is not worthy of success or for some reason should not attain success may operate to keep one from striving for it (Horner, 1973, 1974). In the past, females more than males may have suffered undue anxiety about succeeding in intellectual, business, and even leisure pursuits because success was equated with an aggressive—and therefore masculine—self (Horner, 1973).

Illusory correlation, sometimes combined with irrational beliefs, can play a role in developing and maintaining a distorted or inaccurate self-perception or self-concept. People who suffer from eating disorders, for example, have been found as a group to harbor distorted self-concepts; in many instances, they perceive themselves as heavier than they are in reality (Bruch, 1962; Cash & Brown, 1987; Garner et al., 1976; Hsu & Sobkiewicz, 1991; Steinhausen & Vollrath, 1992, 1993; Slade, 1985). In order to gauge the accuracy of one's perception of one's own body, as well as the magnitude of body image distortion (if any), a number of different techniques have been used (Garner & Garfinkel, 1981; Gleghorn et al., 1987; Lindholm & Wilson, 1988; Ruff & Barrios, 1986). One innovative technique developed and described by J. Kevin Thompson and his associates (Penner et al., 1991; Thompson, 1990; Thompson & Spana, 1988; Thompson & Thompson, 1986) is called the adjustable light beam apparatus. Using four adjustable beams of light, the width of one's waist, hips, cheeks, and thighs are estimated (see Figure 10–3). By comparing the estimates to the actual measurements, a measure of body image distortion is obtained.

Another source of error when it comes to one's self-concept may be called the *inappropriate reference group error*. Using an inappropriate reference group may lead to disillusionment and unfulfilled expectations regardless of whether the reference group is too "high above" or too "far below" oneself on some critical variable (Marsh & Parker, 1984). For example, it would be appropriate for a member of a class of gifted children to use other children in the class as a reference group rather than children in regular classes or special

FIGURE 10–3 AN OBJECTIVE MEASURE OF SELF-PERCEPTION DISTORTION A number of studies indicate that people with eating disorders also have distorted self-perceptions. Through the use of a device that projects beams of light, a measure of the accuracy of one's physical self-image can be obtained.

education classes. Using children in the regular classes or special education classes as a reference group might lead to a false sense of self-confidence and an unwarranted sense of self-esteem.

SELF-ESTEEM

Self-esteem refers to *one's general estimate of one's value or worth.* Self-concept, self-perceptions, and self-esteem are to some extent all interrelated; one may influence the other (Rogers, 1981; Tesser & Campbell, 1983). Self-esteem and general feelings of self-worth may vary as a function of time, context, role, and new information processed. For example, you may walk into a job interview thinking thoughts like, "There is nobody more qualified for this job than me!" As you take your seat in the reception area, your self-esteem is as high as the smile on your face is wide. However, as you wait to be interviewed and strike up a conversation with the other applicants, you discover that there are other people who are more qualified for the position than you. Your broad smile fades along with your confidence that you are without peer in terms of qualifications for the job. Indeed, your self-esteem might be negatively impacted by meeting highly qualified competitors but boosted by meeting highly unqualified ones (Morse & Gergen, 1970). A similar interplay of social comparison and self-esteem may have been operative in the thinking of the third party candidate during the 1992 presidential campaign. Speculation on that point is presented in *In the News.*

Different roles may be of differential value in contributing to one's overall self-esteem (Burke, 1980; Campbell & Tesser, 1985; Wells & Markwell, 1976). For example, one person's role as "student" may contribute more, as well as more positively, to that person's overall self-esteem than another role of that same individual as "delivery person."

The impact of one's self-esteem on one's general adjustment and overall quality of life cannot be minimized. How people perceive, process, and react to self-relevant feedback and information may depend to some extent on self-esteem (Jones, 1973). For example, if self-esteem is low, one may selectively focus on others' perceptions that are consistent with that negative image, thus acting to keep the self-concept low. A very positive self-concept may lead to high self-esteem and a tendency to selectively focus on others' perceptions that validate this generally positive self-image.

Research has suggested that individual differences in self-esteem may affect behavior in a wide variety of ways including competition, attraction, achievement-oriented behavior, and helping behavior (Wells & Markwell, 1976; Wylie, 1974, 1979). People with low self-esteem are less likely to join groups or to take part in group activities (Jones et al., 1981), and they are especially vulnerable to rejection by others (Rosenberg, 1985). Low self-esteem may also impact negatively on the values one holds (Rokeach, 1968) and on one's ability to genuinely love, like, or accept other people (Baron, 1974; Wylie, 1979).

self-esteem
one's general estimate of one's value or worth.

Social Comparison and the 1992 Presidential Campaign

After musing about becoming a candidate for the office of president of the United States on a nationally televised talk show (*Larry King Live* on Cable News Network), a Texas billionaire businessman named Ross Perot proceeded, to the surprise of just about everyone, including his wife and family, to actually to enter the race—and in relatively short order become a very serious contender. A new and independent political party was hastily organized and enough petitions were quickly gathered to place Perot's name on ballots in all 50 states. By the time the Democrats convened their nominating convention in July 1992, Perot's popularity in the nation was estimated to be in the 30% range—ratings that favorably compared to the incumbent president, George Bush, and the Democratic challenger, Bill Clinton. The story of the day was, "What will happen if no candidate obtains a majority of votes and the election is thrown into the House of Representatives to decide?" Ross Perot's meteoric rise from relative obscurity on the national political scene was truly impressive. But with Perot at the height of his popularity, and the Democrats nominating Bill Clinton at their convention, the story took a dramatic turn. Ross Perot announced that he was dropping out of the race.

Perot's stated reason for withdrawing was that there was no longer a need for his candidacy because the two major political parties had begun to address the political issues that he felt needed to be addressed. Few political analysts accepted Perot's explanation because the two major party candidates were not really addressing the issues any more than they had been when Perot entered the race. Widespread speculation began about the "real" reason Perot dropped out. Some believed that Perot did not like the scrutiny he had been subjected to by the media and by his opponents. Others believed that money was a major factor in Perot's decision. Although a billionaire, Perot did not believe it would be a smart business decision to fund his own campaign to the tune of millions of dollars if he was not reasonably certain that he could win the presidency.

To existing speculation about why Perot pulled out of the race, let's add one that stems from what we know about social comparison theory. Perhaps Perot had soberly compared his own qualifications and leadership ability to that of the two major-party candidates—and as a result seriously questioned whether he belonged in the race. Certainly the timing of Perot's withdrawal from the race would

support such a hypothesis. Perot withdrew at a time when the nationally televised hooplah of the Democratic party's nominating convention was at its peak. The withdrawal speech was given on the morning of the same day that the Democratic convention would climactically end, with Bill Clinton's acceptance of his party's nomination for president.

The postscript to the story is that Perot's decision to withdraw outraged millions of volunteers and paid staffers who had worked so diligently to get his name on the ballot in every state. Headlines and news commentators used words like *quitter* to describe Perot. But within months, Perot was back in the race. According to Perot, he decided to reenter the race due to strong pressure from volunteers across the country for him to do so. Critics, however, saw his reentry as simply a face-saving device. Perot did not want to be branded as a quitter for the rest of his life. It is also the case that Perot seemed to enjoy the limelight—so much that he spent millions of dollars of his own funds for television time. Whether he will seek the limelight again probably depends on many factors, ranging from the mood of the people to his personal self-confidence level.

These relationships are correlational and do not necessarily imply cause-and-effect. It may be, for example, that low self-esteem causes an aversion to joining groups for some people. In other cases, an aversion to joining groups may cause low self-esteem.

SELF-PRESENTATION

self-presentation

the totality of the way one exhibits oneself to others.

Self-presentation may be defined as *the totality of the way one exhibits oneself to others.* Here, *totality* refers not only to external behavior but also to physical characteristics, manner of dress, accessories, associates in one's company, and other such variables. We all try to present ourselves in a manner designed to convey to other people only the information we wish to share. Referring to this phenomenon as "impression management," Goffman (1959, p. 3) observed that an individual may want observers "to think highly of him, or to think that he thinks highly of them, or perceive how in fact he feels towards them, or to obtain no clear-cut impression; he may wish to ensure sufficient harmony so that the interaction can be sustained, or to defraud, get rid of, confuse, mislead, antagonize, or insult them." **Impression management** may be defined as *the conscious control of one's expressive behavior so as to influence others' perceptions*. It frequently entails the selective exposure and suppression of information consistent with "a certain definition of ourselves that we attempt to maintain" (Braginsky et al., 1969, p. 51).

impression management
the conscious control of one's expressive behavior so as to influence others' perceptions.

PHYSICAL APPEARANCE AND DRESS

A key part of self-presentation in any social environment is physical appearance. Clothing, hairstyle, makeup, tattoos, and other adornments may all send messages to others about who we are and what we have done or are capable of doing (Davis, 1985). A best-selling book advised us that there are ways to "dress for success"; presumably, there are ways that one could deliberately or inadvertently dress for failure as well. According to psychoanalyst Ernest Dichter (1985), clothing and other adornments also affect how we feel about ourselves. Wearing an old dress can make one feel old, while donning a new dress can make one feel young, renewed, and rejuvenated. As Dichter put it, "Fashion is one of the oldest fountains of youth" (p. 30). Trying on new clothing, a new hairstyle, or some other new adornment is also exciting for the sense of discovery it provides. For example, simply trying on a biker-style leather jacket may conjure up mental images of one in a biker-type role. By the way, Dichter (1985) believes that wearing leather is associated with sex because leather is another skin; from a psychoanalytic perspective, wearing leather may communicate an unconscious willingness to be naked (p. 37). Your (conscious) reaction to such speculation?

How one appears and what one wears has much to do with the culture one is from (see *Cultural Close-Up* on page 270). During the 1980s, for example, the president of the former Soviet Union, Mikhail S. Gorbachev, attended many black tie affairs sporting a dark business suit. As the leader of the Communist party, Gorbachev had staunchly refused to wear a tuxedo, a type of clothing that communists have always identified with capitalism. However, after Gorbachev was ousted from power in December 1991, his views about tuxedos changed. In May 1992, he accepted an award in New York wearing a tuxedo. The event was noted in a Moscow newspaper as communicating that Gorbachev had been both externally and internally converted to the capitalist way (Schmemann, 1992).

GROUP PROCESSES AND BEHAVIOR

In addition to a personal identity, people develop various group identities as well. As you read, think about your own group identities and how the various social processes described may apply to you personally. *+ THIS AFFECTS YOUR ADJUSTMENT.*

GROUP IDENTITY

A sense of who one is begins to solidify during adolescence. Elements of this sense of personal identity (Erikson, 1968) include a consistency of self-image, a recognized role in society, and a commitment to various ideals. Paralleling personal identity is a sense of **group identity**, or *a sense of close affiliation with other people on the basis of a common variable such as interests, abilities, disabilities, or demographic characteristics*. One's identity as a family member may be among one's earliest group identities. From then onward, people come to see themselves as members of other groups, including groups defined by nationality, religion, or other characteristics. If you have recently joined some student group, you may already have come to appreciate some of the benefits of group membership. Among the benefits of group membership is the opportunity to mingle with people who are experiencing many of the same trials, tribulations, and joys as you are. Perhaps through a pub-

group identity
a sense of close affiliation with other people on the basis of a common variable such as interests, abilities, disabilities, or demographic characteristics.

Cultural
C L O S E - U P

Clothing, Adornments, and Culture

Clothing, adornments, and even the body scars one exhibits or tries to hide all send messages to other people. The contemporary tatoo may have had its origins in the blood stains ancient warriors proudly displayed when they returned from a war or a hunt (Hurlock, 1929). Members of traditional societies frequently molded clothing or adornments from the body parts of the living things they had slain (Spencer, 1892). Wearing a bear's head, a necklace made of some animal's teeth, or the pelt of some animal served many different personal and interpersonal purposes. At a personal level, such adornments might serve as personal mementos of battles fought and won. At an interpersonal level, such adornments were designed to raise one's social status and the esteem with which one was viewed by others. Certainly in climates in which clothing was not necessary to keep warm, it is probably as Thomas Carlyle (1838/1967) speculated, that tatooing and body painting came before clothing. Had a hierarchy of human needs for ancient people ever been developed, Carlyle would have ranked the need for adornment as very basic, right after the need for food and water. As Carlyle put it, "The first spiritual want of a barbarous man is decoration."

In nonliterate societies, the naked body could be adorned or in some way modified for a number of different reasons. According to sociologist Ruth Rubenstein (1985), principal factors in such adornment include group membership, social organization, and indication of social status:

1. *Group membership*
   The Chinook Indians of North America sought to distinguish their offspring by keeping babies' heads pressed against two boards for the first 12 months of life. Because a newborn infant's head has some flexibility, the practice led to a tribe of people that on average had longer and flatter heads than any other group of people (Brain, 1979).
2. *Social organization*
   Different types of body modifications and adornments may be suited to different members of the group, such as adults and children.
3. *Gender distinction*
   Different types of body modifications and adornments are used to introduce children into gender-specific roles.
4. *Rules of social conduct*
   An adornment or modification of the ears or lips, for example, may be symbolic of, and have its origins in what the culture deems to be appropriate behavior regarding listening and speaking.
5. *Indication of social status*
   The chief, elders, and warriors of a tribe may all sport role-specific adornments or body modifications that win respect, admiration, and esteem from fellow tribespeople.
6. *Control of sexual activity*
   Various devices and surgical procedures ranging from sheaths around the penis for males to surgical closing of the vulva in females have been employed for the purpose of regulating sexual activity.
7. *Enhancement of role performance*
   People have traditionally psyched themselves up for events ranging from war to lovemaking by wearing certain clothing or adornments. Sometimes body painting serves a practical purpose as well, as in the case of camouflage.
8. *Enhancement of personal security*
   Clothing and other adornments may thought to be endowed with supernatural properties that will in some way help one to cope or to achieve some end. Rubenstein (1985) notes that after a battle, a warrior of the Jibaro tribe of South America paints his body black in the belief that this will ward off the souls of the slain enemy.

As you read about these traditional uses of clothing, body modification, and adornments, what modern day parallels to such behavior can you identify?

lication of that student group, you derive another benefit of group membership: news and information that is relevant to your particular interests and needs. Group membership also affords feelings of "belonging" and "community."

Worldwide, there are tens of thousands of various organized groups—legal (such as an automobile club, political party, or civic organization), as well as illegal (such as a street gang, organized crime family, or hate group). Some group memberships branch into subgroup memberships. An American Psychological Association member may seek membership in any of that association's dozens of divisions, such as its division of Media Psychology or its division of Exercise and Sports Psychology.

GROUP MEMBERSHIP AND PERSONAL VALUES

Make a list of five groups to which you belong. Now, rank order this listing in terms of which group memberships are most important to you. As you look at your list, ask yourself why you joined these particular organizations. Also, why did you rank order your list as you did?

Most of us enjoy meeting and affiliating with people with whom we share interests, attitudes, beliefs, problems, objectives, or whatever. Perhaps some of the more common kinds of group membership include groups based on political or social beliefs, groups based on the practice of a particular sport or hobby, groups based on one's employment or former employment, and groups based on service or charity to the community. In addition there are fan clubs, video clubs, book clubs, golf clubs (no pun intended), automobile clubs, travel clubs—the list goes on and on. And then there are those offbeat kinds of groups established for people who share a particular physical attribute (Bald-Headed Men of America), a particular psychological attribute (The Procrastinators' Club of America), a combined vocation and avocation (the Diving Dentists Society), the first name Mike, (Mikes of America), or the whole name Jim Smith (the Jim Smith Society).

Regardless of whether we belong to a group that is offbeat or mainstream, our membership in that group says something to ourselves, as well as to other people, about who we are. In that context, take another look at your rank-ordering of your group memberships. What do your group memberships say about who you are?

CONFORMITY

Conformity literally means *similarity in form and character.* When psychologists speak of conformity, they make reference to *similarities in behavior, thinking, outward appearance, or other such factors between two or more people.* Interestingly, conformity can carry with it both connotations of power (as in the case of precision military drills by elite troops) and connotations of powerlessness (as in the case of masses of commuters being crowded into a New York City subway car). Most conformity derives from free choice, although there are situations in which conformity may be imposed upon people as in the case of prison garb and routine.

A series of classic experiments by Solomon Asch (1951) illustrated just how uncomfortable people can be when they do not conform to other people in public. Asch studied conformity by means of an experiment presented to the subjects as having to do with visual perception. The subjects' task was to look at a line and then judge which of several other lines was equal in length. For example, look at the line labeled 1:

(1) _____

Which of the following is the same length as Line 1:

(a) _____

(b) _____

(c) _____

The correct answer is *b,* and you probably wish all of your examination questions had the same level of difficulty as this! But now imagine that you were a subject in Asch's experiment. You are seated in a room with half a dozen or so other people. The experiment begins, and in each of the few such perceptual problems everyone in the room agrees as

conformity
similarity in form and character.

to the length of the stimulus line and the comparison line. Just as you are beginning to think that you are involved in a particularly boring psychology experiment, something strange begins to happen. All of a sudden, your opinion as to the correct response for some of the problems differs from that of the rest of the group! For example, if line 1 was presented, all of the other subjects might respond that the correct answer is *a*. While remaining personally convinced that the correct answer is *b*, you might question your own judgment and wonder if *a* was indeed the correct response.

In the Asch study, the six to eight people who would be seated in the room with you were not really fellow subjects but confederates of the experimenter. At prearranged times, usually in 12 of the 18 problems presented, all members of the group would purposely choose the same wrong response. What would you do under such conditions?

Asch found that 76% of the subjects in his study conformed to the obviously wrong choice of the group at least once; only 24% of the subjects never conformed to the misjudgment of the group. The effect of the group's influence on the individual in this research as well as in a subsequent study (Tanford & Penrod, 1984) was therefore interpreted as being quite strong. People appeared to put more stock in other people's judgment than in their own perceptions! In a control condition of the experiment, in which all the group members were indeed subjects and there were no confederates, no more than 5% of the subjects ever gave the wrong response.

Further research by Asch (1957) reopened the question of whether people really did place more stock in other people's judgment than in their own. When Asch had subjects write down their choice of line in private, conformity to the group of confederates decreased dramatically. The study drew attention to the differences between public compliance and private acceptance. People may conform in public to some widely accepted pattern of behavior or norm, but not accept it in private.

Generalizing from Asch's findings to your own life and your own adjustment, are there any ways that you conform to some norm but privately question or reject such conformity? How might conformity serve the needs of society? How might nonconformity serve the needs of society?

LEADERSHIP

Whether in whole societies, small communities, associations, or other kinds of groups of people, one person or group of people typically goes to the fore to lead. The duties of a leader will of course vary as a function of the objectives of the particular group, but most leaders tend to have two duties in common: (1) to move the group towards achieving its objectives, and (2) to minimize interpersonal conflict between the individual group members. Many laypeople and social scientists alike have wondered about what personality characteristics leaders have in common. Interestingly, research into this matter suggests that no one characteristic or group of characteristics is common to all kinds of leaders; different situations will provide fertile conditions for different types of leaders to go to the fore (Bass, 1981; Geier, 1969). For example, because many American presidents can be described as charismatic, we may be inclined to regard charisma as an attribute common to them all. However, there have been times in history during which other characteristics, perhaps even a lack of charisma, were viewed as most desirable in an American president. Consider in this context an era in this country when the vice president, Spiro Agnew, and soon thereafter the president, Richard Nixon, both resigned from office in disgrace. With the White House wracked by scandal, the office of the president virtually demanded someone whose honesty and trustworthiness was above reproach. In such a climate, a man whose integrity was unquestionable, Gerald Ford, ascended to the presidency. Although Ford was widely viewed as honest and trustworthy, few would describe him as charismatic.

In experimental work in the area of leadership it has also been found that while the views of the leader affect the individual group members, the views of individual group members also affect the behavior of the group leader (Hollander, 1978; Price & Garland, 1981; Scandura & Graen, 1984; Sims & Manz, 1984). Thus, leaders, and in particular democratic leaders in contrast to dictatorial ones, are responsive to the needs and demands of those they lead.

Different combinations of circumstances and conditions may be conducive to different types of leaders rising to power. Unfortunately, there is never any guarantee that the person or people rising to power will use authority benevolently. History is replete with examples of political leaders who have used their power to inflict death and misery on their own people rather than to promote general well-being and the common good. In the recent past, for example, we have witnessed the slaughter of people within Iraq by that country's dictator, Saddam Hussein. Ayatollah Khomeini of Iran and Muammar al-Qaddafi of Libya have participated in state-sponsored terrorist activities that have resulted in innocent civilians being taken hostage and killed. Conditions in post-World War I Germany were ripe for the rise of hate mongers such as Adolf Hitler and his Nazi party. With inflation out of control and social confusion prevailing throughout much of that country, the Nazi message of scapegoating and hate provided a quick and easy—though thoroughly inaccurate—explanation for why conditions in Germany were so poor (Cantril, 1941).

In the wake of the Nazi holocaust, a horrified international community took the unprecedented step of instituting trials for war crimes. How and why could the Nazi politicians, civil servants, soldiers, and citizens obey their government orders to commit such immoral acts? Although extensive analyses of the testimony given at the war crimes trials have been made (see, for example, Arendt, 1963), perhaps the most common defense on the part of the defendants can be paraphrased, "I was just following orders." Indeed, leaders—whether elected or dictators—make rules and issue orders that others must follow, usually under the threat of punishment or some other retribution for disobedience. Perhaps this is as it should be, for as Milgram (1963, p. 371) acknowledged, "Some system of authority is a requirement of all communal living." But what if the leader is mentally ill, malevolent, or impaired in some way? What if obedience to authority results in innocent people being hurt? What if people in authority make rules or issue orders that are unjust or immoral? Dare we decide for ourselves what rules are moral, immoral, or unjust? Dare we *not* decide for ourselves what rules are moral, immoral, or unjust?

OBEDIENCE

Social psychologist Stanley Milgram (1933–1984) conducted a classic but controversial research program on **obedience**, or *the behavior of dutifully carrying out the orders or commands of another.* The studies (Milgram, 1961, 1963, 1965, 1974) employed subjects from many different walks of life and the findings were in part replicated by other researchers in Jordan, West Germany, and Australia (Baron, 1987). In general, such studies suggest that adults (Kilham & Mann, 1974) and children (Shanab & Yahya, 1977) are quite willing to comply to perceived authority, even when the perceived authority does not have the power to punish disobedience.

In one study Milgram (1963) conducted at Yale University, the subjects were 40 males who came from a wide range of educational backgrounds. They had been recruited either by a newspaper ad or by direct mail and had been promised payment of $4.50 (modest even by 1960s standards) for participation in what was billed as a study on learning and memory. Shortly after his arrival at the laboratory, the subject was introduced to a kindly man in his late 40s, "Mr. Wallace," who was represented to be a fellow subject. In reality, Mr. Wallace was a confederate of the experimenter. The subject and Mr. Wallace were given the cover story that the study was an investigation of the effect of punishment on learning. By a drawing of pieces of paper from a hat, one of the subjects would assume the role of Teacher (and punishment administrator), and the other would assume the role of Learner. Actually, *Teacher* was written on both pieces of paper, and Mr. Wallace always claimed to have drawn the paper that said *Learner.* The study was in reality concerned with obedience to authority, and the variable of interest was the degree of the subject's compliance to the experimenter's order. The $4.50 was paid to subjects upon arrival, and subjects were told that this payment was theirs regardless of their performance (Milgram, 1965)—this to help rule out money as a reason for any subjects' compliance to the experimenter's orders.

According to the cover story, Mr. Wallace's task as Learner was to commit to memory a list of word pairs. When Teacher gave him a stimulus word (say, *sit*), Mr. Wallace was to respond with the matched word (say, *chair*) from the list of word pairs he had memorized.

obedience

the behavior of dutifully carrying out the orders or commands of another.

If Mr. Wallace responded incorrectly or failed to respond to a stimulus word, Teacher was to punish Mr. Wallace by administering an electric shock which Mr. Wallace received through a shockplate in the armrest of what looked like an electric chair. In reality, no shocks were ever administered to Mr. Wallace, although a post-experiment interview of subjects indicated that they did indeed believe that shocks had been administered.

As Mr. Wallace was strapped into the electric chair, the experimenter noted that the straps were necessary to prevent excessive movement while Learner was being shocked. Applying electrode paste to Mr. Wallace's wrist, the experimenter explained that this was necessary "to avoid blisters and burns." The experimenter also advised the participants that, "Although the shocks can be extremely painful, they cause no permanent damage." Teacher was then led to a room around the corner from the strapped-in Mr. Wallace where he was given further instructions in the experimental procedure and an introduction to the use of the shock generator instrument panel. The subject would read the stimulus words into an intercom. Mr. Wallace's responses would register on a screen atop the shock generator. The instrument panel of this generator consisted of 30 levers, each labeled in increasing increments from 15 to 450 volts (see Figure 10–4). To better convince the subject that he would be administering real shocks, the experimenter attached a lead to the wrist of the subject and administered a real sample shock of 45 volts to him by depressing the lever labeled *45 Volts* on the shock generator. Subjects were instructed to shock Learner (Mr. Wallace) for each wrong response beginning at the 15-volt level and to move one level higher in shock upon every wrong answer. The absence of a response from Learner was to be treated as an incorrect response. In order to remind the subjects of the voltage that they were administering, the subjects announced the number of volts being administered before depressing the lever.

At two programmed intervals in this experiment, the subject received feedback from Mr. Wallace. After the 300-volt shock was administered, Mr. Wallace was heard to pound on the wall. Subjects typically looked to the experimenter for guidance as to what to do at that point. Using a series of four "prods," the experimenter encouraged the subject to continue administering shocks as required by the experiment. The four standardized prods used by the experimenter, increasingly stronger in wording, were as follows: (1) "Please

FIGURE 10–4 STUDYING OBEDIENCE IN THE LABORATORY On the left is the "shock generator" instrument panel used in Stanley Milgram's classic studies of obedience. It contained numerical designations that ranged from 15 to 450 volts with corresponding verbal designations that read: Slight Shock, Moderate Shock, Strong Shock, Very Strong Shock, Intense Shock, Extreme Intensity Shock, and Danger: Severe Shock. The two switches after Danger: Severe Shock were marked only XXX. Each time the subject depressed a shock lever switch, a bright red light on the panel flashed, an electric buzzing sounded, a blue light labeled *voltage energizer* flashed, and a dial on the "voltage meter" would swing to the right. Post-experiment interviews confirmed that no subject ever suspected that the apparatus was not genuine. On the right, the *Learner* in the experiment, a confederate of the experimenter who was referred to as Mr. Wallace, is strapped into a chair in preparation for the beginning of the study. Actually, Mr. Wallace was a 47-year-old accountant "of Irish-American stock, whom most observers found mild-mannered and likable" (Milgram, 1963). The man with the gray labcoat to the right is the experimenter—who when not acting in this role for Milgram was actually a 31-year-old high school biology teacher. The man on the left assisting in the preparation of Mr. Wallace is one of the subjects who served as a *Teacher* in the study. Copyright 1965 by Stanley Milgram. From the film, *Obedience*, distributed by The Pennsylvania State University Audio Visual Services.

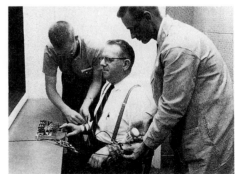

continue" (2) "The experiment requires that you continue"; (3) "It is absolutely essential that you continue"; and (4) "You have no other choice, you *must* go on."

If Teacher proceeded beyond 300 volts, Mr. Wallace did not respond with an answer to the next item but merely pounded on the wall again. After 315 volts, there was no further pounding on the wall, and no further response at all from Mr. Wallace. Given this scenario, how many of the 40 subjects in this experiment would you estimate went all the way to the last lever on the board?

The answer to the question may surprise you; it surprised Milgram. The most extreme shock possible was delivered to Learner by 65% of the subjects (26 of the 40 participants), this when no punishment or penalty of any kind would ensue from disobedience. Another finding surprising to Milgram was the great deal of emotional stress that many subjects experienced while complying with the experimenter's commands. Observed signs of nervous tension included sweating, trembling, stuttering, groaning, lip-biting, nervous laughter, nervous smiling, even uncontrollable seizures. Many of the subjects were clearly uncomfortable with what they were being told to do. Yet neither this extreme discomfort, nor the widespread belief on the part of the subjects that they were administering painful shocks kept them from complying with the experimenter. Why?

FACTORS AFFECTING DESTRUCTIVE OBEDIENCE

In an effort to learn more about the phenomenon of what Milgram called **destructive obedience** (that is, *one person's obedience to another person's orders to harm a third party*), he varied the experiment described above in a number of ways. In one variation, there was much more feedback from Mr. Wallace and it came much earlier on. For example, while being strapped into the electric chair, the subject might overhear Mr. Wallace make mention of his heart condition. Later, Mr. Wallace would beg to be released complaining of his heart bothering him. Despite such circumstances, most subjects complied with the experimenter's urgings to continue the experiment and proceeded to deliver shocks all the way through to the 30th and final shock level.

Perhaps it was the prestige of the Yale University laboratory that was responsible for the findings. After all, what could go wrong if the study was being conducted under the auspices of such a respected institution? To achieve insight into whether the institution might be influencing the findings, Milgram moved the study to a commercial building in the downtown area of the nearby industrial town of Bridgeport, Connecticut. The study was conducted under the auspices of the fictional "Research Associates of Bridgeport" in a three-room office suite that was, according to Milgram, "marginally respectable in appearance." The level of obedience found in the Bridgeport study was less, although not significantly less than that found at Yale; almost half the subjects obeyed the experimenter and proceeded all the way to the 30th shock level. Milgram believed that subjects probably considered one laboratory to be as competent as the next so long as both laboratories met subjects' private criteria for categorization as a bona fide scientific laboratory.

What conditions would militate against destructive obedience? Could Mr. Wallace say or do anything that would stop all subjects from administering shocks? These are questions that Milgram explored in a number of different variations of the experiment. One factor that was found to reduce subject compliance significantly was the opportunity for the subject to view noncompliant models while waiting his turn to be Teacher; watching another subject (actually a confederate of the experimenter) reject the experimenter's commands, gave subjects the confidence to behave in like fashion. The physical closeness of the subject (1) to the experimenter, and (2) to Learner both affected compliance. Obedience to the experimenter declined as greater physical distance was placed between the experimenter and the subject. For example, obedience declined sharply if instead of communicating face-to-face with the subject, the experimenter issued orders over the telephone. In fact, in this condition, some subjects attempted to deceive the experimenter by telling him that they were following directions when in reality they were delivering a lesser level of shock than they reported. Compliance to the experimenter's commands declined even more when the experimenter was totally absent. In that experimental condition, all instructions were given to the subject by means of notes left by the experimenter. Obedience to the experimenter also declined with less physical distance between the subject and

destructive obedience
one person's compliance with the order of another person to harm some third party or parties.

Learner; that is, the closer the physical distance between the subject and Learner, the less the obedience (see Figure 10–5).

After testing nearly 1,000 subjects in different variations of this experiment, Milgram (1965) was neither pleased with what he learned, nor very optimistic about the human condition. He wrote:

> The results, as seen and felt in the laboratory, are to this author disturbing. They raise the possibility that human nature, or—more specifically—the kind of character produced in American democratic society, cannot be counted on to insulate its citizens from brutality and inhumane treatment at the direction of malevolent authority. A substantial proportion of people do what they are told to do, irrespective of the content of the act and without limitations of conscience, so long as they perceive that the command comes from a legitimate authority. If in this study an anonymous experimenter could successfully command adults to subdue a fifty-year-old man, and force on him painful electric shocks against his protests, one can only wonder what government, with its vastly greater authority and prestige, can command of its subjects.

Today, many praise Stanley Milgram's pioneering contribution to our knowledge of humankind. In one obituary of Milgram, this social psychologist was aptly likened to an artist who preferred to take the candid and revealing snapshot of people—an image that is not necessarily pleasing: "Is there any picture of our nature that people have been as eager to reject as the one depicted in those experiments? What artist has done better at making us see who we really are? Which artist ought we miss more?" (Sabini, 1986, p. 1379).

Despite the reverence with which many psychologists continue to view Milgram after his untimely death, Milgram was quickly embroiled in controversy soon after publishing his findings. Some questioned whether what was learned justified the extreme distress some of the subjects experienced. After reading *A Question of Values* on page 278, make your own decision about whether the costs involved in these studies did or did not outweigh the benefit in terms of knowledge gained.

CONFLICT

Most subjects in the Milgram obedience studies found that the experiment they participated in created a conflict in their own minds, a conflict between the opposing interests of the experimenter (helping him to gain scientific knowledge) and the Learner (keeping him from being subjected to harm). **Conflict** in this sense refers to *the simultaneous existence of two mutually exclusive wishes, impulses, or tendencies.* Beyond its use to describe an

FIGURE 10–5 OBEDIENCE AND PROXIMITY This graph illustrates how conditions of increasing proximity between a subject (*Teacher*) and the victim (*Learner*) can decrease destructive obedience—in this case, the average maximum shock subjects inflicted on Learner Mr. Wallace. In the Remote Feedback condition, Mr. Wallace was not seen or heard from by the subject except for pounding on the wall at 300 volts and again at 315 volts. After 315 volts he was no longer heard from at all. The Voice Feedback condition was the same as the Remote Feedback condition except that Mr. Wallace could be heard grunting in response to being shocked at 75 volts. He then made various verbal complaints and demands (such as "I can't stand the pain!" and "Let me out!") as the shock levels grew higher. The third condition, Proximity, was similar to the second except that Mr. Wallace was in the same room with *Teacher* (subject), only 1-1/2 feet from him. The Touch Proximity condition was identical to the third condition, except that Mr. Wallace received a shock only when his hand rested on the shockplate. In this condition, Mr. Wallace not only complained at 150 volts, but also refused to let his hand touch the shockplate. The experimenter ordered the subject to press Mr. Wallace's hand on the plate for every shock thereafter. The percentage of subjects in each condition who were totally obedient to the experimenter and went all the way to level 30 of the shock generator was as follows: Remote = 66% obedience, Voice Feedback = 62.5% obedience, Proximity= 40% obedience, and Touch Proximity = 30% obedience.

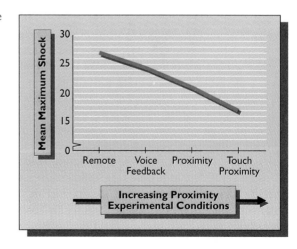

intrapsychic (*in-the-mind*) state, the term *conflict* is also used to describe an interpersonal state in which two or more people (or entities such as nations, organizations, or corporations) disagree, are opposed to one another, or are engaged in mutually aggressive behavior. Differences between people in terms of their values, desires, beliefs, and goals are the raw materials of interpersonal conflict.

Conflict may find behavioral expression in many forms such as verbal exchanges, lack of verbal exchanges ("silent treatment"), physical aggression (see Figure 10–6), and lawsuits. For example, in the business world, a conflict situation which concerns the values of two corporate workers regarding the desirability of having sexual relations may result in the filing of a claim of sexual harassment. In a more global business-related conflict, one organization may attempt to execute what is called a hostile takeover of the other.

Two basic strategies for dealing with interpersonal conflict are: (1) avoiding it and (2) confronting it. Focusing our discussion on the interpersonal variety of conflict that people face every day, let's take a closer look at each of these strategies.

AVOIDING CONFLICT

Many popular books that offer advice for dealing with interpersonal conflict caution against or totally rule out avoidance as a viable strategy. In many of these books, particularly those dealing with management techniques in the workplace, conflict is viewed as a great "opportunity" that will ultimately benefit the parties involved if handled properly. The assumption here is that conflict can be a learning experience for the parties involved, as it encourages the brainstorming of creative solutions. Although this may be true in some special instances, and although it is indeed possible for conflict to create learning opportunities, less optimistic outcomes of conflict must also be considered.

When weighing the merits of various responses to conflict, it is important to consider that interpersonal conflict, whether in business or other situations, typically creates stress, tension, anger, discomfort, and other unpleasant states and feelings in all the parties involved. The magnitude of these negative states and feelings varies, as do behavioral responses to them. Every day, people suffer physically and/or emotionally as a result of interpersonal conflict. In extreme cases, family members, neighbors, acquaintances, fellow workers, and others are even murdered as a result of such conflict. For this reason, avoidance of conflict can sometimes be a viable coping option. For women living under the pain or threat of physical abuse from their husbands, for example, there is something to be said for taking a time-out from the conflict by entering a shelter or other safe haven until some viable strategy can be planned. In some situations, then, avoidance is not only a perfectly viable option, but actually the lifesaving one. In less volatile and less life-threatening situations in which avoidance of conflict will simply prolong the conflict or leave important differences unresolved between the parties, confronting the conflict in a reasonable way may be the more desirable option.

conflict (intrapsychic)
the simultaneous existence of two mutually exclusive wishes, impulses, or tendencies.

intrapsychic
in the mind.

conflict (interpersonal)
a state in which two or more people disagree, are opposed to one another, or are engaged in mutually aggressive behavior.

FIGURE 10–6 CONFLICT IN PARLIAMENT The rules of order were unofficially suspended when this fistfight broke out in Italy's Parliament in May 1992. The "fighting words" uttered made reference to the unceremonious hanging upside down in Milan Square of the Italian dictator Benito Mussolini after he was executed at the end of the Second World War. At the urging of Mussolini's granddaughter, a member of the Neo-Fascist party, her fellow party members stormed the benches of a rival party. How might this conflict have been handled differently? Are there times when physical conflict is the only alternative? Do you think that this might have been one of those times?

A QUESTION OF Values

Research on Obedience to Authority

Milgram (1965) described his experiment to 20 undergraduate students and then asked them these questions:

> In terms of the moral and ethical values most important to you, and taking into account the scientific goals served by the research, how should you perform in the experimental situation? Should you go through to the end of the experiment or should you break off at some point?

Milgram found a clear consensus for defying the experimenter at some point before the 30th level, with break-off points ranging from 0 to 255 (with the average being about 150 volts). For Milgram then, an important question addressed in his research concerned the discrepancy between such widely held values and the actual behavior of the subjects he tested. For other psychologists, however, a more immediate question of values concerned the cost of the knowledge gained from such research and whether the potential risks were worth the potential benefit. Milgram (1963) himself had painted vivid portraits of the distress many of his subjects suffered, including 3 of 40 subjects in one series who suffered "full-blown, uncontrollable seizures" (p. 375):

> I observed a mature and initially poised businessman enter the laboratory smiling and confident. Within 20 minutes he was reduced to a twitching, stuttering wreck, who was rapidly approaching a point of nervous collapse. He constantly pulled on his earlobe, and twisted his hands. At one point he pushed his fist into his forehead and muttered: "Oh God, let's stop it." And yet he continued to respond to every word of the experimenter, and obeyed to the end. (p. 377)

Diane Baumrind (1964) feared that research methodologies such as that employed by Milgram might place subjects in a position where they might suffer emotional pain, humiliation, a destructive alteration in self-image, or an inability to trust authority in the future. She suggested that such procedures represented an abuse of trust that subjects have come to place in scientific researchers. She wrote:

> Unfortunately, the subject is not always treated with the respect he deserves. It has become more commonplace in sociopsychological laboratory studies to manipulate, embarrass, and discomfort subjects. At times the insult to the subject's sensibilities extends to the journal reader when the results are reported. Milgram's (1963) study is a case in point. (p. 422)

Baumrind suggested that Milgram may have justified possible problems caused in his subjects by much the same kind of thinking that his subjects may have used to justify their shocking of innocent victims—thinking that goes, "[T]he discomfort caused the victim is momentary, while the scientific gains resulting from the experiment are enduring" (Milgram, 1963, p. 378). Baumrind allowed that "such a rationale might suffice to justify the means used to achieve his end if that end were of inestimable value to humanity," yet she questioned whether this was the case:

> The behavioral psychologist is not in as good a position to objectify his faith in the significance of his work as medical colleagues at points of breakthrough. His experimental situations are not sufficiently accurate models of real-life experience; his sampling techniques are seldom of a scope which would justify the meaning with which he would like to endow his results; and these results are hard to reproduce by colleagues with opposing theoretical views. Unlike the Sabin vaccine, for example, the concrete benefit to humanity of his particular piece of work, no matter how competently handled, cannot justify the risk that real harm will be done to the subject. (p. 422)

In reply, Milgram (1964) noted that Baumrind confused the unanticipated outcome of the experiment with its basic procedure; neither Milgram, nor any of the people to whom Milgram described the experiment, could have

CONFRONTING CONFLICT

appeasement

resolving conflict by acceding to or giving in to the demands of another.

The strategy of confronting or dealing with conflict may be subdivided into a number of different strategies. For example, one way of dealing with conflict is through **appeasement** or *acceding or giving in to the demands of another.* In the late 1930s, the term appeasement was used to describe the policy of giving Nazi Germany the land she demanded in an ef-

predicted in advance the subjects' extreme tension or other consequences or results of the experiment. Indeed, if subjects would have generally disobeyed the experimenter "at the first sign of the learner's discomfort, the results had been pleasant, and reassuring, and who would protest?" (Milgram, 1964, p. 849). As the experiment progressed, and patterns began to emerge, Milgram then had to decide whether or not to abandon the study. Based on his view that subjects suffered no more than momentary (not long-term or injurious) stress as well as endorsements of the research by the subjects themselves, Milgram proceeded.

In all of the obedience studies, there was an extensive debriefing and "dehoaxing" of subjects which, upon follow-up evaluation, were determined to be effective. Included in the debriefing was an explanation of the experiment, a friendly reconciliation with the unharmed victim (Mr. Wallace), and a conversation with the experimenter that supported the choice made by both defiant and obedient subjects. Obedient subjects were told, for example, that "their behavior was entirely normal and that their feelings of conflict or tension were shared by other participants" (Milgram, 1964, p. 849). Subjects were sent a comprehensive report on the research after it was completed as well as a postexperiment questionnaire. Replies to the questionnaire supported Milgram's

subjective feeling that subjects left the laboratory feeling positive about the experiment: 84% reported that they were glad to have been part of the experiment, 15% were neutral, and only 1.3% reported negative feelings. Approximately 80% of the subjects believed that more such experiments should be carried out, and 74% of the subjects reported that they had learned something of personal importance as a result of having been in the study. One man wrote: "This experiment has strengthened my belief that man should avoid harm to his fellow man even at the risk of violating authority" (Milgram, 1964, p. 850). Contrary to potentially turning off subjects to psychological research, as Baumrind suggested, participation in this study left subjects with a sense that they had participated in meaningful research. As for the stress suffered during it, Milgram commissioned an independent psychiatrist to assess 40 subjects who participated in one of the experiments. He concluded that, although extreme stress had been experienced by several subjects,

> none was found by this interviewer to show signs of having been harmed by his experience. . . . Each subject seemed to handle his task [in the experiment] in a manner consistent with well established patterns of behavior. No evidence was found of any traumatic reactions. (Milgram, 1964, p. 850)

Milgram (1964) rejected any suggestion that he compromised any subject's dignity, and he took full responsibility for his research efforts:

> A concern with human dignity is based on a respect for a man's potential to act morally. Baumrind feels that the experimenter *made* the subject shock the victim. This conception is alien to my view. The experimenter tells the subject to do something. But between the command and the outcome there is a paramount force, the acting person who may obey or disobey. I started with the belief that every person who came to the laboratory was free to accept or to reject the dictates of authority. This view sustains a conception of human dignity insofar as it sees in each man a capacity for *choosing* his own behavior. And as it turned out, many subjects did, indeed, choose to reject the experimenter's commands, providing a powerful affirmation of human ideals. (p. 851)

> If there is a moral to be learned from the obedience study, it is that every man must be responsible for his own actions. This author accepts full responsibility for the design and execution of the study. Some people may feel it should not have been done. I disagree and accept the burden of their judgment. (p. 852)

fort to avoid all-out war. In 1938, British Prime Minister Neville Chamberlain expressed his belief that the Nazis would be appeased by being granted a piece of what was then Czechoslovakia. In a famous, ironic statement, Chamberlain expressed his (mistaken) belief that land conceded to Hitler had brought "peace for our time." But Hitler's hunger for territory and power was voracious and the Nazis would ultimately break almost as many peace treaties as they signed. In addition to being of proven ineffectiveness on a nation-to-nation basis, appeasement is not a very effective conflict resolution strategy on a person-to-person basis. This is because the consequence of appeasement is a *win-lose situation*: There is one clear winner of the conflict and one clear loser. In such a situation, the loser may continue to harbor ill feelings toward the winner and the winner may proceed to act in such fashion as to demand even more from the loser on similar, win/lose terms.

Another substrategy in confronting conflict, one that we have seen with increasing frequency in the corporate world of the 1980s and 1990s, is *absorption* (Leavitt, 1978). Absorption on a large scale occurs in business when stock transfer actions lead to mergers or to a takeover of one company by another. When the corporations being merged into one were formally competitors, as was the case with many merged airlines, banks, and other businesses, competition between them is eliminated. On a somewhat smaller scale, absorption can be seen on a college campus as a method of resolving a dispute between students and the administration. A university may prevent student protests by allowing a contingent of students to participate in administrative decision making, thus absorbing them into the parent organization (Leavitt, 1978).

Perhaps the most widely known approach to confronting a conflict is *compromise*. If the advertised price of a used car is $1,100 and you really want to spend only $900, you could (a) walk away from the deal, (b) give in and pay the full $1,100, or (c) attempt to negotiate downward. Since you are both exactly $100 away from what you believe to be a fair price, the obvious compromise price would be $1,000. You might resent paying the extra $100 and the seller might resent losing an extra $100, but there is no clear winner and no clear loser in such a transaction. The outcome of a compromise approach is a win-win situation (or lose-lose situation, if you prefer to conceptualize it that way) for the parties.

Although compromise may represent a perfect solution in a situation such as that involving an automobile purchase, its value is not always as straightforward in many interpersonal situations. For example, suppose newlyweds Alice and Ralph have a dispute about Alice's mother staying for the weekend. Alice wants Ralph to agree to allow her mother to sleep over 2 nights, Friday and Saturday. Ralph does not want Alice's mother as an overnight house guest. A compromise position would be for Alice's mother to stay over only 1 night. On a strictly logical basis, this is a perfectly reasonable compromise. However, life is not always logical, and such a compromise might be viewed as lose-lose in nature by both Alice and Ralph. Moreover, it might be viewed as a lose-lose-lose situation when considered from the perspective of all of the parties involved, including Alice's mother. Ralph may feel that he has lost the argument because Alice's mother is being allowed to stay overnight. The 1-night compromise may be offensive to Alice, because of the implication that Ralph does not accept her mother. And imagine the reaction of Alice's mother to this explanation of the compromise solution:

> Mom, I know you were planning to stay over 2 nights, but Ralph did not want you to stay over at all. We compromised. You can stay over Friday night but you have to leave by 6 PM on Saturday.

A solution that goes above and beyond mere compromise is required in this situation. This solution, which might be termed a *beyond compromise* solution, is the product of a sincere and focused effort to address the needs of the parties involved. A starting point for arriving at such a solution will be some honest communication between the parties addressed to questions such as these:

- Why does Alice's mother want to stay over for the weekend?
- Why does Alice want her mother to stay over?
- What are Ralph's objections to having Alice's mother over?

It may be, for example, that Ralph finds certain behaviors objectionable that Alice's mother characteristically engages in while staying at their house. Problem-solving efforts may be focused on how best to amicably minimize or eliminate these specific behaviors. Focus would therefore be shifted away from Alice's mother as the problem and to behavior perceived as a problem. By the way, the behavior that is perceived as a problem may be engaged in by Alice's mother or by anyone else in the house during the time that Alice's mother is a house guest. For example, exploration of the issues might reveal that Ralph perceives an undesirable change in Alice's behavior during the time that both women are at home. It may be that in some critical respects Alice abandons her role as "wife" during these parental visits, and reverts to her role as "daughter."

Some tips on resolving interpersonal conflicts are presented in the *Quality of Life* on page 282.

AGGRESSION

In the context of psychology, **aggression** may be defined as *the act of behaving in a hostile fashion with the likely result of physical harm or emotional hurt*. Why do people behave in such fashion? Are there any situational triggers to aggressive behavior? What can be done to prevent aggressive behavior?

aggression

hostile behavior, sometimes with resulting physical or emotional harm.

THEORIES OF AGGRESSION

Just as what we label as *aggressive behavior* in many animals appears to be the result of inborn instincts, so some theorists have sought to explain aggressive behavior in humans as the product of instincts (Lorenz, 1974). It may well be the case that some expressions of aggressive behavior are the residual result of some inborn instinct. However, such an explanation is rejected by most psychologists, in part because it appears to explain everything and in reality explains nothing at all. If all human aggression were merely the product of instinct, there would be very little more to say about it. Anytime aggressive behavior was observed we could simply say it was instinctual. Ultimately, such an explanation would prove unsatisfactory in explaining great interpersonal differences in aggressive behavior. A similar deficiency in explanatory power exists with respect to "aggressive drives" to account for interpersonal differences in aggressive behavior. In circular fashion, someone who emits aggressive behavior would be deemed to be "high in an aggressive drive." Yet the only way a person would be labeled as "high in an aggressive drive" (or "high in an aggression instinct" for that matter) would be by being aggressive.

Leonard Berkowitz (1984) has proposed a cognitively based theory of aggressive behavior that not only accounts for observed aggressive behavior but may also be useful in predicting its occurrence. According to Berkowitz, being confronted with unpleasant situations produces a negative feeling state which in turn may activate a "flight response" (that is, fleeing to get out of the unpleasant situation), or a "fight response" (that is, physical confrontation). Whether either or both of these responses is actually acted on will depend on cognitive factors such as memory and reasoning. For example, if the person who cut you off in traffic turns out to be an imposing, Arnold Schwarzenegger-type, you may reason that you had better moderate what you have to say to him in the interest of your own physical safety.[2]

Perhaps the most widely accepted theory of human aggression is one based on social learning principles (Bandura, 1973; Baron, 1977). According to this view, whether aggressive behavior is emitted, and whether such behavior will be maintained or inhibited in the future, is very much the result of a complex interplay of factors. Included among these interacting factors are all that we learn about aggression and ways of being aggressive, as well as the rewards and punishments for aggression that we perceive as existing within a given situation (see Figure 10–7 on page 284).

SITUATIONAL DETERMINANTS OF AGGRESSIVE BEHAVIOR

A number of factors may contribute to the emission of aggressive behavior. Frustration of one's needs may lead to aggression directed at the person or persons perceived to be frustrating those needs. The perception of verbal or nonverbal provocation such as an insult or a sign of disrespect may lead to aggression. Feelings of powerlessness or vulnerability may directly or indirectly lead to acts of aggression. For example, watching the evening news may give many people the impression that they are in more imminent danger than they actually are of becoming a crime victim. As a result, they may feel powerless and seek

[2]This is particularly the case if you are male. If you are female, you can probably say what you want to him with relative impunity. Some research suggests that males, including the imposing Schwarzenegger-types, are not likely to retaliate physically against females (Hoppe, 1979), especially when the female is physically attractive. (Ohbuchi & Izutsu, 1984)

QUALITY OF *Life*

Techniques of Conflict Resolution

1. *Define the conflict.*
    You have no hope of resolving something that you cannot adequately define. The more detailed and sincere your definition of the conflict is, the better. The more precisely you can identify the specific behaviors and thoughts that are contributing to the conflict, the greater your chances of developing workable solutions. What led up to the conflict? What factors are maintaining it? What are the obstacles to resolving it? Try to answer these types of questions not only from your own perspective but also from that of the other parties involved in the conflict. Ideally, your definition of the conflict—as well as negotiations you make in resolving it—will be devoid of judgments about behavior in insulting or disrespectful terms. Facts will go a long way towards successful conflict resolution. For example, parents who

    tell their teenagers that they do not want them hanging around a particular person will ideally be prepared to explain their concerns. Simply saying something like, "I don't like this person," will not be very compelling to the teenager.

2. *List the consequences of resolving or not resolving the conflict.*
    How will your world be changed for the better if this conflict is resolved? Is it possible that your world will be changed for the worse if this conflict is resolved? If so, how? How will your world be changed for the worse if this conflict is not resolved? Is it possible that your world will be changed for the better if this conflict is not resolved? If so, how? Answer the same type of questions from the perspectives of the other parties involved. Taking the time to analyze all possible consequences of resolving or not resolving the con-

    flict may aid in clarifying the objectives of your resolution efforts. For example, envisioning how your world might be better as a result of resolving this conflict may help keep you focused on the elements necessary for a successful resolution, at least from your own perspective.

3. *Develop alternative courses of action for resolving the conflict.*
    This type of "conflict resolution brainstorming" may be done on your own or in collaboration with the person(s) with whom you are in conflict. An effective conflict resolution brainstorming technique is to begin with points of similarity between the parties involved. Do the parties agree about anything? What do they agree on? Why do they agree on whatever it is that they agree on? From there, discussion can be eased into specific points of disagreement and possible solutions that address the

---

aggressive

1. inclined to behave in a hostile fashion. 2. inclined to behave in a bold or enterprising way.

[3]A gun-purchasing frenzy was one of the consequences of the 1992 riots in Los Angeles (Egan, 1992; Thompson, 1992). In a sense, then, guns empower the people who carry them, and this effect holds true for people from a wide range of socioeconomic status—the gang members and the corporate board member alike.

a firearm to empower them. More firearms are then purchased, and these firearms are kept in homes, businesses, and on one's person.[3] Unfortunately, with some 200 million firearms in the United States, and more being added at the rate of about 4 million per year (Eckholm, 1992a), the homicide rate—and not the crime prevention rate—seems to be ever rising. Cause and effect between an increasing number of guns, and an increasing number of gun-related deaths would be difficult to prove. However, the correlational data are quite compelling with respect to the role of guns in homicide and suicide. In states, such as Texas, having particularly liberal gun laws, death by gunshot is now outpacing death by motor vehicle accident.

PREVENTION OF DESTRUCTIVE AGGRESSION

Like the concept of obedience, which can be conceptualized as being constructive (prosocial) or destructive (antisocial) in nature, aggression too may be thought of as being constructive (as in the case of an *aggressive salesperson* or *aggressive gymnast*) or destructive (as in the case in which people are unjustly harmed as a result). What can be done to curb or prevent destructive aggression?

needs of the concerned parties. Brainstorming is typically *not* effective if undertaken in the middle of a heated argument. If brainstorming turns into argument, it will be useful for one of the parties to signal "Time Out!" Set a date and time in which to resume the discussion when all have some distance on the subject matter.

4. *Carefully analyze the consequences of the various alternative courses of action.*

   Generally speaking, ideal consequences of conflict resolution efforts will include feelings on the part of the parties involved that they have accomplished something worthwhile, that they have not been manipulated or deceived, and that their views have been addressed with genuine concern and respect. In addition to these general consequences, more specific consequences based on the specific nature of the conflict will be components of successful resolution. Try to anticipate the various consequences of alternative courses of action by envisioning various "What if?"-scenarios. For example, "What if I tell Alice's mother she cannot stay for the weekend? What would her mother's reaction be? What would Alice's reaction be? How would I respond to Alice and her mother?"

5. *Agree on a course of action, perhaps on a limited-time or trial basis.*

   Often, there are glitches in proposed resolutions to conflicts. The possibility that there will be a glitch in your proposed solution should be acknowledged from the outset by all of the parties. The course of action taken may in many circumstances best be thought of as temporary, due for review and possible modification on a designated date in the future.

6. *Review the effectiveness of the course of action and the satisfactions and dissatisfactions of the parties.*

   On the appointed review date, explore each other's sources of satisfaction, as well as lingering sources of dissatisfaction. Keep in mind that the problem will only be effectively addressed when all parties are as satisfied as the circumstances will allow. If dissatisfactions run deep, a return to Step 1 in this program may be required.

7. *Fine-tune your course of action to address the effectiveness of the course of action, as well as each of the parties' level of satisfaction.*

   On the basis of your review, you may agree to modify your course of action and, if necessary, set more dates in the future for periodic progress review.

At a societal level, people need more role models for the constructive expression of aggression. There are all too many role models for the expression of destructive aggression in television, films, news and other media. Evidence from social psychological research laboratories (for example, Baron, 1972; Donnerstein & Donnerstein, 1976) suggests that there is promise in conducting more research into how to train people to react in nonaggressive fashion to various sorts of provocation. The problem of violence is so great in American society that it probably warrants the development of a grade-school curriculum in which nonviolent action alternatives are discussed and nonaggressive role models are presented.

Society must also monitor social causes of frustration and discontent and effectively address problems such as unemployment, homelessness, and drug abuse—easier said than done, but such problems must be high on the national agenda. The criminal justice system too must do better. Psychological studies suggest that punishment will only be effective as a deterrent to crime if it is swift, sure, and sufficiently aversive. This means that people who aggress, as well as other criminals, must do so knowing that there is a very good probability that they will be caught. It also means that the punishment once they are caught will be of sufficient severity to deter the behavior. Ideally, of course, punishment is

FIGURE 10–7 LEARNING TO BEHAVE AGGRESSIVELY This 10-year-old got a lesson in firing an M16 at the annual Hill Country Machine Gun Shoot in Helotes, Texas. According to a reporter covering the event, "The parking area was filled with cars sporting bumper stickers proclaiming 'Freedom Wasn't Won with a Registered Gun' and 'The more people I meet, the more bullets I need'" (Belkin, 1990). In addition to learning about the mechanics of operating this weapon, what else might this boy be learning?

catharsis

a venting of anxiety or aggressive impulses.

always a last resort for purposes of modifying behavior; a better approach is providing obtainable incentives and rewards for socially approved behavior.

At an individual level, many people believe that they can constructively dissipate their aggression by watching aggressive sporting events, punching a pillow, exercising, or otherwise draining aggressive impulses safely by means of a process that psychologists call **catharsis** (*a venting of anxiety or aggressive impulses*). But whether any aggression is truly vented during such activities is highly questionable (Feshbach, 1984). More likely, many of these activities probably do little more than produce a temporary fatigue effect. In some instances, such activities may even be instrumental in disposing a person to be *more* aggressive, as in the case of the individual who may be more disposed to aggression after witnessing a heavyweight fight (Phillips, 1983). Additionally, some vicarious and supposedly cathartic activities can increase thinking about aggression (Berkowitz, 1984), or act to desensitize a person to the destructive effects of aggression (Geen, 1981), thus making the individual more prone to an aggressive response upon perceived provocation (Carver et al., 1983).

Also at an individual level, people need to learn and to practice ways of reducing anger, as anger may too often lead to verbal or physical aggression (Hazaleus & Deffenbacher, 1986; Rule & Nesdale, 1976), child abuse (Nomellini & Katz, 1983), or other tragic consequences. We need to understand, for example, that in some cases, bad things happen to good people for no apparent reason. In the face of such injustice, lashing out with anger or aggression usually only worsens one's problems. Strong convictions that any problem or frustration can be worked through along with planned cognitive "escape routes" to regain control during an anger-driven crash course are necessary to defuse anger and potentially aggressive situations (Suinn, 1977). At times, a sense of humor can also be of great value to defuse tense situations. Frustration and other potential anger-causing or aggression-causing feelings are part of everyday life for everyone. We will all be better off if we deal adaptively and effectively with such feelings.

In this chapter, we have shifted the focus from the individual to the individual in society and from one's personal identity to one's group identity. We have begun to look at the processes of social perception and self-perception and at the many possible sources of error within those processes. We have also begun to explore group processes and the ways that people come to help or hurt each other. In the following chapter, this focus on the person in an interpersonal context continues as we look at topics such as friendship, liking, loving, and communication.

SUMMARY

SOCIAL PERCEPTION Our view of ourselves and other people results from the influence of many different but overlapping factors including past experience and culture. We try to maintain consistency in our perceptions and in that process, act to resolve *cognitive dissonance,* or discrepant thoughts and behaviors.

SOURCES OF ERROR IN SOCIAL PERCEPTION *Attribution* refers to a mental assignment of characteristics or causation. Attributions we make about others and ourselves are subject to error. The *fundamental attribution error* refers to a tendency to attribute the causes of another person's behavior to internal factors and the causes of our own behavior to external causes. Attributions may also be inaccurate as a result of many factors, including (1) faulty learning, (2) comparison to an inappropriate reference group, or (3) perceiving exactly what one expects to perceive.

SELF-PERCEPTION *Self-concept* may be defined as the summary statement of all one's accumulated information about oneself including one's interpretation of that information. Many of the same errors that are possible in social perception in general can also occur in self-perception. *Self-esteem* refers to one's general estimate of one's value or worth. Self-concept, self-perceptions, and self-esteem are to some extent all interrelated; one may influence the others. *Self-presentation* may be defined as the totality of the way one exhibits oneself to others.

GROUP PROCESSES AND BEHAVIOR Understanding adjustment entails an understanding of social processes such as group identity, conformity, obedience, leadership, conflict, and aggression. *Group identity* refers to a sense of close affiliation with other people on the basis of a common variable such as interests, abilities, disabilities, or demographic characteristics. In a psychological sense, *conformity* refers to similarities in terms of behavior, thinking, outward appearance, or other such factors between two or more people. Conformity may carry connotations of either power or powerlessness depending upon its context. *Obedience* refers to the behavior of dutifully carrying out the orders or commands of another. *Conflict* refers to the simultaneous existence of two mutually exclusive wishes, impulses, or tendencies. *Aggression* may be defined as the act of behaving in a hostile fashion with the likely result of physical harm or emotional hurt.

Chapter 11

Friendship and Love

O U T L I N E

I remember watching many years ago the beautiful Italian screen star Sophia Loren being interviewed on the *Tonight* show. Having previously seen her in many films, I (mistakenly) felt that I had gotten to know her somewhat. A fantasy I had—one that may well have been shared with millions of other men at the time—was that Sophia and I could be great friends if our paths ever crossed. Yet in listening to her spontaneously answer questions during that television interview, I began to question whether Sophia and I were really ever meant to be. We did not have very much in common. I surprised myself by even being put off as she went on about how superstitious she was and how she always wore something red to ward off evil. A lesson I learned from that interview was that while we can admire screen stars and other celebrities from afar, true friendships, as well as more intimate relationships, require much more.

In this chapter, we will explore why people become friends as well as some of the mysteries of love and interpersonal attraction. We will also discuss that most important ingredient of friendship and love relationships, communication. Before all that, however, some discussion of the human need for affiliation.

THE NEED FOR AFFILIATION

People need other people: societies are built on that simple principle. In addition to veritably relying on others, we may also derive great joy from interacting with other people. Other people can bring a feeling of comfort and security. Especially during stressful times, the presence of others can act to quell anxiety, a fact that has been demonstrated in adults (Schachter, 1959/1976), in infants and children (Ainsworth, 1969; Morris et al., 1976), and even in other species (Bovard, 1959).

The motivation to interact with other people, including the motivation to please or comfort them and to be pleased or comforted by them, has been referred to as the **need for affiliation** (Murray, 1938). The strength of this need is presumed to differ in people. In the workplace, for example, some people seem to thrive on jobs independently executed in solitude, while other people seem to thrive on jobs requiring daily contact with, even strong dependence on, a number of other people. Many different theories exist to explain why people may differ in terms of their need for affiliation (Eidelson, 1980; Weiner, 1972, 1974). Experience, particularly experience during periods of infancy or childhood that have been presumed to be critical in the later development of trust (Erikson, 1963), may play a role, as may genetics and later learning regarding social support.

As we saw earlier (page 72 and pages 183–185), the nature and quality of the social support we receive can affect psychological and physical well-being. According to House (1981), social support may take many forms, including *appraisal support* (help in evaluating a particular situation), *informational support* (help in supplying needed facts for decision making), and *instrumental support* (help with money or other material things). Pagel et al. (1987) remind us that in addition to supplying various forms of social support, the members of our social network are also capable of withholding support. The nature of past experiences with people, and the degree of emotional distress experienced as a result of those experiences, may affect the strength of one's motive to affiliate with other people.

LONELINESS

Loneliness is a condition that results from the frustration of one's need for affiliation. The lonely person desires more interaction or better quality interaction with other people. In this sense, loneliness is clearly not synonymous with being alone. One can feel lonely even while surrounded by thousands of people. If you don't believe that, buy a single ticket to a professional sporting event such as a baseball, basketball, football, or hockey game. As you sit in the stands, you may find yourself not only being a spectator regarding the in-

---

need for affiliation

the motivation to interact with other people, including the motivation to please or comfort them and to be pleased or comforted by them.

teraction on the playing field, but a spectator regarding the interaction of others who have come to enjoy the event with friends and family. Depending upon the level of your own need for affiliation, you may well begin to feel very lonely.

One need not be surrounded by strangers to experience loneliness. Being around family members, friends, or others with whom you do not feel "connected" or supported may also lead to feelings of loneliness. In a poignant response to a newspaper article extolling the virtues of Valentine's Day, Beckwith (1993) argued that, "There are legions of lonely people who, for one reason or another, are virtually always without love." For these people, Valentine's Day served only as "society's thoughtless reminder that, yes, another bitter year has passed and you are still in the cold."

Different types of loneliness have been distinguished (Young, 1982). *Chronic loneliness* is the condition so graphically described above by Beckwith. It is a condition characterized by the inability to develop satisfactory relationships with other people over the course of many years. *Transitional loneliness* refers to loneliness that occurs as a result of some transitional period in life such as a new job or the death of a spouse. *Transient loneliness* refers to a relatively brief episode of loneliness such as one might experience upon entering a room filled with people with whom one is not acquainted. In addition to being categorized by length of time, loneliness may also be categorized in terms of the sphere of one's life in which the deficit of human interaction is perceived. For example, one may not experience feelings of loneliness while at work but experience strong feelings of loneliness at home. Loneliness may be further subcategorized by whether it reflects longings for greater family-, romantic-, or community-related involvement (Schmidt & Sermat, 1983).

Loneliness can be a very painful experience—in the extreme, so painful that it may take daily courage just to survive (Beckwith, 1993). Calls to suicide and depression hotlines, even certain calls to late night radio and television call-in shows, reveal the untold number of people who are lonely at any given time. The good news is that loneliness need not be as final as a court sentence or fatal disease. There are a number of things people can do to lessen greatly, if not eradicate, troubling feelings of loneliness (Moustakas, 1961). One might begin by mentally exploring one's loneliness. How and why did it start? What are the most painful things about it? Are there any benefits of loneliness that may be acting to maintain it? Does one's loneliness reflect elements of self-rejection? Rejection of others? Both? Might a period of loneliness provide an opportunity for personal growth or a greater sense of comfort with oneself? How?

Exactly what remedial action should be taken will of course depend on the nature of the loneliness. For example, if one is married and lonely, one might take steps to enhance communication and the general quality of the relationship with one's spouse. Such steps might entail couples counseling, perhaps in combination with an expansion of activities the couple participates in together. If the loneliness stems from an absence of friends, personal counseling may be helpful in addressing the individual's self-confidence, social skills, and general pessimism about social relationships. Social support in a therapy or counseling situation, combined with role playing of appropriate behaviors in social situations, can be useful preparation as one attempts to widen one's circle of friends and/or enhance the quality of existing relationships.

FRIENDSHIP AND LIKING

What are friends for? The answer to this question may vary as a function of factors such as the stage of life one is in or the particular circumstances one is facing. In early childhood, for example, the people we call friends are typically other children who live nearby who happen to be playmates. As children get older, more than mere physical proximity and a desire to play will be required if two children are to develop friendship. In adults, the need for affiliation may fluctuate greatly with different life circumstances. For example, a new mother may experience a rise in her need for affiliation with other new mothers. "Mommy-and-Me" support groups provide a forum for new parents to share and discuss the problems and joys of being a parent. Friendships may develop from participation in such groups, just as friendships might develop between classmates or office co-workers. Most of us have different types of friendships, with different types of friends, who meet different types of needs.

At a most general level, many people may view friends as people who "are there for you in a time of need." This is true, but friends tend to be much more than that. From childhood onward, friends help mold our self-image and self-esteem by providing us with important feedback about how we present ourselves to the outside world (Smollar & Youniss, 1985). Friends provide us with a basis of social comparison that is more objective than our own judgment. They provide input as to how physically attractive we are in relation to other people, how well we play sports in relation to other people, and how well we relate to other people in general. Friends also provide important feedback regarding our judgments and emotional output—whether we are too harsh or angry with ourselves or someone else and whether we are unrealistically pessimistic or optimistic.

Friends are people through whom we can live vicariously. By relating in exquisite detail what this or that experience was like, friends broaden us, acquainting us with aspects of life we may never live ourselves. Friends are the people we entrust our most personal confidences in, and whom we expect can trust us. Friends are loyal; we expect that they will stand up for us in our absence. Interestingly, some differences in the nature of friendship as a function of gender have been observed. While men typically become friends with other men as a result of shared interests and activities, the focus of friendship for many women is more likely to be discussion of emotionally significant matters (Caldwell & Peplau, 1982; Davidson & Duberman, 1982; Hays, 1985; Sherrod, 1989).

In *Of Friendship,* Emerson wrote, "The only way to have a friend is to be one." In thinking about how good some of your friends are to you, it may be helpful to think about how good a friend you are to them (see *Self-Assessment*). After taking this quiz, here are some questions you may wish to consider in order to gain more insight regarding you and your relationship to your friends: How does what I expect my friends to give me differ from what I have to offer them? Is there a fair exchange? How has my perception of the meaning of friendship changed since I was a child? How might my perception of the meaning of friendship change even more in the next 10 years or so? Under what circumstances can friendship become love?

Our friends are usually people we like, and we seldom seek the friendship of someone we do not like. Liking may take place for many different reasons, and may be only one component of friendship. As you read further, you may find yourself thinking more about why you like your best friend and why your best friend likes you.

FACTORS IN LIKING

Of the many hundreds of reasons people like other people, six general themes have been identified by researchers as being prominent: *proximity* (geographical closeness), *attractiveness, personality, equity, reciprocity,* and *similarity.* Take the first letter from each of these factors and you have the easy-to-remember acronym "PAPERS".

PROXIMITY

Being geographically close allows people to get to know one another and to discover areas of mutual interest. Living near each other, working near each other, attending the same religious services, attending the same school or classes and in general being in close physical proximity to one another increases the odds that a friendship will form.

Research has suggested that favorable attitudes towards someone or something can result merely from repeated exposure to that person or object (Zajonc, 1968; Moreland & Zajonc, 1982). Given such findings, it therefore should come as no surprise that people tend to like, admire, or have favorable attitudes towards radio, television, and screen stars. Repeated exposure to celebrities in the print, on film, and in the electronic media increases both their familiarity and our favorable attitudes towards them. Of course, attitudes may change if such celebrities engage in behavior we find offensive or that otherwise puts us off.

Me in My Role as Friend

Many of us think frequently about how good a friend one or another person is to us, but seldom think about how good a friend we are to them. The items in this exercise tap many of the qualities that people view as key to friendship. Answer them honestly, and then go back and draw some conclusions regarding yourself in your role as someone's friend. *Instructions:* Think of your relationship with one friend and then respond to all of the items with either *True* or *False*. Then think of your relationship with another friend and respond to the items again. Are your answers different for each of these relationships? Why? How could you be a better friend to each of these two people?

1. If my friend tells me something in confidence, I keep it in confidence.
2. I am loyal to my friend.
3. I truly like my friend and my friend knows it.
4. My friend values the emotional support I offer.
5. I am honest to my friend.
6. I always have time for my friend.
7. My friend can always turn to me for help.
8. I am eager to hear about my friend's successes.
9. I can be counted on to stand up for my friend when he or she is not around.
10. I tend to be interested in what my friend is interested in.

It is also possible for geographical proximity to engender negative attitudes, especially when close contact affords a glimpse of behavior that angers, repulses, or is otherwise perceived as unpleasant (see Table 11–1). Family members come in conflict with each other, neighbors feud with neighbors, even heads of neighboring nations may socially shun, if not be hostile towards, one another. As an example of the latter case, relations between the United States and Cuba have been cool, if not hostile, ever since the dictator Fidel Castro seized power there in 1959. In 1960, Castro's Communist government nationalized about one billion dollars in United States-owned properties. In response, the United States broke

TABLE 11–1 ANNOYING HUMAN BEHAVIOR

Over 60 years ago, Cason (1930) attempted to derive a comprehensive list of things that people find annoying. From a total of about 21,000 common annoyances as reported in interviews with people, he distilled the list down to 507 specific items, most of them the result of human behavior. On a kind of "annoyance scale" that ranged from a low of 0 to a high of 30, he then had over 1,000 male and female subjects rate the 507 annoyances. Some of the most annoying behaviors were:

Annoyance	Average Score	
	Males	Females
A person coughing in my face	28.5	29.3
A person in an automobile I am driving telling me how to drive	23.0	18.5
A person picking his or her teeth	15.3	21.3
A woman smoking a cigarette in public	16.5	18.3
Being held very close by my dancing partner	6.8	19.3
A beggar asking me for some money in a public place	14.0	10.8

In your opinion, do you think things have changed since the publication of this study in 1930? If so, how? What behaviors would you add to this list?

diplomatic relations with Cuba. The lack of cordiality between the two neighbors was reflected in the behavior of its two leaders at a world conference (see Figure 11–1). As you can probably attest from personal experience, people who do not like one another typically do not go out of their way to communicate with one another, even if they are in relatively close proximity. More detailed consideration of communication is presented later in this chapter.

ATTRACTIVENESS

Physical attractiveness is a definite asset in many spheres of social interaction, be it making friends, getting dates, or getting hired (Byrne et al., 1968; Green et al., 1984; Reis et al., 1980). As compared to nonattractive people, attractive people tend to be perceived more positively with respect to variables that are totally unrelated to physical attractiveness (Brigham, 1980; Dion et al., 1972). For example, physically attractive people may be perceived as more mentally stable than nonattractive people (Feingold, 1992; Jones et al., 1978; Unger et al., 1982). Such unjustified positive attributions seem to rub off, even on people who merely associate with people who are physically attractive (Kernis & Wheeler, 1981). Perhaps because of prior positive experiences with such a rub-off effect, people tend to welcome friendships with physically attractive people.

PERSONALITY

Are you more attracted to a person who most people would judge to be sincere, understanding, and trustworthy, or one who is insincere, narrow-minded, and not trustworthy? In general, people viewed as being more pleasant, positive, and agreeable tend to be more liked than people who are unpleasant, negative, and disagreeable (Anderson, 1968; Folkes & Sears, 1977; Kaplan & Anderson, 1973). Sometimes, whether due to sheer fascination or the vicarious sense of excitement provided, we may associate with people who have all of the "wrong" personality characteristics. However, when it comes to having a true friendship, most of us prefer our friends to be sincere, understanding, trustworthy—and in possession of as many other positive personality traits as possible.

EQUITY

social exchange theory
a social psychological theory regarding the principle of equity in the trading of social resources between two or more people.

A popular theory in social psychology is that of **social exchange**, or *the trading of social resources between two or more people*. The *social resources* traded may range from the abstract

FIGURE 11–1
A FAILURE TO COMMUNICATE In June 1992, while the world leaders at the Earth Summit in Rio de Janeiro were assembling for a group photo, the Cuban Communist dictator, Fidel Castro, had occasion to pass in front of the president of the United States, George Bush. Given the strong political differences that existed between the two men, as well as the fact that each had a long history of denouncing the other, it came as little surprise that the two leaders did not acknowledge each other's presence.

and intangible (such as love, loyalty, approval, or physical attractiveness) to much more concrete but nonetheless socially desirable things (such as bank accounts, material goods, or corporate secrets). In friendships, dating situations, marriage, and other social relationships, people tend to seek **equity**, or *a fair and equal exchange*, in the social exchanges that are made. For example, one very physically attractive person may seek an equally physically attractive person as a spouse. Alternatively, one very physically attractive person may seek a nonphysically attractive but high status person as a spouse. In such a case, equity would be achieved as a result of the trade-off between one person's good looks and the other's high status. Think now of your relationship with one of your current or former friends or dates. According to social exchange theory, what social trade-offs were made by each party? In your view, did equity exist in the relationship? Why or why not?

RECIPROCITY

As used in the social psychology literature, **reciprocity** refers to the *mutuality of attitudes and/or behavior between two or more people*. With reference to attraction and liking, *reciprocity* refers to the fact that people tend to like people who like them, and tend to dislike people who dislike them. We have a tendency to like people who show signs of interest in us (Gold et al., 1984; Hays, 1984), positively evaluate us (Byrne, 1971), and/or flatter us (Drachman et al., 1978). We have a tendency to dislike people who speak negatively of us, or speak negatively of people in general (Amabile, 1983). High levels of cooperative or competitive attitudes emitted by one person in a social interaction have been found to elicit the same attitudes in the other person (Black & Higbee, 1973; Kuhlman & Marshello, 1975; Rosenbaum, 1980). In a general sense, such findings suggest that people tend to "reap what they sow," or "get as good as they give" when it comes to interpersonal relationships: cooperation breeds cooperation and competition breeds competition.

SIMILARITY

People tend to like other people who are similar to themselves. Typically, the more similar people are on a wide range of variables, including physical attractiveness, attitudes, and values, the better the chance that liking will occur (Buss, 1984; Lesnik-Oberstein & Cohen, 1984). High levels of similarity have been found in dating and married couples on variables such as physical attractiveness (Folkes, 1982), facial features (Hinsz, 1989), even weight (Schafer & Keith, 1990). Keep in mind, however, that social exchange factors may also enter into such relationships; similarity may go by the wayside in certain relationships because certain nonsimilar attributes (such as physical attractiveness and wealth) are being traded off.

In general, "opposites attract" may be true for magnetic poles, but it tends not to be true when it comes to interpersonal relationships. People—"Dead-heads," as they are called—who would make a special effort to attend a Grateful Dead concert, for example, are probably unlikely to associate very much with, let alone date, fall in love with, or have many friends among people whose taste in music runs more to classical recitals and symphony performances. This is so because similarity between people in political outlook, musical taste, attitudes, values, and other preferences tends to be mutually pleasing; such similarity leads to a kind of social validation of one's world view (Sanders, 1982). Still, there is much to be said for cultural diversity within one's circle of friends (Gormly, 1979; Snyder & Franklin, 1980).

Because liking and friendship are so intertwined, all of the PAPERS factors relevant to liking are also relevant to interpersonal attraction in general, including romantic relationships.

ATTRACTION AND LOVE

In the mid-1970s, the National Science Foundation (NSF) granted two researchers $84,000 to study love from a sociological and psychological perspective. When Senator William Proxmire of Wisconsin got wind of this use of taxpayer money, he issued a press release arguing that "falling in love is not a science" and that the contemplation of such

subjects was better left in the hands of a poet like Elizabeth Barrett Browning. For Proxmire, some things in life should remain a mystery; he personally did not care to know anything about love from the perspective of social science. A reply to Proxmire by James
Reston, published in *The New York Times*, acknowledged that love will forever remain a
mystery in spite of any research. However, as Reston put it, if we could learn more about
"our pattern of romantic love, marriage, disillusions, divorce—and the children left behind—it would be the best investment of federal money since Jefferson made the Louisiana
Purchase."

There are people who would like to cherish romantic notions of love and attraction
unencumbered by any research on them. There are also people who believe that love and
attraction are legitimate areas for scientific inquiry. Which best describes your own viewpoint? Why?

INTERPERSONAL ATTRACTION

For the starry-eyed, incurable romantic, attraction and love can grow from a fleeting meeting of eyes across a crowded room. Indeed, such an occurrence is entirely possible. Then
again, the attraction could wind up lasting little longer than the fleeting eye meeting. To
understand why, let's play out a hypothetical scenario involving two young people we will
call Nicole and Scott:

> Scott, Nicole, and hundreds of other people are attending a fund-raising gala for a new
> hospital. Scott's and Nicole's eyes meet across a crowded room. Magnetic attraction be-
> tween them fixates their gaze. The physical attraction between them is electric, chemical,
> and all but overwhelming. Neither one of them perceives much else. The band's rendition
> of "We've Only Just Begun" has faded in the background. Nicole sees only Scott. Scott has
> completely lost track of the fact that the open bar will be closing in 10 minutes. While
> most of the assembled company feasts on the Viennese table, Nicole and Scott feast only
> on the sight of each other. Visually immersed in each other, they slowly but deliberately
> gravitate to within earshot of one another. Still, they interact only nonverbally, first with a
> shy smile. The verbal interaction that follows is noteworthy only for its simplicity. A soft
> and simple exchange of "Hellos" followed by silence. They gaze into each others' eyes, now
> from a distance of only inches.

By this point, there are any number of things that could potentially put the kibosh on
the relationship. What might some of those things be?

As in all social interactions, at least four different types of attributions are probably
being made by the two people in our scenario. These include attributions one makes concerning another person, and attributions one makes concerning oneself (see Figure 11–2).
For example, Nicole is making attributions about Scott as well as about herself. Some of
her attributions regarding Scott made from close up may include those related to his physical appearance (she had no way of knowing how yellow his teeth were from across the
room), his health (Scott is terribly congested and breathes with a loud, raspy wheeze), and
his political preference (Nicole is a staunch Republican and Scott is wearing a lapel pin

**FIGURE 11–2 ATTRIBUTIONS IN A SOCIAL
ENCOUNTER** In a social encounter, four general
types of attributions are typically made. These include
(1) attributions regarding the self based on feedback
from the other, and (2) attributions regarding the other
party. The other party in the interaction is also making
self-attributions (3), as well as attributions regarding the
other person (4).

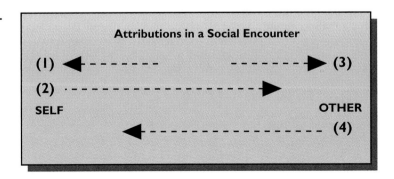

asking for support of the Socialist Workers' party candidate for mayor). After a few minutes of conversation, Nicole learns that Scott *is* the Socialist Workers' party candidate for mayor.

In turn, Scott is making attributions about Nicole, and, like Nicole, wondering about things that did not occur to him from across the crowded room. For example, the pitch of Nicole's voice is so high it reminds Scott of chalk grating on a chalkboard. Additionally, just as Nicole is making attributions about herself during the interaction, so Scott is making attributions about himself. For example, Scott has sized up Nicole as someone who is used to the finer things in life. He is wondering whether she would feel entirely comfortable in his 1981 Chevette with its broken passenger-side door lock. Scott may also see before him a very long commute should he enter into a dating relationship with Nicole. Nicole lives in a part of town that is a good 2 hours' drive from Scott's home. Even if Scott was inclined to make the 4-hour round trip commitment to a dating relationship there is no guarantee that Nicole would be willing to do the same, or that the Chevette wouldn't overheat enroute.

Now it is time for you to rewrite the Nicole and Scott scenario. Take it from the point that their eyes first meet from across the crowded room. What factors would have to be present in order for the two parties to "click"? Think about it before reading on.

Research indicates that many of the PAPERS factors (discussed above) are likely to play a role in the process of interpersonal attraction. Proximity, or what one early researcher referred to as *propinquity,* is certainly a factor. In a paper entitled "Residential Propinquity as a Factor in Marriage Selection," Bossard (1932) observed that most couples applying for marriage licenses in Philadelphia were likely to live only a few blocks from each other. Over 60 years later, geographic proximity (or propinquity) is still thought to be a key variable in interpersonal attraction and love.

In general, we tend to be attracted to people who are similar to ourselves in many ways. Fairy tales like *Beauty and the Beast* may be wonderfully entertaining, but they have little basis in social reality. A classic study by sociologists Ernest Burgess and Paul Wallin (1953) provided the first demonstration for what has come to be known as the **matching hypothesis**, the view that *people tend to become romantically involved with other people who are comparable to themselves in terms of physical attractiveness and other variables.* Burgess and Wallin showed that loving couples tend to be relatively matched on numerous variables, including physical appearance, physical health, mental health, popularity, and varied aspects of family background (ranging from demographic variables such as race, religion, and socioeconomic status, to other variables such as the happiness of their parents' marriages).

matching hypothesis
the tendency for people to become romantically involved with other people who are comparable to themselves in terms of physical attractiveness and related variables.

WHAT'S "SEXY"?

In your mental rewriting of the Nicole and Scott saga, you may well have used the word "sexy" in describing how one or both of these parties viewed the other. But what exactly is "sexy"? Is it something about the way one looks? The way one speaks? The way one behaves? The power or material things one possesses? Is it all of these? None of these?

"Sexiness," much like beauty, truth, and other attributes, is in the eye of the beholder. It is a complex and multifaceted attribute; no one variable makes one person sexy and another not sexy (Brown et al., 1986). What is considered sexy and physically attractive will vary not only as a matter of individual preferences, but also as a function of time, place, and culture. For example, in the not too distant past, native Hawaiians believed that excess body weight improved a woman's beauty and nobility. The physical ideal for female beauty was quite different from today's (see Figure 11–3).

Is drinking beer sexy? Is smoking cigarettes sexy? Is having coffee sexy? In each case, it would seem that there is nothing inherently sexy in any of these activities. Still, as a result of exposure to advertisements that pair beer drinking, cigarette smoking, and coffee drinking with attractive, flirting, "party people," one might certainly come to believe that these activities are themselves sexy activities. In one set of commercials for a very-high-alcohol content malt liquor, Billy Dee Williams is pictured with a group of attractive women as the message "It Works Every Time" is conveyed. What the manufacturer does not advertise is that alcohol is a central nervous system depressant that can impair a male's ability to attain and sustain an erection. In this context, "It May Not Work Every Time" might

FIGURE 11–3 A CULTURAL IDEAL FOR BEAUTY The native Hawaiian ideal of feminine beauty and grace was once embodied by Princess Ruth Keelikolani of Hawaii.

be more truthful advertising. One of the newer product entries to the "sell-it-with-sex" approach is coffee (see Figure 11–4).

Sexiness can be described a bit more precisely in terms of the physiological effect one person can have on another. From a physiological perspective, finding someone sexy typically entails both (1) a rise in one's level of arousal (as measured by heartbeat, breathing, and other such indices) either when in the presence of the person or when simply thinking about the person, and (2) a cognitive labeling of this raised level of arousal as sexual attraction (Dutton & Aron, 1974). What is required for one to cognitively label another as sexy will vary with factors such as one's prior learning and the cultural context in which the evaluation is being made. The same behavior in different cultural contexts may or may not be sexy (see *Cultural Close-Up*).

Sexiness, however defined, may be one part of romantic love.

THE NATURE OF LOVE

There are many different types of love, all involving intense affection (such as the love between a parent and a child) and some involving romance and sexual attraction (such as the powerful feelings experienced by Shakespeare's lovers Romeo and Juliet). Focusing on the latter, romantic variety, Elaine Hatfield (1988; Walster & Walster, 1978) dichotomized love into *passionate love* and *companionate love*.[1] **Passionate love** is *the product of emotional arousal plus a cognitive label of "love."*

Hatfield's definition of passionate love draws on Schachter's theory about the cognitive labeling of arousal (see page 170). According to this view, love is essentially physiological arousal (increased heartbeat and respiration, etc.) coupled with a cognitive label that attributes that arousal to being in love. Of course, the same type of physiological arousal could exist in a person and not be attributed to love; it could even be attributed to hate. Under ordinary circumstances, how one labels the physiological arousal experienced is the complex result of a number of factors including learning history and current environmental conditions.

Schachter's theory can be interpreted as having implications for a wide range of observed phenomena associated with love and dating relationships. For example, can you think of how this theory might be used to explain the appeal of scary movies or amusement parks for dating couples? Scary movies and amusement parks are two of many possible situations in which one's level of arousal will probably be raised. As you watch the movie or ride a roller coaster, your heart will beat faster, your respiration will increase, and you will experience other signs of physiological arousal. Should one attribute or associate

passionate love

from a cognitive perspective, the product of emotional arousal plus a cognitive label of love.

[1]Elaine Hatfield was one of the recipients of that $84,000 NSF grant for research on love mentioned earlier. At the time, she was a sociology professor married to a fellow sociology professor, G. William Walster. The Walsters collaborated on a rather comprehensive book on the subject of love (Walster & Walster, 1978), and both were considered to be among the world's foremost experts on the subject. Yet soon after their book was published, the Walsters divorced.

FIGURE 11–4 COFFEE AND ROMANCE Sharon Maughan and Tony Head have flirted their way through numerous commercials for the *Taster's Choice* brand of instant coffee. Yet as Maslin (1992) observed, "viewers are being asked to buy a lot more than processed coffee. These ads are also selling sophistication (as manifested by flowers, sculpture, modern furniture, etc.) and romance (Sharon and Tony end their first date on a near-kiss, though he is by then on a three-cup coffee bender)." Are viewers buying? Sales of the product have risen by 10% since the flirtatious couple began their ongoing saga of breathless exchanges and pregnant pauses in 1990.

Cultural

Hand-Kissing in Cultural Perspective

It was once quite fashionable in European society for a man to kiss the hand of a woman he was courting or a woman of high status to whom he was introduced. How fashionable is it today? Not very, according to journalist Frieda Garmaise. Garmaise (1984) writes that in Poland, hand kissing was once practiced only by the aristocracy. In modern-day Poland, hands are probably too busy making a living to be kissed. In modern-day Germany, hand-kissing carries with it historical connotations of militarism and is therefore to be avoided. Garmaise believes that a Frenchman will kiss a hand, but that hand will most likely be his own, not that of a woman. Here she refers to the French gesture for approval of a particular food or wine—done by placing the tips of one's fingers to one's lips and kissing them. Hand kissing never caught on in England and has always been thought of as distasteful.

Similarly, hand kissing has never really caught on in the United States. As Garmaise put it, once American men kiss a woman's hand, "they've kissed everything else" (p. 88).

Although hand kissing appears to be a lost art, having different meanings and role implications as a function of culture, it still occurs from time to time. Today, it can probably most generally be interpreted as an effort to be charming in a very old-fashioned way.

The contemporary woman who has her hand unexpectedly kissed by a man may feel somewhat awkward, and perhaps even be at a loss for words as a result. This happened to Garmaise at the conclusion of an interview with Ricardo Montalban. The actor spontaneously took her hand and kissed it saying, "You are very charming." The somewhat flustered Garmaise responded, "I'll bet you say that to all the girls." Montalban replied, "I do."

this heightened arousal to one's date (and not its true source), positive feeling towards the date may be increased.

Schachter's theory as applied to passionate love also explains why, as folk wisdom has it, "there is a thin line between love and hate." Consider in this context Noreen, who is engaged to, and passionately in love with, Rufus. Noreen will continue to consider herself in love with Rufus so long as she (1) continues to feel physiologically aroused in his presence, and (2) cognitively labels this arousal love. But what if the arousal Noreen experiences in thinking about or seeing Rufus is tainted by negative information? The negative information may prompt Noreen to cognitively relabel the arousal she is experiencing. For example, what if Noreen receives a reliable account of Rufus's irresponsible behavior at his bachelor party? The physiological arousal she experiences may qualitatively be the same as that she experienced and labeled love, although the feelings may now instead be labeled rage or some other such emotion.

Companionate love is *the product of affection, less the intense arousal and passion of passionate love*. Hatfield believes that in marriage, the heat of passionate love undergoes a transformation into the warmth and comfort of companionate love. Positive arousal is still present, but the novelty of the situation has worn off and the degree of positive arousal has

companionate love
the product of affection, in contrast to the intense arousal and passion of passionate love.

stabilized at a level lower than that experienced during passionate love. Some couples stubbornly try to keep their marriages forever passionate, and a few may even succeed. Other couples, after the initial passions have died down, opt for a relationship based primarily on companionate love. Still other couples opt for a mixture of passionate and companionate love. Sometimes one partner wants one of these types of relationship while the other wants the other type. In such circumstances it will be essential for the parties to be able to communicate their needs and feelings effectively, the goal being to address each party's concerns.

From one psychological perspective then, **romantic love**, whether passionate or companionate, may be defined as *a state of physiological arousal coupled with the cognitive label that one is in love*.

STERNBERG'S TRIANGULAR THEORY

Have you ever wondered whether the romantic love you have experienced was "true," "consummate," or "complete"? Robert J. Sternberg's **triangular theory of love** may be of some assistance. According to Sternberg (1986, 1987, 1988a, 1988b; Sternberg & Barnes, 1988), a love can be assessed with respect to its three major components: *decision/commitment, intimacy,* and *passion* (see Figure 11–5). Consummate or "true" love exists when all three of these elements are present. Other types of love relationships exist, including passionate and companionate love as conceived by Sternberg, when the three basic elements of love are present in varying magnitudes. An explanation of the role of each of these three elements in love, as well as an illustration of some of the "love triangles" they may form, follows.

DECISION/COMMITMENT

In the context of a love relationship, **decision/commitment** refers to *an intention to maintain the relationship*. In the short term, commitment refers to the decision that one is, in fact, in love. In the long-term, commitment refers to one's resolve to make the relationship work. How certain are you that other people could not come between you and your loved one? How certain are you that circumstances (such as a job-mandated relocation) could not come between you and your loved one? How willing are you to end your relationship

romantic love

a state of physiological arousal coupled with the cognitive label that one is "in love."

decision/commitment

in the context of Sternberg's triangular theory, an intention to maintain a love relationship.

FIGURE 11–5 LOVE AND THE "DIP" Take the first letters of decision/commitment, intimacy, and passion, and you have the acronym "DIP". An additional aid to remembering Sternberg's three components of love might be the mental image of two lovers dancing, with the man "dipping" the woman.

with this person? How long do you foresee the relationship with this person lasting? These are the types of questions one asks oneself when thinking about the decision/commitment element of love. The critical importance of commitment in marriage is evident from the fact that most marriage vows contain some reference to commitment, such as the vow to stay together "in sickness and in health as long as you both may live." Commitment can be further analyzed into value-related components (see *A Question of Values*).

A QUESTION OF  Values

Values and Commitment

The word *commitment* with reference to personal relationships has been used in many different ways (Becker, 1960; Leik & Leik, 1977, Rusbult, 1980, 1983). For example, as Johnson (1978, 1982), and others (Stanley & Markman, 1992) have observed, commitment may be thought of as having at least two components or different meanings: (1) personal dedication, and (2) constraint. Commitment in the sense of dedication is implied when we speak, for example, of being "committed to getting a final grade of A in your psychology course." Commitment in the sense of constraint is implied when we speak, for example, of being "committed to working 4 hours a day, 6 days a week, at the book store." For Stanley and Markman (1992), *personal dedication* refers to

> the desire of an individual to maintain or improve the quality of his or her relationship for the joint benefit of the participants. It is evidenced by a desire (and associated behaviors) not only to continue in the relationship, but also to improve it, to sacrifice for it, to invest in it, to link personal goals to it, and to seek the partner's welfare, not simply one's own. (p. 595)

These authors refer to *constraint commitment* as forces that compel individuals to maintain relationships irrespective of personal dedication, and "favor relationship stability by making termination of a relationship more economically, socially, personally, or psychologically costly" (p. 596). They further point out that in the context of engagement and marriage, personal dedication and constraint commitment are not necessarily independent:

> High personal dedication during engagement increases constraint as the couple expresses their dedication by committing themselves to marriage, children, joint possessions, and so forth. More is invested, others expect and want the relationship to continue, more complicated procedures are required to end the relationship, and alternatives may become less attractive. Simply put, today's dedication is tomorrow's constraint. (p. 597)

The dedication-constraint distinction is not always made explicit in considerations of commitment to personal relationships. Yet the distinction seems important to the extent that each of these aspects of commitment may have relevance to the values underlying an individual's perception of, and attitudes towards, marital commitment. For example, we may speak of someone being committed to a marriage, and simply assume that we are referring to values such as loyalty and selflessness. However, from a constraint commitment perspective, commitment to a marriage may be symptomatic of underlying values such as selfishness and preservation of wealth. One can be committed to a marriage only because a divorce would be financially disastrous.

Stanley and Markman (1992) also note that commitment as a result of constraint need not have a negative connotation. Constraint will only have a negative connotation to couples if personal dedication or general satisfaction with marriage has diminished. Constraints may be useful in helping couples to maintain a long-term perspective while weathering day-to-day conflicts. These authors further observed that, "When you ask couples what is important in their relationships, they often mention commitment. Yet, compared to other key constructs . . . commitment has been under-researched" (p. 605). Through their own research and a test they developed called the Commitment Inventory, Stanley and Markman have enriched our understanding of what is meant by commitment and of the different values that may underlie the use of that term.

INTIMACY

intimacy

in the context of Sternberg's triangular theory of love, a state of closeness, warmth, bondedness, and connectedness in which the parties are disposed to sharing with each other aspects of their most personal, private, and innermost selves.

Intimacy may be defined as *a state of closeness, warmth, bondedness, and connectedness in which the parties are disposed to sharing with each other aspects of their most personal, private, and innermost self.* As in the case of love in general, it may be useful to dichotomize intimacy into *passionate* and *companionate* varieties, the former being the more physical, sexualized variety, and the latter being the more cognitive type. Being able to share one's most personal thoughts and feelings as if the other person will understand is one element of intimacy. Quality of communication between the parties, quality of emotional support given and received, quality of physical and financial support given and received, and overall level of personal/social comfort in being together all impact on the level of intimacy inherent in a relationship.

PASSION

passion

in the context of Sternberg's triangular theory of love, a powerful, emotion-driven zeal that can be positive or negative in nature.

From literature, and perhaps from firsthand experience, **passion** can be understood as *powerful, emotion-driven zeal that can be positive or negative in nature.* One can experience love, hate, or any other emotion as a deep and overwhelming gut-level feeling. Alternatively, such emotions can be experienced less passionately, with feelings one might more aptly label as desire or enthusiasm. The amount of passion that exists in a relationship can be gauged by the answers to a number of different questions regarding one's lover. How sexually arousing do you find this person? How often do you find yourself thinking about her/him? How comfortable do you feel being in close physical contact with this person? If you see a film, television show, or other such presentation about two people who are deeply and passionately in love, how much do you identify with those people in terms of your own relationship?

LOVE TRIANGLES

Conceptualizing each of the three key elements of love as points in a triangle, Sternberg discusses how each of the points, singly or in combination, may characterize the nature of a love relationship (see Figure 11–6). For example, one who has resolved to be married by a certain time in one's life—with or without true love—may become involved in a relationship that Sternberg calls *empty love;* it is love based on commitment to the relationship, but passion and intimacy are lacking. A relationship built on intimacy alone is a *liking* relationship according to Sternberg. A relationship built on passion alone is *infatuation.*

FIGURE 11–6   THE THREE SIDES OF LOVE In Sternberg's triangular theory of love, the type of love relationship one has is gauged by the comparative amounts of decision/commitment, intimacy, and passion.

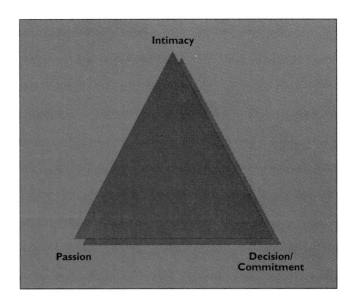

Sternberg defines the various points in between the anchoring points as *companionate love* (between intimacy and commitment with passion lacking), *romantic love* (between intimacy and passion with commitment lacking), and *fatuous love* or *infatuation* (between decision/commitment and passion with intimacy lacking).

In geometry, two triangles are said to be congruent when they coincide exactly when superimposed on each other. One may also speak of congruency in love relationships with reference to Sternberg's model. According to Sternberg, a perfect love relationship exists when one individual's "love triangle" is perfectly congruent with that of the other person (see Figure 11–7). Of course, very few things in life, even love relationships, can be said to meet the standard of absolute perfection. The closer the triangles are to congruency, the better the love relationship. The further away the triangles are from congruency, the worse the love relationship.

Pondering whether one is in love or not can be a confusing venture, filled with vague, unsystematic, perhaps even competing thoughts. Although criticized for its lack of completeness (Murstein, 1988), Sternberg's theory can be quite useful as a guide for logically sorting out thoughts and feelings relating to love, a nonlogical phenomenon.

BEGINNING A RELATIONSHIP

The unmarried population in the United States has climbed from 47 million in 1975 to 68 million in 1985 (Bennet, 1989). Many members of this population are, to use the title of an old song, *Looking for Love*. For those who are indeed seeking out intimacy and romance, where and how will they find it?

DATING IN AMERICA

How people meet and court prospective mates has changed over time in this country. While dating or getting together in groups is the norm today in the United States, it was not always that way. In colonial America, a man had to obtain permission both from the woman he wished to court and the woman's parents. The couple may have been chaperoned at their meetings by parents or others or allowed to meet only at public functions, and then only under some elder's watchful eye. When the man was permitted to visit the woman's house, it was usually after the chores of the day were done and there was not much time for socializing; most families retired for the night soon after supper. In instances when the man had came from very far away, or when inclement weather would prevent his return home that same evening, the courting couple would be permitted to talk, keep warm, and spend the evening and night together "bundling" (see Figure 11–8 on page 302). If the couple wanted to marry, it was customary for the young man to ask the young woman's father for his daughter's hand in marriage.

Dating first emerged in the late 1800s as the result of a number of factors. The industrial revolution had spurred the growth of cities, and city life meant closer proximity between males and females of courting age at home, in school, and in factories. The increased opportunity for unsupervised social contact led to more informal meetings between couples. The invention of the telephone meant that couples could keep in contact, even from far away, and make plans to meet. The invention of the automobile further revolutionized dating as it provided not only a means of transportation during dating but also a private environment for time together.

Today, there are probably more opportunities than ever before for men and women to meet and date. In a bygone era, many schools, athletic facilities, and other institutions were segregated by sex. Increasingly, however, many facilities that were once closed to one sex or the other, including health clubs and many other organizations, are open to both men and women. Even some fraternities and sororities have become coeducational (see Figure 11–9 on page 303). Dating today is far more informal than it used to be, and it is as appropriate for a woman to ask a man out as it is for a man to ask a woman out. Whereas paying for the movie, restaurant, or other entertainment on a date was once the man's obligation, greater economic equality between the sexes means that couples today are more apt to divide such costs. Some things have not changed, however; a primary objective in dating for the marriage-minded single person remains screening for possible mate selection.

FIGURE 11–7 LOVE GEOMETRY These sets of triangles illustrate a continuum of relationships from perfect to poor. If you are in a love relationship, how would you draw your set of triangles? Why?

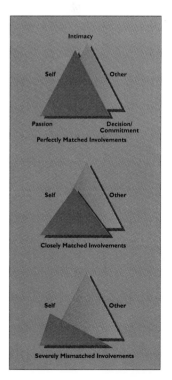

FIGURE 11–8 BUNDLING A colonial custom called "bundling" permitted a courting couple to extend a date, even sleep together—in a manner of speaking. The two would get into a "bundling" bed and talk late into the night with the lights on—that is, with candles lit. Only outer garments were removed and what was called a "bundling" board might be placed between them. Alternatively, the woman might "bundle up" in a sack that was tied at the neck, this to help physically enforce a strict social barrier against any sexual activity. As roads and transportation improved, and it was possible for male courters to return to their homes on the same evening, courting moved from the bundling bed to a couch in the parlor (Doten, 1938).

THE OLD-FASHIONED CENTER-BOARD
The Pennsylvania Germans invented all kinds of ways and means to get the courting couples together — and all kinds of knick-knacks to keep them apart when they got together! Girls were safer in the old days, in bed with their beaux, than they are today roaming the world over in search of adventure!

MEETING YOUR MATCH

There are many ways that people meet other people. One of the most popular is by third-party introduction (Knox & Wilson, 1981). Someone—a friend, a relative, a friend of a friend, etc.—who knows each of you arranges the meeting. If you are particularly shy, you might wish to arrange what I call a *rendezvous à trois*. No, that is not some kind of kinky encounter, but rather *a meeting of three* at which you, the person making the introduction, and the person you are being introduced to all meet together. The presence of the person who knows you both will help ease the awkwardness of the situation and pave the way for a first encounter during which you can learn more about each other in a more relaxed way.

Another method of third-party introduction is through the use of a commercial matchmaking service. Such services have been on the rise in recent years, especially since people are marrying later than ever and may have fewer and fewer single friends or others in their social network who can help them meet prospective mates (Ahuvia & Adelman, 1990, 1992). Additionally, concerns about contracting a sexually transmitted disease (Castro, 1987), fear of becoming a victim of crime (Deal & Wampler, 1986), and a desire for social support in the early stages of dating (Adelman, 1987) may all be factors that discourage more independent and casual methods of meeting people. Although little research has been done on formal matchmaking services, the available data is not encouraging. The marriage rate of clients ranges from 5% to 20%, with negative outcomes such as wasted time, wasted money, and lowered self-esteem an ever-present possibility (Adelman & Ahuvia, 1991). On the positive side, it is a slim but nonetheless real possibility that such a service will help you meet the "right" person. At the very least, your network of friends and potential "referral sources" will increase. Additionally, you may find that the use of such a service helps to clarify your own thoughts, attitudes, beliefs, and perceptions about being single (Adelman & Ahuvia, 1991).

In any blind date, whether third-party-arranged or not, and whether in the company of the third-party or not, it is generally a good idea for the initial meeting to be arranged for some brief occasion or period of time (such as the time of a drink, rather than of lunch or dinner). The meeting can always be mutually extended, whereas abruptly cutting it short may lead to unnecessary hurt or anger.

Another way of meeting people is through membership in organizations that (1) interest you, and that (2) meet frequently. Psychology may interest you but it would not be prudent to count on your membership in the American Psychological Association (APA) as a means of meeting the love of your life. The APA holds only one meeting per year and that meeting is in a different city every year. For meeting people, singles groups such as those sponsored by local religious organizations or private concerns, special interest groups (such as a poetry reading group, a community theatre, or a local environmental interest group), and adult education classes of interest (ceramics? music? computer? foreign language?) may all prove to be good choices. Even if you do not meet the person you hope to meet, you will still probably have met some interesting people, and perhaps even learned a great deal in the bargain.

For the less adventuresome, there is the possibility of meeting through the written word. Personal ads in newspapers or magazines or personal ads by telephone voice mail will get you many replies if you word your ad in an appealing manner. Of course, what is appealing in a personal ad is culturally relative. In our country, phrases like "nonsmoker" and "likes to take long walks" appear with great frequency in such ads. In Algiers, Algeria, where a severe housing shortage coexists with a military curfew, an advertiser like one 36-year-old woman will entice many potential suitors with her mention of "average looks and my own apartment" (Hedges, 1993).

Traditional pen-pal clubs are still very much around (Henneberger, 1992), although they must now compete with the more contemporary and fashionable mode of electronic pen-palism: the computer network (Markoff, 1990). Variously referred to as electronic mail, computer conferencing, and electronic bulletin boards, a mushrooming number of computer networks are providing electronic meeting places for people who have access

FIGURE 11–9 COED FRATERNITIES In response to allegations of sexism and discrimination, the all-male fraternity house was abolished at Middlebury College in Vermont as of January 1990. The fraternity houses were all on school property and the school threatened to reclaim the houses if women were denied admission. Other colleges and universities have either already taken, or are seriously contemplating similar action. Proponents of the all-male fraternity argue that it encourages male-bonding in a way that will be threatened if not diluted by a coeducational environment. Yet as argued by one of the female members of a fraternity at Trinity College in Hartford, Connecticut, the coeducational environment has definite social advantages for students in terms of getting to know people as people rather than as sex objects. She said that in the traditional fraternity/sorority arrangement, "Men and women cannot help but view each other as sexual partners." By contrast, in a coeducational environment, the men and women "respect each other as people" ("The Idea of Coeducational Fraternities," 1990).

to a computer and a modem. Meeting through such an electronic medium has its advantages over a traditional pen-pal relationship because there is an opportunity for immediate feedback. It is even possible to dialogue through this electronic medium. Keep in mind, however, that unlike traditional letter writing, you enjoy no privacy on a computer network: anyone hooked into the same network can read what you and your keyboard pal write.

For the more adventuresome, there is the possibility of meeting people in the fashion that is referred to in French as *en passant* or *in passing*. By chance, for example, the person standing in back of you on a line to enter a movie theater may have attracted your eye and be someone you would like to know more about. What do you say? What do you do? You have a relatively short period of time to initiate some sort of interaction if you are ever going to learn more about this person. Walster and Walster (1978) and others (see Cunningham, 1989) list a number of ice-breaking strategies you may wish to employ: (1) complimenting the other person (as in, "I like that jacket"), (2) asking the person for assistance or information (as in, "Is it supposed to rain today?"), or (3) disclosing something about yourself (as in, "I really am shy and I don't know what I'm doing here"). The conversation can be kept going by shifting the focus from yourself to the other person. In some circumstances, however, nothing you can do will get the conversation initiated or maintained. Expect that too and do not interpret it as a personal rejection; there are times when you too do not wish to speak to anyone.

You can help the *en passant* method along in some subtle ways, as well as some ways that are not so subtle. On the subtle list, purchase or adopt a dog and then walk it in a park or area frequented by other people walking their dogs; the dog will attract the attention not only of other dogs, but of their owners as well. Also on the subtle list, carry a controversial book with you at all times, one that might prompt comments or conversation (Brown, 1963). Among the not-so-subtle ideas for meeting people is the wearing of some attention-getting apparel. When Elaine Walster wore a T-shirt that read, "My body is my own, but I share," she found many strangers striking up conversations with her (Walster & Walster, 1978, p. 31).[2]

We have all heard or read about horror stories when it comes to dating and to crime. No one is immune from tragedy. For this reason, it is important *not* to immediately become involved, or to go anywhere with, people you meet *en passant* or under circumstances that are in any way suspicious. The first few dates with someone who is known to neither you nor anyone you know should be in public places. On those dates, take the opportunity to find out as much as you can about the person—not only in the interest of determining whether this is someone you want to continue seeing, but also in the interest of determining whether this is someone you can trust. Meeting *en passant* may seem very inviting and romantic, and it may well be. However, the realistic possibility of harm from someone you really do not know exists. It is an unhappy reality of everyday life that people are harmed by people they do and do not know well. Dating and meeting new people can truly be one of the joys of life. In a perfect world, we would not have to worry about this activity or take safety precautions when engaging in it. But we do not live in a perfect world. The person who is right for you will understand and appreciate all of your reasonable safety-related concerns.

ENDING A RELATIONSHIP

From one perspective, love may be likened to a living thing that grows and thrives or withers and dies. Some people marry their childhood sweethearts, having never dated anyone else, nor ever having wanted to date anyone else. However, given that most of us do a fair amount of dating and may have more than one love relationship before committing to one person, we need to be prepared for the possible termination of such a relationship. This means acknowledging from the beginning that you or the person with whom you are entering into a relationship might in the future find the relationship unfulfilling and/or find someone else more attractive, desirable, or more "right" for you for any number of reasons. Keeping this simple fact in mind from the outset may inoculate one against the stress and emotional pain of a breakup when and if it subsequently occurs (Meichenbaum, 1973,

[2]That same slogan may not prove as effective in the 1990s. Can you think of a better one?

emotional pain of a breakup when and if it subsequently occurs (Meichenbaum, 1973, 1974, 1977).

Why do relationships break up? One analysis of 103 breakups before marriage of couples who had described themselves as being in love indicated that boredom with the relationship, differences in interest, and differences in background were fairly common causes (Hill et al., 1976). In general, committing to the relationship before one knew enough about one's partner in the relationship was seen as being a major cause of pre-marital breakups (Hill et al., 1976). Unrealistic expectations regarding the relationship may also do it in. Contrary to popular portrayals of couples in a love relationship, each person is likely to criticize the other, perhaps even more than they would criticize non-intimate friends (Davis, 1985). For the relationship to run smoothly, criticism must be communicated, received, and acted on in a manner that is palatable to each of the parties.

Because people typically invest so much of themselves in trying to make a relationship work, because they have dreamed their private dreams about what the future of a loving relationship might be like, and because their hopes for the relationship may have been unrealistically high to begin with, the ending of a love relationship can be a very painful and highly emotional experience. Consequently, many people keep their relationships sputtering along, well after both parties would have been better off ending it and moving on. Other people have unfortunately gone to other extremes and tried to obtain a sense of satisfaction by hurting or exacting some kind of retribution from the former lover. Depending on the rejected person's mental health, maturity, resources, and other factors, the retribution sought may take many different forms and vary greatly in terms of sophistication (see *In the News* on page 306).

A dating relationship is fraught with many potential sources of conflict (Braiker & Kelley, 1979; Surra & Longstreth, 1990), perhaps more than many people anticipate from the outset. If loving couples are to remain loving couples in the long run, they must cultivate conflict resolution skills, as well as other skills related to effective communication.

COMMUNICATION

In a world in which effective communication between people is so vitally important, it seems somewhat surprising that education in communication is not widely incorporated into grade school and college curriculums. Most people assume that they were born with the ability to communicate. While this assumption is in one sense correct, it is also true that communication can be improved greatly with training. In some professions, courses are devoted to teaching effective communication skills. Psychologists in specialty areas such as counseling and clinical psychology, for example, may receive formal education and training in active listening, active reception of nonverbal communication, and training in interviewing.

THE PROCESS OF COMMUNICATION

Communication may be defined as *an exchange of messages by verbal and/or nonverbal means*. Means through which messages may be exchanged include face-to-face/person-to-person contact, face-to-face/person-to-intermediary (such as a translator) contact, letters, faxes, exchange of video- or audiotapes, and so forth. Some of these means provide for both verbal and nonverbal transmission and reception of messages, while others provide only for the transmission and reception of verbal messages. Communication entails an *exchange* of messages, or an imparting and receipt of a message. The *message* in a communication may express a statement, a fact, an opinion, a thought, a question, a belief, an order, a riddle, a prophecy, a threat, or whatever it is the person sending the message wishes to convey. **Effective communication** is said to exist when *the message that the source wishes to convey is received by the person or persons targeted to receive that message.*

communication
an exchange of messages by verbal and/or nonverbal means.

effective communication
an exchange of messages such that the message that the source wishes to convey is received by the person or persons targeted to receive that message.

The Turbulence of Unrequited Love

The Phantom of the Opera is a dramatic tale about unrequited love and the turbulence of such unreturned passion. Unfortunately, both the dramatic media and the news media provide us with an overabundance of such violently passionate role models. Perhaps because it is conflict that drives drama—and sells movie tickets as well as newspapers—people tend to have little exposure to role models who respond adaptively and in civilized fashion to a relationship breakup. Interestingly, one case reported in newspapers may suggest to some that it is also possible to be almost *too* civilized when it comes to a break-up. Margolick (1992) described

the case of a 44-year-old corporate attorney and a 21-year-old restaurant hostess who became engaged about 4 months after they first met. However, the next several months were stormy and the woman broke off the engagement. The attorney responded with a lawsuit demanding $40,310.48 based on his former fiancée's breach of promise to marry. On its face, the lawsuit was an action to recover every penny of courtship costs, including items such as a one-carat diamond engagement ring ($5,200), a Notre Dame umbrella, and $7.99 for a Patsy Cline cassette. However, as the woman herself noted, the lawsuit seemed to serve as a means of keeping their relationship going. It was the only way left to the man for communicating with his former fiancée. Three days before filing the lawsuit, the man wrote in a letter to her, "I am still willing to marry you on the conditions hereinbelow set forth. . . ." The conditions included a commitment to marry within 45 days of her receipt of the letter. The woman resented having to spend her own money for legal representation to respond to this lawsuit. She said, "I think he's trying to use this as a way to make me say 'O. K . . . I'll marry you' . . . But there's nothing romantic about it. I can't imagine telling my children as a bedtime story that mommy and daddy got married

because of a lawsuit" (Margolick, 1992). On the advice of her attorney, the woman is keeping the ring and other gifts pending the outcome of the lawsuit.

A lawsuit is certainly a rare, but nonetheless civil way of exacting payment from the rejecting party—or "maintaining a relationship," depending upon how you look at it. Too often, it is some illegal, violent, or hurtful act to which a former lover resorts. The outcome of such action ranges from trivial to tragic, but is always negative and usually lose/lose in nature; no one wins, each party loses. Personal or couples counseling is the option to consider before doing anything that may not only lose you your love but also lose you your liberty. Should you ultimately decide to terminate a relationship with someone, you expect that the person will accept your decision, however reluctantly, and then move on. Similarly, if someone decides, for whatever reason, to terminate a relationship with you, the best course of action will also be to accept it and move on. Because love is a mental attribution harbored in one's being and only given freely, it cannot be compelled. Even thinking thoughts about compelling love from another should prompt the person thinking such thoughts to seek counseling.

VERBAL COMMUNICATION

The ability to communicate verbally with precision, clarity, and a richness of vocabulary distinguishes the human species from other species. Words communicated between people may be designed to convey different sentiments and messages ranging, for example, from social support ("Happy birthday!"), to helpful advice ("Take two aspirin and call me in the morning"), to life-changing information ("You have been accepted into the program"), to life-or-death information ("This nation is now in a state of war"). Words spoken between people can have consequences so momentous that they can influence the very survival of the planet. Such was the case in October 1962 when two nuclear superpowers, the United States and the former Soviet Union, brought the world to the very brink of global nuclear annihilation. Numerous safeguards against the outbreak of nuclear war have been implemented since that crisis. Included were policies for better communication between Washington and Moscow and the installation of a "hotline" telephone that instantly linked the two heads of state.

NONVERBAL COMMUNICATION

I forgive you. You look marvelous! I'm very happy. These messages may be imparted verbally or nonverbally. In some circumstances, for example, a hug and a kiss may mean, "I forgive you." A wide-eyed, admiring gaze may convey, "You look marvelous!" A broad smile or laugh, even tears of joy, may impart the message, "I'm very happy." In fact, as we know from everyday experience, many nonverbal variables such as facial expressions, hand gestures, eye movements, mouth movements, tone of voice, even perspiration can convey various kinds of messages (Ekman, 1985; Izard, 1982; Rosenthal et al., 1979). Simple changes in tone of voice—such as attaching sarcasm when uttering the word *great* in "I thought it was great"—can change a message from praise to condemnation. Because nonverbal communication is often perceived as more spontaneous than verbal communication (Verderber & Verderber, 1989), the nonverbal message may be perceived as the more gut-level or genuine.

Nonverbal messages are easily overinterpreted or misinterpreted because there are few rules when it comes to their interpretation. For example, gestures that involve physical touching may vary greatly in terms of their interpretation by the person receiving such messages. In different situations and contexts, and depending upon where and how a person is physically touched, touching may represent a display of anger, affection, admiration, respect, disrespect, dominance, or sexual interest. Perhaps the value of nonverbal communication is the extent to which it may be used as a basis for hypothesis testing; an inferred message may be confirmed or disconfirmed by verbal means.

Like verbal communication, nonverbal communication must be interpreted within its own cultural context (Hall, 1959). Ever-changing cultural norms exist for many aspects of nonverbal behavior including dress, personal space, and eye contact. Prolonged eye contact, for example, can, in different cultures, signal attraction or dislike depending upon other aspects of one's facial expression. Deviation from cultural nonverbal norms by people unfamiliar with a culture may send confusing signals. Sticking one's tongue out at someone in this culture is usually interpreted as a juvenile sign of contempt. Yet engaging in that same behavior in Tibet may be a simple greeting (Ekman, 1975).

BARRIERS TO EFFECTIVE COMMUNICATION

Many barriers to effective communication exist. Categorized broadly, there are physical, psychological, cultural, and situational obstacles.

PHYSICAL OBSTACLES

Developmental disabilities, physical injury to the brain, and temporary injuries or conditions affecting the mouth (such as a dental appliance or the prolonged effects of a dental anesthetic), the eyes, the ears, or other organs may all physically impede communication. Additionally, communication may be impeded by illness, headaches, and other physical conditions that take away from concentration or otherwise impede active listening.

PSYCHOLOGICAL OBSTACLES

Potential psychological obstacles to effective communication run the gamut from being "too close" to or "too distant" from what is being communicated. When one is too close, good judgment may take a backseat to personal involvement in the communication. When one is too distant, there may not be sufficient interest to maintain effective communication. People may or may not be motivated to impart or receive messages clearly for a variety of reasons. In a two-party communication, for example, one party may not trust the other, like the other, want to be influenced by the other, or find the other to be a credible source (Wood & Eagly, 1981). Effective communication can be short-circuited by positive feelings such as fondness, liking, or loving. In such instances, one person may fear inflicting emotional hurt on the other and refrain from communicating what a more neutral party would communicate. Alternatively, one person may fear some negative consequence (such as abandonment, rejection, alienation, or physical harm) if effective communication was to take place. Preoccupation with some theme may prove to be an obstacle to effective communication. For example, a person who suspects a loved one of infidelity may be so preoccupied with that thought that the person will relentlessly keep the focus on that topic. More generally, one might be so preoccupied with one's own self-interest that anything communicated that is not directly relevant to that interest is ignored. Another psychological obstacle to communication is simple carelessness. A carelessly spoken word or phrase may instantly and inadvertently shut down communication.

CULTURAL OBSTACLES

Verbal and nonverbal communication between people may be impeded by different meanings that various cultures assign to specific words or nonverbal gestures. When these culture-specific messages get "lost in the translation," the consequence may be ambiguity about what the actual intent of the parties are. For example, nonverbal customs between merchants and customers in Asian countries differ from such customs in this country. In recent years in the United States, there have been a rash of tragic misunderstandings between Asian-Americans who own stores in minority neighborhoods and their clientele. According to an Asian-American business owner and community activist, Glenda Joe (1992), many of the difficulties arise from misinterpreted communications between the parties. For example, Joe points out that merchant rudeness is high among customers' complaints regarding Asian-American merchants. Yet many Koreans, for example, have been taught not to speak to strangers and not to be overly familiar in business. This attitude, combined with a tendency on the part of clerks not to express appreciation for patronage, may be interpreted as rudeness by American customers.

In friendship, intimate, or other relationships in which the parties come from two different cultural backgrounds, effective communication is particularly important if behavior dictated by cultural custom is not to be misinterpreted. For example, Marin and Marin (1991) point out that after a love relationship has broken up, Hispanics brought up in more traditional Hispanic homes will be less likely than Anglos to enter into a friendship relationship with the former lover. Becoming friends with a former lover is thought to potentially impair one's relationship with one's future spouse. It is thought that it may cause jealousy or future problems with loyalty. In a dating relationship involving an Anglo and an Hispanic that sours, it is conceivable that the Anglo might want to continue the relationship as friends while the Hispanic might not. Unless cultural teachings are communicated, the situation may needlessly lead to misunderstanding and hurt feelings.

SITUATIONAL OBSTACLES

In general, physical proximity or nearness facilitates the ability of one party to influence another (Milgram, 1974). You may have experienced this effect for yourself when on a cross-country or international trip; somehow, the advice of a parent or friend given from thousands of miles away may pale in impact to the advice given to you by that same person when they are but a few inches away. Distance, then, can be an obstacle to effective communication. A marriage in which one or both parties must spend a great deal of time on the road as part of their employment responsibilities is not conducive to the development of effective communication and intimacy between the parties. Another type of situational barrier to effective communication concerns the physical environment in which communication is conducted. For example, the library or the study hall are typically not the ideal places to conduct private and meaningful student-to-student conversations, because these are public areas reserved for silent, independent study. Similarly, the classroom is designed for group learning, not private, student-to-student communication. Private, student-to-student communication within the environs of a classroom is unfair to fellow students, because it makes it more difficult for the instructor to communicate effectively with the rest of the class. Meaningful and effective student-to-student communications can be conducted in a variety of settings, such as parks, cafés, automobiles, apartments, and similar settings, where privacy can be assured and distractions can be kept to a minimum.

GUIDELINES FOR EFFECTIVE COMMUNICATION

How can people communicate more effectively with one another? Perhaps the first step in becoming a more effective communicator is to recognize that different types of communications are appropriate for different types of settings and situations. For example, highly personal and revealing kinds of communications are appropriate with family members and very close friends. By contrast, highly personal and revealing kinds of communications are generally inappropriate in the workplace, in the classroom, and in other situations in which one's relationship to the people involved is, broadly speaking, business in nature (note here that a student's "business" in the classroom is learning). Because humor is a highly individual matter, attempts at humor can be reacted to with many responses that range from positive to negative. Accordingly, very playful and joking types of communication are typically better reserved for friends, family, and other situations in which the people know you well and you know them well. It is certainly possible to use humor effectively in situations with strangers, co-workers, fellow students, and business clients, although whether your humor will be appreciated is a question you must be prepared to gamble on. Even professional comedians have been known to offend individuals or groups of individuals with their humor—with the result being a costly lawsuit!

By its very nature, effective communication between people cannot take place in an environment that is not conducive to the parties being able to devote their undivided attention to one another. For this reason, choose a time and a place to communicate that presents as few competing influences as possible. Beyond the physical environment, a "climate" for communication or *rapport* between the parties must also be created. This climate is one in which the parties are relating in an honest, direct fashion, and each one is withholding judgment on the other's thoughts until all sides of a question or argument have been presented.

If cultural differences exist between the parties, sensitivity to these differences will go a long way towards ensuring a climate of mutual respect. If you have questions about any of the parties' culture-based preferences or concerns, it may be a good idea to raise such issues for discussion diplomatically. In addition to engaging in some self-questioning in advance with regard to situational and environmental variables, it may also be a good idea to question yourself with respect to any possible psychological obstacles you may have going into the discussion. What obstacles exist? Why do they exist? How can they be dealt with in order to make communication between the parties maximally effective?

With these types of cautions stated at the outset, some very general guidelines for effective communication are presented in the *Quality of Life*.

QUALITY OF  Life

Effective Communication

Effective communication entails what might be termed "active reception" of messages as well as "speaking your mind."

Active Reception

The method of listening in class that was described in Chapter 1 (page 21) can be usefully built on and then generalized to other situations as well. It can be built on by adding *active observation* skills to the active listening skills. Active observation entails an attempt to discern not only the verbal messages that are being sent, but the nonverbal ones as well. When active listening is combined with such active observation, the result is *active reception,* a process of actively attending to, even anticipating, a communication.

One technique of active reception is to begin an interaction with a self-posed question such as, "What is this person trying to say to me verbally and nonverbally?" Test your hypotheses about what is being conveyed to you by rephrasing in your own words whatever messages you believe you are being sent, and then find out from the speaker whether your understanding is correct.

In active reception, you too are sending nonverbal messages back to the individual speaking as that person speaks. The message you are sending back is that you are attending to what is being said, processing it, and evaluating it. You need not agree with everything that is being said, but for effective communication to take place, you should at least understand it. You communicate to the speaker that you are listening by your eye contact, facial expressions, posture, and the questions and comments you offer in reply.

Of course, active reception is but half of the effective communication equation. The other half of that equation concerns imparting the message that you wish to impart.

Speaking Your Mind

In everyday conversation, the phrase *speaking your mind* may carry with it the connotation of speaking bluntly, candidly, or dealing with something that has been bothering you by "getting it off your chest." In the context of effective communication, however, speaking your mind does not necessarily carry with it any such connotations. Rather the phrase refers, quite literally and simply, to communicating effectively to another whatever it is that is on your mind. Here are five guidelines which you may find helpful:

1. *Know what you want to communicate.*
   Help your listener to focus on what you are saying by making certain that you know what you want to say. In most instances, the more succinctly you can make your point the better.
2. *Know how you want to communicate whatever it is you wish to communicate.*
   People have many different communication styles. Some use a relaxed, homespun approach, while other people make their case similar to the way that a lawyer might in court. What communication style works best for you? How can you best incorporate your own personal assets—your charm, wit, or whatever—to maximize the effectiveness of your presentation?
3. *Anticipate what the other party might have to say and how the other party might attempt to communicate to you.*
   By anticipating the words and actions of the other party you will be preparing as best you can to question the logic or advisability of the positions being advocated. What are the areas of agreement and disagreement between you, if any? If you disagree, what is the basis for the disagreement? What is the purpose of the communication for the other party? What can you do to help the other party achieve this purpose by the time that the communication between you is concluded? If you cannot or will not help the other party in this way, for what specific reasons will you not?
4. *Be aware of the nonverbal presentation you are making as well as the verbal one.*
   Just as you might be attempting to read the nonverbal messages the other party is sending you, so the other party may be trying to read your nonverbal messages. You may choose to be either an "open book" (in which the nonverbal cues you deliberately send are easily interpreted) or "poker-faced" with respect to the nonverbal messages you deliberately impart. In both cases, the intent is the same: to provide as little basis as possible for the other party's misinterpretation of your nonverbal behavior.
5. *Conclude communications by leaving the door open for future communications.*
   Rarely does it pay to burn one's bridges and attempt to close off communication forever. Even if you vehemently disagree with the other party, it is usually a better strategy to withdraw, regroup, rearm yourself with new information, and go back and communicate more effectively on another day.

SUMMARY

THE NEED FOR AFFILIATION People rely on other people, enjoy other people, and derive a sense of comfort and security from other people. The motivation to interact with other people, including the motivation to please or comfort them and be pleased or comforted by them, has been referred to as the *need for affiliation*. The strength of this need varies in different people and different theories have been advanced to explain why. *Loneliness* is a condition that results from the frustration of one's need for affiliation.

FRIENDSHIP AND LIKING Friends are people we like, and six factors have been found to be prominent in liking: proximity, attractiveness, personality, equity, reciprocity, and similarity. The acronym "PAPERS" was introduced as an aid to remembering these factors.

ATTRACTION AND LOVE There are many different types of love, all involving intense affection (such as the love between a parent and a child) and some involving romance and sexual attraction (such as the powerful feelings experienced by Shakespeare's lovers Romeo and Juliet). Focusing on the romantic variety, some theorists have drawn a distinction between *passionate love* and *companionate love*. Passionate love is the product of emotional arousal plus a cognitive label of "love." Companionate love is the product of affection, less the intense arousal and passion of passionate love.

COMMUNICATING *Communication* may be defined as an exchange of messages by verbal and/or nonverbal means. *Effective communication* is said to exist when the message that the source wishes to convey is received by the person or persons targeted to receive that message. All communication must be considered within a cultural context and mixing cultural contexts in communication leads to misinterpretation. Nonverbal messages are particularly prone to misinterpretation. Other potential obstacles to effective communication are physical, psychological, or situational in nature.

Human Sexuality

O U T L I N E

For what reasons do people engage in sex?

Jot down your thoughts in response to this question before reading on. The list of possible motivations is probably longer than most people might first think (Nass et al., 1981; Neubeck, 1972).

It is through human sexuality that many wide-ranging objectives, from procreation to procrastination, can be accomplished. For some people, sex and love are inextricably intertwined; sex is a physical expression of powerful emotions and feelings. Some people use sex to keep boredom away, keep from doing unpleasant things, or keep depression at bay. Sex is undertaken by some people for the sole purpose of reproduction. Sex may be used as an expression of reconciliation or forgiveness. It may be used as a gift, as a weapon, or as a bargaining tool. Some people seek out sexual experiences, at least in part, for the sense of accomplishment or conquest such experiences provide. In prostitution, the motivation of the prostitute may range from simple financial gain to a desire to express anger and contempt at people. The motivation of the prostitute's client may range from simple sexual relief to self-destruction. In coercive or forced sex, the motivation on the part of the person forcing the sexual activity may in reality not be very sexual at all; sex may simply be a means to dominate, humiliate, hurt, or otherwise abuse the victim. In some situations, difficult questions are raised regarding the ability of someone to consent to engage in sexual activity. For example, in the course of a much-publicized rape trial involving a 21-year-old, developmentally disabled woman, experts testified that the woman appeared to have given consent to sexual activity as a gesture of friendship (Hanley, 1992a), but may not have been intellectually capable of truly understanding her consent (Hanley, 1992b).

Regardless of individual motivations to engage in it, sex is undeniably a part of human life. It is an aspect of life that has at once both fascinated and challenged personality theorists, educators, members of the clergy, clinicians, developmental psychologists, comparative psychologists, and other professionals who approach its study from varied vantage points. Its fascination for the general public is well documented in the form of a never-ending stream of gossip in the popular media.

As with virtually all of the major topics covered in this book, human sexuality may be discussed from many different perspectives. In this chapter, we will examine selected aspects of human sexuality from a biological perspective, and then devote the remainder of the chapter to a consideration of various behavioral aspects. Along the way, many values- and culture-related issues will be raised.

A BIOLOGICAL PERSPECTIVE

Biological factors, including one's genetic inheritance and the state of one's physical and mental health, play a great role in the nature, quality, and level of satisfaction one experiences as a sexual person. Let's look at some of those factors, beginning "at the beginning."

THE GENETIC BASIS OF HUMAN SEXUALITY

The origins of a person who is genetically programmed to be either a man or a woman can be traced back to the moment of conception. At conception, the father's sperm united with a female egg or *ovum* and formed what is called a *zygote*. The ovum was genetically encoded with a pair of chromosomes designated as *XX*, while the sperm was genetically encoded with a pair of chromosomes designated as *XY*. The resulting zygote contained 23 chromosomes from the sperm and 23 chromosomes from the ovum, or a total of 46 chromosomes in all. If an *X* chromosome from the mother combined with an *X* chromosome from the father, the result was an *XX* chromosome pattern, indicative of biologically female offspring. If an *X* chromosome from the mother combined with a *Y* chromosome from the father, the result was an *XY* chromosome pattern, indicative of biologically male offspring.

Although most people are born either male or female, and with a total of 46 chromosomes, relatively rare exceptions do occur. Factors such as one or both parents' exposure to drugs or other agents (such as excessive radiation), illness, genetic abnormalities, genetic disease, or advanced age, as well as numerous other factors, may lead to the birth of a child who has more or less than 46 chromosomes. Variations in chromosomal number and structure, as well as other abnormalities, may also lead to atypical sexual development. Atypical sexual development may manifest itself in internal and/or external ways. For example, although a male child may possess the typical *XY* configuration of chromosomes, he may have the outward appearance of a female. Alternatively, atypical sex-related development may progress internally and not be readily visible from outward appearances. Internal, atypical sex-related development may affect organs such as the ovaries, the testes, even the brain. It has been found, for example, that insufficient prenatal levels of the hormone androgen in a biologically male child result in a brain that resembles that of a female (Plapinger & McEwen, 1978; MacLusky & Naftolin, 1981; McEwen, 1981).

MALE SEXUAL ANATOMY

Anatomy is *the science of the structure of organisms.* The term **sexual anatomy** is used here to refer to *bodily organs involved in reproduction and/or potential sources of sexual pleasure.* The word **genital**, derived from the Latin word meaning *to beget* or *to produce,* usually refers to *an external and visible reproductive organ.* Genital is most frequently used in either of its two plural forms, *genitals* or *genitalia.* The presentation below of the anatomy of males and females focuses on the genitals. Keep in mind that other parts of the body, such as the mouth, the hands, even the brain, could also be discussed in terms of this open-ended definition of sexual anatomy.

The anatomy of a normal male's penis and testes is presented in Figure 12–1. The *penis* is *the male organ used in copulation and urination.* In the process of excreting urine, urine travels from the bladder through a tube called the *urethra* and exits the body via the *meatus* or opening in the penis. *Semen, the ejaculate of sperm and other cells,* also travels through the urethra and out the opening in the penis. Semen and urine are never mixed due to gatekeeper-type muscles called *sphincters* which regulate the entry of semen and urine into the urethra. The tip of the penis, referred to as the *glans,* contains many more nerve endings than the shaft and, as a result, is extremely sensitive to stimulation. Also particularly sensitive to stimulation are the *coronal ridge* at the top of the penis and the *frenulum* on the underside of the penis where the glans meets the shaft.

The *foreskin* is a thin layer of skin covering the penis. In a surgical procedure called *circumcision,* the foreskin covering the glans is removed. Circumcision is routinely performed in accordance with the religious laws of Judaism, and other religious groups. Experts disagree about whether circumcision also has health benefits. At the very least, circumcision does have a hygiene benefit. In uncircumcised males, a substance called *smegma* will typically build up under the glans. Uncircumcised men must take extra care to make certain that smegma, which is actually a mixture of dead skin cells, dirt, bacteria, and bodily secretions, is thoroughly washed away. If not regularly removed, smegma may cause infection of the foreskin or glans.

anatomy
the science of the structure of organisms.

sexual anatomy
bodily organs involved in reproduction and/or potential sources of sexual pleasure.

genital
from the Latin meaning *to beget* or *to produce,* an external and visible reproductive organ. Plural form is either *genitals* or *genitalia.*

FIGURE 12–1   THE PENIS AND THE TESTES

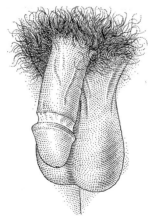 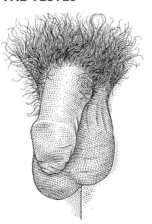

The physical appearance of a circumcised penis (foreskin of the glans has been surgically removed)

The physical appearance of an uncircumcised penis (foreskin of the glans is intact)

On average, the length of the penis in the nonerect (flaccid) state is slightly under 4 inches. The length of the penis in the erect state varies much less than the size of the penis in the nonerect state; the penis that is smaller in the flaccid state may become proportionately larger when aroused than the penis that is larger in the flaccid state. For this reason, Masters and Johnson (1966) referred to erection as "the great equalizer." Masters and Johnson also noted that the concern of many men regarding the size of their own genitals—as well as feelings of masculine inadequacy that may accompany those concerns—is usually unfounded. Although penile size, either in the aroused or nonaroused state, may indeed have a psychological impact on a female sexual partner, the actual physical impact is minimal. This is so because there are relatively few sensory nerve endings in the inner two-thirds of the vagina; most of the sensation derived from penile stimulation is perceived only from the first third of the vagina and its surrounding area. In a very rare medical condition called *micropenis*, a fully developed penis reaches less than 1 inch in length. When due to a deficiency in the hormone testosterone, micropenis can be effectively treated by hormone injections.

A **gonad** is *a gamete-producing organ*. A **gamete** is *a cell containing chromosomal material that is capable of producing a zygote upon union with a gamete from the opposite sex*. In the male, the *testes* are the gonads. In the female, the *ovaries*, another paired organ, are the gonads. The testes hang just below the penis, and one testis (the singular form of testes) typically hangs slightly lower than the other. The testes are surrounded by a thin layer of skin called the *scrotum*. The scrotum has muscles in it which can either draw the testes closer to the body or let them hang freely away from the body. Because gamete (sperm) production can be halted by excesses in temperature, such movement of the scrotum serves a protective function, among other functions. In a cold environment, the testes will be drawn closer to the body, thus providing extra warmth. In a hot environment, the testes will hang freely, thus exposing a maximum amount of surface area and allowing a maximum amount of heat dissipation. In addition to producing sperm beginning with the onset of puberty, the testes also produce the hormone testosterone.

Folded against each testis is a network of tubing called the *epididymis*. After being produced in the testes, sperm cells spend weeks maturing as they slowly travel through the epididymis. From the epididymis, the sperm exits the testis via another relatively long tubular structure called the *vas deferens*.[1] From the vas deferens, the sperm cells will eventually be expelled during sexual activity through the urethra. The *prostate gland* produces a fluid that helps transport and nourish the sperm cells. Along with the seminal fluid produced by the seminal vesicles, the fluid produced by the prostate gland will also be expelled from the penis during **ejaculation** (*the discharge of seminal fluid, also referred to as semen, that occurs during sexual activity*). Although it takes only one lone sperm to fertilize an egg, each ejaculation produces many more times that amount. A sperm count of between 40 to 120 million per ejaculation is considered normal.

THE MALE SEXUAL RESPONSE CYCLE

What follows is a brief description of what physiologically takes place from the time of arousal to the time of orgasm. Keep in mind, however, that beginning with the varied stimuli that people find arousing and ending with the stimulus that produces orgasm, a number of intervening factors can be discussed. A wealth of very varied factors—personal values, social customs, social learning, physical fatigue level, degree of one's comfort or feelings of security, diet, and environmental temperature among them—may play a role in the physiology of an individual sexual response.

It has been said that the brain is the largest sex organ. Certainly, sexual arousal does not take place without the brain's participation. In fact, a male may consider himself sexually aroused without any visible reaction at all on the part of the genitals. It is usually only as the arousal intensifies that the more visible aspects of arousal become noticeable.

As described by William H. Masters and Virginia E. Johnson (1966), the male and female sexual response cycles go through the same four stages: excitement, plateau, orgasm, and resolution. The *excitement stage* begins with mental and/or physical stimulation, usually accompanied by an erection of the penis. Erection is actually caused by increased blood flow to the penis. Factors such as anxiety, guilt, and fatigue may negatively affect the

---

gonad

a gamete-producing organ.

gamete

a cell containing chromosomal material that is capable of producing a zygote upon union with a gamete from the opposite sex.

ejaculation

the discharge of seminal fluid that occurs during sexual activity.

[1]It is the *vas deferens* that is surgically severed in the male sterilization procedure called *vasectomy*.

blood flow with the result being a penis that is only partially erect. During the *plateau stage*, the coronal ridge may become darker in color due to a pooling of blood, and the testes swell, sometimes to nearly twice their size in a nonaroused state. A clear fluid, which sometimes contains active sperm cells, is emitted at this stage. It is this clear fluid that periodically frustrates couples who use "withdrawal" as a means of contraception. With continued stimulation, the point of *orgasm* (also referred to as ejaculation in males, and climax in both males and females) is reached. During this stage, which lasts only for a few seconds, rhythmic muscular contractions propel semen in a gush from the penis. The psychological effects of orgasm may vary. Variables such as the nature of the relationship with the partner, feelings about the partner, time since last orgasm, and prior expectations about the experience may all affect a male or female's postorgasmic mental response.

The *resolution stage* entails a return to the nonaroused state. During this stage, and for a period of time thereafter referred to as the *refractory period*, it will be physiologically impossible for the man to have another orgasm. The length of time of the refractory period varies both between and within men as a function of many factors. It may be as short as a few minutes, especially in younger men, or as long as hours for other men. In general, the length of the male's refractory period tends to grow with age. Variations in this sequence of stages are possible. For example, it sometimes happens that a man stays in the plateau stage for an extended period of time, does not have an orgasm, and subsequently goes to the resolution stage. Such a situation, especially when there was an extended period of arousal, may cause testicular aching (referred to in slang as "blue balls").

MALE SEXUAL DYSFUNCTION AND TREATMENT

Male sexual dysfunction typically occurs at either the excitement, plateau, or orgasm stage of the sexual response cycle. At the excitement stage, a failure of the penis to become erect is variously referred to as *erectile dysfunction* or *impotence*. Erectile dysfunction may be caused by psychological factors, medical factors (such as diabetes), drug taking (including ingestion of alcohol), and other factors. A sexual dysfunction that occurs at the plateau stage is painful intercourse. The cause of the pain may vary; contraceptive devices (including foams or creams) may cause irritation, as may any infection in the penis, the urethra, the testes, or the prostate gland. A male sexual dysfunction associated with the orgasm stage is **premature ejaculation,** a term that for our purposes will be defined simply as *climax that comes too quickly for one or both partners.*

Treatment for male sexual dysfunction, usually referred to simply as *sex therapy*, may employ a wide variety of techniques depending upon the specific dysfunction and its perceived cause (Barlow, 1986; Killman & Auerbach, 1979). In the Masters and Johnson approach, a female/male team of therapists will treat the man and his sexual partner with homework and other assignments demanding increasingly complex sexual activity. The preference of most sex therapists in the Masters and Johnson tradition is to treat couples, although individuals may be accepted for treatment and assigned a sexual partner (referred to as a **surrogate**). Sex therapy will seek to improve the level of sex education and sexual competency of the partners as well as the quality of their overall relationship and communication. One type of exercise innovated by Masters and Johnson is called **sensate focus.** This exercise, usually carried out in the nude, entails each partner pleasuring the other with nongenital touching. Such pleasing physical contact within the context of a situation that is not sexually demanding is presumably therapeutic in that partners explore each other's sensory preferences. The Masters and Johnson treatment approach for sexual dysfunction may also be employed through the use of books, videos, and other non-therapist-applied programs, although the results are likely to be more variable (Mohr & Beutler, 1990).

FEMALE SEXUAL ANATOMY

Like the external appearance of male genitalia, female genitalia may vary greatly in appearance due to individual differences in size, shape, and coloring. Just as there can be no definitive description of how a nose, mouth, or ear should look—there is a great deal of variation, yet all are "normal"—so there can be only a most general description of how sexual organs look. Figure 12–2 is an illustration of the female genitalia, including the *labia*

premature ejaculation

a male sexual dysfunction at the orgasm stage of the sexual response cycle involving a too quick climax.

surrogate

in sex therapy, a sexual partner in place of a spouse

sensate focus

a technique in sex therapy involving non-genital, pleasure-giving touching.

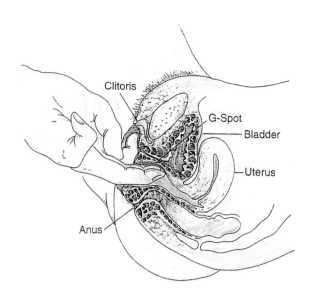

FIGURE 12–2   THE VULVA To ghosts, flying saucers, and other things whose existence remains a matter of heated debate, add a distinct entity in the female anatomy called the "G-spot." The G-spot was named after gynecologist Ernest Grafenberg. He was the first to call the world's attention to an area on the ceiling of the vaginal wall about 1 to 2 inches from the vaginal opening and to discuss its role in human sexuality. Grafenberg (1950) believed that this area was so sensitive that female orgasm, complete with a milk-like ejaculate, could arise from its stimulation. Some have speculated that the fluid observed by Grafenberg and other researchers who followed him was not really an ejaculate but merely drops of urine released involuntarily at the point of orgasm (Alzate, 1985; Goldberg et al., 1983). Such charges have been disputed on the basis of chemical analyses of the "ejaculate" (Zaviac et al., 1988). Although a great deal of research has been conducted on Grafenberg's assertions, whether a veritable female ejaculation occurs, indeed the very existence of the G–spot, remains a matter of controversy (Alzate & Londono, 1984; Davidson et al., 1989; Masters et al., 1989).

majora, the *labia minora*, the *clitoris*, and the entrance to the *vagina* (sometimes referred to as the vaginal vestibule). Collectively, these genitals are referred to as the *vulva*.

The *labia majora* (or "outer lips") of the vulva physically protect the vaginal entrance and urinary opening. The *labia minora* (or "inner lips"), which also serve a protective function, have been likened to the petals of a flower. The top of these "petals" form a fold of skin referred to as the *clitoral hood* because they cover the clitoris. Located just below where the top of the labia minora meet is the *clitoris*, an organ that is exquisitely sensitive to touch, pressure, and temperature. According to Masters and Johnson (1970), the clitoris is the only organ in either sex whose sole function is related to sexual sensations and erotic pleasure. The three structures that comprise the clitoris are the *clitoral glans*, the *clitoral shaft*, and the *crura of clitoris*. The part of the clitoris that is visible when the clitoral hood is lifted is called the clitoral glans, a button-like structure at the tip of the clitoris. Behind the clitoral glans is the clitoral shaft, and behind the clitoral shaft is the crura (Latin for *legs*) of clitoris, which anchor the clitoris to the pubic bone. The crura also contain cavities that become engorged with blood, causing some stiffening of the clitoris during sexual arousal. Although some parallels exist between the clitoris and the penis, important differences exist as well. Unlike a penis, the clitoris has no function in urination and does not lengthen during sexual arousal.

The vagina is a fairly elastic organ which averages about 5 1/2 inches in length in women who have not given birth vaginally. After a vaginal birth, it typically enlarges somewhat and loses some of its original elasticity. The vagina is made of muscle and has an inner *mucosa* lining which is similar to that of the mouth. In the nonaroused state, it could be likened to a deflated balloon. Yet the vagina has many blood vessels going to it and it is capable of expansion, even rhythmic contraction, during sexual intercourse. Only the outer one-third of the vagina has nerve cells going to it, and it is in that area that the Grafenberg spot is thought to exist.

At birth, the external opening of the vagina is usually covered with a thin, elastic tissue referred to as the *hymen*, which is Greek for *membrane*. Usually this structure is naturally perforated, which allows for the free flow of the menses at puberty. An *imperforate hymen* is one that has not been perforated. If not perforated by puberty, a problem will arise due to the blockage of the menstrual flow. The problem is easily remedied with a simple surgical perforation of the hymen. For many years, many people throughout the world believed that an intact hymen at the time of marriage was a sign that a woman was a virgin. We now know that this is not necessarily the case. Occasionally, females are born with a perforated hymen. It is not unusual for a hymen to be perforated by various kinds of sports activity including bicycle or horseback riding. And because this structure is so elastic, it is possible in some instances that even sexual intercourse will not perforate it.

THE FEMALE SEXUAL RESPONSE CYCLE

As observed by Masters and Johnson (1966), women go through the same four stages in a sexual response cycle as men, although what happens physiologically during those stages is quite different. The excitement stage for females is characterized by a flattening and moving apart of the labia majora, a swelling of the labia minora, enlargement of the clitoris as it becomes engorged with blood, a swelling of most of the inner area of the vagina, and lubrication of the vaginal vestibule. Additionally, the nipples of the breast may become erect as the result of muscle contractions. During the plateau phase, the labia minora continue to swell, and may even double or triple in thickness. The swelling of the labia minora cause the labia majora to push apart. Also swelling during the plateau phase is the outer portion of the vagina, an action that causes the opening of the vaginal orifice to narrow by as much as 30%. The clitoral glans, which has become increasingly engorged during the plateau stage, is typically seen by researchers to disappear beneath the clitoral hood. During sexual intercourse, then, the clitoris glans is actually receiving penile stimulation through the clitoral hood; it is therefore only indirectly being stimulated by the penis. The penis thrusts the labia minora back and forth, which impacts on the clitoral hood, which in turn impacts on the clitoral glans (Masters & Johnson, 1966). Masters and Johnson note that manual stimulation of the labia minora, the labia majora, even the area just above the clitoral hood (an area known as the *mons* or "mound") during this stage may yield pleasurable clitoral sensations.

Up until the 1950s or so, few people, including medical authorities, believed that females could have orgasms. This sexist myth probably evolved from the cultural expectation that "proper" women did not derive as much pleasure from sexual activity as men. Women who believed that they had indeed experienced orgasms may not have been eager to share such information for fear of being saddled with some highly undesirable label. Masters and Johnson (1966; 1981) studied female orgasm and noted that descriptions of it typically included references to a momentary sense of suspension, followed by a pleasurable feeling that radiates from the clitoris to the entire pelvic region, sometimes accompanied by vaginal muscular contractions. In addition, the female orgasm is marked by distinctive brain wave patterns (Cohen et al., 1976), as well as by muscular contractions in the uterus and the anal sphincter. A "mild" orgasm may entail only a half-dozen or so such contractions. An "intense" orgasm may entail two or three times that many contractions. A small number of women emit a fluid that is neither urine nor vaginal lubrication at the time of orgasm (Masters & Johnson, 1981).

A key difference between male and female sexual response comes at the stage of resolution. Immediately after orgasm, the male sexual response cycle moves into a refractory period before beginning the cycle anew with arousal. By contrast, immediately after orgasm, the human female is capable of experiencing additional orgasms. In order to be multiorgasmic, two conditions must typically be met: (1) sexual stimulation must be continuing, and (2) sexual interest must be maintained. Relatively few women consistently have multiorgasmic experiences during sexual intercourse, although they may have such experiences during masturbation. This latter fact may be due to factors such as the ease of continuing sexual stimulation and the ease of producing and maintaining highly arousing sexual fantasies.

FEMALE SEXUAL DYSFUNCTION AND TREATMENT

As with males, females may experience dysfunction associated with one or more of the four stages of the sexual response cycle. For example, with respect to the excitement stage, some women (and men) experience disorders of sexual desire. Other people may experience undue fears, anxiety, guilt, or other psychological problems associated with the prospect of having sex, becoming sexually aroused, or losing control. A problem that may occur during the plateau stage is a condition involving an involuntary spasm of the vaginal muscles near the opening of the vagina. This condition, referred to as *vaginismus*, can make intercourse extremely uncomfortable or painful, if not impossible. A dysfunction that may occur at the stage of orgasm, and a relatively common one for many women according to Masters and Johnson, is that of not experiencing an orgasm during intercourse. Some women are not able to experience an orgasm at all, while others are able in response to self-stimulation of their genitals but not as a result of intercourse. Orgasmic failure may result from a number of causes ranging from a male partner who consistently achieves orgasm sooner to lingering feelings of guilt regarding the expression of sexuality (Kelly et al., 1990). Guilt, as well as numerous other psychological variables, including hostility, distrust, and low self-esteem, among others, may contribute to various types of sexual dysfunction (Cotten-Huston & Wheeler, 1983; Killmann et al., 1987; Nichols, 1990; Vance, 1984).

As in sex therapy for males, the exact nature of the treatment program will vary as a function of the specific presenting problem and its presumed cause. And as in therapy with males, there is a preference for treating couples as opposed to individuals. In general, the Masters and Johnson approach to treatment will entail detailed history–taking, with particular attention paid to relevant nonsexual as well as sexual issues (including issues pertaining to the couple's relationship). In private rooms, the couples will engage in sensate focus exercises (see page 317), perhaps in various positions. An example of a more specific treatment technique for the female sexual dysfunction vaginismus will entail the use of exercises designed to relax the muscles around the vagina. These exercises may include voluntary tightening and loosening by the woman. Additional treatment may employ the use of dilators of various size first inserted into the vagina by a physician, and then inserted by the woman herself. As tolerance for the increasingly larger dilators builds, the vagina will soon be able to tolerate a penis in it without going into spasms (Kolodny et al., 1970).

HUMAN SEXUALITY THROUGH THE LIFESPAN

Human sexuality finds expression through the lifespan in various ways ranging, for example, from the toddler's naive self-manipulation of the genitals to sexual intercourse indulged in during late adulthood. From a biological perspective, reproductive capability begins towards the end of puberty, a period of time marked by great physical changes beginning with the appearance of secondary sex characteristics. Largely through the action of hormones, people undergo a transformation that culminates in the physical ability to sexually reproduce. This transformation includes physical changes that are necessary for reproduction, such as the enlargement of the uterus and vagina in the female and the enlargement of the penis and the testes in the male. As a kind of side-effect of the flood of hormones into the system, many other physical changes—some unwelcome—also occur. For example, glands in the armpits begin to produce sweat that emits what many people find to be an unpleasant odor. Glands producing oil become especially active in the region of the face; skin pores blocked as a consequence will result in blackheads. Pimples are blackheads that have become infected. Perhaps the most tumultuous changes during this period are the physically unobservable, emotional ones. The hormones carry with them emotional effects, including mood swings and extreme sensitivity (Schickedanz et al., 1990).

The term primary sex characteristics refers to the internal and external organs necessary for reproduction to take place, and to related processes such as ovulation in females and sperm production in males. An **ovum** is *the female reproductive cell or egg*; its plural form is *ova*. The **ovaries** are *a pair of female organs that produce ova*. **Ovulation** refers to *the process of producing ova*. On average, human female ovulation takes place on a 28-day cycle. This cycle is variously referred to in humans as the *ovarian cycle* or the *menstrual cycle*, and as the *estrus cycle* in other mammals. A by-product of ovulation when impregnation does not take place is the flow of the **menses**, which is *a mixture of blood and dead cells from the uterus*. Normally, a total of only about 2 to 3 ounces of blood is lost during **menstruation** (*the process of menstrual flow*). In the healthy, nonpregnant female, menstruation will occur from 1 to 5 days on a "monthly" (that is, 28-day) cycle from the time of **menarche** (*the first menstruation*) through **menopause** (*the period in which menstruation ceases*). In the United States, the average age of menarche is 12.8 years (Insel & Roth, 1991). Menopause typically occurs some time between the ages of 45 and 50 and may last for about 2 years or so.

ovum

the female reproductive cell or egg. Plural form is *ova*.

ovaries

the female gonads.

ovulation

the process of producing ova.

menses

a mixture of blood and cells from the uterus that is a by-product of ovulation when impregnation does not take place.

menstruation

the process of menstrual flow which typically occurs from 1 to 5 days on a monthly (28-day) basis in the healthy, non-pregnant female.

menarche

the first menstruation, usually between 12 and 13 years of age.

menopause

the age at which menstruation ceases, usually some time between 45 and 50.

Female reproductive capability statistically lessens with age after age 30 (Schneider, 1978) and ceases with menopause . . . well, not entirely. Although the postmenopausal woman is incapable of producing ova, she may be capable of carrying to term a fertilized ova that has been implanted in her uterus (Sauer et al., 1990). Due to the decrease in hormone production that accompanies menopause, the walls of the vagina may become thin and less elastic. The vagina may also shrink somewhat, and be slower to lubricate and lubricate less during sexual arousal. Despite such changes, sexual responsiveness, which typically peaks in a woman's 30s, may remain strong well into the 60s and beyond. Commercially available lubricants are usually advisable to help remedy lubrication problems. Hormone replacement therapy is sometimes recommended to treat painful intercourse as well as many other symptoms brought on by menopause, including **hot flashes** (sudden bouts of sweating and flushing) and progressively increasing brittleness of the bones (Ettinger, 1988). However, there is evidence that hormone replacement therapy may increase the risk of cancer as well as blood clots, hypertension, gallstones, and other problems (Antunes et al., 1979; Goldman & Tosteson, 1991; Greenblatt & Stoddard, 1978; Mack et al., 1976). Although the risks can sometimes be minimized by preventive methods (Bachmann & Gill, 1988), whether the potential dangers of hormone replacement therapy outweigh its potential benefits is an individual matter, and one that must be discussed with a physician. One menopause specialist, Wulf H. Utian, cautions that before hormone replacement therapy is prescribed, the possible presence of numerous conditions (including high levels of fat or cholesterol in the blood, severe varicose veins, very high blood pressure or other circulatory problems, and uterine fibroids) must be evaluated. Utian (1992) cautioned against hormonal replacement therapy for menopausal women with any of the following conditions: (1) any tumor which can be stimulated by the hormone estrogen, such as known or suspected breast or uterine cancer; (2) a strong family history of estrogen-related cancer; (3) unexplained or abnormal genital bleeding, and (4) liver disease.

Male reproductive capability appears to be virtually lifelong. Healthy men in their 80s and 90s are physiologically capable of fathering children. Yet it is also true that male sexual responsiveness typically peaks in the teen years and then declines. With increasing age, sperm production decreases, the angle of the erection lowers, the scrotum hangs lower, and the force and intensity of contractions during ejaculation decreases. Men in their 50s, 60s, and beyond may need more direct physical stimulation to become aroused sexually. Older men may also find an erection more difficult to obtain, and more difficult to sustain once obtained.

Whether or not the equivalent of a female menopause in men takes place is a matter of debate. Some researchers claim to have found a significant drop in the male hormone testosterone in men in their 50s or 60s, while other researchers have been unable to replicate such findings. Surveying the available research, John B. McKinlay, an epidemiologist at Boston University, remains unconvinced that any "male menopause" exists. However, McKinlay (1992) forecasted that, "even though in my perspective there is no epidemiological, physiological or clinical evidence for such a syndrome, I think by the year 2000 the syndrome will exist. There's very strong interest in treating aging men for a profit, just as there is for menopausal women." To McKinlay's statement one might add the political incentive for reducing differences between the sexes; in the interest of equality, then, if one sex has a menopause, the other must have one too. Masters and Johnson and others (Greenblatt et al., 1979; Kolodny, Masters, & Johnson, 1979) did observe that after the age of 60, about 5% of men studied experienced many symptoms similar to female menopause. They reported that the condition responded favorably to male hormone replacement therapy.

Much more common and far less debatable than a male menopause are problems related to an enlarged prostate. About 30% of men in their 40s, 50% of men in their 50s, and 75% of men in their 80s are affected by this problem. The prostate gland is located just under the bladder and it surrounds a portion of the urethra which carries urine from the bladder to the penis. Problems arise when the prostate enlarges and presses against the urethra, impeding the flow of urine (much like pinching a straw will impede the flow of liquid). Symptoms of prostate problems include various urinary difficulties, including sudden urges to urinate, frequent urination, and an interrupted stream of urine. In severe

hot flashes
in menopausal women, sudden bouts of sweating and flushing.

cases, blockage results, a condition that usually requires surgery. Because the prostate can be felt through the rectum, its size and condition can be evaluated by a physician during a routine office visit. A man experiencing such urinary difficulties should schedule an appointment with a physician. Prostate enlargement may be due to normal aging and be treatable, or it may be due to prostate cancer. A simple blood test can identify the existence of prostate cancer.

SEXUAL VALUES, ORIENTATION, AND BEHAVIOR

Chances are good that there are images being shown on one of your cable television stations right at this moment that are highly sexual. Sex-related stories can probably be found in that magazine or newspaper on your coffee table. Yet, curiously, in a society that almost seems to thrive on sex-related communications, most people are quite shy when it comes to discussing their own sexual functioning. Even many married couples have difficulty in broaching this subject with each other.

Modesty about sex in our culture begins early. From birth onward, genitals are referred to as "private parts," and tend to be scrupulously covered up, even when most everything else is not. As children grow old enough to communicate, sex-related topics are the ones that most parents tend to feel awkward or uncomfortable in discussing; they may do so only when they feel they must, and then for only as long as they perceive necessary. Even parents who feel that they can talk to their children about almost anything may find themselves stuttering and stammering when the subject of sex is raised. Perhaps this is because sexual acts are among the most private things that people do. Studies suggest that most people first learn about sex not from parents and not at school, but from peers (Coles & Stokes, 1985; Papini et al., 1988; Thornburg & Aras, 1986).

Sex education in the schools is becoming more widespread (Kenney et al., 1989), although the curricula of individual school districts vary widely (Brooks-Gunn & Furstenberg, 1989; Forrest & Silverman, 1989). Topic coverage will vary depending on the child's developmental level but will typically include sexual anatomy, reproduction and pregnancy, family planning, and sexually transmitted diseases. Factual information provided in such sex education curricula, much like information provided in college textbooks like this, can provide an important base of knowledge for informed sexual decision making. But are such facts all that is needed to act responsibly in sexual decision making? What else is required? How does one achieve a sense of sexual adjustment?

A key component of sexual adjustment is a personal system of values that guides sexual decision making. A personal system of values contains relatively specific implications for what is right and what is wrong when it comes to sexual behavior.

SEXUAL VALUES

Physical attraction between people can exert a powerful influence on behavior and thinking. In the presence of an extremely attractive person, the strong can become weak at the knees, the intelligent can become dumbfounded, and the eloquent can become incoherent. Antoine Bret once said, "The first sigh of love is the last of wisdom."

In an era when acting on sexual urges can readily lead to consequences that range from beautiful and fulfilling to ugly and tragic, the decision to enter into a sexual relationship is probably best not left to chance impulses. In movies and other media, people are often depicted as spontaneously "wandering into" or "finding themselves" in relationships. In real life, there is definitely a time for spontaneity in sexual relationships, but whether that time is when the two parties know relatively little about each other seems, at best, questionable. Too often, people really do not even know themselves all that well sexually—let alone someone else! All of which raises some important questions.

How well do you know yourself in terms of your own values? How did you acquire these values? If you have not given much thought to such questions, now may be a good time to begin. If you have given thought to such questions, now may be a good time to evaluate your own personal comfort level with your convictions. Especially if you are single and not presently involved in a relationship, a tool that you may find useful in helping to define and evaluate your sex-related values is the Forethought-to-Foreplay Quiz (see the *Self-Assessment* feature). The test has no right or wrong answers; you decide what is right and wrong. For further assistance in distilling your own sex-related values, a consultation or two with a member of your school's counseling staff may be helpful. Under some circumstances, open and frank discussions about values and related matters with a sexual partner or prospective sexual partner can also be helpful. Such discussion may be useful not only in clarifying each of your own respective value systems but also in enhancing your overall relationship (Zimmer, 1983).

In addition to sexual values, another element of one's sexual identity is sexual orientation.

SEXUAL ORIENTATION

Sexual orientation refers to *the general nature of one's erotic inclination or preference with respect to the gender of sexual partners.* A **heterosexual orientation** refers to a *general erotic inclination or preference for opposite-sex sexual partners.* A slang term used to describe the heterosexual orientation is the adjective *straight.* A **homosexual orientation** refers to *a general erotic inclination or preference for same-sex sexual partners.* Female homosexuals, also referred to as *lesbians*, are sexually oriented towards other females. Male homosexuals, also referred to as *gays*, are sexually oriented towards other males. A *bisexual orientation* refers to a general erotic inclination towards same-sex as well as opposite-sex sexual partners. Some bisexuals have no particular preference for sexual partners of one sex or the other. Other bisexuals do have a preference for partners of one sex but will occasionally have sex with someone of the other sex.

sexual orientation
the general nature of one's erotic inclination or preference with respect for the gender of sexual partners.

heterosexual orientation
a general erotic inclination or preference for opposite-sex sexual partners.

homosexual orientation
a general erotic inclination or preference for same-sex sexual partners.

SELF-ASSESSMENT

The Forethought-to-Foreplay Test

Instructions: Each of the items below contains one statement regarding a person's sexual attitudes or values. For each item, state whether you agree or disagree with this statement from your own perspective. Explain in depth *why* you agree or disagree with the statement, drawing on past experiences or anticipating future scenarios you could be in. Take your time in responding—there are only 10 items—and draw on your innermost beliefs and values in responding. The more candidly and spontaneously you respond, the closer to learning about your values you get. No one need ever see your answer sheet but you.

Scoring and Interpretation: You get to decide which answers are right or wrong. File away your answers, read them from time to time, and feel free to modify them as you grow in your thinking about sex-related issues.

1. When it comes to sex there is only one rule: "If it feels good for me, do it."
2. I believe that the only acceptable sexual behavior is wholly consensual sexual behavior; no one should be made to engage in sex that is against one's will or undertaken as a result of deception.
3. I have given serious thought both to the type of person I could become sexually involved with and to the circumstances under which that involvement would take place.
4. Love and sex are two different things.
5. I accept and respect myself as a sexual person.
6. Except for purposes of reproduction, sex is basically immoral.
7. I believe the respect one has for one's own body should enter into the decision to initiate a sexual relationship.
8. Peers probably have too great an influence on me in terms of my thoughts about sex and/or my sexual behavior.
9. My religion serves as a guide for me in sexual matters.
10. I believe the parties to a sexual relationship should discuss their prior sexual history and be tested for the HIV (AIDS) virus before entering into that relationship.

Primarily for convenience, sexual orientation is typically categorized as heterosexual, homosexual, or bisexual. Yet as data compiled by Alfred C. Kinsey and his colleagues (1948, 1953) suggest, such discrete categorizations can sometimes be misleading. Some heterosexuals have had varying degrees of homosexual experience. Some homosexuals have had varying degrees of heterosexual experience. For these reasons as well as others, including greater social acceptance of homosexuality in recent years, estimates of number of people by sexual orientation are difficult to make with great accuracy. One recent, large-scale survey of American men reported that only about 1% were exclusively homosexual in orientation and that 2% had had homosexual experiences (Barringer, 1993a). In another recent study, it was reported that 4.4% of American men and 3.6% of American women had had sex with a same-sex partner (Barringer, 1993b). In the past, it has been estimated that between 3 and 6% of the adult population are not strictly heterosexual in sexual orientation (Van Wyk & Geist, 1984).

THE ORIGINS OF SEXUAL ORIENTATION

Views about the origins of sexual orientation have undergone dramatic changes in recent years. A decade or so ago, the proposition that some people are born genetically programmed to be heterosexual and others are born genetically programmed to be homosexual would have been seen by members of the professional and lay community alike as quite revolutionary. The dominant view was that all people were born heterosexual in orientation and that some, as a result of environmental factors or early childhood experiences, then became homosexual in orientation. The details of the process by which an individual made the transformation from heterosexual to homosexual would be different depending upon whether a psychoanalytic, behavioral, or other psychological theory was relied upon for explanation.

Although few professionals would deny that psychological factors may well play a part in the decision of some people to choose a particular sexual orientation, a small but increasing number of studies have begun to suggest that sexual orientation may well have a biological basis. For example, evidence from different laboratories is mounting to support the notion that physiological differences may exist between homosexuals and heterosexuals. Simon LeVay (1992) of the Salk Institute in La Jolla, California, reported that a region of the brain that is involved in the regulation of sexual behavior (the *hypothalamus*) was smaller in homosexual than in heterosexual men. Laura S. Allen and Roger A. Gorski (1992) of the University of California at Los Angeles observed differences between gays and straights in the size of the cord of nerve fibers that serves a communication function between the two halves of the brain (the part of the brain referred to as the *anterior commissure*).

The reported physiological differences, should they be replicated in subsequent studies, are intriguing, but nonetheless open to interpretation. Some, such as psychiatrist Robert P. Cabaj of the University of California at San Francisco, have wondered whether such findings may in part be due to the effect of AIDS on the brain. The researchers who observed the physiological differences employed in their analyses the brains of subjects who had died of AIDS. As Cabaj (1992) put it, "We know that HIV has an affinity for brain cells, and I don't think we can rule out this is having an effect." Others view such research as reminiscent of futile searches in years past for physiological differences between members of different ethnic or other groups. As one researcher put it, "I just don't think sexual orientation is going to be represented in any particular brain structure. It's like looking in the brain for your political party affiliation" (Byne, 1992). Gay advocacy groups find political value in studies that report physiological differences between homosexuals and heterosexuals. They argue that just as people have no control over variables such as their ethnic group membership, they have no control over their sexual orientation. In response to the publication of the Allen and Gorski findings, a spokesperson for the National Gay and Lesbian Task force, a Washington-based advocacy group, commented, "It points out gay people are made this way by nature. It strikes at the heart of people who oppose gay rights and who think we don't deserve our rights because we're choosing to be the way we are" (Bray, 1992). Because the studies are correlational in nature, it is in fact impossible to determine from them whether anatomical differences are a precursor to or are caused by sexual orientation.

Studies employing identical twins as subjects—that is, subjects who have the exact same genetic inheritance—have been inconclusive regarding the issue of homosexuality as a genetically inherited orientation. Some findings suggest it is, while other studies suggest it is not. For example, Kallmann (1952) observed that in every case, when one male twin was homosexual, the other one was also homosexual. Yet other researchers have failed to make comparable observations (for example, Bailey & Pillard, 1991; Eckert et al., 1986). Perhaps it is as Money (1987) has concluded, that genetic factors may play some role in sexual orientation but not necessarily a governing role. Determining just how biological, psychological, social, and other factors may interact to give rise to sexual orientation, is a question researchers continue to explore.

SEXUAL ORIENTATION AND PSYCHOPATHOLOGY

What is considered mental disease or illness often hinges on prevailing societal attitudes. Craig MacAndrew (1969) made this point in "On the Notion that Certain Persons Who Are Given to Frequent Drunkenness Suffer from a Disease Called Alcoholism" as he traced how alcoholism came to be regarded as a disease. In what would be his final work, Elvin M. Jellinek, one of this country's most cited alcoholism researchers, argued that once the medical profession decreed alcoholism to be an illness, "through this fact alone alcoholism becomes an illness, whether a part of the lay public likes it or not, and even if a minority of the medical profession is disinclined to accept the idea" (1960, p. 12).

With this background, it is instructive to consider homosexuality from various perspectives including that of the general public, the medical profession, and the homosexual community. In the 1970s, the general public tended to see homosexuality as "sick" (Pattison, 1974) and "sinful" (Steffensmeier & Steffensmeier, 1974). However, as a popular abnormal psychology textbook of that era noted, gay liberation and other homosexual advocacy groups were at work trying to change such attitudes: "Recently, homosexual organizations such as the Homophile Society, the Mattachine Society, and the Gay Liberation Front have been actively campaigning for social recognition and acceptance" (CRM, 1972, p. 200). As a result of such efforts, homosexuals did achieve greater recognition and acceptance—but not from the general public. The acceptance came from the trustees of the American Psychiatric Association in the form of a vote taken on December 15, 1973. On December 14th, the psychiatric profession had considered homosexuals to be mentally ill sexual deviants. But the next day the trustees voted to abolish that diagnosis from its psychiatric manual (DSM-II).

Psychiatrists who believed that homosexuality did represent a mental disorder promptly began their own lobbying efforts. The result was the appearance in the next version of the diagnostic manual (DSM-III) of what might be termed a compromise diagnosis: *ego dystonic homosexuality*. According to this diagnosis, homosexuality is not a mental disorder unless it is "ego dystonic," that is, alien to, or inconsistent with, the way an individual perceives herself or himself. Stated another way, only if an individual was distressed about homosexual behavior and wished to be more heterosexual in orientation would that individual's homosexuality be considered a mental disorder.

This diagnostic compromise of sorts did not end the controversy among mental health professionals. It may even have intensified it. Dissatisfied that the diagnosis of ego dystonic homosexuality as a mental disorder might act to persuade some homosexuals that they required treatment for their sexual orientation, psychologist Gerald Davison (1976, 1978) argued that the only ethical course of action for therapists would be to withhold such treatment, even from a person seeking it. Others (for example, Sturgis & Adams, 1978) took a more moderate position, questioning the ethics of withholding treatment and cautioning therapists against taking as value-laden a position as Davison's. By and large, therapists who specialize in the treatment of sexual disorders have not refused on ethical grounds to treat homosexuals who wish to change their sexual orientation. A program described by Masters and Johnson (1979) has been quite successful in this regard, reversing the orientation of about two of every three clients who seek treatment, and maintaining that reversal through at least five years (Schwartz & Masters, 1984). Other therapists work to assist clients in fully accepting themselves and their sexual orientations.

Over the 2 decades since the American Psychiatric Association initially stopped listing homosexuality as a mental disorder, how much has changed? Gay and lesbian groups are much better organized than they have ever been before. One consequence of this organization has been a rising number of events in which the homosexual community can publicly express pride in its sexual orientation. These events range from gay pride parades to Olympics-style gay games. However, whether such events arouse general goodwill or ill will on the part of the public is debatable. Public attitudes towards homosexuality have tended to remain negative(Davis & Smith, 1987; Gordon & Snyder, 1989; Renzetti & Curran, 1989). Worse yet, *crimes of violence against gays and lesbians* called **gay bashing** have become all too common (see Figure 12–3). Disapproval and disgust regarding homosexual sexual practices, the advent of the AIDS crisis, and the backlash created by the new openness of homosexuals may all have contributed to this rise of senseless violence (Hays, 1990; Renzetti & Curran, 1989). Further, as the director of the Gay and Lesbian Anti-Violence Project, a nonprofit organization has come to believe, "gay-bashing is a fairly hip thing to do these days. It's a sporting event for a lot of young men" (Foreman, 1990).

gay bashing
a crime of hate and violence against gays and lesbians.

ADJUSTIVE DEMANDS AND CHALLENGES

Coming of age sexually brings its own adjustive demands and challenges. Even for the heterosexual youngster who has never had any doubts regarding sexual orientation, the transition to becoming an adult sexual person may be difficult (Sorenson, 1973). Peer-group members and family members may impart conflicting messages regarding expected sexual behavior and roles. The adolescent who has reason to be uncertain regarding aspects of his or her burgeoning sexuality is probably at higher risk for emotional difficulties. In a longitudinal study of gender characteristics and adjustment, Aube & Koestner (1992) observed that adolescent boys who exhibited interest and behavior more consistent with female than with male peers were likely to experience low self-esteem at age 12 and ad-

**FIGURE 12–3
IN SELF-DEFENSE**

"It used to be that when gay men got together, they talked about all their friends who were dying of AIDS," said one gay man who himself had been attacked in Brooklyn years before, "Now, in addition to that, they talk about who's been beaten up" (cited in Hays, 1990). In response to a rising rate of the bias crime known as gay bashing, unarmed groups of citizens have begun patrolling the streets in major cities such as San Francisco, New York, Houston, and Chicago. Pictured are three members of the New York patrol group called the Pink Panthers. Like other such groups, the Pink Panthers keep in close radio contact with each other and the police to help protect gays, as well as other fellow citizens, from attack.

justment problems in adulthood. Even more ominous is the fact that the "suicide rate among gay teenage boys is estimated to be from 30 to 40%, and that for teenage lesbians 20%, both far above the 10% rate for teenagers overall" (Evall, 1991, p. 364). Fear and anxiety about homosexuality, as well as fear of being found out, may contribute to this disproportionately high suicide rate (Britt, 1992). A fairly constant stream of news stories reflecting controversial questions about the rights of homosexuals in society may contribute to some adolescents' anxiety (see *In the News*).

Efforts to prevent gay teenage suicide may take the form of support services to help adolescents work through their sexual identity, and to cope with any sense of isolation or prejudice they may be experiencing. In San Francisco, the Lavender Youth Recreation and Information Center addresses the queries and concerns of lesbian and gay youths. In South Orange, New Jersey, a gay and lesbian youth group meets at a Presbyterian church for meetings coordinated by Michael Singervalt, a gay school psychologist. According to Singervalt (1992), young people would come to the center "hating who they are" and the group would provide a much needed "safe space where teenagers can explore who they are without pressure."

How comfortable are adult homosexuals with their sexuality? According to one study, about 1 out of 4 gay males and a little more than 1 out of 10 lesbians would want to have been given a "magic heterosexuality pill" if such a hypothetical pill was available when they were born (Bell & Weinberg, 1978). Those numbers dwindled to approximately half in value when the same subjects were asked if they wanted such a pill as an adult. According to Reiss (1980), adult homosexuals are no more or less prone to psychiatric disorders than adult heterosexuals.

IN THE News

Gays, Lesbians, and Human Rights

Monitor your local newspaper for a week or so and chances are good that you will find a story or two that relates to sexual orientation and the rights of gays and lesbians in a predominantly heterosexual society. As compiled from actual news accounts in the print and electronic media, here is a list of some of the questions and issues you may find debated:

■ Should a homosexual group be allowed to march in a St. Patrick's Day parade?
■ Under what circumstances should homosexuals be allowed in the military?
■ Should information about, and tolerance of, homosexuality be taught in the schools?

■ Should homosexuals be denied the right to hold certain jobs, such as teaching in preschools or grade schools?
■ Should homosexual social groups be funded at private or state-sponsored schools?
■ Should homosexuals be allowed to worship in a religious facility of a religion that holds that homosexuality cannot be condoned?
■ Can homosexuals assume roles in the clergy within religions that hold that homosexuality cannot be condoned?
■ Should one partner in a homosexual live-in relationship receive the same death benefits, or other benefits and other rights, accorded a legally married couple?

■ Should gays be allowed into the Boy Scouts?
■ Should lesbians be allowed into the Girl Scouts?

Many people have very strong opinions with regard to such questions. These people might read such a list and respond almost reflexively with a "yes" or "no" answer, expecting that any rational person would agree with their views. Yet, in each case, there are many compelling points worthy of discussion and debate regarding the various rights of all the people involved. What are your thoughts on these and related issues?

SEXUAL BEHAVIOR

Is it normal? Is it legal? Is it pleasurable? Did it occur as the result of mutual consent? Did it result in pregnancy? What exactly happened? These are some of the many questions that have been repeatedly posed through the ages regarding that broad category of actions we refer to as *sexual behavior*. Also through the ages, manuals disseminating how-to advice as well as other information have been available. One of the first and most comprehensive of these manuals was the *Kama Sutra*, written in India some time between the third and fifth century A.D. for members of the Hindu faith, who believed that sex was a religious duty (see Figure 12–4). Such manuals would eventually evolve into storehouses of more secular information, providing tips for enhancing partners' sexual pleasure (for example, Comfort, 1972).

THE DOUBLE STANDARD

double standard

the notion that sex before marriage on the part of men is to be winked-at while the same behavior on the part of women is contemptible.

Many sex manuals and other works dealing with sex, particularly those published prior to the Kinsey studies in the late 1940s, tended to reflect two standards regarding sexual behavior: one standard for men, and another for women. According to this **double standard**, *sex before marriage on the part of men was behavior to be winked-at while the same behavior on the part of women was contemptible.* Back then, on the wedding night, it was the man's role, by virtue of his knowledge and experience in such matters, to take the lead in educating his wife in the pleasures of the flesh (see Figure 12–5). One of the many then-shocking findings of Kinsey et al. (1953) was that about half of the women in the research sample reported having had sexual intercourse prior to marriage. Wedding night images of men gently initiating women into the world of sexual pleasure would never be the same.

Remnants of the double standard may survive today in the form of more negative attitudes towards sexually active women as compared to sexually active men. There is some research that suggests that such attitudes have greatly diminished (Earle & Perricone, 1986; Sprecher, 1989). Yet such findings may in reality not reflect equal acceptance of sexual activity on the part of men and women so much as they reflect equal condemnation. Revived negative attitudes towards sexually active singles—male as well as female—may have been a consequence of the wide publicity given the deadly AIDS crisis which began in the early 1980s. Regardless, as Masters et al. (1982) observed, parental messages consistent with a double standard probably still persist, and such teachings begin relatively early. Girls tend to be cautioned against sex play but boys tend to receive mixed messages

FIGURE 12–4   AN ILLUSTRATION FROM
THE KAMA SUTRA *The Kama Sutra* illustrated several sexual positions, some, apparently, for double-jointed partners.

The Arousing of Desire

The husband therefore should proceed with extreme caution. Let him lie close beside his spouse; let him fondle her, carrying his hand over her face and her arms and shoulders. This is to be done sweetly and reverently as though he feels it a privilege even to touch her. Let him take her into his arms, letting her lie completely relaxed in his embrace, happy in being so close to him, a part of him. Let him exchange kisses with her frequently and let him kiss her not only upon the lips but upon her neck, the shoulders, the throat. Let his hands eventually slip, as Shakespeare says, "lower where the pleasant fountains lie," to her breasts. And all the time let him talk with her using endearing expressions and telling her how much he loves her and how happy is is to know that she and he are united never to be separated. This will help to overcome her bashfulness and fears. By degrees his body may be brought into closer contact with hers; she will feel its warmth and will be stirred and somewhat aroused by this contact. By these gentle actions and honeyed words and with kisses which by now may become more and more ardent in their nature, the husband will soon note a response to his endearments and advances. He may now attempt to fondle other and more intimate portions of her body. This will probably cause some nervousness and fright on the part of the bride. She may attempt to repel him, to push him away and if so he must not persist in his attentions but must desist for the time and make no further advances. He must endeavor to overcome her resistance and her timidity by kisses and caresses but must not object in any way to her rebuffs at the moment. This may be kept up for some time. It is often better to go no further the first night, depending of course upon the spirit in which he was repelled.

Due to nervousness, fright, fear, or possibly to puritanical obsessions or taboos, many a bride has refused sexual union for some days until love and increased desire have become so strong in her as to sweep away all objections and she can no longer resist but submits not only willingly but eagerly. (Clinton, 1935, pp. 100–101)

FIGURE 12–5 HOW TO AROUSE DESIRE ON THE WEDDING NIGHT In a manual entitled *Sex Behavior in Marriage*, which went through several printings through the 1940s, physician Charles A. Clinton (1935) advised readers on topics as diverse as "choosing the proper mate" and "fear of the change of life." The excerpt above came from a section entitled "The Arousing of Desire" in the chapter entitled "The Wedding Night."

along with a more forgiving "boys will be boys" general attitude. One father of a 7-year-old boy who had been involved in a sexual escapade with a female classmate thought it was good that his son was "getting an early start" (Masters et al., 1982, p. 190).

In reading about discussions of human sexuality, in this book or others, one often comes across information in which averages are cited. A reminder is in order at this point that an average is just that—a number that identifies the middle point of some distribution of numbers. Comparing yourself to some reported average number and finding that you are higher or lower than the average should not necessarily be cause for emotional upset. However, should you become concerned as you read in this section—or elsewhere—communicating your concerns with a member of your school's counseling center may prove helpful.

VARIETIES OF SEXUAL BEHAVIOR

Humans are capable of an exceptionally wide range of sexual behaviors. Consider, for example, that Madonna's book *Sex* contains 401 pictures of her including 110 with a man, 25 with a woman, 30 with a pair of male twins, and 1 with a dog (Thomas & Trebbe, 1992). The relatively broad range of sexual fantasies depicted in such books only begin to describe the great amount of variation that exists in human sexual fantasy and behavior. In fact, humans are probably unique among species in this regard. No evidence exists to suggest that, while mating, mammals other than humans engage in sexual fantasies, such as the fantasy of a simultaneous sexual encounter with multiple partners. Also in contrast to other mammals, humans have exhibited a seemingly timeless fascination with the variety of different sexual positions that are possible during intercourse. Most members of the animal kingdom engage in fairly stereotypical sexual patterns. For example, two dogs engaging in sexual intercourse do so in a fairly predictable, rear-entry fashion; for a couple of dogs to inject some originality into this behavior pattern would be truly remarkable.

Beyond a seemingly limitless capacity to cognitively construct sexual scenarios, humans are also capable of a wide range of behaviors that are sexual in a physical/genital sense. **Masturbation** is typically *a solitary form of sexual behavior involving manipulation of*

masturbation

a solitary form of sexual behavior involving manipulation of the genitals, usually to the point of orgasm. Contrast with *mutual masturbation*.

the genitals, usually to the point of orgasm. Masturbation may be accomplished using the hands only or with the aid of diverse devices ranging from electric vibrators to inflatable latex dolls. At one university, 95% of the male students and 85% of the female students reported that they had masturbated in their lifetimes, most having masturbated within the prior 3 months (Person et al., 1990). Masturbation is practiced by married men (Hunt, 1974) and women (Tavris & Sadd, 1977), as well as by older adults (Starr & Weiner, 1981). A nonsolitary variety of masturbation is **mutual masturbation**, wherein *two (or more) individuals manually arouse each other, usually to the point of orgasm*. Mutual masturbation is particularly popular among gay (Masters & Johnson, 1979) and lesbian (Bell & Weinberg, 1978) partners.

Sexual intercourse, otherwise referred to as *coitus* (as well as a seemingly endless array of slang terms), involves *penile-vaginal coupling*. As even the most casual glance through the pages of any sex manual at the local bookstore will reveal, coitus may be accomplished in many different positions, ranging from the comfortable to the acrobatic. What has been called the missionary position (man-on-top, face-to-face) is the position employed with perhaps most frequency, although the female-on-top position may be gaining popularity among Americans (Hunt, 1974).[2] Masters et al. (1982) remind us of our individual uniqueness, in terms not only of anatomy but also of other variables such as personality, past experience, and prevailing mood. These variables, among others, serve as contributing factors regarding the many possible choices couples can make during sexual intercourse. The position of intercourse, the surroundings, the "tempo" of the coital activity, and the events prior and subsequent to intercourse may all be influenced by many such variables.

Foreplay refers to *a wide range of sexually stimulating activities that people engage in prior to having sexual intercourse*. Hugging, kissing, fondling, snuggling, nuzzling, touching, talking, and oral-genital contact are some of the activities that may occur not only before sexual intercourse, but after (**afterplay**) as well. Research using college subjects suggests that women tend to desire longer periods of foreplay and afterplay than men (Denny et al., 1984). **Fellatio** (*oral stimulation of the penis*) and **cunnilingus** (*oral stimulation of the vulva*) is practiced by about 90% or more of married couples (Blumstein & Schwartz, 1983). Oral stimulation of the genitals, sometimes to the point of orgasm, may also be employed by lesbian and gay couples (Martin & Lyon, 1977; Masters & Johnson, 1979). Other sexual practices more common to gay men than any other demographic group are anal intercourse and "fisting." **Anal intercourse** *entails the insertion of the penis into the partner's anus*. "Fisting" refers to the practice of inserting one's hand or fist into the other partner's anus (Lowry & Williams, 1983).

Some varieties of sexual behavior, particularly those favored by gay males, have been outlawed under *sodomy* laws in several states. Deriving from sins perpetrated in the biblical city of Sodom, **sodomy** is *a legal term used to refer to anal intercourse and, in some states, to oral-genital contact*. In 1986, the United States Supreme Court ruled in the case of *Bowers v. Hardwick* that sodomy was not a federally protected constitutional right. The ruling opened the way for states to decide individually whether sodomy should be considered a crime. About half the states in the union currently have sodomy laws on the books, with some of these states specifying that the law applies only to homosexual sodomy (DeAngelis, 1992). Homosexual advocacy groups and other organizations, including the American Psychological Association, have called for the repeal of such statutes on the grounds that they are discriminatory.

DEVIANT SEXUAL BEHAVIOR

As organisms climb the evolutionary scale in complexity, so their sexual and reproductive behavior becomes less reflexive and their sexual options and outlets multiply. Humans are capable of exhibiting an enormously wide range of sexual behavior, some of which is deemed by society to be normal, some of which is deemed to be abnormal or deviant. Sexually deviant behavior ranges from the harmless to the harmful, from the legal to the illegal, from the unspeakable to the prankish. Deviant sexual behavior can present imminent danger to one's own life or the lives of others, as it sometimes does during sex that involves

mutual masturbation
an interpersonal variety of masturbation in which two (or more) individuals manually arouse each other, usually to the point of orgasm. Contrast with *masturbation*.

sexual intercourse
coitus; penile-vaginal coupling.

foreplay
sexually stimulating activities that people may engage in prior to having sexual intercourse. Contrast with *afterplay*.

afterplay
affectionate and sexual activity that people may engage in subsequent to having sexual intercourse.

fellatio
oral stimulation of the penis.

cunnilingus
oral stimulation of the vulva or clitoris.

anal intercourse
a sexual act entailing insertion of the penis into the partner's anus.

sodomy
a legal term used to refer to anal intercourse, and in some states, to oral-genital contact as well.

[2]No one knows for sure how the "missionary position" got its name. Reinisch (1990) speculated that its origins may lie in the name given by Pacific Islanders to the "unusual" man-on-top position of sexual intercourse employed by Western missionaries.

the administration of painful or noxious stimuli. Deviant sexual behavior can be a source of personal accomplishment, pleasure, and excitement—all when it rationally should be a source of of personal disgust, shame, and remorse—as in the case of a sociopathic rapist. Our glimpse at a sample of sexually deviant behavior begins with the non-coercive variety and continues with coercive behavior including rape.

NON-COERCIVE SEXUAL BEHAVIOR

For some people to achieve sexual arousal, what is key is the presence or image of some *thing*, not someone. Such people are said to suffer from a **fetish**, and the object of sexual pleasure is referred to as the *fetishistic object*. Virtually anything can take on the property of a fetishistic object, although articles of clothing such as panties, pairs of pants, and leatherware are popular choices. Fetishists may masturbate or engage in sexual intercourse while viewing, touching, rubbing against, or merely envisioning the fetishistic object. For some fetishists, who are referred to as **transvestites, cross-dressing** (that is, *dressing in the clothing of the opposite sex*) is sexually arousing. Transvestites are almost exclusively male, some of whom are gay, many of whom are heterosexual in orientation. In fact, some transvestites are married men who engage in heterosexual intercourse with their wives only when they are cross-dressed (Wincze, 1977). Some evidence suggests that many adult transvestites received support and encouragement for cross-dressing as children (Stoller, 1967). Transvestites should not be confused with **transsexuals**; the latter group is composed of both *males and females who believe they are trapped in the body of a person of the opposite sex*. Many transsexuals seek surgery to transform themselves from women to men, or men to women.

Coercive deviant sexual behavior has in common with non-coercive deviant sexual behavior a sexual object or outlet of preference that is viewed by society as inappropriate. Society is much more concerned, however, with coercive deviant sexual behavior. The inappropriate sexual object of choice is not an inanimate fetishistic object such as a piece of clothing, but rather a person who is either unwilling to participate or unable to give consent to participate. In the latter category are people who have been drugged, children, and adults with diminished mental capacity—all of whom lack the cognitive capacity to give fully informed consent. One all too common form of coercive sexual behavior is rape.

RAPE

700,000 ACTUALLY OCCURED

Rape generally refers to *nonconsensual sexual intercourse.*[3] Rape is a crime in every state although its legal definition varies from state to state. In general, at least two types of nonconsensual sexual intercourse are prohibited by law. One type is the kind that results from the use of brute force; that crime is referred to as *forcible rape*. Another type of nonconsensual sexual intercourse, *statutory rape*, need not necessarily occur as the result of brute force. Statutory rape involves sex with a person who is a child in the eyes of the law (a minor), and minors are not legally competent to give consent to sex (see page 219).

According to the Justice Department's director of the Bureau of Justice Statistics, an estimated 130,260 rapes occurred in 1990, and 207,610 occurred in 1991 (Dillingham, 1992). Many academic researchers believe that such federal statistics seriously underestimate the number of actual rapes and that the actual number of women who have been raped may be many times higher (Koss, 1992). The government-sponsored National Women's Study published in 1992 confirmed the worst fears of many rape researchers. Based on a telephone survey of 4,008 women who represented a cross-section of women in the United States, it was estimated that about 683,000 women had been raped in this country in 1990 (Johnston, 1992). Who commits these rapes? Some insights into this question from the study data are illustrated in Figure 12–6 on page 332.

Different categorizations of rapists and rape circumstances have been developed through the years. For example, Cohen et al. (1969) identified four types of rapists; men who commit rape with (1) an intent to vent aggression on women, (2) a fantasy that their victim will submit and enjoy it (this is the variety of rapist who will flee if met with strong resistance); (3) a mixture of sexual and aggression feelings; (4) no premeditated intent to commit at the outset (rather, the rape is committed on impulse, typically in the course of

fetish

a disorder in which an object of sexual pleasure or a prerequisite to sexual arousal is some object or thing.

transvestite

a person who achieves sexual arousal by cross-dressing.

cross-dressing

dressing in the clothing of the opposite sex.

transsexuals

males and females who believe they are trapped in the body of a person of the opposite sex.

rape

nonconsensual sexual intercourse.

[3]Rape is most frequently committed by males, and victims are most frequently females. Reports of homosexual rape, in which anal intercourse is forced on a male victim, are common in special situations such as prisons (Groth & Birnbaum, 1979). There have also been reported cases in which a woman was the rapist and a man the victim (Struckman-Johnson, 1988). In some instances, a woman or a gang of women have forced men to perform sexual intercourse—and perform satisfactorily—under the threat of death or castration (Sarrel & Masters, 1982). The discussion here, however, focuses exclusively on heterosexual rape in which the rapist is male and the victim is female.

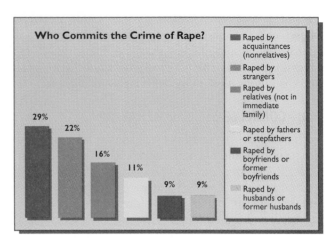

FIGURE 12–6 A PORTRAIT OF RAPISTS Data from the National Women's Study (Johnston, 1992) paint a troubling portrait of coerced sex in this country. Not included in the survey were rapes of female children and adolescents or rapes of boys or men. Consequently, the survey's estimate of 683,000 rapes of women in 1990 was thought to reflect only one-half the actual number of rapes against all people in this country. According to Johnston (1992), women classified as rape victims for survey purposes had to have been the victim of rape, not attempted rape. A rape victim was defined as a woman who had "had sexual contact against her will, where force or the threat of force was used, and where penetration had occurred."

committing some other antisocial act such as burglary). Circumstances surrounding rape, according to one system, can be categorized into one of three categories: (1) the *anger rape*, in which the rapist angrily humiliates the victim in addition to raping her; (2) the *power rape*, in which the need to dominate and prove one's worth and power is primary, while sex is secondary; and (3) the *sadistic rape*, in which a savage, brutalizing, sometimes murderous attack can take place (Groth & Hobson, 1983). According to Groth and Hobson, the sadistic rapist is the one who is most apt to plan and plot the scenario by which the rape will take place. He may feign a need of help, ask directions, offer assistance, or engage in some such activity in order to lure the victim to a site where the torture will occur. Groth (1979) estimated that 5% of all rapes are sadistic rapes, 40% are anger rapes, and 55% are power rapes.

Although some research employing nonincarcerated, sexually aggressive men is available (for example, Lisak & Roth, 1988), most of our knowledge about rapists has come from the study of men who have been caught, tried, found guilty, and imprisoned (Harney & Muehlenhard, 1991). This knowledge base may therefore not be very representa-

FIGURE 12–7 DATE RAPE Orientation at many colleges now includes information about a form of forcible rape called **acquaintance** or **date rape.** Estimates of date rape run as high as 15% of women surveyed although the true incidence may be higher (Koss, 1988). A key factor in date rape appears to be the man's refusal to accept "no" at face value; many date rapists appear to believe that "no" is a gender-appropriate response for a woman that really means "yes" (Muehlenhard & Linton, 1987). Initial dating involving short dates in public places and separate cars or public transportation can help prevent the opportunity for a date rape to occur.

tive given that the vast majority of rapists, especially the men who rape acquaintances and not strangers, never go through the criminal justice system (Gibbs, 1991). Of the rapists who have been studied, few generalizations can be made because they tend to be quite diverse in terms of variables such as intelligence, family background, mental health, and criminal history (Prentky & Knight, 1991).

Rape victims may suffer from a variety of symptoms shortly after the rape. These symptoms may include uncontrollable crying, anxiety, anger, fear, shame, guilt, depression, and a cessation of some activities normally engaged in (Hall & Flannery, 1985; Siegel et al., 1990). If the woman was under medical or psychological care at the time of the rape, or if other factors existed that could compound the trauma of rape, the immediate reaction to the rape may be more severe, and the potential for suicide should be evaluated (Burgess & Holmstrom, 1974). Long-term adjustment to rape is very much an individual matter. About 75% of women who are raped are able to put the emotional trauma behind them within 1 year and to go on with their lives (Calhoun & Atkeson, 1991; Hanson, 1990). For other women, the aftermath of rape may hold in store several varieties of adjustment difficulties, health problems (including the possibility of sexually transmitted disease), and sex-related performance problems (Ellis et al., 1981; Sales et al., 1984; Waigandt et al., 1990; Wyatt et al., 1990).

The fact that rape respects few geographical or cultural boundaries (see *Cultural Close-Up* on page 334), and the fact that it occurs with such shocking frequency in our own country, compels us to think of solutions to this horrible problem. *What do you think should be done?* Jot down a few of your own notes before reading on, and then let's compare notes.

At a national level, it would appear that the culture has to do a better job of conveying to boys and men that rape is wrong, totally unacceptable, not macho, and behavior that will not be tolerated. The criminal justice system needs to do a better job of making sure that any rapes or rape attempts will be answered with a societal response and a mandatory jail/rehabilitation sentence. The message must be conveyed that a woman's "no" means "no"—and that holds true for situations as diverse as a first date and the first wedding night. Such a message can be conveyed effectively in classrooms (Hamilton & Yee, 1990). It can and must also be conveyed in less formal contexts, such as in the popular media, including television programs, movies, music, and music videos. Unfortunately, what is imparted in too much of the popular media seems to run contrary to messages that would promote responsible, consensual, and non-coercive sexual behavior on the part of men.

Paralleling a rape education and sensitivity program for males, a formal curriculum of rape prevention instruction for females would appear desirable. The curriculum might include not only general rape prevention tips but also more personalized and situation-specific guidelines and strategies, such as those outlined in the *Quality of Life* on pages 336–337. Because rapist motivation may vary widely, and because the circumstances under which rape occurs may also vary widely, so a woman's response to a would-be rapist in a particular situation must vary appropriately. People bring to emergency situations a number of important individual differences in strengths and weaknesses (including differences in personality and physical strength, for example), and personalized strategies for coping with different types of situations will exploit each individual's strengths to full advantage. One does not attempt to immobilize a would-be rapist with a kick to the groin, for example, unless one is capable of delivering a truly immobilizing kick. Fleeing the site of a would-be rape is only a viable strategy if there is a place to flee to, and some realistic possibility of escape. If there is no place to flee to, or no realistic possibility of escape, other options, such as persuasion, submission, and physical self-defense must be considered. As frightening, painful, distasteful, and uncomfortable as it may be to anticipate one's response to a possible rape situation, such anticipation, combined with periodic behavioral rehearsal of various types of responses, may one day mean the difference between becoming a victim or not becoming a victim.

SEXUAL HARASSMENT

In 1992, a Stanford University brain surgeon was demoted from his position at the medical school and compelled to undergo sensitivity training. The doctor had been accused of

Cultural

CLOSE-UP

Is Rape a Cultural Universal?

In his exhaustive review of research related to the cultural universality of rape, Craig Palmer (1989) reexamined reports by anthropologists and others who had described a number of societies as rape free. In each case, Palmer was able to find references that would call into question whether the society was indeed free of rape. For example, Sanday (1981) and Broude and Greene (1976) claimed that rape was unknown to the Mbuti Pygmies of the Ituri forest in Africa. In making this assertion, Sanday cited the work of an anthropologist who had lived among the Mbuti and written that he knew of no instances of rape. Palmer pointed out that the full statement of the anthropologist being cited (Turnbull, 1965) read as follows: "I know of no cases of rape, though boys often talk about their intentions of forcing reluctant maidens to their will." Turnbull (1965) further noted that during the female initiation ceremony, a male is supposed to have a female's permission in order for intercourse to take place. "The men say that once they lie down with a girl, however, if they want her they take her by surprise when petting her, and force her to their will" (Turnbull, 1965, p. 137).

As another example, the people of Outer Mongolia have been thought of as living in a rape-free society, based largely on a report by Maiskii (1921). Maiskii asked a well-educated lama what punishment was imposed for rape and the lama replied, "We have no crimes of this nature here. Our women never resist" (Maiskii, 1921, p. 98). Yet as Ho-t'ien (1949, p. 34) noted, "according to Mongol law both theft and rape are punishable by jail sentences."

The Arapesh society of New Guinea, described in detail by Margaret Mead (1935), and others (Minturn et al., 1969) as being a rape-free society is probably not free of rape. Mead (1935, p. 104) described these people as not having "any conception of male nature that might make rape understandable to them." As Palmer (1989) noted, such statements would lead us to believe that rape is a learned behavior and not a cultural universal. But Palmer believes that rape is universal to all cultures, and he cites the following passage from Mead's own work as evidence that it occurs among the Arapesh:

> If a man carries off a woman whom he has not won through seduction, he will not take her at once, in the heat of his excitement over having captured her. Rather he will delay soberly until he sees which way negotiations turn, whether there is a battle over her, what pressure is brought upon him to return her. If she is not to belong to him permanently, it is much safer never to possess her at all. (Mead, 1935, p. 104)

Palmer argued that the passage disproves Mead's claim that rape is incomprehensible to the Arapesh male. Mead's description describes the abduction of a nonconsenting woman for sexual purposes. Implied is the fact that rape will occur if the male does not deem the consequences to be too severe. Palmer also presented evidence contradicting earlier writings that suggested that some societies have never established punishments for rape. He concluded that "rape is a behavior present in all societies despite efforts to influence males to refrain from rape" (p. 12). He cautioned that the evidence in no way suggests that rape is a behavior that is inevitable or genetically encoded. Because rape occurs in every known society, "emphasis should be placed on identifying the ways in which certain cultures are inefficient in discouraging males from raping" and "social reformers need to take great care in retaining those aspects of traditions that restrain males from raping" (p. 12).

insensitivity towards female colleagues and medical students. One female colleague had even resigned, claiming that he propositioned and demeaned her during surgeries ("Stanford Doctor," 1992).

An unmarried 34-year-old woman made history when she filed the first ever sexual harassment lawsuit in Japan against her employer—and made history again when she won her case in April 1992. She had claimed that one of her supervisors had spread rumors that she was promiscuous, which forced her to resign. The Tokyo court ruled that the company and one of its male employees had violated the woman's rights, and it ordered the defendants to pay the woman $12,500. The case was seen as a great victory for the relatively small group of feminists in that country (Weisman, 1992b).

At Duluth Central High School in Minnesota, a female student was upset about bathroom graffiti about her and she requested that the school remove it. When the school did not, the student sued. In 1991, the school settled with the young woman, agreeing to pay her $15,000 for the mental anguish she had suffered (Gross, 1992b).

Each of these cases has something in common, and something in common with hearings held by a United States Senate committee in the matter of the confirmation of Clarence Thomas as a justice of the United States Supreme Court. Thomas had been accused by attorney Anita Hill of **sexual harassment**, a coercive form of sexual behavior which according to one definition, involves *deliberate or repeated unsolicited verbal comments, gestures, or physical contact of a sexual nature that is considered to be unwelcome by the recipient* (U.S. Merit Systems Protections Board, 1981, p. 2). Charges of sexual harassment in the workplace have increased sharply since the highly publicized Thomas confirmation hearings (see Figure 12–8). Yet it is important to understand that sexual harassment is not limited to the workplace. Students can be sexually harassed by instructors, patients can be sexually harassed by doctors, neighbors can be sexually harassed by neighbors. The person being harassed may be male or female, just as the person doing the harassing may be male or female. In general, the person doing the harassing is in some superior or more powerful position compared to the person being harassed.

Sexual harassment has consequences that go far beyond simple kidding around or flirting. Emotional consequences of sexual harassment may include anger, irritability, and other symptoms associated with stress (Loy & Stewart, 1984). In the workplace, such symptoms may lead to absences and decreased work productivity, even resignation or firing—all consequences that potentially carry financial and other negative effects on both the employer and the employee. The actual frequency of sexual harassment in the workplace, especially directed at female workers, is probably much higher than the number of complaints filed suggest (Fain & Anderson, 1987; Lafontaine & Tredeau, 1986). Because court awards for litigated cases of sexual harassment may cost employers millions of dollars, employers have more actively attempted to stop such harassment. In record numbers, employers are seeking to clarify their own definitions and policies regarding sexual harassment and attempting to educate employees about its nature and prevention (see Figure 12–9 on page 338). Sexual harassment in college settings can have momentous consequences. Wital (1993) recalled that when a professor she spurned gave her a *D* in a

sexual harassment

a coercive form of sexual behavior which involves the deliberate or repeated conveyance of unsolicited verbal comments, gestures, or physical contact of a sexual nature considered unwelcome by the recipient.

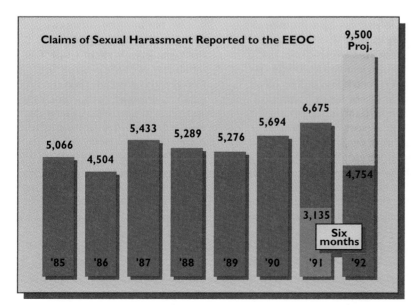

Claims of Sexual Harassment Reported to the EEOC

'85	'86	'87	'88	'89	'90	'91	'92
5,066	4,504	5,433	5,289	5,276	5,694	6,675	3,135 (Six months) + 4,754 = 9,500 Proj.

FIGURE 12–8   CLAIMS OF SEXUAL HARASSMENT The Equal Employment Opportunity Commission (EEOC) is the federal agency charged with enforcing federal discrimination laws. Claims of sexual harassment have been pouring into that agency since the Clarence Thomas confirmation hearings. Although the Senate Judiciary Committee ultimately confirmed Thomas's nomination, the country has not been the same since. As Senator Orrin Hatch (1992), a member of the judiciary committee put it, "The one good thing to come out of the hearing is that everybody—and I mean everybody—is more aware."

Developing a Personal Taxonomy of Rape Prevention Strategies

Effective rape prevention entails advance thinking about scenarios that for many women—and men—are unthinkable. It involves preparing yourself to act as judiciously as possible under various kinds of emergency conditions. It means knowing yourself and knowing what you are capable of doing and not capable of doing. It requires being able to size up a situation calmly and to come to some decision about what is best to do—often in the face of extreme urgency and horrendous pressure.

Different rapists have different motivations and different characteristic methods of raping. Some rapes are perpetrated by individuals, others by gangs. Some rapists are armed, some are not. Some have carefully plotted the rape while others are acting on impulse. Some rapists can be talked out of rape or be intimidated into relinquishing the idea (Byers & Lewis, 1988), while pleas and protests may only make others more excited and violent (Bart & O'Brien, 1985; Hazelwood et al., 1989). Physical resistance will deter some rapists (Ullman & Knight, 1991) but spur others to become more violent and assaultive (Powell, 1991). Different circumstances provide different opportunities. In some circumstances, for example, there may be an opportunity to escape, to enlist help from others, or to buy time. In other circumstances, there are no such opportunities and the options are few. Compliance with the demands of the rapist is also an option. As the health columnist for *The New York Times*, Jane Brody, once advised, "Always remember that it is better to be raped than to risk being permanently injured or killed" (1992, p. C13).

In what follows, you are encouraged to give some thought to the rape prevention strategies that might realistically work for you were you to be targeted for victimization by a rapist or gang of rapists. Which of the following strategies do you think would be personally useful for you, and under what circumstances? This noncomprehensive listing may serve as an aid in the development of your own taxonomy (or *classification system*) for various kinds of preventive, deterrent, or evasive actions.

General Rape Prevention Strategies

Antitheft devices in the home and automobile make good sense for most everyone. A citizens band radio or car phone is invaluable should your car break down on a stretch of highway. Always avoid deserted areas and areas known to be crime hazards, and avoid walking alone at night. Have your keys ready as you approach your home, office, or car, and keep entranceways and surroundings as well lit as possible. When returning to your car or your home, be alert to any atypical activity or signs of something amiss. When returning to your car, make it a habit to look very carefully through the window at the front and rear seats and the front and rear floors to make certain that no one is lying in wait. Never pick up a male or female hitchhiker under any circumstances, even if the hitchhiker appears to require assistance; rather, telephone for assistance from the nearest phone.

Most rapes of females are committed by males known to the female victim. For this reason, a certain degree of prudence and caution must accompany interactions with the opposite sex that could lead to any miscommunication or any possible message that you are ripe for victimization. Avoid sending any messages that might be construed as indicative of sexual interest, if in fact you do not wish to convey such interest. Be attuned to messages of sexual interest on the part of men, and be clear, unambiguous, self-confident, and nonintimidated in your response to them. Look a man straight in the eye and confidently and unambiguously convey "no" to him in no uncertain terms. In dating situations, Elizabeth Powell (1991) noted many things women can do to avoid problems. For example, always take your own car to meet someone versus meeting people in their cars. Trust your instincts. If you feel uncomfortable with someone, or if a person has exhibited signs, however subtle, of disrespect for you, your feelings, or social boundaries, end the date with no second thoughts.

Deterrence through Words

Denver psychologist James Selkin (1992) believes that many rapists seek easy prey—women who will go quietly without screaming or putting up a fight. In such instances, a failure to react with intimidation to a rapist's demands may work in a woman's favor. Mentally and behaviorally rehearse an emotionally and physically strong, self-assured, nonintimidated response to a rapist's demands. Another method of deterrence under certain circumstances is to convince the assailant that a man will be arriving soon or is waiting in some nearby location. If you are not in an isolated area, and there are people nearby, scream, "Fire!" The scream may scare-off the assailant while attracting people closer—people who might unfortunately walk the other way in fear for their own safety if they heard the cry "Rape!"

If the assailant is someone who has tried earlier to become intimate using socially acceptable methods, one strategy is to suggest that you go for coffee or a drink at some nearby establishment to get to know each other better. Once there, call the police or have someone else summon the police. If the assailant will not go to some public place, buy as much time as possible by talking while mentally planning other possible actions that might effectively deter an assault.

Deterrence through Action

Rape may be deterred through physical action that ranges from walking away from the assailant to attempting to physically disable him. Brody (1992) suggests that crying hysterically or "doing something disgusting like vomiting or urinating on the assailant" might be worth a try under some circumstances. If you carry some form of personal protection, whether a cannister of mace or simply a nail file, know how to use it and be mentally prepared to use it if necessary. Explore the limits of your own physical abilities by taking a self-defense course for women. Such a course is probably offered by a local community institution or commercial establishment. You may be surprised to learn that you have sufficient physical ability to deter an assailant. If you do find such training helpful and believe that you are capable of using physical force to deter an attack, keep up your training or take periodic refresher courses.

Edward Welch, a University of Oklahoma campus police officer, advises that if an assailant threatens you with a weapon and orders you to get into a car, your best course of action might be to firmly say, "No," and walk briskly away. According to Welch (1992), the odds are that the assailant will *not* use the weapon against you. On the other hand, according to Welch, the odds are that the assailant *will* use the weapon against you if you do get into the car; in fact, according to Welch, the odds are that you will not survive the attack. If someone has gotten into your car with you, you may judge it to be advantageous to attract attention by driving up a one-way street the wrong way, driving up on somebody's lawn, or purposely getting into a minor fender-bender with another vehicle (preferably a police car!).

In life-or-death situations in which a fatal attack seems imminent, anything you can do to physically incapacitate the assailant, even momentarily, must be attempted. Using whatever can be used as a weapon (including a pin, a pen, keys, a rock, sand, or whatever), attack the assailant where he is most vulnerable. Sensory organs such as the eyes, the ears, and the nose are very vulnerable to attack. If you are grabbed from behind, thrusting the back of the head into the assailant's nose may yield a precious moment or two and an opportunity to call for assistance or to escape.

Nondeterrence as a Strategy

If someone is holding a loaded gun to your head or a knife at your throat, few people, including highly trained martial arts experts, see many options

beyond obeying the assailant's commands. If you find yourself in any situation wherein you judge compliance with the assailant's commands to be the best course of action, summon the police to the crime scene as soon as possible afterward. As Powell (1991) recommends, do not change your clothing or even comb your hair, as precious evidence may lie in your hair, on your clothing, or on your body. Also, although your first impulse may be to put this trauma as far behind you as possible, the police will no doubt ask you for a physical description of the man and the clothes he was wearing. Try to recall and mentally rehearse this description while waiting for the police to arrive. You should be seen by a physician, even if you do not think you were physically injured; it may be that you suffered injuries that you were not even aware of.

The emotional aftermath of rape may be as varied as the individuals who have suffered the trauma. For some, experiencing and reexperiencing a sense of outrage, anger, and vindictiveness may well prove therapeutic. For others, coping with rape entails focusing as much as possible on the present and the future, not the past. As one 20-year-old rape victim put it, "My future is of much greater consequence than my past. And I refuse to be angry. Anger requires energy which I feel can be better directed toward by studies" (Name Withheld, 1993). Counseling with a professional who has expertise in the trauma of rape and a sensitivity to individual coping preferences is highly recommended.

FIGURE 12–9 EDUCAT-ING EMPLOYEES ABOUT SEXUAL HARASSMENT
Using sensitivity trainers and media such as pamphlets and videos, even live reenactments of actual sexual harassment cases employers have sought to educate their employees about the nature and prevention of sexual harassment. In addition, many companies have devised procedures to investigate claims of sexual harassment and hired mediators to hear such claims (Hoffman, 1992).

course, it seriously affected not only her self-esteem and her relationship with other teachers and supervisors, but also her grade–point average and her entire college career.

SEXUALLY TRANSMITTED DISEASES

Comedian Robin Williams met cocktail waitress Michelle Tish Carter in 1984 while performing at a comedy club in Los Angeles. According to Carter's lawyer, Adolph Canelo, the couple had sex, after which Williams asked Carter, "You don't have anything I can take home to my wife, do you?" The attorney said that his client responded "No," and then asked Williams if he had any sexually transmitted diseases. Williams reportedly said that he did not. The couple dated periodically over the next two years, during which, according to Canelo (1992), Carter "only had two isolated sexual incidents with two other famous comedians." When Carter discovered that she had contracted herpes, she brought a lawsuit against Williams for $6.2 million. In court papers, Williams neither denied nor stated that he had herpes, but did acknowledge that he had had a relationship with Carter. Williams stated that Carter had a history of sexual activity with many sexual partners and that any of those partners could have transmitted the herpes virus to her.

It was undisputed that neither of the parties had asked the other about communicable diseases before they had sex. Further, neither party had insisted on the use of condoms. Under such circumstances, argued Williams's lawyer, Philip Ryan, the parties both assumed risk for their own actions. For courts to rule otherwise, said Ryan (1992), would be to create a "judicial ménage à trois" opening the courtroom "to any forlorn lover whose affair has come to an unexpected end." The Williams case, which Ryan described as one of "financial attraction," was settled out of court for an undisclosed amount one week before it was to go to trial. Yet the case seems useful as a point of departure for thinking about the obligations people have—legally or ethically—before agreeing to have sex with one another. What are those obligations?

Many courts throughout the country have held that a person who is infected with a sexually transmittable disease has a legal obligation to inform the partner or prospective partner of that condition. This is not always as straightforward as it sounds, however. Herpes, for example, is a recurrent disease that is usually only transmittable when it is in an active stage. Yet many people are unaware when they have an active, transmittable case of herpes. And judges have not been very specific about how and under what circumstances notice must be given to the other party. As Robert L. Rabin (1992), a Stanford University Law School professor, put it, the courts "haven't exactly spelled out a kind of Miranda warning" when it comes to two people discussing the possibility of having sex.

In another highly publicized duty-to-warn case, it was never even suggested that the person who brought the lawsuit ever contracted any sexually transmitted disease from the defendant. The defendant in that case was the estate of actor Rock Hudson, who had died of AIDS. The lawsuit was brought by Hudson's gay lover, Marc Christian. Despite the fact that no transmission of disease had occurred, merely putting an individual at risk of contracting a disease without that person's consent was sufficient for the court to assign liability. Christian was awarded $5.5 million from Hudson's estate.

With this background regarding some of the intriguing legal and ethical aspects of behavior involving sexually transmittable diseases, let's proceed to a consideration of some of the psychological and medical aspects of such behavior. The primary focus of our discussion will be AIDS and what people can do to prevent its sexual transmission.

AIDS

AIDS is an acronym for *acquired immunodeficiency syndrome*. As its name implies, it is a disease that affects the efficiency or effectiveness of one's immune system. The immune system is a term that collectively describes the body's natural defenses against disease. When the immune system becomes deficient or defective, the body becomes highly susceptible to various diseases and infections—and death results. AIDS is said to be *acquired* because it is transmitted by means of a virus—a virus called *human immunodeficiency virus*, or HIV for short. Viruses, HIV among others, may take several different forms or *strains*. Viruses may be transmitted from one person to another in various ways. For example, HIV as well as many other viruses can be passed from an infected pregnant woman to her fetus. About 2,000 infants annually are currently born with HIV (Gwinn et al., 1991) and that number is expected to rise as a function of an increasing number of cases in the adult population (Altman, 1992a; Crossette, 1992; Mann, 1992). Infected mothers may also infect their children through breast feeding (Glasner & Kaslow, 1990). HIV may be transmitted from contact with infected blood, as when infected blood is given in a transfusion or otherwise allowed entry into the body (such as an accidental squirt into the eyes of medical personnel). Drug addicts or others who self-administer drugs with a shared needle that is injected either into a vein (intravenous) or under the skin are at very high risk for contracting AIDS. One drug user can contract AIDS from another if that other, HIV-infected drug user was a prior user of the same needle.

HIV can be transmitted sexually from one infected partner to another through sexual intercourse, anal intercourse, or oral sex (Perry et al., 1989; Spitzer & Weiner, 1989). Because HIV lives in the blood and other secretions, including vaginal secretions, it is possible for a noninfected person to contract the virus through the insertion of the hand or any part of it into the vagina or anus of an infected person. A tiny cut on any part of the hand could provide a convenient port of entry to the virus. Whether AIDS can be transmitted through "deep" or "French" kissing with an infected person is a matter of controversy. Although a case of transmission in this manner has yet to be documented, it is possible in theory, especially if both parties have even minor cuts or abrasions in their mouths or gums (Hein et al., 1989). Pending definitive evidence then, deep kissing with a person known to be HIV-infected is not advisable. For reasons not well understood, some HIV-infected people may be more contagious than others, while some people not infected with HIV (such as people who have had other sexually transmitted diseases) may be more susceptible to the virus than are others (Rosenthal, 1990).

Perhaps because relatively little is known about AIDS, many myths about it, as well as myths about how it can be contracted, have been circulated. AIDS is *not* transmitted via toilet seats, swimming pools, eating utensils, water fountains, telephones, or clothing used by an infected person (Gordon & Snyder, 1989). AIDS has not been shown to be transmitted via mosquito bites when the mosquito has previously bitten an infected person, or via a sneeze by an infected person. It is *not* true that you can get AIDS by giving blood. In the United States and other countries, sterile needles are used once only in the extraction of blood and then thrown away. Risk associated with donated blood is borne by the person receiving the donated blood, not the person donating the blood. This risk to the recipient of donated blood was especially high before the nation's blood supply was routinely

FIGURE 12–10 MAGIC JOHNSON'S INFLUENCE ON SEXUAL BEHAVIOR
On November 7, 1991, basketball star Magic Johnson announced that he was infected with HIV. A study conducted by the Centers for Disease Control and Prevention between July 1991 and February 1992, suggested that the announcement may have acted to lower the rate of high risk sexual behavior ("Magic Johnson Talks," 1993).

screened for the AIDS virus. Today, all donated blood is carefully screened. Still, the chances of being infected with AIDS as a result of a blood transfusion have been estimated to be about 1 in 75,000 (Altman, 1992b).

AIDS is diagnosed in different ways but the most common evaluation procedure is a blood test. In 1991, an estimated 41 million units of blood were tested for HIV (Berry, 1992). When a person is infected with HIV, the immune system produces an antibody to the virus which can be identified in blood as well as in other bodily fluids, including saliva and urine. Identification of the antibody to HIV may occur years before the virus actually causes AIDS (Eckholm, 1991). Simple diagnostic AIDS tests that rely on the identification of HIV antibodies from urine and saliva samples are actively being developed and should be available soon ("A Simpler Test," 1992).

The first symptoms of AIDS, which may appear upwards of 11 years subsequent to exposure to HIV, are all related to signs of problems with one's immune system. Such symptoms may mimic those seen in common colds or flus, including fever, chills, swollen glands, extreme fatigue, and night sweats. More specific signs commonly associated with AIDS include a pneumonia-producing infection called PCP (*Pneumocystis carinii*) and/or a rare form of cancer, Kaposi's sarcoma, characterized by the appearance of painless purplish or brown spots that do not go away. These spots may appear anywhere on the body, including areas not immediately visible such as areas inside the nose, mouth, or rectum.

If you have reason to believe that you may have been exposed to HIV, you may wish to consult a physician and be tested. It is advisable that such testing be done in the strictest confidence. Unfortunately, a diagnosis of AIDS can not only be personally devastating but socially and financially devastating if social acquaintances and co-workers learn of it; a great deal of ignorance still surrounds AIDS and people who are diagnosed as having it are the brunt of such ignorance. Should you test positive for AIDS, your physician can offer you advice on preventing other diseases and associated problems. Your physician may also start you on some medication that may slow the progress of AIDS. The outlook for treatment, however, is not encouraging at this writing. New strains of HIV have been discovered which are resistant to the beneficial effects of drugs such as AZT (*zidovudine*). It is believed that some of these new strains may have arisen in people who were infected by AIDS patients who were taking AZT ("New HIV Strains," 1993). As AIDS researcher Wendell Ching of UCLA Medical School explained, "People usually are infected with various strains of HIV. Once they start taking AZT, the resistant strains are the ones that survive" (1993, p. A18). If such a person spreads the virus to another person, the person contracting the virus contracts an AZT-resistant strain of the virus.

Since a July 1981 study of 30 cases of what was then referred to as "gay pneumonia," AIDS has mushroomed onto the national and international scene in epidemic proportions. Currently, about 10 million people are infected with HIV worldwide and that number is expected to rise to 40 million by the year 2000 (Eckholm, 1992b). It has been estimated that about 80,000 American children will be left motherless as a result of AIDS by the year 2000 ("Toll of American AIDS Orphans," 1992). These are statistics that too often gloss over the many tragic and poignant stories of human torment that the scourge of AIDS writes: lovers having to say goodbye to lovers, friends saying goodbye to friends, parents saying goodbye to children, children saying goodbye to parents (Bondy, 1992; Navarro, 1992; Nichols & Ostrow, 1984; Schmalz, 1992). Many people, particularly gay men, have seen dozens of close friends die in fairly rapid succession (Rosenthal, 1992). Exposure to so many deaths in so short a period of time has prompted therapists to search for alternatives to traditional methods of grieving (see Figure 12–11). Death statistics only begin to reflect the great financial toll AIDS takes not only on the savings of stricken individuals but also on society in general. Millions of taxpayer dollars are spent annually not only for treatment and medication but also for AIDS-related research, counseling, and education (Leary, 1992b; Mundell & Friedman, 1992). With those expenditures come some emotional controversies, such as how best to educate school children regarding AIDS (Dao, 1992b).

Although AIDS is almost always fatal and has no cure at this time, its transmission via sexual activity is preventable. Methods of preventing the contraction of HIV, as well as other diseases, are discussed after a brief look at some other sexually transmitted diseases. The individual infected with HIV can take care to prevent transmission of it to others by (1) not donating blood, sperm, or organs; (2) carefully disposing of any material that has become contaminated with blood as a result of menstruation or other causes; (3) not sharing needles, razor blades, toothbrushes, or any item that can become contaminated with blood; (4) not breastfeeding; and (5) practicing abstinence or "safer sex."

Note that although the term *safe sex* is widely used in the popular media, it may convey a false sense of security and foster misconceptions about how safe sex can actually be. The term typically refers, for example, to practices such as the use of latex condoms. Although latex condoms do protect against HIV, it is also true that they may be not used correctly and may come off or break during sex. For such reasons, the term *safer sex* seems preferable to *safe sex*.

FIGURE 12–11 DEALING WITH GRIEF THROUGH ANCIENT RITUALS At an AIDS conference in Amsterdam, psychologist Terry Tafoya, an American Indian, demonstrated wearing full Indian garb, how ancient rituals can be used therapeutically to deal with the grief of multiple losses. According to Tafoya (1992) and his colleagues, rituals such as calling out the names of people who have died as a drum beats in the background may help survivors restore a sense of order and control in their lives. Tafoya reminds his audience that "sorrow shared is halved and joy shared is doubled."

OTHER SEXUALLY TRANSMITTED DISEASES

AIDS has virtually eclipsed other sexually transmitted diseases in terms of media coverage, but it is not the only condition sexually active people have to worry about. Many diseases can be transmitted via sexual contact, and Table 12–1 provides a summary of information about a sample of them. It has been estimated that some 56 million people in this country—that is, one in five Americans—are infected with a sexually transmitted viral disease such as herpes, hepatitis B, gonorrhea, and chlamydia (Barringer, 1993c). The 56 million figure *excludes* people infected with HIV.

Knowing or suspecting that one has contracted a sexually transmitted disease can lead to a number of different emotions, including fear, anger, and shame. Given the way that sexually transmitted diseases tend to be widely viewed, such responses are understandable and need to be talked through. A danger, however, is that such emotions can prompt various types of maladjustive behavior, such as reluctance on the part of one or both parties to see a physician. If such reluctance is strong enough, it is not unknown for only one partner to visit a physician, get a prescription, and then share the medication with the other partner. While such a procedure assures the anonymity of the second party, it also ensures that neither partner will get well. In fact, if the prescription was for an antibiotic, such a procedure would cure neither person and make the condition more difficult to treat in both. Taking only half of a prescribed regimen of antibiotics may create a partial immunity to the antibiotic. If you or a sexual partner believe that you may have contracted some sexually transmitted disease, you must both see a physician and you must both be prescribed medicine, which you must both take as per the orders of the prescribing doctor.

TABLE 12–1 DESCRIPTION OF SOME SEXUALLY TRANSMITTED DISEASES

Disease	Method of Contraction	Symptoms
Chlamydia (Chlamydia trachomatis)	Chlamydia is a bacterial disease in which bacteria grow in mucous membranes, including the moist linings of the mouth, vagina, urethra, and anal canal. It can be contracted through sexual contact in these areas.	In men, slight watery discharge from penis and painful urination. In women, painful urination, painful inflammation of the oviducts, and discharge from the uterus, although many women are asymptomatic. Gay men who are infected rectally may be asymptomatic. About 30% of heterosexual men are asymptomatic. A potentially major complication of chlamydia infection in women is pelvic inflammatory disease (PID), which may present as pain in one or both sides, especially when sneezing or coughing. PID is the leading cause of sterility in young women.
Syphilis	Syphilis is a bacterial disease in which bacteria grow in mucous membranes, including the moist linings of the mouth, vagina, urethra, and anal canal. It can be contracted through sexual contact in these areas.	Within 10 to 90 days, and typically about 3 weeks after infection, a **chancre** (*a sore resembling a whitish pimple that is about the size of a dime*) will appear at the site of infection. The chancre is painless and may not be noticed, especially if it appears within the vagina, the urethra, or the rectum. The chancre will disappear in weeks. If the bacteria is not treated, a second stage of the disease will occur about 6 weeks after infection. At this time, symptoms may mimic those of the flu, including fever, sore throat, headache, swollen glands, and a general feeling of illness. In addition, other symptoms, such as a rash on the palms of the hands, soles of the feet, mucous membranes, or other parts of the body may be present. Left untreated, relapses of these conditions, sometimes with hair loss, may occur, especially within the first year of infection. In the third stage, syphilis attacks the central nervous system and/or internal organs and can lead to a variety of symptoms, even death.
Gonorrhea	Gonorrhea is a bacterial disease in which bacteria grow in mucous membranes, including the moist linings of the mouth, vagina, urethra, and anal canal. It can be contracted through sexual contact in these areas.	In men, first symptoms may appear about 5 days after sexual contact with an infected person. Painful urination and a discharge of a watery, yellowish-white or yellowish-green substance occurs in about 70% of cases. Most women will show no symptoms, but when there are symptoms, they are similar to those in men: painful or uncomfortable urination and a discharge. After 2 months, the infection may cause other symptoms in women including vaginal bleeding and cramps in the lower abdomen and fever. In the throat, gonorrheal infection may be experienced as a sore throat, and tonsils may develop pus. In the rectum, symptoms include pus in the feces and rectal irritation and itching. As with other infections, symptoms may also include swollen glands and fever. A potentially major complication of gonorrheal infection in women is pelvic inflammatory disease (PID), which may present as pain in one or both sides, especially when sneezing or coughing. PID is the leading cause of sterility in young women.
Herpes (Herpes simplex, type 1; Herpes simplex, type 2)	Herpes is a viral infection that may occur in any of several forms, each having different symptoms. The two forms discussed here may be transmitted through sexual activity in the broadest sense, including activity such as kissing, touching, and any skin-to-skin contact.	The symptoms of herpes simplex (type 1) are cold sores or related infections (such as fever blisters) around the mouth. Herpes simplex (type 2) is characterized by a painful and/or itchy rash, similar in appearance to cold sores, on or near the genitals or other parts of the body. In addition, both types of infection may be accompanied by other symptoms, including swollen lymph glands, fever, and muscle aches. After the initial outbreak of a herpes infection, outbreaks may recur from time to time. Recurrences may be triggered by different factors in different people, but exposure to sunlight, temperature extremes, and stress are thought to be key factors. A third type of herpes infection which is also capable of sexual transmission, CMV (cytomegalovirus), produces no symptoms. Its presence should be screened for in pregnant women because it can be harmful to the fetus.
Genital warts (condyloma)	Genital warts are transmitted by any of many possible strains of a highly contagious virus. Transmission occurs as a result of physical contact with the affected person or with physical contact with material, such as a towel, that can harbor the virus.	At least 4 to 6 weeks from the time of contact, and sometimes as long as 2 to 3 months from that time, warts (which vary in appearance much as other warts that are not sexually transmitted may vary in appearance) begin growing in the affected area. In males, they may appear near the opening of the penis and spread to the urethra. In gay males, the warts may also appear near the opening of the anus and spread to inside the rectum. In females, genital warts may appear in the area of the vulva and the surrounding region, including the perineum (the area between the vulva and the anus).

Diagnosis	Treatment	Incidence

Because symptoms may be similar to gonorrhea, gonorrhea is usually ruled out first. Diagnosis of chlamydia can be made by the growth of a tissue culture or by a test of antibodies. Pregnant women may be screened and treated to prevent infection of babies, which can occur at the time of birth.

Selected antibiotic medication and abstinence from sex during the entire course of treatment. Left untreated, this disease can cause damage to reproductive organs, including sterility.

Chlamydia is the most common sexually transmitted bacterial infection, with from 3 to 4 million new cases being reported annually in the United States.

Syphilis is diagnosed in its earliest stage by examination of a specimen from the chancre. Syphilis is diagnosed in its second stage by means of different types of blood tests, including one developed by the Venereal Disease Research Laboratory (VDRL).

Syphilis responds to treatment with penicillin as well as with other drugs such as tetracycline and erythromycin. Different doses and schedules of treatment are prescribed based on which stage the disease is in. Four weeks after a course of treatment, a follow-up test to make certain that the bacteria have been completely eradicated is usually conducted. Additional follow-up tests will be conducted once every 3 months thereafter for 1 year.

About 100,000 new cases are reported annually.

A sample of the discharge is subjected to analysis. Many different strains of gonorrheal infection exist and different strains will require different treatment. For example, while some forms of gonorrhea can be treated with penicillin, others, such as those linked to travel to Southeast Asia, are antibiotic-resistant.

Gonorrhea is usually treated with drugs such as penicillin, tetracycline, or other antibiotics. If left untreated, it can cause various conditions, including some that lead to sterility. An infected mother can pass an eye infection to her infant (which can cause blindness if not treated) during the baby's passage through the birth canal.

Between 1 and 2 million new cases are reported annually.

Most diagnoses of both types of herpes simplex are made on the basis of visual inspection of the sores as well as on the reported history. If doubt remains as to whether the infection is indeed herpes, a sample of the tissue is taken when it is actively infected and analyzed. Such analysis is highly recommended for pregnant women who believe that they are among the more than 20 million people in the United States who are infected with herpes.

A drug called acyclovir has been used with varying degrees of success in different people to treat herpes simplex, type 2. The drug has value for some people, particularly when used to treat the initial infection. The long term effects of acyclovir itself are not known. Many other treatments have been tried, including zinc and other ointments, yet none have proven to be curative. For all practical purposes, no cure exists for either type of herpes simplex at the present time. Interventions are most frequently limited to relieving the symptoms of infection, such as itching and pain.

In excess of 500,000 new cases annually.

Diagnosis of genital warts is frequently made upon visual inspection of the wart. In some cases, especially when there is a question of whether the diagnosis is genital warts or syphilis in the second stage, laboratory tests on samples of the warts must be done. Of the some 60 strains of genital warts that it is possible for humans to contract, 12 have been implicated as causative in cervical cancer if left untreated.

Treatment may entail removal of the warts using various surgical procedures, including laser therapy and freezing. The application of highly toxic agents such as podophyllin may be employed to "burn" the wart off. Injection of the drug alpha interferon into the warts has shown promise, and this procedure, first approved by the Federal Drug Administration in 1989, has been used increasingly.

Incidence in the general population of sexually active people is thought to rival other highly contagious diseases that can be transmitted sexually or otherwise. Between 20% to 30% of all sexually active Americans may have genital warts (Blakeslee, 1992b).

PREVENTING SEXUALLY TRANSMITTED DISEASES

Most sexually transmitted diseases are transmitted from an infected person to a noninfected person by a virus, bacteria, or other microorganism that finds a port of entry in the non-infected person during intimate contact. Practicing safer sex involves preventing the transmission/contraction of such diseases by physical, chemical, or other means. For all sexual contact involving the penis, including sexual intercourse, anal intercourse, and oral-genital stimulation, a latex condom is recommended. When used in sexual or anal intercourse, the condom should be coated with a spermicide containing nonoxynol-9 or octoxynol. The use of a dental dam (a flat piece of latex rubber used by oral surgeons) to cover the vagina prior to cunnilingus parallels the practice of using a latex condom to cover the penis during fellatio (Reinisch, 1990).

Recognizing the myth of safe sex, Ellen Hopkins, a feminist and a contributing editor to *Rolling Stone* magazine, has argued a compelling case for sexual abstinence:

> Our teen-ager knows that before going to bed with someone, she and the guy are supposed to exchange detailed sexual histories. Tandem AIDS tests are next, and if both can forge a monogamy pact, they will use condoms (and a more reliable form of birth control like the pill) for six months and then get tested again.
>
> Does our teen-ager hammer out these elaborate social contracts every time Cupid calls? Of course not . . .
>
> I once thought I'd tell my young son that anything goes—so long as he used condoms. Now I'm not so sure. (Hopkins, 1992, p. 21)

sexual outercourse

sexual behavior that does not involve contact with potentially infectious bodily fluids.

Unless one can be absolutely certain that a potential sexual partner is not infected with HIV or some other sexually transmittable infection, sexual abstinence is the "safest sex." If one finds sexual abstinence an impossibility, what has been called **sexual outercourse—***sexual behavior that does not involve contact with potentially infectious bodily fluids*—is a low-risk alternative to more traditional varieties of sexual activity. Sexual outercourse activities include caressing, massage, even mutual masturbation by manual or other stimulation (including rubbing or the use of mechanical devices) during which bodily fluids do not come in contact with potential ports of entry.

In a world where one sexual error can mean a lessened quality of life, if not a much abbreviated life, the potential joy of more intimate sexual contact must be weighed against the potential risks of contracting a curable but bothersome disease . . . or worse.

SUMMARY

A BIOLOGICAL PERSPECTIVE Biological factors, including the nature of one's genetic inheritance and the state of one's physical and mental health, play a great role in the nature, quality, and level of satisfaction one experiences as a sexual person. Male sexual dysfunctions such as erectile dysfunction, impotence, and premature ejaculation may be caused by psychological factors (such as anxiety), medical factors (such as diabetes), drug taking (including ingestion of alcohol), as well as by other factors. Female sexual dysfunctions such as vaginismus and failure to experience orgasm may also be caused by psychological, medical, and/or other factors. Both female and male sexual dysfunctions may be treated with a Masters-and-Johnson-type approach to treatment. In this approach, treatment is administered by a male and female therapist team who may employ sensate focus exercises, homework assignments, and a variety of behavioral techniques to treat the dysfunction.

SEXUAL VALUES, ORIENTATION, AND BEHAVIOR
A key component of sexual adjustment is a personal system of values that guides sexual decision making. *Sexual orientation* refers to the general nature of one's erotic inclination or preference with respect to the gender of sexual partners. A *heterosexual orientation* refers to a general erotic inclination or preference for opposite-sex sexual partners. A *homosexual orientation* refers to a general erotic inclination or preference for same-sex sexual partners. A *bisexual orientation* refers to a general erotic inclination towards same-sex and opposite-sex sexual partners. Just how biological, psychological, social, and other factors may interact to give rise to sexual orientation is a question researchers continue to explore. Humans are capable of an exceptionally wide range of sexual behaviors, and like beauty and truth, exactly what one finds sexually arousing is very much in the eye of the beholder.

SEXUALLY TRANSMITTED DISEASES Diseases that are passed from one person to another by means of sexual activity, including genital-genital contact, oral-genital contact, and other such means, are referred to as *sexually transmitted diseases*. AIDS (acquired immunodeficiency syndrome), chlamydia, syphilis, gonorrhea, herpes, and genital warts are some of many sexually transmitted diseases. Sexual abstinence is really the only way of protecting oneself from sexual transmission of most of these diseases. Methods of "safer sex," including the use of latex condoms, are not foolproof and may instill a false sense of security.

Marriage and Family

O U T L I N E

Marriage ceremonies range from somber to silly although the decision to marry, and who to marry, is critically important. Because of the far-reaching consequences of this decision, a great deal of serious thought, preferably including the counsel of worldly friends or professionals you trust, should precede engagement or wedding plans.

If you are not married now, you have probably given some thought to whether a wedding is in your future. And if you envision yourself married in the future, you have also probably given some thought to the type of person you want as your spouse. You may even be presently engaged or have a good idea about whom you think you will marry. In what follows, two questions are posed: *Is marriage right for you?* and *Who is right for you?* Although these questions may well be quite familiar to you, you may find your answers to them becoming a bit more focused as you read on. Later in this chapter, we will discuss a number of family-related issues, as well as issues related to divorce, remarriage, and marriage alternatives.

MARRIAGE

IS MARRIAGE RIGHT FOR YOU?

From all outward appearances, some married people seem as if they could not be happier. They love their families, feel good about themselves, and believe that the day they got married was the day they really started "living life." From a health perspective, it has been shown that married people as a group tend to be healthier than singles, and have a longer life expectancy (Verbrugge, 1979). Married men tend to be healthier, both mentally and physically, than never-married men (Bernard, 1982). Of course, it is difficult to know whether marriage has some kind of health-enhancing effect or whether people in better health are somehow the ones most likely to marry.

On the other side of the coin from the "happily married" people are legions of people of divorced, confirmed-single, or other status who want no part of marriage. Mae West, a sexy film star of the 1940s, once quipped that marriage is an institution, but, "Who wants to live in an institution?" In fact, when it comes to marriage, there are some people who scrupulously avoid such "institutionalization." Today, relatively fewer people are getting married than in the past. Further, the average age at which they are marrying is rising (see Figure 13–1). The number of years of an adult American's lifetime spent in marriage has decreased (Espenshade, 1985). According to current census data, about one in four Americans aged 18 or older have never married. By comparison, in 1970, only about 1 in 6 Americans in this age group had never married. In 1991, almost 18% of American men in the 35 to 39 age group had never been married—an increase of roughly 8% since 1980. About 12% of the women in the 35 to 39 age group had never been married in 1991, as compared to about 6% in 1980.

The factors operating to encourage or discourage marriage may be both environmental and psychological. At an environmental level, for example, a poor economy coupled with uncertain employment or unemployment is not conducive to marriage. In 1991, the country was in the midst of a recession, a fact noted by Robert J. Willis, director of the Economics Research Center at the University of Chicago's National Opinion Research Center. Commenting on the census data, Willis (1992) said, "My own hunch is that the decline in marriage rates has something to do with the recession. Marriages tend to be accelerated or postponed depending on the state of the economy."

At a psychological level, there are a number of factors that may motivate one to shy away from marriage. Marriage entails commitment and there are some people who have no wish to be "committed." Commitment entails trust and it is possible that many people who avoid commitment have suffered lapses of trust either with their own family while growing up or with a former lover (Lutwak, 1985). The negative consequences of allow-

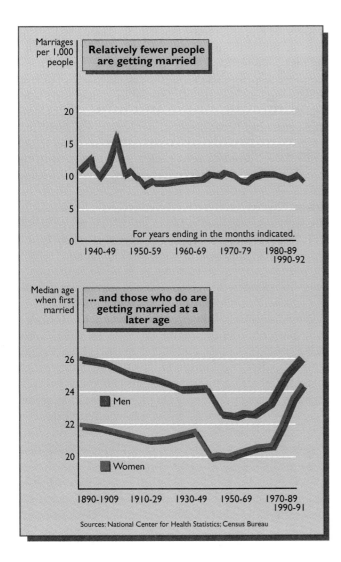

FIGURE 13–1 CENSUS DATA ON MARRIAGE
The top graph shows a decline and flattening out of the number of people getting married in recent years. The bottom graph shows an upward trend in the age at which people are first getting married.

ing oneself to care for or love another may be perceived as outweighing the positive consequences. Included among the negative consequences are vulnerability, the potential for pain, and the loss of one's sense of independence, freedom, and self.

If you are currently considering marriage, you may wish to think about your own ability to commit to someone, as well as other aspects of your personality that may affect how satisfied you would be when married. Marriage entails responsibility, communication, adaptability, and affection, among other things. For example, do you enjoy spending a lot of time socializing with your friends and meeting new people? Do you enjoy spending a lot of your time by yourself? Do you have difficulty sharing things you possess or time reserved for yourself? If you enjoy a lot of socializing with your friends as well as meeting new people, the single as opposed to the married lifestyle might be better suited to your needs. The same is true if you prefer to spend a great deal of your time on your own. Marriage also entails a great deal of sharing and it is ill-suited to perpetuating "what's mine is mine and what's yours is yours" attitudes. Further, at least according to social exchange theory, marital satisfaction derives from a sense of equity; the partners should perceive that they are contributing equally to the relationship in a material or emotional way, as well as in other ways (Ammons & Stinnet, 1980).

MARRIAGE MOTIVATION

In terms of optimizing one's chances for a happy, mutually fulfilling marriage, there are many "right" reasons for marrying. People marry to consummate one's love for one another, to establish a legal and moral basis for having and raising children, to commit to lifelong companionship and a life of mutual sharing of thoughts, feelings, and experiences. In surveys, when people are asked why they got married or what is important to them in marriage, *love* tends to be an almost reflexive response. Yet despite the great importance of love to marriage, it is important to understand that how people respond to such surveys is to some extent dictated by what is socially acceptable. Ever since childhood, most of us have been taught that love and marriage go together. For this reason, love is certainly among the most socially desirable reasons for people to get married. Responding, "I married for love," not only wins social approval, but presents people making such a proclamation with an image of themselves that is much more pleasing than saying, for example, "I married for money."

In fact, people marry for diverse reasons, and the actual reasons may be denied or deemphasized in surveys dealing with marriage. For example, in one survey of about 75,000 married female readers of *Redbook,* it was reported that only about 1 in 10 respondents rated financial security as essential to marriage (Tavris & Jayaratne, 1976). Common experience tells us that financial security in marriage is probably more important than this magazine article suggests. In research on the sources of marital conflict, finance-related concerns typically place high on the list (Geiss & O'Leary, 1981). In two studies that employed divorced people as subjects, divorced wives mentioned financial problems as a causal factor in their divorce in over 30% of the cases (Burns, 1984; Cleek & Pearson, 1985). Although wealth provides neither a guarantee of marital satisfaction nor a guarantee against finance-related difficulties (Pittman & Lloyd, 1988; Schaningner & Buss, 1986), a lack of financial resources can seriously depress chances for marital success (Komarovsky, 1977). Expectations of financial security are probably one component of the motivation to marry, although not always one that will be readily acknowledged in popular surveys.

The clinical psychology literature is replete with case studies of people who married for the "wrong" reasons. Experience tells us that marrying solely for financial security or solely for the purpose of getting out of the house are not good reasons for getting married. It would also be a mistake to marry to spite or hurt someone, to show gratitude or respect to someone, to prove one's own worth, to avoid condemnation, to avoid desperation, or to fulfill someone else's expectations. Can you think of any other "wrong" reasons why people marry? Why would you advise people against marrying for such reasons?

CULTURAL PRESSURE AND INCENTIVES TO MARRY

Virtually every culture throughout the world encourages its people to marry and multiply. That fact is true in our own country, as any single person who has ever been asked repeatedly, "So when are you getting married?" can well attest. Beyond such informal pressure to marry, government as well as private organizations offer many incentives to marry. The primary governmental incentive comes in the form of tax benefits, including tax deductions for dependents. Married couples also enjoy fringe benefits given to employees, such as family health insurance, as well as visiting rights at hospitals and prisons. Married couples who have children technically share equal rights with respect to their child, whereas this is not necessarily the case when the couple is not married. Rituals associated with marriage are among the oldest known sociolegal ceremonies, although the form such rituals take may vary widely by culture (see Figure 13–2).

Although cultural pressure to marry still exists in the United States, there is far less of such pressure than there has been in the past. In a bygone era, when women were not as much a part of the work force as they are now, there was more pressure on them to marry for financial security. The relaxation of cultural prohibitions regarding sexual behavior between consenting adults and the wide availability of birth control devices have also contributed to lessening culture pressure to marry. Marriage prompted by an unexpected pregnancy still occurs, although with far less frequency than in years past. Beyond sexual gratification, contemporary couples contemplating marriage typically expect intellectual and emotional gratification from the relationship (Rubin, 1988) and the single person may be very selective regarding such criteria (Bernard et al., 1991).

FIGURE 13–2 THE PRINCE AND THE HARVARD GRADUATE In a traditional wedding ceremony that dates back hundreds of years, Masako Owada married Crown Prince Naruhito of Japan in 1993. Masako was given a six-week course in "princess studies" in preparation for the event to supplement her Harvard education. When Masako eventually ascends to the crown, she will become the first Empress of Japan to have worked as a research assistant for a professor in the United States (Gordon, 1993).

WHO IS RIGHT FOR YOU?

No one, perhaps not even you, can predict who is "right" for you. It sometimes happens that people spend years dating one type of person only ultimately to marry another type of person. Experience teaches us, however, that the person whom you marry may well meet all or many of the PAPERS criteria discussed in Chapter 11. Whether a potential spouse meets some of these criteria, such as proximity and attractiveness, is immediately evident. However, the extent to which a potential spouse meets the remaining criteria can only be learned in the process of courtship. As you go beyond your first few contacts as a dating couple, the level of the dialogue will ideally gravitate from impersonal to increasingly personal topics of conversation. From conversations about daily activities (details about school or work), types of food enjoyed, and feelings about smoking, for example, the content may move towards more personally meaningful topics. Throughout, an informal evaluation is in progress regarding many of those PAPERS criteria, including personality, equity, reciprocity, and similarity.

To focus on the *S* (for *Similarity*) in the PAPERS acronym, it has been suggested that similar attitudes and values about things that are important to the individuals make for stronger marital compatibility and less stress in adjustment to marriage (Lasswell & Lasswell, 1987; Nahemow, 1983). Accordingly, one might expect a lower marriage success rate for spouses of different cultures as compared to spouses from the same culture. Indeed, this has been the case.

INTERMARRIAGE

Intermarriage is a general term used to describe *a marriage between people of two different heritages.* An **intercultural marriage** is a general term used to describe *a marriage between people of different cultures.* An **interfaith marriage** is *a marriage between two people of different religious faiths.* An **interracial marriage** is *a marriage between two people of different races.* It has been found that interfaith marriages and interracial marriages have a higher divorce rate than marriages between people of the same religious faith and/or the same race (Heer,

intermarriage
a general term used to describe a marriage between people of two different heritages.

intercultural marriage
a general term used to describe a marriage between people of different cultures.

interfaith marriage
a marriage between two people of different religious faiths.

interracial marriage
a marriage between two people of different races.

FIGURE 13–3 A MARRIAGE MADE—OR AT LEAST PARTIALLY SPENT—IN HEAVEN In September of 1992, American astronauts Mark Lee and Jan Davis became the first married couple ever to fly in space. Talk about similarity and shared interests!

1974; Shulruff, 1992). In one national study, it was found that the probability that a couple would still be together after 10 years of marriage was far less for interracial than for same-race marriages. According to Heer (1974), a marriage in which both partners were white had a 90% chance of remaining intact after 10 years. By contrast, a black husband and white wife had a 63% chance of remaining together. A white husband and black wife were found to have a 47% chance of remaining together.

Interestingly, even married couples who are practitioners of the same religion may experience the same kind of values-related difficulties as couples in various kinds of intermarriage if one spouse is more religious than the other. For example, in one Illinois divorce case involving a Jewish couple, the mother, an Orthodox Jew, had rather strict rules regarding dress, diet, synagogue attendance, and other matters. She did not want to share child custody with her ex-husband because this would mean a relaxation of religious rules on weekends and at other times while their child was with the father. The judge referred the couple to an experimental program at the DePaul University College of Law called the Interfaith Mediation Project. There, with the assistance of trained mediators, the divorcing Jewish couple was able to settle their dispute (Shulruff, 1992).

Many of the problems that arise in intermarried couples are only indirectly attributable to factors such as religion or race. At their root, the problems may stem from differences in values that exist between different cultures. A great deal of intercultural variation exists regarding attitudes and values concerning an extraordinarily wide range of variables. Couples may learn after marriage that they have significantly different, culturally based views on matters as diverse as money, personal hygiene, material possessions, sex, gender roles, and attitudes towards elders and in-laws. Perceived violations of one's culturally ingrained expectations can quickly become the subject of an emotionally heated confrontation. Sufficient advance communication about these and other values-related issues, not merely blind expectations, will go a long way towards preventing mutual disappointment in marriage.

It has been speculated that children of intermarriage have more potential adjustive demands and challenges facing them than children of single heritage marriages. They may encounter rejection from one or more of the groups with which they seek identity and may in general have greater difficulty establishing a sense of personal identity (Gordon, 1964; Henriques, 1974; McDermott & Fukunaga, 1977; Piskacek & Golub, 1973; Washington, 1970). They may be subject to competing patterns of socialization, which in turn may predispose them to maladjustment (Bronfenbrenner, 1986; Higgins, 1985; Maccoby, 1980; Smither & Rodriguez-Giegling, 1979).

Intermarriage in American society is increasing (Alba & Golden, 1986; Lieberson & Waters, 1985). In some culturally diverse states such as Hawaii, for example, it has been estimated that as many as 50% of all marriages are intermarriages (Hawaii State Department of Health, 1987; Labov & Jacobs, 1986). Although such marriages have the potential to be as fulfilling as same-heritage marriages—if not more fulfilling due to the added and enriching benefits of exposure to another's heritage—intermarriage may demand more effort if the marriage is to last. The couple must work to keep communication lines between them open when culture-related differences threaten to close them. The couple may also have to work to keep communication lines open with family and friends who may not approve of the marriage.

SOME QUESTIONS FOR DISCUSSION

If failed expectations play a role in failed relationships, then one component of a success prescription is extended communication prior to marriage. Many people ask more questions about a car they are planning to purchase than about a relationship they hope to forge for life. The *Self-Assessment* feature below lists a number of questions you may want to raise either in your own mind prior to marriage or for discussion between you and your prospective mate.

SELF-ASSESSMENT

A Premarital Checklist

Prior to interviewing caterers, here is a brief list of some of the relatively obvious questions you may wish to consider.

1. *Do you trust this person implicitly?*
   Trust is an extremely important, yet seldom talked about, variable in marriage. Marriage is an extremely weighty social and legal commitment and it is absolutely essential that you trust a prospective spouse as much or more than the family member or friend you currently trust the most.
2. *How will the marriage function financially?*
   Who is bringing what to the marriage? How will housing, food, transportation, telephone, insurance, and related living expenses be paid every month? Will you have single or joint checking accounts? To what extent will personal assets (such as one's car) become shared assets? How will each partner's earnings, savings, investments, past credit card debts, and/or other assets and liabilities be handled once you become legally married? What expectations for the future, if any, do you have of your spouse financially?
3. *What expectations, if any, do you have of your future spouse sexually?*
4. *What are your feelings about having children after you are married?*
   If you or your prospective spouse have different desires regarding family size, or if one of you is incapable for some reason of having children, such issues will ideally be discussed prior to marriage. A related issue concerns child care if the decision is made to have children. What priorities do you and your spouse-to-be have regarding work, employment, and child care?
5. *What are your feelings about continuing your education?*
   If you or your prospective spouse wishes to do so, how will this be accomplished?

6. *How do each of you envision spending your leisure time?* What types of things do you envision doing as a couple? What types of things do you envision doing individually, without your spouse?
7. *How do you plan to handle everyday household chores such as cooking, cleaning, raking leaves, food shopping, and so forth?*
   How will such roles and obligations be decided?
8. *What expectations do you have about where you will live?* Is there a possibility that either of you might be transferred to some other geographical area as a result of work? What would the consequences of such a transfer be? What if one or both of you has a job that requires extensive travel and time away from home?
9. *How good are each of you at resolving conflicts when they come up?* How are conflicts typically resolved? Are the mechanisms for conflict resolution that seem to be in place mutually satisfactory?
10. *What other expectations do you have regarding yourself and your prospective spouse as marital partners? What other expectations does your prospective spouse have?*

These are just some of the many types of questions that need to be thought about and discussed when thinking seriously about marriage. If you or your prospective spouse believe that a professional could be useful in more thorough exploration of these or other issues, a consultation with an expert in premarital evaluation would be a very wise investment. You may also wish to consider some sort of premarital educational program. Markman et al. (1988) described one such program which covers areas such as communication skills, problem-solving skills, and sexual education. This program, as well as other such programs, have shown promise in preventing future divorce.

Ideally, part of the courtship process will involve not only getting to know a lot about your prospective spouse but also getting to know a lot about your prospective in-laws (your prospective spouse's family). A common myth among many single people is that the spouse's family does not matter because you are marrying the person, not the family. But as anyone married for some time can tell you, there may well be a grain of truth in the fact that you are marrying the person's family, not merely the person. In marriage, one spouse is frequently drawn into the goings-on within the other spouse's family. Further, your in-laws are the people with whom you may be spending holidays every year, as well as some portion of your leisure time. If there is physical illness, mental illness, drug abuse, or other types of problems plaguing your intended's family, the time to learn about it and discuss it is before, not after, the marriage vows. If there are problems to be resolved between an intended spouse and prospective in-laws, those problems will ideally be addressed before, not after, marriage.

ADJUSTMENT IN MARRIAGE

For someone used to living the single life, marriage requires some major changes and adjustment. The changes begin with a whole new identity for you as well as for your former boyfriend or girlfriend; that of *husband* or *wife*. For women, getting married may also entail getting used to being called "Mrs." and to a new last name. But beyond replacing monograms on towels and having new checks printed, lie truly major changes in identity, complete with changes in roles. Exactly what those new roles are may well be the subject of negotiation over time.

When setting up house together, one of the first tasks newlyweds face is assigning domestic responsibilities. Two variables that research has found to be influential in shaping a household's division of labor are (1) the power of the respective parties in the relationship, including each member's resources, earnings, and potential earnings, and (2) each member's gender-related attitudes regarding what is appropriate as a role in marriage. When wives who function in traditional gender-related work roles hold nontraditional ideas about such roles, the potential for marital dissatisfaction grows (McHale & Crouter, 1992).

A CRASH COURSE IN WHAT TO ANTICIPATE

If you have never before been married, prepare for change. Based on my own personal experience, and that of my wife's, here are a dozen changes of varying significance that you may anticipate:

1. *Changes in Tidiness*
   Forget about leaving the mayonnaise jar on the counter just because you are in a hurry. Mom is no longer around to clean up for you. You will have to take responsibility for cleaning up the mess you make.
2. *Changes in "Reporting"*
   Remember when you used to just run out of the house at will to go shopping? Those days are gone. As a courtesy, spouses tell each other where they are going (as in "I'm going shopping, honey") whenever they are going to be away for some time.
3. *Changes in Phone Habits*
   You may have fond memories of talking on the phone for hours to that person you eventually married. Little did you know at the time that that person was also capable of talking to dozens of other people on the phone for hours. A second phone line may be a sound investment in marital bliss.
4. *Changes in Sleep Patterns*
   Should you choose to sleep in the same bed, as many newlyweds do, you may find that you do not get as much sleep as you used to. No, the sleep deprivation is not necessarily due to all the sex you are having with your spouse. Rather, it has more to do with getting used to somebody sleeping in your bed on a regular basis. It may also have to do with your spouse's insomnia, sleeping schedule, television watching habits, illumination or temperature preferences, and/or an uncontrollable, incurable, and unstoppable tendency to snore powerfully.

5. *Changes in Temperature*

   Your body temperature may not change as a function of marriage but the temperature of your home might. You may be used to a certain temperature that your spouse finds oppressively hot or cold. You may be used to sleeping with the window open and a cool breeze blowing on your face. Your spouse may prefer sleeping with the windows bolted shut and any "breeze" coming only from an air conditioner.

6. *Changes in Your Television Viewing Habits*

   Sure, you probably own more than one television and, in theory, you could both watch different shows. However, some times may seem right to watch television together and there is going to have to be compromise about what to watch. You may despise reruns of *Murder, She Wrote,* for example, but find yourself sitting through them occasionally just to be accommodating. Of course, there's always the video-recorder, so you don't have to miss anything.

7. *Changes in Privacy*

   Once you are married, most aspects of your life—including those you once believed were the most private aspects imaginable—may well become public knowledge to your spouse.

8. *Lessening of Closet Space*

   Along with your privacy, it is a good bet that you can kiss a lot of your closet space good-bye. Because many couples just starting out cannot afford a home of the size they would like, space is at a premium. Some of your things will either have to be disposed of or put into storage. Marriage sometimes means sacrifice . . . literally!

9. *Changes in Eating Habits*

   In your single days, you ate whatever you wanted, whenever you wanted, wherever you wanted. Meals may become much more regimented. Be prepared by rehearsing questions like, "What would you like for dinner tonight?", "What time would you like to eat?" and "Where did you put the menu for that Chinese take-out place?"

10. *Changes in Socialization*

    Social meetings with your single friends may lessen in frequency after marriage, while socialization with married friends may increase. Of course, if your spouse and the spouse of your married friend do not quite hit it off, you may find that the time you spend socializing with that married friend also decreases.

11. *Changes in Pet-Lover Status*

    My wife spent most of her adult life fearing dogs. When her friends heard that her fiancé owned a German shepherd, they could not believe it. Yet, my wife has come to love Sheena. Marriage does wonderful things to people.

12. *Changes in Sharing*

    As a single person you may share your house, your car, your computer, or anything of value with anyone because that's what you want to do. In marriage, you share just about everything because you are more or less obliged to do so. If there is one car between you, for instance, it is no longer *my* car or *your* car, it is *our* car—and *we* use it whenever *we* need to use it.

If you are not married, expect to add other changes to your own personal list depending upon the unique nature of your relationship. If you are married, you can probably add another dozen or so changes based on your own experience. Some of the changes require relatively little in the way of adjustment. For example, changes in room temperature at night can be adjusted for by sleeping with more or less clothing on. Other changes, such as changes in privacy, may require more creative problem-solving.

PARENTHOOD AND FAMILY LIFE

"For most adult humans, parenthood is still the ultimate source of the sense of meaning. For most adults the question 'What does life mean?' is automatically answered once they have children; better yet, it is no longer asked" (Gutmann, 1975, p. 170). Erikson (1963) seemed to agree, and he wrote that a basic human need was the need to create and nourish children. Survey and other research suggests that many more conscious, noninstinctual motives may also be at work in one's motivation to parent.

In their national survey of men and women who were either parents or nonparents, Hoffman and Manis (1979) found that a desire for love and close ties to others ranked high among the reasons given for having children. Other reasons commonly given included the desire for the stimulation and novelty that children bring to an adult's life, the desire for a creative outlet and a sense of achievement, and the desire to develop oneself and to extend one's links to the community. Some survey respondents perceived parenting as the ultimate test of one's maturity and stability; for them, becoming a responsible parent was an indication that a person has reached maturity. A more recent survey of 600 male and female unmarried college graduates between the ages of 21 and 30 found that only 8% of the sample wanted a child-free marriage. Asked why they would want to have children, most of the responses were categorized by the researchers as being "narcissistic" in nature. Included were responses that made reference to personal fulfillment, having someone to love, and having "a little person like me" (Caron & Wynn, 1992, p. 484).

FAMILY PLANNING

Contemporary reproductive knowledge and technology have greatly diminished the role of chance in the process of having a baby. Now more than ever, a couple can plan to have a baby or plan not to have a baby.

FERTILITY

fertile
capable of reproducing.

fertility
the condition of being fertile.

fertilization
see *conception.*

pregnancy
the state of having a fertilized ovum.

infertility
inability to impregnate or to become impregnated.

To be **fertile** means to be *capable of reproducing,* **fertility** refers to *the condition of being fertile,* and **fertilization** refers to *the union of an ovum with a sperm* or *conception.* **Pregnancy** refers to *the state of having a fertilized ovum* and a woman whose ovum has been fertilized is said to be *pregnant.* For our purposes, a woman who is physically capable of being impregnated and carrying the baby to term and a man who is capable of physically impregnating a woman are both considered fertile.[1] **Infertility,** which refers to the *inability to impregnate or to become impregnated,* may be a temporary or permanent condition. Female infertility may be caused by a number of problems, including failure to ovulate, blockage of passageways the ova must travel through, drugs, injury, poor nutrition, radiation or other environmental variables, birth defects, and damage to reproductive tissue as a result of a sexually transmitted disease or other infection. Male infertility may also be caused by a number of problems, including a low number or low quality of sperm, which in turn may be caused by many factors. Birth defects, injury, the aftermath of sexually transmitted diseases or other infections (such as mumps in adulthood), drugs, radiation or other environmental variables, and endocrine disorders are all capable of causing such difficulties. Extremes of temperature can affect sperm count, as can frequency of ejaculation.

For many couples, the challenge of parenting begins long before conception. This is so because infertility among couples has been rising to rates that are about triple what they were in the 1960s (Mazor, 1980). Infertility problems are due to the female's infertility in about 60% of the cases, with male infertility problems accounting for the remaining 40% of the cases (Mosher & Pratt, 1982). Paralleling these mysterious rises in infertility rates have been great strides in the medical technology used to diagnose and treat the condition. Although available, this technology does not come cheaply and is seldom covered by insurance. Still, approximately 50% of all infertile couples seek medical treatment for the problem, and about 1.6 million physician office visits for fertility services were made in 1984 (U. S. Congress, 1988). Depending upon the problem, the physician may be able to prescribe medication and/or perform or recommend various types of procedures in order to facilitate the possibility of conception (see the *Quality of Life* on page 358).

The fertile couple who wishes to conceive a child has the options of letting fertilization result by chance or of actively planning the conception. If the latter course is chosen, the couple will optimize their chances by having sexual intercourse during the time of ovulation. For a woman having a regular 28-day menstrual cycle, ovulation will typically occur some time between Day 10 (assuming 5 days of menstruation, and referring to the 5th day after menstruation ceases), and Day 17 in the cycle. Another natural technique for more

[1]More precise definitions of fertility typically make reference to the quality and/or quantity of the gametes, as well as to other variables (Glass & Ericsson, 1982).

precisely estimating the optimal time for intercourse is the *basal body temperature* method (Kolodny et al., 1979). This method entails tracking the woman's body temperature, preferably by means of an accurate digital thermometer capable of recording fractional changes in body temperature. Just prior to ovulation, the woman's body temperature may dip slightly. Just subsequent to ovulation, the body temperature may rise slightly. Sexual intercourse about 12 hours subsequent to this rise in temperature is advisable. Other natural methods, as well as over-the-counter tests, are also available for more precisely determining when intercourse is most likely to result in a fertilized ovum.

In addition to an awareness of when intercourse should be attempted, a couple seeking to conceive should also be aware of how best to optimize the chances of conception. In this context, sexual intercourse in a position that guarantees the deposit of the ejaculate in the vagina and places the least burden on the sperm in terms of gravitational pull is generally advisable. The prone, man-on-top, face-to-face position, with the woman's legs raised towards her chest is sometimes recommended because this position helps the ejaculated sperm better defy gravity and move upward. After ejaculation, the man should not withdraw immediately. Also, it is advisable for the woman to remain relatively still on her back for upwards of an hour or so. It is also advisable for men to refrain from ejaculating for at least 48 hours prior to intercourse, in order that the highest possible sperm count be maintained. Based on one's own medical history, a physician or fertility specialist can best provide more detailed and personalized information for when and how to conceive.

CONTRACEPTION

Knowledge of human reproduction may also be marshaled in the service of lessening the probability that conception will take place. A "natural," or "fertility awareness," method of contraception is based on the simple principle that both a sperm and an ovum must be present simultaneously for conception to take place. For the woman having a regular 28-day menstrual cycle, refraining from sexual intercourse between Day 10 and Day 17 can be a useful first step in a contraceptive or pregnancy prevention program. However, sperm may be capable of fertilizing ova for as long as 7 days after being deposited in the vagina. For this reason, the only "safe" days for intercourse in a natural pregnancy prevention program are Days 18 through 28, and then Days 1 through 3 (the first 3 days of the menstrual period). For the woman having a regular 28-day menstrual cycle, then, Days 4 through 17 would be "unsafe" in terms of conception. The "safe" and "unsafe" days for women having irregular cycles will vary, and use of techniques such as the basal body temperature method and commercially available fertility testing kits is recommended in order to more precisely determine days when ovulation occurs. In addition to, or in place of, such natural, fertility awareness approaches to contraception, other methods may also be employed.

The use of linen sheaths draped over the penis as a disease prevention technique was described in the sixteenth century by the Italian anatomist Fallopius. The contraceptive value of such sperm-blocking techniques would become widely recognized within the next two centuries, and primitive condoms, usually made from the internal organs of sheep, began to be marketed in Europe. In the mid-1800s, when methods of rubber processing were revolutionized, condoms made of rubber first began to be mass produced. These condoms, or *rubbers,* as people referred to them, did not initially receive the widespread public acceptance that they enjoy today. In fact, the federal Comstock Laws of 1873 restricted the interstate sale of condoms and other such items that the government deemed to be obscene. People purchased condoms in rather secretive fashion at sites ranging from barber shops to gasoline filling stations. In the 1920s, in an effort to counter the aura of obscenity that surrounded their product, the manufacturer of Trojan brand condoms (Youngs Rubber, bought in 1985 by the Carter Wallace Company), proudly proclaimed that Trojans would be sold only in drug stores. Today, condoms are sold in a wide variety of outlets, including barber shops (once again), and even beauty shops (see Figure 13–4 on page 360).

Since the mid-1800s, the number of contraceptive methods widely available to the general public has mushroomed. Yet all these many different methods can be grouped into three, sometimes overlapping, general categories: (1) *barrier methods,* which physically and/or chemically block sperm from uniting with ova; (2) *hormonal methods,* which alter biochemistry, thus preventing conception or the attachment of the fertilized ovum to the

QUALITY OF *Life*

Reproduction and Biosocial Innovation

For the couple having fertility problems, as well as for others seeking to have a child, a number of methods are either currently available or on the horizon (Edwards, 1991). These methods include *in vitro* fertilization, cryopreservation, ovum transfer, artificial insemination, surrogacy, genetic engineering, ectogenesis, and cloning.

In vitro fertilization

In this process, an egg gathered by a technician and sperm that have been inspected and appropriately prepared come to union within a petri dish. Up to four such fertilized eggs, then referred to as embryos are implanted within a woman's womb—this in an effort to simulate the natural odds that any one of the embryos will grow to maturity. Fertility drugs may be used if they are deemed helpful in aiding the implantation, and multiple births are a possible outcome of such procedures.

Cryopreservation

Cryopreservation refers to the freezing of embryos. It is a procedure most typically used in conjunction with *in vitro* fertilization. If embryos attached to the womb are for any reason not carried to term, embryos that have been cryopreserved (frozen) can be thawed and used. Some clinicians prefer cryopreserved to fresh embryos because they believe that if embryos survive cryopreservation, they are more likely to result in a live birth. Cryopreserved embryos may also be used in the future for "embryo adop-

tion," as they may stay preserved for hundreds, perhaps even thousands of years (Lieber, 1989).

Ovum transfer

Despite the use of fertility drugs and other such interventions, some women are unable to carry an embryo to term. Ovum transfer entails the placement of the donor woman's fertilized ovum (an embryo), into the womb of a recipient woman, where it will be carried to term. The procedure is accomplished through the use of a specially devised catheter and is therefore nonsurgical.

Artificial insemination

Using donated sperm from either an identified or anonymous donor, fertilization takes place via the mechanical insertion of semen into the woman. Long used in animal husbandry, the procedure is particularly valuable in humans when a couple wishes to conceive but the male has a low sperm count, a premature ejaculation problem, or related problems with impregnation. The procedure is also useful for males who opt to preserve their semen in a sperm bank for possible use at a later date. Men going off to war or other hazardous duty, men undergoing chemical or radiation treatment, and men choosing to have a vasectomy may all opt to have their sperm frozen in a sperm bank for possible future use. Artificial insemination is also more frequently being used by lesbian couples who wish to have a

child but no sexual contact with a man.

Surrogacy

Surrogacy is more of a legal arrangement than a medical procedure. Artificial insemination is typically used to fertilize the egg of a "surrogate mother" who agrees to carry to term a baby, usually for a couple in which the female has an infertility problem. The term "surrogate mother" is also used to refer to a woman carrying an embryo to term who has had implanted in her womb an embryo created by the couple who have contracted with her to carry it. Surrogacy is an option for women who are either infertile or unwilling to carry a baby to term for medical, cosmetic, or career-related reasons. In recent years, relatives of an infertile couple, including sisters, mothers, and even grandmothers, have acted as surrogate mothers.

Genetic engineering

As the process of human conception increasingly takes place outside the body, scientists have had an opportunity to manipulate what the final product will be. Some experimentation with human genetic material has already begun, primarily on medical grounds. However, as Edwards (1991) has noted, there are currently no barriers to prevent such technology from being used for eugenic purposes. It has already become possible to genetically alter the sex of the embryo (Ewing,

wall of the uterus; and (3) *surgical methods*, which alter the anatomy in a way so as to make fertilization impossible. Table 13–1 on page 360 lists some contraceptive techniques illustrative of each of these three categories. Each method of contraception carries its own unique benefits and risks. If you are sexually active, take a moment now to ask yourself which method of contraception is best for you.

1988) and over 500 clinics in India have been set up for just that purpose (Wichterich, 1988). Given the cultural preference in that country for male children, and the fact that the family of a female is still expected to award a dowry upon marriage, one can presume that few embryos will be changed from male to female. According to Mahoney (1992) a significant, shockingly disproportionate number of abortions done in that country subsequent to amniocentesis are on female fetuses. One Bombay hospital even advertised openly, "Pay 5,000 rupees now or pay 50,000 as dowry later."

Ectogenesis

Imagine not only conceiving a person outside the human body, but also bringing it to term in a kind of artificial uterus, also outside of the body. Ectogenesis refers to the process of bringing a fertilized ovum to term in just that way. Although the technology for ectogenesis does not currently exist, scientists foresee a day when it will. The closest thing to ectogenesis we currently have are incubators and related technology capable of keeping alive premature babies having birth weights of less than one pound (Walters, 1982).

Cloning

Perhaps the most astounding and ethically problematic form of all the new or proposed genetic technologies is cloning. In theory, the procedure of cloning entails using cells from one organism to create an exact duplicate of that organism. Scientists have already made unnecessary the need for sexual contact between two people to produce a child. If human cloning were to become a reality, even the need for genetic material from two people would be eliminated; only the genetic material from one person would be necessary. Already, frogs, salamanders, and fruit flies have been cloned (Edwards, 1991). What benefits could you see in cloning human beings? What problems do you foresee? In general, how do you feel about biosocial innovations in reproductive methods? Why do you feel that way?

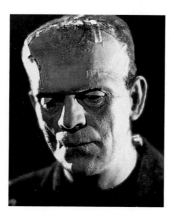

Is it meaningful to speak of this man's mother, father, grandfather, or grandmother? Some believe that terms such as these, as well as the related concepts of family and kinship may all become meaningless if present biosocial trends continue (Edwards, 1991).

in vitro fertilization
the process of uniting a sperm and egg in a laboratory and then implanting the zygote within a woman's womb.

cryopreservation
in the medical specialty of human fertility, the freezing of embryos, usually in conjunction with in vitro fertilization.

artificial insemination
a procedure in which fertilization takes place via the mechanical insertion of donated sperm from either an identified or anonymous donor into a woman.

surrogacy
an arrangement typically made between a fertile woman and an infertile person or couple for the fertile woman to carry a baby to term.

genetic engineering
the deliberate manipulation and alteration of genetic material.

ectogenesis
in theory, a technological process for conceiving and bringing to term a person outside the human body through the use of an artificial placenta.

cloning
the process of using cells from one organism to create an exact duplicate of that organism.

Questions about contraception can perhaps best be answered by a three-way conversation between you, your partner, and a physician or counselor who is knowledgeable about (1) contraceptive alternatives, and (2) the medical and behavioral history of you and your partner. Some of the questions you may wish to raise include: How effective, in theory, is the method in preventing unwanted pregnancy? How effective, in practice, is the

FIGURE 13–4 HAIRSTYLING AND CONDOMS In 1986, the surgeon general of the United States announced that, except for sexual abstinence, the use of latex rubber condoms represented the only effective method of preventing the transmission of the virus that causes AIDS during sex. That announcement, as well as other news, such as Magic Johnson's revelation in 1990 that he had contracted the AIDS virus from heterosexual sex, compelled people in record numbers to think anew about condoms as both a contraceptive and disease-prevention device (Hochman, 1992). With the new respectability accorded condoms, they have been given away free by schools, public health agencies, and private organizations. They are also being sold in a wide variety of settings. This photo was snapped at a hair salon in South Carolina where condoms wrapped like lollipops are available to customers.

TABLE 13–1 CONTRACEPTIVE TECHNIQUES

Type of Method	Specific Techniques
Barrier Method	Male Condom Female Condom Diaphragm Cervical Cap Intrauterine device (IUD) Sponge Spermicidal jelly, cream, or foam
Hormonal Method	Birth control pills "Morning after" pills Injectable progestin Implanted progestin Vaginal ring
Surgical Method	Vasectomy* Removal of the uterus Tying of the fallopian tubes
*Other**	Natural Withdrawal Douche Abstinence

Vasectomy, a surgical technique that has been the preferred birth control method for millions of men, has recently been linked to a higher rate of risk for prostate cancer (Altman, 1993).

**Natural* refers to methods of fertility awareness and to the idea that certain days during the menstrual cycle are "safe" for having intercourse while other days are "unsafe." *Withdrawal* refers to the removal of the penis from the vagina just prior to ejaculation. This method is perhaps better referred to as a "nonmethod" of contraception because fluid containing live sperm may be emitted from the penis prior to ejaculation. Upwards of 25% of women who rely exclusively on this method of contraception become pregnant annually. *Douching,* or propelling fluid into the vagina immediately after sexual intercourse, is another nonmethod of contraception, even when the douche contains a spermicide (Shapiro, 1988). Sperm may be on its way up the vaginal vestibule seconds after ejaculation. The injection of douche may actually serve to propel sperm farther rather than to retard their progress.

method in preventing unwanted pregnancy? Is the method fully reversible if conception should be viewed as desirable at some future time? What possible side effects or other unwanted effects does the method have? How consistent is this method of birth control with the behavior and lifestyle of the people who will be using it?

According to data from the Ortho Pharmaceutical Company (Hochman, 1992), for American women between the ages of 15 and 44, preferred contraceptive methods include birth control pills (28%), surgical procedures (25%), condoms (17%), withdrawal (6%), diaphragm (3%), fertility awareness (3%), and all other methods (18%), including abstinence, cervical cap, douching, intrauterine device, sponge, and spermicides.

ABORTION

Spontaneous abortion, synonymous with **miscarriage**, may be defined as *a natural termination of pregnancy.* Spontaneous abortions end an estimated 10% to 40% of all pregnancies (Insel & Roth, 1991). **Abortion** refers to *an artificially induced termination of pregnancy, usually by chemical, mechanical, or surgical means.* Abortion is sometimes mistakenly referred to as a method of contraception. Because abortion takes place after conception has taken place, it is not, by definition, a method of contraception.

Anti-abortion groups have long challenged the morality and legality of abortion. In 1973, the Supreme Court of the United States ruled in the case of *Roe v. Wade* that abortion was a constitutionally guaranteed right, although the Court prescribed strict standards to govern the procedure. Those restrictions were in essence tightened by a ruling of the Court in the 1989 case of *Webster v. Reproductive Health Services.* As cases that impact on abortion rights continue to be raised, the fate of abortion as a legal means of terminating a pregnancy rests in no small way with the nine justices who sit on the Supreme Court. In turn, the composition of the Court is in part determined by the president, who appoints new justices to the Court when sitting justices retire or die. During the 12-year period from 1980 to 1992, the administrations of Ronald Reagan and George Bush sought to appoint justices who shared their publicly stated anti-abortion values.

Also during this period, the number of abortions in proportion to live births began to decline in the United States. According to the Federal Centers for Disease Control and Prevention, contemporary women in America, as compared to women in the late 1970s, are more apt to have a baby than an abortion (see Figure 13–5). Exactly what accounts for the decline in the abortion rate has been a matter of speculation. On the one hand, fewer abortions may reflect a total reduction in the number of unwanted pregnancies as a result of factors such as more effective sex education efforts and greater use and improved quality of contraceptive technology. On the other hand, fewer abortions may also have resulted from increased acceptance of anti-abortion groups' message or from the perpetration of illegal violence on abortion clinic property, personnel, and patients, thus limiting patients' access to facilities that perform abortion (Barringer, 1992). In the past 15 years, over 100 clinics have been bombed or set on fire, and over 400 have been vandalized ("The Death of Dr. Gunn," 1993). In March 1993, anti-abortion extremists sprayed eight California clin-

spontaneous abortion
see *miscarriage.*

miscarriage
a natural termination of pregnancy, also referred to as a spontaneous abortion. Contrast with *abortion.*

abortion
an artificially induced termination of pregnancy, usually by chemical, mechanical, or surgical means.

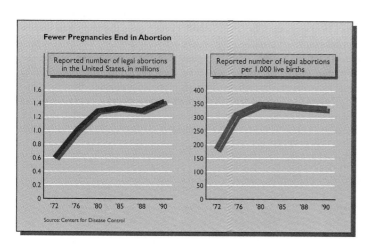

FIGURE 13–5 DECLINING AMERICAN ABORTIONS RATES According to data from the federal Centers for Disease Control and Prevention, as illustrated in graph on left, the actual number of abortions being done in this country has more than doubled since 1972. However, the ratio of abortions to live births has shown a slight decline since 1980 (refer to graph on right). In 1989, there were 359 abortions per 1,000 live births. In 1990, there were 344 abortions per 1,000 live births. Currently about 79% of all abortions are performed on unmarried women (Barringer, 1992).

ics with butyric acid, a caustic and putrid chemical. The spraying caused the hospitalization of four health care workers for respiratory problems (Rohter, 1993). That same week, David Gunn, a 47-year-old physician, was shot dead during an anti-abortion demonstration at the Florida clinic he had founded. The shooting, the first of its kind in the United States, prompted a new round of soul-searching and values-related questioning with respect to abortion-related issues on the part of many thoughtful people, regardless of their stand on the abortion issue (see *A Question of Values*).

A QUESTION OF Values

Abortion

Few issues in the history of this country have been as emotion-charged and controversial as the issue of abortion. Anti-abortion advocates, such as J. C. Willkie, president of the National Right to Life Committee, Inc., argue that human life begins at the moment of conception and that abortion represents a violation of the right of equal protection under the law for all living things. According to Willkie (1991, p. 171), "A woman has a right to her own body, but to say that the little passenger residing within her is part of her body is to utter a biologic absurdity". By contrast, Kate Michelman, executive director of the National Abortion Rights Action League, argues that women themselves, not politicians or anyone else, are the only people who ethically can be allowed to make choices regarding pregnancy, childbirth, and abortion. She argues that her group is pro-choice, not pro-abortion, and that, "As difficult as it is morally for some people to accept abortion, we feel there is a greater wrong in forcing a woman to undergo the demanding, intimate, and at times, life-threatening experiences of pregnancy and childbirth" (Michelman, 1991 p. 169).

Women who, for whatever reason, may be contemplating abortion quickly become caught up not only in the storm of social controversy surrounding the procedure but in personal tur-

moil as well. In cases in which it is not deemed a medical necessity to save the life of the mother, the mere contemplation of an abortion may be emotionally wrenching. Acting to compound such stress are many difficult legal and ethical questions about which reasonable and sincere people may differ on the basis of their own strongly held values. Stress surrounding a contemplated abortion has been compounded yet further as a result of escalating violence against abortion clinics, their patients, and their staff. In 1985, patients at a Manhattan clinic, some still groggy from anesthetic, were evacuated and forced to stand in the rain as police responded to a bomb threat. In the years since, many clinics have actually been bombed or set afire.

Some groups seeking to stop abortion through legal as well as illegal means have made a policy of terrorizing physicians who perform the procedure. In one campaign referred to as "No Place to Hide" by the group Operation Rescue, photographs of physicians who perform abortions were distributed on "Wanted"-type posters along with personal information, including their home telephone numbers. Such physicians may then be confronted with threats either in person, by phone, or by other means if they do not submit to the group's demands. Although the right of anti-

abortion advocates to be heard is undisputed, critics of such groups believe that the Reagan and Bush administrations allowed them to over-step their rights to the point where they are infringing on others' constitutionally guaranteed right to obtain or perform an abortion.

Lewis (1993) writes that all individuals are constitutionally guaranteed the right to choose their own religious beliefs, but they may not constitutionally attempt to force those beliefs on anyone else. He views the violence being perpetrated on abortion clinics as the work of religious fanatics who would compel others to accept their interpretation of the Bible. Yet, the very same activities Lewis condemns are viewed by others as desperate but nonetheless necessary to stop the loss of human life.

People on both sides of this important issue do not agree on much. Perhaps one thing they can agree on is the advisability of thinking ahead when and if one makes the choice to be sexually active. Important values-related questions are better raised at that time, long before the time when other even more complex and troublesome values-related issues—those related to the mother, the unborn child, the father, and society in general—urgently beg resolution.

WHAT IS A FAMILY?

In its most traditional sense, a **family** is *a group of people joined by both a marital bond and a consanguineal (that is, blood-related) bond* (Murdock, 1949). According to the United States Census Bureau, a **family** consists of *any two or more related people living in one household.* Yet a wide diversity of groups of "two or more related people" currently exist in this country and others as households. For example, in Denmark, homosexual marriage has been legal since 1992. Examples of different groups of people who consider themselves to be a family, with or without the legal status of a family can be quite broad. Some examples:

1. A **married heterosexual couple that is voluntarily childless.** A married male and female who elect not to have children.
2. A **married homosexual couple that is childless.** Two legally married people of the same sex who have no children as a result of a prior heterosexual marriage, or who have elected not to adopt, or, in the case of lesbians, elected not to have a child by a male.
3. A **married heterosexual couple that is involuntarily childless.** A married male and female who have been trying unsuccessfully to have children, perhaps due to fertility problems.
4. A **cohabiting heterosexual couple that is voluntarily childless.** A nonmarried male and female who are living together and who have elected not to have children.
5. A **cohabiting homosexual couple that is childless.** Two people of the same sex living together who have no children as a result of a prior heterosexual marriage, or who have elected not to adopt, or, in the case of lesbians, elected not to have a child by a male.
6. A **cohabiting heterosexual couple that is involuntarily childless.** A male and female living together who have been trying unsuccessfully to have children, perhaps due to fertility problems.
7. A **single (formerly married) parent family in which child is blood relative.** A divorced parent and his or her own child or children.
8. A **single (not formerly married) parent family in which child is blood relative.** A parent who has never been married and her or his own child or children.
9. A **single (formerly married) parent family in which child is not a blood relative.** A divorced parent and a child (or children) who is not a blood relative.
10. A **single (not formerly married) parent family in which child is not a blood relative.** A parent who has never been married and child (or children) who is not a blood relative.
11. **Three or more cohabiting partners.** Also referred to as a *multilateral family,* all of the people in this relationship have a sense of being married to, or analogously committed to, more than one of the other partners.
12. **Two males and two females in which each person is "married" to all persons of the opposite sex.** This kind of arrangement has also been referred to as a *group marriage.*

This listing only begins to impart a sense of the diversity in families that exist today and is not comprehensive. The types of families listed could be further broken down to more specific types, and additional types could be added. In some cultures, such as that of Native Americans, the term *family* itself may be somewhat misleading since it is the tribe, and not a group of individuals within it, that has traditionally been the primary source of identification. The role of individual families within the tribe varies from tribe to tribe, as does the role of relatives such as grandparents (Red Horse et al., 1979).

We speak of a **nuclear family** with reference to *the traditional mother/father/child family.* **Extended family** incorporates *the nuclear family plus any relatives who live in the household.* A **patriarchal family** is one in which *the father has primary authority,* and a **matriarchal family** is one in which *the mother has primary authority.* A **blended** or **reconstituted family** describes *a family that has been "made whole" again after a divorce or the death of a spouse.* If children are involved, a **stepfamily** *results from a reconstituted family.* A **polygamous family** is the general term used to describe *a family in which one spouse has two or more mates.*

family
any two or more related people living in one household.

nuclear family
the traditional mother/father/child family.

extended family
the nuclear family plus relatives who live in the same household.

patriarchal family
a family in which the father has primary authority.

matriarchal family
a family in which the mother has primary authority.

blended family
see *reconstituted family.*

reconstituted family
a family that has been made whole again after a divorce or the death of a spouse.

stepfamily
the result of a reconstituted family including children.

polygamous family
a family in which one spouse has two or more mates.

Biosocial innovations, such as those described in the *Quality of Life* Application on page 362, hold the promise or specter—depending upon how one views it—of totally new types of families, ones in which babies are genetically tailored to order. For some, such notions summon images from Mary Wollstonecraft Shelley's novel *Frankenstein*, the ghoulish tale of biotechnology run amuck. The man/monster featured in that tale was fashioned from various body parts and given life by "Dr." Victor Frankenstein.[2] Edwards (1991) observed that Frankenstein's abiding desire to learn the secrets of life for the purpose of creating life is shared by many contemporary genetic engineers. If current social trends and biosocial innovations continue to progress at a dizzying pace, the "traditional family" as envisioned by Murdock (1949) will become a vanishing breed. In fact, some of the nontraditional families listed above may appear traditional when compared to families having as many as five parents (see Figure 13–6).

ANOTHER CRASH COURSE

Earlier in this chapter, a crash course in what to anticipate from marriage was presented. Here, also courtesy of Susan R. Cohen (my wife) and yours truly, is a list of changes you can expect after the birth of your first child:

1. *Changes in Worry Patterns*
   Even before your child is born, you will begin to worry about the child's safety and well-being. Such worry is natural and may subside by the time your child moves out of your house . . . but perhaps not (Pillemer & Suitor, 1991).

2. *Changes in Sleep*
   Newborn children do not have an eight-hour work day. They work at getting to know the world on a random schedule that may run a full 24 hours per day. When they are not being incredibly cute, they are crying. Sometimes they cry because they are hungry. Sometimes they cry because their diapers need changing. Sometimes they cry for reasons known only to them. All of this is a not so fancy way of saying that you can expect to be up to feed and comfort your newborn infant at odd hours, catching sleep when you can.

3. *More Changes in Socialization Patterns*
   Remember the change in your socialization habits that took place as a result of your transformation from single to married status? Things get much worse. Relatively simple things like going out to visit friends, going to a restaurant, or going out to a movie have become complicated by the need for competent and reliable child care. Phrases such as the following may become a staple of everyday conversation: "Then who is going to babysit?", "Does that restaurant allow children?", and "Where is the car seat?"

4. *Change from Employed Status to Unemployed Status*
   If child care is not available, or if your preference is to take care of your own newborn child, a spouse who may have been gainfully employed prior to the birth may elect to take on the duties of full-time child care.

[2]Hollywood took dramatic license with Mary Shelley's novel by conferring the title of "Dr." on Frankenstein in the original (1931) film. In subsequent films, scriptwriters have likewise referred to the mad scientist as "Doctor." Yet according to Shelley's book first published in 1818, the world's first bioengineer had never earned any doctorate. Victor Frankenstein was a sophomore dropout from Inglostadt University.

FIGURE 13–6 A FAMILY PORTRAIT: BABY AND PARENTS In this hypothetical family portrait, the nurturing mother and nurturing father contracted with a female genetic donor to provide an ovum, and with a sperm bank to fertilize that ovum. They also contracted with a carrying mother to carry the embryo to term.

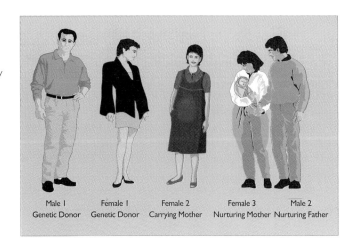

| Male 1 | Female 1 | Female 2 | Female 3 | Male 2 |
| Genetic Donor | Genetic Donor | Carrying Mother | Nurturing Mother | Nurturing Father |

5. *Change in Sexual Relationship*

After the birth of your first child you may find that feeding schedules, work schedules, and other schedules, along with sheer fatigue, begin to exert a strong effect on your sexual relationship.

6. *Change in Your Life Focus*

The birth of your first child may prompt a change in life focus away from you, your spouse, and your jobs to your child. This change may become manifest in several ways. When friends call and ask, "What's new?", you may find yourself speaking about your child. When you go shopping, years of conditioned thinking about what you can buy yourself may go by the wayside as you find yourself wondering what to get the baby.

7. *Change in Others' Life Focus*

Complementing your own change in life focus will be a change on the part of other people as well. You will find, for example, that your mother-in-law wants to sleep over more often. Your father-in-law begins searching stores to find one of those "Ask Me About My Grandson (or Grandaughter)" bumper stickers. More people will come to visit—not you, but your baby. You will even take on a new identity—that of [*insert name of baby here*]'s mother or father.

8. *Change in the Number of Calls to Your Own Parents and In-Laws*

Your mother-in-law wanting to sleep over more often is not actually all that bad. Your mother-in-law (as well as your father-in-law and your own parents) have, after all, valuable experience and insights to share about child rearing. Parents and grandparents can be great sources of support during the often stressful transition to parenthood (Bond & Wagner, 1988; McCubbin et al., 1980). In one study, it was observed that almost two-thirds of the maternal grandmothers were at their daughter's side shortly after delivery (Hansen & Jacob, 1992). In that study, it was also found that grandparents were typically "on call" at short notice for their children. Grandparents who respected their children's wishes for autonomy while remaining available to them were perceived as providing the greatest support.

Given these and other considerations, some time off from work shortly after the birth of a child is advisable. Such parental leave time can be supported by arguments grounded in sound social, psychological, medical, and economic policies (Trzcinski & Finn-Stevenson, 1991; Zigler & Frank, 1988).

THE CHALLENGES AND DEMANDS OF PARENTING

The challenges involved in parenting begin with decisions about matters such as bottle- or breast-feeding the infant—and only multiply thereafter. In the days, weeks, months, and years to follow, there will be countless more decisions to be made, including those regarding every conceivable aspect of the child's physical, emotional, social, and intellectual well-being and development. If the child is developmentally or physically disabled, chronically ill, or has other special needs, the process of parenting can be even more demanding (Turner-Henson et al., 1992). Regardless of the child's physical or mental health, the stresses of the transition to parenthood may lead to a decrease in marital satisfaction (Belsky & Rovine, 1990). The discrepancy that exists between prebirth expectations regarding parenthood and the actual experience of parenthood may contribute to such stress (Belsky et al., 1986; Kach & McGhee, 1982; Kalmuss et al., 1992; Ruble et al., 1988).

THE JOYS OF FAMILY LIFE

The sources of joy and pleasure in family life are many. If you were fortunate enough to grow up in a loving home, you know many of these joys and pleasures from firsthand experience. You know that the family serves as "home base" for many people; it is the source of one's strength and of unswerving emotional support. On the subject of love, Shakespeare wrote in *Romeo and Juliet* that the more one gives, the more one has. Although he was speaking of romantic love, the same is true of familial love; demonstrating love for a family member enriches not only the other but the self.

In a classic study entitled *The Joys and Problems of Child Rearing,* Arthur Jersild and his colleagues reported on the results of in-depth interviews with 544 parents. Jersild et al. (1949) paint a warm and optimistic picture of the great pleasures that parenting can bring in terms affection, companionship, and the shared wonder of discovery. Their conclusion seems as timely today as nearly a half-century ago: "Perhaps no other circumstance in life offers so many challenges to an individual's powers, so great an array of opportunities for appreciation, such a varied emotional and intellectual stimulation" (p. 122).

SOURCES AND SYMPTOMS OF STRESS AND CONFLICT

Alcoholism. Extramarital affairs. Persistent quarreling. The death of a family member. Many sources and symptoms of conflict and stress may exist in or befall a marriage (or any other intimate relationship). Three examples of such problems are presented below. These and many other potential problems are all overlapping in many instances. For example, financial difficulties may be a causal factor in family conflict and spouse abuse.

FINANCIAL DIFFICULTIES

An abundance of research suggests that economic hardship and financial pressure can impact negatively on marital satisfaction (Clark-Nicolas & Gray-Little, 1991; Conger et al., 1990; Lorenz et al., 1991), physical health (Zick & Smith, 1991), and the general emotional health of children (Elder et al., 1985; Institute of Medicine, 1989; Takeuchi et al., 1991) and adults (Brenner, 1973; Brown & Harris, 1978; Catalano & Dooley, 1977; Cohn, 1978; Dohrenwend & Dohrenwend, 1969; Feather & Barber, 1983; Kasl & Cobb, 1979; Mirowsky & Ross, 1986; Oliver & Pomicter, 1981; Williams, 1990).

In two-parent households, both parents may hold jobs in an effort to keep pace with living expenses. Although more money is brought in, there are many economic as well as other costs associated with such an arrangement (Hanson & Ooms, 1991). Some possible additional costs include those of child care, transportation, clothing, laundry, food away from home, union or other dues, and so forth. In one analysis of such work-related costs, it was found that one woman's salary of $199.00 per week represented only $107.41 per week after such costs were deducted (Perzeszty, 1986). The costs associated with working can easily be even more financially and emotionally burdensome in a single-parent household.

WORK AND FAMILY ROLE CONFLICTS

In an era when both marital partners are likely to be employed outside the home, an issue of increasing concern has been roles and division of labor within the household (Benin & Agostinelli, 1988; Suitor, 1991). Wives tend to shoulder a disproportionate amount of household responsibility through the lifespan of a marriage, although this disparity tends to decrease after the childbearing years (Cowan et al., 1985; Rexroat & Shehan, 1987). Conflicts regarding division of household labor can contribute to marital dissatisfaction which in turn can result in divorce. A household in which one person is the breadwinner and the other is the homemaker may act to inhibit divorce (Huber & Spitze, 1980), especially if both people are satisfied with their roles. Gary Becker has argued that such marked division of labor acts to keep couples together because breaking up would in many instances necessitate drastic lifestyle changes that neither party would want. Becker (1981) believes that egalitarian marital relationships, such as those found in dual-career marriages, are more unstable than more traditional relationships. In marriages in which each partner is a wage earner and roles and household duties are defined arbitrarily, it is much easier for the couple to part company. Of course, whether an individual decides to stay or leave a marriage will depend on a number of factors (discussed subsequently).

Daily stress, including job-related stress or dissatisfaction with a homemaker or other role in a marriage, can have a negative effect on cognition and mood, thus acting to impact negatively on marital satisfaction and the general quality of family life (Barling, 1990; Barling & Rosenbaum, 1986; Bolger et al., 1989; DeLongis et al., 1988; Forehand et al., 1987; Guelzow et al., 1991; Henggeler & Borduin, 1981; Hock & DeMeis, 1990; Holahan & Gilbert, 1979; Jouriles et al., 1979; Lerner & Galambos, 1985; Locksley, 1980;

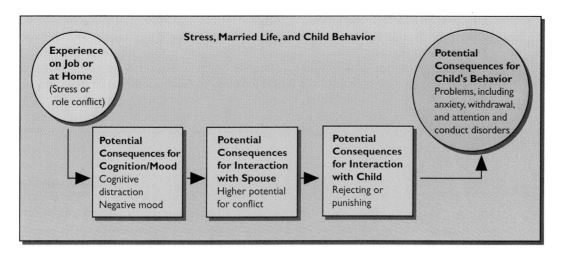

FIGURE 13–7   STRESS, MARRIED LIFE, AND CHILD BEHAVIOR The findings and implications from several research studies strongly suggest that stress on the job and conflicts about one's role at home may adversely impact on cognition and mood, which in turn may adversely impact both the quality of the marital relationship and the quality of care given to children. Poor parental care may play a causal role in emotional and behavioral difficulties. The model pictured above is a highly simplified rendering of a very complex, and as yet not fully understood process.

MacEwen & Barling, 1991; Menaghan & Parcel, 1990 Orthner & Axelson, 1980; Parry, 1987; Repetti, 1989; Rook et al., 1991; Spitze, 1988; Stone, 1987; Stuckey et al., 1982). As illustrated in Figure 13–7, such stress or dissatisfaction can ultimately affect even the emotional adjustment and behavior of one's children.

SPOUSE ABUSE

It has been estimated that over 1.5 million wives in this country are severely beaten by their husbands annually (Straus & Gelles, 1986), and such figures may underestimate the number of actual cases (Egley, 1991). Women in cohabiting relationships are even more likely than wives to be battered (Stets & Straus, 1989), although the reasons for this are not at all clear (Stets, 1991). In other countries, where fewer cultural restraints on wife battering exist, the number of tragic and senseless beatings women are subjected to is probably higher proportionately than the already high rate in this country (see Figure 13–8).

Unfortunately, sympathy for battered women may be difficult to come by in light of widespread tendencies to blame the victim for staying with, going back to, or not walking

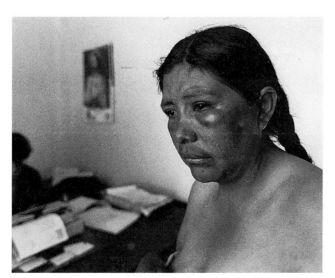

FIGURE 13–8   A VICTIM OF DOMESTIC VIOLENCE A woman from the Aymara culture in Bolivia files a complaint against her husband at a government office in the city of La Paz. According to Erika Hinojoza, a forensic physician in that country, "In the Aymara culture, the woman is the property of the man and he can do with her what he likes . . . He doesn't like the way she prepared his meal or doesn't like the way she keeps the house, so he starts hitting her. If you beat your wife it's a test of manhood" (Hinojoza, 1992, p. A4). In our own country, the American Medical Association reported that in 1990, husbands or boyfriends were responsible for the killing of nearly one-third of all women murdered. The organization warned that nearly 25% of all women will be abused by a current or former partner. In June 1992, it began recommending routine screening of all female patients for signs of domestic violence ("Doctors are Advised," 1992).

out on an abusive husband or lover (Cohn & Sugarman, 1980; Dutton & Painter, 1981). Years of exploration have addressed the question of why abused women stay with abusers. Proposed explanations, none of them entirely satisfactory, have included reference to (1) the victims' economic dependency, (2) the victims' tendencies to place blame on themselves, not the batterers, and (3) a vicious circle of abuse leading to lowered self-esteem on the part of the victim which, in turn, leads to greater abuse (Frieze, 1987; Porter, 1981; Strube & Barbour, 1983).

Whereas others have asked, "Why does a woman stay with an abusive partner?", Tracy Bennett Herbert and her colleagues asked a slightly different question: "*How* does a woman stay with an abusive partner?" (Herbert et al., 1991, p. 313). To the extent that they are generalizable, Herbert et al.'s data suggest that the key to understanding battered women may lie with the cognitive strategies they employ to cope with the abusive situation. Women involved in abusive relationships tended to see more positive things about the relationships than an outside observer might who is more objective. In essence, these women cognitively structured their situation "in such a way as to view their relationship in a positive light" (p. 321). Such cognitive structuring was highly specific; that is, the entire relationship was not distorted. The women could, for example, be very realistic about the prospect of abuse in the future; over 80% of them believed that the abuse would recur.

Although outsiders might formulate an image of abusing men as monsters, there are reports that paint pictures of some of them as "nice guys" who can be quite charming (Ganley & Harris, 1978; Purdy & Nickle, 1982), relatively unassertive (Douglas et al., 1984; Rosenbaum & O'Leary, 1981), dependent on their partners (Hilberman & Munson, 1977–1978), and sincerely apologetic after an episode of abuse (Walker, 1979). In short, they may indeed have some redeeming features in spite of their abusive tendencies. Herbert et al. (1991) suggest that abused women may place a mental spotlight on those features and not focus as much as they should on the "darker" side.

A treatment implication from Herbert et al.'s research concerns the need to focus therapeutic efforts with battered clients on their appraisals of the men with whom they are involved. An objective in therapy will be to cognitively restructure those appraisals, at least to the point where they resemble those shared by any realistic outside observer. The extent to which violence in a domestic relationship is rationalized as usual, unavoidable, or legitimate may prove another useful area of exploration in therapeutic work with both victims and batterers (Williams, 1992). Because there is a strong tendency for domestic violence to recur and in some cases to become progressively more severe over time (Pressman, 1984), victims must be strongly encouraged to seek professional and/or legal assistance at the very first sign that their spouses or lovers are batterers—this despite any promises, protests, excuses, apologies, or vows never to do it again on the part of the batterers.

WHEN MARRIAGE ENDS

When expectations of marital bliss are not met, marital partners have a number of options. They can individually, jointly, or with the assistance of some third party (such as a professional counselor) reevaluate their expectations, their communication, their roles, and other aspects of their marriage. Perhaps their expectations regarding marriage were unrealistically high. Perhaps they never really communicated meaningfully with one other—a problem that appears to be quite common among people dissatisfied with their marriage (Burns, 1984; Cleek & Pearson, 1985). If talking it over, with or without a professional counselor, does not help, physical separation and/or a divorce might be the next step for some people. For other people, religious or moral convictions or perceived financial or other consequences of a divorce will keep them in what Heaton and Albrecht (1991) termed a "stable unhappy marriage."

The National Center for Health Statistics projects that approximately one-half of all marriages in the United States that began in the 1980s will end in divorce. Some projections regarding the divorce rate in this country have been even higher (Martin & Bumpass, 1989). In addition to dissolution by divorce, other marriages will end as a result of death.

Still other marriages will end as a result of abandonment, separation (legal and otherwise), annulment, or other circumstances (such as one of the partners being listed as missing in action in war). Regardless of how a marriage eventually ends, there are one or two former spouses who must adjust to no longer being married. Below we take a closer look at some of the adjustive demands of divorce and widowhood.

ADJUSTIVE DEMANDS OF DIVORCE

The number of divorces in this country has been steadily rising since the late 1800s (see Figure 13–9). Although no one can say with certainty why, a list of contributing factors would include women's liberation from financial dependence on men, more men and women together in the workplace (with consequently higher probability of extramarital affairs), increasing sources of social support for divorced people, increasing religious tolerance for divorce, decreasing social stigma attached to divorce, and a growing widespread impatience with suffering silently through a bad marriage. In general, the barriers to divorce have been weakening for some time (Goode, 1963).

For many people, the very prospect of divorce is painful. The decision to proceed may therefore be agonized over for months, even years (Melicher & Chiriboga, 1985). Wide-ranging possible consequences of a divorce concerning, for example, one's children, personal well-being, financial outlook, and prospects for remarriage may all be considered. The process of divorce itself may prove to be emotionally and financially draining. Divorce entails emotionally and legally extricating oneself from a relationship in which a strong commitment, common resources, and a lifetime of shared experiences may have once existed. It entails physical and emotional distancing from the person with whom one's most intimate thoughts and pledges may have been shared. Often, such a process entails not only sadness but also anger. At its worst, the process of divorce is a contentious struggle not only for marital freedom, but also for money, material possessions, power, and custody. In a divorce in which the parties are openly hostile towards one another, the unstated objective of the parties' lawyers may be to inflict as much emotional and financial hurt as possible on the opposing side. In addition to a severe emotional and social toll, a hostile divorce may be costly in terms of valuable time robbed from personal or business-related matters. Meeting with attorneys, negotiating positions, making depositions, reading depositions, and evaluating the depositions made by others can be a tremendously time-consuming process.

In the wake of such stressful proceedings may lie depression and other social and emotional problems for divorcing parents (Ilfeld, 1977; Schaefer & Burnett, 1987) as well as children (Wallerstein, 1991). Loss of the parents' social support may take place when former friends and relatives take sides. Loss of prized possessions may also be the consequence of a divorce. What may be desirable but difficult to lose are the many associations

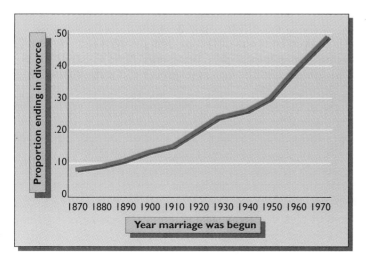

FIGURE 13–9 DIVORCE IN AMERICA These data from Cherlin (1981) illustrate that about one of every three marriages begun in the 1950s ended in divorce. By contrast, almost one of every two marriages begun in the 1970s ended in divorce. Couples who marry in their teenage years are much more likely to have their marriages end in divorce than couples who marry in their late 20s or later (Booth & Edwards, 1985; Hanson & Tuch, 1984). The latter finding may be due at least in part to more realistic expectations regarding marriage on the part of the older couples.

to different things that a couple builds up over the course of a marriage. The longer a couple knew each other before the divorce, and the more intense their relationship, the more reminders there may be of that relationship in the everyday environment (Huber & Spitze, 1980). Songs the couple listened to together, places the couple went or talked about going to, even people the couple used to get together with are all capable of triggering memories. These memories may have attached to them strong negative feelings such as anger, depression, guilt, humiliation, and sadness. Alternatively, the memories may have attached to them strong positive feelings, in which case they may trigger ambivalence or doubt about having gone through with the divorce.

Divorce may hold unhappy consequences for minor children involved. As compared to divorces having no children involved, divorces involving children may be more bitter and result in less friendly postdivorce relations between the parties (Masheter, 1991). A number of studies have suggested that the children of divorce are at higher risk than children in intact families for emotional and behavioral disorders (Caspi & Elder, 1988; Cowan et al., 1989; Dawson, 1991; Easterbrooks, 1987; Kline et al., 1981). In addition, children of divorce are at higher risk for the trauma of abduction, either at the hands of a noncustodial parent (or a parent who fears an unsatisfactory custody or visitation judgment) or of some relative or ally of a parent (Agopian, 1981). Abduction in this context is defined differently in different states (Hoff, 1986). Depending on the definition employed, upwards of 350,000 children may be abducted annually (Finkelhor et al., 1991). For our purposes, we will define **abduction** broadly as *the deprivation of parental access to a child in violation of law, formal agreements, or informal arrangements.*

Abduction has not been extensively studied although there is a sense that it has been increasing in recent years (Finkelhor et al., 1991). Factors that may contribute to a rise in abductions include a general rise in the number of divorces involving children, the number of legal contests involving custody, and the number of working women. Courts are no longer as disposed as they once were to award custody to the woman. Further, men's greater emotional involvement in childrearing—in part a consequence of the women's movement (Finkelhor et al., 1991)—has meant that they are not as willing as they once were to give child custody to their wives. Some divorce courts are so backed up that a divorce proceeding may take 2 to 3 years to be heard (Peterson, 1992). Abduction may occur before or after the case is heard. Abduction may have many different motives, ranging from a desire to protect the child from the real or imagined prospect of child abuse to retaliation against a loving parent. According to Finkelhor et al. (1991), more social emphasis needs to be placed on the prevention of abduction. This might be accomplished, for example, by the institution of child custody crisis hotlines to help people negotiate solutions in urgent situations.

Given the great frequency of divorce, some researchers have begun to search for a model of how divorce, if it is to take place, can best be accomplished (Abelsohn, 1992; Ahrons & Rodgers, 1987; Kelly, 1988). Abelsohn (1992) explored some of the coping and problem-solving strategies used by a family that was not referred for clinical services and considered to have "successfully" separated. One strategy was the temporary withdrawal of the ties between the spouses while parental ties were maintained. Such withdrawal involved "the healthy use of initial avoidance and distancing from the other to allow for personal growth and grounding outside of the spousal relationship" (Abelsohn, 1992, p. 79). For family members who are overwhelmed by the consequences of divorce, counseling is recommended.

In addition to couples divorcing from each other, a new type of divorce may be on the horizon: a child divorcing a parent. In the past, when parents have either neglected, abused, or otherwise failed to adequately take care of their children, the state has stepped in and placed the child in its care. The exact form of the care offered varies by state although it typically involves either a state-run institution of some sort or placement in a foster home. In 1992, a Florida court terminated the parental rights of a 12-year-old boy's natural mother as a result of legal action brought by the boy. The case was historic in that it was the first time that family rights were terminated as a result of a lawsuit brought by a child (see *In the News*).

abduction

in developmental psychology and law, the deprivation of parental access to a child in violation of law, formal agreements, or informal arrangements.

Child Divorces Parents

In April 1992, "Gregory K.," then 11 years old, filed court papers asking that all ties to his natural parents be severed so that he could be legally adopted by the foster parents he had been living with since October of 1991. In May 1992, Gregory's natural father signed away all legal rights to his son. However, Gregory's biological mother, "Rachel K.," a 30-year-old waitress, argued that she had given up her son to the foster care system because of poverty, and only with the state of Florida's promise that she could regain custody when she was financially able. Rachel's attorney argued that a minor did not have the right to bring a lawsuit according to state law—and no minor had ever done so before—but a Florida court rejected that argument. The court cited the Florida state constitution which declares that all people are entitled to access to the courts and related legal rights. A lawyer for the National Child Rights Alliance believed that allowing the child to move forward as the plaintiff in a lawsuit might serve as a precedent for other cases. Rachel's attorney argued that the court's decision to allow a minor to bring a lawsuit "raises questions about everything from guardians' control of a child's money to a child's right to sign a contract" (Rohter, 1992a).

The trial was held in late September 1992. Gregory's attorneys argued that Rachel's parental rights should be terminated because she had abused and neglected Gregory for most of his life. They argued that she was an unfit parent due to her drug abuse, lesbianism, and promiscuity. One witness testified as to the promiscuity. Another witness testified that she had observed Rachel smoke marijuana in front of her children and, on one occasion, smack Gregory on the head. The state testified that Gregory had only lived with his natural mother for approximately 7 months during the prior 8 years, and had been placed in foster care on three occasions. Representatives of the state also offered their opinion that it would not be in the best interest of Gregory for him to be returned to Rachel. Gregory's foster father, an attorney with eight children currently in the family, argued, "Let the law protect real families, not families in name only." Rachel's attorneys argued that the state of Florida must respect "the right of natural families to be together" above all else. Two experts at the trial testified that Rachel had improved her life and could provide a nurturing home. Testifying on her own behalf, Rachel denied the charges of child abuse, neglect, drug abuse, promiscuity, and homosexuality.

The court ruled in favor of the 12-year-old plaintiff and ordered the rights of his natural mother terminated so that Gregory could be legally adopted by his foster parents. The victory for Gregory left legal experts wondering whether the interests of the American family had actually been strengthened or weakened as a result (DePalma, 1992). Rohter (1992b) noted that the case "raised but did not answer the most elusive question that faces those immersed in all aspects of foster care: When is a family beyond reclaiming?" Rachel's attorney wondered aloud whether Gregory truly understood all the legal papers he had signed, and she said she would appeal the court's decision.

The afterword of the Gregory K. case and the thousands of cases like it has yet to be written. There are currently nearly half a million children in foster care; poverty, the AIDS crisis, and drug abuse is causing that number to swell. A number of states have in place "family preservation" programs wherein a social service caseworker may be assigned to a single family for 4 to 6 weeks and be available to that family 24 hours a day. The idea is for the caseworker to help get the family up and running on its own by providing intensive services that range from budgeting guidance to child guidance. Currently, however, only about 247 million dollars are spent annually in such efforts to help keep families together, while about 2.3 billion dollars are spent on foster care programs (Rohter, 1992b).

ADJUSTIVE DEMANDS OF WIDOWHOOD

Widowhood refers to *the state of, or the time period spent, surviving a spouse. A widow* is a female whose husband has died and a *widower* is a male whose wife has died. We often think of widows and widowers as being advanced in years, and most indeed are. Yet because death by causes such as disease, accident, homicide, suicide, and natural disaster do not respect age, any married person can be thrust into widowhood.

widowhood
the state of, or the time period spent, being single as the result of the death of a spouse.

How the surviving member of the former couple reacts to and copes with the death of the spouse will depend on a multitude of factors, including the survivor's own attitudes and beliefs regarding death and mortality, the social support available to the survivor, the financial support available to the survivor, the cause and mode of the spouse's death, the age of the spouse at death, the nature and quality of the relationship that the couple enjoyed, and cultural expectations. In some cases, the death of a spouse may be viewed as a horrible injustice. In others, particularly in those cases involving a disease that inflicts a slow and painful process of dying, death may be viewed as a blessing. In some cases, the spouse may be able readily to accept the partner's loss. In others, acceptance of the loss may be so traumatic that the spouse will have to deny it. For example, in one instance known to the author, the surviving woman coped with the death of her husband by pretending that he was simply away on a business trip and would return. This fantasy helped the woman to adjust to her immediate needs, and with time, the reality of what had happened set in.

At a very practical level, many marriages entail division of responsibilities such that, for example, one partner takes primary responsibility for financial management while the other tends to matters involving home maintenance. Upon the death of one partner, the sometimes overwhelming burden of taking care of the shopping, the cooking, the cleaning, the financial management, the home maintenance, and all other duties rests on the surviving partner (Morgan, 1976). Adjustment to the death of a spouse seems to improve if, during their time together, each partner had a multitude of roles and responsibilities in the marriage (Hershberger & Walsh, 1990).

In addition to coping with the grief of the loss, the surviving spouse has many constant and ever-present reminders of the spouse and their life together ranging from material possessions (such as photographs) to mental associations (such as things discussed at meal times or comments made while watching certain television shows). The death of a spouse when the couple has dependent children has additional adjustive consequences, including all the adjustments one must make to being a single parent. Finally, the death of one's spouse compels one to confront one's own mortality. In practical terms, this may mean making contingency plans for the care of the children in the event of one's own death.

There are an estimated 13.5 million widowed people in the United States, about 11 million of whom are women ("Marital Status," 1990). If at some point a widowed person again wishes to mate, feelings of guilt must sometimes be overcome in order to do so. If the surviving spouse has children, the children may view the surviving parent's pursuit of a new love as a betrayal to the deceased parent. Social support groups help to ease widowed people back into intimate relationships with other people.

REMARRIAGE

The rising incidence of divorce has brought with it a complementary rise in the ranks of the remarried; approximately one-third of all married people in this country have been married at least once before (Kargman, 1983). Remarriage may bring with it a host of new adjustive demands. The specific nature of these demands will be a consequence of a number of factors, such as the personality and past experiences of the remarried partners as well as the personality and past experiences of the children of the partners if either of them has custody of children from a prior marriage.

ADJUSTIVE DEMANDS OF REMARRIAGE

In a family with children, the loss of a parent through either divorce or death will bring with it redefinition of the child-parent relationship, as well as the roles each person plays in the family. New routines may be established in the family, and it may take as long as several years for these routines to indeed become routine (Hetherington, 1989). The timing of the custodial spouse's dating since becoming single, as well as dating frequency, number of dating partners, and related variables may all impact not only on the custodial parent/child relationship, but also on the stepparent/stepchild relationship. Traditional wisdom has it that the earlier courtship behavior of the custodial spouse begins, the more the degree of disruption to a divorced family goes up (Rodgers & Conrad, 1986). Yet this view has been challenged by the finding that longer intervals of time in a mother-custody household were associated with more difficulties in stepfather-stepchild relationships (Montgomery et al., 1992). The latter observation was made on the basis of longitudinal research with 57 remarried families. The researchers noted a great deal of diversity in patterns of courting for remarriage, which may at least partially account for the unexpected findings.

People seeking to remarry often embark on their new search for a mate with a more defined image of the type of person they would like to marry. If, for example, they were happily married but widowed the first time around, they may seek someone who shared many of the characteristics of their first spouses. If they were unhappily married and divorced, they may seek people who specifically did not share some of the characteristics of the first spouses. In either situation, the potential for finding the ideal is slim. Because no two people are alike, widows or widowers seeking people much like former spouses are unlikely to find them. And while it is possible for the divorced person to meet someone who does not share some particular problem with the first spouse, this is no guarantee that the individual does not have other kinds of problems that will require an equal or greater amount of adjustive energy.

Complicating the courtship of those seeking to remarry are the sometimes conflicting interests of family members, including parents, children, and even ex-spouses who may have their own ideas about appropriateness of a prospective mate. A prospective stepparent may view prospective stepchildren with great favor and anticipation or with great resign, as they must be part of a "package deal" (Cherlin, 1978; Hetherington et al., 1985; Kurdek & Fine, 1991).

Remarriage carries the potential for erroneous expectations and misinterpretation of communications that are primarily based on learning that occurred in a previous marriage. For example, in a previous marriage, the couple might have habitually gone to the market for food shopping together. While one of the spouses from this marriage might seek to perpetuate this pleasant experience in the new marriage, the other spouse might find it awkward to do food shopping jointly and prefer to do it alone. In the previous marriage, for example, the partners might have signaled a desire to have sex by hugging and kissing in bed. In the new marriage, this nonverbal behavior on the part of one of the partners may be repeatedly misinterpreted by the other as a prelude to sexual activity; all the new spouse may wish to convey by hugging and kissing is simple affection. Because of the vivid memories of emotional suffering in a prior marriage, getting over needless apprehension and oversensitivity with respect to the current spouse may present an adjustive challenge. For example, if a man was formerly married to an alcoholic, the mere thought of his wife enjoying a cocktail before dinner might be anxiety-provoking. In short, if there is to be any chance for smooth sailing in remarriage, the excess baggage of the previous marriage must be left at the dock.

Issues related to finances can plague any marriage, but they are particularly apt to be a focus of concern in remarriage. This is so because one or the other of the parties may be paying alimony (in some states this is referred to as maintenance) and/or child support to the former spouse. The amount of money going to the former spouse, usually on a monthly basis, may be a source of contention for both the former as well as the current spouse. For the current spouse, it may be perceived as a burdensome drain of money. For the former spouse, it may be perceived as a pittance of what is realistically needed to support the divorced family. Bitter conflicts and jealousies may erupt with respect to money, especially when money is wrongly used as the index of how much parents love their estranged children. Depending upon the specifics of the situation, different types of economic strategies may serve to ease the money-related conflicts, jealousies, and other negative feelings that may erupt (Fishman, 1983).

ADJUSTIVE DEMANDS IN STEPFAMILIES

The family network of what has been variously termed a *stepfamily* and a *reconstituted family* can be quite complex—complete with stepparents, stepchildren, stepgrandparents, stepuncles, stepaunts, and stepcousins. With all of these steppeople in the picture, it is all too easy for one person to figuratively step on the toes of another, either by accident or intention (see

Figure 13–10). The situation becomes further complicated when the remarried parents have children of their own (thus creating what are referred to as half-siblings), or when grandparents, uncles, aunts, or other relatives also divorce and remarry.

To better appreciate the many adjustive demands that may be placed on the various members of a newly created stepfamily, consider a term that you have probably heard mentioned with reference to dynamics within the primary family. **Sibling rivalry** refers to *an ongoing state of competitiveness that exists between brothers and sisters*. At an early age, the siblings may vie for parental attention. As they get older, they may vie against each other for other reasons, including personal pride. Siblings may try to out-do each other by proving that they are tougher, smarter, more popular, or otherwise superior in some way.

Stepsibling rivalry is in some respects similar, and in some respects much worse. Siblings may resent their parents' divorce, maintain loyalty to the noncustodial parent, and be dissatisfied with the new family and living arrangements that have been thrust upon them. They therefore have very little motivation to work to make things in the new home run smoothly—and they may well invest effort in seeing to it that things do *not* work out (Amato, 1987). Whereas children may have previously had their own rooms and bathrooms, as well as their own toys, for example, the new situation may mean they must now share living quarters as well as their toys with one or more strangers who are members of their "instant family." More than that, the children must share the affections of their biological parent, and any slights of them in favor of the stepsiblings will be readily perceived and the cause for hurt feelings. In many instances, remarried parents will treat their stepchildren more leniently than they do their biological children in an effort to win, or guard against alienating, the affection of the stepchildren (Roosevelt & Lofas, 1977). Relationships among stepsiblings as they grow into adulthood have not received a great deal of research attention (Coleman & Ganong, 1990). From the scant research available, it seems that step-siblings and half-siblings do continue to consider each other as family but may not see each other as often as full siblings (White & Riedmann, 1992). Having no full siblings may act as an encouragement to keep in better contact with step- and half-siblings.

Perhaps the most trying and difficult of all the relationships within a stepfamily network is the relation between stepparent and stepchild (Pasley & Ihinger-Tallman, 1987; White & Booth, 1985). Children may take a "you're not really my parent" attitude towards the stepparent, just as the stepparent may take a "you're not really my child" attitude towards the child. In fact, the nature of the relationship between the adult and the child in a stepfamily lacks a widely accepted social definition and must therefore be defined by the parties involved (Pink & Wampler, 1985). From school, fairy tales (such as *Cinderella*), the media, or other sources, children may have even developed negative images of "evil" stepparents (Bryan et al., 1986). Even when children learn from firsthand experience that the new parent is not evil, they will still have neither experience nor any model for dealing

FIGURE 13–10 A STEPFAMILY TREE This diagram presumes that the re-marrying bride and groom each have custody of children from their former marriage, as well as living parents, and living siblings who are married with children of their own. It also assumes that they have a living ex-spouse with custody of at least one of their children. The diagram becomes geometrically complicated by factors such as more than one prior marriage on the part of the bride or groom, remarriage on the part of the ex-spouse, or remarriage on the part of the bride or groom's parents or siblings. Given such a complex network of relationships, with all of the competing interests inherent within it, a stepfamily situation has great potential for domestic conflict (Berstein & Collins, 1985).

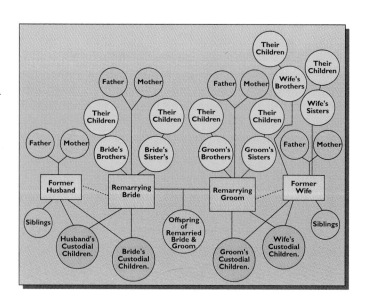

with a person who is neither parent nor friend. The parents might therefore be well-advised to seize the initiative, especially with older children, and acknowledge even before the marriage that there may be some awkwardness with respect to their roles. They might then proceed to outline their mutual expectations regarding what it means to be stepparent and a stepchild. It may have to be acknowledged, for example, that the natural parent's ex-spouse may have had ideas about raising children that are quite different from those of the stepparent (Kompara, 1980). Ideally, these differences will be discussed by the stepparent and stepchildren as they come up, and workable solutions will be agreed upon. In the interest of making the home environment as good as it can be for everyone concerned, an agreement to talk over differences as they arise is basic to the evolution of a successful stepfamily situation.

REMARRIAGE IN LATER LIFE

The average life expectancy for men is 71.8 years. Women tend to live about 6.5 years longer than that. According to 1990 Census Bureau data, a little more than 7% of the population is between the ages of 65 and 74. By the year 2010, the Census Bureau projects that about 12% of the population will be between the ages of 65 and 84. Roughly 70% of men aged 75 and older and 25% of women aged 75 and older are married and living with their spouses.

Companionship—and yes, sex—are important components of the lifestyle of the older married person ("Late-Life Love," 1992). It sometimes comes as a surprise to some younger people that many older people are involved in—and indeed relish—sexual activity. Yet based on data from two studies of some 5,700 people over the age of 60, sociologist Andrew Greeley reported that 37% of the married respondents made love once a week or more, and 16% of these respondents made love several times a week. About two-thirds of the sexually active respondents reported that they engaged in regular sexual experimentation. One-third of the respondents reported showering together. What is your reaction to these findings? Greeley (1992) speculated that some people may actually be offended by them due to the "image of passionate love between older people as grotesque" in our society. The primary obstacle to sex in the aged is disease or other conditions which physically prohibit it.

Older people may meet, fall in love, and marry in settings as diverse as senior centers, hospitals, and retirement homes (Bennet, 1992; see Figure 13–11)—sometimes over the objections of their adult children. Robert Butler (1992), chair of the department of geriatrics and adult development at Mount Sinai Medical Center in New York, described the benefits of such late-blooming relationships this way: "You have someone to look after you, to get you a hot meal when you're sick, to get you to the emergency room—and then there's the much harder thing to evaluate called affection."

FIGURE 13–11 NEWLYWEDS Evelyn and Solomon Werner, married in January 1992 when both were in their early 70s. The couple first met in a Bronx nursing home and then moved together to a Brooklyn nursing home, where they were married. The couple honeymooned in their private room at the home. Both had previously suffered strokes which physically weakened them, but as the director of the Brooklyn nursing home observed, love seems to have had a beneficial effect: "It really helped them. She was almost bedridden, and so was he" (Oberlander, 1992). Bennet (1992) reported that, "Neither can quite remember who popped the question, although each is pretty sure it was the other."

ALTERNATIVES TO MARRIAGE

Some people have spent a good part of their lives growing up dreaming of a large wedding. Other people have attributed relatively little importance to such matters and at some point decided to focus their energies on careers or other pursuits. Still other people would really like to be married but find it difficult to do so for various reasons (not having met the right person, not being financially prepared for marriage, and so forth). Census data indicate that about one in every five people in the United States over the age of 18 has never been married. However, one must look beyond that broad label of *single* to better understand the 20% or so of our adult population who have always been single. As Stein (1981) observed, single people may vary greatly in terms of their commitment to a single lifestyle. Just as there are confirmed bachelors who have made a deliberate and conscious choice to remain single, there are single people who have made an equally deliberate and conscious choice to marry. Some fraction of singles are exclusively gay or lesbian in sexual orientation and will probably never enter into a traditional marriage. Other people may be single by chance, single by choice, or not really single in the non-census sense because they are living with a lover. With this caution regarding the broad diversity of people clumped together in census data as single, let's consider some very general aspects of the single lifestyle.

REMAINING SINGLE

Many of the previously discussed factors acting to delay the age at which one first marries have had the effect of making the single lifestyle more socially acceptable than ever before. Some of these factors include the women's liberation movement, the sexual revolution, the lengthened period of economic dependency on parents, and the media. The 1960s witnessed the flourishing of the women's liberation movement, which in part had the effect of sending more women into the workplace. Through the 1970s and 1980s, social acceptance of the single career woman has risen increasingly. Today, a woman's choice not to marry is likely to be more respected than ever by her friends, family, neighbors, and co-workers (Thornton & Freedman, 1982). The greater social acceptance of a woman's right to remain single has spilled over into increasing social acceptance of single men as well. Whereas men who were intent on remaining single may have once been viewed as too attached to their parents or otherwise deviant (Cargan & Melko, 1982), the single lifestyle is increasingly recognized as having its own rewards.

Another factor contributing to greater social acceptance of the single lifestyle has been the sexual revolution. Just decades ago, premarital sexual intercourse enjoyed far less social acceptance than it does today. Motivation to marry was based at least in part on the desire to consummate one's love for another with sexual union. Today, the focus of social prohibition against premarital intercourse probably stems more from a disease-prevention perspective than it does from an appeal to simple morality.

In a bygone era, high school graduation signaled not only the end of high school, but also that the graduate would soon be working full time, moving out of the house, and getting married. All of that began to change in the 1950s when more and more people began thinking about—and were increasingly encouraged by the government to think about—higher education. The primary stimulus for the government's heightened interest in educational issues was something that happened in the former Soviet Union, not in this country. On October 4, 1957, Moscow launched a satellite called *Sputnik* into space and also launched a race to space between that country and this one. In order to be competitive, the United States would need educated and trained scientists. One year after the Soviet launch, Congress passed the *National Defense Education Act* which, in part, provided for student loans and offered other incentives for enrollment in higher education. As more and more high school graduates went on to college and graduate or professional school, the time span during which these students were dependent on their parents increased. Also acting to increase the time of grown children's dependency on parents are the consequences of a poor economy and personal financial needs; adult children are reluctant if not unable to leave their parents' home under such conditions (Ward et al., 1992).

Added legitimacy for lengthened singledom and the singles lifestyle in general comes from books, magazine articles, television, films, and other popular media. In many of these depictions, the time spent by singles engaged in exciting and diverse activities is disproportionate to the time spent home alone feeling lonely—this despite the fact that both fun and loneliness may in reality be part of the single lifestyle.

At a psychological level, remaining single can be fulfilling to the extent that it can provide one with a sense of self-sufficiency and a feeling of being entirely in control of one's life. The single person is typically freer than the married person to pursue career paths that entail a great deal of travel. Because there is no family to support or care for, the single person might opt for a career or an assignment that is a bit more hazardous than the person would have chosen had the person been married. Romantically, the single person has traditionally been free to experience a variety of passionate experiences. Of course, given the AIDS crisis, even many singles are now opting for monogamous relationships.

SINGLE PARENTHOOD

Never-married singles share with married people many of the same motivations to parent. An additional motivation, shared only with married people who are not happily married, would be the desire to have someone they can love in their immediate families. The dream of having a child of their own can be realized by single people in many ways. A fertile woman may be inseminated by laboratory means, or by a man she contracts with to father her child (in or out of a laboratory setting). Similarly, a single man may contract with a woman to have his baby. A single person may adopt a child, although many agencies may be reluctant to place a child with a single parent, especially when they have an ample number of qualified two-parent families on their waiting list.

Whether a single parent is a single parent by choice or has become one as a result of divorce or widowhood, many potential problems will be similar. In an age of dual-career marriages when every bit of two incomes may be needed to keep a household going, one of the most important issues for the single parent is adequacy of income. Single parents must be financially able to care for themselves and their children, a task that may quickly become extremely difficult should a costly medical condition strike either parent or child. Census estimates indicate that about one-third of all single-parent families in which the head-of-household is a woman fall below the poverty line. Because single parents must typically work full time to support themselves and their children, they may, depending upon their children's ages, require someone or some agency to care for their children when they are at work. If they cannot make arrangements with a relative or neighbor to do this, they will have to contract with an agency for such services, and these services, if not provided by the employer, can be expensive.

Parents who are on their own may find that they do not have as much time as they would like to tend to household duties (Burden, 1986). Communication and general quality of interaction with their children may be negatively impacted by all the demands on their time (Colletta, 1985; Dornbusch et al., 1985). Classes in what is called "family life education" are offered at many facilities throughout the country, and for the single parent not too overburdened to take one, such a class often provides help and coping tips (Porter & Chatelain, 1981; Smith & Smith 1981). Support groups devoted to the needs of single parents, such as Parents Without Partners, may also be of great value in helping the single parent cope, and perhaps even to meet other single parents. Most single parents have not lost their need or desire for adult companionship and romance, a fact acknowledged by such organizations. At the very least, the social support a single parent obtains through a support group or other organizations helps to buffer not only the stress of single parenthood but also the emotional hurt a single parent might experience as a result of views expressed by some in the name of "family values" and the "traditional" family.

LIVING TOGETHER

Many people categorized as single in census data are actually involved in a love relationship and living with the people they love. For some segment of that population, living together is a prelude to getting married. For another segment of that population, living together is a prelude only to whatever life next holds in store; the parties may not have any intention to marry. Other people in that rather broad category of singles may be sharing a residence with roommates, apartmentmates, or housemates. Below we briefly survey some of the adjustive demands on single people in these types of relationships.

RESIDENCE-SHARING SINGLES

A single person may share a house, apartment, room, or other residence for any number of different reasons. For example, the person may wish to rent an apartment in a luxurious complex that caters to the single lifestyle and one or more apartmentmates may be necessary to share the monthly rent. The apartmentmates may be friends or they may not. In addition to the financial advantage of such a living arrangement, there are social advantages. Provided the residence-sharers are friends, they may form a support network for one another, and facilitate the meeting of possible dates through their own social acquaintances. Additionally, fellow residence-sharers can provide each other with a greater sense of security than a single person might have living alone. There are other people sleeping in the residence overnight, and other people to whom you can report your whereabouts and schedule to should someone need to find you in an emergency.

Perhaps the primary negative aspect of a residence-sharing arrangement is a lack of privacy, especially in common areas such as the kitchen, the living room, and the bathroom, if one is shared. Moreover, the situation can quickly turn nightmarish if the residence-sharers do not get along or cannot trust one another implicitly. Such an arrangement may entail substantial up-front outlays of cash in terms of security deposits and rent in advance. It is therefore essential that you be able to trust any person with whom you co-sign a lease because you will both be held equally responsible under the law for damage or other unexpected outcomes while your lease is in effect. In addition, residence-sharers who cannot live in relative harmony with each other can make life miserable for one another in many different ways (for example, by playing the stereo loudly, having friends over at all hours of the night, and so forth). Living in this or any other dysfunctional environment may cloud an individual's judgment, making marriage appealing as an escape route from an intolerable living situation. In reality, such problems may seem mild by comparison to the problems experienced in marriage, if marriage is motivated primarily by a desire to escape.

LIVE-IN LOVERS

At some point in the lives of lovers who find themselves carrying bags filled with personal belongings to one another's home to stay for the night, the idea of living together may emerge. The idea of cohabiting (living together) might be proposed as a way of experiencing a trial marriage of sorts. The notion of a trial marriage makes sense to many contemporary students—so much so that, in many instances, it is seen as one stage in courtship. Because marriage is such a major undertaking, it would seem as if a preview of behavior in an actual domestic situation might increase the chances for marital success. Unfortunately, a wealth of research suggests that the opposite is true; living together prior to marriage increases the risk of marital dissolution (Balakrishnan et al., 1987; Bennett et al., 1988; Bumpass et al., 1991; Bumpass & Sweet, 1989; DeMaris & Rao, 1992; Hoem & Hoem 1992; Kelly & Conley, 1987; Newcomb, 1987; Trussel et al. 1992). In one study, it was found that couples who had cohabited prior to marriage perceived their likelihood of divorce to be greater than couples who had not cohabited prior to marriage. Further, the longer the cohabitation prior to marriage, the higher was the perceived likelihood of divorce (Thomson & Colella, 1992). In another study, it was shown that more than one cohabitation prior to marriage was a better predictor of marital dissolution than one cohabitation with the person who eventually became the subject's spouse. For cohabitation only with one's future spouse, the odds of marital dissolution did not differ significantly from those of people who had never cohabited before marriage (Teachman & Polonko, 1990).

Why might couples who live together before marriage be more prone to divorce? The answer is open to speculation, but people who cohabit as a kind of trial or test, without a strong commitment to marriage may simply be people who are either not very committed to the institution of marriage to begin with, or not very committed to the particular relationship (Teachman et al., 1991). If a person is not very committed to marriage or to a particular relationship, that individual may be prone to extramarital affairs or other behavior that will wind up destroying the marriage. Perhaps as compared to noncohabitors, cohabitors may be more prone to a deviant lifestyle in general (Booth & Johnson, 1988), or be less disposed to fulfilling conventional role expectations for married people (DeMaris & Leslie, 1984). It is also possible that the ability to delay the gratifications of marriage until one is actually married is an ability that is critical to marital success.

Social obstacles to cohabitation prior to marriage have declined (Bumpass, 1990). On the basis of his analysis of data from a study that employed a national sample of over 13,000 people, Robert Schoen (1992) noted that more recent, first-time cohabitors may, from a statistical perspective, have no more of a chance of marital dissolution than noncohabitors. Schoen wondered whether the disproportionately high rate of marriage failure among cohabitors will diminish as cohabitation prior to marriage becomes more common. In addition to age of the cohabitor, other factors, such as ethnic, racial, or national background may also prove to be key to understanding the effects of prior cohabitation on marriage.

DOMESTIC PARTNERSHIPS

In relatively few communities nationwide, an option available to unmarried heterosexual couples as well as to homosexual couples living together is to register as "domestic partners." Formal registration as domestic partners extends to each of the partners some rights that were previously granted automatically to married couples. The specific rights granted differ from city to city. For example, in Cambridge, Massachusetts, domestic partners have visiting rights at hospitals and jails and may become eligible for a partner's insurance benefits. In Sacramento, California, the domestic partnership ordinance provides for hospital visiting rights and bereavement leave from work.

Our families can serve as a great source of personal fulfillment. As we will see in the next chapter, work can serve a similar purpose—in addition to keeping food on the family table.

SUMMARY

MARRIAGE The decision to marry, as well as whom to marry, is among life's most important decisions. Many multifaceted concerns regarding one's motivation and the appropriateness of one's prospective spouse will ideally be given due consideration prior to marriage. Once married, many adjustments will have to be made and new roles will have to be negotiated.

PARENTHOOD AND FAMILY LIFE A basic human need is to create and nourish children. A number of technical and biosocial innovations has greatly enhanced the modern couple's chances of having or not having a baby as they so desire. In the process, the concepts of family and kinship as we presently know them may go by the wayside. Parenthood may bring with it many joys, including the joy of giving and receiving affection and companionship. Parenthood, as well as married life in general, may also bring with it conflict and stress. Alcoholism, extramarital affairs, persistent quarreling, the death of a family member, financial difficulties, and spouse abuse are all possible sources as well as symptoms of stress and conflict.

WHEN MARRIAGE ENDS When expectations of marital bliss are not met, counseling or a divorce may be the next step. Some couples will elect to stay in what has been called a "stable unhappy marriage" due to strong religious beliefs or other concerns about the consequences of a divorce. Divorce may precipitate emotional or behavior disorders in the children involved. Researchers suggest that divorce be a carefully planned process. *Widowhood* refers to the state of, or the time period spent, being single as the result of the death of a spouse. Social support groups help to ease widowed people back into relationships with other people.

REMARRIAGE The rising incidence of divorce has brought with it a complementary rise in the ranks of the remarried; approximately one-third of all married people in this country have been married at least once before. Remarriage may bring with it many new adjustive demands and challenges, including those regarding the establishment of new routines with one's new spouse and satisfactory relations with, between, and among stepchildren.

ALTERNATIVES TO MARRIAGE Alternatives to marriage include remaining single, living together with no intention of marrying, living together with the intention of marrying, and forming a domestic partnership. Each of these alternatives has its own unique advantages and disadvantages, and the nonmarried lifestyle has acquired increasing acceptance in recent years.

Chapter 14

Work, Play, and Retirement

O U T L I N E

Industrial/organizational (I/O) psychology is *that branch of psychology that deals with the application of the principles and methods of psychology to business organizations and people at work.* I/O psychologists study many varied aspects of occupations and jobs from the perspective of both employees and employers.

In this chapter, we will survey a sampling of some of the areas studied by I/O psychologists, including work-related adjustive challenges and demands, and even some challenges and demands related to play and leisure.

WORK

Work and the exchange of goods and services that flow from work are necessary from a societal perspective. People have different talents and abilities that can be pressed into the service of the greater good. The person skilled in carpentry builds a piece of furniture or a house for the physician, and the physician tends to the physical health of the carpenter and other patients. Work is central to one's own sense of identity. People make various kinds of attributions about others as well as themselves based on the type of work they do. We can pat ourselves on the back and experience a supreme sense of satisfaction for a job well done. We can also feel like crawling into the nearest hole when the work that we did failed to meet reasonable expectations of ourselves or others.

occupation

a vocation, profession, or other activity that one regularly works at, keeps busy at, and/or earns one's livelihood through.

Occupation may be defined as *a vocation, profession, or other activity that one regularly works at, keeps busy at, and/or earns one's livelihood through.* A **job** may be defined as *a task, an undertaking or an activity performed for pay.* For example, *plumber* is an *occupation,* one that may entail various kinds of *jobs,* such as unclogging drains, installing toilets, and repairing leaky faucets.

job

a task, an undertaking, or an activity performed for pay.

WHY PEOPLE WORK

Jacqueline Kennedy Onassis, widow of President John F. Kennedy and of the Greek multimillionaire Aristotle Onassis, is a very wealthy woman who does not need to work for a living. Despite that fact, Mrs. Onassis has held a position for many years as a book editor at the Doubleday Publishing Company. Why does Mrs. Onassis go to work? More generally, why does anyone work? Once having taken a job, what motivates one to do well at it?

Many different theories about why people work and why some people are better workers than others have been proposed. If some of the explanations discussed below sound familiar—and they should—it is because they represent adaptations of other theories with which you have already become acquainted.

THE TRAIT THEORY PERSPECTIVE

intrinsic motivation

internal incentives for action, in contrast to external or extrinsic ones.

Deci (1975) argued that some people seem to do well at whatever they do because of **intrinsic motivation** or *internal motivation.* Intrinsic motivation can be contrasted to *external* or **extrinsic motivation.** Deci viewed intrinsically motivated people as more apt to look to themselves for the mental reward of a job well done, than to the environment for tangible reinforcers.

extrinsic motivation

external incentives for action, in contrast to internal or intrinsic ones.

The notion that some people are more intrinsically motivated than others has great common-sense appeal, but it has proven to be resistant to experimental demonstration for a number of reasons (Dyer & Parker, 1975; Mawhinney, 1979; Scott, 1976). One such reason is that it is difficult to develop a test that measures work motivation. In Wherry and South's (1977) Worker Motivation Scale, for example, respondents indicate the degree to which they engage in various motivation-related thoughts and behavior. Items such as "I like to expend a lot of energy" are responded to on a scale that ranges from "almost always" to "almost never." On such tests, it is generally quite easy for the respondent to figure out which is the "motivated" response and then to respond accordingly. In addition to the ease with which the trait of motivation to work can be faked on such a test, another problem is the vagueness of some of the terms. For example, what is "a lot" of energy to one person may be "very little" energy to another person.

Trait theory has a great deal of appeal as a simple way of explaining why some people work and why some people are better workers than others. Unfortunately, trait-related explanations of work behavior (such as, "She works hardest at the job because she has the most work-related motivation") do not carry a great deal of practical utility. Further, there is a certain circularity inherent in such observations; it is almost like saying, "She works hardest because she's the hardest worker."

THE BEHAVIORAL PERSPECTIVE

From the behavioral perspective, motivation is a learned phenomenon, and it can be increased, decreased, or made to remain the same through rewards (such as a pay raise, paid day-care, commissions, and perks) and punishments (such as verbal reprimands, threatening memos, and transfer of one's office to the basement). Payment based on piecework is an example of the behavioral perspective in a work setting (Yukl & Latham, 1975); the more pieces (of whatever) that the worker produces, finishes, or otherwise manipulates to the employer's specification, the more money the worker is paid. Entrepreneurial behavior is another area where this perspective has clear application. An **entrepreneur** is *someone who organizes business ventures, usually taking personal financial interest in their success.* Small-business owners are entrepreneurs; the harder they work, the more they sell, and the more money they make—although it does not always work that way (see Figure 14–1).

entrepreneur
one who organizes and/or invests in business ventures.

The behavioral principle of social learning also has a clear application to employment settings. People learn about occupations from role models, among other ways. Many children follow in the occupational steps of a parent in part because the parent served as a role model. Children may follow in their parents' footsteps in occupations as diverse as police officer, lawyer, physician, and funeral director. Recognizing that we all need role models but that some children have had few appropriate ones in their environment, psychologist Spencer Holland started a program for providing role models to children in the Washington area (Saul, 1992). The program was called Project 2000 because that is the year the third-grade children in the initial program are scheduled to graduate from high school. The program provided for appropriate role models to visit the school, help in teaching, and answer occupation-related questions for inner-city youth. Project 2000 has since spread to

FIGURE 14–1 ENTREPRENEUR AT WORK Ui Man Chung is a 58-year-old Korean immigrant and owner of a liquor store in South Central Los Angeles. Mr. Chung believes he made a wise investment when he bought the store in 1987; the business has been good to him (Sims, 1992). However, one of the hazards of being an entrepreneur are market forces and other forces that are out of one's control. For Mr. Chung, many such forces may act to limit the amount of liquor he sells in the future. Members of the clergy and community activists are calling on customers to use restraint in the purchase of alcoholic beverages. These same groups are pressuring legislators to limit by law the number of hours liquor stores can remain open daily. Additionally, there is the ever-present factor of racial tension and hostility between Asians and inner city residents. In the past, such tensions have led to boycotts and violence.

other grades, as well as to a number of other cities in states such as Florida, Maryland, Missouri, and New Jersey (see Figure 14–2).

Although the use of incentives in the context of a behaviorally oriented work program may have a place as a management tool (Jablonsky & DeVries, 1972; Nord, 1969; Potter 1980; Schneier, 1974), some cautions regarding the organizational use of incentives have been noted. For example, not all people find the same incentives equally rewarding (Mawhinney, 1975). A free trip to Europe for the top salesperson may be a great incentive to many in a company's salesforce, but a nightmare for the salesperson having a fear of flying. Also, research on the use of behavioral methods in the workplace have tended to focus on worker productivity rather than on cognitive aspects of the long-term effects of using such methods. The long-term effects of incentive programs may include changes in worker attitudes (Heiman, 1975). There are also ethical issues to be reckoned with when organizations are run from a strictly behavioral perspective. For example, when management controls the value of the reinforcers that workers earn, workers might be placed in a situation in which they must work to near exhaustion to obtain the reinforcers. Should the worker become ill or die in the process, the organization may be considered blamable. In summary, then, some aspects of a behaviorally based approach to work, such as the use of social learning of roles, have been used quite successfully in many different situations. Other aspects of a behaviorally based approach to work, such as the use of incentive programs, may also be quite effective, but must be used judiciously.

THE COGNITIVE PERSPECTIVE

From a cognitive perspective, the motivation to work stems from cognitive variables such as one's beliefs, values, and expectancies. A cognitive theory of worker motivation that has received a great deal of research attention is *expectancy theory*. As set forth by Victor H. Vroom (1964), this theory holds that workers act in a manner that is consistent with their expectancies regarding what their labor will earn them. Will increased effort lead to an increase in performance? Will an increase in performance lead to favorable outcomes such as raises, a private office, or perks? These are the kinds of questions that Vroom believed people consider as they decide how much effort to exert on the job. Expectancy theory provides one way of understanding why people in some types of positions (say, salespeople), may exert more on-the-job effort than people in other types of positions (say, toll-col-

FIGURE 14–2
ROLE MODELS AND EMPLOYMENT Juan Simpson (right) is an executive with a pharmaceutical company affiliated with the Johnson & Johnson corporation. His company gives him one afternoon off each week to participate in Project 2000 to serve as a role model for children who are typically fatherless and from the inner city. Simpson was surprised to find that some of the children "think it's normal for adult males to spend some time in jail." He stated, "We want to let these children know what it's like to succeed . . . Our purpose is to show them they have a choice" (Saul, 1992).

lectors). Salespeople may harbor cognitive images or expectancies of one day making the big sale (and earning the big commission), while the toll collector has no such imagery and thoughts to provide motivation. In general, a number of studies provide support for expectancy theory, although certain technical aspects of it (such as how certain variables are measured and calculated) remain controversial (Muchinsky, 1983).

THE HUMANISTIC PERSPECTIVE

Many published theories of work motivation have greater or lesser degrees of similarity to Abraham Maslow's hierarchical theory (see page 53–54). Such theories may propose, for example, that after certain basic needs are met, the individual works to meet certain higher-order needs. One theory of work motivation that has ties to Maslow's theory is Clayton Alderfer's *existence/relatedness/growth* or *ERG* theory. Alderfer (1972) focused on what he called existence, relatedness, and growth needs in the workplace. He believed that all or none of these needs could be operating in workers. *Existence needs* include basic physiological and shelter needs, and these needs are met by pay. *Relatedness needs* include needs for social support, a sense of belonging, and respect, and these are met by the social environment in the workplace. *Growth needs* include needs for personal development and using one's ability to the fullest. The ERG theory differs from Maslow's hierarchical theory because Alderfer's theory is not hierarchical; that is, one need is not necessarily "higher" than another. Further, Alderfer believed that needs could be gratified in different ways, and that some needs could be exchanged for others. For example, jobs that deprive workers of relatedness needs by forcing them to work in isolation might be compensated for by higher salary (existence needs) or prestige and recognition (growth needs). Although ERG theory has received some support (Wanous & Zwany, 1977), it has not been viewed as one of great practical utility in the workplace (Campbell & Pritchard, 1976).

THE DEVELOPMENTAL PERSPECTIVE

The evolution of an adult's motivation and attitudes towards work may be studied developmentally. The developmental psychologist would be interested in attitudes towards work expressed by one's parents and how those attitudes may have influenced the child's motivation to work. Did parents convey the idea that one works to earn money to buy things? Did parents convey anything to their children about the intrinsic satisfaction work can provide? Did parents convey to children that they should feel good or feel bad about going to work? What was the child's first job? Was this experience with work a satisfactory one, or one that made the child feel cynical about the adult work world? Was it a job in which the child was given genuine responsibility? Or was it a job in which the child was given menial tasks to do for very little compensation? Did the child feel exploited at work? Under what circumstances was the employment terminated? These are some of the work-related questions that may be raised from a developmental perspective.

Too often a child's first exposure to the adult world of work is not a very satisfactory one. Richard M. Lerner (1992b) believes that "highly repetitive and mindless jobs like those in fast-food restaurants often make adolescents cynical about the world of adult work. The tasks are routine and regimented. The workers feel, and in fact are, completely replaceable." Lerner recommends that parents teach children the intrinsic value of work by, for example, letting the child accompany them to work on occasion, if possible. He also recommends introducing a child to the world of work through volunteer activities for nonprofit entities rather than through menial, low-paying jobs (see Figure 14–3 on page 386).

OTHER PERSPECTIVES

Many other ways of looking at worker motivation have been developed. For example, according to *equity theory* as set forth by J. Stacy Adams, worker motivation is influenced by the perceived balance of "inputs" (what the worker brings or applies to a job) and "outputs" (what the worker gets out of the job in terms of salary, benefits, and so forth). According to this view, workers make such input and output evaluations regarding their own work, and then compare these evaluations to other workers. Adams (1965) believes that a sense of equity (or lack thereof) regarding one's inputs and outputs has a strong influence on the worker's motivation.

FIGURE 14–3   VOLUNTEER WORK AS A FIRST JOB Volunteer work may be preferable to other types of labor as a child's first introduction to the adult world of work. In contrast to many low-pay, menial jobs available to children, volunteer work may offer an opportunity to obtain valuable training and experience. It may foster the development of the child's capacity for empathy and sensitivity. It may provide the child with a sense that his or her work is truly valued. Depending on the particular work setting, the child may also profit intellectually and socially from exposure to culturally diverse people. Praising such benefits of volunteer work for children, Richard M. Lerner (1992b), director of the Institute for Children, Youth, and Families at Michigan State University, advises parents that, "As a long-term investment, and if you can afford it, it's probably worth your while to pay your child out of your own pocket the amount he would earn at a part-time minimum-wage job. It's an investment both in your child's future and in the quality of life in your community."

J. Richard Hackman and G. R. Oldham (1976) advanced a theory of work motivation that focuses on various characteristics of jobs. One such characteristic is the number and quality of the *skills* needed to perform the job. The more skills, and the greater the skill required, the more the worker is likely to find the work personally meaningful. A master craftsperson who constructs guitars and violins by hand, for example, is likely to be very personally involved in the work. Another job characteristic is *task identity,* or how identified the worker is with the whole task. Hackman and Oldham believe that the work will be most personally meaningful when the worker has responsibility for the whole product or service and less personally meaningful with only partial responsibility, as in assembly line work. *Task significance* refers to how important or socially valued the task performed is. Airline pilots and surgeons have jobs with more task significance than, for example, pizza delivery people (although try telling that to someone waiting for a pizza). People with high-task-significance jobs are likely to find their work personally meaningful. Personal meaningfulness as well as other factors in the Hackman and Oldham theory are thought to contribute to outcomes such as high intrinsic motivation, high-quality work performance, high worker satisfaction, and low absenteeism.

The great number of existing theories about why people work has been described as "a blessing and a curse" (McCormick & Ilgen, 1980); each has a contribution to make to our understanding of work behavior, yet none on its own satisfactorily accounts for such behavior. These theories have been shown to have greater or lesser degrees of applicability to different types of work. For example, a behavioral perspective may provide the best frame of reference for understanding the motivation of a hot dog vendor, an entrepreneur, or a farm laborer paid on a piecework basis; the relationship between the worker's output and the financial rewards are very clear in such instances. Yet the application of the behavioral perspective to other kinds of work, including volunteer and low-pay positions occupied by highly qualified people, is much less straightforward. In your own opinion, what theory of work motivation would provide the best frame of reference for understanding why one would want to become a spiritual counselor in a nonprofit religious agency? What drives the "starving artist"? What is the motivation for taking a job (such as, for example, toll collecting), in which the rewards may not be as dependent on worker output as they are in other jobs?

CHOOSING AN OCCUPATION AND A COMPANY

In the previous chapter, we discussed momentous considerations regarding the matching of people with people. Here we discuss issues related to matching people to occupations and companies. As a result of factors such as genetic inheritance and learning, we all seem to develop unique patterns of abilities, interest, fears and values.

MATCHING THE PERSON TO THE OCCUPATION

What types of things interest you? Are you interested in photography? Food preparation? Weather? Medical science? Law? Are you more of a "people person," or someone who likes to work independently? In the 1920s, after attending a seminar on measuring people's interests, psychologist Edward K. Strong, Jr., began exploring the relationship between patterns of interest and career choice. Strong developed a test that was first published in 1928 and has subsequently been revised several times. The test, called the Strong Vocational Interest Blank (SVIB), is designed to compare the test-taker's pattern of interests with the pattern of interests of groups of people working in different occupations. After taking "the Strong" (as it is frequently referred to by counselors), test-takers can learn about their own pattern of interests and how this pattern compares to those of people from various occupational groups. Is the test-taker's pattern of interests more similar to that of college professors, architects, pilots, broadcasters, athletic trainers, bus drivers, computer programmers, or military personnel? This is the type of question the Strong can answer. It is important to emphasize that the Strong is only a test of interests; it is not a measure of vocational abilities. The test may suggest, for example, that your pattern of interests is shared by surgeons. Yet if you lack the fine motor coordination that a surgeon must possess, an alternative career choice would be prudent. The Strong is administered by trained counselors who will also provide you with a detailed interpretation of the results.

Values must also be given adequate consideration in vocational decisions as they typically play a role not only in attracting people to a particular occupation, but in maintaining job-related satisfaction (see *A Question of Values* on page 388).

Less discussed than interests and values, but no less important as a factor in vocational choice, are the fears different people harbor. Many people who might otherwise pursue a career as a physician avoid that profession due to anxiety or fear related to the sight of blood. Also, the prospect of tending to people who are ill and in some cases near death may also be frightening. Today, such fears are compounded by the hazards of contracting potentially fatal diseases such as AIDS, tuberculosis, and hepatitis. In fact, fear of contracting disease has dramatically altered the way medicine today is practiced. Robert M. Wachter, a professor of medicine at the University of California at San Francisco, has studied the effect on the practice of medicine of diseases such as AIDS and tuberculosis. Wachter (1992) believes that, "It is human nature for people to fear for their own health. In any contact with patients, one is always going to have to weigh the risk to themselves over the care they are going to provide for the patient . . . I worry that people are not providing the medical care they would like to be providing."

A more general approach to matching an individual to a particular occupation by focusing on interests, attitudes, values, traits, and related factors can be found in research on personality and vocational choice. Perhaps the most popular of the many different classification systems for personality and vocational choice is the one developed by John Holland (see Table 14–1 on page 389). Based on this classification system of "personal orientations," a self-administered and self-interpreted test called Self-Directed Search (Holland, 1985) is available for help in discovering one's ideal work setting.

Opportunity is another factor to keep in mind when considering occupations. You may, for example, aspire to be an auto assembly line worker. However, if the economic climate is such that the auto companies are closing plants and laying off workers, it would be prudent to revise your aspirations. Reading a daily newspaper or keeping up with the news through radio and television is a good way to begin thinking about where employment, as well as entrepreneurial opportunities, are. Presently, there appears to be a lot of growth in environment-related companies. Environmental professionals are needed worldwide to help deal with problems caused by hazardous wastes (Cortese, 1992). Chapter 15 contains much more food for thought about environment-related occupational opportunities.

Career opportunities are often the product of personal diligence, sometimes the product of chance, and sometimes the product of both. Consider the path taken to stardom by many Hollywood celebrities. Screenwriter William Goldman (1983) notes, for example, that Robert Redford may never have achieved stardom without landing the role of Paul Newman's sidekick in *Butch Cassidy and the Sundance Kid*. Marlon Brando was offered, but turned down, the part of the Sundance Kid. Steve McQueen and Warren Beatty were also offered the part, and they turned it down. Had any of these stars said "Yes," according to Goldman, "Redford might well have remained what one studio executive said to me he was

Values and Employment

To help discover what was important about work to a population of rural, unskilled women and men, Champagne (1969) devised a test that consisted of items like those illustrated below.

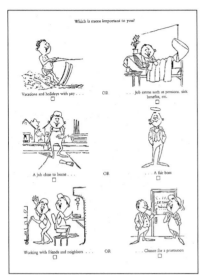

Of the 12 values assessed, "steady job" was found to be most important, and "working with friends and neighbors" was found to be the least important. Champagne cautioned that these two factors were respectively most and least important in terms of attracting workers to a position, but not necessarily in maintaining them in the position: "what prompts a person to accept a job is not necessarily the same as what prompts a person to retain a job or do well in it" (p. 268).

If you intend to work for a company, are your values consistent with the values of that company? For example, if you strongly believe that tobacco companies should not be selling cigarettes, could you take a position at a tobacco company? What about an advertising, public relations, or law firm that represents a tobacco company? Are your values consistent with the particular duties you will be called upon to perform? For example, if you are considering a sales position, could you—would you—sell something that you really did not believe in? The job description for many foreign corporations includes bribery as one technique of doing business; are you prepared to bribe a potential client upon the orders of the company that employs you?

Values are also an important consideration when it comes to many other aspects of a job description, from every day schedules to vacations and sick leave. Many firms offer only 2 weeks or so of paid vacation per year to start; is that acceptable to you? If you enjoy traveling extensively every summer, you may wish to explore occupations, such as teaching, in which a benefit is summer vacation with pay. Is a 9-to-5 job important to you, or do you prefer a position in which you can make your own hours? Why? Are you seeking a position that entails extensive travel, or would you prefer one with little or no travel? Why? Is it important to you that your employment be in a particular part of the country? Why? How long a commute are you willing to make each day to work? Why? Examining the answer to the *Why?* part of each of these questions, and many more questions like them, may help you to discover more about yourself and what you value.

when talk of hiring him first came up: 'He's just another California blond—throw a stick at Malibu, you'll hit six of them.'"

Occupational opportunity may rear its head on a more everyday level, as well. For example, friends or relatives of yours may find that they are doing much better than they had anticipated in a particular business; opportunity knocks on your door when you are asked to join their blossoming young company as either an employee or a partner. On occasion, an individual having a very prized position in a company must vacate the position as a result of unforeseen circumstances either positive (a generous inheritance makes work unnecessary) or negative (incapacity by accident makes work impossible). By sheer chance, you happen to be in the right place at the right time and win the vacated position. But chance cannot be counted on. You need to count on your dedication and hard work. You need to count on yourself and your best efforts both in making a work-related choice, and then in making that choice work.

CONDUCTING YOUR OWN OCCUPATIONAL RESEARCH

Ask children what they want to be when they grow up and most will name occupations such as doctor, nurse, or policeman. Precious few, if any, children are likely to express in-

TABLE 14-1 PERSONAL ORIENTATION AND OCCUPATION

Holland (1985) discussed the types of occupations that he believes provide the best match for people having six different types of "personal orientations" he defined: a realistic orientation, an investigative orientation, an artistic orientation, a social orientation, an enterprising orientation, and a conventional orientation.

Personal Orientation	Occupation
The individual having a *realistic orientation* prefers clearly defined jobs and tasks and does not like occupations that rely heavily on verbal or social skills.	People having a realistic orientation may be best suited for occupations such as bookkeeper, engineer, or auto mechanic.
An *investigative orientation* is characterized by an interest in exploration, in contrast to an interest in manipulating things or interacting with people.	People having an investigative orientation may be best suited for occupations such as chemist, physicist, or computer programmer.
People having a strong *artistic orientation* perceive themselves as being highly creative and having a strong need to express this creativity.	People having an artistic orientation may be best suited for occupations such as writer, musician, artist, or chef.
As its name implies, a *social orientation* is characterized by an interest in working with people.	People having a social orientation may be best suited for occupations such as psychologist, teaching, or nursing.
The *enterprising orientation* is seen in people who perceive themselves as having superior interpersonal and persuasive skills.	People having an enterprising orientation may best be suited for occupations such as sales, agenting, or public relations.
A *conventional orientation* is characterized by strong conformity to social norms, usually coupled with superior clerical and mathematical ability.	People having a conventional orientation may best be suited for occupations such as clerk, word processor, and Internal Revenue Service agent.

terest in fields such as physical therapy, insurance, rug shampooing, or dry cleaning (although they might be more disposed to do so if one or both of their parents happens to be in any of these fields). Children up to the age of 11 or so have had relatively little detailed exposure to many occupational fields, in or out of school. Further, they are in a stage of vocational choice that has been referred to as a *fantasy period,* not one that is in any way based on their abilities. From the age of 11 through the age of 17 or so, children move into a second phase of occupational choice called the *tentative period* (Ginzberg, 1966). Here, interests, then interests and abilities, and then interest, abilities, and values, will all play a part in occupational choice. The final stage in this three-stage process is the *realistic period,* wherein the individual recognizes that in addition to interest, ability, and values, employment requires opportunity in the form of a willing employer. The realistic choice stage may be repeated periodically throughout life, as when an individual changes careers many times.

Perhaps the ideal time to begin exploring varieties of occupational choice in an informal yet systematic way is during the tentative period. Watching television news and business programs, or reading (or skimming) a daily newspaper that has a business section can provide a stimulus to learn more about various kinds of occupations. Reading the newspapers in 1992, one might have seen a notice of the corporate presidential appointment of Sandy Grushow at the Fox Entertainment Group ("New Head," 1992). In 1983, at age 23, Grushow began his work career as an intern at Fox Television. As the term is typically used in the business world, an **intern** is an *entry-level, earn-while-you-learn (in some cases even nonpaid) position in which the individual is exposed to varied aspects of a business or industry.*

intern

an entry-level, earn-while-you-learn (in some cases even non-paid) position in which the individual is exposed to varied aspects of a business, industry, or profession.

Typically, the intern's duties include all of the things that none of the regular employees care to do, such as running errands, making photocopies, preparing coffee, and so forth. In December 1992, Fox announced Grushow's presidential appointment, saying that the 32-year-old would have responsibility for all shows produced by that network.[1] Reading of such career advancement opportunity might well serve as an inspiration for students who wish to enter the field of broadcasting.

Whether in the tentative or realistic period of career search, a number of government- and privately published resources at your campus or community library are readily available to better acquaint you with various aspects of different careers. The reference librarian can assist you in finding answers to specific questions. Information on salaries in different types of work, such as that presented in Table 14–2, can be obtained from Department of Labor publications. Some of the many other government publications that you may find useful include the *Guide for Occupational Exploration,* the *Dictionary of Occupational Titles,* the *Handbook for Analyzing Jobs, Franchising in the Economy,* and *Flexible Workstyles,* all published by the Department of Labor. The United States Army publishes a *Career and Education Guide.* Various special interest groups have their own publications regarding careers in various areas. For example, you can obtain literature on careers in psychology from the American Psychological Association in Washington, D.C., and from certain state psychological associations. A Washington-based group called the National Commission on Working Women of Wider Opportunities for Women published a volume called *Workforce 2000,* which discusses job opportunities in the twenty-first century. As noted in that and other publications, the law has provided that, for all intents and purposes, gender is no obstacle to any career you wish to pursue. A number of popular books are also self-help sources for career search (for example, Kennedy & Laramore, 1988; Michelozzi, 1992).

Many professions and occupations have specialty areas within them that are either growing or are relatively stagnant. If you are seriously considering any of these professions or occupations, it will be important to investigate the prospects of the specific specialty area that you are considering. For example, if you are thinking about a career in medicine, you might want to think twice about psychiatry. Insurance companies have greatly cut back on the extent to which they are willing to reimburse for psychotherapeutic services. Boris Rifkin (1990), a psychiatrist at Yale University School of Medicine, observed, "For the first time, psychiatrists have to justify their very existence to those who pay their patients' bills, to government, to other physicians; it's demoralizing." [2] Contemporary psychiatrists have many competitors who also offer psychotherapy (without medication). Among these competitors are not only bona fide mental health professionals (such as licensed psychologists and licensed social workers), but also many unlicensed people who hold themselves out to the public as "therapists," "psychotherapists," "psychoanalysts," or other legally unregulated titles (see page 230). Psychologists in some states have been granted hospital admitting privileges, and there is a move afoot for psychologists to obtain additional education that would earn them medication-prescribing privileges. Even in the face of such

[1]Not every career progresses in such linear fashion. Further, the broadcasting and entertainment industries are known for meteoric rises—as well as falls.

[2]Figure 9–1 on page 232 graphically illustrates how little growth there has been in psychiatry relative to other professions.

TABLE 14–2 A SAMPLING OF OCCUPATIONS AND SALARIES In the wake of the 1992 presidential debates between Bill Clinton, George Bush, and Ross Perot, Cronin (1992) observed that Clinton may have struck a nerve when he said, "None of us can promise any of you that what you do now for a living is absolutely safe from now on." In addition to there being no guarantee of job security or availability, there is also no guarantee that salaries will steadily rise. These data from the Bureau of Labor Statistics compare 1983 average weekly salaries (adjusted for inflation to indicate what they would purchase in 1991) with 1991 average weekly salaries.

Job	1983 ($91)	1991	Change	Job	1983 ($91)	1991	Change
Architects	$680	$623	–8.4%	Machinists	$522	$476	–8.7%
Automobile mechanics	400	385	–3.8	Mail carriers	580	580	0.0
Bank tellers	279	281	0.9	Marketing/advertising/pub. rel. managers	778	784	0.7
Bartenders	269	249	–7.4	Mechanical engineers	814	836	2.7
Bookkeeping/accounting/auditing clerks	343	345	0.7	Nurses	541	634	17.3
Carpenters	429	425	–0.9	Office machine repair people	479	468	–2.4
Cashiers	231	218	–5.5	Operations and systems researchers/analysts	803	755	–6.0
Chemists	694	687	–1.0	Personnel/labor relations managers	669	752	12.4
Child care workers	98	132	34.3	Physicians	685	984	43.6
Clergy	431	459	6.4	Police officers/detectives	553	595	7.6
Clinical laboratory technologists/technicians	441	461	4.5	Professors/college teachers	670	756	12.8
Computer programmers	646	662	2.5	Real estate salespeople	524	517	–1.4
Economists	822	732	–11.0	Salespeople, apparel	231	246	6.6
Editors/reporters	523	593	13.4	Secretaries	344	359	4.3
Farm workers	246	239	–2.8	Sewing machine operators	311	326	4.7
Financial managers	672	743	10.6	Social workers	453	466	2.8
Hairdressers/cosmetologists	262	263	0.3	Taxicab drivers/chauffeurs	332	339	2.2
Insurance salespeople	520	513	–1.4	Teachers, elementary school	493	537	8.9
Janitors/cleaners	299	292	–2.4	Travel agents	522	408	–21.8
Lawyers	853	1,008	18.1	Truck drivers (heavy trucks)	445	429	–3.6
Librarians	522	521	–0.1	Waiters/waitresses	221	218	–1.5

developments, psychiatrist Melvin Sabshin, the medical director of the American Psychiatric Association, remains optimistic regarding the future of psychiatry as a profession. Sabshin (1990) believes that the long-term prospects for psychiatry will improve as the biological basis of more mental disorders becomes known.

Reading about various occupations, perhaps even seeing videos about them (if available), can provide useful points of departure for the person in search of a career. After identifying some possible occupational choices, the next step might be a trip to the type of worksite or office where the work you are considering is being done. You may even consider taking some kind of summer internship position in the office, just for the opportunity of a closer look. For example, if you are considering a career as an attorney, a summer internship position in a law office may prove very instructive. There you will find that there are many different types of lawyers, and contrary to what is portrayed in the popular media, very few of them spend the majority of their time in court. Rather, most lawyers may spend their time drafting or reading documents and discussing legal matters with clients or fellow attorneys.

Different companies have different policies and procedures which, by inference, reflect the organization's philosophies regarding its workers. Psychologist Douglas McGregor described two different approaches to management and organizational behavior that carry implications for whether democratic or dictatorial policies towards workers are in effect. In the *Theory X* approach to management, people are viewed as having an innate dislike of work and a tendency to avoid taking responsibility for their work-related behavior. The Theory X manager or organization must therefore be very directive, using threats and punishment if necessary to control the worker and enforce the organization's goals. The Theory X manager or organization would have no reason to involve workers in management decisions because the workers would only opt for whatever would make things easiest for them. By contrast, in the *Theory Y* approach to management, work is as natural as other activities, and may be pursued primarily for the satisfaction it affords the worker. The manager operating from the perspective of Theory Y appreciates that workers are responsible, self-disciplined, and proud of what they do on the job. According to McGregor (1960), workers will remain committed to their work to the extent that they continue to receive the rewards they value from doing it. The Theory Y manager or organization welcomes worker input regarding management, and presumes that workers are industrious, responsible, and creative.

A third type of organizational approach to management, one practiced by many Japanese corporations, is referred to as *Theory Z* (Ouchi, 1981). In this approach, a corporation is seen as almost an extension of an employee's family, not merely as a place to work. The Theory Z approach to management works in Japan, where employment with a corporation has traditionally been a lifetime proposition. Aspects of this approach have been adopted by many American organizations, and in fact overlap with McGregor's notion of a Theory Y managerial approach. Still, the Japanese may have become more accustomed than most Americans would be to increased integration of their corporate and private lives. In researching employment opportunities, you may find it desirable to find out whether a company's policies are more Theory X, Y, or Z in nature.

If possible, one component of your occupational research might be a personal meeting with someone who actually does whatever it is you aspire to do. If you are fortunate enough to arrange such a meeting, what might you ask that person? Some useful information could be obtained from questions such as the following: How do you spend an average day? What are the greatest sources of satisfaction in your work? What are the greatest sources of frustration in your work? Why would you recommend this line of work to others? Why would you not recommend this line of work to others? What are some of the things that nobody really knows about this type of work? Why would you recommend this particular company over others? What are some of the things that "outsiders" do not know about this company?

PROFESSIONAL AND ENTREPRENEURIAL PURSUITS

A **profession** may be defined as *a vocation that requires advanced education in the liberal arts or sciences, and/or training and experience in a specialized field of study.* Each of the states has

profession
a vocation that requires advanced education in the liberal arts or sciences and/or training and experience in a specialized field of study.

their own requirements for the licensing, certification, or registration (all different forms of credentialing) of people who hold themselves out to the public as professionals in a given area. Physicians, psychologists, and attorneys are some of the occupational titles that may come readily to mind when you think of the term *professional,* but there are dozens more. For example, *masseuse* (massage therapist) is a licensed profession in New York State. Information on professions can be obtained from the associations or other organizations that represent the professionals that you are interested in learning more about.

Entrepreneurial pursuits, such as setting up one's own business, is another employment option. There are many routes to becoming an entrepreneur (see for example Figure 14–4). If you think you might be interested in an entrepreneurial career, you may find helpful many publications of the United States Small Business Administration (USSBA; PO Box 15434, Fort Worth, TX 76119). USSBA publications, as well as other publications related to entrepreneurial careers, can often be found in your local community library. A middle ground between the go-it-alone route of the entrepreneur and relying totally on a corporation for one's livelihood is to develop some business idea while working for a corporation. The corporation one works for might even help fund the idea in exchange for some interest in the profits derived. This relatively new type of work relationship between

FIGURE 14–4   ONE WOMAN'S ROUTE TO AN ENTREPRENEURIAL CAREER

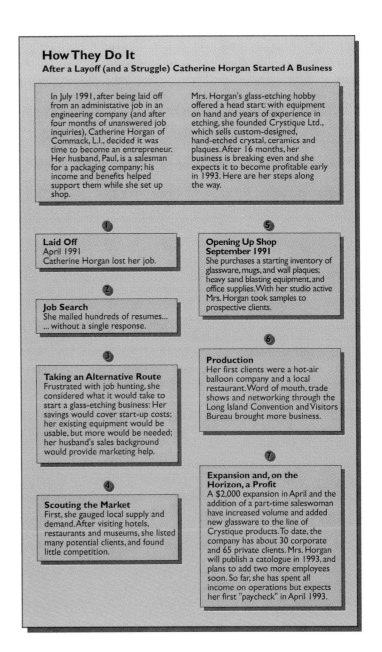

How They Do It
After a Layoff (and a Struggle) Catherine Horgan Started A Business

In July 1991, after being laid off from an administative job in an engineering company (and after four months of unanswered job inquiries), Catherine Horgan of Commack, L.I., decided it was time to become an entrepreneur. Her husband, Paul, is a salesman for a packaging company; his income and benefits helped support them while she set up shop.

Mrs. Horgan's glass-etching hobby offered a head start: with equipment on hand and years of experience in etching, she founded Crystique Ltd., which sells custom-designed, hand-etched crystal, ceramics and plaques. After 16 months, her business is breaking even and she expects it to become profitable early in 1993. Here are her steps along the way.

① Laid Off
April 1991
Catherine Horgan lost her job.

② Job Search
She mailed hundreds of resumes... ... without a single response.

③ Taking an Alternative Route
Frustrated with job hunting, she considered what it would take to start a glass-etching business: Her savings would cover start-up costs; her existing equipment would be usable, but more would be needed; her husband's sales background would provide marketing help.

④ Scouting the Market
First, she gauged local supply and demand. After visiting hotels, restaurants and museums, she listed many potential clients, and found little competition.

⑤ Opening Up Shop
September 1991
She purchases a starting inventory of glassware, mugs, and wall plaques; heavy sand blasting equipment, and office supplies. With her studio active Mrs. Horgan took samples to prospective clients.

⑥ Production
Her first clients were a hot-air balloon company and a local restaurant. Word of mouth, trade shows and networking through the Long Island Convention and Visitors Bureau brought more business.

⑦ Expansion and, on the Horizon, a Profit
A $2,000 expansion in April and the addition of a part-time saleswoman have increased volume and added new glassware to the line of Crystique products. To date, the company has about 30 corporate and 65 private clients. Mrs. Horgan will publish a catologue in 1993, and plans to add two more employees soon. So far, she has spent all income on operations but expects her first "paycheck" in April 1993.

a company and an employer is referred to as *intrapreneurial* in nature. An **intrapreneur** may be defined as *a company employee who is developing or managing some independent project while receiving salary and/or other support for the project from the company*. Intrapreneurs benefit because they enjoy virtually all of the satisfactions of entrepreneurs, but very little risk. Companies benefit from intrapreneurial relations because they retain valued employees (who might leave to become entrepreneurs) and valued ideas (which are not brought to their competitors for consideration). Relatively few companies are open to intrapreneurial relationships at the present time, but this is not necessarily due to any iron-clad policies against it. Many more companies may become receptive to intrepreneurial relations as they become convinced some would-be intrepreneur's idea is valuable and worthy of development.

intrapreneur
a person who is developing or managing some independent project for an employer while still receiving salary and/or other support for this independent project from the employer.

GETTING HIRED

Having made a vocational choice, and assuming that this choice entails getting hired by some type of company (in contrast to, say, starting your own business), the next step is landing the position you want. In recent years, upwards of 9 million people have been in the job market at any time, according to the Bureau of Labor Statistics (Cronin, 1992). Given that you will have stiff competition for most any job you apply for, it is important to resolve from the outset not to become discouraged easily. Sometimes, the speed at which qualified applicants get hired depends more on the health of the economy than it does on an individual's credentials. Persistence in applying for the positions you feel qualified for is what is necessary under such conditions.

On-campus job fairs are an excellent starting point for students seeking employment. The companies represented at such fairs are in the market to hire, and many may have fast-track executive programs for college graduates. Go to such fairs prepared to make a positive impression by dressing appropriately, knowing something about the companies that will be represented there, and projecting self-confidence. Perhaps most importantly, be prepared to ask a number of thoughtful questions about companies you may wish to work for and about their available openings. Further, you may wish to ask the representatives if it would be possible to arrange a meeting with someone who works for the company locally (if that is possible) to learn more about what a career at that company might be like. Many people prepare resumes in advance of job fairs and leave them with company representatives. However, keep in mind that after discussing a particular position with a representative, you might want your resume to better reflect one or another area of your experience. For this reason, you might consider asking representatives for their cards and then mailing your resume at a later date. Depending on the number of job-seekers and the number of corporate representatives, it sometimes happens that you must wait a relatively long time to speak to someone, and then will be able to talk only for a few minutes or so. Again, it is important not to be discouraged or to project anything other than enthusiasm to the company representative. The time spent waiting for the interview will be more than well worth it should it pay off with a job offer. In one study in the New York City area, about 35% of the students who attended a job fair and subsequently responded to a questionnaire reported that they had found work through the event (Thomas, 1992).

Family and friends may be other people to network with in your job search. Sometimes even the name of someone who knows someone— anyone, even a receptionist—at a company can turn out to be the contact that wins you consideration for some position. Answering classified advertising is a very common route to employment, one traveled by many people. For success, a good cover letter and resume is essential. Some tips on preparing that cover letter and resume, as well as on interviewing for a job, are presented in the *Quality of Life* on pages 394–396.

Beyond evaluation of your resume and a personal evaluation by means of an interview, many companies may require that you undergo more extensive evaluation with respect to job-related skills and other variables. This evaluation may take the form of paper-and-pencil ability tests, or job-related performance tests (such as a word-processing test for word processors). Companies also administer what are collectively called **integrity tests,** or *honesty measures* to some 15 million employees or prospective employees annually (Gavzer,

integrity test
an instrument most typically administered in employment settings designed to assess the honesty of employees or prospective employees.

QUALITY

Success in Job Hunting

Perhaps the two most basic components of a job search are (1) a resume to be sent to a prospective employer, and (2) a cover letter to accompany the resume. For many jobs, if the cover letter and resume pass muster with the prospective employer, the next step is a personal interview. What information should be in the resume? What does one say in the cover letter to accompany the resume? How does one behave during the interview? These are the types of questions briefly addressed below.

The Resume

There is no one standard resume because resumes are as unique as the individuals they represent. The resumes of older, highly experienced people will typically look quite different in form and other respects than the resumes of people seeking their first full-time jobs. The person just entering the job market might include a section on high school electives, hobbies, and/or interests. By contrast, the more experienced person might have a resume that focuses on a chronological listing of variables such as education and work experience. Also, the resumes of many older job applicants may contain reference to education or experience in diverse settings or occupations. What both resumes will have in common with every other resume ever written is the fact that they are selling tools. Resumes are designed to sell a potential employee to a potential employer. To better understand this point, think of those brochures you get in the mail trying to sell you on a particular product or service. Some of those brochures have more visual appeal than others, some have more useful or engaging information than others, some have a better product or

service to sell, and some are simply better at getting people to buy whatever it is that they are selling. If you are serious about getting a job, you must be serious about making your resume look as good as it possibly can.

One of many possible forms you may wish to employ is presented in the sample resume below. This hypothetical individual, Harrison Clark, is applying for his first full-time position. Note that in this resume, the individual's name, address, and telephone number are centered at the top. Mr. Clark aspires to become a certified public accountant and he is applying for a position as an accounting trainee. He would like the person reading this to obtain a quick picture of his qualifications in brief, his work experience, his community experience, and his education. Employers interested in pursuing someone for a position will typically request references, and it has become fairly customary for the last line in a resume to say that references are available upon request.

In the interest of giving your resume its best shot at being read and seriously considered, you want it to look as aesthetically pleasing as possible. For this reason, having it professionally set on a word processor and printed on fine quality paper by a laser printer is an excellent investment. For the person just starting out, there is seldom a need for the resume to be longer than one page in length. Every word in it, as well as its companion cover letter, should be spelled correctly. Further, all the grammar must be correct. Remember that your resume is your selling tool, and you may not get another chance with a particular company if this tool does not speak extremely well of you. Other sample forms that resumes may take can be

found in career search resource books such as Michelozzi (1992).

The Cover Letter

Although resumes may take different forms, most still convey certain standard types of information (such as education and experience). The cover letter provides you with an opportunity to show some "personality," indicate that you are serious about your career, and show that you can be business-like, courteous, and engaging. The cover letter to accompany Harrison Clark's resume follows. Note that this letter fulfills two key purposes of a cover letter: (1) to act as a link between the resume and the prospective employer, and (2) to end by suggesting some specific next steps. The link may be a reference to how you came to write the letter and send in a resume. That link might be a personal referral, as is the case in the sample letter, or something else, such as a classified ad. The link can be strengthened with material that clearly shows that you know something about the company, and that you are qualified and interested in working there. In the sample letter, Clark demonstrates that he shares the company's values with respect to providing *pro bono* (free, for the public good) professional services. He ends by saying he will follow up with a phone call. Other, somewhat less assertive endings include, "I am looking forward to hearing from you," or something like, "Would it be possible to arrange for an interview during the week of (fill in)?"

The Interview

For some prospective employees, an interview is perceived as an obstacle to be overcome in order to get the job. Perhaps a better way of thinking about an interview is as an opportunity to learn more about the company and the position(s) being offered. After all, an employment interview is usually a two-way street with both parties having the opportunity to pose questions to one another. The interviewer comes prepared with questions and is also prepared to answer the interviewee's questions. You must come prepared to answer the interviewer's questions. In addition, it is advisable to have prepared in advance a number of your own questions about the company and the position being offered. It is not only the quality of your answers that will impress the interviewer. Your

questions may signal to the interviewer that you have given a great amount of consideration to the position and all that it entails.

What kinds of questions might the interviewer ask? Be prepared for both specific and open-ended questions. If you are just out of school, some specific questions might be asked about your education (the courses you took—which you particularly liked, and why), part-time and summer employment (how it prepared you for the world of work), and other aspects of your past experience that you would bring to the position. You might be

asked about your ambitions and expectations with a question such as, "Where do you see yourself in this company 5 years from now?" More open-ended questions you should be prepared to answer include, "Tell me about yourself," "Tell me about your strengths and weaknesses," and "Why would you like to work for this company?" The interviewer might ask an open-ended question like, "How do you generally get along with people?" Most work involves human relations and you may score some points by re-

(continued)

Sample cover letter to accompany resume

> 0000 Beverly Drive
> Beverly Hills, California 90210
> (213) 555-1111
> April 16, 1996
>
> Mr. Leopold L. Smith, CPA
> Director of Human Resources
> Smith, Jones, Johnson & Brown
> Pico-Rivera Professional Building
> Pico, California 90321
>
> Dear Mr. Smith:
>
> While working as a volunteer at the El Cohone office of Americares, I had occasion to meet Mr. Angel Wences from your Pico office. Over the last four years, Mr. Wences has sent me copies of your company's annual report, as well as literature that describes the charitable works that the company is involved in. I have been most impressed with your firm, and believe wholeheartedly in the policy of giving back something to the community from corporate profits. I am writing to request an interview for a position as an Accounting Trainee.
>
> Until their bankruptcy in 1996, I worked every summer since 1993 as an Assistant Bookkeeper at Crestfallen Gem Company, a retail sales outlet for precious and semi-precious gems. During the bankruptcy, my ability to work quickly and efficiently combined with my ability to communicate clearly earned me extra responsibility. The firm made me the primary liaison between it and the Los Angeles County Sheriff's office.
>
> Although I have relatively little formal work experience, I do feel that I learn quickly and could be an asset to your company. I learned conversational Spanish during my junior high and high school years, and have sufficient fluency to be able to effectively assist with Spanish-speaking clients. One of the reasons I took the position at Ralph's in Los Alamitos was the opportunity to hone my fluency in that language. While president of the Accounting Club in high school, I helped organize a program that offered Spanish-speaking community residents free assistance in preparing their income tax returns. A Latino merchants' organization awarded me and each of the other students involved certificates of appreciation.
>
> I have always been good with numbers, and my interest in accounting has grown with every course I have taken in this area. I plan to pursue a master's degree in accounting part time while working full time. I know that your firm encourages such continuing education, which is yet another reason why I would like to work there. Further, I believe in the pro bono work you provide to the community, and I could make a contribution in assisting in those efforts. I will follow up with a call next week in the hope that we can set an interview date.
>
> Sincerely,
>
> *Harrison Clark*
>
> Harrison Clark

Sample resume of person applying for first full-time job

> **HARRISON CLARK**
> 0000 Beverly Drive
> Beverly Hills, California 90210
> (213) 555-1111
>
> **POSITION OBJECTIVE:**
> Accounting Trainee (with eventual CPA)
>
> **QUALIFICATIONS IN BRIEF:**
> BA in Business with Honors. AA in Business with Honors.
> Voted "Most Likely to Succeed" in high school. Class Treasurer for junior and senior years in high school. President of the Accounting Club. Working knowledge of Spanish.
>
> **WORK EXPERIENCE:**
> 1993-1996 (summers)
> Crestfallen Gem Company, El Segundo, CA
> Assistant Bookkeeper
> Assisted company bookkeeper by entering data related to net profits and losses; also assisted in bankruptcy proceedings.
>
> Summer, 1992
> Ralph's Market, Los Alamitos, CA
> Cashier
> Rang up groceries and balanced drawer; won "Employee of the Month" (August, 1993)
>
> **COMMUNITY EXPERIENCE:**
> December 1992–February 1993
> Americares, El Cohone, CA
> Volunteer
> Assisted in packaging of food and other emergency relief supplies for shipment to Somalia.
>
> **EDUCATION:**
> 1988-1992
> Beverly Hills High School, Beverly Hills, CA
> Voted "Most Likely to Succeed." Senior Class Treasurer, President of Accounting Club during junior year. Vice President of Spanish Club during sophomore year. Participated in chess club in sophomore through senior years, and in intramural fencing during junior and senior years.
>
> 1992-1994
> Los Alamitos Community College, Los Alamitos, CA
> AA in Business with Honors. Class President (1993-1994)
>
> 1994-1996
> California State University at Chico, Chico, CA
> BA in Business with Honors. Class valedictorian
>
> **REFERENCES:**
> Available upon request.

QUALITY OF Life

Success in Job Hunting *(continued)*

sponding with a brief vignette that demonstrates your good human relations skills. Michelozzi (1992) points out that a theme underlying virtually most everything the interviewer asks is, "Can you do the job?" She advises that "It's not fair to expect to be hired if you can't do the job well" (Michelozzi, 1992, p. 204). On the other hand, if you *can* do the job well, then each of your answers, as well as your behavior throughout the interview, must reflect that confidence.

Effective interview behavior includes listening actively (see page 21, and pages 305–310). Communicate with your eye contact, posture, and speech that you are sincerely interested in getting the

job and doing well at it. Exude confidence, but avoid being overbearing. Avoid being defensive, even if your prior work experience has been limited. When interviewing for an entry-level position, many of the applicants may have even less work experience than you do. Avoid harsh criticisms of former employers, teachers, or others in authority. A general objective is to convey to the interviewer that you can be an asset to the company. When the issue of salary is raised, newcomers to the working world should simply convey that they hope to receive a fair and equitable return for their effort. It is perfectly appropriate to inquire about how raises are determined and how

people advance in the company. Avoid making salary the focus of the interview. Rather, the focus of the interview must not stray very far from your qualifications to fill the available position. When the interviewer terminates the interview, shake hands firmly and leave without lingering. Especially if you do not have much experience at job interviewing, it will be very useful to role-play some sample job interviews, with a friend playing the role of interviewer. Ultimately, all you can do is your best. With effort, however, there will come a time when both you and an employer you want to work for agree that a good match exists between you.

1990). These tests can be divided into two types: tests that attempt to measure honesty through direct questions (such as, "Do you usually tell the truth?") and tests that attempt to measure honesty through indirect, personality-related questions (Sackett et al., 1989). Although the number of integrity tests is soaring, a study commissioned by the American Psychological Association (1991) found only a few of these tests to be valid. In addition to integrity testing, drug testing is also becoming more common in the workplace.

ON THE JOB

In the wake of the Industrial Revolution, most employers tended in many respects to draw little distinction between their machines and their employees; the objective was to get as much work as possible from each. Labor laws were gradually passed to prevent abuse of workers. However, employers only first began to appreciate the benefits of treating their employees in more humane fashion as a result of research on the relationship between psychological variables and worker productivity.

PRODUCTIVITY

productivity
the creation of goods or services to produce value or wealth.

Productivity refers to *the creation of goods or services to produce value or wealth.* With high, as opposed to low, productivity among the people they employ, business and industry can produce more goods and services with fewer employees. For example, a bank teller who handles 40 customers per hour on average is more productive than a bank teller who can handle only 20 customers per hour. Banks who have faster tellers can hire fewer of them, keep labor costs down, and be more competitive in the banking industry.

At a national level, productivity is a key factor in how fast a country's standard of living rises. At the level of the individual business, employers seek to keep worker productivity high so that the business will reap maximum profits; money from profits may be reinvested into the business to hire new employees, purchase new technology, or otherwise make the business more competitive in the marketplace. At the level of the individual worker, high productivity can contribute to one's sense of self-esteem as well as to one's satisfaction with one's job.

A series of studies that began in 1924 at the Western Electric Company plant in Hawthorne, Illinois, yielded important findings regarding worker productivity and related variables. These "Hawthorne Studies" (Roethlisberger & Dickson, 1939) were carried out over the course of 12 years in a joint research project of the Western Electric Company and researchers from Harvard University. The initial study was designed to determine the effect of workplace lighting on productivity. To their great surprise, the researchers found that productivity increased regardless of the lighting level. The researchers observed increased productivity when the illumination level was constant (as when the researchers first came), when the level was intensely bright (almost too bright to work in), and when the level was very dim (as dim as in working by moonlight). What could account for these amazing findings?

The researchers concluded that the workers had considered themselves quite special: they had observers from the prestigious Harvard University in their plant. Productivity apparently increased because the employees wanted to impress the researchers with how hard they could work. For the time that the researchers' presence at the plant remained a novelty, productivity was higher than usual. However, when the novelty began to wear off, productivity reverted back to its previous level. The finding that *novelty in the workplace (such as the presence of observers) could affect worker productivity* in such a fashion is referred to today as the **Hawthorne Effect.** References to this phenomenon in field studies may still be found in the contemporary I/O psychology literature. Depending on the source of the novelty, a *Hawthorne effect* may last only for days, or for as long as a year or two.

Subsequent experiments carried out by the Hawthorne researchers explored many aspects of psychology in the workplace, such as the relationship between productivity and variables such as worker and supervisory attitudes. Although the Hawthorne Studies have been criticized for their methodology, this series of studies served as an important stimulus in shifting the focus of I/O psychology away from corporate balance sheets and onto the human needs, satisfactions, stresses, and motivations of the company's employees and managers. Anyone reading even the initial reports of the Hawthorne Studies might wonder, "If the presence of researchers from Harvard could make workers feel special and raise productivity, what else might be done to make workers feel special?"

JOB SATISFACTION

Job satisfaction may be defined as *a pleasurable or positive emotional state resulting from the appraisal of one's job or job experiences* (Locke, 1976). The term may also be thought of as a shorthand way of describing workers' global level of gratification with respect to dozens of diverse elements or facets of their everyday employment. Two people in two different jobs may have the same global level of job satisfaction, but for very different reasons. To understand the specific reasons for this global level of satisfaction, it is important to examine what is called *job facet satisfaction,* or the level of satisfaction derived from many diverse, individual components of the job. The quality of the food in the employee commissary, the ease of the commute to and from work, the degree to which one finds the work personally meaningful and gratifying, the boss's manner and tone of voice, the salary paid and the company benefits provided, the sense of ease one feels around co-workers, the company's policy regarding child-care, and the amount of work one must actually do are some of the individual job facets that contribute to a global level of job satisfaction. A number of tests have been developed to measure both global job satisfaction and job facet satisfaction, although none has proven to be entirely satisfactory from a technical perspective (Buckley et al., 1992).

Job satisfaction may have many consequences. Great dissatisfaction with one's job or feelings of being powerless to do anything about it may negatively impact on one's mental and physical health (Karasek & Theorell, 1990; Kavanaugh et al., 1981; Kornhauser, 1965; Matteson & Ivancevich 1987; Wolf 1986). The extent to which one is satisfied or dissatis-

Hawthorne Effect
a phenomenon that refers to a change in worker productivity as a function of a change in working conditions.

job satisfaction
a pleasurable or positive emotional state resulting from the appraisal of one's job or occupational experiences.

fied with a job may also influence the manner in which the employee relates to co-workers (Motowidlo, 1984). The relationship between job satisfaction and productivity is complex. Although it seems logical that high job satisfaction leads to high productivity and low job satisfaction leads to low productivity, research has not borne out such assumptions (Gray & Starke, 1984). It is possible that workers may be highly productive even when dissatisfied with their jobs if they fear losing their jobs for lack of productivity. The relationship between job satisfaction and variables such as absenteeism is equally complex; there too, few generalizations can be made. We might logically assume that high job satisfaction leads to low absenteeism and that low job satisfaction leads to high absenteeism. Again, no such relationship has been clearly established through research (Youngblood, 1984).

Regardless of the actual relationship between job satisfaction and productivity for a particular job, it seems fair to assume that many American employers and employees believe that one should feel a sense of satisfaction at work. Muchinsky (1983, p. 317) notes that our work ethic was "developed as part of the fabric of American life style, a work ethic formulated on the 'pursuit of happiness' to which work contributes." In "the land of opportunity" and "the land of the free," we are prone to expect that only prisoners compelled to make license plates are dissatisfied with their jobs. In fact, general level of job satisfaction may be high for some types of jobs (such as professional work) and lower for others (such as blue-collar work). A large-scale study that employed over 4,700 full-time employees polled annually from 1972 through 1978 indicated that most workers—about 85% to 89% of them—reported being either "somewhat satisfied" or "very satisfied" with their jobs (Weaver, 1980). Other surveys have also shown global level of job satisfaction to be in the 80% or higher range (Smither, 1988).

Many people who are dissatisfied at work are dissatisfied with their lives in general (Tait et al., 1989). For those who are specifically dissatisfied with their jobs, however, different types of intervention may help increase the level of satisfaction. In a *motivator-hygiene* model of job satisfaction proposed by Frederick Herzberg (Herzberg et al., 1959), *motivator needs* (similar to Abraham Maslow's notion of self-actualization needs) are the needs that must be met for job satisfaction to occur. Merely meeting what Herzberg calls *hygiene needs* (basic physiological needs) with a paycheck will not result in job satisfaction. Other researchers have pointed to various factors that may be able to play a role in increasing job satisfaction. Increases in pay (Lawler, 1971), diversification of work (Lawler, 1969), job restructuring for the purpose of making the job more intellectually challenging (Hackman & Oldham, 1976), institution of flexible hours (Ralston et al., 1985), and institution of flexible compensation and benefit systems (Tane & Treacy, 1984) may all contribute to a greater sense of satisfaction with one's job.

JOB STRESS

In a world of "good stress" and "bad stress" (see page 150), references to job stress usually refer to the bad variety. A person who earns a living as a daredevil may experience a great deal of stress prior to performing some death-defying act, but this stress is largely good; if it were largely bad, the daredevil might long ago have gotten into another line of work. What potential sources of stress exist in the workplace? Exercise some generative thought by listing all the sources you can think of before reading on.

Some sources of stress at the workplace include (1) the overall feeling that one has chosen or somehow drifted into the wrong occupation; (2) a conflict in values with the values inherent in one's work; (3) interpersonal conflicts with co-workers or superiors; (4) too much work to do; (5) too little work to do; (6) work tasks that are boring, repetitive, or simply not stimulating; (6) unfavorable physical conditions at the worksite; (7) unfavorable market conditions in the marketplace; (8) a feeling of being exploited by one's employer with respect to pay and/or benefits; (9) a feeling that one's efforts or abilities are not sufficiently recognized, appreciated, or rewarded; (10) advances in new technology in the field which seem overwhelming and difficult to keep up with; (11) physical illness or injury which impairs one's ability to do work at the same level as prior to the illness or injury; or (12) racial, ethnic, sexual, or other varieties of discrimination, prejudice, or bias in the workplace. Additionally, there are always those unanticipated events that can cause great stress at a worksite (see Figure 14–5).

As is the case with chronic job dissatisfaction, chronic stress at work may be harmful to one's physical or mental health. In Japan, "working to death" is more than an idiom; according to law, it is a reality. *Karoshi* is the Japanese word for "death by overwork," and if *karoshi* can be proven, the government will compensate the family of the victim. Claims of *karoshi* usually involve blue-collar workers. In July 1992, however, a Japanese executive who was found dead in a hotel room was ruled to be a *karoshi* victim. The man, a 47-year-old executive with a trading company, who was fluent in Russian, had been escorting some Russian clients visiting Japan. Court papers filed by the executive's widow indicated that the victim had spent 115 days on the road in the year prior to his death. In the week just before he died, the victim had put in long hours and had been unable to take a day off. The Japanese government officially recognizes about 30 cases of *karoshi* annually. According to an organization called the National Defense Council for Victims of Karoshi, as many as 10,000 Japanese work themselves to death each year ("Japan Says," 1992).

Two stress-related phenomena that are common to the American workplace are *workaholism* and *burnout*. **Workaholism** may be defined as *a condition characterized by spending inordinate time at work*. From outward appearances, the "workaholic" seems to be addicted to work, much like an alcoholic is addicted to alcohol. However, outward appearances can be deceiving. In some cases, the addiction model may be inappropriate because the workaholic genuinely loves the work and the long hours at work only add to feelings of personal fulfillment, utility, and happiness. For other workaholics, the need to work long hours is perhaps better characterized as a compulsion—one driven by insecurity, anxiety, an unhappy homelife, a need to compensate for perceived deficiencies, or other such factors. It is in the latter cases that workaholism can present problems, not only to the worker but also to the worker's friends and family (Machlowitz, 1980). One psychoanalytically oriented consumer researcher, Ernest Dichter, believed that an inability to remove oneself from work was due to factors such as guilt and a fear of death: "Unconsciously, leisure time represents to them a foretaste of passive retirement and perhaps even death" (Dichter, 1981, p. x).

Burnout may be defined as *a condition caused by overwork in which an individual becomes less productive, less motivated, and less energetic with respect to work*. Depression, apathy, irritability, fault finding, and social withdrawal are some of the symptoms victims of burnout may exhibit (Freudenberger, 1977). Sometimes the burnout victim will follow work guidelines strictly by the book because the mental energy required for flexibility and creativity

workaholism

a condition characterized by spending an inordinate and disproportionate time at work.

burnout

a condition caused by overwork in which an individual becomes less productive, less motivated, and less energetic with respect to work.

FIGURE 14–5 JOB STRESS IN WINDOW WASHING Experienced Manhattan window washers like 28-year-old Ivor Hanson, a Vassar graduate and musician, do not suffer from fear of heights. Yet even they can experience extraordinary job stress at times. On one occasion, a ledge Hanson was using for support crumbled, leaving him supported only by his safety belt. How did he cope? According to Hanson (1992), "What you do when something like that happens or when the fear grabs you, is you concentrate as hard as you can on the exact position of your body . . . Then you just focus on the job, the window, the sponges, the squeegee, the $6 you are going to get for each window."

in problem solving has long been spent. Victims of burnout may require time away from the job, perhaps with counseling, in order to reassess their motivation to work, as well as the costs and benefits of their work habits.

Stress at the workplace, like stress from other sources, can be symptomatically dealt with through the use of strategies and techniques such as those described in Chapters 7 and 9. However, beyond treating the symptoms, it will be essential to analyze and deal with the specific causes of stress. Psychologically based antistress techniques such as meditation or systematic desensitization will be of little value, for example, if the source of stress at work is an offensive chemical in the office carpeting. For this reason, it is essential to evaluate what it is about the work that is causing the problem. Taking appropriate action may range from having a talk with a manager, preparing and sending out resumes, or calling a local carpet retailer. Stress in one form or another is an element of virtually all occupations. Adjusting to it in the workplace entails not allowing it to be your downfall but rather using it as a stimulus for personal growth and development.

PEOPLE AT WORK

career

a sequence of positions occupied by a person during the course of a lifetime.

I/O psychologist Donald E. Super conceptualized career development in terms of a series of stages. For Super, **career** may be defined simply as *a sequence of positions occupied by a person during the course of a lifetime* (Super & Hall, 1978, p. 334). These "positions" parallel a stage of growth from birth to age 14 or so, a stage of exploration from age 15 to 24, and an *establishment* stage from age 25 to 44, during which people try to establish themselves in a particular occupation. According to Super (1957, 1985, 1988), after establishment comes *maintenance* between the ages of 45 to 65. Thereafter comes the *decline* stage, during which there is a lessening of vocational activity and ultimately a cessation of it.

As Super freely acknowledged himself, and as is true with all stage theories (see page 141), many exceptions to this career development theory exist. Ronald Reagan had his career peak with his election to the presidency of the United States at an age 5 years after Super's system would classify him as in decline. Some people begin careers much earlier than Super would predict; other people, much later. Also, Super's original theory, like others conceived in the 1950s, focused primarily on men's patterns of career development. Super acknowledged that women might follow other paths, such as a *stable homemaking pattern* or an *interrupted pattern,* the latter characterized by sporadic periods of employment outside the home. Indeed, as other researchers have found, career paths have tended to be far more random for women than for men (Larwood & Gattiker, 1984). Some issues related to women in the workplace were covered in Chapter 4. Here let's briefly look at a sample of other issues relevant to people at work.

ETHNIC, RACIAL, AND RELIGIOUS MINORITIES

The Bureau of Labor Statistics estimates that from the period 1990 to 2005, 26 million more people will enter the labor force. Of these people, about 46% will be white, 28% will be Hispanic, 16% will be black, and 10% will be Asian. Concerns regarding this work force have been expressed from many different perspectives. From an economic perspective, it is feared that the work force will lack the skills, education, and training to be competitive in the world marketplace (Greenhouse, 1992). Marc Tucker (1992), president of a private research group called the National Center on Education and the Economy, observed that, "The level of poverty among kids in this country is more than twice that of any industrial country with which we compete. It's not reasonable to expect those who grow up in poverty to achieve world-class levels in school and in the workplace." Bill Brock (1992), a former secretary of labor, believes that the poor education received by many Americans, particularly minority group members, will translate into "a lower standard of living for all Americans, not just blacks and Hispanics." A Labor Department commission estimated that 60% of all Americans between the ages of 21 and 25 lacked reading and writing skills needed for the workplace. A study conducted by the National Urban League found that only 31% of African-American adults read at the 11th grade level, as compared to 68% of whites (Greenhouse, 1992).

In an effort to better educate and train Americans for the workplace challenges of to-morrow, economists, educators, and legislators have proposed a wide variety of programs, including student loans, not only for high school graduates but also for blue-collar work-ers who have been in the work force for many years. Wider availability of worker retrain-ing programs, such as those that have worked successfully in California (Kilborn, 1992b), is another proposal that is currently being discussed. Apprenticeship programs, complete with a wide range of new technical and professional certifications, may be another route to keeping the American work force competitive.

Citing experts in the field of labor and economics, Greenhouse (1992) writes that "the profound changes in the work force expected in the next decade point to an increased in-terdependence between America's whites and nonwhites." Increased interdependence may foster greater sensitivity to the needs and perspectives of people from different cultures. Al-though job discrimination on the basis of race, ethnic background, or religion is illegal, it is still known to go on—sometimes in extremely subtle ways (see *Cultural Close-Up* on page 402). Perhaps increased minority representation in the work force, along with the greater need for interdependence that will result, will be useful in minimizing if not eliminating such discriminatory practices.

CHILDREN IN THE WORKPLACE

Abuse of children in the workplace was an immediate consequence of the Industrial Rev-olution. The exploitation of children as workers at the turn of the century was addressed by the imposition and enforcement of strict child labor laws. Today, some 4 million chil-dren between the ages of 14 to 18 are legally employed. An estimated 2 million children are illegally employed, according to Philip J. Landrigan, chair of the Department of Com-munity Medicine at New York's Mount Sinai Medical Center. Landrigan (1992) attributes the growth of legal and illegal child labor in this country to (1) poor economic conditions requiring families to send children to work; (2) increased immigration by people from countries where child labor is routine and expected; and, (3) a decrease in federal budgets for policing workplaces for violation of child labor laws. The number of children in the labor force and the number of hours children work may also rise in a very good economy. Under such conditions, business requires more help quickly and children can provide a ready and cheap supply of labor (Newman, 1992).

Historian David Rosner believes that Americans have been very ambivalent about child labor laws. According to Rosner (1992), "We see work as redemptive and as a morally le-gitimate method of self-improvement." However, even if many people in society harbor a view of employment as good for children, few would disagree that the work that children are called upon to do, and the worksite itself, must be safe. In fact, in too many instances, the jobs children are given, or the worksite itself, is not safe (see Figure 14–6). Federal

FIGURE 14–6   CHILDREN IN HAZARDOUS OCCUPATIONS A study by the Massachusetts Depart-ment of Public Health found that the annual injury rate for children was 3.5 times higher than that for adults (Davis, 1992). Children may suffer burns, deep cuts, amputations, or other severe injuries while working, according to a study by the National Institute for Occupational Safety and Health. That study also reported that several hundred children a year are killed on the job. One 14-year-old child fell asleep while working a farmer's field and was run over by a truck. A 17-year-old was killed while illegally operating a machine that crushes cardboard boxes. A 15-year-old was killed when he was pulled inside a bakery doughmaking machine. Greater policing of worksites by more inspectors is necessary if this workplace abuse of children is to be curbed.

Career and Workplace Constraints of Observant Jews

Sandy Koufax, the Jewish Hall-of-Famer and Cy Young award-winning pitcher for the Dodgers from 1955 to 1966, once refused to play a World Series game because it fell on the religious holiday of *Yom Kippur* (the Day of Atonement). A comprehensive exploration of some lesser known, though no less momentous, career constraints on *observant Jews* (Jews who strictly follow the laws of the Five Books of Moses in the Old Testament) was provided by Fred A. Mael (1991). The discussion below is based, after Mael (1991), on behavioral and attitudinal constraints on career advancement that affect observant Jews. As you read, think about how other groups of people might also be constrained in the workplace as a result of their religious beliefs and practices.

Jewish law prohibits work (including using electricity, riding by motorized vehicle, using a computer, and so forth) on the Sabbath, which lasts from sundown on Friday to sundown on Saturday. An early release from work on Friday afternoons may be necessary so that a worker may be home by the time the Sabbath begins, especially in time zones and places where sundown occurs late in the afternoon. In addition to being restricted from work during the Sabbath, most observers are also excluded from corporate social events held on Saturdays (including picnics, sports, or other events held on Saturdays) due to restrictions against travel. Observant Jews are faced with many of the same problems when any of the 13 work-restricted holidays fall on a weekday/work day. In some organizations, a person wishing to take a religious holiday off must use a vacation day to do so. Yet as Mael (1991) points out, the religious workers in such settings "can never accumulate sufficient time for the discretionary activities or vacations that provide rejuvenation for other workers."

Jewish dietary laws prescribe that only kosher food can be eaten. A widely held view is that kosher food is food that has been blessed by a rabbi; this is a myth. Kosher food is simply food that has been prepared in accordance with Jewish law. In the case of meat, beef and poultry must be slaughtered in a prescribed manner, and pork in any form may not be consumed. Meat and dairy foods cannot be mixed or prepared or eaten with the same plates or utensils. Shellfish, like pork, is prohibited. The businessperson who wishes to consume only kosher food may be at a disadvantage when it comes to entertaining clients, attending banquets, or engaging in other business-related functions where nonkosher food is served. There are many kosher restaurants, but these tend to be concentrated in the few cities having large Jewish populations. Packaged kosher food is another alternative, as are fresh fruits and fresh vegetables.

---

child labor laws provide that children under the age of 16 may only work certain hours, and may not work at certain hazardous jobs such as construction, roofing, mining, and logging. In a study of 1988 census data, economist Charles Jeszeck (1992) determined that at least 166,000 children were either working at occupations that they were not allowed to work at by law (such as construction) or working too many hours. The danger of a child being injured or killed at worksites will remain as long as society remains ambivalent about child labor laws. Stopping the needless injury and death of children will entail making the enforcement of child labor laws a high priority.

AIDS IN THE WORKPLACE

Despite widespread efforts to educate the public and professionals regarding the nature of AIDS and the transmission of the virus (HIV) that causes it, a great deal of ignorance about this disease continues to exist (Peterson, 1991; Wiener & Siegal, 1990). In the workplace, one consequence of this ignorance for the AIDS sufferer may be an additional and needless burden of emotional hurt. While some co-workers may treat the infected person with compassion, others may take extraordinary (and unnecessary) precautions against contracting the disease, sometimes even expressing anger at the infected person for continu-

Because of the need to attend synagogue on the Sabbath and the prohibition against traveling to the synagogue by motorized vehicle, many observant Jews live near their place of worship. Also, the children in the family may attend a religious school. These two factors, combined with the desire to live in a community where kosher food and restaurants are readily available, make long-term job relocation difficult if not a virtual impossibility for many observant Jews. Unfortunately, unwillingness to relocate may be an impediment to corporate advancement (Brett, 1982).

In addition to Sabbath- and holiday-related constraints, dietary constraints, and geographic constraints, observant Jews may also have restraints placed on them as a consequence of their appearance. Custom dictates that male Jews wear something on their head to acknowledge the everpresent existence of the Lord. When not wearing a hat, a small cloth head-covering called a *yarmulke* (also referred to as a skullcap or *kippah*) may be worn. Yet wearing a skullcap has been found to impair one's chances of corporate advancement (Zweigenhaft, 1984) and is "rarely, if ever, accepted in corporate life as appropriate for those aspiring to executive careers" (Korman, 1988, p. 39). Much the same holds true for the wearing of beards, another Jewish tradition which is rejected by most of the American business community. For some, Jews remain permanent outsiders to high-level positions in powerful American corporations (Quinn et al., 1968; Slavin & Pradt, 1982). In order to succeed, many Jews have played down their Jewishness. Of 219 Jewish directors of *Fortune 500* companies, few identified themselves as Jews (Zweigenhaft & Domhoff, 1982).

Mael (1991) argues persuasively that the internal constraints observant Jews face are all easily surmountable in the business world, while the external constraints, such as prejudice, are not. Some companies and other organizations avoid employing Jews in an effort to comply with the demands of Arab clients (Korman, 1988; Volkman, 1982). This practice is illegal but persists, perhaps because there are typically too few Jews employed in an organization to establish a case for systematic bias; the company may simply claim that the individual did not fit the corporate image. Yet as Mael (1991) points out, observant Jews can "accept current lost opportunities as a relatively small price to pay for their beliefs. The real losers are those organizations who would willingly forego bright, hardworking individuals with excellent credentials, or who would let such persons stagnate in jobs below their potential."

ing to come to work (Anonymous, 1992). Co-workers may be reluctant to make or receive calls with a phone used by an AIDS-infected person, to drink from the same water cooler, to eat at the same table, to eat treats brought to work and offered by the person, or to socialize at corporate events with the infected person. For co-workers, the witnessing of someone's decline due to a disease such as AIDS, or due to any other comparably degenerative disease for that matter, may serve as a daily but unwelcome reminder of one's own mortality and/or other losses by disease one may have suffered. In short, the workplace becomes unpleasant because the usual denial mechanisms regarding such death-related thoughts are hampered.

In addition to unrealistic concerns co-workers may have about contracting AIDS through some as yet undiscovered method of transmission, there are also very real problems that must be dealt with. For example, performance on the job may be affected by the disease, or by side effects of medication taken to treat the disease. If the infected person's performance begins to slip, the manager "needs to address the performance changes directly and discuss alternatives in the context of the employee's rights and the organization's commitment to reasonable accommodation and necessary productivity" (Macks & Emery, 1992, p. 564).

On the heels of a Centers for Disease Control and Prevention (CDC) education program called "America Responds to AIDS," the CDC launched a "Business Responds to AIDS" program in December 1992. This program was designed to promote worker understanding of the disease and support for infected employees. A Manager's Kit available from the CDC contains posters and pamphlets on a variety of AIDS-related topics. For example, because people with AIDS are covered by the Americans with Disabilities Act of 1990, employers are legally bound to "reasonably accommodate" such workers on the job. Other independent organizations are available to assist companies with policy or procedure questions related to AIDS in the workplace.[3]

UNEMPLOYMENT

unemployment

the condition of being involuntarily out of work.

Unemployment as the term is being used here refers to *the condition of being out of work as a result of factors beyond one's control;* unemployment does not refer to a choice not to work. For most of us, it is easier to appreciate the negative physical and emotional stresses of work than the negative physical and emotional stresses of being out of work. In fact, there is a natural temptation to equate being out of work with vacation time. Initially, a person suddenly unemployed may well think of unemployment in much the same way as a vacation. According to Powell and Driscoll (1973), in this first stage of unemployment, the unemployed person views the newly freed time as an opportunity to travel, relax, catch up on things, or work at hobbies. However, this initial reaction to being unemployed may last only a month or so. Soon the individual has a strong desire to return to work and job-seeking behavior begins. Should job seeking not result in a job, the unemployed person may enter a period characterized by self-doubt. Now, job-seeking behavior becomes sporadic if it occurs at all. If unable to remain motivated to seek a job in the face of adversity, the unemployed worker enters a final stage of prolonged unemployment. According to Powell and Driscoll (1973), this stage involves radical changes in attitudes towards society and work. During this last and final stage, a very real danger is that the person will totally withdraw and become a homeless person. For many people laid off in the recession that began in the late 1980s, especially white collar workers, the spiral downward described by Powell and Driscoll (1973) is a reality. Many of these former executives retain all of the trappings of success, but as we have seen so often, appearances can be deceiving (see Figure 14–7).

Regardless of whether one is employed to earn a living or one is employed for any other reason, suddenly becoming unemployed can bring with it several kinds of very serious consequences and adjustive challenges. Severe emotional upset, physical symptoms and illness, sleep difficulties, drug abuse, child abuse, alcoholism, and/or marital and family disruption may all be linked to unemployment (Banks & Jackson, 1982; Liem & Rayman, 1980; Price, 1992; Rayman, 1992). Even if the firing or lay-off is the result of forces that are completely beyond the individual's control, feelings of guilt or misgivings about having taken the job in the first place may result. The loss of identity and feeling of rootlessness that accompanies a firing or lay-off can sometimes be so severe as to be a primary

[3]Workplace education resources for AIDS-related information may be found at agencies such as:

The Centers for Disease Control and Prevention AIDS Hotline
800–342-AIDS; 800–243–7889

National AIDS Clearinghouse Business Responds to AIDS Resource Service
800–458–5231

The National Leadership Coalition on AIDS
1730 M Street, Suite 905 Washington, DC 20036
202–429–0930

American Red Cross, Workplace HIV/AIDS Program
1709 New York Avenue NW
Washington, DC 20006
202–434–4074

Equal Employment Opportunity Americans with Disabilities Act (ADA) Helpline
800–669-EEOC
800–800–3302 (hearing impaired)

FIGURE 14–7 MEMBERS OF THE UNEMPLOYED CORVETTE OWNERS ASSOCIATION Members of this club of formerly highly paid executives posed by their cars for this photo in 1992. For them, and thousands of people like them, the stress of unemployment can be great. As Cowan and Barron (1992) observed, "After selling the boat and letting the athletic club membership lapse, they are scrounging for spare change, letting the car repairs go, and wondering how many mortgage payments they can miss before the bank forecloses." Unemployed white-collar workers may become more defensive and self-critical than blue-collar workers, who may adapt more readily to changing job market conditions. Describing laid-off white-collar workers he has treated, psychiatrist David Robbins (1992) said that they had been left with "a pervasive sense of betrayal."

factor in death by suicide or heart attack (Boor, 1980; Craig, 1989). Unemployment may have the indirect effect of landing some people in jail because they feel compelled to commit crimes to obtain money and/or to wreak revenge on society.

How can one best cope with being unemployed? As in treating depression, activity may be one of the best remedies. For the jobseeker, constructive activity will consist of keeping one's eyes and ears open to opportunities and acting quickly when an appropriate one arises. Avoid blaming yourself; in all probability you were not the cause of the lay-off (and even if you were, there is nothing you can do about it but do better next time). Funnel the anger you may harbor regarding your job loss into constructive activities such as job-seeking activities, developing new business ideas, engaging in volunteer work, or taking up a new sport or exercise. If need be, think about retraining for a career in some area where greater opportunities are available. If a community support group for unemployed persons is available, join it. If not, you may wish to be instrumental in starting one. Develop a "business plan" to put yourself "back in business" and make it a rule that there will be no let-up in effort until you are on your way. Try to keep in contact with the same friends you kept in contact with when employed. Too often, a blow to one's pride or embarrassment about being unemployed causes one to feel uncomfortable in the presence of others. This is unfortunate because a period of unemployment is when people most need social support and a broadening of their social network.

PLAY

We all have a need to entertain or amuse ourselves—that is, to play. Much like work, play may manifest itself in many varied ways. Playing box games, playing video games, playing cards and other games of chance, playing sports, watching television, going mountain biking, listening to the radio, visiting a museum, sightseeing abroad, working out, doing crossword puzzles, going fishing, driving a recreational vehicle or snowmobile, going boating, going hunting, going scuba diving, playing catch with a pet, playing peek-a-boo with an infant, listening to music, making music, and going to a rock concert are some of the many varied activities that people partake of in their leisure time. Many games and sports have their origins in friendly competition between workers. For example, the American sport of rodeo developed as a result of competition between cowboys as to who was the best rider, roper, and so forth. Below we briefly explore some observations regarding play, the psychology of leisure, and adjustment.

THE RELATIONSHIP OF WORK TIME TO LEISURE TIME

Like the motivation to work, the motivation to play can be very complex and resistant to simplistic explanations. One view of adult play is that it helps to relieve tension that has accumulated at work and elsewhere. An alternative view is that how one works and plays are completely independent of one another (Dubin, 1958; Kabanoff, 1980). Which view makes more sense to you from your own experience? If you are having difficulty with the answer to this question, you are probably not alone; either or both views may be correct. Perhaps there is no general rule that can be applied to all cases. Rather, as several researchers have concluded, differences in personality, motivation, perceptions, prior learning experiences, and other factors may all account for varying relationships between work and play (Kabanoff & O'Brien, 1980; Kando & Summers, 1971). Some people, for example, are extremely "job-centered." They give relatively little thought to vacation or other leisure activities, and express little need to vent any work-related frustration in play. At the other end of the spectrum are people who see work as a means to play. If these people were independently wealthy, they might not work at all. Somewhere between these two extremes are people who fit the description of a "work hard/play hard" type.

Some people view leisure as a time for personal growth. These people may use their leisure time in activities that others might consider work—reading, visiting museums, or taking a noncredit course. For other people, leisure time is time to "veg out," as they say— to loll on a beach or do anything at all regardless of its social value. These broad general-

leisure time

time spent engaging in a non-work/noncompensated activity.

izations regarding the respective role that work and play may occupy in one's life only begin to describe the complexities entailed in understanding the psychology of leisure (Neulinger, 1981). Moreover, for some people, many college athletes among them, the line between work and play can sometimes seem very thin (see Figure 14–8).

LEISURE TIME AND VACATIONING

In their study of the psychology of leisure travel, Edward J. Mayo and Lance P. Jarvis reported that Americans spend over 120 billion dollars annually on leisure-related activities, and more than half of those dollars are spent on domestic or international travel. Mayo and Jarvis (1981) discussed how the vacation destination one chooses, as well as how one gets there, may be a function of many varied factors. Perceptions are one important factor, including perceptions regarding the various airlines, hotel chains, and destination sites. Motivation to travel is another key variable. Some people travel for education and culture, while others travel for relaxation and pleasure. Learning factors such as generalization may enter into travel plans. For example, if you enjoyed the time you spent at *Disneyland* in Anaheim, you might also enjoy *Disney World* in Orlando or *EuroDisney* in France. Personality factors may enter into the decision as well. For example, a publication of the Canadian Government Travel Bureau (1971) describes Canadian Winter vacationers as "active," Spring vacationers as "reflective," and Autumn vacationers as "emotionally stable, passive." Also in that publication, air vacationers are described as "very active" and "very confident," train vacationers are described in terms as "reflective," "passive," and "aloof," and bus vacationers are described as "dependent," "apprehensive," and "sensitive." What kind of traveler are you, and what kind of vacation might be best for you?

ADAPTIVE AND MALADAPTIVE USE OF LEISURE TIME

Whether leisure time is used in travel, personal growth activities, "mindless" entertainment, or no activities at all is very much a matter of personal preference. Leisure time ideally provides a sense of renewal; for some people this may be achieved by exercising on a treadmill, for others, by swinging in a hammock. What you do not want is to have your leisure time work *against* you. Stated another way, you want to use your leisure time in a way that makes your life pleasant and easier, not unpleasant and harder. Consider in this context the case of Laurie Palmer, a mother, grandmother, and intensive care nurse for

FIGURE 14–8   MORE WORK THAN PLAY Kabanoff (1980) characterized leisure as, among other things, an activity that is performed in a nonwork context, personally meaningful, and performed in the absence of monetary compensation. On its face, playing college basketball may meet these as well as the other criteria listed by Kabanoff. But from the stress reflected in the faces of these Miami University of Ohio players, one would hardly conclude that these men are involved in leisure activity. The photo was snapped in the closing moments of their 68–63 loss to North Carolina in March 1992.

whom rollerblading is a preferred mode of aerobic exercise and tension release (see Figure 14–9). According to Hays (1992), after two previous clashes with police who had ordered her to skate on the sidewalk, not in the road, Palmer was arrested and charged with the misdemeanor of disorderly conduct. Palmer claimed that in the interest of pedestrian safety, it was not prudent for her to skate on the sidewalk. A representative of the In-Line Skating Association had argued in other such cases that the "transportation profile of somebody that's in-line skating is more like a person on a bicycle than a person on foot, in terms of speed, maneuverability, and ability to stop" (Cooper, 1992). In short, Palmer claimed that she had a right to roller-blade on the road. The police maintained that she represented a traffic hazard, and was violating the rights of motorists.

The Palmer case may not seem like a very important one in the grand scheme of all the things that are happening around us. Still, it is a useful reminder that leisure time is best spent in activities that will relieve stress, not add it. Continuing to skate on the road in defiance of the police orders could certainly cause a rollerblader a great deal of personal stress and difficulty. Could you think of a possible compromise in the Palmer case? What would you do if you were in her shoes (or rollerblades)? Would you continue to rollerblade in the street if this subjected you to arrest and a possible jail sentence?

RETIREMENT

The period of young adulthood is usually defined as ranging from the age of about 20 or so to 40. Some time about midway through that period, many adults will reassess their lives and careers (Levinson et al., 1978). This reassessment will typically entail an evaluation of the extent to which one's interests, abilities, values, and objectives are being fulfilled or have a reasonable chance of being fulfilled in the future (Havighurst, 1982). Women may be more apt to reconsider their priorities with respect to work and family (Craig, 1989). For some people, much of this period may be spent experimenting with various occupations. For others, such as people who began their work career in their late teens or early 20s in government jobs (such as the local fire department, the state police, or the military), the end of this developmental period may actually represent a new beginning. For them, it may be time to think about retirement. This is so because many government workers (as well as employees of private corporations having comparable benefits) are entitled to retire after 20 to 25 years of service. These employees may even be entitled to retire sooner if their employer has an early-retirement program in effect. In some private companies, early-retirement programs have been instituted not as an employee option, but as a cost-cutting measure designed to trim the payroll. So whether by choice, by chance, or simply by "putting one's time in on the job," the number of people who have become eligible for retirement in their 40s and 50s is probably higher today than it ever has been. Whether these people, or older people, can afford to retire is another matter. Let's briefly consider some of the costs and benefits of retirement from several perspectives.

THE COSTS OF RETIREMENT

From a financial standpoint, leaving the workforce may indeed be a costly proposition. While one's expenses either remain constant or rise, income drops from whatever the salary was while working to whatever the retirement pension is. The amount of money received from a retirement pension is typically some fraction of what the full-time pay was at the time of retirement. Further, inflation may eat away at the actual buying power of these pension dollars. A catastrophic illness can be financially devastating to savings (depending of course upon the quality of the individual's health coverage). The terms of retirement and early retirement programs differ from employer to employer. For some employers, such as the New York City police and fire departments, employees may retire with a pension as early as they desire after having put in some amount of time (say, 20 years) on the job. It sometimes happens, then, for example, that an employee who began working at such a job at the age of 21 is retired from that job by age 41. In other occupations, such as many teaching positions, the employee may be entitled to similar benefits except that there is a

FIGURE 14–9 ROLLER-BLADING AND THE RELEASE OF STRESS Laurie Palmer rollerblades an average of about 15 miles each day. Yet her clashes with police and their repeated prohibitions against her rollerblading in traffic might cause one to wonder how tension-relieving this practice can actually be.

retirement
1. cessation of working for compensation at a specific occupation, profession, or job.
2. cessation of a working-for-compensation lifestyle.

prohibition against receiving any pension until reaching some minimum retirement age (such as age 55). Thus when an individual "retires" without having reached this minimum retirement age, "retirement" may represent retirement in name only; usually the person must still work for a living.

In addition to financial costs, retirement carries with it social and psychological costs. The very word *retirement* carries with it connotations of inactivity and withdrawal. The verb *to retire* is synonymous with *to go to bed,* as in, "She retired for the evening." We also use the verb *to retire* in baseball jargon in which it means *to put out* (as in, "The pitcher retired the batter"). In other uses of the word, *to retire* is synonymous with *to go away*.

But in more ways than just the connotation of the word, retirement is in fact a time of withdrawing or moving away from well-established patterns in life. The camaraderie shared for years with fellow employees—at work, at a local spot after work, at parties, and at other times—suddenly ends. The role of company "insider" is abruptly exchanged for the role of company "outsider." One's self-image as a productive, contributing, useful member of society may transform to one that is far less desirable. In extreme cases, especially when retirement is accompanied by depression, retirees may see themselves as nonproductive, noncontributing, spent individuals who are a drain on public funds and societal resources. Careful preretirement planning can help prevent such postretirement depression. Counseling and courses designed to help retirees gradually make the transition from *employed* to *retired* typically focus on the formulation of new objectives and new activities to become involved in. In general, the objective is to help the individual to appreciate retirement as a next stage in life rather than to see it as a withdrawal from it.

THE BENEFITS OF RETIREMENT

Perhaps the most obvious benefit of retirement is the windfall of time the retired person has to engage in nonwork activities. Different people will use this time in vastly different ways (see Figure 14–10), while others may not really use the time at all, but simply try to pass it. In many cases, the difference between actively using one's time and merely trying to pass the time is the difference between a successful and an unsuccessful retirement.

Like most students, your thoughts may be preoccupied with many things, and retirement is not likely to be one of them. Your more immediate concerns might center on pulling a good grade in your psychology course, your social plans for Saturday night, or how to raise money for purchases you wish to make. Still, a thought or two, however fleeting, about your future retirement can be beneficial. Many of the activities you enjoy partaking of today may be the same activities you will enjoy partaking of in retirement. For example, if you enjoy playing tennis or golf, you might take a moment to visualize yourself happily playing tennis or golf in retirement. Giving an occasional thought to retirement far in advance of it, realistically planning for it when the time is right, and coming to look forward to it as it becomes imminent may well help diminish some of the potentially high costs cited above.

FIGURE 14–10 GETTING A KICK OUT OF RETIREMENT Retirement time can be play time. The retired man on the left pursues his passion for building and flying model planes. The women at the right, ranging in age from mid-50s to late 70s are part of an amateur dance troupe called the Calendar Girls, begun as an outgrowth of a dance class. The group charges $100 per performance to help defray the cost of transportation, costumes, and stereo equipment.

Erikson (1963) theorized that middle adulthood (about age 40 to age 60) is a time when many people begin a search for meaning in their lives. The meaning that they seek is twofold in that it concerns both themselves as well as future generations. "What have I done with my life?" "Has my being here made a difference?" These are the types of questions people may ask themselves in their search for a sense of what Erikson called **generativity**—*a sense that one's works will stand the test of time and positively influence future generations.* Such works may be done in the context of business life (as in the invention or development of a new product or process) or in nonbusiness pursuits. Retired people may be able to achieve a sense of generativity through personal participation in political groups, volunteer organizations, or by providing for monetary support of such organizations. One relatively common way of fulfilling one's needs for generativity is through the provisions of a will. People with children and/or grandchildren may also achieve a sense of generativity through teaching the children skills, helping them through some crisis, or helping to shape their system of values. Even if one has not satisfied one's generative needs during one's working days, retirement supplies one with the time to address these needs.

In this and the previous chapters in this unit, we have covered issues related more to interpersonal than personal adjustment. In the next and final chapter, we expand still further to consider the concept of adjustment from a global, environmental perspective.

generativity
according to Erik Erikson, a sense that one's work will stand the test of time and positively influence future generations.

SUMMARY

WORK Work is necessary for each of us to have the goods and services we want, and it is central to our sense of identity. Many different theories about why people work have been advanced. Ideally, matching an individual to a job entails matching the individual's personality, abilities, values, and interests to the demands and challenges of a particular position. Routes to getting hired, each with their own pros and cons, include job fairs, published want ads, unsolicited query writing, and networking with friends and family. Once one has been hired, some of the variables that may become important include productivity, the amount of job satisfaction and job stress experienced. *Unemployment* refers to the condition of being out of work as a result of factors beyond one's control. For most of us, it is easier to appreciate the negative physical and emotional stresses of work than the negative physical and emotional stresses of being out of work. Still, unemployment may bring with it serious consequences, such as severe emotional upset, physical symptoms and illness, sleep difficulties, drug abuse, child abuse, alco-

holism, and/or marital and family disruption. As in the treatment of depression, activity may be one of the best remedies for the adjustive demands and challenges of being unemployed.

PLAY In addition to other needs, we all have a need to entertain or amuse ourselves—that is, to play. Like the motivation to work, the motivation to play can be very complex and resistant to simplistic explanations. One view of adult play is that it helps to relieve tension that has accumulated at work and elsewhere. An alternative view is that how one works and plays are completely independent of one another.

RETIREMENT Retirement and the benefit of free time carries with it several costs, such as reduced income and the psychological and social consequences of being retired. Many of the decisions people make when they are younger will influence how they will feel about themselves in their later, retirement years.

Chapter 15

Adjustment and the Environment

O U T L I N E

Adjustment, as we have seen throughout this book, can be studied from different perspectives with diverse methods and many varied kinds of objectives. From the perspective of the individual, we can study, for example, the changes in thought, feelings, and behavior that accompany adjustive efforts across situations. From an interpersonal perspective, we can study, for example, the effect of different people and situations on adjustment. From a multicultural perspective, we can study, for example, adjustment of different cultural groups, across and within national, state, or local boundaries. In this chapter, our view of adjustment broadens considerably. To borrow a term from photography, we will "zoom out" from the close shot of people in the context of their immediate surroundings to a long shot of populations in the context of their planet. It is from this broader perspective that we can most meaningfully comprehend adjustment in its most global sense.

PSYCHOLOGY AND THE BIOSPHERE

To this point, we have focused primarily on the study of individuals and groups in various situations and cultural contexts. Yet the study of adjustment in the most general sense would seem to demand at least some consideration of another broad class of variables—variables which tend to be neither as readily available for research purposes as human subjects nor as geographically accessible as a local school, workplace, or shopping mall. This broad class of variables pertains to the earth's **biosphere**, or *the totality of the earth, including its land, water, atmosphere, and any element capable of sustaining life.* "Humankind has altered or transformed virtually every element of the biosphere," according to B. L. Turner (Turner et al., 1990), the director of a program at Clark University that is devoted to the study of how human beings have transformed the earth. Such alterations and transformations have had momentous consequences, some so negative that they may in turn necessitate very drastic and unpleasant forms of human adjustment in the future (see Figure 15–1).

HEALTH, QUALITY OF LIFE, AND ENVIRONMENTAL PSYCHOLOGY

The health and general quality of life of people all over the world depend in no small way on the health of the earth and the life-sustaining nature of its land, water, and atmosphere. Pages of reference citations could be cited to support a simple fact that every reader of these words knows intuitively: pollution of the air, land, and water can reap the most horrific consequences, ranging from anxiety, to disease, to loss of life (Travis et al., 1989). The mere threat of environmental contamination or catastrophe can cause extreme mental distress. It is not comforting to learn, for example, that many experts now believe that nuclear plants are vulnerable to terrorist bombings (Wald, 1993).

Our health and general quality of life is currently endangered by numerous threats to the biosphere (Meadows et al., 1992). "How can one person do anything about such threats?" you may ask. A first step in problem solving is to acquire a basic understanding of exactly what the problems are. Developing what has been called **environmental literacy** (*knowledge of basic elements of the environment including global threats to the stability of the environment*) is therefore a prerequisite to confronting an environmental crisis. Next steps entail action that will effectively address the environmental challenges. Before reading further, you may wish to check your own acquaintance with a variety of environment-related issues by answering the questions in the *Self-Assessment* exercise.

In the vast body of research literature contained in the field of psychology, the term *environment* has been used in diverse ways. It has decidedly *not* been used to refer to variables such as the "physical integrity of the ozone layer" or "the remaining square mileage of the world's tropical rain forests." For our purposes, let's define **environment** as *elements of one's surroundings that may influence the development, behavior and/or adjustment of organisms.* This rather broad definition can accommodate most of the varied ways *environment*

biosphere
elements of the earth that have a role in sustaining life, including the land, water, and atmosphere.

environmental literacy
knowledge of basic elements of the earth's environment, including global threats to its well-being.

environment
elements of the surroundings that may influence the development, behavior, and/or adjustment of organisms.

FIGURE 15–1 FUTURE ADJUSTMENT? An outer layer of ozone around the earth prevents people from being exposed to deadly ultraviolet radiation from the sun. In recent years, chemicals released into the atmosphere have greatly depleted the earth's protective ozone layer. Should such depletion continue, the environmental advocacy group Greenpeace offered this jarring vision of things to come. People would have to wear suits to protect them from harmful radiation whenever they ventured into the sunlight. Awareness of the diminished ozone layer as well as the other environmental hazards discussed in this chapter, may help prevent the need for such extreme "adjustment" in the future.

and related terms have been used in the psychology literature. For example, "candy used as a positive reinforcer," "father absent in the home," "second-hand smoke in the workplace," and "the physical intactness of the earth's ozone layer" all qualify as *environmental variables* according to this definition.

Many environmental variables share an important reality: they can significantly impact one's personal health, well-being, quality of life, and/or emotional adjustment. For this reason, whether environmental variables are millimeters or miles away in physical distance from an individual, they can have great relevance to personal adjustment.

Environment in the term *environmental psychology* has traditionally referred to the social or interpersonal environment. This is not surprising when you consider, as McAndrew (1993, p. 4) observed, that it is "to social psychology as much as to any other area that environmental psychologists trace their disciplinary origins."

THE SOCIAL PSYCHOLOGICAL TRADITION

Environmental psychology and its precursor *ecological psychology* (Barker & Wright, 1955) were terms used by social psychologists to refer to the study of how physical settings influenced behavior. In contrast to social psychologists who drew conclusions based on laboratory research, the pioneers of environmental psychology envisioned a discipline in which insights would be gained largely from observation of people in their natural habitats. From a contemporary perspective, it seems fair to say that environmental and ecological psychology as initially conceived had more kinship with the types of variables employed in the Hawthorne studies (see page 357) than they did with the types of variables discussed by contemporary environmentalists and ecologists. Since the coining of the terms *environmental psychology* and *ecological psychology*, a number of new specialty areas within the larger field of psychology has come into existence. Much that was written by the pioneers of environmental psychology—Roger Barker, Herbert Wright, and Paul Gump (1974, 1978)—might more properly be subsumed today in the literature of specialty areas such as community psychology, educational psychology, industrial/organizational psychology, or human factors psychology (see Figure 15–2 on page 415). **Community psychology** is concerned with *the study of people and their relationships to community institutions.*

community psychology
the study of people and their relationships to community institutions.

SELF-ASSESSMENT

The Environmental Literacy Test

Here are a dozen questions which you can use to informally gauge your knowledge about various aspects of the planet you live on as well as about some current environmental issues.

1. The current world population is about
   - a. 1 billion
   - b. 2 billion
   - c. 10 billion
   - d. 20 billion
   - e. 50 billion

2. It has been estimated that by the year 2050, the world population will be
   - a. 2 billion
   - b. 10 billion
   - c. 20 billion
   - d. 50 billion
   - e. 75 billion

3. Soil used in the croplands of the northeastern United States and some eastern provinces of Canada is considered to be
   - a. the highest quality in the world
   - b. useless for planting many crops like sugar beets
   - c. under stress
   - d. underutilized
   - e. capable only of growing radishes

4. The United Nations has estimated that each year an area of tropical forest disappears from the earth that is greater in area than
   - a. Florida
   - b. Puerto Rico
   - c. Canada
   - d. the Bronx
   - e. the Houston Astrodome

5. If all the water in the world amounted to 25 gallons, about this much water would be available for human use:
   - a. 1 gallon
   - b. 1 teaspoon
   - c. 1/2 gallon
   - d. 1/2 teaspoon
   - e. 10 gallons

6. The average worldwide catch of fish has increased from about 21.5 million tons in 1950, to this amount at present:
   - a. over 30 million tons
   - b. over 50 million tons
   - c. over 75 million tons
   - d. over 100 million tons
   - e. over 200 million tons

7. In a study conducted by *Consumer Reports* magazine, this percentage of the swordfish on supermarket shelves was found to be contaminated with mercury:
   - a. 22.5%
   - b. 45%
   - c. 67.5%
   - d. 90%
   - e. 8%

8. It has been estimated that every hour of every day, these many species of plant or animal life are made extinct:
   - a. 4
   - b. 3
   - c. 2
   - d. 1
   - e. 0

9. It has been estimated that this percentage of all species of plant and animal life existing today will be extinct within the next 30 years:
   - a. 20% will be extinct
   - b. 15% will be extinct
   - c. 10% will be extinct
   - d. 5% will be extinct
   - e. 1% will be extinct

10. Although Western medical experts can find no evidence to support the claim, a Chinese folk remedy
    - a. for impotence employs powdered rhinoceros horn
    - b. for eruptions under the toenail employs powdered tiger bones
    - c. for malaria employs powdered tiger bones
    - d. all of the above
    - e. none of the above

11. The tiger and the black rhinoceros are
    - a. two of many species that are at the brink of extinction
    - b. two of many species that overpopulate southern Africa
    - c. two of many species that Michael Jackson keeps in his yard
    - d. none of the above
    - e. (b) and (c) only

12. The United States Environmental Protection Agency has estimated that this many Americans will contract skin cancer in the next 50 years as a direct result of the thinning of the earth's ozone layer:
    - a. 1 million people
    - b. 4 million people
    - c. 8 million people
    - d. 10 million people
    - e. 12 million people

Answer Key to Self-Assessment: 1. b; 2. b; 3. c; 4. a; 5. d; 6. d; 7. d; 8. b; 9. d; 10. d; 11. a; 12. e

---

human factors psychology
the field in which psychologists are involved in designing working environments in which humans can perform to optimal levels of their abilities.

Human factors psychology has been characterized as *the field in which psychologists "are involved in designing working environments in which humans can perform to the optimal levels of their abilities"* (Smither, 1988, p. 8).

The social psychological heritage of environmental psychology is evident in contemporary publications. Environmental psychology was defined in a recently published textbook (*Environmental Psychology*), after social psychologist Harold Proshansky (1990), as "*the*

FIGURE 15–2 ENVIRONMENTAL PSYCHOLOGY, CIRCA 1950 As described by Barker (1990), Gump (1990), and others (for example, Wicker, 1979), environmental psychology had its beginnings with the founding of The Midwest Psychological Field Station in Oskaloosa, Kansas, in 1947. Social psychologists Roger Barker and Herbert Wright founded the field station in an effort to study "real people" in a "real-world" environment (Kaminski, 1989). Here one of the field station's observers takes notes regarding some "real children" at play.

discipline that is concerned with the interactions and relationships between people and their environments" (McAndrew, 1993, p. 2 emphasis in the original). McAndrew (1993, p. 2) wrote that, "Proshansky rightly points out every physical environment is also a social environment and that it is sometimes impossible to separate these two aspects of environments."

What some might describe as a new genre of environmental research is addressed to more global issues than that conducted by the pioneers of environmental psychology. Included, for example, are studies on topics such as psychological aspects of outdoor air pollution (de Boer et al., 1987; Evans et al., 1988; Rotton & Frey, 1984), indoor air pollution (Abrritti et al., 1992; Finnegan & Pickering, 1986; Samet et al., 1988); energy problems (Kempton et al., 1992; Neuman, 1986; Stern, 1992), and numerous other environment-related variables (Durlak & Reich, 1987; Grasmick et al., 1991; Hopper & Nielsen, 1991; Stern, 1992). The physical and behavioral correlates of environment-related sources of stress are being studied (Baum et al., 1983; Logue et al., 1981; Robertson et al., 1985; Shore et al., 1986; Stone & Levine, 1986), as are possible cultural differences in response to such stress (Palinkas et al., 1992). The correlates of variables such as environmentalism, personality, and politics have also drawn research attention (Ray, 1975, 1980; Steger et al., 1989; Stewart & Healy, 1986; Van Liere & Dunlap, 1981; Wiltfang & McAdam, 1991; Wysor, 1983). Compelling calls to provide students with more environment-related education have been made (Cortese, 1992; Weis, 1992; Yambert & Donow, 1986).

HEALTH AND ADJUSTMENT

People in this country are healthier than they have ever been and living longer than they have ever lived before. This happy fact not only masks a horrible reality but also obscures urgent adjustive challenges. As you may conclude as you read on, we are, in a sense, living on borrowed time and cannot be complacent about our collective health and well-being. Adjustment in the most global sense needs to be made if a healthy future is to be assured for generations to come.

For decades, humans have been making major changes for the worse to their land, water, and atmosphere. Usually, species that impair or destroy their own environments, including their food supply, can be expected to die off. However, given our unique intellectual and other endowments, human beings have evidenced an uncanny ability to adjust, even to the most aversive environmental changes. Despite the fact that the quality of many aspects of our biosphere, including the air we breathe, has generally worsened, the numbers of human beings on this planet has steadily increased, not decreased. This is so for many reasons, including advances in medical technology, nutrition, and other areas, which have in essence outpaced the deadly effects of environmental contamination.

Humans have a great capacity for flexibility and adjustment. We have fashioned elaborate communication, transportation, and other technologies that allow for great flexibility in terms of needed resources. In the past, however, such ingenuity has been a curse to most other forms of life, as well as to the biosphere in general. As one geographical area became depleted of wanted resources, another area was quickly targeted. Technology acted to render variables such as distance or climate no obstacle when it came to obtaining these needed resources. What was too often overlooked, however, were the consequences of such actions on other life forms and on the biosphere in general. Entire ecosystems were thoughtlessly destroyed in missions to extract one resource or another from the earth. The word **ecosystem** refers to *the environment and the organisms within it considered as a unit*. A related word, **ecology**, refers to *the relationship between the environment and organisms*. If timber was needed for lumber or other products, for example, little thought was given to the forest as an ecosystem—that is, a system of plant, animal, and insect life—and it was summarily cleared. Similarly, if there was a desire to raise a type of animal or plant life that was not native to a particular area, the decision to import the new species was typically devoid of any consideration regarding the existing balance of nature. In this context you may recall the imported gypsy moths and the inestimable damage they did to thousands of acres of trees (p. 61). In short, humankind's consideration of the value of ecosystems has historically been secondary to economic and related concerns—with the results in some instances being environmental havoc.

Current trends in worldwide population growth, exhaustion or pollution of resources, extinction of species, and other such environment-related factors have set off alarms in the minds of many scientists. As you will see as you read on, great concern exists about the earth's capacity to adapt to the demands placed on it. An environmental crisis having the consequence of a worsened quality of life for all living things is now a reality. The *Environmental Literacy Test* on page 414 provided some hints regarding various aspects of this crisis. More details, as well as some strategies for change, follow.

ecosystem

the environment and the organisms within it considered as a unit.

ecology

the relationship between the environment and organisms.

CRITICAL ENVIRONMENTAL CHALLENGES

As the population of the earth continues to grow, greater demands are placed on the earth to support this growth. Can the earth keep pace with the demands that are placed on it? Environmental experts disagree on this important question. Some have argued that humans are remarkably adaptive organisms who are capable of stretching what appear to be finite limits into near-infinite limits (Sinai, 1992). Others have argued, perhaps more persuasively, that the earth's capacity for growth, and human beings' capacity for change, is not infinite. Based on computer simulation, Meadows et al. (1992) predicted that if human beings do not make drastic changes in their environment-related behavior by the year 2030 or 2040 or so, the result will be a permanently impoverished environment and a generally lower standard of living. An increasing world population, decreasing croplands, a decreasing usable water supply, and the other factors briefly discussed below are the elements fueling environmentalists' concerns. At times, such problems may seem remote—problems that are "over there" and not really our own. All things considered, however, these problems do not have traditional geographic boundaries.

INCREASING POPULATION

In 1800, only about 1 billion people inhabited our planet (see Figure 15–3). Within the following 150 years, that figure had doubled. By 1950, better nutrition, health practices, and disease-fighting drugs and medical technology had combined to make a significant impact on life expectancies. Due to these factors, the worldwide population began to rise much more dramatically than it ever had in any other period in history. From 2 billion people in 1950, the population soared to an estimated 5.5 billion in 1992. By the year 2050, it has been estimated that the world population will be about 10 billion people.

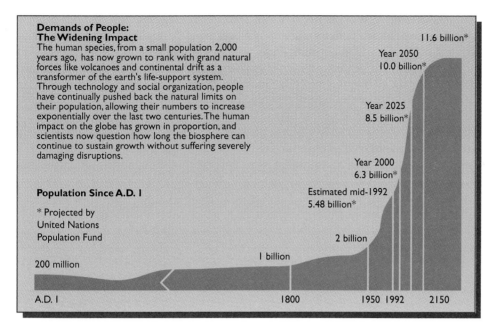

**Demands of People:
The Widening Impact**
The human species, from a small population 2,000 years ago, has now grown to rank with grand natural forces like volcanoes and continental drift as a transformer of the earth's life-support system. Through technology and social organization, people have continually pushed back the natural limits on their population, allowing their numbers to increase exponentially over the last two centuries. The human impact on the globe has grown in proportion, and scientists now question how long the biosphere can continue to sustain growth without suffering severely damaging disruptions.

Population Since A.D. 1

* Projected by
United Nations
Population Fund

200 million

1 billion

2 billion

Estimated mid-1992
5.48 billion*

Year 2000
6.3 billion*

Year 2025
8.5 billion*

Year 2050
10.0 billion*

11.6 billion*

A.D. 1   1800   1950 1992   2150

FIGURE 15–3   THE WORLD POPULATION It has been estimated that about 200 million people populated the earth in the year 1 A.D. According to United Nations Population Fund projections, the world population will be about 10 billion by the year 2050. Currently, the vast majority of the world's population, about 77%, is from developing countries. By the year 2025, it has been estimated that about 84% of the world's population will come from developing countries and 16% from industrialized nations.

Increasing population is not necessarily a change for the worse. In fact, depending on one's perspective, increasing population may be seen as a cause for celebration due, for example, to increased business opportunities. Increasing population only represents a change for the worse when it is out of control to the extent that the biosphere is incapable of supporting it. In many developed nations, **zero population growth** (*a rate of growth in which the number of people remains relatively stable*) has become the rule. The same cannot be said of many developing countries, where the per person birth rate may be twice (or more) that of many developed countries. In those countries, overpopulation threatens the health and quality of life for all people. A question increasingly posed by the people of more developed nations concerns the extent of the contribution they are willing to make, if any, to help in sorely overpopulated areas of the world.

zero population growth
a rate of growth at which the number of people remains relatively stable.

DECREASING CROPLANDS

Soil may become unsuitable for farming as a result of prior use of the land in farming or grazing or of other factors such as pollution. There are now large areas of the world, particularly in Africa and India, where the number of people in the area probably exceeds the ability of local agriculture to provide food for the people. In some areas where croplands are being actively cultivated, including the northeastern United States and much of Europe, the soil is very acidic and considered to be under stress. As a general rule, cropland (as measured on a per-person basis) is declining. Food production, however, by the grace of factors such as advances in agricultural methods, has been boosted. Yet, in many developing nations, such as most recently in Somalia, we have already witnessed the horror of people dying every day of starvation. Although temporary relief in the form of food and supplies has been shipped to Somalia and other developing countries, problems of distribution and crime still hamper such distribution efforts worldwide. For people with compassion, the crisis of mass numbers of people starving to death daily is not something that can easily be ignored. Agonizing decisions about where and how to apportion food resources—as well as who will pay for such apportionment—are already being made now, and may have to be made more frequently in the future.

DECREASING USABLE WATER SUPPLY

Stevens (1992, p. C7) observed that, "If all the water in the world amounted to 25 gallons, about half a teaspoon would be available for human use." Water is used extensively in agriculture and by industry, as well as more everyday uses such as washing, bathing, and drinking. In some areas of the world, water is in chronically low supply, and this shortage presents a great obstacle to farmers and would-be farmers. Beyond lack of rainfall and other such natural difficulties in obtaining fresh water, industry-driven pollution presents another problem. Since the early days of the industrial revolution, rivers were viewed by captains of industry as a convenient place to draw water and to discharge their industrial waste. Year after year of this type of pollution has reduced once mighty rivers to dried up river banks or whimpering streams. The sadness engendered by this environmental toll is reflected in one river-watcher's firsthand account of a recent look at two American rivers, the Colorado and the Mississippi:

> Because Mexicans have complained about the quality of the Colorado when it enters their country, the United States has erected a treatment plant. So the Colorado is monitored by computer, just like a patient on life support. Traces of pollutants are precisely regulated when they cross the border: if salinity [salt] levels, for example, are deemed excessive, engineers dilute the river with snowmelt released from dams upstream. And if the river is judged too pure, too clean, the technicians pump in runoff collected from fields in the Southwest. With everything under control, there is rarely a ripple. By most definitions the river has become a ditch.
>
> The currents of the lower Mississippi have the opposite problem: overflow. From my vantage point in downtown New Orleans, I had the impression the river could not just overrun its anguished banks but also burst through them from underneath. And for someone accustomed to the Mississippi in Minnesota, where the river is fiercely blue, the sediment-choked southern end is appalling. In New Orleans, having drained the fields and industries of the nation's midsection, the torrent moves almost as a single brown mass. The river's urgent force is menacing, as if the channel knows there should be no delay in burying its load deep in the sea. (Uehling, 1992, p. 35)

Polluted water causes marine life to either sicken or die. Fish may become sick from pollutants directly, or may consume other marine life that has consumed pollutants. The result is that humans who eat fish previously exposed to pollutants—however exposed—may well become ill. A 1991 survey of fish sold in supermarkets published by *Consumer Reports* indicated that 90% of the swordfish tested was contaminated with mercury, and 25% of the swordfish contained a toxic substance known as PCBs. Almost half of all the salmon tested contained PCBs. Clams were found to have high lead levels, and some even contained the poison arsenic. Although PCBs have been banned, these chemicals can be found in landfills. They find their way through the soil into rivers and eventually to the ocean. Once in the ocean, they act to kill fish by suppressing their immune system functions. Other effects of PCBs in fish include the suppression of reproductive function and the proliferation of infection.

INCREASING TEMPERATURES: GLOBAL WARMING

Scientists believe that the planet's climate is generally getting warmer. The warming is believed to be due to an increase of carbon dioxide gas in the atmosphere. Carbon dioxide gas in the atmosphere traps and holds heat. A great increase in the amount of carbon dioxide in the atmosphere has been recorded since the days of the industrial revolution. This is so because carbon dioxide is released into the atmosphere when fuels such as natural gas, oil, coal, and timber are burned. Continued widespread use of such fuels will lead to a warming of the earth's climate, many scientists believe. Such global warming may be disruptive at best, and catastrophic at worst. Projected consequences range from uncomfortable changes in climate to the transformation of fertile lands to dustbowls to the melting of polar icecaps. Some countries may disappear under water if global warming intensifies.

Another factor related to global warming and more carbon dioxide being released into the atmosphere is deforestation.

DECREASING TROPICAL FORESTS

extraction farming
the process of harvesting products from the land without destroying the land in the process.

For the most part, tropical forests exist in developing nations where they tend to be viewed not as ecosystems to be preserved but as economic resources to be exploited. Forests are sold for their wood, while their potential for what has been called **extraction farming** (*the* *process of harvesting products from the land without destroying the land in the process*) may be largely ignored. The loss of forests, tropical or otherwise, for any reason (such as clearing for home sites or cropland) or by any cause (such as forest fires or pollution) further contributes to global warming because trees capture and retain carbon dioxide. According to estimates from the United Nations, an amount of tropical forest that is greater in total area than the state of Florida disappears from the earth every year. Forests also contribute to the biosphere by holding soil in place and by providing a home for many different species.

DECREASING BIODIVERSITY

Entire species of life, both plant and animal, are either annihilated or endangered by many human endeavors (such as the deliberate clearing of forests to build housing), malevolent actions (such as acts of war by hostile nations), and accidents (such as forest fires). Edward O. Wilson, a science professor and curator at Harvard University's Museum of Comparative Zoology, has estimated that every hour of every day, 3 species are eliminated, and that 20% of the species existing today will be extinct within the next 30 years. Wilson (1992) tells us that there are many species as yet undiscovered, and that there are even new species still evolving. However, advanced technology has meant that the pace at which humans are destroying species is rapid. Today, tropical rain forests house about half of all of Nature's species and they are threatened by overpopulation and its consequences (such as the need for food-producing land, timber for housing, and so forth). Environment-related issues are often couched in the media as being obstacles to human progress (as in "Jobs versus the Environment" or "Housing versus the Environment" types of stories). When the environment is pitted in this manner against issues such as housing, or pocketbook issues such as jobs, the environment tends to lose. Politicians know this and most will seldom take a stand against economy-related issues in favor of environment-related ones. Yet the pitting of economic against environmental interests may at least in some instances be misleading; the two may be entirely compatible (see *A Question of Values* on page 420).

Perhaps of particular interest to psychologists is the fact that some species are being annihilated for little reason other than sheer superstition. For example, according to a widespread folk remedy in China, tiger bones are thought to be useful in treating conditions as diverse as ulcers, malaria, burns, and eruptions under the toenail. Powdered rhinoceros horn is believed by the Chinese to enhance male sexual potency. Such claims of medicinal value for tiger bones and rhinoceros horn are absolutely without merit, according to Western medical experts. Still, the tiger and the black rhinoceros are on the brink of extinction due, in part, to widespread demand in China for their bones and horns. In 1976, the estimated population of the black rhinoceros in the wild in Africa was 65,000. Today there are fewer than 2,000 of these creatures in the wild and they are fiercely hunted by poachers. In Africa, the world population of mountain gorilla has dwindled to between 600 and 650 and they are highly imperiled (Steklis, 1993). In our own country, the Steller sea lion was listed as endangered in 1990 (see Figure 15–4 on page 422). Unfortunately, the mere listing of a species as endangered is not sufficient to save it. By the time the species is so listed, its numbers may well have dwindled to the point where it cannot be saved. The United States Fish and Wildlife Service endangered species office has a backlog of 3,600 species that are candidates for extinction. Some have become extinct while on that waitlist or while bureaucrats debate whether they should be listed as endangered (Luoma, 1993).

CONSERVATION VERSUS UTILIZATION

A great controversy concerning endangered wildlife in Africa is brewing. If *an area of land is set aside for the purpose of conserving a particular species* (**conservation**), the land and the species may be viewed by the surrounding villagers as a white man's indulgence. Resentment spills over into acts of vandalism and poaching. An alternative to conservation has been a strategy called utilization. In **utilization**, *game parks are treated "not as museums but as local industries that generate income for the human residents through tourism, trophy hunting, sales of breeding stock to private game ranches, marketing of venison, and other ventures that enlist the locals as partners in preservation"* (Keller, 1992). In utilization, hunters might be

conservation
the practice of setting aside an area of land for the purpose of conserving a particular species. *Contrast with utilization.*

utilization
the practice of treating game parts as revenue producers for conservation through activities such as tourism, trophy hunting, and the sale of breeding stock to game ranches.

A QUESTION OF

Environment versus Economics?

There is a proverb that goes, "It's an ill wind that blows nobody good." Can you think of what that proverb means? How might that proverb be applied to the environmental dilemmas now plaguing the earth?

The proverb might be paraphrased as, "Something truly bad must happen for absolutely no one to benefit from it," or "Even in most catastrophes, there are some people who benefit." The proverb would seem to have applicability to the global environmental crisis. Whereas many people believe that the pitting of environmental interests against economic ones is a harsh reality of life, other people have found a way for environmental and economic interests to coexist. For example, air pollution limits in Japan and Germany are almost four times as strict as those in the United States, according to Moore (1992). Cleaning up the air in those countries, according to Moore, has helped Japan and Germany to become first and second in terms of having the cleanest and most efficient

power plants and steel mills. The distinction of producing cars with the best fuel efficiency also goes to Japan (Toyota), who is first in this area, followed by Germany (Volkswagen). Moore notes that pollution-cutting programs in Germany have led to healthy profits and little waste:

> The Germans have adopted regulations mandating a wide range of pollution-cutting measures from industries and citizens. One program requires car makers to pick up and recycle vehicles that in the U. S. would be junked. BMWs, Mercedeses and Volkswagens now roll off the assembly line with bar-coded parts to speed disassembly, sorting and recycling. Soon, this policy will be extended to computers and cameras, then to everything from cardboard boxes to yogurt containers . . . In six years, every power plant in the country is required to reduce air pollution by 90 percent, with most using scrubbers that remove acid rain-

causing pollutants. Scrubber byproducts (considered waste to be thrown away in the U.S.) are dried and made into gypsum board and construction mortar in Germany. The Germans, in other words, literally build homes out of pollution. The system is so successful that Knauf Gypsum, a German company, opened a plant in Britain with 1991 sales of $48 million . . . America, once the world's environmental leader, is now a follower. To claim otherwise is not only untrue but a disservice to our children. Sadly, it is they who will pay—with their health, their quality of life and their jobs. (Moore, 1992, p. 33)

Some may take issue with Moore's assertions, especially in states such as California, where pollution-cutting regulations and standards are among the toughest in the world. Also there has been movement on the part of some American companies to turn a profit in environmentally friendly ways. For ex-

charged a hefty fee to kill a member of an endangered species. As Keller (1992) put it, a big game hunter "might pay $100,000 for the chance to kill one of the planet's 2,000 surviving black rhinos." According to this plan, the black rhino to be killed would be one that is older and incapable of reproducing. The $100,000 would be used, in part, to provide protection for the younger rhinos. Already, such plans are in effect. Officials at African game preserves believe that utilization is a sound idea whose time has come. They may refrain from such practices more for appearance's sake than anything else. As one member of the African Wildlife Foundation has said, "Biologically there's nothing to lose. Politically, there's everything to lose."

INCREASING ULTRAVIOLET RADIATION

A layer of the earth's atmosphere called the stratosphere contains the chemical ozone. Ozone acts as a shield against the sun's harmful ultraviolet rays. If ozone were not in the stratosphere to shield us against the sun's harmful ultraviolet rays, the results would be catastrophic. Exposure to unscreened ultraviolet radiation would cause, among other things, skin cancer, eye problems (ranging from cataracts to blindness), and an overall weakening

ample, the McGaw company of Irvine, California, has pioneered the manufacture of environmentally safe intravenous bags for use by hospitals. The bags do not contain polyvinyl chlorides and can therefore be recycled. The company had revenue of $300 million in 1991, with two-thirds of that money coming from recyclable intravenous bags. A Connecticut firm called Environmental Data Resources (EDR) is also doing its share to try and make "an ill wind blow good." The company searches out records to determine where government and private toxic waste disposal, storage, or treatment sites are. The information is sold to companies that have an interest in knowing where such sites are, such as banks lending money to finance real estate deals. As of 1992, EDR's revenue was growing at upwards of 50% a month (Burrow, 1992).

Many opportunities exist for the development of new and environmentally safe technology. For example, as an alternative to asthma inhalers that contain ozone-depleting chemicals, dry powder inhalers have recently become available in Sweden and the Netherlands. Citrus-based solvents are gradually replacing those that contain ozone-depleting CFCs. And CFCs will one day be eliminated from home refrigerators, thanks to the development of solar technology, and systems that use water and alcohol, helium, or other alternative refrigerants.

Too often, an environment-versus-economics issue seems to raise questions about one's values. In truth, however, most of us value both economic and environment-related considerations. Joan Martin-Brown, chief of the Washington office of the United Nations Environmental Program, wrote that,

> The either-or options of jobs or the environment, economic growth or the environment, technology or the environment, are false dichotomies, intellectually bankrupt formulations of reality, which are as cruel in their effects as demanding that we operate in the world as if it were flat. Today there are enormous debts on the world's economic book reflecting the loss of ecosystemic capacities, and economic obligations requiring staggering amounts of money to reclaim nature's capacity...The environmental scientist is, today, the best hope to regenerate the world's economy. (Martin-Brown, 1992, p. 1102)

It is not always readily apparent, especially in the short-term, how the interests of the environment and jobs, the environment and economic growth, and the environment and technology are consistent with one another. Yet, sometimes it seems that too little effort is placed in seeing how such interests can be complementary, especially for the long term. After all, there will ultimately be little interest in economic issues if the earth is so depleted of its essential resources and integrity that its very ability to support human life hangs in the balance.

of our immune systems. It would be impossible to take a walk in the sunshine safely without 100% skin and eye coverage.

Chlorofluorocarbons (or CFCs) have been found to destroy ozone in the earth's stratosphere. CFCs used to be found in many aerosol products (hairspray, spray deodorants, spray paint, and spray cleaners) until their use was banned for such purposes in this country and Canada. However, spray products containing CFCs are still legally manufactured and used throughout much of the rest of the world. Further, CFCs and other ozone-destroying chemicals may sometimes be used in this country in the manufacture of food and drink containers, cleaning solvents (primarily used for industrial applications), auto air conditioning, and home refrigerators.

CFC takes about 20 years to rise to the stratosphere where the particles break apart and release chlorine, which destroys ozone. The result is a thinning of the earth's ozone layer, and an increase in ultraviolet radiation reaching the earth. Because CFC production peaked in the mid-1980s, we have yet to see the full impact of them on the earth's ozone layer—and on human health. Another source of ozone destruction are varieties of manufactured halon gas that are used in fire extinguishers. Although they are far less concentrated in the atmosphere than CFCs, halon gases may be 10 to 40 times more powerful

FIGURE 15–4 VANISHING SPECIES There are fewer than 7,000 tigers left in the wild throughout the world. They are fiercely hunted, with poachers even killing them in tiger preserves visited by tourists (Browne, 1992). As their numbers dwindle, the chances that males will mate with fertile females decline. A population of 140,000 sea lions in an Alaskan rookery has shrunk to an estimated population of 25,000. Mountain gorillas are hunted by poachers. As grotesque as it sounds, their heads are sought as souvenirs, and their hands are chopped off and sold as ashtrays.

than CFCs in destroying ozone. The chemical reaction between ozone and halon not only destroys the molecule of ozone, but acts as a catalyst to additional ozone-destroying chemical reactions.

The U.S. Environmental Protection Agency has predicted that over the next 50 years, 12 million Americans will suffer skin cancer as a direct result of the thinning of the earth's ozone layer. Worldwide, the potential impact of increased ultraviolet radiation could be enormous and multifaceted. In addition to taking a human toll, increased ultraviolet radiation will negatively affect animals, crops, trees, plants, and marine life, especially marine life that exists near the surface of the water. Phytoplankton, a minute form of life that is at the base of the fish food chain, is one such species that may be affected. Increased ultraviolet radiation may destroy phytoplankton. With reduced phytoplankton, the numbers of fish that eat phytoplankton may be reduced, as may the numbers of other fish, higher up the food chain, that eat fish that eat fish that eat phytoplankton. One consequence of reduced phytoplankton may therefore be reduced variety of fish for people to eat.

INCREASING ENERGY DEMAND AND AIR POLLUTION

Increasing demand for energy is a natural consequence of a growing population, particularly in developing nations. But what form of energy will be used to meet that demand, and what will the impact on the environment be? Various forms of energy exist, each form carrying with it various advantages and disadvantages. For example, wood was humankind's first source of energy and there was in abundant—usually nearby—supply for purposes such as heating and cooking. The situation changed dramatically at the time of the Industrial Revolution, when wood began to be used in other ways, including a process that produced metals from metal ores.

With forests rapidly being cleared of wood, other forms of energy, such as coal, began to enjoy widespread use for purposes such as cooking, heating, and transportation. Recoverable coal has always been in abundant supply in this country. However, the many benefits of this relatively inexpensive fuel source must be weighed against other concerns, such as those related to convenience, the environment, and health. When mined from below the surface of the earth, for example, care must be taken to protect the health of the miners, not only from the hazards of a mine collapse but also from the more long-term health risks that come with daily exposure to coal dust. Mining for coal below the surface of the earth may also affect the fertility of the soil above and the purity of the water supply that feeds nearby wells. Mining for coal at surface level using a process called strip mining can strip the affected area of fertile soil if great care and expensive techniques are not used. Interstate transportation of coal does not present a hazard, although storage of it may. Burning coal is thought to release sulfur and other impurities into the air in sufficient quantity to cause an environmental phenomenon known as "acid rain" (see Figure 15–5).

Earlier in the twentieth century, the lower cost and greater convenience of petroleum products, such as oil, natural gas, gasoline, and kerosene, made them the fuel of choice for home use. Currently, petroleum products represent the world's most-consumed energy source. However, neither the price nor the supply of the oil and natural gas that is used to make these products has been stable in recent years. The world's largest deposits of oil are in the Middle East, a politically unstable part of the world. In 1960, four oil-producing countries from that region, along with the oil-rich South American nation of Venezuela, formed the Organization of Petroleum Exporting Countries (OPEC). Since that time, OPEC, acting as a group or as individual member nations, has wrought havoc on the world's economy by fixing oil prices and by withholding or releasing for sale huge quantities of oil.

Not only have petroleum products proven to be unstable in price and supply; waste products from their production and burning pollute the air we breathe and other elements of the biosphere. Pollution from the refining of oil in this country was at its height in the early days of the industry. Technical expertise was in its infancy, and legal regulation was nonexistent. Today, the amount of petroleum-related pollution, mostly in the form of the toxic chemical sulfur discharged into the atmosphere, is highly regulated. Still, because it is expensive to remove sulfur from petroleum products, the sulfur waste content of spent petroleum products remains relatively high. In an effort to help keep its air clean in the face of millions of cars emitting billions of particles of sulfur and other pollutants, the state of California has enacted extremely strict emission standards with which manufacturers of new automobiles must comply. Beyond pollution caused by emissions from autos, furnaces, and other petroleum-burning sources, there are other potential sources of pollution associated with petroleum. It is highly volatile, and its transportation by land can be hazardous. In recent years, we have also witnessed how hazardous to the environment the transportation of petroleum products can be (see Figure 15–6 on page 424). Oil spills at sea can be not only devastating to ecosystems but also to human health (they may result in breathing, skin, and other problems) and human relationships (see *Cultural Close-Up*).

FIGURE 15–5 THE EFFECTS OF ACID RAIN Automobiles burn gasoline to drive their engines. Power plants burn coal and/or other fuels to provide electricity. The waste products of such combustion, as well as other sources, spew environmentally harmful chemicals such as sulfur dioxide into the atmosphere. These deadly chemicals react with sunlight, moisture, and other elements of the atmosphere to produce precipitation that is very high in sulfuric acid and other acids. This "acid rain" and "acid snow" can be highly corrosive, as illustrated by the effects on the stone in this supporting column of Chicago's Field Museum.

FIGURE 15–6   DEATH IN THE WAKE OF AN OIL SPILL The Shetland Islands near Scotland are internationally known for the soft, fine wool that is sewn into Shetland sweaters. In January 1993, the Islands were the site of an oil spill which endangered not only their sheep but also wildlife, including birds and salmon, an important part of the local economy. A tanker carrying 26 million gallons of oil ran aground near the cliffs of one of the islands, and began spewing its cargo. The oil fouled the pastures where the sheep feed and contaminated the water and beaches where birds, seals, fish, and other wildlife live. Within three days of the accident, over 500 birds were found dead and over 100 were injured (Schmidt, 1993).

C L O S E - U P

Environmental Disaster and Cultural Group Membership

On March 24, 1989, the Exxon supertanker *Valdez* ran aground in Alaskan waters. Within hours, thousands of gallons of crude oil were pouring into Prince William Sound, polluting the water, polluting beaches, and in general, threatening the region's ecosystem. Palinkas and his colleagues (1992) observed that the environmental disaster also took a human toll throughout the affected region, as reflected by a significant rise in visits to community clinics for medical and mental health care. A similar rise in physical and mental health symptoms had been observed in the wake of other disasters (Baum et al., 1983; Logue et al., 1981; Robins et al., 1986; Shore et al., 1986).

Palinkas et al. (1992) examined differences in stress, coping, and depressive symptoms after the Exxon *Valdez* oil spill as a function of ethnic differences. They wondered what differential effect, if any, the spill would have on native Alaskans versus people of Euro-American origin. Since these researchers did not have any baseline

(pre-*Valdez* disaster) on the two groups of interest, they could not draw cause-and-effect conclusions about what they found. However, they interpreted their findings as suggesting that cultural differences may play an important role in determining the psychosocial impact of such a disaster. The oil spill probably had a greater impact on the natives as compared to the Euro-Americans in the sense that it impacted not only subsistence activities (such as fishing for food) but also all of the cultural and social traditions that are associated with such activities (Fienup-Riordan, 1983). The impact of the oil spill could not solely be measured in economic terms. Rather, it impacted on the affected native Alaskans' sense of identity. As one native Alaskan put it,

> When we worry about our subsistence way of life, we worry about losing our identity . . . it [subsistence] is that spirit that makes you who you are, makes you think the way you do and act the way you do and how you

perceive the world and relate to the land. Ninety-five percent of our cultural tradition is now subsistence . . . it's what we have left of our tradition. (Palinkas et al., 1992, p. 292)

Another finding from the Palinkas et al. study concerned the relationship between stress and extra income earned by native Alaskans for participating in clean-up operations. The influx of cash resulted not only in a significant increase in household income but in an increase in stress as well. The increased money, among other things, served to socially differentiate the·workers from their brethren who were not employed in the clean-up and who did not profit economically. A similar phenomenon had been observed in the late 1970s and early 1980s when an influx of cash derived from commercial salmon fishing enriched some members of a native community that had formerly been relatively homogeneous in an economic sense (Palinkas, 1987).

Processing of petroleum products may cause sickening, acrid odors to emanate from the grounds of the oil refinery into neighboring residential neighborhoods. In some instances, the damage caused by an oil refinery near a residential area has gone beyond acrid odors (see Figure 15–7).

Alternatives to petroleum products and coal are currently available and may one day replace these two natural resources as the primary source of the world's energy. More on these alternatives will be presented later in the chapter.

"SICK BUILDINGS"

New terms reflecting greater sensitivity to the problems of our indoor environment have come into our vocabulary in recent years. The term **sick building** refers to *a structure, usually a non-industrial office building or complex, that is known to be or is capable of making people who work in it ill.* The term **sick building syndrome** refers to *the physical problems suffered by people as a result of working in, or otherwise being exposed to, the indoor environment of a sick building.* Some of the specific types of physical problems that have been reported singly or in combination are headaches, dizziness, fatigue, skin rashes, nausea, wheezing, sinus congestion, and irritations of the eye, nose, and throat (Finnegan et al., 1984; Robertson et al., 1985). People who exhibit this syndrome become sick shortly after entering a sick building, and typically recover a few hours after leaving it. They do not exhibit the symptoms when they are away from the building for prolonged periods of time such as during business trips, weekends, holidays, or vacations.

Exactly what causes people to become sick from sick buildings is not known. Ventilation, insulation, illumination, carpeting, pollution of outside or indoor air, indoor temperature and humidity, even psychosocial factors have been explored as possible causes (Abrritti et al., 1992; Finnegan & Pickering, 1986; Samet et al., 1988; Skov et al., 1989), although the causes may vary in different sick buildings. It may be that stringent building codes prompting energy efficiency enacted during the time of the OPEC oil embargo of 1973 were too restrictive in terms of allowing fresh air into buildings. Whatever the cause, the problem appears to be widespread. According to a senior health scientist with the Occupational Safety and Health Administration, from 800,000 to 1.2 million buildings in the United States may be classified as sick, and from 20 million to 70 million people may be affected as a result ("On Healthy Indoor Air," 1992). James E. Woods, a professor of building construction at the Virginia Polytechnic Institute, has estimated that the cost of sick buildings in terms of lost worker productivity runs into tens of billions of dollars (Shaman, 1992).

sick building
a structure, usually a nonindustrial office building or complex, that is known to make, or is capable of making, people who work in it ill.

sick building syndrome
a constellation of respiratory and other types of problems suffered by people as a result of working in, or otherwise being exposed to, the indoor environment of a sick building.

ADJUSTMENT IN THE GLOBAL SENSE

For people who have never before seriously thought about environmental issues, the exposure to all the weighty issues we have presented in this chapter may be a bit overwhelming. Unfortunately, most of us have a great deal of (depressing) things to learn about

FIGURE 15–7 A CASE OF ENVIRONMENTAL CONTAMINATION These people represent some of the 400 families who live near an oil refinery in Ponca City, Oklahoma. As a group, the families brought a lawsuit against the oil refinery company, which they claimed had contaminated the environment. When testing confirmed that cancer-causing agents had seeped into the water table around the refinery, the oil company offered monetary settlements to its neighbors in return for their moving away. Although the total dollar amount paid out by the oil company has not been made public, it was estimated to be between 23 and 27 million dollars (Suro, 1990).

our biosphere. However, it is precisely because people do have such a marvelous ability to change, adjust, and adapt their behavior to a wide range of situations that there is cause for optimism. Some of the things that can be done and already are being done in the areas of education, research, and intervention are discussed below.

EDUCATION

A conservationist from the nation of Senegal named Baba Dioum has said, "In the end we will conserve only what we love, we will love only what we understand, and we will understand only what we are taught." If Dioum is correct, the key to conservation in the broadest sense—that is, conservation of our biosphere—lies in education. Awareness of the concerns about the environment that need to be addressed is a prerequisite to constructive attitude and behavior change. Education about environmental issues can take place formally or informally.

FORMAL EDUCATION

Formal education in environmental issues is offered at many universities and professional schools, even in grade schools. Yet there has been a growing feeling on the part of many academicians that a much greater commitment to the spread of environmental literacy is required if the biosphere is to survive, let alone prosper. In October 1990, a meeting of educators took place in the town of Talloires, France. The meeting was attended by 22 university presidents from 13 countries, as well as by internationally respected environmental leaders. Its purpose was to consider ways that universities could contribute to an environmentally sustainable future. The meeting concluded with the drafting and signing by all 22 of the university presidents of the Talloires Declaration, a document that set forth in writing a strong commitment to respond to what was described as an "urgent challenge." Soon after that meeting, the Declaration would be endorsed by a growing list of over 100 university presidents from over 30 countries, as well as by the Conference of European Rectors (an organization that represents nearly 500 university heads in Europe). An excerpt from the Talloires Declaration is reprinted in Figure 15–8.

A meeting in San Antonio, Texas, in August 1991 brought together directors and faculty members of undergraduate environmental studies programs from major research centers, state institutions, and private colleges and universities throughout the United States. Although coming from diverse settings, the participants were agreed on a number of points. The educators agreed that a need existed for a commitment to educate the general student population about environmental issues. They also agreed that there was a need to educate environmental science majors. One participant at that meeting, Judith S. Weis, observed that the number of students in environmental science programs has grown rapidly in recent years, and that the growing enrollments "call for a greater variety of courses, more faculty in both traditional and new subjects, and more opportunities for fieldwork" (Weis, 1992, p. 1297). Weis further observed that graduates of environmental science programs are uniquely qualified and have a number of employment options open to them in government agencies, consulting firms, and nonprofit advocacy organizations.

The dean of environmental programs at Tufts University, Anthony D. Cortese, is a strong advocate of environmental literacy as a first step towards constructive behavior change. Cortese (1992, p. 1110) believes that, "the diverse and diffuse nature of human activities that are transforming the environment clearly requires that society use every possible tool to change the behavior of individuals and institutions." Towards this end, society will have a great need for environmentally literate people from many different backgrounds:

> Demographers are needed to understand the trends in population growth and to develop the strategies to stabilize the population at levels that are environmentally and economically sustainable. Attorneys and policy specialists are needed to develop government and industry policy and laws to protect the environment. Scientists are needed to understand the natural world, the effects of human activity on the environment, the fate and transport of pollutants in the environment, and the efficacy of environmental improvement strategies. Health specialists should help understand the effects of pollution on human health

FIGURE 15–8   THE TALLOIRES DECLARATION

University heads must provide the leadership and support to mobilize internal and external resources so that their institutions respond to this urgent challenge. We, therefore, agree to take the following actions:

1. Use every opportunity to raise public, government, industry, foundtion, and university awareness by publicly addressing the urgent need to move toward an environmentally sustainable future.
2. Encourage all universities to engage in education, research, policy formation, and information exchange on population, environment, and development to move toward a sustainable future.
3. Establish programs to produce expertise in environmental management, sustainable economic development, population, and related fields to ensure that all univeresity graduates are environmentally literate and responsible citizens.
4. Create programs to develop the capability of university faculty to teach environmental literacy to all undergraduate, graduate, and professional school students.
5. Set an example of environmental responsibility by establishing programs of resource conservation, recycling, and waste reduction at the universities.
6. Encourage the involvement of government (at all levels), foundations, and industry in supporting university research, education, policy formation, and information exchange in environmentally sustainable development. Expand work with nongovernmental organizations to assist in finding solutions to environmental problems.
7. Convene school deans and environmental practitioners to develop research, policy, information exchange programs, and curricula for an environmentally sustainable future.
8. Establish partnerships with primary and secondary schools to help develop the capability of their faculty to teach about population, environment, and sustainable development issues.
9. Work with the U.N. Conference on Environment and Development, the U.N. Environment Programme, and other national and international organizations to promote a worldwide university effort toward a sustainable future.
10. Establish a steering committee and a secretariat to continue this momentum and inform and support each other's efforts in carrying out this declaration.

and advise the public on strategies to reduce health hazards. Engineers are needed to develop technologies and products that will minimize the generation of pollution and waste and restore contaminated environments. Economists are needed to evaluate the costs to society of pollution and resource destruction, as well as to assist in the allocation of resources needed for environmental improvement. Geographers and planners are needed to develop socially, culturally, politically, and economically appropriate solutions to regional, U.S., and worldwide environmental problems. (Cortese, 1992, pp. 1109–1110)

In all probability, curriculum requirements regarding coverage of environmental issues as early as grade school will one day be a nationwide reality. In developing nations, the need is currently most urgent for education related to topics such as birth control, agricultural production, and agricultural and biological conservation. In developed nations, where an informed citizenry is so critical to the survival of the biosphere, there is a crucial need for exposure not only to the everyday bits and pieces of our various environmental dilemmas but also for a basic understanding of how these parts relate to the whole.

INFORMAL EDUCATION

For adults, informal environmental education is available primarily in the form of presentations in the print (newspapers, books, magazines) and electronic (television, radio) media. Other possible sources of informal environmental education range from lectures organized by environmental advocacy groups to environmentally oriented recreational activities (such as whale-watches).

A growing number of resources are becoming available to help parents educate their children about environmental issues. For example, there is a trend in the manufacturing of children's toys to be not only environmentally sound for disposal but also environmentally educational. One manufacturer called the Nature Company, for example, distributes nationally sold toys with names like *The Ecology Kit* and *Earthlab*. *The Ecology Kit* makes tasks like measuring household water usage fun, while *Earthlab* helps children understand topics as complicated as acid rain. Jigsaw puzzles feature varieties of endangered species. Games that teach environmental lessons are also proliferating. In *The Green Game* you win by answering environment-related questions correctly. The object of the *Captain Planet and the Planeteers* game (manufactured completely from recycled materials) is to clean up environmental disasters caused by villains with names like "Sly Sludge."

In addition to toys and games used as teaching tools, there are museum and other institutional exhibits in many areas of the country offering environmental themes and tours. A growing number of environmental themes are also in evidence in fiction and nonfiction children's books. For example, *Hey! Get Off Our Train* (Burningham, 1990) is a delightful tale that introduces children to endangered species. *Miss Rumphius* (Cooney, 1982) is about a woman who acts on her grandfather's suggestion to beautify the world. Children will also be entertained as well as educated by books such as *Antarctica* (Cowcher, 1990) and *Rain Forest* (Taylor, 1992).

RESEARCH

If an environmentally sustainable future is to be realized, research in any of many diverse academic areas—agriculture, animal husbandry, energy, marine biology, molecular biology, manufacturing, mineralogy, and psychology, to name but a few—will almost certainly play a key role. Let's take a brief look at two types of research from an environmental perspective: technological research and behavioral research.

TECHNOLOGICAL RESEARCH

The future challenges for technological research are many. A partial listing of these challenges would include the following:

- the challenge of developing more and more products that are made of recyclable materials, not materials that will one day be destined for landfill mountains;
- the challenge of developing refrigeration and other materials that do not rely on ozone-depleting chemicals;
- the challenge of developing safe and effective methods of toxic and nuclear waste disposal;
- the challenge of developing highly fuel-efficient engines and machines, or engines and machines that run on plentiful or renewable forms of energy;
- the challenge of ending air, land, and water pollution from a variety of sources ranging from pesticide use to the dumping of industrial wastes; and
- the challenge of adapting to the consequences of global warming.

Yet even the most spectacular technological advances, in these or other areas, have their limits. For example, research is capable of showing the way to restoring fertility to soil and increasing crop yields. No amount of research, however, can ever restore extinct animal or plant species that once thrived on that soil. If we in fact value biodiversity, other kinds of research—behavioral research—complemented by other strategies, such as legislation having strong enforcement contingencies, are all needed to help cut everyday losses in the biodiversity that presently exists.

BEHAVIORAL RESEARCH

A growing number of psychological studies have enriched our understanding of how people from different segments of society perceive and respond to environment-related issues and phenomena. Researchers have helped us to better understand college students' perceptions and attitudes regarding the environment (Wysor, 1983), citizens' responses to unanticipated sources of environmental stress (Stone & Levine, 1986), and the role of psychological variables such as shame and embarrassment in deterring noncompliance with environment-related legislation (Grasmick et al., 1991). Stern (1992) provided an overview of psychological findings with respect to energy conservation and the implications of those findings for energy policy. From Neuman's (1986) exploration of the role of values in commitment to energy conservation we are surprised to learn that values do not necessarily play as dominant a role as one might have thought. Other research has focused on aspects of the measurement of environmental concern (Ray, 1975; Van Liere & Dunlap, 1981), the role of personality development in shaping political commitment (Stewart & Healy, 1986), the possible role of self-perception in engaging in pro-environment behavior (Hopper & Nielsen, 1991), and the social costs and benefits of environmental activism (Wiltfang & McAdam, 1991).

Psychological studies addressed to the problem of air pollution suggest that people may mistakenly rely on visual cues to evaluate air quality (Barker, 1976) and that pollution may impair performance on complicated tasks (Weiss, 1983). There is also evidence to suggest an association between higher amounts of air pollution and higher degrees of measured anxiety (Evans et al., 1988), increased aggression (Rotton et al., 1979), decreased interpersonal attraction (Rotton et al., 1978), increased admission rates to psychiatric hospitals (Briere et al., 1983; Stahilivetz et al., 1979), increased crime (Rotton & Frey, 1985), and increased 911 calls (Rotton & Frey, 1984).

Behavioral research better equips us for designing strategies of effective and constructive behavior and attitude change. There is some research to suggest, for example, that it is individuals having a high **internal locus of control**—*the belief that they themselves, as opposed to others or chance, can influence outcomes*—who are more likely to be actively involved in environment-related issues. If this is the case, perhaps we need to think about ways to environmentally empower people, that is, to make them believe and feel that their actions can make a difference. In one Dutch study, it was found that angry callers to a telephone hotline on air pollution were more desirous of more information about air pollution than a matched group of noncallers. The noncallers tended to rationalize, deny, or otherwise avoid the problem (de Boer et al., 1987). If this is the case, perhaps we need to think about ways to make people more aware, if not angry, about environmental issues, thus better setting the stage for constructive action.

Behavioral research can help us to plan strategies and design techniques that will effectively modify widespread behavior patterns that are environmentally maladaptive. For example, based on studies involving the classical conditioning of aversions to taste (Garcia & Koelling, 1966), Gustavson et al. (1974) demonstrated how learning principles might be brought to bear on real-life animal control problems. In this case, the experimenters made coyotes ill by providing tainted sheep carcasses for them to eat from. Once having been made sick from the tainted sheep, coyotes no longer stalked sheep as a food source. Because the coyotes stopped stalking their sheep, farmers stopped killing coyotes. All things considered, making coyotes temporarily sick in an effort to keep their species alive provided a very humane solution to a very difficult problem.

Environmentally-oriented behavioral research can help us to achieve a better general understanding of how people relate to their environment and how the problems we face are conceptualized in the minds of individuals. In this context, Martin-Brown (1992) reminds us that while the environmentally destructive impact of technologies associated with war are obvious, the equally destructive impact of many peace-time technologies, including technologies that produce simple consumer goods—but impact negatively on the environment—are not well understood. Perhaps behavioral research can help us better understand the public mind-set with respect to such environmental issues.

internal locus of control
a personality variable relating to the degree people believe that they control their own fate.

INTERVENTION

In addition to education and research, action is also urgently necessary to ensure our environmentally sustainable future. Below we briefly survey some of the actions that can be taken by governments, business, groups of people, and individuals.

GOVERNMENTAL INTERVENTION

Through its laws, regulations, policies, incentive programs, and international treaties and agreements, government has immense power to influence what the future face of the earth will be like (see Figure 15–9). This does not mean, however, that it is always easy

FIGURE 15–9 PRESERVING A PIECE OF THE ENVIRONMENT The Key Largo National Marine Sanctuary in Florida, like our national parks, is there for all of us to enjoy. The sanctuary was established to protect the only living barrier reef in the United States. The reef contains beautiful coral, tropical fish, and exotic underwater plant life. Laws protect the sanctuary from divers who chip off pieces of the coral for souvenirs, boats that drop anchor on it, and other such threats. Here, a sanctuary officer signals a diver who unlawfully touched the coral to surface. The offending diver will be issued a ticket that carries with it a monetary fine ("Undersea Police," 1990).

to discern what the "right" laws, regulations, policies, and incentive programs are. Nor does it mean that even if the "right" laws, regulations, policies, and incentive programs were known that the government will always be able or willing to go against existing interests and institute them. For example, expectations were high during the Jimmy Carter presidency (1977–1981) that alternative energy sources, such as solar energy (energy from the sun) or wind energy (as produced by windmills), would be encouraged by the government by means of incentive programs. At that time, the nation was reeling from the shock of long gasoline lines caused by oil shortages resulting from an OPEC-sponsored oil boycott. However, the comprehensive energy program that was signed into law during the Carter administration supported private energy development, including nuclear sources of energy. There was little incentive to develop solar, wind, or other such nondepletable energy sources. The federal government's support of nuclear energy has been increasingly questioned through the years by consumer and environmental advocacy groups.

International cooperation is necessary to address many of the environmental problems now plaguing the earth. When international cooperation is agreed to, and the nations involved deliver on their pledges, dramatic results can sometimes be seen. For example, in a 1987 agreement that is referred to as the Montreal Protocol, the United States and 22 other nations agreed to halt completely the production of ozone-destroying halon gases by the year 2000. The Protocol set forth a schedule for decreased production of these gases. As of 1992, a study of the rate of halon accumulation in the earth's atmosphere suggested that the rate was about half that of 1987—a very favorable finding according to many environmentalists. However, since new quantities of halon gas may be stockpiled, and since old, stockpiled quantities of the gas may be released, it is important to keep in mind that we are not out of the woods yet. All things considered, however, the Montreal Protocol, according to one scientist, has been "politically and environmentally an extraordinary success story" ("An Easing of Threat," 1992).

To be effective, international treaties affecting the environment must be signed by *all* relevant parties. For example, it would do no good for the United States and England to enter into a pact to ban whaling for certain species of whale if other whaling nations, such as Japan and Norway, did not also enter into the agreement. Unfortunately, in the area of nuclear weapons testing, there are ample agreements between the United States and the former Soviet Union, but few agreements between the United States, the former Soviet

Union, and other countries that have nuclear weapon capability such as China and India. In 1990, Washington and Moscow signed a treaty limiting underground tests of atomic bombs to nuclear devices that have a yield of 150 kilotons. China, not a party to that treaty, conducted an underground nuclear test in May 1992 with a device that was estimated to have a yield of 1,000 kilotons (one megaton). For comparison purposes, a 150 kiloton bomb has about 70 times the explosive power of the atomic bomb that was dropped on Hiroshima during World War II. As reported by Crossette (1992), "The Chinese test comes on the heels of persistent reports that Beijing is selling missile technology to Middle Eastern nations..." If the reports are correct, the Middle Eastern nations that China has been selling to will, or already now have, nuclear weapons capabilities. Equally ominous in this regard is North Korea's withdrawal from a treaty it signed to halt the spread of nuclear weapons (Holmes, 1993). The withdrawal has prompted its neighbor and longtime foe, South Korea, to debate whether it should begin work on its own nuclear bomb (Sanger, 1993).

CORPORATE INTERVENTION

Often, America's corporations are depicted in the news media as being on the wrong side of environmental issues—dumping wastes into rivers or manufacturing products that are environmentally detrimental. Perhaps that is so because it is difficult to get publicity for engaging in environmentally sound policies. Yet many companies are becoming environmentally distinguished corporate citizens of the world. Corporations are developing environmentally "friendly" policies, such as using only recyclable packaging, paper, and other products where possible and instituting energy-saving policies (such as ride-share programs). Ben & Jerry's Homemade, Inc., an ice cream manufacturer based in Vermont, donates a portion of is pretax profits to environmental causes. The Coca-Cola Company and its subsidiary brands (such as *Minute Maid* juices) frequently become involved in proenvironment causes. One such project was a tree-planting program in Redwood National Park in California. Moosehead Breweries of Canada was involved in a promotion whereby, upon the request of the individual consumer, it would donate $1 to the National Fish and Wildlife Foundation for every six-pack of *Moosehead* brand beer sold (with a minimum guaranteed contribution of $100,000). A number of corporations have sponsored various kinds of environmental education programs in Scholastic Magazines. For example, the S. C. Johnson Company sponsored a series called "The Living Planet," and the Procter and Gamble Company sponsored a program called "Waste Not." Scholastic Magazines likes to think that such corporate-sponsored environmental awareness programs help an estimated 23 million children to improve not only their grade-point average but their "green-point average."

Corporate America, and more specifically pharmaceutical companies, are most likely to be the savior of the world's tropical forests—this because it is probably in the companies' own best interest to save this precious natural resource. Plants from tropical forests yield valuable medicinal products—so valuable that forest land is thought to be worth more intact than cleared for purposes such as farming or the sale of timber (Dold, 1992). Here is yet another instance when a long-term economic interest is pitted against a quick short-term one while the health of the environment hangs in the balance.

GROUP INTERVENTION

Writing in the early 1970s, psychologist George Albee observed that a dehumanization of the physical environment goes hand-in-hand with a dehumanization of the social environment. Albee (1973, pp. 34–35) wrote of "morally destructive forces" responsible for the pollution and destruction of the environment, and the transformation of cities into a "hideous blight." He argued that we have been "proselytized and propagandized into thinking that wasteful, meaningless consumption is the highest end of living," and that such a philosophy devalues interpersonal relationships. The products of such thinking, according to Albee, are "dehumanized and irrational consumers unresponsive or refractory to violence and suffering whose fragmented emotional lives lead increasing numbers to go out of control."

In a sense, Albee's words have been prophetic. Yet in the relatively recent past, we have begun to witness a grass-roots upsurge of interest in what might be termed "morally constructive" forces. There has emerged on the scene hundreds of new citizens groups whose philosophy is anything but wanton consumerism and whose mission it is to save the environment. Joining more established advocacy groups such as the Sierra Club and the Audubon Society have been groups such as American Rivers, Inc., the Environmental Defense Fund, Earth First, Friends of Conservation, Friends of the Earth, and the World Wildlife Fund, to name but a few. The groups differ widely not only in the types of causes they support, but in the methods they use (see Figure 15–10).

When it comes to advancing environmental causes, however, perhaps the most influential group is ultimately consumers. By supporting environment-friendly products or services, and by not supporting products or services that are environmentally harmful, consumers can send a powerful message for real change in environment-related policy. Consider in this context the boycott urged by the Humane Society of the United States (HSUS) in the matter of Norway's violation of a 1986 International Whaling Commission (IWC) order for a worldwide moratorium on all commercial whaling. The IWC's order came in response to studies that showed that various species of whale were threatened with extinction. Whether there is truly a need to kill whales is open to question. Whales once served as a source of meat, oil, and other such products. However, such products are today more plentiful and more cheaply obtained from other sources. The HSUS believes that Norway's motivation to begin whaling anew may have to do with the fact that whale meat is prized by the Japanese and it can sell for $200 or more a pound in Japanese markets. According to the United States government, Norway violated the IWC order in 1992 by conducting whaling under the guise of scientific research (HSUS, 1993). The HSUS responded to Norway's violation of the IWC's order with a "No way to Norway" campaign urging consumers to boycott everything from Jarlsberg cheese to Norwegian Cruise Lines to various Norwegian fish products, such as salmon and sardines. Short of military intervention, which will probably not happen, the only action that will compel violators of international agreements to rethink their actions is economic in nature.

FIGURE 15–10   TAKING A STAND BY SITTING DOWN Members of an environmental group called Earth First use techniques such as sit-ins at logging sites in order to stop the cutting and shipping of redwood trees in Northern California. While other environmental activist groups, such as the Sierra Club and the Audubon Society use more traditional methods (such as lobbying politicians, lawsuits, and letter writing) to achieve their goals, Earth First is among those groups that believe more confrontational methods must be employed if the environment is to be saved. To quote one Earth Firster who trains volunteers in nonviolent strategies of protest, "There is a need for an extreme element . . . The holocaust against the environment and its species is the same as any holocaust against humans . . . Civil rights for the environment are inseparable from civil rights for humans, since the environment provides us with our life support systems" (Bregger, 1990). Do you agree?

INDIVIDUAL INTERVENTION

What can one person do?

If you have been asking yourself that question as you contemplate what may seem like an overwhelming clean-up task, take heart: there are a number of things one person can do to make a real difference. A sample of things one can do is listed in the *Quality of Life*.

In this chapter we have presented capsule summaries of a number of environment-related issues. In all instances, these issues are very complex, and no simple solutions exist to dealing with them. Therefore, if any of the topics was of particular interest to you, some outside reading is recommended to help you gain a better appreciation of the complexity of the problem, as well as of alternative solutions. If you think, for example, that you might like to learn more about the biodiversity crisis, you may want to read E. O. Wilson's *The Diversity of Life*. In that book, Wilson (1992) likens the diversity of life on earth to our cultural heritage. He notes that while society goes to great lengths to preserve ancient artworks and artifacts, it has mistakenly not placed the same value on our living cultural heritage. Certain species will die off on their own, of course; that is Nature's way. But how can we justify to our descendants, for example, the killing and extinction of elephants for their ivory? The killing and extinction of tigers for the use of their bones in worthless folk remedies? The killing and extinction of rhinoceroses for the use of their horns in worthless folk remedies? The massive and senseless annihilation of life that is currently underway cries out for solution.

Perhaps the most important thing one person can do for the environment is to maintain an awareness of the issues involved and to support political candidates, private corporations, and governmental policies that are sincere in their efforts to preserve our environment for future generations. Whales are magnificent animals (see Figure 15–11), as are tigers, rhinoceroses, gorillas, elephants, and other endangered species. Preserving them, as well as less magnificent animals such as endangered insects and other elements of our biosphere, must be given the highest priority. Because of the seemingly infinite ability humankind has to adjust, we no doubt could adapt to a world without whales, tigers, or clean air, water, or land. But it is to be hoped that those are adjustments that neither we nor any generation to follow us will ever have to make.

**FIGURE 15–11
MAGNIFICENT TO BEHOLD, AND NEVER TO BE FORGOTTEN**
Whales breathe oxygen from the air and must surface to do so. In recent years, with their numbers in the world's oceans declining rapidly, a new industry of whale-watching tours has been born. Dunne (1992) described his experience on such a trip, including how "the sound of exultation from the crowd" eclipsed the usually audible sound of the whale exhaling. Here is his description of what happened aboard the boat he was on with some 90 other whale-watchers when the whale emerged again: "It surfaced again, impossibly close, and this time the animal's appearance was greeted by cheers, squeals and shouts and laughter. Then it sounded for the last time, with its tail raised in a

QUALITY OF  *Life*

What One Person Can Do

Here are 10 things you can probably do right now to help the environment:

1. *Dispose of all trash properly.* Be especially carefully with plastic you wrap a sandwich with and take to the beach, the plastic used in the packaging of six-packs of canned beverages, and any kind of styrofoam. This kind of packaging has been responsible for the slow and agonizing death of many animals ranging from whales to pelicans to turtles. Diving birds can mistake styrofoam for food or become hopelessly enmeshed in plastic. Part of a turtle's diet is jellyfish and turtles cannot distinguish plastic bags from jellyfish. They eat plastic and die soon thereafter of blocked intestines.

2. *If you drive, only have your oil changed at establishments that recycle old motor oil.* Currently, only about 10% of all old motor oil is recycled. The remaining 90% is either dumped in landfills or burned. Also, make sure to have your car tuned once a year; tune-ups can save as much as 900 pounds of carbon dioxide gas from getting into the atmosphere.

3. *Take every opportunity to conserve energy.* Shut lights that are not in use. Replace incandescent bulbs with compact fluorescent ones. Patch air leaks around windows and doors with weather-stripping. Take shorter showers, use low-flow showerheads to conserve hot water, and do laundry in cold water. Reuse plastic bags if possible. Reuse supermarket bags. In the car, shut off the engine while parked. Keep your car's automobile tires properly inflated as this will improve gasoline mileage.

4. *Support recycled products.* Right now it is possible to buy everything from recycled paper to recycled doormats (the latter constructed from discarded rubber tires). Recycled products make great novelty gifts. For example, if you look hard enough, you may be able to find personally monogrammed cuff-links made from old typewriter keys! Use recycled paper, if possible.

5. *Write letters to companies and government officials expressing your dissatisfaction regarding action or policies that are not environmentally friendly.* For example, you might write to manufacturers of ozone-depleting products asking them to develop new alternatives or switch to some existing alternative. Such action is beginning to persuade automobile manufacturers to install more environmentally friendly air conditioners in cars.

6. *Avoid purchasing products that are harmful to the environment.* For example, avoid products that use ozone depleting chemicals such as CFCs, hydrochlorofluorocarbons (HCFCs), or halon gas. Halon gas may be found in fire extinguishers. CFCs and HCFCs may be found in refrigerators, industrial cleaners and foams, and aerosol products that are manufactured outside the United States and Canada.

7. *Recycle.* Participate in your community's efforts to recycle aluminum, glass, and newspapers. If your community does not currently have such a program, lobby to get one. Volunteer to be part of group clean-ups or start a group clean-up campaign in your area. In one such operation in 1991, a group of over 118,000 volunteers worked on 3,800 miles of the United States coastline and picked up 2.5 million pounds of trash.

8. *Volunteer.* For example, volunteer to be part of a group that plant trees or donate the money for a tree to some organization that plants trees.

9. *Write for literature from various environmental advocacy groups and join one or more that have objectives that you share.*

10. *Support television presentations, films, books, and other media that support environmental causes.* For example, if you have not seen the film *Gorillas in the Mist,* why not rent it this weekend?

Gorillas in the Mist is the true-life tale of Dian Fossey (above) who was mysteriously slain while working in Rwanda to conserve the world's population of mountain gorillas. According to H. Dieter Steklis, Fossey's successor, the world's population of mountain gorillas is highly imperiled. Due to a civil war in Rwanda, workers at the research center Fossey established were forced to abandon it in February 1993. Steklis (1993) wrote, "Conserving this species and its habitat depends on finding a way, perhaps through the United Nations, to buffer the gorillas from the dangerous instability of national politics. I am afraid that our not-so-distant giant relatives are not high on the world's agenda of problems to solve."

SUMMARY

PSYCHOLOGY AND THE BIOSPHERE The study of adjustment in the most general sense demands some consideration of the broad class of variables related to the *biosphere,* or the totality of the earth, including its land, water, atmosphere, and any element capable of sustaining life. Human alterations to the biosphere have had momentous consequences, some so negative that they may in turn necessitate very drastic adjustments on the part of humankind in the future.Environmental issues have very direct relevance to every individual's health, behavior, physical and emotional well-being, and general quality of life.

CRITICAL ENVIRONMENTAL CHALLENGES The quality of life and health of people all over the world depends in no small way on the health of the earth and of the life-sustaining nature of its land, water, and atmosphere. Worldwide population growth, exhaustion or pollution of resources, extinction of species, and other such environment-related factors have increasingly set off alarms in the minds of many scientists. If current trends continue, an environmental crisis yielding a worsened quality of life for all people, as well as all other living inhabitants of the planet, seems a certainty. In this sense, one's personal well-being and adjustment is intertwined with the well-being of the earth—its land, its water, its atmosphere, and its diversity of life.

ADJUSTMENT IN THE GLOBAL SENSE Adjustment in the global sense requires education, research, and intervention. Environmental education can take place formally in classrooms and informally in the print and electronic media. Other possible sources of informal environmental education include lectures organized by environmental advocacy groups, institutional exhibitions, and environmentally oriented recreational activities. Technological research can aid in the development of a wide range of environmentally friendly products and processes. Behavioral research better equips us for designing strategies of effective and constructive behavior and attitude change. In addition to education and research, action by the government, businesses, private groups, and individuals will also be necessary to ensure an environmentally sustainable future for ourselves and for future generations.

Behavioral Science Research: What It Is, How It's Done, and How It's Used

OUTLINE

A *hypnotist on a television or radio talk show brags that, on the basis of "scientific research," 100% of the people he has treated for smoking have stopped completely.*

Advertisements for audiotapes that contain embedded subliminal messages about losing weight claim that, on the basis of "scientific research," such tapes are superior to more conventional weight loss and diet programs.

Psychologists and others with training in behavioral science might take a dim view of such claims. Even the best stop-smoking programs, using hypnosis and/or other related techniques, have success rates that seldom go beyond 20% or so. Claims of self-help effectiveness using audiotapes containing embedded subliminal messages are even more dubious. There is, in fact, no research conducted by independent investigators to show that such tapes deliver on the promises their manufacturers make for them. But most people have little or no training in psychology and are ill-equipped to gauge the accuracy of psychology-related claims. It is

little wonder that the selling of self-help audiocassettes is a multi-million dollar industry—this despite the fact that their effectiveness is questionable at best.

The subject of this chapter is not stop-smoking programs, subliminal cassettes, or other kinds of services and products sold in the name of self-help. The subject of this chapter is research in behavioral science. An understanding of some basic aspects of how research in psychology is conducted is essential to an understanding of personal adjustment. This is because our knowledge about personal adjustment has been built on a base of research studies. By becoming acquainted with the rationale and methods of scientific research, you will be better able to evaluate critically the research studies reported in this and other textbooks. Also, such knowledge may be helpful in terms of making you a more informed consumer of psychology-related news stories and other presentations in the popular media as well as of advertisements for psychology-related products and services.

WHAT IS "SCIENTIFIC RESEARCH"?
A PHILOSOPHY OF SCIENCE

philosophy
a viewpoint about something.

In the context of the expression *philosophy of science*, **philosophy** may be defined simply as *a viewpoint about something*. You no doubt have your own viewpoint or philosophy about different things. For example, if someone were to ask you about your "philosophy of friendship," you could probably readily describe the personal meaning you attach to words like "friend" and "friendship." But what if someone asked you about your "philosophy of science"? Could you just as readily describe the personal meaning that words like "science" and "scientific" have for you?

philosophy of science
a set of assumptions about pathways to knowledge.

A **philosophy of science** refers to *assumptions about pathways to knowledge*. How is new knowledge discovered? What tools and methods are appropriate in the search for new knowledge? What constitutes evidence of new knowledge? What test of proof must evidence undergo before it is accepted as new knowledge? These are the types of questions you must grapple with if your goal is to develop your own philosophy of science.

In many areas of science, such as medical science, veterinary science, and earth science, different paths to the development of new knowledge have evolved. In this chapter we will focus primarily on behavioral science and the rationale and methods used by scientists who study behavior (psychologists, sociologists, and others) in their quest for new knowledge.

TYPES OF RESEARCH IN BEHAVIORAL SCIENCE

There are many ways that behavioral research can be categorized. Perhaps the most general typology is in terms of "basic research," "applied research," and "program evaluation research."

C L O S E - U P

Scientific Research Around the World

Some cities offer wonderful shopping. Others offer world class vacation settings. And yet other cities are known for the industrial or consumer goods produced in them. Moscow does not fit into any of these categories. Still, it does hold at least one record. According to a 1993 issue of Science Watch, the newsletter published by the Philadelphia-based Institute for Scientific Information, more scientific research papers originated from Moscow than any other city in the world. Following Moscow on the "top 10" list of prolific research cities was London, followed by Boston/Cambridge, Tokyo, New York, Paris, Los Angeles, Bethesda (Maryland),

Philadelphia, and Osaka. Although in tenth place in terms of number of published papers, Osaka was the fastest growing research city, exhibiting a 57.3% increase in scientific papers over the previous ten years. Tokyo, with its 41.1% increase in papers for the same period, was the second fastest growing city in terms of scientific research.

Of course, as any scientist will tell you, sheer number of papers published does not necessarily reflect on the quality of research being produced in a city. Still, as Broad (1993, p. C5) put it, "a large number of papers suggests that the level of scientific activity may be quite high."

What factors do you think might account for observed differences between cities in levels of scientific activity. How might cultural differences play a part in such differences, and in the growth or decline of such activity?

BASIC RESEARCH

Simply stated **basic research** in behavioral science is concerned with *the gathering of knowledge about behavior.* In a manner of speaking, basic research is research in its purest form, a gathering of knowledge for the sake of gathering knowledge. *Not* implied in basic research is the gathering of knowledge for the sake of immediately pressing it into use to serve people.

basic psychological research investigation for the general purpose of gathering knowledge about behavior and thinking.

Some hypothetical titles of articles that might typify basic research are:

"The Effect of Rewriting Stimulus Material on Memory Retention"

"New Visual Illusions and the Eye of the Beholder"

"200 Different Taste Stimuli and Subjects' Report of Taste Experience"

APPLIED RESEARCH

As its name implies, **applied research** in behavioral science is concerned with *the use of principles of behavior in finding solutions to practical concerns.*

In many instances, basic research on a particular topic inspires applied research. For example, the basic research study on memory cited above might serve as the inspiration for an applied research study having a title such as, "Helping College Students Learn with supplemented SQ3R." The basic research study that dealt with the perception of visual illusions might inspire an applied research study by military psychologists having a title like, "The Effectiveness of Traditional Camouflage and Proposed New Ways to Camouflage a Tank." Basic research on human subjects' taste experiences with a variety of taste stimuli

applied psychological research

behavioral investigation for the purpose of finding solutions to practical concerns.

or sensations might stimulate a wide range of applied research. Some of these investigations might have titles such as the following:

"How Specially Flavored Chewing Gum and Hard Candy is Used by Workers Having Routine Jobs to Overcome Boredom in a Manufacturing Setting"

"Satisfying Nicotine Cravings with Various Oral Stimuli"

"The Use of A Foul-Tasting Solution Applied to Fingernails in the Treatment of Nailbiting."

PROGRAM EVALUATION RESEARCH

program evaluation research

investigation that has as its objective the assessment of the effectiveness, efficiency, or value of various kinds of institutionalized procedures in the public, private, or government sector.

Program evaluation research has as its objective *the assessment of the effectiveness, efficiency, or value of various kinds of institutionalized procedures in the public or private sector.* Some sample titles of research involving program evaluation might be:

"Effectiveness of Methods Used at the Betty Ford Clinic: A One-Year Study"

"A Comparison of Participants in Project Head Start for Preschool Children and Matched Nonparticipants 20 Years Later"

"Capital Punishment as a Deterrent to Crime in the State of Florida"

Researchers may employ different research methods, regardless of the particular type of research (basic, applied, program evaluation) they are conducting. Some of the methods psychologists commonly use to develop new knowledge are *experiments, natural observation, surveys,* and *case studies.* Before we discuss each of these research methods in somewhat greater depth, consider the fact that the quality of research, just as the quality of most other things in life, can vary.

QUALITY IN RESEARCH

All research is not created equal. Some research may be better planned, executed, analyzed, and/or interpreted than other research. Some research may be better than other research simply because the findings derived from it are more representative Consider the following research question: What topics are of greatest interest to students in North America who take a course in introductory psychology?

Researcher 1 attempts to answer this question by administering the questionnaire in Figure AP-1 to all of the students in your class. Researcher 2 attempts to answer this question by administering the questionnaire to a representative sample of introductory psychology students in the United States. Researcher 3 attempts to answer this question by admi
nistering the questionnaire to a representative sample of introductory psychology students in the United States and Canada. All other things being equal (such as the competence of the three researchers), it is a good bet that the best answer to the research question will be provided by Researcher 3, simply because the findings will be most representative of "North American students."

Who is to judge which research study is superior to another? What are the criteria to be used in making such evaluations?

peer review

a stage in the research publication process during which the research undergoes evaluation by experts in the subject matter.

Scholarly journals, books, papers presented at scientific meetings, and other such outlets for research can be thought of as a running record of contributions to behavioral science. Manuscripts submitted for publication in such outlets typically undergo a process called **peer review** or *evaluation by experts in the area of the proposed contribution.* The manuscript will only be considered worthy to be published when the reviewers (or a majority of them) agree that the research represents a bona fide contribution to knowledge.

The criteria used in making the judgment that something is suitable for publication may vary somewhat from one research outlet to the next. We might expect, however, that a proposed contribution to knowledge will meet certain minimal requirements, such as requirements we will refer to as *objectivity, replicability,* and *evidence.*

INTEREST SURVEY FOR INTRODUCTORY PSYCHOLOGY

Instructions:

Please rank in order the following topics typically covered in introductory psychology from 1 through 20 where
1 = your most favorite topic and
20 = your least favorite topic

Topic	Fill-in Rank Order Number Here
Abnormal behavior	_____
Adjustment	_____
Biological psychology	_____
Consciousness	_____
Developmental psychology	_____
Emotion	_____
Environmental psychology	_____
Health psychology	_____
Human development	_____
Instinctive behavior	_____
Intelligence	_____
Language and communication	_____
Learning	_____
Motivation	_____
Perception	_____
Personality theory	_____
Psychological assessment	_____
Psychotherapy	_____
Sensation	_____
Social psychology	_____

FIGURE AP-1

THE REQUIREMENT OF OBJECTIVITY

Behavioral scientists, such as psychologists, share with other scientists, such as biologists, training that helps to prepare them to use their education and experience in the service of adding to human knowledge. And just as all apprentice craftspeople learn about accepted methods and tools of a trade, so all beginning scientists learn about accepted methods and tools of conducting and reporting research. In general, for a reported finding to be accepted as a scientific fact, it must, at a minimum, evidence a reasonable degree of **objectivity**. That is, the primary findings must indeed be *factual, and not the product of the researcher's opinions, hunches, prejudices, or desires.*

The results of a taste test pitting Coke against Pepsi will probably be taken more seriously if the test is conducted by an independent researcher rather than by the sales manager for Coca-Cola. The sales manager for Coca-Cola would be presumed to have a great personal interest in the outcome of the research. Scientists have learned that it is possible for an experimenter's hope or expectancy about the outcome of research to become a self-fulfilling prophecy. Researchers, even teachers and others, may "find" what they expect to find, sometimes even when another more neutral party might find something else entirely (Rosenthal, 1966, 1967, 1969; Rosenthal & Jacobson, 1968).

It is true that in many scientific investigations, the researcher conducting the study has a vested interest in achieving one or another outcomes. For example, future funding for additional research might hinge on the results of the present experiment. Still, the scientist must design the research to safeguard against possible sources of **bias** or *prejudice* in the study.

objectivity
an attitude and ethic in scientific research regarding the factual nature of published findings.

bias
prejudice.

In a taste test study, as in other studies, bias may enter the research in a wide range of ways. Some of these potential sources of bias may be deliberate. Some of them are not deliberate. Some are very subtle. One example of a deliberate source of bias in a taste test study would be coaxing subjects into conceding that one or another beverage tastes better. A potentially inadvertent and more subtle form of bias might enter the experiment in the form of the temperature at which the two products are served. If one of the two beverages is served at a temperature that is warmer than it should be, it is a good bet it will be the loser in the taste test.

Having objectivity as a goal in research does not in any way mean that scientific research is value-free. Scientists, like everyone else, have their own value systems which, whether they like it or not, inevitably enter into their work. For example, researchers who have devoted their lives to cancer research have, by the very nature of the work they have chosen, made a decision with respect to what they value; they value life. Still, the way that they conduct individual research studies should ideally be objective and to the extent that it is humanly possible, value-free. Variables such as pride, even the threat of loss of employment, must not prevent them from reporting that they have made no progress at all, if that is indeed the case.

THE REQUIREMENT OF REPLICABILITY

Scientists require that research be **replicable** or *repeatable by other experimenters who follow the same procedures as the original experimenter.*

Consider, for example, one study of patients with **Alzheimer's disease**, *a neurological disorder, typically but not necessarily seen in persons of advanced age, characterized by memory loss and other symptoms.* The researcher reports that Alzheimer's patients tend to evidence impairment in their sense of smell. When other researchers studying similar patients in other settings confirm that patients having Alzheimer's disease tend to develop **olfactory** (*sense of smell*) impairments, this observation will be on its way toward widespread acceptance as a scientific fact. Eventually, evaluation of the sense of smell may become part of any routine examination of a person suspected of having Alzheimer's disease. There is, by the way, suggestive evidence that olfactory impairment does occur in Alzheimer's patients (Serby et al., 1991).

Many instances occur in which one researcher fails to replicate the findings reported by another researcher. Should one failure to replicate invalidate the findings of the original study? No. There are many possible explanations for a single failure to replicate. For example, the researcher attempting the replication may have wittingly or unwittingly failed to follow critical aspects of the procedures reported by the original experimenter. It may be the case that some subtleties in the experimental procedure used by the original experimenter were never published. Contacting the original experimenter and learning about such subtleties would be the only way to ensure an exact replication. The experimenter failing to replicate the original research might have collected data that could—for lack of a more detailed explanation here—be deemed a "fluke" (that is, a finding that occurred by chance). The experimenter failing to replicate the original research might have been plagued by faulty equipment, incompetent assistants, or other factors that interfered with the conduct of the experiment, the collection of data, or the analysis of the findings. Of course, if a number of different researchers report a failure to replicate a particular finding, the original study would itself be called into question or viewed as the fluke. In general, it is expected that scientists using the same methods, procedures, and/or tools as described in an original study will obtain the same or substantially similar results.

THE REQUIREMENT OF EVIDENCE

Evidence may be defined as *information or observations by which probability or proof can be established.* In addition to being replicable, a purported contribution to knowledge must be backed by acceptable evidence. No claim of discovery of new knowledge will be accepted simply on faith. A world-renowned group of scientists may issue an opinion, for example, stating a particular belief. Such a statement may be taken quite seriously by colleagues as food for thought, but it will not be accepted as scientific fact without satisfactory evidence.

Exactly what constitutes acceptable evidence may vary depending upon, for instance, academic discipline and individual aspects of the situation. In law, for example, there is a different standard of proof for civil and criminal cases. In civil cases, what is needed to prove something is "a preponderance of the evidence." A stricter criteria for proof is applied in criminal cases, where what needs to be demonstrated is "guilt beyond a reasonable doubt." Similarly, different standards of proof may also be applied with respect to evidence offered in behavioral science research. In recent years, courts, too, have struggled with questions regarding the acceptability of scientific research and opinions as evidence in trials (see *In the News*).

In various disciplines, different ways and means of presenting evidence for the purpose of demonstrating that a particular conclusion is true have evolved. In mathematics, for example, evidence proving that *a*/2=.5*a* is true could be marshaled through the use of a series of mathematically provable assumptions. In law, there are traditional rules of evidence which govern what may or may not be considered in the judge's or jury's decision-making process. In behavioral science, too, there have evolved accepted procedures for establishing that something is true or most likely true. Perhaps most important in this context, however, is the behavioral scientist's demand that evidence be **empirical** in nature, that is, *derived from observable facts or experience.*

empirical
derived from observable facts or experience.

In what follows, we will survey some of the general types of research and research methods that have become traditional in behavioral science. Our objective is to impart a conceptual understanding of the research process; a better understanding of the *concept* of research as that term is used in behavioral science. Most of the coverage will be on experimentation as a research method. It is through experiments that behavioral scientists are capable of obtaining the strongest or most compelling kind of empirical evidence.

THE EXPERIMENTAL METHOD

What kind of mental pictures does the term *scientific experiment* conjure? For many students, this term conjures images of a person in a white laboratory coat pouring multicolored chemicals from one test tube into another and noting the reaction. In principle, this image is accurate in conveying three general components of experimentation:

1. *The experimenter is doing something that may have an effect on the outcome of the phenomena under observation.* In this case, the experimenter is mixing chemicals.
2. *The experimenter's behavior has a purpose and things are being manipulated to answer some question or test some idea.* Although we may not know exactly why the experimenter is mixing chemicals, it is a fair assumption that this activity is purposive; the experimenter hopes to find something out by engaging in this activity.
3. *The experimenter is observing and recording the effect of whatever it is that has been done.* In this case, the experimenter notes the consequence of mixing a particular group of chemicals.

In such chemical research, the outcome of interest to the experimenter might be a particular change in the properties of one of the chemicals being mixed. In behavioral research, the outcome of interest always concerns a change in behavior. To understand why this is so, and to become acquainted with what is actually involved in the experimental method as applied in behavioral science, let's begin at the beginning: the **experimental design** or *planning of an experiment.*

experimental design
planning of an experiment.

DESIGNING THE EXPERIMENT

A responsible architect designs a bridge, house, or other structure so that it will be soundly constructed and of value to the people who will use it. A responsible researcher designs research so that it too will be "soundly constructed" and of value to all who might use it. For a house, there are some essential elements of the architectural design that must be included (walls, ceiling, floor, and a door). For an experiment, there are also some essentials of an experimental design. An outline of these essentials and notes on the vocabulary of research follow.

Research as Evidence

Under what circumstances should a court admit research into evidence? How widely accepted by other members of the scientific community should the research be before it is acceptable as evidence in a federal court? Should judges make judgments regarding whether juries should hear about certain types of research? Alternatively, should juries hear whatever research each side desires to present and make its own judgment regarding the soundness of the research?

These are the types of questions raised by the landmark case of *Daubert v. Merrell Dow Pharmaceuticals,* argued before the Supreme Court of the United States in April 1993 (Greenhouse, 1993a). The *Daubert* case had its origins with the prescription of a drug called *Bendectin* to relieve nausea during pregnancy. When the plaintiffs' children were born with birth defects, the plaintiffs sued the manufacturer of the drug, claiming that the drug was responsible for the birth defects. Attorneys for the plaintiffs came to court armed with research that they claimed would prove that *Bendectin* causes birth defects. However, the trial judge refused to admit the research into evidence, ruling that it failed to meet the criteria necessary to be admissible. Ultimately, the judge found in favor of the defendant, Merrell Dow Pharmaceuticals. The plaintiffs appealed the verdict to the next highest court, which like its predecessor, ruled in favor of the defendant. The plaintiffs next appealed to the Supreme Court of the United States. A question before the Supreme Court was whether the judge in the original trial acted properly by not allowing the research to be admitted into evidence.

A major precedent regarding the admissibility of research into evidence was the 1923 case of *Frye v. United States.* In *Frye,* the Court held that a research study, or a particular method of research, will be admissible into evidence when the research study or method enjoys general acceptance. A less rigorous standard for admissibility of research was set forth by Congress in 1975, in the *Federal Rules of Evidence* (FRE). Rule 702 of the FRE opened the door to expert witnesses testifying as to the admissability of research and research methods. An expert might offer an opinion to a jury concerning the acceptability of a research study or method, regardless of whether the opinion represented the opinion of other experts. The 702 Rule was designed to assist juries in their fact-finding mission and to help them better understand issues involved in research.

The plaintiffs in the *Daubert* case argued to the Supreme Court that the 702 rule was "trampled" by the trial judge who blatantly abused judicial power. Merrell Dow argued that the lower court ruled correctly, and that high standards of evidence admissibility were necessary to protect juries from "scientific shamans who, in the guise of their purported expertise, are willing to testify to virtually any conclusion to suit the needs of the litigant with resources sufficient to pay their retainer."

In June 1993, the Supreme Court of the United States charged federal judges with the responsibility of insuring that "any and all scientific testimony or evidence admitted is not only relevant but reliable." The ruling replaced the prevailing policy of admitting into evidence scientific testimony that had won general acceptance in the scientific community. According to this new, "gatekeeper" policy, "judges could either keep evidence from the jury or take from the jury the power to reach a judgment if the scientific evidence admitted at trial turned out to be insufficient ot permit a 'reasonable juror' to reach a conclusion" (Greenhouse, 1993b, p. A13). The Supreme Court ordered that the *Daubert* case be re-tried in a lower court, with the judge acting as the "gatekeeper" of what qualifies as scientific knowledge. According to this policy, factors such as general acceptance in the scientific community or publication in a peer-reviewed journal were only "relevant" factors for a judge to consider. Justices Wiliam H. Rehnquist and John Paul Stevens dissented with the majority warning that the gatekeeper policy endorsed by the majority might have the effect of requiring judges to be "amateur scientists."

The Supreme Court's ruling in *Daubert* may have a ripple effect regarding many other cases in which the issue of admissability of research is key. For example, in some criminal cases, notably rape cases, questions have been raised regarding the admissability of techniques—so-called "DNA fingerprinting" methods—that employ genetic material for positive identification of accused rapists. In civil cases, such as medical malpractice cases, there have also been bitter disputes about what types of testimony a jury should be allowed to hear as they weigh the evidence. In the words of one law professor at Georgetown University in Washington, the Supreme Court's ruling in *Daubert,* "could affect almost every piece of litigation in the Federal courts from this point foward" (Rothstein, 1993, p. A12).

THEORY

For our purposes a **theory** may be defined as *a group of organized principles which may be used to explain and predict certain phenomena.* A theory provides a kind of structure that can systematically accommodate all that is known about a particular phenomenon, as well as all that may become known about it in the future. If you have ever read a detective story or watched a police drama on television, you probably have great familiarity with the idea of theorizing why this or that suspect had motive to commit a particular crime. "The son did it for the inheritance!" "The lover did it in a jealous rage!" "The daughter did it as retaliation for childhood abuse inflicted upon her!" "A former employee who protested his dismissal did it!" These are some of many theories that might be advanced to account for why a victim was murdered.

Behavioral scientists use theory in an effort to account for observed phenomena. For example, in March of 1964 a woman named Kitty Genovese was brutally attacked for over a half-hour as neighbors looked on in horror but did not call the police or come to her aid. The homicide prompted two psychologists (Latané & Darley, 1970) to begin a program of behavioral research designed to determine the conditions under which people will aid other people in emergency situations. Data from such research is still helping to mold a theory of altruism (pro-social behavior). Contrary to what most people tend to believe on the basis of common sense, Darley and Latané's theory predicted that the more people around under certain conditions, the less chance that someone will come to a victim's aid. According to the Darley and Latané (1968), this is so because responsibility tends to be "diffused" in an emergency; that is, who should take responsibility for action is not clear, and each person might believe another to be the one to take action (Latané & Nida, 1981).

HYPOTHESIS

An experiment, like other forms of research, is designed to test a **hypothesis**, *a premise, assertion, or proposition, usually derived from a theory, that is subject to proof.* **Hypothesis testing** refers to *the process of conducting research designed to examine the validity of a particular proposition or series of propositions.*

As an exercise in developing hypotheses (the plural of *hypothesis*), consider a **hypothetical** (that is, *made-up for the purpose of example*) theory called "the pleasure theory." According to this theory, organisms act in a way so as to maximize pleasure and reduce stress, or minimize pain and annoyance. Many hypotheses about human behavior might flow from this theory. Can you think of any?

Some of the many thousands of possible hypotheses that might be derived from our pleasure theory are:

Partaking of a dessert of one's choice is generally preferable to drinking tabasco sauce straight from a jar.

The greater one's ability to postpone immediate gratification, the more likely it is that one will enter a learned profession.

Time spent receiving a sensual back massage is generally preferable to a comparable amount of time standing on line at the Department of Motor Vehicles.

People who habitually bite their fingernails must do so because they find such activity pleasurable or stress-relieving.

One logical extension of the last of these hypotheses might be:

If fingernail biting were to be made nonpleasurable or non-stress-relieving, then people who habitually bite their fingernails would stop doing it.

Suppose now that a psychologist wishes to test this last hypothesis. The psychologist, whose hobby happens to be chemistry, has concocted a colorless, harmless, but foul-tasting and long-lasting solution called "No-Nail-Bite" (NNB). The psychologist reasons that if the fingernails of nailbiters were treated with NNB, they might be cured of this habit as a result of the repeated contact with the foul-tasting substance. "Make it unpleasant to bite your nails, and you'll stop biting your nails," the psychologist believes. One way of stating this hunch in the form of a research hypothesis might be:

theory
a group of organized principles which may be explanatory and/or predictive with respect to certain phenomena.

hypothesis
a premise, assertion, or proposition, usually derived from a theory, that is subject to proof.

hypothesis testing
conducting research designed to examine the validity of a particular proposition or series of propositions.

hypothetical
made-up for the purpose of example.

NNB applied to the fingernails of people who habitually bite their nails results in significantly less nailbiting behavior.

For reasons of precision, behavioral scientists would probably *not* state the research hypothesis quite that way.[1] Rather, a formal statement of the psychologist's research hypothesis might look more like this:

NNB applied to the fingernails of people who habitually bite their nails results in no significant difference in nailbiting behavior.

Does the second version of the research hypothesis impress you as more negative than the first? If so, your impression is accurate. Still, the second version is more representative of the way that research hypotheses in behavioral science are characteristically stated. The second version characterizes what is called the **null hypothesis**, or *the proposition that no significant difference exists as a result of the experimenter's treatment.*

Should the experiment prove such statements to be untrue, the null hypothesis is said to be *rejected* or discarded. For the psychologist who would like to prove that NNB is indeed effective in modifying habitual nailbiting behavior, one element of success would be satisfactory proof that the null hypothesis could be rejected. If, on the other hand, the evidence from the experiment proved that NNB is indeed ineffective in treating the problem of fingernail biting, then the null hypothesis would not be rejected. The research purist will note that as a matter of custom, an experimenter is seldom, if ever said to "accept" the null hypothesis; rather, one speaks in terms of rejecting it or failing to reject it.

SUBJECTS AND METHOD

Subject is a term used to refer to *the human or nonhuman participant in an experiment or other behavioral study whose behavior will be observed and analyzed by the experimenter.* Examples of descriptions of subjects you might find in the pages of psychology journals are

300 Sprague-Dawley laboratory rats.

50 children from the Chicago school district between the ages of 10 and 12 with a diagnosis of attention deficit disorder (ADD).

200 students enrolled in a course in introductory psychology at Oshkosh Community College, participating in the experiment in return for extra course credit.

If an experimenter uses 300 laboratory rats supplied by the Sprague-Dawley Company, does this mean the experimenter's objective in conducting the research is to make a statement that is applicable only to the 300 Sprague-Dawley rats used in the experiment? Would you suppose that a study conducted with 50 ADD children from Chicago is conducted for the sole purpose of finding something out about 50 ADD children from Chicago? Or what about a study conducted with 200 students enrolled in a course in introductory psychology at Oshkosh Community College? Would you suppose that the experimenter's interest is limited to how these subjects perform with respect to the experiment?

Perhaps the best answer to each of the questions is "probably not." The experimenter usually hopes to *generalize* from the specific facts found in a particular study to facts that are more universal in nature. *The single subject or group of subjects that a researcher works with in a particular experiment (or other research project)* is referred to as the **sample**. And just as a swatch of fabric is in a sense a sample of an entire suit, so the group of subjects in a particular research project may be viewed as a sample of a larger whole. *The larger whole in this context* is referred to as the **population**. In the study we made reference to earlier regarding North American students' preferences regarding topics in introductory psychology, the students who actually completed the survey for the research study would constitute the sample. All students in North America who take a course in introductory psychology would constitute the population. In a Coke versus Pepsi taste test, the group of subjects who participate in the experiment would collectively be referred to as the sample, while all the people who drink Coke and Pepsi would be the population.

There are techniques researchers may use to ensure that the findings of research using a particular sample of subjects will be reasonably generalizable to the population of interest. Here we will simply emphasize that an objective in most research is to learn something

null hypothesis

used in research, the proposition that no significant difference exists as a result of the experimenter's treatment.

subject

in behavioral science research, the human or nonhuman participant in an experiment or other behavioral study whose behavior will be observed and analyzed by the experimenter.

sample

the single subject or group of subjects that a researcher works with to investigate a hypothesis in a particular experiment or other research project.

population

in scientific research, the larger group from which the sample was drawn to whom the experimenter wishes to generalize.

[1]Discussion of these reasons can get quite technical and are better left to books devoted to discussion of research methods.

that is generalizable to the targeted population, rather than something specific to the subjects in any given study.

In some instances, experimenters do not use the subjects they would prefer to use in a particular experiment. The desired subjects may be unavailable, or the cost of gaining their participation in the experiment may be prohibitive. As an example, consider a hypothetical 30-minute film entitled *On the Need for Corporate Responsibility in the Proper Disposal of Toxic Waste*. And let us say that this film was produced at great expense by a group of socially minded environmentalists who have targeted it for distribution to the presidents of America's 500 leading corporations. It is the producers' hope that the film will be effective in modifying corporate leaders' attitudes regarding the disposal of toxic waste. The environmentalists have hired a psychologist who is an expert in measuring attitude change to report to them regarding the actual effectiveness of the film in modifying attitudes.

The psychologist designs a study that may be summarized as follows:

1. The subjects will be any 100 presidents of America's 500 currently leading corporations as listed in *Fortune* magazine.
2. On Day 1 of the study, all subjects will complete a specially devised Attitudes Towards the Environment Questionnaire (ATEQ), which includes many items tapping the respondents' attitudes and beliefs regarding corporate disposal of toxic waste.
3. On Day 7 of the study, all subjects will view the *On the Need for Corporate Responsibility . . .* film.
4. On Day 14 of the study, all subjects will again complete the ATEQ.
5. The resulting **data** (the plural form of **datum** meaning *information*) will be analyzed to determine if exposure to the film had any effect on the subjects' attitudes toward the environment and the disposal of toxic waste.

data
plural form of *datum* meaning information.

Stated in terms of the null hypothesis, the experimenter's hypothesis is that *no significant difference in attitudes toward disposal of toxic wastes by corporations will be observed as a result of exposure to the film*. As you might expect, the environmentalists who produced the film will be rooting for a rejection of the null hypothesis! They invested their time, money, and expertise in producing the film, and they would like to see some attitude shift on the part of those who view it.

Ideally, the psychologist would like to use as subjects for this study all 500 presidents of America's leading 500 corporations. Realizing that this may be a bit ambitious, the psychologist has somewhat arbitrarily settled for a sample of 20% of this population, or any 100 presidents. Unfortunately, the psychologist will probably find that even obtaining the participation of 100 corporate presidents is overly optimistic. The reality of the situation is that it will probably be impossible to get even a few, if any, of these very busy corporate leaders to participate in the research. Among other reasons, they are scattered around the country and their schedules leave little or no time for such projects. Additionally, the political sensitivity of participating in a study of corporate environmental attitudes might prompt many corporate heads to shy away from participation.

As an alternative to conducting the research with the people who would be ideal for the study, an attempt might be made to recruit local business people to participate. Should the psychologist fail in that attempt as well, the psychologist might recruit subjects in other ways such as by placing an ad for subjects in a newspaper. The term **convenience sample** is used to refer to *subjects that are readily attainable (though not always the most appropriate) for use in a research study*. Have you any idea what single group of people has served as the sample in more psychology studies than any other group of people? If you guessed introductory psychology students, you are correct. Through the use of incentives such as extra course credit and the promise of learning something firsthand about research, it is introductory psychology students who, one might say, have been the most convenient of all convenience samples for psychological research.

convenience sample
subjects that are readily attainable, though not always the most appropriate, for use in a research study.

One question that inevitably arises when a convenience sample is used is the question concerning the generalizability of the findings. For example, if introductory psychology students were used in the toxic waste film study, how generalizable do you think the findings would be to *Fortune 500* company presidents? One way of approaching this difficult question would be to consult the published literature that is available on such presidents and see where areas of commonality exist with the people used in the study's convenience sample. In truth, however, generalizing the results of data obtained with the use of a convenience sample to some population that on its face bears little resemblance to the convenience sample is usually a very risky business.

Whether using a convenience sample or any other sample, a question arises: How many subjects need to be recruited? The answer will vary according to a number of factors. The general rule is that the experiment requires a sufficient number of subjects to answer the questions asked by the experimenter. In some areas of behavioral science, many experiments are undertaken with as few as one subject. Pick up a copy of the *Journal of the Experimental Analysis of Behavior* at your university library, and you will see that many of the studies reported in it were conducted with a single subject. On the other hand, few if any of the studies reported in journals such as the *Journal of Personality and Social Psychology* will report single-subject research. You will, however, see great variation in the number of subjects reported in the various studies. The number of subjects used in what is called a **pilot** (or *a preliminary or exploratory*) **study** will typically be a fraction of the number of subjects used in a follow-up study to the pilot study.

There exist many different types of experimental designs and the number of subjects used in a particular experiment may vary as a function of the type of experimental design being employed. For example, all other things being equal, what is called a *repeated measures design* tends to require fewer subjects for an experiment than what is called an *independent groups design*. In a repeated measures design, there is at least one group of subjects (although there may be more than one group), all subjects are exposed to the experimental treatment, and at least two measures on each subject are taken (one measurement prior to exposure to the treatment, and the other after exposure to the treatment). The previously described experiment involving exposure to the toxic waste film is an example of a simple repeated measures design. All subjects are exposed to the experimental treatment (in this case, the showing of the toxic waste film), and attitudes regarding this topic are assessed prior to the "treatment," and then again after the "treatment" (see Figure AP–2).

In an independent groups experimental design, there are at least two groups of subjects (and usually more), and at least one of the groups is not exposed to the experimental treatment or condition. Had the toxic waste film experiment been designed to be conducted with independent groups, at least two groups of subjects would be required. One group would be exposed to the experimental treatment (that is, they would be shown the film on toxic waste), while the other group might be shown a film that had absolutely nothing to do with toxic waste. *A group of subjects who are not exposed to the experimental treatment* is called a **control group**. A control group is used in experimentation to "control for" or "verify the effects" of the treatment. In a repeated measures design, each subject serves, in essence, as his or her own control.

Regardless of the experimental design, experimenters typically anticipate some **attrition** or *reduction in the total number of subjects employed during the course of an experiment*. Generally, the greater the number of days human subjects are involved in an experiment, the greater the subject attrition the experimenter must plan on. Attrition is a fact of research life due to a number of factors ranging from subjects' competing obligations, to sickness, to simple irresponsibility. One method of coping with the problem of attrition is through over-recruiting subjects for participation in an experiment. In the context of a description of an experiment, **method** refers to the *procedures, techniques, and/or measures employed and the order in which they were used*. Suppose now that you wanted to design an experiment to explore the effectiveness of No-Nail-Bite solution (NNB) in stopping habitual nailbiters from biting. . . How would you design such a study? Would you use an independent groups design? A repeated measures design? Who would be your subjects? Describe the method you would use before reading on.

An overview of one approach to an experiment designed to explore the effectiveness of NNB is presented in Table AP–1. This approach outlines an independent groups design. The study you designed may have employed repeated measures; either can provide useful information in the pursuit of information regarding the effectiveness of NNB.

As noted in Table AP–1, the NNB study design calls for the researcher to recruit a total of 100 subjects; 25 subjects will be assigned to each of 4 groups. Group 1 will consist of

pilot study

in scientific research, a preliminary or exploratory investigation.

attrition

in research, usually a reference to a reduction or dropping-out of participating subjects.

control group

a group of subjects not exposed to the experimental treatment who will be compared to subjects who were exposed to the experimental treatment.

attrition

reduction in the total number of subjects employed during the course of an experiment.

method

in scientific research, the procedures, techniques, and/or measures employed and the order in which they are used.

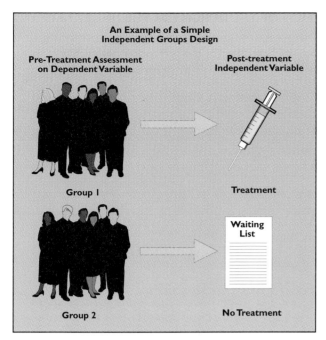

**An Example of a Simple
Independent Groups Design**

**Pre-Treatment Assessment
on Dependent Variable**

**Post-treatment
Independent Variable**

Group 1

Treatment

Group 2

Waiting
List

No Treatment

FIGURE AP-2 An *independent groups design* is sometimes also referred to as a "between groups design" since the comparisons of interest are *between* the two or more groups of subjects in the study. A *repeated measures design* is sometimes also referred to as a "within groups design" since the comparisons of interest are *within* single subjects.

Each type of experimental design has advantages and disadvantages. For example, a repeated measures design typically requires fewer subjects than an independent groups design, and may be more sensitive to changes as a result of treatment than an independent groups design. However, the results of an experiment that employs an indepedent groups design may in some ways better parallel what happens in the "real world" than the findings from a comparable experiment that employed a repeated measures design (Greenwald, 1976).

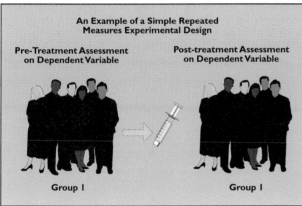

**An Example of a Simple Repeated
Measures Experimental Design**

**Pre-Treatment Assessment
on Dependent Variable**

**Post-treatment Assessment
on Dependent Variable**

Group 1

Group 1

25 nailbiters who will be treated with NNB solution. Stated another way, the "treatment" these 25 subjects will receive will be an application of NNB to all of their fingernails. On Day 1 of the experiment, members of Group 1 will have all of their fingernails measured and be instructed, "Please do not cut, manicure, or otherwise touch or bite your nails until instructed that you may do so by the experimenter." Members of Group 1 will be asked to report to the experimenter on Day 10 to have their fingernails measured again.

Group 2 will consist of 25 subjects who will be treated with a solution that is actually only plain tap water. The "treatment" these 25 subjects will receive will be an application of plain tap water to all of their fingernails. On Day 1 of the experiment, members of Group 2 will have all of their fingernails measured and then receive the same instructions as the members of Group 1: "Please do not cut, manicure, or otherwise touch or bite your nails until instructed that you may do so by the experimenter." Members of Group 2 will be asked to report to the experimenter on Day 10 to have their fingernails measured again.

Group 3 will consist of 25 subjects who will be placed on a waiting list for treatment. During the course of the actual study, however, no member of Group 3 will receive any treatment. Members of Group 3 will, however, receive the same instructions as the members of Groups 1 and 2: "Please do not cut, manicure, or otherwise touch or bite your nails until instructed that you may do so by the experimenter." Members of Group 3 will be asked to report to the experimenter on Day 1 and then again on Day 10 to have their fingernails measured.

TABLE AP-1 OVERVIEW OF THE DESIGN FOR THE NNB EXPERIMENT

1. An independent groups design under double-blind conditions will be used.

2. A total of 120 subjects will be recruited by means of an ad in the campus newspaper, and one-quarter of the total number of subjects will be assigned to each of 1 of 4 conditions:

    (1) experimental (NNB) treatment group

    (2) placebo treatment group

    (3) wait list/instructions only group and

    (4) wait list/no instructions group.

    It is anticipated that subject attrition during the course of the experiment will be equal to no more than 5 subjects from each of the four groups. It is further anticipated that the data will be analyzed on a total of no less than 100 subjects, including 25 subjects from each of the four groups.

3. All subjects will have the length of their fingernails measured by a technician on Day 1 of the study, and measured again on Day 10.

4. All subjects (except the subjects in Group 4) will be instructed not to cut, manicure or otherwise touch their nails for the 10 days that the study is being conducted.

5. All subjects will be paid $50 and debriefed at the end of the study.

6. The average length of fingernail growth for each of the groups will be compared to the average length of fingernail growth for each of the remaining groups by means of appropriate statistical tests.

7. NNB will be considered to have been proven successful in this experiment if the null hypothesis can be rejected at the .05 level of significance. Note that the meaning of rejection of the null hypothesis at the ".05 level of significance" is explained subsequently under the heading, "The Concept of Confidence Level."

blind

in scientific research, a condition of unawareness as to aspects of the study on the part of one or more of the parties to the research. Compare to *double-blind*.

double-blind

in scientific research, a condition of unawareness as to aspects of the study on the part of both the experimenter and the subject.

placebo

in scientific research, an inactive substance usually administered to control for the effect of an active substance.

Like Group 3, Group 4 will also consist of 25 subjects who will be placed on a waiting list for treatment. During the course of the actual study, members of Group 4 will receive neither treatment nor instructions. Members of Group 4 will be asked to report to the experimenter on Day 1 and then again on Day 10 to have their fingernails measured. They will receive no instructions as to the care of their nails during the 10-day period.

All subjects will be **blind** or *unaware of the treatment condition to which they were assigned.* Subjects in Group 1 and Group 2 will not know whether they are being treated with a solution that contains the active ingredient (NNB) or plain tap water. Subjects in Group 3 will be unaware that they have been assigned to a "waiting list/instructions only" treatment condition. Subjects in Group 4 will be unaware that they have been assigned to a "waiting list/no instructions" treatment condition.

In addition to all subjects being blind to their treatment condition, all technicians working for the experimenter will be blind to the treatment condition subjects have been assigned to. This means, for example, that any or all of the technicians involved in taking measurements of fingernails will not know whether they are measuring the fingernails of someone who has been treated with NNB, treated with water, or someone who has been placed on a waiting list for treatment (with or without instructions). With *both the experimenters and the subjects blind to the subjects' treatment condition,* the study is said to be conducted under **double-blind** conditions. All other things being equal, double-blind studies are preferable to *single-blind* studies (that is, studies in which only the subjects are blind to their treatment condition). As was noted earlier, there is evidence that if experimenters are aware of who was assigned to which group, the experimenter's expectancies concerning how the results should come out may actually influence the findings.

In the NNB experiment, tap water is being used as a **placebo** (*an inactive substance*) to control for the effect of NNB (the solution with the active ingredient). To understand why a control such as water might be used in the experiment, suppose that at the end of the 10-day experiment all of the subjects in Groups 1 and 2 seemed to have stopped biting their nails (as evidenced by the fingernail measurements taken), while the subjects in Groups 3 and 4 seemed to have continued to bite their nails. Would you consider NNB a successful treatment for nailbiting? Hardly! If plain tap water could achieve the same results as NNB, there is nothing very special about NNB. In fact, such a finding in this study might prompt the experimenter to test other hypotheses, such as: *Providing nailbiters with any kind of treatment for their nailbiting will stop them from nailbiting.*

Group 3 could be referred to as the "instructions-only control group." This group is included to control for the effect of the instruction given to subjects not to touch their nails for the 10 days that the experiment will be conducted. Should there be evidence that the subjects in Groups 1, 2, and 3 (but not Group 4) all stopped biting their nails, it may well be that the experimenter's instruction not to touch the fingernails during the course of the study was in itself sufficient to curb nailbiting behavior. But what if there was evidence at the end of the study that *all* subjects in all of the groups (even the no-instructions group) succeeded in stopping their nailbiting behavior?

One interpretation of such a finding might be that simply participating in a research study on nailbiting curbs nailbiting behavior. Another explanation might relate to the way that subjects were selected for participation in the study in the first place. Perhaps the method of selecting subjects was not rigorous enough in that "hard core" fingernail biters were not identified. Alternatively, there may have been some bias, however subtle, that allowed for the selection of subjects who were atypically high in motivation to stop biting their nails.

VARIABLES

Another term that is key in discussions of behavioral research is **variable**, which, simply put, is *anything that can vary*. Age, eye color, gender, loudness of music, race, length of one's hair, and length of one's nails are variables. Treatment group (such as treated/untreated), diagnostic category (such as alcoholic/cocaine abuser/normal), intelligence (such as below, at, or above average intelligence), muscular coordination (such as good, fair, poor), and political party (such as Republican/Democrat or Republican/Democrat/Liberal or Republican/Democrat/Liberal/Conservative) are but a few of the many examples of things that might be variables in a study.

In an experiment, the experimenter manipulates one or more variables in a situation, and then observes the effect of that manipulation on one or more other variables. Stated a bit more technically, the experimenter manipulates what is called the independent variable, and then notes the effect on a dependent variable. **Independent variable** may be defined simply as *a variable manipulated by the experimenter, such as an experimental treatment.* A **dependent variable** may be defined simply as *an observable and/or measurable response to a variable manipulated by the experimenter,* such as a response to an experimental treatment. In advance of an experiment, the experimenter makes decisions about the nature, magnitude, or strength of independent variables. The nature, magnitude, or strength of dependent variables may be dependent upon the independent variable(s) employed in the study.

In the toxic waste film study, the independent variable is "exposed/not exposed to toxic waste film." The dependent variable is "attitude towards corporate toxic waste disposal methods." In the NNB study, the independent variable might be termed "treated/not treated with NNB solution on fingernails." What would the dependent variable be?

In experimental investigations, scientists typically prefer dependent variables that can be measured or quantified. In fact, descriptions of the majority of dependent variables in the scientific literature begin with the phrase "the number of. . . ." Some examples of dependent variables include "the number of seconds," "the number of points on an attitude (or other) test," and "the number of presses on a bar." In the NNB study, the dependent variable would be "the number of millimeters all subjects' fingernails grew over the course of 10 days."

In general, the experimental method demands that only the variable(s) of interest to the experimenter be systematically varied. All other possible sources of variation must either be controlled for or allowed to vary in a **random** or *nonsystematic* way. For the NNB study, this would mean that only the application of NNB to the fingernails should be systematically varied by the experimenter. Certain things related to that treatment variable, such as the temperature of the NNB solution when it is applied to the fingernails, can readily be controlled by the experimenter. The date on which the study will be run can be controlled for by the experimenter—and this may sometimes prove a factor of some

variable
anything that can vary, such as age, eye color, gender, loudness of music, race, length of one's hair, and so forth.

independent variable
a variable manipulated by the experimenter.

dependent variable
an observable and/or measurable response to a variable manipulated by the experimenter.

random
nonsystematic

ethics
principles of conduct generally considered to be "right,"

importance. For example, conducting the NNB experiment during the week of final examinations might prove a more challenging test of the effectiveness of NNB then conducting the same study during the first week of a new semester. This is because nailbiters typically bite their nails in response to increased stress, and one source of stress for most students is final examinations.

Many variables cannot, however, be controlled for by the experimenter and must therefore be allowed to vary randomly. For example, anxiety-provoking events and situations that happen to occur in the private lives of subjects might prompt some subjects to bite their nails with greater frequency than they otherwise would. During the course of the 10 days that the NNB study is conducted, it might rain constantly—providing yet another source of stress to individual subjects who tend to feel "down" when there is a lack of bright sunshine for a prolonged period of time.

One procedure experimenters employ in their efforts to ensure that variables out of their control will vary randomly is *random assignment of subjects to groups*. For the NNB experiment, one way of ensuring random assignment to treatment condition would be an assignment based solely on the order in which the individual was recruited for the study. One student would be assigned to the NNB treatment group, the next to Group 2, the next to Group 3, the next to Group 4, the next to Group 1, and so forth. It would *not* be a random procedure to assign, for example, all the people who were recruited by phone to one group and all the people who were recruited in-person to another group. There may be, for example, differences in anxiety level between people who apply by phone or in-person, and these differences may in some way affect the findings.

ETHICAL CONSIDERATIONS

Ethics are *principles of conduct generally considered to be "right," "proper," or "good."* For psychologists, what is and is not considered ethical in research has been embodied in a number of publications of the American Psychological Association (APA). Through many specific principles guiding research with human subjects, there is repeated emphasis on the need for respect and concern for the subjects' dignity and welfare. Through many specific principles guiding research with animal subjects, there is repeated emphasis on the need to safeguard the welfare of the animals and in every way possible treat them humanely. Whether research is being conducted with human or animal subjects, ethical principles dictate that the scientist report what was done and what was found accurately. Unfortunately, this has not always been the case (see *A Question of Values*).

Ethical guidelines do not necessarily have the force of law behind them (though some, such as prohibitions against animal cruelty, do have the force of law behind them in most states). Still, most psychologists would agree that anyone who conducts psychological research should have a knowledge of APA ethical principles and should design and conduct experiments accordingly.

CONDUCTING THE EXPERIMENT

Even before the experiment begins, there is typically much that the experimenter has to do. In the NNB study, for example, some of the things the experimenter will have to do is recruit and screen subjects, train technicians, and set up procedures to ensure that both subjects and technicians will be "blind" regarding treatment condition.

RECRUITING AND SCREENING SUBJECTS

Having decided who (or what) the subjects in a research study will be, the experimenter then specifies the criteria by which individual subjects will be deemed *qualified* or suitable for participation. For example, in the NNB study, the experimenter has decided to use nailbiters as subjects. But nailbiters represent a very wide-ranging group in terms of age and other variables. One of the experimenter's first tasks, then, is to narrow the field a bit and to specify exactly what will be meant by the term *nailbiter*. Stated another way, the experimenter must provide an **operational definition** of nailbiting, or *the meaning of a particular term for the purposes of the research*. For research purposes, experimenters may operationally define any term in any way that they believe will best serve the objectives

A QUESTION OF

Fame and Recognition versus Honesty and Integrity

Fraud may be defined as *a deception deliberately practiced in order to secure unfair or unlawful gain.* In newspapers, we may read about how one person or corporation defrauded another in order to reap some financial benefit. In movies, we may see a dramatization of a law enforcement officer "planting" drugs or a gun on someone in order to support some fraudulent charge against the person. Rarely do we read about, or even see in a dramatization, fraud practiced by scientists. Does it exist? If so, why does it exist? How is fraud in science dealt with? What can be done to prevent it?

As in other areas of human endeavors, fraud is an unfortunate reality in science. It may take the form of a report of a scientist doing something that in reality wasn't done. It may take the form of a report of finding something that in reality was not found. It may take the form of depriving someone else of the credit he or she rightfully deserves. We would all like to believe that such incidents of fraud in scientific research are very, very rare. Yet in a survey of 1,500 members of the American Association for the Advancement of Science (1992), about 27% of the respondents reported that they believed that they had personally witnessed some type of fraud on the part of a peer. Equally, if not more disturbing, 37% of these survey respon-

dents expressed the belief that fraud in science was on the rise, and only 2% of the respondents expressed the belief that fraud in science was declining.

Scientists, like other professionals, may find themselves under pressure to "produce." When scientists fail to produce for whatever reason—such as an inability to adjust to pressure, an inability to think creatively, or simply an inability to competently perform their duties—fraud may result.

Allegations of fraud in science are a very serious business as lives and reputations may well be at stake. Charging fraud can expose the person making the charge to counterclaims of defamation which may result in costly and time-consuming litigation. Whether or not fraud was actually committed may be left to some "blue-ribbon panel" of scientists to decide. That is what happened, for example, when Dr. Robert C. Gallo of the National Cancer Institute was charged with committing either an error or fraud in claiming that he co-discovered the AIDS virus with Dr. Luc Montagnier of the Pasteur Institute in Paris. In 1984, the laboratories headed by Gallo and Montagnier were cooperating with one another in an effort to isolate the AIDS virus. When the charge was made that Gallo had used a sample sent from Montagnier's laboratory to claim credit for isolating the AIDS

virus, a panel of experts from the National Institutes of Health undertook the task of trying to reconstruct what the truth of the matter was. This task involved hours of interviewing Gallo and his staff, as well as going over the details from dozens of Gallo's laboratory notebooks regarding his experiments. In late December 1992, after conducting an investigation that lasted over three years, the Federal Office of Research Integrity concluded that Gallo had committed scientific misconduct (Hilts, 1992a). According to the report, Gallo falsely reported a critical finding in a 1984 paper. In so doing, the report went on, Gallo "impeded potential AIDS research progress" in order to win credit for himself.

Prevention of fraud is essential if we are to be able to rely on and act on the findings scientists report to us. Towards that end, mechanisms for detecting, reporting, and ultimately stopping fraud must exist, as must counseling and support services for any scientist who might contemplate such a breach of the public trust. The majority of the respondents in the American Association for the Advancement of Science study (1992) believed that fraud-related problems are best handled at the institution in which they occur rather than by government organizations.

of the study. However, the final report of the study must contain the operational definitions of all key terms and a clear description of all of the procedures used. Such clear definitions and descriptions are important not only for readers seeking to understand and interpret the findings, but also for other researchers who may want to attempt a replication.

In the NNB study, the definition of *nailbiter* could range from one that is all-inclusive (such as "people who report that they bite their fingernails") to one that is fairly narrow with a provision for visual verification (such as "people who report that they have bitten off one or more of their own fingernails within the last day and who present visible evidence of missing at least one nail"). In this case, let us say that the psychologist has chosen an operational definition of nailbiting that is somewhere in the middle between the two examples given above: "undergraduate students between the ages of 18 and 21 who report that they have bitten at least one fingernail within the 30-day period prior to responding to the ad."

The experimenter is well aware that undergraduate students may range in age below 18 and far beyond 21. Why then place limits?

In this case, the experimenter has limited the age range primarily to *control for,* or to regulate the influence of, age as a factor in this experiment. It may be, for example, that the fingernails of 20-year-olds grow at a different rate from the fingernails of 60-year-olds. Thus, if subjects of wide-ranging age were included in the study, the results of the study might be **confounded** (that is, *made confusing or more difficult to interpret*) by age as a factor. The experimenter will have enough questions to answer without having to worry about, "Did the number of millimeters the subjects' nails grow during the course of the 10-day study have more to do with nailbiting behavior or the age of the subject?"

The psychologist recruits nailbiting subjects for the NNB study by means of an ad in the campus newspaper which reads in part: "Students between the ages of 18 and 21 who bite their fingernails wanted for study of new treatment for nailbiting. All participants will be paid $50 for the 10-day study."

The experimental design calls for a brief preexperiment interview to determine if in fact people who responded to the ad qualify as nailbiters according to the experimenter's operational definition of nailbiting. Through this process of **screening** or *sifting out who is and is not qualified to participate in an experiment,* subjects will be selected for participation in the study. Also at this time, subjects may be told something about the study and what the experimenter is trying to do. This is done to obtain the subject's **informed consent** to participate in the study, meaning that *the subject willingly agrees to participate in the study after being told about it.* In some types of experiments, the NNB experiment being one of them, it is not always possible to disclose every aspect of what will be done prior to the study. For example, a disclosure such as, "You are in the wait list/instructions-only treatment condition," might bias the results. Decisions as to what is or is not ethical must sometimes be made on a case-by-case basis. Ideally such decisions will be made in consultation with respected colleagues who are knowledgeable about the application of ethical principles, or an institution's research review board.

TRAINING TECHNICIANS

All experiments involve some kind of measurement. The particular measures used will of course vary widely with the objectives of different research projects. A sampling of the various types of measures used in behavioral research is presented in Table AP–2. Some measures, such as a paper-and-pencil survey with easy-to-follow directions, require little or no training to administer. Other measures, such as a test of intelligence, may require a great deal of training to administer depending upon the particular test used.

In the NNB study, physical measurements of fingernail length will have to be made by the technicians. Because the study's findings will hinge on the precision with which these measurements are made, the experimenter has decided to train one technician to conduct such measurements precisely. Only when that technician has met the criteria of precision in measurement set by the experimenter can the study get under way. If additional technicians are to be trained, they too will have to demonstrate their ability to measure precisely in accordance with the experimenter's standards.

OTHER ACTIVITIES

During the experiment, the researcher may be involved in a great variety of quality control activities to ensure that the experiment is indeed carried out according to the experimental design. Sometimes, after beginning an experiment, a researcher may discover unanticipated problems, such as the failure of a particular apparatus, which will bring the research to an abrupt halt for "debugging."

As the experiment draws to a close, another activity that experimenters engage in when conducting research with human subjects is **debriefing**. A debriefing may be defined as *a disclosure to a research subject, typically at the end of the research or the end of the individ-*

TABLE AP-2   MEASURES COMMONLY USED IN PSYCHOLOGICAL RESEARCH

Type of Measure	Explanation
Psychological tests	Intelligence tests, personality tests, and tests of interest and aptitude are but a few of the types of tests that may be used as measures in psychological research with human subjects.
Performance tests	In psychological research with nonhuman subjects, such as laboratory rats, some measure of behavioral accomplishment, such as pressing down on a bar, may be the measure employed by the researcher. With human subjects, a performance test may also take many different forms, such as presenting a spontaneous speech on a given topic.
Physical measurements	As their name implies, physical measurements involve measuring some physical aspect of the subject. Measuring the length of one's fingernails in a study on nailbiting behavior is an example of one type of physical measurement. Measuring the amount of tissue regenerated during the course of an experiment might be another type of physical measurement.
Psychophysiological measurements	Included here are measures of physical processes that the subject has no voluntary control over such as blood pressure and heart rate.
Self-report measures	Included here are all kinds of written and/or oral assessments of an individual's opinions, beliefs, feelings, sensations, and impressions.
Unobtrusive measures	These are measures that are "nonreactive" in that they "do not require the cooperation of a respondent" (Webb, et al., 1966, p. 2). Research on the amount of whiskey consumption in small towns, for example, might be carried out using the number of empty bottles disposed of as an unobtrusive measure.

ual subject's participation in the research, of details regarding the objectives, procedures, and findings of the research. If there was any deception involved in the experiment, the experimenter will explain to the subject why such deception was necessary in order to carry out the experiment. Debriefing is an important element of behavioral research because it may be educational for the subject, and, it is hoped, helps to maintain positive attitudes towards such research on the part of the public. In the NNB study, subjects' debriefing would include disclosure of which treatment condition the subject was assigned to and the rationale for using four treatment conditions.

ANALYZING, INTERPRETING, AND REPORTING THE FINDINGS

In the wake of an experiment, there are data to be analyzed and interpreted. After the NNB study, for example, the experimenter will have accumulated 1,000 measures of fingernail length (the measurement of all 10 fingernails of each of the 100 subjects) taken on Day 1 of the experiment, and another 1,000 such measures taken on Day 10 of the experiment. These data will have to be analyzed in order to assist the experimenter in gauging the effectiveness of NNB as a treatment for nailbiting. More specifically, the experimenter will compare the average length of fingernail growth for the subjects in each of the groups. Then, as planned in the experimental design from the start, "NNB will be deemed successful if the null hypothesis can be rejected at the .05 level of significance." *What does that mean?!* Stated succinctly, it means that *statistical methods* (discussed subsequently) will be used to help the experimenter make sense of the collected data.

Interpretation of findings can be a difficult task, and the more variables that are operative in a particular experiment, the more difficult interpretation can be. Beyond the question of whether NNB is effective as a treatment for nailbiting, the experimenter may want to tackle interpretation of the findings with regard to other variables that were operative in the study. For example, what was the effect of using these particular subjects? Would the results have been different if older or younger subjects had been used? What was the effect of using this particular method to measure the effectiveness of NNB? Would the conclusions have been the same if a simple measure of self-report of nailbiting had been used? What was the effect of paying all subjects $50 for their participation in the study? Would the same results have been obtained if all subjects had been paid $5? $500? These may all be questions for future researchers.

Once data have been analyzed and experimenters have formulated some interpretation for why they found what they did, the next step would be to report the findings in an acceptable way in some outlet for research. Usual outlets for research are scientific journals and presentations at professional meetings. Unusual outlets for research would include radio or television talk shows and magazines targeted to the general public or nonscientists. The research report will usually include references to the professional and/or lay literature. Note that in the body of the research report itself, just as in the body of this text, reference is usually made to the author and the year of publication (for example, "Rogers, 1939"). The term *et al.,* meaning "and others," may be used if there are other authors' names that are not listed. At or near the end of the research article (and books as well—see pages 469 to 516 herein) are complete reference citations. When the reference is to a newspaper or magazine article in which there is no listing of an author's name, the title of the article, and the year of its publication may be listed. For professional journals, a complete reference citation includes the name of the author, the title of the article, the name of the journal the article was published in, the volume number of the journal that the article was published in, and the page numbers of the article. For a book, a reference citation will include the author's name, the year of publication, the title of the book, the city the publisher is (or was) located in, and the name of the publisher.

OTHER RESEARCH METHODS

Suppose an insurance company is interested in determining whether a family of four has a better chance of surviving a 55-mile-per-hour collision in a top-of-the-line Mercedes Benz or a top-of-the-line Volvo. And let's suppose further that they wished to conduct an experiment using live subjects, not dummies, to test this hypothesis: "There is no difference in safety between a Mercedes and a Volvo in a 55-mile-per-hour collision." Can you picture the newspaper ad that would be used to recruit subjects for such an experiment?

> Wanted. Family of four to crash luxury car into brick wall at 55 miles-per-hour. No experience necessary. Will train. Good pay and benefits.

We might expect that there would be no takers regardless of the "good pay and benefits." Either the company will have to settle for the use of crash dummies in the experiment or not conduct the experiment. But perhaps there is some alternative to experimentation that can be used to answer the question. In fact there is. A research method that involves analysis of past accident reports involving the Volvo and Mercedes models of interest might be all that is needed to answer the insurance company's questions.

Depending on the objectives of the research and other factors, experimental or nonexperimental research methods may be employed. The primary difference between these two approaches to research is the control the experimenter has. You will recall that in experimental research, the experimenter is manipulating the independent variable and noting the effect of this manipulation on the dependent variable. In nonexperimental research, the researcher may be viewed less as a "manipulator" and more as an "observer" watching variables at work. Some nonexperimental approaches to research are briefly discussed below.

FIELD OBSERVATION

field observation

the systematic viewing of an organism in its own natural setting.

One example of nonexperimental research is **field observation**, which may be defined as *the systematic viewing of an organism in its own natural setting*. If you have ever watched a nature documentary wherein a camera records the action of some animal in its native habitat, you have a sense of what field observation (also referred to as *field study*) is all about. Psychologists may use field observation techniques to observe people as well. Suppose, for example, you were interested in researching this hypothesis: "Middle school students spend less time eating lunch than high school students." You might design an experiment that involved serving lunch to a representative number of middle school and high school students and then comparing the results. A far less complex and costly, and all-around better approach to the same question, would be field observation. Observers in cafeterias at selected middle schools and high schools would time the number of minutes students spent actually eating lunch and then would report back to the researcher.

CASE STUDIES

Another type of nonexperimental research method involves compiling materials from a variety of sources in order to make educated inferences. This type of research method is called the **case study** approach, and it may be defined as *a research method that entails making inferences or conclusions from the collection of data from different sources (as wide-ranging as hospital, police, and other official records, family album photos, writings, possessions, etc.).* In medical science, case studies are used extensively to learn about the course a particular disease may take. Similarly, in behavioral science, case studies are used to better understand patterns of behavior that typically occur in groups of people diagnosed with a particular behavior disorder. For example, extensive case studies have been compiled on people diagnosed with different sub-types of schizophrenia. The case study material helps shed much needed light on the course this disorder may take, with or without treatment.

case study research
a nonexperimental research method that entails making inferences or conclusions from a collection of data from varied sources.

CORRELATIONAL RESEARCH

What is the relationship between fatality in a 55-mile-per-hour crash and ownership of a Volvo? What is the relationship between performance on this job interview and performance on the job? Is there a relationship between alcohol consumption and aggression? Is there a relationship between violence on television and violence in society? These are but a few of the types of questions that might be addressed through what are referred to as *correlational* studies. **Correlation** is *a statistical tool used to determine the nature and the magnitude of the relationship between two variables.*

correlation
a statistical tool used to determine the nature and the magnitude of the relationship between two variables.

When the relationship between two variables is strong, a *high* correlation is said to exist. For example, we usually expect a strong or high correlation between the price we pay for something and quality. We expect that the more we pay, the higher the quality. The less we pay, the lower the quality. The price/quality relationship is an example of a high, *positive* correlation; as one variable varies up or down, so the other variable varies right along with it in the same direction. In a high, *negative* correlation, as one variable varies up or down, the other variable varies right along with it but in the *opposite* direction. Can you think of a relationship between two things that is representative of a high, negative correlation? What about the relationship between miles on a car and the price the car can fetch in the marketplace? As one variable, say miles on the car, goes up, the other variable, the value of the car in the marketplace, goes down.

An important point to keep in mind about correlational research methods is that, at best, these methods tell us something about the strength and direction of the relationship between things. Correlation is *not* synonymous with causation. To illustrate, there is a high positive correlation between hat size and cognitive abilities in human children from birth through age 6. Does this mean that increases in the size of the head are alone responsible for human children's remarkable growth in cognitive abilities between birth and age 6? Of course not. Such a correlation only indicates that a relationship exists between hat size and cognitive abilities. It does not tell us what—if anything—causes this relationship.

Figure AP–3 contains an Associated Press story that appeared in hundreds of newspapers around the country in mid-September 1992. This article describes correlational research that focused on alcohol drinking among college students. The headline tells us that the researchers found that students at small colleges tended to drink more than their counterparts at larger schools. Also contained in the article is the correlational finding that "students with low grades consume about three times as many drinks as those on the honor roll" ("Study Finds Students," 1992, p. L33). The latter finding is useful in illustrating another point about correlational research. Although correlational studies do not yield find-

Study Finds Students at Small Colleges Drink More

WASHINGTON, Sept. 19 (AP)—Students at small colleges drink more alcohol than their colleagues at larger schools, a study based on a survey of more than 56,000 students shows.

The study also found that students with low grades consume about three times as many drinks as those on the honor roll.

The survey results, based on data collected at 56 four-year schools and 22 community colleges during the 1989–90 school year, were analyzed by researchers from Southern Illinois University and the College of William and Mary.

They said their report was intended to help campus leaders understand the frequency of drug and alcohol use as they design programs to combat such activities. "It's the largest sample that's ever been done," said one researcher, Cheryl A. Presley. "Here is the information for them to make better decisions."

Average of 7 Drinks a Week

The information about drinking on small campuses was particularly significant, said Ms. Presley and her colleague, Philip W. Meilman.

At four-year schools with enrollments of less than 2,500, students under 24 years old averaged seven drinks a week, as against 4.59 drinks at campuses with 20,000 students or more.

"Small schools tend to be located in rural environments where there is less to do, so people may turn to drinking more," Mr. Meilman siad. "There's a tendency to conform to existing social norms."

The study did not establish a causal link between drinking and low grades but found a strong correlation.

Students who were getting D's and F's were averaging nearly 11 drinks a week, while students with A's were consuming 3.4, the study reported.

The survey also made these findings:

• About 42 percent of students said they had gone on a drinking binge at least once in the past two weeks, defined as consuming five or more drinks.

• 66 percent of all students wanted alcohol available at social events on or near campus, but only 13 percent wanted drugs. Among daily drinkers, 49 percent said they would like to have drugs available.

• Twenty-seven percent of students said they smoked marijuana in the past year and 6.1 percent said they used cocaine.

As expected, alcohol was popular on all the campuses: 86 percent of the respondents said they used it in the last year, and 45 percent said they drank on a weekly or more frequent basis.

ings that establish causal relationships, such studies may be useful in suggesting the exploration of causal relationships through other research methods, such as experimentation. After reading the article, consider the question, "Is there a causal relationship between alcohol consumption and grades in college students?" How might you go about answering this question by means of an experiment?

OTHER ALTERNATIVES TO EXPERIMENTATION

Suppose that an environmental psychologist is interested in studying a community's reaction to an impending nuclear meltdown disaster at a local power plant. The psychologist is particularly interested in investigating whether it is really possible to safely evacuate 200,000 people under emergency conditions within a 50-mile radius of the power facility. Such research conducted as an experiment would require that virtually everyone in the entire community surrounding the facility be deceived by false media reports of an impending meltdown. In this instance, a mere sampling of the people evacuating town would not be sufficient to mimic the crowded roadways, panic, and other conditions that would prevail in a real emergency. Do you think the potential gains in knowledge from conducting such an experiment would outweigh the possible risks of conducting it?

The answer to this question is arguable. Some may view as ethically unconscionable the sense of horror, fear, and panic, that such news would elicit in many thousands of unsuspecting, nonconsenting "subjects." Others might concede that such an experiment would be highly disruptive, but also argue that such research would ultimately benefit the community in terms of better preparing it for a real emergency in the future.

For me, the argument *against* conducting such an experiment seems the more compelling. Participation in *any* psychological experiment should never carry with it risks such as sudden death—which is exactly what might happen as a result of cardiac arrest in "subjects" having preexisting heart problems were the study to be conducted. Some alternatives to conducting such an experiment might be (1) a computer simulation of what would happen under such circumstances, (2) a research program that entails maintaining readiness to observe systematically what happens when and if a threat of a meltdown actually occurs naturally, and (3) role playing, or *the* planned staging of such an event with the full knowledge and consent of community members.

Figure AP–4 provides an overview of the research process and the research methods that may be employed in that process. Regardless of which research method is used, **raw data** (that is, *information collected in unanalyzed form*) will be generated. This information may take the form of pages of numbers. It may take the form of "yes" or "no" answers to one or more questions. It may take the form of a videotape of particular behavior that must be further analyzed. Regardless of form, some strategy and techniques will be necessary for transforming the raw data of scientific research into a more meaningful, interpretable form. Statistical methods are used to do just that (among other things). A brief introduction to some basic concepts regarding statistical methods will round out our overview of research methods in psychology.

STATISTICAL METHODS

A **statistic** may be defined as *any numerical piece of data*. In its plural form (*statistics*), as well as in the term **statistical methods**, reference is being made to *strategies, tools, and techniques for gathering, describing, analyzing, and drawing conclusions about data*. Two general types of statistical methods are *descriptive statistics* and *inferential statistics*.

DESCRIPTIVE STATISTICS

Some *statistical methods are used for the purpose of describing data*, and these methods are called **descriptive statistics**. A descriptive statistic that is probably familiar to you is the

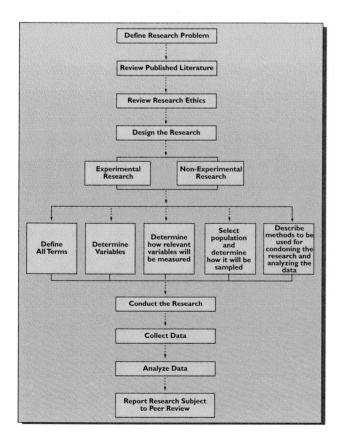

FIGURE AP–4 A MODEL OF THE RESEARCH PROCESS As shown by this relatively simple model, the research process entails at the outset activities such as defining the research problem, review of the published literature, review of the relevant research ethics, and the design of how the research will be conducted. Will the research take the form of an experiment? Will it take some other form? Regardless, terms and variables will have to be defined, as will the population to be studied. Additionally, all of the methods used in conducting the research and analyzing the data obtained should be specified at the outset.

average. The arithmetic average (or *mean* as it is typically referred to in the context of data analysis) is one of several descriptive statistics that may be used to obtain what is technically referred to as a "measure of central tendency." In a set of data that reads, 1, 2, and 3, the average or mean, as you are probably aware, is equal to 2. There are statistics other than the mean to describe a measure of central tendency. And there are many other kinds of descriptive statistics that can be used to describe data. Suffice it to say here that *descriptive statistics describe data.* Should you decide to pursue more advanced training in psychology, you will learn more about the various ways that data can be described.

INFERENTIAL STATISTICS

inferential statistics

in scientific research, methods used for the purpose of making conclusions, predictions, or interpretations from study findings. Contrast with *descriptive statistics.*

Beyond simply describing data, researchers generally want to make reasonable conclusions, predictions, or interpretations from their findings. Stated another way, they want to be able *to infer something about what data may mean;* to do this, researchers use strategies, tools, and techniques that are collectively referred to as **inferential statistics**. One type of inference commonly made by researchers concerns whether a treatment method was or was not effective. Should you decide to pursue more advanced study in psychology or other social sciences, you will probably take a research methods course in which you will learn more about descriptive and inferential statistics.

THE CONCEPT OF CONFIDENCE LEVEL

Statistical methods are used by researchers as a tool to aid in decisions regarding the null hypothesis. But what criteria are applied in making such judgments? For example, if a treatment is found to be effective in 70 out of 100 people, shall the experimenter conclude that the treatment is effective or ineffective? Should the null hypothesis be rejected? What if the treatment is effective in 55 of 125 people? 85 of 363 people? 25 of 42 people? *What kind of ratio is necessary for the researcher to be confident that the treatment is indeed effective?*

confidence level

a criterion usually expressed in the form of a probability, that will be used to accept or reject a hypothesis.

In addressing such questions, a knowledge of the concept of "confidence level" in research will be helpful. A **confidence level** may be defined as *a criterion, usually expressed in the form of a probability, that will be used to accept or reject a hypothesis.* In a way, it is an expression that reflects the researcher's "level of confidence" in rejecting (or failing to reject) the null hypotheis. It is through statistical analyses of the research data—a description of which is beyond the scope of this chapter—that the effectiveness of a treatment will be determined. Stated differently, it is with the aid of statistical analyses that the experimenter will determine whether or not the observed findings in a given sample of a certain size could have been obtained entirely as a matter of chance. For example, consider an experiment in which iced tea was used to treat schizophrenia. Over the course of this experiment, one group of institutionalized schizophrenics drank a glass of iced tea daily. One matched group of subjects was deprived of iced tea. Another matched groups of subjects drank a placebo solution of colored/flavored water that looked and tasted like iced tea. Given that behavioral scientists know of no curative properties of iced tea, what might we expect? One thing that we might expect is that any observed improvement in the condition of the schizophrenics administered the iced tea was not actually due to the treatment (iced tea). Rather any observed improvement in the condition of that group over the other two groups would probably be due more to chance than to the effectiveness of iced tea in treating schizophrenia.

Statistical analysis of data help researchers to make judgments about whether what they observe could have occured as a result of chance alone, or whether something else (such as an effective treatment) appears to be operative. For some researchers to feel comfortable about rejecting the null hypothesis, they will need statistical reassurance that the result that they obtained in the research could have occurred by chance alone less than 1 time in 10. These researchers want to be "9 in 10" confident in rejecting the null hypothesis. For other researchers—more demanding in terms of the proof they require—such statistical reassurance would require odds of 1 time in 100; to reject the null hypothesis, the results obtained would be found to occur by chance alone less than one time in a hundred.

Other, yet more demanding researchers—some would say unreasonably demanding—might require even greater statistical reassurance before rejecting the null hypothesis. Before rejecting the null hypothesis, they might require that the observed finding could have occurred by chance alone less than 1 time in 1000.

In accordance with accepted practice in science, the criterion that will be used to reject the null hypothesis—that is, the confidence level—is set at the beginning, and not the end of a research study. Through statistical analysis of the data, the researcher will determine whether rejection of the null hypothesis is warranted on the basis of this pre-set criterion.

Although researchers may set virtually any confidence level that they care to select, there are two confidence levels that are traditionally used in psychology. One of these confidence levels—perhaps the more common one judging from studies reported in the literature— is variously referred to in published research as the "0.5 level" or the ".05 level of significance." Whether described in any of these terms, or in other, yet more technical ones, the **.05 level of significance** refers to *a finding that could have occurred by chance alone less than 5 times in 100*. Stated another way, the ".05 level" rerers to *a finding that could have occurred by chance alone less than 5 times in 100*. Stated another way, the ".05 level" refers to a finding that could have occurred by chance alone less than 1 time in 20.

The confidence level variously described as the ".01 level" or the **.01 level of significance** refers to *a finding that could have occurred by chance alone less than 1 time in 100*. The .01 level may be described variously as more "rigorous" or "conservative" than the .05 level. To understand why, let's illustrate with reference to the data from the NNB study. Using the .01 level of signficance, for NNB to be proven signficantly effective as a treatment, its superiority would have to be demonstrated statistically with data indicating that the results could have occurred by chance less than 1 time in 100. By contrast, using the .05 level of significance, it would have had to be shown statistically that the results could have occurred by chance less than 5 times in 100. Whether or not the obtained findings would be deemed to be "significant," would depend on the confidence level that was set at the outset. Findings shown to meet the pre-set level of significance are, logically enough, considered "significant." Findings that do not meet the pre-set level of signifiance are said to be "not significant."

.05 level of significance
a finding that could have occurred by chance alone less than 5 times in 100.

.01 level of significance
a finding that could have occurred by chance alone less than 1 time in 100.

THE USES OF RESEARCH

Every day we are bombarded with claims in the media and elsewhere of findings that are purported to be "scientific" in nature. In advertising, for example, we might be told that, based on scientific research, loyal beer drinkers of one brand actually preferred another brand in a taste test. Polled as to their general satisfaction with their automobiles, owners of one particular brand report much higher levels of satisfaction than owners of another brand of automobile. Participants in one self-help weight control group are purported to lose weight faster or more safely than participants in a competing weight control program. The list goes on.

Few consumers have the knowledge, background, experience, or training to make an informed evaluation of various advertising claims. The assertion, for example, that 51% of people who regularly buy Brand X beer (the best-selling beer in the country) prefer Brand Y beer in a taste test may sound quite persuasive. But is such a finding really "scientific"?

Without knowing more, perhaps the best answer to this question is probably not. Ask any beer drinker why they are loyal to a particular brand of beer and they will reflexively supply a one-word response: "taste". In truth, however, other factors may be involved. Loyalty to a particular brand of beer may be based, at least to some degree, for example, on the image of the person who drinks the beer as created and conveyed in advertising for the beer. In reality, it may be the case that Brand X is virtually unrecognizable by taste alone from Brand Y (see Figure AP–5). For any given taste test then, it might be possible to obtain a preference of 51% (or more) for either of the two beers under scrutiny. Consequently, the taste preference difference of 51% and 49% may in a scientific sense amount to no real

FIGURE AP-5

"I buy this brand of beer because I strongly identify with the kind of people they show in their commercials. You know, the beach, the vollyball, the Swedish bikini team..."

difference at all. It is also true that there are a number of sometimes subtle factors that may influence the outcome of a taste test (see, for example, Buchanan & Morrison, 1984; Morrison, 1981; Ringold, 1992).

USE OF RESEARCH BY BEHAVIORAL SCIENTISTS

In the short term, the "users" of behavioral research published in outlets such as professional journals tend to be behavioral scientists. A published study may provide answers to questions other researchers have independently been seeking, and/or inspire other researchers to ask more questions about phenomena under study. Published research may also have far-reaching implications for human welfare in terms of enhanced ability to diagnose, treat, or prevent some kinds of psychological disorders. As an example, consider the possible uses of new published findings concerning bulimia nervosa.

bulimia

an eating disorder characterized by disturbed self-perception, excessive exercise, and binging and purging for the purposes of weight control. Also referred to as *bulimia nervosa*.

Bulimia nervosa is *an eating disorder that is usually characterized by binge-eating, purging (vomiting), and over-concern with body shape and weight.* People who are afflicted with this disorder are referred to as *bulimics*. In a study entitled "Body Dissatisfaction in Bulimia Nervosa: Relationship to Weight and Shape Concerns and Psychological Functioning," Garfinkel et al. (1992) reported the results of a survey they conducted with 524 bulimics in Toronto and New York. On a test called the Eating Disorder Inventory, the bulimics evidenced very high levels of dissatisfaction with their own bodies. The authors of the study suggested that body dissatisfaction (as distinguished from mere overconcern with body shape and weight) be used in the future as one of the criteria in the diagnosis of bulimia nervosa.

What possible use or consequence might such research have? Some of the many possible consequences are as follows:

- It will stimulate other researchers to conduct similar surveys to see if the findings are true and replicable.
- It will ultimately lead to the addition of "dissatisfaction with one's own body" as a criterion used to diagnose bulimia nervosa.
- It will lead to more discussion of issues related to body dissatisfaction in the therapy of bulimics.
- It will lead to more sensitivity to issues related to body dissatisfaction in programs designed to prevent bulimia.

If you were a professional psychologist reading such a study in a professional journal, how might *you* use or respond to these findings?

USE OF RESEARCH BY NONPROFESSIONALS

In an oft-cited presidential address to the American Psychological Association in 1969, George A. Miller urged psychologists to promote human welfare by "giving psychology away." As Miller (1969) saw it, the responsibility of psychologists was not to apply psychology but to "give it away to the people who really need it." The result of this give-away would be what Miller referred to as "the practice of valid psychology by nonpsychologists" and a "psychological revolution." Much of what Miller said and subsequently emphasized again 11 years later (Miller, 1980) was inspirational. He envisioned psychology being brought to varied settings such as the workplace for use by supervisors to get more productivity from workers, and the inner city, so that mothers could learn how to foster psychological growth in their children.

Browsing through bookstores, listening to talk radio, or watching talk show television today, George Miller might be struck by the great amount of psychology being "given away" on any given day. But would George Miller be proud? Is the psychological expertise of popular media figures like Dr. Ruth Westheimer (see Figure 16–6), for example, what Miller envisioned in his oft-quoted address? Is the psychology being "given away" on talk shows like those hosted by Phil Donahue, Oprah Winfrey, Joan Rivers, Sally Jessy Raphael, and Geraldo Rivera what Miller had in mind?

It would seem that there are some fundamental differences between Miller's sincere but somewhat idealistic objectives and the goals of the media through which the "give-away" is supposed to take place. Perhaps the most basic difference is the desire on the part of psychologists to educate and the desire of the for-profit-media to entertain. Psy-

FIGURE AP–6 DR. RUTH WESTHEIMER As she is known to millions, "Dr. Ruth" (who is *not* a psychologist but a sex therapist), gives away advice on human sexuality. But how good is the advice? Was her rise to media prominence based on her brilliance with respect to sexual matters? Or was it based more on the premise that people would find it entertaining to watch a little old lady with an accent talk about sex-related matters? Randomly changing cable stations on the evening of December 25th, 1992, the author happened to catch an appearance of Dr. Ruth on a CNBC call-in program called, *Real Personal*. One caller thought she had experienced a female ejaculation but Dr. Ruth shrugged-off the ejaculate the woman observed as urine. In fact, as we saw in Chapter 12 (Human Sexuality), this is a very controversial matter. While some believe that the so-called female ejaculate is urine released involuntarily at the point of orgasm (Alzate, 1935; Goldbert et al., 1983), others have chemically analyzed the ejaculate and found it not to be urine (Zaviacic et al., 1988). Another female caller complained to Dr. Ruth that her boyfriend's penis was too small to satisfy her. Without even asking what most people would probably regard as the most obvious question about size (essential information under the circumstances), Dr. Ruth advised the caller to somehow bring the man for a consultation with a urologist—without telling him where they were going!

chologists hope to impart information, while the philosophy of a talk show is to quickly curtail anything that might be viewed as boring by members of a mass media audience. Counseling conducted by professional therapists and counselors in consultation rooms takes time. Counseling conducted over the airwaves may be accomplished in the space of whatever time is remaining before the next commercial break. The selling of audio-tapes with so-called "subliminal messages" on them for the purposes of self-help—and profit to the seller—is a multi-million-dollar a year industry. Yet the only psychologists who seem to endorse this technology are those affiliated in some way with the companies who are selling such tapes. Psychologists who have independently evaluated the claims made by marketers of subliminal audiotapes have not been satisfied that the claims are valid (Holender, 1986; Merikle, 1988, 1992; Pratkanis & Greenwald, 1988; Synodinos, 1988).

The next time you read about or hear someone discussing psychology-related research in the popular media, perhaps some of the material on research methods that you read about in this chapter will come to mind. Critically examine what is being represented. One tool for such examination is the checklist of questions presented in this chapter's *Quality of Life* section. Encourage people you know also to think critically about exactly what is "scientific" about representations regarding "scientific research" in the popular media.

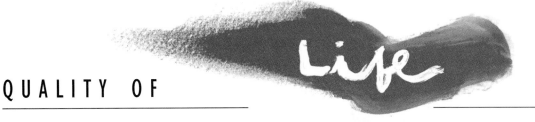

QUALITY OF

Psychology in the Popular Media

Conducting scientific research is infinitely more complicated than the thumbnail sketch provided in this chapter. However, even from this relatively simple description, perhaps you have formed a sense of some of the many elements that make scientific research "scientific." As you read about studies represented as scientific in books, magazines, and newspapers, or hear about them on radio or television talk shows, you may wish to ask questions such as the following:

1. In your opinion, did the researcher meet the requirement of objectivity?
2. Is the research reported in sufficient detail to be replicable by others? Do you think other re-

sponsible researchers would find the same thing?
3. Has the researcher proven whatever is being claimed? What is the claim of proof actually based on? What statistical tests were conducted? What was the researcher's pre-set confidence level?
4. What theory was the research based on?
5. What was the hypothesis?
6. Who were the subjects and how appropriate was this selection of subjects in light of the questions being asked in the research?
7. What variables were operative in the research? How might the results have been different if different variables were operative?

8. What training, if any, were the people who ran the experiment given?
9. If the research was an experiment, was it conducted under single- or double-blind conditions?
10. If the research was a case study, what was your impression of how balanced the selection of materials for presentation were?
11. If the research was field observation, did you have the sense that the researcher was able to carry it out without influencing whatever it was that was being observed?
12. Whatever form the research took, did it ring true to you? Why or why not?

SUMMARY

WHAT IS "SCIENTIFIC RESEARCH"? Exactly what constitutes "scientific research" will vary with one's *philosophy of science*, or assumptions about how new knowledge is discovered. This chapter outlines some basic assumptions psychologists make about pathways to knowledge.

TYPES OF RESEARCH IN BEHAVIORAL SCIENCE Three types of research in behavioral science are *basic research*, *applied research*, and *program evaluation research*. Basic research describes studies undertaken solely for the purpose of gathering new knowledge. *Applied research* describes studies undertaken in order to discover or confirm findings that can be put to use in the service of concerns or problems. *Program evaluation research* describes studies undertaken to assess the effectiveness, efficiency, or value of institutionalized procedures in the public or private sector.

QUALITY IN RESEARCH All research is not created equal; from the conception of the idea to the conduct of a particular research project to the writing of the final report, a number of different variables may affect the quality of the study. In general, research must be objective and replicable. *Objectivity* refers to a factual report of the findings that is free of the researcher's opinions, hunches, prejudices, or desires. *Replicability* refers to the repeatability of the findings; other researchers using the same methods should be able to replicate the original researcher's findings. In addition, the researcher must present evidence that the scientific community will deem satisfactory to support conclusions.

THE EXPERIMENTAL METHOD One way new knowledge is discovered in psychology is through experimentation. There are many considerations in experimentation including, among others, ethical issues, issues regarding the design or structure of the experiment, issues regarding the methods that will be used, and issues regarding the *subjects*—the people, or other organisms or things (such as crash test dummies) that will be "experimented on."

OTHER RESEARCH METHODS In addition to experiments, new knowledge is gathered by other means, such as *field observation, case studies,* and *correlational studies. Field observation* refers to systematic viewing of organisms in their own natural environment. *Case studies* are compilations of information and materials, usually from a variety of sources, used to make informed judgments about a person or group of people. *Correlational studies* provide a measure of the relationship between two variables.

STATISTICAL METHODS A *statistic* is any numerical piece of data and statistical methods refer to the strategies, tools, and techniques for gathering, describing, analyzing, and drawing conclusions about data. Some statistical methods are used primarily to describe data and these are called *descriptive statistics*. Other statistical methods are used primarily to make inferences or predictions about populations and these are called *inferential statistics*.

THE USES OF RESEARCH Research is used by scientists to develop new knowledge. It may also be used by commercial enterprises to promote sales of products. An informed consumer understands research to the extent that claims regarding findings made on the basis of "scientific research" can be critically evaluated.

REFERENCES

A Simpler Test Uses Only Saliva. (1992, April 12). *The New York Times,* p. F11.

Abel, E. (1983). *Marihuana, tobacco, alcohol and reproduction.* Boca Raton, FL: CRC Press.

Abelsohn, D. (1992). A "good enough" separation: Some characteristic operations and tasks. *Family Processes, 31,* 61–83.

Abrritti, G., et al. (1992). High prevalence of sick building syndrome in a new air-conditioned building in Italy. *Archives of Environmental Health, 47,* 16–22.

Achenbach, T. (1980). DSM-III in light of empirical research on the classification of child psychopathology. *Journal of the American Academy of Child Psychiatry, 19,* 395–412.

Ackerman, A. (1992, May 7). Cited in S. Slesin. Children at play saving the earth. *The New York Times,* pp. C1, C6.

Ackerman, M. (1987). Child sexual abuse: Bona fide or fabricated? *American Journal of Family Law, 2,* 181–185.

Adams, A., Carnine, D., & Gersten, R. (1982). Instructional strategies for studying context area texts in the intermediate grades. *Reading Research Quarterly, 18,* 27–53.

Adams, J. S. (1965). Inequity in social exchange. In L. Berkowitz (Ed.), *Advances in experimental social psychology* (Vol. 2) (pp. 276–300). New York: Academic Press.

Adelman, M. (1987, May/June). *Love's urban agent: Social support and the matchmaker.* Paper presented at the Iowa Conference on Personal Relationships, Iowa City, IA.

Adelman, M. (1988). Cross-cultural adjustment: A theoretical perspective on social support. *International Journal of Intercultural Relations, 12,* 183–204.

Adelman, M., & Ahuvia, A. C. (1991). Mediated channels for mate seeking: A solution to involuntary singlehood? *Critical Studies in Mass Communication, 8,* 273–279.

Ader, R., & Cohen, N. (1984). Behavior and the immune system. In W. D. Gentry (Ed.), *Handbook of behavioral medicine* (pp. 117–173). New York: Guilford.

Adjamine, P. (1992, June 6). A dog who taught the lesson of hope [Editorial]. *The New York Times,* p. A22.

Adler, A. (1927/1965). *Understanding human nature.* Greenwich, CT: Fawcett.

After a Layoff (and a Struggle) Catherine Horgan Started a Business. (1992, December 5). *The New York Times,* p. 34L.

Agnew, R. (1990). Adolescent resources and delinquency. *Criminology, 28,* 535–565.

Agopian, M. (1981). *Parental child stealing.* Lexington, MA: D. C. Heath.

Aguilar, R., Bellido, C., & Auguilar, E. (1987). Differences in prepuberal neonatally estrogenized or androgenized male rats. *Andrologia, 19,* 183–187.

Ahrons, C., & Rodgers, R. (1987). *Divorced families: A multidisciplinary developmental view.* New York: Norton.

Ahsen, A., & Lazarus, A. A. (1972). Eidetics: An internal behavior approach. In A. A. Lazarus (Ed.), *Clinical behavior therapy.* New York: Brunner/Mazel.

Ahuvia, A. C., & Adelman, M. B. (1990). *A descriptive study of a matchmaking service.* Unpublished manuscript, University of Michigan/Northwestern University, Ann Arbor, Evanston.

Ahuvia, A. C., & Adelman, M. B. (1992). Formal intermediaries in the marriage market: A typology and review. *Journal of Marriage and the Family, 54,* 452–463.

Ainsworth, M. D. S. (1969). Object relations, dependency, and attachment: A theoretical review of the infant-mother relationship. *Child Development, 40,* 969–1025.

Ainsworth, M. D. S. (1973). The development of infant-mother attachment. In B. M. Caldwell & H. N. Ricciuti (Eds.), *Review of child development research* (Vol. 3) (pp. 1–94). Chicago: University of Chicago Press.

Ainsworth, M. D. S., Blehar, M. C., Waters, E., & Wall, S. (1978). *Patterns of attachment: A psychological study of the strange situation.* Hillside, NJ: Erlbaum.

Alavanja, M. (1993, March 30). Presentation at a meeting of the American Cancer Society, March, 1993, in San Diego, CA. Cited in Lung Cancer and Fat Level, *The New York Times,* p. C8.

Alba, R. D., & Golden, R. M. (1986). Patterns of ethnic marriage in the United States. *Social Forces, 65,* 202–223.

Albee, G. W. (1968). Models, myths, and manpower. *Mental Hygiene, 52,* 168–180.

Albee, G. W. (1973). The sickness model of mental disorder means a double standard of care. In O. Milton, & R. G. Wahler (Eds.), *Behavior disorders* (pp. 27–42). Philadelphia: Lippincott.

Albert, E. M. (1963). Women of Burundi: A study of social values. In D. Paulme (Ed.), *Women of tropical Africa* (pp. 179–215). Berkeley, CA: University of California Press.

Alberti, R. E., & Emmons, M. L. (1970). *Your perfect right.* San Luis Obispo, CA: Impact.

Alberti, R. E., & Emmons, M. L. (1974). *Your perfect right* (2nd ed.). San Luis Obispo, CA: Impact.

Alderfer, C. P. (1972). *Existence, relatedness, and growth: Human needs in organizational settings.* New York: Free Press.

Allen, K. M. (1985). *The human-animal bond.* Metuchen, NJ: Scarecrow Press.

Allen, K. M., Blascovich, J., Tomaka, J., & Kelsey, R. M. (1991). Presence of human friends and pet dogs as moderators of autonomic responses to stress in women. *Journal of Personality and Social Psychology, 61,* 582–589.

Allen, L. S., & Gorski, R. A. (1990). Sex difference in the bed nucleus of the stria terminalis of the human brain. *Journal of Comparative Neurology, 302,* 697–706.

Allen, L. S., & Gorski, R. A. (1992). Report in the *Proceedings of the National Academy of Sciences,* August 1, 1992. Cited in N. Angier, (1992, August 1), Researchers find a second anatomical idiosyncracy in brains of homosexual men. *The New York Times,* p. L7.

Allen, L. W., Hines, M., Shryne, J. E., & Gorski, R. A. (1989). Two sexually dimorphic cell groups in the human brain. *Journal of Neuroscience, 9,* 497–506.

Allen, S., & Wollman, J. (1987). *How to be funny.* New York: McGraw-Hill.

Allison, D., & Heshka, S. (1993). Literature review cited in Adler, T. (1993). Study: Data don't support "emotional eating" theory. *The APA Monitor, 23* (6), 17.

Allport, G. W. (1937). *Personality: A psychological interpretation.* New York: Holt.

Allport, G. W. (1954). *The nature of prejudice.* Garden City, NY: Doubleday.

Allport, G. W. (1961). *Pattern and growth in personality.* New York: Holt, Rinehart and Winston.

Allport, G. W., & Odbert, H. S. (1936). Trait-names: A psycholexical study. *Psychological Monographs, 47* (Whole No. 211).

Allred, K. D., & Smith, T. W. (1989). The hardy personality: Cognitive and physiological responses to evaluative threat. *Journal of Personality and Social Psychology, 56,* 257–266.

Altman, L. K. (1992a, April 19). Ashe received a transfusion before blood supply was tested for H. I. V. *The New York Times,* p. B15.

Altman, L. K. (1992b, July 21). Women worldwide nearing higher rate for AIDS than men. *The New York Times,* p. C3.

Altman, L. K. (1993, February 17). 2 new studies link vasectomy to higher prostate cancer risk. *The New York Times,* p. C12.

Alzate, H. (1985). Vaginal eroticism: A replication study. *Archives of Sexual Behavior, 14,* 529–537.

Alzate, H., & Londono, M. L. (1984). Vaginal erotic sensitivity. *Journal of Sex and Marital Therapy, 10,* 48–56.

Amabile, T. M. (1983). Brilliant but cruel: Perceptions of negative evaluators. *Journal of Experimental Social Psychology, 19,* 146–156.

Amato, P. R. (1987). Family process in one-parent, step-parent, and intact families: The child's point of view. *Journal of Marriage and the Family, 47,* 319–334.

Amelang, M., & Borkenau, P. (1982). [On the factor structure and external validity of some questionnaire scales measuring dimensions of extraversion and neuroticism]. *Zeitschrift fur Differentielle und Diagnostische Psychologie, 3,* 119–146.

American Association for the Advancement of Science. (1992, December 31). Cited in P. J. Hilts. Federal inquiry finds misconduct by a discoverer of the AIDS virus. *The New York Times,* pp. A1, A20.

American College of Obstetricians and Gynecologists. (1990). *ACOG guide to planning for pregnancy, birth, and beyond.* Washington, DC: Author.

American Psychiatric Association. (1987). *DSM-III-R.* Washington, DC: Author.

American Psychological Association. (1991). *Questionnaires used in the prediction of trustworthiness in pre-employment selection decisions: An APA Task Force Report.* Washington, DC: Author.

American Psychological Association. (1993a, January). Call for book proposals for test instruments. *APA Monitor,* p. 12.

American Psychological Association, Office of Ethnic Minority Affairs. (1993b). Guidelines for providers of psychological services to ethnic, linguistic, and culturally diverse populations. *American Psychologist, 48,* 45–48.

Ames, M. A., & Houston, D. A. (1990). Legal, social, and biological definitions of pedophilia. *Archives of Sexual Behavior, 19,* 333–342.

Amler, R. W., & Doll, H. B. (1987). *Closing the gap: The burden of unnecessary illness.* New York: Oxford University Press.

Ammons, P., & Stinnet, N. (1980). The vital marriage: A closer look. *Family Relations, 29,* 37–42.

An Easing of Threat to Ozone Reported. (1992, October 6). *The New York Times,* p. C5.

Andersen, S. M., & Ross, L. (1984). Self-knowledge and social inference: 1. The impact of cognitive/affective and behavioral data. *Journal of Personality and Social Psychology, 46,* 294–307.

Anderson, J. R. (1985). *Cognitive psychology and its implications* (2nd ed.). San Francisco: W. H. Freeman.

Anderson, N. H. (1968). Likableness ratings of 555 personality trait words. *Journal of Personality and Social Psychology, 9,* 272–279.

Anderson, R. K., Hart, B. L., & Hart, L. (1984). *The pet connection: Its influence on our health and quality of life.* St. Paul, MN: Globe.

Anderson, S. & Gantt, W. H. (1966). The effect of person on cardiac and motor responsivity to shock in dogs. *Conditional Reflex, 1,* 181–189.

Andreason, N. C., & Black, D. W. (1991). *Introductory textbook of psychiatry.* Washington, DC: American Psychiatric Press.

Angelbeck, J. H., & DuBrul, E. F. (1983). The effect of neonatal testosterone on specific male and female patterns of phosphoylated cytosolic proteins in the rat preoptic-hypothalamus, cortex and amygdala. *Brain Research, 264,* 277–283.

Angell, M. (1988, September/October). Cited in Barber, J. Worried sick. *Equinox.*

Angier, N. (1992a, October 1). Gains made in effort to map the human genetic makeup. *The New York Times,* pp. A1, A22.

Angier, N. (1992b, June 9). A clue to longevity found at chromosome tip. *The New York Times,* p. C1.

Anonymous. (1992). Staff reaction to AIDS in the workplace. *Families in Society, 73,* 559–563.

Antoni, M. H., Bagget, L., Ironson, G., LaPerriere, A., August, S., Klimas, N., Schneiderman, N., & Fletcher, M. A. (1991). Cognitive-behavioral stress management intervention buffers distress responses and immunologic changes following notification of HIV-1 seropositivity. *Journal of Consulting and Clinical Psychology, 39,* 906–915.

Antoni, M. H., Schneiderman, N., Fletcher, M. A., & Goldstein, D. A. (1990). Psychoneuroimmunology and HIV-1. *Journal of Consulting and Clinical Psychology, 58,* 38–49.

Antunes, C. M., et al. (1979). Endometrial cancer and estrogen use: Report of a large case-control study. *The New England Journal of Medicine, 300,* 9–13.

Apfelbaum, M. (1993, January 24). Cited in R. Cohen. Dieting a la Paris: Foie gras, wine and chocolate. *The New York Times,* p. 10L.

Applebome, P. (1992, April 18). Gingrich tries to avoid heat of voter outrage he fanned. *The New York Times,* pp. A1, L8.

Arendt, H. (1963). *Eichmann in Jerusalem.* New York: Viking.

Armstrong, T. (1985) *The radiant child.* Wheaton, IL: Quest.

Aronson, E. (1990). Applying social psychology to desegregation and energy conservation. *Personality and Social Psychology Bulletin, 16,* 118–132.

Asch, S. E. (1951). Effects of group pressure upon the modification and distortion of judgment. In H. Guetzkow (Ed.), *Groups, leadership, and men.* Pittsburgh: Carnegie.

Asch, S. E. (1957). An experimental investigation of group influence. In Walter Reed Army Institute of Research (Ed.), *Symposium on preventive and social psychiatry.* Washington, DC: U. S. Government Printing Office.

Atkinson, D. R., Maruyama, M., & Matsui, S. (1978). The effects of counselor race and counseling approach on Asian Americans' perceptions of counselor credibility and utility. *Journal of Counseling Psychology, 25,* 76–83.

Atkinson, J., & Huston, T. L. (1984). Sex role orientation and division of labor early in the marriage. *Journal of Personality and Social Psychology, 46,* 330–345.

Attneave, C. L. (1984). Themes striving for harmony; Conventional mental health services and American Indian traditions. In S. Sue & T. Moore (Eds.), *The pluralistic society: A community mental health perspective.* New York: Human Services Press.

Aube, J., & Koestner, R. (1992). Gender characteristics and adjustment: A longitudinal study. *Journal of Personality and Social Psychology, 63,* 485–493.

Averill, J. R., & Rosen, M. (1972). Vigilant and nonvigilant coping strategies and psychophysiological stress reactions during anticipation of electric shock. *Journal of Personality and Social Psychology, 23,* 128–141.

Avery, D. H., Khan, A., Dager, S. R., Cohen, S., Cox, G. B., & Dunner, D. L. (1991). Morning or evening bright light treatment of winter depression. *Biological Psychiatry, 29,* 117–126.

Bachmann, G., & Gill, J. (1988). Endocrine and metabolic changes of menopause. *Medical Aspects of Human Sexuality, 74* (2), 81.

Back, K. W. (1972, July). The group can comfort but it can't cure. *Psychology Today, 6,* 28–35.

Bailey, J. M., & Pillard, R. (1991). A genetic study of male sexual orientation. *Archives of General Psychiatry, 48,* 1089–1096.

Bajardi, S. E. (1992, October 16). Why we need genetic privacy (editorial). *The New York Times,* p. A30.

Baker, R. (1992, March 28). Going to the dogs. *The New York Times,* p. L23.

Baker, S. P., & Fisher, R. S. (1980). Childhood asphyxiation by choking or suffocation. *Journal of the American Medical Association, 244,* 1343–1346.

Balakrishnan, T. R., Rao, K. V., Lapierre-Adamcyk, E., & Krotki, K. J. (1987). A hazard model analysis of the covariates of marriage dissolution in Canada. *Demography, 24,* 395–406.

Bandura, A. (1965). Influence of a model's reinforcement contingencies on the acquisition of imitative responses. *Journal of Personality and Social Psychology, 1,* 589–595.

Bandura, A. (1969). *Principles of behavior modification.* New York: Holt, Rinehart & Winston.

Bandura, A. (1973). *Aggression: A social learning analysis.* Englewood Cliffs, NJ: Prentice-Hall.

Bandura, A. (1977). *Social learning theory.* Englewood Cliffs: NJ: Prentice-Hall.

Bandura, A. (1979). The social learning perspective: Mechanisms of aggression. In H. Toch (Ed.), *Psychology of crime and criminal justice.* New York: Holt, Rinehart & Winston.

Bandura, A. (1982). Self-efficacy mechanism in human agency. *American Psychologist, 37,* 122–147.

Bandura, A. (1986). *Social foundations of thought and action: A social-cognitive theory.* Englewood Cliffs, NJ: Prentice-Hall.

Banks, M. H., & Jackson, P. R. (1982). Unemployment and the risk of minor psychiatric disorder in young people: Cross-sectional and longitudinal evidence. *Psychological Medicine, 12,* 789–798.

Banning, A. (1989). Mother-son incest: Confronting a prejudice. *Child Abuse and Neglect, 13,* 563–570.

Barber, J. (1988, September/October). Worried sick. *Equinox.*

Bardin, C. W., & Catterall, J. F. (1981). Testosterone: A major determinant of extragenital sexual dimorphism. *Science, 211,* 1285–1294.

Barker, M. (1976). Planning for environmental indices: Observer appraisals of air quality. In K. Craik & E. Zube (Eds.), *Perceiving environmental quality* (pp. 175–204). New York: Plenum.

Barker, R. G. (1990). Settings of a professional lifetime. In I. Altman & K. Christensen (Eds.), *Environment and behavior studies: Emergence of intellectual traditions.* New York: Plenum.

Barker, R. G., & Wright, H. F. (1955). *Midwest and its children: The psychological ecology of an American town.* New York: Row, Peterson.

Barling, J. (1990). *Employment, stress and family functioning.* Chichester, England: Wiley.

Barling, J., & Rosenbaum, A. (1986). Work stressors and wife abuse. *Journal of Applied Psychology, 71,* 346–348.

Barlow, D. H. (1986). Causes of sexual dysfunction: The role of anxiety and cognitive interference. *Journal of Consulting and Clinical Psychology, 54,* 140–148.

Barlow, D. H., Craske, M. G., Cerny, J. A., & Klosko, J. S. (1985). The phenomenon of panic. *Journal of Abnormal Psychology, 94,* 320–328.

Baron, P. H. (1974). Self-esteem, ingratiation, and evaluation of unknown others. *Journal of Personality and Social Psychology, 30,* 104–109.

Baron, R. A. (1972). Reducing the influence of an aggressive model: The restraining effects of peer censure. *Journal of Experimental Social Psychology, 8,* 266–275.

Baron, R. A. (1977). *Human aggression.* New York: Plenum.

Baron, R. A. (1987). *Social psychology.* Boston: Allyn & Bacon.

Barrett, J. E., Rose, R. M., & Klerman, G. L. (Eds.). (1979). *Stress and mental disorder.* New York: Raven.

Barringer, F. (1992a, May 31). As American as apple pie, dim sum or burritos. *The New York Times,* p. E2.

Barringer, F. (1992b, December 19). Rate of abortions is lowest since 70's. *The New York Times,* p. L9.

Barringer, F. (1993a, April 15). Sex survey of American men finds 1% are gay. *The New York Times,* pp. A1, A18.

Barringer, F. (1993b, April 25). Polling on sexual issues has its drawbacks. *The New York Times,* p. L23.

Barringer, F. (1993c, April 1). Viral sexual deseases are found in 1 of 5 in U.S. *The New York Times,* pp. A1, B9.

Bart, P. B., & O'Brien, P. B. (1985). *Stopping rape: Successful survival strategies.* Elmsford, NY: Pergamon.

Bartsch, W., & Voight, K. D. (1984). Endocrine aspects of aging in the male. *Maturitas, 6,* 243–251.

Basedow, R. H. (1925). *The Australian aboriginal.* Cited in Richter, C. P. (1957). On the phenomenon of sudden death in animals and man. *Psychosomatic Medicine, 19,* 191–198.

Basow, S. A. (1992). *Gender: Stereotypes and roles* (3rd ed.). Pacific Grove, CA: Brooks/Cole.

Bass, B. M. (1981). *Stogdill's handbook of leadership: A survey of theory and research.* New York: Free Press.

Baudelaire, C. P. (Translated by E. Fox). (1971). *Artificial paradises: On hashish and wine as means of expanding individuality.* New York: Herder & Herder.

Baum, A., Gatchel, R. J., & Schaefer, M. (1983). Emotional behavior and psychophysiological effects of chronic stress at Three Mile Island. *Journal of Consulting and Clinical Psychology, 51,* 565–572.

Baum, M. J., Stockman, E. R., & Lundell, L. A. (1985). Evidence of proceptive without receptive defeminization in male ferrets. *Behavioral Neuroscience, 99,* 742–750.

Baumeister, R. F. (1989). *Masochism and the self.* Hillsdale, NJ: Erlbaum.

Baumeister, R. F. (1990). Suicide as escape from self. *Psychological Review, 97,* 90–113.

Baumrind, D. (1964). Some thoughts on ethics of research: After reading Milgram's "Behavioral Study of Obedience." *American Psychologist, 19,* 421–423.

Baumrind, D. (1967). Child-care practices anteceding three patterns of preschool behavior. *Genetic Psychology Monographs, 75,* 43–88.

Baumrind, D. (1971). Current patterns of parental authority. *Developmental Psychology, 4,* 1–103.

Baxter, L. R., Schwartz, J. M., Bergman, K. S., et al. (1992). Caudate glucose metabolic rate changes with both drug and behavior therapy for obsessive-compulsive disorder. *Archives of General Psychiatry, 49,* 681–689.

Bayer, R., & Spitzer, R. (1982). Edited correspondence of the status of homosexuality in DSM-III. *Journal of the History of the Behavioral Sciences, 18,* 32–52.

Beals, R. L., & Hoijer, H. (1965). *An introduction to anthropology* (3rd ed.). New York: Macmillan.

Bean, F., & Tienda, M. (1987). *The Hispanic population of the United States.* New York: Russell Sage Foundation.

Beck, A. (1976). *Cognitive therapy and the emotional disorders.* New York: International Universities Press.

Beck, A., et al. (1990). *Cognitive therapy of personality disorders.* New York: Guilford.

Beck, A. T., & Weishaar, M. (1989). Cognitive therapy. In A. Freeman, K. M. Simon, L. E. Beutler, & H. Arkowitz (Eds.), *Comprehensive handbook of cognitive therapy* (pp. 21–36). New York: Plenum.

Becker, G. (1981). *A treatise on the family.* Cambridge, MA: Harvard University Press.

Becker, H. S. (1960). Notes on the concept of commitment. *American Journal of Sociology, 66,* 32–40.

Becker, M. H. (1985). Patient adherence to prescribed therapies. *Medical Care, 23,* 539–555.

Becker, P. (1992, May 24). Power pets find space in the executive suite. *The New York Times,* p. F21.

Beckwith, P. (1993, March 8). Let's remember the loveless once a year [Letter to the editor]. *The New York Times,* p. A16.

Belkin, L. (1990, May 28). Bored with the usual fireworks? Try this. *The New York Times,* p. A1.

Bell, A. P., & Weinberg, M. S. (1978). *Homosexualities: A study of diversity among men and women.* New York: Simon & Schuster.

Bell, C. (1987). Preventive strategies for dealing with violence among Blacks. *Community Mental Health Journal, 23,* 217–228.

Bell, C. (1990, August 18). Cited in Homicide is top cause of death from on-job injury for women. *The New York Times,* p. A8.

Belsky, J., & Rovine, M. (1990). Patterns of marital change across the transition to parenthood: Pregnancy to three years postpartum. *Journal of Marriage and the Family, 52,* 5–19.

Belsky, J., Ward, M. J., & Rovine, M (1986). Prenatal expectations, postnatal experiences, and the transition to parenthood. In R. Ashmore, R. D. & D. M. Brodinsky (Eds.) (1986). *Thinking about the family: Views of parents and children* (pp. 119–145). Hillsdale, NJ: Erlbaum.

Bem, D. (1972). Self-perception theory. In L. Berkowitz (Ed.), *Advances in experimental social psychology* (Vol. 6). New York: Academic Press.

Bem, S. L. (1974). The measurement of psychological androgyny. *Journal of Consulting and Clinical Psychology, 42,* 151–162.

Bem, S. L. (1975a). Sex role adaptability: One consequence of psychological androgyny. *Journal of Personality and Social Psychology, 31,* 634–643.

Bem, S. L. (1975b). Androgyny vs. the tight little lives of fluffy women and chesty men. *Psychology Today, 9*(4), 58–62.

Bem, S. L. (1981). Gender schema theory: A cognitive account of sex typing. *Psychological Review, 88,* 354–364.

Bem, S. L. (1983). Gender schema theory and its implications for child development: Raising gender-aschematic children in a gender-schematic society. *Signs, 8,* 598–616.

Bem, S. L. (1985). Androgyny and gender schema theory: A conceptual and empirical integration. In B. T. Sonderegger (Ed.), *Nebraska symposium on motivation 1984: Psychology and gender* (Vol. 32). Lincoln: University of Nebraska Press.

Bem, S. L., Martyna, W., & Watson, C. (1976). Sex typing and androgyny: Further explorations of the expressive domain. *Journal of Personality and Social Psychology, 34,* 1016–1023.

Benin, M. H., & Agostinelli, J. (1988). Husbands' and wives' satisfaction with the division of labor. *Journal of Marriage and Family, 50,* 349–361.

Bennet, J. (1989, February 13). The data game. *The New Republic,* pp. 20–22.

Bennet, J. (1992, September 6). Romantic hearts do not wither: Among the elderly, love and marriage eternally spring. *The New York Times,* pp. L49, L55.

Bennett, N. G., Blanc, A. K., & Bloom, D. E. (1988). Commitment and the modern union: Assessing the link between premarital cohabitation and subsequent marital stability. *American Sociological Review, 53,* 127–138.

Benson, H. (1992). *The wellness book.* New York: Birch Lane Press.

Berenbaum, H., Snowhite, R., & Oltmanns, T. F. (1987). Anhedonia and emotional responses to affect evoking stimuli. *Psychological Medicine, 17,* 677–684.

Berger, J. (1990, September 25). College paper article called blatant anti-Semitism. *The New York Times,* p. B4.

Berger, L. (1981). Childhood injuries: Recognition and prevention. *Current Problems in Pediatrics, 12,* 1–59.

Berkowitz, L. (1984). Some effects of thoughts on anti- and prosocial influences of media events: A cognitive-neoassociation analysis. *Psychological Bulletin, 95,* 410–427.

Bernard, A. C., Adelman, M. B., & Schroeder, J. E. (1991). Two views of consumption in mating and dating. In R. H. Holman & M. R. Solomon (Eds.), *Advances in consumer research,* Vol. 17. Provo, UT: Association for Consumer Research.

Bernard, J. (1982). *The future of marriage* (2nd ed.). New Haven: Yale University Press.

Bernard, M. (Ed.). (1991). *Using rational-emotive therapy effectively.* New York: Plenum.

Bernard-Bonnin, A. C., Gilbert, Rousseau, E., Masson, P., & Maheux, B. (1991). Television and the 3- to 10-year-old child. *Pediatrics, 88,* 48–54.

Berry, J. W. (1990). Psychology of acculturation: Understanding individuals moving between cultures. In R. W. Brislin (Ed.), *Applied Cross-Cultural Psychology.* Newbury Park, CA: Sage.

Berry, K. M. (1992, April 12). The business of tracking deadly viruses. *The New York Times,* p. F11.

Berstein, B. E., & Collins, S. K. (1985). Remarriage counseling: Lawyer and therapists' help with the second time around. *Family Relations, 34,* 387–391.

Besharov, D. J. (1985). "Doing something" about child abuse: The need to narrow the grounds for state intervention. *Harvard Journal of Law and Public Policy, 8,* 539–589.

Betzig, L. B. (1986). *Despotism and differential reproductive success: A Darwinian view of human history.* Chicago: Aldine.

Birns, B. (1964). Individual differences in human neonate responses to stimulation. *Child Development, 43,* 1171–1190.

Bishop, K. (1990, May 6). Disbelieving and defiant, students vow: No men. *The New York Times,* p. L24.

Black, T. E., & Higbee, K. L. (1973). Effects of power, threat, and sex on exploitation. *Journal of Personality and Social Psychology, 27,* 382–388.

Blakeslee, S. (1992b, January 22). An epidemic of genital warts raises concern but not alarm. *The New York Times,* p. C12.

Blakeslee, S. (1992a, September 16). Behavior therapy can change how the brain functions, researchers say. *The New York Times,* p. A20.

Blanchard, E. B., Andrasik, F., Guarnieri, P., Neff, D. F., & Rodichok, L. D. (1987). Two-, three-, and four-year follow-up on the self-regulatory treatment of chronic headache. *Journal of Consulting and Clinical Psychology, 55,* 257–259.

Blanchard, E. B., et al. (1986). A controlled comparison of thermal biofeedback and relaxation training of essential hypertension: I. Short-term and long-term outcome. *Behavior Therapy, 17,* 563–579.

Bledsoe, C. (1990). Transformations in sub-Saharan African marriage and fertility. *Annals, AAPSS, 510,* 115–125.

Bliss, E. L. (1984). A symptom profile of patients with multiple personalities, including MMPI results. *The Journal of Nervous and Mental Disease, 172,* 197–202.

Bloch, D. P. (1989). Using career information with dropouts and at-risk youth. *Career Development Quarterly, 38,* 160–171.

Blum, K. (1984). *Handbook of abusable drugs.* New York: Gardner.

Blum, R. (1987). Contemporary threats to adolescent health in the United States. *Journal of the American Medical Association, 257,* 3390–3395.

Blumenthal, R., Hanley R., Mitchell, A., Tabor, M. B. W., & Treaster, J. B. (1993, May 26). Fitting the pieces of terrorism: Accounts trace the planning of the Trade Center explosion. *The New York Times,* pp. A1, B1, B4.

Blumstein, P., & Schwartz, P. (1983). *American couples: Money, work, sex.* New York: Morrow.

Bohlen, C. (1992, June 14). Russians ask, "What country do I live in?" *The New York Times,* p. A1.

Bohlen, C. (1993, January 29). Diptheria epidemic sweeps Russia. *The New York Times,* p. A8.

Boker, J. R. (1974). Immediate and delayed retention effects of interspersing questions in written instructional passages. *Journal of Educational Psychology, 66,* 96–98.

Bolger, N., DeLongis, A., Kessler, R. C., & Wethington, E. (1989). Effects of daily stress on negative mood. *Journal of Personality and Social Psychology, 57,* 808–818.

Bond, L. A. & Wagner, B. M. (Eds.). (1988). *Primary prevention of psychopathology.* Beverly Hills, CA: Sage.

Bond, M. H. (Ed.). (1988). *The cross-cultural challenge to social psychology.* Newbury Park, CA: Sage.

Bondy, F. (1992, November 17). AIDS death tears at figure-skating world. *The New York Times,* pp. A1, B16.

Boor, M. (1980). Relationships between unemployment rates and suicide rates in eight countries, 1962–1976. *Psychological Reports, 60,* 562–564.

Booth, A., & Edwards, J. N. (1985). Age at marriage and marital instability. *Journal of Marrige and the Family, 47,* 67–75.

Booth, A., & Johnson, D. (1988). Premarital cohabitation and marital success. *Journal of Family Issues, 9,* 255–272.

Boring, E. G. (1950). *A history of experimental psychology* (2nd ed.). New York: Appleton-Century-Crofts.

Borkovec, T. D., & Grayson, J. B. (1980). Consequences of increasing the functional impact of internal emotional stimuli. In K. Blankstein, P. Pliner, & J. Polivy (Eds.), *Assessment and modification of emotional behavior.* New York: Plenum.

Borkovec, T. D., & Hennings, B. L. (1978). The role of physiological attention-focusing in the relaxation treatment of sleep disturbance, general tension, and specific stress reaction. *Behavior Research and Therapy, 16,* 7–19.

Borysenko, J. (1990). *Guilt is the teacher, love is the lesson.* New York: Warner Books.

Bossard, J. (1932). Residential propinquity as a factor in marriage selection. *American Journal of Sociology, 38,* 219–224.

Bovard, E. W. (1959). The effects of social stimuli on the response to stress. *Psychological Review, 66,* 267–277.

Bowlby, J. (1969). *Attachment*. New York: Basic Books.

Bradshaw, J. (1990). *Home coming: Reclaiming and championing your inner child*. New York: Bantam.

Braff, D. L., et al. (1981). Impaired speed of visual information processing in marijuana intoxication. *American Journal of Psychiatry, 138*, 613–617.

Braginsky, B. M., Braginsky, D. D., & Ring, K. (1969). *Methods of madness*. New York: Holt, Rinehart & Winston.

Braham, R. (1992, November 10). Quoted in Gardner, S. Agency is fighting violence in teen-age dating. *The New York Times*, p. NJ13.

Braiker, H. B., & Kelley, H. H. (1979). Conflict in the development of close relationships. In R. L. Burgess & T. L. Huston (Eds.), *Social exchange in developing relationships* (pp. 135–168). Orlando, FL: Academic Press.

Brain, R. (1979). *The decorated body*. New York: Harper & Row.

Brandon, S. (1981). The history of shock treatment. In *Electroconvulsive therapy: An appraisal*. Oxford: Oxford University Press.

Braude, M. C., & Ludford, J. P. (Eds.). (1984). *Marijuana effects on the endocrine and reproductive system*. NIDA Research Monograph 44, Department of Health and Human Services.

Braun, B. G. (Ed.). (1988). *Treatment of multiple personality disorder*. Washington, DC: American Psychiatric Press.

Bray, G. A. (1986). Effects of obesity on health and happiness. In K. D. Brownell & J. P. Foreyt (Eds.), *Handbook of eating disorders* (pp. 3–44). New York: Basic Books.

Bray, R. (1992, August). Cited in N. Angier, Researchers find a second anatomical idiosyncracy in brains of homosexual men. *The New York Times*, p. L7.

Bregger, L. (1990, June 19). Cited in Bishop, K. Militant environmentalists planning Summer protests to save redwoods. *The New York Times*, p. A18.

Brenner, H. (1973). *Mental illness and the economy*. Cambridge, MA: Harvard University Press.

Brentar, J., & McNamara, J. R. (1991). The right to prescribe medicine: Considerations for professional psychology. *Professional Psychology: Research and Practice, 22*, 179–187.

Bretherton, I. (1985). Attachment theory: Retrospect and prospect. In I. Bretherton & E. Waters (Eds.), Growing points of attachment theory and research. *Monographs of the Society for Research in Child Development, 50* (1 & 2, Serial No. 209).

Brett, J. M. (1982). Job transfer and well being. *Journal of Applied Psychology, 67*, 450–463.

Briere, J., Downes, A., & Spensley, J. (1983). Summer in the city: Urban weather conditions and psychiatric-emergency room visits. *Journal of Abnormal Psychology, 92*, 77–80.

Brigham, J. C. (1980). Limiting conditions of the "physical attractiveness stereotype": Attributions about divorce. *Journal of Research in Personality, 14*, 365–375.

Brislin, R. (1993). *Understanding culture's influence on behavior*. Fort Worth, TX: Harcourt Brace Jovanovich.

Britt, H. (1992, July 2). Gay and lesbian teen-age suicide toll is high. *The New York Times*, p. A18.

Britton, B. K., & Tesser, A. (1991). Effects of time-management practices on college grades. *Journal of Educational Psychology, 83*, 405–410.

Broad, W. J. (1993, February 2). Shortages in Moscow? Not of science papers. *The New York Times*, p. C5.

Brock, B. (1992, June 7). Cited in S. Greenhouse. The coming crisis of the American work force. *The New York Times*, p. F14.

Brody, J. E. (1992, April 29). How to outwit a rapist: rehearse. *The New York Times*, p. C13.

Bronfenbrenner, U. (1986). Ecology of the family as a context of human development: Research perspectives. *Developmental Psychology, 22*, 723–742.

Brooks, J. (1992, April 16). Quoted in Advice on cutting infant death risk. *The New York Times*, p. A21.

Brooks-Gunn, J., & Furstenberg, F. F. (1989). Adolescent sexual behavior. *American Psychologist, 44*, 249–257.

Broome, B. J. (1983). The attraction paradigm revisited. Response to dissimilar others. *Human Communication Research, 10*, 137–151.

Broude, G., & Greene, S. (1976). Cross-cultural codes on twenty sexual attitudes and practices. *Ethnology, 15*, 409–429.

Brown, G. W., & Harris, T. (1978). *Social origins of depression*. New York: Free Press.

Brown, H. G. (1963). *Sex and the single girl*. New York: Geis.

Brown, R. E. (1985). Hormones and paternal behavior in vertebrates. *American Zoologist, 25*, 895–910.

Brown, T. A., Cash, T. F., & Noles, S. W. (1986). Perceptions of physical attractiveness among college students: Selected determinants and methodological matters. *Journal of Social Psychology, 126*, 305–316.

Browne, M. W. (1992, September 22). Folk remedy demand may wipe out tigers. *The New York Times*, p. C2.

Brownell, K. (1991). Dieting and the search for the perfect body: Where physiology and culture collide. *Behavior Therapy, 22*, 1–12.

Bruch, H. (1962). Perceptual and conceptual disturbances in anorexia nervosa. *Psychosomatic Medicine, 24*, 187–194.

Bruggeman, E. (1992, March 24). Genetic engineering needs strict regulation [Letter to the editor]. *The New York Times*, p. A20.

Bryan, L. R., Coleman, M., Ganong, L., & Bryan, S. H. (1986). Person perception: Family structure as a cue for stereotyping. *Journal of Marriage and the Family, 48*, 169–174.

Buber, M. (1957). *Pointing the way*. New York: Harper & Row.

Buchanan, B. S., & Morrison, D. G. (1984). Taste tests: Psychophysical issues in comparitive test design. *Psychology & Marketing, 1*, 69–91.

Buckley, M. R., Carraher, S. M., & Cote, J. A. (1992). Measurement issues concerning the use of inventories of job satisfaction. *Educational and Psychological Measurement, 52*, 529–543.

Buell, S. J., & Coleman, P. D. (1981). Quantitative evidence for selective growth in normal human aging but not in senile dimentia. *Brain Research, 214*, 23–41.

Bullard, S. (1993, January 10). Tolerance begins in the home. *The New York Times*, Section 4A, p. 50.

Bumpass, L. L. (1990). What's happening to the family? Interactions between demographic and institutional change. *Demography, 27*, 483–498.

Bumpass, L. L., Martin, T. C., & Sweet, J. A. (1991). The impact of family background and early marital factors on marital disruption. *Journal of Family Issues, 12*, 22–42.

Bumpass, L. L., & Sweet, J. A. (1989). National estimates of cohabitation: Cohort levels and union stability. *Demography, 26*, 615–625.

Burack, J. (1992, July). Paper presented at the Eighth International Conference on AIDS, Amsterdam.

Burden, D. S. (1986). Single parents and the work setting: The impact of multiple job and homelife responsibilities. *Family Relations, 35*, 37–43.

Burgess, A. W., & Holmstrom, L. L. (1974). Rape trauma syndrome. *American Journal of Psychiatry, 131*, 981–986.

Burgess, E. W., & Wallin, P. (1953). *Engagement and marriage.* Philadelphia: Lippincott.

Burke, P. J. (1980). The self: Measurement requirements from an interactionist perspective. *Social Psychology Quarterly, 43,* 18–29.

Burks, N., & Martin, B. (1983). Everyday problems and life-change events: Ongoing versus acute sources of stress. *Journal of Human Stress, 11,* 27–35.

Burningham, J. (1990). *Hey! Get off our train.* New York: Crown.

Burns, A. (1984). Perceived causes of marriage breakdown and the conditions of life. *Journal of Marriage and the Family, 46,* 551–562.

Burros, M. (1992a, June 17). Gene-spliced foods: Is it safe soup yet? *The New York Times,* pp. C1, C4.

Burros, M. (1992b, August 12). Eating well. *The New York Times,* p. C3.

Burrow, C. (1992, October 4). The toxic waste detective finds many eager clients. *The New York Times,* p. F8.

Burton, H. J., Kline, S. A., Lindsay, R. M., & Heidenheim, A. P. (1986). The relationship of depression to survival in chronic renal failure. *Psychosomatic Medicine, 48,* 261–269.

Bush to ease rules on products made by altering genes. (1992, February 25). *The New York Times,* p. A1.

Buss, D. M. (1984). Toward a psychology of person-environment (PE) correlation: The role of spouse selection. *Journal of Personality and Social Psychology, 47,* 361–377.

Bustad, L. K. (1979). How animals make people human and humane. *Modern Veterinary Practice, 60,* 707–710.

Butler, R. (1992, September 6). Cited in J. Bennet. Romantic hearts do not wither: Among the elderly, love and marriage eternally spring. *The New York Times,* pp. L49, L55.

Butterfield, F. (1992a, April 1). Therapy in suicide case defended by psychiatrist. *The New York Times,* p. A16.

Butterfield, F. (1992b, April 2). Analyst spoke of desire for client, court is told. *The New York Times,* p. A14.

Butterfield, F., & Mydans, S. (1992, April 12). Paths of patient and his therapist cross on dark journey leading to death. *The New York Times,* p. A38.

Byers, E. S., & Lewis, K. (1988). Dating couples' disagreements over the desired level of sexual intimacy. *Journal of Sex Research, 24,* 15–29.

Byne, W. (1992, August 1). Cited in N. Angier. Researchers find a second anatomical idiosyncracy in brains of homosexual men. *The New York Times,* p. L7.

Byrne, D. (1971). *The attraction paradigm.* New York: Academic Press.

Byrne, D., London, C., & Reeves, K. (1968). The effects of physical attractiveness among college students: Selected determinants and methodological matters. *Journal of Social Psychology, 126,* 305–316.

Cabaj, R. P. (1992, August 1). Cited in N. Angier. Researchers find a second anatomical idiosyncracy in brains of homosexual men. *The New York Times,* p. L7.

Caldwell, M. A., & Peplau, L. A. (1982). Sex differences in same-sex friendship. *Sex Roles, 8,* 721–732.

Calhoun, K. S., & Atkeson, B. M. (1991). *Treatment of rape victims: Facilitating social adjustment.* New York: Pergamon.

Camel, J. E., Withers, G. S., & Greenough, W. T. (1986). Persistence of visual cortex dendritic alterations induced by post-weaning exposures to a "superenriched" environment in rats. *Behavioral Neuroscience, 100,* 810–813.

Camera in school bathroom curbs vandalism but sets off debate. (1992, March 25). *The New York Times,* p. A21.

Cammermeyer, M. (1992, May 31). Cited in T. Egan. Dismissed from Army as lesbian, colonel will fight homosexual ban. *The New York Times,* p. L18.

Campbell, A. A. (1947). Factors associated with attitudes toward Jews. In T. M. Newcomb & E. L. Hartley (Eds.), *Readings in social psychology.* New York: Holt.

Campbell, A. M. G., Evans, M., Thompson, J. L. G., & Williams, M. J. (1971). Cerebral atrophy in young cannabis smokers, *Lancet, 2,* 1219–1224.

Campbell, J. D., & Tesser, A. (1985). Self-evaluation maintenance processes in relationships. In S. Duck & D. Perlaman (Eds.), *Understanding personal relationships: An interdisciplinary approach* (Vol. 1, pp. 107–135). Beverly Hills, CA: Sage.

Campbell, J. P., & Pritchard, R. D. (1976). Motivation theory in industrial and organizational psychology. In M. D. Dunnette (Ed.), *Handbook of industrial and organizational psychology.* Skokie, IL: Rand McNally.

Camper, D. (1992, April 13). Adolescents, at risk: The nation's future is also its shame [Editorial]. *The New York Times,* p. A18.

Campos, J. J., Langer, A., & Krowitz, A. (1970). Cardiac responses on the visual cliff. In M. Lewis & L. A. Rosenblum (Eds.), *The development of affect* (pp. 149–182). New York: Plenum.

Campus Journal: A book is read as biased at Wellesley. (1993, April 28). *The New York Times,* p. A19.

Canadian Convicted in Anti-Semitism Case. (1992, July 11). *The New York Times,* p. L3.

Canadian Government Travel Bureau. (1971). *1969 vacation trends and recreation patterns.* Ottawa, Canada: Author.

Canelo, A. (1992, August 9). Cited in J. Hoffman. Pillow talk. *The New York Times,* p. V8.

Cannon, W. B. (1942). "Voodoo" death. *American Anthropologist, 44,* 169–181.

Cantor, N., & Mischel, W. (1977). Traits as prototypes: Effects on recognition memory. *Journal of Personality and Social Psychology, 35,* 38–48.

Cantor, N., & Mischel, W. (1979). Prototypes in person perception. In L. Berkowitz (Ed.), *Advances in experimental social psychology* (Vol. 12, pp. 3–52). San Diego: Academic Press.

Cantril, H. (1941). *The psychology of social movements.* New York: Wiley.

Cantril, H., & Hunt, W. A. (1932). Emotional effects produced by the injection of adrenalin. *American Journal of Psychology, 44,* 300–307.

Caplan, P. J. (1987). The psychiatric association's failure to meet its own standards: The dangers of self-defeating personality disorder as a category. *Journal of Personality Disorders, 1,* 178–182.

Carey, W. B. (1985). Interactions of temperament and clinical conditions. *Advances in Developmental and Behavioral Pediatrics, 6,* 83–115.

Cargan, L., & Melko, M. (1982). *Singles: Myths and realities.* Beverly Hills, CA: Sage.

Carlyle, T. (1967). *Sartor resartus.* New York: Dutton. (Originally published in 1838, London: Dent & Sons).

Caron, S. L., & Wynn, R. L. (1992). The intent to parent among young unmarried college graduates. *Families in Society, 73,* 480–487.

Carrington, P. (1977). *Freedom in meditation.* New York: Doubleday.

Carskadon, M. A., & Dement, W. C. Normal human sleep: An overview. In M. H. Kryger, T. Roth, & W. C. Dement (Eds.), *Principles and practice of sleep medicine* (pp. 3–13). Philadelphia: W. B. Saunders.

Carver, C. S., Ganellen, R., Froming, W., & Chambers, W. (1983). Modeling: An analysis in terms of category accessibility. *Journal of Experimental Social Psychology, 19*, 403–421.

Cash, T. F., & Brown, T. A. (1987). Body image in anorexia nervosa and bulimia nervosa: A review of the literature. *Behavior Modification, 11*, 487–521.

Cason, H. (1930). Common annoyances: A psychological study of everyday aversions and irritations. *Psychological Monographs, 40* (2), 1–218.

Caspi, A., & Elder, G. H. (1988). Emergent family patterns: The intergenerational construction of problem behavior and relationships. In R. Hinde & J. Stevenson-Hinde (Eds.), *Understanding family dynamics.* New York: Oxford University Press.

Cassileth, B. (1988, September/October). Cited in J. Barber. Worried sick. *Equinox.*

Castro, J. (1987, May). Paying for peace of mind. *Time,* p. 26.

Catalano, R., & Dooley, D. (1977). Economic predictors of depressed mood and stressful life events in a metropolitan community. *Journal of Health and Social Behavior, 18*, 292–307.

Cathcart, C. (1993, January 24). Cited in M. Marriott. Rap's embrace of "nigger" fires bitter debate. *The New York Times,* pp. A1, A31.

Cattell, R. B. (1957). *Personality and motivation: Structure and measurement.* Yonkers, NY: World Book.

Cattell, R. B., & Krug, S. E. (1986). The number of factors in the 16 PF: A review of the evidence with special emphasis on methodological problems. *Educational and Psychological Measurement, 46*, 509–522.

CDC (Centers for Disease Control). (1991). Forum on youth violence in minority communities: Setting the agenda for prevention. *Public Health Reports, 106*, 225–253.

CDC (Centers for Disease Control). (1992). Sexual behavior among high school students—United States, 1990. *Morbidity and Mortality Weekly Report, 40* (51,52), 885–888.

Ceci, S. J., & Bruck, M. The suggestibility of the child witness: A historical review and synthesis. *Psychological Bulletin.*

Ceci, S. J., Ross, D. F., & Toglia, M. P. (1987). Suggestibility of children's memory: Psycholegal implications. *Journal of Experimental Psychology, 116*, 38–49.

Chaga, E. (1993). Cited in N. C. Nash, (1993). A slaying stuns Brazil: It's right out of the soaps. *The New York Times,* January 1, 1993, p. A4.

Chagnon, N. A. (1979). Is reproductive success equal in egalitarian societies? In N. A. Chagnon & W. Irons (Eds.), *Evolutionary biology and human social behavior: An anthropological perspective* (pp. 374–401). North Scituate, MA: Duxbury.

Chagnon, N. A. (1988). Male Yanomamo manipulations of kinship classifications of female kin for reproductive advantage. In L. Betzig, P. Turke, & M. B. Mulder (Eds.), *Human reproductive behavior: A Darwinian perspective* (pp. 291–318). Cambridge: Cambridge University Press.

Chaiken, S., & Baldwin, M. W. (1981). Affective-cognitive consistency and the effect of salient behavioral information on self-perception of attitudes. *Journal of Personality and Social Psychology, 41*, 1–12.

Chait, L. D., Fishman, M. W., & Schuster, C. R. (1985). "Hangover" effects the morning after marijuana smoking. *Drug and Alcohol Dependence, 15*, 229–238.

Champagne, J. E. (1969). Job recruitment of the unskilled. *Personnel Journal, 48*, 259–268.

Chan, S. (1992, April 13). Asian families in transition: Cultural conflicts and adjustment problems. In R. A. Javier (Chair), *Our families in crisis: A multicultural and multiethnic perspective.* Second annual conference at St. John's University, Jamaica, NY.

Chari-Bitron, A. (1976). Effect of delta-9-THC on blood cell membranes and on alveolar macrophages. Cited in Russell, G. K. (1983). *Marijuana today* (revised edition). New York: The Myrin Institute, Inc. for Adult Education.

Charkaborty, A., Das, S., & Mukherji, A. (1983). Koro epidemic in India. *Transcultural Psychiatry Research Review, 20*, 150–151.

Chartrand, S. (1993, March 29). Patents. *The New York Times,* p. D2.

Cheatham, H. (1990). Empowering Black families. In H. Cheatham & J. Stewart (Eds.), *Black families* (pp. 373–393). New Brunswick, NJ: Transaction.

Cherlin, A. (1978). Remarriage as an incomplete institution. *American Journal of Sociology, 84*, 634–650.

Cherlin, A. J. (1981). *Marriage, divorce, remarriage.* Cambridge, MA: Harvard University Press.

Chermayeff, J. C. (1992, May 7). Cited in S. Slesin. Children at play saving the earth. *The New York Times,* pp. C1, C6.

Cheung, F. K., & Snowden, L. R. (1990). Community mental health and ethnic minority populations. *Community Mental Health Journal, 26*, 277–291.

Ching, W. T. W. (1993). Cited in New H. I. V. strains resist AIDS drugs (1993). *The New York Times,* January 1, 1993, p. A18.

Choate, R. (1975). *Testimony before the House Subcommittee on Communications, United States House of Representatives.* Washington, DC: Council on Children, Media and Merchandising.

Cholesterol at 20. (1993, February 17). *The New York Times.*

Chomsky, C. (1969). *The acquisition of syntax in children from 5 to 10.* Cambridge, MA: MIT Press.

Chopich, E. J., & Paul, M. (1990). *Healing your aloneness: Finding love and wholeness through your inner child.* New York: Harper & Row.

Christoffel, K. K. (1990). Violent death and injury in U.S. children and adolescents. *American Journal of Diseases of Childhood, 144*, 697–706.

Clark, D. M. (1986). A cognitive approach to panic. *Behaviour Research and Therapy, 23*, 35–44.

Clark, D. M., Salkovskis, P. M., Gelder, M., Koehler, C., Martin, M., Anastasiades, P., Hackman, A., Middleton, H., & Jeavons, A. (1988). Tests of a cognitive theory of panic. In I. Hand & H. U. Wittchen (Eds.), *Panic and phobias 2.* Berlin: Springer.

Clark, M., & Gelman, D. (1987, January 12). A user's guide to hormones. *Newsweek,* pp. 50–59.

Clark-Nicolas, P., & Gray-Little, B. (1991). Effect of economic resources on marital quality in black married couples. *Journal of Marriage and the Family, 53*, 645–655.

Clarke, J. I., & Dawson, C. (1989). *Growing up again.* New York: Harper & Row.

Clayton, R. R., & Voss, H. L. (1977). Shacking up: Cohabitation in the 1970s. *Journal of Marriage and the Family, 39*, 273–283.

Cleary, P. J. (1980). A checklist for life event research. *Journal of Psychosomatic Research, 24*, 199–207.

Cleek, M. B., & Pearson, T. A. (1985). Perceived causes of divorce: An analysis of interrelationships. *Journal of Marriage and the Family, 47*, 179–183.

Clinton, C. A. (1935). *Sex behavior in marriage.* New York: Pioneer Publications.

Clinton, W. (1992, November 12). Cited in T. L. Friedman, Clinton to open military's ranks to homosexuals. *The New York Times,* pp. A1, A22.

Cobb, S. (1976). Social support as a moderator of life stress. *Psychosomatic Medicine, 38,* 300–314.

Cohen, F. (1979). Personality, stress and the development of physical illness. In G. C. Stone, F. Cohen, N. E. Adler & associates (Eds.), *Health psychology—A handbook.* San Francisco: Jossey-Bass.

Cohen, H., Rosen, R. C., & Goldstein, L. (1976). Electroencephalographic laterality changes during human sexual orgasm. *Archives of Sexual Behavior, 5,* 189–199.

Cohen, L., & Roth, S. (1984). Coping with abortion. *Journal of Human Stress, 10,* 140–145.

Cohen, L. A. (1987, November). Diet and cancer. *Scientific American,* pp. 42–48.

Cohen, L. H., Sargent, M. M., & Sechrest, L. B. (1986). Use of psychotherapy research by professional psychologists. *American Psychologist, 41,* 198–206.

Cohen, M., Seghorn, T., & Calmas, W. (1969). Sociometric study of the sex offender. *Journal of Abnormal Psychology, 74,* 249–255.

Cohen, R. (1993, January 24). Dieting a la Paris: Foie gras, wine and chocolate. *The New York Times,* p. 10L.

Cohen, R. J. (1976a). Is dying being worked to death? *American Journal of Psychiatry, 133,* 575–577.

Cohen, R. J. (1976b). Dr. Cohen replies. *American Journal of Psychiatry, 133,* 1348–1349.

Cohen, R. J. (1976c). *Cognition/Behavior Survey.* New York: Author.

Cohen, R. J. (1977). Socially reinforced obsessing: A reply. *Journal of Consulting and Clinical Psychology, 45,* 1166–1171.

Cohen, R. J. (1978). The case of Mary and the issue of control. In C. W. McLemore (Chair), *Religion and psychotherapy.* Symposium presented at the 86th annual convention of the American Psychological Association, Toronto, Ontario, Canada.

Cohen, R. J. (1979a). *Malpractice: A guide for mental health professionals.* New York: The Free Press.

Cohen, R. J. (1979b). *Binge! It's not a state of hunger...It's a state of mind.* New York: Macmillan.

Cohen, R. J. (1993). *Professional psychology and its public image* (Book in preparation). Chicago: University of Chicago Press.

Cohen, R. J., & Mariano, W. E. (1982). *Legal guidebook in mental health.* New York: The Free Press.

Cohen, R. J., Montague, P., Nathanson, L. S., & Swerdlik, M. E. (1988). *Psychological testing: An introduction to tests & measurement.* Mountain View, CA: Mayfield Publishing.

Cohen, R. J., & Smith, F. J. (1976). Socially reinforced obsessing: Etiology of a disorder in a Christian Scientist. *Journal of Consulting and Clinical Psychology, 44,* 142–144.

Cohen, R. J., Swerdlik, M., & Molstre, J. A. (1977). College students' attitudes toward New York State's drug law as a function of geographical location. *Journal of Drug Education, 7,* 37–42.

Cohen, R. J., Swerdlik, M. E., & Smith, D. K. (1992). *Psychological testing and assessment: An introduction to tests and measurement* (2nd ed.). Mountain View, CA: Mayfield Publishing.

Cohen, S. (1980). *The substance abuse problem.* New York: Haworth Press.

Cohen, S. (1982). Mind, memory, motivation, and marijuana. In The American Council for Drug Education (Ed.), *Marijuana: The national impact on education.* Rockville, MD: The American Council for Drug Education.

Cohen, S. (1986). Psychosocial models of the role of social support in the etiology of physical disease. *Health Psychology, 7,* 269–297.

Cohen, S., & Syme, S. L. (Eds.). (1985). *Social support and health.* New York: Academic Press.

Cohen, S., & Tashkin, D. P. (1981). *Marijuana smoking and its effects on the lungs.* New York: The American Council for Drug Education.

Cohen, S., Tyrrell, D. A. J., & Smith, A. P. (1991). Psychological stress and susceptibility to the common cold. *New England Journal of Medicine, 325,* 606–612.

Cohen, S., Tyrrell, D. A. J., & Smith, A. P. (1993). Negative life events, perceived stress, negative affect, and susceptibility to the common cold. *Journal of Personality and Social Psychology, 64,* 131–140.

Cohen, S., & Williamson, G. M. (1991). Stress and infectious disease in humans. *Psychological Bulletin, 109,* 5–24.

Cohen, S., & Wills, T. A. (1985). Stress, social support, and the buffering hypothesis. *Psychological Bulletin, 98,* 310–357.

Cohn, E., & Sugarman, D. B. (1980). Marital abuse: Abusing the one you love. *Victimology, 5,* 203–212.

Cohn, R. M. (1978). The effects of employment status change on self attitudes. *Social Psychology, 41,* 81–93.

Coleman, L. (1989). Medical examination for sexual abuse: Are we being told the truth? *Family Law News, 12*(2).

Coleman, M., & Ganong, L. H. (1990). Remarriage and stepfamily research in the 1980s: Increased interest in an old family form. *Journal of Marriage and the Family, 52,* 925–940.

Coles, R., & Stokes, G. (1985). *Sex and the American teenager.* New York: Harper & Row.

Colletta, N. D. (1985). Stressful lives: The situation of divorced mothers and their children. *Journal of Divorce, 6,* 19–31.

Collins, W. A., Sobol, B. L., Westby, S. (1981). Effects of adult commentary on children's comprehension and inferences about a televised aggressive portrayal. *Child Development, 52,* 158–163.

Colman, T. S. (1992, May 10). The jury said, "I'm white, and you're wrong" [Letter to the editor]. *The New York Times,* p. E16.

Colombo, J., Mitchell, D. W., Coldren, J. T., & Atwater, D. (1990). Discrimination learning during the first year: Stimulus and positional cues. *Journal of Experimental Psychology: Learning, Memory, and Cognition, 16,* 98–109.

Comas-Diaz, L., & Griffith, E. H. (1988). *Clinical guidelines in cross-cultural mental health.* New York: Wiley.

Comfort, A. (1972). *The joy of sex.* New York: Crown.

Coming to America. (1992, May 17). *The New York Times,* p. A18.

Committee on Sports Medicine. (1989). Anabolic steroids and the adolescent athlete. *Pediatrics, 83,* 138–140.

Compton, D. R., Dewey, W. L., & Martin, B. R. (1990). Cannibis dependence and tolerance production. *Advances in Alcohol & Substance Abuse, 9,* 129–147.

Comstock, G., Chaffee, S., Katzman, N., McCombs, M., & Roberts, D. (1978). *Television and human behavior.* New York: Columbia University Press.

Conger, R. D., et al. (1990). Linking economic hardship to marital quality and instability. *Journal of Marriage and the Family, 52,* 643–656.

Congressional Budget Office. (1990). *Preliminary cost estimate for the homeless outreach act of 1990.* Unpublished manuscript. Washington, DC: National Law Center on Homelessness and Poverty.

Cook, S. W. (1985). Experimenting on social issues: The case of school desegregation. *American Psychologist, 40,* 452–460.

Cooney, B. (1982). *Miss Rumphius.* New York: Viking.

Cooper, A. J., et al. (1990). A female sex offender with multiple paraphilias: A psychologic, physiologic (laboratory sex arousal) and endocrine case study. *Canadian Journal of Psychiatry, 35,* 334–337.

Cooper, D. (1992, September 23). Cited in L. Hays. Rollerblading leads woman to court. *The New York Times,* p. B5.

Cortese, A. D. (1992). Education for an environmentally sustainable future. *Environment, Science, & Technology, 26,* 1108–1114.

Corwin, D., Berlinger, L., Goodman, G., Goodwin, J., & White, S. (1987). Child sexual abuse and custody disputes: No easy answers. *Journal of Interpersonal Violence, 2,* 91–105.

Costa, P. T., Jr., (1991). Clinical use of the five-factor model: An introduction. *Journal of Personality Assessment, 57,* 393–398.

Costa, P. T., Jr., & McCrae, R. R. (1989). *The NEO-PI/NEO-FFI manual supplement.* Odessa, FL: Psychological Assessment Resources.

Cotten-Houston, A. L., & Wheeler, K. A. (1983). Preorgasmic group treatment: Assertiveness, marital adjustment and sexual function in women. *Journal of Sex and Marital Therapy, 9,* 296–302.

Covino, D. (1992, March 27). Cited in R. D. Givhan. Doc Hollywood's "primal screen" therapy. *New York Daily News,* p. 43.

Cowan, A. L., & Barron, J. (1992, November 22). Executives the economy left behind. *The New York Times,* pp. F1, F6.

Cowan, C. P., et al. (1985). Transition to parenthood: His, hers, and theirs. *Journal of Family Issues, 6,* 451–482.

Cowan, P. A., Cowan, C. P., & Heming, G. (1989, April). *From parent adaptation in pregnancy to children's adaptation in kindergarten.* Paper presented at the biennial meeting of the Society for Research in Child Development, Kansas City, MO.

Cowcher, H. (1990). *Antarctica.* New York: Farrar, Straus, & Giroux.

Cowell, A. (1992, November 15). Italy poll sees rising feeling against Jews. *The New York Times,* p. A15.

Coyne, J. C. (1976). The place of informed consent in ethical dilemmas. *Journal of Consulting and Clinical Psychology, 44,* 1015–1017.

Cartwright, R. D., Lloyd, S., Nelson, J. B., & Bass, S. (1983). The traditional-liberated woman dimension: Social stereotype and self-concept. *Journal of Personality and Social Psychology, 44,* 581–588.

Cordua, G. D., McGraw, K. O., & Drabman, R. S. (1979). Doctor or nurse: Children's perception of sex-typed occupations. *Child Development, 50,* 590–593.

Corea, G. (1992). *The invisible epidemic: The story of women and AIDS.* New York: HarperCollins.

Craig, G. J. (1989). *Human development* (5th ed.). Englewood Cliffs, NJ: Prentice-Hall.

Crews, D. (1984). Gamete production, sex hormone secretion, and mating behavior uncoupled. *Hormones and Behavior, 18,* 22–28.

Crick, F., & Mitchison, G. (1983). The function of dream sleep. *Nature, 304,* 408–416.

CRM (Communications Research Machines, Inc.) (1972). *Abnormal psychology: Current perspectives.* Del Mar, CA: CRM Books.

Crocker, J., & Major, B. (1989). Social stigma and self-esteem: The self-protective properties of stigma. *Psychological Review, 96,* 608–630.

Cronin, A. (1992, November 15). The bottom line: A reality check on salaries. *The New York Times,* p. E2.

Crossette, B. (1992, May 9). Study sees rise in child death rates. *The New York Times,* p. A4.

Crusco, A. H., & Wetzel, C. G. (1984). The Midas touch: The effects of interpersonal touch on restaurant tipping. *Personality and Social Psychology Bulletin, 10,* 512–517.

Cunningham, M. R. (1989). Reactions to heterosexual opening gambits: Female selectivity and male responsiveness. *Personality and Social Psychology Bulletin, 15,* 27–41.

Cuomo's Freudian Slips: Desire, or Just Fatigue? (1992, April 1). *The New York Times,* p. A20.

Current, W. (1992, April 12). Cited in B. P. Noble. Testing Employees for Drugs. *The New York Times,* p. F27.

Cushman, J. H., Jr. (1992, November 14). Top military officers object to lifting homosexual ban. *The New York Times,* p. L9

Custrini, R. J., & Feldman, R. S. (1989). Children's social competence and nonverbal encoding and decoding of emotions. *Journal of Clinical Child Psychology, 18,* 336–342.

Cutler, W. B., Garcia, C. R., & Krieger, A. M. (1979). Sexual behavior frequency and menstrual cycle length in mature premenopausal women. *Psychoneuroendocrinology, 4,* 297–309.

Cutler, W. B., Preti, G., Huggins, G. R., Erickson, B., & Garcia, C. R. (1985). Sexual behavior frequency and biphasic ovulatory type menstrual cycles. *Physiology & Behavior, 34,* 805–810.

Cutrona, C. E., Russell, D., & Rose, J. (1986). Social support and adaptation to stress by the elderly. *Psychology and Aging, 1,* 47–54.

Dabbs, J. M., Jurkovic, G. J., & Frady, R. L. (1991). Salivary testosterone and cortisol among late adolescent male offenders. *Journal of Abnormal Child Psychology, 19,* 469–478.

Dabbs, J. M., & Morris, R. (1990). Testosterone, social class, and antisocial behavior in a sample of 4,462 men. *Psychological Science, 1,* 209–211.

Daley, R. M. (1992, June 16). Quoted in Terry, D. Basketball title brings Chicago night of looting. *The New York Times,* p. A16.

Daly, M., & Wilson, M. (1983). *Sex, evolution, and behavior* (2nd ed.). North Scituate, MA: Duxbury.

Damon, W. (1980). Patterns of change in children's social reasoning: A two-year longitudinal study. *Child Development, 51,* 1010–1017.

D'Andrade, R. G. (1966). Sex differences and cultural institutions. In E. E. Maccoby (Ed.), *The development of sex differences.* Stanford: Stanford University Press.

Dao, J. (1992a, May 25). Ghanaians hail a surrogate king: Immigrants elect a cultural leader to preserve traditions. *The New York Times,* p. L23.

Dao, J. (1992b, May 28). School board bars material about AIDS. *The New York Times,* p. B1.

Darley, J. M., & Latané, B. (1968). Bystander intervention in emergencies: Diffusion of responsibility. *Journal of Personality and Social Psychology, 44,* 20–33.

Darwin, C. (1874). *Descent of man and selection in relation to sex.* New York: A. L. Burt.

Davidson, K. J., Darling, C., & Conway-Welch, C. (1989). The role of the Grafenberg spot and female ejaculation in the female orgasmic response: An empirical analysis. *Journal of Sex and Marital Therapy, 15,* 102–119.

Davidson, L. R., & Duberman, L. (1982). Friendship: Communication and interactional patterns in same-sex dyads. *Sex Roles, 8,* 809–822.

Davis, F. (1985). Clothing and fashion as communication. In M. R. Solomon (Ed.), *The psychology of fashion* (pp. 15–27). Lexington, MA: Lexington Books.

Davis, J. A., & Smith, T. (1987). *General social surveys, 1972–1987: Cumulative data.* Storrs, CT: University of Connecticut, Roper Center for Public Opinion Research.

Davis, K. E. (1985). Near and dear: Friendship and love compared. *Psychology Today, 19*(2), 22–30.

Davis, L. (1992, June 21). Cited in G. Kolata. More children are employed, often perilously. *The New York Times*, pp. A1, A22.

Davison, G. C. (1976). Homosexuality: The ethical challenge. *Journal of Consulting and Clinical Psychology, 44,* 157–162.

Davison, G. C. (1978). Not can but ought: The treatment of homosexuality. *Journal of Consulting and Clinical Psychology, 46,* 170–172.

Dawson, D. A. (1991). Family structure and children's health and well-being: Data from the 1988 National Health Interview Survey on child health. *Journal of Marriage and the Family, 53,* 573–584.

Deal, J. K., & Wampler, K. S. (1986). Dating violence: The primacy of previous experience. *Journal of Social and Personal Relationships, 3,* 457–471.

DeAngelis, T. (1992). Ky. high court repeals sodomy law. *The APA Monitor, 23(12),* 1, 30.

Deaux, K., & Lewis, L. L. (1984). Structure of gender stereotypes: Interrelationships among components and gender label. *Journal of Personality and Social Psychology, 46,* 991–1004.

Deaux, K., & Major, B. (1987). Putting gender into context: An interactive model of gender-related behavior. *Psychological Review, 94,* 369–389.

de Boer, J., van der Linden, J., & van der Plight, J. (1987). Air pollution and coping. In H. S. Koelga (Ed.), *Environmental annoyance: Characterization, measurement, and control.* Amsterdam: Elsevier.

de Bono, E. (1970). *Lateral thinking: Creativity step by step.* New York: Harper & Row.

Delabarre, E. B. (1899). Cited in O. Ray (1978) *Drugs, society, and human behavior* (2nd ed.). St. Louis: Mosby.

Dell, P. F. (1988). Professional skepticism about multiple personality. *Journal of Nervous and Mental Disease, 176,* 528–531.

DeLongis, A., Coyne, J. C., Dakof, G., Folkman, S., & Lazarus, R. S. (1982). Relationship of daily hassles, uplifts and major life events to health status. *Health Psychology, 1,* 119–136.

DeLongis, A., Folkman, S., & Lazarus, R. S. (1988). The impact of daily stress on health and mood: Psychological and social resources as mediators. *Journal of Personality and Social Psychology, 54,* 486–495.

DeMaris, A., & Leslie, G. R. (1984). Cohabitation with the future spouse: Its influence upon marital satisfaction and communication. *Journal of Marriage and the Family, 46,* 77–84.

DeMaris, A., & Rao, K. V. (1992). Premarital cohabitation and subsequent marital stability in the United States: A reassessment. *Journal of Marriage and the Family, 54,* 178–190.

Dement, W. C. (1974). *Some must watch while some must sleep.* San Francisco: W. H. Freeman.

DeNelsky, G. Y. (1991). Prescription privileges for psychologists: The case against. *Professional Psychology: Research and Practice, 22,* 188–193.

Dennis, W. (1973). *Children of the crèche.* New York: Appleton-Century-Crofts.

Denny, N., Field, J., & Quadagno, D. (1984). Sex differences in sexual needs and desires. *Archives of Sexual Behavior, 13,* 233–245.

DeParle, J. (1993, April 22). Free-vaccine plan creates unusual array of skeptics. *The New York Times*, pp. A1, A19.

Depue, R. A., & Monroe, S. M. (1986). Conceptualization and measurement of human disorder in life stress research: The problem of chronic disturbance. *Psychological Bulletin, 99,* 36–51.

Derogatis, L. R. (1982). Self-report measures of stress. In L. Goldberger & S. Breznitz (Eds.), *Handbook of stress: Theoretical and clinical aspects.* New York: Free Press.

Dershewitz, R. A., & Williamson, J. W. (1977). Prevention of childhood household injuries: A controlled clinical trial. *American Journal of Public Health, 67,* 1148–1153.

DeVries, R. (1970). The development of role-taking as reflected by behavior of bright, average, and retarded children in a social guessing game. *Child Development, 41,* 759–770.

DeWitt, K. (1992, April 17). Survey shows U.S. children write seldom and not well. *The New York Times*, p. A12.

Diamond, E. (1982). The role of anger and hostility in essential hypertension and coronary heart disease. *Psychological Review, 92,* 410–433.

Dichter, E. (1981). Foreword. In E. J. Mayo & L. P. Jarvis, *The psychology of leisure travel* (pp. ix–xi). Boston: CBI Publishing.

Dichter, E. (1985). Why we dress the way we do. In M. R. Solomon (Ed.), *The psychology of fashion* (pp. 29–37). Lexington, MA: Lexington Books.

Dietz, W. H., Jr., & Gortmaker, S. L. (1985). Do we fatten our children at the television set? Obesity and television viewing in children and adolescents. *Pediatrics, 75,* 807–812.

Digman, J. M. (1990). Personality structure: Emergence of the five factor model. *Annual Review of Psychology, 41,* 417–440.

Digman, J. M., & Takemoto-Chock, N. K. (1981). Factors in the natural language of personality: Re-analysis, comparison, and interpretation of six major studies. *Multivariate Behavioral Research, 16,* 149–170.

Dillingham, S. D. (1992, April 24). Cited in D. Johnston. Survey shows number of rapes far higher than official figures. *The New York Times*, p. A14.

DiMatteo, M. R., & DiNocola, D. D. (1982). *Achieving patient compliance.* New York: Pergamon.

Dime-Meenan, S. (1992, April 4). To relieve the suffering of mental illness [Editorial]. *The New York Times*, A22.

Dimsdale, J. E. (1988). A perspective on Type A behavior and coronary disease. *New England Journal of Medicine, 318,* 110–112.

Dion, K. K., et al. (1972). What is beautiful is good. *Journal of Personality and Social Psychology, 24,* 285–290.

Doctors are Advised to Screen Women for Abuse. (1992, June 17). *The New York Times*, p. A26.

Dogoloff, L. I. (1987). *Fair Oaks Hospital Psychiatry Letter, 5(9),* 44–49.

Dohrenwend, B. P., & Dohrenwend, B. S. (1969). *Social status and psychological disorder.* New York: Wiley.

Dohrenwend, B. P., & Shrout, P. E. (1985). "Hassles" in the conceptualization and measurement of life-stress variables. *American Psychologist, 40,* 780–785.

Dohrenwend, B. S., Dohrenwend, B. P., Dodson, M., & Shrout, P. (1984). Symptoms, hassles, social supports and life events: Problem of confounded measures. *Journal of Abnormal Psychology, 93,* 222–230.

Dold, C. (1992, April 28). Tropical forests found more valuable for medicine than other uses. *The New York Times*, p. C4.

Dollard, J., & Miller, N. E. (1950). *Personality and psychotherapy.* New York: McGraw-Hill.

Donahue, D. (1992, October 21). A silly charade in the flesh. *USA Today*, pp. D1, D2.

Donnerstein, E., & Donnerstein, M. (1976). Research in the control of interracial aggression. In R. G. Green & E. C. O'Neal (Eds.), *Perspectives on aggression.* New York: Academic Press.

Dornbusch, S. M., Carlsmith, J. M., Bushwall, S. J., Ritter, P. L., Leidman, H., Historf, A. H., & Gross, R. T. (1985). Single parents, extended households, and the control of adolescents. *Child Development, 56,* 326–341.

Doten, D. (1938). *The art of bundling.* New York: Farrar.

Douglas, M. A., Alley, J., Daston, A. P., Svaldi-Farr, J., & Samson, M. (1984, August). *Court-involved batterers and their victims: Characteristics and ethnic differences.* Paper presented at the 92nd annual meeting of the American Psychological Association, Toronto, Ontario, Canada.

Drachman, D., de Carufel, A., & Insko, C. A. (1978). The extra credit effect in interpersonal attraction. *Journal of Experimental Social Psychology, 14,* 458–465.

Driskell, J. L., & Kelly, E. L. (1980). A guided notetaking and study skills system for use with university freshmen predicted to fail. *Journal of Reading, 1,* 4–5.

Dryfoos, J. G. (1990). *Adolescents at risk: Prevalence and prevention.* London: Oxford University Press.

Dubin, R. (1958). *The world of work: Industrial society and human relations.* Englewood Cliffs, NJ: Prentice-Hall.

Dugger, C. W. (1992, March 17). As calls to child-abuse line soar to highest since '87, expansion is planned. *The New York Times,* p. B3.

Dunne, P. (1992, August 30). In the natural state. *The New York Times,* p. NJ17.

Durkheim, E. (1951). *Suicide: A study of sociology.* New York: Free Press. (Originally published in 1897).

Durkin, K. (1985). Television and sex-role acquisition. 3: Counterstereotyping. *British Journal of Social Psychology, 24,* 211–222.

Durlak, J. A., & Reich, J. N. (1987). Preventive interventions in the environment. *Prevention in Human Services, 5,* 279–299.

Dutton, D., & Painter, S. L. (1981). Traumatic bonding: The development of emotional attachments in battered women and other relationships with intermittent abuse. *Victimology, 6,* 139–155.

Dutton, D. G., & Aron, A. P. (1974). Some evidence for heightened sexual attraction under conditions of high anxiety. *Journal of Personality and Social Psychology, 30,* 510–517.

Dweck, C. S., Goetz, T. E., & Strauss, N. L. (1980). Sex differences in learned helplessness: IV. An experimental and naturalistic study of failure generalization and its mediators. *Journal of Personality and Social Psychology, 38,* 441–452.

Dyer, L., & Parker, D. F. (1975). Classifying outcomes in work motivation research: An examination of the intrinsic-extrinsic dichotomy. *Journal of Applied Psychology, 60,* 455–458.

Eagly, A. H., & Steffen, V. J. (1984). Gender stereotypes stem from the distribution of men and women into social roles. *Journal of Personality and Social Psychology, 46,* 735–754.

Earle, J. R., & Perricone, P. J. (1986). Premarital sexuality: A ten-year study of attitudes and behavior on a small university campus. *Journal of Sex Research, 22,* 304–310.

Earls, F. (1981). Temperament characteristics and behavior problems in 3-year-old children. *Journal of Nervous and Mental Disease, 169,* 367–373.

Earls, F., & Jung, K. G. (1987). Temperament and home environment characteristics as causal factors in the early development of childhood psychopathology. *Journal of the American Academy of Child and Adolescent Psychiatry, 26,* 491–498.

Easterbrooks, M. A. (1987, April). *Early family development: Longitudinal impact of marital quality.* Paper presented at the biennial meeting of the Society for Research in Child Development, Baltimore.

Easterbrooks, M. A., & Goldberg, W. A. (1985). Effects of early maternal employment on toddlers, mothers, and fathers. *Developmental Psychology, 21,* 774–783.

Eccles, J. S. (1985). Sex differences in achievement patterns. In T. Sonderegger (Ed.), *Nebraska symposium on motivation.* Lincoln: University of Nebraska Press.

Eccles, J. S., Midgley, C., Wigfield, A., Buchanan, C. M., Reuman, D., Flanagan, C., & Iver, D. M. (1993). Development during adolescence. *American Psychologist, 48,* 90–101.

Echterling, L. G., & Emmerling, D. A. (1987). Impact of stage hypnosis. *American Journal of Clinical Hypnosis, 29,* 149–154.

Eckenrode, J. (1984). Impact of chronic and acute stressors on daily reports of mood. *Journal of Personality and Social Psychology, 46,* 907–918.

Eckerman, C. O., Davis, C. C., & Didow, S. M. (1989). Toddlers' emerging ways of achieving social coordination with a peer. *Child Development, 60,* 440–453.

Eckerman, C. O. & Stein, M. R. (1982). The toddler's emerging interactive skills. In K. H. Rubin & H. S. Ross (Eds.), *Peer relationships and social skills in childhood* (pp. 41–71). New York: Springer-Verlag.

Eckerman, C. O., & Stein, M. R. (1990). How imitation begets imitation and toddlers' generation of games. *Developmental Psychology, 26,* 370–378.

Eckert, E. D., et al. (1986). Homosexuality in monozygotic twins reared apart. *British Journal of Psychiatry, 148,* 421–425.

Eckholm, E. (1991, November 17). Facts of life: More than inspiration is needed to fight AIDS. *The New York Times,* pp. E1, E3.

Eckholm, E. (1992a, March 8). Ailing gun industry confronts outrage over glut of violence. *The New York Times,* pp. A1, A30.

Eckholm, E. (1992b, June 28). AIDS, fatally steady in the U.S., accelerates worldwide. *The New York Times,* p. E5.

Edinger, J. D., & Jacobsen, R. (1982). Incidence and significance of relaxation treatment side effects. *The Behavior Therapist, 5,* 137–138.

Edwards, D. A. (1969). Early androgen stimulation and aggressive behavior in male and female mice. *Physiology and Behavior, 4,* 333–338.

Edwards, D. P., et al. (1991). Mechanisms controlling steroid receptor binding to specific DNA sequences. *Steroids, 56,* 271–278.

Edwards, J. N. (1991). New conceptions: Biosocial innovations and the family. *Journal of Marriage and the Family, 53,* 349–360.

Egan, K. J., Kogan, H. N., Garber, A., & Jarrett, M. (1983). The impact of psychological distress on the control of hypertension. *Journal of Human Stress, 9*(4), 4–10.

Egan, T. (1992, May 14). Los Angeles riots spurring big rise in sales of guns. *The New York Times,* pp. A1, A20.

Egley, L. C. (1991). What changes the societal prevalence of domestic violence? *Journal of Marriage and the Family, 53,* 885–897.

Ehlers, A., Margraf, J., Taylor, C. B., & Roth, W. T. (1988). Cardiovascular aspects of panic disorder. In T. Elbert, W. Langosch, A. Steptoe, & D. Vaitl (Eds.), *Behavioural medicine in cardiovascular disorders.* Chichester, United Kingdom: Wiley.

Eidelson, R. J. (1980). Interpersonal satisfaction and level of involvement: A curvilinear relationship. *Journal of Personality and Social Psychology, 39,* 460–470.

Eisenberg, R. B., Coursin, D. B., & Rupp, N. R. (1961). Habituation to an acoustic pattern as an index of differences among neonates. *Journal of Auditory Research, 6,* 239–248.

Eisenbruch, M. (1992). Toward a culturally sensitive DSM: Cultural bereavement in Cambodian refugees and the traditional healer as taxonomist. *The Journal of Nervous and Mental Disease, 180,* 8–10.

Ekman, P. (1975). The universal smile: Face muscles talk every language. *Psychology Today, 9*(4), 35–39.

Ekman, P. (1985). *Telling lies: Clues to deceit in the marketplace, politics, and marriage.* New York: Norton.

Ekman, P., & Friesen, W. V. (1975). *Unmasking the face.* Englewood Cliffs, NJ: Prentice-Hall.

Ekman, P., Levenson, R. W., & Friesen, W. V. (1983). Emotions differ in autonomic activity. *Science, 221,* 1208–1210.

Elder, G. H., Nguyen, T. V., & Caspi, A. (1985). Linking family hardship to children's lives. *Child Development, 56,* 361–365.

Elliott, G. R., & Eisdorfer, C. (Eds.). (1982). *Stress and human health: Analysis and implications of research.* New York: Springer.

Ellis, A. (1958). Rational psychotherapy. *Journal of General Psychology, 59,* 35–49.

Ellis, A. (1959). Requisite conditions for basic personality change. *Journal of Consulting Psychology, 23,* 538–549.

Ellis, A. (1962). *Reason and emotion in psychotherapy.* New York: Lyle Stuart.

Ellis, A. (1965). *Sex without guilt.* New York: Grove Press.

Ellis, A. (1967). Rational-emotive psychotherapy. In D. Arbuckel (Ed.), *Counseling and psychotherapy.* New York: McGraw-Hill.

Ellis, A. (1978). Religion and psychopathology. In C. W. McLemore (Chair), *Religion and psychotherapy.* Symposium presented at the 86th annual convention of the American Psychological Association, Toronto, Ontario, Canada.

Ellis, A. (1988). *How to stubbornly refuse to make yourself miserable about anything—yes, anything!* Seacaucus, NJ: Lyle Stuart.

Ellis, A. (1991). Using RET effectively: Reflections and interview. In M. Bernard (Ed.), *Using rational-emotive therapy effectively* (pp. 1–33). New York: Plenum.

Ellis, E. M., Atkeson, B. M., & Calhoun, K. S. (1981). Sexual dysfunction in victims of rape. *Women and Health, 5,* 39–47.

Emmelkamp, P. M. G., & Wessels, H. (1975). Flooding in imagination vs. flooding in vivo: A comparison with agoraphobics. *Behavior Research and Therapy, 13,* 7–15.

Endicott, N. A. (1989). Psychosocial and behavioral factors in myocardial infarction and sudden cardiac death. In S. Cheren (Ed.), *Psychosomatic medicine: Theory, physiology, and practice* (Vol. 2) (pp. 611–660). Madison, CT: International Universities Press.

Engebretson, T. O., & Matthews, K. A. (1992). Dimensions of hostility in men, women, and boys: Relationships to personality and cardiovascular responses to stress. *Psychosomatic Medicine, 54,* 311–323.

Engel, G. L. (1977). The need for a new medical model: A challenge for biomedicine. *Science, 196,* 126–129.

Entwisle, D. R., & Alexander, K. L. (1990). Beginning school math competence: Minority and majority comparisons. *Child Development, 61,* 454–471.

Epstein, S., & Katz, L. (1992). Coping ability, stress, productive load, and symptoms. *Journal of Personality and Social Psychology, 62,* 813–825.

Erhardt, A. A., & Baker, S. W. (1974). Fetal androgens, human central nervous system differentiation, and behavior sex differences. In R. C. Friedman, R. M. Richart, & R. L. Vandewiele (Eds.), *Sex differences in behavior.* New York: Wiley.

Erikson, E. H. (1963). *Childhood and society.* New York: Norton.

Erikson, E. H. (1963). *Childhood and society* (2nd ed.). New York: Norton.

Erikson, E. H. (1968). *Identity, youth, and crisis.* New York: Norton.

Erickson, M. H., & Rossi, E. L. (1989). *The February man.* New York: Brunner/Mazel.

Erlanger, S. (1993, April 8). Russian officials say little radiation is released in nuclear plant accident. *The New York Times,* p. A8.

Eron, L. D., & Peterson, R. A. (1982). Abnormal behavior: Social approaches. In M. R. Rosenzweig & L. W. Porter (Eds.), *Annual Review of Psychology, 33,* 231–265.

Eskenazi, G. (1992, July 28). 13-year-old easily takes a gold in diving. *The New York Times,* pp. B9, B10.

Espenshade, T. J. (1985). The recent decline of American marriage: Blacks and whites in comparative perspective. In K. Davis (Ed.), *Contemporary marriage: Comparative perspectives on a changing institution* (pp. 53–90). New York: Russell Sage.

Etaugh, C. F., & Harlow, H. (1975). Behaviors of male and female teachers as related to behaviors and attitudes of elementary school children. *Journal of Genetic Psychology, 127,* 163–170.

Ettinger, B. (1988). Prevention of osteoporosis: Treatment of estradiol deficiency. *Obstetrics and Gynecology, 72,* 12s-17s.

Evall, J. (1991). Sexual orientation and adoptive matching. *Family Law Quarterly, 25,* 364.

Evans, G. W., Colome, S. D., & Shearer, D. F. (1988). Psychological reactions to air pollution. *Environmental Research, 45,* 1–15.

Ewing, C. M. (1988). Tailored genes: IVF, genetic engineering, and eugenics. *Reproductive and Genetic Engineering, 1,* 31–40.

Eyer, D. E. (1993). *Mother-infant bonding: A scientific fiction.* New Haven: Yale University Press.

Eysenck, H. J., & Eysenck, M. (1984). *Personality and individual differences.* London: Plenum.

Fabiano, J. (1992, September 18). Cited in F. Butterfield. Psychiatrist in sex abuse case offers her license. *The New York Times,* p. A12.

Fabrega, Jr., H. (1992). Diagnosis interminable: Toward a culturally sensitive DSM-IV. *The Journal of Nervous and Mental Disease, 180,* 5–7.

Fagot, B. I., Leinbach, M. D., & O'Boyle, C. (1992). Gender labeling, gender stereotyping, and parenting behaviors. *Developmental Psychology, 28,* 225–230.

Fain, T. C., & Anderson, D. L. (1987). Sexual harassment: Organizational context and diffuse status. *Sex Roles, 17,* 291–311.

Fantino, E., Kasdon, D., & Stringer, N. (1970). The Yerkes-Dodson law and alimentary motivation. *Canadian Journal of Psychology, 24,* 77–84.

Farber, E. (1987). The adolescent who runs. In B. S. Brown & A. R. Mills (Eds.), *Youth at high risk* (Department of Health and Human Services Publication No. ADM 87–1537). Washington, DC: U.S. Government Printing Office.

Farber, E., Kinast, C., McCoard, W., & Faulkner, D. (1984). Violence in families of adolescent runaways. *Child Abuse and Neglect, 8,* 295–299.

Farnsworth, C. H. (1993, February 2). Anti-woman bias may bring asylum. *The New York Times,* p. A8.

Farnsworth, N. R., & Cordell, G. A. (1976). New potential hazard regarding the use of marijuana: Treatment of plants with liquid fertilizers. *Journal of Psychedelic Drugs, 8,* 151–155.

Fay, A. (1976). The drug modality. In A. A. Lazarus (Ed.), *Multimodal behavior therapy* (pp. 65–85). New York: Springer.

FBI (Federal Bureau of Investigation). (1987). *Crime in the United States: 1986.* Washington, DC: US Department of Justice.

FBI (Federal Bureau of Investigation). (1989). *Uniform crime reports for the United States, 1988.* Washington, DC: Author.

Feather, N. T., & Barber, J. G. (1983). Depressive reactions and unemployment. *Journal of Abnormal Psychology, 92,* 185–195.

Fehr, K. O. B., & Kalant, H. (Eds.). (1983). *Addiction Research Foundation/World Health Organization Meeting on Adverse Health and Behavioral Consequences of Cannabis Use.* Toronto: Addiction Research Foundation.

Feifel, H. (1990). Psychology and death: Meaningful rediscovery. *American Psychologist, 45,* 537–543.

Feingold, A. (1992). Good-looking people are not what we think. *Psychological Bulletin, 111,* 304–341.

Feitel, B., Margetson, N., Chamas, J., & Lipman, C. (1992). Psychosocial background and behavioral and emotional disorders of homeless and runaway youth. *Hospital and Community Psychiatry, 43,* 155–159.

Feltz, D. L. (1990, June 28). Quoted in L. Kutner. If you want to coach, or watch. *The New York Times,* p. C8.

Fenton, W. S., McGlashan, T. H., & Heinssen, R. K. (1988). A comparison of DSM-III and DSM-III-R schizophrenia. *American Journal of Psychiatry, 145,* 1446–1449.

Feshbach, S. (1984). The catharsis hypothesis, aggressive drive, and the reduction of aggression. *Aggressive Behavior, 10,* 91–101.

Feshback, S., & Weiner, B. (1982). *Personality.* Lexington, MA: Heath.

Festinger, L. (1954). A theory of social comparison processes. *Human Relations, 7,* 117–140.

Festinger, L. (1957). *A theory of cognitive dissonance.* Stanford, CA: Stanford University Press.

Fienup-Riordan, A. (1983). *The Nelson Island Eskimo: Social structure and ritual distribution.* Anchorage: Alaska Pacific University.

Finchilescu, G. (1988). Interracial contact in South Africa within the nursing context. *Journal of Applied Social Psychology, 18,* 1207–1221.

Fine, P., McIntire, M. S., & Fain, P. R. (1986). Early indicators of self-destruction in childhood and adolescence: A survey of pediatricians and psychiatrists. *Pediatrics, 77,* 557–568.

Fingerhut, L., Ingram, D., & Feldman, J. (1992). Firearm and nonfirearm homicide among persons 15 through 19 years of age. *Journal of the American Medical Association, 267,* 3048–3053.

Fingerhut, L., & Kleinman, J. (1989). Trends and current status in childhood mortality: United States 1900–1985. *Vital Health Statistics, 26,* 1–44.

Finkelhor, D., et al. (1990). Sexual abuse in a national survey of adult men and women: Prevalence, characteristics, and risk factors. *Child Abuse and Neglect, 14,* 19–28.

Finkelhor, D., Hotaling, G., & Sedlak, A. (1991). Children abducted by family members: A national household survey of incidence and episode characteristics. *Journal of Marriage and the Family, 53,* 805–817.

Finkelhor, D., & Russell, D. (1984). Women as perpetrators: Review of the evidence. In D. Finkelhor (Ed.), *Child sexual abuse: Theory and research.* New York: Free Press.

Finkelstein, S. (1989). Adverse effects after exposure to lay hypnosis in group setting: A case report. *American Journal of Clinical Hypnosis, 32,* 107–109.

Finnegan, M. J., & Pickering, C. A. C. (1986). Building-related illness. *Clinical Allergy, 16,* 389–405.

Finnegan, M. J., Pickering, C. A. C., & Burge, P. S. (1984). Sick building syndrome: Prevalence studies. *British Medical Journal, 289,* 1573–1575.

Fiore, J., Becker, J., & Coppel, D. B. (1983). Social network interactions: A buffer or a stress. *American Journal of Community Psychology, 11,* 423–439.

Fischer, P. J. (1989). Estimating prevalence of alcohol, drug, and mental health problems in the contemporary homeless population: A review of the literature. *Contemporary Drug Problems, 16,* 333–390.

Fischer, P. J., & Breakey, W. R. (1991). The epidemiology of alcohol, drug, and mental disorders among homeless persons. *American Psychologist, 46,* 1115–1128.

Fischer, S. M. (1992, December 13). An outbreak of anti-Semitic incidents. *The New York Times,* pp. NJ1, NJ4.

Fischman, M. W. (1987). Type A on trial. *Psychology Today, 21*(2), 42–50.

Fisher, J. D., Nadler, A., & Whitcher-Alagna, S. (1982). Recipient reactions to aid. *Psychological Bulletin, 91,* 27–54.

Fisher, L. M. (1992, July 7). Cygnus joins nicotine-patch fray. *The New York Times,* p. D4.

Fishman, B. (1983). The economic behavior of stepfamilies. *Family Relations, 32,* 359–366.

Fiske, S. T., & Taylor, S. E. (1984). *Social cognition.* Reading, MA: Addison-Wesley.

Fitzgerald, L. F., & Crites, J. O. (1980). Toward a career psychology of women: What do we know? What do we need to know? *Journal of Counseling Psychology, 27,* 44–62.

Flavell, J. H. (1977). *Cognitive development.* Englewood Cliffs, NJ: Prentice-Hall.

Foa, E. B., Steketee, G., & Young, M. C. (1984). Agoraphobia: Phenomenological aspects, associated characteristics, and theoretical considerations. *Clinical Psychology Review, 4,* 431–457.

Folkes, V. S. (1982). Forming relationships and the matching hypothesis. *Personality and Social Psychology Bulletin, 8,* 631–636.

Folkes, V. S., & Sears, D. O. (1977). Does everybody like a liker? *Journal of Experimental Social Psychology, 13,* 505–519.

Foltz, K. (1990, March 26). In ads, men's image becomes softer. *The New York Times,* p. D12.

Food Facts Just a Phone Call Away. (1992, October 3). *The New York Times,* p. L11.

Forehand, R., McCombs, A., & Brody, G. H. (1987). The relationship between parental depressive mood states and child functioning. *Behavior Research and Therapy, 9,* 1–20.

Foreman, M. (1990, September 3). Cited in C. L. Hays. Anti-gay attacks increase and some fight back. *The New York Times,* pp. L23, L26.

Forrest, J. D., & Silverman, J. (1989). What public school teachers teach about preventing pregnancy, AIDS and sexually transmitted diseases. *Family Planning Perspectives, 15,* 65–72.

Forsyth, D. R., & McMillan, J. H. (1981). Attributions, affect, and expectations: A test of Weiner's three-dimensional model. *Journal of Educational Psychology, 73,* 393–403.

Fowler, R. D. (1992). Solid support needed for animal research [editorial]. *The APA Monitor, 23* (6), 2.

Fox, L. H., Brody, L., & Tobin, D. (1985). The impact of early intervention programs upon course-taking and attitudes in high school. In S. F. Chipman, L. R. Brush, & D. M. Wilson (Eds.), *Women and mathematics: Balancing the equation.* London: Erlbaum.

Fox, M. W. (1975). Pet-owner relations. In R. S. Anderson (Ed.), *Pet animals and society* (pp. 37–53). London: Baillere Tindall.

Frances, A. J., Widiger, T. A., & Pincus, H. A. (1989). The development of DSM-IV. *Archives of General Psychiatry, 46,* 373–375.

Franks, C. M. (1976). Foreword. In A. A. Lazarus (Ed.), *Multimodal behavior therapy* (pp. viii–ix). New York: Springer.

Freedman, D. G. (1965). An ethological approach to the genetical study of human behavior. In S. G. Vandenberg (Ed.), *Methods and goals in human behavior genetics.* New York: Academic Press.

Freiberg, P. (1991, February). APA pro bono program serves homeless people. *APA Monitor,* p. 34.

French, A. P., Schmid, A. C., & Ingalls, E. (1975). Transcendental meditation, altered reality testing and behavioral change: A case report. *Journal of Nervous and Mental Disease, 161,* 55–58.

Freud, M. (19—). *Glory reflected.* London: Angus and Robertson.

Freud, S. (1900/1953). *The interpretation of dreams.* In J. Strachey (Ed.), *Sigmund Freud: The standard edition of the complete psychological works.* London: Hogarth Press.

Freud, S. (1901/1960). *Psychopathology of everyday life.* In J. Strachey (Ed.), *The standard edition of the complete psychological works of Sigmund Freud* (Vol. 6). London: Hogarth Press. (Originally published as *Psycho-pathology of everyday life* in 1901).

Freud, S. (1913/1959). Further recommendations in the technique of psychoanalysis. In E. Jones (Ed.) and J. Riviere (trans.), *Collected papers* (Vol. 2). New York: Basic Books. (Originally pulished in 1913).

Freud, S. (1933). *New introductory lectures on psycho-analysis.* New York: Carlton House.

Freud, S. (1952). *A general introduction to psycho-analysis.* New York: Washington Square Press. [Reprinted from original 1924 edition].

Freudenberger, H. J. (1977). Burn-out: The organizational menace. *Training and Development Journal, 31* (7), 26–27.

Fried, P. A., Watkinson, B., & Willin, A. (1984). Marijuana use during pregnancy and decreased length of gestation. *American Journal of Obstetrics and Gynecology, 150,* 23–27.

Friede, A. M., Carey, V., Azzara, M. A., Gallagher, S. S., & Guyer, B. (1985). The epidemiology of injuries to bicycle riders. *Pediatric Clinics of North America, 32,* 141–151.

Friedman, H. L. (1992). Changing patterns of adolescent sexual behavior: Consequences for health and development. *Journal of Adolescent Health, 13,* 345–350.

Friedman, H. S., & DiMatteo, R. (1989). *Health psychology.* Englewood Cliffs, NJ: Prentice-Hall.

Friedman, M., & Rosenman, R. (1959). Association of specific overt behavior pattern with blood and cardiovascular findings. *Journal of the American Medical Association, 169,* 1286.

Friedman, M., & Rosenman, R. (1974). *Type A behavior and your heart.* New York: Knopf.

Friedman, S. (1992, November 15). Fitting the therapy to the patient's needs. *The New York Times,* p. NJ3.

Friedmann, E., Katcher, A. H., Lynch, J. J., & Messent, P. R. (1983). Social interaction and blood pressure. *Journal of Nervous and Mental Disease, 171,* 461–465.

Friedmann, E., Katcher, A. H., Lynch, J. J., & Thomas, S. A. (1980). Animal companions and one-year survival of patients after discharge from a coronary care unit. *Public Health Reports, 95,* 307–312.

Frieze, I. H. (1987). Perceptions of battered wives. In I. H. Frieze, D. Bar-Tal, & J. Carroll (Eds.), *New approaches to social problems: Applications of attribution theory.* San Francisco: Jossey-Bass.

Frieze, I. H., Olson, J. E., & Russell, J. (1991). Attractiveness and income for men and women in management. *Journal of Applied Social Psychology, 21,* 1039–1057.

Funk, S. C., & Houston, B. K. (1987). A critical analysis of the Hardiness Scale's validity and utility. *Journal of Personality and Social Psychology, 53,* 572–578.

Furnham, A., & Bochner, S. (1986). *Culture shock: Psychological reactions to unfamiliar environments.* London: Methuen.

Furnham, A., & Duignan, S. (1989). The selective recall of attitude consistent information: A study concerning sex differences. *Psychologia, 32,* 112–119.

Gabbard, K., & Gabbard, G. O. (1987). *Psychiatry and the cinema.* Chicago: University of Chicago Press.

Gaertner, S. L., Mann, J. A., Dovidio, J. F., & Murrell, A. J. (1990). How does cooperation reduce intergroup bias: The benefits of recategorization. *Journal of Personality and Social Psychology, 59,* 692–704.

Gage, M. G., & Anderson, R. K. (1985). Pet ownership, social support, and stress. *Journal of the Delta Society, 2,* 64–71.

Galaburda, A. M., Corsiglia, J., Rosen, G. C., & Sherman, G. F. (1987). Planum temporale asymmetry: Reappraisal since Geschwind and Levitsky. *Neuropsychologia, 25,* 853–868.

Ganellen, R. J., & Blaney, P. H. (1984). Hardiness and social support as moderators of the effects of life stress. *Journal of Personality and Social Psychology, 47,* 156–163.

Ganley, A. L., & Harris, L. (1978, August). *Domestic violence: Issues in designing and implementing programs for male batterers.* Paper presented at the annual meeting of the American Psychological Association, Toronto, Ontario, Canada.

Garbarino, J. (1988). Preventing childhood injury: Developmental and mental health issues. *American Journal of Orthopsychiatry, 58,* 25–45.

Garcia, J., & Koelling, R. A. (1966). Relation of cue to consequence in avoidance learning. *Psychonomic Science, 4,* 123–124.

Garcia-Preto, N. (1992, April 13). Hispanic families in crisis: A cultural and ethnic view. In R. A. Javier (Chair), *Our families in crisis: A multicultural and multiethnic perspective.* Second annual conference at St. John's University, Jamaica, NY.

Garcia-Segura, L. M., Olmos, G., Tranque, P., & Naftolin, F. (1987). Rapid effects of gonadal steroids upon hypothalamic neuronal membrane ultrastructure. *Journal of Steroid Biochemistry, 27,* 1–3.

Gardner, L. K. (1971). The therapeutic relationship under varying conditions of race. *Psychotherapy: Theory, Research & Practice, 8,* 78–87.

Gardner, R. (1989). *Sex abuse hysteria: Salem Witch Trials revisited.* Longwood, NJ: Creative Therapeutics Press.

Gardner, S. (1991, November 10). Agency is fighting violence in teen-age dating. *The New York Times,* p. NJ13.

Garfinkel, P. E., Goldbloom, D., Davis, R., Olmsted, M. P., Garner, D. M., & Halmi, K. A. (1992). Body dissatisfaction in bulimia nervosa: Relationship to weight and shape concerns and psychological functioning. *International Journal of Eating Disorders, 11,* 151–161.

Garland, A. F., & Zigler, E. (1993). Adolescent suicide prevention: Current research and social policy implications. *American Psychologist, 48,* 169–182.

Garmaise, F. (1984). The refined art of hand kissing. *Republic, 5*(10), 88.

Garner, D. M., & Garfinkel, P. E. (1981). Body image in anorexia nervosa: Measurement, theory, and clinical implications. *International Journal of Psychiatry in Medicine, 11,* 263–284.

Garner, D. M., Garfinkel, P. E., Stancer, H. C., & Moldofsky, H. (1976). Body image disturbances in anorexia nervosa and obesity. *Psychosomatic Medicine, 38,* 327–336.

Garrity, K. & Degelman, D. (1990). Effect of server introduction on restaurant tipping. *Journal of Applied Social Psychology, 20,* 168–172.

Garvey, C. (1977). *Play.* Cambridge, MA: Harvard University Press.

Gates, H. L., Jr. (1992, June 3). Cited in F. Butterfield. Afro-American studies get new life at Harvard. *The New York Times,* p. B7.

Gavzer, B. (1990, May 27). Should you tell all? *Parade Magazine,* pp. 4–7.

Geen, R. G. (1981). Behavioral and physiological reactions to observed violence: Effects of prior exposure to aggressive stimuli. *Journal of Personality and Social Psychology, 40,* 868–875.

Geier, J. G. (1969). A trait approach to the study of leadership in small groups. *Journal of Communication, 17,* 316–323.

Geiss, S. K., & O'Leary, K. D. (1981). Therapist rating of frequency and severity of marital problems: Implications for research. *Journal of Marital and Family Therapy, 7,* 515–520.

Gendlin, E. T. (1988). Carl Rogers (1902–1987). *American Psychologist, 43,* 127–128.

Gerin, W., Pieper, C., Levy, R., & Pickering, T. G. (1992). Social support in social interaction: A moderator of cardiovascular reactivity. *Psychosomatic Medicine, 54,* 324–326.

Geschwind, N., & Galaburda, A. M. (1985a). Cerebral lateralization: Biological mechanisms, associations, and pathology: I. A hypothesis and a program for research. *Archives of Neurology, 42,* 428–459.

Geschwind, N., & Galaburda, A. M. (1985b). Cerebral lateralization: Biological mechanisms, associations, and pathology: II. A hypothesis and a program for research. *Archives of Neurology, 42,* 521–552.

Geschwind, N., & Galaburda, A. M. (1985c). Cerebral lateralization: Biological mechanisms, associations, and pathology: III. A hypothesis and a program for research. *Archives of Neurology, 42,* 634–654.

Gibbs, N. (1991, June 3). When is it rape? *Time,* pp. 48–54.

Gibson, E. J., Tighe, T. J., & Walk, R. D. (1957). Behavior of light- and dark-reared rats on a visual cliff. *Science, 126,* 80–81.

Gibson, E. J., & Walk, R. D. (1960). The "visual cliff." *Scientific American, 202* (4), 64–72.

Gilder, G. (1986). *Men and marriage.* New York: Pelican.

Gilligan, C. (1977). In a different voice: Women's conceptions of the self and of morality. *Harvard Educational Review, 47,* 481–517.

Gilligan, C. (1982). *In a different voice: Psychological theory and women's development.* Cambridge, MA: Harvard University Press.

Ginzberg, E. (1966). *The development of human resources.* New York: McGraw-Hill.

Glaberson, W. (1992, April 5). A new twist on lost youth: The mall rats. *The New York Times,* pp. A1, A31.

Glaser, R., Kiecolt-Glaser, J. K., Speicher, C. E., & Holliday, J. E. (1985). Stress, loneliness and changes in herpesvirus latency. *Journal of Behavioral Medicine, 8,* 401–402.

Glasner, P. D., & Kaslow, R. A. (1990). The epidemiology of human immunodeficiency virus infection. *Journal of Consulting and Clinical Psychology, 58,* 13–21.

Glass, L. L., Kirsch, M. A., & Parris, F. N. (1977). Psychiatric disturbances associated with Erhard Seminars Training: I. A report of cases. *American Journal of Psychiatry, 134,* 245–247.

Glass, R. H., & Ericsson, R. (1982). *Getting pregnant in the 1980's.* Berkeley: University of California Press.

Glasser, W. (1965). *Reality therapy.* New York: HarperCollins.

Glasser, W. (1981). *Stations of the mind.* New York: HarperCollins.

Glasser, W. (1984). *Take effective control of your life.* New York: HarperCollins.

Gleghorn, A., Penner, L., Powers, P., & Schulman, R. (1987). The psychometric properties of several measures of body image. *Journal of Psychopathology and Behavioral Assessment, 9,* 203–218.

Goffman, E. (1959). *The presentation of self in everyday life.* New York: Anchor.

Gold, J. A., Ryckman, R. M., & Mosely, N. R. (1984). Romantic mood induction and attraction to a dissimilar other: Is love blind? *Personality and Social Psychology Bulletin, 10,* 358–368.

Goldberg, B. (1992, April 26). Cited in G. Kolata. A parents' guide to kids' sports. *The New York Times Magazine,* Part 2, pp. 12–15, 40, 44, 46.

Goldberg, D. C., et al. (1983). The Grafenberg spot and female ejaculation: A review of initial hypotheses. *Journal of Sex and Marital Therapy, 9,* 27–37.

Goldberg, I. D., Roghmann, K. J., McInery, T. K., & Burke, J. D. (1984). Mental health problems among children seen in pediatric practice: Prevalence and management. *Pediatrics, 73,* 278–293.

Goldberg, L. R. (1981). Language and individual differences: The search for universals in personality lexicons. In L. Wheeler (Ed.), *Review of personality and social psychology* (Vol. 2). (pp. 141–165). Beverly Hills: Sage.

Goldberg, L. R. (1982). From ace to zombie: Some explorations in the language of personality. In C. D. Spielberger & J. N. Butcher (Eds.), *Advances in personality assessment* (Vol. 1) (pp. 203–234). Hillsdale, NJ: Erlbaum.

Goldberg, V. (1992, March 8). Photography and the sin of voyeurism. *The New York Times,* pp. H1, H37.

Goldgaber, D., Lerman, M. I., McBride, O. W., Saffiotti, U., & Gajdusek, D. C. (1987). Characterization and chromosomal localization of a cDNA encoding brain amyloid of Alzheimer's disease. *Science, 235,* 877–880.

Goldman, L., & Tosteson, A. N. A. (1991). Uncertainty about post-menopausal estrogen: Time for action, not debate. *The New England Journal of Medicine, 325,* 800–802.

Goldman, W. (1983). *Adventures in the screen trade.* New York: Warner Books.

Gonzales, M., et al. (1983). Interactional approach to interpersonal attraction. *Journal of Personality and Social Psychology, 44,* 1192–1197.

Gonzales, M. H., David, J. M., Loney, G. L., LuKens, C. K., & Junghans, C. M. (1983). Interactional approach to interpersonal attraction. *Journal of Personality and Social Psychology, 44,* 1192–1197.

Good, G. E., Gilbert, L. A., & Scher, M. (1990). Gender aware therapy: A synthesis of feminist therapy and knowledge about gender. *Journal of Counseling and Development, 68,* 376–380.

Good, T. L., Sikes, J. N., & Brophy, J. E. (1973). Effects of teacher sex and student sex on classroom interaction. *Journal of Educational Psychology, 65,* 74–87.

Goode, W. J. (1963). *World revolutions and family patterns.* New York: Free Press.

Goodman, G. S., & Reed, R. S. (1986). Age differences in eyewitness testimony. *Law and Human Behavior, 10,* 317–332.

Goodtracks, J. (1973). Native American noninterference. *Social Work, 18* (11), 30–34.

Goodwin, F. K., & Jamison, K. R. (1987). Bipolar disorders. In R. E. Hales, & A. J. Frances (Eds.), *American Psychiatric Associa-*

tion annual review (Vol. 6). Washington, DC: American Psychiatric Press.

Gordon, A. (1993, March 17). My student, the princess. *The New York Times*, p. A2.

Gordon, A. I. (1964). *Intermarriage*. Boston: Beacon Press.

Gordon, M. (1992, March 19). Analyzing the analyst's couch. *The New York Times*, pp. C1, C6.

Gordon, M. R. (1993, April 24). Pentagon report tells of aviators' debauchery. *The New York Times*, pp. A1, A9.

Gordon, S., & Snyder, C. W. (1989). *Personal issues in human sexuality: A guidebook for better sexual health* (2nd ed.). Boston: Allyn & Bacon.

Gore, S. (1978). The effect of social support in moderating the health consequences of unemployment. *Journal of Health and Social Behavior, 19*, 157–165.

Gormly, A. V. (1979). Behavioral effects of receiving agreement or disagreement from a peer. *Personality and Social Psychology Bulletin, 5*, 267–270.

Gottlieb, A. N., & Mayer, J. D. (1988, April). *Taxonomies of advice*. Poster presented at the 59th annual meeting of the Eastern Psychological Association, Buffalo, NY.

Grafenberg, E. (1950). The role of the urethra in female orgasm. *International Journal of Sexology, 3*, 145–148.

Graham, M. (1993, March). Unprotected children. *Atlantic*, pp. 20, 22–23, 28–29.

Graham, P., Rutter, M., & George, S. (1973). Temperamental characteristics as predictors of behavior disorders in children. *American Journal of Orthopsychiatry, 43*, 328–339.

Granny dumping by the thousands [Editorial]. (1992, March 29). *The New York Times*, p. E16.

Grasmick, H. G., Bursik, Jr., R. J., & Kinsey, K. A. (1991). Shame and embarrassment as deterrents to noncompliance with the law: The case of an antilittering campaign. *Environment and Behavior, 23*, 233–251.

Grass Grows More Acceptable. (1973, September 10). *Time*.

Gray, J. L., & Starke, F. A. (1984). *Organizational behavior: Concepts and applications* (3rd ed.). Columbus, OH: Merrill.

Greeley, A. M. (1992, October 4). Cited in Happiest couples in study have sex after 60. *The New York Times*, p. L23.

Green, A. (1986). True and false allegations of sexual abuse in child custody disputes. *Journal of the American Academy of Child Psychology, 25*, 449–456.

Green, B. L. (1986). On the confounding of "hassles," stress and outcome. *American Psychologist, 41*, 714–715.

Green, L. (1982). A learned helplessness analysis on problems confronting the Black community. In S. M. Turner and R. T. Jones (Eds.), *Behavior modification in black populations: Psychosocial issues and empirical findings*. New York: Plenum.

Green, L. W., Tryon, W. W., Marks, B., & Huryn, J. (1986). Periodental disease as a function of life events stress. *Journal of Human Stress, 12* (1), 32–36.

Green, S. K., Buchanan, D. R., & Heuer, S. K. (1984). Winners, losers, and choosers: A field investigation of dating initiation. *Personality and Social Psychology Bulletin, 10*, 502–511.

Greenberger, E., & Goldberg, W. A. (1989). Work, parenting, and the socialization of children. *Developmental Psychology, 25*, 22–35.

Greenblatt, R., et al. (1979). Update on the male and female climacteric. *American Geriatrics Society, 27*, 481–490.

Greenblatt, R. B., & Stoddard, L. D. (1978). The estrogen-cancer controversy. *Journal of the American Geriatrics Society, 26*, 1–8.

Greene, B. A. (1985). Considerations in the treatment of black patients by white therapists. *Psychotherapy, 22*, 389–393.

Greene, B. A. (1992, April 13). African-American families: The crisis is survival. In R. A. Javier (Chair), *Our families in crisis: A multicultural and multiethnic perspective*. Second annual conference at St. John's University, Jamaica, NY.

Greenhouse, L. (1993, March 31). Court hears case on science rules. *The New York Times*, p. A19. (a)

Greenhouse, L. (1993, June 29). Justices put judges in charge of deciding reliability of scientific testimony. *The New York Times*, p. A13. (b)

Greenhouse, S. (1992, June 7). The coming crisis of the American work force. *The New York Times*, p. F14.

Greenough, W. T., Black, J. E., & Wallace, C. S. (1987). Experience and brain development. *Child Development, 58*, 539–559.

Greensher, J., & Mofenson, H. C. (1985). Injuries at play. *Pediatric Clinics of North America, 32*, 127–139.

Greenson, R. (1964). *The technique and practice of psychoanalysis*. New York: International Universities Press.

Greenwald, A. G. (1976). Within-subjects designs: To use or not to use? *Psychological Bulletin, 83*, 314–320.

Greenwald, M. K., Cook, E. W. III, & Lang, P. J. (1989). Affective judgment and psychophysiological response: Dimensional covariation in the evaluation of pictorial stimuli. *Journal of Psychophysiology, 3*, 51–64.

Griesinger, W. (1845). *Pathologie und therapie der psychischen krankheiten*. (*The pathology and therapy of psychic disorders*).

Grin, T. R., Nelson, L. B., & Jeffers, J. B. (1987). Eye injuries in childhood. *Pediatrics, 80*, 13–17.

Grinberg-Levin, Z., & Berry, G. (1988). Parental mediation, the child and television: Securing positive psycho-social messages from the medium. In R. Baruch & P. Vesin (Eds.), *Channeling children's anger: Proceedings of the International Conference*. Paris: Centre International de l'Enfance.

Grinspoon, L. (1977). *Marijuana reconsidered* (2nd ed.). Cambridge, MA: Harvard University Press.

Gross, J. (1992a, March 29). Collapse of inner-city families creates America's new orphans. *The New York Times*, pp. A1, A20.

Gross, J. (1992b, July 31). Suffering in silence no more: Fighting sexual harassment. *The New York Times*, pp. A1, D10.

Groth, A., & Hobson, W. (1983). The dynamics of sexual assault. In L. Schlesinger & E. Revitch (Eds.), *Sexual dynamics of antisocial behavior*. Springfield, IL: Charles C Thomas.

Groth, A. N. (1979). *Men who rape*. New York: Plenum Press.

Groth, A. N., & Birnbaum, H. J. (1979). *Men who rape: The psychology of the offender*. New York: Plenum Press.

Grove, C. L., & Torbiorn, I. (1986). A new conceptualization of intercultural adjustment and the goals of learning. In R. M. Paige (Ed.), *Cross-cultural orientation: New conceptualizations and applications* (pp. 71–109). Chicago: University of Chicago Press.

Gruson, L. (1992, April 22). Gains in deciphering genes set off effort to guard data against abuses. *The New York Times*, p. C12.

Guelzow, M. G., Bird, G. W., & Koball, E. H. (1991). An exploratory path analysis of the stress process for dual-career men and women. *Journal of Marriage and the Family, 53*, 151–164.

Guilford, J. P. (1959). *Personality*. New York: McGraw-Hill.

Gump, P. V. (1974). Operating environments in open and traditional schools. *School Review, 84*, 575–593.

Gump, P. V. (1978). School environments. In I. Altman & J. F. Wohlwill (Eds.), *Children and the environment*. New York: Plenum.

Gump, P. V. (1990). A short history of the Midwest Psychological Field Station. *Environment and Behavior, 22*, 436–457.

Gunderson, J. (1983). DSM-III diagnoses of personality disorders. In J. P. Frosch (Ed.), *Current perspectives on personality disorders* (pp. 20–39). Washington, D. C.: American Psychiatric Press.

Gupta, S., Grieco, M. D., & Cushman, P. (1974). Impairment of rosette-forming T-lymphocites in chronic marihuana smokers. *New England Journal of Medicine, 291*, 874–876.

Gustavson, C. R., Garcia, J., Hankins, W. G., & Rusiniak, K. W. (1974). Coyote predation control by aversive conditioning. *Science, 184*, 581–583.

Gutmann, D. (1975). Parenthood: A key to the comparitive study of the life cycle. In N. Daton & L. H. Ginsberg (Eds.), *Life-span developmental psychology: Normative life crises* (pp. 167–184). New York: Academic Press.

Gwartney-Gibbs, P. A. (1986). The institutionalization of premarital cohabitation: Estimates from marriage license applications, 1970 and 1980. *Journal of Marriage and the Family, 48*, 423–434.

Gwinn, M., et al. (1991). Prevalence of HIV infection in childbearing women in the United States: Surveillance using newborn blood samples. *Journal of the American Medical Association, 265*, 1704–1708.

Haberman, C. (1992, May 13). What makes "Samson" run amok? He's manic in Jerusalem. *The New York Times*, p. A13.

Hackman, J. R., & Oldham, G. R. (1976). Motivation through the design of work: Test of a theory. *Organizational Behavior and Human Performance, 16*, 250–279.

Hagen, C. (1992, May 10). The power of a video image depends on the caption. *The New York Times*, p. H32.

Hall, E. J., & Flannery, P. J. (1985). Prevalence and correlates of sexual assault experiences in adolescents. *Victimology: An International Journal, 9*, 398–406.

Hall, E. T. (1959). *The silent language*. Garden City, NY: Doubleday.

Hall, M. H. (1968). The psychology of universality: A conversation with the president of the American Psychological Association. *Psychology Today, 2*, 34–37, 54–57.

Hall, N. (1988, September/October). Cited in J. Barber. Worried sick. *Equinox*.

Hall, S. S. (1989, June). A molecular code links emotions, mind and health. *Smithsonian*; pp. 62–71.

Halleck, S. L. (1976). Discussion of "Socially Reinforced Obsessing." *Journal of Consulting and Clinical Psychology, 44*, 146–147.

Hamburg, D. A., Elliott, G. R., & Parron, D. L. (1982). *Health and behavior: Frontiers of research in the behavioral sciences*. Washington, DC: National Academy Press.

Hamilton, D. L., & Gifford, R. K. (1976). Illusory correlation in interpersonal perception: A cognitive basis of stereotypic judgments. *Journal of Experimental Social Psychology, 12*, 392–407.

Hamilton, M., Kolotkin, R. L., Cogburn, D. F., Moore, D. T., & Watterson, K. (1990). *The Duke University Medical Center book of diet and fitness*. New York: Fawcett Columbine.

Hamilton, M., & Yee, J. (1990). Rape knowledge and propensity to rape. *Journal of Research in Personality, 24*, 111–122.

Hammond, R. (1991). *Dealing with anger: Givin' it, takin' it, workin' it out*. Champaign, IL: Research Press.

Hammond, R., & Yung, B. (1991). Preventing violence in at-risk African American youth. *Journal of Health Care for the Poor and Underserved, 2*, 359–373.

Hammond, W. R., & Yung, B. (1993). Psychology's role in the public health response to assaultive violence among young African-American men. *American Psychologist, 48*, 142–154.

Hampson, E. (1990). Variations in sex-related cognitive abilities across the menstrual cycle. *Brain and Cognitions, 14*, 26–43.

Hampton, R. (1986). Family violence and homicide in the Black community: Are they linked? In *Report of the Secretary's Task Force on Black and Minority Health* (Vol. 5, pp. 69–96). Washington, DC: US Department of Health and Human Services.

Hanley, R. (1992a, December 9). Counselor says woman in abuse case sought affection to gain friends. *The New York Times*, B6.

Hanley, R. (1992b, December 19). Psychiatrist calls woman "bewildered" and helpless in Glen Ridge sex case. *The New York Times*, p. L29.

Hannigan, T. P. (1990). Traits, attitudes, and skills that are related to intercultural effectiveness and their implications for cross-cultural training: A review of the literature. *International Journal of Intercultural Relations, 14*, 89–111.

Hansen, L. B., & Jacob, E. (1992). Intergenerational support during the transition to parenthood: Issues for new parents and grandparents. *Families in Society, 73*, 471–479.

Hanson, S. L., & Ooms, T. (1991). The economic costs and rewards of two-earner, two-parent families. *Journal of Marriage and the Family, 53*, 622–634.

Hanson, I. (1992, September 16). Cited in M. T. Kaufman. At work, high above the fast track. *The New York Times*, p. B3.

Hanson, R. K. (1990). The psychological impact of sexual assault on women and children: A review. *Annals of Sex Research, 1*, 485–499.

Hanson, S. L., & Tuch, S. A. (1984). The determinants of marital instability: Some methodological issues. *Journal of Marriage and the Family, 46*, 631–642.

Hanzlick, R. (1984). Deaths among the homeless: Atlanta, Georgia. *Morbidity and Mortality Weekly Report, 36* (19), 297–299.

Harlow, C. (1989). *Injuries from crime* (Bureau of Justice Statistics, Special Report No. NCJ-116811). Washington, DC: U.S. Department of Health and Human Services.

Harlow, C. (1991). *Female victims of violent crime* (Bureau of Justice Statistics, Special Report No. NCJ-126826). Washington, DC: U.S. Department of Justice.

Harlow, H. F. (1958). The nature of love. *American Psychologist, 13*, 673–685.

Harlow, H. F. (1959). Love in infant monkeys. *Scientific American, 200* (6), 68–74.

Harlow, H. F., & Harlow, M. K. (1962). Social deprivation in monkeys. *Scientific American, 207* (5), 136–146.

Harney, P. A., & Muehlenhard, C. L. (1991). Rape. In E. Grauerholz & M. A. Koraleski (Eds.), *Sexual coercion: A sourcebook on its nature, causes, and prevention* (pp. 3–16). Lexington, MA: Lexington Books.

Harris, D. M., & Guten, S. (1979). Health protective behavior: An exploratory study. *Journal of Health and Social Behavior, 20*, 17–29.

Harvey, J. H., Town, J. P., & Yarkin, K. L. (1981). How fundamental is "the fundamental attribution error"? *Journal of Personality and Social Psychology, 40*, 346–349.

Harvey, W. (1628). *Exercitatio anatomica de motu cordis et sanguinis in animalibus* [Anatomical essay on the motion of the heart and blood in animals].

Harwood, R. L., & Miller, J. G. (1991). Perceptions of attachment behavior: A comparison of Anglo and Puerto Rican mothers. *Merrill-Palmer Quarterly, 37*, 583–599.

Hatch, O. G. (1992, July 31). Cited in J. Gross. Suffering in silence no more: Fighting sexual harassment. *The New York Times*, pp. A1, D10.

Hatfield, E. (1988). Passionate and companionate love. In R. J. Sternberg & M. L. Barnes (Eds.), *The psychology of love*. New Haven, CT: Yale University Press.

Havighurst, R. J. (1982). The world of work. In B. Wolman (Ed.), *Handbook of developmental psychology*. Englewood Cliffs, NJ: Prentice-Hall.

Hawaii State Department of Health. (1987). *Statistical report*. Honolulu: Author.

Hawkins, D. (1990). Explaining the Black homicide rate. *Journal of Interpersonal Violence, 5*, 151–163.

Hawkins, R. P. (1989). Developing potent behavior change technologies: An invitation to cognitive behavior therapists. *The Behavior Therapist, 12*, 126–131.

Haynes, R. B., Taylor, D. W., & Sackett, D. L. (1979). *Compliance in health care*. Baltimore: Johns Hopkins University Press.

Haynes, S. G., Feinleib, M., & Kannel, W. B. (1980). The relationship of psychosocial factors to coronary heart disease in the Framingham study: III. Eight year incidence of coronary heart disease. *American Journal of Epidemiology, 111*, 37–58.

Hays, C. L. (1990, September 3). Anti-gay attacks increase and some fight back. *The New York Times*, pp. L23, L26.

Hays, C. L. (1992, September 23). Rollerblading leads woman to court. *The New York Times*, p. B5.

Hays, R. B. (1984). The development and maintenance of friendship. *Journal of Social and Personal Relationships, 1*, 75–98.

Hays, R. B. (1985). A longitudinal study of friendship development. *Journal of Personality and Social Psychology, 52*, 511–524.

Haywood, T. W., Grossman, L. S., & Cavanaugh, Jr., J. L. (1990). Subjective versus objective measurements of deviant sexual arousal in clinical evaluations of alleged child molesters. *Psychological Assessment: A Journal of Consulting and Clinical Psychology, 2*, 269–275.

Hazaleus, S. L., & Deffenbacher, J. L. (1986). Relaxation and cognitive treatments of anger. *Journal of Consulting and Clinical Psychology, 54*, 222–226.

Hazelwood, R. R., Reboussin, R., & Warren, J. I. (1989). Serial rape: Correlates of increased aggression and the relationship of offender pleasure to victim resistance. *Journal of Interpersonal Violence, 4*, 65–78.

Hazleton, L. (1992, March 29). Really cool cars. *The New York Times*, Section 6, pp. 34–39, 73.

Hearing of Appeal on Press-Leak Order. (1993, April 8). *The New York Times*, p. B2.

Hearn, J., & Morgan, D. (Eds.). (1990). *Men, masculinities and social theory*. London: Unwin Hyman.

Hearn, M. D., Murray, D. M., & Luepker, R. V. (1989). Hostility, coronary heart disease, and total mortality: A 33-year follow-up study of university students. *Journal of Behavioral Medicine, 12*, 105–121.

Heatherton, T. F., & Baumeister, R. F. (1991). Binge eating as an escape from self-awareness. *Psychological Bulletin, 110*, 86–108.

Heatherton, T. F., Herman, C. P., & Polivy, J. (1991). Effects of physical threat and ego threat on eating behavior. *Journal of Personality and Social Psychology, 60*, 138–143.

Heatherton, T. F., Herman, C. P., & Polivy, J. (1992). Effects of distress on eating: The importance of ego involvement. *Journal of Personality and Social Psychology, 62*, 801–803.

Heaton, T. B., & Albrecht, S. L. (1991). Stable unhappy marriages. *Journal of Marriage and the Family, 53*, 747–758.

Hechinger, F. M. (1992). *Fateful choices*. New York: Hill & Wang.

Hedges, C. (1993, May 9). Looking for love (shhh!) in ads. *The New York Times*, p. V3.

Heer, D. M. (1974). The prevalence of black-white marriages in the United States, 1960 and 1970. *Journal of Marriage and the Family, 36*, 246–258.

Heesacker, M., & Prichard, S. (1992). *In a Different Voice*, revisited: Men, women, and emotion. *Journal of Mental Health Counseling, 14*, 274–290.

Heide, F. J. (1981). *Relaxation-induced anxiety: A psychophysiological investigation*. Unpublished doctoral dissertation. The Pennsylvania State University, University Park, PA.

Heide, F. J., & Borkovec, T. D. (1983). Relaxation-induced anxiety: Paradoxical anxiety enhancement due to relaxation training. *Journal of Consulting and Clinical Psychology, 51*, 171–182.

Heide, F. J., & Borkovec, T. D. (1984). Relaxation-induced anxiety: Mechanisms and theoretical implications. *Behavior Research and Therapy, 22*, 1–12.

Heilman, M. E., Block, C. J., Martell, R. F., & Simon, M. C. (1989). Has anything changed? Current characterizations of men, women, and managers. *Journal of Applied Psychology, 74*, 935–942.

Heilman, M. E., Martell, R. F., & Simon, M. C. (1988). The vagaries of sex bias: Conditions regulating the undervaluation, equivaluation, and overvaluation of female job applicants. *Organizational Behavior and Human Decision Process, 41*, 98–110.

Heiman, G. W. (1975). A note on "Operant conditioning principles extrapolated to the theory of management." *Organizational Behavior and Human Performance, 13*, 165–170.

Hein, K., et al. (1989). *AIDS: Trading fears for facts*. Mount Vernon, NY: Consumers Union.

Hellekson, C. J., Kline, J. A., & Rosenthal, N. E. (1986). Phototherapy of seasonal affective disorder in Alaska. *American Journal of Psychiatry, 143*, 1035–1037.

Heller, K., Swindle, R. W., & Dusenbury, L. (1986). Component social support processes: Comments and integration. *Journal of Consulting and Clinical Psychology, 54*, 466–470.

Hembree, W. C., Nahas, G. G., & Huang, H. F. S. (1979). Changes in human spermatoza associated with high dose marihuana-smoking. In G. G. Nahas & W. D. M. Paton (Eds.), *Marihuana: Biological effects*. Elmsford, NY: Pergamon.

Henggeler, S. W., & Borduin, C. M. (1981). Satisfied working mothers and their preschool sons. *Journal of Family Issues, 2*, 322–335.

Henig, R. M. (1993a, March 30). New vaccine method using DNA protects mice against flu. *The New York Times*, p. C3.

Henig, R. M. (1993b, March 3). The immunity myth. *The New York Times*, p. A25.

Henneberger, M. (1992, October 28). From warm letters to cold warring, romance fades. *The New York Times*, pp. B1, B5.

Henriques, F. (1974). *Children of conflict: A study of interracial sex and marriage*. New York: Dutton.

Henslin, J. M. (1993). *Sociology*. Boston: Allyn & Bacon.

Herbert, T. B., & Cohen, S. (1993). Depression and immunity: A meta-analytic review. *Psychological Bulletin, 113*, in press.

Herbert, T. B., Silver, R. C., Ellard, J. H. (1991). Coping with an abusive relationship: I. How and why do women stay? *Journal of Marriage and the Family, 53*, 311–325.

Hershberger, P. J., & Walsh, W. B. (1990). Multiple role involvements and the adjustment to conjugal bereavement: An exploratory study. *Omega, 21*, 91–102.

Herzberg, F., Mausner, B., & Snyderman, B. B. (1959). *The motivation to work*. New York: Wiley.

Hetherington, E. M. (1989). Coping with marital transitions: Winners, losers, and survivors. *Child Development, 60*, 1–14.

Hetherington, E. M., Cox, M., & Cox, R. (1985). Long-term effects of divorce and remarriage on the adjustment of children. *Journal of the American Academy of Child Psychiatry, 24,* 518–530.

Hier, M. (1993). Publication of the Simon Wiesenthal Center, 9670 West Pico Boulevard, Los Angeles, CA 90035.

Higgins, E. T., & Bargh, J. A. (1987). Social cognition and social perception. In M. R. Rosenzweig & L. W. Porter (Eds.), *Annual reviews of psychology* (Vol. 38, pp. 369–425). Palo Alto, CA: Annual Reviews.

Higgins, M. K. (1985). *From slavery to vagrancy in Brazil: Crime and social control in the third world.* New Brunswick, NJ: Rutgers University Press.

Hilberman, E., & Munson, K. (1977–1978). Sixty battered women. *Victimology, 2,* 460–470.

Hill, C. T., Rubin, Z., & Peplau, L. A. (1976). Breakups before marriage: The end of 103 affairs. *The Journal of Social Issues, 32,* 147–168.

Hilts, P. J. (1992, December 31). Federal inquiry finds misconduct by a discoverer of the AIDS virus. *The New York Times,* pp. A1, A20.

Hilts, P. J. (1992, June 10). More teen-agers being slain by guns. *The New York Times,* p. A19.

Himmelfarb, S. (1992, June 1). Graduates fell anxious, not just about jobs. *The New York Times,* p. A16.

Hingson, R., et al. (1982). Effects of maternal drinking and marijuana use on fetal growth and development. *Pediatrics, 70,* 539–546.

Hinojoza, E. (1992, March 30). Cited in N. C. Cash. Bolivia is helping its battered wives to stand up. *The New York Times,* p. A4.

Hinsz, V. B. (1989). Facial resemblance in engaged and married couples. *Journal of Social and Personal Relationships, 6,* 223–229.

Hoch, P. H. (1943). Clinical and biological interrelations between schizophrenia and epilepsy. *American Journal of Psychiatry, 99,* 507–511.

Hochhauser, M., & Fowler, H. (1975). Cue effects of drive and reward as a function of discrimination difficulty: Evidence against the Yerkes-Dodson law. *Journal of Experimental Psychology: Animal Behavior Processes, 1,* 261–269.

Hochman, D. (1992, November 29). A safe-sex product in need of a marketing plan. *The New York Times,* p. F10.

Hock, E., & DeMeis, D. K. (1990). Depression in mothers of infants: The role of maternal employment. *Developmental Psychology, 26,* 285–291.

Hockenberry, J. (1992, April 13). Limited seating on Broadway [Editorial]. *The New York Times.*

Hodgman, C. H., & Roberts, F. N. (1982). Adolescent suicide and the pediatrician. *Journal of Pediatrics, 101,* 118–123.

Hoem, B., & Hoem, J. M. (1992). The disruption of marital and nonmarital unions in contemporary Sweden. In J. Trussell, R. Hankinson, & J. Tilton, (Eds.), *Demographic applications of event history analysis* (pp. 61–93). Oxford: Clarendon Press.

Hoff, P. M. (1986). *Legal remedies in parental kidnapping cases: A collection of materials.* Washington, DC: American Bar Association.

Hoffman, C., & Hurst, N. (1990). Gender stereotypes: Perception or rationalization? *Journal of Personality and Social Psychology, 58,* 197–208.

Hoffman, J. (1992, November 1). Pull up a chair, boys. Can you take dictation? *The New York Times,* p. E3.

Hoffman, L. (1982). Foreword. In S. Rosen (1982), *My voice will go with you: The teaching tales of Milton H. Erickson.* New York: Norton.

Hoffman, L. (1987). The effects on children of maternal and paternal employment. In N. Gerstel & H. Gross (Eds.), *Families and work.* Philadelphia: Temple University Press.

Hoffman, L. W., & Manis, J. D. (1979). The value of children in the United States: A new approach to the study of fertility. *Journal of Marriage and the Family, 41,* 583–596.

Hoffman, M. L. (1984). Moral development. In M. H. Bronstein & M. E. Lamb (Eds.), *Developmental Psychology: An advanced textbook* (pp. 279–324). Hillsdale, NJ: Erlbaum.

Hofman, M. A., & Swaab, D. F. (1991). Sexual dimorphism of the human brain: Myth and reality. *Experimental and Clinical Endocrinology, 98,* 161–170.

Hogan, R. (1975). Theoretical egocentrism and the problem of compliance. *American Psychologist, 30,* 533–540.

Hogan, R. (1983). Socioanalytic theory of personality. In M. M. Page (Ed.), *1982 Nebraska symposium on motivation: Personality* (pp. 55–89). Lincoln: University of Nebraska Press.

Holahan, C. K., & Gilbert, L. A. (1979). Conflict between major life roles: Women and men in dual career couples. *Human Relations, 32,* 451–467.

Holender, D. (1986). Semantic activation without conscious identification in dichotic listening, parafoveal vision, and visual masking: A survey and appraisal. *Behavioral and Brain Sciences, 9,* 1–23.

Holland, J. L. (1985). *Self-Directed Search, 1985 Revision.* Odessa, FL: Psychological Assessment Resources.

Hollander, E. P. (1978). *Leadership dynamics: A practical guide to effective relationships.* New York: Free Press.

Holmes, S. A. (1993, March 18). U.S. rebukes North Koreans for scrapping nuclear pact. *The New York Times,* p. A6.

Holmes, T. H. (1979). Development and application of a quantitative measure of life change magnitude. In J. E. Barrett, R. M. Rose, & G. L. Klerman (Eds.), *Stress and mental disorder.* New York: Raven.

Holmes, T. H., & Masuda, M. (1974). Life change and illness susceptibility. In B. S. Dohrenwend & B. P. Dohrenwend (Eds.), *Stressful life events: Their nature and effects.* New York: Wiley.

Holmes, T. H., & Rahe, R. H. (1967). The Social Readjustment Rating Scale. *Journal of Psychosomatic Research, 11,* 213–218.

Holmes, T. S., & Holmes, T. H. (1970). Short-term intrusions into the life-style routine. *Journal of Psychosomatic Research, 14,* 121–132.

Holroyd, K. A., & Lazarus, R. S. (1982). Stress, coping and somatic adaptation. In L. Goldberger & S. Breznitz (Eds.), *Handbook of stress: Theoretical and clinical aspects.* New York: Free Press.

Homme, L. E. (1965). Perspectives in psychology: Control of coverants, the operants of the mind (Vol. 24). *Psychological Record, 15,* 501–511.

Homme, L. E., & Tosti, D. T. (1965). Contingency management and motivation. *Journal of the National Society for Programmed Instruction, 4,* 14–16.

Hooker, W. D., & Jones, R. T. (1987). Increased susceptibility to memory intrusions and the Stroop interference effect during acute marijuana intoxication. *Psychopharmacology, 91,* 20–24.

Hopkins, E. (1992, December 26). Sex is for adults. *The New York Times,* p. 21.

Hoppe, C. M. (1979). Interpersonal aggression as a function of subject's sex, sex role identification, opponent's sex, and degree of provocation. *Journal of Personality, 47,* 317–329.

Hopper, J. R., & Nielsen, J. M. (1991). Recycling as altruistic behavior. *Environment and Behavior, 23,* 195–220.

Horejsi, C., Craig, B. H. R., & Pablo, J. (1992). Reactions by Native American parents to child protection agencies: Cultural and community factors. *Child Welfare, 51,* 369–377.

Horner, M. (1974). Toward an understanding of achievement-related conflicts in women. In J. Stacey, S. Bereaud, & J. Daniels (Eds.), *And Jill came tumbling after: Sexism in American education.* New York: Dell. pp. 43–63.

Horner, M. S. (1973). A psychological barrier to achievement in women: The motive to avoid success. In D. C. McClelland & R. S. Steele (Eds.), *Human motivation* (pp. 222–230). Morristown, NJ: General Learning Press.

Horney, K. (1945). *Our inner conflicts.* New York: Norton.

Horney, K. (1950). *Neurosis and human growth: The struggle toward self-realization.* New York: Norton.

Horney, K. (1980). *The adolescent diaries of Karen Horney.* New York: Basic Books.

Horowitz, F. D. (1969). Learning, developmental research, and individual differences. In L. P. Lipsitt & H. W. Reese (Eds.), *Advances in child development and behavior* (Vol. 4). New York: Academic Press.

Horowitz, M. (1976). *Stress response syndromes.* New York: Aronson.

Horowitz, M. (1979). Psychological response to serious life events. In V. Hamilton & D. M. Warburton (Eds.), *Human stress and cognition: An information processing approach* (pp. 237–265). Chichester, England: Wiley.

Ho-t'ien, M. (1949). *Culture and ethos of Kaska Society.* New Haven: Yale University Press.

House, J. S. (1981). *Work, stress, and social support.* Reading, MA: Addison-Wesley.

House, J. S., Landis, K. R., & Umberson, D. (1988). Social relationships and health. *Science, 241,* 541–545.

House of Representatives (1990). *No place to call home: Discarded children in America. A report of the Select Committee on Children, Youth, and Families.* Washington, DC: U.S. Government Printing Office.

Hovland, C. I., & Sears, R. R. (1940). Minor studies in aggression. VI: Correlation of lynchings with economic indices. *Journal of Psychology, 9,* 301–310.

Hoyenga, K. B., & Hoyenga, K. T. (1993a). *Gender-related differences: Origins and outcomes.* Needham Heights, MA: Allyn & Bacon.

Hoyenga, K. B., & Hoyenga, K. T. (1993b). *A manual to accompany Gender-Related Differences: Origins and outcomes.* Needham Heights, MA: Allyn & Bacon.

Hsu, L. K. G., & Sobkiewicz, T. A. (1991). Body image disturbance: Time to abandon the concept for eating disorders. *International Journal of Eating Disorders, 10,* 15–30.

HSUS (Humane Society of the United States). (1992, June). *Close-up report.* Washington, DC: Author.

HSUS. (1993). *Close-up report: Slaughter on the high seas.* Washington, DC: HSUS.

Huber, J., & Spitze, G. (1980). Considering divorce: An expansion of Becker's theory of marital instability. *American Journal of Sociology, 86,* 75–89.

Hughes, C. C. (1985). The genital retraction taxon: Commentary. In R. C. Simon & C. C. Hughes (Eds.), *The culture-bound syndromes: Folk illness of psychiatric and anthropological interest.* Dordrecht: Reidel.

Hull, J. G., van Treuren, R. R., & Virnelli, S. (1987). Hardiness and health: A critique and alternative approach. *Journal of Personality and Social Psychology, 53,* 518–530.

Humphries, C. (1986). *An investigation of stress and stress outcomes among mortgage company employees as a function of implementation of a computerized information management system.* Unpublished doctoral dissertation, University of Miami, FL.

Hunt, M. (1974). *Sexual behavior in the 1970's.* New York: Dell.

Hurlock, E. B. (1929). *The psychology of dress.* New York: Ronald Press.

Huston, A. C., Wright, J. C., Rice, M. L., Kerkman, D., & St. Peters, M. (1990). Development of television viewing patterns in early childhood: A longitudinal investigation. *Developmental Psychology, 26,* 409–420.

Hyde, J. S. (1990). *Understanding human sexuality* (4th ed.). New York: McGraw-Hill.

Hyde, J. S., & Linn, M. C. (1988). Gender differences in verbal ability: A meta-analysis. *Psychological Bulletin, 104,* 53–69.

Hymowitz, K. S. (1993, March 25). Multiculturalism is anti-culture. *The New York Times,* p. A23.

Impastato, D. J. (1960). The story of the first electroshock treatment. *American Journal of Psychiatry, 116,* 1113–1114.

Insel, P. M., & Roth, W. T. (1991). *Core concepts in health.* Mountain View, CA: Mayfield Publishing.

Institute of Medicine. (1988). *Homelessness, health and human needs.* Washington, DC: National Academy Press.

Institute of Medicine/National Academy of Sciences. (1982). *Marijuana and health.* Washington, DC: National Academy Press.

Interior Dept.'s Drug Testing Found Mismanaged. (1992, November 22). *The New York Times,* p. L32.

Irons, W. (1979). Cultural and biological success. In N. A. Chagnon & W. Irons (Eds.), *Evolutionary biology and human social behavior: An anthropological perspective* (pp. 257–272). North Scituate, MA: Duxbury.

Irwin, M., Daniels, M., Smith, T. L., Bloom, E., Weiner, H. (1987). Impaired natural killer cell activity during bereavement. *Brain Behavior Immunology, 1,* 98–104.

Ivey, A. E., Ivey, M. B., & Simek-Morgan, L. (1993). *Counseling and psychotherapy: A multicultural perspective.* Needham Heights, MA: Allyn & Bacon.

Izard, C. E. (1971). *The face of emotion.* New York: Appleton-Century-Crofts.

Izard, C. E. (1982). The psychology of emotion comes of age on the coattails of Darwin. *Contemporary Psychology, 27,* 426–429.

Jablonsky, S. F., & DeVries, D. L. (1972). Operant conditioning principles extrapolated to the theory of management. *Organizational Behavior and Human Performance, 7,* 340–358.

Jacklin, C. N. (1989). Female and male: Issues of gender. *American Psychologist, 44,* 536–545.

Jacklin, C. N., Maccoby, E. E., & Doering, C. M. (1983). Neonatal sex-steroid hormones and timidity in 6–18 month-old boys and girls. *Developmental Psychobiology, 16,* 163–168.

Jacklin, C. N., Wilcox, K. T., & Maccoby, E. E. (1988). Neonatal sex steroid hormones and cognitive abilities at six years. *Developmental Psychobiology, 21,* 567–574.

Jackson, A. M. (1973). Psychotherapy: Factors associated with the race of the therapist. *Psychotherapy: Theory, Research, and Practice, 10,* 273–277.

Jackson, A. M. (1983). The Black patient and traditional psychotherapy: Implications and possible extensions. *Journal of Community Psychology, 11,* 303–307.

Jacobsen, F. M., Wehr, T. A., Skewer, R. A., Sack, D. A., & Rosenthal, N. E. (1987). Morning versus midday phototherapy of seasonal affective disorder. *American Journal of Psychiatry, 144,* 1301–1305.

Jacobson, E. (1938). *Progressive relaxation.* Chicago: University of Chicago Press.

Jacobson, N. S. (1991). Behavioral versus insight-oriented marital therapy. *Journal of Consulting and Clinical Psychology, 59,* 142–145.

James, C. (1992, October 25). The empress has no clothes. *The New York Times Book Review,* p. 7.

James, S. P., Wehr, T. A., Sack, D. A., Parry, B. L., Rosenthal, N. E. (1985). Treatment of seasonal affective disorder with light in the evening. *British Journal of Psychiatry, 147,* 424–428.

James, W. (1890). *The principles of psychology.* New York: Holt.

Janis, I. L. (1972). *Victims of groupthink.* Boston: Houghton Mifflin.

Japan says an executive worked himself to death. (1992, July 16). *The New York Times,* p. D4.

Jeffrey, D. B., & Lemnitzer, N. (1981). Diet, exercise, obesity and related health problems: A macroenvironmental analysis. In Kromhaut, D., Bosschieter, E. B., & de Lezenne Coulander, C. (1985). The inverse relation between fish consumption and 20-year mortality from coronary heart disease. *New England Journal of Medicine, 312,* 1205–1209.

Jellinek, E. M. (1960). *The disease concept of alcoholism.* New Haven: Hillhouse Press.

Jemmott, J. B., III, & Locke, S. E. (1984). Psychosocial factors, immunologic mediation, and human susceptibility to infectious diseases: How much do we know? *Psychological Bulletin, 95,* 78–108.

Jemmott, J. B., III, & Magloire, K. (1988). Academic stress, social support, secretory Immunoglobin A. *Journal of Personality and Social Psychology, 55,* 803–810.

Jenkins, C. D., Zyzanski, S. J., & Rosenman, R. H. (1976). Risk of new myocardial infarction in middle-age men with manifest coronary heart disease. *Circulation, 53,* 342–347.

Jenkins, C. D., Zyzanksi, S. J., & Rosenman, R. H. (1979). *Jenkins Activity Survey: Manual.* San Antonio, TX: Psychological Corporation.

Jersild, A. T., Woodyard, E. S., del Solar, C., Osborne, E. G., & Challman, R. C. (1949). *Joys and problems of child rearing.* New York: Bureau of Publications, Teachers College, Columbia University.

Jessor, R. (1992). Risk behavior in adolescence: A psychosocial framework for understanding and action. In D. E. Rogers & E. Ginzburg (Eds.), *Adolescents at risk: Medical and social perspectives* (pp. 19–34). Boulder, CO: Westview Press.

Jessor, R. (1993). Successful adolescent development among youth in high-risk settings. *American Psychologist, 48,* 117–126.

Jeszeck, C. (1992, June 21). Cited in G. Kolata. More children are employed, often perilously. *The New York Times,* pp. A1, A22.

Jobes, D. A., Berman, A. L., & Josselson, A. R. (1987). Improving the validity and reliability of medical-legal certifications of suicide. *Suicide and Life-Threatening Behavior, 17,* 310–325.

Joe, G. (1992, October 25). Cited in V. Byrd. Easing the cultural tension at the neighborhood store. *The New York Times,* p. F8.

Joffe, L. S., Vaughn, B. E., Barglow, P., & Benveniste, R. (1985). Biobehavioral antecedents in the development of infant-mother attachment. In M. Reite & T. Field (Eds.), *The psychobiology of attachment and separation.* New York: Academic Press.

Johnson, J. T. (1987). The heart on the sleeve and the secret self: Estimations of hidden emotions in self and acquaintances. *Journal of Personality, 55,* 563–582.

Johnson, M. P. (1978). *Personal and structural commitment: Sources of consistency in the development of relationships.* Paper presented at the Theory Construction and Research Methodology Workshop, National Council on Family Relations annual meeting, Philadelphia.

Johnson, M. P. (1982). The social and cognitive features of the dissolution of commitment to relationships. In S. Duck (Ed.), *Personal relationships: Dissolving personal relationships* (pp. 51–73). New York: Academic Press.

Johnson, R. K., Smiciklas-Wright, H., Crouter, A. C., & Willits, F. K. (1992). Maternal employment and the quality of young children's diets: Empirical evidence based on the 1987–1988 nationwide food consumption survey. *Pediatrics, 90,* 345–249.

Johnston, D. (1992, April 24). Survey shows number of rapes far higher than official figures. *The New York Times,* p. A14.

Jones, D. P., & McGraw, J. M. (1987). Reliable and fictitious accounts of sexual abuse to children. *Journal of Interpersonal Violence, 2,* 27–45.

Jones, E. (1953). *The life and works of Sigmund Freud.* New York: Basic Books.

Jones, E. (1961). *The life and works of Sigmund Freud.* New York: Basic Books.

Jones, E. E. (1986). Interpreting interpersonal behavior: The effect of expectancies. *Science, 234,* 41–46.

Jones, E. E., & Nisbett, R. E. (1971). *The actor and the observer: Divergent perceptions of the causes of behavior.* Morristown, NJ: General Learning Press.

Jones, J. M. (1990, August). *Developing psychology's agenda on homelessness.* Paper presented at the miniconvention on homelessness, 98th Annual Convention of the American Psychological Association, Boston, MA.

Jones, J. M., Levine, I. S., & Rosenberg, A. A. (1991). (Eds.). Homelessness [Special issue]. *American Psychologist, 46,* 1105–1264.

Jones, R. T., & Haney, J. L. (1984). A primary preventive approach to the acquisition and maintenance of fire emergency responding: Comparison of external and self-instruction strategies. *Journal of Community Psychology, 12,* 180–191.

Jones, R. T., & Kazdin, A. E. (1984). Teaching children how and when to make emergency telephone calls. *Behavior Therapy, 11,* 509–521.

Jones, S. C. (1973). Self and interpersonal evaluations: Esteem theories versus consistency theories. *Psychological Bulletin, 79,* 185–199.

Jones, W. H., Freeman, J. A., & Goswick, R. A. (1981). The persistence of loneliness: Self and other determinants. *Journal of Personality, 49,* 27–48.

Jones, W. H., Hansson, R., & Phillips, A. L. (1978). Physical attractiveness and judgments of psychotherapy. *Journal of Social Psychology, 105,* 79–84.

Joslyn, W. D. (1971). Androgen-induced social dominance in infant female rhesus monkeys. *Journal of Child Psychology and Psychiatry, 84,* 35–44.

Jouriles, E. N., Murphy, C. M., & O'Leary, K. D. (1979). Effects of maternal mood on mother-son interaction patterns. *Journal of Abnormal Child Psychology, 17,* 513–526.

Juarez, R. (1985). Core issues in psychotherapy with the Hispanic child. *Psychotherapy, 22,* 441–448.

Judge in Florida voids statutory rape law. (1992, July 25). *The New York Times,* p. L9.

Judson, G. (1992, May 24). Student parking, at a price: To foster better behavior, school makes driving a privilege. *The New York Times,* pp. L35, L41.

Jung, C. G. (1923). *Psychological types.* London: Rutledge & Kegan Paul.

Juraska, J. M., Fitch, J. M., & Washburne, D. L. (1989). The dendritic morphology of pyramidal neurons in the rat hippocampal CA3 area. II. Effects of gender and the environment. *Brain Research, 479,* 115–119.

Jussim, L. (1986). Self-fulfilling prophecies: A theoretical and integrative review. *Psychological Review, 93,* 429–445.

Kabagarama, D. (1993). *Breaking the ice.* Boston: Allyn & Bacon.

Kabanoff, B. (1980). Work and nonwork: A review of models, methods, and findings. *Psychological Bulletin, 88,* 60–77.

Kabanoff, B., & O'Brien, G. E. (1980). Work and leisure: A task attribute analysis. *Journal of Applied Psychology, 65,* 596–609.

Kach, J., & McGhee, P. (1982). Adjustment to early parenthood: The role of accuracy of pre-parenthood expectations. *Journal of Family Issues, 3,* 375–388.

Kalinowsky, L., & Hippius, H. (1969). *Pharmacological, convulsive and other somatic treatments in psychiatry.* New York: Grune & Stratton.

Kallmann, F. J. (1952). Comparative twin study on the genetic aspects of male homosexuality. *Journal of Nervous and Mental Disease, 115,* 283–298.

Kalmuss, D., Davidson, A., & Cushman, L. (1992). Parenting expectations, experiences, and adjustment to parenthood: A test of the violated expectations framework. *Journal of Marriage and the Family, 54,* 516–526.

Kamarck, T. W., Manuck, S. B., & Jennings, J. R. (1990). Social support reduces cardiovascular reactivity to psychological challenge: A laboratory model. *Psychosomatic Medicine, 52,* 42–58.

Kaminski, G. (1989). The relevance of ecologically oriented conceptualizations to theory building in environment and behavior research. In E. H. Zube & G. T. Moore (Eds.), *Advances in environment, behavior, and design* (Vol. 2). New York: Plenum.

Kandel, D. B., Davies, M., Karus, D., & Yamaguchi, K. (1986). The consequences in young adulthood of adolescent drug involvement. *Archives of General Psychiatry, 43,* 746–754.

Kando, T., & Summers, W. (1971). The impact of work on leisure. *Pacific Sociological Review, 14,* 310–327.

Kanner, A. D., Coyne, J. C., Schaefer, C., & Lazarus, R. S. (1981). Comparison of two modes of stress measurement: Daily hassles and uplifts versus major life events. *Journal of Behavioral Medicine, 4,* 1–39.

Kantorovich, N. V. (1928). An attempt of curing alcoholism by associated reflexes. *Novoye Refleksologii nervnoy i Fiziologii Sistemy, 3,* 436–435.

Kantrowitz, R., & Ballou, M. (1992). A feminist critique of cognitive-behavioral therapy. In L. Brown & M. Ballou (Eds.), *Theories of personality and psychopathology: Feminist reappraisals* (pp. 70–87). New York: Guilford.

Kaplan, H. I. (1985). History of psychosomatic medicine. In H. I. Kaplan & B. J. Saddock (Eds.), *Comprehensive textbook of psychiatry/IV* (4th edition). Baltimore: Williams & Wilkins.

Kaplan, M. (1983). A woman's view of DSM-III. *American Psychologist, 38,* 786–792.

Kaplan, M. F., & Anderson, N. H. (1973). Information integration theory and reinforcement theory as approaches to interpersonal attraction. *Journal of Personality and Social Psychology, 28,* 301–312.

Kaplan, P., Fox, K., & Huckeby, B. (1991, April). *Are faces sensitizing?* Paper presented at the biennial meeting of the Society for Research in Child Development. Seattle, WA.

Kaplan, P. S., Fox, K. B., Huckeby, E. R. (1992). Faces as reinforcers: Effects of pairing condition and facial expression. *Developmental Psychobiology, 25,* 299–312.

Karasek, R. A., Jr., & Theorell, T. (1990). *Healthy work: Stress, productivity, and the reconstruction of working life.* New York: Basic Books.

Kargman, M. W. (1983). The revolution in divorce law. *The Family Coordinator, 22,* 245–248.

Kashima, Y., & Triandis, H. C. (1986). The self-serving bias in attributions as a coping strategy: A cross-cultural study. *Journal of Cross-Cultural Psychology, 17,* 83–97.

Kasl, S., & Cobb, S. (1979). Some mental health consequences of plant closings and job loss. In L. A. Ferman & J. P. Gordus (Eds.), *Mental health and the economy.* Kalamazoo, MI: Upjohn Institute for Employment Research.

Kassovic, J. (1979). Paper presented at the 1979 meeting of the American Folklore Society in Los Angeles. Cited in C. Rubenstein. Gallows humor and religious fallout. *Psychology Today,* 1980 (April), p. 33.

Katcher, A. H., & Beck, A. M. (1983). *New perspectives on our lives with companion animals.* Philadelphia: University of Pennsylvania Press.

Katcher, A. H., & Friedmann, E. (1980). Potential health value of pet ownership. *Comprehensive Continuing Education, 1* (2), 117–121.

Katcher, A. H., Segal, H., & Beck, A. M. (1984). Contemplation of an aquarium for the reduction of anxiety. In R. K. Anderson, B. L. Hart, & L. A. Hart (Eds.), *The pet connection: Its influence on our health and quality of life* (pp. 171–178). Minneapolis: University of Minnesota Press.

Katz, M., & Konner, M. (1981). The role of the father: An anthropological perspective. In M. Lamb (Ed.), *The role of the father in child development.* New York: Wiley.

Katz, R. C., & Singh, N. N. (1986). Reflections on the ex-smoker: Some findings on successful quitters. *Journal of Behavioral Medicine, 9,* 191–202.

Kaurov, G. (1993, April 8). Quoted in S. Erlanger. Russian officials say little radiation is released in nuclear plant accident. *The New York Times,* p. A8.

Kavanaugh, M. J., Hurst, M. W., & Rose, R. (1981). The relationship between job satisfaction and psychiatric health symptoms for air traffic controllers. *Personnel Psychology, 34,* 691–707.

Kay, M. (1977). Health and illness in a Mexican-American barrio. In E. H. Spicer (Ed.), *Ethnic medicine in the Southwest.* Tucson: University of Arizona Press.

Keller, B. (1992, December 27). Africa thinks about making wildlife pay for its survival. *The New York Times,* p. E3.

Keller, S. E., Bartlett, J. A., Schleifer, S. J., Johnson, R. L., Pinner, E., & Delaney, B. (1991). HIV-relevant sexual behavior among a healthy inner-city heterosexual adolescent population in an endemic area of HIV. *Journal of Adolescent Health, 12,* 44–48.

Kelley, H. H. (1950). The warm-cold dimension in first impressions of a person. *Journal of Personality, 18,* 431–439.

Kelly, C., & Goodwin, G. C. (1983). Adolescents' perception of three styles of parental control. *Adolescence, 18,* 567–571.

Kelly, E. L., & Conley, J. J. (1987). Personality and compatibility: A prospective analysis of marital stability and marital satisfaction. *Journal of Personality and Social Psychology, 52,* 27–40.

Kelly, G. A. (1955). *The psychology of personal constructs.* (2 vols.). New York: Norton.

Kelly, J. B. (1988). Longer-term adjustment in children of divorce: Converging findings and implications for practice. *Journal of Family Psychology, 2,* 119–140.

Kelly, M. P., Strassberg, D. S., & Kircher, J. R. (1990). Attitudinal and experiential correlates of anorgasmia. *Archives of Sexual Behavior, 19,* 165–177.

Kemeny, M. E., Cohen, F., Zegans, L. S., & Conant, M. A. (1989). Psychological and immunological predictors of genital herpes recurrence. *Psychosomatic Medicine, 51,* 195–208.

Kempton, W., Darley, J. M., & Stern, P. C. (1992). Psychological research for the new energy problems: Strategies and opportunities. *American Psychologist, 47,* 1213–1223.

Kendell, R. E. (1988). Priorities for the next decade. In J. Mezzich & M. von Cranach (Eds.), *International classification in psychiatry* (pp. 332–340). New York: Cambridge University Press.

Kennedy, J. L., & Laramore, D. (1988). *Joyce Lain Kennedy's career book.* Lincolnwood, IL: VGM Career Horizons.

Kennedy, R. (1976). Self-induced depersonalization syndrome. *The American Journal of Psychiatry, 133,* 1326–1328.

Kennedy, R. S., Bittner, A. C., Harbeson, M., & Jones, M. B. (1982). Television computer games: A "new look" in performance testing. *Aviation, Space and Environmental Medicine, 53,* 49–53.

Kenney, A. M., Guardad, S., & Brown, L. (1989). Sex education and AIDS education in the schools. *Family Planning Perspectives, 21,* 56–64.

Keogh, B. (1982). Children's temperament and teachers' decisions. In R. Porter & G. Collins (Eds.), *Temperamental differences in infants and young toddlers* (pp. 269–279). London: Pitman.

Keppel, D. (1992, June 16). Mutant foods create risks we can't yet guess [editorial]. *The New York Times,* p. A24.

Kernberg, O. F. (1984). *Severe personality disorders: Psychotherapeutic strategies.* New Haven, CT: Yale University Press.

Kernis, M. H., & Wheeler, L. (1981). Beautiful friends and ugly strangers: Radiation and contrast effects in perceptions of same-sex pairs. *Personality and Social Psychology Bulletin, 4,* 479–482.

Kessler, R. C., Kendler, K. S., Heath, A., Neale, M. C., & Eaves, L. J. (1992). Social support, depressed mood, and adjustment to stress: A genetic epidemiologic investigation. *Journal of Personality and Social Psychology, 62,* 257–272.

Kettl, P. A., & Bixler, E. O. (1991). Suicide in Alaska natives, 1979–1984. *Psychiatry, 54,* 55–63.

Kiecolt-Glaser, J. K. (1989, June). Cited in Hall, S. A molecular code links emotions, mind and health. *Smithsonian.*

Kiecolt-Glaser, J. K., Dura, J. R., Speicher, C. E., Trask, O. J., & Glaser, R. (1991). Spousal caregivers of dementia victims: Longitudinal changes in immunity and health. *Psychosomatic Medicine, 53,* 345–362.

Kiecolt-Glaser, J. K., Garner, W., Speicher, C. E., Penn, & Glaser, R. (1984). Psychosocial modifiers of immunocompetence in medical students. *Psychosomatic Medicine, 46,* 7–14.

Kiecolt-Glaser, J. K., & Glaser, R. (1985). Stress and immune function in humans. In R. Ader, D. L. Felten, & N. Cohen (Eds.), *Psychoneuroimmunology.* San Diego: Academic Press.

Kihlstrom, J. F., & Cantor, N. (1983). Mental representations of the self. In L. Berkowitz (Ed.), *Advances in experimental social psychology* (Vol. 17, pp. 1–47). San Diego: Academic Press.

Kihlstrom, J. F., Cantor, N., Albright, S. J., Chew, B. R., Klein, S. B., & Niedenthal, P. M. (1988). Information processing and the study of the self. In L. Berkowitz (Ed.), *Advances in experimental social psychology* (Vol. 21, pp. 145–178). San Diego: Academic Press.

Kilborn, P. T. (1992a, November 29). As pay for nurses increases, so does the number of men entering the field. *The New York Times,* p. L22.

Kilborn, P. T. (1992b, November 27). Innovative program in California aids those with outdated skills. *The New York Times,* pp. A1, D17.

Kilham, W., & Mann, L. (1974). Level of destructive obedience as a function of transmitter and executant roles in the Milgram obedience paradigm. *Journal of Personality and Social Psychology, 29,* 696–702.

Killman, P. R., & Auerbach, R. (1979). Treatments of premature ejaculation and psychogenic impotence: A critical review of the literature. *Archives of Sexual Behavior, 8,* 81–100.

Killman, P. R., et al. (1987). The treatment of secondary orgasmic dysfunction II. *Journal of Sex and Marital Therapy, 13,* 93–105.

Kimmel, M. S. (1987). *Changing men: New directions in research on men and masculinity.* Newbury Park, CA: Sage.

King is arrested for 3d time since videotaped beating. (1992, July 17). *The New York Times,* p. A21.

Kinsey, A. C., Pomeroy, W. B., & Martin, C. E. (1948). *Sexual behavior in the human male.* Philadelphia: Saunders.

Kinsey, A. C., Pomeroy, W. B., Martin, C. E., & Gebhard, P. H. (1953). *Sexual behavior in the human female.* Philadelphia: Saunders.

Kinsman, R. A., Dirks, J. F., Jones, N. F., & Dahlem, NW. W. (1980). Anxiety reduction in asthma: Four catches to general application. *Psychosomatic Medicine, 42,* 397–405.

Kinzer, S. (1991, November 17). The neo-Nazis: How quickly they remember. *The New York Times,* pp. E1, E4.

Kinzer, S. (1992, September 28). Youth adrift in a new Germany turn to neo-Nazis. *The New York Times,* p. A3.

Kirsch, M. A., & Glass, L. L. (1977). Psychiatric disturbances associated with Erhard Seminars Training: II. Additional cases and theoretical considerations. *American Journal of Psychiatry, 134,* 1254–1258.

Klaiber, E. L., et al. (1982). Estrogens and central nervous system function: Electroencephalography, cognition, and depression. In R. C. Friedman (Ed.), *Behavior and the menstrual cycle.* New York: Marcel Dekker.

Kleinfield, N. R. (1993, April 29). For girls only: Glimpse of workaday world. *The New York Times,* pp. A1, B8.

Kleinhauz, M., & Beran, B. (1981). Misuses of hypnosis: A medical emergency and its treatment. *International Journal of Clinical and Experimental Hypnosis, 29,* 148–161.

Kleinhauz, M., & Eli, I. (1987). Potential deleterious effects of hypnosis in the clinical setting. *American Journal of Clinical Hypnosis, 29,* 155–159.

Kleinman, A. (1980). *Patients and healers in the context of culture.* Berkeley: University of California Press.

Kline, M., Johnston, J. R., & Tschann, J. M. (1991). The long shadow of marital conflict: A model of children's postdivorce adjustment. *Journal of Marriage and the Family, 53,* 297–309.

Kline, P., & Barrett, P. (1983). The factors in personality questionnaires among normal subjects. *Advances in Behaviour Research and Therapy, 5,* 141–202.

Kneeling with death haunted a life. (1990, May 6). *The New York Times,* p. A32.

Knox, E., & Wilson, K. (1981). Dating behavior of university students. *Family Relations, 30,* 255–258.

Knudsen, D. D. (1991). Child sexual coercion. In E. Grauerholz & M. A. Koralewski (Eds.), *Sexual coercion: A sourcebook on its nature, causes, and prevention* (pp. 17–28). Lexington, MA: Lexington Books.

Kobasa, S. C. (1979a). Personality and resistance to stress. *American Journal of Community Psychology, 7,* 413–423.

Kobasa, S. C. (1979b). Stressful life events, personality, and health: An inquiry into hardiness. *Journal of Personality and Social Psychology, 37,* 1–11.

Kobasa, S. C. (1982a). Commitment and coping in stress resistance among lawyers. *Journal of Personality and Social Psychology, 42,* 707–717.

Kobasa, S. C. (1982b). The hardy personality: Toward a social psychology of health. In G. S. Sanders & J. Suls (Eds.), *Social psychology of health and illness.* Hillsdale, NJ: Erlbaum.

Kobasa, S. C. (1984). How much stress can you survive? *American Health, 3* (9), 64–77.

Kobasa, S. C., Maddi, S. R., & Kahn, S. (1982). Hardiness and health: A prospective study. *Journal of Personality and Social Psychology, 42,* 168–177.

Koch, S., & Leary, D. E. (Eds.). *A century of psychology as a science.* Washington, DC: American Psychological Association. (Originally published in 1985 by McGraw-Hill).

Kohlberg, L. (1966). A cognitive-developmental analysis of children's sex-role concepts and attitudes. In E. E. Maccoby (Ed.), *The development of sex differences* (pp. 82–173). Stanford, CA: Stanford University Press.

Kohlberg, L. (1969). Stage and sequence: The cognitive developmental approach to socialization. In D. A. Goslin (Ed.), *Handbook of socialization theory and research* (pp. 347–480). Chicago: Rand McNally.

Kohlberg, L. (1976). Moral stages and mobilization. In T. Lickona (Ed.), *Moral development and behavior* (pp. 219–249). New York: Holt, Rinehart and Winston.

Kohlberg, L., & Ullian, D. Z. (1974). In R. C. Friedman, R. M. Richart, & R. L. Vande Wiele (Eds.), *Sex differences in behavior* (pp. 209–222). New York: Wiley.

Kohn, P. M., Lafreniere, K., & Gurevich, M. (1990). The Inventory of College Students' Recent Life Experiences: A decontaminated hassles scale for a special population. *Journal of Behavioral Medicine, 13,* 619–630.

Kolata, G. (1992a, April 15). Chief says panel backs courts' use of a genetic test. *The New York Times,* pp. A1, A23.

Kolata, G. (1992b, April 26). A parents' guide to kids' sports. *The New York Times Magazine,* Part 2, pp. 12–15, 40, 44, 46.

Kolodny, R. C. et al. (1974). Depression of plasma testosterone levels after chronic intensive marijuana use. *New England Journal of Medicine, 291,* 872–874.

Kolodny, R. C., Masters, W. H., & Johnson, V. E. (1979). *Textbook of sexual medicine.* Boston: Little, Brown.

Komarovsky, M. (1977). The effects of poverty upon marriage. In J. E. DeBurger (Ed.), *Marriage today: Problems, issues, and alternatives.* Cambridge, MA: Schenkman.

Kompara, D. R. (1980). Difficulties in the socialization process of stepparenting. *Family Relations, 29,* 69–73.

Koocher, G. P. (1973). Childhood, death, and cognitive development. *Developmental Psychology, 9,* 369–375.

Korman, A. K. (1988). *The outsiders: Jews and corporate America.* Lexington, MA: Lexington Books.

Kornhauser, A. (1965). *Mental health of the industrial worker: A Detroit study.* New York: Wiley.

Koss, M. P. (1988). Stranger and acquaintance rape: Are there differences in the victim's experience? *Psychology of Women Quarterly, 12,* 1–24.

Koss, M. P. (1992, April 24). Cited in D. Johnston. Survey shows number of rapes far higher than official figures. *The New York Times,* p. A14.

Kotila, L. (1992). The outcome of attempted suicide in adolescence. *Journal of Adolescent Health, 13,* 415–417.

Krantz, D. S., & Glass, D. C. (1984). Personality, behavior patterns, and physical illness: Conceptual and methodological issues. In W. D. Gentry (Ed.), *Handbook of behavioral medicine* (pp. 38–86). New York: Guilford.

Krantz, D. S., & Manuck, S. B. (1984). Acute psychophysiologic reactivity and risk of cardiovascular disease: A review and methodologic critique. *Psychological Bulletin, 96,* 435–464.

Kristof, N. D. (1993, April 25). China's crackdown on births: A stunning, and harsh, success. *The New York Times,* p. A1, A12.

Kromhaut, D., Bosschieter, E. B., & de Lezenne Coulander, C. (1985). The inverse relation between fish consumption and 20-year mortality from coronary heart disease. *New England Journal of Medicine, 312,* 1205–1209.

Kryger, M. H., Roth, T., & Dement, W. C. (Eds.). (1989). *Principles and practice of sleep medicine.* Philadelphia: W. B. Saunders.

Kübler-Ross, E. (1969). *On death and dying.* New York: Macmillan.

Kuhlman, D. M., & Marshello, A. F. J. (1975). Individual differences in game motivation as moderators of pre-programmed strategy effects in prisoner's dilemma. *Journal of Personality and Social Psychology, 32,* 922–931.

Kunjufu, J. (1986). *Countering the conspiracy to destroy Black boys: Vol II.* Chicago: African American Images.

Kurdek, L. A., & Fine, M. A. (1991). Cognitive correlates of satisfaction for mothers and stepfathers in stepfather families. *Journal of Marriage and the Family, 53,* 565–572.

Kuriansky, J. (1991, November 17). Cited in J. Shaheen. As symbol for others, dance troupe finds age is no barrier. *The New York Times,* pp. NJ1, NJ10.

Kurstak, E., Lipowski, A. J., & Morozov, P. V. (Eds.). (1987). *Viruses, immunity, and mental disorders.* New York: Plenum Medical Books.

La Barre, W. (1954). *The human animal.* Chicago: University of Chicago Press.

Labaton, S. (1993, February 7). Few women have resumes that job at Justice Dept. *The New York Times.*

Labov, T., & Jacobs, J. A. (1986). Intermarriage in Hawaii, 1950–1983. *Journal of Marriage and the Family, 48,* 279–284.

Lafontaine, E., & Tredeau, L. (1986). The frequency, sources, and correlates of sexual harassment among women in traditional male occupations. *Sex Roles, 15,* 433–442.

Lai, J. Y., & Linden, W. (1992). Gender, anger expression style, and opportunity for anger release determine cardiovascular reaction to and recovery from anger provocation. *Psychosomatic Medicine, 54,* 297–310.

Lambert, W. E., & Taylor, D. M. (1990). *Coping with cultural and racial diversity in urban America.* New York: Praeger.

Landale, N. S., & Fennelly, K. (1992). Informal unions among mainland Puerto Ricans: Cohabitation or an alternative to legal marriage? *Journal of Marriage and the Family, 54,* 269–280.

Landale, N. S., & Forste, R. (1991). Patterns of entry into cohabitation and marriage among mainland Puerto Rican women. *Demography, 28,* 587–607.

Landfield, P., Cadwallader, L. B., & Vinsant, S. (1988). Quantitative changes in hippocampal structure following long-term exposure to Delta-9-tetrahydrocannabinol: Possible mediation by glucorticoid systems. *Brain Research, 443,* 47–62.

Landis, C., & Hunt, W. A. (1932). Adrenalin and emotion. *Psychological Review, 39,* 467–485.

Landrigan, P. J. (1992, June 21). Cited in G. Kolata. More children are employed, often perilously. *The New York Times*, pp. A1, A22.

Landrine, H. (1992). Clinical implications of cultural differences: The referential versus the indexical self. *Clinical Psychology Review, 12*, 401–415.

Larwood, L., & Gattiker, U. (1984, August). *A comparison of the career paths used by successful men and women.* Paper presented at the meeting of the American Psychological Association, Toronto, Ontario.

Lasswell, M., & Lasswell, T. (1987). *Marriage and the family* (2nd ed.). Belmont, CA: Wadsworth.

Laszlo, J. (1993, March 30). Cited in Lung cancer and fat level. *The New York Times*, p. C8.

Latané, B., & Darley, J. M. (1970). *The unresponsive bystander: Why doesn't he help?* New York: Appleton-Century-Crofts.

Latané, B., & Nida, S. (1981). Ten years of research on group size and helping. *Psychological Bulletin, 89*, 308–324.

Late-life love. (1992). *Harvard Health Letter, 18*(1), pp. 1–3.

Lavie, P., Hefez, A., Halperin, G., & Enoch, D. (1979). Long-term effects of traumatic war-related events on sleep. *American Journal of Psychiatry, 136*, 175–178.

Lawler, E. E., III. (1969). Job design and employee motivation. *Personnel Psychology, 22*, 426–435.

Lawler, E. E., III. (1971). *Pay and organizational effectiveness: A psychological view.* New York: McGraw-Hill.

Lawson, C. (1990, May 3). 4th-grade lament: "Everyone's dating." *The New York Times*, p. C1.

Lawson, C. (1992, May 28). Parents and AIDS: Rage and tears. *The New York Times*, p. C1.

Lawton, M. P., Moss, M., & Moles, E. (1984). Pet ownership: A research note. *Gerontologist, 24*, 208–210.

Lazarus, A. A. (1965). A preliminary report on the use of directed muscular activity in counter-conditioning. *Behavior Research and Therapy, 2*, 301–303.

Lazarus, A. A. (1971). *Behavior therapy and beyond.* New York: McGraw-Hill.

Lazarus, A. A. (1973). Multimodal behavior therapy: Treating the BASIC ID. *The Journal of Nervous and Mental Disease, 156*, 404–411.

Lazarus, A. A. (1976a). Psychiatric problems precipitated by transcendental meditation. *Psychological Reports, 39*, 601–602.

Lazarus, A. A. (1976b). *Multi-modal behavior therapy.* New York: Springer.

Lazarus, A. A. (1987). The multimodal approach with adult outpatients. In N. S. Jacobson (Ed.), *Psychotherapists in clinical practice.* New York: Guilford.

Lazarus, A. A. (1989a). *The practice of multimodal therapy.* Baltimore: Johns Hopkins University Press.

Lazarus, A. A. (1989b). Multimodal therapy. In R. J. Corsini & D. Wedding (Eds.), *Current psychotherapies.* Itasca, IL: Peacock.

Lazarus, A. A. (1992a). The multimodal approach to the treatment of minor depression. *American Journal of Psychotherapy, 46*, 50–57.

Lazarus, A. A. (1992b). When is couples therapy necessary and sufficient? *Psychological Reports, 70*, 787–790.

Lazarus, A. A., Beutler, L. E., & Norcross, J. C. (1992). *Psychotherapy, 29*, 11–20.

Lazarus, A. A., & Fay, A. (1975). *I can if I want to.* New York: Warner Books.

Lazarus, A. A., & Mayne, T. J. (1990). Relaxation: Some limitations, side effects, and proposed solutions. *Psychotherapy, 27*, 261–266.

Lazarus, R. S. (1983). The costs and benefits of denial. In S. Breznitz (Ed.), *The denial of stress* (pp. 1–30). New York: International Universities Press.

Lazarus, R. S., & Folkman, S. (1984). *Stress, appraisal and coping.* New York: Springer.

Lazarus, R. S., & Folkman, S. (1987). Transactional theory and research on emotions and coping. *European Journal of Personality, 1*, 141–169.

Leary, W. E. (1990, June 9). Gloomy report on the health of teenagers. *The New York Times*, p. 24.

Leary, W. E. (1992, June 9). Gloomy report on the health of teenagers. *The New York Times*, p. 24.

Leary, W. E. (1992, May 13). Surprising costs found for H.I.V. *The New York Times*, p. A18.

Leary, W. E. (1993, March 30). Gains reported in transferring genetic material to mice. *The New York Times*, p. C3.

Leavitt, H. J. (1978). *Managerial psychology* (4th ed.). Chicago: University of Chicago Press.

Leavy, R. L. (1983). Social support and psychological disorder: A review. *Journal of Community Psychology, 11*, 3–21.

Lefebre, L. B. (1963). Existentialism and psychotherapy. *Review of Existential Psychology and Psychiatry, 3*, 271–285.

Leflore, L. (1988). Delinquent youths and family. *Adolescence, 23*, 629–647.

Lehrer, P. M., Hochron, S. M., McCann, B., Swartzman, L., & Reba, P. (1986). Relaxation decreases large-airway but not small-airway asthma. *Journal of Psychosomatic Research, 30*, 13–25.

Leik, R. K., & Leik, S. A. (1977). Transition to interpersonal commitment. In R. L. Hamblin & J. H. Kunkel (Eds.), *Behavioral theory in sociology* (pp. 299–322). New Brunswick, NJ: Transaction Books.

Lelliott, P., Marks, I., McNamee, G., & Tobena, A. (1989). Onset of panic disorder with agoraphobia. *Archives of General Psychiatry, 46*, 1000–1004.

Lemberger, L., et al. (1970). Marihuana: Studies on the disposition and metabolism of delta-9-tetrahydrocannibinol in man. *Science, 170*, 1320–1322.

Leone, C., & Ensley, E. (1985). Self-generated attitude change: Another look at the effects of thought and cognitive schemata. *Representative Research in Social Psychology, 15*, 2–9.

Lerner, J. V., & Galambos, N. L. (1985). Maternal role satisfaction, mother-child interaction, and child temperament: A process model. *Developmental Psychology, 21*, 1157–1164.

Lerner, R. M. (1992b, May 28). Cited in L. Kutner. A first job can provide value beyond just money. *The New York Times*, p. C12.

Lesnik-Oberstein, M., & Cohen, L. (1984). Cognitive style, sensation seeking, and assortive mating. *Journal of Personality and Social Psychology, 46*, 112–117.

Lester, D. (1986). *The murderer and his murder: A review of research.* New York: AMS Press.

LeVay, S. (1992, August 1). Cited in N. Angier. Researchers find a second anatomical idiosyncracy in brains of homosexual men. *The New York Times*, p. L7.

Levenson, J. L., & Bemis, C. (1991). The role of psychological factors in cancer onset and progression. *Psychosomatics, 32*, 124–132.

Leventhal, H., & Tomarken, A. J. (1986). Emotion: Today's problems. *Annual Review of Psychology, 37*, 565–610.

Levin, D. P. (1992, May 25). Bitter memories of anti-Semitism live on in a Michigan parish. *The New York Times*, p. A7.

LeVine, R. A., & White, M. (1987). Parenthood in social transformation. In J. B. Lancaster, J. Altmann, A. S. Rossi, & L. R. Sherrod (Eds.), *Parenting across the life span: Biosocial dimensions.* New York: Aldine de Gruyter.

Levinson, D. J., Darrow, C. N., Klein, E. B., Levinson, M. H., & McKee, B. (1978). *The seasons of a man's life.* New York: Ballantine.

Levitan, S. (1990). *Programs in aid of the poor* (6th ed.). Baltimore, MD: Johns Hopkins University.

Levoy, G. (1989, October). Inexplicable recoveries from incurable diseases: The search to find the cause of 3,500 spontaneous remissions. *Longevity.*

Levy, G. D., & Carter, D. B. (1989). Gender-schema, gender constancy, and gender-role knowledge: The roles of cognitive factors in preschoolers' gender-role stereotype attributions. *Developmental Psychology, 25,* 444–449.

Lewis, A.(1993, March 12). Right to life. *The New York Times*, A29.

Lewy, A. J., Sack, R. L., Frederickson, R. H., Reaves, M., Denney, D., Zielske, D. (1983). The use of bright light in the treatment of chronobiologic sleep and mood disorders: The phase-response curve. *Psychopharmacology Bulletin, 9,* 523–525.

Lieber, J. (1989, June). A piece of yourself in the world. *Atlantic Monthly,* pp. 76–80.

Lieberson, S., & Waters, M. (1985). Ethnic mixtures in the United States. *Sociology and Social Research, 70,* 43–53.

Liebowitz, M. R., Gorman, J. M., Fryer, A. J., & Klein, D. F. (1985). Social phobia: Review of a neglected anxiety disorder. *Archives of General Psychiatry, 42,* 729–736.

Liem, R., & Rayman, P. (1982). Health and social costs of unemployment. *American Psychologist, 37,* 1116–1123.

Light, K. C., Dolan, C. A., Davis, M. R., & Sherwood, A. (1992). Cardiovascular responses to an active coping challenge as predictors of blood pressure patterns 10 to 15 years later. *Psychosomatic Medicine, 54,* 217–230.

Lindholm, L., & Wilson, G. T. (1988). Body image assessment in patients with bulimia nervosa and normal controls. *International Journal of Eating Disorders, 7,* 527–539.

Linn, M. C., & Hyde, J. S. (1989). Gender, mathematics, and science. *Educational Researcher, 18* (8), 17–19, 22–27.

Lipp, M. R., & Benson, S. G. (1972). Physician use of marijuana, alcohol, and tobacco. *American Journal of Psychiatry, 129,* 612–616.

Lipton, E. L., Steinschneider, A., & Richmond, J. B. (1961). Autonomic function in the neonate: IV. Individual differences in cardiac reactivity. *Psychosomatic Medicine, 23,* 472–484.

Lisak, D., & Roth, S. (1988). Motivational factors in nonincarcerated sexually aggressive men. *Journal of Personality and Social Psychology, 55,* 795–802.

Littlewood, R. (1991, April). *DSM-IV and culture: Is the classification valid?* Paper presented at the NIMH/American Psychiatric Association, Pittsburgh, PA.

Locke, E. A. (1976). The nature and causes of job satisfaction. In M. D. Dunnette (Ed.), *Handbook of industrial and organizational psychology.* Chicago: Rand-McNally.

Locksley, A. (1980). On the effects of wives' employment on marital adjustment and companionship. *Journal of Marriage and the Family, 42,* 337–345.

Logue, J. N., Hansen, H., & Struening, E. (1981). Some indications of the longterm health effects of a natural disaster. *Public Health Reports, 96,* 67–79.

London, P. (1976). Psychotherapy for religious neuroses? Comments on Cohen and Smith. *Journal of Consulting and Clinical Psychology, 44,* 145–147.

Longo, D. J., & Clum, G. A. (1989). Psychosocial factors affecting genital herpes recurrences: Linear vs. mediating models. *Journal of Psychosomatic Research, 33,* 161–166.

Lorenz, F. O., Conger, R. D., Simon, R. L., Whitbeck, L. B., & Elder, G. H., Jr. (1991). Economic pressure and marital quality: An illustration of the method of variance problem in the causal modeling of family processes. *Journal of Marriage and the Family, 53,* 375–388.

Lorenz, K. (1974). *Civilized man's eight deadly sins.* New York: Harcourt Brace Jovanovich.

Lott, B. (1981). A feminist critique of androgyny: Toward the elimination of gender attributions for learned behavior. In C. Mayo & N. M. Henley (Eds.), *Gender and nonverbal behavior.* New York: Springer.

Lott, B. (1985). The potential enhancement of social/personality psychology through feminist research and vice versa. *American Psychologist, 40,* 155–164.

Low, B. S. (1989). Cross-cultural patterns in the training of children: An evolutionary perspective. *Journal of Comparative Psychology, 103,* 311–319.

Lowry, T. P., & Williams, G. R. (1983). Brachioproctic eroticism. *Journal of Sex Education and Therapy, 9,* 50–52.

Loy, P. H., & Stewart, L. P. (1984). The extent and effects of the sexual harassment of working women. *Sociological Focus, 17,* 31–43.

Loya, F., Garcia, P., Sullivan, J., Vargas, L., Mercy, J., & Allen, N. (1986). Conditional risks of homicide among Anglo, Hispanic, Black, and Asian victims in Los Angeles, 1970–1979. In *Report of the Secretary's Task Force on Black and Minority Health, Vol. 5,* 137–144.

Luborsky, L., Todd, T. C., & Katcher, A. H. (1973). A self-administered social assets scale for predicting physical and physiological illness and health. *Journal of Psychosomatic Research, 17,* 109–120.

Ludwick-Rosenthal, R., & Neufeld, R. W. J. (1988). Stress management during noxious medical procedures: An evaluative review of outcome studies. *Psychological Bulletin, 104,* 326–342.

Lundberg, G. (1992, June 10). Quoted in P. J. Hilts. More teenagers being slain by guns. *The New York Times*, p. A19.

Lundin, R. W. (1972). *Theories and systems of psychology.* Lexington, MA: D. C. Heath.

Luoma, J. R. (1993, March 16). Listing of endangered species said to come too late to help. *The New York Times*, p. C4.

Luthe, W., & Schultz, J. H. (1969). *Autogenic training: Medical applications.* New York: Grune & Stratton.

Lutwak, N. (1985). Fear of intimacy among college women. *Adolescence, 77,* 15–20.

Lynch, J. J. (1985). *The language of the heart.* New York: Basic Books.

Lynch, J. J., Fregin, G. F., Mackie, J. B., & Monroe, R. R. (1974). The effect of human contact on the heart activity of the horse. *Psychophysiology, 11,* 472–478.

Lynch, J. J., & McCarthy, J. F. (1967). The effect of petting on a classically conditioned emotional response. *Behavior Research and Therapy, 5,* 55–62.

Lynch, J. J., & McCarthy, J. F. (1969). Social responding in dogs: Heart rate changes to a person. *Psychophysiology, 5,* 389–393.

Lyne, B. (1992, September 27). Women at the top: Role models or relics? *The New York Times*, p. F27.

Lytton, H., & Romney, D. M. (1991). Parents' differential social-ization of boys and girls: A meta-analysis. *Psychological Bulletin, 109,* 267–296.

MacAndrew, C. (1969). On the notion that certain persons who are given to frequent drunkenness suffer from a disease called al-coholism. In S. C. Plog & R. B. Edgerton (Eds.). *Changing per-spectives in mental illness* (pp. 483–501). New York: Holt, Rinehart and Winston.

Maccoby, E. (1980). *Social development.* New York: Harcourt Brace Jovanovich.

MacEwen, K. E., & Barling, J. (1991). Effects of maternal employ-ment experiences on children's behavior via mood, cognitive difficulties, and parenting behavior. *Journal of Marriage and the Family, 53,* 635–644.

Machlowitz, M. (1980). *Workaholics: Living with them, working with them.* Reading, MA: Addison-Wesley.

MacHovec, F. J. (1988). Hypnosis complications, risk factors, and prevention. *American Journal of Clinical Hypnosis, 31,* 40–49.

Mack, T. M., et al. (1976). Estrogens and Endometrial cancer in a retirement community. *The New England Journal of Medicine, 294,* 1262–1267.

Macks, J., & Emery, A. (1992). AIDS in the workplace: Another view. *Families in Society, 73,* 563–567.

MacLean, P. A. (1991, April). Tee'd off: Women golfers learning that swinging a club can be easier than joining one. *Women's Sports & Fitness,* pp. 43–48.

MacLeod, R. B. (1959). Review of *Cumulative record* by B. F. Skin-ner. *Science, 130,* 34–35.

MacLusky, N., & Naftolin, F. (1981). Sexual differentiation of the central nervous system. *Science, 211,* 1294–1303.

Madonna (1992). *Sex.* New York: Warner Books.

Mael, F. A. (1991). Career constraints of observant Jews. *Career De-velopment Quarterly, 39,* 341–349.

Magic Johnson talks; risky sex falls. (1993, January 29). *The New York Times,* p. A16.

Mahama, E. (1992, June 20). Quoted in F. Butterfield. Boston's mayor cites crowd size in concert melee. *The New York Times,* p. 6L.

Mahoney, M. J. (1974). *Cognition and behavior modification.* Cam-bridge, MA: Ballinger.

Mahoney, M. J., & Mahoney, K. (1976). *Permanent weight control.* New York: Norton.

Mahoney, R. (1992, March/April). On the trail of the world's "miss-ing women." *Ms.*

Maiskii, I. (1921). *Sovremennaia Mongolia.* Gosudarstvennoe Iz-datel'stvo, Irkutskoe Otedelenie: Irkutsk.

Maiter, D., Koenig, J. I., & Kaplan, L. M. (1991). Sexually dimor-phic expression of the growth hormone-releasing hormone gene is not mediated by circulating gonadal hormones in the adult rat. *Endocrinology, 128,* 1709–1716.

Major, B., Cozzarelli, C., Sciacchitano, A. M., Cooper, M. L., Testa, M., & Mueller, P. M. (1990). Perceived social support, self-effi-cacy, and adjustment to abortion. *Journal of Personality and So-cial Psychology, 59,* 452–463.

Malgady, R. G., Rogler, L. H., & Costantino, G. (1987). Ethnocul-tural and linguistic bias in mental health evaluation of Hispan-ics. *American Psychologist, 42,* 228–234.

Mann, J. (1992, June 4). Cited in L. K. Altman. Researchers report much grimmer AIDS outlook. *The New York Times,* pp. A, B10.

Mannes, E., & Carter, H. (Writers). (1992). *Frontline: Who is David Duke?* PBS report aired on WNET (New York), March 3, 1992.

Mansfield, P. K., Hood, K. E., & Henderson, J. (1989). Women and their husbands: Mood and arousal fluctuations across the men-strual cycle and days of the week. *Psychosomatic Medicine, 51,* 66–80.

Marano, L. (1992, November 10). Quoted in S. Gardner. Agency is fighting violence in teen-age dating. *The New York Times,* p. NJ13.

Marañon, G. (1924). Contribution a l'étude de l'action emotive de l'adrenaline. *Revue Francaise Endocrinologie, 2,* 301–325.

Marcia, J. E. (1966). Development and validation of ego-identity status. *Journal of Personality and Social Psychology, 3,* 551–558.

Marcus, H. R., & Kitayama, S. (1991). Culture and the self: Im-plications for cognition, emotion, and motivation. *Psychological Review, 98,* 224–253.

Marcus, J., Maccoby, E. E., Jacklin, C. N., & Doering, C. H. (1985). Individual differences in mood in early childhood: Their rela-tion to gender and neonatal sex steroids. *Developmental Psy-chology, 18,* 327–340.

Marcus, T. L., & Corsini, D. A. (1978). Parental expectations of preschool children as related to child gender and socioeco-nomic status. *Child Development, 49,* 243–246.

Margolick, D. (1992, September 11). Lawyer, hereafter broken heart, sues to mend it. *The New York Times,* p. B8.

Margolick, D. (1993, February 10). At bar meeting, muttering about justice slot. *The New York Times,* p. A20.

Margolis, L., & Runyan, C. (1983). Accidental policy: An analysis of the problem of unintentional injuries of childhood. *Ameri-can Journal of Orthopsychiatry, 53,* 629–644.

Marin, G., & Marin, B. V. (1991). *Research with Hispanic popula-tions.* Beverly Hills, CA: Sage.

Marital status of the population. In *Statistical abstract of the United States 1990, 110,* 43. Washington,D.C.: Government Printing Office.

Markman, H. J., Floyd, F. J., Stanley, S. M., & Staraasli, R. D. (1988). Prevention of marital distress: A longitudinal investiga-tion. *Journal of Consulting and Clinical Psychology, 56,* 210–217.

Markoff, J. (1990, May 13). Some computer conversation is chang-ing human contact. *The New York Times,* pp. A1, A20.

Markus, H. (1980). The self in thought and memory. In D. M. Wegner & R. R. Vallacher (Eds.), *The self in social psychology* (pp. 102–130). New York: Oxford University Press.

Marmor, J. (1976). Some psychodynamic aspects of the seduction of patients in psychotherapy. *The American Journal of Psycho-analysis, 36,* 319–323.

Marquis, J. N. (1991). A report on seventy-eight cases treated by eye movement desensitization. *Journal of Behavior Therapy and Experimental Psychiatry, 22,* 187–192.

Marriott, M. (1993, January 24). Rap's embrace of "nigger" fires bitter debate. *The New York Times,* pp. A1, A31.

Marsh, H. W., & Parker, J. W. (1984). Determinants of student self-concept: Is it better to be a relatively large fish in a small pond even if you don't learn to swim well? *Journal of Personality and Social Psychology, 47,* 213–231.

Marshall, G. D. (1976). The affective consequences of "inade-quately explained" physiological arousal. (Doctoral disserta-tion, Stanford University). *Dissertation Abstracts International, 37* (2-B), 1041.

Marshall, G. D., & Zimbardo, P. G. (1979). Affective consequences of inadequately explained arousal. *Journal of Personality and So-cial Psychology, 37,* 970–985.

Martin, B. (1975). Parent-child relations. In F. D. Horowitz (Ed.), *Review of child development research* (Vol. 4) (pp. 463–540). Chicago: University of Chicago Press.

Martin, C. L., & Little, J. K. (1990). The relation of gender understanding to children's sex-typed preferences and gender stereotypes. *Child Development, 61,* 1891–1904.

Martin, D., & Lyon, P. (1977). *Lesbian/woman.* New York: Bantam.

Martin, R. A., & Lefcourt, H. M. (1983). Sense of humor as a moderator of the relation between stressors and moods. *Journal of Personality and Social Psychology, 45,* 1313–1324.

Martin, T. C., & Bumpass, L. L. (1989). Recent trends in marital disruption. *Demography, 26,* 37–52.

Martin-Brown, J. (1992). Rethinking technology in the future. *Environment, Science, and Technology, 26,* 1100–1102.

Marziali, E. A., & Pilkonis, P. A. (1986). The measurement of subjective response to stressful life events. *Journal of Human Stress, 12,* 5–12.

Masheter, C. (1991). Postdivorce relationships between ex-spouses: The roles of attachment and interpersonal conflict. *Journal of Marriage and the Family, 53,* 103–110.

Maslach, C. (1979). Negative emotional biasing of unexplained physiological arousal. *Journal of Personality and Social Psychology, 37,* 953–969.

Maslin, J. (1992, November 22). Steamy TV: Coffee opera. *The New York Times,* p. V9.

Maslow, A. H. (1935a). Appetites and hungers in animal motivation. *Journal of Comparative Psychology, 20,* 75–83.

Maslow, A. H. (1935b). Individual psychology and the social behavior of monkeys and apes. *International Journal of Individual Psychology, 1,* 47–59.

Maslow, A. H. (1936). The role of dominance in the social and sexual behavior of infrahuman primates. I: Observations at Vilas Park Zoo. *Journal of Genetic Psychology, 48,* 261–277.

Maslow, A. H. (1937). Dominance-feeling, behavior and status. *Psychological Review, 44,* 404–420.

Maslow, A. H. (1939). Dominance-feeling, personality and social behavior in women. *Journal of Social Psychology, 10,* 3–39.

Maslow, A. H. (1940). Dominance-quality and social behavior in infrahuman primates. *Journal of Social Psychology, 11,* 313–324.

Maslow, A. H. (1962). *Toward a psychology of being.* Princeton, NJ: Van Nostrand.

Maslow, A. H. (1964). *Religion, values, and peak-experiences.* Columbus, Ohio: Ohio State University Press.

Maslow, A. H. (1966). *The psychology of science.* New York: Harper & Row.

Maslow, A. H. (1970). *Motivation and personality* (2nd ed.). New York: Harper & Row.

Maslow, A. H. (1971). *The farther reaches of human nature.* New York: Viking.

Maslow, A. H., & Harlow, H. (1932). Delayed reaction tests on primates at Bronx Park Zoo. *Journal of Comparative Psychology, 14,* 97–101.

Mason, J. W. (1975). A historical view of the stress field, Part II. *Journal of Human Stress, 1,* 22–36.

Masters, W. H., & Johnson, V. E. (1966). *Human sexual response.* Boston: Little, Brown.

Masters, W. H., & Johnson, V. E. (1970). *Human sexual inadequacy.* Boston: Little, Brown.

Masters, W. H., & Johnson, V. E. (1979). *Homosexuality in perspective.* Boston: Little, Brown.

Masters, W. H., & Johnson, V. E. (1981, April 4). *Facts and fallacies in sexual physiology.* Paper presented at the Fifth National Meeting of the American Association of Sex Educators, Counselors, and Therapists, San Francisco.

Masters, W. H., Johnson, V. E., & Kolodny, R. C. (1982). *Human Sexuality.* Boston: Little, Brown.

Masters, W. H., Johnson, V. E., & Kolodny, R. C. (1989). *Human sexuality* (4th ed.). New York: HarperCollins.

Masuda, M., & Holmes, T. H. (1967). Magnitude estimations of social readjustments. *Journal of Psychosomatic Research, 11,* 219–225.

Matlin, M. (1987). *The psychology of women.* New York: Holt, Rinehart and Winston.

Matsuda, L., Lolait, S. J., Brownstein, M. M., Young, A. C., & Bonner, T. I. (1990). Structure of a cannabinoid receptor and functional expression of the cloned CDNA. *Nature, 346,* 561–564.

Matteson, M. T., & Ivancevich, J. M. (1987). *Controlling work stress: Effective human resource and management strategies.* San Francisco: Jossey-Bass.

Matthews, K. A. (1982). Psychological perspectives on the Type-A behavior pattern. *Psychological Bulletin, 91,* 293–323.

Maultsby, M. C. (1982). A historical view of Blacks' distrust of psychiatry. In S. M. Turner & R. T. Jones (Eds.), *Behavior modification in black populations: Psychosocial issues and empirical findings.* New York: Plenum.

Mavissakalian, M. R., Perel, J. M. (1989). Imipramine dose-response relationship in panic disorder with agoraphobia. *Archives of General Psychiatry, 46,* 127–131.

Mawhinney, T. C. (1975). Operant terms and concepts in the description of individual work behavior: Some problems of interpretation, application, and evaluation. *Journal of Applied Psychology, 60,* 704–712.

Mawhinney, T. C. (1979). Intrinsic and extrinsic work motivation: Perspectives from behaviorism. *Organizational Behavior and Human Performance, 24,* 411–440.

Mayo, E. J., & Jarvis, L. P. *The psychology of leisure travel.* Boston: CBI.

Mazor, M. D. (1980). Psychosexual problems of the infertile couple. *Medical Aspects of Human Sexuality, 14* (12), 32–49.

McAndrew, F. T. (1993). *Environmental psychology.* Pacific Grove, CA: Brooks/Cole.

McCann, B. S., & Matthews, K. A. (1988). Influences of potential for hostility, Type A behavior, and parental history of hypertension on adolescent's cardiovascular responses during stress. *Psychophysiology, 25,* 503–511.

McCarty, D., Argeriou, M., Huebner, R. B., & Lubran, B. (1991). Alcoholism, drug abuse, and the homeless. *American Psychologist, 46,* 1139–1148.

McCarty, P. A. (1986). Effects of feedback on the self-confidence of men and women. *Academy of Management Journal, 29,* 840–847.

McConaghy, M. J. (1979). Gender permanence and the genital basis of gender: Stages in the development of constancy of gender. *Child Development, 50,* 1223–1226.

McCormick, E. J., & Ilgen, D. R. (1980). *Industrial psychology* (7th ed.). Englewood Cliffs, NJ: Prentice-Hall.

McCrae, R. (1984). Situational determinants of coping responses: Loss, threat and challenge. *Journal of Personality and Social Psychology, 49,* 710–721.

McCrae, R. R. (1991). The five-factor model and its assessment in clinic settings. *Journal of Personality Assessment, 57,* 399–414.

McCrae, R. R., & Costa, P. T., Jr. (1987). Validation of the five-factor model of personality across instruments and observers. *Journal of Personality and Social Psychology, 52,* 81–90.

McCubbin, H. I., Patterson, J. M., Comeau, J. K., Joy, C. B., Cauble, A. E., & Needle, R. H. (1980). Family stress and coping: A decade review. *Journal of Marriage and the Family, 42,* 855–871.

McDermott, J. F., & Fukunaga, D. (1977). Intercultural family interaction patterns. In W-S Tseng, J. F. McDermott, & T. W. Maretzki (Eds.), *Adjustment to intercultural marriage.* Honolulu: University of Hawaii Press.

McEwen, B. (1981). Neural gonadal steroid actions. *Science, 211,* 1303–1311.

McEwen, B. S. (1991). Non-genomic and genomic effects of steroids on neural activity. *Trends in Physiological Sciences, 12,* 141–147.

McFadden, R. D. (1992, December 6). New York Jews' fears amid racial anguish. *The New York Times,* p. A1.

McFarlane, J., Martin, C. L., & Williams, T. M. (1988). Women versus men and menstrual versus other cycles. *Psychology of Women Quarterly, 12,* 201–223.

McGinnis, J. M. (1991). Health objectives for the nation. *American Psychologist, 46,* 520–524.

McGlashan, T. H., Levy, S. T., & Carpenter, W. T. (1975). Integration and sealing over. *Archives of General Psychiatry, 32,* 1269–1272.

McGoldrick, M. (1992, April 13). Italian and Irish families: Cultural and ethnic issues. In R. A. Javier (Chair), *Our families in crisis: A multicultural and multiethnic perspective.* Second annual conference at St. John's University, Jamaica, NY.

McGoldrick, M., Pearce, J. K., & Giordano, J. G. (Eds.). (1982). *Ethnicity and family therapy.* New York: Guilford.

McGregor, D. (1960). *The human side of enterprise.* New York: McGraw-Hill.

McGuire, J. (1992, November 12). Cited in E. Schmitt. Challenging the Military. *The New York Times,* pp. A1, A22.

McGuire, P. (1993, March 2). Let's stop guessing about women's health [Editorial]. *The New York Times,* p. A20.

McGuire, W. J., & McGuire, C. V. (1986). Differences in conceptualizing self versus other people as manifested in contrasting verb types used in natural speech. *Journal of Personality and Social Psychology, 51,* 1135–1143.

McHale, S., & Crouter, A. C. (1992). You can't always get what you want: Incongruence between sex-role attitudes and family work roles and its implications for marriage. *Journal of Marriage and the Family, 54,* 537–547.

McInery, T., & Chamberlin, R. W. (1975). Is it feasible to identify infants who are at risk for later behavior problems? *Clinical Pediatrics, 17,* 233–238.

McKelvey, T. (1992, April 26). A fiery death comes back to haunt Poland. *The New York Times,* p. H26.

McKinlay, J. B. (1992, May 20). Cited in N. Angier. A male menopause? Jury is still out. *The New York Times,* p. C14.

McKinlay, J. B., McKinlay, S. M., & Beaglehole, R. (1989). A review of the evidence concerning the impact of medical measures on recent mortality and morbidity in the United States. *International Journal of Health Services, 19,* 181–208.

McLarin, K. J. (1993, April 29). Left behind, some boys feel left out. *The New York Times,* p. B8.

McLemore, C. W., & Court, J. H. (1977). Religion and psychotherapy—ethics, civil liberties, and clinical savvy: A critique. *Journal of Consulting and Clinical Psychology, 45,* 1172–1175.

McNamara, R. S. (1992, October 14). One minute to doomsday [Editorial]. *The New York Times,* p. A25.

Mead, M. (1935). *Sex and temperament in three primitive societies.* New York: William Morrow.

Meador, B. D., & Rogers, C. R. (1973). Client-centered therapy. In R. Corsini (Ed.), *Current psychotherapies* (pp. 119–165). Itasca, IL: Peacock.

Meadows, D. H., Meadows, D. L., & Randers, J. (1992). *Beyond the limits.* New York: Chelsea Green Publishing Company.

Meduna, L. J. (1936). *Die konvulsions therapie der schizophrenie.* Marhold: Halle.

Meece, J. L., Parsons, J. E., Kaczala, C. M., Goff, S. B., & Futterman, R. (1982). Sex differences in math achievement: Toward a model of academic choice. *Psychological Bulletin, 91,* 324–348.

Meer, J. (1984). Pet theories. *Psychology Today, 18,* 60–67.

Meichenbaum, D. (1973). Cognitive factors in behavior modification: Modifying what clients say to themselves. In C. M. Franks & G. T. Wilson (Eds.), *Annual review of behavior therapy: Theory and practice* (pp. 415–431). New York: Brunner-Mazel.

Meichenbaum, D. (1974). *Cognitive behavior modification.* Morristown, NJ: General Learning Press.

Meichenbaum, D. (1977). *Cognitive behavior modification: An integrative approach.* New York: Plenum.

Melges, F. T., et al. (1970). Temporal disintegration and depersonalization during marihuana intoxication. *Archives of General Psychiatry, 23,* 204–210.

Melicher, J., & Chiriboga, D. A. (1985). Timetables in the divorce process. *Journal of Marriage and the Family, 47,* 701–708.

Melton, R. F. (1978). Resolution of conflicting claims concerning the effect of behavioral objectives on student learning. *Review of Educational Research, 48,* 291–302.

Menaghan, E. G., & Parcel, T. L. (1990). Parental employment and family life: Research in the 1980's. *Journal of Marriage and the Family, 52,* 1079–1098.

Mercy, J., Goodman, R., Rosenberg, M., Allen, N., Loya, F., Smith, J., & Vargas, L. (1986). Patterns of homicide victimization in the city of Los Angeles, 1970–1979. *Bulletin of the New York Academy of Medicine, 62,* 427–445.

Merikle, P. M. (1988). Subliminal auditory messages: An evaluation. *Psychology & Marketing, 5,* 355–372.

Merikle, P. M. (1992). Toward improved reading comprehension. *Psychology & Marketing, 9,* 81–83.

Mezzich, J. E., Fabrega, H., & Kleinman, A. (1992). Cultural validity and DSM-IV [Editorial]. *The Journal of Nervous and Mental Disease, 180,* 4.

Michaud, T. (1992, June 7). Cited in M. Winerip. A wild streak is uncovered at Princeton. *The New York Times,* p. A31.

Michelman, K. (1991). Restrictions mean suffering and death. In P. M. Insel & W. T. Roth, *Core concepts in health* (pp. 169–170). Mountain View, CA: Mayfield Publishing.

Michelozzi, B. N. (1992). *Coming alive from nine to five: The career search handbook.* Mountain View, CA: Mayfield Publishing.

Michels, R. (1984). A debate of DSM-III: A first rebuttal. *American Journal of Psychiatry, 141,* 548–551.

Milburn, N., & D'Ercole, A. (1991). Homeless women: Moving toward a comprehensive model. *American Psychologist, 46,* 1161–1169.

Milgram, S. (1961, January 25). *Dynamics of obedience: Experiments in social psychology.* Washington, DC: National Science Foundation Report.

Milgram, S. (1963). Behavioral study of obedience. *Journal of Abnormal and Social Psychology, 67,* 371–378.

Milgram, S. (1964). Issues in the study of obedience: A reply to Baumrind. *American Psychologist, 19,* 848–852.

Milgram, S. (1965). Some conditions of obedience and disobedience to authority. *Human Relations, 18,* 57–75.

Milgram, S. (1974). *Obedience to authority.* New York: Harper.

Miller, G. A. (1962). *Psychology.* New York: Harper & Row.

Miller, G. A. (1969). Psychology as a means of promoting human welfare. *American Psychologist, 24,* 1063–1065.

Miller, G. A. (1980). Giving psychology away in the 80's. *Psychology Today, 13* (1), 38.

Miller, J. (1992, May 7). Cited in Young black men [Editorial]. *The New York Times,* p. A26.

Miller, J. G., & Bersoff, D. M. (1992). Culture and moral judgment: How are conflicts between justice and interpersonal responsibilities resolved? *Journal of Personality and Social Psychology, 62,* 541–554.

Miller, L. B., & Dyer, J. L. (1976). Four preschool programs: Their dimensions and effects. *Monographs of the Society for Research in Child Development, 40*(5 & 6).

Miller, S. (1980). When is a little knowledge a dangerous thing? Coping with stressful events by monitoring vs. blunting. In S. Levine & H. Ursin (Eds.), *Coping and health.* New York: Plenum Press.

Miller, S., & Mangan, C. E. (1983). Interacting effects of information and coping style in adapting to gynecological stress: When should the doctor tell all? *Journal of Personality and Social Psychology, 45,* 223–236.

Millon, T. (1981). *Disorders of personality, DSM-III: Axis II.* New York: Wiley.

Minturn, L., Grosse, M., & Haider, S. (1969). Cultural patterning of sexual beliefs and behavior. *Ethnology, 8,* 301–318.

Mirowsky, J., & Ross, C. E. (1986). Social patterns of distress. *Annual Review of Sociology, 12,* 23–45.

Mischel, W. W. (1966). A social-learning view of sex differences in behavior. In E. E. Maccoby (Ed.), *The development of sex differences.* Stanford, CA: Stanford University Press.

Missildine, W. H. (1983). *Your inner child of the past.* New York: Pocket Books.

Mitchell, A. (1993, March 28). Letter explained motive in bombing, officials now say. *The New York Times,* pp. A1, L35.

Mo, K. M., Li, L. S., & Ou, L. W. (1987). Report of koro epidemic in Leizhou Peninsula, Hainan Island. *Chinese Journal of Neuropsychiatry, 20,* 232–234.

Moghaddam, F. M., & Solliday, E. A. (1991). "Balanced multiculturalism" and the challenge of peaceful coexistence in pluralistic societies. *Psychology and Developing Societies, 3,* 51–72.

Mogul, K. M. (1992). Ethics complaints against female psychiatrists. *American Journal of Psychiatry, 149,* 651–653.

Mohr, D. C., & Beutler, L. E. (1990). Erectile dysfunction: A review of diagnostic and treatment procedures. *Clinical Psychology Review, 10,* 123–150.

Money, J. (1987). Sin, sickness or status—homosexual gender identity and psychoneuroendocrinology. *American Psychologist, 42,* 384–399.

Monroe, S. M. (1982). Life events assessment: Current practices, emerging trends. *Clinical Psychology Review, 2* (4), 435–453.

Monroe, S. M. (1983). Major and minor life events as predictors of psychological distress: Further issues and findings. *Journal of Behavioral Medicine, 6,* 189–205.

Montagu, A. (1965). *Man's most dangerous myth: The fallacy of race.* New York: Meridian.

Montgomery, M. J., Anderson, E. R., Hetherington, E. M., & Clingempell, W. G. (1992). Patterns of courtship for remarriage: Implications for child adjustment and parent-child relationships. *Journal of Marriage and the Family, 54,* 686–698.

Mooradian, A. D., Morley, J. E., & Korenman, S. G. (1987). Biological actions of androgens. *Endocrine Reviews, 8,* 1–28.

Moore, A. S. (1992, September 27). Cited in B. Lyne. Women at the top: Role models or relics? *The New York Times,* p. F27.

Moore, C. (1992, September 25). Bush's nonsense on jobs and the environment [Editorial]. *The New York Times,* p. A33.

Moreland, R. L., & Zajonc, R. B. (1982). Exposure effects in person perception: Familiarity, similarity, and attraction. *Journal of Experimental Social Psychology, 18,* 395–415.

Morgan, J. P. (1992, April 12). Cited in B. P. Noble. Testing employees for drugs. *The New York Times,* p. F27.

Morgan, L. A. (1976). A reexamination of widowhood and morale. *Journal of Gerontology, 31,* 687–695.

Morris, W. N., et al. (1976). Collective coping with stress: Group reactions to fear, anxiety, and ambiguity. *Journal of Personality and Social Psychology, 33,* 674–679.

Morrison, A. M., & Von Glinow, M. A. (1990). Women and minorities in management. *American Psychologist, 45,* 200–209.

Morrison, D. G. (1981). Triangle taste tests: Are subjects who respond correctly lucky or good? *Journal of Marketing, 45* (Summer), 111–119.

Morrow, K. B., & Sorell, G. T. (1989). Factors affecting self-esteem, depression, and negative behaviors in sexually abused female adolescents. *Journal of Marriage and the Family, 51,* 677–686.

Morse, S., & Gergan, K. J. (1970). Social comparison, self-consistency, and the concept of self. *Journal of Personality and Social Psychology, 16,* 148–156.

Mosher, P. W. (1993, April 20). What Freud meant by "infantile amnesia" [Letter to the editor]. *The New York Times,* p. A28.

Mosher, W. D., & Pratt, W. F. (1982). Reproductive impairments among married couples in the United States. *Vital and Health Statistics, 23* (11), 1–51.

Moss, D. C. (1988). "Real" dolls too suggestive: Do anatomically correct dolls lead to false abuse charges? *American Bar Association Journal, 74* (December 1).

Motowidlo, S. J. (1984). Psychometric properties of subordinate ratings of managerial performance. *Personnel Psychology, 37,* 687–702.

Mott, T., Jr. (1987). Adverse reactions in the use of hypnosis. *American Journal of Clinical Hypnosis, 29,* 147–148.

Moustakas, C. E. (1961). *Loneliness.* Englewood Cliffs, NJ: Prentice-Hall.

Muchinsky, P. M. (1983). *Psychology applied to work.* Homewood, IL: Dorsey.

Muehlenhard, C. L., & Linton, M. A. (1987). Date rape and sexual aggression in dating situations: Incidence and risk factors. *Journal of Counseling Psychology, 34,* 186–196.

Mueller, D., & Wasser, V. (1977). Implications of changing answers on objective test items. *Journal of Educational Measurement, 14,* 9–13.

Mukhopadhyay, C. C., & Higgens, P. J. (1988). Anthropological studies of women's status revisited: 1977–1987. *Annual review of anthropology, 17,* 461–495.

Mundell, W. A., & Friedman, J. (1992, November 22). Financing to meet AIDS's true costs. *The New York Times,* p. F11.

Murdock, G. P. (1949). *Social structure.* New York: Free Press.

Murdock, G. P., & Provost, C. (1973). Factors in the division of labor by sex: A cross-cultural analysis. *Ethology, 12,* 203–225.

Murray, H. A. (1938). *Explorations in personality.* Cambridge: Harvard University Press.

Murstein, B. I. (1988). A taxonomy of love. In R. J. Sternberg & M. L. Barnes (Eds.), *The psychology of love.* New Haven: Yale University Press.

Muschel, I. J. (1984). Pet therapy with terminal cancer patients. *Social Casework, 65,* 451–458.

Mydans, S. (1993a, March 26). An electric courtroom duel in Los Angeles beating case. *The New York Times,* p. A14.

Mydans, S. (1993b, February 15). Haunted still, jurors in beating trial give warning to possible successors. *The New York Times,* p. A8.

Mydans, S. (1993c, April 18). 2 of 4 officers found guilty in Los Angeles beating. *The New York Times,* pp. A1, A32.

Mydans, S. (1993d, April 18). Verdict in Los Angeles: Points of evidence, not emotion. *The New York Times,* p. L33.

Myers, A. M., & Gonda, G. (1982). Utility of the masculinity-femininity construct: Comparison of traditional and androgyny approaches. *Journal of Personality and Social Psychology, 43,* 514–523.

Nachman, E. P. (1992, May 1). For the disabled, theater needn't be tragic [editorial]. *The New York Times,* p. A34.

Nadal, R. A. (1992, December 2). Toll on leadership [Letter to the editor]. *The New York Times,* p. A22.

Nadel, J. (1986). *Imitation et communication entre jeune enfants.* [Imitation and communication between young children]. Paris: Presses Universitaires de France.

Nadler, A., Fisher, J. D., & Itzhak, S. B. (1983). With a little help from my friend: Effect of single or multiple act aid as a function of donor and task characteristics. *Journal of Personality and Social Psychology, 44,* 310–321.

Nadler, A., Fisher, J. D., & Streufert, S. (1974). The donor's dilemma: Recipients' reaction to aid from friend or foe. *Journal of Applied Social Psychology, 4,* 275–285.

Nahas, G. G. (1976). *Marijuana: Chemistry, biochemistry and cellular effects.* New York: Springer.

Nahemow, N. (1983). Mate selection. *Medical Aspects of Human Sexuality, 17,* 106–123.

Name Withheld. (1993, May 11). A rape victim victimized by activists. *The New York Times,* p. A20.

Namka, L. (1989). *The doormat syndrome.* Deerfield Beach, Florida: Health Communications, Inc.

Nasar, S. (1992, October 18). Women's progress stalled? Just not so. *The New York Times,* pp. F1, F10.

Nash, N. C. (1993, January 1). A slaying stuns Brazil: It's right out of the soaps. *The New York Times,* p. A4.

Nass, G. D., Libby, R. W., & Fisher, M. P. (1981). *Sexual choices: An introduction to human sexuality.* Monterey, CA: Wadsworth.

National Academy of Sciences, Institute of Medicine. (1982). *Marijuana and health.* Washington, DC: National Academic Press.

National Center for Health Statistics. (1985). *Health: United States, 1985* (DHHS Pub. No. (PHS) 86–1232). Washington, DC: US Government Printing Office.

National Center for Health Statistics. (1992). *Unpublished data tables from the NCHS Mortality Tapes, FBI-SHR.* Atlanta, GA: Centers for Disease Control.

National Institute on Drug Abuse. (1983). *Population projections, based on the national survey of drug abuse, 1982.* Rockville, MD: National Institute on Drug Abuse.

Navarro, M. (1992, May 6). Left behind by AIDS. *The New York Times,* pp. B1, B10.

Neer, M. C. G. (1990, June 28). Quoted in L. Kutner. If you want to coach, or watch. *The New York Times,* p. C8.

Nelson, M. (1992, April 26). Cited in G. Kolata. A parents' guide to kids' sports. *The New York Times Magazine,* Part 2, pp. 12–15, 40, 44, 46.

Nelson, M. R. (1988). Issues of access to knowledge: Dropping out of school. In L. N. Tanner (Ed.), *Critical issues in curriculum.* Chicago: University of Chicago Press.

Neubeck, G. (1972). The myriad motives for sex. *Sexual Behavior, 2* (7), 51–56.

Neulinger, J. (1981). *The psychology of leisure* (2nd ed.). Springfield, IL: Charles C Thomas.

Neuman, K. (1986). Personal values and commitment to energy conservation. *Environment and Behavior, 18,* 53–74.

New Head of Fox Unit. (1992, December 1). *The New York Times,* p. D17.

New H.I.V. strains resist AIDS drugs. (1993, January 1). *The New York Times,* p. A18.

New Riots, Old Story, Panel Finds. (1992, October 4). *The New York Times,* p. 36.

New York League for the Hard of Hearing. (1993). *Warning: Noise can damage your hearing.* New York: Author.

Newcomb, M. D., & Bentler, P. M. (1988). Impact of adolescent drug use and social support on problems of young adults: A longitudinal study. *Journal of Abnormal Psychology, 97,* 64–75.

Newcomb, M. D. (1987). Cohabitation and marriage: A quest for independence and relatedness. In S. Oskamp (Ed.), *Family processes and problems: Social psychological aspects.* Newbury Park, CA: Sage.

Newcomb, M. D., & Bentler, P. M. (1988). Impact of adolescent drug use and social support on problems of young adults: A longitudinal study. *Journal of Abnormal Psychology, 97,* 64–75.

Newcomb, M. D., & Bentler, P. M. (1989). Substance use and abuse among children and teenagers. *American Psychologist, 44,* 242–248.

Newcomb, M. D., & McGee, L. (1991). *Journal of Personality and Social Psychology, 61,* 614–628.

Newman, J. (1992, June 21). Cited in G. Kolata. More children are employed, often perilously. *The New York Times,* pp. A1, A22.

Newton, J. E., & Ehrlich, W. W. (1966). Coronary blood flow in dogs: Effect of person. *Conditional Reflex, 1,* 81.

Nezu, A. M., Nezu, C. M., & Blissett, S. E. (1988). Sense of humor as a moderator of the relation between stressful events and psychological distress: A prospective analysis. *Journal of Personality and Social Psychology, 54,* 520–525.

Ngui, P. W. (1969). The koro epidemic in Singapore. *Australia/New Zealand Journal of Psychiatry, 3,* 263–266.

Nicassio, P. M., & Wallston, K. A. (1992). Longitudinal relationships among pain, sleep problems, and depression in rheumatoid arthritis. *Journal of Abnormal Psychology, 101,* 514–520.

Nichols, M. (1990). Lesbian relationships: Implications for the study of sexuality and gender. In D. P. McWhirter, S. A. Sanders, & J. M. Reinisch (Eds.), *Homosexuality/heterosexuality: Concepts of sexual orientation* (pp. 350–364). New York: Oxford.

Nichols, S. E., & Ostrow, D. G. (1984). *The psychiatric implications of AIDS.* Washington, DC: American Psychiatric Press.

Nielsen, A. C. Co. (1990). *1990 report on television.* Northbrook, IL: AC Nielsen Company.

No more math phobia. (1992, October 25). *The New York Times,* p. F2.

Nogee, J. L. (1992, May 10). Mass media's fault [Editorial]. *The New York Times,* p. E16.

Nomellini, S., & Katz, R. C. (1983). Effects of anger control training on abusive parents. *Cognitive Therapy and Research, 7,* 57–68.

Norcross, J. C. (1989). Commentary: Eclecticism misrepresented and integration misunderstood. *Psychotherapy, 27,* 297–300.

Nord, W. (1969). Beyond the teaching machine: The neglected area of operant conditioning in the theory and practice of management. *Organizational Behavior and Human Performance, 4,* 375–401.

Norman, W. T. (1963). Toward an adequate taxonomy of personality attributes: Replicated factor structure in peer nomination personality ratings. *Journal of Abnormal and Social Psychology, 66,* 574–583.

Novaco, R. (1975). *Anger control: The development and evaluation of an experimental treatment.* Lexington, MA: Heath.

Oakley, A. (1985). Social support in pregnancy: The "soft" way to increase birthweight? *Social Science and Medicine, 21,* 1259–1268.

Oberklaid, F., Sewell, J., Sanson, A., & Prior, M. (1991). Temperament and behavior of preterm infants: A six-year follow-up. *Pediatrics, 87,* 854–861.

Oberlander, J. (1992, September 6). Cited in J. Bennet. Romantic hearts do not wither: among the elderly, love and marriage eternally spring. *The New York Times,* pp. L49, L55.

Ohbuchi, K., & Izutsu, T. (1984). Retaliation by male victims: Effects of physical attractiveness and intensity of attack of female attacker. *Personality and Social Psychology Bulletin, 10,* 216–224.

Ojemann, G. A. (1991). Cortical organization of language. *Journal of Neuroscience, 11,* 2281–2287.

O'Keefe, A. M., & McCullough, S. J. (1979). Physician domination in the health care industry: The pursuit of antitrust redress. *Professional Psychology, 10,* 605–618.

Okun, B. (1992). Object relations and self-psychology: Overview and feminist perspective. In L. Brown & M. Ballou (Eds.), *Theories of personality and psychopathology: Feminist reappraisals* (pp. 20–45). New York: Guilford.

Oliver, J. M., & Pomicter, C. (1981). Depression in automotive assembly line workers as a function of unemployment variables. *American Journal of Community Psychology, 9,* 507–512.

Oliver, W. (1989a). Black males and social problems: Prevention through Afrocentric socialization. *Journal of Black Studies, 20,* 15–39.

Oliver, W. (1989b). Sexual conquest and patterns of Black-on-Black violence: A structural-cultural perspective. *Violence and Victims, 4,* 257–271.

Olson, D. H., Portner, J., & Lavee, Y. (1985). *Family adaptability and cohesion evaluation scale.* St. Paul, MN: Author, University of Minnesota.

Olweus, D., Mattsson, A., Schalling, D., & Low, H. (1980). Testosterone, aggression, physical and personality dimensions in normal adolescent males. *Psychosomatic Medicine, 42,* 253–269.

Omizo, M. M., & Williams, R. E. (1981). Biofeedback training can calm the hyperactive child. *Academic Therapy, 17,* 43–46.

On healthy indoor air, and avoiding suits. (1992, May 15). *The New York Times,* p. B20.

O'Neill, M. (1992, March 11). New mainstream: Hot dogs, apple pie and salsa. *The New York Times,* pp. C1, C6.

Opposite mental effects are found in twin drugs. (1993, April 1). *The New York Times,* p. D23.

Orthner, D. K., & Axelson, L. J. (1980). The effects of wife employment on marital sociability. *Journal of Comparative Family Studies, 11,* 531–545.

Ory, M., & Goldberg, E. (1983). Pet ownership and life satisfaction in elderly women. In A. Katcher & A. Beck (Eds.), *New perspectives on our life with companion animals* (pp. 803–817). Philadelphia: University of Pennsylvania Press.

O'Shea, J. S. (1986). Childhood accident prevention strategies. *Forensic Science International, 30,* 99–111.

Osler, W. (1892). *Lectures on angina pectoris and allied states.* New York: Appleton-Century-Crofts.

Ouchi, W. C. (1981). *Theory Z: How American business can meet the Japanese challenge.* Reading, MA: Addison-Wesley.

Paffenbarger, R. S., Hyde, R. T., Wing, A. L., et al. (1993). The association of changes in physical-activity level and other lifestyle characteristics with mortality among men. *The New England Journal of Medicine, 328,* 538–545.

Pagel, M. D., Erdly, W. W., & Becker, J. (1987). Social networks: We get by with (and in spite of) a little help from our friends. *Journal of Personality and Social Psychology, 53,* 793–804.

Paige, R. M. (1990). International students: Cross-cultural psychological perspectives. In R. W. Brislin (Ed.), *Applied cross-cultural psychology.* Newbury Park, CA: Sage.

Pak, R. C. K., Tsim, K. W. K., & Cheng, C. H. K. (1985). The role of neonatal and pubertal gonadal hormones in regulating the sex dependence of the hepatic microsomal testosterone 5-reductase activity in the rat. *Journal of Endocrinology, 106,* 71–79.

Palinkas, L. A. (1987). Points of stress and modes of adjustment in southwest Alaska. *Human Organ, 46,* 292–304.

Palinkas, L. A., Russell, J., Downs, M. A., & Peterson, J. S. (1992). Ethnic differences in stress, coping, and depressive symptoms after the Exxon *Valdez* oil spill. *The Journal of Nervous and Mental Disease, 180,* 287–295.

Palmer, C. (1989). Is rape a cultural universal? A re-examination of the ethnographic data. *Ethnology, 28,* 1–16.

Palmer, J. D., Udry, J. R., & Morris, N. M. (1982). Diurnal and weekly, but no lunar rhythms in human copulation. *Human Biology, 54,* 111–121.

Papini, D., et al. (1988). An evaluation of adolescent patterns of sexual self-disclosure to parents and friends. *Journal of Adolescent Research, 3,* 387–401.

Pareles, J. (1991, November 10). Tales from the dark side, spun by a reluctant outlaw. *The New York Times,* pp. 26, 28.

Pareles, J. (1992, July 30). The disappearance of Ice-T's "Cop Killer." *The New York Times,* p. C13.

Parham, T. (1990). *Do the right thing: Racial discussion in counseling psychology.* Paper presented at the annual meeting of the American Psychological Association, Boston, MA.

Park, Y. (1992, May 22) Cited in S. Mydans. A target of rioters, Koreatown is bitter, armed and determined. *The New York Times,* pp. A1, A22.

Parke, R. D., & Slaby, R. G. (1983). The development of aggression. In P. H. Mussen (Ed.), *Handbook of child psychology* (Vol. 4). New York: Wiley.

Parker, R. (1989). Poverty, subculture of violence, and type of homicide. *Social Forces, 67,* 983–1007.

Parry, A. (1935). The menace of marihuana. *American Mercury, 36,* 487–488.

Parry, G. (1987). Sex-role beliefs, work attitudes and mental health in employed and non-employed mothers. *British Journal of Social Psychology, 26,* 47–58.

Parsons, T. (1978). *Action theory and the human condition.* New York: Free Press.

Parsons, T. (1979). Definitions of health and illness in light of the American values and social structure. In E. G. Jaco (Ed.), *Pa-*

tients, physicians and illness: A sourcebook in behavioral science and health. New York: Free Press.

Parten, M. B. (1932). Social participation among pre-school children. *Journal of Abnormal and Social Psychology, 27,* 243–269.

Pasley, K., & Ihinger-Tallman, M. (Eds.). (1987). *Remarriage and stepparenting.* New York: Guilford.

Patterson, C. H. (1989). Eclecticism in psychotherapy: Is it possible? *Psychotherapy, 26,* 157–161.

Patterson, C. H. (1990). On misrepresentation and misunderstanding. *Psychotherapy, 27,* 301.

Pattison, E. M. (1974). Confusing concepts about the concept of homosexuality. *Psychiatry, 47,* 340–349.

Paykel, E. S. (1974). Life stress and psychiatric disorder. In B. S. Dohrenwend, & B. P. Dohrenwend (Eds.), *Stressful life events: Their nature and effects.* New York: Wiley.

Peabody, D. (1984). Personality dimensions through trait inferences. *Journal of Personality and Social Psychology, 46,* 384–403.

Pennebaker, J. W., & Roberts, T. (1991, August). *Towards a his and hers theory of emotion: Gender differences in visceral perception.* Paper presented at the meeting of the American Psychological Association, San Francisco, CA.

Penner, L. A., Thompson, J. K., & Coovert, D. L. (1991). Size estimation among anorexics: Much ado about very little? *Journal of Abnormal Psychology, 100,* 90–93.

Perkins, D. V. (1982). The assessment of stress using life events scales. In L. Goldberger & S. Breznitz (Eds.), *Handbook of stress: Theoretical and clinical aspects.* New York: Free Press.

Perls, F. S. (1969). *Gestalt therapy verbatim.* Lafayette, CA: Real People Press.

Perry, D. G., & Bussey, K. (1979). The social learning theory of sex differences: Imitation is alive and well. *Journal of Personality and Social Psychology, 37,* 1699–1712.

Perry, S., Jacobsberg, L., & Fogel, K. (1989). Orogenital transmission of human immunodeficiency virus (HIV). *Annals of Internal Medicine, 111,* 951–952.

Person, E. S., et al. (1990). Gender differences in sexual behaviors and fantasies in a college population. *Journal of Marriage and the Family, 15,* 187–198.

Pert, C. (1989, June). Cited in Hall, S. S. A molecular code links emotions, mind and health. *Smithsonian,* pp. 62–71.

Perzeszty, A. (1986). Annual price survey: Family budget costs. *Supplement to Family Budget Standard.* New York: Community Council of Greater New York.

Petersen, B. H., Graham, J., Lemberger, L., & Dalton, B. (1974). Studies of the immune response in chronic marihuana smokers. Cited in G. K. Russell. (1983). *Marijuana today* (revised edition). New York: The Myrin Institute, Inc. for Adult Education.

Peterson, C., Seligman, M. E. P., & Vaillant, G. E. (1988). Pessimistic explanatory style is a risk factor for physical illness: A thirty-five year longitudinal study. *Journal of Personality and Social Psychology, 55,* 23–27.

Peterson, I. (1992, April 14). Breaking up is *really* hard to do. *The New York Times,* pp. B1, B4.

Peterson, K. J. (1991). Social workers' knowledge about AIDS. *Social Work, 36,* 31–37.

Peterson, L., & Roberts, M. C. (1992). Complacency, misdirection, and effective prevention of children's injuries. *American Psychologist, 47,* 1040–1044.

Petrovic, S. (1993, July 6). Cited in Sudetic, C. (1993, July 6). This can't be Bosnia, there's too much laughing. *The New York Times,* p. A4.

Phillips, D. P. (1983). The impact of mass media violence on U.S. homicides. *American Sociological Review, 48,* 560–568.

Piaget, J. (1965). *The moral judgment of the child.* (M. Gabain, Trans.). New York: Free Press.

Piaget, J., & Inhelder, B. (1969). *The psychology of the child.* New York: Basic Books.

Pickering, T. G., & Gerin, W. (1990). Cardiovascular reactivity in the laboratory and the role of behavioral factors in hypertension: A critical review. *Annals of Behavioral Medicine, 12,* 3–16.

Piedmont, R. L., & Weinstein, H. P. (1993). A psychometric evaluation of the new NEO-PIR facet scales for agreeableness and conscientiousness. *Journal of Personality Assessment, 60,* 302–318.

Pieper, M. H., & Pieper, W. J. (1992). It's not tough, it's tender love: Problem teens need compassion that the "tough love" approach to child-rearing doesn't offer them. *Child Welfare, 51,* 369–377.

Pillemer, K., & Suitor, J. J. (1991). "Will I ever escape my child's problems?" Effects of adult children's problems on elderly parents. *Journal of Marriage and the Family, 53,* 585–594.

Pincus, H. A., Frances, A., Davis, W. W., First, M. B., & Widiger, T. A. (1992). DSM-IV and new diagnostic categories: Holding the line on proliferation. *American Journal of Psychiatry, 149,* 112–117.

Pink, J. E. T., & Wampler, K. S. (1985). Problem areas in stepfamilies: Cohesion, adaptibility, and the step-father-adolescent relationship. *Family Relations, 34,* 327–335.

Pinkert, T. M. (Ed.). (1985). *Current research on the consequences of maternal drug abuse.* NIDA Research Monograph 59, Department of Health and Human Services.

Piskacek, V., & Golub, M. (1973). Children of interracial marriage. In I. R. Stuart & L. E. Abt (Eds.), *Interracial marriage: Expectations and reality.* New York: Grossman.

Pittman, F. (1990, May/June). The masculine mystique. *Family Therapy Networker,* pp. 40–52.

Pittman, J. F., & Lloyd, S. A. (1988). Quality of family life, social support, and stress. *Journal of Marriage and the Family, 50,* 53–67.

Pittman, R. B., & Haughwout, P. (1987). Influence of high school size on dropout rate. *Educational Evaluation and Policy Analysis, 9,* 337–343.

Plapinger, L., & McEwen, B. S. (1978). Gonadal steroid-brain interactions in sexual differentiation. In J. B. Hutchison (Ed.), *Biological determinants of sexual behavior* (pp. 111–122). New York: Wiley.

Pleck, J. H. (1984). Men's power with women, other men, and society. In P. P. Rieker & E. Carmen (Eds.), *The gender gap in psychotherapy* (pp. 79–89). New York: Plenum.

Poche, C., Brouwer, R., & Swearingen, M. (1981). Teaching self-protection to young children. *Journal of Applied Behavior Analysis, 14,* 169–176.

Poll of sex in military finds troops made more than war. (1992, October 4). *The New York Times,* p. L23.

Pollard, C. A., Pollard, H. J., & Corn, K. J. (1989). Panic onset and major events in the lives of agoraphobics: A test of contiguity. *Journal of Abnormal Psychology, 98,* 318–321.

Pollard, J. K. III. (1987). *Self-parenting.* Malibu, CA: Generic Human Studies Publishing.

Ponsonby, A-L., Dwyer, M. B., Gibbons, L. E., Cochrane, J. A., & Wang, Y-G. (1993). Factors potentiating the risk of sudden infant death syndrome associated with the prone position. *The New England Journal of Medicine, 329,* 377–382.

Porter, C. A. (1981, June). *The interrelation of attributions, coping, and affect in battered women.* Paper presented at the annual meeting of the Canadian Psychological Association, Toronto, Ontario, Canada.

Porter, N. L., & Chatelain, R. S. (1981). Family life education for single parent families. *Family Relations, 33,* 309–315.

Potter, B. A. (1980). *Turning around: The behavioral approach to managing people.* New York: American Management Association.

Powell, C. L. (1992, November 14). Cited in J. H. Cushman, Jr. Top military officers object to lifting homosexual ban. *The New York Times,* p. L9

Powell, D. H., & Driscoll, P. F. (1973). Middle class professionals face unemployment. *Society, 10* (2), 18–26.

Powell, E. (1991). *Talking back to sexual pressure.* Minneapolis: CompCare Publishers.

Powell, L. H., Friedman, M., Thoresen, C. E., Gill, J. J., & Ulmer, D. K. (1984). Can the Type A behavior pattern be altered after myocardial infarction? A second year report from the recurrent coronary prevention project. *Psychosomatic Medicine, 46,* 293–313.

Pratkanis, A. R., & Greenwald, A. G. (1988). Recent perspectives on unconscious processing: Still no marketing applications. *Psychology & Marketing, 5,* 337–353.

Prentky, R. A., & Knight, R. A. (1991). Identifying critical dimensions for discriminating among rapists. *Journal of Consulting and Clinical Psychology, 59,* 643–661.

Pressman, B. (1984). *Family violence: Origins and treatment.* Guelph, Ontario: Children's Aid Society of the City of Guelph and the County of Wellington.

Price, J., Desmond, S., & Smith, D. (1991). A preliminary investigation of inner city adolescents' perceptions of guns. *Journal of School Health, 61,* 255–269.

Price, K. H., & Garland, H. (1981). Compliance with a leader's suggestions as a function of perceived leader/members competence and potential reciprocity. *Journal of Applied Social Psychology, 66,* 329–336.

Price, R. H. (1992, March 25). Cited in J. E. Brody. Overcoming the trauma of losing your job. *The New York Times,* p. C12.

Prior, M., Garino, E., Sanson, A., & Oberklaid, F. (1987). Ethnic influences on "difficult" temperament and behavioural problems in infants. *Australian Journal of Psychology, 39,* 163–171.

Proshansky, H. M. (1990). The pursuit of understanding: An intellectual history. In I. Altman & K. Christensen (Eds.), *Environment and behavior studies: Emergence of intellectual traditions.* New York: Plenum.

Puk, G. (1991). Treating traumatic memories: A case report on the eye movement desensitization procedure. *Journal of Behavior Therapy and Experimental Psychiatry, 22,* 149–151.

Purdy, F., & Nickle, N. (1982). Practice principles for working with groups of men who batter. *Social Work with Groups, 4,* 111–122.

Quadrel, M. J., Fischoff, B., & Davis, W. (1993). Adolescent (in)vulnerability. *American Psychologist, 48,* 102–116.

Quay, H. (1986). A critical analysis of DSM-III as a taxonomy of psychopathology of childhood and adolescence. In T. Millon & G. Klerman (Eds.), *Contemporary directions in psychopathology: Toward the DSM-IV* (pp. 151–165). New York: Guilford.

Quindlen, A. (1993, March 10). Gynocide. *The New York Times,* p. A19.

Quinn, R. P., Kahn, R. K., Tabor, J. M., & Gordon, L. K. (1968). *The chosen few: A study of discrimination in executive selection.* Ann Arbor: University of Michigan, Institute of Social Research.

Quinn, S. (1980). *A mind of her own: The life of Karen Horney.* New York: Summit Books.

Rabin, R. L. (1992, August 9). Cited in J. Hoffman. Pillow talk. *The New York Times,* p. V8.

Rabinovitz, J. (1992, August 16). Dispute on Bronx sidewalk leads to fatal shots. *The New York Times,* p. L44.

Rabkin, J. G., & Streuning, E. L. (1976). Life events, stress, and illness. *Science, 194,* 1013–1020.

Rachels, J. (1990). *Created from animals: The moral implications of Darwinism.* New York: Oxford University Press.

Rachman, S. J., & Hodgson, R. J. (1980). *Obsessions and compulsions.* Englewood Cliffs, NJ: Prentice-Hall.

Rafaelsen, O. J., Bech, P., Christiansen, J., Christrup, H., Nyboe, J., & Rafaelsen, L. (1973). Cannabis and alcohol: Effects on simulated car driving. *Science, 179,* 920–923.

Rafferty, Y., & Shinn, M. (1991). The impact of homelessness on children. *American Psychologist, 46,* 1170–1179.

Ragland, D. R., & Brand, R. J. (1988). Type A behavior and mortality from coronary heart disease. *New England Journal of Medicine, 318,* 65–69.

Rahe, R. H., & Arthur, R. J. (1978). Life changes and illness studies: Past history and future directions. *Journal of Human Stress, 4,* 3–15.

Rahe, R. H., & Holmes, T. H. (1965). Social, psychologic and psychophysiologic aspects of inguinal hernia. *Journal of Psychosomatic Research, 8,* 487–491.

Rahe, R. H., Meyer, M., Smith, M., Kjaer, G., & Holmes, T. H. (1964). Social stress and illness onset. *Journal of Psychosomatic Research, 8,* 35–44.

Ralston, D. A., Anthony, W. P., & Gustafson, D. J. (1985). Employees may love flextime, but what does it do to the organization's performance? *Journal of Applied Psychology, 70,* 272–279.

Ramey, L. (1980). Homicide among Black males. *Public Health Reports, 95,* 549–561.

Ramsey, C. N., Jr., Abell, T. C., & Baker, L. C. (1986). The relationship between family functioning, life events, family structure, and the outcome of pregnancy. *Journal of Family Practice, 22,* 522–527.

Randel, W. P. (1965). *The Ku Klux Klan.* Philadelphia: Chilton Books.

Rapee, R. (1987). The psychological treatment of panic attacks: Theoretical conceptualization and review of evidence. *Clinical Psychology Review, 7,* 427–438.

Raskin, D. C., & Yuille, J. C. (1987). Problems of evaluating interviews of children in sexual abuse cases. In S. J. Ceci, M. P. Toglia, & D. F. Ross (Eds.), *New perspectives on the child witness.* New York: Springer-Verlag.

Raskin, D. C., & Yuille, J. C. (1989). Problems in evaluating interviews of children in sexual abuse cases. In S. J. Ceci, M. P. Toglia, & D. F. Ross (Eds.), *Adults' perceptions of children's testimony* (pp. 184–207). New York: Springer-Verlag.

Ravo, N. (1992, April 15). Topless bars for a crowd in pin stripes. *The New York Times,* pp. C1, C12.

Ray, J. J. (1975). Measuring environmentalist attitudes. *Australian and New Zealand Journal of Sociology, 11* (2), 70–71.

Ray, J. J. (1980). The psychology of environmental concern: Some Australian data. *Personality and Individual Differences, 1,* 161–173.

Ray, O. (1978). *Drugs, society, and human behavior* (2nd ed.). St. Louis: Mosby.

Rayman, P. M. (1992, March 25). Cited in J. E. Brody. Overcoming the trauma of losing your job. *The New York Times*, p. C12.

Razran, G. H. S. (1934). Conditioned withdrawal responses with shock as the conditioning stimulus in adult human subjects. *Psychological Bulletin, 31*, 111–143.

Red Horse, J. G., Lewis, R., Feit, M., & Decker, J. (1979). Family behavior of urban American Indians. *Social Casework, 59*, 67–72.

Redlich, F. C., & Freedman, D. X. (1966). *The theory and practice of psychiatry*. New York: Basic Books.

Reeb, K. G., Graham, A. V., Zyzanski, S. J., & Kitson, G. C. (1987). Predicting low birth weight and complicated labor in urban black women: A biopsychosocial perspective. *Social Science and Medicine, 25*, 1321–1327.

Reinisch, J. M. (1990). *The Kinsey Institute new report on sex: What you must know to be sexually literate*. New York: St. Martin's Press.

Reis, H. T., Nezlek, J., & Wheeler, L. (1980). Physical attractiveness in social interaction. *Journal of Personality and Social Psychology, 38*, 604–617.

Reisenzein, R. (1983). The Schachter theory of emotion: Two decades later. *Psychological Bulletin, 94*, 239–264.

Reiss, B. F. (1980). Psychological tests in homosexuality. In J. Marmor (Ed.), *Homosexual behavior* (pp. 296–311). New York: Basic Books.

Reitzfeld, R. (1990, March 26). Cited in Foltz, K. In ads, men's image becomes softer. *The New York Times*, p. D12.

Reker, G. T., & Wong, P. T. P. (1985). Personal optimism, physical and mental health: The triumph of successful aging. In J. E. Birren & J. Livingston (Eds.), *Cognition, stress and aging*. Englewood Cliffs, NJ: Prentice-Hall.

Renner, M. J., & Rosenzweig, M. R. (1987). *Enriched and impoverished environments: Effects on brain and behavior*. New York: Springer Verlag.

Renzetti, C. M., & Curran, D. J. (1989). *Women, men, and society: The sociology of gender*. Boston: Allyn & Bacon.

Repetti, R. L. (1989). Effects of daily workload on subsequent behavior during marital interaction: The roles of social withdrawal and spouse support. *Journal of Personality and Social Psychology, 57*, 651–659.

Rescorla, R. A. (1988). Pavlovian conditioning: It's not what you think it is. *American Psychologist, 43*, 151–160.

Rest, J. R. (1983). Morality. In P. H. Mussen (Ed.), *Handbook of child psychology: Vol. 3. Cognitive development*. New York: Wiley.

Rexroat, C., & Shehan, C. (1987). The family life cycle and spouse's time in housework. *Journal of Marriage and the Family, 43*, 941–956.

Rey, J. (1988). DSM-III-R: Too much too soon? *Australian and New Zealand Journal of Psychiatry, 126*, 983–987.

Rice, M. E., Quinsey, V. L., & Harris, G. T. (1991). Sexual recidivism among child molesters released from a maximum security psychiatric institution. *Journal of Consulting and Clinical Psychology, 59*, 381–386.

Richardson, J. T. E. (1991). The menstrual cycle and student learning. *Journal of Higher Education, 62*, 317–340.

Richardson, L. (1992, September 2). No cookie-cutter answers in "Mommy Wars." *The New York Times*, pp. B1, B5.

Richter, C. P. (1957). On the phenomenon of sudden death in animals and man. *Psychosomatic Medicine, 19*, 191–198.

Rider college puts spotlight on prejudice. (1993, February 16). *The New York Times*, p. B6.

Riding, A. (1992a, June 22). Paris asked to admit Vichy's crimes against Jews. *The New York Times*, p. A10.

Riding, A. (1992b, April 1). 500 years after expulsion, Spain reaches out to Jews. *The New York Times*, p. A14.

Rifkin, B. (1990, May 17). Cited in D. Goleman. New paths to mental health put strains on some healers. *The New York Times*, pp. A1, B12.

Rindfuss, R. R. & VandenHeuvel, A. (1990). Cohabitation: Precursor to marriage or alternative to being single? *Population and Development Review, 16*, 703–726.

Ringold, D. J. (1992). Consumer response to product withdrawal: The reformulation of Coca-Cola. In R. J. Cohen, *Sixty-five exercises in psychological testing and assessment* (pp. 191–198). Mountain View, CA: Mayfield Publishing.

Rivara, F. P., Reay, D. T., & Bergman, A. B. (1989). Analysis of fatal pedestrian industries in King County, WA, and prospects of prevention. *Public Health Reports, 104*, 293–297.

Robb, S. S., & Stegman, C. E. (1983). Companion animals and elderly people: A challenge for evaluators of social support. *Gerontologist, 23*, 277–282.

Robbins, D. B. (1992, November 22). Cited in A.L. Cowan, & J. Barron. Executives the economy left behind. *The New York Times*, pp. F1, F6.

Roberts, G. C. (1990, June 28). Quoted in L. Kutner. If you want to coach, or watch. *The New York Times*, p. C8.

Roberts, M. C., Fanurik, D., & Layfield, D. A. (1987). Behavioral approaches to prevention of childhood injuries. *Journal of Social Issues, 43*, 105–118.

Roberts, M. C., & Turner, D. S. (1986). Rewarding parents for their children's use of safety seats. *Journal of Pediatrics Psychology, 11*, 25–36.

Roberts, S. (1990). Murder, mayhem, and other joys of youth. *The Journal of NIH Research, 2*, 67–72.

Robertson, A. S., Burge, P. S., Hedge, A., et al. (1985). Comparison of health problems related to work and environmental measurements in two office buildings with different ventilation systems. *British Medical Journal, 291*, 373–376.

Robertson, M. J. (1991). Homeless women with children: The role of alcohol and other drug abuse. *American Psychologist, 46*, 1198–1204.

Robins, L. N., & Helzer, J. E. (1986). Diagnosis and clinical assessment: The current state of psychiatric diagnosis. *Annual Review of Psychology, 37*, 409–432.

Robins, L. N., et al. (1986). Impact of disaster on previously assessed mental health. In J. H. Shore (Ed.), *Disaster stress studies: New methods and findings*. Washington, DC: American Psychiatric Press.

Robinson, F. P. (1941). *Effective behavior*. New York: Harper & Row.

Robinson, L. A., Berman, J. S., & Neimeyer, R. A. (1990). Psychotherapy for the treatment of depression: A comprehensive review of controlled outcome research. *Psychological Bulletin, 108*, 30–49.

Robles, F. E. (1992, April 7). Cited in L. Belkin. Fear of disease changing how doctors work. *The New York Times*, pp. A1, B2.

Rodgers, R. H., & Conrad, L. M. (1986). Courtship for remarriage: Influences on family reorganization after divorce. *Journal of Marriage and the Family, 48*, 767–775.

Rodin, J. (1986). Aging and health: Effects of the sense of control. *Science, 233*, 1271–1276.

Rodin, M. J. (1987). Who is memorable to whom: A study of cognitive disregard. *Social Cognition, 5*, 144–165.

Rodney King arrested in dispute. (1992, June 27). *The New York Times*, p. 6L.

Rodriguez, J. G. (1990). Childhood injuries in the United States: A priority issue. *American Journal of Diseases of Children, 144*, 625–626.

Rodriguez-Sierra, J. F., Howard, J. L., Pollard, G. T., & Hendricks, S. E. (1984). Effect of ovarian hormones on conflict behavior. *Psychoneuroendocrinology, 9*, 293–300.

Roethlisberger, F. J., & Dickson, W. J. (1939). *Management and the worker: An account of a research program conducted by the Western Electric Company.* Cambridge, MA: Harvard University Press.

Rogers, C. R. (1939) *The clinical treatment of the problem child.* Boston: Houghton Mifflin.

Rogers, C. R. (1942). *Counseling and psychotherapy.* Boston: Houghton Mifflin.

Rogers, C. R. (1951). *Client centered therapy.* Boston: Houghton Mifflin.

Rogers, C. R. (1961). *On becoming a person: A therapist's view of psychotherapy.* Boston: Houghton Mifflin.

Rogers, C. R. (1969). *Freedom to learn: A view of what education might become.* Columbus, Ohio: Charles E. Merrill Publishing.

Rogers, C. R. (1970). *Carl Rogers on encounter groups.* New York: Harper & Row.

Rogers, C. R. (1972). *On becoming partners: Marriage and its alternatives.* New York: Delacourte.

Rogers, C. R. (1980). *A way of being.* Boston: Houghton Mifflin.

Rogers, C. R., & Dymond, R. F. (Eds.). (1954). *Psychotherapy and personality change.* Chicago: University of Chicago Press.

Rogers, C. R., & Skinner, B. F. (1956). Some issues concerning the control of human behavior: A symposium. *Science, 124*, 1057–1066.

Rogers, R. W., & Deckner, C. W. (1975). Effects of fear appeals and physiological arousal upon emotion, attitudes and cigarette smoking. *Journal of Personality and Social Psychology, 32*, 225–230.

Rogers, T. B. (1981). A model of the self as an aspect of the human information-processing system. In N. Cantor & J. F. Kihlstrom (Eds.), *Personality, cognition, and social interaction* (pp. 193–214). Hillsdale, NJ: Erlbaum.

Rohsenow, D. J., & Smith, R. E. (1982). Irrational beliefs as predictors of negative affective states. *Motivation and Emotion, 6*, 299–301.

Rohter, L. (1992a, July 10). Boy wins right to sue parents for separation. *The New York Times*, p. A13.

Rohter, L. (1992b, October 4). To save or end a troubled parent's rights. *The New York Times*, p. E1.

Rohter, L. (1993, March 11). Doctor is slain during protest over abortions. *The New York Times*, pp. A1, B10.

Rokeach, M. (1968). *Beliefs, attitudes, and values: A theory of organization and change.* San Francisco: Jossey-Bass.

Rook, K., Dooley, D., & Catalano, R. (1991). Stress transmission: The effects of husbands' job stressors on the emotional health of their wives. *Journal of Marriage and the Family, 53*, 165–177.

Rook, K. S. (1984). The negative side of social interaction: Impact on psychological well-being. *Journal of Personality and Social Psychology, 46*, 1097–1108.

Roosevelt, R., & Lofas, J. (1977). *Living in step.* New York: McGraw-Hill.

Root, M. P. P. (1985). Guidelines for facilitating therapy with Asian American clients. *Psychotherapy, 22*, 349–356.

Rosaldo, M. Z. (1974). The use and abuse of anthropology: Reflections on feminism and cross-cultural understanding. *Signs: Journal of Women in Culture and Society, 5*, 389–417.

Rosch, E. (1978). Principles of categorization. In E. Rosch & B. B. Lloyd (Eds.), *Cognition and categorization* (pp. 27–48). Hillsdale, NJ: Erlbaum.

Rosen, S. (1982). *My voice will go with you: The teaching tales of Milton H. Erickson.* New York: Norton.

Rosenbaum, A., & O'Leary, K. D. (1981). Marital violence: Characteristics of abusive couples. *Journal of Consulting and Clinical Psychology, 49*, 63–71.

Rosenbaum, M. E. (1980). Cooperation and competition. In P. B. Paulus (Ed.), *The psychology of group influence.* Hillsdale, NJ: Erlbaum.

Rosenbaum, S. (1990, August 19). Schools feel impact of children of drug abusers. *The New York Times*, pp. NJ1, NJ12.

Rosenberg, M. (1979). *Conceiving the self.* New York: Basic Books.

Rosenberg, M. (1985). Self-concept and psychological well-being in adolescence. In R. L. Leahy (Ed.), *The development of the self.* Orlando, FL: Academic Press.

Rosenman, R. H., Brand, R. J., Jenkins, C. D., Friedman, M., Straus, R., & Wurm, M. (1975). Coronary heart disease in the Western Collaborative Group Study: Final followup experience of 8 1/2 years. *Journal of the American Medical Association, 233*, 872–877.

Rosenman, R. H., & Chesney, M. A. (1982). Stress, Type A behavior and coronary disease. In L. Goldberger & S. Bresnitz (Eds.), *Handbook of stress: Theoretical and clinical aspects.* New York: The Free Press.

Rosenthal, E. (1990, August 28). The spread of AIDS: A mystery unravels. *The New York Times*, pp. C1, C2.

Rosenthal, E. (1992, December 6). To a drumbeat of losses to AIDS, a rethinking of traditional grief. *The New York Times*, pp. A1, A32.

Rosenthal, E. (1993a, March 15). Claims and counterclaims on vaccine costs generate heat but little light. *The New York Times*, p. A16.

Rosenthal, E. (1993b, March 28). Patients in pain find relief, not addiction, in narcotics. *The New York Times*, pp. A1, A24.

Rosenthal, R. (1966). *Experimenter effects in behavioral research.* New York: Appleton-Century-Crofts.

Rosenthal, R. (1967). Covert communication in the psychological experiment. *Psychological Bulletin, 67*, 356–367.

Rosenthal, R. (1969). Interpersonal expectations: Effects of the experimenter's hypothesis. In R. Rosenthal & R. L. Rosnow (Eds.), *Artifacts in behavioral research.* New York: Academic Press.

Rosenthal, R., & Jacobson, L. (1968). *Pygmalion in the classroom: Teacher expectation and pupils' intellectual development.* New York: Holt, Rinehart & Winston.

Rosenthal, R., et al. (1979). The PONS test: Measuring sensitivity to nonverbal cues. In S. Weitz (Ed.), *Nonverbal communication* (2nd ed.). New York: Oxford University Press.

Rosenzweig, M. R. (1984). Experience, memory, and the brain. *American Psychologist, 39*, 365–376.

Rosenzweig, M. R., Bennett, E. L., & Diamond, M. C. (1972, February). Brain changes in response to experience. *Scientific American*, pp. 22–29.

Rosenzweig, S. (1993). *Freud, Jung, and Hall the King-Maker: The Historic Expedition to America (1909).* Seattle: Hogrefe & Huber.

Rosner, D. (1992, June 21). Cited in G. Kolata. More children are employed, often perilously. *The New York Times*, pp. A1, A22.

Ross, L. (1977). The intuitive psychologist and his shortcomings: Distortions in the attribution process. In L. Berkowitz (Ed.), *Advances in experimental social psychology* (Vol. 10). New York: Academic Press.

Roth, S., & Cohen, L. J. (1986). Approach, avoidance, and coping with stress. *American Psychologist, 41,* 813–819.

Rothstein, P. (1993, June 30). Cited in N. Angier, "Ruling on scientific evidence: A just burden." *The New York Times*, p. A12.

Rotheram-Borus, M. J., Koopman, C., & Ehrhardt, M. J. (1991). Homeless youths and HIV infection. *American Psychologist, 46,* 1188–1197.

Rotton, J., Barry, T., Frey, J., & Soler, E. (1978). Air pollution and interpersonal attraction. *Journal of Applied Social Psychology, 8,* 57–71.

Rotton, J., & Frey, J. (1984). Psychological costs of air pollution: Atmospheric condition, seasonal trends, and psychiatric emergencies. *Population and Environment, 7,* 3–16.

Rotton, J., & Frey, J. (1985). Air pollution, weather, and violent crime: Concomitant time-series analysis of archival data. *Journal of Personality and Social Psychology, 49,* 1207–1220.

Rotton, J., Frey, J., Barry, T., Milligan, M., & Fitzpatrick, M. (1979). The air pollution experience and physical aggression. *Journal of Applied Social Psychology, 9,* 347–412.

Rubenstein, R. P. (1985). Color, circumcision, tatoos, and scars. In M. R. Solomon (Ed.), *The psychology of fashion* (pp. 243–254). Lexington, MA: Lexington Books.

Rubin, K. H., Maioni, T. L., & Hornung, M. (1976). Free play behaviors in middle-and lower-class preschoolers: Parten and Piaget revisited. *Child Development, 47,* 414–419.

Rubin, Z. (1988). Preface. In R. J. Sternberg & M. L. Barnes (Eds.), *The psychology of love.* New Haven: Yale University Press.

Ruble, D. N., Fleming, A. S., Hackel, L. S., & Stangor, C. (1988). Changes in the marital relationship during the transition to first time motherhood: Effects of violated expectations concerning division of household labor. *Journal of Personality and Social Psychology, 55,* 78–87.

Ruble, D. N., & Stangor, C. (1986). Stalking the elusive schema: Insights from the developmental and social-psychological analysis of gender schemas. *Social Cognition, 4,* 227–261.

Rudenstine, N. L. (1992, June 5). Cited in race problem is addressed at harvard. *The New York Times*, p. A14.

Ruff, G. A., & Barrios, B. A. (1986). Realistic assessment of body image. *Behavioral Assessment, 8,* 237–252.

Rule, B. G., & Nesdale, A. R. (1976). Emotional arousal and aggressive behavior. *Psychological Bulletin, 83,* 851–863.

Rule, S. (1992, May 26). Rappers say the riots were no surprise to their listeners. *The New York Times*, p. C13.

Rusbult, C. E. (1980). Commitment and satisfaction in romantic associations: A test of the investment model. *Journal of Experimental Social Psychology, 16,* 172–186.

Rusbult, C. E. (1983). A longitudinal test of the investment model: The development (and deterioration) of satisfaction and commitment in heterosexual involvements. *Journal of Personality and Social Psychology, 45,* 101–117.

Russell, G. K. (1983). *Marijuana today* (revised edition). New York: The Myrin Institute, Inc. for Adult Education.

Rutter, M. (1974). *The qualities of mothering: Maternal deprivation reassessed.* New York: Aronson.

Rutter, M., & Shaffer, D. (1980). DSM-III: A step forward or back in terms of the classification of child disorders? *Journal of the American Academy of Child Psychiatry, 19,* 371–394.

Ryan, P. (1992, August 9). Cited in J. Hoffman. Pillow talk. *The New York Times*, p. V8.

Sabini, J. (1986). Stanley Milgram (1933–1984). *American Psychologist, 41,* 1378–1379.

Sabshin, M. (1990, May 17). Cited in D. Goleman. New paths to mental health put strains on some healers. *The New York Times*, pp. A1, B12.

Sackett, P. R., Burris, L. R., & Callahan, C. (1989). Integrity testing for personnel selection: A review and critique. *Personnel Psychology, 37,* 221–245.

Sagan, C. (1979). *Broca's brain.* New York: Random House.

Sales, E., Baum, M., & Shore, B. (1984). Victim readjustment following assault. *Journal of Social Issues, 40,* 117–136.

Salmony, S. E., & Smoke, R. (1985, August). *Psychodynamics of the Ku Klux Klan.* Paper presented at the 93rd annual meeting of the American Psychological Association, Los Angeles, CA.

Salomon, G. (1977). Effects of encouraging Israeli mothers to co-observe "Sesame Street" with their five-year-olds. *Child Development, 48,* 1146–1151.

Saltzman, A. (1991, July 17). Trouble at the top. *U.S. News & World Report*, pp. 40–48.

Samet, J. M., Marbury, M. C., & Spengler, J. D. (1988). Health effects and sources of indoor air pollution. II. *American Review of Respiratory Diseases, 137,* 221–242.

Sampson, H. A., Mendelson, L., & Rosen, J. P. (1992). Fatal and nearfatal anaphylactic reactions to food in children and adolescents. *The New England Journal of Medicine, 327,* 380–384.

Sampson, R. (1987). Urban Black violence: The effect of male joblessness and family disruption. *American Journal of Sociology, 93,* 348–405.

Samuels, R. C. (1992, June 5). Imagine what it's like to go to the movies in a wheelchair [Editorial]. *The New York Times*, p. A28.

Sanday, P. (1981). The socio-cultural context of rape: A cross-cultural study. *Journal of Social Issues, 37,* 5–27.

Sanders, G. S. (1982). Social comparison as a basis for evaluating others. *Journal of Research in Personality, 16,* 21–31.

Sanderson, W. C., Rapee, R. M., & Barlow, D. H. (1989). The influence of an illusion of control on panic attacks induced via inhalation of 5.5% carbon dioxide-enriched air. *Archives of General Psychiatry, 46,* 157–162.

Sandler, I. N., & Barrera, M., Jr. (1984). Toward a multimethod approach to assessing the effects of social support. *American Journal of Community Psychology, 12,* 37–52.

Sandomir, R. (1992, June 5). A tragedy of manners at the movies. *The New York Times*, pp. C1, C30.

Sanger, D. E. (1990, June 30). In palace woods, a Japanese wedding. *The New York Times*, p. L3.

Sanger, D. E. (1992, October 15). Japan's plan to ship plutonium has big and little lands roaring. *The New York Times*, pp. A1, A6.

Sanger, D. E. (1993, March 19). South Korea, wary of the North, debates building a nuclear bomb. *The New York Times*, p. A8.

Sanson, A., Oberklaid, F., Pedlow, R., & Prior, M. (1991). Risk indicators: Assessment of infancy predictors of pre-school behavioural maladjustment. *Journal of Child Psychology and Psychiatry, 32,* 609–626.

Sarason, I. G., Johnson, J. H., & Siegel, J. M. (1978). Assessing the impact of life changes: Development of the Life Experiences Survey. *Journal of Consulting and Clinical Psychology, 46,* 932–946.

Sarrel, P., & Masters, W. (1982). Sexual molestation of men by women. *Archives of Sexual Behavior, 11,* 117–131.

Satinsky, D., & Frerotti, A. (1981). Biofeedback treatment for headache: A two-year follow-up study. *American Journal of Clinical Biofeedback, 4,* 62–65.

Sauer, M. V., Paulson, R. J., & Lobo, R. A. (1990). A preliminary report on oocyte donation extending reproductive potential to women over 40. *The New England Journal of Medicine, 323,* 1157–1160.

Saul, L. (1992, March 22). Executives inspire inner-city students. *The New York Times,* p. 10NJ.

Scandura, T. A., & Graen, B. B. (1984). Moderating effects of initial leader-member exchange status on the effects of a leadership intervention. *Journal of Applied Psychology, 69,* 428–436.

Scarr, H. (1993, May 9). Cited in F. Barringer. Ethnic pride confounds the census. *The New York Times,* p. E3.

Schacht, T. (1985). DSM-III and the politics of truth. *American Psychologist, 40,* 513–521.

Schachter, S. (1959/1976). *The psychology of affiliation.* Stanford, CA: Stanford University Press.

Schachter, S. (1964). The interaction of cognitive and physiological determinants of emotional state. In L. Berkowitz (Ed.), *Advances in experimental social psychology* (Vol. 1). New York: Academic Press.

Schacter, S., & Singer, J. (1962). Cognitive, social and physiological determinants of emotional state. *Psychological Review, 69,* 379–399.

Schachter, S. C., Ransil, B. J., & Geschwind, N. (1987). Associations of handedness with hair color and learning disabilities. *Neuropsychologia, 25,* 269–276.

Schafer, D. W. (1986). Recognizing multiple personality patients. *American Journal of Psychotherapy, 40,* 500–510.

Schafer, R. B., & Keith, P. M. (1990). Matching by weight in married couples: A life cycle perspective. *Journal of Social Psychology, 130,* 657–664.

Schaningner, C. M., & Buss, W. C. (1986). A longitudinal comparison of consumption and finance handling between happily married and divorced couples. *Journal of Marriage and the Family, 48,* 129–136.

Scheier, M. F., & Carver, C. S. (1985). Optimism, coping and health: Assessment and implications of generalized expectancies. *Health Psychology, 4,* 219–247.

Scheier, M. F., Weintraub, J. K., & Carver, C. S. (1986). Coping with stress: Divergent strategies of optimists and pessimists. *Journal of Personality and Social Psychology, 51,* 1257–1264.

Scher, M. (1990). Effect of gender role incongruities on men's experience as clients in psychotherapy. *Psychotherapy, 27,* 322–326.

Schickedanz, J. A., Hansen, K., & Forsyth, P. D. (1990). *Understanding children.* Mountain View, CA: Mayfield Publishing.

Schiess, M. C., Joels, M., & Shinnick-Gallagher, P. (1988). Estrogen priming affects active membrane properties of medial amygdala neurons. *Brain Research, 440,* 380–385.

Schleifer, S. J., Keller, S. E., Canerino, M., Thornton, J. C., Stein, M. (1983). Suppression of lymphocyte stimulation following bereavement. *Journal of the American Medical Association, 250,* 374–377.

Schmalz, J. (1992, December 20). Covering AIDS and living it: A reporter's testimony. *The New York Times,* pp. E1, E5.

Schmeck, H. M., Jr. (1977, March 11). Cancer therapy role seen for marijuana. *The New York Times,* p. A11.

Schmemann, S. (1992, May 15). Gorbachev's tux? Moscow could care less. *The New York Times,* p. A3.

Schmidt, N., & Sermat, V. (1983). Measuring loneliness in different relationships. *Journal of Personality and Social Psychology, 44,* 1038–1047.

Schmidt, W. E. (1993, January 10). Hope is expressed on Shetland spill. *The New York Times,* p. L7.

Schmitt, E. (1992, November 12). Challenging the military. *The New York Times,* pp. A1, A22.

Schneider, D. J. (1973). Implicit personality theory: A review. *Psychological Bulletin, 79,* 294–309.

Schneider, D. J., & Blankmeyer, B. L. (1983). Prototype salience and implicit personality theories. *Journal of Personality and Social Psychology, 38,* 841–856.

Schneider, E. L. (Ed.) (1978). *The aging reproductive system.* New York: Raven Press.

Schneier, C. E. (1974). Behavior modification in management: A review and critique. *Academy of Management Journal, 17,* 528–548.

Schnellmann, J., & Gibbons, J. L. (1984, August). *The perception by women and minorities of trivial discriminatory actions in the classroom.* Paper presented at the annual meeting of the American Psychological Association, Toronto, Ontario, Canada.

Schoemer, K. (1992, March 12). Twisted humor of children's cartoon gains a cult [Review]. *The New York Times,* pp. C17, C24.

Schoen, R. (1992). First unions and the stability of first marriages. *Journal of Marriage and the Family, 54,* 281–284.

Schroeder, D. H., & Costa, P. T., Jr. (1984). Influence of life events stress on physical illness: Substantive effects or methodological flaws. *Journal of Personality and Social Psychology, 46,* 853–863.

Schultz, D. P. (1969). *A history of modern psychology.* New York: Academic Press.

Schuman, H., Steeh, C., & Bobo, L. (1985). *Racial attitudes in America: Trends and interpretations.* Cambridge, MA: Harvard University Press.

Schwartz, F. N. (1989, January/February). Management women and the new facts of life. *Harvard Business Review,* 65–76.

Schwartz, G. E. (1982). Testing the biopsychosocial model: The ultimate challenge facing behavioral medicine? *Journal of Consulting and Clinical Psychology, 50,* 1040–1052.

Schwartz, M., & Masters, W. H. (1984). The Masters and Johnson treatment program for dissatisfied homosexual men. *American Journal of Psychiatry, 141,* 173–181.

Scott, A. I. F. (1989). Which depressed patients will respond to electroconvulsive therapy? The search for biological predictors of recovery. *British Journal of Psychiatry, 154,* 8–17.

Scott, W. E. (1976). The effects of extrinsic rewards on "intrinsic motivation." *Organizational Behavior and Human Performance, 15,* 117–129.

Searcy, E., & Eisenberg, N. (1992). Defensiveness in response to aid from a sibling. *Journal of Personality and Social Psychology, 62,* 422–433.

Sears, R. R., Maccoby, E. E., & Levin, H. (1957). *Patterns of child rearing.* New York: Harper & Row.

Seefeldt, V. (1992, April 26). Cited in G. Kolata. A parents' guide to kids' sports. *The New York Times Magazine,* Part 2, pp. 12–15, 40, 44, 46.

Seeman, T. E., Kaplan, G. A., Knudsen, L., Cohen, R., & Guralnik, J. (1987). Social network ties and mortality among the elderly in the Alameda County study. *American Journal of Epidemiology, 126,* 714–723.

Seligman, M. E. P. (1975). *Helplessness: On depression, development, and death.* San Francisco: Freeman.

Selkin, J. (1992, April 29). Cited in J. E. Brody. How to outwit a rapist: rehearse. *The New York Times,* p. C13.

Selye, H. (1956). *The stress of life.* New York: McGraw-Hill.

Selye, H. (1974). *Stress without distress.* New York: Lippincott.

Selye, H. (1976). *The stress of life* (2nd edition). New York: Mc-Graw-Hill.

Selye, H. (1980). The stress concept today. In I. L. Kutash et al. (Eds.), *Handbook on stress and anxiety: Contemporary knowledge, theory, and treatment.* San Francisco: Jossey-Bass.

Serbin, L. A., & Sprafkin, C. (1986). The salience of gender and the process of sex-typing in three-to-seven-year-old children. *Child Development, 57,* 1188–1209.

Serby, M., Larson, P., & Kalkstein, D. (1991). The nature and course of olfactory deficits in Alzheimer's disease. *American Journal of Psychiatry, 148,* 781–782.

Shaman, D. (1992, April 12). Seeking remedies for indoor-air-pollution problems. *The New York Times,* p. NJR13.

Shanab, M. E., & Yahya, K. A. (1977). A behavioral study of obedience in children. *Journal of Personality and Social Psychology, 35,* 530–536.

Shapiro, F. (1989a). Eye movement desensitization: A new treatment for the post traumatic stress disorder. *Journal of Behavior Therapy and Experimental Psychiatry, 20,* 211–217.

Shapiro, F. (1989b). Efficacy of the eye movement desensitization procedure in the treatment of traumatic memories. *Journal of Traumatic Stress, 2,* 199–223.

Shapiro, F. (1990). Eye movement desensitization procedure: A new treatment for anxiety and related traumata. *California Psychologist, 33,* No. 3.

Shapiro, F. (1991). Eye movement desensitization and reprocessing procedure. *Behavior Therapist, 14,* 133–135.

Shapiro, H. I. (1988). *The new birth-control book: A complete guide for women and men.* Englewood Cliffs, NJ: Prentice-Hall.

Sheehy, G. (1976). *Passages.* Toronto: Bantam.

Shekelle, R. B., Hulley, S. B., Neaton, J. D., Billings, J. H., Borhani, N. O., Gerace, T. A., Jacobs, D. R., Lasser, N. L., Mittlemark, M. B., & Stamler, J. (1985). The MRFIT behavior pattern study: II. Type A behavior and incidence of coronary heart disease. *American Journal of Epidemiology, 122,* 559–570.

Shelton, R. (1968). *Kloran.* Birmingham, AL: Imperial Press.

Sherman, G. F., Galaburda, A. M., & Geschwind, N. (1985). Cortical anomalies in brains of New Zealand mice: A neuropathologic model of dyslexia. *Proceedings of the National Academy of Sciences, USA, 82,* 8072–8074.

Sherrod, D. (1989). The influence of gender on same-sex friendships. In C. Hendrick (Ed.), *Review of personality and social psychology: Vol. 10. Close relationships.* Newbury Park, CA: Sage.

Shinn, M., Lehmann, S., & Wong, N. W. (1984). Social interaction and social support. *Journal of Social Issues, 40,* 55–76.

Shinn, M. & Weitzman, B. C. (1990). Research on homelessness: An introduction. *Journal of Social Issues, 46,* 1–12.

Shontz, F. C. (1975). *The psychological aspects of physical illness and disability.* New York: Macmillan.

Shore, J. H., Tatum, E. L., & Vollmer, W. M. (1986). Psychiatric reactions to disaster: The Mount St. Helen experience. *American Journal of Psychiatry, 143,* 590–595.

Shulruff, L. I. (1992, October 23). When a child-custody tug-of-war is on religion. *The New York Times,* p. B16.

Shumaker, S. A., & Brownell, A. (1984). Toward a theory of social support: Closing conceptual gaps. *Journal of Social Issues, 40,* 11–36.

Sidanius, J., Cling, B. J., & Pratto, F. (1991). Ranking and linking as a function of sex and gender role attitudes. *Journal of Social Issues, 47,* 131–149.

Siegel, B. (1991, May). A capsule of hope. *Longevity.*

Siegel, J. M. (1990). Stressful life events and use of physician services among the elderly: The moderating role of pet ownership. *Journal of Personality and Social Psychology, 58,* 1081–1086.

Siegel, J. M., & Kuykendall, D. H. (1990). Loss, widowhood, and psychological distress among the elderly. *Journal of Consulting and Clinical Psychology, 58,* 519–524.

Siegel, J. M., et al. (1990). Reactions to sexual assault: A community study. *Journal of Interpersonal Violence, 5,* 229–246.

Silverblatt, I. (1988). Women in states. *Annual Review of Anthropology, 17,* 427–460.

Simkins, L., et al. (1990). Characteristics predictive of child sex abusers' response to treatment: An exploratory study. *Journal of Psychology & Human Sexuality, 3,* 19–55.

Sims, C. (1992, November 29). Under siege: Liquor's inner-city pipeline. *The New York Times,* pp. F1, F5.

Sims, H. P., & Manz, C. C. (1984). Observing leader verbal behavior: Toward reciprocal determinism in leadership theory. *Journal of Applied Psychology, 69,* 222–232.

Sinai, A. (1992, May 5). Cited in Stevens, W. K. Humanity confronts its handiwork: An altered planet. *The New York Times,* pp. C1, C6-C7.

Singer, J. L. (1990). *Use TV to your child's advantage.* New York: Acropolis Press.

Singer, J. L., Singer, D. G., Desmond, R., Hirsch, B., Nicol, A. (1988). Family mediation and children's cognition, aggression, and comprehension of television: A longitudinal study. *Journal of Applied Developmental Psychology, 9,* 329–347.

Singervalt, M. (1992, September 20). Cited in L. Lynwander. For gay youths, a "safe space." *The New York Times,* pp. NJ1, NJ9.

Skinner, B. F. (1938). *The behavior of organisms.* New York: Appleton-Century-Crofts.

Skinner, B. F. (1948). *Walden Two.* New York: Macmillan.

Skinner, B. F. (1950). Are theories of learning necessary? *Psychological Review, 57,* 193–216.

Skinner, B. F. (1953). *Science and human behavior.* New York: Macmillan.

Skinner, B. F. (1967). Autobiography. In E. G. Boring and G. Lindzey (Eds.), *A history of psychology in autobiography, Vol. 5* (pp. 387–413). New York: Appleton-Century-Crofts.

Skov, P., et al. (1989). Influence of personal characteristics, job-related factors, and psychosocial factors on the sick building syndrome. *Scandinavian Journal of Work Environment Health, 15,* 286–295.

Slade, P. D. (1985). A review of body-image studies in anorexia nervosa and bulimia nervosa. *Journal of Psychiatric Research, 19,* 255–265.

Slap, G. B., Vorters, D. F., Khalid, N., Margulies, S. R., & Forke, C. M. (1992). Adolescent suicide attempters: Do physicians recognize them? *Journal of Adolescent Health, 13,* 286–292.

Slavin, S. L., & Pradt, M. S. (1982). *The Einstein syndrome: Corporate anti-Semitism in America today.* Lanham, MD: University Press of America.

Sloane, L. (1992, May 30). A study suggests ways to eliminate playground hazards. *The New York Times,* p. L48.

Smith, B. D., Meyers, M., & Kline, R. (1989). Parietal processing of affect and cognition: Cerebral organization in strongly lateralized left-handed subjects. *Biological Psychology, 29,* 11–26.

Smith, B. D., Meyers, M., Kline, R., & Bozman, A. (1987). Hemispheric asymmetry and emotion: Lateralized parietal processing of affect and cognition. *Biological Psychology, 25,* 11–26.

Smith, C., & Lapp, L. (1991). Increases in number of REMS and REM density in humans following an intensive learning period. *Sleep, 14,* 325–330.

Smith, J., Mercy, J., & Rosenberg, M. (1986). Suicide and homicide among Hispanics in the Southwest. *Public Health Reports, 101,* 265–270.

Smith, R. M., & Smith, C. W. (1981). Childrearing and single-parent fathers. *Family Relations, 30,* 411–417.

Smith, S. (1983). Interactions between pet dog and family members: An ethological study. In A. K. Katcher & A. M. Beck (Eds.), *New perspectives on our lives with companion animals* (pp. 29–36). Philadelphia: University of Pennsylvania Press.

Smither, R., & Rodriguez-Giegling, M. (1979). Marginality, modernity, and anxiety in Indo-Chinese refugees. *Journal of Cross-Cultural Psychology, 10,* 469–477.

Smither, R. D. (1988). *The psychology of work and human performance.* New York: Harper & Row.

Smollar, J., & Youniss, J. (1985). Adolescent self-concept development. In R. L. Leahy (Ed.), *The development of the self.* Orlando, FL: Academic Press.

Snyder, C. R., & Fromkin, H. L. (1980). *Uniqueness: The human pursuit of difference.* New York: Plenum.

Snyder, M. (1984). When belief creates reality. *Advances in Experimental Social Psychology, 18,* 247–305.

Snyder, S. H. (1970, December 13). What we have forgotten about pot. *The New York Times Magazine,* pp. 27, 121, 124, 130.

Sobel, D. (1990, August 20). B. F. Skinner, the champion of behaviorism, is dead at 86. *The New York Times,* pp. A1, B10.

Soder, D. (1992, May 24). Cited in P. Becker. Power pets find space in the executive suite. *The New York Times,* p. F21.

Solomon, G. F. (1989, June). Cited in Hall, S. S. A molecular code links emotions, mind and health. *Smithsonian,* pp. 62–71.

Solomon, G. F., Amkraut, A., & Rubin, R. T. (1985). Stress, hormones, neuroregulation and immunity. In S. R. Burchfield (Ed.), *Stress: Psychological and physiological interactions.* New York: Hemisphere.

Somers, V. K., Dyken, M. E., Mark, A. L., & Abboud, F. M. (1993). Sympathetic-nerve activity during sleep in normal subjects. *New England Journal of Medicine, 328,* 303–307.

Sonestein, F. L., Pleck, J. H., & Ku, L. C. (1991). Levels of sexual activity among adolescent males in the United States. *Family Planning Perspectives, 23,* 162–167.

Sorenson, R. C. (1973). *Adolescent sexuality in contemporary America: Personal values and sexual behavior, ages thirteen to nineteen.* New York: World.

Spanos, N. P., Weekes, J. R., & Bertrand, L. D. (1985). Multiple personality: A social psychological perspective. *Journal of Abnormal Psychology, 93,* 277–284.

Spencer, H. (1892). *The principles of sociology* (Vol. 2). New York: D. Appleton.

Spielberger, C. D., & Frank, R. G. (1992). Injury control: A promising field for psychologists. *American Psychologist, 47,* 1029–1030.

Spitz, R. A. (1965). *The first year of life: A psychoanalytic study of normal and deviant object relations.* New York: International Universities Press.

Spitze, G. (1988). Women's employment and family relations: A review. *Journal of Marriage and the Family, 50,* 595–618.

Spitzer, P. G., & Weiner, N. J. (1989). Transmission of HIV infection from a woman to a man by oral sex. *Journal of the American Medical Association, 320,* 251.

Spitzer, R. L. (1985). DSM-III and the politics-science dichotomy syndrome: A response to Thomas E. Schacht's "DSM-II and the politics of truth." *American Psychologist, 40,* 522–526.

Spranger, S. A., Fahrenbach, W. H., & Bethea, C. L. (1991). Steroid action on estrogen and progestin receptors in monkey pituitary cell cultures. *Endocrinology, 128,* 1907–1917.

Sprecher, S. (1989). Premarital sexual standards for different categories of individuals. *Journal of Sex Research, 26,* 232–248.

Stahilevitz, M., Strahilevitz, A., & Miller, J. (1979). Air pollution and the admission rate of psychiatric patients. *American Journal of Psychiatry, 136,* 205–207.

Stampfl, T. G., & Levis, D. J. (1967). Essentials of implosive therapy: A learning theory-based psychodynamic behavioral therapy. *Journal of Abnormal Psychology, 72,* 496–503.

Stanford doctor to get training in sensitivity. (1992, March 23). *The New York Times,* p. B7.

Stanley, S. M., & Markman, H. J. (1992). Assessing commitment in personal relationships. *Journal of Marriage and the Family, 54,* 595–608.

Starr, B. D., & Weiner, M. B. (1981). *The Starr-Weiner report on sex and sexuality in the mature years.* New York: Stein & Day.

Stecklis, H. D. (1993, March 17). Abandoned in the mist. *The New York Times,* p. A21.

Steffensmeier, D., & Steffensmeier, R. (1974). Sex differences in reactions to homosexuals: Research continuities and further developments. *Journal of Sex Research, 10,* 52–67.

Steger, M. A., Pierce, J. C., Steel, B. S., & Lovrich, N. P. (1989). Political culture, postmaterial values, and the new environmental paradigm. *Political Behavior, 11,* 233–254.

Stein, P. (1981). *Single life: Unmarried adults in social context.* New York: St. Martin's Press.

Steinberg, L. (1991). *You and your adolescent.* New York: Harper Perennial.

Steinhausen, H.-C., & Vollrath, M. (1992). Semantic differential for the assessment of body image and perception of personality in eating disordered patients. *International Journal of Eating Disorders, 12,* 83–91.

Steinhausen, H.-C., & Vollrath, M. (1993). The self-image of adolescent patients with eating disorders. *International Journal of Eating Disorders, 13,* 221–227.

Steketee, G., & Foa, E. B. (1985). Obsessive-compulsive disorder. In D. H. Barlow (Ed.), *Clinical handbook of psychological disorders* (pp. 69–144). New York: Guilford Press.

Steklis, H. D. (1993, March 17). Abandoned in the mist. *The New York Times,* p. A21.

Stephen, R., & Zweigenhaft, R. L. (1986). The effect on tipping of a waitress touching male and female customers. *The Journal of Social Psychology, 126,* 141–142.

Stern, P. C. (1992). What psychology knows about energy conservation. *American Psychologist, 47,* 1224–1232.

Sternberg, R. J. (1986). A triangular theory of love. *Psychological Review, 93,* 119–135.

Sternberg, R. J. (1987). Liking versus loving: A comparative evaluation of theories. *Psychological Bulletin, 102,* 331–345.

Sternberg, R. J. (1988a). *The triangle of love: Intimacy, passion, commitment.* New York: Basic Books.

Sternberg, R. J. (1988b). Triangulating love. In R. J. Sternberg & M. L. Barnes (Eds.), *The psychology of love.* New Haven: Yale University Press.

Sternberg, R. J., & Barnes, M. L. (1988). An introduction to the psychology of love. In R. J. Sternberg & M. L. Barnes (Eds.), *The psychology of love.* New Haven: Yale University Press.

Stets, J. E. (1991). Cohabiting and marital aggression: The role of social isolation. *Journal of Marriage and the Family, 53,* 669–680.

Stets, J. E., & Straus, M. A. (1989). The marriage license as a hitting license: A comparison of assaults in dating, cohabiting, and married couples. In M. A. Pirog-Good & J. E. Stets (Eds.), *Violence in dating relationships: Emerging social issues.* New York: Praeger.

Stevens, W. K. (1992, May 5). Humanity confronts its handiwork: An altered planet. *The New York Times,* pp. C1, C6-C7.

Stevenson, R. L. (1886). *The strange case of Dr. Jekyll and Mr. Hyde.*

Stewart, A. J., & Healy, Jr., J. M. (1986). The role of personality development and experience in shaping political commitment: An illustrative case. *Journal of Social Issues, 42,* 11–31.

Stokes, J. B. (1977). Comment on "Socially reinforced obsessing: Etiology of a disorder in a Christian Scientist." *Journal of Consulting and Clinical Psychology, 45,* 1071–1088.

Stoller, R. J. (1967). Transvestites' women. *American Journal of Psychiatry, 124,* 333–339.

Stone, A. A. (1987). Event content in a daily survey is differentially associated with concurrent mood. *Journal of Personality and Social Psychology, 52,* 56–58.

Stone, R. A., & Levine, A. G. (1986). Reactions to collective stress: Correlates of active citizen participation at Love Canal. *Prevention in Human Services, 4* (1985–1986 Fall/Winter), 153–177.

Stott, D. (1971). The child's hazards in utero. In J. G. Howells (Ed.), *Modern perspectives in international child psychiatry.* New York: Brunner-Mazel.

Strain, J. J., et al. (1991). Cost offset from a psychiatric consultation-liaison intervention with elderly hip fracture patients. *American Journal of Psychiatry, 148,* 1044–1049.

Strain, J. S. (1978). *Psychological interventions in medical practice.* New York: Appleton-Century-Crofts.

Straus, M. A., & Gelles, R. J. (1986). Societal change and change in family violence from 1975 to 1985 as revealed by two national surveys. *Journal of Marriage and the Family, 48,* 465–479.

Streissguth, A. P., Barr, H. M., Sampson, P. D., Darby, B. L., & Martin, D. C. (1989). IQ at age 4 in relation to maternal alcohol use and smoking during pregnancy. *Developmental pregnancy, 25,* 3–11.

Strong, M. (1992, March 22). 40 Chernobyls waiting to happen [Editorial]. *The New York Times,* p. E15.

Strube, M. J., & Barbour, L. S. (1983). Adjustment to threatening events: A theory of cognitive adaptation. *American Psychologist, 38,* 1161–1173.

Struckman-Johnson, C. (1988). Forced sex on dates: It happens to men, too. *The Journal of Sex Research, 24,* 234–241.

Stuart, R. B. (1978). *Act thin, stay thin.* New York: Norton.

Stuckey, M. F., McGhee, P. E., & Bell, N. J. (1982). Parent-child interaction: The influence of maternal employment. *Developmental Psychology, 18,* 636–644.

Student who stabbed teacher has a warning. (1992, June 23). *The New York Times,* p. A14.

Study finds students at small colleges drink more. (1992, September 20). *The New York Times,* p. L33.

Sturgis, E. T., & Adams, H. E. (1978). The right to treatment: Issues in the treatment of homosexuality. *Journal of Consulting and Clinical Psychology, 46,* 165–169.

Sudetic, C. (1993, July 6). This can't be Bosnia, there's too much laughing. *The New York Times,* p. A4.

Sue, D., & Sue, S. (1990). *Counseling the culturally different* (2nd ed.). New York: Wiley.

Sue, S. (1981). *Counseling the culturally different: Theory and practice.* New York: Wiley.

Sue, S. & Zane, N. (1987). The role of culture and cultural techniques in psychotherapy. *American Psychologist, 42,* 37–45.

Suinn, R. M. (1977). *Anxiety management training manual.* Fort Collins, CO: Rocky Mountain Behavioral Sciences Institute.

Suitor, J. J. (1991). Marital quality and satisfaction with the division of household labor across the family life cycle. *Journal of Marriage and the Family, 53,* 221–230.

Sulkowicz, K. (1992, March 19). Cited in Gordon, M. Analyzing the analyst's couch. *The New York Times,* pp. C1, C6.

Sullivan, E. V. (1977). A study of Kohlberg's structural theory of moral development: A critique of liberal science ideology. *Human Development, 20,* 352–376.

Sumner, B., Mintz, E., & Brown, P. (1986). Interviewing persons hospitalized with interpersonal violence-related injuries: A pilot study. In *Report of the Secretary's Task Force on Black and Minority Health* (Vol. 5, pp. 267–311). Washington, DC: U.S. Department of Health and Human Services.

Sunwanlert, S., & Coates, D. (1979). Epidemic koro in Thailand: Clinical and social aspects. *Transcultural Psychiatry Research Review, 16,* 64–66.

Super, D. E. (1957). *The psychology of careers.* New York: Harper & Row.

Super, D. E. (1985). Career and life development. In D. Brown & L. Brooks (Eds.), *Career choice and development.* San Francisco: Jossey-Bass.

Super, D. E. (1988). Vocational adjustment: Implementing a self-concept. *Career Development Quarterly, 36,* 351–357.

Super, D. E., & Hall, D. T. (1978). Career development: Exploration and planning. *Annual Review of Psychology, 29,* 333–372.

Suro, R. (1990, April 4). Refinery's neighbors count sorrows, and riches. *The New York Times,* p. A14.

Surra, C. A., & Longstreth, M. (1990). Similarity of outcomes, interdependence, and conflict in dating relationships. *Journal of Personality and Social Psychology, 59,* 501–516.

Swedo, S. E., Pietrini, P., Leonard, H. L., et al. (1992). Cerebral glucose metabolism in childhood-onset obsessive-compulsive disorder: Revisualization during pharmacotherapy. *Archives of General Psychiatry, 49,* 690–694.

Sweet, A. A., & Loizeaux, A. L. (1991). Behavioral and cognitive treatment methods: A critical comparative review. *Journal of Behavior Therapy and Experimental Psychiatry, 22,* 159–185.

Synodinos, N. E. (1988). Review and appraisal of subliminal perception within the context of signal detection theory. *Psychology & Marketing, 5,* 317–336.

Szasz, T. (1960). The myth of mental illness. *American Psychologist, 15,* 113–118.

Tafoya, T. (1992, December 6). Cited in E. Rosenthal. To a drumbeat of losses to AIDS, a rethinking of traditional grief. *The New York Times,* pp. A1, A32.

Tait, M., Padgett, M. Y., & Baldwin, T. T. (1989). Job and life satisfaction: A reevaluation of the strength of the relationship and gender effects as a function of the date of the study. *Journal of Applied Psychology, 74,* 502–507.

Tajfel, H. (1970). Experiments in intergroup discrimination. *Scientific American, 223,* 96–102.

Takanishi, R. (Guest Editor). (1993). Special issue: Adolescence. *American Psychologist, 48,* 85–216.

Takeuchi, D. T., Williams, D. R., & Adair, R. K. (1991). Economic stress in the family and children's emotional and behavioral problems. *Journal of Marriage and the Family, 53,* 1031–1041.

Tako, C. (1992, April 5). Quoted in Glaberson, W. A new twist on lost youth: The mall rats. *The New York Times,* pp. A1, A31.

Tane, L. D., & Treacy, M. E. (1984, April). Benefits that bend with employees' needs. *Nation's Business,* pp. 80–82.

Tanfer, K. (1987). Patterns of premarital cohabitation among never-married women in the United States. *Journal of Marriage and the Family, 49,* 483–497.

Tanford, S., & Penrod, S. (1984). Social influence model: A formal integration of research on majority and minority influence processes. *Psychological Bulletin, 95,* 189–225.

Tardiff, K., & Gross, E. (1986). Homicide in New York City. *Bulletin of the New York Academy of Medicine, 62,* 413–426.

Tashkin, D. P., Calvarese, B., & Simmons, M. (1978). Respiratory status of 75 chronic marijuana smokers: Comparison with matched controls. *American Review of Respiratory Disease, 117,* 261 (abstract).

Taub, J. M., & Berger, R. J. (1974). Diurnal variations in mood as asserted by self-report and verbal content analysis. *Journal of Psychiatric Research, 10,* 83–88.

Tavris, C., & Jayaratne, T. E. (1976, June). How happy is your marriage? What 75,000 wives say about their most intimate relationship. *Redbook,* pp. 90–92, 132, 134.

Tavris, C., & Sadd, S. (1977). *The Redbook report on female sexuality.* New York: Delacorte.

Taylor, B. (1992). *Rain forest.* New York: Dorling Kindersley.

Taylor, D. M. (1991). The social psychology of racial and cultural diversity: Issues of assimilation and multiculturalism. In A. G. Reynolds (Ed.), *Bilingualism.* Hillsdale, NJ: Erlbaum.

Taylor, J. (1992, August 13). Quoted in S. Mydans. Painting of heroic size shows Nixon to match. *The New York Times,* p. A16.

Taylor, S. E. (1981). Categorization approach to stereotyping. In D. L. Hamilton (Ed.), *Cognitive processes in stereotyping and intergroup behavior* (pp. 83–114). Hillsdale, NJ: Erlbaum.

Taylor, S. E. (1986). *Health psychology.* New York: Random House.

Teachman, J. D., & Polonko, K. A. (1990). Cohabitation and marital stability in the United States. *Social Forces, 69,* 207–220.

Teachman, J. D., Thomas, J., & Paasch, K. (1991). Legal status and the stability of coresidential unions. *Demography, 28,* 571–586.

Teen-agers and AIDS: The risk worsens. (1992, April 14). *The New York Times,* p. L3.

Terr, L. (1988). Anatomically correct dolls: Should they be used as a basis for expert testimony? *Journal of the American Academy of Child and Adolescent Psychiatry, 27,* 254–257.

Terry, D. (1992, May 3). Decades of rage created crucible of violence. *The New York Times,* A1, A24.

Tesser, A., & Campbell, J. (1983). Self-definition and self-evaluation maintenance. In J. Suls & A. Greenwald (Eds.), *Psychological perspectives on the self* (Vol 2, pp. 1–31). Hillsdale, NJ: Erlbaum.

Testa, M. A., Anderson, R. B., Nackley, J. F., et al. (1993). Quality of life and antihypertensive therapy in men: A comparison of captroril with enalapril. *New England Journal of Medicine, 328,* 907–913.

Texas set to execute first woman since 1863. (1992, June 21). *The New York Times,* p. A17.

The Death of Dr. Gunn [Editorial]. (1993, March 12). *The New York Times,* p. A28.

The experience at Occidental. (1992, April 12). *The New York Times,* p. F27.

The idea of coeducational fraternities is catching on in the northeast. (1990, April 8). *The New York Times,* p. 39.

The Rabbi at Sing Sing. (1992, April 22). *The New York Times,* p. B5.

Thoits, P. A. (1986). Social support as coping assistance. *Journal of Consulting and Clinical Psychology, 54,* 416–423.

Thomas, K., & Trebbe, A. (1992, October 21). People. *USA Today,* p. 2D.

Thomas, T. L. (1992, April 10). Cited in CUNY students adjust expectations at job fair. *The New York Times,* pp. B1, B2.

Thompson, A. (1992, June 28). Post-riot L. A.'s gun-toting liberals. *The New York Times,* p. F23.

Thompson, J. K. (1990). *Body image disturbance: Assessment and treatment.* Elmsford, NY: Pergamon Press.

Thompson, J. K., & Spana, R. E. (1988). The adjustable light beam method for the assessment of size estimation accuracy: Description, psychometric, and normative data. *International Journal of Eating Disorders, 7,* 521–526.

Thompson, J. K., & Thompson, C. M. (1986). Body size distortion and self-esteem in asymptomatic, normal weight males and females. *International Journal of Eating Disorders, 5,* 1061–1068.

Thomson, E., & Colella, U. (1992). Cohabitation and marital stability: Quality or commitment? *Journal of Marriage and the Family, 54,* 259–267.

Thornburg, H. D., & Aras, Z. (1986). Physical characteristics of developing adolescents. *Journal of Adolescent Research, 1,* 47–78.

Thorndike, E. L. (1898). Animal intelligence. *Psychological Review Monograph Supplement, 2* (4, Whole No. 8).

Thorndike, E. L. (1905). *The elements of psychology.* New York: Seiler.

Thorndike, E. L. (1931). *Human learning.* New York: Appleton-Century-Crofts.

Thorne, F. C. (1973). Eclectic psychotherapy. In R. Corsini (Ed.), *Current psychotherapies.* Itasca, IL: Peacock.

Thornton, A., & Freedman, D. (1982). Changing attitudes toward marriage and single life. *Family Planning Perspectives, 14,* 297–303.

Three Feathers Associates. (1987, January/February). *Indian Child Welfare Network,* p. 1.

Three Feathers Associates. (1989, August/September). The status of American Indian families. *Indian Child Welfare Digest,* pp. 11–12.

Tien, A. Y., & Anthony, J. C. (1990). Epidemiological analysis of alcohol and drug use as risk factors for psychotic experiences. *Journal of Nervous and Mental Disease, 178,* 473–480.

Toll of American AIDS orphans put at 80,000 by end of decade. (1992, December 23). *The New York Times,* p. B6.

Totman, R., Kiff, J., Reed, S. E., & Craig, J. W. (1980). Predicting experimental colds in volunteers from different measures of recent life stress. *Journal of Psychosomatic Research, 24,* 155–163.

Toufexis, A., Garcia, C., & Kalb, B. (1986, January 20). Dieting: The losing game. *Time,* pp. 54–60.

Trainer, F. E. (1977). A critical analysis of Kohlberg's contributions to the study of moral thought. *Journal for the Theory of Social Behavior, 7,* 41–63.

Travis, C. B., McLean, B. E., & Ribar, C. (1989). *Environmental toxins: Psychological, behavioral, and sociocultural aspects, 1973–1989.* Washington, DC: American Psychological Association.

Treaster, J. B. (1992, June 14). 20 years of war on drugs, and no victory yet. *The New York Times,* p. E7.

Treaster, J. B. (1993a, February 16). For children of cocaine, fresh reasons for hope. *The New York Times,* pp. A1, B4.

Treaster, J. B. (1993b, April 4). Drug use by younger teen-agers appears to rise, counter to trend. *The New York Times,* pp. A1, B8.

Trotter, R. (1983). *Alcohol, drug abuse, and mental health problems of the homeless: Proceedings of a roundtable.* Rockville, MD: Alcohol, Drug Abuse and Mental Health Administration.

Trussel, J., Rodriguez, G., & Vaughan, B. (1992). Union dissolution in Sweden. In J. Trussell, R. Hankinson, & J. Tilton (Eds.), *Demographic applications of event history analysis* (pp. 38–60). Oxford: Clarendon Press.

Tryer, P. (1988). What's wrong with DSM-III personality disorders? *Journal of Personality Disorders, 2,* 281–291.

Trzcinski, E., & Finn-Stevenson, M. (1991). A response to arguments against mandated parental leave: Findings from the Connecticut Survey of Parental Leave Policies. *Journal of Marriage and the Family, 53,* 445–460.

Tseng, W. S., et al. (1988). A sociocultural study of koro epidemic in Guangdong, China. *American Journal of Psychiatry, 145,* 1538–1543.

Tseng, W. S., et al. (1992). Koro epidemics in Guangdong, China: A questionnaire survey. *The Journal of Nervous and Mental Disease, 180,* 117–123.

Tseng, W. S., & Hsu, J. (1970). Chinese culture, personality formation and mental illness. *International Journal of Psychiatry, 16,* 5–14.

Tsim, K. W. K., Pak, R. C. K., & Cheng, C. H. K. (1985). Prolactin receptor in rat liver: Sex differences in estrogenic stimulation and imprinting of the responsiveness to estrogen by neonatal androgen in male rats. *Molecular and Cellular Endocrinology, 40,* 99–105.

Tucker, M. (1992, June 7). Cited in S. Greenhouse. The coming crisis of the American work force. *The New York Times,* p. F14.

Tucker, R. K., Marvin, M. G., & Vivian, B. (1991). What constitutes a romantic act? An empirical study. *Psychological Reports, 69,* 651–654.

Tupes, E. C., & Christal, R. E. (1961). *Recurrent personality factors based on trait ratings* (USAF ASD Tech. Rep. No. 61–97). Lackland Air Force Base, TX: U.S. Air Force.

Turiel, E. (1974). Conflict and transition in adolescent moral development. *Child Development, 45,* 14–29.

Turke, P. W., & Betzig, L. L. (1985). Those who can do: Wealth, status, and reproductive success on Ifaluk. *Ethology and Sociobiology, 6,* 79–87.

Turnbull, C. M. (1965). *Wayward servants: The two worlds of the African Pygmies.* Westport, Connecticut.

Turner, B. L., II, Kates, R. W., & Clark, W. C. (1990). *The earth as transformed by human action.* New York: Cambridge University Press.

Turner, S. M., & Beidel, D. C. (1989). Social phobia: Clinical syndrome, diagnosis, and comorbidity. *Clinical Psychology Review, 9,* 3–18.

Turner, S. M., Beidel, D. C., Dancu, C. V., & Keys, D. J. (1986). Psychopathology of social phobia and comparison to avoidant personality disorder. *Journal of Abnormal Psychology, 95,* 389–394.

Turner-Henson, A., Holaday, B., & Swan, J. H. (1992). When parenting becomes caregiving: Caring for the chronically ill child. *Family and Community Health, 15* (2), 19–30.

Twenty percent in U.S. hold bias against jews. (1992, November 22). *The New York Times,* p. L34.

Tyler, F. (1992, April 13). Ethnic validity: A model for families on uncharted seas. In R. A. Javier (Chair), *Our families in crisis: A multicultural and multiethnic perspective.* Second annual conference at St. John's University, Jamaica, NY.

Tyler, P. E. (1992, May 4). Soviets' secret nuclear dumping raises fears for arctic waters. *The New York Times,* pp. A1, A8.

Uehling, M. D. (1992, October 4). Beauty and the bleak: Visiting damaged landscapes can sharpen appreciation of what is still untouched. *The New York Times,* Section 5, p. 35.

Ullman, S. E., & Knight, R. A. (1991). A multivariate model for predicting rape and physical injury outcomes during sexual assaults. *Journal of Consulting and Clinical Psychology, 59,* 724–731.

Uncle Sam's groceries: how dietary recommendations have changed. (1992, May 3). *The New York Times,* p. E2.

Undersea police protect fragile reef off florida. (1992, June 16). *The New York Times,* p. A6.

Unger, R. K. (1979). Toward a redefinition of sex and gender. *American Psychologist, 34,* 1085–1094.

Unger, R. K., Hilderbrand, M., & Madar, T. (1982). Physical attractiveness and assumptions about social deviance: Some sex-by-sex comparisons. *Personality and Social Psychology Bulletin, 8,* 293–301.

U. S. Bureau of the Census. (1991, March). The Hispanic population in the United States. *Current Population Reports,* Series P-20, No. 449. Washington, DC: U.S. Government Printing Office.

U. S. Congress, Office of Technology Assessment. (1988). *Infertility: Medical and social choices* (OTA-BA-358). Washington, DC: U. S. Government Printing Office.

US Consumer Product Safety Commission. (1980). *Baby walkers: Fact sheet 66 revised.* Washington, DC: Author.

U.S. Department of Justice. (1991). *Criminal victimization, 1990* (Special Report No. NCJ-122743). Washington, DC: Bureau of Justice Statistics.

U.S. health study to involve 160,000 women at 16 centers. (1993, March 31). *The New York Times,* p. A21.

United States Government. (1974). *Marihuana-hashish epidemic and its impact on the United States security.* Washington, DC: U.S. Government Printing Office.

United States Government. (1975). *Marihuana and health: Sixth annual report to the U.S. Congress from the Secretary of Health, Education, and Welfare* (Publication No. (ADM) 77-443). Washington, DC: U.S. Government Printing Office.

U.S. Merit Systems Protection Board. (1981). *Sexual harassment in the federal workplace: Is it a problem?* Washington, DC: Office of Merit Systems Review and Studies.

Utian, W. H. (1992, May 19). Cited in J. E. Brody. Can drugs "treat" menopause? Amid doubt, women must decide. *The New York Times,* pp. C1, C8.

Uzgiris, I. C. (1984). Imitation in infancy: Its interpersonal aspects. In M. Perlmutter (Ed.), *Minnesota Symposium on Child Psychology* (Vol. 17, pp. 1–32). Hillsdale, NJ: Erlbaum.

Vaillant, G. E. (1977). *Adaptation to life.* Boston: Little, Brown.

Vance, C. (1984). *Pleasure and danger: Exploring female sexuality.* London: Routledge & Kegan Paul.

Vandenberg, B. (1978). Play and development from an ethological perspective. *American Psychologist, 33,* 724–738.

Van den Bergh, B. R. H., Mulder, E. J. H., Visser, G. H. A., Poelmann-Weesjes, G., Bekedam, D. J., & Prechtl, H. F. R. (1989). The effect of (induced) maternal emotions on fetal behaviour: A controlled study. *Early Human Development, 19,* 9–19.

Van Italie, T. B. (1979). Obesity: Adverse effects on health and longevity. *American Journal of Clinical Nutrition, 32,* 2723–2733.

Van Liere, K. D., & Dunlap, R. E. (1981). Environmental concern: Does it make a difference how it's measured? *Environment and Behavior, 13,* 651–676.

Van Wyk, P. H., & Geist, C. S. (1984). Psychosocial development of heterosexual, bisexual, and homosexual behavior. *Archives of Sexual Behavior, 13,* 505–544.

Verbrugge, L. (1979). Marital status and health. *Journal of Marriage and the Family, 41,* 267–285.

Verderber, K. S., & Verderber, R. F. (1989). *Inter-act: Using interpersonal communication skills* (2nd ed.). Belmont, CA: Wadsworth.

Verhovek, S. H. (1990, March 23). Albany tale: Commissioner to Knishener. *The New York Times,* pp. B1, B3.

Verhovek, S. H. (1993, April 20). Scores die as cult compound is set afire after F.B.I. sends in tanks with tear gas. *The New York Times,* pp. A1, A20.

Vice President calls corporation wrong for selling rap song. (1992, June 20). *The New York Times,* p. L9.

Volkman, E. (1982). *A legacy of hate: Anti-Semitism in America.* New York: Franklin Watts.

Von Korff, M., Ormel, J., Katon, W., & Lin, E. H. B. (1992). Disability and depression among high utilizers of health care: A longitudinal analysis. *Archives of General Psychiatry, 49,* 91–100.

Vroom, V. H. (1964). *Work and motivation.* New York: Wiley.

Wachter, R. M. (1992, April 7). Cited in L. Belkin. Fear of disease changing how doctors work. *The New York Times,* pp. A1, B2.

Wadden, T. A., Foster, G. D., Letizia, K. A., & Stunkard, A. J. (1992). A multicenter evaluation of a proprietary weight reduction program for the treatment of marked obesity. *Archives of Internal Medicine, 152,* 961–966.

Waelder, R. (1940). Cited in G. Watson (Chair), Areas of agreement in psychotherapy: A symposium. *American Journal of Orthopsychiatry, 10,* 698–709.

Wagenheim, J. (1990, September/October). The secret life of men. *New Age Journal,* pp. 40–45.

Waigandt, A., et al. (1990). The impact of sexual assault on physical health status. *Journal of Traumatic Stress, 3,* 93–102.

Wald, M. L. (1992a, September 20). As nuclear plants close, costs don't shut down. *The New York Times,* p. E18.

Wald, M. L. (1992b, September 23). Shoreham's nuclear fuel may be headed abroad. *The New York Times,* p. B5.

Wald, M. L. (1992c, October 3). Nuclear plants held hostage to old fuel. *The New York Times,* p. L6.

Wald, M. L. (1992d, July 30). Vital gauge in reactor found prone to error. *The New York Times,* pp. A14.

Wald, M. L. (1993, March 21). Nuclear plants said to be vulnerable to bombings. *The New York Times,* p. 21.

Walk, R. D. (1966). The development of depth perception in animals and human infants. *Monographs of the Society for Research in Child Development, 31,* 82–108.

Walk, R. D. (1969). Two types of depth discrimination by the human infant with five inches of visual depth. *Psychonomic Science, 14,* 253–254.

Walk, R. D., & Gibson, E. J. (1961). A comparative and analytical study of visual depth perception. *Psychological Monographs, 75,* No. 15.

Walker, L. E. (1979). *The battered woman.* New York: Harper & Row.

Walker-Andrews, A. (1988). Infants' perception of the affordances of expressive behaviors. In C. Rovee-Collier (Ed.), *Advances in infancy research* (Vol. 5) (pp. 173–221). Norwood, NJ: Ablex.

Wallach, M. A., & Wallach, L. (1983). *Psychology's sanction for selfishness: The error of egoism in theory and therapy.* San Francisco: W. H. Freeman.

Wallerstein, J. S. (1991). The long-term effects of divorce on children: A review. *Journal of the American Academy of Child and Adolescent Psychiatry, 30,* 349–360.

Wallston, B. S., Alagna, S. W., DeVellis, B. M., & DeVellis, R. F. (1983). Social support and physical health. *Health Psychology, 2,* 367–391.

Walster, E., & Walster, G. W. (1978). *A new look at love.* Reading, MA: Addison-Wesley.

Walters, W. A. W. (1982). Cloning, ectogenesis, and hybrids: Things to come? In W. A. W. Walters & P. Singer (Eds.), *Test-tube babies.* Melbourne: Oxford University Press.

Wanous, J. P., & Zwany, A. (1977). A cross-sectional test of need hierarchy theory. *Organizational Behavior and Human Performance, 18,* 78–97.

Ward, R., Logan, J., & Spitze, G. (1992). The influence of parent and child needs on coresidence in middle and later life. *Journal of Marriage and the Family, 54,* 209–221.

Washington, J. R. (1970). *Marriage in black and white.* Boston: Beacon Press.

Waterman, J., & Lusk, R. (1986). Scope of the problem. In K. Mac-Farlane et al. (Eds.), *Sexual abuse of young children: Evaluation and treatment* (pp. 3–14). New York: Guilford.

Watson, D. (1982). The actor and the observer: How are their perceptions of causality divergent? *Psychological Bulletin, 92,* 682–700.

Watson, J. B. (1913). Psychology as the behaviorist views it. *Psychological Review, 20,* 158–177.

Watson, R. I. (1963). *The great psychologists from Aristotle to Freud.* Philadelphia: J. B. Lippincott.

Weaver, C. (1980). Job satisfaction in the United States in the 1970s. *Journal of Applied Psychology, 65,* 364–368.

Webb, D. (1992, August 5). Children need more calcium, a study suggests. *The New York Times,* p. C4.

Webb, D. (1993, January 13). Fat in the diet: The myths die hard. *The New York Times,* p. C4.

Webb, E. J., Campbell, D. T., Schwartz, R. D., & Sechrest, L. (1966). *Unobtrusive measures: Nonreactive research in the social sciences.* Chicago: Rand McNally.

Webb, W. (Ed.). (1982). *Biological rhythms, sleep, and performance* (pp. 87–110). Chichester, England: Wiley.

Webb, W., & Campbell, S. S. (1983). Relationships in sleep characteristics of identical and fraternal twins. *Archives of General Psychiatry, 40,* 1093–1095.

Wehr, T. A., Skwerer, R. G., Jacobsen, F. M., Sack, D. A., Rosenthal, N. E. (1987). Eye versus skin phototherapy of seasonal affective disorder. *American Journal of Psychiatry, 144,* 753–757.

Weinberger, M., Hiner, E. L., & Tierney, W. M. (1987). In support of hassles as a measure of stress in predicting health outcomes. *Journal of Behavioral Medicine, 10,* 19–31.

Weiner, B. (1972). *Theories of motivation.* Chicago: Markham/Rand McNally.

Weiner, B. (1974). *Cognitive views of human motivation.* New York: Academic Press.

Weiner, R. D., & Coffey, C. E. (1988). Indications for use of electroconvulsive therapy. In A. J. Frances & R. E. Hales (Eds.), *American Psychiatric Press review of psychiatry* (Vol. 7). Washington, DC: American Psychiatric Press.

Weis, J. S. (1992). Undergraduate environmental science report. *Environment, Science and Technology, 26,* 1296–1297.

Weisheit, R. A. (1990). Domestic marijuana growers: Mainstreaming deviance. *Deviant Behavior, 11,* 107–129.

Weisman, S. R. (1992a, April 27). How do Japan's students do it? They cram. *The New York Times,* pp. A1, A8.

Weisman, S. R. (1992b, March 17). Landmark harassment case in Japan. *The New York Times,* p. A3.

Weiss, B. (1983). Behavioral toxicology and environmental health science. *American Psychologist, 38,* 1174–1187.

Weiss, M., & Mirin, S. M. (1987). *Cocaine.* Washington, DC: American Psychiatric Press.

Weissberg, M., Berentsen, M., Cote, A., Cravey, B., & Heath, K. (1982). An assessment of the personal, career, and academic needs of undergraduate students. *Journal of College Student Personnel, 23,* 115–122.

Welch, E. (1992, April 29). Cited in J. E. Brody. How to outwit a rapist: rehearse. *The New York Times,* p. C13.

Wells, L. E., & Markwell, G. (1976). *Self-esteem.* Beverly Hills, Ca: Sage.

West, C. (1993). *Race matters.* New York: Beacon Press.

Westen, D. (1985). *Self and society: Narcissism, collectivism, and the development of morals.* NY: Cambridge University Press.

Westman, J. C. (Ed.). (1973). *Individual differences in children.* New York: Wiley.

Wetherington, E., & Kessler, R. C. (1986). Perceived support, received support and adjustment to stressful life events. *Journal of Health and Social Behavior, 27,* 78–89.

Whelan, E. M., & Stare, F. J. (1990). Nutrition. *Journal of the American Medical Association, 263,* 2661–2663.

Wherry, R. J., & South, J. C. (1977). A worker motivation scale. *Personnel Psychology, 30,* 613–636.

White, J., & Parham, T. (1990). *The psychology of Blacks.* Englewood Cliffs, NJ: Prentice-Hall.

White, L. K., & Booth, A. (1985). The quality and stability of remarriages: The role of step-children. *American Sociological Review, 50,* 689–698.

White, L. K., & Riedmann, A. (1992). When the Brady Bunch grows up: Step/half- and fullsibling relationships in adulthood. *Journal of Marriage and the Family, 54,* 197–208.

White, S. H. (1965). Evidence for a hierarchical arrangement of learning processes. In L. P. Lipsitt & C. C. Spiker (Eds.), *Advances in child development and behavior* (Vol. 2) (pp. 187–220). New York: Academic Press.

Whitely, B. E., Jr. (1983). Sex role orientation and self-esteem: A critical meta-analysis. *Journal of Personality and Social Psychology, 44,* 765–788.

Whiting, B., & Edwards, O. P. (1988). *Children of different worlds.* Cambridge, MA: Harvard University Press.

Whitley, B. E., Jr., & Frieze, I. H. (1985). Children's causal attributions for success and failure in achievement settings: A meta-analysis. *Journal of Educational Psychology, 77,* 608–616.

Whitman, A. (1980, September 17). Jean Piaget dies in Geneva at 84. *The New York Times,* pp. A1, D27.

Whitney, C. R. (1992a, November 25). To be a Jew in Germany is to plead: End the hate. *The New York Times,* p. A6.

Whitney, C. R. (1992b, December 15). Russian carries on like the bad old days, then says it was all a ruse. *The New York Times,* A16.

Wichterich, C. (1988). From the struggle against "overpopulation" to the industrialization of human reproduction. *Reproductive and Genetic Engineering, 1,* 21–30.

Wicker, A. W. (1979). *An introduction to ecological psychology.* Pacific Grove, CA: Brooks/Cole.

Widiger, T. A., Frances, A. J., Pincus, H. A., & Davis, W. W. (1990). DSM-IV literature reviews: Rationale, process, and limitations. *Journal of Psychopathology and Behavioral Assessment, 12,* 189–202.

Widiger, T. A., Frances, A. J., Pincus, H. A., Davis, W. W., & First, M. B. (1991). Toward an empirical classification for the DSM-IV. *Journal of Abnormal Psychology, 100,* 280–288.

Wiener, L. S., & Siegel, K. (1990). Social workers' comfort in providing service to AIDS patients. *Social Work, 35,* 18–25.

Wiggins, J. S. (1979). A psychological taxonomy of trait-descriptive terms: The interpersonal domain. *Journal of Personality and Social Psychology, 37,* 395–412.

Wilbur, C. B. (1986). Psychoanalysis and multiple personality disorder. In B. G. Braun (Ed.), *Treatment of multiple personality disorder.* Washington, DC: American Psychiatric Press.

Wilford, J. N. (1992, March 24). Letters to a supporter record Einstein's search for proof. *The New York Times,* pp. C1, C10.

Wilkerson, I. (1992, September 4). Hurricane haunts children long after winds have died. *The New York Times,* pp. A1, A10.

Willet, W. C., et al. (1990). Relation of meat, fat, and fiber intake to the risk of colon cancer in a prospective study among women. *The New England Journal of Medicine, 323,* 1664–1672.

Williams, D. (1990). Socioeconomic differentials in health: A review and redirection. *Social Psychology Quarterly, 53,* 81–99.

Williams, J. E., & Best, D. L. (1982). *Measuring sex stereotypes: A thirty-nation study.* Beverly Hills: Sage.

Williams, K. R. (1992). Social sources of marital violence and deterrence: Testing an integrated theory of assaults between partners. *Journal of Marriage and the Family, 54,* 620–629.

Williams, R. B., Jr., Lane, J. D., Kuhn, C. M., Melosh, W., White, A. D., & Schanberg, S. M. (1982). Type A behavior and elevated physiological and neuroendocrine responses to cognitive tasks. *Science, 218,* 438–485.

Williams, R. M., Jr. (1970). *American society: A sociological interpretation* (3rd ed.). New York: Knopf.

Williams, S. R. (1986). *Essentials of nutrition and diet therapy* (4th ed.). St. Louis: Times Mirror/Mosby.

Willke, J. C. (1991). The fetus is life itself. In P. M. Insel & W. T. Roth, *Core concepts in health* (pp. 170–171). Mountain View, CA: Mayfield Publishing.

Willis, R. J. (1992, July 17). Cited in F. Barringer. Rate of marriage continues decline. *The New York Times,* p. A20.

Willis, R. J., & Michael, R. T. (1988). *Innovation in family formation: Evidence on cohabitation in the United States.* Paper presented at the IUSSP seminar on "The Family, the Market, and the State in Aging Societies." Sendai City, Japan.

Wilson, E. O. (1992). *The diversity of life.* Cambridge, MA: Belknap Press/Harvard University Press.

Wilson, G., & Cox, D. (1983). Personality of pedophile club members. *Personality and Individual Differences, 4,* 323–329.

Wilson, M., & Daly, M. (1985). Competitiveness, risk taking, and violence: The young male syndrome. *Ethology and Sociobiology, 6,* 59–73.

Wilson-Brewer, R., Cohen, S., O'Donnell, L., & Goodman, I. (1991). *Violence prevention for young adolescents: A survey of the state of the art.* New York: Carnegie Council on Adolescent Development.

Wilson-Brewer, R., & Jacklin, B. (1990). *Violence prevention strategies targeted at the general population of minority youth* (Background paper prepared for the Forum on Youth Violence in Minority Communities: Setting the Agenda for Prevention). Newton, MA: Education Development Center, Inc.

Wiltfang, G. L., & McAdam, D. (1991). The costs and risks of social activism: A study of sanctuary movement activism. *Social Forces, 69,* 987–1010.

Wincze, J. P. (1977). Sexual deviance and dysfunction. In D. C. Rimm & J. W. Somervill (Eds.), *Abnormal psychology* (pp. 343–379). New York: Academic Press.

Winerip, M. (1992, June 7). A wild streak is uncovered at Princeton. *The New York Times,* p. A31.

Wingard, D. L., & Cohen, B. A. (1990). Variations in disease-specific sex-morbidity and mortality ratios: United States vital statistics data and prospective data from Alameda County Study. In M. G. Ory & H. R. Warner (Eds.), *Gender, health and longevity: Multidisciplinary perspectives.* New York: Springer.

Wirz-Justice, A., et al. (1989). Phototherapy in Switzerland: "Mehr licht." In C. Thompson & T. Silverstone (Eds.), *Seasonal affective disorder* (pp. 169–185). London: Clinical Neuroscience Publishers.

Wistrich, R. S. (1992). *Anti-Semitism: The longest hatred.* New York: Pantheon.

Witztum, E. (1992, May 13). Cited in C. Haberman. What makes "Samson" run amok? He's manic in Jerusalem. *The New York Times,* p. A13.

Wolf, S. (1986). Common and grave disorders identified with psychological stress. In S. Wolf & A. J. Finestone (Eds.), *Occupational stress: Health and performance at work.* Littleton, MA: PSG Publishing.

Wolfe, J. (1991). Abuse and trauma in women: Broadening the social context. *American Psychologist, 45,* 1386–1387.

Wolfson, A., Lacks, P., & Futterman, A. (1992). Parent training of infant sleeping patterns. *Journal of Consulting and Clinical Psychology, 60,* 41–48.

Wolpe, J., & Abrams, J. (1991). Post-traumatic stress disorder overcome by eye-movement desensitization: A case report. *Journal of Behavior Therapy and Experimental Psychiatry, 22,* 39–43.

Woman convicted in father dumping. (1992, December 4). *The New York Times,* p. A24.

Women on Words and Images. (1972). *Dick and Jane as victims: Sex stereotyping in children's readers.* Princeton, NJ: Author.

Wong, D. L. (1987). False allegations of child abuse: The other side of the tragedy. *Pediatric Nursing, 13,* 329–333.

Wood, W., & Eagly, A. H. (1981). Stages in the analysis of persuasive messages: The role of causal attributions and message comprehension. *Journal of Personality and Social Psychology, 40,* 246–259.

Woodworth, R. S. & Sheehan, M. R. (1964). *Contemporary schools of psychology* (3rd ed.). New York: Ronald Press.

World Health Organization. (1986). *Young people's health: A challenge for society. Report of a WHO study group on young people and health for all by the year 2000* (Technical Report Series 731). Geneva: World Health Organization.

Wright, J. C., & Vlietstra, A. G. (1975). The development of selective attention: From perceptual exploration to logical search. In H. W. Reese (Ed.), *Advances in child development and behavior* (Vol. 10) (pp. 195–239). New York: Academic Press.

Wright, S. C., Taylor, D. M., & Moghaddam, F. (1990). Responding to membership in a disadvantaged group: From acceptance to collective protest. *Journal of Personality and Social Psychology, 58,* 994–1003.

Wu, T-C., Tashkin, D. P., Djahed, B., & Rose, J. E. (1988). Pulmonary hazards of smoking marijuana as compared with tobacco. *New England Journal of Medicine, 318,* 347–351.

Wyatt, G. E., Notgrass, C. M., & Newcomb, M. (1990). Internal and external mediators of women's rape experiences. *Psychology of Women Quarterly, 14,* 153–176.

Wylie, R. (1974). *The self-concept* (Vol. 1). Lincoln: University of Nebraska Press.

Wylie, R. (1979). *The self-concept* (Vol. 2). Lincoln: University of Nebraska Press.

Wysor, M. S. (1983). Comparing college students' environmental perceptions and attitudes. *Environment and Behavior, 15,* 615–645.

Yambert, P. A., & Donow, C. F. (1986). Are we ready for ecological commandments? *Journal of Environmental Education, 17,* 13-?

Yap, P. M. (1951). Mental diseases peculiar to certain cultures: A survey of comparative psychiatry. *Journal of Mental Science, 19,* 313–327.

Yeaton, W. H., & Bailey, J. S. (1978). Teaching pedestrian safety skills to young children: An analysis and one year follow-up. *Journal of Applied Behavior Analysis, 11,* 315–329.

Yerkes, R. M., & Dodson, J. D. (1908). The relationship of strength of stimulus to rapidity of habit formation. *Journal of Comparative and Neurological Psychology, 18,* 459–482.

Yetman, N. R. (Ed.). (1991). *Majority and minority: The dynamics of race and ethnicity in American life* (5th ed.). Boston: Allyn & Bacon.

Yonas, A. (Ed.). (1988). *Perceptual development in infancy: The Minnesota Symposium on Child Psychology* (Volume 20). Hillsdale, NJ: Erlbaum.

Young, J. E. (1982). Loneliness, depression and cognitive therapy: Theory and application. In L. A. Peplau & D. Perlman (Eds.), *Loneliness: A sourcebook of current theory, research and therapy.* New York: Wiley.

Young, W. C., Goy, R. W., & Phoenix, C. H. (1964). Hormones and sexual behavior. *Science, 143,* 212–218.

Youngblood, S. A. (1984). Work, nonwork, and withdrawal. *Journal of Applied Psychology, 69,* 106–117.

Youth Indicators. (1988). *Trends in the well-being of American youth.* Washington, DC: U.S. Government Printing Office.

Yu, L. C., & Wu, S. (1988). Effects of length of stay in the United States on how the Chinese fulfilled their filial obligations. In L. L. Adler (Ed.)., *Cross-cultural research in human development.* New York: Praeger.

Yukl, G. A., & Latham, G. P. (1975). Consequences of reinforcement schedules and incentive magnitudes for employee performance: Problems encountered in an industrial setting. *Journal of Applied Psychology, 60,* 294–298.

Zajonc, R. B. (1968). Attitudinal effects of mere exposure. *Journal of Personality and Social Psychology Monographs Supplement, 9,* 1–27.

Zajonc, R. B. (1980). Feeling and thinking: Preferences need no inferences. *American Psychologist, 35,* 151–175.

Zajonc, R. B. (1984). On the primacy of affect. *American Psychologist, 39,* 117–123.

Zaviacic, M., et al. (1988). Concentrations of fructose in female ejaculate and urine: A comparative biochemical study. *Journal of Sex Research, 24,* 319–325.

Zeiss, A. M. (1980). Aversiveness versus change in the assessment of life stress. *Journal of Psychosomatic Stress, 24,* 15–19.

Zick, C. D., & Smith, K. R. (1991). Marital transitions, poverty, and gender differences in mortality. *Journal of Marriage and the Family, 53,* 327–336.

Zigler, E., & Frank, M. (1988). *The parental leave crisis: Toward a national policy.* New Haven, CT: Yale University Press.

Zimmer, D. (1983). Interaction patterns and communication skills in sexually distressed and normal couples: Two experimental studies. *Journal of Sex and Marital Therapy, 9,* 251–265.

Zimmerman, M. (1983). Methodological issues in the assessment of life events: A review of issues and research. *Clinical Psychology Review, 3,* 339–370.

Zimmerman, M. (1988). Why are we rushing to publish DSM-IV? *Archives of General Psychiatry, 45,* 1135–1138.

Zucker, K. J., & Green, R. (1992). Psychosexual disorders in children and adolescents. *Journal of Child Psychology and Psychiatry, 33,* 107–151.

Zuckerman, M. (1971). Dimensions of sensation seeking. *Journal of Consulting and Clinical Psychology, 36,* 45–52.

Zuckerman, M. (1972). *Manual and research report for the Sensation Seeking Scale (SSS).* Newark, DE: University of Delaware.

Zuckerman, M. (1978). Sensation seeking. In H. London & J. Exner (Eds.), *Dimensions of personality* (pp. 487–559). New York: Wiley.

Zuckerman, M. (1979). *Sensation seeking: Beyond the optimal level of arousal.* Hillsdale, NJ: Erlbaum.

Zuckerman, M. (1984). Sensation seeking: A comparative approach to a human trait. *The Behavioral and Brain Sciences, 7,* 413–471.

Zuniga, M. E. (1988). Assessment issues with Chicanas: Practical implications. *Psychotherapy, 25,* 288–293.

Zweigenhaft, R. L. (1984). *Who gets to the top? Executive suite discrimination in the eighties.* New York: American Jewish Committee Institute of Human Relations.

Zweigenhaft, R. L., & Domhoff, G. W. (1982). *Jews in the Protestant establishment.* New York: Praeger.

GLOSSARY

A

abduction
in developmental psychology and law, the deprivation of parental access to a child in violation of law, formal agreements, or informal arrangements.

abnormtal
from the Latin *abnormis*, meaning departing from normal or away from the rule.

abnormal behavior
overt action or covert thinking that is statistically rare in the population, counter to the prevailing cultural and/or subcultural norms, and usually harmful to the well-being of oneself or others.

abortion
an artificially induced termination of pregnancy, usually by chemical, mechanical, or surgical means (compare to *spontaneous abortion* or *miscarriage*).

absorption
a conflict resolution strategy that entails incorporation of the conflicting source in whole or in part, as in a corporate takeover.

abstract
the element of a research report that contains a brief, general summary of the research question addressed; the method used, the findings, and implications.

acculturation
an ongoing process by which an individual's thoughts, behaviors, and values develop in relation to the general thinking, behavior, and values of a particular cultural group.

acid rain
precipitation high in sulfuric acid and other acids that results from chemical reactions that occur when fossil fuels are burned.

acid snow
the same as acid rain but formed at lower temperatures.

acquaintance rape
see *date rape.*

active listening
a type of listening that entails one's undivided attention to whatever one is attending to; it includes anticipation or visualization.

actualization
in humanistic theory, the inborn tendency of personal growth that results in an adjusted person; when thwarted, maladjustment is presumed to result.

adaptive
an adjective describing a rational process that yields constructive thoughts or behaviors.

adaptive coping
contending with stress in a manner such that the source of the stress is maturely and effectively addressed as a result and the stress is thereby lessened, eliminated, or made more tolerable.

addiction
a condition of physiological or psychological dependence.

adjustive challenges
factors originating within the self, such as the mobilization of ability, energy, and resources to respond constructively to change. Contrast with *adjustive demands.*

adjustive demands
factors originating primarily in the environment that prompt us to respond constructively to change. Contrast with *adjustive challenges.*

adjustment
change or adaptation made in response to a new situation or a new perception of a situation.

adjustment disorder
a condition diagnosed when a maladaptive or excessive response to a stressor occurs within three months of the stressful event or when everyday functioning has been profoundly impaired by the stressful event.

adrenaline
a hormone that arouses the sympathetic nervous system.

affect
expression of emotion.

afterplay
sexual, affectual, or other activities that people may engage in subsequent to having sexual intercourse. Contrast with *foreplay*.

aggression
hostile behavior, sometimes with resulting physical or emotional harm.

agoraphobia
fear of venturing outdoors or into open spaces.

AIDS
an acronym for the disease acquired immunodeficiency syndrome.

altruistic behavior
helping another, presumably with no expectation of personal gain.

Alzheimer's disease
a neurological disorder, typically but not necessarily, seen in persons of advanced age, that is characterized by memory loss and other symptoms.

amnesia
loss of memory related to one's identity.

anabolic steroid
a synthetic male hormone frequently abused by bodybuilders, athletes, and others who seek chemical assistance in building up muscle quickly.

anal intercourse
a sexual act entailing insertion of the penis into the partner's anus.

analysand
in psychoanaltyic psychotherapy, the person being analyzed by the psychoanalyst.

anatomy
the science of the structure of organisms.

androgyny
the coexistence in one person of both masculine and feminine thoughts, behavior, emotions, and physical appearance as culturally stereotyped.

antecedent
in behavioral parlance, that which causes, cues, or prompts a particular behavior or thought.

anthropomorphic
human-like or person-like.

antibody
the general term used to describe protein molecules in the blood that defend the body against invading pathogens.

anti-Semitism
political, social, and economic prejudice, discrimination, and aggression against Jews.

antisexist men's movement
a radical perspective on male thinking and behavior patterns that holds that such patterns are the product of biological instincts that have not kept pace with cultural evolution.

antisocial
disapproved of by society and/or not sanctioned by law.

antisocial personality disorder
a condition characterized by disrespect for others and the authority of the law.

anxiety
a state of fear, dread, uncertainty, nervousness, or concern.

APA
as used in this text, an abbreviation for American Psychological Association. May also be used as an abbreviation for American Psychiatric Association.

aphasia
From the Greek for "without speech," the general name for a condition wherein one is physically unable to communicate. See also *expressive aphasia* and *receptive aphasia*.

appeasement
resolving conflict by acceding to or giving in to the demands of another.

applied psychological research
behavioral investigation for the purpose of finding solutions to practical concerns.

appraisal support
a type of social support that specifically relates to assistance in evaluating situations.

approach-approach conflict
conflict arising as the result of the desirability of approaching two or more positive alternatives.

approach-avoidance conflict
conflict arising as a result of the mixed feelings—both positive and negative—that keep a person from feeling good about approaching or avoiding something.

arousal
the state of nervous system activation.

artificial insemination
a procedure in which fertilization takes place via the mechanical insertion of donated sperm from either an identified or anonymous donor into a woman.

assertiveness
maintaining or defending one's rights yet not being hostile.

assimilation

incorporation of information into one's fund of information and experience.

asymptomatic

not manifesting signs of a disease or disorder.

attachment

in developmental psychology, the emotional ties that develop between the infant and others.

attrition

in research, usually a reference to a reduction or dropping-out of participating subjects.

attribution

derived from the verb *to attribute* (mentally assign), a social psychological term that refers to an inferred characteristic and/or causation.

auto-immune disease

a condition such as lupus, for example, wherein the body misidentifies some of its own cells as pathogens and proceeds to produce antibodies to destroy them.

aversion therapy

in behavior therapy, a process in which an unpleasant stimulus is applied or a positive reinforcer is removed in an effort to lessen the positive appeal of an undesirable behavior.

avoidance-avoidance conflict

conflict arising as the result of the undesirability of two or more negative alternatives.

B

basal body temperature method

a natural technique for estimating the optimal time for intercourse for conception that entails tracking the woman's body temperature.

basic anxiety

according to psychoanalyst Karen Horney, a condition resulting from poor social conditions and/or a poor parent-child relationship.

BASIC ID

an acronym from multimodal behavior therapy that stands for *behavior, affect, sensation, imagery, cognition, interpersonal,* and *drugs.*

basic psychological research

investigation for the general purpose of gathering knowledge about behavior and thinking.

behavior

action or conduct of an organism that may be observable or unobservable to others.

behavior genetics

the study of biological mechanisms of variation and hereditary transmission that affect behavior.

behavior therapy

an approach to therapy based on the principle that, because most behavior is learned, maladaptive behavior can be extinguished or unlearned and replaced by more adaptive alternatives.

behavioral coping

a process of using action in addition to thoughts as a means of diminishing, eliminating, or helping oneself to feel better about the negative affect associated with stress. Contrast with *cognitive coping.*

behavioral exercise

in behavior and cognitive-behavior therapy, a task that the client is assigned by the therapist.

behavioral observation

watching an individual or group of people for psychodiagnostic, psychotherapeutic, or research purposes, typically while maintaining some kind of record of what is observed.

behavioral science

the observation, description, identification, experimental investigation, and/or theoretical explanation of behavior-related phenomena.

bias

prejudice.

bibliotherapy

the use of books in a psychotherapeutic context, as in learning some moral from a story.

biodiversity

the diversity of plant and animal species of life.

biofeedback

an abbreviation for *biological feedback* which refers to the internal monitoring of bodily processes amplified through some type of external output such as light or sound.

biopsychosocial perspective

a view of how biological, psychological, and social factors may independently or in combination affect wellness and illness.

biosphere

elements of the earth that have a role in sustaining life, including the land, water, and atmosphere.

biotechnology

the application of biological science for commercial or industrial objectives.

bipolar disorder
a mood disorder that involves the expression of affectual extremes, including "highs" as well as "lows." Contrast with *unipolar disorder*.

bisexual orientation
a general erotic inclination towards same-sex as well as opposite-sex sexual partners. Synonymous with *bisexuality*.

blended family
see *reconstituted family*.

blind
in scientific research, a condition of unawareness as to aspects of the study on the part of one or more of the parties to the research. Compare to *double-blind*.

blunted affect
a condition of limited capacity to respond emotionally.

brainstorming
problem solving, especially the seeking of creative solutions, engaged in jointly by two or more people who have a shared objective.

branching
growth and interconnections in a nervous system.

bright light treatment
the systematic and regular exposure to intense illumination for therapeutic purposes. Also referred to as *bright light therapy* and *phototherapy*.

broad spectrum behavior therapy
a name used to describe the specific approach to cognitive-behavior therapy developed by Arnold Lazarus prior to his development of multimodal behavior therapy.

Broca's area
a region in the left, frontal brain that is involved in speech production; named for the French surgeon Paul Broca.

bulimia
an eating disorder characterized by disturbed self-perception, excessive exercise, and binging and purging for the purposes of weight control. Also referred to as *bulimia nervosa*.

bundling
the antiquated colonial custom practiced by courting couples that entailed keeping warm, socializing, and sleeping together with clothes on, sometimes in a bed expressly designed for that purpose.

burnout
a condition caused by overwork in which an individual becomes less productive, less motivated, and less energetic with respect to work.

C

career
a sequence of positions occupied by a person during the course of a lifetime.

case history
see *case study*.

case study
a compilation of biographical data on one person drawn from diverse sources including, among others, official government records, school records, police reports, medical and psychological records, employment records, family albums, family videotapes, and interview data.

case study research
a nonexperimental research method that entails making inferences or conclusions from a collection of data from varied sources.

catatonic schizophrenia
a subtype of schizophrenia characterized by extreme, sometimes curious motor behavior ranging from excited movement to the assumption of odd poses for long periods of time without moving.

catharsis
a venting of anxiety or aggressive impulses.

central nervous system
consists of the brain and the spinal cord.

CFC
see *chlorofluorocarbon*.

chancre
a syphilitic sore resembling a whitish pimple that is about the size of a dime. See also *syphilis*.

child abuse

harm to a minor caused by an adult as a result of intentional infliction of physical or emotional injury, the creation of conditions that create risk of such harm, or the act of committing or allowing a sexual offense.

child neglect

harm to a minor caused by the failure of an adult responsible for the child's care to provide the child with food, clothing, shelter, supervision, or other such necessities.

child proofing

acting to help prevent injury to young children in an environment such as the home by using devices such as plastic outlet protectors or by keeping all medicines, cleaners, insecticides, and other potentially harmful items out of access to the child.

chlamydia

a sexually tranmitted bacterial disease wherein bacteria grow in mucous membranes including the moist linings of the mouth, vagina, urethra, and anal canal.

chlorofluorocarbon

a class of chemicals known to destroy ozone in the earth's stratosphere.

chromosome

a substance within the cells of plants and animals that is responsible for the determination and transmission of hereditary characteristics.

circumcision

a surgical procedure in which the foreskin is removed from the penis.

classical conditioning

a process in which relationships between events are learned such that behavior comes to be elicited by a conditioned stimulus due to a prior pairing of the conditioned stimulus with an unconditioned stimulus.

claustrophobia

fear of closed spaces.

client-centered therapy

a humanistic approach to psychotherapy developed by Carl Rogers; a precursor to what Rogers subsequently called person-centered therapy.

clinical psychologist

although specific credentials vary from state to state, people having this occupational title typically hold a doctoral degree in clinical psychology and background, training, and experience that prepares them for psychotherapeutic work and/or research with a very wide range of clientele, including severely mentally disordered individuals.

cloning

the process of using cells from one organism to create an exact duplicate of that organism.

coercive deviant sexual behavior

1. the criminal act of compelling a person to engage in a sexual act against that person's will (as in rape). 2. the criminal act of engaging in a sexual act with a person, such as a child, who, in the eyes of the law, is not sufficiently mature to give informed consent to such activity.

cognition

mental activity, including thinking and feeling.

cognitive-behavior therapy

in general, a modified and expanded variety of behavior therapy that allows for more therapeutic focus on unobservable mental processes.

cognitive behavioral

a reference to a model of behavior that is more mentalistic in nature than one that is strictly behavioral.

cognitive coping

a process of using thoughts as a means of diminishing, eliminating, or helping oneself to feel better about the negative affect associated with stress. Contrast with *behavioral coping*.

cognitive dissonance

an unpleasant mental state owing to the simultaneous existence of two or more thoughts that have contradictory implications for behavior.

cognitive restructuring

in cognitive and cognitive-behavior therapy, the therapeutic technique of changing patterns of thought. See also *thought*.

cognitive therapy

a cognitive-behavioral approach to therapy developed by Aaron Beck.

coitus

sexual intercourse.

collective monologue

people, usually young children, apparently talking to one another but in reality not listening or reacting to what each other is saying.

communication

an exchange of messages by verbal and/or nonverbal means. Contrast with *effective communication*.

community psychology
the study of people and their relationships to community institutions

companionate love
the product of affection, in contrast to the intense arousal and passion of passionate love.

compromise
a conflict resolution strategy that entails each side making concessions in order to settle differences.

compulsion
an urge or impulse, usually perceived as irresistible, to engage in some type of behavior.

conception
the union of an ovum with a sperm.

concrete operations
In Piaget's theory, mental activities and logic applied with reference to specific (or "concrete") types of examples.

conditioning
a type of learning that entails the acquisition of relatively specific patterns of response to the presence of well-defined stimuli.

condyloma
see *genital warts*.

confidence level
a criterion, usually expressed in the form of a probability, that will be used to accept or reject a hypothesis.

conflict
1. an intrapsychic state in which two or more mutually exclusive wishes, impulses, or tendencies simultaneously exist. 2. an interpersonal state in which two or more people (or entities such as nations, organizations, or corporations) disagree, are opposed to one another, or are engaged in mutually aggressive behavior. See also *approach-approach conflict*, *approach-avoidance conflict*, and *avoidance-avoidance conflict*.

conformity
similarity in form and character.

consequences
what happens as a result of engaging in a particular behavior.

conservation
the practice of setting aside an area of land for the purpose of conserving a particular species. *Contrast with utilization.*

construct
an informed, scientific idea that is fabricated or "constructed" to describe or explain behavior.

contingency
an event incidental to another event.

contingency contracting
in behavior and cognitive-behavior therapy, the technique of devising an agreement regarding the client's behavior and the consequences of that behavior, including rewards and punishments, for therapeutic purposes. See also *token economy*.

contraception
pregnancy prevention.

contraindications
in psychotherapy, reasons for not using a particular technique. Opposite of *indications*.

control for
in scientific research, to regulate the influence of.

control group
a group of subjects not exposed to the experimental treatment who will be compared to subjects who were exposed to the experimental treatment.

convenience sample
subjects that are readily attainable, though not always the most appropriate, for use in a research study.

cope
contend, adapt, or adjust.

correlation
1. a statistical tool used to determine the magnitude of the relationship between two variables. 2. a reference to a relationship between variables.

counseling
guidance or advice giving.

counseling psychologist
an occupational title for a person who typically holds a doctoral degree in counseling psychology, and background, training, and experience that focuses on everyday problems in living, including school-related problems, occupational and career choices dilemmas, marital and family-related difficulties, and so forth.

counterculture
a group that subscribes to values, norms, and sanctions that are inconsistent with the dominant culture (literally, "against culture" in social orientation).

counter-transference
in psychoanalytic psychotherapy, a process by which the feelings the therapist has for one person are presumed to be projected to the client. See also *transference*.

critical thinking
the active employment of judgment capabilities and evaluative skills in the thought process.

cross-dressing
dressing in the clothing of the opposite sex.

cryopreservation
in the medical specialty of human fertility, the freezing of embryos, usually in conjunction with *in vitro fertilization*.

cultural universal
a lesson or concept taught by all known cultures.

culture
the socially transmitted behavior patterns, beliefs, and products of human work of a particular population, community, or group of people.

culture-defining group
in sociology, a reference to the majority group in a culture, in contrast to a minority group. Contrast with *non-culture defining group*.

cunnilingus
oral stimulation of the vulva or clitoris.

cure
recovery from disease or a restoration of health.

customs
behavior arising from cultural tradition.

D

data
plural form of *datum* meaning information.

date rape
forcible sexual intercourse perpetrated by an acquaintance of the violated individual.

debriefing
a disclosure by a researcher to a research subject regarding the study's objectives, procedures, and/or findings, typically at the time the research is terminated and/or at the time an individual subject's participation in the research is terminated.

decision/commitment
in the context of Sternberg's triangular theory, an intention to maintain a love relationship.

defect
a physical or mental fault or disability that impairs normal functioning.

deficit
deficiency, usually with reference to some basic cognitive, behavioral, or social ability.

delusion
false belief.

denial
a cognitive coping mechanism that entails consciously attempting to repress or block out the source of the anxiety as if it had never happened.

dependent variable
an observable and/or measurable response to a variable manipulated by the experimenter.

depressant
a category of drugs so named because they depress central nervous system activity and make the user feel drowsy, less jittery, and/or euphoric.

depression
see *mood disorder* and *major depression*.

descriptive statistics
in scientific research, methods used for the purpose of describing data. Contrast with *inferential statistics*.

design
in the context of experimentation and research in general, a reference to the planning and/or structure of the research.

destructive obedience
one person's compliance with the order of another person to harm some third party or parties.

diagnosis
a classification derived as a result of an attempt to identify or distinguish a disease, disorder, or deficit on the basis of signs and symptoms.

discrimination
preferential, exclusionary, or differential behavior towards a person or group of people on the basis of race, religion, ethnic origin, gender, or other factors related to the person's or group of people's group membership.

disease
an abnormal biological condition that impairs normal functioning and arises from factors such as infection, inherent weakness, or environmental agents.

diseases of adaptation
a term stress researcher Hans Selye used to refer to conditions arising as a result of the body's attempt to cope with stress. See also *psychosomatic disease*.

disorder
1. a maladaptive behavior and/or thought pattern. 2. an upset of usual physical or mental functioning. 3. disease.

disorganized schizophrenia

a subtype of schizophrenia characterized by fragmented, sometimes chaotic thought patterns, usually accompanied by hallucinations and delusions.

displacement

process by which psychic energy is shunted from one object to another.

dissociative disorder

a general term used to describe a condition characterized by a loss of association between identity, consciousness, and memory, as in amnesia and multiple personality disorder.

distress

as conceived of by stress researcher Hans Selye, the variety of stress that carries with it unpleasurable and harmful consequences.

divorce

1. dissolution of a marriage. 2. dissolution of a legal parent-child relationship.

doctoral degree

an academic degree which, in the mental health field, may take various forms, including Doctor of Philosophy (PhD), Doctor of Psychology (PsyD), Doctor of Education (EdD), Doctor of Social Work (DSW), and Medical Doctor (MD).

double-blind

in scientific research, a condition of unawareness as to aspects of the study on the part of both the experimenter and the subject.

double standard

the notion that sex before marriage on the part of men is to be winked at while the same behavior on the part of women is contemptible.

Down syndrome

a genetic disorder marked by mental disability, heart defects, and other physical abnormalities.

dramatic play

in developmental psychology, play engaged in by a child that involves spontaneously produced plots or dramas.

drugs

biologically active agents.

DSM

a general abbreviation for any edition of the American Psychiatric Association's *Diagnostic and Statistical Manual (DSM) of Mental Disorders*.

DSM-IV

an abbreviation for the fourth and most current revision of the American Psychiatric Association's *Diagnostic and Statistical Manual of Mental Disorders*.

dynamic

of or pertaining to energy or force, usually used with reference to mental energy exchanges. 2. a model of personality and thought processes based on energy exchanges in the mind, as in psychoanalytic theory.

E

ecological psychology

see *environmental psychology*.

ecology

the relationship between the environment and organisms.

ecosystem

the environment and the organisms within it considered as a unit.

ectogenesis

in theory, a technological process for conceiving and bringing to term a person outside the human body through the use of an artificial placenta.

effective communication

an exchange of messages such that the message that the source wishes to convey is received by the person or persons targeted to receive that message. Contrast with *communication*.

ego

in psychoanalytic theory, the mental structure that controls the id and the superego.

ego dystonic homosexuality

a diagnosis that first appeared in DSM-III wherein homosexuality was not deemed a mental disorder unless it was alien to or inconsistent with the way an individual perceives herself or himself.

ejaculation

the discharge of seminal fluid that occurs during sexual activity.

Electra complex

in psychoanalytic theory, a period during the phallic stage of development during which girls experience incestuous urges towards their fathers. Contrast with *Oedipal complex*.

electroconvulsive treatment or therapy

see *electroshock treatment or therapy*.

electroshock treatment or therapy

the passing of an electrical current through the brain which causes a convulsion for therapeutic purposes.

empathy

in person-centered therapy, an active state of perceiving how another feels, almost as if one were the other.

empirical

derived from observable facts or experience.

empty love

in the context of Sternberg's triangular theory, a love relationship based on commitment but lacking in passion and intimacy.

encounter group

a humanistic, group approach to personal growth and awareness typically derived from different types of confrontation.

endangered species

animal and plant species threatened with or near extinction.

endocrine system

a system of glands including the hypothalamus, the pituitary, the thyroid, the parathyroids, the adrenals, the pancreas, and the ovaries in the female, and the testes in the male.

endorphin

a morphine-like substance produced by the body which may be released into the bloodstream in response to or in anticipation of pain.

entrepreneur

one who organizes and/or invests in business ventures.

environment

elements of the surroundings that may influence the development, behavior, and/or adjustment of organisms.

environmental literacy

knowledge of basic elements of the earth's environment, including global threats to its well-being.

environmental psychology

a specialty area within psychology that focuses on the relationship between people and the biosphere.

equity theory

a theory of work motivation that holds that worker motivation is influenced by the perceived balance of what the worker brings or applies to a job and what the worker gets out of the job in terms of salary and/or other benefits.

erectile dysfunction

see *impotence*.

Erhard Seminars Training

an encounter group business run by non-mental health professionals (also known as e*st* and the *Forum*).

epidemic

the rapid or extensive spread of a disease, especially a contagious disease.

epidemiology

the medical science that explores the origins and distribution of disease within a population as well as the conditions that influence the spread or severity of the disease.

equity theory

see *social exchange theory*.

error of expectancy

an attributional error made as the result of what one anticipates.

est

see *Erhard Seminars Training*.

estrogen

female sex hormone.

estrus cycle

the schedule according to which ova are produced in mammals other than humans.

ethics

principles of conduct generally considered to be "right," "proper," or "good."

ethnicity

the quality of belonging to a group with a common religious, linguistic, or ancestral heritage.

euphoria

a feeling of elation, happiness, bliss, or well-being.

eustress

as defined by stress researcher Hans Selye, a pleasurable type of stress, such as that experienced when racewalking.

evidence

information or observation by which probability or proof can be established.

exceptional

advanced or backward with respect to average development.

existence/relatedness/ growth (ERG) theory

a theory of work motivation proposed by Clayton Alderfer that is based on Abraham Maslow's hierarchy of needs.

existential psychotherapy

loosely based on the writings of philosophers known as existentialists, an approach to therapy that focuses on global issues regarding human existence, including the demands and challenges of contemporary living.

expectancy of therapeutic gain
in counseling or psychotherapy, a belief that a positive outcome will result from a course of counseling or psychotherapy.

expectancy theory
as set forth by Victor Vroom, a theory of work motivation that holds that workers act in a manner that is consistent with what they believe their labor will earn them.

experimental analysis of behavior
the study of how operants are conditioned and extinguished.

experimental design
planning of an experiment. See *design*.

expressive aphasia
a communication disorder wherein one understands another's communication but has difficulty responding. Contrast with *receptive aphasia*.

extended family
the nuclear family plus relatives who live in the same household.

extinguish
eliminate a behavior or thought.

extraction farming
the process of harvesting products from the land without destroying the land in the process.

extrinsic motivation
external incentives for action, in contrast to internal or intrinsic ones.

eye movement desensitization
a modification of the classic, muscle-relaxation method of systematic desensitization that was expressly designed for the treatment of post-traumatic stress syndrome.

F

family
any two or more related people living in one household.

fantasizing
see *imagining*.

fellatio
oral stimulation of the penis.

fertile
capable of reproducing.

fertility
the condition of being fertile.

fertilization
see *conception*.

fetish
the achievement of sexual arousal as a result of the presence or image of some thing versus someone.

fetishistic object
a nonhuman object of sexual pleasure.

field observation
the systematic viewing of an organism in its own natural setting.

field study
see *field observation*.

fine motor skills
abilities involving relatively small muscle movements, such as tying one's shoe or pouring milk.

fixation
in psychoanalytic theory, an ego defense mechanism in which emotional development is arrested in response to fear of failure or punishment.

flat affect
a condition wherein there is little or no emotional response to stimuli that would normally induce emotional changes.

flight of ideas
a condition symptomatic of the mood disorder, *mania*, in which there is a rapid stream of different thoughts and images.

flooding
an *in vivo* form of implosive therapy that entails increasing exposure to anxiety-provoking stimuli. Contrast with *implosion*.

forcible rape
rape conducted by brute force. Contrast with *statutory rape*.

foreplay
sexually stimulating activities that people may engage in prior to having sexual intercourse. Contrast with *afterplay*.

foreskin
the thin layer of skin covering the glans of the penis which may be removed during circumcision.

formal psychological thought
in Piaget's theory, a cognitive stage of development typically reached at the age of 12 or so characterized by the ability to generalize from specific things or experiences.

Forum
see *Erhard Seminars Training*.

fraternal twins
two siblings who share the same father and mother and who were carried to term together in the mother's uterus but who developed from separate fertilized eggs.

fraud
in scientific research, a deliberately practiced deception in order to secure unfair or unlawful gain.

free association

a psychoanalytic technique, designed to make the unconscious conscious, in which patients say everything that comes to mind without censoring anything.

Freudian slip

a slip of the tongue presumed to betray an unconscious thought or feeling.

frustration

a source of stress resulting from the prevention, blocking, or thwarting of efforts or wishes to achieve a desired objective.

fully functioning person

in person-centered therapy, an adjusted individual.

functional conditions

presenting symptoms that have no known biological, genetic, or physiological basis. Contrast with *organic conditions*.

fundamental attribution error

an error of social perception regarding the tendency of people to explain their own behavior in terms of external or environmental causes while explaining the behavior of others in terms of internal or personal causes.

G

G-spot

an area on the ceiling of the vaginal wall about 1 to 2 inches from the vaginal opening believed by gynecologist Ernest Grafenberg (for whom it is named) to be exquisitely sensitive to sexual stimulation.

gamete

a cell containing chromosomal material that is capable of producing a zygote upon union with a gamete from the opposite sex.

gay

male homosexual.

gay bashing

a crime of hate and violence against gays and lesbians.

gender

1. biological sex 2. cultural, social, and psychological aspects, in contrast to purely biological ones, of being male or female.

gender identity

the sense that one is female or male.

gender identity disorder

a rare condition in which a child develops the gender identity of a person of the opposite sex.

gender roles

culturally defined expectations of behavior formed on the basis of sex.

gender schema theory

a theory of gender role development that blends elements of cognitive developmental theory with social learning theory.

gender stereotype

a belief about a person or group of people based solely on the sex of that person or group of people.

gene

a substance that typically occupies a fixed location on a chromosome and has responsibility for the determination and transmission of hereditary characteristics.

general adaptation syndrome

according to Hans Selye, an internal sequence of events that takes place in response to stress.

general paresis

the loss of certain voluntary and reflexive motor capabilities as well as the development of other mental and behavioral deficits, as seen in later stages of syphilis.

generalized anxiety disorder

a DSM diagnosis characterized by anxiety and related symptoms that has lasted for a minimum of 6 months and cannot be linked to a single event or circumstance in one's life.

generative thinking

the goal-oriented intellectual production of new or creative ideas.

generativity

as conceived of by Erik Erikson, a sense that one's life work will stand the test of time and positively influence future generations.

genetic engineering

the deliberate manipulation and alteration of genetic material.

genetics

the study of the biological mechanisms of variation and hereditary transmission in living organisms.

genital

from the Latin meaning to beget or to produce, an external and visible reproductive organ. Plural form is either *genitals* or *genitalia*.

genital warts
a virus transmitted sexually and by other means that results in warts appearing at or near the infected area, usually within about 6 weeks of the time of infection. Also referred to as *condyloma*.

genocide
the systematic annihilation of a group of people based on their religious or political beliefs, racial or ethnic origin, or other such factors.

genuineness
in person-centered therapy, an honest experiencing of the moment and the absence of a false front.

gestalt therapy
an approach to psychotherapy that has as its objective an increase in one's self-awareness and self-acceptance through an "unblocking" of various sensory and cognitive obstacles.

gland
an organ that extracts from the blood specific substances in order to manufacture other substances.

gonad
a gamete-producing organ.

gonorrhea
a sexually transmitted bacterial disease.

good samaritanism
see *altruistic behavior*.

granny dumping
the abandonment of the elderly by relatives who are unable or unwilling to maintain their care.

gross motor skills
abilities involving large muscle movements, such as running, jumping, hopping, skipping, throwing, climbing, kicking, pushing, and pulling.

group identity
a sense of close affiliation with other people on the basis of a common variable such as interests, abilities, disabilities, or demographic characteristics.

groupthink
a small-group phenomenon involving a drive for consensus that is so strong that innovative alternatives tend to be suppressed.

guided imagery
in cognitive therapy, a technique that involves the client imagining different scenarios at the direction of the therapist.

H

hallucinations
sensory experiences of things that are not really there.

hallucinogens
a category of drugs so named because they may dramatically alter perception, sometimes to the point of inducing sensory registration of stimuli that are not really there.

hardiness
a constellation of personality characteristics thought to decrease or buffer the illness-related effects of stressful life events.

health psychology
a growing specialty area in psychology seeking to understand how psychological variables can influence illness or disease.

hebephrenic schizophrenia
a former subtype of schizophrenia (now diagnosed as *disorganized schizophrenia*) characterized by incessant giggling, laughing, or silliness and little concern about personal appearance and hygiene.

hermaphrodite
a person born with tissue from the testes (usually characteristic of males only) and with tissue from the ovaries (usually characteristic of females only).

herpes
the general name for a sexually transmitted viral infection that may occur in any of several different forms including cold sores, fever blisters, and painful or itchy skin rashes.

heterosexual orientation
a general erotic inclination or preference for opposite-sex sexual partners.

hierarchy
a graded series.

HIV
an abbreviation for human immunodeficiency virus, the virus that causes AIDS.

homelessness
a condition that has been defined in different studies in various ways ranging from living in sheltered institutions, including jails and homeless shelters, to living in public settings, such as streets, parks, and beaches.

homeostasis
bodily equilibrium.

homosexual orientation
a general erotic inclination or preference for same-sex sexual partners.

homosexuality
sexual attraction to people of the same sex, as in the case of gays and lesbians.

hormone
a chemical messenger produced by one tissue that travels through the blood to affect another tissue.

hot flashes
in menopausal women, sudden bouts of sweating and flushing.

human factors psychology
the field in which psychologists are involved in designing working environments in which humans can perform to optimal levels of their abilities.

humanism
a view of human behavior and cognition that tends to focus on ideals, potential, moral dilemmas, and other aspects of living that are uniquely human.

humor
1. in general, a quality of being funny or laughable. 2. in the psychology of adjustment, a cognitive coping mechanism that may be used to confront a stressful situation yet still allow for the expression of positive affect with respect to it.

hymen
a thin, elastic membrane that usually, although not always, covers the external opening of the vagina at birth.

hyperstress
as defined by stress researcher Hans Selye, a condition involving an excessive demand on one's coping ability.

hypnoanalysis
see *hypnotherapy.*

hypnoanalyst
see *hypnotherapist.*

hypnosis
an altered state of consciousness in which there is heightened suggestibility.

hypnotherapist
1. broadly refers to a therapist who employs hypnosis as a therapeutic technique. 2. one of many occupational titles that carry no legal standing and that are used by licensed as well as unlicensed persons who hold themselves out to the public as mental health professionals.

hypnotherapy
psychotherapy in which hypnosis is primary among the therapeutic tools employed.

hypostress
as defined by stress researcher Hans Selye, a condition involving too little stress, as in boredom.

hypothesis
a premise, assertion, or proposition, usually derived from a theory, that is subject to proof.

hypothesis testing
conducting research designed to examine the validity of a particular proposition or series of propositions.

hypothetical
made-up for the purpose of example.

I

id
in psychoanalytic theory, the mental structure governing one's instincts.

ideal self
the person one would like to be.

identical twins
two siblings who have exactly the same genetic inheritance because they developed from the same fertilized egg.

identification
a process of association with another to the point of emulation of the other's behavior and/or thinking.

identity
according to Erik Erikson, a consistency in one's self-image, a recognized role in society, and a commitment to various ideals.

identity diffusion
according to Erik Erikson, a state in which a person exhibits no particular commitment to life goals or values and little motivation to develop any such commitment.

illusory correlation error
an attributional error based on an observer's belief that a relationship exists between two aspects of another person's behavior, appearance, or other variables.

imagining
a cognitive coping mechanism that entails visualizing how things might have been done differently, how one would have liked things to occur, or how in fact they might occur in the future.

immune system
an organism's natural system of external and internal defenses against pathogens.

immunization
a process that stimulates the formation of protective antibodies to infectious organisms.

implosion
a behavior therapy technique that entails the exaggerated imaginal exposure to the feared or anxiety-producing stimuli. Contrast with *flooding*.

impotence
a failure of the penis to become erect at the excitement stage of the sexual response cycle.

impression management
the conscious control of one's expressive behavior so as to influence others' perceptions.

incidence
the current rate of new cases of illness (or accidents or other events) in a specified population over a specified period of time.

independent variable
a variable manipulated by the experimenter.

indications
in psychotherapy, reasons for using a particular technique. Opposite of *contraindications*.

industrial/organizational (I/O) psychology
that branch of psychology that deals with the application of the principles and methods of psychology to business organizations and people at work.

infancy
the period between birth and 2 years of age.

infantile amnesia
in psychoanalytic theory, the absence, in adulthood, of many childhood memories after the age of 2 and up to at least the age of 6.

infatuation
in the context of Sternberg's triangular theory, love that is built on passion alone.

inferential statistics
in scientific research, methods used for the purpose of making conclusions, predictions, or interpretations from study findings. Contrast with *descriptive statistics*.

infertility
inability to impregnate or to become impregnated.

informational support
a type of social support that specifically relates to assistance in supplying needed facts for decision making.

informed consent
in research, a term applied to a subject's consent to participate in a study after having had details about various aspects of the study disclosed by the experimenter.

in-group/out-group phenomenon
the tendency for one to view as outsiders all people who are not members of the same group.

instinct
an inborn, unlearned condition or motivating process, as in hunger.

instrumental conditioning
the learning of relationships between an organism's own actions and the consequences of those actions in a particular context.

instrumental support
a type of social support that specifically relates to assistance with money or other material things.

integrity test
an instrument most typically administered in employment settings designed to assess the honesty of employees or prospective employees.

intercultural marriage
a general term used to describe a marriage between people of different cultures.

interfaith marriage
a marriage between two people of different religious faiths.

intermarriage
a general term used to describe a marriage between people of two different heritages.

intern
an entry-level, earn-while-you-learn (in some cases even non-paid) position in which the individual is exposed to varied aspects of a business, industry, or profession.

internal locus of control
a personality variable relating to the degree people believe that they control their own fate.

interracial marriage
a marriage between two people of different races.

interview
a technique for gathering information by means of discussion.

intimacy
in the context of Sternberg's triangular theory of love, a state of closeness, warmth, bondedness, and connectedness in which the parties are disposed to sharing with each other aspects of their most personal, private, and innermost selves.

intrapreneur
a person who is developing or managing some independent project for an employer while still receiving salary and/or other support for this independent project from the employer.

intrapsychic
in the mind.

intrinsic motivation
internal incentives for action, in contrast to external or extrinsic ones.

invasive procedures
procedures that directly impact upon bodily tissues (such as injections and electroshock treatment) and that may legally be performed only by medical doctors, not psychologists.

in vitro fertilization
the process of uniting a sperm and egg in a laboratory and then implanting the zygote within a woman's womb.

in vivo
living or live, as in *in vivo* systematic desensitization, during which live anxiety-provoking objects, in contrast to imaginal ones, are employed.

J

job
a task, an undertaking, or an activity performed for pay. Contrast with *occupation*.

job facet satisfaction
the level of satisfaction derived from many diverse, individual components of a job or occupation.

job satisfaction
a pleasurable or positive emotional state resulting from the appraisal of one's job or occupational experiences.

job sharing
two or more people sharing a particular job with prorated salaries and benefits.

K

karoshi
in Japanese, death by overwork.

koro
an Asian psychiatric disorder characterized by the delusion that one's genitals are shrinking and by related symptoms.

L

latency period
in psychoanalytic theory, the period of development after the third or phallic stage and before the fourth or genital stage.

learning
a process that brings about a relatively enduring change in behavior or knowledge as a result of experience.

leisure
time spent engaging in a non-work, non-compensated activity.

lesbian
female homosexual.

.01 level of significance
a finding that could have occurred by chance alone less than 1 time in 100.

.05 level of signifance
a finding that could have occurred by chance alone less than 5 times in 100.

libido
in psychoanalytic theory, sexual energy.

lifestyle
an individual or group's relatively consistent day-to-day patterns of living.

love
see *companionate love, passionate love, empty love* and *romantic love*.

M

major depression
a DSM diagnosis characterized by symptoms such as changes from usual physical functioning, including changes in eating or sleeping patterns, crying, irritability, lessened motivation to achieve, lessened motivation to relate socially, negative thought patterns, and/or general slowing of movement or speech.

maladaptive
an adjective describing a typically irrational process that does not yield constructive thoughts or behavior.

maladaptive coping
contending with stress in a manner such that the source of the stress is ineffectively or inadequately addressed and the stress either remains or is compounded as a result.

mania
a mood disorder characterized by highly emotional behavior—elation, anger, or sadness—combined with high energy, and rapid, usually faulty, thinking.

masturbation
a solitary form of sexual behavior involving manipulation of the genitals, usually to the point of orgasm. Contrast with *mutual masturbation*.

matching hypothesis
the tendency for people to become romantically involved with other people who are comparable to themselves in terms of physical attractiveness and related variables.

matriarchal family
a family in which the mother has primary authority.

medical model
a model of understanding and treatment in which the presenting problem is conceptualized as symptomatic of an underlying disorder.

menarche
the first menstruation, usually between 12 and 13 years of age.

menopause
the age at which menstruation ceases, usually some time between 45 and 50.

menses
a mixture of blood and cells from the uterus that is a by-product of ovulation when impregnation does not take place.

menstrual cycle
the schedule on which ova are produced in humans. Contrast with *estrus cycle*.

menstruation
the process of menstrual flow which typically occurs from 1 to 5 days on a monthly (28-day) basis in the healthy, non-pregnant female.

mental status examination
a face-to-face interview in which the interviewer evaluates the interviewee on numerous variables, such as judgment and memory, in order to derive a diagnosis and/or behavioral assessment.

metabolism
the process by which the body breaks down substances.

method
in scientific research, the procedures, techniques, and/or measures that were used, and the order and way in which they were employed.

micropenis
a rare medical condition, usually due to a deficiency in testosterone, in which the fully developed penis reaches less than one inch in length.

middle childhood
the period of life defined as from age 7 to age 12.

minor
the legal term for a person who has not reached adulthood as defined by law.

miscarriage
a natural termination of pregnancy, also referred to as a spontaneous abortion. Contrast with *abortion*.

mnemonic devices
(note on pronunciation: the *m* is silent and *mnemonic* sounds like *ni-mon-ik*). memory-enhancing devices such as rhymes or acronyms.

modality profile
in multimodal behavior therapy, a listing of the seven (BASIC ID) modalities along with specific areas of concern derived from history taking.

model
1. a representation of some person, place, object, or process, devised to facilitate general understanding and specific information about operation, utility, and structure. 2. in social learning terms, the object of imitation.

mood
an average of affect over a period of time.

mood disorder
an emotion-related problem of behavior and thinking of such magnitude that everyday functioning is impaired.

moral anxiety
in psychoanalytic theory, a fear of the superego, usually characterized by feelings of guilt or shame, as in the case of disturbing sexual or aggressive urges or fantasies.

moral development
the process by which people acquire and practice principles of right, good, proper, and/or ethical conduct.

motor skills
proficiency related to placing the body in motion. See also *gross motor skills* and *fine motor skills*.

multimodal behavior therapy
an eclectic system of psychotherapy devised by Arnold A. Lazarus.

multiple personality disorder (MPD)
a condition characterized by the development of one or more different identities in the same individual.

mutual masturbation
an interpersonal variety of masturbation in which two (or more) individuals manually arouse each other, usually to the point of orgasm. Contrast with *masturbation*.

N

need for affiliation
the motivation to interact with other people, including the motivation to please or comfort them and to be pleased or comforted by them.

negative affect
an unpleasant state of tension that may take the form of anxiety or feelings of dread.

negative reinforcer
a stimulus that is avoided or terminated after an operant behavior is emitted and that tends to increase the frequency with which the operant behavior is emitted.

negativistic
doing exactly the opposite of what one is directed to do.

negligence
an unintentional breach of the duty of care owed to another person.

nervous system
the brain, the spinal cord, and the entire network of nerves "wired" to it, including the electrical and chemical activity that goes on within it.

neurosis
literally, "nerve related disease," a now antiquated term used to refer to nonpsychotic mental disorder. See also *neurotic anxiety*.

neurotic anxiety
in psychoanalytic theory, a fear of one's own id and instinctual impulses.

neurotransmitter
a substance within the brain that is involved in the transmission of nerve impulses.

non-culture defining group
in sociology, a reference to the minority groups in a culture in contrast to the majority group.

non-directive counseling
a now antiquated term for a humanistic approach to counseling and psychotherapy devised by Carl Rogers. See also *client-centered therapy* and *person-centered therapy*.

norepinephrine
a hormone secreted during stress.

norms
1. in sociology, guidelines for most aspects of everyday living. 2. with reference to psychological testing and assessment, a standard used to compare test scores.

nuclear family
the traditional mother/father/child family.

null hypothesis
used in research, the proposition that no significant difference exists as a result of the experimenter's treatment.

O

obedience
the behavior of dutifully carrying out the orders or commands of another.

obesity
a condition said to exist when body fat exceeds 20% of total weight in men or 30% of total weight in women.

objectivity
an attitude and ethic in scientific research regarding the factual nature of published findings.

obsession
a mental preoccupation, usually with the same or similar thoughts being thought repeatedly.

obsessive-compulsive disorder (OCD)
a DSM diagnosis in which either obsessive thoughts or compulsive behavior or both are present.

occupation
a vocation, profession, or other activity that one regularly works at, keeps busy at, and/or earns one's livelihood through. Contrast with *job*.

Oedipal complex
in psychoanalytic theory, a period during the phallic stage of development during which boys experience incestuous urges towards their mother (a parallel to the *Electra complex* in girls).

olfactory
referring to the sense of smell.

operant
an observable behavior that, once emitted, has an observable effect on the environment.

operant conditioning

B. F. Skinner's nonmentalistic term for instrumental conditioning, a learning process whereby the probability or frequency of emission of a particular response is altered as a result of a change in the consequences of emitting that response.

operants of the mind

in cognitive-behavior theory and therapy, a way of conceptualizing cognitions or thoughts.

operational definition

in scientific research, the meaning of a particular term for the purposes of a particular study.

opportunistic disease

a condition arising from a weakened immune system as a result of a disease such as AIDS.

optimism

a general tendency to envision the future as favorable. Opposite of *pessimism*.

organic conditions

presenting symptoms that have a biological, genetic, or physiological basis. Contrast with *functional conditions*.

orgasm

a point in the sexual response cycle referred to as ejaculation in males and climax in both females and males.

ovarian cycle

see *menstrual cycle*.

ovaries

the female gonads.

ovum

the female reproductive cell or egg. Plural form is *ova*.

ovum transfer

a procedure that entails the placement of a donor woman's fertilized ovum (an embryo), into the womb of a recipient woman, where it will be carried to term.

ovulation

the process of producing ova.

ozone layer

a level of the earth's atmosphere called the stratosphere that contains the chemical ozone, which acts as a shield against the sun's harmful ultraviolet rays.

P

panic attack

a condition of relatively brief duration, not precipitated by the victim being the focus of others' attention, in which the victim experiences behavioral, cognitive, and physical terror with symptoms such as shortness of breath or related breathing difficulties, dizziness, shaking, trembling, sweating, nausea, and/or fear of dying or losing control.

panic disorder

diagnosed as a consequence of a sufferer's report of frequent panic attacks and/or the fear that panic attacks will recur.

PAPERS

an acronym for six key factors in liking: *proximity* (geographical closeness), *attractiveness, personality, equity, reciprocity,* and *similarity*.

parallel play

a type of play in which children may appear to be playing with each other but are actually playing by themselves and not interacting.

paranoid schizophrenia

a subtype of schizophrenia characterized by highly systematized delusions, usually of persecution, sometimes accompanied by hallucinations.

paraphilia

a mental disorder characterized by the choice of an inappropriate sexual object, as in pedophilia.

paraprofessionals

in the mental health field, providers of mental health services who have had relatively little formal training from professional mental health providers.

parasympathetic nervous system
the branch of the peripheral nervous system that reverses the effects of the sympathetic nervous system.

passion
in the context of Sternberg's triangular theory of love, a powerful, emotion-driven zeal that can be positive or negative in nature.

passionate love
from a cognitive perspective, the product of emotional arousal plus a cognitive label of *love*.

pathogen
a harmful or potentially harmful agent such as a virus or a bacteria.

pathology
disease process.

patriarchal family
a family in which the father has primary authority.

Pavlovian conditioning
see *classical conditioning*.

pedophilia
sexual abuse of children by adults.

peer review
a stage in the research publication process during which the research undergoes evaluation by experts in the subject matter.

perception
the process whereby sensory stimuli are organized and interpreted into meaningful cognitions.

period prevalence
in epidemiology, prevalence for a narrowly specified period of time. Contrast with *prevalence*.

peripheral nervous system
tissue that connects the central nervous system to the rest of the body.

person-centered therapy
a humanistic approach to counseling and psychotherapy devised by Carl Rogers.

personal growth
change in the self for the better.

personality
an individual's unique constellation of psychological traits and states.

personality disorder
a condition characterized by inflexible and maladaptive psychological traits that causes significant impairment in the person's functioning in social, occupational, or other contexts.

personality type
any distinguishable, relatively enduring way in which one group of personality traits varies from another group of personality traits.

pessimism
a general tendency to envision the future as unfavorable. Opposite of *optimism*.

phallic symbol
in psychoanalytic theory, an object in fantasy or a dream presumed to represent or symbolize genitalia.

philosophy
a viewpoint about something.

philosophy of science
a set of assumptions about pathways to knowledge.

phobia
irrational fear characterized by the generation of great anxiety and avoidance behavior.

phobic disorder
the condition of being phobic.

phobic objects
stimuli that are irrationally feared and capable of producing avoidance behavior.

phototherapy
see *bright light treatment*.

phytoplankton
a minute form of life that is at the base of the fish food chain.

piblokto
a psychiatric condition once common in the Arctic characterized by behavior such as imitating the sounds of animals and running or throwing oneself wildly.

pilot study
in scientific research, a preliminary or exploratory investigation.

placebo
in scientific research, an inactive substance usually administered to control for the effect of an active substance.

pleasure principle
in psychoanalytic theory, a striving to seek pleasure and avoid pain.

pluralistic society
a social group comprised of people from many different cultures.

polygamist
one who practices polygamy.

polygamous family
a family in which one spouse has two or more mates.

polygamy
the practice of having more than one spouse.

polygenic
deriving from more than one gene.

population
in scientific research, the larger group from which the sample was drawn to whom the experimenter wishes to generalize.

positive reinforcer
a reinforcer that increases the probability or rate of the operant behavior that precedes its administration.

positive thinking
a process of interpreting information in its best possible light, anticipating and mentally working towards the best possible outcome, and/or focusing on whatever is best or most hopeful.

post-traumatic stress disorder
a variety of anxiety disorder caused by a reaction to a severe life stressor such as a natural disaster, a rape or other violent crime, or military combat.

prayer
in terms of the psychology of adjustment, a cognitive coping mechanism that entails appealing to a higher, spiritual authority for some wish to be granted.

pregnancy
the state of having a fertilized ovum.

prejudice
preconceived judgments and opinions.

premature ejaculation
a male sexual dysfunction at the orgasm stage of the sexual response cycle involving a too quick climax.

prenatal
before birth.

preoperational thought
in Piaget's theory of cognitive development, the period of time between age 2 and age 7 in which the child has not yet acquired the ability to perform logical operations on thoughts.

pressure
burdensome internal or external demands regarding thoughts, feelings, or behavior.

prevalence
the current rate of illness (or accidents or other events) in a specified population, including new, presently existing, or treated (or deceased) cases. Contrast with *period prevalence*.

primary sex characteristics
qualities necessary for reproduction, such as ovulation and menstruation in females and sperm production and ejaculation in males.

pro bono
free or for the public good, as in *pro bono* legal, psychological, medical, or other professional services.

problem solving
a cognitive coping mechanism that entails mentally searching for alternative solutions, also referred to as *brainstorming* when engaged in by two or more people having a common objective.

productivity
the creation of goods or services to produce value or wealth.

profession
a vocation that requires advanced education in the liberal arts or sciences and/or training and experience in a specialized field of study.

prognosis
a statement regarding the probable course of a disease.

program evaluation research
investigation that has as its objective the assessment of the effectiveness, efficiency, or value of various kinds of institutionalized procedures in the public, private, or government sector.

projection
in psychoanalytic theory, an ego defense mechanism that entails the process of causally attributing anxiety generating from the id or superego to the external world.

propinquity
proximity, usually referred to in the context of factors that enter into liking.

prosocial
approved by society and deemed to be beneficial in nature.

pseudohermaphrodite
a person who has sexual organs that in appearance only are similar to those of the opposite sex.

psychiatrist
a medical doctor who specializes in the treatment of mental and behavioral disorders.

psychiatry
a specialty area within medicine that deals with the research, diagnosis, treatment, and prevention of mental disorders.

psychic energy
the type of energy Freud believed to be involved in psychological activity, analogous to mechanical energy for mechanical activity.

psychoactive substance use disorder

a DSM diagnosis applied when, for a minimum of one month, an individual continues to use some drug (1) while aware that such usage may cause or aggravate psychological, social, or physical problems, or (2) in situations where its use is clearly dangerous to oneself and/or others, as in using it before operating heavy machinery.

psychoanalysis

a method of psychotherapy originated by Sigmund Freud.

psychoanalyst

1. in psychoanalytic psychotherapy, the person conducting therapy with the analysand(s). 2. an occupational title with no legal standing that may be used by licensed as well as unlicensed persons holding themselves out to the public as mental health professionals.

psychoanalytic theory

refers both to the theory of personality that Freud developed and to the theory underlying Freud's system of therapy.

psychodynamic

of or pertaining to mental energy exchanges.

psychogenic disease or disorder

see *psychosomatic disease or disorder.*

psychological test

a gauge, device, or procedure used to measure psychological variables.

psychological trait

any distinguishable, relatively enduring way in which one individual varies from another.

psychologist

in general, an individual have doctoral level training in psychology although exceptions do exist, as in the case of school psychologists legally permitted to use the title "psychologist" within the confines of a school setting.

psychology

the study of mental processes and behavior.

psychology of adjustment

changes in thoughts, feelings, and behavior that contribute to effective adaptation.

psychoneuroimmunology

the study of how the nervous system interacts with the endocrine and immune systems.

psychopathology

disease of the mind.

psychophysics

the study of how physical stimuli are perceived.

psychophysiological disease or disorder

see *psychosomatic disease or disorder.*

psychophysiological measure

a device or means for assessing physical processes that the subject has no voluntary control over, such as blood pressure and heart rate.

psychosexual stages

in psychoanalytic theory, periods in maturation linked to the discharge of sexual energy in various ways.

psychosomatic disease or disorder

terms used to describe physical conditions that result from infection or weakness and are thought to be caused, maintained, or affected in intensity by psychological factors.

psychotherapist

1. in general, refers to a counselor or therapist in the mental health field. 2. an occupational title having no legal standing that may be used by licensed as well as unlicensed persons holding themselves out to the public as mental health professionals.

psychotherapy

literally, "therapy of the mind or soul"; the psychological treatment of mental and behavioral disorders.

psychotherapy outcome study

research on the effectiveness of various approaches to psychotherapy.

psychotropic medication

drugs that have as their targeted site of action the psyche or mind.

puberty

a period of life marked by a number of hormonal and physiological changes beginning with the appearance of secondary sex characteristics and ending with the transformation of a child into an adult capable of reproduction.

punisher

in experimental research, an aversive or unpleasant stimulus, such as electric shock, or a condition involving the withdrawal of something the organism finds positively reinforcing.

punishment

the condition of having an aversive or unpleasant stimulus administered or some favored thing being withdrawn as a consequence of the emission of a particular behavior.

R

race

any group of people classified together on the basis of genetic characteristics that are more or less distinct.

racism

notions of the superiority of one race over another.

random

nonsystematic.

rape

nonconsensual sexual intercourse.

rapid eye movement (REM) sleep

sleep characterized by quick, side-to-side movement of the eyes that is highly correlated with dreaming.

rapport

in interviewing, assessment, counseling or psychotherapy, the working relationship or alliance.

rational-emotive therapy

a cognitive-behavioral approach to therapy developed by Albert Ellis.

rational thinking

a cognitive coping mechanism that entails the use of logic and reasoning to address the source of anxiety.

rationalization

1. a cognitive coping mechanism that entails justifying the stress in some way. 2. in psychoanalytic theory, an ego defense mechanism that entails the process of finding an excuse in the real world to justify something that might be frowned upon by the superego.

raw data

in scientific research, information that has been collected in unanalyzed form.

reaction formation

in psychoanalytic theory, an ego defense mechanism that entails dealing with the anxiety aroused by one instinct by thinking or acting on its opposite.

reality anxiety

in psychoanalytic theory, a fear arising from something that actually exists in the external world.

reality principle

in psychoanalytic theory, seeking gratification through appropriate means with appropriate objects.

reality therapy

a cognitive-behavioral approach to therapy developed by William Glasser.

receptive aphasia

a communication disorder wherein one has difficulty comprehending another's communications but can express oneself freely. Contrast with *expressive aphasia.*

reciprocity

a social psychological concept that refers to the mutuality of attitudes and/or behavior between two or more people.

reconstituted family

a family that has been made whole again after a divorce or the death of a spouse.

reference group

people with respect to whom some social comparison is made.

refractory period

a stage in the sexual response cycle after orgasm when it is physiologically impossible to have another orgasm.

regression

in psychoanalytic theory, an ego defense mechanism that involves moving backward in level of emotional development.

reinforcement

in general, describes the operation of contingently related stimulus events or consequences that tend to increase the probability or rate of emission of operant behaviors.

reinforcer

a general term for any stimulus—such as a food pellet or a jolt of electric shock—received by the organism after it emits an operant behavior such as pressing a bar in a Skinner box. See also *positive reinforcer* and *negative reinforcer.*

relapse

a regression back into illness after whole or partial recovery.

relaxation

a general term for a state of calmness that may be achieved through a variety of means including cognition and imagination, muscle tensing/untensing, and deep breathing.

religion

a system of expressing belief in a higher power that is believed to have created the universe and continues to oversee it.

remission

a condition in which the symptoms of a disease have abated.

repeated measures design

in experimental research such as a before-and-after study, an experiment structured so that comparisons of interest are made within single subjects.

replicable

with reference to scientific research, repeatable by other experimenters who follow the same procedures as the original experimenter.

repression
in psychoanalytic theory, an ego defense mechanism in which anxiety-provoking material is forced out of consciousness and/or maintained out of consciousness.

response prevention
a behavioral treatment technique for treating compulsions wherein the client is prohibited from engaging in the compulsive behavior.

retirement
cessation of working for compensation at a specific occupation, profession, or job.

reverse tolerance
a condition in which less and less of a drug is required by a regular user of it to achieve the same effect.

role
expected behavior in the context of a particular situation.

role conflict
a state in which two or more expected behaviors in a particular situation are at odds with each other.

role model
a person who emits behavior that is emulated and imitated by another person or by groups of people.

romantic love
a state of physiological arousal coupled with the cognitive label that one is "in love."

S

safe sex
a term that refers to practices such as "sexual outercourse" and the use of latex condoms during sexual intercourse, although no sex is truly "safe."

sample
the single subject or group of subjects that a researcher works with to investigate a hypothesis in a particular experiment or other research project.

sanction
a culturally mandated social consequence for adherence or nonadherence to a culture's guidelines; positive sanctions express social approval and negative sanctions express social disapproval.

Satyagraha
the doctrine of nonviolent persuasion taught by Gandhi in India and adopted by Martin Luther King, Jr., in the United States.

schizophrenia
literally, split mind, a psychotic condition characterized by severe disturbances in thought, behavior, and/or emotion.

science
the observation, description, identification, experimental investigation, and/or theoretical explanation of natural phenomena.

screening
sifting out, as in screening qualified subjects to participate in a study or screening qualified job applicants with a test.

scrotum
the thin layer of skin surrounding the testes.

secondary sex characteristics
somatic qualities associated with sexual maturation but not necessary for reproduction, such as pubic and underarm hair.

sedentary lifestyle
a way of life that entails a great deal of sitting with little or no exercise.

self-actualization
a relatively rare state in which one's complete potential has been attained.

self-concept
the summary statement of one's accumulated information about oneself including one's interpretation of that information.

self-efficacy
one's judgments and perceptions regarding how effective one's actions are likely to be with respect to particular situations.

self-esteem
one's general estimate of one's value or worth.

self-ideal discrepancy
the difference between how one sees oneself and how one would like to see oneself.

self-perception theory
a theory that holds that inferences about one's own internal states may be drawn from one's own outward behavior.

self-presentation
the totality of the way one exhibits oneself to others.

self-report measure
written and/or oral assessment of an individual's opinions, beliefs, feelings, sensations, and impressions.

senility

a condition characterized by diminished cognitive abilities, including memory loss, usually due to advanced age but sometimes due to disease.

sensate focus

a technique involving non-genital, pleasure-giving touching.

sensation seeking

the need for varied, novel, and complex sensations and experiences and the willingness to take physical and social risks for the sake of such experiences.

sensitivity training

1. a group approach to personal growth by becoming more physically, mentally, or socially aware. 2. a general name for a specific type of counseling sometimes court-ordered for remedial purposes, as in the case of sensitivity training for a person who has engaged in sexual harassment.

sensorimotor

1. a contraction of sensory and motor that refers to coordination between perception and movement 2. in Piaget's theory, the name for the period of the first 2 years of development.

sex education

formal coursework covering topics such as sexual anatomy, reproduction and pregnancy, family planning, and sexually transmitted diseases.

sex therapy

professional treatment for sexual dysfunction.

sexism

a gender-related form of prejudice that derives from a basic view that one sex is superior to the other.

sexual anatomy

bodily organs involved in reproduction and/or potential sources of sexual pleasure.

sexual disorder

according to the DSM, either a sexual dysfunction or paraphilia.

sexual dysfunction

an inability or impairment in achieving sexual satisfaction.

sexual harassment

a coercive form of sexual behavior which involves the deliberate or repeated conveyance of unsolicited verbal comments, gestures, or physical contact of a sexual nature considered unwelcome by the recipient.

sexual intercourse

coitus; penile/vagina coupling.

sexual orientation

the general nature of one's erotic inclination or preference with respect to the gender of sexual partners.

sexual outercourse

sexual behavior that does not involve contact with potentially infectious bodily fluids.

sexual response cycle

as described by William H. Masters and Virginia E. Johnson, the human sexual response cycle that consists of the following four stages in both males and females: excitement, plateau, orgasm, and resolution.

shaken baby syndrome

a potentially fatal form of child abuse that entails shaking of a baby by its arms or shoulders which in turn causes a tear in its fragile blood vessels.

sibling rivalry

an ongoing state of competitiveness that exists between brothers and sisters in the same family. See also *stepsibling rivalry*.

sick building

a structure, usually a nonindustrial office building or complex, that is known to make, or is capable of making, people who work in it ill.

sick building syndrome

a constellation of respiratory and other types of problems suffered by people as a result of working in, or otherwise being exposed to, the indoor environment of a sick building.

sign

an observable manifestation, such as a weak reflex response of any of many diseases or disorders. See also *symptom* and *syndrome*.

simple phobia

irrational fears of specific objects and/or situations.

smegma

a substance that may build up under the glans of the penis in uncircumcised men if not regularly removed by washing.

social exchange theory

a social psychological theory regarding the principle of equity in the trading of social resources between two or more people.

social learning

a general term used to describe learning that occurs as a result of watching or observing the behavior of others.

social phobia

fear of interacting with people.

social perception

the process, act, or faculty of becoming aware of other people in relation to oneself.

social support
understanding, acceptance, empathy, advice, guidance, and/or expressions of care, concern, agreement, trust, and love from friends, family, community caregivers, or others in one's social environment.

social worker
in a clinic or psychiatric setting, a person who holds either a bachelor's degree, a master's of social work (MSW) degree, or a doctoral (PhD or DSW) degree. State licensing requirements include clinical training in a mental health facility.

socioeconomic
a contraction of the words *social* and *economic*, typically used to refer to one's status or class in society (such as "lower class" or "upper class"), which, in turn, is typically tied to family income and number of people in the family.

sodomy
a legal term used to refer to anal intercourse, and in some states, to oral-genital contact as well.

spontaneous abortion
see *miscarriage*.

SQ3R
a study method acronym for Survey, Question, Read, Recite, and Review. See also *supplemented SQ3R*.

state
a transitory exhibition of a trait.

statistic
any numerical piece of data.

statistical methods
strategies, tools, and techniques for gathering, describing, analyzing, and drawing conclusions about data. See also *descriptive statistics* and *inferential statistics*.

statistics
1. plural of statistic 2. see *statistical methods*.

statutory rape
the criminal act of sex with a minor which may or may not be forcible rape.

stepfamily
the result of a reconstituted family including children.

stepsibling rivalry
an ongoing state of competitiveness that exists between stepsiblings in the same family complicated by loyalties to or dissatisfactions concerning the custodial and noncustodial parents.

stereotype
a belief about a person or a group of people that is based primarily on the basis of perceptions regarding the group to which the individual belongs.

stimulant
a category of drugs that in general act to increase heart rate, respiration rate, and blood pressure and tend to make people feel more alert and, in some cases, euphoric than they would feel without them.

strains
different forms viruses may take.

stress
mental and/or physical strain resulting from anxiety, work, or adjustive demands or challenges.

stressor
something capable of causing stress.

stroke
a cutting off of blood to a site in the brain, usually due to a clot in an artery.

subculture
a group that can be distinguished from the dominant culture by its unique sets of values, norms, and sanctions.

subject
in behavioral science research, the human or nonhuman participant in an experiment or other behavioral study whose behavior will be observed and analyzed by the experimenter.

sudden infant death syndrome (SIDS)
a disease in which an apparently healthy baby unexpectedly dies in its sleep as a result of a mysterious respiratory failure.

superego
in psychoanalytic theory, the keeper of the mind's morals and values.

supplemented SQ3R
the SQ3R study system supplemented with three additional *R*'s: Rewrite, Remember, and Record. See also *SQ3R*.

surrogacy
an arrangement typically made between a fertile woman and an infertile person or couple for the fertile woman to carry a baby to term.

surrogate
1. in Harry Harlow's experiments with monkeys, an inanimate mother substitute made of cloth or wire. 2. a paid sexual partner for the purpose of treating a patient when a spouse is not available for such purposes. 3. a fertile woman paid to carry a baby to term.

sympathetic nervous system
the branch of the peripheral nervous system that gears up the body to respond to stress and danger.

symptom

an observed manifestation of one or more known diseases or disorders. See also *sign* and *syndrome*.

syndrome

a pattern of symptoms that characterize a particular disease or disorder.

syphilis

a potentially fatal sexually transmitted bacterial disease characterized by the appearance of a chancre at the site of infection within 10 to 90 days from the time of infection.

systematic desensitization

in behavior and cognitive-behavior therapy, a technique for progressively overcoming anxiety in response to some anxiety-provoking stimulus by pairing relaxation with the presentation of the anxiety-provoking stimulus.

T

taboo

something prohibited by the culture.

talking cure

a reference to psychotherapy, usually psychoanalysis as practiced by Freud.

taxonomies

classification systems.

telomere

a hairlike piece of genetic material whose length has been found to decrease with age.

temperament

emotional and behavioral dispositions presumed to be inborn.

test

a gauge, device, or procedure used to measure. See also *psychological test*.

test anxiety

worry or stress associated with taking an examination.

testes

the male gonads.

testosterone

male sex hormone.

theory

a group of organized principles which may be explanatory and/or predictive with respect to certain phenomena.

Theory X

a directive and authoritarian approach to management based on the belief that workers basically dislike work and have a tendency to avoid responsibility for their work-related behavior.

Theory Y

a democratic approach to management based on the belief that work is as natural as other activities and may be pursued primarily for the satisfaction it affords the worker.

Theory Z

an approach to management that originated in Japan that is based on the proposition that the worksite is a kind of extension of an employee's family.

therapist

see *psychotherapist*.

thought

from a cognitive-behavioral perspective, an intermediary between one's internal and external world.

time management

using one's hours to one's maximum advantage.

toddler

a child between the ages of 1 and 2, the age at which toddling, a precursor to walking, typically begins.

token economy

an institutional application of contingency contracting that entails the use of rewards such as tokens, gold stars, or other such "currency," exchangable for material goods, services, or privileges.

tolerance

a situation wherein the body begins to tolerate a particular dosage of a drug and increasingly higher dosages are needed to achieve the same effects.

tort

a legal wrong.

toxin

poisonous material.

trait
a characteristic.

transactional model of stress
a theory that focuses on the unique aspects of the interaction between the person and the environment as the determinants of stress.

transference
in psychoanalytic psychotherapy, a process by which feelings the client has for one person are presumed to be projected to the therapist.

transsexual
male or female who believe they are trapped in a body of the opposite sex.

transvestite
an individual who dresses in the clothes of, and takes on the appearance and mannerisms of, a person of the opposite sex.

triangular theory of love
Sternberg's theory which assesses love's three major components: decision/commitment, intimacy, and passion.

Type A behavior or personality
a pattern of behavior characterized by impatience, competitiveness, and feelings of time pressure and presumed to place people at high risk for a heart attack.

Type B behavior or personality
a mellow and "laid back" pattern of behavior presumed to place people at less risk for a heart attack than *Type A behavior*.

U

unconditional positive regard
in person-centered therapy, an interpersonal environment wherein there is unqualified acceptance, valuing, and prizing of the inherent worth of an individual.

unemployment
the condition of being involuntarily out of work.

unipolar disorder
a mood disorder that involves only one affectual extreme, such as depression at the low end of the spectrum or mania at the high end. Contrast with *bipolar disorder*.

unobtrusive measures
assessments that are nonreactive in that they do not require the cooperation of a respondent.

utilization
the practice of treating game parks as revenue producers for conservation through activities such as tourism, trophy hunting and the sale of breeding stock to game ranches.

V

vaccine
minute amounts of inactive or live organisms or toxins introduced into the body for the purpose of bringing about immunization to a disease.

value system
one's priorities with respect to values.

values
that which one believes in and/or prizes.

variable
anything that can vary, such as age, eye color, gender, loudness of music, race, length of one's hair, and so forth.

vasectomy
a method of contraception that entails the severing of the male's vas deferens, thus blocking the path of sperm cells to the urethra.

videotherapy
using videos psychotherapeutically, as in the case of learning some moral from a story told in a film.

visual cliff
an apparatus used to study depth perceptions in human infants and other species.

voyeurism
a condition characterized by acting on recurrent and powerful sexual urges or fantasies to watch unsuspecting people, usually strangers, disrobe, be in the nude, or engage in sexual activity.

vulva
female genitalia including the labia majora, labia minora, clitoris, and the vaginal vestibule.

W

waxy flexibility
a term used to characterize the phenomenon of melted candle-like limbs typically observed in people who have a diagnosis of catatonic schizophrenia.

Wernicke's area
named for the German neurologist Carl Wernicke, an area of the brain thought to be involved in hearing.

widow
a female whose husband has died.

widower
a male whose wife has died.

widowhood
the state of, or the time period spent, being single as the result of the death of a spouse.

withdrawal
1. the unpleasant feelings or thoughts one experiences when one refrains from using a drug for which a physiological or psychological dependence has been established. 2. an unreliable method of contraception that entails removal of the penis from the vagina just prior to ejaculation.

word association
a psychotherapeutic and assessment technique whereby the therapist or assessor provides a stimulus word and clients respond with the first word or words that come to mind.

workaholism
a condition characterized by spending an inordinate and disproportionate time at work.

Y

Yerkes-Dodson principle
a notion about the optimal degree of pressure for a particular task.

Z

zero population growth
a rate of growth at which the number of people remains relatively stable.

zygote
a sperm united with an ovum.

PHOTO CREDITS

NAME INDEX

Abelsohn, D., 370
Abrams, J., 242
Abrritti, G., 415, 425
Achenbach, T., 223
Ackerman, M., 120
Adams, A., 18
Adams, H.E., 325
Adams, J.S., 385
Adelman, M., 103, 302, 303
Adelman, M.B., 302
Ader, R., 69, 70
Adjamine, P., 176
Adler, A., 31
Agnew, R., 134
Agnew, S.T., 272
Agopian, M., 370
Agostinelli, J., 366
Aguilar, R., 89
Ahrons, C., 370
Ahsen, A., 190
Ahuvia, A.C., 302, 303
Ainsworth, M.D.S., 123, 288
Alavanja, M., 75
Alba, R.D., 352
Albee, G.W., 210, 431
Albert, E.M., 103
Alberti, R.E., 196
Albrecht, S.L., 368
Alderfer, C.P., 385
Alexander, K.L., 135
Allen, K.M., 177
Allen, L.S., 89, 324
Allen, S., 54
Allison, D.B., 181
Allport, G.W., 29, 111
Allred, K.D., 70
Altman, L.K., 360
Alzate, H., 318, 464
Amabile, T.M., 293
Amato, P.R., 374

Amelang, M., 29
American Association for the
    Advancement of Science, 453
American College of Obstetricians
    and Gynecologists, 80, 119
American Psychological Association,
    214, 229, 396
Ames, M.A., 220
Amler, R.W., 72
Ammons, P., 349
Andersen, S.M., 266
Anderson, D.L., 97, 335
Anderson, J.R., 18
Anderson, N.H., 292
Anderson, R.K., 177
Anderson, S., 177
Angelbeck, J.H., 88
Angell, M., 68
Angier, N., 60
Antoni, M.H., 69
Antunes, C.M., 321
Apfelbaum, M., 76
Applebome, P., 131
Aras, Z., 322
Arendt, H., 273
Argeriou, M., 107
Aron, A.P., 296
Aronson, E., 114
Arthur, R.J., 157
Asch, S.E., 271, 272
Atkeson, B.M., 333
Atkinson, D.R., 186
Atkinson, J., 95
Attneave, C.L., 186
Atwater, W.O., 74
Aube, J., 326
Auerbach, R., 317
Averill, J.R., 191
Avery, D.H., 255
Axelson, L.J., 366

Bachmann, G., 321
Back, K.W., 249
Bailey, J.M., 325
Baird, Z., 99
Bajardi, S.E., 59, 60
Baker, R., 10
Baker, S.W., 92
Balakrishnan, T.R., 378
Baldwin, M.W., 266
Ballou, M., 197
Bandura, A., 48, 49, 180, 239, 244,
    247, 250, 281
Banks, M.H., 404
Banning, A., 220
Barber, J., 70
Barber, J.G., 366
Barbour, L.S., 367
Bardin, C.W., 89
Bardot, B., 93, 94
Bargh, J.A., 265
Barker, M., 429
Barker, R.G., 413, 415
Barling, J., 366
Barlow, D.H., 217, 317
Barnes, M.L., 298
Baron, P.H., 267
Baron, R.A., 273, 281, 283
Barrera, M., Jr., 184
Barrett, J.E., 157
Barrett, P., 29
Barringer, F., 203, 324, 341, 361
Barrios, B.A., 266
Barron, J., 404
Bart, P.B., 336
Bartsch, W., 89
Basedow, R.H., 149
Basow, S.A., 92, 101
Bass, B.M., 272
Baum, A., 415, 424
Baum, M.J., 88

Baumeister, R.F., 181
Baumrind, D., 127, 278
Baxter, L.R., 217
Bayer, R., 223
Beals, R.L., 103
Beck, A., 209, 239
Beck, A.M., 177
Beck, A.T., 238
Becker, G., 366
Becker, H.S., 300
Becker, M.H., 73
Becker, P., 177
Beckwith, P., 289
Beidel, D.C., 216
Belkin, L., 284
Bell, A.P., 327, 330
Bell, C., 100, 134
Belsky, J., 365
Bem, D., 265
Bem, S.L., 92, 101
Bemis, C., 68
Benin, M.H., 366
Bennet, J., 301, 375
Bennett, N.G., 378
Benson, H., 193
Bentler, P.M., 138
Beran, B., 198
Berenbaum, H., 90
Berger, J., 109
Berger, L., 124
Berger, R.J., 89
Berkowitz, L., 281, 284
Bernard, A.C., 350
Bernard, J., 348
Bernard, M., 239
Bernard-Bonnin, A.C., 131
Bernays, M., 32
Berry, J., 103
Berry, K.M., 340
Bersoff, D.M., 103
Berstein, B.E., 374
Besharov, D.J., 120
Best, D.L., 90
Betzig, L.B., 91
Betzig, L.L., 91
Beutler, L.E., 317
Bewrry, G., 132
Birns, B., 122
Bishop, K., 158
Bixler, E.O., 164
Black, T.E., 293
Blakeslee, S., 217, 343
Blanchard, E.B., 253
Blaney, P.H., 70

Blau, F., 97
Bliss, E.L., 223
Bloch, D.P., 136
Blum, R., 138
Blumstein, P., 330
Bochner, S., 103
Bohlen, C., 65, 164
Boker, J.R., 18
Bolger, N., 366
Bond, L.A., 365
Bond, M.H., 103
Bondy, F., 341
Boor, M., 404
Booth, A., 374, 378
Boring, E.G., 33
Borkenau, P., 29
Borkovec, T.D., 73, 240
Borysenko, J., 144
Bossard, J., 295
Bovard, E.W., 288
Bowlby, J., 123
Bradshaw, J., 144
Braginsky, B.M., 269
Braham, R., 140
Braiker, H.B., 305
Brain, R., 270
Brand, R.J., 71
Brandon, S., 254
Braun, B.G., 222
Bray, G.A., 75
Bray, R., 325
Breakey, W.R., 107
Bregger, L., 432
Brenner, H., 366
Brentar, J., 255
Bret, A., 322
Brett, J.M., 403
Breuer, J., 33
Briere, J., 429
Brigham, J.C., 292
Brislin, R., 88
Britt, H., 327
Britton, B.K., 15
Brock, B., 400
Brody, J.E., 336, 337
Bronfenbrenner, U., 352
Brooks, J., 119
Brooks-Gunn, J., 322
Brophy, J.E., 100
Broude, G., 334
Brown, G.W., 366
Brown, H.G., 304
Brown, R.E., 88
Brown, T.A., 266, 295

Browne, M.W., 422
Brownell, 184
Brownell, K., 77
Bruch, H., 266
Bruck, M., 120
Bruggeman, E., 61
Bryan, L.R., 374
Buber, M., 249
Buckley, M.R., 397
Buell, S.J., 62
Bullard, S., 112
Bulloch, K., 69
Bumpass, L.L., 367, 378
Burack, J., 216
Burden, D.S., 377
Burgess, A.W., 333
Burgess, E.W., 295
Burke, P.J., 267
Burks, N., 166
Burningham, J., 428
Burns, A., 350, 368
Burns, G., 143
Burros, M., 60
Burrow, C., 421
Burton, H.J., 216
Bush, G., 268, 292, 361, 390
Buss, D.M., 293
Buss, W.C., 350
Bussey, K., 91
Bustad, L.K., 177
Butler, R., 375
Byers, E.S., 336
Byne, W., 324
Byrne, D., 292, 293

Cabaj, R.P., 324
Caldwell, M.A., 290
Calhoun, K.S., 333
Camel, J.E., 62
Campbell, A.A., 110
Campbell, J., 267
Campbell, J.P., 385
Campbell, S.S., 79
Camper, D., 133
Campos, J.J., 122
Canadian Government Travel
    Bureau, 406
Canelo, A., 338
Canon, W.B., 149
Cantor, N., 265
Cantril, H., 154, 273
Caplan, P.J., 223
Carey, W.B., 122
Cargan, L., 376

Tucker, K.F., 163
Tucker, M., 400
Tucker, R.K., 92
Turiel, E., 130
Turke, P.W., 91
Turnbull, C.M., 334
Turner, B.L., II, 412
Turner, S.M., 216
Turner-Henson, A., 365
Tyler, F., 105

Uehling, M.D., 415
Ullian, D.Z., 91
Ullman, S.E., 336
Unger, R.K., 88, 292
U.S. Congress, 356
U.S. Department of Justice, 134
U.S. Merit Systems Protection
    Board, 335
Utian, W.H., 321
Uzgiris, I.C., 48

Vaillant, G.E., 68
Vance, C., 320
Vandenberg, B., 124
Van den Bergh, B.R.H., 118
Van Italie, T.B., 75
Van Liere, K.D., 415, 429
Van Wyk, P.H., 324
Vecchio, M.A., 165
Verbrugge, L., 348
Verderber, K.S., 307
Verderber, R.F., 307
Vlietstra, A.G., 128
Voight, K.D., 89
Volkman, E., 403
Vollrath, M., 266
Von Glinow, M.A., 96
Von Korff, M., 216
von Leibniz, G., 32
Vroom, V.H., 384

Wachter, R.M., 388
Wadden, T.A., 76
Waelder, R., 250
Wagenheim, J., 98, 100
Wagner, B.M., 365
Waigandt, A., 333
Wald, M.L., 413
Walk, R.D., 121, 122
Walker, L.E., 367
Walker-Andrews, A., 122
Wallach, L., 130
Wallach, M.A., 130

Wallerstein, J.S., 367
Wallin, P., 295
Wallston, B.S., 184
Wallston, K.A., 216
Walster, E., 297, 304
Walster, G.W., 297, 304
Walters, W.A.W., 359
Wampler, K.S., 302, 374
Wanous, J.P., 385
Ward, R., 376
Washington, J.R., 352
Waterman, J., 220
Waters, M., 352
Watson, D., 260
Watson, J.B., 40, 45, 50, 52
Weaver, C., 398
Webb, D., 95, 132
Webb, E.J., 455
Webb, W., 78, 79
Wehr, T.A., 255
Weinberg, M.S., 327, 330
Weinberger, M., 166
Weiner, B., 191, 288
Weiner, M.B., 330
Weiner, N.J., 339
Weiner, R.D., 253
Weinstein, H.P., 29
Weis, J.S., 415, 426
Weishaar, M., 238
Weisman, S.R., 161, 335
Weiss, M., 119
Weissberg, M., 15
Welch, E., 337
Wells, L.E., 267
Wessels, H., 244
West, C., 111
West, M., 348
Westen, D., 142
Westman, J.C., 122
Wetherington, E., 183,
    184
Wetzel, C.G., 6
Wheeler, K.A., 320
Wheeler, L., 292
Whelan, E.M., 75
White, J., 197
White, L.K., 374
White, M., 126
White, S.H., 128
Whitely, B.E., Jr., 101
Whiting, B., 90, 103
Whitley, B.E., Jr., 263
Whitman, C., 62
Whitney, C.R., 109

Wichterich, C., 359
Wicker, A.W., 415
Widiger, T.A., 211, 212
Wiener, L.S., 402
Wiggins, J.S., 29
Wilkerson, I., 207
Willet, W.C., 75
Williams, B.D., 295
Williams, D., 366
Williams, G.R., 330
Williams, J.E., 90
Williams, K.R., 367
Williams, R.B., Jr., 71
Williams, R.E., 253
Williams, R.M., Jr., 104
Williams, S.R., 75
Williamson, G.M., 67
Williamson, J.W., 124
Willis, R.J., 348
Willke, J.C., 362
Wills, T.A., 184
Wilson, E.O., 419, 433
Wilson, G., 220
Wilson, G.T., 266
Wilson, K., 302
Wilson, M., 91, 134
Wilson-Brewer, R., 134
Wiltfang, G.L., 415, 429
Wincze, J.P., 331
Wingard, D.L., 74
Wirz-Justice, A., 255
Wistrich, R.S., 108
Wolfe, J., 100
Wolfson, A., 119
Wollman, J., 54
Wolpe, J., 242
Wong, D.L., 120
Wood, W., 304
Woods, J.E., 425
Woodworth, R.S., 40
World Health Organization,
    141
Wright, H.F., 413, 415
Wright, J.C., 128
Wright, S.C., 114
Wu, S., 103
Wyatt, G.E., 333
Wylie, R., 267
Wynn, R.L., 356
Wysor, M.S., 415, 428

Yahya, K.A., 273
Yambert, P.A., 415
Yap, P.M., 213

SUBJECT INDEX

Abandonment
  child's fear of, 37
  of the elderly, 9, 10
Abduction, 370
Abnormal behavior, 202, 205
  behavioral model of, 208
  biological model of, 205–206
  biopsychosocial model of,
    210–211
  causes of, 205–211
  classification and diagnosis of,
    211–212, 214
  cognitive model of, 208–209
  current issues in diagnosing,
    223–224
  humanistic model of, 209, 210
  integrative perspective on,
    205
  labeling, 224
  medical model of, 206
  versus normal behavior,
    202–204
  psychoanalytic model of, 208
  psychosocial model of, 204–205,
    207–210
  sociocultural perspective on,
    203–204
  statistical perspective on, 202
  varieties of, 214–223
Abortion, 219, 361
  Catholicism and, 10–11
  controversial issue of, 361, 362
  declining rates of, 361
  pro-choice arguments, 362
  spontaneous, 361
Absenteeism, 398
Absorption, in business, 280
Abstract concepts, 125
Abuse, 233–234. *See also* Alcohol
    abuse; Child abuse; Drug use
    and abuse; Spouse abuse

Abused children, 123, 137
  as abusers, 120
Academic skills
  early programs for, 126
  in middle childhood years, 130
Acculturation, 103
Accuracy error, 264
Acquired immunodeficiency
    syndrome (AIDS). *See* AIDS
Acquiring the relevant
    competencies, 192
Active listening, 21, 310
Active reception, 310
Actualization, 51
Adaptation
  diseases of, 67
  play and, 124
Adaptive, 169
Adaptive coping, 174
Adaptive state. *See* Resistance stage,
    in stress
Addiction, 81–82
Adjustive challenges, 7, 8, 9
  prenatal, 118–123
Adjustive demands, 7, 8, 9
Adjustment
  behavioral sciences and, 3
  change and, 6–12
  culture and, 5–6, 102–114
  developmental perspective on,
    117–144
  divorce and, 368–370
  in the global sense, 412, 425–434
  health and, 64–72, 415–416
  maladjustment and, 7
  marriage and, 354–355
  ongoing process of, 7
  psychology of, 2–12
  research related to, 13
  sexual, 322–323
  social support and, 184–185

values and, 3–5, 6
Adjustment disorders, 214–215
Adolescence, 133–141
  cognitive development in,
    133–136
  dating in, 139, 140–141
  deaths in, 139, 140
  dress codes in, 137, 140
  drugs and alcohol use in, 138
  family and, 137
  health in, 141
  identity in, 137, 142
  language codes in, 137
  peers in, 136–137, 141
  physical development in, 133
  puberty, 133, 140, 320
  risk behavior in, 132–133,
    138–141
  sexual behavior in, 141
  sexually transmitted diseases in,
    140–141
  social development in, 136–138
  socioeconomic perspective on,
    136
  suicide in, 140
  teenage pregnancy, 135, 141
  transition to adulthood, 142
  violence in, 132–135, 138–140
Adoption, by singles, 377
Adornments, culture and, 270
Adrenal glands, 63
Adrenaline, 63, 154–155
Adulthood, 141–144
  aging process, 142–143
  confronting mortality, 143–144
  transition to, 141–142
  see also Elderly
Advertising
  critical thinking and, 12–13
  personal, 304
  sex in, 296

Assessment
    methods of, 28, 212–214
    see also Psychological tests
As You Like It (Shakespeare), 11
Attachment, development of, 123
Attitudes, sexual, 322–323, 328
Attraction, 293–305
    interpersonal, 294–296
    matching hypothesis, 295
    opposites and, 293
    sexual, 296, 297, 322
    see also Liking; Love
Attractiveness
    cultural ideal of, 296
    and liking, 292, 293
    physical, 295
Attribution, 260–261
    fundamental attribution error,
        263–265
    social comparison as basis for,
        264
    in social encounters, 294–295
    unjustified positive, 292
Auditory discrimination, 122
Authoritarian parent, 127
Authoritative parent, 127
Authority, obedience to, 273,
        278–279
Averages, 460
    citing of, 329
Aversion therapy, 244
Avoidance-avoidance conflict, 159
Aymara culture, domestic violence
    in, 367
AZT (zidovudine), 340

Barbiturates, 80
Basal body temperature, 357
Basic anxiety, 39
BASIC ID, 189, 245
Basic research, 439
Batterers, 139–140, 367
Behavior
    antecedents of, 240–242
    consequences of, 240–242
    contingencies and, 240–242
Behavior genetics, 60
Behavior therapy
    fear of snakes and, 240
    obsessive-compulsive disorders
        and, 217
    pedophilia and, 240, 244
    perspective on, 208, 209, 228,
        239–245, 247–248, 251

post-traumatic stress disorder
    and, 242, 243
    for weight loss, 76
Behavioral observation, 212–213,
    240
Behavioral perspective, 40–50
    on abnormal behavior, 208,
        209
    evaluation of, 49–50
    on multiple personality, 223
    on work motivation, 383–384,
        386
    see also Behaviorism
Behavioral research
    quality in, 440–443
    types of, 438–440
    see also Research, 428–429,
        437–465
Behavioral sciences
    and adjustment, 3
    objective of, 3
    uses of research in, 463
Behaviorism
    B. F. Skinner, 45–48
    John Watson, 45
Behavior-related phenomena, 3
Behavior Therapy and Beyond
    (Lazarus), 245
Belongingness, need for, 53
Bias
    cultural, 61, 185–186
    in research, 441–442
Bibliotherapy, 243
Bigotry, 106
Binge eating, 181
Biofeedback, 253
Biologically based therapy,
    252–256
    perspective on, 255–256
Biological perspective
    on abnormal behavior, 205–206
    on genetics, 59–60
    on schizophrenia, 221
    on sexuality, 314–322
Biology, and gender, 88–89
Biopsychosocial perspective
    on abnormal behavior, 210–211
    endocrine system and, 62–63
    genetics and, 58–62
    on health, 83–84
    immune system and, 63–64
    nervous system and, 62
    on values, 82–84
    on weight loss, 76–77

Biosphere, psychology and,
    412–416
Biotechnology, 61, 363–364
    risks in, 61
Birth defects, 444
Bisexual orientation, 323–324
Blended family, 363
Blind, in research, 450–451
Blunted affect, 215
Body image, 266
Bone mass, 142
Bowers v. Hardwick, 330
Brain
    damage to, 62, 205
    environment and, 62
    hormones and, 89
    and psychological adjustment, 62
    and sexual response, 316, 324
    tumors of, 62
Brainstorming, 180, 194
    to resolve conflict, 282–283
Branching, 62
Bright light treatment, 255
Bulimia nervosa, 35, 463
Bundling, 301, 302
Burnout, 399–400
Business
    absorption in, 280
    attribution in, 260
    environment and, 431
Butch Cassidy and the Sundance Kid
    (film), 389

Caffeine, 80
Calories, 74, 75, 78, 79
Cancer, 74, 75, 84
    prostate, 322
    skin, 422
Cannibalism, 103
Capital punishment, 47, 163
Captain Planet and the Planeteers
    (game), 428
Carbohydrates, 74, 75
Cardiovascular disease, 71
Career, 400
Career development theory, 400
Cartoons, 131, 132
Case study method, 39, 213–214
Case study research, 457
Castration anxiety, 36, 38
Catatonic schizophrenia, 221, 222,
    254
Catharsis, 284
CAT scans, 9

Impulsiveness, in preschool years, 126
Inappropriate affect, 176
Incentive programs, 384
Incest, 103
Incidence, 212
Indecent Proposal (film), 90
Independent groups design, 448
Independent variable, 451–452
Industrial/organization (I/O) psychology, 382, 413
Infancy, 118, 123, 133
  abuse in, 120
  cognitive development in, 122
  emotional development in, 122–123
  first two years, 119–123
  motor development in, 119–122
  sleep in, 119
  social development in, 123
  toilet training in, 127
Infant-caregiver relationship, 119
Infantile amnesia, 39
Infantile sexuality, 36, 38
Infatuation, 299, 300
Inferential statistics, 460
Infertility, 356
Informed consent, 254, 454
In-group/out-group phenomenon, 111
Injuries
  with exercise, 78
  from falls, 125
  in preschool years, 124–125
  prevention of, 124–125
"Inner child," 144
Insanity, legal plea of, 210
Insight-oriented approaches, 248
Instinct, 34, 40, 281
Instrumental conditioning, 43–48
  devices used in studies of, 44
  law of effect, 43
  reinforcers, 46
  Skinner's behaviorism, 45
  social learning, 48–49
  Watson's behaviorism, 45
Integrative perspective, on abnormal behavior, 205
Integrity tests, 393–395
Intelligence, 28
Intercultural marriage, 351, 352
Interfaith marriage, 351, 352
Intermarriage, 351–353
Internal locus of control, 429

Internship, 389–390
Interpretation of Dreams, The (Freud), 31
Interracial marriage, 351–352
Interviews, 212
  job, 393, 394–396
  mental status examinations, 212
Intimacy, 12, 299
Intrapreneur, 393
Intrapsychic, 276–277
Invasive procedures, 230
Inventory of College Students' Recent Life Experiences (ICSRLE), 166
In vitro fertilization, 358–359
Irrational thinking, 161, 162, 239
Italian culture, 186

Jenkins Activity Survey (JAS), 71
Job, 382
  characteristics of, 386
  discrimination and, 401, 402–403
  fairs, 393
  interviews, 393, 394–396
Job facet satisfaction, 397
Job satisfaction, 397–398
  motivator-hygiene model of, 398
  and productivity, 397–398
Job search, 394–396, 404
  cover letter, 393, 394
  resumés in, 393, 394
Job security, 390, 391
Job-sharing, 102
Joys and Problems of Child Rearing, The (Jersild), 365
Judgment
  loss of, 66
  moral, 130
  poor, 215

Kama Sutra, 328
Kaposi's sarcoma, 340
Karoshi, 398–399
Koro epidemic, 213, 223
Ku Klux Klan (KKK), 104–105, 111, 113

Labor, domestic division of, 90, 354, 366
Laboratory research, 50
  punishment in, 47
Lashley jumping stand, 45
Latency period, 38–39
Lateral thinking, 13

Law
  insanity and, 210
  rule of, 4
Law of effect, 43
Leaders
  characteristics of, 272
  duties of, 272
  political, 273, 274
Leadership, 272–273
Learned helplessness, 150
Learning, 40
  flash cards, 23
  method of *loci* and, 23
  and phobic disorders, 217
  social, 48–49
  see also Conditioning
Learning or experiential history, 207, 209
Leisure time, 8, 405–407
  adaptive and maladaptive use of, 406–407
  relationship of work time to, 405–406
  vacationing, 406
  see also Retirement
Lesbians, 323
Levels of statistical significance, 461–462
Libido, 36, 38
Life changes, 157–158
Life expectancy, 72, 375
Lifestyle, 74
  and health, 72–82
  in middle childhood, 130
  and perception, 167
  sedentary, 183
  single, 376–379
Liking, 289–293
  factors in, 290–293
  and intimacy, 299
  see also Attraction; Friendship
Limit-setting, in childhood, 126
Listening
  active, 21, 310
  to boring material, 21
  in class, 21
Live-in lovers, 378–379
Loneliness, 194, 288–289
  chronic, 289
  transitional, 289
  types of, 289
Los Angeles, civil unrest in, 112–113

Psychoanalysis, 208, 250
  after Freud, 39–40
  in humanistic perspective, 51
  perspective on, 238
  in psychoanalytic perspective, 31,
    33, 50
Psychoanalytic perspective, 31–40
  on abnormal behavior, 208
  on multiple personality,
    222–223
  on personality, 34–39
  see also Psychoanalysis
Psychoanalytic theory, 31–32,
  34–39
Psychodynamic, 34. See also
  Psychoanalytic perspective;
  Psychoanalytic theory
Psycho (film), 223
Psychogenic disease, 67. See also
  Psychosomatic disease
Psychological assessment. See
  Assessment
Psychological "filters" in stress
  perception model, 169
Psychological perspectives, 27–55
  behavioral, 40–50
  biological, 59
  biopsychosocial, 58–64, 83–84
  humanistic, 50–55
  psychoanalytic, 31–40
Psychological tests, 28, 31, 214,
  455. see also Assessment
Psychologist, 195, 229, 230,
  390–391
Psychology, 2
  of adjustment, 2–12
  scope of, 2
Psychology as the Behaviorist Views It
  (Watson), 45
Psychology of Personal Constructs, The
  (Kelly), 208
Psychology of Science, The (Maslow),
  52
Psychoneuroimmunology, 69–70
Psychopathology, 165, 206
  medical model of, 206
  perception and, 165
  sexual orientation and, 325
  societal attitudes as determinant
    of, 325
  see also Abnormal behavior
Psychopathology of Everyday Life, The
  (Freud), 33
Psychophysics, 32

Psychosexual stages (Freud's), 36, 38
Psychosocial perspective, on
  abnormal behavior, 204–205,
  207–210
Psychosomatic disease, 67
  types of, 67, 69
  see also Health, mind-body
    connection
Psychotherapist. See Therapists
Psychotherapy, 228. See also
  Therapy
Psychotherapy outcome studies, 233
Psychotropic medication, 252–253
Psylocybin, 81
Puberty, 133, 140, 320. See also
  Adolescence
Public policy
  on child safety, 124
  and environmental issues,
    429–431
  on granny dumping, 10
  and the homeless, 107
  on urban violence, 134
Punishers, 47
Punishment, 47
  capital, 47, 163
  corporal, 47, 126
  as deterrent to crime, 283–284
  distinguished from negative
    reinforcement, 47
  and learning, 47
  legal forms of, 47
  as means of behavioral control, 47
Puzzle boxes, 44

Questions
  asking, in class, 23–24
  asking, in job interviews, 395

Race, 108
Racism, 108
  institutionalized, 112
  roots of, 109–111
Random assignment, 452
Random in research, 452
Rape, 331–333
  circumstances surrounding, 332,
    333
  court cases, 444
  cultural universality of, 333, 334
  date, 332, 336
  forcible, 331
  prevention strategies, 332, 333,
    336–337

  sadistic, 332
  statistics, 331–332
  statutory, 219, 331
  taxonomy of, 336
  victims of, 314, 333, 337
Rapid eye movement (REM) sleep,
  66, 243
Rapists, 331–333
Rapport, 228
Rational-emotive therapy (RET),
  239
Rationalization, 37, 179
Reaction formation, 37
Reality anxiety, 35
Reality principle, 35
Reality therapy, 36, 239
Reasoning
  impaired ability, 221
  in preschool years, 125
  see also Moral development
Reciprocity, and liking, 293
Reconstituted family, 363, 373
Reference group, 264, 266
Reflexes, infant, 121, 122
Reflexive behavior, 40
Refractory period, 317, 319
Regression, 37
Reinforcement, 46–48
Reinforcer, 46, 48
  negative, 46, 48
  positive, 46, 48
Relatedness needs, 385
Relationship
  beginning a, 301–304
  cultural influences on, 308
  ending a, 305, 306
  sexual, 322–323
  see also Friendship; Liking; Love
Relaxation-induced anxiety, 72, 73
Relaxation training, 73, 193, 253
Religion, 108
  and coping with stress, 180
  role conflicts and, 10–11
  stereotyping on basis of, 108
Religious cults, 4
Remarriage, 372–375
  adjustive demands of, 372–373
  in later life, 375
Remission, 206
Ren and Stimpy Show (TV), 132
Rendezvous à trois, 302
Repeated measures design, 448
Replicability in research, 442
Repression, 35, 37